Southwest USA

DATE DUE

Utah
p385

Southwestern
Colorado
p353

Arizona
p109

New Mexico
p235

PLAN YOUR TRIP

NEON COWBOY, LAS VEGAS
P62

DOUG MCKINLAY / GETTY IMAGES ©

NATIVE AMERICAN ART
P524

DANITA DELIMONT / GETTY IMAGES ©

ON THE ROAD

RALPH LEE HOPKINS / GETTY IMAGES ©

Contents

COLORADO RIVER, GRAND
CANYON P160

MILLION DOLLAR HIGHWAY
P377

JOHN ELK III / GETTY IMAGES ©

GRAND CANYON NATIONAL
PARK P160

ANN CECIL / GETTY IMAGES ©

Contents

UNDERSTAND

SURVIVAL GUIDE

SPECIAL FEATURES

Welcome to Southwest USA

The Southwest is America's playground, luring adventurous travelers with thrilling red-rock landscapes, the legends of shoot-'em-up cowboys and the kicky delights of green-chile stew.

The Great Outdoors

Beauty and adventure are a fun-loving team in the Southwest. They crank up the white-water, unleash the singletrack, add blooms to the trail and drape a sunset across the red rocks. This captivating mix of scenery and possibility lures travelers who want to rejuvenate physically, mentally and spiritually. The big draw is the Grand Canyon, a two-billion-year-old wonder that shares its geologic treasures with a healthy dose of fun. In Utah the red rocks will nourish your soul while thrashing your bike, while in southern Colorado ice climbing and mountain biking excite. Take a scenic drive, an art walk or a lazy slide down a shimmery dune in New Mexico, or chase the neon lights in Vegas.

This Is the Place for History

The Southwest wears its history on its big, sandy sleeve. Ancient cultures left behind cliff dwellings and petroglyphs, while their descendants live on in reservations and pueblos. Navajos and Apaches arrived next, followed by Spanish conquistadors. Then the missionaries left a string of stunning missions in their wake. Mormon religious refugees arrived with Brigham Young in the Salt Lake Valley, and their cities have flourished. The lure of gold and copper drew prospectors, and vast tracts of land drew cattlemen.

Multicultural Meanderings

It's the multicultural mix – Native American, Hispanic, Anglo – that makes a trip to the Southwest unique. There are 19 Indian pueblos in New Mexico, and the Navajo Reservation alone covers more than 27,000 sq miles. Monument Valley and Canyon de Chelly, two of the most striking geologic features in the Southwest, are protected as sacred places. Tribal traditions and imagery influence art across the region. The Spanish and Mexican cultures are also a part of daily life, from the food to the language to headlines about immigration.

Local Food & Drink

Green-chile sauces in New Mexico. Sonoran dogs in Tucson. Steak in Colorado. Regional specialties are pleasingly diverse in the Southwest and sampling homegrown fare is half the fun of a trip. Top restaurants are increasingly focused on fresh and locally grown fare – anyone up for a little foraging? A crop of new microbreweries has opened across the region, and Arizona wines are also winning fans.

Why I Love Southwest USA

By Amy C Balfour, Author

Because I never get bored. Deserts, mountains, red-rock canyons. Wherever I hike in the Southwest, I know there will always be a cool new view around the bend. But it's not just the scenery that's compelling. Behind every beautiful landscape there is, inevitably, an interesting story or bit of history that adds to the richness of the experience. And outdoor fun? Seriously, there are enough adventures here to fill several lifetimes. Yep, the Southwest – it's worth an extended visit.

For more about our authors, see page 576

Above: Spider Rock Overlook (p193)

Southwest USA

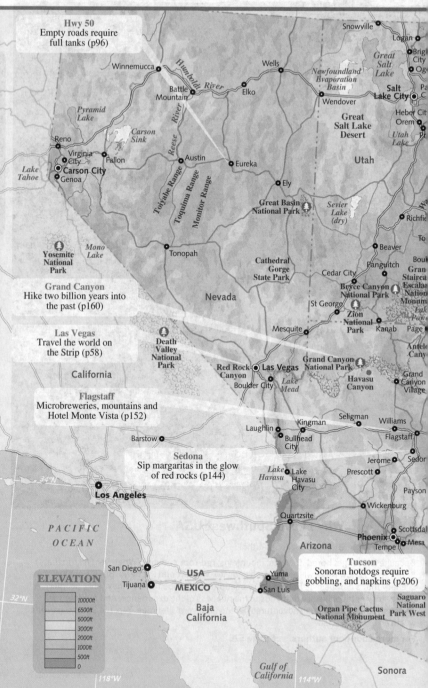

Hwy 50
Empty roads require full tanks (p96)

Snowville

Logan

Brig
City

Oge

Great Salt Lake

Salt Lake City

Pa
C

Winnemucca

Wells

Newfoundland Evaporation Basin

Heber Cit

Orem

Pr

Battle Mountain

Elko

Wendover

Humboldt River

Pyramid Lake

Carson Sink

Great Salt Lake Desert

Utah Lake

Reno

Reese River

Virginia City

Fallon

Austin

Eureka

Utah

Wa

Richfie

Carson City

Lake Tahoe

Genoa

Toiyabe Range

Toquima Range

Monitor Range

Ely

Sevier Lake (dry)

To

Great Basin National Park

Beaver

Yosemite National Park

Mono Lake

Tonopah

Cathedral Gorge State Park

Panguitch

Cedar City

Boul

**Gran
Stairca
Escala
Nation
Monum

*Lak
Pow

Grand Canyon
Hike two billion years into the past (p160)

Nevada

Bryce Canyon National Park

St George

Zion National Park

Kanab

Page

Las Vegas
Travel the world on the Strip (p58)

Death Valley National Park

Mesquite

Ante
Cany

California

Red Rock Canyon

Las Vegas

Grand Canyon National Park

Grand Canyon Village

Boulder City

Lake Mead

Havasu Canyon

Flagstaff
Microbreweries, mountains and Hotel Monte Vista (p152)

Seligman

Williams

Laughlin

Kingman

Flagstaff

Barstow

Bullhead City

Sedona
Sip margaritas in the glow of red rocks (p144)

Jerome

Sedor

Lake Havasu

Lake Havasu City

Prescott

Payson

34°N

Los Angeles

Wickenburg

Quartzsite

PACIFIC OCEAN

Scottsda

Phoenix

Mesa

Arizona

Tempe

ELEVATION

San Diego

USA

MEXICO

Yuma

Tucson
Sonoran hotdogs require gobbling, and napkins (p206)

Tijuana

San Luis

Saguaro National Park West

	10000ft
	6500ft
	5000ft
	3000ft
	2000ft
	1000ft
	500ft
	0

32°N

Baja California

Organ Pipe Cactus National Monument

Sonora

Gulf of California

118°W

114°W

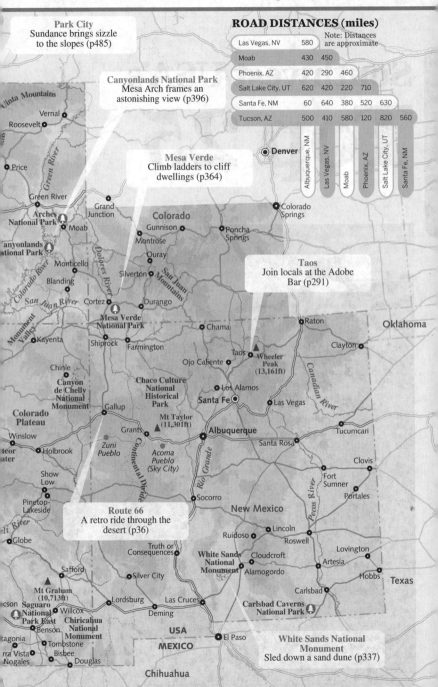

Park City
Sundance brings sizzle
to the slopes (p485)

Canyonlands National Park
Mesa Arch frames an
astonishing view (p396)

Mesa Verde
Climb ladders to cliff
dwellings (p364)

Taos
Join locals at the Adobe
Bar (p291)

Route 66
A retro ride through the
desert (p36)

**White Sands National
Monument**
Sled down a sand dune (p337)

ROAD DISTANCES (miles)

	Albuquerque, NM	Las Vegas, NV	Moab	Phoenix, AZ	Salt Lake City, UT	Santa Fe, NM
Las Vegas, NV	580					
Moab	430	450				
Phoenix, AZ	420	290	460			
Salt Lake City, UT	620	420	220	710		
Santa Fe, NM	60	640	380	520	630	
Tucson, AZ	500	410	580	120	820	560

Note: Distances
are approximate

Southwest USA's
Top 25

Grand Canyon National Park

1 The sheer immensity of the canyon (p160) is what grabs you first: it's a two-billion-year-old rip across the landscape that reveals the earth's geologic secrets with commanding authority. But it's Mother Nature's artistic touches – from sun-dappled ridges and crimson buttes to lush oases and a ribbonlike river – that hold your attention and demand your return. As Theodore Roosevelt said, this natural wonder is 'unparalleled throughout the rest of the world.'

Sedona

2 The beauty of the red rocks hits you on an elemental level. Yes, the jeep tours, crystal shops and chichi galleries add to the fun, but it's the crimson buttes – strange yet familiar – that make Sedona (p144) unique. Soak up the beauty by hiking to Airport Mesa, cycling beneath Bell Rock or sliding across Oak Creek. New Agers might tell you to seek out the vortexes, which allegedly radiate the earth's power, but even nonbelievers can appreciate the sacred nature of this breathtaking tableau.

RALPH LEE HOPKINS / GETTY IMAGES ©

CHEYENNE ROUSE / GETTY IMAGES ©

Las Vegas

3 As you awake from your in-flight nap – rested, content, ready for red-rock inspiration – here comes Vegas (p62) on the horizon, like a showgirl looking for trouble. As you leave the airport and glide under the neon of the Strip, she puts on a dazzling show: dancing fountains, a spewing volcano, the Eiffel Tower. But her most dangerous charms lie in the gambling dens – seductive lairs where the fresh-pumped air and bright colors share one goal: separating you from your money. Step away if you can for fine restaurants, Cirque du Soleil and a shark-filled reef.

Old West Towns of Arizona

4 If you judge an Old West town by the quality of its nickname, then Jerome, once known as the Wickedest Town in the West, and Tombstone, the Town Too Tough to Die, are the most fascinating spots in Arizona. While the moniker for Bisbee (p227) – Queen of the Copper Camps – isn't quite as intriguing, the town shares key traits with the others: a rough-and-tumble mining past, a remote location capping a scenic drive, and a quirky cast of entrepreneurial citizens putting their spin on galleries, B&Bs and restaurants. Top left: Bisbee

Santa Fe

5 Although Santa Fe (p257) is more than 400 years old, she's still kicking up her heels like a teenager. On Friday night, art lovers flock to Canyon Rd to gab with artists, sip wine and explore more than 100-plus galleries and shops. Art and history partner within a consortium of museums, with international crafts, Native American art, world-class collections and a history museum competing for attention. And oh, the food and shopping. With that crystal blue sky as a backdrop, dining and shopping on the Plaza isn't just satisfying, it's sublime.
Top right: New Mexico Museum of Art (p259)

Route 66

6 As you step up to the counter at the Snow Cap Drive-In in Seligman, Arizona, you know a prank is coming – a squirt of fake mustard or ridiculously incorrect change. And though it's all a bit hokey, you'd be disappointed if the owner forgot to 'get you'. It's these kitschy, down-home touches that make the Mother Road (p36) so memorable. Begging burros, the Wigwam Motel, the neon signs of Tucumcari – you gotta have something to break up the scrubby Southwest plains.
Bottom right: Hackberry (p200)

Angels Landing

7 The climb to Angels Landing in Zion National Park may be the best day hike in North America. The 2.2-mile trail (p448) crosses the Virgin River, hugs a towering cliffside, snakes through a narrow canyon and up Walter's Wiggles (a series of sharp switchbacks) then traverses a thin ridge – where steel chains and the encouragement of strangers are your only friends. Your reward after reaching the 5790ft summit? A lofty view of Zion Canyon. This hike offers beauty, adventure and the shared community of travelers who love the outdoors. Below: Walter's Wiggles

Moab

8 Moab (p401) is the mountain-biking capital of the world, where the desert slickrock surrounding the town makes a perfect 'sticky' surface for knobbly tires. Challenging trails ascend steep bluffs, twist through forests and slam over 4WD roads into the wilds of canyon country. And you'll surely redefine adventure after treading the roller-coaster rock face of the 12.7-mile Slickrock Bike Trail. There's a reason why some Moab hotels have showers for bikes. One trip and you'll be hooked. Top left: Cycling, Slickrock Bike Trail

WITOLD SKRYPCZAK / GETTY IMAGES ©

MICHAEL BENANAV / GETTY IMAGES ©

Mesa Verde National Park

9 You don't just walk into the past at Mesa Verde (p364), the site of 600 ancient cliff dwellings. You scramble up 10ft ladders, scale a 60ft rock face, and crawl through a 12ft tunnel. Yes, it's interactive exploring at its most low tech, but it's also one of the most exhilarating adventures in the Southwest. It's also a place to puzzle out the clues left by its former inhabitants – Ancestral Puebloans vacated the site in AD 1300 for reasons still not fully understood.

Flagstaff

10 Flagstaff (p152) is finally the perfect mountain town. For years this outdoorsy mecca – hiking, biking, skiing and stargazing – fell short of perfection due to the persistent blare of passing trains, up to 125 daily. Today, the horns have been silenced and travelers can finally enjoy a decent night's sleep. Well rested? Stay longer to walk the vibrant downtown, loaded with ecofriendly restaurants, indie coffee shops, genial breweries and atmospheric hotels. It's a liberal-minded place fueled by students at North Arizona University – and it's ready to share the fun. Bottom right: Hotel Monte Vista (p155)

Monument Valley & Navajo Nation

11 'In Beauty May I Walk' is a Navajo prayer. Beauty comes in many forms on the Navajo's sprawling reservation, but it makes its most famous appearance at Monument Valley (p192), a majestic cluster of rugged buttes and stubborn spires. Beauty swoops in on the wings of birds at Canyon de Chelly, a valley where farmers till the land near age-old cliff dwellings. Elsewhere, beauty is in connections, from the docent explaining Navajo clans to the cafe waiter offering a welcoming smile. Top: Canyon de Chelly (p193)

Taos

12 With its snowy peaks, crisp blue skies and steep-walled gorge, Taos (p291) makes a dazzling first impression. Its rebellious, slightly groovy temperament springs from a long line of local artists, writers and innovators. See for yourself on a tour of the eye-catching Earthships, or at one of the 80-plus art galleries, or with a drink at the quirky Adobe Bar. Ski slopes, hiking trails and white-water rapids lure outdoor adventurers while Taos Pueblo and diverse museums offer cultural distraction. One guarantee? You'll never get bored in Taos. Bottom: Taos' Earthships

JOHN & LISA MERRILL / GETTY IMAGES ©

RICHARD CUMMINS / GETTY IMAGES ©

Carlsbad Caverns National Park

13 As the elevator drops, it's hard to comprehend the ranger's words. Wait, what? We're plunging the length of the Empire State Building? I'm not sure that's such a great idea. But then the doors open, and look: there's a subterranean village (p349) down here. A snack bar, water fountains, restrooms and, most impressive, the 255ft-high Big Room where geologic wonders line a 2-mile path. But you're not the only one thinking it's cool – 250,000 Mexican free-tailed bats roost here from April to October, swooping out to feed at sunset.

Rafting

14 Rafting the Colorado River (p169) through the Grand Canyon is a once-in-a-lifetime journey, but rafting in the Southwest isn't limited to bucket-list expeditions that last for a week or more. For a mellow float, take a relaxing ride on the Green River outside Moab, or look for wildlife alongside the Colorado River in Utah's Westwater Canyon. For an adrenaline rush, smash through Class V rapids on the Rio Grande through the Taos Box. Low-key, scenic or wild – the rafts and rivers here are worth a ride.

Top right: Colorado River, Grand Canyon National Park

Tucson

15 Like so many towns in Arizona, Tucson (p206) sprawls. Yet it still manages to feel like a cohesive whole that's wonderfully eclectic. From the pedestrian-friendly anchor of 4th Ave, you can walk past indie clothing boutiques and live-music clubs that balance cowboy rock with East Coast punk. You can stop to eat at the place where the chimichanga originated, and then see a show at a Gothy burlesque club. With wheels, you can follow the saguaros to their namesake park then catch a sunset at Gates Pass. Conclude with a Sonoran hotdog, a taste of delicious excess that epitomizes the city's multicultural heritage.

RON AND PATTY THOMAS / GETTY IMAGES ©

White Sands National Monument

16 Frisbee on the dunes, colorful umbrellas in the sand, kids riding wind-blown swells – the only thing missing at this beach (p337) is the water. But you don't really mind its absence, not with 275 sq miles of gypsum draping the landscape with a hypnotic whiteness that rolls and rises across the southern New Mexico horizon. A 16-mile scenic drive loops past one-of-a-kind views, but to best get a handle on the place, full immersion is key: buy a disc at the gift store, trudge to the top of a dune, run a few steps and...wheee!

Salt Lake City

17 Big-city fun. Small-town charm. Proximity to outdoor adventure. Looking for a city with all three? To echo city founder Brigham Young: 'This is the place.' Just look around. Outdoorsy tourists and new residents are swooping in for world-class hiking, climbing and skiing. In the process they're infusing this Mormon enclave with rebel spirit. For decades the populace was like its streets: orderly and square, with the Mormon influence keeping change at bay. But no more. Today the city (p464) hums with bustling brewpubs, eclectic restaurants and a flourishing arts scene. Top right: Temple Square (p465)

Phoenix

18 Sometimes you just have to ask: what about me? Phoenix (p111) answers that question with a stylish grin. Golfers have their pick of more than 200 courses. Posh resorts cater to families, honeymooners and even dear old Fido. The spas are just as decadent, offering aquatic massages, citrusy facials and healing desert-clay wraps. Add in world-class museums, patio-dining extraordinaire, chichi shopping and more than 300 days of sunshine, and it's easy to condone a little selfishness. Bottom right: Spa, Scottsdale

Arches & Canyonlands National Parks

19 More than 2000 sandstone arches cluster within just 119 sq miles at Arches (p413), a cauldron of geologic wonders that includes a balanced rock, a swath of giant fins and a span that's emblazoned on Utah license plates. Just north is the stunning Canyonlands, a forbidding and beautiful maze of plateaus, mesas and canyons. How to understand the power of the landscape? As eco-warrior Edward Abbey has said, 'you can't see anything from the car.' So get out, breathe in and walk. Below: Arches National Park

Microbreweries

20 Local breweries are the center of the action in outpost towns such as Durango, Flagstaff and Moab. And though microbreweries (p537) are spread far and wide across the region, these watering holes share a few commonalities: convivial drinkers, flavorful craft brews and cavernous drinking rooms that smell of malt and adventure. And when it comes to memorable beer names, Wasatch Brew Pub & Brewery in Park City earns kudos for its Polygamy Porter tagline: Why Have Just One? Bottom: Wasatch Brew Pub (p491), Park City

Park City

21 Park City (p485), how'd you get to be so cool? Sure, you hosted events in the 2002 Winter Olympics, and you're home to the US Ski Team, but it's not just the snow sports. There's the Sundance Film Festival, which draws enough glitterati to keep the world abuzz. We're also digging the stylish restaurants; they serve fine cuisine but never take themselves too seriously. Maybe that's the key – it's a world-class destination comfortable with its small-town roots. Top: Wasatch Mountains, near Park City

Pueblos

22 Nineteen Indian pueblos are scattered across New Mexico. These adobe villages – often rising stories above the ground – offer a glimpse into the cultures of some of America's longest-running communities. Not all are tourist attractions, but several offer unique experiences that may be among your most memorable in the Southwest. Marvel at the mesa-top views at Acoma (p324), shop for jewelry at Zuni and immerse yourself in history at Taos Pueblo – where the fry bread at Tiwa Kitchen makes a tasty distraction. Bottom: Acoma Pueblo

DANITA DELIMONT / GETTY IMAGES ©

MINT IMAGES - DAVID SCHULTZ / GETTY IMAGES ©

Iwy 50: the Loneliest Road in America

23 So you want to drop off the grid? Are you sure? Test your resolve on this desolate strip of pavement that stretches across the white-hot belly of Nevada. The highway (p96) passes through a poetic assortment of tumbleweed towns following the route of the Overland Stagecoach, the Pony Express and the first transcontinental telephone line. Today, it looks like the backdrop for a David Lynch film, with scrappy ghost towns, hardscrabble saloons, singing sand dunes and ancient petroglyphs – keeping things more than a little off-kilter.

Native American Art

24 Native American art continues to thrive in the Southwest. While designs often have a ceremonial purpose or religious significance, the baskets, rugs and jewelry that are crafted today often put a fresh spin on the ancient traditions – in Phoenix's Heard Museum (p114), dedicated to Southwest cultures, you'll even see pottery emblazoned with a Harry Potter theme. From Hopi kachina dolls and Navajo rugs to Zuni jewelry and the baskets of the White Mountain Apaches, art is a window into the heart of the native Southwest peoples.

San Juan Mountains

25 Adventure lovers, welcome home. The San Juans (p371) are a steep, rugged playground renowned for mountain biking, hut-to-hut hiking and high-octane skiing. But it's not all about amped-up thrills in the towns lining US 550, also known as the San Juan Byway (or the Million Dollar Hwy between Ouray and Silverton). Both glitzy and gritty, secluded Telluride draws travelers to its outdoor festivals while Ouray lures 'em in with hot springs and ice climbing. In summer a historic train chugs into Silverton daily from Durango. Enjoy shimmering yellow aspens in the fall.

Need to Know

For more information, see Survival Guide (p543)

Currency
US dollar ($)

Language
English

Visas
Generally not required for stays up to 90 days for countries in the Visa Waiver Program. ESTA required (apply online in advance).

Money
ATMs widely available in cities and towns, less prevalent on Native American land. Credit cards accepted in most hotels and restaurants.

Cell Phones
Only GSM multiband models work in the US. Cell-phone reception can be nonexistent in remote or mountainous areas.

Time
Arizona, Colorado, New Mexico and Utah are on Mountain Time (GMT/UTC minus seven hours). Nevada is on Pacific Time (GMT/UTC minus eight hours). Arizona doesn't observe Daylight Savings Time (DST).

When to Go

Salt Lake City
GO Jan–Dec

Las Vegas
GO May–Sep

Grand Canyon
GO May–Sep

Santa Fe
GO May–Oct

Phoenix
GO Oct–May

Desert, dry climate
Warm to hot summers, mild winters
Mild to hot summers, cold winters

High Season
(Jun–Aug, Nov–Feb)

➡ Enjoy warm temperatures and sunny skies in New Mexico, Utah and northern Arizona.

➡ In winter hit the slopes in Arizona, Utah, New Mexico and Colorado or giddyap at southern Arizona dude ranches.

Shoulder Season
(Mar–May, Sep–Oct)

➡ In fall, check out colorful aspens and cottonwoods in southern Colorado and northern New Mexico.

➡ Cooler temperatures and lighter crowds on the Grand Canyon South Rim.

Low Season
(Nov–Feb, Jun–Aug)

➡ National parks in Utah and northern Arizona clear out as the snow arrives.

➡ In summer locals flee the heat in southern Arizona. Rates plummet at top resorts in Phoenix and Tucson.

Useful Websites

National Park Service (www.nps.gov) Current information about national parks.

Lonely Planet (www.lonelyplanet.com/usa/southwest) Summaries, travel news, links and traveler forum.

Recreation.gov (www.recreation.gov) Camping reservations on federally managed lands.

American Southwest (www.americansouthwest.net) Comprehensive site for national parks and natural landscapes.

Grand Canyon Association (www.grandcanyon.org) Online bookstore with helpful links.

Important Numbers

Country code	☎1
International access code	☎011
Emergency	☎911
National sexual assault hotline	☎800-656-4673
Statewide road conditions	☎511

Exchange Rates

Australia	A$1	$0.89
Canada	C$1	$0.91
Europe	€1	$1.28
Japan	¥100	$0.92
Mexico	10 pesos	$0.76
New Zealand	NZ$1	$0.82
UK	£1	$1.64

For current exchange rates see www.xe.com.

Daily Costs

Budget:
Less than $100

➡ Campgrounds and hostels: $18–$45

➡ Food at markets, *taquerías*, sidewalk vendors: $3–$10

➡ Bus, local shuttle: free to $5

Midrange:
$100–$250

➡ Mom-and-pop motels, low-priced chains: $50–$90

➡ Diners, good local restaurants: $10–$30

➡ Museums, national and state parks: $5–$25

➡ Car rental from $30 per day

Top End:
More than $250

➡ Boutique hotels, B&Bs, resorts, park lodges: from $170

➡ Upscale restaurants: $30–$75 plus wine

➡ Jeep tour, outdoor outfitter; top shows: from $90

➡ Rent a convertible: from $60 per day

Opening Hours

Opening hours vary throughout the year. Many attractions open longer in high season. We've provided high-season hours.

Banks 8:30am to 4:30pm Monday to Thursday, to 5:30pm Friday; some open 9am to 12:30pm Saturday

Bars 5pm to midnight, to 2am Friday and Saturday

Restaurants Breakfast 7am to 10:30am Monday to Friday, brunch 9am to 2pm Saturday and Sunday, lunch 11:30am to 2:30pm Monday to Friday, dinner 5pm to 9:30pm, later Friday and Saturday

Stores 10am to 6pm Monday to Saturday, noon to 5pm Sunday

Arriving in Southwest USA

McCarran International Airport (Las Vegas, NV, p553) Shuttles: $11 to the Strip. Available at exits seven to 13 by baggage claim in Terminal 1. Available on Level Zero in Terminal 3. Taxis: $17 to $20 to the Strip; 30 minutes in heavy traffic.

Sky Harbor International Airport (Phoenix, AZ, p553) Shuttles: $13 to downtown, $17 to Old Town Scottsdale. Taxis: $20 to $30 to downtown, $25 to $30 to Old Town Scottsdale.

Getting Around

Car This is the best option for travelers who want to leave urban areas to explore national parks and more remote areas. Drive on the right.

Train Amtrak can be slow due to frequent delays. Travel by train can be a scenic way to travel between Los Angeles and a few tourist-track cities in Arizona and New Mexico.

Bus Cheaper and slower than trains; can be a good option for travel to cities not serviced by Amtrak.

Shuttle Commercial outfitters provide guided tours and van transportation to many national parks and scenic areas from nearby cities.

Helicopter Fly round-trip between Las Vegas and Hualapai Reservation and Skywalk.

For much more on **getting around**, see p553

If You Like...

Geology

The Southwest's geologic story starts with oceans, sediment and uplift, continues with a continental collision and more oceans, then ends with wind, water and erosion.

Grand Canyon A 277-mile river cuts through two-billion-year-old rock with geologic secrets that are layered and revealed within a mile-high stack. (p160)

Chiricahua National Monument A rugged wonderland of rock chiseled by rain and wind into pinnacles, bridges and balanced rocks. (p230)

White Sands National Monument The white and chalky gypsum sand dunes are, simply put, mesmerizing. (p337)

Arches National Park Sweeping arcs of sandstone create windows on the snowy peaks and desert landscapes. (p413)

Carlsbad Caverns An 800ft plunge to a subterranean wonderland. (p349)

Kartchner Caverns Step into the cavern's pristine confines for an educational tour. (p231)

Bisti Badlands Wander past multicolored hoodoos and balanced rocks. (p317)

Wildlife

You'd be surprised how much wildlife you can see from your car – roadrunners, coyotes, elk, maybe a condor too.

Bird-watching Southern Arizona is the place to be in April, May and September. Migrating birds are attracted to its riparian forests. (p224)

Valles Caldera National Preserve Dormant crater of a supervolcano is home to New Mexico's largest elk herd. (p283)

Gila National Forest Javelina, bear and trout live in this remote and rugged corner of New Mexico. (p423)

California condors This prehistoric bird, recently on the verge of extinction, is making a comeback near the Vermilion Cliffs. (p164)

Arizona-Sonora Desert Museum Education-minded wildlife repository spotlights desert creatures. (p209)

Hiking

As you descend the South Kaibab Trail past two billion years of geologic history, it's easy to feel insignificant. The Southwest is a rambler's para-

dise, with scenery to satisfy every type of craving: mountain, riparian, desert and red rock.

Grand Canyon trails The Rim Trail offers inspiring views, but to really appreciate the age and immensity of the canyon you have to hike into its depths. (p160)

Rio Grande del Norte National Monument Hike down sheer cliffs in the Wild Rivers area to reach the confluence of the Rio Grande and the Red River in this new national monument. (p289)

Zion National Park Slot canyons, hidden pools and lofty scrambles make this stunner Utah's top national park for hiking. (p445)

Piestewa Peak Stroll past saguaros and scale a 2608ft peak in the scrubby heart of Phoenix. (p122)

Red-rock country Hike to vortexes in Sedona (p144), hoodoos in Bryce Canyon (p432) and slender spans in Arches (p413) and Canyonlands National Parks (p396).

Art

Petroglyphs etched onto rocks. Georgia O'Keeffe's cow-skull paintings. Black-and-white photographs by Ansel Adams. The

Southwest has inspired self-expression in all its forms. Today, former mining towns have re-emerged as artists communities, and you'll find galleries and studios lining 1800s-era main streets.

Santa Fe Sidewalk artisans, chichi galleries and sprawling museums are framed by crisp skies and the Sangre de Cristos. (p257)

Heard Museum The art, craftsmanship and culture of Southwestern tribes earn the spotlight at this engaging Phoenix museum. (p114)

Abiquiú (p285) and **Ghost Ranch** (p286) Captivating red-rock landscapes that Georgia O'Keeffe claimed as her own.

Bellagio Gallery of Fine Art Art? On the Las Vegas Strip? You betcha, and the exhibits here draw from top museums and collections. (p63)

Jerome This former mining town lures weekend warriors with artist cooperatives, an art walk and one-of-a-kind gift shops. (p142)

Regional Tastes

Up for a bit of culinary adventuring? Try some of the dishes associated with various cities, cultures and climates. Most of them are utterly delicious – and often quite decadent.

Green chile Sold at roadside stands statewide in September and October. Restaurants boast about their green-chile-topped burgers.

Navajo taco Chili-topped fry bread served at Navajo restaurants and trading posts. Dig in at the Cameron Trading Post. (p160)

PLAN YOUR TRIP IF YOU LIKE...

Top: Carlsbad Caverns National Park (p349)
Bottom: Roadrunner

Sonoran dog This Tucson specialty is a bacon-wrapped hot dog with cheese, pinto beans, salsa and more. Try one at El Guero. (p216)

Prickly pear margarita Bright-pink elixir infused with syrup from the prickly pear cactus. Enjoy one with a view at El Tovar. (p173)

Unique Historic Sights

Across the Southwest, dinosaurs left footprints, ancient civilizations left cliff dwellings and Apache warriors left lasting legacies. Many sights have barely changed over the centuries, making it easy to visualize how history unfolded.

Dinosaur National Monument Touch a 150-million-year-old fossil at one of the largest fossil beds in North America, discovered in 1909. (p501)

Mesa Verde Climb up to cliff dwellings that housed Ancestral Puebloans more than 700 years ago. (p364)

Fort Bowie Hike 1.5 miles into the past on your way to the fort at the center of the Apache Wars. (p231)

Picacho Peak State Park On April 15, 1862 this desolate place witnessed the westernmost battle of the Civil War. (p218)

Golden Spike National Historic Site Union Pacific Railroad and Central Pacific Railroad met here on May 10, 1869, completing the transcontinental railroad. (p479)

Water Adventures

Thank the big dams – Hoover, Glen Canyon and Parker – for the region's big lakes and their splashy activities. Hurtle over white water, paddle over ripples or slide through a plastic tube – there's something here to fit your speed.

Grand Canyon Rafting the Colorado through the Big Ditch is the Southwest's most thrilling, iconic expedition. (p169)

Pools and theme parks Las Vegas pools are playgrounds for adults; Phoenix water parks are ideal splash grounds for kids. (p74)

Big lakes Water-skiers zip across Lake Mead (p91) and houseboaters putter below crimson rocks on Lake Powell (p186).

Moab rivers The Colorado and Green Rivers offer rafting, canoeing and kayaking. (p404)

Fly-fishing at McPhee Lake This Dolores, CO, reservoir has the best catch ratio in the Southwest. (p370)

Old West

The legend of the Wild West has been America's grandest tale, capturing the imagination of writers, singers, filmmakers and travelers around the world.

Lincoln Billy the Kid's old stomping – and shooting – ground during the Lincoln County War. (p344)

Tombstone Famous for the Gunfight at the OK Corral, this dusty town is also home to Boothill Graveyard (p225) and the Bird Cage Theater (p226).

Whiskey Row This block of Victorian-era saloons has survived fires and filmmakers. (p136)

Virginia City Sip beer in the Bucket of Blood Saloon then stroll the streets of this National Historic Landmark, site of the Comstock Lode silver strike. (p105)

Steam train Channel the Old West on the steam-driven train that's chugged between Durango and Silverton for 125 years. (p359)

Different Cultures

Cowboys and miners followed on the heels of several vibrant cultures that had already laid claim to the region. Descendants of these early inhabitants (Native Americans, Spanish and Mexican settlers, and Mormons) still live in the region, giving the Southwest a multicultural flair evident in its art, food and festivals.

Hopi Reservation The past and present merge atop the Hopi's long-inhabited mesas, the center of their spiritual world. (p194)

Temple Square Trace the history of Mormon pioneers and their leaders on a 10-acre block in Salt Lake City. (p465)

National Hispanic Cultural Center Galleries and a stage spotlight Hispanic arts. (p245)

Pueblos Multilevel adobe villages, some up to 1000 years old, are home to a diverse array of Native American tribes in northern New Mexico. (p240)

Canyon de Chelly Learn about the history and traditions of the Navajo on a guided tour into this remote but stunning canyon. (p193)

Film Locations

From glowing red buttes to scrubby desert plains to the twinkling lights of Vegas, the landscape glows

Stegosaurus, Dinosaur Quarry (p501)

with undeniable cinematic appeal. It's simultaneously a place of refuge, unknown dangers and breathtaking beauty.

Monument Valley Stride John Wayne–tall beneath the iconic red monoliths that starred in seven of the Duke's beloved Westerns. (p192)

Las Vegas Bad boys and their hijinks brought Sin City back to the big screen in *Oceans Eleven* and *The Hangover.* (p62)

Moab and around Directors of *Thelma & Louise* and *127 Hours* shot their most dramatic scenes in nearby parks. (p401)

Butch Cassidy and the Sundance Kid Cassidy roamed southwestern Utah; Grafton ghost town is the site of the movie's bicycle scene. (p438)

Very Large Array Twenty-seven giant antenna dishes look to the stars in extraterrestrial-themed

movies such as *Contact* and *Cocoon.* (p325)

Wine & Microbrews

Celebrate your adventures with a post-workout toast at brewpubs, microbreweries and wineries scattered across the region.

Polygamy Porter Lip-smacking Utah microbrew with a catchy slogan: 'Why have just one?' Try one, or two, at the Wasatch Brew Pub. (p491)

Alpine Pedaler Hop on this 14-passenger bicycle and pedal to breweries in Flagstaff. (p158)

Verde Valley wine country Home to an inviting Arizona wine trail that winds past wineries and vineyards in Cottonwood, Jerome and Cornville. (p135)

San Juan Brewfest Hosted by the knobby-tired mountain town of Durango, CO. (p360)

Napoleon's More than 100 types of champagne? *Mais oui* at this 19th-century French theme bar. (p83)

Kitsch & Offbeat

There's a lot of empty space in the Southwest and this empty space draws the weird out of people: dinosaur sculptures, museums of the bizarre, and festivals that spotlight cannibals and desert creativity.

Route 66 This two-lane ode to Americana is dotted with wacky roadside attractions, especially in western Arizona. (p36)

Burning Man A temporary city in the Nevada desert attracts

61,000 for a week of self-expression and blowing sand. (p107)

Roswell, NM Did a UFO crash outside Roswell in 1947? A museum and a UFO festival explore whether the truth is out there. (p345)

Ogden Eccles Dinosaur Park Roadside dinosaurs at their kitschy, animatronic best. (p494)

Wacky museums View the death mask of John Dillinger in Bisbee, a prostitute's 'crib' in Tombstone and towering neon signs in Las Vegas.

Small Towns

The small towns of the Southwest may have been settled by ornery miners, greedy cattle barons and single-minded Mormon refugees, but today you'll find artist communities, outdoorsy outposts and a warm hello.

Bisbee One-time mining town which merges artsy, grungy and quirky with thoroughly engaging flair. (p227)

Torrey Mecca for outdoor lovers headed into Capital Reef National Park. Also home to pioneer buildings, a bad-movie festival and the fantastic Cafe Diablo. (p425)

Billy the Kid Highway Named for the outlaw, this scenic byway swoops past shoot-'em-up

Lincoln, Smokey Bear's Capitan and woodsy Ruidoso. (p39)

Ouray Hooray for Ouray, an ice-climber's paradise in winter and a haven for hikers in summer that sits beside the Million Dollar Hwy. (p377)

Wickenburg Channels the 1890s with an ice-cream parlor, an Old West museum, home-cooked-breakfast joints and several dude ranches on the range. (p134)

Spas & Resorts

When it comes to lavish resorts, the Southwest serves up everything except an oceanfront view.

Truth or Consequences Built over hot springs adjacent to Rio Grande, the bathtubs and pools here bubble soothing, hydro-healing warmth. (p327)

Ten Thousand Waves The soaking tubs at this intimate Japanese spa are tucked on a woodsy hillside. (p273)

Phoenix & Scottsdale Honeymooners, families, golfers – there's a resort for every type of traveler within a few miles of Camelback Rd.

Las Vegas Many four- and five-star hotels – Encore, Bellagio, Venetian – offer resortlike amenities. (p76)

Sheraton Wild Horse Pass Resort & Spa This resort on the Gila Indian Reservation

embraces its Native American heritage with style. (p125)

Shopping

High-quality Native American jewelry and crafts make shopping in the Southwest unique. Beautiful landscapes attract artists galore and their paintings make wonderful gifts. There's plenty of upscale shopping, but save five dollars for that kitschy key chain from Route 66.

Trading posts Scattered across the Southwest, these were the first go-to shops for Native American crafts.

Scottsdale Manolo up: we don't have malls in Scottsdale, we have promenades, commons and fashion squares. (p131)

Santa Fe boutiques Eclectic specialty stores dot downtown and 100-plus galleries hug Canyon Rd. (p278)

The Strip Over-the-top goes over-the-top at Vegas' designer-label malls: Crystals (p87) at City Center and the Shoppes at Palazzo. (p87)

Singing Wind Bookshop Indie bookstore has everything you'll ever want to read about the Southwest, and a whole lot more. (p232)

Month by Month

January

Start the New Year swooshing down mountain slopes in New Mexico, Utah and yes, even Arizona. Artsy events such as film festivals and poetry readings will turn your mind from the cold. Snowbirds keep warm in Phoenix and Yuma.

☆ Cowboy Poetry

Wranglers and ropers gather in Elko, NV, for a week of poetry readings and folklore performances. Started in 1985, this event has inspired cowboy poetry gatherings across the region.

🏃 Ice Climbing

Billed as 'The Biggest Ice Festival in North America,' this mid-January party offers chills and thrills with four days of climbing competitions, clinics and microbrew beer – all in Ouray, CO.

🎬 Sundance Film Festival

Hollywood moves to Park City in late January when aspiring filmmakers, actors and industry buffs gather for a week of cutting-edge films.

February

Wintery sports not your thing? Hit an urban center for indoor distractions such as shopping, gallery-hopping or attending the symphony. If your family wants to rope and ride on a dude ranch, now is the time to finalize reservations in southern Arizona.

🔒 Tucson Gem & Mineral Show

The largest mineral and gem show in the US is held over the second full weekend in February. More than 250 dealers sell jewelry, fossils, crafts and lots and lots of rocks. Lectures, seminars and a silent auction round out the weekend.

March

March is spring-break season in the US. Hordes of rowdy college students descend on Arizona's lakes while families head to the region's national parks. Lodging prices may jump in response. Skiers will want to enjoy their last runs in Telluride.

🏃 Spring Training

Major league baseball fans have it good in March. Arizona hosts the preseason Cactus League when some of the best pro teams play ball in Phoenix and Tucson.

👁 Wildflower-Viewing

Depending on rainfall, spring is wildflower season in the desert. Check www.desertusa.com for wildflower bloom reports at your favorite national and state parks.

April

Nature preserves lure birders, who scan for migrating favorites. Spring is also the season for outdoor art and music festivals. Runners might consider the Salt Lake City marathon.

☆✩ Native American Powwow

More than 3000 Native American dancers and singers from the US and Canada come together in late April in Albuquerque, NM, to compete at the Gathering of Nations Powwow. There's also an Indian market with more than 800 artists and craftspeople.

May

As the school year winds down, May is a good time to enjoy pleasant weather and lighter crowds at the Grand Canyon and other national parks. Southern Arizona starts to heat up, so get that shopping spree done before Phoenix starts to melt. Memorial Day weekend marks the start of summer fun.

🏃 Route 66 Fun Run

Classic cars, not joggers, 'run' down Route 66 between Seligman and Golden Shores in western Arizona in early May. Roadster enthusiasts can check out the cars, vans and buses at the Powerhouse Visitor Center parking lot in Kingman on Saturday afternoon.

☆✩ Cinco de Mayo

Mexico's 1862 victory over the French in the Battle of Puebla is celebrated on May 5 with parades, dances, music, arts and crafts, and street fairs. And lots of Mexican beer.

June

School is out! High season begins across most of the Southwest. Look for rodeos, and food and music festivals. Inner tubers can now get their float on.

☆✩ Utah Shakespearean Festival

The play's the thing in Cedar City, where visitors can enjoy a dramatic 'Shakesperience' with performances, literary seminars and educational backstage tours from mid-June to mid-October.

☆ Telluride Bluegrass Festival

In mid-June you can catch the high lonesome sounds of bluegrass in the beauty of mountain-flanked Telluride. Favorites such as Old Crow Medicine Show, Sam Bush and Emmylou Harris keep festivarians happy.

July

Summer is in full swing, with annual 4th of July celebrations reminding us that the season is almost halfway over. If you've always wanted to luxuriate in a fancy Phoenix spa, now's your chance. The 100°-plus heat drives away tourists, so it's a fantastic time to score awesome deals. Mountain bikers can hit the trails at ski resorts in Utah and Colorado.

☆✩ Independence Day

Cities and towns across the region celebrate America's birth with rodeos, music, parades and fireworks on the 4th of July. For something different, drive Route 66 to Oatman for the 4th of July sidewalk egg fry.

☆✩ UFO Festival

Held over the 4th of July weekend, this festival beams down on Roswell, NM, with an otherworldly costume parade, guest speakers and workshops.

☆✩ Spanish Market

This weekend festival draws huge crowds to Santa Fe in late July. More than 350 approved artists exhibit and sell handmade traditional Spanish Colonial arts and crafts, including small religious devotionals such as *retablos*, handcrafted furniture and metalwork.

August

This is the month to check out Native American culture, with art fairs, markets and ceremonial gatherings in several cities and towns. Popular parks such as the Grand Canyon will likely be booked up, but you can grab your tents and water jugs for dispersed camping in nearby national forests and on the Bureau of Land Management (BLM) acreage.

✨ Navajo Festival of Arts & Culture

Artists, dancers and story-tellers share the customs and history of the Diné in Flagstaff on a weekend in early August.

✨ Santa Fe Indian Market

Only the best get approved to show their work at Santa Fe's most famous festival, held the third week of August on the historic plaza. Wander past exhibits by more than 1100 artists from 220-plus tribes and pueblos.

☆ August Doin's – World's Oldest Continuous Rodeo

Steer wrestling and bar-rel racing are on tap the third weekend of August in Payson, where the annual rodeo has been held for 130 continuous years.

September

It's back to school for the kiddies, which means lighter crowds at the national parks. Fall is a particularly nice time for an overnight hike to the bottom of the Grand Canyon. Leaf-peepers may want to start planning fall drives in northern mountains.

✨ Burning Man

In 2013 more than 61,000 people attended this out-door celebration of self-expression known for its elaborate art displays, bar-ter system, blowing sand

and final burning of the man. This temporary city rises in the Nevada desert before Labor Day.

🍺 Beer Tasting

Mountain bikers, micro-brews, an outdoorsy town and a late-August weekend. The only thing missing is a beer festi... oh wait, there is one. The San Juan Brewfest in Durango serves samples from 50 mostly regional breweries.

October

Shimmering aspens bring road-trippers to Colorado and northern New Mexico for the annual fall show. Keep an eye out for goblins, ghouls and ghost tours as Halloween makes its annual peek-a-boo appearance on October 31.

✨ Sedona Arts Festival

This fine-art show, which has 125 artists exhibiting, overflows with jewelry, ceramics, glass and sculp-tures. It's in mid-October at Sedona's Red Rock High School.

✨ International Balloon Fiesta

Albuquerque, NM, hosts the world's biggest gather-ing of hot-air balloons. The daily mass liftoffs inspire childlike awe.

✨ Navajo Nation Fair

The country's largest Na-tive American fair, with a rodeo, a parade, dances,

songs, arts, crafts and food, is held in mid-October in Window Rock, AZ.

November

✨ Dia de los Muertos

Mexican communities honor dead ancestors on November 2 with costumed parades, sugar skulls, graveyard picnics, candle-light processions and fabu-lous altars.

✨ Festival of the Cranes

The Rocky Mountain Sand hill Crane spends the win-ter at Bosque del Apache National Wildlife Refuge. Mark the return of this red-crested bird with tours and workshops the weekend before Thanksgiving.

December

It's Christmas season in the Southwest, which means nativity pageants and holiday lights displays. It's also high season at resorts across the region, from Phoenix to ski towns.

✨ Festival of Lights

Some 6000 luminaries twinkle in Tlaquepaque Arts & Crafts Village in mid-December in Sedona, with Santa Claus and live music.

Itineraries

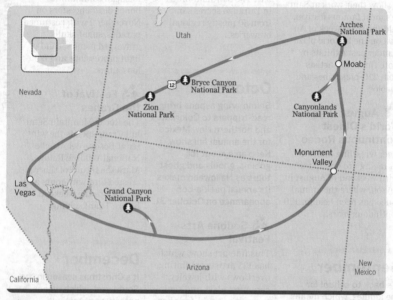

Vegas, Grand Canyon & Southern Utah Loop

2 WEEKS

Want the biggest bang for your buck, and for your two-week vacation? Drive this scenic loop, which swings past the Southwest's most famous city, canyon and scenery.

Start in **Las Vegas** and dedicate two days to traveling the world on the Strip. When you've soaked up enough decadence, head east to canyon country – **Grand Canyon** country, that is. Spend a couple of days exploring America's most famous park. For a once-in-a-lifetime experience, descend into the South Rim on a mule and spend the night at Phantom Ranch on the canyon floor.

From the Grand Canyon head northeast through **Monument Valley**, with scenery straight out of a Hollywood Western, to the national parks in Utah's southeast corner – they're some of the most visually stunning in the country. Hike the shape-shifting slot canyons of **Canyonlands National Park**, watch the sun set in **Arches National Park**, or mountain-bike sick slickrock outside **Moab**. Then drive Hwy 12, a spectacular stretch of pavement sweeping in **Bryce Canyon National Park**, followed by **Zion National Park** on Hwy 9. Continue west to I-15 and follow it south to Las Vegas.

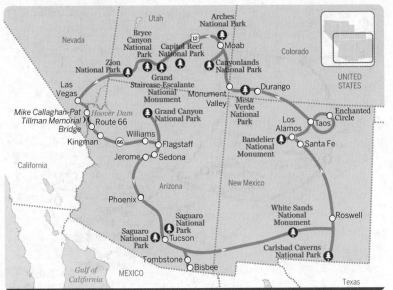

Grand Tour
4 WEEKS

Grab cowboy boots or walking shoes and get ready to ride. This trip covers geographic, historic and scenic highlights. If you're curious and outdoorsy, this trip is for you.

Roll the dice for two days on the **Las Vegas Strip** then cross the new **Mike Callaghan-Pat Tillman Memorial Bridge**. Be sure to ogle **Hoover Dam** as you swoop into Arizona. Next is **Route 66**, which chases trains and Burma-Shave signs as it unfurls between **Kingman** and **Williams**. Regroup in funky **Flagstaff** before venturing into **Grand Canyon National Park**, where a hike is a must-do. After three days, end the week among the red rocks of **Sedona.**

Head south for shabby-chic in **Jerome**. Drive to **Phoenix** for two days of shopping and museums. Next mellow out on 4th Ave, **Tucson**, study cacti at **Saguaro National Park** and fancy yourself a gunslinger in **Tombstone**. End the week in charming **Bisbee**.

Next is New Mexico: sled down sand dunes in **White Sands National Monument**, spend a day exploring caves at **Carlsbad Caverns National Park**, then head to **Roswell** to ponder its UFO mysteries. Spend two days in **Santa Fe**, a foodie haven and art-fiend magnet. Atomic-age secrets are revealed at **Los Alamos**, followed by laid-back musings of hippies and ski bums just north in **Taos**. Drive the luscious **Enchanted Circle** then chill with a microbrew and bike ride in **Durango**. Ponder the past inside cliff dwellings at **Mesa Verde National Park**, then be equally amazed by the towering red buttes at **Monument Valley**.

For the most stunning wilderness in the US, spend your last week in Utah's national parks. Use **Moab** as a base to visit **Canyonlands National Park** and **Arches National Park**. From Moab follow Hwy 12 back to Las Vegas, stopping at **Capitol Reef National Park**, **Grand Staircase-Escalante National Monument**, the spires of **Bryce Canyon National Park** and the sheer, red-rock walls at **Zion National Park**.

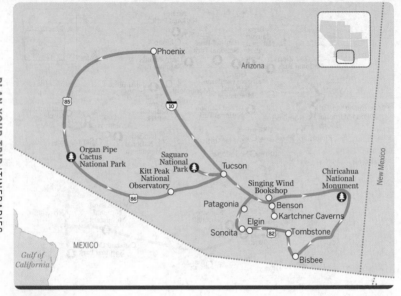

12 DAYS Southern Arizona

Explore the Old West and the New West on this crazy-eight loop that swings past legendary mining towns, art galleries and pretty wineries. There's plenty of desert scenery too.

This adventure starts in **Phoenix**, where a multitude of posh spas, top museums and upscale dining and shopping options will have you primed for exploring. Escape the urban crush with a long drive south on Hwy 85 to the lonely but rejuvenating **Organ Pipe Cactus National Park**. Hike, explore and relax for two days. From there, head along Hwy 85 to Hwy 86. Follow this lonely two-lane road east to lofty **Kitt Peak National Observatory**, site of 24 optical telescopes – the largest collection in the world. Take a tour or reserve a spot for nighttime stargazing.

Just northeast, laid-back **Tucson** is a pleasant place to chill out for a day or two. Indie shops line 4th Ave, and Congress St is the place to catch live music. Stop and smell the cacti in **Saguaro National Park** before spending the night in **Benson**, a good launchpad for the pristine **Kartchner Caverns** and the gloriously eclectic **Singing Wind Bookshop**. Wander the odd rock formations at **Chiricahua National Monument** then loop south on Hwys 191 and 181 for eye-catching galleries, great restaurants and an interesting mine tour in **Bisbee**. And you can't drive this far south without swinging by **Tombstone** for a reenactment of the shootout at the OK Corral. From Tombstone, Hwy 82 unfurls across sweeping grasslands, the horizon interrupted by scenic mountain ranges (known in these parts as sky islands).

Enjoy a day of wine-tasting in the villages of **Elgin** and **Sonoita** capped off with a slice of Elvis-inspired pizza in **Patagonia**. Close the loop with a drive west on I-10, swinging back through Tucson to grab a Sonoran dog before the return to Phoenix.

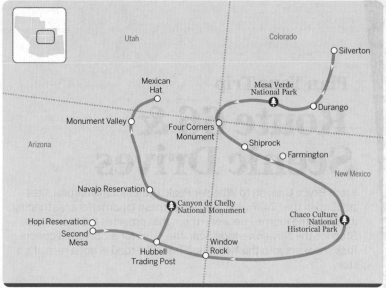

Four Corners – A Native American Journey

1 WEEK

Native American culture and history are in the spotlight on this trip though the Four Corners region, where Colorado, New Mexico, Arizona and Utah meet. Climb into cliff dwellings, buy a kachina (Hopi spirit doll) and drive through the sunset glory of Monument Valley.

Start in **Durango** and spend a day exploring the historic mining town. The next day, ride the narrow-gauge railway to **Silverton** and quaff a beer at a Durango microbrewery on your return. Climb ladders into the haunting ruins at **Mesa Verde National Park** before heading to Arizona, stopping on the way at the revamped **Four Corners Monument** – check out that snazzy new plaza – to snap a cheesy picture with your hands and feet in four different states.

As you head into New Mexico, ogle **Shiprock**, a stunning, ragged red-rock formation. Spend the night at a motel in nearby **Farmington** or enjoy a snooze inside Kokopelli's Cave, a B&B room 70ft underground – complete with hot tub. A dusty, rutted drive leads to the isolated **Chaco Culture National Historical Park**, an amazing architectural sight. Stay near **Window Rock**, the capital of the Navajo Reservation, and be sure to check out the namesake rock. The old-world **Hubbell Trading Post** was the reservation's lifeline when it was established in the 1870s. Detour (65 miles each way) to **Second Mesa**, the heart of the **Hopi Reservation**, where you will find artisans and the Hopi Cultural Center.

Next up? The relatively verdant **Canyon de Chelly National Monument**, an inhabited, cultivated canyon with hogans (traditional home of the Navajo) and sheep herds. Remember to breathe as you approach the otherworldly **Monument Valley**. Drive the 17-mile loop around the towering buttes then spend the night at the View Hotel; you'll want to spend time – a lot of time – gaping at the monuments from your balcony. Finish the trip with a drive north to **Mexican Hat** in Utah – trust us, you can't miss it.

Plan Your Trip

Route 66 & Scenic Drives

From Bryce Canyon to Wheeler Peak, eye-catching natural sites abound in the Southwest. And while these landmarks are stunning, it's often the journey between them that provides the memories. Stop for the Navajo vendor. Scan the skies for a California condor. Toss sneakers into the New Shoe Tree. The road is not a race, it's a story.

Buckle Up

Route 66

A classic journey through small-town America; 758 to 882 miles depending on segments driven.

Hwy 89 & 89A: Wickenburg to Sedona

Old West meets New West on this drive past dude ranches, mining towns, art galleries and stylish wineries; 120 miles.

Billy the Kid Highway

This outlaw loop shoots through Billy the Kid's old stomping grounds; 84 miles.

Hwy 12

See cinematic rock formations in the southern wilds of Utah, with delicious dining along the way; 124 miles.

Hwy 50: The Loneliest Road

This off-the-grid ramble mixes quirky, historic and lonesome in tumbleweed Nevada; 320 miles.

High Road to Taos

A picturesque mountain romp between Santa Fe and Taos; 85 miles.

Route 66

'Get your kitsch on Route 66' might be a better slogan for the scrubby stretch of Mother Road running through Arizona and New Mexico. Begging burros. Lumbering dinosaurs. A wigwam motel. It's a bit offbeat, but the folks along the way sure seem glad that you're stopping by.

Why Go?

History, scenery and the open road. This alluring combination is what makes a road trip on Route 66 so fun. From Topock, AZ, heading east, highlights include the begging burros of Oatman, the Route 66 Museum in Kingman and an eclectic general store in tiny Hackberry. Kitsch roars its dinosaury head at Grand Canyon Caverns (p200), luring you 21 stories underground for a tour and even an overnight stay. Burma-Shave signs spout amusing advice on the way to Seligman, a funny little village that greets travelers with retro motels, a roadkill cafe and a squirt of fake mustard at the Snow Cap Drive-In.

Next up is Williams, a railroad town lined with courtyard motels and brimming with small-town charm. Route 66 runs parallel to the train tracks through Flagstaff, passing the wonderful Museum Club (p158), a cabin-

Million Dollar Highway (p377)

like roadhouse where everyone's having fun. From here, must-sees include Meteor Crater and the 'Take it Easy' town of Winslow where there's a girl, my Lord, in a flatbed Ford, commemorating the Eagles song. Snap a photo of the famous corner then savor a spectacular dinner in the Turquoise Room (p233) at La Posada hotel. Finish Arizona in kitschy style with a snooze in a concrete tipi in Holbrook.

In New Mexico, Route 66 runs uninterrupted through Gallup, passing near the restored 1926 Spanish Colonial El Morro Theatre (p319) and right by the 1937 El Rancho hotel (p320) – John Wayne slept here!. Next up? Albuquerque, where a stop by Frontier for green-chile stew is a delicious pit stop. Then it's on to Santa Rosa's scuba-ready Blue Hole (p350) followed by the neon signs of Tucumcari, comforting reminders of civilization as dusk falls over the lonesome plains.

When to Go

The best time to travel Route 66 is from May to September, when the weather is warm and you'll be able to take advantage of more outdoor activities.

The Route (882 miles)

This journey starts in Topock, AZ, then continues northeast to Kingman. After crossing I-40, Route 66 travels east and cuts through Flagstaff, Winslow and Holbrook. In New Mexico, it passes through Gallup and Grants before entering Albuquerque, Santa Rosa and Tucumcari.

Time

Even if you're racing down the Mother Road, this trip will still take about two days because the route is primarily two lanes and there are lots of stoplights in the cities. If you have some time, it's best explored over the course of a week.

Hwy 89 & 89A: Wickenburg to Sedona

Hwy 89 and its sidekick Hwy 89A are familiar to Arizona road-trippers because they cross some of the most scenic and distinct regions in the center of the state. This section travels from Wickenburg over

Route 66 & Scenic Drives

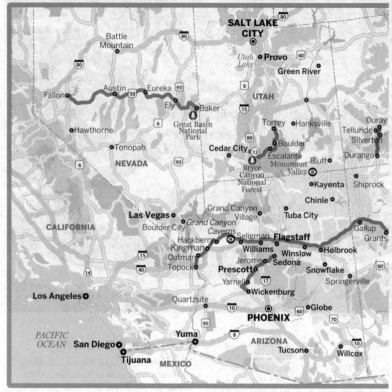

the Weaver and Mingus Mountains before rolling into Sedona.

Why Go?

This is our favorite drive in Arizona. It may not be the prettiest or the wildest, but the trip is infused with a palpable sense of the Old West, like you've slipped through the swinging doors of history. But the route's not stuck in the 19th century. Weekend art walks, a burgeoning wine trail, stylish indie shops and top-notch restaurants all add 21st-century spark.

For those interested in cowboy history, Wickenburg and its dude ranches are a good place to spend some time. Hwy 89 leaves town via Hwy 93 and soon tackles the Weaver Mountains, climbing 2500ft in 4 miles. The road levels out at mountain-topping Yarnell, 'where the desert breeze meets the mountain air,' then swoops easily past grassy buttes and grazing cattle in

the Peeples Valley. From here, highlights include Prescott's Whiskey Row, towering Thumb Butte and the unusual boulders at Granite Dells.

Follow Hwy 89A and hold on tight to your seat. This serpentine section of road brooks no distraction, clinging tight to the side of Mingus Mountain. If you dare, glance east for stunning views of the Verde Valley. The zigzagging road reaches epic proportions in Jerome, a former mining town cleaved into the side of Cleopatra Hill. Pull over for art galleries, tasting rooms, quirky inns and an unusually high number of ghosts. Hwy 89A then drops into Clarkdale, Tuzigoot National Monument (p143) and Old Town Cottonwood.

On the way to the red rocks of Sedona and Oak Creek Canyon, detour to wineries on Page Springs Rd or loop into town via the Red Rock Loop Rd past Cathedral Rock.

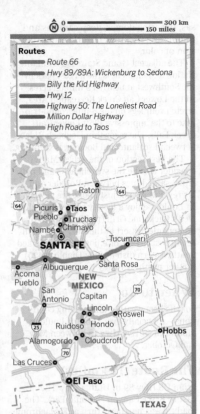

Routes
- Route 66
- Hwy 89/89A: Wickenburg to Sedona
- Billy the Kid Highway
- Hwy 12
- Highway 50: The Loneliest Road
- Million Dollar Highway
- High Road to Taos

When to Go

This route is best traveled in spring, summer and fall to avoid winter snow – although you might see a few flakes in the mountains in April. In the dead of summer, you won't want to linger in low-lying, toasty Wickenburg.

The Route (120 miles)

From Wickenburg, follow Hwy 93 to Hwy 89 then drive north to Prescott. North of town pick up Hwy 89A, following it to Sedona.

Time

This trip takes about a half-day to drive without stopping, assuming you don't get stuck behind a slow-moving recreational vehicle. To fully enjoy the scenery and towns, give yourself four to five days.

Billy the Kid Highway

Named for the controversial outlaw famous for his role in the Lincoln County War, the Billy the Kid National Scenic Byway loops around his old stomping grounds in the rugged mountains of Lincoln National Forest in central New Mexico.

Why Go?

This mountain-hugging loop provides a cool respite from the heat and hustle-bustle of Roswell and Alamogordo. For a primer on Billy the Kid, also known as William Bonney, head to Lincoln, population 50. This one-road hamlet was the focal point of the Lincoln County War, a bloody rivalry between two competing merchants and their gangs in the late 1870s. Billy took an active role in the conflict and evidence of his involvement can be seen today at the courthouse: a bullet hole left in the wall after he shot his way to freedom during a jailbreak. From here, you can visit Smokey Bear's grave in Capitan, hike up Sierra Blanca Peak, or take in a bit of horse racing at Ruidoso Downs.

When to Go

Although there's skiing in the area in winter, the best time for a scenic drive is summer, when average temperatures hover between 77°F (25°C) and 82°F (28°C). It's also a pleasant time to enjoy hiking and fly-fishing in the surrounding national forest.

The Route (84 miles)

From Roswell, follow Hwy 70 west to Hwy 380, following it through Hondo, Lincoln and Capitan before looping south on Hwy 48 to Ruidoso. Then take Hwy 70 east to close the loop at Hondo.

Detour

From Ruidoso, a spectacular 40-mile drive south travels through the Mescalero Apache Indian Reservation (p341), where you're still likely to see Native American cowboys riding the range, and on to Cloudcroft, home to a historic hilltop hotel and great hiking.

HISTORY OF ROUTE 66

Launched in 1926, Route 66 stretched from Chicago to Los Angeles, linking a ribbon of small towns and country byways as it rolled across eight states. The road gained notoriety during the Great Depression, when migrant farmers followed it west from the Dust Bowl across the Great Plains. Its nickname, 'Mother Road', first appeared in John Steinbeck's novel about the era, *The Grapes of Wrath*. Things got a bit more fun after World War II, when newfound prosperity prompted Americans to get behind the wheel and explore. Sadly, just as things got going, the Feds rolled out the interstate system, which eventually caused the Mother Road's demise. The very last town on Route 66 to be bypassed by an interstate was Arizona's very own Williams, in 1984.

Time

If you're not stopping, this route should take about half a day. To see the sights, including Cloudcroft, allow three days.

Hwy 12

Arguably Utah's most diverse and stunning drive, Hwy 12 winds through a remote and rugged canyon land, linking several national and state parks – and destination restaurants – in the state's red-rock center.

Why Go?

With its mesmerizing mix of crimson canyons, sprawling deserts, thick forests and lofty peaks, Hwy 12 works well for adventurous explorers. The trip kicks off at Bryce Canyon National Park where gold-and-crimson spires set the stage for the color-infused journey to come.

Traveling east, the first highlight is Kodachrome Basin State Park, home to petrified geysers and red, pink and white sandstone chimneys. Pass through tiny Escalante then pull over for Head of the Rocks Overlook which is atop Aquarius Plateau. From here, you'll see giant me-

sas, towering domes, deep canyons and undulating slickrock unfurl in an explosion of color.

The adjacent Grand Staircase-Escalante National Monument is the largest park in the Southwest at nearly 1.9 million acres. At the Lower Calf Creek Recreation Area, stretch your legs on the 6-mile round-trip hike to the impressive 126ft Lower Calf Creek Falls. The razor-thin Hogback Ridge, between Escalante and Boulder, is stunning.

The best section of the drive? Many consider it to be the switchbacks and petrified sand dunes between Boulder and Torrey. But it's not just about the views. In Boulder enjoy a locally sourced meal at Hell's Backbone Grill (p427) followed by homemade dessert at the Burr Trail Grill & Outpost (p427), or enjoy a flavor-packed Southwestern dish at Cafe Diablo (p425) further north in Torrey.

When to Go

For the best weather and driving conditions – especially over 11,000ft Boulder Mountain – drive Hwy 12 between May and October.

The Route (124 miles)

From US Hwy 89 in Utah, follow Hwy 12 east to Bryce Canyon National Park. The road takes a northerly turn at Kodachrome Basin State Park then continues to Torrey.

Time

Although the route could be driven in a few hours, two to three days will allow for a bit of exploration.

Highway 50: The Loneliest Road

Stretching east from Fallon, NV, to Great Basin National Park and the Nevada state line, remote Highway 50 follows some of America's most iconic routes – the Pony Express, the Overland Stagecoach and the Lincoln Highway – across the heart of the state.

Why Go?

Why would you drive the Loneliest Road in America? As mountaineer George Mallory said about Everest: 'Because it's there.' And yes, Mallory disappeared while attempting the feat, but the lesson still applies. You drive Highway 50 because something might just...happen. So point your ride toward Fallon, a former pioneer town now home to the US Navy's TOPGUN fighter-pilot school. From here, listen for the singing dunes at Sand Mountain Recreation Area (p96), then pull over and hike to the ruins of a Pony Express station.

Just east of Austin (population 192) look for petroglyphs, then yell 'Eureka!' for the tiny town that coughed up $40 million in silver in the 1800s. Next, check out the beehive-shaped buildings at Ward Charcoal Ovens State Historic Park (p97) near Ely, where charcoal was created to use in the silver smelters. End this trip with a 12-mile scenic drive up Wheeler Peak inside Great Basin National Park. After ascending 4000ft, the end-of-trip reward is an expansive view of the Great Basin Desert.

When To Go

Your best bet is summer. Sections of the road get hit with snow and rain in winter and early spring; in a few towns the road requires 4WD and chains during the worst conditions. Spring can be nice driving east, for views of snowcapped peaks.

The Route (320 miles)

From Fallon, NV – about 75 miles east of Lake Tahoe – follow Hwy 50 east to Austin, Eureka, Ely and then Great Basin National National Park, bordering Utah.

Time

The Loneliest Road can be driven in less than a day but to check out a few sites and the national park, allow for two or three.

Million Dollar Highway

Stretching between old Colorado mining towns Ouray and Silverton is one of the most gorgeous alpine drives in the US. Part of the 236-mile San Juan Skyway, this section of US 550 is known as the Million Dollar Highway, most likely because its roadbed is filled with ore.

Why Go?

Twenty-five miles of smooth, buttery pavement twists over three mountain passes, serving up views of Victorian homes, snowcapped peaks, mineshaft headframes and a gorge lined with rock. But the allure isn't just the beauty – there is also the thrill of driving. Hairpin turns, occasional rock slides and narrow, mountain-hugging pavement flip this Sunday-afternoon drive into a Nascar-worthy adventure.

Charming Ouray sits at nearly 7800ft, surrounded by lofty peaks. It also fronts the Uncompahgre Gorge, a steep, rocky canyon famous for its ice climbing. While here, take a hike or soak in the town's hot springs. From Ouray, the Million Dollar Hwy – completed in 1884 after three years of construction – hugs the side of the gorge, twisting past old mines that pock the mountainsides. Stay vigilant for the masochistic, spandex-clad cyclists pumping over the passes on the ribbon-thin road. In Silverton, step away from the car and enjoy the aspen-covered mountains or watch the steam-powered Durango & Silverton Narrow Gauge Railroad (p359)

ROADSIDE ODDITIES: ROUTE 66

Grand Canyon Caverns tour and underground motel room (p200) A guided tour 21 stories below the earth's surface loops past mummified bobcats, civil-defense supplies and an $800 motel room.

Burma-Shave signs Red-and-white ads from a bygone era line the roadside, offering tongue-in-cheek advice for life.

Seligman's Snow Cap Drive-In (p201) Juan Delgadillo opened this prankish burger joint and ice-cream shop in 1953.

Meteor Crater (p232) A fiery rock slammed into the earth 50,000 years ago, leaving a 550ft-deep pockmark that's nearly 1 mile across.

Holbrook's Wigwam Motel (p233) Concrete wigwams will flash you back to the 1950s with retro hickory logpole furniture.

chug into town. End with a microbrew in mountain-biking hot spot Durango.

When to Go

In winter, Red Mountain Pass south of Ouray may close if there is too much snow; at other times you may need chains. You might even see snow on the ground in summer, though it likely won't be on the road.

The Route (25 miles)

From Ouray, follow Hwy 550 south to Silverton.

Detour

The drive between Ouray and Telluride is 50 miles – if you take the paved route. If you're feeling adventurous and have a 4WD (don't try it otherwise), consider the un-paved 16-mile road over Imogene Pass. On this old mining road you'll cross streams, pass through alpine meadows, negotiate one of the state's highest passes and even drive by the old mine itself. But we should mention one thing: this 'shortcut' takes three hours. Still game? If so, plan to spend the night in mountain-flanked Telluride. The hiking here is superb and in summer there are tons of festivals.

Time

Travel time depends on who's traveling in front of you and weather conditions, but at a minimum allow yourself half a day to drive it. If you have time, spend two to three days exploring the region.

High Road to Taos

This picturesque byway in northern New Mexico links Santa Fe to Taos, rippling through a series of adobe villages and mountain-flanked vistas in and around the Truchas Peaks.

Why Go?

Santa Fe and Taos are well-known artists communities, lovely places brimming

with galleries, studios and museums that are framed by turquoise skies and lofty mountains. These two stunning cities are linked by an artistically pleasing byway: the High Road to Taos, a wandering route that climbs into the mountains.

In Nambé, hike to waterfalls or simply meditate at Lake Nambé. From here, the road leads north to picturesque Chimayo. Ponder the crutches left in the El Santuario de Chimayo (p287; the 'Lourdes of America') or admire fine weaving and wood carving in family-run galleries. Near Truchas, a village of galleries and century-old adobes, you'll find the High Road Marketplace (p288). This cooperative on SR 676 sells a variety of artwork by area artists.

Further up Hwy 76, original paintings and carvings remain in good condition inside the Church of San José de Gracia (p288), considered one of the finest surviving 18th-century churches in the USA. Next is the Picuris Pueblo (p289), once one of the most powerful pueblos in the region. This ride swoops through Peñasco, a gateway to the Pecos Wilderness. The town is also the home of the engagingly experimental Peñasco Theatre (p290). From here, follow Hwy 75 and 518 to Taos.

When to Go

The high season is summer, but you can catch blooms in spring and see changing leaves in the fall. Winter is not the best time to visit due to the mountains on this route.

The Route (85 miles)

From Santa Fe, take 84/285 north to Pojoaque and turn right on Hwy 503, toward Nambé. From Hwy 503, turn left onto Juan Medina Rd. Continue to Chimayo then drive north on Hwy 76. Turn right onto Hwy 75. At Hwy 518 turn left towards Taos.

Time

You can spend a half-day enjoying just the scenery, or two days checking out the history and galleries as well.

Plan Your Trip

Southwest USA Outdoors

The Southwest earns its reputation as the USA's land of adventure with a dizzying array of outdoor landscapes. Plunging canyons, lofty peaks, prickly deserts and red-rock formations galore. Where to start? Pick an outdoor town – Moab, Flagstaff, Durango – in a multisport region and launch yourself into the wild.

Hiking

Planning

It's always hiking season somewhere in the Southwest. When temperatures in Phoenix hit the 100s (about 40°C), cooler mountain trails beckon in Utah and New Mexico. When highland paths are blanketed in snow, southern Arizona provides balmy weather. Parks near St George in south-western Utah offer pleasant hiking possibilities well into midwinter. Of course, hardy and experienced backpackers can always don cross-country skis or snowshoes and head out for beautiful wintertime mountain treks.

More and more people venture further from their cars and into the wilds these days, so logistics isn't the only reason for careful planning. Some places cap the number of backpackers due to ecological sensitivity or limited facilities. Reservations are essential in highly visited areas such as the Grand Canyon and during the busy spring and fall months in more seasonal areas like Canyonlands National Park. Consider going to the less heavily visited Bryce Canyon National Park or Bureau of Land Management (BLM) lands and state parks, for a backpacking trip during busy months. Not only are they less restrictive than the national

Best Short Hikes to Big Views

South Kaibab Trail to Cedar Ridge South Rim, Grand Canyon National Park

Bright Angel Point Trail North Rim, Grand Canyon National Park

Angels Landing Zion National Park

Spider Rock Overlook Canyon de Chelly National Monument

Best Wildlife Watching

Birds Patagonia-Sonoita Creek Preserve and Ramsey Canyon Preserve, AZ

Elk Jemez Trail, Valles Caldera, New Mexico

Eagles Mesa Canyon near Durango, CO

Bears Gila National Forest, NM and southern Colorado mountains

Best Water Activities

Tubing Virgin River, Springdale, UT or Salt River, AZ

Rafting Rio Grande near Taos, NM; the Colorado and Green Rivers in Moab, UT; Colorado River through Grand Canyon National Park

Splashing Beneath Havasu Falls, Havasupai Reservation, Arizona

Fly fishing Dolores, Colorado

parks, but usually you can just show up and head out.

Backcountry areas are fragile and cannot support an inundation of human activity, especially when the activity is insensitive or careless. The key is to minimize your impact, leaving no trace of your visit and taking nothing but photographs and memories. To avoid erosion and damage, stay on main trails.

Safety

The climate is partly responsible for the epic nature of the Southwestern landscape. The weather is extraordinary in its unpredictability and sheer, pummeling force – from blazing sun to blinding blizzards and deadly flash floods. When there's too much water – the kind of amounts necessary to scour a slot canyon smooth – drownings can occur.

Too little water combined with unforgiving heat leads to crippling dehydration. A gallon (3.8L) of water per person per day is the recommended minimum in hot weather.

Sun protection (brimmed hats, dark glasses and sunblock) is vital to a desert hiker. Know your limitations, pace yourself accordingly and be realistic about your abilities and interests.

Solo travelers should always let someone know where they are going and how long they plan to be gone. At the very least, use sign-in boards at trailheads or ranger stations. Travelers looking for hiking companions can inquire or post notices at ranger stations, outdoors stores, campgrounds and hostels.

RIO GRANDE DEL NORTE NATIONAL MONUMENT

Want to be first on the scene? Then get your hiking boots and paddles to this new national monument (p289), established in 2013. Stretching north from Taos along the Rio Grande, it's a wildlife corridor offering top-notch hiking and white-water rafting, plus plenty of solitude. Picture a river-carved gorge, volcanic cones, wide plains, untrammeled trails...need we go on?

Mountain Biking & Cycling

As with hiking and backpacking, perfect cycling weather can be found at any time of year in different parts of the Southwest. Southern Arizona is a perfect winter destination; Tucson, considered a bicycle-friendly city, has many bike lanes and parks with bike trails. In spring and fall, Utah's Moab is an incredibly popular destination for mountain bikers who want to ride on scenic slickrock trails.

In southern Colorado, the area around Durango has numerous trails as do Crested Butte and the Four Corners area. Hut-to-hut biking is also available in the San Juan Mountains.

Cycling on the South Rim of the Grand Canyon is a fun way to explore the park. The development of the cyclist-friendly Greenway Trail and the opening of a bike-rental shop at the visitor center make this easier than ever.

Local bike shops in all major and many minor cities rent bikes and provide maps and information. Visitor information offices and chambers of commerce usually have brochures with detailed trail maps.

Black Canyon of the Gunnison National Park

A dark, narrow gash above the Gunnison River leads down a 2000ft-deep chasm that's as eerie as it is spectacular. Head to the 6-mile-long South Rim Rd, which takes you to 11 overlooks. To challenge your senses, cycle along the smooth pavement running parallel to the rim.

The nearest town to this area is Montrose. For more information contact **Black Canyon of the Gunnison National Park** (☑970-641-2337; www.nps.gov/blca; 7-day admission per vehicle/pedestrians & cyclists $15/7)

Carson National Forest

Carson contains an enormous network of mountain-bike and multiuse trails between Taos, Angel Fire and Picuris Peak. The nearest town is Taos, where you can rent bikes from **Gearing Up Bicycle Shop** (p295) for $35 per day. For more information contact **Carson National Forest** (☑575-758-6200; www.fs.usda.gov/carson).

Top: Grand Canyon National Park (p160)

Bottom: Rafting, Colorado River (p169)

JOHN ELK / GETTY IMAGES ©

NATIONAL PARKS & MONUMENTS

PARK	FEATURES	ACTIVITIES
Arches NP	sandstone arches, diverse geologic formations	hiking, camping, scenic drives
Black Canyon of the Gunnison NP	rugged deep canyon, ancient rocks	rock climbing, rafting, hiking, horseback riding
Bosque del Apache NWR	cottonwood forest along Rio Grande, cranes & geese in winter	birding
Bryce Canyon NP	eroded hillsides, red & orange hoodoos & pillars	camping, hiking, scenic drives, stargazing, cross-country skiing
Canyon de Chelly NM	ancient cliff dwellings, canyons, cliffs	guided hiking and backpacking, horseback riding, scenic overlooks
Canyonlands NP	sandstone formations at confluence of Green & Colorado Rivers	rafting, camping, mountain biking, backpacking
Capitol Reef NP	buckled sandstone cliffs along the Waterpocket Fold	mountain biking, hiking, camping, wilderness, solitude
Carlsbad Caverns NP	underground cave system, limestone formations, bat flight in evening	ranger-led walks, spelunking (experienced only), backpacking
Dinosaur NM	fossil beds along Yampa & Green Rivers, dinosaur fossils & exhibits	hiking, scenic drives, camping, rafting
Grand Canyon NP	canyon scenery, geologic record, remote wilderness, condors	rafting, hiking, camping, mountain biking, road cycling
Grand Staircase-Escalante NM	desert wilderness, mountains, canyons, wildlife	mountain biking, hiking, camping, solitude
Great Basin NP	desert mountains, canyons, wildlife, fall colors	hiking, camping
Mesa Verde NP	Ancestral Puebloan sites	hiking, cross-country skiing
Monument Valley Navajo Tribal Park	desert basin with sandstone pillars & buttes	scenic drive, guided tours, horseback riding
Natural Bridges NM	premier examples of stone architecture	hiking, camping, sightseeing
Organ Pipe Cactus NM	Sonoran Desert, cactus bloom May & Jun	cactus-viewing, scenic drives, mountain biking
Petrified Forest NP	Painted Desert, fossilized logs	scenic drives, backcountry hiking
Red Rock Canyon NCA	unique geologic features close to Las Vegas, waterfalls	scenic drives, hiking, rock climbing
Saguaro NP	desert slopes, giant saguaro, wildflowers, Gila woodpeckers, wildlife	cactus-viewing, hiking, camping
San Pedro Riparian NCA	forty miles of protected river habitats	birding, picnicking, fishing, horseback riding
Sunset Crater Volcano NM	dramatic volcanic landscape	hiking, sightseeing
White Sands NM	white sand dunes, specially adapted plants & animals	scenic drives, limited hiking, moonlight bicycle tours, walks
Zion NP	sandstone canyons, high mesas	hiking, camping, scenic drives, backpacking, rock climbing

NP – National Park; NWR – National Wildlife Refuge; NM – National Monument; NCA – National Conservation Area

Kaibab National Forest

One of the premier mountain-biking destinations in Arizona is the 800-plus-mile Arizona Trail. A popular section that's great for families is the Tusayan Bike Trail System, east of the town of Tusayan. It's a pretty easy ride mostly on an old logging road that cuts through the Kaibab National Forest to the South Rim of the Grand Canyon. If you ride or walk the trail into the park, you have to pay the $12 entrance fee that's good for seven days. For more information contact the **Tusayan Ranger Station** (☎928-638-2443; www.fs.usda.gov/kaibab).

Moab

Bikers from around the world come to pedal the steep slickrock trails and challenging 4WD roads winding through woods and into canyon country around Moab. The legendary Slickrock Trail is for experts only. This 12.7-mile, half-day loop will kick your butt. Intermediate riders can learn to ride slickrock on Klondike Bluffs Trail, a 15.6-mile round-trip that passes dinosaur tracks. For a family-friendly ride, try the 8-mile Bar-M Loop.

Full-suspension bikes start at around $43 a day at Rim Cyclery (p404) – check out its museum.

Visit www.go-utah.com/Moab/Biking and www.discovermoab.com/biking.htm for excellent Moab biking information. Both have loads of easy-to-access pictures, ratings and descriptions about specific trails.

Snow Sports

All five states offer snow sports on some level. Yes, you can even ski in Arizona. Southwestern Colorado is riddled with fabulous ski resorts, while the Lake Tahoe area reigns in Nevada. In New Mexico head to the steeps at Taos and in Utah the resorts outside Salt Lake City – the host of the 2002 Winter Olympic Games.

Downhill Skiing & Snowboarding

Endless vistas, blood-curdling chutes, sweet glades and ricocheting half-pipes: downhill skiing and boarding are epic, whether you're hitting fancy resorts or local haunts. The season lasts from late November to April, depending on where you are.

Salt Lake City and nearby towns hosted the 2002 Winter Olympics, and have rip-roaring routes to test your metal edges. Slopes are not crowded at Snowbasin, where the Olympic downhill races were held. The terrain here is, in turns, gentle and ultra-yikes. Nearby Alta is the quintessential Utah ski experience: unpretentious and packed with powder fields, gullies, chutes and glades.

New Mexico's Taos Ski Valley is easily one of the most challenging mountains in the US, while the Santa Fe ski area, just 15 miles outside town, allows you the chance to ski in the morning and shop Canyon Rd galleries come afternoon.

In Colorado you'll want to head to Telluride or Crested Butte. For extreme skiing, try Silverton. All three are wonderfully laid-back, old mining-turned-ski towns, offering the opportunity to ride some of the best powder in the state by day, then chill in some of the coolest old saloons at night. For something completely local and low-key, check out family-run Wolf Creek. For more details about where to ride powder in the state visit www.coloradoski.com. The website lists 'ski and stay' specials and provides resort details and snow reports.

The Lake Tahoe area, straddling the Nevada–California border, is home to nearly a dozen ski and snowboard resorts.

And then there's Arizona. Yes, you can ski. The snow isn't anything to write home about, but the novelty value may be. Head to the Arizona Snowbowl (p153) outside Flagstaff.

Ski areas generally have full resort amenities, including lessons and equipment rentals (although renting in nearby towns can be cheaper). Got kids? Don't leave them at home when you can stash them at ski school for a day. For 'ski, fly and stay' deals check out web consolidators and the ski areas' own websites.

ACCESSIBLE ADVENTURES

If you're disabled but want to run white water, canoe, rock climb or Nordic ski, head to Salt Lake City–based Splore (p405), which runs outdoor trips in the area.

Cross-Country & Backcountry Skiing

Backcountry and telemark skiing are joining cross-country skiing and snowshoeing as alternative ways to explore the untamed Southwestern terrain.

A must-ski for cross-country aficionados? Utah's serene Soldier Hollow (p496), which was the Nordic course used in the 2002 Winter Olympics. It's accessible to all skill levels.

The North and South Rims of the Grand Canyon both boast cross-country trails. The North Rim is much more remote. On the south side, you'll find several trails of easy to medium difficulty groomed and signed within the Kaibab National Forest.

The San Juan Hut Systems consist of a great series of shelters along a 60-mile route in Colorado from Telluride to Ouray – the scenery is fantastic.

Rock Climbing

Tolkien meets Dr Seuss in the Southwest, a surreal landscape filled with enormous blobs, spires, blobs on spires and soaring cliffs. While southern Utah seems to have the market cornered on rock climbing, the rest of the region isn't too shabby when it comes to the vertical scene. Just keep an eye on the thermometer – those rocks can really sizzle during summer. Help keep climbing spaces open by respecting access restrictions, whether they are set by landowners harried by loud louts or because of endangered, cliff-dwelling birds that need space and silence during nesting season.

Southwestern Utah's Snow Canyon State Park offers more than 150 bolted and sport routes. Zion Canyon has some of the most famous big-wall climbs in the country, including Moonlight Buttress, Prodigal Son, Touchstone and Space Shot. In southeastern Utah, awesome destinations include Moab and Indian Creek.

Otherwise, make a swift approach to central Arizona's Granite Mountain Wilderness, which attracts rock climbers in warmer months. Pack your rack for the rocky reaches of Taos Ski Valley or pack your picks for the Ouray Ice Park, where a 2-mile stretch of the Uncompahgre Gorge has become world renowned for its sublime ice formations. Chicks with Picks (p376) makes it easy for women to get involved.

Caving & Canyoneering

Much of the Southwest's most stunning beauty is out of sight, sitting below the earth's surface in serpentine corridors of stone that make up miles of canyons and

---

FLASH FLOODS: A DEADLY DESERT DANGER

Flash floods, which occur when large amounts of rain fall suddenly and quickly, are most common during the 'monsoon months' from mid-July to early September, but heavy precipitation in late winter can also cause these floods. They occur with little warning and reach a raging peak in minutes. Rainfall occurring miles away is funnelled from the surrounding mountains into a normally dry wash or canyon and a wall of water several feet high can appear seemingly out of nowhere. There are rarely warning signs – perhaps you'll see some distant rain clouds – but if you see a flash flood coming, the only recommendation is to reach higher ground as quickly as possible.

Floods carry a battering mixture of rocks and trees and can be extremely dangerous. A swiftly moving wall of water is much stronger than it appears; at only a foot high, it will easily knock over a strong adult. A 2ft-high flood sweeps away vehicles.

Heed local warnings and weather forecasts, especially during the monsoon season. Avoid camping in sandy washes and canyon bottoms, which are the likeliest spots for flash floods. Campers and hikers are not the only potential victims; every year foolhardy drivers driving across flooded roads are swept away. Flash floods usually subside fairly quickly. A road that is closed will often be passable later on the same day.

HORSEBACK RIDING

WHERE	WHAT	INFORMATION
Southern Arizona dude ranches	cowboy up in Old West country; most ranches close in summer due to the heat	www.azdra.com
Grand Canyon South Rim, AZ	low-key trips through Kaibab National Forest; campfire ride	www.apachestables.com
Santa Fe, NM	themed trail rides; sunsets	www.bishopslodge.com
Telluride, CO	all-season rides in the hills	www.ridewithroudy.com
Durango, CO	day rides and overnight camping in the Weminuche Wilderness	www.vallecitolakeoutfitter.com

caves. Visit Carlsbad Caverns National Park and not only will you feel swallowed whole by the planet, you'll be amply rewarded with a bejeweled trove of glistening, colorful formations.

Canyoneering adventures vary from pleasant day hikes to multiday technical climbing excursions. Longer trips may involve technical rock climbing, swimming across pools, shooting down waterfalls and camping. Many experienced canyoneers bring inflatable mattresses to float their backpacks and sleep on.

Arizona and Utah offer some of the best canyoneering anywhere. The first canyoneers in the huge gashes of the Colorado Plateau were Native Americans, whose abandoned cliff dwellings and artifacts mark their passage. See for yourself at the many-fingered Canyon de Chelly, which is accessible with a Navajo guide intimately familiar with its deep mazes.

The Grand Canyon is the mother of all canyoneering experiences, attracting thousands to its jaw-dropping vistas.

Then there are slot canyons, hundreds of feet deep and only a few feet wide. These must be negotiated during dry months because of the risk of deadly flash floods. Always check with the appropriate rangers for weather and safety information. The Paria Canyon, carved by a tributary of the Colorado River on the Arizona–Utah border, includes the amazing Buckskin Gulch, a 12-mile-long canyon, hundreds of feet deep and only 15ft wide for most of its length. Perhaps the best-known (though now highly commercialized) slot canyon is Antelope Canyon, near Lake Powell. You can also drive through magical Oak Creek Canyon, with dramatic red, orange and white cliffs sweetened with aromatic pine.

A nimbus of giant cottonwoods crowd the creek.

Zion National Park offers dozens of canyoneering experiences for day hikers and extreme adventurers, with weeping rocks, tiny grottoes, hanging gardens and majestic, towering walls.

Water Sports

Water in the desert? You betcha. In fact, few places in the US offer as much watery diversity as the Southwest. Bronco-busting rivers share the territory with enormous lakes and sweet trickles that open into great escapes. If you're into diving, check out Blue Hole (p350) near Santa Rosa, NM. It has an 81ft-deep artesian well; blue water leads into a 131ft-long submerged cavern.

Boating

Near the California–Arizona state line, a series of dammed lakes on the lower Colorado River is thronged with boaters year-round. Area marinas rent canoes, fishing boats, speedboats, water-skiing boats, Jet Skis and windsurfers. On the biggest

---

TOP SPOTS FOR WHITE-WATER RAFTING

Grand Canyon National Park AZ

Cataract Canyon Moab, UT

Westwater Canyon Moab, UT

Taos Box Pilar, NM

Animas River Durango, CO

RANKING RAPIDS

White-water rapids are rated on a class scale of I to V, with Class V being the wildest and Class I being nearly flat water. Most beginner trips take rafters on Class III rivers, which means you'll experience big rolling waves and some bumps along the way, but nothing super technical. In Class IV water you can expect to find short drops, big holes (meaning giant waves) and stronger undertows, making it a bit rougher if you get thrown off the boat. Class V rapids are the baddest of all and should only be attempted by strong swimmers with previous white-water experience – you should expect to be thrown out of the boat and perhaps sucked under for a few moments. You'll need to know what to do and not panic.

Tip: if you do get thrown, float through the rapid, lying on your back – your life vest will keep you afloat. Point your feet downriver and keep your toes up. Protect your head and neck with your arms (don't leave them loose or they can get caught in rocks).

The I to V class system applies to all Southwestern rivers except for the section of the Colorado River running through the Grand Canyon. This portion is just too wild to play by traditional rules and requires its own scale system – from Class I to Class X – to classify its 160-plus rapids. Many of the Grand's rapids are ranked Class V or higher; two merit a perfect 10.

lakes – especially Arizona's Lake Powell in the Glen Canyon National Recreation Area near the Grand Canyon and Lake Mead in the Lake Mead National Recreation Area near Las Vegas – houseboat rentals sleep six to 12 people and allow exploration of remote areas difficult to reach on foot.

The thrill of speed mixed with alcohol makes popular houseboat areas dangerous for kayakers and canoeists. If you're renting a big rig, take the same care with alcohol as you would when driving a car. Travel at a speed that is safe based on the conditions, which include the amount of traffic on the water and the likelihood of underwater hazards (more common when water levels drop). Carbon monoxide emitted by houseboat engines is a recently recognized threat. Colorless and odorless, the deadly gas is heavier than air and gathers at water level, creating dangerous conditions for swimmers and boaters. In recent years, several swimmers have drowned after being overcome by carbon monoxide.

Swimming & Tubing

Most lakes and many reservoirs in the Southwest allow swimmers. The exception will be high-traffic areas of the bigger lakes, where swimming is very dangerous due to the number of motorboats. It's not unusual to see locals swimming in rivers during the hot summer months, and tubing on creeks throughout the Southwest is popular. If you happen to see a bunch of people riding down a creek, and wish to join, just ask where they go for their tires – where there's tubing in this region there is usually an entrepreneur renting tubes from a van in the nearest parking lot. Swimming in lakes and rivers is generally free but if you are in a state or national park or on a reservoir, you may have to pay an entrance fee to enter the property itself.

Plan Your Trip

Travel with Children

The Southwest is a blast for families, with entertaining attractions for all ages: national parks, aquariums, zoos, science museums, theme parks, lively campgrounds, and hiking and biking in outrageously scenic places. Geology, history and wildlife are accessible in concrete ways at every turn, making the Southwest as educational as it is fun.

Southwest USA for Kids

Why visit the Southwest with your family? Because it's fun. Yes, the long drives, harsh desert landscape and oppressive summer heat can be daunting, but the rewards for families far outweigh the challenges. These rewards can be found in simple activities – splashing in the creek in New Mexico's Jemez Mountains, picnicking on the edge of the Grand Canyon in Arizona or watching an old Western on the big screen at Parry Lodge's Old Barn playhouse in Kanab, UT.

Education comes easy too, with docents at museums, rangers in the parks and interpretative signage along numerous trails. Most national parks in the Southwest have a free Junior Ranger Program, with activities geared to children. Ask for details at the visitor center or check the park website before your trip for details.

Lodging

Hotels and motels typically offer rooms with two beds, which are ideal for families. Some have cribs and rollaway beds, sometimes for a minimal fee (these are usually portable cribs which may not work for all children). Ask about suites, adjoining rooms and rooms with microwaves or refrigerators. Some hotels offer 'kids stay

Best Regions for Kids

Las Vegas & Nevada

Children are not allowed in the gaming areas, but roller coasters and animal exhibits cater to the kiddies. For outdoor adventure, head to Great Basin National Park or Valley of Fire State Park.

Arizona

Families can bike the Greenway near Grand Canyon Village and study saguaros outside Tucson. Water parks lure kids to Phoenix, while dude ranches, ghost towns and cliff dwellings are only a scenic drive away.

New Mexico

Swoop up a mountain on the Sandia Peak Tramway, drop into Carlsbad Caverns or scramble to the Gila Cliff Dwellings.

Southwestern Colorado

Chug through the San Juan Mountains on a historic steam train, relax in Ouray's hot springs or go hiking, fishing, or skiing in low-key Telluride.

Utah

National parks sprawl across swaths of red-rock country, offering fantastic hiking, biking and rafting. In the mountains, skis, alpine slides or snow tubes are equally fun.

free' programs for children up to 12, and sometimes up to 18 years old. Many B&Bs don't allow children, so ask before booking.

Full-scale resorts with kids programs, lovely grounds, full service and in-house babysitting can be found throughout the region, but particularly in Phoenix and, to a lesser degree, Tucson. For the real Western-immersion cowboy experience, complete with trail rides through the chamisa, cattle wrangling and beans 'n' corn bread round the fire, stay at a dude ranch, such as the Flying E Ranch (p134) in Wickenburg, AZ.

If it's late and you don't want surprises, head to a chain motel or hotel. Hilton is at the high end of the scale, while Motel 6 and Super 8, usually the least expensive, offer minimal services. Best Western is notoriously inconsistent. Your best bets are Holiday Inn Express, Fairfield Inn & Suites and Drury Inn & Suites, which usually offers free popcorn and soda in the evening.

Beautiful campsites perfect for car-camping are easily found in national and state forests, and parks throughout the region. It's flexible, cheap, and kids love it.

Dining

While the Southwest offers the usual fast-food suspects, you may find yourself driving mile after mile without a neon-lit fast-food joint anywhere. Be prepared with snacks and a cooler packed with picnic items. Many lodgings offer free breakfast.

Don't sacrifice a good meal or attractive ambience because you have kids. All but a handful of upscale restaurants welcome families and many provide crayons and children's menus. To avoid the dilemma of yet another fried meal, ubiquitous on kids' menus, simply ask for small adaptations to the standard menu, such as grilled chicken with no sauce, a side of steamed vegetables or rice with soy sauce.

Children's Highlights

Outdoor Adventure

➡ Explore Grand Canyon National Park in Arizona.

➡ Swoosh down a red-rock waterslide at Red Rock State Park in Oak Creek Canyon, AZ.

➡ Chug into the San Juan Mountains on the Durango & Silverton Narrow Gauge Railroad in Colorado. (p359)

➡ Ride horses at Ghost Ranch, New Mexico. (p286)

➡ Ski the slopes at Wolf Mountain in Utah. (p494)

Museums & Theme Parks

➡ Take in coyotes, cacti and demos at the Arizona-Sonora Desert Museum. (p209)

➡ Check out the Seismosaurus in the Age of Super Giants Hall at the Museum of Natural History & Science in Albuquerque, NM.

➡ Visit with local artists and scientists at the Santa Fe Children's Museum in New Mexico. (p262)

➡ Relive the rootin', tootin' Old West with gold panning, burro rides and shoot-outs at Rawhide Western Town & Steakhouse in Mesa, AZ. (p121)

➡ Have fun at Thanksgiving Point in Salt Lake City, UT, which has 55 acres of gardens, a petting farm, a movie theater and golf. (p473)

Wacky Attractions

➡ Take a photo of the burros that loiter in the middle of downtown Oatman, AZ.

➡ Marvel at the fake dinosaurs and mummified bobcats at Grand Canyon Caverns in Arizona – Route 66 kitsch at its best. (p200)

➡ Gaze at the world's most comprehensive collection of rattlesnake species at the Rattlesnake Museum in Albuquerque, NM. (p241)

➡ Discover the truth, and lots of wild theories, at the International UFO Museum & Research Center in Roswell, NM. (p345)

➡ Visit Mexican Hat in Utah – hey, that rock looks like a sombrero!

Native American Sites

➡ Climb four ladders to a ceremonial cave that combines education with adventure at Bandelier National Monument in New Mexico. (p284)

➡ Explore ancient living history inside Taos Pueblo, NM, a multistory pueblo village dating to the 1400s.

➡ Discover Acoma Pueblo in New Mexico, also known as Sky City, which sits atop a mesa 7000ft above sea level. (p324)

➡ Climb into cliff dwellings in Mesa Verde National Park in southwestern Colorado for hands-on learning at its best.

➡ Match the names to the butte – Mittens, Eagle Rock – at Monument Valley Navajo Tribal Park in Arizona. (p192)

Mesa Verde National Park (p364)

Transportation

Car-Seat Laws

Child-restraint laws vary by state and are subject to change. The requirements listed here may be incomplete or outdated and should be verified before departure.

Arizona law states that children under the age of five must be properly secured in a child-restraint device. Children five to seven years must use a booster seat unless they are 4ft 9in or taller. Children aged between eight and 15 years must wear a seat belt.

In Colorado, infants under the age of one year and weighing less than 20lb must be in a rear-facing infant seat in the back seat. Children aged one to three years and between 20lb and 40lb must be in a car seat. Four- to seven-year-olds must use a booster. Seat belts are required for children aged eight to 15, in both the front and back seats. Anyone 16 or older who is the driver or is a passenger in the front seat must wear a seat belt.

Nevada requires children aged five and under, and those weighing less than 60lb, to use a child seat.

In New Mexico, infants under one year must be restrained in a rear-facing infant seat in the back seat, children aged one to four or weighing less than 40lb must use a child safety seat, and five- and six-year-olds and kids weighing less than 60lb must use a booster seat.

Utah law requires children under eight years old or shorter than 4ft 9in to sit in a car seat; children who are not yet eight but who are 4ft 9in or taller can use the car seat belt alone.

Most car-rental agencies rent rear-facing car seats (for infants under one), forward-facing seats (for one to four years old or up to a certain height/weight) and boosters for $9 to $12 per day, but you must reserve these in advance. Clarify the type of seat when you make the reservation as each is suitable for specified ages and weights only.

Flying

Children under two can fly free on most airlines when sitting on a parent's lap. Remember to bring a copy of your child's birth certificate – if the airline asks for it and you don't have it, you won't be able to board. Ask about children's fares and reserve seats together in advance. Other passengers have no obligation to switch seats and sometimes have no qualms about refusing to do so. Southwest Airlines' open seating policy helps avoid this.

Planning
Planning Ahead

Perhaps the most difficult part of a family trip to this region will be deciding where

to go and avoiding the temptation to do too much. Distances are deceptive and any one state could easily fill a two-week family vacation. Choose a handful of primary destinations, such as major cities and national parks, to serve as the backbone of your trip. Then sit down with the map and connect these dots with a flexible driving plan.

Book rooms at the major destinations and make advance reservations for horseback rides, rafting trips, scenic train rides and educational programs or camps, but allow a couple of days between each to follow your fancy.

What to Bring

If you plan on hiking, you'll want a front baby carrier or a backpack with a built-in shade top. These can be purchased or rented from outfitters throughout the region. Older kids will need sturdy shoes and, for playing in streams, water sandals.

Other things you'll want to include are towels, rain gear, a snuggly fleece or heavy sweater (even in summer, desert nights can be cold; if you're camping, bring hats) and bug repellent. To avoid children's angst at sleeping in new places and to minimize concerns about bed configurations, bring a travel playpen/bed for infants, and sleeping bags for older children.

Regions at a Glance

Las Vegas works best for travelers seeking urban adventures, from fine dining to late-night club-hopping. Head to Nevada's mountains and deserts for outdoor thrills. Arizona offers nightlife and culture in Phoenix and Tucson, but the state earns bragging rights at the Grand Canyon. Its mining towns and Native American sites are also a draw, attracting cultural explorers to the deserts and mountains. New Mexico is a top spot for artists, but its chile-infused cuisine and Pueblo culture lure crowds too. Peak baggers and cyclists love Colorado's lofty San Juan Mountains while Mesa Verde wins praise from history buffs. And potheads love, well, all of it, man. Utah draws hikers and cyclists with red-rock parks, sandstone trails and delicate natural grace.

Las Vegas & Nevada

Nightlife
Dining
Offbeat

Casinos

The flashy casinos on the Las Vegas Strip are self-contained party caves where you can hold 'em, fold 'em, sip cocktails, shake your booty and watch contortionists and comedians.

Cornucopias

In Vegas, food is about both quantity and quality. Stretch your budget and your waistline at the ubiquitous buffets or dine like royalty at a chef-driven sanctuary.

Out There

From Hwy 50 (the Loneliest Road) to Hwy 375 (the Extraterrestrial Hwy), Nevada is wild and wacky. Caravan to the Black Rock Desert in September for Burning Man, a conflagration of self-expression.

p58

Arizona

Culture
Adventure
Scenery

Native Americans

From craftwork to cliff dwellings to sprawling reservations, tribal traditions flourish across the state. Tribal history and art are also unique.

Hiking & Rafting

Want to take it easy? Hike a desert interpretative trail or kayak a human-made lake. To ramp it up, head to canyon country to clamber over red rocks or bounce over white-capped rapids.

Canyons & Arches

After the continents collided, Mother Nature got involved with the decorating. Crumbly hoodoos, graceful spans, glowing buttes and crimson ridges – do you have batteries for the camera?

p109

56

PLAN YOUR TRIP REGIONS AT A GLANCE

New Mexico

Art
Culture
Food

Santa Fe

Vendors on the Plaza. Galleries on Canyon Rd. The Georgia O'Keeffe Museum. Art is all around us. The city itself is a living work of art, framed by mountains and crisp blue skies.

Pueblos

Nineteen Native American pueblos are clustered in the western and north-central regions of the state. They share similarities, but their histories, customs and craftwork are distinctly fascinating.

Red & Green

New Mexican food comes with a chile-infused twist. Red or green – chiles are not just for salsas but are an integral part of the whole. Pinto beans. Posole. *Carne adobada* (marinated pork chunks). Isn't this why you're here?

p235

Southwestern Colorado

Adventure
Scenery
History

Tracks & Racks

You got stuff? Skis, snowboards, bikes, fishing poles? Then start unpacking. The San Juan Mountains are a primo place to clear the roof racks and dirty up your gear.

Peaks & Ponderosas

When it comes to alpine scenery in the US, few places are more sublime than the San Juan Skyway: craggy peaks, steep canyons and glorious meadows. Just don't drive off the road.

Holes in the Rock

The Mesa Verde cliff dwellings offer a fascinating glimpse into the lives of the ancient Puebloans. Up in the San Juan Mountains, the mining past is recalled in Victorian homes and the abandoned claims.

p353

Utah

Outdoors
Ancient Sites
History

Room to Roam

When it comes to large, all-natural playgrounds, Utah takes the lead. From sprawling national parks to empty Bureau of Land Management (BLM) expanses, the place is ready-made for big adventures – often with a sandstone backdrop.

Rock On

Dinosaurs roamed the earth and trilobites swam the seas, leaving footprints and fossils as calling cards. Elsewhere, cliff dwellings and rock art remind us we weren't the first inhabitants.

Mormons

The Mormons arrived in the 1840s, building temples, streets, farms and communities. Get some background at Temple Sq in Salt Lake City, then explore downtown.

p385

On the Road

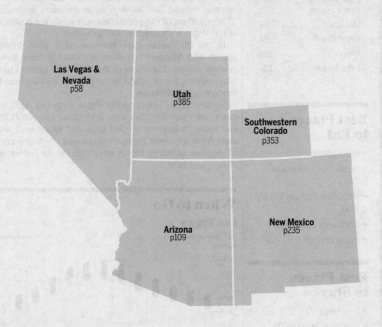

Las Vegas & Nevada

Best Places to Eat

➡ Raku (p81)

➡ Andiamo Steakhouse (p79)

➡ Old Granite Street Eatery (p103)

➡ Container Park (p81)

➡ Bouchon (p80)

Best Places to Stay

➡ Encore (p77)

➡ Golden Nugget (p77)

➡ Vdara (p76)

➡ Tropicana (p76)

➡ Tahoma Meadows B&B Cottages (p107)

Why Go?

From ski boots to stilettos, Nevada is a paradox, a place of contrasts and contradictions, which could make packing tricky. Vast, empty and the driest state in the nation, it's only recently coming into its own as an outdoors destination. Three-quarters of the population surrounds the desert star of Las Vegas, a glittering world unto itself.

In this libertarian state, freedom rules. Rural brothels coexist with Mormon churches, slot machines and Basque cowboy culture. The ghost of the Wild West persists in old silver-mining towns, while Vegas polishes its own brand of modern-day lawlessness.

Seeking thrills? Start on the Vegas Strip, but don't hesitate to step into Nevada's wide wilderness. The cobalt lakes and snowy mountains around Reno and Tahoe are a world away from the Great Basin expanses and the lonely curves of Highway 50, where fighter jets pierce the sky...or was that alien spacecraft?

When to Go

Las Vegas

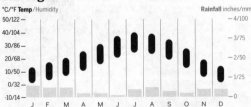

Apr–May Southern Nevada is balmy by day and pleasantly cool at night.

Dec Sin City deals in excess, yet it's never more buck wild than at Christmas.

Jun–Aug While temps soar, low season in Las Vegas means great hotel deals.

Vegas Planning

Planning a Vegas trip can be strangely counterintuitive, because Vegas refuses to play by the rules of most cities. First off: though parking is widely free, it's not time or cost-effective to rent a car unless you'll be doing a lot of day trips. Stick to taxis, walking and the good bus/monorail system while exploring the city. Dinner reservations are often necessary; note that many high-end restaurants, bars and nightclubs enforce a dress code.

DON'T MISS

Even if late nights, gambling and neon aren't your style, cut loose and cruise Las Vegas' infamous **Strip** for at least a day or two: chill out poolside at a 4-star resort, hit the clubs, and splurge on steak and martinis in Rat Pack style. While you're there, don't miss a **Cirque du Soleil show**.

In a state known for lovably bizarre small towns, the prize for the most unique is a toss-up between **Virginia City**, where the gold rush and the Wild West live on, or spirited **Elko**, with its Basque restaurants and cowboy poetry festival.

For incomparable outdoor bliss, **Lake Tahoe** offers fairy-tale ski slopes come winter and pristine beaches in summer. If untamed wilderness strikes your fancy, you'll want to get lost in the vast **Great Basin National Park** or brave the eerily deserted **US Highway 50**, nicknamed the 'Loneliest Road in America.'

Finally, the hottest place in Nevada is also home to one of the Southwest's most unique annual events: the **Burning Man** festival, where iconoclasts, rebels, artists, soul-seekers and the irrepressibly curious celebrate and create in the shimmering heat of the Black Rock Desert.

Tips for Drivers

➡ Most drivers speed across Nevada on interstate highways I-80 or I-15.

➡ It takes less than two hours to drive 125 miles from Primm, on the California state line, to Mesquite near the Utah border via I-15; the best overnight stop along this route is Las Vegas.

➡ When driving across the state on I-80, Winnemucca and Elko are the most interesting places to pull off for a night's sleep.

➡ Note that US Hwy 95 may be the quickest route between Las Vegas and Reno, but it's still a full day's drive without much to see or do along the way.

➡ For road conditions, call ☎ 877-687-6237 or visit www.nvroads.com.

TIME ZONE

Nevada is in the Pacific Time Zone (eight hours behind GMT). The exception is West Wendover, which is on Mountain Time.

Fast Facts

➡ **Population** 2.8 million

➡ **Area** 109,800 sq miles

➡ **Sales tax** 6.85%

➡ **Las Vegas to Grand Canyon, AZ** 275 miles, 4½ hours

➡ **Highest point** Boundary Peak (13,147ft)

➡ **Lowest point** Colorado River at California border (481ft)

You Have Company

Las Vegas has more hotel rooms than anywhere in the world.

Resources

➡ **Nevada Commission on Tourism** (☎ 800-638-2328; www.travelnevada.com)

➡ **Las Vegas Convention & Visitors Authority** (www.visitlasvegas.com)

➡ **VEGAS.com** (www.vegas.com)

➡ **Nevada Division of State Parks** (☎ 775-684-2770; www.parks.nv.gov)

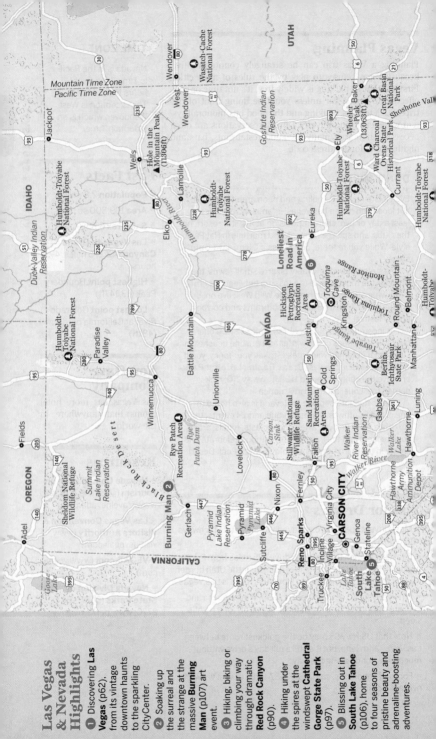

Las Vegas & Nevada Highlights

1 Discovering **Las Vegas** (p62), from its vintage downtown haunts to the sparkling CityCenter.

2 Soaking up the surreal and the strange at the massive **Burning Man** (p107) art event.

3 Hiking, biking or climbing your way through dramatic **Red Rock Canyon** (p90).

4 Hiking under the spires at the windswept **Cathedral Gorge State Park** (p97).

5 Blissing out in **South Lake Tahoe** (p106), home to four seasons of pristine beauty and adrenaline-boosting adventures.

⑥ Driving through the vast, naked landscape of the **Loneliest Road in America** (p96).

History

You ask, what history? It's true that, unlike the rest of the ruin-laden Southwest, traces of early history are scarce in the Silver State.

Contrary to Hollywood legend, there was much more at the dusty crossroads than a gambling parlor and some tumbleweeds the day mobster Ben 'Bugsy' Siegel rolled in and erected a glamorous tropical-themed casino, the Flamingo, under the searing sun.

In 1855, Mormon missionaries built and then abandoned a fort in the Las Vegas valley, where a natural-springs oasis flowed. In 1859 the richest vein of silver ever discovered in the USA, the Comstock Lode, was struck at Virginia City, which became the most notorious boomtown in the West. President Abraham Lincoln ratified Nevada as a state in 1864.

After the completion of the railroad, Las Vegas finally boomed in the 1920s. Gambling dens, brothels and saloons soon sprang up beside the tracks, especially in Las Vegas' infamous Block 16 red-light district, which survived Nevada's bans on gambling and the supposedly 'dry' years of Prohibition.

The legalization of gambling in 1931, and the sudden lessening of the divorce residency requirement to six weeks, guaranteed an influx of jet-setting divorcees and taxable tourist dollars that carried Vegas through the Great Depression. WWII brought a huge air-force base and big aerospace bucks, plus a paved highway to Los Angeles. Soon after, the Cold War justified the Nevada Test Site. Monthly above-ground atomic blasts shattered casino windows in Las Vegas, while the city's official 'Miss Atomic Bomb' beauty queen graced tourism campaigns.

A building spree sparked by the Flamingo in 1946 led to mob-backed tycoons upping the glitz ante at every turn. Big-name entertainers, like Frank Sinatra, Liberace and Sammy Davis Jr, arrived on stage at the same time as topless French showgirls in the 'Fabulous Fifties.'

Since then, Sin City continues to exist chiefly to satisfy the desires of visitors. Once North America's fastest-growing metropolitan area, the housing crisis hit residents here especially hard. Now among the glittering lights of the Strip, you'll spot unlit, vacant condominium towers that speak to a need for economic revival. Yet Vegas has always been a boom or bust kind of place, and if history is any judge, the city will double down and resume its winning streak in no time.

Nevada Scenic Routes

For those who love wild and lonely places, almost all of Nevada's back roads are scenic routes. Nicknamed the 'Loneliest Road in America,' famous Highway 50 bisects the state. Request the *Hwy 50 Survival Guide* from the Nevada Commission on Tourism (☑ 800-638-2328; www.travelnevada.com) to find out how to get a free souvenir pin and a signed certificate from the governor.

Plenty of shorter scenic routes abound in Nevada. The Las Vegas Strip is the USA's only nighttime scenic byway. Around Las Vegas, Red Rock Canyon, the Valley of Fire, Lake Mead and the Spring Mountains there are scenic drives too. Lesser-known routes around Nevada include the Ruby Mountains outside Elko; stairway-to-heaven Angel Lake Rd via Wells; and, near Reno, the Pyramid Lake Scenic Byway and the Mt Rose Hwy, which winds down to Lake Tahoe.

LAS VEGAS

POP 600,000 / ELEV 2000FT

Vegas remains the ultimate escape. Where else can you party in ancient Rome, get hitched at midnight, wake up in Egypt and brunch under the Eiffel Tower? Double down with the high rollers, browse couture or tacky souvenirs, sip a neon 3ft-high margarita or a frozen vodka martini from a bar made of ice – it's all here for the taking.

Ever notice that there are no clocks inside casinos? Vegas exists outside time, a sequence of never-ending buffets, ever-flowing drinks and adrenaline-fueled gaming tables. It's safe to say that the landscape is a constantly shifting paradox of boom and bust, where sophistication meets smut. Changeability is all part of the charm.

After exploring the dreamland of the Strip, head downtown to explore Vegas' nostalgic beginnings, a renaissance of indie shops and cocktail bars where local culture thrives, then detour to find intriguing museums that investigate Vegas' gangster, atomic-fueled past.

To get your bearings: the Strip, a stretch of Las Vegas Blvd, is the center of gravity in Sin City. Roughly 4 miles long, the Strip is capped by Circus Circus Las Vegas at the north end and Mandalay Bay at the south end near the airport. Whether walking or driving, distances on the Strip are deceiving.

Downtown, the original town center at the north end of Las Vegas Blvd, is incredibly compact and can be explored with a minimum of fuss. Its main drag is fun-loving Fremont St. McCarran International Airport is southeast of the Strip, off I-215.

◉ Sights

The action in Vegas centers on casinos, but there are some unique museums along with thrill rides and amusements guaranteed to get your adrenaline pumping.

◉ The Strip

Ever more spectacular, the world-famous (or rather, infamous) Strip is constantly reinventing itself. As the cliché goes, it's an adult Disneyland, dealing nonstop excitement. Every megaresort is an attraction in its own right, with plenty on offer besides gambling. The unwritten rule is that casino hotels are open for business 24/7/365.

Major tourist areas are safe. However, Las Vegas Blvd between downtown and the Strip gets shabby, along with a desolate area along Las Vegas Blvd known as the 'Naked City'.

Cosmopolitan CASINO
(Map p64; ☑702-698-7000; www.cosmopolitan-lasvegas.com; 3708 Las Vegas Blvd S; ◷24hr) Hipsters who thought they were too cool for Vegas finally have a place to go where they don't need irony to endure – or enjoy – the aesthetics of the Strip. Like the new Holly-

wood 'It' girl, the Cosmopolitan casino looks absolutely fabulous at all times. A steady stream of ingenues and entourages parade through the lobby, along with anyone else who adores contemporary art and design.

Bellagio CASINO
(Map p64; ☑888-987-6667; www.bellagio.com; 3600 Las Vegas Blvd S; ◷24hr) This posh European-style casino has high-limit gaming tables and 2400 slot machines with very comfortable seats but highly unfavorable odds. A stop on the World Poker Tour, Bellagio's tournament-worthy poker room offers 24-hour tableside food delivery for card sharks.

★CityCenter LANDMARK
(Map p64; www.citycenter.com; 3780 Las Vegas Blvd S) We've seen this symbiotic relationship before (think giant hotel anchored by a mall 'concept') but the way that this futuristic-feeling complex places a small galaxy of hypermodern, chichi hotels in orbit around the glitzy Crystals (p87) shopping center is a first. The uber-upscale spread includes the subdued, stylish Vdara (p76), the hush-hush opulent **Mandarin Oriental** (Map p64; www.mandarinoriental.com; 3752 Las Vegas Blvd S) and the dramatic architectural showpiece **Aria** (Map p64; ☑702-590-7111; www.aria.com; 3730 Las Vegas Blvd S; ◷24hr), which has a sophisticated casino providing a fitting backdrop to its many drop-dead gorgeous restaurants.

LAS VEGAS IN...

One Day

Cruise the infamous Strip, starting with a ride on the glass elevator at Mandalay Bay (p69) to rooftop lounge views. Tour the sites of New York–New York (p68) and take in the Eiffel Tower Experience (p66) before dining at Paris Las Vegas (p68). Peruse the conservatory and fountains at the Bellagio (p63) before ogling the frescoes and luxe Forum Shops of Caesars Palace (p67). Catch the exploding volcano at the Mirage (p67) and take a load off with a gondola ride at the Venetian (p66).

Two Days

Shake off the Rabelaisian fete of the night before at a brunch buffet. Indulge at a spa or chill poolside at your hotel before rolling west to Red Rock Canyon (p90) for a sunset hike. On the way back to town, enjoy a casual dinner off the Strip, then finish the night with live music and SoCal crowds at the Hard Rock (p73) or at a coveted Cirque du Soleil (p85) show.

Three Days

Spend the morning shopping and the afternoon at one of Vegas' quirky attractions, such as the Mob Museum (p71) or Burlesque Hall of Fame (p72). Stick around downtown after dark to see where it all began. Visit the trippy Fremont Street Experience (p71) before testing your blackjack luck at the Golden Nugget (p71). After midnight, let it ride on the Strip one last time, grabbing a bite or a nightcap at the Peppermill's Fireside Lounge (p82) before sunrise. Still have energy? The after-hours party at Drai's (p84) rages till past dawn.

The Strip

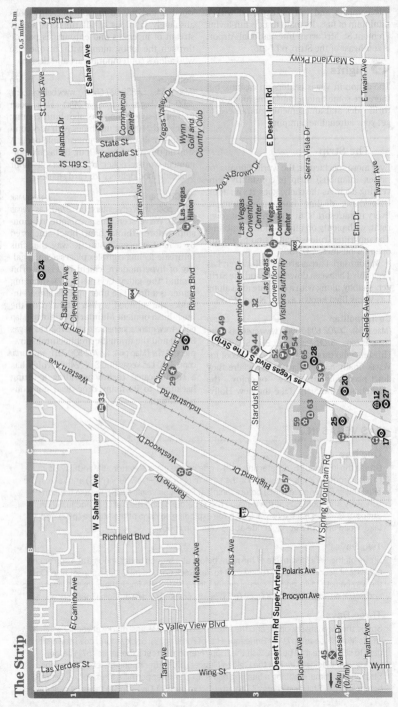

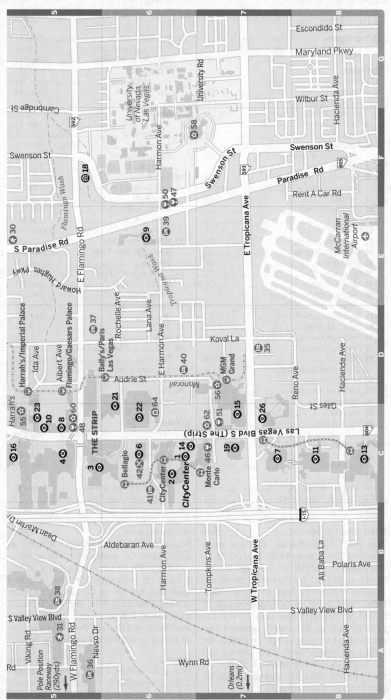

The Strip

Eiffel Tower Experience   TOWER

(Map p64; ☑888-727-4758; Paris Las Vegas; adult/child 12yr & under/family $10.50/7.50/32, after 7:15pm $15.50/10.50/47; ◎9:30am-12:30am Mon-Fri, to 1am Sat & Sun, weather permitting) Families and lovers flock to Vegas' ersatz Eiffel Tower, lining up for grated views from a wind-blown observation deck. It's cheaper to take a ride on the tower's elevators during the day, but nighttime panoramas of the Strip, with casinos' neon signs glowing and the Bellagio's dancing fountains lit up, are worth paying extra. Get free admission on your birthday with photo ID.

Mirage Volcano   LANDMARK

(Map p64; Mirage; ◎shows 8pm-midnight; ♿) **FREE** When the trademark artificial volcano erupts with a roar out of a 3-acre lagoon, it inevitably brings traffic on the Strip to a screeching halt. Be on the lookout for wisps of smoke escaping from the top, signaling that the fiery Polynesian-style inferno, with a soundtrack by a Grateful Dead drummer and an Indian tabla musician, is about to begin.

Venetian   CASINO

(Map p64; ☑702-414-1000; www.venetian.com; 3355 Las Vegas Blvd S; ◎24hr) The Venetian's regal 120,000-sq-ft casino has marble floors, hand-painted ceiling frescoes and 120 table games, including a high-limit lounge and an elegant no-smoking poker room, where women are especially welcome (unlike at many other poker rooms in town).

Palazzo Casino CASINO
(Map p64; ☎ 702-607-7777; www.palazzo.com; 3325 Las Vegas Blvd S; ⏰24hr) Slightly smaller than the Venetian, but equally lavish, this casino has the usual spread of high-limit table games and slot machines.

Caesars Palace CASINO
(Map p64; ☎ 702-731-7110; www.caesarspalace. com; 3570 Las Vegas Blvd S; ⏰24hr) Despite recent upgrades that have lent the once-gaudy Palace a more sophisticated air, some of the resort's original features from the swinging '60s have survived. Out front are the same spritzing fountains that daredevil Evil Knievel made famous when he jumped

them on a motorcycle on December 31, 1967 (and ended up with a shattered pelvis and a fractured skull. More than two decades later, his son Robby repeated the attempt – more successfully).

Mirage CASINO
(Map p64; ☎ 702-791-7111; www.mirage.com; 3400 Las Vegas Blvd S; ⏰24hr) Inside, the Mirage's paradisiacal setting is replete with a huge **rain forest atrium** under a conservatory dome filled with jungle foliage, meandering streams and soothing cascades. Woven into the tropical waterscape are scores of bromeliads enveloped in sunlight and fed by a computerized misting system. Tropical scents also waft through the hotel lobby, which features a 20,000-gallon saltwater **aquarium** filled with 60 species of coral-reef critters from Fiji to the Red Sea, including puffer fish, tangs and pygmy sharks.

New York–New York
CASINO

(Map p64; ☑702-740-6969; www.newyorknewyork.com; 3790 Las Vegas Blvd S; ⊙24hr) Opened in 1997, the mini-megalopolis of New York–New York features scaled-down replicas of the Big Apple's landmarks, such as the **Statue of Liberty** and a miniature **Brooklyn Bridge**, out front. Rising above are perspective-warping replicas of the Chrysler, Empire State and Ziggurat buildings. Wrapped around the hotel's flashy facade is the pièce de résistance: the **Big Apple roller coaster** (Map p64; 1 ride/day pass $14/25; ⊙11am-11pm Sun-Thu, 10:30am-midnight Fri & Sat; ⚐), with cars resembling NYC taxicabs.

Paris Las Vegas
CASINO

(Map p64; ☑702-946-7000; www.parislasvegas.com; 3655 Las Vegas Blvd S; ⊙24hr) Welcome to the City of Light, Vegas-style. This mini version of the French capital may not exude the true charm of Paris – it feels like a themed section of Disney World's Epcot – but efforts to emulate the city's great landmarks, including a 34-story Hotel de Ville replica and famous facades from the Paris Opera House and the Louvre, make it a fun stop for families and Francophiles who've yet to see the real thing.

Circus Circus
CASINO

(Map p64; ☑702-734-0410; www.circuscircus.com; 2880 Las Vegas Blvd S; ⊙24hr; ⚐) If you're cruising the bedraggled north Strip, don't overlook Circus Circus. Granted, it's pretty hard to miss, what with the enormous clown-shaped marquee and tent-shaped casino under a gaudily striped big top. From the outside, this sprawling resort looks pretty cheesy – and it *is*. It's also overrun by kids, baby strollers and hilariously immature adults.

Excalibur
CASINO

(Map p64; ☑702-597-7777; www.excalibur.com; 3850 Las Vegas Blvd S; ⊙24hr) This medieval caricature, complete with crayon-colored towers and a faux drawbridge, epitomizes gaudy Vegas. Inside the mock castle, casino walls are hung with coats of arms and cheap stained-glass imitations depicting valiant knights and lovely damsels. Buried in the Fun Dungeon arcade are Ye Olde carnival games such as skee-ball and joystick joys. The **Tournament of Kings** dinner show is a demolition derby with hooves and sticky fingers. Parents beware: this place looks more child friendly than it actually is.

Flamingo
CASINO

(Map p64; ☑702-733-3111; www.flamingolasvegas.com; 3555 Las Vegas Blvd S; ⊙24hr) In 1946 the Flamingo was the talk of the town. Its original owners – all members of the East Coast mafia – shelled out millions to build this unprecedented tropical gaming oasis in the desert. It was prime gangster Americana, initially managed by the infamous mobster Benjamin 'Bugsy' Siegel, who named it after his girlfriend, dancer Virginia Hill (nicknamed 'the Flamingo' for her red hair and long legs).

Flamingo Wildlife Habitat
GARDENS

(Map p64; ☑702-733-3349; 3555 Las Vegas Blvd S, Flamingo; ⊙8am-dusk, pelican feedings 8am & 2:30pm; ⚐) **FREE** Slip away from the madness to the Flamingo's wildlife habitat, out behind the Flamingo casino. Over a dozen acres of pools, gardens, waterfalls and waterways are filled with swans, exotic birds and ornamental koi (carp). Here Chilean flamingos and African penguins wander

---

ⓘ GAMBLER'S SURVIVAL GUIDE

➜ The house always wins – eventually. Except for poker, all casino games pit the player against the house, which always has a statistical edge. Think of gambling only as entertainment – for which you do pay a fee.

➜ Always sign up for free player clubs at the casinos – they're located at the information desk on the casino floor.

➜ On a budget? Drink free cocktails while you're gambling and hit the buffets at lunch – you probably won't need to eat much the rest of the day.

➜ Take advantage of the introductory lessons in poker, blackjack and craps offered at some casinos.

➜ Don't be afraid to ask the dealer for advice on strategy or odds.

➜ If you're winning, it's polite to give your dealer a 'toke' (tip).

➜ As for the famous saying, 'what happens in Vegas stays in Vegas,' it's often true – especially in regard to your cash.

LAS VEGAS FOR CHILDREN

Look past the smoke and glitter and you will notice a range of family-friendly attractions and activities. Most casinos have virtual-reality and video game arcades. At New York–New York, a roller coaster shoots out of a fake Big Apple skyline, while Circus Circus has the **Adventuredome** (p74) theme park and free acrobat shows. Teens will get a thrill from the **Stratosphere Tower** (p74) and its adrenaline-pumping rides. Cirque du Soleil's show Mystère welcomes all-ages audiences, while the shows Kà, Zarkana, Michael Jackson ONE and the Beatles LOVE can be fun for children ages five and up. For an educational experience, make time to head out to the **Springs Preserve** (p74), also home of the Nevada State Museum, or the hands-on **Discovery Children's Museum** (p73) in Symphony Park. Mandalay Bay's walk-through **Shark Reef Aquarium** (p69) is entertaining,

around, and palm trees and jungle plants flourish in the middle of the desert.

Luxor
CASINO

(Map p64; ☑ 702-262-4000; www.luxor.com; 3900 Las Vegas Blvd S; ☻24hr) Named after Egypt's splendid ancient city on the east bank of the Nile, the landmark Luxor once had the biggest wow factor on the south Strip. While the theme easily could have produced a pyramid of gaudiness, instead it resulted in a relatively refined shrine to Egyptian art, architecture and antiquities. Some of the more outrageous kitsch has gone the way of the pharaohs, though – in efforts to modernize, the Luxor was 'de-themed' some years ago.

Mandalay Bay
CASINO

(Map p64; ☑ 702-632-7777; www.mandalay-bay.com; 3950 Las Vegas Blvd S; ☻24hr) The 1950s-era Hacienda resort was imploded on New Year's Eve 1996 to clear the way for Mandalay Bay. This casino resort's upscale tropical theme may be subtle, but its grand opening – during which Jim Belushi, Dan Aykroyd and John Goodman cruised through the front doors on motorcycles – certainly wasn't. Today, a Harley-Davidson crew might look out of place in the regal ivory-hued lobby or on the swish casino floor.

Not trying to be any one fantasy, posh Mandalay Bay's standout attractions are many, and include the multilevel **Shark Reef Aquarium** (Map p64; ☑ 702-632-4555; www.sharkreef.com; adult/child 5-12yr $18/12; ☻10am-10pm daily late May–early Sep, 10am-8pm Sun-Thu, to 10pm Fri & Sat early Sep–late May, last admission 1hr before closing; ☑), a walk-through aquarium where overarching windows reveal thousands of tropical fish and a shallow pool that lets you pet pint-sized sharks. Down the resort's romantically lit passageways lie a pair of top-tier spas. World-class chefs have also staked out claims at M-Bay,

including atop one of the gold-tinted hotel towers.

Eleven acres, 2700 tons of imported California sand, 6ft waves in a 1.6-million-gallon wave pool...at **Mandalay Bay Beach**, kids float along the lazy river on inner tubes and surf competitions are held on artificial waves. When the stress of gambling in the air-conditioned beachside casino becomes too much, retire to a rooftop cabana villa or unwind at Moorea Beach Club, where sultry topless sunbathing happens in summer.

Wynn & Encore Casinos
CASINO

(Map p64; ☑ 702-770-7000; www.wynnlasvegas.com; 3131 S Las Vegas Blvd; ☻24hr) Inside the Wynn's elegant, sprawling casino is a popular poker room that lures pros around the clock. Not far away are slot machines from a penny up to $5000 per pull, a classy race and sports book, and a full spread of table games (mostly high minimum bets), including seasonal poolside blackjack by the cabana bar. Neighboring Encore's casino looks like a carbon copy of Wynn's, with outdoor casino tables standing ready in summer next to the resort's swimming pool.

MGM Grand
CASINO

(Map p64; ☑ 702-891-1111; www.mgmgrand.com; 3799 Las Vegas Blvd S; ☻24hr) Owned by movie company Metro-Goldwyn-Mayer, the MGM Grand liberally borrows Hollywood themes. Check out the casino resort's Strip-side entrance, where flashing LED screens and computerized fountains add extra theatrics to the 100,000lb, 45ft-tall bronze lion statue – naturally, it's the largest bronze statue in the country. Star-worthy 'Maximum Vegas' attractions include Cirque du Soleil's martial-arts-inspired spectacular Kà (p86) and the massive **MGM Grand Garden Arena** (Map p64; ☑ 877-880-0880; www.mgmgrand.com/entertainment; ticket prices vary; ☻box office 9am–

TOP POKER HOT SPOTS

With the rules of Texas Hold'em a frequent conversation starter these days, it's obvious poker is the hottest game in town.

Wynn Las Vegas (p69) Vegas' most posh poker room.

Bellagio (p63) World Poker Tour stop.

Golden Nugget Classy carpet joint with nonsmoking tables.

Hard Rock (p73) Poker lounge with bottle service, iPod docking stations and free lessons lure in the young and the hip.

8:30pm), which stages championship boxing and mega concerts by pop stars.

Treasure Island Casino CASINO
(Map p64; Treasure Island; ⏰24hr) TI's extralarge, always-busy casino is less wholesome than it once was: one-armed Playboy bandits await where playful pirates, plastic doubloons and chests full 'o' booty once reigned. Slot machines and gaming tables are tightly grouped, but no one seems to mind – the place is relentlessly packed.

Tropicana CASINO
(Map p64; ☎800-462-8767; www.troplv.com; 3801 Las Vegas Blvd S; ⏰24hr) Open since 1957, the Trop has had half a century to sully its shine, lose its crowds and go the way of the Dunes and the Sands – ashes to ashes, dust to dust. But thanks to a massive face-lift and a chic new Miami-meets-Havana theme, it just keeps hanging in there. Out back, the tropically inspired pool complex has multilevel lagoons, streaming waterfalls and classic swim-up blackjack tables. After dark, get your yuks at the **Laugh Factory** comedy club.

Stratosphere CASINO
(Map p64; ☎702-380-7777; www.stratospherehotel.com; 2000 Las Vegas Blvd S; tower entry adult/child $18/10, all-day pass incl unlimited thrill rides $34, SkyJump from $110; ⏰casino 24hr, tower & thrill rides 10am-1am Sun-Thu, to 2am Fri & Sat, weather permitting; 🅿) Las Vegas has many buildings over 20 stories tall, but only the Stratosphere exceeds 100. Atop the 1149ft-high tapered tripod tower, vertiginous indoor and outdoor viewing decks afford Vegas' best 360-degree panoramas. There you'll also find **Top of the World** (Map p64; ☎702-380-7711; www.topoftheworldlv.com; 2000 Las Vegas Blvd S, 106th fl, Stratosphere Tower; mains lunch $25-34, dinner $40-79; ⏰11am-11pm), a revolving restaurant, and the jazzy **Level 107** (p82) cocktail lounge. To get to the top of Vegas' lucky landmark, ride one of America's fastest elevators, lifting you 108 floors in a mere 37 ear-popping seconds.

Planet Hollywood CASINO
(Map p64; www.planethollywoodresort.com; 3667 Las Vegas Blvd S) Lest you mistake that Planet Hollywood is to Hollywood what the Hard Rock is to rock and roll, two steps into the casino will instantly clear up the difference. We're not sure what the inordinate number of scantily clad women gyrating on poles above the table games have to do with the movies, but if that's your thing, plunk down your cash on blackjack in the Pleasure Pit. The coolest movie stuff actually hangs in some of the most inconspicuous places, like by the elevators or in the hallways: go figure.

Quad CASINO
(Map p64; ☎702-731-3311; www.thequadlv.com; 3535 Las Vegas Blvd S; ⏰24hr) What was once the Imperial Palace, with a blue-neon-roofed pagoda facade and a faux–Far East theme, has become a theme-free boxy casino hotel called the Quad. On the casino floor, celebrity impersonators still do double duty as 'dealertainers,' jumping up from the blackjack tables to show off their song-and-dance skills. Also inside you'll find the resurrected, lucky leprechaun-themed **O'Sheas** casino, packed with low rollers and college students.

LINQ & High Roller LANDMARK
(Map p64; ☎800-223-7277; www.thelinq.com; 3545 Las Vegas Blvd S; High Roller ride before/after 5:50pm $25/35; ⏰High Roller noon-2am daily; monorail Flamingo or Harrah's/Quad) A mammoth open-air dining, entertainment and retail complex, the $550-million LINQ project has transformed what was once a lackluster stretch of the center Strip between the Flamingo and Quad casino hotels. Eclectic shops, buzzing bars, trendy restaurants, live-music venues and even a bowling alley line the pedestrian promenade, where you'll also find the **High Roller**, a 550ft-tall observation wheel.

Viva Las Vegas Wedding Chapel
WEDDING CHAPEL

(☑800-574-4450, 702-384-0771; www.vivalasvegasweddings.com; 1205 Las Vegas Blvd S) Even if you're not contemplating tying the knot, it's worth a peek inside this little assembly-line wedding chapel of loooovvvee to see if anyone is getting married. The public is welcome to attend the themed weddings: kitschy as all get-out too, they range from Elvis' 'Blue Hawaii' and 'Pink Caddy' to 'Twilight,' 'Gangster' and 'Gladiator' themes. Book ceremonies in advance.

⊙ Downtown

Think Vegas doesn't have real grit or soul? Come downtown and think again. The original spirit of Las Vegas looms large here. Serious gamblers, colorful locals and rowdy tourists come to play $5 blackjack and drink giant daiquiris amid the swirling neon and open-air shows on Fremont St. Expect a retro feel, cheaper drinks and lower table limits.

Note that the areas between downtown and the Strip and Fremont St east of downtown can be rather unsavory.

★ Mob Museum
MUSEUM

(Map p72; ☑702-229-2734; www.themobmuseum.org; 300 Stewart Ave; adult/child 11-17yr $20/14; ⊙10am-7pm Sun-Thu, to 8pm Fri & Sat; ☐Deuce) It's hard to say what's more impressive: the museum's physical location in a historic federal courthouse where mobsters sat for federal hearings in 1950–51, the fact that the board of directors is headed up by a former FBI Special Agent, or the thoughtfully curated exhibits telling the story of organized crime in America. In addition to hands-on FBI equipment and mob-related artifacts, the museum boasts a series of multimedia exhibits featuring interviews with real-life Tony Sopranos.

Downtown Grand
CASINO

(Map p72; ☑701-719-5100; www.downtowngrand.com; 206 N 3rd St; ⊙24hr; ☐Deuce, SDX) Reborn from the shell of the Lady Luck casino, the Downtown Grand is a shiny new player on the downtown gambling scene. Just north of Fremont St, the urban-chic casino combines chandeliers and 'street dice' gamblers placing bets outdoors, weather permitting. The diminutive casino holds about 600 slot machines and 30 table games. A quirky bunch of bars and restaurants includes a rooftop pool bar serving food in picnic baskets.

Fremont Street Experience
OUTDOORS

(Map p72; www.vegasexperience.com; Fremont St, btwn Main St & Las Vegas Blvd; ⊙hourly dusk-midnight; ☐Deuce, SDX) FREE A five-block pedestrian mall topped by an arched steel canopy and filled with computer-controlled lights, the Fremont Street Experience, between Main St and Las Vegas Blvd, has brought life back to downtown. Every evening, the canopy is transformed by hokey six-minute light-and-sound shows enhanced by 550,000 watts of wraparound sound and a larger-than-life screen lit up by 12.5 million synchronized LEDs. Soar through the air on zip lines strung underneath the canopy from Slotzilla (Map p72; ☑844-947-8342; www.vegasexperience.com; rides from $20; ⊙noon-midnight Sun-Thu, to 2am Fri & Sat), a 12-story, slot-machine-themed platform.

El Cortez
CASINO

(Map p72; ☑702-385-5200; www.elcortezhotelcasino.com; 600 E Fremont St; ⊙24hr; ☐Deuce) Head to the unabashedly retro El Cortez, Vegas' oldest continuously operating casino, on the National Register of Historic Places. Going strong since 1941, it's one of the only carpet joints left where the slot machines are the real thing. If you hit the jackpot, you'll enjoy the clatter of actual coins – none of that newfangled paper ticket nonsense.

Golden Nugget
CASINO

(Map p72; ☑702-385-7111; www.goldennugget.com; 129 E Fremont St; ⊙24hr; ☐Deuce, SDX) Check out the polished brass and white leather seats in the casino: day or night, the Golden Nugget is downtown's poshest address. With classy eateries and a swimming pool famous for its shark tank, the Golden Nugget outshines the competition. This swank carpet joint rakes in a moneyed downtown crowd with a 38,000-sq-ft casino populated by table games and slot machines with the same odds as at Strip megaresorts. The nonsmoking poker room hosts daily tournaments.

VEGAS IN FILM

⊳ *Casino*, Martin Scorsese

⊳ *Ocean's Eleven*, Steven Soderbergh

⊳ *Leaving Las Vegas*, Mike Figgis

⊳ *Fear and Loathing in Las Vegas*, Terry Gilliam

⊳ *The Hangover*, Todd Phillips

Downtown Las Vegas

Main Street Station

CASINO

(Map p72; ☑702-387-1896; www.mainstreetcasino. com; 200 N Main St; ⊙24hr; ☐SDX) This fili-greed casino re-creates Victorian opulence with its unique design, detailed craftwork and an extensive antiques collection. Pick up a brochure at the hotel's front desk and take a self-guided tour of the *objets d'histoires*. Highlights include exquisite bronze chandeliers (originally from an 1890s Coca-Cola building in Austin, Texas), a graffiti-covered chunk of the Berlin Wall (now supporting a urinal in the men's restroom) and an art nouveau chandelier from Paris' Figaro Opera House. Outside on Main St stands the private rail car once used by Buffalo Bill Cody.

Binion's

CASINO

(Map p72; ☑702-382-1600; www.binions.com; 128 E Fremont St; ⊙24hr; ☐Deuce, SDX) Binion's gambling hall and hotel was opened in 1951 by notorious Texan gambler Benny Binion, who wore gold coins for buttons on his cowboy shirts and spurred the transformation of Fremont St casino hotels from sawdust gambling halls to classy carpet joints. Benny was among the first to offer free drinks for slot-machine players and airport limo rides for high rollers. Today, what appeals most about this bedraggled downtown property is its genuine country-and-western flavor.

Burlesque Hall of Fame

MUSEUM

(Map p72; ☑888-661-6465; www.burlesquehall.com; 520 E Fremont St; suggested donation $5; ⊙usually noon-5pm Wed-Sun; ☐Deuce) Set amid the funky artist workshops, gallery spaces and yoga studios of the Emergency Arts complex, this tiny two-room museum pays homage to the history of burlesque performance in the USA. Gawk at fab sequined outfits and photos of some of the genre's sultriest stars from yesteryear. Enter from **Beat** (Map p72; ☑702-385-2328; www.thebeatlv.com; 520 E Fremont St, Emergency Arts; ⊙7am-midnight Mon-Fri, from 9am Sat, 9am-5pm Sun; ☎; ☐Deuce) coffee house.

Downtown Las Vegas

Discovery Children's Museum MUSEUM
(Map p72; ☎702-382-5437; www.discoverykidslv.org; 360 Promenade Pl, Symphony Park; admission $12; ⏱10am-5pm Mon-Sat, noon-5pm Sun Jun-early Sep, hours vary rest of year; 🚼; 🚍SDX) Designed for toddlers to preteens, the Discovery Children's Museum has undergone a major overhaul and reopened in a state-of-the-art building in Symphony Park. Highlights include 'The Summit,' a 12-story tower of interactive activities and play space, plus themed educational and entertaining exhibits such as Eco City, Water World, Toddler Town, Fantasy Festival, Patents Pending and Young at Art.

◎ Off the Strip

National Atomic Testing Museum MUSEUM
(Map p64; ☎702-794-5151; www.nationalatomic testingmuseum.org; 755 E Flamingo Rd, Desert Research Institute; adult/child 7-17yr $14/12; ⏱10am-5pm Mon-Sat, noon-5pm Sun; 🚍202) Fascinating multimedia exhibits focus on science, technology and the social history of the 'Atomic Age,' which lasted from WWII until atmospheric bomb testing was driven underground in 1961 and a worldwide ban on nuclear testing was declared in 1992. View historical footage of atomic testing and examine southern Nevada's past, present and future, from Native American ways of life to the environmental legacy of atomic testing. Don't miss the cool museum shop near the ticket booth, a Nevada Test Site guard-station replica.

Hard Rock CASINO
(Map p64; ☎702-693-5000; www.hardrockho tel.com; 4455 Paradise Rd; ⏱24hr; 🚍108) The world's original rock-and-roll casino houses what may be the most impressive collection of rock-star memorabilia ever assembled under one roof. Priceless items being watched over by security guards suited up like bouncers are concert attire worn by Elvis, Britney Spears and Prince; a display case filled with Beatles mementos; Jim Morrison's handwritten lyrics to one of The Doors' greatest hits; and dozens of leather jackets and guitars formerly owned by everyone from the Ramones to U2.

The Hard Rock's sexy, see-and-be-seen scene is perfect for rock stars and entourage wannabes alike. Especially favored by Southern Californians, this party hotel opens on to a circular casino with a competitive spread of table games, a state-of-the-art race and sports book, a busy poker room and the glowing Peacock high-limit gaming salon.

Trendy restaurants include the rule-breaking **Culinary Dropout** (Map p64; ☎702-522-8100; www.hardrockhotel.com; 4455 Paradise Rd, Hard Rock; mains brunch $8-14, lunch & dinner $14-32; ⏱11am-11pm Mon-Thu, 11am-midnight Fri, 10am-midnight Sat, 10am-11pm Sun; 🚍108) and Fú for pan-Asian plates, plus contemporary classics such as Nobu sushi bar and Mr Lucky's diner. Raucous bars and music venues range from an intimate lounge space called Vinyl and the floating poolside Palapa Bar, to the renowned **Joint** (p85) concert theater and glamorous Body English, a cavernous subterranean nightclub.

There's seasonal swim-up blackjack at the Nirvana Pool, and rollicking Rehab pool parties on summer weekends at Paradise Beach. For hip hangover cures, head to the hotel's **Reliquary Spa & Salon** (Map p64; ☑ salon 702-693-5522, spa 702-693-5520; www.hardrockhotel.com; 4455 Paradise Rd, Hard Rock; spa & fitness center day pass hotel guests/nonguests $25/50; ☺ spa 8am-8pm, salon 10am-7pm Tue-Sat, 10am-5pm Sun & Mon; ▣108). To act like a real rock star, get a spontaneous tattoo at Hart & Huntington Tattoo and pick up naughty bedroom toys at Love Jones before retreating to a plush HRH Tower suite outfitted in silver-studded velvet and cool leather.

Springs Preserve   MUSEUM, PARK

(☑702-822-7700; www.springspreserve.org; 333 S Valley View Blvd; adult/child 5-17yr $19/11; ☺10am-6pm; ▣; ▣104) 🌿 On the site of the natural springs (which ran dry in 1962) that fed *las vegas* (the meadows), where southern Paiutes and Spanish Trail traders camped, and later Mormon missionaries and Western pioneers settled the valley, this educational complex is an incredible trip through historical, cultural and biological time. The touchstone is the Desert Living Center, demonstrating sustainable architectural design and everyday eco-conscious living.

🏃 Activities

Adventuredome   THEME PARK

(Map p64; www.adventuredome.com; Circus Circus; per ride $5-8, day pass over/under 48in tall $30/17; ☺10am-6pm daily, later on weekends & May-Sep; ▣) Enclosed by over 8000 pink-glass panes, Circus Circus' indoor amusement park is packed with thrills. Must-rides

include the double-loop, double-corkscrew Canyon Blaster and the gravity-defying El Loco that packs a whopping -1.5 Gs of vertical acceleration. Older kids get a rock-climbing wall, bungee-jumping area, mini-golf and 4D special-effect 'ridefilms.' Clowns perform free shows throughout the day.

Gold Coast Bowling Alley   BOWLING

(Map p64; ☑702-367-4700; www.goldcoastcasino.com; 4000 W Flamingo Rd, Gold Coast; per game $2-3.25, shoe rental $3; ☺24hr; ▣; ▣202) A 70-lane bowling alley with pool tables and video arcade games, this family-friendly place rock outs with cosmic bowling (think crazy lights, fog and disco balls) on weekend nights. 'Graveyard' bowling in the wee hours costs just a buck a game.

Pole Position Raceway   RACING

(☑702-227-7223; www.polepositionraceway.com; 4175 S Arville St; 1-week membership $6, per race $22-26; ☺11am-10pm Sun-Thu, to midnight Fri & Sat; ▣202) Dreamed up by Nascar and Supercross champs and modeled on Formula 1 road courses, this European-style raceway boasts the USA's fastest indoor go-karts – up to 45mph! All drivers must be at least 48in tall and wear close-toed shoes (rentals available for a fee).

Stratosphere Tower   TOWER

(Map p64; ☑702-380-7777; www.stratospherehotel.com; Stratosphere; elevator adult/concession $18/15, incl 3 thrill rides $33, all-day pass $34, SkyJump from $110; monorail Sahara) The world's highest thrill rides await, a whopping 110 stories above the Strip. Big Shot straps riders into completely exposed seats that zip up the tower's pinnacle, while Insanity spins

COOL POOLS

Mirage (p67) The lush tropical pool is a sight to behold, with waterfalls tumbling off cliffs, deep grottoes and palm-tree studded islands for sunbathing. Feeling flirty? Check out the topless Bare lounge.

Mandalay Bay (p69) Splash around an artificial sand-and-surf beach built from imported California sand and boasting a wave pool, lazy-river ride, casino and DJ-driven topless Moorea Beach Club.

Caesars Palace (p67) Corinthian columns, overflowing fountains, magnificent palms and marble-inlaid pools make the Garden of the Gods Oasis divine. Goddesses proffer frozen grapes in summer, including at the topless Venus pool lounge.

Golden Nugget (p71) Downtown's best pool offers lots of fun and zero attitude. Play poolside blackjack, or sip on a daiquiri in the Jacuzzi and watch the sharks frolic in the nearby aquarium.

riders out over the tower's edge. Views from xScream are good, but the ride itself is a dud. If you want an adrenaline rush, save your dough for the SkyJump instead.

Spas & Gyms

Qua Baths & Spa SPA
(Map p64; ☏ 866-782-0655; Caesars Palace; fitness center day pass $25, incl spa facilities $45; ☉ 6am-8pm) Qua evokes the ancient Roman rituals of indulgent bathing. Try a signature 'bath liqueur,' a personalized potion of herbs and oils poured into your own private tub. The women's side includes a tea lounge, a herbal steam room and an arctic ice room where artificial snow falls. On the men's side, there's a barber spa and big-screen sports TVs.

Bathhouse SPA
(Map p64; ☏ 702-632-4760, 877-632-9636; www. mandalaybay.com; Mandalay Bay; 1-/3-/5-day gym pass $15/35/65; ☉ 6am-8:30pm) Seducing both sexes, this $25-million minimalist, Asian-inspired spa offers redwood saunas, eucalyptus steam rooms and essential-oil baths. It's a quieter, more intimate alternative to the grander Spa Mandalay. Hotel guests can use the spa facilities by buying a day pass ($25); nonguests must purchase a spa treatment to enter.

➤ Courses

Stripper 101 DANCE
(Map p64; ☏ 702-260-7200, 866-932-1818; www. stripper101.com; 3663 Las Vegas Blvd S, Miracle Mile Shops, V Theater; tickets from $40; ☉ hours vary) In a cabaret setting complete with strobe lights, cocktails and feather boas, these (non-nude) pole-dancing classes are popular with bachelorettes.

☞ Tours

Haunted Vegas Tours BUS
(Map p64; ☏ 866-218-4935, 702-677-6499; www. hauntedvegastours.com; 99 Convention Center Dr, Royal Resort; 2½hr tour $100; ☉ usually 9:30pm) A pizza party and (borrowed) 'ghost finder' dowsing rods are included on this paranormal hunt at three hot spots around town, including a reputedly haunted house and a creepy park. Tickets include admission to **Madame Tussauds** (Map p64; ☏ 866-841-3739, 702-862-7800; www.madametussauds.com/lasvegas; Venetian; adult/child 4-12yr $30/20; ☉ usually 10am-9pm; ♿) wax museum.

Vegas Mob Tour BUS
(Map p64; ☏ 702-807-8036; www.vegasmobtour. com; 99 Convention Center Dr, Royal Resort; 3hr tour $75; ☉ by reservation only) Created with input from real-life mobsters and historians, this bus tour delves into the mafia underworld of Sin City's past, including celebrity scandals, mobster assassinations and other dirty laundry. Tickets include pizza and admission to downtown's Mob Museum (p71).

✪ Festivals & Events

For more information about special events, contact the Las Vegas Convention & Visitors Authority (p88).

First Friday CULTURAL
(Map p72; www.firstfridaylasvegas.com; ☉ 5-11pm) Between 5pm and 11pm on the first Friday of each month, a carnival of 10,000 art lovers, hipsters, indie musicians and sundry hangers-on wander around the downtown arts and antiques district for First Friday evenings. These giant block parties come alive with gallery openings accompanied by performance art, music, fortune-tellers and tattoo artists.

Viva Las Vegas MUSIC
(Map p64; www.vivalasvegas.net) Ultimate rockabilly weekend downtown in mid-April.

Las Vegas Pride CULTURAL
(www.lasvegaspride.org) Annual events include Las Vegas Pride in May, and gay rodeo events, too.

Helldorado Days CULTURAL
(www.elkshelldorado.com) Historic Old West hoedown, rodeo and barbecue near Fremont St in May.

World Series of Poker CASINO
(www.worldseriesofpoker.com) High rollers, casino dealers, Hollywood celebs and internet stars vie for millions from early June to mid-July.

National Finals Rodeo RODEO
(www.nfrexperience.com) Ten days of cowboys at the Thomas & Mack Center in December.

⌖ Sleeping

Pricewise, Vegas hotels jump like the stock market. Bargains in summer, midweek and *after* holidays can be shockingly good – even at luxe properties. During midweek, rooms can cost 50% less than on weekends. Note that the best deals are often found via hotel websites. Don't be surprised when you find a 'resort' fee (from $25) on your bill. Valet (add tip) and self-parking are free.

The Strip

Reasonable deals are more common at older properties.

New York–New York
CASINO HOTEL $

(Map p64; ☎ 866-815-4365, 702-740-6969; www.newyorknewyork.com; 3790 Las Vegas Blvd S; weekday/weekend r from $50/110; P ✳ @ ☞ ≋) A favorite of college students, these decent digs are rather tiny (just what one would expect in NYC).

Treasure Island
CASINO HOTEL $

(Map p64; ☎ 800-944-7444, 702-894-7111; www.treasureisland.com; 3300 Las Vegas Blvd S; weekday/weekend r from $50/99; P ✳ @ ☞ ≋) Breezily renovated rooms are comfortable enough, although on-site dining and amenities are only so-so. Good value for the location.

Vdara
HOTEL $$

(Map p64; ☎ 866-745-7767, 702-590-2111; www.vdara.com; 2600 W Harmon Ave; weekday/weekend ste from $119/179; P ⊖ ✳ @ ☞ ≋) 🌿 Cool sophistication, generously proportioned apartments and warm hospitality merge seamlessly at this nongaming, nonsmoking, all-suites hotel at CityCenter.

Planet Hollywood
CASINO HOTEL $$

(Map p64; ☎ 866-919-7472, 702-785-5555; www.planethollywoodresort.com; 3667 Las Vegas Blvd S; weekday/weekend r from $59/160; P ✳ ☞ ≋ ✳) Ultracontemporary rooms contain black lacquer furnishings, club chairs and plush beds with leather headboards.

Tropicana
CASINO HOTEL $$

(Map p64; ☎ 800-462-8767, 702-739-2222; www.troplv.com; 3801 Las Vegas Blvd S; weekday/weekend r from $75/120; P ✳ @ ☞ ≋) Keeping its tropical vibe going since the 1950s, the vintage Trop's multimillion-dollar renovation pays off with Miami-chic rooms painted in sunset hues.

Aria
CASINO HOTEL $$

(Map p64; ☎ 866-359-7757, 702-590-7757; www.arialasvegas.com; 3730 Las Vegas Blvd S; r weekday/weekend from $129/189; P ✳ @ ☞ ≋) This sleek 4000-room casino hotel at CityCenter has no theme. Instead it's all about soothing design, spacious lodgings and deluxe amenities.

Venetian
CASINO HOTEL $$

(Map p64; ☎ 866-659-9643, 702-414-1000; www.venetian.com; 3355 Las Vegas Blvd S; weekday/weekend ste from $149/289; P ✳ @ ☞ ≋) Ve-

gas' own 'Most Serene Republic' features huge suites with sunken living rooms and countless luxuries from deep soaking tubs to pillow menus.

Caesars Palace
CASINO HOTEL $$

(Map p64; ☎ 866-227-5938, 702-731-7110; www.caesarspalace.com; 3570 Las Vegas Blvd S; weekday/weekend r from $90/125; P ✳ @ ☞ ≋ ✳) Expect towers of oversized rooms with marble bathrooms, Nobu boutique hotel and the Garden of the Gods pool complex.

Mirage
CASINO HOTEL $$

(Map p64; ☎ 800-374-9000, 702-791-7111; www.mirage.com; 3400 Las Vegas Blvd S; weekday/weekend r from $95/130; P ✳ @ ☞ ≋) Remodeled rooms are delightfully contemporary, with bold color palettes, plush beds and geometrically patterned carpets.

Mandalay Bay
CASINO HOTEL $$

(Map p64; ☎ 877-632-7800, 702-632-7777; www.mandalaybay.com; 3950 Las Vegas Blvd S; weekday/weekend r from $105/130; P ✳ @ ☞ ≋) The upscale Mandalay Bay casino hotel, exclusive **Four Seasons** (Map p64; ☎ 702-632-5000; www.fourseasons.com/lasvegas; Mandalay Bay; weekday/weekend r from $229/289; P ✳ @ ☞ ≋) hotel and boutique **Delano** (www.delanolasvegas.com; Mandalay Bay; P ✳ @ ☞ ≋) hotel offer variety at the Strip's southernmost resort.

Quad
CASINO HOTEL $$

(Map p64; ☎ 800-351-7400, 702-731-3311; www.thequadlv.com; 3535 Las Vegas Blvd S; weekday/weekend r from $80/160; P ✳ @ ☞ ≋) Unbeatable location next to the new LINQ complex with newly renovated but still cheap rooms.

Paris Las Vegas
CASINO HOTEL $$

(Map p64; ☎ 877-796-2096, 702-946-7000; www.parislasvegas.com; 3655 Las Vegas Blvd S; weekday/weekend r from $60/135; P ✳ @ ☞ ≋ ✳) Standard rooms are far from Parisian, but upgraded Red Luxury Rooms, some with lipstick-shaped sofas, evoke Moulin Rouge.

MGM Grand
CASINO HOTEL $$

(Map p64; ☎ 877-880-0880, 702-891-1111; www.mgmgrand.com; 3799 Las Vegas Blvd S; weekday/weekend r from $70/140; P ✳ @ ☞ ≋) Vegas' biggest hotel, with high-end **Skylofts** (Map p64; ☎ 877-646-5638, 702-891-3832; www.skyloftsmgmgrand.com; MGM Grand; ste from $1000; P ✳ @ ☞ ≋), apartment-style **Signature** (Map p64; ☎ 877-727-0007, 702-797-6000; www.signaturemgmgrand.com; 145 E Harmon Ave; weekday/weekend ste from $95/170; P ✳ @ ☞ ≋) suites and the Strip's most mammoth pool complex.

PROSTITUTION IN NEVADA

Prostitution is illegal only in Clark and Washoe Counties (including Las Vegas and Reno), yet illegal prostitution runs rampant (*especially* in Las Vegas) under the guise of strip clubs, escort services and massage parlors.

Remember that not only is paying for sex through these seemingly innocuous channels illegal and punishable by law, but anyone who does so may be contributing to Nevada's sex-trafficking problem. Shared Hope International has targeted Vegas as one of the biggest hubs for sex trafficking in the US.

Legalized, heavily regulated brothels are found in Nevada's more rural counties. Don't expect a romantic Old West bordello, though; most are just a few double-wide trailers behind a scary barbed-wire fence on the side of a lonesome highway.

Encore
CASINO HOTEL $$$

(Map p64; ☑877-321-9966, 702-770-7100; www.wynnlasvegas.com; 3131 Las Vegas Blvd S; weekday/weekend ste from $199/249; P❋@☞≋) Newer than its sister resort Wynn, Encore offers similarly lavish yet even more spacious suites amid gorgeous surrounds.

Palazzo
CASINO HOTEL $$$

(Map p64; ☑866-263-3001, 702-607-7777; www.palazzo.com; 3325 Las Vegas Blvd S; weekday/weekend ste from $199/349; P❋@☞≋) Enormous suites come with the Venetian's signature sunken living rooms and Roman tubs; Prestige Suites enjoy VIP check-in with complimentary champagne.

Bellagio
CASINO HOTEL $$$

(Map p64; ☑888-987-6667, 702-693-7111; www.bellagio.com; 3600 Las Vegas Blvd S; weekday/weekend r from $169/239; P❋@☞≋) Romantic and artistically designed, Bellagio is a lakeside monument to nouveau riche opulence.

Cosmopolitan
CASINO HOTEL $$$

(Map p64; ☑855-435-0005, 702-698-7000; www.cosmopolitanlasvegas.com; 3708 Las Vegas Blvd S; r/ste from $160/220; P❋@☞≋❋) Frequented by style-conscious clientele, the arty, cool Cosmo wins the contest for the Strip's hippest hotel rooms.

Downtown

Avoid rent-by-the-hour fleapits by sticking close to the Fremont Street Experience.

Golden Nugget
CASINO HOTEL $

(Map p72; ☑800-634-3454, 702-385-7111; www.goldennugget.com; 129 E Fremont St; weekday/weekend r from $49/89; P❋@☞≋) Pretend to relive the fabulous heyday of Vegas in the 1950s at this swank Fremont St address. Upgrade to a Rush Tower room.

El Cortez Cabana Suites
HOTEL $

(Map p72; ☑800-634-6703, 702-385-5200; http://elcortezhotelcasino.com; 651 E Ogden Ave; weekday/weekend r from $40/80; P❋@☞) Across the street from the 1940s casino, mod suites decked out in mint green hide fab retro tiled bathrooms with walk-in showers.

Main Street Station
CASINO HOTEL $

(Map p72; ☑702-387-1896, 800-713-8933; www.mainstreetcasino.com; 200 N Main St; weekday/weekend r from $35/70; P❋@☞) With tiled foyers, Victorian sconces and marble-trimmed hallways, the hotel has turn-of-the-century charm; bright, cheerful rooms have plantation shutters.

East of the Strip

Don't get stuck at chain cheapies near the airport or the city's convention center.

Hard Rock
CASINO HOTEL $

(Map p64; ☑800-473-7625, 702-693-5000; www.hardrockhotel.com; 4455 Paradise Rd; weekday/weekend r from $45/89; P❋@☞≋) Sexy, oversized rooms and HRH suites at this shrine to rock and roll pull in the SoCal party crowd. Free Strip shuttles for guests.

Rumor
BOUTIQUE HOTEL $$

(Map p64; ☑877-997-8667, 702-369-5400; www.rumorvegas.com; 455 E Harmon Ave; weekday/weekend ste from $60/120; P❋@☞≋❋) Opposite the Hard Rock, a sultry, nightclub-cool atmosphere infuses mod suites, some with whirlpool tubs and white leather sofas.

Motel 6 Tropicana
MOTEL $

(Map p64; ☑800-466-8356, 702-798-0728; www.motel6.com; 195 E Tropicana Ave; weekday/weekend r from $35/60; P❋@☞≋) Tiny rooms may be basic, but this all-American motel is within walking distance of the Strip. On weekends, you won't find cheaper rooms for miles.

Platinum Hotel
HOTEL $$

(Map p64; ☎877-211-9211, 702-365-5000; www.
theplatinumhotel.com; 211 E Flamingo Rd; weekday/
weekend ste from $135/170; P⊕❋@🖰❄)
This nongaming and nonsmoking hotel
near the Strip charms guests with a wellness
spa and sanctuary-like suites with kitchens
and Jacuzzi tubs.

West of the Strip

Some off-strip hotels may provide free shut-
tles to the Strip.

Orleans
CASINO HOTEL $

(☎702-365-7111, 800-675-3267; www.orleanscasi-
no.com; 4500 W Tropicana Ave; weekday/weekend r
from $45/95; P❋@🖰❄) Tastefully appoint-
ed French-provincial rooms are good-value
'petite suites,' with fitness-center access, on-
site childcare, a movie theater and a bowling
alley.

Artisan Hotel
BOUTIQUE HOTEL $

(Map p64; ☎800-554-4092, 702-214-4000; www.
artisanhotel.com; 1501 W Sahara Ave; weekday/
weekend r from $35/90; P❋@🖰❄) Suites are
themed around different artists' works at
this weird Gothic baroque fantasy. Swingers
and couples might appreciate the free in-
room porn channel.

Palms & Palms Place
CASINO HOTEL $

(Map p64; ☎702-942-7777, 866-942-7770; www.
palms.com; 4321 W Flamingo Rd; weekday/weekend
r from $59/99; P❋@🖰❄) Spacious rooms
and outrageous party suites get easy access
to the Palms' nightlife scene. Palms Place
condos let you flaunt your VIP status.

Rio
CASINO HOTEL $

(Map p64; ☎866-746-7671, 702-252-7777; www.
riolasvegas.com; 3700 W Flamingo Rd; weekday/
weekend ste from $30/80; P❋@🖰❄🖰)
Carnaval-themed all-suites hotel just off
the Strip, which attracts families, poker
players and bachelor/ette parties. Free, fre-
quent Strip shuttles and a rooftop zip line
are bonuses.

Greater Las Vegas

Hotels may offer free Strip shuttles.

South Point
CASINO HOTEL $

(☎866-796-7111, 702-796-7111; www.southpointca-
sino.com; 9777 Las Vegas Blvd S; weekday/weekend
r from $45/70; @🖰❄) Encompassing a cine-
plex, bowling alley and big rooms with com-

fy beds, this tidy casino hotel is flung south
of the Strip, near an outlet mall.

Red Rock
CASINO HOTEL $$

(☎866-767-7773, 702-797-7777; www.redrock.
sclv.com; 11011 W Charleston Blvd; weekday/
weekend r from $95/140; P❋@🖰❄) At this
upscale casino hotel, forget about the far-
away Strip and spend your time outdoors
by the resort pool or at nearby Red Rock
Canyon.

✖ Eating

Sin City is an unmatched culinary adventure, with celebrity chefs in nearly every
casino. Yet sometimes the hype is just that.
Always book ahead for upscale and popular
casino restaurants, especially on weekends.
OpenTable (www.opentable.com) offers free
restaurant reservations via its website and
mobile app; it's handy for finding last-minute
table availability. For a local slant, see **Eater
Vegas** (http://vegas.eater.com).

✖ The Strip

For a good range of budget options, head to
New York–New York, where Greenwich Village bursts with tasty, budget-saving options.

Stripburger
BURGERS $

(Map p64; ☎702-737-8747; www.stripburger.com;
3200 Las Vegas Blvd S, Fashion Show; menu $4-
14; ⊙11am-11pm Sun-Thu, to midnight Fri & Sat;
🖰) This shiny silver, open-air diner in the
round serves up all-natural (hormone free
etc) beef, chicken, tuna and veggie burgers,
atomic cheese fries, thick milkshakes, buckets of beer and fruity cocktails, with elevated
patio tables overlooking the Strip.

Tacos El Gordo
MEXICAN $

(Map p64; ☎702-641-8228; http://tacoselgor-
dobc.com; 3049 Las Vegas Blvd S; menu $2-10;
⊙9pm-3am Sun-Thu, to 5am Fri & Sat; 🚌Deuce,
SDX) This Tijuana-style taco shop from
SoCal is just the ticket when it's way late,
you've got almost no money left and you're
desperately craving *carne asada* (beef) or
adobada (chile-marinated pork) tacos in
hot, handmade tortillas. Adventurous eaters order the authentic *sesos* (beef brains),
cabeza (roasted cow's head) or tripe (intes-
tines) variations.

Jean Philippe Patisserie
BAKERY, DESSERTS $

(Map p64; www.jpchocolates.com; Bellagio; snacks
& drinks $4-11; ⊙7am-11pm Mon-Thu, to midnight
Fri-Sun; 🖰) As certified by the *Guinness*

A CUT ABOVE

High stakes and steaks go hand in hand in Vegas, though greener alternatives have never been greater. Whether you like it rare or well-done, celebrity or local, retro or mod, and your background music Frank Sinatra or Lady Gaga, Vegas is still pretty much a carnivore's dream.

Gordon Ramsay Steak (Map p64; ☎702-946-4663, 877-346-4642; www.gordonramsay.com; Paris Las Vegas; mains $32-105, tasting menu without/with wine pairings $145/220; ◷4:30-10:30pm daily, bar to midnight Fri & Sat) Carnivores, leave Paris behind and stroll through a miniaturized Chunnel into British chef Gordon Ramsay's steakhouse. Ribboned in red and and domed by a jaunty Union Jack, this is one of the top tables in town. Fish, chops and signature beef Wellington round out a menu of Himalayan salt room-aged steaks. No reservation? Sit at the bar instead.

Stripsteak (Map p64; ☎702-632-7414; www.michaelmina.net; Mandalay Bay; mains $39-75; ◷5:30-10:30pm, lounge from 4pm) *Esquire* magazine once named chef Michael Mina's butter-poached bone-in top loin one of the USA's very best steaks. The chef's minimalist steakhouse knifes into an exceptional menu of all-natural Angus and American Kobe beef, taste-awakening appetizers like ahi tuna and hamachi poppers, and classic side dishes with a twist, from truffle mac 'n' cheese to soy-glazed green beans. Reservations essential.

STK (Map p64; ☎702-698-7990; http://togrp.com/togrp-stk; Cosmopolitan; mains $29-59; ◷5:30-11pm Sun-Thu, to midnight Fri & Sat) With the motto 'Not your daddy's steakhouse' and flush with fashionistas, high rollers and hipsters, Cosmo's STK rocks a nightclub vibe with DJs that you'll either love or hate. Faux animal-skin fabrics, white leather banquettes and cinematic lighting appeal to swinging bachelor/ette parties. The mostly solid steakhouse menu is spiced up with creative tastes such as jalapeno onions and bacon butter.

Andiamo Steakhouse (Map p72; ☎702-388-2220; www.thed.com; 301 E Fremont St, The D; mains $23-79; ◷5-11pm; 🚌 Deuce, SDX) Of all the old-school steakhouses inside downtown's carpet joints, the current front-runner is Joe Vicari's Andiamo Steakhouse. Upstairs from the casino, richly upholstered half-moon booths and impeccably polite waiters set the tone for a classic Italian steakhouse feast of surf-and-turf platters and house-made pasta, followed by a rolling dessert cart. Extensive Californian and European wine list. Reservations recommended.

N9NE (Map p64; ☎702-933-9900; www.palms.com; 4321 W Flamingo Rd, Palms; mains $28-72; ◷5:30-10pm Sun-Thu, to 11pm Fri & Sat; 🚌202) The Palms' dramatically lit steakhouse lets A-list celebs lounge inside a semiprivate curtained dining space in the middle of a see-and-be-seen dining room. At edgy, mod tables and booths, the beautifully aged steaks and chops keep on coming, along with everything else from oysters Rockefeller to mushrooms stuffed with Alaska king crab and Gruyère cheese. Reservations essential. Dress to impress.

Cut (Map p64; ☎702-607-6300; www.wolfgangpuck.com; Grand Canal Shoppes at the Palazzo; mains $39-119; ◷5:30-10pm Sun-Thu, to 11pm Fri & Sat, lounge from 5pm daily) Peripatetic chef Wolfgang Puck strikes again and this time he's on fire – or 1200°F (649°C) in the broiler, to be exact. Modern earth-toned furnishings with stainless-steel accents and dried-flower arrangements complement a surprisingly smart menu, which dares to infuse Indian spices into Kobe beef and accompany Nebraska corn-fed steaks with Argentinean *chimichurri* sauce or Point Reyes blue cheese.

World Records, the world's largest chocolate fountain cascades inside the front windows of this champion pastry-maker's shop, known for its fantastic sorbets, gelati, pastries and chocolate confections. Coffee and espresso are above the Strip's low-bar average.

Earl of Sandwich DELI $
(Map p64; www.earlofsandwichusa.com; Planet Hollywood; menu $2-7; ◷24hr; ♿) Penny-pinchers sing the praises of this super-popular deli next to the casino, which pops out sandwiches on toasted artisan bread, tossed salads, wraps and a kids' menu, all with quick

service, unbeatable opening hours and some of the lowest prices on the Strip.

Roxy's Diner
DINER $$

(Map p64; ☑ 702-380-7777; www.stratospherehotel.com; 2000 Las Vegas Blvd S, Stratosphere; mains $8-14; ⊙ 24hr; 🖼) At this '50s-style rockand-roll diner, waitstaff drop everything to perform song-and-dance numbers straight out of *Grease*. It's fun, and the menu tastes about right for the prices. Super-thick milkshakes come with silver sidecars, just like when you were a kid.

Bouchon
FRENCH $$$

(Map p64; ☑ 702-414-6200; www.bouchonbistro.com; Venezia Tower, Venetian; mains breakfast & brunch $12-26, dinner $19-51; ⊙ 7-10:30am Mon-Fri, 8am-2pm Sat & Sun, 5-10pm daily) Napa Valley wunderkind Thomas Keller's rendition of a Lyonnaise bistro features a seasonal menu of French classics. The poolside setting complements the oyster bar (open 3pm to 10:30pm daily) and an extensive raw seafood selection. Decadent breakfasts and brunches, imported cheeses, caviar, foie gras and a superb French and Californian wine list all make appearances. Reservations essential.

Joël Robuchon
FRENCH $$$

(Map p64; ☑ 702-891-7925; www.joel-robuchon.com/en; MGM Grand; tasting menu per person $120-425; ⊙ 5:30-10pm Sun-Thu, to 10:30pm Fri & Sat) The acclaimed 'Chef of the Century' leads the pack in the French culinary invasion of the Strip. Adjacent to the high-rollers' gaming area, Robuchon's plush dining rooms, done up in leather and velvet, feel like a dinner party at a 1930s Paris mansion. Complex seasonal tasting menus promise the meal of a lifetime – and they often deliver.

Jaleo
SPANISH, TAPAS $$$

(Map p64; ☑ 702-698-7950; www.jaleo.com; Cosmopolitan; shared plates $5-35; ⊙ noon-midnight; 🖼) The Vegas version of pioneering Spanish chef José Andrés' flagship restaurant in DC brings modern tapas to a light-hearted setting with a rustic-chic look: recycled wooden tables with mismatched chairs, whimsical glassware and colorful details left and right. Try the potent sangria and a few traditional small plates or more innovative tastes like gin-and-tonic Pacific oysters. Reservations essential.

Nobu
JAPANESE, FUSION $$$

(Map p64; ☑ 702-785-6628; www.noburestaurants.com; Caesars Palace; shared plates $5-60,

lunch mains $22-50, dinner tasting menus $90-500; ⊙ lunch 11am-3pm Sat & Sun, dinner 5-11pm daily) Iron Chef Matsuhisa's new sequel to his NYC establishment is almost as good as the original. The setting is postmodern Zen, with glowing yellow lanterns, private dining 'pods' and sociable teppanyaki grill tables. Stick with Nobu's classics such as black cod with miso, South American–influenced *tiradito* (a lighter version of ceviche), spicy edamame and fusion sushi rolls. Reservations essential. If you can't afford a full meal, grab one of the 300-odd seats in the lounge and order cocktails and appetizers.

Sage
AMERICAN $$$

(Map p64; ☑ 702-590-8690; Aria, CityCenter; mains $35-54, tastings menus $59-150; ⊙ 5-11pm Mon-Sat) Chef Shawn McClain brings seasonal Midwestern farm-to-table cuisine to the Strip. The backlit mural over the bar almost steals the scene, but creative twists on meat-and-potatoes classics – imagine pork terrine with blue corn succotash and salsa verde – and seafood and pasta also shine. After dinner, sip absinthe poured from a rolling cart. Reservations essential; business casual dress.

Social House
ASIAN, SUSHI $$$

(Map p64; ☑ 702-736-1122; www.angelmg.com; Crystals, CityCenter; prix-fixe lunch $20-25, shared plates $5-50, dinner mains $25-50; ⊙ noon-5pm & 6-10pm daily) You won't find a sexier sushi bar and pan-Asian grill anywhere on the Strip. Low-slung tatami cushions, faded Japanese woodblock prints and a sky terrace inside Crystals mall add up to a seductively date-worthy atmosphere. Be thrilled by the imported sake list. Dinner reservations recommended.

Hash House a Go Go
AMERICAN $$$

(Map p64; ☑ 702-254-4646; www.hashhouseagogo.com; 3535 Las Vegas Blvd S, Quad; mains breakfast & lunch $8-16, dinner $17-39; ⊙ 24hr, closed 11pm-7am last Wed of month; 🖼) Fill up on this SoCal import's 'twisted farm food,' which has to be seen to be believed. The pancakes are as big as tractor tires, while farm-egg scrambles and house-made hashes could knock over a cow. Meatloaf, pot pies, chicken 'n' biscuits and wild-boar sloppy joes are what's for dinner, but it's more popular for breakfast and brunch.

Mesa Grill
SOUTHWESTERN $$$

(Map p64; ☑ 702-731-7731; www.mesagrill.com; Caesars Palace; mains brunch & lunch $13-24, dinner $32-50; ⏰11:30am-2:30pm Mon-Fri, 10:30am-3pm Sat & Sun, 5-11pm daily; 🅿) While star chef Bobby Flay doesn't cook on the premises, his bold signature menu of spicy Southwestern fare is usually satisfying, whether it's a New Mexican green-chile cheeseburger, blue-corn pancakes with barbecued duck, or ancho-chile-and-honey-glazed salmon. Lunch and weekend brunch are better value than dinner.

🍴 Downtown

Fremont St is the neon-illuminated land of cheap and bountiful buffets, retro cafes and authentic ethnic hideaways.

Container Park   FAST FOOD $
(Map p72; 🅿702-637-4244; http://downtown-containerpark.com; 707 E Fremont St; menu $3-9; ⏰11am-11pm Sun-Thu, to 1am Fri & Sat) With food-truck-style menus, outdoor patio seating and late-night hours, food vendors inside the cutting-edge Container Park sell something to satisfy everyone's appetite. When we last stopped by, the ever-changing lineup included Pinche's Tacos for Mexican flavors, Pork & Beans for piggy goodness, Southern-style Big Ern's BBQ, raw-food and healthy vegan cuisine from Simply Pure and Bin 702 wine bar. After 9pm only over-21s are allowed.

Grotto   ITALIAN $$
(Map p72; 🅿702-385-7111; www.goldennugget.com; 129 E Fremont St, Golden Nugget; pizzas $14-17; ⏰11am-midnight Sun-Thu, to 1am Fri & Sat; 🚌Deuce, SDX) At this Italian trattoria covered in painted murals, you'll be drawn to the sunlight-filled patio next to the Nugget's shark-tank waterslide and swimming pool.

Wood-oven-fired, thin-crust pizzas (the only thing on the menu we can recommend) are accompanied by a 200-bottle list of Italian wines. Happy hour runs 2pm to 6pm daily.

Wild   PIZZERIA, AMERICAN $$
(Map p72; 🅿702-778-8800; http://eatdrinkwild.com; 150 Las Vegas Blvd N, Ogden; pizzas $9-26, brunch prix-fixe menu $18; ⏰7am-7pm Mon-Sat; 🅿; 🚌Deuce) 🌿 At sidewalk level in a high-rise condo complex, this gluten-free pizzeria sources farm-fresh ingredients that are sustainably harvested. Up the feel-good factor with a fruit smoothie from the juice bar or with a side salad of kale and smoked tofu. Pizza flavors are rule-breaking, from white-truffle ricotta to chicken tikka masala. The unique beer and wine list encourages socializing.

🍴 East & West of the Strip

Pan-Asian delights and several food trucks – part of Vegas' new food craze – await around the Spring Mountain Rd strip malls of Chinatown.

Veggie Delight   VEGETARIAN $
(Map p64; 🅿702-310-6565; www.veggiedelight.biz; 3504 Wynn Rd; menu $3-10; ⏰11am-9pm; 🅿) This Buddhist-owned, Vietnamese-flavored vegetarian and vegan kitchen mixes up chakra color-coded Chinese herbal tonics and makes *banh mi*–style sandwiches, hot pots and noodle soups.

Raku   JAPANESE $$
(🅿702-367-3511; www.raku-grill.com; 5030 W Spring Mountain Rd; shared dishes $2-12; ⏰6pm-3am Mon-Sat; 🚌203) At the place where LA chefs come to dine when they're in town,

---

THE BEST OF BUFFET WORLDS

The adage 'you get what you pay for' was never truer: most large casino hotels in Nevada lay on all-you-can-eat buffets, but look before you buy. Not all are created equal. It's OK to peruse the offerings before putting down your money.

Vegas' best buffets, all of which are open for three meals a day (unless otherwise noted), include the following:

Wicked Spoon Buffet (3708 Las Vegas Blvd S, Cosmopolitan; per person $26-40; ⏰8am-2pm & 5-9pm Mon-Fri, 8am-9pm Sat & Sun; 🌐)

Le Village Buffet (🅿702-946-7000; Paris Las Vegas; buffet per adult $22-34, child 4-8yr $13-20; ⏰7am-10pm; 🅿🌐)

Spice Market Buffet (Planet Hollywood; buffet per adult $22-36, per child 4-12yr $13-20; ⏰7am-11pm; 🅿🌐)

House of Blues Gospel Brunch (🅿702-632-7600; www.houseofblues.com; Mandalay Bay; adult/child under 11yr $50/27; ⏰seatings 10am & 1pm Sun; 🌐)

Japanese owner-chef Mitsuo Edo crafts small plates blossoming with exquisite flavors. You'll find yourself ordering just one more thing, again and again, from the menu of *robata*-grilled meats, homemade tofu and seasoned vegetables. Make reservations a few days in advance or angle for the tiny bar.

Also in the same Chinatown strip mall, try desserts-only Sweets Raku, Tokyo-style sushi bar Kabuto and casual, family-friendly Monta Ramen.

Lotus of Siam
THAI $$

(Map p64; ☑ 702-735-3033; www.saipinchutima. com; 953 E Sahara Ave; mains $9-30; ☺ 11:30am-2:30pm Mon-Fri, 5:30-10pm daily; ☑; ☐ SDX) Saipin Chutima's authentic northern Thai cooking has won almost as many awards as her distinguished European and New World wine cellar. Renowned food critic Jonathan Gold once called it 'the single best Thai restaurant in North America.' Although the strip-mall hole-in-the-wall may not look like much, foodies flock here. Reservations essential.

Firefly
TAPAS $$

(Map p64; ☑ 702-369-3971; www.fireflylv.com; 3824 Paradise Rd; shared plates $5-12, mains $15-20; ☺ 11:30am-midnight; ☐ 108) Firefly is always packed with a fashionable local crowd, who come for well-prepared Spanish and Latin American tapas, such as *patatas bravas*, chorizo-stuffed empanadas and vegetarian bites like garbanzo beans seasoned with chili, lime and sea salt. A backlit bar dispenses the house specialty sangria – red, white or sparkling – and fruity mojitos. Reservations recommended. Show up for happy hour from 3pm to 6pm Monday through Thursday (till 5pm on Friday).

Alizé
FRENCH $$$

(Map p64; ☑ 702-951-7000; www.alizelv.com; 4321 W Flamingo Rd, 56th fl, Ivory Tower, Palms; mains $46-66, tasting menu without/with wine pairings $135/230; ☺ 5:30-10pm; ☐ 202) Chef André

> ### VEGAS HAPPY HOURS
>
> When the slots have gobbled your cash, skip the pricey pomegranate mojito with hand-crushed ice served by a bronzed model in a satin corset. For happy hour on the cheap, check out:
>
> ➡ Double Down Saloon (p85)
>
> ➡ Lavo
>
> ➡ Frankie's Tiki Room (p85)

Rochat's top-drawer gourmet room is named after a gentle Mediterranean trade wind. Enjoyed by nearly every table, panoramic floor-to-ceiling views of the glittering Strip are even more stunning than the haute French cuisine and a remarkably deep wine cellar. Reservations essential. Upscale dress code.

Drinking & Nightlife

The Strip

One of Vegas' dark secrets: the Strip is packed with over-the-top ultralounges where wannabe fashionistas sip overpriced mojitos and poseur DJs spin mediocre Top-40 mash-ups. Head to these places instead to avoid the deadly combination of alcohol and boredom.

Level 107 Lounge
LOUNGE

(Map p64; ☑ 702-380-7685; www.topoftheworldlv. com; 2000 Las Vegas Blvd S, 107th fl, Stratosphere Tower; ☺ 4pm-4am) There's just no place to get any higher in Las Vegas – without the approval of an air traffic controller – than the lounge overlooking the revolving Top of the World restaurant. Come during happy hour (4pm to 7pm daily) for two-for-one cocktails, half-price appetizers and striking sunset views.

Fireside Lounge
LOUNGE

(Map p64; www.peppermilllasvegas.com; 2985 Las Vegas Blvd S, Peppermill; ☺ 24hr) Don't be blinded by the outlandishly bright neon outside. The Strip's most spellbinding retro hideaway awaits at the pint-sized Peppermill casino. Courting couples adore the sunken fire pit, fake tropical foliage and 64oz goblet-sized 'Scorpion' cocktails served by waiters in black evening gowns.

Double Barrel Roadhouse
BAR

(Map p64; www.sbe.com/doublebarrel; 3770 Las Vegas Blvd S, Monte Carlo; ☺ 11am-2am) With a Strip-view patio, this double-decker bar and grill anchors the new pedestrian district between the Monte Carlo and New York–New York casino hotels. Staff pour stiff housemade wine coolers into mason jars, cook up Southern comfort food and cheer the live rock bands on stage.

Mix Lounge
LOUNGE

(Map p64; 64th fl, Mandalay Bay; cover after 10pm $20-25; ☺ 5pm-midnight Sun-Tue, to 3am Wed-Sat) High atop one of M-Bay's hotel towers, this is *the* place to go for sunset cocktails. The glassed-in elevator has amazing views on the ride up to the rooftop, and that's before you even glimpse the mod interior design with chocolate brown leather sofas or the roofless balcony opening up soaring views of the Strip, desert and mountains.

Todd English P.U.B. PUB

(Map p64; www.toddenglishpub.com; Crystals, CityCenter; ⏰11am-2am Mon-Fri, from 9:30am Sat & Sun) Twice-daily happy hours (3pm to 6pm, and 10pm until midnight) with half-price pints and cheap wings, oysters and sliders keep barstools filled at this cozy brick-walled pub with an outdoor patio. The kitchen closes at 11:30pm daily.

Red Square BAR

(Map p64; ☑702-632-7407; Mandalay Bay; ⏰4:30-10pm Sun-Thu, to midnight Fri & Sat) How very post-perestroika: a headless Lenin invites you to join your comrades for a tipple behind the blood red curtains of this Russian restaurant. Behind the solid-ice bar are caviar bowls and more than 200 vodkas mixed with infusions and into cocktails. Sable coats are kept on hand for visiting the private vodka vault. Happy hour runs from 4pm to 7pm daily.

Mandarin Bar & Tea Lounge LOUNGE, BAR

(Map p64; Mandarin Oriental, CityCenter; ⏰lounge 10am-10pm daily, bar 5pm-2am Fri & Sat, to 11pm Sun) With glittering Strip views from the panoramic windows of the hotel's 23rd-floor 'sky lobby,' this sophisticated lounge serves exotic teas by day and champagne cocktails by night. Make reservations for afternoon tea (from $36, available 1pm to 5pm daily).

Lavo LOUNGE

(Map p64; ☑702-791-1800; http://lavolv.com; Palazzo; cover free-$20; ⏰6pm-1am Tue-Thu, 7pm-2am Fri & Sat) After nibbling on modern Italian bites and drinks on the spacious Strip-side terrace, head upstairs to the plush library-esque lounge with a small dance floor, where DJs spin Top 40 hits some nights. Weekend party brunches (10am until 4pm every Saturday, except during summer) with unlimited champagne mimosas are an ultra-trendy destination for the clubbing set. Happy hour runs from 6pm to 8pm Tuesday through Saturday.

Napoleon's BAR

(Map p64; Paris Las Vegas; ⏰4pm-1am) Whisk yourself off to the never-never land of 19th-century France, with a mosaic floor and overstuffed sofas as luxurious as the menu of 100 types of bubbly, including vintage Dom Pérignon for big spenders. Dueling pianos draw a crowd; there's no cover charge, but expect a two-drink minimum.

Tryst CLUB

(Map p64; ☑702-770-7300; www.trystlasvegas. com; Wynn; cover $20-50; ⏰10:30pm-4am Thu-Sat) Groove the night away at this opulent subterranean dance club, situated on a faux lagoon under a waterfall. Let your sugar daddy treat you to over-the-top cocktails like the gold-sprinkled Ménage á Trois. Older men in suits often outnumber the glam young things on the dance floor. You'll have a better time on nights when superstar DJs spin.

Marquee CLUB

(Map p64; ☑702-333-9000; www.marqueelasvegas. com; Cosmopolitan; ⏰10pm-5am Thu-Sat & Mon) The Cosmopolitan's glam nightclub cashes in on its multimillion-dollar sound system and a happening dance floor surrounded by towering LED screens displaying light projections that complement electronic dance music (EDM) tracks hand picked by famous-name DJs. From late spring through early fall, Marquee's megapopular daytime pool club heads outside to a lively party deck overlooking the Strip, with VIP cabanas and bungalows.

Surrender CLUB

(Map p64; ☑702-770-7300; www.surrendernight-club.com; Encore; cover $20-40; ⏰10:30pm-4am Wed, Fri & Sat) Even the club-averse admit that this is an audaciously gorgeous place to hang out, with its saffron-colored silk walls, mustard banquettes, bright-yellow patent-leather entrance and a shimmering wall-art snake coiled behind the bar. Play blackjack or just hang out by the pool after dark during summer. EDM and hip-hop DJs and musicians pull huge crowds.

XS CLUB

(Map p64; ☑702-770-0097; www.xslasvegas. com; Encore; cover $20-50; ⏰9:30pm-4am Fri & Sat, from 10:30pm Sun & Mon) XS is *the* hottest nightclub in Vegas – at least for now. Its extravagantly gold-drenched decor and over-the-top design means you'll be waiting in line for cocktails at a bar towered over by ultra-curvaceous, larger-than-life golden statues of female torsos. Famous-name electronica DJs make the dance floor writhe, while high rollers opt for VIP bottle service at private poolside cabanas.

ⓘ VEGAS CLUBBING 101

Brave the velvet rope – or skip it altogether – with these nightlife survival tips we culled from the inner circle of Vegas club bouncers, VIP hosts and concierges.

➡ Dress to impress for chances of entering without an extended delay. Men especially need to look sharp in top-tier nightlife venues – that means collared shirts, nice pants and leather shoes, not athletic wear.

➡ Avoid that long line by booking ahead with a club promoter such as Chris Hornak of **Free Vegas Club Passes** (www.freevegasclubpasses.com).

➡ Look for club promoters, usually on the casino floor giving out passes for expedited entry and free drinks, especially to well-dressed ladies.

➡ Ask your hotel concierges for clubbing suggestions – they almost always have free passes for clubs, or can make you table reservations (at the usual rates) with the club's VIP host.

➡ At combo restaurant-nightclub complexes, a dinner reservation might not only get you on the club guest list, but also get the cover charge waived, a free drink ticket and possibly a VIP host to walk you in.

➡ To see a different side of the scene, show up for less crowded 'industry nights' early in the week when locals get in free.

➡ Bottle service may be expensive, but it usually waives cover charges (and waiting in line) for your group, plus you get to chill at the table – invaluable 'real estate,' in club speak.

Drai's
CLUB

(Map p64; ☑ 702-737-0555; www.drais.net; 3595 Las Vegas Blvd S, Cromwell; cover $20-50; ☉ nightclub 10am-5pm Thu-Sun year-round, pool club 10am-7pm Fri-Sun usually May-Sep) Feel ready for an after-hours party scene straight outta Hollywood? Or maybe you just wanna hang out all day poolside, then shake your booty on the petite dance floor while DJs spin hip-hop, mash-ups and electronica? This multi-venue club has you covered pretty much all day and night. Dress to kill: no sneakers, tank tops or baggy jeans. Drai's after-hours DJ parties are legendary, and keep going until 10am on club nights.

Krave
CLUB

(Map p64; ☑ 702-677-1740; www.kravelasvegas.com; 3765 Las Vegas Blvd S; cover $20; ☉ 10:30pm-5am Fri & Sat) Currently Krave is the only gay-oriented nightclub on the Strip, although it keeps changing locations. For now a warehouse-sized dance space inside the old Empire Ballroom is packed wall-to-wall with hard-bodied go-go dancers, booth seating and VIP tables.

🍸 Downtown

Want to chill out with the locals? Head to one of these go-to favorites, and watch for new bastions of hipness as they open up along Fremont St.

Chandelier Bar
COCKTAIL BAR

(Map p64; Cosmopolitan; ☉24hr) Towering high in the center of Cosmopolitan, this ethereally designed cocktail bar is inventive yet beautifully simple, with three levels connected by romantic curved staircases, all draped with glowing strands of glass beads. The 2nd level is headquarters for molecular mixology (order a martini made with liquid nitrogen), while the 3rd specializes in floral and fruit infusions.

Downtown Cocktail Room
LOUNGE

(Map p72; ☑ 702-880-3696; www.thedowntownlv.com; 111 Las Vegas Blvd S; ☉4pm-2am Mon-Fri, 7pm-2am Sat; ☐ Deuce) With a serious list of classic cocktails and house-made inventions, this low-lit speakeasy is undeniably romantic, and it feels decades ahead of downtown's old-school casinos. The entrance is ingeniously disguised: the door looks like just another part of the wall until you discover the sweet spot you have to push to get in. Happy hour runs 4pm to 8pm weekdays.

Beauty Bar
BAR

(Map p72; ☑ 702-598-3757; www.thebeautybar.com; 517 Fremont St; cover free-$10; ☉10pm-4am; ☐ Deuce) Swill a cocktail or just chill with the cool kids inside the salvaged innards of a 1950s New Jersey beauty salon. DJs and live bands rotate nightly, spinning everything from tiki lounge tunes, disco and '80s hits to punk, metal, glam and indie rock. Check the website for special events like 'Karate Karaoke.' There's often no cover charge.

🍸 Off the Strip

Double Down Saloon   BAR
(Map p64; www.doubledownsaloon.com; 4640 Paradise Rd; ⊙24hr; 🚍108) This dark, psychedelic gin joint appeals to the lunatic fringe. It never closes, there's never a cover charge, the house drink is called 'ass juice' and it claims to be the birthplace of the bacon martini. When live bands aren't terrorizing the crowd, the jukebox vibrates with New Orleans jazz, British punk, Chicago blues and surf-guitar king Dick Dale.

Frankie's Tiki Room   BAR
(☎702-385-3110; www.frankiestikiroom.com; 1712 W Charleston Blvd; ⊙24hr; 🚍206) At the only round-the-clock tiki bar in town, insanely inventive tropical cocktails are rated in strength by skulls on the menu. Renowned tiki designers, sculptors and painters have their work on display all around, and the souvenir tiki mugs are crazy cool. Walk in wearing a Hawaiian shirt on 'Aloha Friday' between 4pm and 8pm, and your first drink is half-off.

Ghostbar   LOUNGE
(Map p64; ☎702-942-6832; www.palms.com; 4321 W Flamingo Rd, 55th fl, Ivory Tower, Palms; cover $10-25; ⊙8pm-4am; 🚍202) A clubby crowd, often thick with pop-culture celebs and pro athletes, packs the Palms' sky-high watering hole. DJs spin hip-hop and house while wannabe gangsters and Jersey girls sip pricey cocktails. The plush mansion decor and 360-degree panoramas are to die for. Dress to kill. Happy hour goes until 10pm nightly.

Hofbräuhaus   BAR
(Map p64; www.hofbrauhauslasvegas.com; 4510 Paradise Rd; ⊙11am-11pm Sun-Thu, to midnight Fri & Sat) This Bavarian beer hall and garden is a replica of the original in Munich. Celebrate Oktoberfest year-round with premium imported suds, fair fräuleins and live oompah bands nightly.

⭐ Entertainment

For events, Ticketmaster (☎800-745-3000; www.ticketmaster.com) sells tickets.

Live Music
Joint   MUSIC, COMEDY
(Map p64; ☎888-929-7849; www.hardrockhotel.com; 4455 Paradise Rd, Hard Rock; most tickets $40-200; 🚍108) Concerts at the Hard Rock's

scaled-down music venue, holding just 4000 people, feel like private shows, even when rock royalty like the Red Hot Chili Peppers and David Bowie are in town. Intimate acoustic shows happen inside Vinyl lounge (cover charge varies, from nothing up to $40), off the main casino floor.

Pearl   MUSIC, COMEDY
(Map p64; ☎702-944-3200; www.palms.com; 4321 W Flamingo Rd, Palms; most tickets $50-100; 🚍202) A shining beacon for pop divas and rock bands, the Palms' 2500-seat concert hall has a sophisticated sound system. Comedy kingpins and modern rockers from Gwen Stefani to Morrissey have burned up this stage, with most seats only 120ft or less away from the performers. Live albums are minted at the state-of-the-art recording studio.

House of Blues   LIVE MUSIC
(Map p64; ☎702-632-7600; www.houseofblues.com; Mandalay Bay; ⊙box office 9am-9pm) Live blues is definitely not the only game at this imitation Mississippi Delta juke joint. Big-name touring acts entertain the standing-room-only audiences with soul, pop, rock, metal, country, jazz and even burlesque. For some shows, you can skip the long lines to get in by eating dinner in the restaurant beforehand, then showing your same-day receipt.

Production Shows & Comedy
Buy same-day discount tickets for a variety of shows at Tix 4 Tonight (☎877-849-4868; www.tix4tonight.com; 3200 Las Vegas Blvd S, Fashion Show; ⊙10am-8pm), with additional locations on the Strip and downtown.

Beatles LOVE   THEATER
(Map p64; ☎702-792-7777, 800-963-9634; www.cirquedusoleil.com; Mirage; tickets $79-180; ⊙7pm & 9:30pm Thu-Mon; ♿) Another smash hit from Cirque du Soleil, Beatles LOVE started as the brainchild of the late George Harrison. Using Abbey Road master tapes, the show psychedelically fuses the musical legacy of the Beatles with Cirque's high-energy dancers and signature aerial acrobatics. Come early to photograph the trippy, rainbow-colored entryway and grab drinks at Abbey Road bar, next to Revolution Lounge.

Michael Jackson ONE   THEATER
(Map p64; ☎800-745-3000, 877-632-7400; www.cirquedusoleil.com; Mandalay Bay; tickets from $69; ⊙7pm & 9:30pm Sat-Wed) Cirque du Soleil's musical tribute to the King of Pop

EMERGENCY ARTS

A coffee shop, an art gallery, working studios and a de facto community center of sorts, all under one roof and right smack downtown? The **Emergency Arts** (www.emergen-cyartslv.com; 520 E Fremont St) **FREE** building is home to Beat coffeehouse, a friendly bastion of laid-back cool, with strong coffee and fresh baguette sandwiches against a soundtrack of vintage vinyl spinning on old turntables. It also holds the retro-fabulous Burlesque Hall of Fame (p72). If you're aching to meet some savvy locals who know their way around town, this is your hangout spot. After 7pm they serve beer and wine, and the space transforms into a 21-plus venue.

blasts onto M-Bay's stage with showstopping dancers and lissome acrobats and aerialists all moving to a soundtrack of MJ's hits, moon-walking all the way back to his breakout platinum album *Thriller*. No children under five years old allowed.

O   THEATER
(Map p64; ☑888-488-7111, 702-693-8866; www.cirquedusoleil.com; Bellagio; tickets $99-155; ⊙7:30pm & 10pm Wed-Sun) Phonetically speaking, it's the French word for water (*eau*). With a lithe international cast performing in, on and above water, Cirque du Soleil's *O* tells the tale of theater through the ages. It's a spectacular feat of imagination and engineering, and you'll pay dearly to see it – it's one of the Strip's few shows that rarely sells discounted tickets.

Kà   THEATER
(Map p64; ☑800-929-1111, 702-531-3826; www.cirquedusoleil.com; MGM Grand; adult $69-150, child 5-12yr $35-75; ⊙7pm & 9:30pm Tue-Sat; 👪) Cirque du Soleil makes this sensuous story of imperial twins, mysterious destinies, love and conflict one of the Strip's hottest tickets. Instead of a stage, there's a $200-million grid of moving platforms elevating a frenzy of martial-arts-styled performances. Children under five years old are not allowed.

Improv   COMEDY
(Map p64; ☑855-234-7569, 702-777-2782; www.improv.com; 3475 Las Vegas Blvd S, Harrah's; from $30; ⊙8:30pm & 10pm Tue-Sun) The Vegas franchise of this NYC-based chain has the Big Apple's signature red-brick backdrop. The spotlight is firmly cast on touring stand-up headliners of the moment, often polished by recent late-night TV appearances.

Cinemas

United Artists Showcase Theatre 8   CINEMA
(Map p64; ☑702-740-4511; www.regmovies.com; 3769 Las Vegas Blvd S, Showcase Mall; adult/child

3-11yr $11.50/8; 👪) It's the only place to see first-run movies on the Strip, which means it's always packed. Although it's hardly the city's most modern cinema, stadium seating and digital sound bring it up to date. Afternoon matinee shows are discounted for adults.

Brenden Theatres & IMAX   CINEMA
(Map p64; ☑702-507-4849; www.brendentheatres.com; 4321 W Flamingo Rd, Palms; adult/child 3-12yr $10.50/7, IMAX $17/14; 🚌202) Showing new Hollywood releases, as well as independent festival-circuit features and documentaries, the swankiest off-Strip movieplex is fitted with IMAX and Dolby 3D Digital Cinema and Dolby Atmos sound, plus rocker-chair stadium seating for superior sightlines. Matinee shows before 6pm are discounted for adults.

Sports

Although Vegas doesn't have any professional sports franchises, it's a sports-savvy town. You can wager on just about anything at most casinos' race and sports books.

For auto racing, including Nascar, Indy racing, drag and dirt-track races, check out the mega-popular **Las Vegas Motor Speedway** (☑800-644-4444; www.lvms.com; 7000 Las Vegas Blvd N, off I-15 Fwy).

The **Thomas & Mack Center** (☑702-739-3267, 866-388-3267; www.unlvtickets.com; S Swenson St at Tropicana Ave, UNLV campus) hosts wrestling, boxing and pro rodeo events.

Strip Clubs

Prostitution may be illegal, but myriad places offer the illusion of sex on demand. Unescorted women are usually not welcome at popular strip clubs.

Spearmint Rhino   STRIP CLUB
(Map p64; ☑702-796-3600; www.spearmintrhinolv.com; 3344 S Highland Dr; cover $30; ⊙24hr) Fall in love, if only for two minutes (the length of an average lap dance, that is). Strip-club connoisseurs rave about the Rhino.

Treasures STRIP CLUB

(Map p64; ☑ 702-257-3030; www.treasureslasvegas.com; 2801 Westwood Dr; cover $30-35; ☺4pm-6am Sun-Thu, to 9am Fri & Sat) Treasures gets raves as much for its four-star steaks as it does for its faux-baroque interior and glam dancers. Good happy hour from 4pm to 8pm with cheap beer and a free buffet.

🏛 Shopping

The Strip has the highest-octane shopping action, with both chain and designer stores. Downtown offers vintage and retro-inspired cool. Cruise west of the Strip for XXX adult goods and trashy lingerie. East of the Strip, near the University of Nevada, Maryland Parkway is chockablock with hip, bargain-basement shops catering to college students.

🏛 The Strip

Crystals MALL

(Map p64; www.crystalsatcitycenter.com; 3720 Las Vegas Blvd S; ☺10am-11pm Sun-Thu, to midnight Fri & Sat) Design-conscious Crystals is the most striking shopping center on the Strip. Win big at blackjack? Waltz inside Christian Dior, Dolce & Gabbana, Prada, Hermès, Harry Winston, Paul Smith or Stella McCartney showrooms at CityCenter's shrine to haute couture. For sexy couples with unlimited cash to burn, Kiki de Montparnasse is a one-stop shop for lingerie and bedroom toys.

Forum Shops MALL

(Map p64; www.simon.com; Caesars Palace; ☺10am-11pm Sun-Thu, to midnight Fri & Sat) Caesars' fanciful nod to ancient Roman marketplaces houses 160 designer emporia, including catwalk wonders Armani, DKNY, Jimmy Choo, John Varvatos and Versace; trendsetting jewelry and accessory stores; and one-of-a-kind specialty boutiques such as Agent Provocateur lingerie, Bettie Page pin-up fashions, MAC cosmetics and Kiehl's bath-and-body shop. Don't miss the spiral escalator, a grand entrance for divas strutting off the Strip.

Houdini's Magic Shop CHILDREN

(Map p64; www.houdinis.com; New York–New York; ☺10am-midnight Mon-Thu, to 1am Fri & Sat, 9am-midnight Sun) Let yourself be roped into this real-deal magic shop by the staff who perform illusions and card tricks out front for sometimes inebriated passersby (they're easy marks). Magician memorabilia and DIY magic kits are sold inside. There are other locations at MGM Grand, Planet Hollywood's Miracle Mile Shops and the Grand Canal Shoppes at the Venetian.

Grand Canal Shoppes at the Palazzo MALL

(Map p64; www.grandcanalshoppes.com; Palazzo; ☺10am-11pm Sun-Thu, to midnight Fri & Sat) Don't be surprised to find Hollywood celebrities inside this high-design shopping mall. Anchored by the three-story department store Barneys New York, the Palazzo's shops are dazzling: Canali for tailor-made Italian apparel, London fashion imports Chloe and Thomas Pink and luxury US trendsetters such as Diane von Furstenberg. Bauman Rare Books carries rare, signed editions and antiquarian titles.

Le Boulevard MALL

(Map p64; Paris Las Vegas; ☺most shops 10am-11pm Sun-Thu, to midnight Fri & Sat) Along a winding cobblestone replica of the Rue de la Paix, leading onto a promenade that connects to Bally's casino hotel, popular stops include L'Apothecaire beauty shop; Les Eléments home decor; Les Enfants, for French children's fashions and toys; La Cave wine seller; Davidoff Boutique cigar shop; and Presse newsstand.

Linq MALL

(Map p64; www.thelinq.com; 3545 Las Vegas Blvd S; ☺daily) On the Strip's brand-new pedestrian promenade, handpicked unique boutiques beckon. Browse the latest LA fashions at Kitson, don the perfect hat at Goorin Bros, find funky eyewear at Chilli Beans and lace up limited-edition kicks from 12a.m. Run. Print your oh-so cute selfie on paper, canvas or metal at the Polaroid Fotobar, which has a small photography museum upstairs.

Wynn Esplanade MALL

(Map p64; www.wynnlasvegas.com; 3131 Las Vegas Blvd S) Wynn has lured high-end retailers like Oscar de la Renta, Jean-Paul Gaultier, Chanel and Manolo Blahnik to a giant concourse of consumer bliss.

Miracle Mile Shops MALL

(Map p64; ☑ 888-800-8284, 702-866-0703; www.miraclemileshopslv.com; 3663 Las Vegas Blvd S, Planet Hollywood; ☺10am-11pm Sun-Thu, to midnight Fri & Sat) This sleekly redesigned shopping mall is still a staggering 1.2 miles long. With 170 retailers, the focus is on contemporary chains, especially urban apparel, jewelry and gifts. Standout shops include Bettie Page for 1940s and '50s pinup and vintage-style dresses; Brit import H&M; LA denim king True Religion; and Vegas' own rock-star boutique, Stash, for both women and men.

Fashion Show

MALL

(Map p64; www.thefashionshow.com; 3200 Las Vegas Blvd S; ⊙10am-9pm Mon-Sat, 11am-7pm Sun;) Nevada's largest shopping mall is an eye-catcher: topped off by 'the Cloud,' a silver multimedia canopy resembling a flamenco hat, Fashion Show harbors more than 250 chain shops and department stores. Hot European additions to the mainstream lineup include British clothier Topshop (and Topman for men). Live runway shows happen hourly from noon to 5pm on Friday, Saturday and Sunday.

Downtown

Container Park

MALL

(Map p72; ☑702-637-4244; http://downtowncontainerpark.com; 719 E Fremont St; ⊙10am-9pm Mon-Sat, to 8pm Sun) An incubator for up-and-coming fashion designers and local artisans, the edgy Container Park stacks pop-up shops on top of one another. Wander along the sidewalks and catwalks while searching out handmade jewelry, contemporary art and clothing at a half-dozen specialty boutiques. What you'll find on any given day is a whimsical toss-up.

❶ Information

EMERGENCY

Police (☑702-828-3111; www.lvmpd.com) For ambulance, fire and police emergencies, dial ☑911.

INTERNET ACCESS

Wi-fi is available in most hotel rooms (about $15 per day, sometimes included in the 'resort fee') and there are internet kiosks with attached printers in most hotel lobbies. Free wi-fi hot spots are found at some chain coffee shops, casual restaurants and off-Strip at the airport and convention center.

MEDIA

Available in hotel rooms and at the airport, free tourist magazines like *Las Vegas Magazine* plus *Showbiz Weekly* and *What's On* contain valuable discount coupons and listings of attractions, entertainment, nightlife, dining and more.

MEDICAL SERVICES

Harmon Medical Center (☑702-796-1116; www.harmonmedicalcenter.com; 150 E Harmon Ave; ⊙8am-8pm Mon-Fri) Discounts for uninsured patients; limited translation services available.

Sunrise Hospital & Medical Center (☑702-731-8000; http://sunrisehospital.com; 3186 S Maryland Pkwy; ⊙24hr) Specialized children's

trauma services are available at a 24-hour emergency room.

University Medical Center (UMC; ☑702-383-2000; www.umcsn.com; 1800 W Charleston Blvd; ⊙24hr) Southern Nevada's most advanced trauma center has a 24-hour ER.

Walgreens (www.walgreens.com) Downtown (☑702-385-1284; 495 E Fremont St; ⊙store 24hr, pharmacy 9am-5pm; ☐ Deuce) Multiple locations on the Strip; The Strip (☑702-739-9645; 3765 Las Vegas Blvd S; ⊙store 24hr, pharmacy 8am-10pm, clinic 9am-5:30pm).

MONEY

Every casino and bank and most convenience stores have ATMs. Fees imposed by casinos for foreign-currency exchange and ATM transactions (which usually carry a $5 fee) are much higher than at banks.

Travelex Currency Services (☑702-369-2219; www.travelex.com; 3200 Las Vegas Blvd S, Fashion Show; ⊙10am-9pm Mon-Sat, 11am-7pm Sun) Changes currencies at competitive rates.

Tipping

Dealers expect to be tipped (or 'toked') only by winning players, typically with a side bet that the dealer collects if the bet wins. Buffet meals are self-serve, but leave a couple of dollars per person for the waitstaff who bring your drinks and clean your table. Valet parking is usually free, but tip $2–5 when the car keys are handed back to you.

POST

Post office (Map p72; www.usps.com; 201 Las Vegas Blvd S; ⊙9am-5pm Mon-Fri) Downtown.

TOURIST INFORMATION

Las Vegas Convention & Visitors Authority (LVCVA; Map p64; ☑702-892-7575, 877-847-4858; www.lasvegas.com; 3150 Paradise Rd; ⊙8am-5:30pm Mon-Fri; monorail Las Vegas Convention Center)

USEFUL WEBSITES

Eater Vegas (www.vegas.eater.com) The latest news about Sin City's chefs and new restaurants. Posts a regularly updated list of the city's top 38 eateries.

Las Vegas Review-Journal (www.lvrj.com) Daily paper with a weekend guide, *Neon*, on Friday.

Las Vegas Weekly (http://lasvegasweekly.com) Free weekly with good entertainment and restaurant listings.

Qvegas (www.qvegas.com) To plug into the city's current scene, QVegas offers online downloads of the monthly magazine.

Vegas.com (www.vegas.com) Travel information with booking service.

❶ Getting There & Away

AIR

Las Vegas is served by **McCarran International Airport** (LAS; Map p64; ☑702-261-5211; www.mccarran.com; 5757 Wayne Newton Blvd; 🛜), just a crapshoot from the south end of the Strip, and a few smaller general aviation facilities around the city. McCarran ranks among the USA's 10 busiest airports. Many domestic airlines use Terminal 1; international, charter and some domestic flights depart from Terminal 3. Free trams link outlying gates. There are ATMs, a full-service bank, a post office, first-aid and police stations, free wi-fi internet access and slot machines with reputedly bad odds.

BUS & TRAIN

The nearest Amtrak station to Las Vegas is in Kingman, AZ. Greyhound may provide connecting Thruway motor-coach service to Las Vegas ($38–$87, three hours). To reach the Strip, catch a southbound SDX bus (two-hour pass $6).

Long-distance Greyhound buses arrive at the downtown **Greyhound Bus Station** (Map p72; ☑702-384-9561; www.greyhound.com; 200 S Main St; ⊙24hr; ⏹SDX), adjacent to the Plaza and a quick walk from other casino hotels on the Fremont Street Experience.

CAR & MOTORCYCLE

The main roads into and out of Las Vegas are I-15 and US Hwy 95. US Hwy 93 leads southeast from downtown to Hoover Dam; I-215 goes by McCarran International Airport. It's a 165-mile drive (2½ hours) to Utah's Zion National Park, 275 miles (4½ hours) to Arizona's Grand Canyon Village and 270 miles (four hours) to Los Angeles. Along the I-15 corridor to/from California, Highway Radio (98.1FM, 99.5FM) broadcasts traffic updates every 30 minutes.

❶ Getting Around

Gridlock along the Strip makes navigating the city's core a chore. The best way to get around is on foot, along with the occasional air-con taxi, monorail or bus ride.

TO/FROM THE AIRPORT

Some casino hotels both on and off the Strip offer free airport shuttle buses for guests. Public shuttle buses and vans charge about $7 to $8 per person to the Strip, $8.50 to $9 to downtown or off-Strip hotels. Often delayed by making multiple stops, these airport shuttles operate 24 hours. **Bell Trans** (☑800-274-7433; www.belltrans. com) offers competitive rates.

You'll pay at least $20 plus tip for a taxi to the Strip – tell your driver to use surface streets, not the I-15 Fwy airport connector tunnel ('long-hauling'), since fare gouging is common.

CAR & MOTORCYCLE
Rental

Trying to decide whether to rent a car in Vegas? The biggest pro: all of the attractions in Vegas have free self-parking and valet parking available. The biggest cons: car rentals in Las Vegas are more expensive than elsewhere in the Southwest, and using a car to navigate the Strip (especially in the evening) offers zero efficiency.
Hertz (☑800-654-3131; www.hertz.com)

Traffic

Traffic often snarls, especially during morning and afternoon rush hours and at night on weekends around the Strip. Work out in advance which cross street will bring you closest to your destination and try to utilize alternate routes like Industrial Rd and Paradise Rd. Tune to 970AM for traffic updates. If you're too drunk to drive, call **Designated Drivers** (☑702-456-7433; http://vegas. designateddriversinc.com; ⊙24hr)to pick you up and drive your car back to your hotel; fees vary, depending on mileage.

PUBLIC TRANSPORTATION

Buses from Regional Transportation Commission of Southern Nevada (RTC; ☑800-228-3911, 702-228-7433; www.rtcsnv.com/transit; Deuce & SD X 2/24/72hr bus pass $6/8/20)operate from 5am to 2am daily, with Strip and downtown routes running 24/7 every 15 to 20 minutes.

Double-decker Deuce buses to/from downtown stop every block or two along the Strip. Quicker SDX express buses stop outside some Strip casino hotels and at the Fashion Show, the city's convention center and a few off-Strip shopping malls. Have exact change or bills ready when boarding or buy a pass before boarding from ticket vending machines at bus stops.

Many off-Strip casino hotels offer limited free shuttle buses to/from the Strip, usually reserved for hotel guests (sometimes free, but a surcharge may apply).

Free air-conditioned trams shuttle between some Strip casino hotels. One connects the Bellagio, CityCenter and the Monte Carlo. Another links Treasure Island and the Mirage. A third zips between Excalibur, Luxor and Mandalay Bay. Trams run all day and into the evening, usually stopping from late-night until the early-morning hours.

The fast, frequent monorail (☑702-699-8299; www.lvmonorail.com; single-ride $5,24/48/72hr pass $12/22/28; ⊙7am-midnight Mon, to 2am Tue-Thu, to 3am Fri-Sun) stops at the MGM Grand, Bally's/Paris, the Flamingo, Harrah's/Quad, Las Vegas Convention Center, Las Vegas Hilton and the former Sahara (now SLS), a 13-minute route.

TAXI

It's illegal to hail a cab on the street. Taxi stands are found at casino hotels and malls. A lift from one end of the Strip to the other runs about $20, plus tip (10-15%). Some accept credit cards. By law, the maximum number of passengers is five, and all companies must have at least one wheel-chair-accessible van. Call **Desert Cab** (☑702-386-9102), **Western Cab** (☑702-736-8000) or **Yellow/Checker/Star** (☑702-873-2000).

AROUND LAS VEGAS

You might be surprised to discover geologic treasures in Nevada's amazing wind- and water-carved landscape, all within a short drive of surreal facsimiles of Ancient Rome and belle epoque Paris. While Las Vegas may be the antithesis of a naturalist's vision of America, it's certainly close to some spectacular outdoor attractions. For iconic desert landscapes, Red Rock Canyon and Valley of Fire State Park are just outside the city limits. Straddling the Arizona–Nevada state line are Hoover Dam, just outside Boulder City, and the cool oasis of Lake Mead National Recreation Area.

☞ Tours

Hoover Dam package deals can save ticketing and transportation headaches, while adventure outfitters ease logistical hassles for many outdoor excursions. Some tours include free pick-ups and drop-offs from Strip casino hotels. Check free Vegas magazines for deals.

Red Rock Canyon

The startling contrast between Las Vegas' artificial neon glow and the awesome natural forces in this national conservation area can't be exaggerated. Created about 65 million years ago, the canyon is more like a valley, with a steep, rugged red-rock escarpment rising 3000ft on its western edge, dramatic evidence of tectonic-plate collisions. Today this outdoor playground buzzes with rock climbers, hikers and wildlife-watchers. Summer days are blazing hot in the Mojave Desert, so it's better to visit during the cooler spring and fall seasons.

Mountain biking is allowed only on paved roads, not dirt trails. About 2 miles east of the visitor center off NV Hwy 159 is a Bureau of Land Management (BLM) campground, closed at the time of writing. Check on its status before going at www.blm.gov.

◉ Sights

Red Rock Canyon
Visitor Center VISITOR CENTER
(☑702-515-5350; www.redrockcanyonlv.org; ☺8:30am-4:30pm; ♿) Near the start of the scenic loop drive, stop here for natural-history exhibits and information on hiking trails, rock-climbing routes and 4WD routes. Red Rock Canyon Interpretive Association operates the nonprofit bookstore and organizes outdoor activities, including geology, birding and wildflower walks (advance reservations may be required).

Scenic Loop Drive SCENIC DRIVE
(entry per car/bicycle $7/3; ☺6am-8pm Apr-Sep, to 7pm Mar & Oct, to 5pm Nov-Feb) A 13-mile, one-way scenic drive passes by some of the canyon's most striking features. From roadside parking areas you can access hiking trails and rock-climbing routes, or simply be mesmerized by the vistas. Cyclists are allowed on all paved roads, but should watch out for dangerous potholes and distracted drivers!

☆ Activities & Tours

Las Vegas Cyclery CYCLING
(☑702-596-2953; http://lasvegascyclery.com; 10575 Discovery Dr; bicycle rental per day $40-100; ☺10am-7pm Mon-Fri, 9am-6pm Sat, 10am-4pm Sun) Rent high-quality road and mountain bikes in suburban Summerlin, 10 miles west of the Strip. Ask about guided cycling and mountain-biking tours of Red Rock Canyon.

Cowboy Trail Rides HORSEBACK RIDING
(☑702-387-2457; www.cowboytrailrides.com; off Hwy 159; tours $69-329; ♿) To ride 'em cowboy, make reservations for a good ol' Western horseback ride along Fossil Ridge on the canyon rim or a sunset trip on the canyon floor followed by a BBQ cookout.

Scoot City Tours TOUR
(☑702-699-5700; www.scootcitytours.com; per 2 people $250; ☺8am & 1pm daily Apr-Oct, 1pm Nov-Mar) An alternative to ho-hum bus and van tours, drive your own three-wheeled scooter-car around the canyon's scenic loop drive on a semiguided group tour. It can be very cold in winter. Drivers must be at least 21 years old; no passengers under 8 years old allowed.

WORTH A TRIP

VALLEY OF FIRE STATE PARK

A masterpiece of desert scenery filled with psychedelically shaped sandstone outcroppings, this **park** (☑702-397-2088; www.parks.nv.gov; per vehicle $10) on the north edge of Lake Mead wows. It's amazing that this fantasyland of wondrous shapes carved in psychedelic sandstone by the erosive forces of wind and water is also a relaxing escape that's only 55 miles from Vegas.

Hwy 169 runs right past the **visitor center** (☑702-397-2088; ☺8:30am-4:30pm), which offers information on hiking and has excellent desert-life exhibits. It also sells books and maps, and has information about ranger-led activities like guided hikes and stargazing.

Take the winding scenic side road out to **White Domes**, 11 miles round-trip. En route you'll pass **Rainbow Vista**, followed by the turnoff to **Fire Canyon** and **Silica Dome** (incidentally, where Captain Kirk perished in *Star Trek: Generations*).

Spring and fall are the best times to visit; daytime summer temperatures typically exceed 100°F (more than 37°C). The valley is at its most fiery at dawn and dusk, so consider grabbing a first-come, first-served site in the campgrounds (tent/RV sites $20/30). The fastest way here from Las Vegas is to drive I-15 north to NV Hwy 169, taking about an hour.

❶ Getting There & Away

The park is 18 miles west of the Strip. There is no public transportation. To get here from the Strip, take I-15 south, exit at Blue Diamond Rd (NV Hwy 160), and drive westward, veering right onto NV Hwy 159. On the return trip, keep driving east on Hwy 159, which becomes Charleston Blvd, continuing east to I-15 and Las Vegas Blvd.

Spring Mountain Ranch State Park

South of Red Rock Canyon's scenic loop drive, a side road leaves Hwy 159 and enters the petite **Spring Mountain Ranch State Park** (☑702-875-4141; http://parks.nv.gov; entry $7-12; ☺8am-dusk, visitor center 10am-4pm), abutting the cliffs of the Wilson Range. The ranch was established in the 1860s and has had various owners including the eccentric billionaire Howard Hughes. Popular with picnicking families on weekends, today it's a verdant place, with white fences and an old red ranch house, which has historical exhibits. Call for schedules of guided ranch tours, moonlight canyon hikes and outdoor summer theater performances.

Lake Mead & Hoover Dam

Even those who challenge, or at least question, the USA's commitment to damming the US West have to marvel at the engineering and architecture of the Hoover Dam. Set amid the almost unbearably dry Mohave Desert, the dam towers over Black Canyon and provides electricity for the entire region.

Hoover Dam created Lake Mead, which boasts 700 miles of shoreline, while Davis Dam created the much smaller Lake Mohave, which straddles the Arizona border. Black Canyon, the stretch of the Colorado River just below Hoover Dam, links the two lakes. All three bodies of water are included in the Lake Mead National Recreation Area, created in 1964.

◉ Sights

★**Hoover Dam**   HISTORIC SITE
(☑866-730-9097, 702-494-2517; www.usbr.gov/lc/hooverdam; off Hwy 93; admission & 30min tour adult/child 4-16yr $15/12, with 1hr tour $30; ☺9am-6pm Apr-Oct, to 5pm Nov-Mar; ⛟) Straddling the Arizona–Nevada border, the graceful concrete curve of the art deco–style Hoover Dam redefines the stark landscape. The massive 726ft structure is one of the world's tallest dams. Originally named Boulder Dam, this New Deal public works project, completed ahead of schedule and under budget in 1936, was the Colorado River's first major dam.

At the height of the Depression, thousands of men and their families migrated here to build the dam. They worked in excruciating conditions, dangling hundreds of feet above the canyon in 120°F (about 50°C) desert heat. Hundreds lost their lives.

Guided tours begin at the visitor center, with a video of original construction footage. An elevator takes visitors 50 stories below to view the dam's massive generators, which could each could power a city of 100,000 people.

Children under eight are not permitted on the more extensive dam tour (one hour) that visits the dam passageways. Parking at the site costs $10.

Boulder City/Hoover Dam Museum
MUSEUM

(🖉702-294-1988; www.bcmha.org; 1305 Arizona St, Boulder Dam Hotel, Boulder City; adult/child & student $2/1; ⊙10am-5pm Mon-Sat; 🖼) You'll enjoy the dam tour more if you stop at this small but engagingly hands-on museum first. It's upstairs at the historic Boulder Dam Hotel, where Bette Davis, FDR and Howard Hughes once slept. Exhibits focus on Depression-era America and the tough living conditions endured by the people who came to build the dam. A 20-minute film features historic footage of the project.

Mike O'Callaghan–Pat Tillman Memorial Bridge
BRIDGE

(Hwy 93) Featuring a pedestrian walkway with perfect views upstream of Hoover Dam, this bridge is definitely not recommended for anyone with vertigo. Mike O'Callaghan was governor of Nevada from 1971 to 1979. NFL star Pat Tillman was a safety for the Arizona Cardinals when he enlisted as a US Army Ranger in 2002. He was slain by friendly fire during a battle in Afghanistan in 2004. Top army commanders, who promoted the fabrication that he'd been killed by enemy forces, covered up the circumstances surrounding his death.

🏃 Activities

Popular year-round activities in **Lake Mead National Recreation Area** (🖉info desk 702-293-8906, visitor center 702-293-8990; www.nps.gov/lake; 7-day entry per vehicle $10; ⊙24hr, visitor center 9am-4:30pm Wed-Sun; 🖼) include swimming, fishing, boating, water-skiing and kayaking. The splendid scenic drive winds north along Lakeshore Dr and Northshore Rd, passing viewpoints, hiking and birding trailheads, beaches and bays, and full-service marinas.

Don't overlook a simple stroll around charming, serene Boulder City, the only casino-free town in Nevada. Originally erected to house workers constructing the Hoover Dam, casinos were outlawed to prevent distractions from their monumental task.

Lake Mead Cruises
BOAT TOUR

(🖉702-293-6180; www.lakemeadcruises.com; Lakeshore Rd; 90min midday cruise per adult/child 2-11yr $26/13; ⊙noon & 2pm Apr-Oct, schedules vary Nov-Mar; 🖼) Sail away on board triple-decker, Mississippi-style paddle wheelers, which are most importantly air-conditioned. Lunch and dinner cruises aren't worth the extra money. Cruises depart from Hemenway Harbor, near the lake's southern end.

★ Desert Adventures
KAYAKING

(🖉702-293-5026; www.kayaklasvegas.com; 1647a Nevada Hwy, Boulder City; full-day Colorado River kayak $169; ⊙9am-6pm Apr-Oct, 10am-4pm Nov-Mar) With Lake Mead and the Black Canyon of the Colorado River just a short drive away, would-be river rats should check in here for guided kayaking and stand up paddling (SUP) tours. Experienced paddlers can rent canoes and kayaks for DIY trips.

All Mountain Cyclery
CYCLING, KAYAKING

(🖉702-453-2453; http://allmountaincyclery.com; 1404 Nevada Hwy, Boulder City; mountain-bike rentals per day $40-75, half/full-day tour $180/200; ⊙11am-6pm Mon, 10am-6pm Tue-Fri, 9am-6pm Sat, 9am-4pm Sun) Bounce along singletrack in Bootleg Canyon on a guided mountain-biking tour, or get a real workout with an all-day excursion that includes Lake Mead kayaking. Mountain bike rentals and shuttle available.

Bootleg Canyon Flightlines
OUTDOORS

(🖉702-293-6885; www.flightlinezbootleg.com; 1512 Industrial Rd, Boulder City; 2hr tour $159) This thrilling aerial adventure is like zip-lining, but with a paragliding harness. Morning tours see the coolest temps, while late-afternoon tours may catch sunset over the desert. Riders must weigh between 75lb and 250lb (fully dressed) and wear close-toed shoes.

Black Canyon River Adventures
RAFTING

(🖉800-455-3490, 702-294-1414; www.blackcanyonadventures.com; Hacienda Hotel & Casino, Hwy 93, Boulder City; 5hr tour adult/child 5-12yr $92/58; 🖼) Motor-assisted Colorado River raft floats launch beneath Hoover Dam, with stops for swimming and lunch.

Hiking

While most visitors come to Lake Mead for the water, there are a handful of hiking trails too, most of which are short. At Grapevine Canyon near Lake Mohave, for instance, a quarter-mile jaunt takes you to a petroglyph panel, but if you want you can boulder-hop further up the gorge, which cups a ribbon-like stream trickling down from a spring. Longer routes include a 3.7-mile trail along a historic railway line with five tunnels that links the Alan Bible Visitor Center to Hoover Dam. The most challenging hike in the park follows a 3-mile trail down 800ft to a set of hot springs in a slot off Black Canyon. This one's not recommended in summer.

🛏 Sleeping

Boulder Dam Hotel
HOTEL $

(📞702-293-3510; www.boulderdamhotel.com; 1305 Arizona St; incl breakfast r $89-94, ste $99; ✳@🛜) For a peaceful night's sleep worlds away from the madding crowds and neon of Vegas, this gracious Dutch Colonial–style hotel has welcomed illustrious guests since 1933. Relax with a cocktail at the art deco jazz lounge on-site.

NPS Campgrounds
CAMPGROUND $

(📞702-293-8906; tent & RV sites $10) It's first-come, first-served at these campgrounds found on Lake Mead at Boulder Beach, Callville Bay, Echo Bay and Las Vegas Bay.

Cottonwood Cove Motel
MOTEL $$

(📞702-297-1464; www.cottonwoodcoveresort.com; r $131) On Lake Mohave, this motel has rooms with sliding glass doors overlooking a swimming beach.

🍴 Eating

You'll find only basic restaurants at the Temple Bar, Boulder Beach and Echo Bay marinas on Lake Mead, and at Cottonwood Cove and Katherine Landing on Lake Mohave. Other lakeshore marinas have convenience stores for snacks and drinks.

Coffee Cup
DINER $

(📞702-294-0517; www.worldfamouscoffeecup.com; 512 Nevada Way, Boulder City; mains $6-10; ⏰6am-2pm; 🚸) At this classic downtown diner, lines snake outside the door just for a chance to fork into waffles with design-it-yourself fillings like peanut butter, coconut or bacon, or the Mexican pork chile-verde omelet with crispy hash browns. Breakfast served all day.

Milo's Cellar
CAFE $$

(📞702-293-9540; www.miloswinebar.com; 538 Nevada Hwy, Boulder City; mains $9-14; ⏰11am-10pm Sun-Thu, to 11pm Fri & Sat) Downtown Milo's dependably delivers deli sandwiches,

WORTH A TRIP

PIONEER SALOON

Seven miles west of Jean, near the California border, have a mini Wild West adventure in the almost ghost town of Goodsprings where the tin-roofed **Pioneer Saloon** (📞702-874-9362; http://pioneersaloon.info; ⏰11am-late) dates from 1913. Riddled with bullet holes, it still serves up cold beers atop an antique cherrywood bar. Admire the vintage poker table and movie-star memorabilia.

fresh salads and gourmet cheese and meat platters to sidewalk tables outside its lively wine and beer bar.

Dillinger
BURGERS $$

(📞702-293-4001; www.thedillinger.com; 1224 Arizona St, Boulder City; mains $8-13; ⏰11am-10pm) After a day of mountain biking, hiking or kayaking, what sounds better than a burger and a cold beer? Head to this downtown 'drinkery' and order the name-sake Dillinger burger topped with bacon and beef brisket, with sweet-potato fries on the side.

ℹ Information

Alan Bible Visitor Center (📞702-293-8990; www.nps.gov/lake; Lakeshore Scenic Dr, off US Hwy 93; ⏰9am-4:30pm Wed-Sun) This visitor center is about 4 miles west of Hoover Dam. Excellent source of information on area recreation and desert life.

Katherine Landing Ranger Station (📞928-754-3272; off AZ Hwy 68, Bullhead City; ⏰8:30am-4pm) In Arizona, 3 miles north of Davis Dam.

Nevada Welcome Center (📞702-294-1252; www.visitbouldercity.com; 100 Nevada Hwy, Boulder City; ⏰8am-4:30pm) Near Hoover Dam.

ℹ Getting There & Away

From the Strip, take I-15 south to I-215 east to I-515/US 93 and 95 and continue over Railroad Pass, staying on US Hwy 93 past Boulder City. As you approach the dam, park in the multilevel parking lot ($10, cash only; open 8am to 6pm) before you reach the visitor center. Or continue over the Arizona state line and park for free on the roadside (if you can find a space), then walk back over the top of the dam to the visitor center.

Mt Charleston

Up in the Humboldt-Toiyabe National Forest, the Spring Mountains form the western boundary of the Las Vegas valley, with higher rainfall, lower temperatures and fragrant pine, juniper and mountain mahogany forests.

Just past the NV Hwy 158 turnoff and campground, the **information station** (✆702-872-5486; www.fs.usda.gov/htnf; Kyle Canyon Rd; ◷hours vary) has free trail guides, brochures and outdoor activity information.

The village of Mt Charleston gives access to several hikes, including the demanding 16.6-mile round-trip **South Loop Trail** up Charleston Peak (elevation 11,918ft), starting from Cathedral Rock picnic area. The easier, 2.8-mile round-trip **Cathedral Rock Trail** offers canyon views.

Mt Charleston Lodge (✆702-872-5408, 800-955-1314; www.mtcharlestonlodge.com; 1200 Old Park Rd; cabins $108-295; 🐾) has a chalet-style **dining room** (mains $11-24; ◷8am-9pm Sun-Thu, 8am-10pm Fri & Sat) and rustic, romantic log cabins with fireplaces, Jacuzzi tubs and private decks.

Heading back downhill, turn left onto Hwy 158, a curvy alpine road that passes even more trailheads and **campgrounds** (✆877-444-6777, 518-885-3639; www.recreation.gov; tent & RV sites $15-25; ◷mid-May–Oct, some year-round). At NV Hwy 156 (Lee Canyon Rd), turn either right to return to US Hwy 95 or left to reach **Las Vegas Ski & Snowboard Resort** (✆702-385-2754, snow report 702-593-9500; www.skilasvegas.com; half-day pass adult/child $50/30; ◷usually mid-Nov–Apr; ♿), which has four lifts, 11 trails (longest run 3000ft) and a half-pipe and terrain park for snowboarding.

Mesquite

POP 19,570 / ELEV 1600FT

Just over an hour's drive northeast of Las Vegas via I-15, **Mesquite** (✆877-637-7848; www.visitmesquite.com) is another Nevada border town stuffed full of casino hotels, all banking on slot-machine-starved visitors from Utah and Arizona. Escape the casinos by overnighting at the **Falcon Ridge Hotel** (✆844-746-0678; www.hiexpress.com/mesquite; 1030 W Pioneer Blvd; d $80; ❋ 🛜 ❄), down the street from **Sushi Masa** (✆702-346-3434; 155 Pioneer Blvd; mains $6-18; ◷10am-10pm) where even Californians rave about the sushi lovingly crafted by the talented Japanese chef.

GREAT BASIN

Geographically speaking, nearly all of Nevada lies in the Great Basin – a high desert characterized by rugged mountain ranges and broad valleys that extends into Utah and California. Far from Nevada's major cities, this land is largely empty, textured only by peaks covered by snow in winter. It's big country out here – wild, remote and quiet. Anyone seeking the 'Great American Road Trip' will savor the atmospheric small towns and quirky diversions tucked away along these lonely highways. Each of the main routes used by drivers to cut across the state is described here, covering interesting places to stop along the way, plus some unusual detours.

Along Highway 95

US Hwy 95 runs vaguely north–south through western Nevada. Although it's hardly a direct route, it's the fastest way to get from Las Vegas to Reno – and still, it's a full day's drive of 450 miles, so get an early start. The highway zigzags to avoid mountain ranges and passes through old mining centers that are not much more than ghost towns today.

Beatty

POP 1010 / ELEV 3300FT

From Las Vegas, it's 1¾ hours to broken-down Beatty, the northeastern gate-

---

SEEING A NEVADA TEST SITE

About 65 miles northwest of Las Vegas, starkly scenic US Hwy 95 rounds the Spring Mountains and passes a side road signposted 'To Mercury.' Behind barbed wire lies the **Nevada National Security Site** (✆702-295-0944; www.nv.energy.gov/outreach/tours.aspx) FREE, where over 900 atmospheric and underground nuclear explosions were detonated between 1951 and 1992. Free public bus tours depart monthly, usually from Las Vegas' National Atomic Testing Museum (p73), but you must apply for reservations as far in advance as possible.

AREA 51 & THE EXTRATERRESTRIAL HWY

Die-hard UFO fans and conspiracy theorists won't want to miss the way-out-there trip to Area 51, where some believe secret government research into reverse-engineering alien technology takes place. It's located off of Hwy 95, about 127 miles north of Las Vegas.

Coming from Tonopah, drive east along US Hwy 6 for 50 miles, then follow NV Hwy 375, aka the 'Extraterrestrial Hwy,' for another hour to the roadside pitstop of Rachel. Have burgers and beer or spend the night at the **Little A'le' Inn** (✆775-729-2515; www. littlealeinn.com; 1 Old Mill Rd, Alamo; RV sites with hookups $15, r $45-150; ☺restaurant 8am-9pm; ✸❋☎✸).

Sky-watchers gather further east at the 29-mile marker on the south side of Hwy 375.

way to Death Valley National Park. The **chamber of commerce** (✆775-553-2424, 866-736-3716; www.beattynevada.org; 119 Main St; ☺9:30am-2:30pm Tue-Sat) is downtown. Four miles west of town, off NV Hwy 374, is the mining ghost town of **Rhyolite** (www. rhyolitesite.com; donation appreciated; ☺24hr), where you can see a 1906 'bottle house' and the skeletal remains of a three-story bank. Next door, the bizarre **Goldwell Open Air Museum** (✆702-870-9946; www.goldwellmuseum.org; ☺24hr) **FREE** stars Belgian artist Albert Szukalski's spooky *The Last Supper*. Five miles north of town, past the sign for Angel's Ladies brothel, **Bailey's Hot Springs** (✆775-553-2395; hot springs $8, tent/RV sites $15/25; ☺8am-8pm) offers private mineral pools at a 1906 former railroad depot.

Goldfield & Tonopah

Another hour's drive further north, Goldfield became Nevada's biggest boomtown after gold was struck here in 1902. A few precious historic structures survive today, including the Goldfield Hotel, a restored firehouse (now a museum) and the county courthouse, with its Tiffany lamps. Another survivor, the rough-and-tumble **Santa Fe Saloon** (✆775-485-3431; 925 N 5th Ave; ☺hours vary), is a hoary watering hole.

Almost 30 miles further north, huge mine headframes loom above Tonopah, a historic silver-mining town that clings to its remaining population in a bereft yet beautiful setting. The **Central Nevada Museum** (✆775-482-9676; www.tonopahnevada. com; 1900 Logan Field Rd; ☺9am-5pm Tue-Sat) **FREE** has a good collection of Shoshone baskets, early photographs, mining relics and mortician's instruments. The **Tonopah Historic Mining Park** (✆775-482-9274; www. tonopahhistoricminingpark.com; 520 McCulloch

Ave; admission free, walking tours adult/child $5/4; ☺9am-5pm daily Apr-Sep, 10am-4pm Wed-Sun Oct-Mar) lets you explore an underground tunnel and peer into old silver-mine shafts. At night, it's dark enough for **stargazing** (www.tonopahstartrails.com).

Hawthorne
POP 3270 / ELEV 4330FT

The desert surrounding Hawthorne is oddly dotted with concrete bunkers storing millions of tons of explosives from a WWII-era military-ammunition depot bizarrely turned into a golf course.

Heading north, Hwy 95 traces the shrinking shoreline of **Walker Lake State Recreation Area** (✆775-867-3001; www. parks.travelnevada.com; tent sites $6; ☺24hr) **FREE**, a popular picnicking, swimming, boating, camping and fishing spot that's evaporating fast. Alt-US Hwy 95 is the scenic route to Reno, joining I-80 westbound at Fernley.

Along Highway 93

US Hwy 93 is the oft-deserted route from Las Vegas to Great Basin National Park, a 300-mile trip taking over five hours. Expect to pass by mining ghost towns and wide open rangeland populated by more cattle than humans.

Pahranagat Valley

North of I-15, US Hwy 93 parallels the eastern edge of the Desert National Wildlife Range, where bighorn sheep can be spotted. About 90 miles outside of Las Vegas, the road runs by **Pahranagat National Wildlife Refuge** (✆775-725-3417; www.fws.gov/refuge/Pahranagat; ☺24hr) **FREE**, where spring-fed lakes surrounded by cottonwoods are a major stopover for migratory birds, and a public rest area provides a good stopover for a bathroom break and a shaded picnic lunch.

Caliente

POP 1130 / ELEV 4400FT

Past Alamo and Ash Springs, US Hwy 93 leads to a junction, where you turn east through some desolate countryside to Caliente, a former railroad town with a Mission-style 1923 railway depot that makes for a cool photo op. Locals rave about **Pioneer Pizza** (☑775-726-3215; 127 N Spring St; mains $8-19; ☺10am-8pm Tue-Sat), though competition might not be so fierce: it's the only pizza within 100 miles. South of town via NV Hwy 317, **Rainbow Canyon** is known for its colorful cliffs and petroglyphs.

East of US Hwy 395, take a backcountry drive along NV Hwy 372 to **Spring Valley State Park** (☑775-962-5102; http://parks.nv.gov; entry $7, tent & RV sites $14-30) or **Echo Canyon State Park** (☑775-962-5103; http://parks.nv.gov; entry $7, tent/RV sites $17/27), both offering boating and fishing on artificial reservoirs.

Along Highway 50

The nickname says it all: on the **Loneliest Road in America** barren, brown desert hills collide with big blue skies. The highway goes on forever, crossing solitary terrain. Towns are few and far between, with the only sounds being the whisper of wind or the rattle and hum of a truck engine. Once part of the coast-to-coast Lincoln Hwy, US Hwy 50 follows the route of the Overland Stagecoach, the Pony Express and the first transcontinental telegraph line.

Fallon

POP 8600 / ELEV 3960

Look up into the sky and you might spot an F-16 flying over Fallon, home of the US Navy's TOPGUN fighter-pilot school. Dragsters and classic hot rods compete at the **Top Gun Raceway** (☑775-423-0223; www.topgun-raceway.com; adult/child 6-12yr $10/5) between March and November.

Besides the usual pioneer relics, the **Churchill County Museum & Archives** (☑775-423-3677; www.ccmuseum.org; 1050 S Maine St; ☺10am-5pm Mon-Sat, closes 1hr earlier Dec-Feb) FREE also displays an interesting replica of a Paiute hut and sponsors twice-monthly guided tours ($1) of Hidden Cave. The cave is near **Grimes Point Archaeological Area** (☑775-885-6000; www.blm.gov/nv; ☺24hr) FREE, about 10 miles east of Fallon, where a marked trail leads past boulders covered by Native American petroglyphs. Northeast of town, off Stillwater Rd (NV Hwy 166), **Stillwater National Wildlife Refuge** (☑775-428-6452; www.fws.gov/refuge/Stillwater; ☺24hr) FREE is a haven for over 280 species of birds, best seen during the **Spring Wings Festival** (www.springwings.org) in mid-May.

Sand Mountain Recreation Area

About 25 miles southeast of Fallon off US Hwy 50, this **recreation area** (☑775-885-6000; www.blm.gov/nv; 7-day permit $40, admission free Tue & Wed; ☺24hr) boasts sand dunes that 'sing,' occasionally producing a low-pitched boom. The best time to hear it is on a hot, dry evening when the dunes are not covered with screeching off-road vehicles and whooping sandboarders. Pony Express station ruins have been excavated at the small Sand Springs Desert Study Area. Designated campsites with vault toilets (no water) are free.

Cold Springs

Midway between Fallon and Austin, there's a historical marker on the south side of the highway. There a windswept 1½-mile walking path leads to the haunting ruins of **Cold Springs Pony Express Station**, built in 1860 but quickly replaced by a stagecoach stop and then the transcontinental telegraph line. It's just about the best place on US Hwy 50 to be carried away by the romance of the Old West. In fact, the mountain vistas alone are worth stopping for, at least to stretch your legs.

Austin

POP 200 / ELEV 6600FT

Although it looks pretty interesting after hours of uninterrupted basin-and-range driving, there's not much to this mid-19th-century boomtown – really, just a few frontier churches and atmospherically decrepit buildings along the short main street.

What most people come to Austin for is to play outdoors. Mountain biking is insanely popular; the **chamber of commerce** (☑775-964-2200; www.austinnevada.com; 122

Main St; ⊙9am-noon Mon-Thu) can recommend routes. The **USDA Forest Service Austin Ranger District office** (☑775-964-2671; www.fs.fed.us/htnf; 100 Midas Canyon Rd, off US Hwy 50; ⊙7:30am-4:30pm Mon-Fri) has info on camping, hiking trails and scenic drives, including the trip to **Toquima Cave**, where you can see rock art by ancient Shoshones.

Inside a former hotel moved here in pieces from Virginia City in 1863, the **International Cafe & Saloon** (www.internationalcafeandsaloon.com; 59 Main St; meals $4-12; ⊙6am-8pm) is one of Nevada's oldest buildings. The **Toiyabe Cafe** (☑775-964-2301; 150 Main St; mains $4-12; ⊙6am-9pm May-Sep, 6am-2pm Oct-Apr) is known for its breakfasts.

North of US Hwy 50 at Hickison Summit, about 24 miles east of Austin, **Hickison Petroglyph Recreation Area** (☑775-635-4000; www.blm.gov/nv; ⊙24hr) **FREE** has panoramic lookout points; a self-guided, ADA-accessible trail for viewing the petroglyphs; and a free primitive campground (vault toilets, no water).

Eureka

POP 610 / ELEV 6500FT

Eureka! In the late 19th century, $40 million worth of silver was extracted from the hills around Eureka. Pride of place goes to the **county courthouse** (☑775-237-5540; 10 S Main St; ⊙8am-noon & 1-5pm Mon-Fri) **FREE**, with its handsome pressed-tin ceilings and walk-in vaults, and the beautifully restored **opera house** (☑775-237-6006; 31 S Main St; ⊙8am-noon & 1-5pm Mon-Fri), dating from 1880, which hosts an art gallery and summer folk-music concerts. The **Eureka Sentinel Museum** (☑775-237-5010; 10 N Monroe St; ⊙10am-6pm daily May-Oct, Tue-Sat Nov-Apr,) **FREE** displays yesteryear newspaper technology and some colorful examples of period reportage. Budget motels and cafes line Main St.

Ely

POP 4260 / ELEV 6440FT

The biggest town for miles around, Ely deserves an overnight stop. Its old downtown has beautiful regional-history murals and awesome vintage neon signs.

East of downtown's gambling strip, marked by the 1929 Hotel Nevada and Jailhouse Casino, the **White Pine County Tourism & Recreation Board** (☑775-289-3720; www.elynevada.net; 150 Sixth St; ⊙8am-5pm Mon-Fri) provides visitor information on zany

CATHEDRAL GORGE STATE PARK

Awe, then ahhh: this **park** (☑775-728-4460; http://parks.nv.gov; Hwy 93; entry $7; ⊙visitor center 9am-4:30pm) is one of our favorite state parks not just in Nevada, but in the whole USA. Fifteen miles north of Caliente, just past the turnoff to Panaca, Cathedral Gorge State Park really does feel like you've stepped into a magnificent, many-spired cathedral, albeit one whose dome is a view of the sky. Miller Point Overlook has sweeping views, with several easy hikes into narrow side canyons.

Sleep under the stars at the first-come, first-served **campsites** (tent/RV sites $17/27) set amid badlands-style cliffs.

town events like Cocktails and Cannons and the annual Bathtub Races. Ask about the mysterious **Ghost Train** and the **Ely Renaissance Village** (www.elyrenaissance.com; 150 Sixth St; ⊙10am-4pm Sat Jul-Sep), a collection of 1908 period homes built by settlers from France, Slovakia, China, Italy and Greece.

Ely was established as a mining town in the 1860s, but the railroad didn't arrive until 1907. The interesting **East Ely Railroad Depot Museum** (http://museums.nevadaculture.org; 1100 Ave A; adult/child under 18yr $2/free; ⊙8am-4:30pm Wed-Sat) inhabits the historic depot. There, the **Nevada Northern Railway** (☑775-289-2085, 866-407-8326; www.nevadanorthernrailway.net; adult/child 4-12yr from $27/16; ⊙Apr-Dec) offers 90-minute excursion rides on trains pulled by historic steam engines.

Off US Hwy 93 south of town via signposted dirt roads, **Ward Charcoal Ovens State Historic Park** (☑775-728-4460; http://parks.nv.gov/ww.htm; entry $7, tent & RV sites $14, yurts $20) protects a half-dozen beehive-shaped structures dating from 1876 that were once used to make charcoal to supply the silver smelters.

We love the old-style charm and welcome of the **Bristlecone Motel** (☑800-497-7404; www.bristleconemotelelynv.com; 700 Avenue I; r $70; 🐾), with staff that goes the extra mile and sparkling rooms.

Ely's casinos have mostly ho-hum eateries, some open 24 hours. The **Silver State Restaurant** (☑775-289-8866; 1204 Aultman St; mains $6-18; ⊙6am-9pm) is an authentic diner-style coffee shop, where the waitresses call you 'hon' and comfort food is the only thing on the menu (cash only). **La Fiesta** (700 Ave H; lunch special under $8, mains $9.25-26; ⊙11am-9pm; ☑) serves up cheesy enchiladas and frozen margaritas.

Great Basin National Park

Near the Nevada–Utah border, this uncrowded **national park** (☑775-234-7331; www.nps.gov/grba; ⊙24hr) **FREE** encompasses 13,063ft Wheeler Peak, rising abruptly from the desert, creating an awesome range of life zones and landscapes within a very compact area. The peak's narrow, twisting scenic drive is open only during summer, usually from June through October. Hiking trails near the summit take in superb country made up of glacial lakes, groves of ancient bristlecone pines (some over 5000 years old) and even a permanent ice field. The summit trail is an 8.2-mile round-trip trek, with a vertical ascent of nearly 3000ft.

Back below, the main park **visitor center** (☑775-234-7331; ⊙8am-4:30pm) sells tickets for guided tours ($8 to $10) of **Lehman Caves**, which are brimming with limestone formations. The temperature inside is a constant 50°F (10°C), so bring a sweater.

The park's four developed **campgrounds** (☑775-234-7331; www.nps.gove/grba; primitive camping free, tent & RV sites $6-25) are open during summer; only Lower Lehman Creek is available year-round. Next to the visitor center, a simple cafe stays open from May through October. The nearby village of Baker has a gas station, a basic restaurant and sparse accommodations.

Along I-80

I-80 is the old fur-trappers' route, following the Humboldt River from northeast Nevada to Lovelock, near Reno. It's also one of the earliest emigrant trails to California. Transcontinental railroad tracks reached Reno in 1868 and crossed the state within a year. By the 1920s, the Victory Hwy traveled the same route, which later became the interstate. Although not always the most direct route across Nevada, I-80 skirts many of the Great Basin's steep mountain ranges. Overnight stops in the Basque-flavored country around Elko or Winnemucca will give you a true taste of cowboy life.

Lovelock

POP 1900 / ELEV 3980

Couples in love who want to leave a piece of their romance in Nevada would be advised to stop by the quiet town of Lovelock, a 90-minute drive northeast of Reno. Behind the **Pershing County Courthouse** (☑775-273-7213; 400 S Main St; ⊙8am-5pm Mon-Fri), inspired by Rome's pantheon, you can symbolically lock your passion on a chain for all eternity in **Love Lock Plaza** (www.loverslock.com). At the 1874 **Marzen House** (☑775-273-4949; 25 Marzen Lane; ⊙1:30-4pm May-Oct) **FREE**, a small historical museum displays mementos of local sweetheart Edna Purviance, Charlie Chaplin's leading lady. A country-style diner, the **Cowpoke Cafe** (☑775-273-2444; 995 Cornell Ave; meals from $5; ⊙6am-9pm Mon-Fri, to 3pm Sat) serves from-scratch buffalo burgers, brisket sandwiches and homemade desserts like red velvet cake.

Unionville & Around

POP 20 / ELEV 1540FT

This rural late-19th-century ghost town's big claim to fame is that Mark Twain tried his hand (albeit unsuccessfully) at silver mining here. Take a stroll by the writer's old cabin and the Buena Vista schoolhouse, pioneer cemetery and old-fashioned covered bridge. Further west along I-80, **Rye Patch State Recreation Area** (☑775-538-7321; www.parks.nv.gov; entry $7, tent/RV sites $14/27) offers swimming, fishing and boating.

Winnemucca

POP 7400 / ELEV 4300FT

A travelers' stop since the days of the Emigrant Trail, even Butch Cassidy dropped by Winnemucca to rob a bank. Named after a Paiute chief, the biggest town on this stretch of I-80 is also a center for the state's Basque community, descended from 19th-century immigrant shepherds.

◉ Sights & Activities

Unassuming Winnemucca boasts a vintage downtown full of antique shops and a number of Basque restaurants, in keeping with the town's fascinating Basque heritage. Get information on the town's annual June Basque Festival at the **Winnemucca Visitors Center & Chamber of Commerce** (☑775-623-5071; www.winnemucca.nv.us; 50 W

THE NAKED BARSTOOL

While sultry – or, more often, seedy – establishments employing scantily clad women are practically as commonplace across Nevada as casinos themselves, there's one consolation that even the flesh-wary can count on: that it's the employees, not the customers, who you might view in various states of undress. Not so at Winnemucca's **The Mineshaft Bar** (www.themineshaftbar.com; 44 W Railroad St; ⊙24hr), which bills itself as 'Nevada's only clothes-optional bar.' You know it's a serious dive when its website features the competing slogans 'Hard Rock Music for Hard Rock Miners,' and 'Where T and A is A-OK.' Weekend nights aren't for the faint of heart or the easily offended: think metal bands, wet T-shirt contests and girl-on-girl kissing contests.

Winnemucca Blvd; ⊙8am-noon & 1-5pm Mon-Fri, 9am-noon Sat, 11am-4pm Sun), along with a self-guided downtown walking-tour brochure and information on horseback riding at local ranches. Wannabe cowboys and cowgirls should check out the **Buckaroo Hall of Fame** – full of cowboy art and folklore – while taxidermy fans will want to check out the big-game museum in the lobby.

About 50 miles north of town, the Santa Rosa Mountains offer rugged scenery, hiking trails and camping in the **Humboldt-Toiyabe National Forest**.

Humboldt County Museum   MUSEUM
(www.humboldtmuseum.com; cnr Jungo Rd & Maple Ave; ⊙9am-4pm Mon-Fri, 1-4pm Sat) FREE North of the river in a former church, the Humboldt County Museum shows off antique cars, farming implements and beautiful Paiute baskets.

BLM Winnemucca
Field Office   TOURIST INFORMATION
(✆775-623-1500; www.blm.nv.gov; 5100 E Winnemucca Blvd; ⊙7:30am-4:30pm Mon-Fri) East of town, off Highland Dr at the end of Kluncy Canyon Rd, the **Bloody Shins Trails** are part of a burgeoning mountain biking trail system. Stop by this field office for more information.

🛏 Sleeping & Eating

Winnemucca's main drag has abundant motels and a few casino hotels with 24-hour restaurants.

Town House Motel   MOTEL $
(✆775-623-3620, 800-243-3620; www.town-house-motel.com; 375 Monroe St; r $70-80; 🛜) The family-owned Town House Motel has tidy budget rooms equipped with microwaves and minifridges.

Winnemucca Inn   HOTEL $$
(✆775-623-2565; www.winnemuccainn.com; 741 W Winnemucca Blvd; r from $109-125) Offers spacious, well-equipped rooms with a bustling casino, 24-hour restaurant and children's arcade.

Delizioso Global Coffee   CAFE $
(✆775-625-1000; 508a W Winnemucca Blvd; $2-5; ⊙5am-5pm Mon-Fri, 6am-1pm Sat; 🛜) To fuel up for what will likely be a long drive in any direction, delightful Delizioso Global Coffee offers creative espresso drinks like the 'Winnemocha' and fresh scones amid a fanciful forestlike interior.

Griddle   CAFE $$
(www.thegriddle.com; 460 W Winnemucca Blvd; mains $6-15; ⊙7am-2pm) Don't miss a stop at the Griddle, one of Nevada's best retro cafes, serving up fantastic breakfasts, diner classics and homemade desserts since 1948.

Third Street Bistro   CAFE $$
(✆775-623-0800; 45 E Winnemucca Blvd; mains $7-12; ⊙7am-2pm Mon-Sat) Locals adore the Third Street Bistro for its homebaked goods, tasty soups and excellent Philly cheesesteaks for lunch in a genteel atmosphere.

Martin Hotel   BASQUE $$$
(www.themartinhotel.com; 94 W Railroad St; dinner $17-32; ⊙11:30am-2pm Mon-Fri, 4-9pm nightly; 🍴) Those overnighting should plan their evening around dinner at the Martin Hotel, where ranchers, locals and weary travelers have come since 1898 to enjoy family-style Basque meals under pressed-tin ceilings.

Elko

POP 18,300 / ELEV 5070FT

Though small, Elko is the largest town in rural Nevada and a kind of charming center of cowboy culture. There's a calendar of Western cultural events and a museum big on buckaroos, stagecoaches and the Pony Express. Its other cultural influence is Basque; in fact, Basque shepherds and Old West cattlemen had some violent conflicts over grazing rights in the late 19th century.

The **National Basque Festival** (www.elkobasque.com) is held around July 4, with games, traditional dancing and even Elko's own 'Running of the Bulls.'

⊙ Sights & Activities

The **visitor center** (☎775-738-4091, 800-248-3556; www.elkocva.com; 1405 Idaho St; ⊙hours vary) is inside a historic ranch house. For information on summer art walks and wine walks, see www.elkodowntown.com.

South of Elko, the **Ruby Mountains** are a superbly rugged range, nicknamed Nevada's Alps for their prominent peaks, glacial lakes and alpine vegetation. The village of **Lamoille** has basic food and lodging, and one of the most photographed rural churches in the USA. Just before the village, Lamoille Canyon Rd branches south, following the forested canyon for 12 miles past cliffs, waterfalls and other glacial sculptures to the Ruby Crest trailhead at 8800ft.

Northeastern Nevada Museum   MUSEUM
(☎775-738-3418; www.museumelko.org; 1515 Idaho Ave; adult/youth 13-18yr/child 3-12yr $5/3/1; ⊙9am-5pm Mon-Sat, 1-5pm Sun) The Northeastern Nevada Museum has excellent displays on pioneer life, Pony Express riders, Basque settlers and modern mining techniques. Free monthly tours of the nearby Newmont gold mine usually start here; call ☑775-778-4068 for reservations.

Western Folklife Center   ARTS CENTER
(www.westernfolklife.org; 501 Railroad St; adult/child 6-18yr $5/1; ⊙10am-5:30pm Mon-Fri, to 5pm Sat) Aspiring cowboys and cowgirls should visit the Western Folklife Center & Wiegland Gallery, which hosts the remarkably popular Cowboy Poetry Gathering in January.

🛏 Sleeping & Eating

A popular overnight stop for truckers and travelers, Elko has over 2000 rooms that fill up fast, especially on weekends. Chain motels and hotels line Idaho St, particularly east of downtown. Of the chains, we like the comfy **Hilton Garden Inn** (☎775-777-1200; www.hiltongardeninn.com; 736 Idaho St; r $139; P❄@🖥🏊); the best budget choice is the locally run **Thunderbird Motel** (☎775-738-7115; www.thunderbirdmotelelko.com; 345 Idaho St; s/d $78/89; P❄🖥🏊🐕).

Stray Dog Pub & Café   PUB $
(☑775-753-4888; 374 5th St; mains $7-12; ⊙dinner 3-9pm Mon-Sat, bar open late) For decent pizza and local Nevada beer, sidle up to the bar at the Stray Dog Pub & Café, decked out with old bikes and surfboards.

The Coffee Mug   DINER $
(☑775-738-5999; 576 Commercial St; mains $8-12; ⊙6am-9pm) For local color, try this easygoing diner with a long counter of stools, good breakfasts and heaping portions. Their *carne asada* tacos stand out.

Cowboy Joe   CAFE $
(☑775-753-5612; 376 5th St; $2-6; ⊙5:30am-5:30pm Mon-Fri, 6am-5:30pm Sat, 7am-noon Sun; 🖥) A great small-town coffeehouse with cute namesake paraphernalia for sale, friendly service and an eponymous signature drink that will keep you going till Reno.

Star Hotel   BASQUE $$
(www.elkostarhotel.com; 246 Silver St; lunch $6-12, dinner $15-32; ⊙11am-2pm & 5-9pm Mon-Fri, 4:30-9:30pm Sat) If you've never sampled Basque food, the best place in town for your inaugural experience is the Star Hotel, a family-style supper club located in a 1910 boardinghouse for Basque sheepherders.

The irrepressibly curious will not want to miss a peek behind the restaurant, where Elko's small 'red light' district of legal brothels sits, including 'Inez's Dancing and Diddling,' perhaps the most bizarrely named business – tawdry or not – in the state.

Wells

POP 1300 / ELEV 5630FT

Sports fans should know that heavyweight boxer Jack Dempsey started his career here, as a bouncer in the local bars. After strolling around the rough-edged **Front Street historic district** today, you can imagine how tough that job must've been. The **Trail of the '49ers Interpretive Center** (☑775-752-3540; www.wellsnevada.com; 395 S 6th St; ⊙hours vary) **FREE** tells the story of mid-19th-century pioneers on the Emigrant Trail to California.

Southwest of town, scenic byway NV Hwy 231 heads into the mountains, climbing alongside sagebrush, piñon pine and aspen trees past two **campgrounds** (☑877-444-6777; www.recreation.gov; tent & RV sites $16-32;

⊗Jun-Oct). After 12 miles, the road stops at cobalt blue **Angel Lake** (8378ft), a glacial cirque beautifully embedded in the East Humboldt Range. Along NV Hwy 232, further south of Wells, a large natural window near the top of **Hole in the Mountain Peak** (11,306ft) is visible from the road.

West Wendover

POP 4410 / ELEV 4460FT

If you just can't make it to Salt Lake City tonight, stop in West Wendover, where ginormous **casino hotels** (☑800-537-0207; www.wendoverfun.com; r $69-299) with 24-hour restaurants line Wendover Blvd. Over on the Utah side, **Historic Wendover Airfield** (www.wendoverairbase.com; 345 Airport Apron, Wendover; admission by donation; ⊗8am-6pm) is a top-secret WWII-era US Air Force base, where the Enola Gay crew trained for dropping the atomic bomb on Japan. The **Bonneville Speed Museum** (☑775-664-4400; 1000 E Wendover Blvd, Wendover; adult/child $2/1; ⊗10am-6pm Jun-Nov) documents attempts to set land-speed records on the nearby Bonneville Salt Flats, where 'Speed Week' time trials in the third full week of August draw huge crowds every year.

RENO-TAHOE AREA

A vast sagebrush steppe, the western corner of the state is carved by mountain ranges and parched valleys. It's also the place where modern Nevada began. It was the site of the state's first trading post, pioneer farms and the famous Comstock silver lode, which spawned Virginia City, financed the Union during the Civil War and earned Nevada its statehood. Today, Reno and the state capital, Carson City, are far from the Wild West rawness still extant in the Black Rock Desert, reached via Pyramid Lake. For pampering all-seasons getaways, it's a short drive up to emerald Lake Tahoe, right on the California border.

Reno

POP 225,220 / ELEV 4500FT

An easygoing but bipolar city of big-time gambling and top-notch outdoor adventures, Reno resists pigeonholing. The 'Biggest Little City in the World' has something to raise the pulse of adrenaline junkies,

WORTH A TRIP

PYRAMID LAKE

A piercingly blue expanse in an otherwise barren landscape 25 miles north of Reno on the Paiute Indian Reservation, Pyramid Lake is a stunning standalone sight, with shores lined with beaches and eye-catching tufa formations. Closer to its east side, iconic pyramid-like Anaho Island is a bird sanctuary for American white pelicans. The area offers permits for camping (primitive campsites per vehicle per night $9) and fishing (permit $9) at outdoor suppliers and CVS drugstore locations in Reno, as well as at the **ranger station** (☑775-476-1155; http://plpt.nsn.us/rangers; 2500 Lakeview Dr; ⊗9am-1pm & 2-6pm Thu-Mon) on SR 445 in Sutcliffe.

hard-core gamblers and city people craving easy access to wide open spaces.

◉ Sights

National Automobile Museum MUSEUM
(☑775-333-9300; www.automuseum.org; 10 S Lake St; adult/child 6-18yr $10/4; ⊗9:30am-5:30pm Mon-Sat, 10am-4pm Sun; ⊕) Stylized street scenes illustrate a century's worth of automobile history at this engaging car museum. The collection is enormous and impressive, with one-of-a-kind vehicles – including James Dean's 1949 Mercury from *Rebel Without a Cause,* a 1938 Phantom Corsair and a 24-karat-gold-plated DeLorean – and rotating exhibits bringing in all kinds of souped-up or fabulously retro rides.

Nevada Museum of Art MUSEUM
(☑775-329-3333; www.nevadaart.org; 160 W Liberty St; adult/child 6-12yr $10/1; ⊗10am-5pm Wed & Fri-Sun, to 8pm Thu) In a sparkling building inspired by the geological formations of the Black Rock Desert north of town, a floating staircase leads to galleries showcasing temporary exhibits and eclectic collections on the American West, labor and contemporary landscape photography.

University of Nevada, Reno UNIVERSITY
Pop into the flying-saucer-shaped **Fleischmann Planetarium & Science Center** (☑775-784-4811; http://planetarium.unr.nevada.edu; 1650 N Virginia St; planetarium adult/child under 12yr $7/5; ⊗noon-7pm Mon-Thu, to 9pm Fri, 10am-9pm Sat, to 7pm Sun; ⊕) for a window

> ℹ️ **RENO AREA TRAILS**
>
> For the local lowdown on regional hiking and biking trails, including the Mt Rose summit trail and the Tahoe-Pyramid Bikeway, download the Truckee Meadows Trails guide (www.washoecounty.us). Another good resource is the Galena Creek Trails System trail map (www.galenacreekvisitorcenter.org/trail-map.html).

on the universe during star shows and feature presentations. Nearby is the **Nevada Historical Society Museum** (☎775-688-1190; http://museums.nevadaculture.org; 1650 N Virginia St; adult/child under 17yr $4/free; ⊙10am-5pm Tue-Sat), which includes permanent exhibits on neon signs, local Native American culture and the presence of the federal government.

👁 Virginia St

Wedged between the I-80 and the Truckee River, downtown's N Virginia St is casino central. South of the river it continues as S Virginia St. Many hotel casinos are open 24 hours.

Circus Circus   CASINO
(www.circusreno.com; 500 N Sierra St; ⊙24hr; 🚼) The most family-friendly of the bunch, Circus Circus has free circus acts to entertain kids beneath a giant, candy-striped big top, which also harbors a gazillion carnival and video games that look awfully similar to slot machines.

Silver Legacy   CASINO
(www.silverlegacyreno.com; 407 N Virginia St; ⊙24hr) A Victorian-themed place, the Silver Legacy is easily recognized by its white landmark dome, where a giant mock mining rig periodically erupts into a fairly tame sound-and-light spectacle.

Eldorado   CASINO
(www.eldoradoreno.com; 345 N Virginia St; ⊙24hr) The Eldorado has a kitschy Fountain of Fortune that probably has Italian sculptor Bernini spinning in his grave.

Harrah's   CASINO
(www.harrahsreno.com; 219 N Center St; ⊙24hr) Founded by Nevada gambling pioneer William Harrah in 1946, it's still one of the biggest and most popular casinos in town.

Peppermill   CASINO
(www.peppermillreno.com; 2707 S Virginia St; ⊙24hr) About 2 miles south of downtown, this place dazzles with a 17-story Tuscan-style tower.

Atlantis   CASINO
(www.atlantiscasino.com; 3800 S Virginia St; ⊙24hr) Modeled on the legendary underwater city, with a mirrored ceiling and tropical flourishes like indoor waterfalls and palm trees.

🏃 Activities

Reno is a 30- to 60-minute drive from Tahoe ski resorts, and many hotels and casinos offer special stay and ski packages. In summer there's a class III whitewater rafting run on the Truckee River suitable for families.

Truckee River Whitewater Park   WATER SPORTS
(www.reno.gov) Mere steps from the casinos, the park's Class II and III rapids are gentle enough for kids riding inner tubes, yet sufficiently challenging for professional freestyle kayakers. Two courses wrap around Wingfield Park, a small river island that hosts free concerts in summertime. **Tahoe Whitewater Tours** (☎775-787-5000; www.truckeewhitewaterrafting.com; 400 Island Ave; rafting adult/child $68/58) and **Wild Sierra Adventures** (☎866-323-8928; www.wildsierra.com; 11 N Sierra St; tubing $29) offer kayak trips and lessons.

Historic Reno Preservation Society   WALKING TOUR
(☎775-747-4478; www.historicreno.org; tours $10) Dig deeper with a walking or biking tour of the city highlighting subjects including architecture, politics and literary history.

🎉 Festivals & Events

Reno River Festival   SPORTS
(www.renoriverfestival.com) The world's top freestyle kayakers compete in a mad paddling dash through Whitewater Park in mid-May. Free music concerts as well.

Tour de Nez   SPORTS
(www.tourdenez.com) Called the 'coolest bike race in America,' the Tour de Nez brings together pros and amateurs for five days of races and partying in July.

Hot August Nights   CULTURAL
(www.hotaugustnights.net) Catch the *American Graffiti* vibe during this seven-day celebration of hot rods and rock and roll in early August. Hotel rates skyrocket to their peak.

🛏 Sleeping

Lodging rates vary widely depending on the day of the week and local events. Sunday through Thursday are generally the best; Friday is somewhat more expensive and Saturday can be as much as triple the mid-week rate. In the summer months, there's gorgeous high-altitude camping at **Mt Rose** (📞877-444-6777; www.recreation.gov; Hwy 431; RV & tent sites $17-50; ⊙mid-Jun-Sep).

Wildflower Village   MOTEL, B&B **$**
(📞775-747-8848; www.wildflowervillage.com; 4395 W 4th St; dm $34, motel $63, B&B $142; P❋@🐾) Perhaps more of a state of mind than a motel, this artists colony on the west edge of town has a tumbledown yet creative vibe. Individual murals decorate the facade of each room, and you can hear the freight trains rumble on by. Frequent live music and poetry readings at its cafe and pub, and bike rentals available.

Sands Regency   HOTEL **$**
(📞775-348-2200; www.sandsregency.com; 345 N Arlington Ave; r Sun-Thu from $39, Fri & Sat from $85; P❋🛜🐾) With some of the largest standard digs in town, rooms here are decked out in a cheerful tropical palette of upbeat blues, reds and greens – a visual relief from standard-issue motel decor. The 17th-floor gym and Jacuzzi are perfectly positioned to capture the drop-dead panoramic mountain views. An outdoor pool opens in summer. Empress Tower rooms are best.

Peppermill   CASINO HOTEL **$$**
(📞866-821-9996, 775-826-2121; www.peppermill-reno.com; 2707 S Virginia St; r Sun-Thu $59-129, Fri & Sat $79-209, resort fee $16; P❋@🛜🐾) 🐾 With a dash of Vegas-style opulence, the ever-popular Peppermill boasts Tuscan-themed suites in its newest 600-room tower, and plush remodeled rooms throughout the rest of the property. The three sparkling pools (one indoor) are dreamy, with a full spa on hand. Geothermal energy powers the resort's hot water and heat.

🍴 Eating

Reno's dining scene goes far beyond the casino buffets.

Peg's Glorified Ham & Eggs   DINER **$**
(www.eatatpegs.com; 420 S Sierra St; mains $7-14; ⊙6:30am-2pm; 🐾) Locally regarded as the best breakfast in town, Peg's offers tasty grill food that's not too greasy.

★**Old Granite Street**
Eatery   NEW AMERICAN **$$**
(📞775-622-3222; www.oldgranitestreeteatery.com; 243 S Sierra St; dinner mains $12-26; ⊙11am-10pm Mon-Thu, to 11pm Fri, 10am-11pm Sat, to 3pm Sun) A lovely well-lit place for organic and local comfort food, old-school artisanal cocktails and seasonal craft beers, this antique-strewn hot spot enchants diners with its stately wooden bar, water served in old liquor bottles and lengthy seasonal menu. Forgot to make a reservation? Check out the iconic rooster and pig murals and wait at a communal table fashioned from a barn door.

Silver Peak
Restaurant & Brewery   BREWPUB **$$**
(www.silverpeakrestaurant.com; 124 Wonder St; lunch $8.50-11, dinner $10-23; ⊙restaurant 11am-10pm Sun-Thu, to 11pm Sat & Sun, pub open 1hr later) Casual and pretense-free, this place hums with the chatter of happy locals settling in for a night of microbrews and great eats, from pizza with barbecue chicken to shrimp curry and filet mignon.

Louis' Basque Corner   BASQUE **$$**
(📞775-323-7203; 301 E 4th St; dinner menu $10-27; ⊙11am-9:30pm Tue-Sat, 4-9:30pm Sun-Mon) Get ready to dine on lamb, rabbit, sweet breads and more lamb at a big table full of people you've never met before. A different set-course menu is offered every day, posted in the window.

🍷 Drinking & Nightlife

Jungle   CAFE, WINE BAR
(www.thejunglereno.com; 246 W 1st St; ⊙coffee 6am-midnight, wine 3pm-midnight Mon-Thu, 3pm-2am Fri, noon-2am Sat, noon-midnight Sun; 🛜) A side-by-side coffee shop and wine bar with a cool mosaic floor and riverside patio all rolled into one. The wine bar has weekly tastings, while the cafe serves breakfast bagels and lunchtime sandwiches ($6 to $8) and puts on diverse music shows.

Imperial Bar & Lounge   BAR
(www.imperialbarandlounge.com; 150 N Arlington Ave; ⊙11am-2am Fri & Sat, to 10pm Sun-Thu) A classy bar inhabiting a relic of the past – this building was once an old bank, and in the middle of the wood floor you can see cement where the vault once stood. Sandwiches and pizzas go with 16 beers on tap and a buzzing weekend scene.

St James Infirmary
BAR

(445 California Ave) With an eclectic menu of 120 bottled varieties and 18 on tap, this bar will leave beer aficionados short circuiting with delight. Red lights blush over black-and-white retro banquettes and a wall of movie and music stills. The bar hosts sporadic events, including jazz and bluegrass performances.

Edge
CLUB

(www.edgeofreno.com; 2707 S Virginia St, Peppermill; admission $20; ⊙ Thu & Sat from 10pm, Fri from 7pm) The Peppermill reels in the nighthounds with a big glitzy dance club, where go-go dancers, smoke machines and laser lights may cause sensory overload. If so, step outside to the lounge patio and relax in front of cozy fire pits.

☆ Entertainment

The free weekly *Reno News & Review* (www.newsreview.com) is your best source for listings.

Knitting Factory
LIVE MUSIC

(☑ 775-323-5648; http://re.knittingfactory.com; 211 N Virginia St) This midsized music venue books mainstream and indie favorites.

ℹ Information

An **information center** sits near the baggage claim at Reno-Tahoe Airport.

Reno-Sparks Convention & Visitors Authority Visitor Center (☑ 775-682-3800; www.visitrenotahoe.com; 135 N Sierra St; ⊙ 9am-6pm) Also has an airport desk.

ℹ Getting There & Away

Reno-Tahoe International Airport (RNO; www.renoairport.com; ☜) About 5 miles southeast of downtown, the Reno-Tahoe International Airport is served by most major airlines.

North Lake Tahoe Express (☑ 866-216-5222; www.northlaketahoeexpress.com) Operates a shuttle ($45 one way, six to eight daily, 3:30am to midnight) to and from the airport to multiple North Shore Lake Tahoe locations including Truckee, Squaw Valley and Incline Village. Reserve in advance.

RTC Intercity Bus (www.rtcwashoe.com; intercity $5)

Greyhound (☑ 775-322-2970; www.greyhound.com; 155 Stevenson St) Buses run daily service to Truckee, Sacramento and San Francisco ($45, seven hours).

Amtrak (☑ 800-872-7245, 775-329-8638; www.amtrak.com; 280 N Center St) The once-daily westbound *California Zephyr* route ($51-176, 7½ hours) operated by Amtrak has daily service to Truckee, Sacramento and San Francisco ($45, seven days). The train has a bus connection from Emeryville for passengers to San Francisco ($61, 7½ hours).

ℹ Getting Around

The casino hotels offer frequent free airport shuttles for their guests (and don't ask to see reservations).

The local **RTC Ride buses** (☑ 775-348-7433; www.rtcwashoe.com; per ride $2) blanket the city, and most routes converge at the RTC 4th St Station downtown. Useful routes include the RTC Rapid line for S Virginia St, 11 for Sparks and 19 for the airport. The free Sierra Spirit bus loops around all major downtown landmarks – including the casinos and the university – every 15 minutes from 7am to 7pm.

Carson City

POP 55,275 / ELEV 4800FT

Is this the most underrated town in Nevada? We're going to double down and say yes. An easy drive from Reno or Lake Tahoe, it's a perfect stop for lunch and a stroll around the quiet, old-fashioned downtown. Expect handsome antique buildings and pleasant tree-lined streets centered around the 1870 **Nevada State Capitol** (cnr Musser & Carson; ⊙ 8am-5pm Mon-Fri) **FREE** where the governor's door is always open – you'll just have to charm your way past his assistant. Note the silver dome, which fittingly symbolizes Nevada's 'Silver State' status.

US Hwy 395 from Reno becomes the town's main drag, called Carson St. Look for the Cactus Jack neon sign letting you know you've reached downtown. About a mile further south, the **Carson City Convention & Visitors Bureau** (☑ 800-638-2321, 775-687-7410; www.visitcarsoncity.com; 1900 S Carson St; ⊙ 9am-4pm) has information about mountain-biking trails and hands out a historical walking-tour map of the Kit Carson Trail, with interesting podcasts that you can download online.

Several historic attractions and museums are worth visiting. Housed inside the 1869 US Mint building, the **Nevada State Museum** (www.nevadaculture.org; 600 N Carson St; adult/child under 18yr $8/free; ⊙ 8:30am-4:30pm Tues-Sun) puts on rotating exhibits of Native American, frontier and mining history. Train buffs shouldn't miss the **Nevada State Railroad Museum** (☑ 775-687-6953; http://museums.nevadaculture.org; 2180 S Carson St; adult/child under 18yr $6/free; ⊙ 9am-5pm Thu-Mon), displaying some 65 train cars and locomotives, most predating 1900. For made-in-Nevada artisan crafts, shop at the **Brewery Arts Center** (☑ 775-883-1976; www.breweryarts. org; 449 W King St; ⊙ 10am-4pm Mon-Sat).

Lunch, sip and linger at fetching, art-filled **Comma Coffee** (www.commacoffee.com; 312 S Carson St; breakfast $6-8, lunch $8-10; ⊙ 7am-8pm Mon & Wed-Sat, to 10pm Tue; 🛜🖊🖼), where eavesdropping may fetch you the inside scoop from Nevada lobbyists discussing a new bill over lattes, wine and great salads and soups. Nosh on English pub classics in red velvet booths at the **Firkin and Fox** (www.thefirkinandfox.com; 310 S Carson St; mains $10-15; ⊙ 11am-midnight Sun-Thu, to 2am Fri & Sat) downtown in the historic St Charles Hotel. For homemade cinnamon rolls, grab a table at **Mom & Pops** (224 S Carson St; mains $6-9; ⊙ 7am-2pm), a classic diner. Another option very popular with the locals is **Red's** (Old 395 Grille; ☑ 775-887-0395; 1055 S Carson St; mains $8-16; ⊙ 11am-9pm), serving St Louis–style BBQ with slow smoked ribs and beans, plus burgers and salads.

Virginia City

POP 855 / ELEV 6150FT

Twenty-five miles south of Reno, Virginia City is the site where the legendary Comstock Lode was struck, sparking a silver bonanza that began in 1859 and stands as one of the world's richest strikes. During the 1860s gold rush, Virginia City was a high-flying, rip-roaring Wild West boomtown. Newspaperman Samuel Clemens, alias Mark Twain, spent some time in this raucous place during its heyday and vividly captured the Wild West shenanigans in a book called *Roughing It.*

Sure, Virginia City can feel a bit like a high-elevation theme park, but it's still fun to visit. The high-elevation town is a bona fide National Historic Landmark, with a main street of Victorian buildings, wooden sidewalks and historic saloons. The main drag is C St; check out the **visitor center** (☑ 800-718-7587, 775-847-7500; www.visitvirginiacitynv.com; 86 S C St; ⊙ 9am-5pm Mon-Sat, 10am-4pm Sun) inside the historic Crystal Bar. They have information on seasonal stagecoach and trolley rides.

◎ Sights

Way It Was Museum   MUSEUM
(☑ 775-847-0766; 113 N C St; adult/child 11yr & under $3/free; ⊙ 10am-6pm) One of the town's star attractions is the quirky Way It Was Museum. It's a fun, old-fashioned place

offering good background information on mining the lode.

Mackay Mansion   HISTORIC BUILDING
(☑ 775-847-0173; 129 South D St; adult/child $5/free; ⊙ 10am-5pm Tue-Sun summer, hours vary winter) Stop by the Mackay Mansion to see how the mining elite once lived.

Virginia & Truckee Railroad   HISTORIC SITE
(☑ 775-847-0380; www.virginiatruckee.com; F & Washington Sts; 35min narrated tour adult/child 5-12yr $11/5; 🖼) From May through October, the Virginia & Truckee Railroad offers vintage steam-train excursions.

🛏 Sleeping

Sugarloaf Mountain Motel   MOTEL $
(☑ 775-847-0551; 430 S C St; r $60-100) Inside a 1870s boarding house, Sugarloaf Mountain Motel is welcoming and historical. It gets raves for hosts Jim and Michelle's friendly hospitality.

★ **Gold Hill Hotel & Saloon**   HOTEL $$
(☑ 775-847-0111; www.goldhillhotel.net; 1540 Main St; r $45-225; 🅿🏵🛜) A mile south of town via NV Hwy 342, the cool Gold Hill Hotel & Saloon claims to be Nevada's oldest hotel, and feels like it, with a breezy, old-fashioned charm and atmospheric bar boasting a great wine and spirits selection. Some rooms have fireplaces, original tubs and views of the Sierras.

Silverland Inn & Suites   HOTEL $$
(☑ 775-847-4484; www.silverlandusa.com; 100 N E St; r $98-142; 🅿🏵🛜🏊🐾) The renovated rooms at Silverland Inn & Suites will appeal to those who prefer modern (if nondescript)

OLD-TIME SALOONS

Drink like the miners of yesteryear at one of the many Victorian-era watering holes that line C street. We like the longtime family-run **Bucket of Blood Saloon** (www.bucketofbloodsaloonvc.com; 1 S C St; ⊙ 10am-7pm) which serves up beer and 'bar rules' at its antique wooden bar ('If the bartender doesn't laugh, you are not funny'). More about the setting than the food, **Palace Restaurant & Saloon** (www.palacerestaurant1875.com; 54 South C St; mains $7-12; ⊙ hours vary) is full of town memorabilia and serves up breakfasts and lunches.

digs. Has a sunny pool and hot-tub area with mountain views.

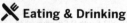 Eating & Drinking

Firehouse BBQ
BARBEQUE $

(☎775-847-4774; 171 S C St; mains $8-12) For gorgeous 100-mile views of the surrounding valleys, have an ice-cream cone on the back porch of the Firehouse BBQ where the friendly owners serve up burgers and pulled-pork sandwiches.

Cafe del Rio
MEXICAN $$

(www.cafedelriovc.com; 394 S C St; mains $11-16; ⊙11am-8pm Wed-Sat, 10am-7pm Sun) Locals agree that the best food in Virginia City is probably at Cafe del Rio, serving a nice blend of *nuevo* Mexican and Southwest cuisine, including brunch.

Roasting House
CAFE

(55 N Ave C; ⊙7am-4pm Mon-Fri, 9:30am-5pm Sat, noon-4pm Sun) Get your caffiene fix at the Roasting House, a micro roaster on the main strip.

Genoa

POP 940 / ELEV 4800FT

Imagine a pretty little cowboy town not gone to seed. The village of Genoa sits at the edge of Carson Valley, beneath the Sierra Nevada mountains. Founded by Mormons, it was the first European settlement at the western edge of the former Utah Territory. It's a quiet, attractive setting for those looking for a scenic getaway. Bring your own playing cards, as entertainment options are slim.

Cramped with old-timey appeal, the Genoa Saloon (☎775-782-3870; ⊙10am-10pm) claims to be the oldest bar in the state (since 1863), and it certainly looks the part. Bands play there on weekends. The Genoa Courthouse Museum (☎775-782-4325; www.genoanevada.org/genoamuseum.htm; 2304 Main St; adult/child $3/2; ⊙10am-4:30pm May-Oct) contains the original jail and a collection of woven Washo baskets. Wander through the early settlement of Mormon Station State Historic Park (☎775-782-2590; entry $7-12; ⊙10am-4pm Wed-Sun) to look at pioneer artifacts.

The town's biggest attraction is about 2 miles south of town, off NV Hwy 206: David Walley's Hot Springs & Spa (☎775-782-8155; www.1862hotsprings.com; 2001 Foothill Rd; pools, sauna & work-out room day pass $30; ⊙7am-9:30pm) is a huge complex that offers respite from traveling Nevada's dusty roads.

There are also a few homey B&Bs sprouting up in the area; though wedding season keeps them busy, they could be worth a shot.

Black Rock Desert

North of Pyramid Lake, NV Hwy 447 continues straight as an arrow for about 60 miles to the dusty railway town of Gerlach, with a gas station, a motel, a cafe and a few bars. Its motto is 'Where the pavement ends, the West begins.' Bruno's Country Club (☎775-557-2220; 445 Main St; meals $6-16; ⊙hours vary) is famous for its meaty ravioli in cheese sauce. Outside Gerlach, world land-speed records have been set on the dry, mud-cracked playas of the Black Rock Desert (☎775-557-2900; www.blackrockfriends.org). Although most people only visit during the Burning Man festival, this vast wilderness is primed for outdoor adventures year-round.

Lake Tahoe

Shimmering in myriad blues and greens, Lake Tahoe is the nation's second-deepest lake and a spot of true pine-scented wonder. Driving the circumference of its spellbinding 72-mile scenic shoreline certainly gives you quite a workout behind the wheel. To best enjoy the trip, take your time.

The north shore is quiet and upscale; the west shore, rugged and old-timey; the east shore, undeveloped; and the south shore, busy and tacky with aging motels and flashy casinos. The horned peaks surrounding the lake, which straddles the California–Nevada state line, are four-season playgrounds.

Tahoe gets packed in summer, on winter weekends and holidays, when reservations are essential. Lake Tahoe Visitors Authority (☎800-288-2463; www.tahoesouth.com; 169 Hwy 50, Stateline, NV; ⊙9am-5pm Mon-Fri) and North Lake Tahoe Visitors' Bureaus (☎888-434-1262; www.gotahoenorth.com) can help with accommodations and tourist information. There's camping in state parks (☎800-444-7275; www.reserveamerica.com) and on USFS lands (☎518-885-3639; www.recreation.gov; campsites $17-48; 🕸).

South Lake Tahoe & West Shore

With retro motels and eateries lining busy Hwy 50, South Lake Tahoe gets crowded. Gambling at Stateline's casino hotels, just across the Nevada border, attracts thou-

BURNING MAN

For one week at the end of August, **Burning Man** (www.burningman.com; admission $380) explodes onto the sunbaked Black Rock Desert, and Nevada sprouts a third major population center – Black Rock City. Over 50,000 revelers attend the event, which originated in 1986.

An experiential art party that climaxes in the immolation of a towering stick figure, Burning Man is a whirlwind of outlandish theme camps, dust-caked bicycles, bizarre bartering, costume-enhanced nudity and a general relinquishment of inhibitions. Think alternate universe. Movement principals include radical inclusion, gifting, decommodification, self-expression and civic responsibility. Attendees are known as 'burners' and indeed, fire is a huge component of the events and exhibits, with burn platforms preventing environmental damage.

Festivities take place on a large, uninhabited 'beach' (sans ocean) maintained by the Bureau of Land Management. With a proposed Leave No Trace ethic, participants are encouraged to do their part. There's mounted solar arrays for energy. The festivities begin on the last Monday in August and end on Labor Day.

sands, as does the world-class ski resort of **Heavenly** (☎775-586-7000; www.skiheavenly.com; 3860 Saddle Rd, South Lake Tahoe; adult/youth 13-18yr/child 5-12yr $99/89/59; ⊙9am-4pm Mon-Fri, 8:30am-4pm Sat, Sun & holidays; ⊕). In summer a trip up Heavenly's gondola (adult/child $45/27) guarantees fabulous views of the lake and **Desolation Wilderness**. This starkly beautiful landscape of raw granite peaks, glacier-carved valleys and alpine lakes is a favorite with hikers. Get maps, information and overnight **wilderness permits** (☎877-444-6777; www.recreation.gov; per adult $5-10) from the **USFS Taylor Creek Visitor Center** (☎530-543-2674; www.fs.usda.gov/ltbmu; Visitor Center Rd, off Hwy 89; ⊙8am-5:30pm late May-Oct). It's 3 miles north of the 'Y' intersection of Hwys 50/89, at **Tallac Historic Site** (www.tahoeheritage.org; Tallac Rd; optional tour adult/child $10/5; ⊙10am-4pm daily mid-Jun–Sep, Fri & Sat late May–mid-Jun; ⊕; **FREE**, which preserves early 20th-century vacation estates. **Lake Tahoe Cruises** (☎800-238-2463; www.zephyrcove.com; adult/child from $49/15) ply the 'Big Blue' year-round.

Cheerful chatter greets you at **Sprouts** (3123 Harrison Ave; mains $7-10; ⊙8am-9pm; ⊕⊕), an energetic, mostly organic cafe that gets extra kudos for its smoothies. A healthy menu will have you noshing happily on satisfying soups, rice bowls, sandwiches, burrito wraps, tempeh burgers and fresh salads.

For a great-value motel, check out **Big Pines Mountain House** (☎530-541-5155; www.thebigpines.com; 4083 Cedar Ave; r incl breakfast $50-129; ⊕@⊙⊕⊕), with a heated pool, decent breakfasts and snack baskets in

rooms. Hwy 89 threads northwest along the thickly forested west shore to **Emerald Bay State Park** (☎530-541-6498; www.parks.ca.gov; per car $10; ⊙late May-Sep), where granite cliffs and pine trees frame a fjordlike inlet, truly sparkling green. A steep 1-mile trail leads down to **Vikingsholm Castle** (tour adult/child $10/8; ⊙11am-4pm late May-Sep). From this 1920s Scandinavian-style mansion, the 4.5-mile Rubicon Trail ribbons north along the lakeshore past an old lighthouse and petite coves to **DL Bliss State Park** (☎530-525-7277; www.parks.ca.gov; per car $10; ⊙late May-Sep; ⊕), offering sandy beaches.

Further north, **Tahoma Meadows B&B Cottages** (☎530-525-1553; www.tahomameadows.com; 6821 W Lake Blvd, Tahoma; cottages incl breakfast $99-389; ⊙⊕) has true backwoods hospitality, hosted by its longtime owner. There is a variety of darling country cabins (pet fee $20), evening wine and cheese for guests and fresh country breakfasts.

North & East Shores

The north shore's commercial hub, **Tahoe City** is great for grabbing supplies and renting outdoor gear. It's not far from **Squaw Valley** (☎530-452-4331; www.squaw.com; 1960 Squaw Valley Rd, off Hwy 89, Olympic Valley; adult/youth 13-22yr/child under 13yr $114/94/66; ⊕), a megasized ski resort that hosted the 1960 Winter Olympics. Après-ski crowds gather for beer and burgers at woodsy **Bridgetender Tavern** (www.tahoebridgetender.com; 65 W Lake Blvd; ⊙11am-11pm, to midnight Fri & Sat) back in town. For breakfast, everyone heads to the friendly **Fire Sign Cafe** (www.firesigncafe.com;

1785 W Lake Blvd; mains $7-13; ⏰7am-3pm; 🅿🚻) for down-home omelets, blueberry pancakes, eggs Benedict with smoked salmon, fresh made-from-scratch pastries and other carbo-loading bombs, plus organic coffee. In summer hit the outdoor patio. Lines are usually very long, so get there early.

In summer swim or kayak at Tahoe Vista or Kings Beach. Spend a night at **Franciscan Lakeside Lodge** (☎530-546-6300; www.franciscanlodge.com; 6944 N Lake Blvd; cabins $93-399; 🛜🏊), where simple cabins, cottages and suites have kitchenettes. East of Kings Beach, which has cheap, filling lakeshore eateries, Hwy 28 barrels into Nevada. Try your luck at the gambling tables or catch a live-music show at the **Crystal Bay Club Casino** (☎775-833-6333; www.crystalbaycasino.com; 14 Hwy 28, Crystal Bay). But for more happening bars and bistros, drive further to Incline Village.

With pristine beaches, lakes and miles of multiuse trails, **Lake Tahoe-Nevada State Park** (www.parks.nv.gov; per car $7-12) is the east shore's biggest draw. Summer crowds splash in the turquoise waters of Sand Harbor. The 15-mile **Flume Trail** (☎775-298-2501; www.flumetrailtahoe.com; 1115 Tunnel Creek Rd; bike rental per day $35-60, shuttle $10-15), a mountain-biker's holy grail, starts further south at Spooner Lake.

Truckee & Around

POP 16,180 / ELEV 5820FT

North of Lake Tahoe off I-80, Truckee is not in fact a truck stop but a thriving mountain town, with organic coffee shops, trendy boutiques and dining in downtown's historical district. Ski bunnies have several area resorts to pick from, including glam **Northstar California** (☎530-562-1010; www.northstarcalifornia.com; 5001 Northstar Dr, off Hwy 267, Truckee; adult/youth 13-22yr/child 5-12yr $116/96/69; ⏰8:30am-4pm; 🚻); kid-friendly **Sugar Bowl** (☎530-426-9000; www.sugarbowl.com; 629 Sugar Bowl Rd, off Donner Pass Rd, Norden; adult/youth 13-22yr/child 6-12yr $82/70/30; ⏰9am-4pm; 🚻), cofounded by Walt Disney; and **Royal Gorge** (☎530-426-3871; www.royalgorge.com; 9411 Pahatsi Rd, off I-80 exit Soda Springs/Norden, Soda Springs; adult/youth 13-22yr $29/22; ⏰9am-5pm; 🚻🏊), a paradise for cross-country skiers.

West of Hwy 89, Donner Summit is where the infamous Donner Party became trapped during the fierce winter of 1846–47. Led astray by their guidebook, less than half survived – by cannibalizing their dead friends. The grisly tale is chronicled at the museum inside **Donner Memorial State Park** (www.parks.ca.gov; Donner Pass Rd; per car $8; ⏰museum 10am-5pm, closed Tue & Wed Sep-May; 🚻), where Donner Lake is popular with swimmers and windsurfers.

Eco-conscious **Cedar House Sport Hotel** (☎530-582-5655; www.cedarhousesporthotel.com; 10918 Brockway Rd; r incl breakfast $180-280; 🅿🛜❄ 🐾 is green building–certified and has an outdoor hot tub and stylishly modern boutique rooms (pet fee $50). For live jazz and wine, **Moody's Bistro & Lounge** (☎530-587-8688; www.moodysbistro.com; 10007 Bridge St; lunch mains $12-18, dinner mains $13-32; ⏰11:30am-9:30pm) sources locally ranched meats and seasonal produce. Down pints of 'Donner Party Porter' at **Fifty Fifty Brewing Co** (www.fiftyfiftybrewing.com; 11197 Brockway Rd; ⏰11am-9pm, to 9:30pm Fri & Sat) 🐾 across the tracks. Across from the Amtrak station, **Squeeze In** (www.squeezein.com; 10060 Donner Pass Rd; mains $8-15; ⏰7am-2pm; 🚻) dishes up near-perfect burgers and lumberjack breakfasts in a colorful setting with colorful handwritten notes plastered on the walls.

ⓘ Getting There & Around

TO/FROM THE AIRPORT

North Lake Tahoe Express (☎866-216-5222; www.northlaketahoeexpress.com; one way/round-trip $45/85) Connects Reno's airport with Truckee, Squaw Valley and north-shore towns.

South Tahoe Express (☎866-898-2463, 775-325-8944; www.southtahoeexpress.com; adult/child 4-12yr one way $30/17) Runs frequent shuttles from Nevada's Reno-Tahoe International Airport to Stateline.

BUS & TRAIN

Amtrak Depot (www.amtrak.com; 10065 Donner Pass Rd) Truckee's Amtrak Depot has daily trains to Sacramento ($41, 4½ hours) and Reno ($15, 1½ hours) and twice-daily Greyhound buses to Reno ($22, one hour), Sacramento ($51, 2½ hours) and San Francisco ($45, six hours).

BlueGO (☎530-541-7149; www.tahoetransportation.org; fare/day pass $2/5) Operates a summer-only trolley up the west shore to Tahoma, connecting with TART.

Tahoe Area Regional Transit (TART; ☎800-736-6365, 530-550-1212; www.placer.ca.gov/tart; fare/day pass $1.75/3.50) Runs local buses to Truckee and around the north and west shores.

CAR

Tire chains are often required in winter on I-80, US 50, Hwy 89 and Mt Rose Hwy, any or all of which may close during and after snowstorms.

Arizona

Best Views

➜ Mather Point (p165)

➜ Red Rock Crossing (p145)

➜ Horseshoe Bend (p187)

➜ View Hotel (p192)

➜ Spider Rock Overlook (p193)

Best Places to Stay

➜ El Tovar (p172)

➜ Grand Canyon Lodge (p183)

➜ Motor Lodge (p138)

➜ Enchantment Resort (p149)

➜ View Hotel (p192)

Why Go?

Arizona is made for road trips. Yes, the state has its show-stoppers – Monument Valley, the Grand Canyon, Cathedral Rock – but it's the drives between these icons and others that really breathe life and context into a trip. For a dose of mom-and-pop friendliness, follow Route 66 into Flagstaff. To understand the sheer will of Arizona's mining barons, take a twisting drive through rugged Jerome. Native American history becomes contemporary as you drive past the inhabitants of a mesa-top Hopi village dating back 1000 years.

Controversies about hot-button issues – immigration, gay rights – have grabbed headlines recently, but these legislative issues are perhaps best left to the politicians, here only temporarily. The majestic beauty of the Grand Canyon, the saguaro-dotted deserts of Tucson, the sunset glow of Camelback Mountain and the red rocks of Sedona...they're here for the duration.

When to Go
Phoenix

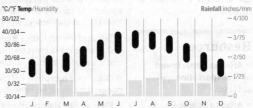

Jan–Mar	Jun–Aug	Sep & Oct
Visit dude ranches in southern Arizona. Cross-country ski in Kaibab National Forest.	High season for the Grand Canyon, Monument Valley and Sedona.	Hike down to Phantom Ranch from the Grand Canyon's South Rim.

TIME ZONE

Arizona is on Mountain Time (seven hours behind GMT) but is the only Western state not to observe daylight saving time from spring to fall. The exception is the Navajo Reservation, which – in keeping with those parts of the reservation located in Utah and New Mexico – does observe daylight saving time. The small Hopi Reservation, which it surrounds, follows Arizona.

Fast Facts

→ **Population** 6.6 million

→ **Area** 113,635 sq miles

→ **Sales Tax** 5.6%

→ **Phoenix to Grand Canyon Village** 235 miles, 3½ hours

→ **Phoenix to Tucson** 116 miles, 1¾ hours

→ **Kingman to Holbrook** 240 miles, 3¼ hours

State Flower

The saguaro cactus blooms in May and June. It is illegal to harm a saguaro in Arizona.

Resources

→ **Arizona Department of Transportation** www.az511.gov

→ **Arizona Scenic Roads** www.arizonascenicroads.com

→ **Arizona Office of Tourism** www.visitarizona.com

Arizona Planning

Although the summer months (June to early September) are a popular time to visit Grand Canyon National Park, it's the opposite in the southern part of the state where the heat can be unbearable at that time of year. Save trips to Phoenix and southern Arizona for the spring. A good rule of thumb is to gauge the climate by the altitude. The lower you are, the hotter and drier it will be.

For Grand Canyon trips, make reservations for lodging, overnight mule rides and white-water rafting a year in advance, particularly if you plan to visit in summer.

DON'T MISS

Grand Canyon Visitor Center on the South Rim has been revamped. Read the interpretive exhibits for background then stroll to Mather Point on the pedestrian-friendly plaza. You'll also find bike rentals here, an increasingly popular way to explore the park. Inside, the introductory film *Grand Canyon: A Journey of Wonder* plays regularly. On the back terrace of Lookout Studio in Grand Canyon Village, attend a ranger-led **Condor Talk** and look for the giant birds soaring nearby.

The expansive **Musical Instrument Museum** in Phoenix will wow your ears with music from guitars, gongs, lutes and thumb pianos – it's an amazing array of global instruments engagingly shared with visitors. If any sense of wonder still lingers in your soul – or you're traveling with kids – visit the new **Mini Time Machine Museum of Miniatures** in Tucson. From dragons to dollhouses, it's all small and it's all cool.

Tips for Drivers

→ The main east–west highway across northern Arizona is the 400-mile stretch of I-40, which roughly follows the path of Historic Route 66. It's the interstate to take if you're headed for the Grand Canyon or the Navajo Reservation. I-10 enters western Arizona at Blythe and travels about 400 miles to New Mexico via Phoenix and Tucson.

→ South of Phoenix, the I-8 coming east from Yuma joins the I-10. The I-8 is the most southerly approach from California, and it's a lonely highway indeed.

→ Cell phone reception, FM radio, lodging and gas are almost nonexistent along I-8 between Yuma and Gila Bend.

→ Phoenix Sky Harbor International Airport and Las Vegas' McCarran International Airport are major gateways, but Tucson also receives its share of flights.

→ Greyhound and Amtrak do not typically stop at national parks in Arizona, nor do city buses and trains.

History

Native American tribes inhabited Arizona for centuries before Spanish explorer Francisco Vásquez de Coronado led an expedition from Mexico City in 1540. Settlers and missionaries followed in his wake, and by the mid-19th century the US controlled Arizona. The Indian Wars, in which the US Army battled Native Americans to protect settlers and claim land for the government, officially ended in 1886 with the surrender of Apache warrior Geronimo.

Railroad and mining expansion followed and people started arriving in ever larger numbers. After President Theodore Roosevelt visited Arizona in 1903 he supported the damming of its rivers to provide year-round water for irrigation and drinking, thus paving the way to statehood: in 1912 Arizona became the last of the 48 contiguous US states to be admitted to the Union.

The state shares a 250-mile border with Mexico and an estimated 250,000 immigrants crossed it illegally in 2009. After the mysterious murder of a popular rancher near the border in 2010, the legislature passed a controversial law requiring police officers to ask for identification from anyone they suspect of being in the country illegally. While the constitutionality of the request for immigration papers was upheld, key provisions of the law, known as SB 1070, were struck down by the US Supreme Court.

Arizona Scenic Routes

Dozens of scenic roads crisscross the state. Some of Arizona's best drives are included in the monthly magazine **Arizona Highways** (www.arizhwys.com), created in 1925 to cover them all and still going strong. For additional ideas, visit www.arizonascenicroads.com.

Wickenburg to Sedona (Hwy 89A) Tremendous views of the Mogollon Rim and a grand welcome to Red Rock Country.

Oak Creek Canyon (Hwy 89A) Winds northeast from Sedona through dizzyingly narrow walls and dramatic rock cliffs before climbing up to Flagstaff.

Grand Canyon North Rim Parkway (Hwy 67) Runs from Jacob Lake south to the North Rim via the pine, fir and aspen of Kaibab National Forest.

Monument Valley (Hwy 163) Stupendous drive past crimson monoliths rising abruptly from the barren desert floor northeast of Kayenta.

OFF THE BEATEN TRACK

ARIZONA DETOURS

Fort Bowie National Historic Site (p231) Hike to a fort built during the Apache Wars.

V-Bar-V Heritage Site (p133) More than 1000 petroglyphs.

Fairbank Historic Site (p226) Wander a ghost town near the San Pedro River.

Pause-Rest-Worship Church (p205) Rest your soul in this tiny ode to faith.

Grand Canyon Caverns (p200) Limestone caves hold Cold War emergency supplies and the bones of a prehistoric sloth.

Sky Island Parkway Traverses ecozones equivalent to a trip from Mexico to Canada as it corkscrews up to Mt Lemmon (9157ft), northeast of Tucson.

Vermilion Cliffs to Fredonia (Hwy 89A) Climbs through the remote Arizona Strip from fiery red Vermilion Cliffs up the forested Kaibab Plateau.

GREATER PHOENIX

URBAN POP 1,567,924 / ELEV 1117FT

The Southwest's most populous city isn't great with first impressions, but give this desert metropolis a chance. Just when you've dismissed the place as a faux-dobe wasteland of cookie-cutter subdivisions, bland shopping malls and water-gobbling golf courses, you're pulled short by a golden sunset setting the urban peaks aglow. Or a stubborn desert bloom determined to make a go of it in the dry, scrubby heat. Or maybe it's the mom-and-pop breakfast joint drawing crowds and thumbing its nose at the ubiquitous chains that dominate the landscape.

It's these little markers of hope – or defiance – that let travelers know there's more substance here than initially meets the eye. And with more than 300 days of sunshine a year – hence the nickname 'Valley of the Sun' – exploring is an agreeable proposition (except in June, July and August when the mercury tops 100°F, or about 38°C).

Culturally, Phoenix offers an opera, a symphony, several theaters, and three of the state's finest museums: the Heard Museum,

Arizona Highlights

1 Bike the Greenway and the road to Hermits Rest at **Grand Canyon National Park** (p160)

2 Hike to a historic fort at **Fort Bowie National Historic Site** (p231)

3 Bounce over red rocks on a jeep tour in **Sedona** (p144)

4 Revel in the surreal majesty of the towering buttes in **Monument Valley Navajo Tribal Park** (p192)

5 Swoop in for bird-watching and wine tasting in **Patagonia** (p222)

6 Peek over the edge to see the Colorado River far, far below at **Horseshoe Bend** (p187)

7 Cowboy up for a dude ranch ride in **Wickenburg** (p134)

8 Listen to drums, lutes and thumb pianos at the **Musical Instrument Museum** (p116) in Phoenix

9 Walk in beauty at **Canyon de Chelly National Monument** (p193)

10 Embrace the kitsch of Route 66 in **Seligman** (p201)

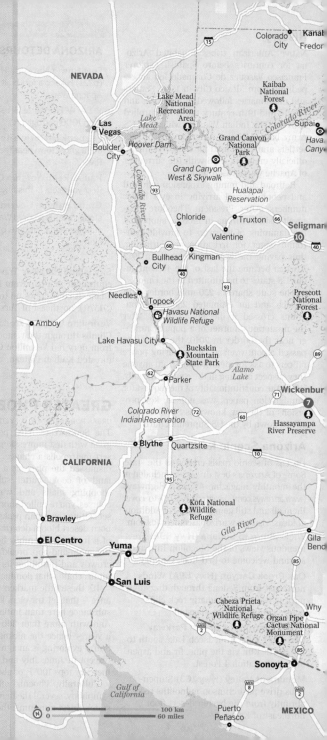

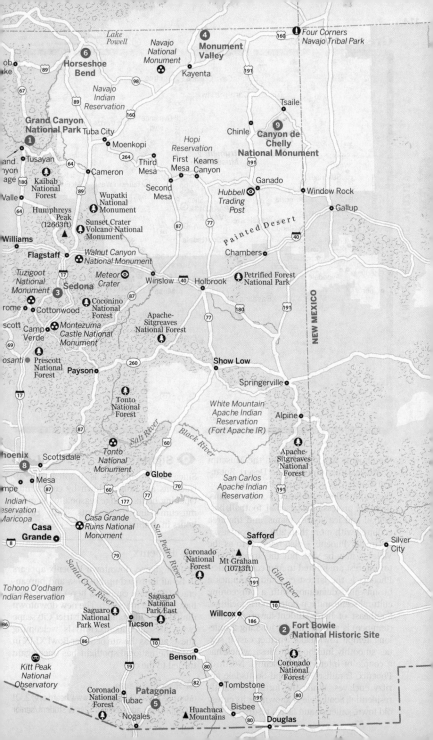

Greater Phoenix

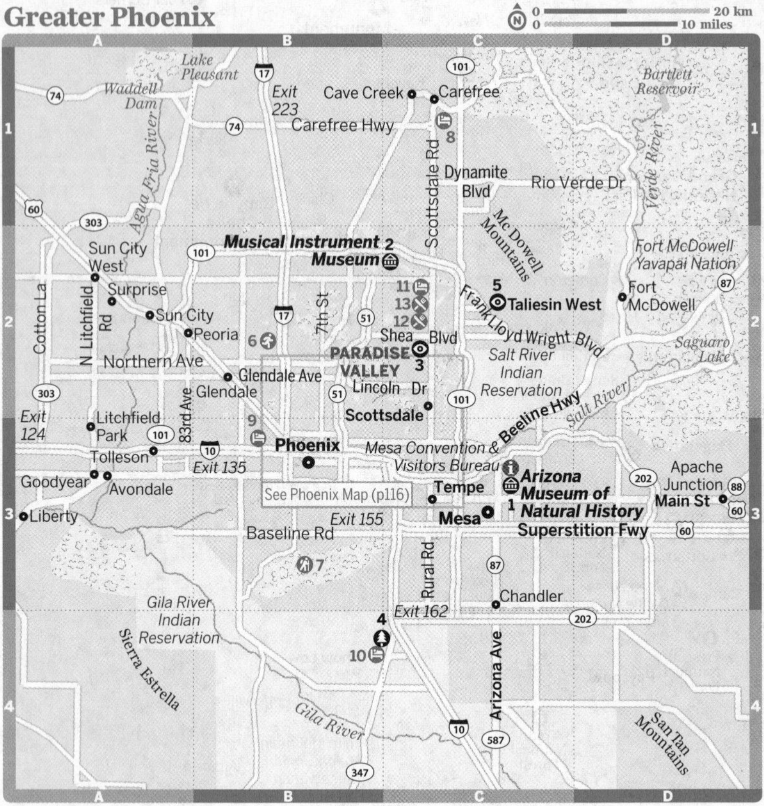
0 20 km
0 10 miles
Lake Pleasant
Waddell Dam
Agua Fria River
Exit 223
Cave Creek
Carefree
Carefree Hwy
Bartlett Reservoir
Verde River
Scottsdale Rd
Dynamite Blvd
Rio Verde Dr
McDowell Mountains
Musical Instrument Museum
Sun City West
Surprise
Sun City
Peoria
Cotton La
N Litchfield Rd
Northern Ave
Glendale Ave
Glendale
83rd Ave
7th St
Shea Blvd
PARADISE VALLEY
Lincoln Dr
Scottsdale
Taliesin West
Frank Lloyd Wright Blvd
Fort McDowell Yavapai Nation
Fort McDowell
Saguaro Lake
Salt River Indian Reservation
Salt River
Beeline Hwy
Exit 124
Litchfield Park
Tolleson
Exit 135
Phoenix
Mesa Convention & Visitors Bureau
Arizona Museum of Natural History
Goodyear
Avondale
Liberty
See Phoenix Map (p116)
Tempe
Mesa
Apache Junction
Main St
Exit 155
Baseline Rd
Superstition Fwy
Rural Rd
Chandler
Gila River Indian Reservation
Exit 162
Sierra Estrella
Gila River
Arizona Ave
San Tan Mountains

the Phoenix Art Museum and the Museum of Musical Instruments. The Desert Botanical Garden is a stunning introduction to the region's flora and fauna. For sports fans, there are professional baseball, football, basketball and ice hockey teams, and the area is dotted with more than 200 golf courses.

Greater Phoenix – also referred to as the Valley – may be vast, but the areas of visitor interest are limited to four communities. Phoenix is the largest city and combines a businesslike demeanor with a burgeoning cultural scene and top-notch sports facilities. Southeast of here, student-flavored Tempe (tem-pee) is a lively district hugging 2-mile-long Tempe Town Lake. Further east it segues smoothly into ho-hum Mesa, which has a couple of interesting museums. North of Phoenix, Paradise Valley and Scottsdale are ritzy enclaves. While the former is mostly residential, Scottsdale is known for its cutesy old town, galleries and lavish resorts.

Sights

Since the Phoenix area is so spread out, attractions are broken down by community. Opening hours change seasonally for many museums and restaurants, with earlier hours in summer.

Phoenix

At first glance, downtown Phoenix appears to be all buttoned-up business and bureaucracy (the state capitol is here), but it does have a spring in its step. The new downtown dining-and-entertainment district Cityscape (www.cityscapephoenix.com) is welcoming guests and, as the site of Super Bowl XLIX in 2015, the national spotlight has once again turned to the city.

★ Heard Museum MUSEUM

(Map p120; ☎602-252-8848; www.heard.org; 2301 N Central Ave; adult/child 6-12yr & student/senior

Greater Phoenix

pieces were a gift from Barry Goldwater). The Heard emphasizes quality over quantity and is one of the best museums of its kind in America.

The moving Boarding School Experience gallery examines the controversial federal policy of removing Native American children from their families and sending them to remote boarding schools in order to 'Americanize' them.

Keep a lookout for unexpected treasures – like the Harry Potter bowl tucked amongst more traditional pottery. Guided tours run at noon, 2pm and 3pm at no extra charge. Overall, allow two to three hours to explore. Also check out the busy events schedule, the well-stocked bookstore and the superb gift shop.

Parking is free. Valley Metro light-rail stops beside the downtown museum at Encanto/Central Ave.

★ **Desert Botanical Garden**   GARDENS
(Map p116; ☑480-941-1225; www.dbg.org; 1201 N Galvin Pkwy; adult/child 3-12yr/student/senior $22/10/12/20; ☉8am-8pm Oct-Apr, 7am-8pm May-Sep) Blue bells and Mexican gold poppies are just two of the colorful showstoppers blooming from March to May along the Desert Wildflower Loop Trail at this well-nurtured botanical garden, a lovely place to reconnect with nature while learning about desert plant life. Looping trails lead past an astonishing variety of desert denizens, arranged by theme (including a Sonoran Desert nature loop and an edible desert garden).

$18/7.50/13.50; ☉9:30am-5pm Mon-Sat, 11am-5pm Sun; ⊞) This extraordinary museum spotlights the history, life, arts and culture of Native American tribes in the Southwest. Visitors will find art galleries, ethnographic displays, a get-creative kids exhibit and an unrivaled Hopi kachina gallery (many of the

---

PHOENIX IN...

One Day

Before the day heats up, hike to the top of Camelback Mountain (p122) then refuel at Matt's Big Breakfast (p126). Afterward, head to the Heard Museum (p114) for a primer on Southwestern tribal history, art and culture. If it's not too hot, take a stroll through the exquisite Desert Botanical Garden (p115); otherwise, steer toward your hotel pool or Wet 'n' Wild Phoenix (p124) to relax and cool off. Wrap up the day with a sunset cocktail and mountain views at Edge Bar (p129) before reporting to dinner at Pizzeria Bianco (p126) or Dick's Hideaway (p126).

Two Days

On day two, head to Taliesin West (p119) to learn about the fertile mind of architectural great Frank Lloyd Wright, then grab a gourmet sandwich at the Herb Box (p127) before browsing the galleries and souvenir shops of Old Town Scottsdale (p119). In the afternoon hit the pool and, if you've got one, see a masseuse back at your hotel ahead of getting all dressed up for a gourmet dinner at Kai Restaurant (p127). Families might prefer an Old West afternoon of cowboys and shoot 'em ups at Rawhide (p121) followed by casual Mexican cuisine at Tee Pee (p126).

Phoenix

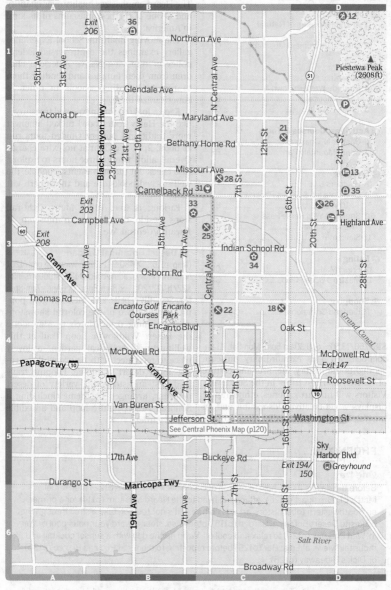

It's pretty dazzling year-round, but the flowering spring season is the busiest and most colorful time to visit. Another highlight is December's nighttime luminarias, when plants are draped in thousands of twinkling lights.

Admission is free the second Tuesday of the month (8am to 4pm).

★ **Musical Instrument Museum** MUSEUM
(Map p114; ☎ 480-478-6000; www.themim.org; 4725 E Mayo Blvd; adult/child 13-19yr/under 13yr

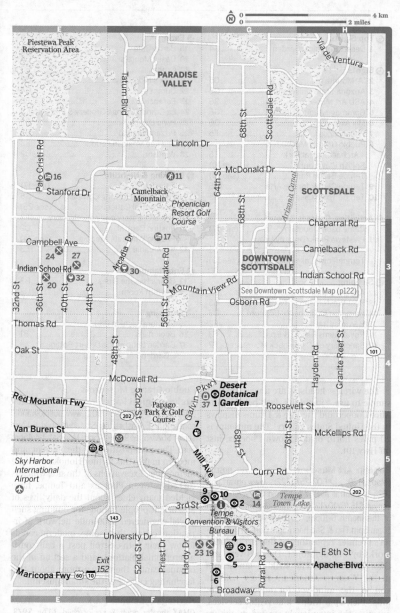

$18/14/10; ⊕9am-5pm Mon-Sat, 10am-5pm Sun, to 9pm first Fri of the month) From Uganda thumb pianos to Hawaiian ukuleles to Indonesian boat lutes, the ears have it at this lively museum that celebrates the world's musical instruments. More than 200 coun-

tries and territories are represented within five regional galleries, where music and video performances begin as you stop beside individual displays. You can also bang a drum in the Experiences Gallery and listen to Taylor Swift rock out in the Artist Gallery.

Phoenix

The wireless headsets are a necessity, but simple to use – just don't dash between the Alice Cooper and the Fife & Drums displays in the United States gallery! The museum is 20 miles north of downtown Phoenix, just off Hwy 101.

Phoenix Art Museum   MUSEUM

(Map p120; ☑ 602-257-1222; www.phxart.org; 1625 N Central Ave; adult/child 6-17yr/student/senior $15/6/10/12, free Wed 3-9pm & 1st Fri of the month 6-10pm; ☺10am-9pm Wed & Fri, 10am-5pm Thu & Sat, noon-5pm Sun; ☑) Arizona's premier repository of fine art includes works by Claude Monet, Diego Rivera and Georgia O'Keeffe. The striking landscapes in the Western American gallery will get you in the mind-set for adventure. Got kids? Pick up a Kidpack at visitor services, examine the ingeniously crafted miniature period Thorne Rooms or visit the PhxArt-Kids Gallery.

There are free guided tours offered at noon, 1pm and 2pm daily and on Wednesdays at 6pm.

Pueblo Grande Museum & Archaeological Park   MUSEUM

(Map p116; ☑ 602-495-0901; www.pueblogrande. com; 4619 E Washington St; adult/child 6-17yr/senior $6/3/5; ☺9am-4:45pm Mon-Sat, 1-4:45pm Sun) The juxtaposition of the ancient and modern makes this former Hohokam village memorable. Excavations at the site, which is tucked between Phoenix and Tempe, have yielded many clues about the daily lives of an ancient people famous for building such a well-engineered 1000-mile network of irrigation canals that some modern canals follow their paths. Stroll past a ball court, a ceremonial platform and a section of the original canals then learn more about this fascinating culture at the small museum.

Heritage & Science Park   PLAZA

(IMAX theater adult & senior/child 3-17yr $9/8, planetarium $8/7) Imagine thundering hooves and creaking stagecoaches as you amble around Historic Heritage Square (Map p120; ☑ park office 602-262-5071, recording 602-262-5029; www.phoenix.gov; 115 N 6th St), a cluster of stately Victorians. To view the interior of one of the homes, join a tour of the 1895 **Rosson House** (Map p120; ☎602-262-5070; www.rossonhousemuseum.org; tours adult/child 6-12yr/senior $7.50/4/6; ⊗10am-4pm Wed-Sat, noon-4pm Sun, also Tue Jun-Aug). For more modern distractions, beeline to the **Arizona Science Center** (Map p120; ☎602-716-2000; www.azscience.org; 600 E Washington St; adult/child 3-17yr/senior $17/12/15; ⊗10am-5pm; ⊛), a high-tech, interactive temple of discovery where kids can slide through a stomach or lie on a bed of nails before winding down at the five-story IMAX theater or the planetarium.

⊙ Scottsdale

Scottsdale sparkles with self-confidence, her glossy allure fueled by good looks, charm and money. Distractions include a pedestrian-friendly downtown, chic hotels and a vibrant food and nightlife scene. For a list of permanent and temporary public art displays, which are often quite intriguing, visit www.scottsdalepublicart.org.

A free trolley links Old Town Scottsdale with Scottsdale Fashion Square Mall via the new Scottsdale Waterfront, a retail and office complex on the Arizona Canal. At the eastern end of the pedestrian walkway along the waterfront, look for the 100ft-long **Soleri Bridge**, a stainless steel wonder by artist and architect Paoli Soleri. The bridge is also a solar calendar.

Old Town Scottsdale   NEIGHBORHOOD
Tucked among the glitzy malls and chichi bistros is Old Town Scottsdale, a Wild West–themed enclave filled with cutesy buildings, covered sidewalks and stores hawking mass-produced 'Indian' jewelry and Western art. One building with genuine history is the 1909 Little Red School House, now home of the **Scottsdale Historical Museum** (☎480-945-4499; www.scottsdalemuseum.

org; 7333 E Scottsdale Mall; ⊗10am-5pm Wed-Sun Oct-May, to 2pm Wed-Sun Jun & Sep) **FREE**, where low-key exhibits highlight Scottsdale's origins and early history. Old Town is centered on Main St and Brown Ave.

In a cleverly adapted old movie theater, the **Scottsdale Museum of Contemporary Arts** (☎480-874-4666; www.smoca.org; 7374 E 2nd St; adult/student/child 15yr & under $7/5/free, free Thu and after 5pm Fri & Sat; ⊗noon-5pm Sun, Tue & Wed, noon-9pm Thu-Sat) showcases global art, architecture and design, including James Turrell's otherworldly Knight Rise skyspace in the sculpture garden. The museum is across from the local performing arts center.

Taliesin West   ARCHITECTURE
(Map p114; ☎480-860-2700; www.franklloydwright. org; 12621 Frank Lloyd Wright Blvd; Insights Tour adult/child 4-12yr $36/17; ⊗tours 9am-4pm, closed Tue & Wed Jun-Aug) Frank Lloyd Wright was one of the seminal American architects of the 20th century. Taliesin West was his desert home and studio, built between 1938 and 1940. Still home to an architecture school and open to the public for guided tours, it's a prime example of organic architecture with buildings incorporating elements and structures found in surrounding nature.

During the popular Insights Tour, a docent leads visitors to Wright's office with its slanted canvas roof, the grand stone-walled living room where you can sit on original Wright-designed furniture, and the half-sunken Cabaret Theater. This informative tour feels much quicker than its 90 minutes. Shorter and longer tours are also available.

Cosanti   ARCHITECTURE
(Map p114; ☎480-948-6145; www.arcosanti.org/cosanti; 6433 E Doubletree Ranch Rd; donation appreciated; ⊗9am-5pm Mon-Sat, 11am-5pm Sun) The home and studio of Frank Lloyd Wright student Paolo Soleri, who died in 2013, this

---

DON'T MISS

ART WALKS

Phoenix has worked its way up the ladder of art cities that matter. Scottsdale in particular teems with galleries laden with everything from epic Western oil paintings to cutting-edge sculpture and moody Southwestern landscapes. Every Thursday evening some 100 of them keep their doors open until 9pm for **Art Walk** (www.scottsdalegalleries.com; ⊗7-9pm), which centers on Marshall Way and Main St.

The vibe is edgier and the setting more urban during **First Fridays** (www.artlinkphoenix. com; ⊗6-10pm), which draws up to 20,000 people to the streets of downtown Phoenix on the first Friday of every month, primarily for art but also for music, poetry slams and other events.

unusual complex of cast-concrete structures was a stepping stone for Soleri's experimental Arcosanti village, 65 miles north. Cosanti is also where Soleri's signature bronze and ceramic bells are crafted. You're free to walk around, see the bells poured (usually between 9am and 11am weekdays but call to confirm) and browse the gift shop. Located about 9 miles south of Taliesin West.

Tempe

Sandwiched between downtown Phoenix and Mesa, just south of Scottsdale, Tempe is a fun and energetic district enlivened by the 60,000 students of **Arizona State University** (ASU; Map p116; www.asu.edu). Founded in 1885, the vast campus is home to Sun Devil Stadium, performance venues, galleries and museums.

ASU Art Museum   MUSEUM
(Map p116; ☑ 480-965-2787; http://asuartmuseum. asu.edu; 51 E Tempe St, cnr Mill Ave & 10th St; ⊙11am-5pm Tue-Sat year-round, to 8pm Tue May-Aug) FREE This airy, contemporary gallery space has eye-catching art and intriguing exhibits. Architecture fans can tour the circu-

Central Phoenix

lar **Gammage Auditorium** (Map p116; ☑ box office 480-965-3434, tours 480-965-6912; www.asugammage.com; 1200 S Forest Ave, cnr Mill Ave & Apache Blvd; admission free, performances from $20; ⊘1-4pm Mon-Fri Oct-May), Frank Lloyd Wright's last major building. A popular performance venue, it stages primarily Broadway-style musicals and shows.

Mill Ave   NEIGHBORHOOD
(Map p116) Along the western edge of Arizona State University, Mill Ave is Tempe's main drag and lined with restaurants, bars and a mix of national chains and indie boutiques. For cool metro and mountain views, huff it up for half a mile to the top of **'A' Mountain** (Map p116), so-called because of the giant letter 'A' painted there by ASU students. It's officially known as Tempe Butte or Hayden Butte; the trailhead is on E 3rd St, near Mill Ave.

Mill Ave spills into **Tempe Town Lake** (Map p116; www.tempe.gov/lake), a 2-mile-long recreational pond created by reclaiming the long-dry Salt River in the 1990s. Have a picnic at **Tempe Beach Park** (Map p116)

and watch kids letting off steam at the waterfalls, rock slides and shallow pools of the ingenious **Splash Playground** (Map p116; ⊘10am-7pm daily Jun & Jul, Sat & Sun Aug; 🚼) **FREE**. There's no swimming in the lake, but **Tempe Town Lake Boat Rentals** (Map p116; ☑480-303-9803; http://boats4rent.com; 72 W Rio Salado Pkwy; pedalboats/single kayaks/stand-up paddleboard/pontoon for 2hr $30/30/35/115) rents human-powered and motorized watercraft. Free outdoor concerts and festivals bring crowds to the park on weekends. For indoor entertainment, the lakeshore has the shiny lakefront **Tempe Center for the Arts** (Map p116; www.tempe.gov/tca; 700 W Rio Salado Pkwy).

To get around downtown Tempe on weekdays, use the free Orbit bus (p132) that runs along Mill Ave and around the university every 15 minutes Monday to Saturday and every 30 minutes on Sunday.

◎ Mesa

Founded by Mormons in 1877, low-key Mesa is one of the fastest-growing cities in the nation and the third-largest city in Arizona with a population of about 450,000.

★**Arizona Museum of
Natural History**   MUSEUM
(Map p114; ☑480-644-2230; www.azmnh.org; 53 N MacDonald St; adult/child 3-12yr/student/senior $10/6/8/9; ⊘10am-5pm Tue-Fri, 11am-5pm Sat, 1-5pm Sun; 🚼) Even if you're not staying in Mesa, this museum is worth a trip, especially if your kids are into dinosaurs (and aren't they all?). In addition to the multilevel Dinosaur Mountain, there are loads of life-size casts of the giant beasts plus a touchable apatosaurus thighbone. Be warned: we saw one small child shrieking in abject terror at it all. Other exhibits highlight Arizona's colorful past, from a prehistoric Hohokam village to an eight-cell territorial jail.

**Rawhide Western Town &
Steakhouse**   THEME PARK
(Map p114; ☑480-502-5600; www.rawhide.com; 5700 W N Loop Rd, Chandler; admission free, per attraction or show $5, unlimited day pass $15; ⊘5-10pm Thu-Sun Jun & Jul, hours vary rest of year; 🚼) Every 'howdy' sounds sincere at this re-created 1880s frontier town located about 20 miles south of Mesa on the Gila River Indian Reservation. Test your mettle on a mechanical bull or a stubborn burro, ride a cutesy train, pan for gold and join in all

Downtown Scottsdale

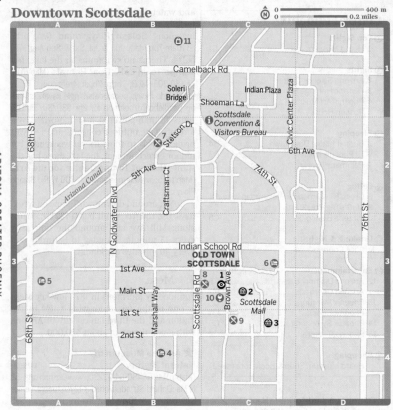

sorts of other hokey-but-fun shenanigans. The steakhouse has rattlesnake and Rocky Mountain oysters (bull testicles) for adventurous eaters and mesquite-grilled slabs of beef for everyone else. Parking costs $5.

🏃 Activities

In Phoenix, it's actually pretty easy to take a walk on the wild side and escape the urban jungle. Find maps and trail descriptions for Camelback Mountain, Piestewa Peak and South Mountain Park at www.phoenix.gov.

Camelback Mountain   HIKING
(Map p116; ☎ 602-261-8318; www.phoenix.gov; ☉ sunrise-sunset) This 2704ft mountain sits smack in the center of the Phoenix action. Two trails, the Cholla Trail (6131 E Cholla Ln) and the Echo Canyon Trail (4925 E McDonald Dr) climb about 1200ft to the summit. The newly renovated Echo Canyon Trail is extremely popular and fills very early, even with 135 parking spots.

Piestewa Peak/Dreamy Draw Recreation Area   HIKING
(Map p116; ☎ 602-261-8318; www.phoenix.gov; Squaw Peak Dr; ☉ trails 5am-11pm, last entry 6:59pm) Dotted with saguaros, ocotillos and other local cacti, this convenient summit was previously known as Squaw Peak. It was renamed for local Native American soldier Lori Piestewa who was killed in Iraq in 2003. Be forewarned: the trek to the 2608ft summit is hugely popular and the park can get jammed on winter weekends. Parking lots northeast of Lincoln Dr between 22nd and 24th Sts fill early. Dogs are allowed on some park trails but not the Summit Trail.

The peak is bordered by two recreation areas, Phoenix Mountains (2701 E Squaw Peak), where the Summit Trail begins, and Dreamy Draw (2421 E Northern Ave).

South Mountain Park   HIKING
(Map p114; ☎ 602-262-7393; www.phoenix.gov; 10919 S Central Ave, Phoenix; ☉ 5am-11pm, last

Downtown Scottsdale

⊙ Sights
1 Old Town Scottsdale C3
2 Scottsdale Historical Museum..............C3
3 Scottsdale Museum of
    Contemporary Arts C4

🛏 Sleeping
4 Bespoke Inn, Cafe & Bicycles B4
5 Hotel Valley Ho..A3
6 The Saguaro C3

✕ Eating
7 Herb Box B2
8 Sugar Bowl...C3
9 The Mission..C4

🍸 Drinking & Nightlife
10 Rusty Spur Saloon..................................C3

🛍 Shopping
11 Scottsdale Fashion Square B1

entry 7pm) At more than 25 sq miles, this local favorite is larger than Manhattan. The 51-mile trail network (leashed dogs allowed) dips through canyons, over grassy hills and past granite walls, offering city views and access to Native American petroglyphs.

Cactus Adventures   BIKING
(☎480-688-4743; www.cactusadventures.com; half-day rental from $55; ⊙hours vary) Cactus Adventures rents bikes for use at South Mountain and offers guided hiking and biking tours at various parks. For rentals, they will meet you at the trailhead.

Ponderosa Stables   HORSEBACK RIDING
(☎602-268-1261; www.arizona-horses.com; 10215 S Central Ave, Phoenix; 1/2/3hr rides $33/55/75, min 2 riders for 3hr rides; ⊙7am-6pm Apr-Aug, 8am-6pm Sep-Mar) This outfitter leads rides through South Mountain Park. Reservations required for most trips.

Salt River Recreation   TUBING
(☎480-984-3305; www.saltrivertubing.com; 1320 N Bush Hwy; tubes & shuttle $17, cash only; ⊙9am-6:30pm May-late Sep; 🚸) On this trip, you'll float in an inner tube on the Lower Salt River through the stark Tonto National Forest. The launch is in northeast Mesa, about 15 miles north of Hwy 60 on Power Rd. Floats are two, three or five hours long, including the shuttle-bus ride back.

Kids must be at least 4ft tall and at least eight years old. Hours vary after Labor Day.

🎊 Festivals & Events

Fiesta Bowl   SPORTING EVENT
(☎480-350-0911; www.fiestabowl.org; 1 Cardinals Dr, Glendale) The most popular event in Phoenix is the Fiesta Bowl football game held in early January at the University of Phoenix Stadium. It's preceded by one of the largest parades in the Southwest.

Arizona State Fair   FAIR
(www.azstatefair.com; 1826 W McDowell Rd; adult/child 5-13yr $10/5) This fair lures folks to the Arizona State Fairgrounds the last two weeks of October and first week of November with a rodeo, livestock displays, a pie-eating contest and concerts.

🛏 Sleeping

Greater Phoenix is well stocked with hotels and resorts, but you won't find many B&Bs, cozy inns or charming, low-cost mom-and-pop motels. Overall, the lowest rates will be found at national chain hotels, a few of which are mentioned here. Prices plummet in summer, and you'll see plenty of Valley residents taking advantage of super-low prices at their favorite resorts when the mercury rises.

🛏 Phoenix

HI Phoenix Hostel   HOSTEL $
(Map p120; ☎602-254-9803; www.phxhostel.org; 1026 N 9th St; dm from $23, s/d $35/45; ❄@🛜) Fall back in love with backpacking at this small hostel with fun owners who know Phoenix and want to enjoy it with you. The 22-bed hostel sits in a working-class residential neighborhood and has relaxing garden nooks. Check-in is from 8am to 10am and 5pm to 10pm. Cash or travelers check only.

Budget Lodge Downtown   MOTEL $
(Map p120; ☎602-254-7247; www.blphx.com; 402 W Van Buren St; r incl breakfast $63-70; 🅿❄🛜) The Budget Lodge doesn't have time for sassiness or charisma. It's got a job to do, and it does it well: providing a clean, low-cost place to sleep. Rooms have a microwave and fridge.

La Quinta Inn & Suites
Phoenix I-10 West   HOTEL $
(Map p114; ☎602-595-6451; www.lq.com; 4929 W McDowell Rd; r $79-89, ste $119-129; 🅿❄@🛜) If you want a no-hassle, low-cost hotel that's easily accessible from the airport and the I-10, try this welcoming La Quinta. For tasty fast food, El Pollo Loco is next door. No pet fee.

PHOENIX FOR CHILDREN

Phoenix Zoo (Map p116; ☑602-273-1341; www.phoenixzoo.org; 455 N Galvin Pkwy; adult/child 3-13yr $20/14; ⊙9am-5pm mid-Jan–May, 7am-2pm Jun-Aug, 9am-5pm Sep & Oct, 9am-4pm Nov–mid-Jan; ♠) If your child loves animals, head to the Phoenix Zoo. A wide variety of critters, including rare ones, are housed in several distinct and natural-looking environments. Watch giraffes nibble on a lofty lunch in the African savanna, then walk through Monkey Village – those squirrel monkeys are darn cute.

Castles n' Coasters (Map p114; ☑602-997-7575; www.castlesncoasters.com; 9445 E Metro Pkwy; unlimited rides $25; ⊙hours vary; ♠) Older kids will enjoy Castles n' Coasters, a big amusement park by the Metrocenter Mall about 20 miles northwest of downtown, near exit 207 off I-17. There's a coaster (or ride) for everyone.

Wet 'n' Wild Phoenix (☑623-201-2000; www.wetnwildphoenix.com; 4243 W Pinnacle Peak Rd, Glendale; over/under 42in tall $40/30, senior $30; ⊙10am-6pm Sun-Wed, 10am-10pm Thu-Sat Jun & Jul, varies May, Aug & Sep; ♠) Cool off in summer with pools, tube slides, wave pools, waterfalls, floating rivers and other splash zones. It's located in Glendale, 2 miles west of I-17 at exit 217, about 30 miles northwest of downtown Phoenix. Parking is $8.

Hampton Inn Phoenix-Biltmore   HOTEL $$
(Map p116; ☑602-956-5221; www.hamptoninn.com; 2310 E Highland Ave; r/ste incl breakfast from $179/219; P❋❂@❂❂) It's Hampton Inn, so you know the drill: hearty free breakfasts, freshly washed duvets and an efficient front desk. So why choose this one? It's close to the Biltmore Fashion Park and some of Phoenix's buzziest new restaurants. The free hotel shuttle runs within a 3-mile radius.

Royal Palms Resort & Spa   RESORT $$$
(Map p116; ☑602-840-3610; www.royalpalmshotel.com; 5200 E Camelback Rd; r/stes/casitas from $519/529/559; P❋@❂❂❂) Camelback Mountain is the photogenic backdrop for this posh and intimate resort, which was once the winter retreat of New York industrialist Delos Cook. Today, it's a hushed and elegant place, dotted with Spanish Colonial villas, flower-lined walkways and palms imported from Egypt. Pets can go Pavlovian for soft beds, personalized biscuits and walking services. The $30 daily resort fee covers wi-fi, the fitness center and gratuities. Parking is an additional $15.

Palomar Phoenix   HOTEL $$$
(Map p120; ☑877-488-1908, 602-253-6633; www.hotelpalomar-phoenix.com; 2 E Jefferson St; r $309-429, studios & ste $359-369; P❋@❂❂❂) Shaggy pillows, antler-shaped lamps and portraits of blue cows. Yep, whimsy takes a stand at the 242-room Palomar, and we like it. Rooms are larger than average and pop with fresh, modern style. All come with yoga mats, animal-print robes and pillowtop beds with Italian frette linens. And did we mention the nightly wine reception? The hotel anchors downtown's new CityScape dining and entertainment district and the lofty outdoor pool and lounge offer the requisite views. Rates are slightly lower on weekends. Parking is $22 per night.

Arizona Biltmore Resort & Spa   RESORT $$$
(Map p116; ☑800-950-0086, 602-955-6600; www.arizonabiltmore.com; 2400 E Missouri Ave; r $289-329, ste from $439; P❋@❂❂❂) With architecture inspired by Frank Lloyd Wright, the Biltmore is perfect for connecting to the magic of yesterday: when Irving Berlin penned 'White Christmas' in his suite and Marilyn Monroe splashed around in the pool. It boasts more than 700 discerning units, two golf courses, several pools, a spa, a kids' club and more luxe touches. The daily resort fee is $28; self-parking is $12 per night. Pets require a $100 deposit per stay, with $50 refundable.

🛏 Scottsdale

Sleep Inn   HOTEL $$
(Map p114; ☑480-998-9211; www.sleepinnscottsdale.com; 16630 N Scottsdale Rd; r incl breakfast $129-134; P❋@❂) It's part of a national chain, but this Sleep Inn wins for its extensive complimentary breakfast, afternoon cookies, friendly staff and proximity to Taliesin West. There's also a laundry and free 24hr hotel shuttle that runs within 5 miles of the hotel.

★Hotel Valley Ho   BOUTIQUE HOTEL $$$
(☑480-248-2000; www.hotelvalleyho.com; 6850 E Main St; r $249-299, ste $439-609; P❋@❂❂❂) Everything's swell at the Valley Ho, where

mid-century modern gets a 21st-century twist. This jazzy joint once bedded Bing Crosby, Natalie Wood and Janet Leigh, and today it's a top pick for movie stars filming on location in Phoenix. Bebop music, upbeat staff and eye-magnets like the 'ice fireplace' recapture the Rat Pack vibe, and the theme travels well to the balconied rooms.

★**Bespoke Inn, Cafe & Bicycles** B&B $$$
(☑ 480-664-0730; www.bespokeinn.com; 3701 N Marshall Way; r incl brunch from $319; P ❋ @ ⦿ ❄ ❉) Ooh la la. Are we in the English countryside or downtown Scottsdale? At this breezy B&B guests can nibble chocolate scones in the chic cafe, loll in the infinity edge pool or pedal the neighborhood on Pashley city bikes. Rooms are plush with handsome touches like handcrafted furniture and nickel bath fixtures. Gourmet brunch served at the on-site restaurant Virtu. Book early.

Boulders RESORT $$$
(Map p114; ☑ 480-488-9009; www.theboulders.com; 34631 N Tom Darlington Dr, Carefree; casitas $249-299, villas $529-779; P ❋ @ ⦿ ❄ ❉) Tensions evaporate upon arrival at this desert oasis that blends into a landscape of natural rock formations – and that's before you've put in a session at the on-site spa or settled in at one of the four pools. Basically, everything here is calculated to make life better. Outdoor programs include hiking, rock climbing and stargazing with an astronomer. Complimentary yoga classes are offered daily. For extra privacy book an individual casita, to which you will be whisked on a golf cart past the 18-hole Jay Morris–designed championship golf course. Daily resort fee is $30. Weekend rates can drop as low as $129 in summer.

Sanctuary on Camelback
Mountain RESORT $$$
(Map p116; ☑ 480-948-2100; www.sanctuaryon-camelback.com; 5700 E McDonald Dr; r $399-559, houses $1900-4000; P ❋ @ ⦿ ❄ ❉) Draped across the northern slopes of Camelback Mountain, this luxe resort and spa feels like a hideaway of the gods. Mountain suites, spa casitas, private homes – no matter your choice, you will feel pampered, protected and deserving. Lodgings are decorated with the beautiful warm tones of the desert. Enjoy a cocktail at Edge, a sleek outdoor watering hole with sweeping views of the Valley. The daily resort fee is $26; pets are $100 per visit. Travelers with their children in tow may be happier elsewhere.

Hermosa Inn BOUTIQUE HOTEL $$$
(Map p116; ☑ 602-955-8614; www.hermosainn.com; 5532 N Palo Cristi Rd; r & casitas $260-440; P ❋ ⦿ ❄ ❉) The signage is discreet but the flowers are not at this gorgeous retreat. The 34 rooms and casitas give off soothing vibes thanks to Spanish Colonial decor that makes perfect use of color and proportion. There's an excellent restaurant on site. The pet fee is $75 per stay, per pet.

The Saguaro HOTEL $$$
(☑ 480-308-1100; www.jdvhotels.com; 4000 N Drinkwater Blvd; r $169-229, ste 249-669; P ❋ ⦿ ❄ ❉) Embrace your inner hipster at this candy-bright hideaway beside Old Town Scottsdale. When compared to more established Scottsdale properties there may be less attention to detail here, and the vibe skews young, but the location is great, there's a palm-dotted pool and the Saguaro's rates are lower than its neighborhood competitors.

🛏 Tempe

Best Western Inn of Tempe HOTEL $$
(Map p116; ☑ 480-784-2233; www.innoftempe.com; 670 N Scottsdale Rd; r incl breakfast from $117; P ❋ @ ⦿ ❄ ❉) This well-kept contender sits right next to the busy 202 freeway but is within walking distance of Tempe Town Lake. ASU and Mill Ave are within staggering distance. The hotel also offers a free airport shuttle. Pets are $10 each per day.

Sheraton Wild Horse
Pass Resort & Spa RESORT $$$
(Map p114; ☑ 602-225-0100; www.wildhorsepass-resort.com; 5594 W Wild Horse Pass Blvd, Chandler; r $259, ste from $334; P ❋ @ ⦿ ❄) At sunset, scan the lonely horizon for the eponymous wild horses silhouetted against the South Mountains. Owned by the Gila River tribe and nestled on their sweeping reservation south of Tempe, this 500-room resort is a stunning alchemy of luxury and Native American traditions. The domed lobby is a mural-festooned roundhouse, and rooms reflect the traditions of local tribes.

The spa offers indigenous body treatments and massages while the award-winning Kai Restaurant serves tribally inspired Southwestern cuisine. That, plus two 18-hole golf courses, an equestrian center, tennis courts, sumptuous rooms and a waterslide modeled after ancient desert ruins round out the appeal.

✕ Eating

Phoenix has the biggest selection of restaurants in the Southwest. Reservations are recommended at the more fashionable places.

✕ Phoenix

★ Matt's Big Breakfast
BREAKFAST $

(Map p120; ☎602-254-1074; www.mattsbigbreakfast.com; 825 N 1st St, at Garfield St; breakfast $5-10, lunch $7-10; ⏱6:30am-2:30pm) First, a warning: even on weekdays lines are often out the door. There are no reservations, so sign your name on the clipboard and expect a 20-minute wait (and bring quarters for the meter). The upside? Best. Breakfast. Ever.

Every regular menu item is great but daily specials – such as eggs scrambled with peppers and chorizo into fluffy-spicy-oh-my-goodness on a bed of mouthwatering crispy home fries – are supremely yummy. A true Phoenix institution.

★ Green New American Vegetarian
VEGAN, VEGETARIAN $

(Map p120; ☎602-258-1870; www.greenvegetarian.com; 2022 N 7th St; mains $6-9; ☙) Whoa, whoa, whoa. Vegan food isn't supposed to taste this good. Or is it? Your expectations will be forever raised after dining at this hip cafe where vegan chef Damon Brasch stirs up savory vegan and vegetarian dishes. The burgers, po-boys and Asian-style bowls taste as good, if not better, than their carnivorous counterparts. Order at the counter then take a seat in the garage-style digs.

For dessert, walk next door to sister restaurant nami (www.tsoynami.com) for pastries and soft serve, all vegan.

Tee Pee Mexican Food
MEXICAN $

(Map p116; ☎602-956-0178; www.teepeemexicanfood.com; 4144 E Indian School Rd; mains $5-14; ⏱11am-10pm Mon-Sat, to 9pm Sun) If you're snobby about Mexican food, you will not be happy at Tee Pee. If, however, you like piping-hot plates piled high with cheesy, messy, American-style Mexican food, then grab a booth at this 40-year-old Phoenix fave. George W Bush ate here in 2004 and ordered two enchiladas, rice and beans – now called the Presidential Special. Dig in!

La Grande Orange Grocery & Pizzeria
CAFE $

(Map p116; ☎602-840-7777; www.lagrandeorangegrocery.com; 4410 N 40th St; breakfast $6-8, lunch $7-10, pizza $12-15; ⏱cafe 6:30am-10pm, pizzeria from 4pm Mon-Thu, from 11am Fri & Sat) Grab a muffin and coffee for breakfast, pop by for a guacamole BLT at lunch, or settle in for a margherita pizza at dinner at this bustling gourmet market, bakery, cafe and pizzeria at the corner of 40th St and E Campbell Ave. In a hurry? Check the online menu then call ahead for curbside service.

★ Dick's Hideaway
NEW MEXICAN $$

(Map p116; ☎602-241-1881; http://richardsonsnm.com; 6008 N 16th St; breakfast $5-20, lunch $12-16, dinner $12-35; ⏱7am-midnight Sun-Wed, to 1am Thu-Sat) At this pocket-sized ode to New Mexican cuisine, grab a small table beside the bar or settle in at the communal table in the side room and prepare for hearty servings of savory, chile-slathered New Mexican fare, from enchiladas to tamales to rellenos. We especially like the Hideaway for breakfast, when the Bloody Marys arrive with a shot of beer. A tip: the unmarked entrance is between the towering shrubs.

Pizzeria Bianco
PIZZA $$

(Map p120; ☎602-258-8300; www.pizzeriabianco.com; 623 E Adams St; pizza $13-18; ⏱11am-9pm Mon, 11am-10pm Tue-Sat) James Beard–winner Chris Bianco is back in the kitchen at his famous downtown pizza joint after stepping back in 2010 due to allergies. But thanks to new medicine and his love of pizza crafting, Bianco has returned in full force, and his thin-crust gourmet pies are as popular as ever. The tiny restaurant is a convenient stop for travelers exploring the adjacent Heritage Square. A second location (Map p116; 4743 N 20th St; ⏱11am-9pm Sun-Thu, to 10pm Fri & Sat), which also serves sandwiches, is in Town & Country mall at the corner of 20th St and Camelback Rd, near Biltmore Fashion Park.

Crudo
ITALIAN $$

(Map p116; ☎602-358-8666; www.crudoaz.com; 3603 E Indian School Rd, Gaslight Square; mains dinner $12-20, brunch $12-14; ⏱5-10pm Tue-Sat, 10am-2pm & 5-9pm Sun) This isn't your mama's Italian. Unless mama mixes up her risotto with squid ink, chiles and tuna. Hot-on-the-scene Crudo, which is tucked in the back of a strip mall, gives Italian dishes a light, modern spin with a few nods to the Old World – crispy pigs ear anyone? We hear they're divine. Creative cocktails lure the after-work crowd to the cozy, chattering bar.

Windsor
AMERICAN $$

(Map p116; ☎602-279-1111; www.windsoraz.com; 5223 N Central Ave; mains $11-19; ⏱11am-11pm

Mon-Thu, 11am-midnight Fri, 9am-midnight Sat, 9am-10pm Sun) We like it here. Maybe it's the buzzy energy of the central bar. Or the no-worries charm of the waitstaff. Or the $5 pitchers at happy hour. And the back wall that's covered in '80s cassette tapes? Pretty darn mesmerizing. With its craft beers and upscale comfort food (the BBQ comes on a buttermilk bun), we'd call this Uptown hotspot a gourmet gastropub. For dessert, savor a Fat Elvis sundae at **Churn** (www.churnaz. com), the attached ice-cream shop.

Barrio Café
MEXICAN $$

(Map p116; ☑ 602-636-0240; www.barriocafe.com; 2814 N 16th St; mains $12-29; ◷ 11am-10pm Tue-Thu, 11am-10:30pm Fri & Sat, 11am-9pm Sun) Barrio's T-shirts are emblazoned with *comida chingona,* which translates as 'fucking good food.' Crude, maybe. To the point, definitely. Barrio makes Mexican food at its most creative: how many menus featuring guacamole spiked with pomegranate seeds or goatmilk-caramel-filled churros have you seen?

Pane Bianco
SANDWICHES $$

(Map p116; ☑ 602-234-2100; 4404 N Central Ave; lunch mains $9-12, dinner mains $12-16; ◷ lunch 11am-4pm Mon-Sat, until 3pm Sun, dinner 4-8pm Mon-Thu, until 9pm Fri & Sat) Part of the Pizzeria Bianco empire, Pane is a top spot for an artisan sandwich. Formerly a take-out place, it expanded in 2012 to include a sit-down restaurant. Enjoy salads and sandwiches at lunch and pizza and a few seasonal specials at dinner.

Durant's
STEAK $$$

(Map p116; ☑ 602-264-5967; www.durantsaz.com; 2611 N Central Ave; lunch $12-26, dinner $22-61; ◷ 11am-10pm Mon-Fri, 5-11pm Sat, 4:30-10pm Sun) This dark and manly place is a gloriously old-school steak house. You will get steak. It will be big and juicy. There will be a potato. The ambiance is awesome too: red velvet cozy booths and the sense that the Rat Pack is going to waltz in at any minute.

✖ Scottsdale

Fresh Mint
VIETNAMESE $

(Map p114; ☑ 480-443-2556; www.freshmint.us.com; 13802 N Scottsdale Rd; lunch mains $8, dinner $6-14; ◷ 11am-9pm Mon-Sat; ⊘) What? Never had kosher Vietnamese vegan? Well, there's always a first time – and if it tastes anything like the food at Fresh Mint, you'll want to get more. If you're skeptical of soy chicken and tofu (served many ways), we understand, but we

respectfully submit that this stuff is as tasty as any bacon cheeseburger.

Sugar Bowl
ICE CREAM $

(☑ 480-946-0051; www.sugarbowlscottsdale.com; 4005 N Scottsdale Rd; ice cream $2.25-9, mains $6-12; ◷ 11am-10pm Sun-Thu, 11am-midnight Fri & Sat; ☖) Get your ice cream fix at this pink-and-white Valley institution. Also serves a full menu of sandwiches and salads.

The Mission
MEXICAN $$

(☑ 480-636-5005; www.themissionaz.com; 3815 N Brown Ave; lunch $9-23, dinner $12-36; ◷ 11am-10pm Sun-Thu, to 11pm Fri & Sat) With its dark interior and glowing votives, we'll call this *nuevo* Latin spot sexy – although our exclamations about the food's deliciousness may ruin the sultry vibe. The tecate-marinated steak taco with lime and avocado is superb and makes for a satisfying light lunch. The guacamole is made table-side, and wins raves. Margaritas and mojitos round out the fun.

Herb Box
AMERICAN $$

(☑ 480-289-6160; www.theherbbox.com; 7134 E Stetson Dr; brunch $7-16, lunch $10-16, dinner $15-28; ◷ 11am-3pm Mon, 11am-9pm Tue-Fri, 9am-10pm Sat, 9am-3pm Sun) It's not just about sparkle and air kisses at this chichi bistro in the heart of Old Town's Southbridge. It's also about fresh regional ingredients, artful presentation and attentive service. For a light, healthy, ever-so-stylish lunch (steak salad, turkey avocado wrap, kale and capicola flatbread), settle in on the patio and toast your good fortune with a blackberry mojito.

Mastro's Ocean Club
SEAFOOD $$$

(Map p114; ☑ 480-443-8555; www.mastrosrestaurants.com; 15045 N Kierland Blvd; mains $28-100; ◷ 5-10pm Sun-Thu, until 11pm Fri & Sat, lounge until 1am) Mastro's is gunning for the title of best seafood in the Valley of the Sun, and we think it may deserve the crown. The allure of the restaurant, part of an upscale chain, is in its incredibly rich, decadent take on everything that swims under the waves. The restaurant is located in Kierland Commons.

✖ Tempe

Essence
CAFE $

(Map p116; ☑ 480-966-2745; www.essencebakery. com; 825 W University Dr; breakfast $6-9.25, lunch $8-9; ◷ 7am-3pm Tue-Sat; ⊘) Look for French toast and egg dishes at breakfast, and salads, gourmet sandwiches and a few Mediterranean specialties at lunch. The eco-minded cafe strives to serve organic, locally grown fare. The popular macaroons are mighty fine.

Casey Moore's   SEAFOOD, PUB GRUB $$

(Map p116; ☑480-968-9935; www.caseymoores. com; 850 S Ash Ave; mans $7-23; ☺11am-2am) Did somebody say oysters? Oh yes they did. And Casey Moore's is the place to slurp them. Part Irish pub, part seafood restaurant, part Tempe institution, Casey's is a fun and friendly place to hang out on a Saturday afternoon. The patio is dog friendly until 5pm; things may get more rambunctious at night. Oysters are from the East Coast, if you're wondering.

★ Kai Restaurant   NATIVE AMERICAN $$$

(☑602-225-0100; www.wildhorsepassresort.com; 5594 W Wild Horse Pass Blvd, Chandler; mains $42-54, tasting menus $135-$225; ☺5:30-9pm Tue-Sat) Native American cuisine soars to new heights at Kai, enhanced and transformed by traditional crops grown along the Gila River. Dinners strike just the right balance between adventure and comfort. Dress nicely (no shorts or hats). It's at the Sheraton Wild Horse Pass Resort & Spa on the Gila River Indian Reservation. Expect creations such as pecan-crusted Colorado lamb with native seeds mole or elk loin with wild mushrooms. Service is unobtrusive yet flawless, the wine list handpicked and the room decorated with Native American art.

✖ Mesa

Landmark   AMERICAN $$

(☑480-962-4652; www.landmarkrestaurant.com; 809 W Main St; lunch $8-13, dinner $11-27; ☺11am-8pm Mon-Thu, to 9pm Fri & Sat, to 7pm Sun) This converted 1908 Mormon church has been a family-owned local mainstay for decades. Lighter eaters, meanwhile, have an entire 'Salad Room' (lunch/dinner $12/15) with over 80 items for grazing, from tomatoes and smoked turkey to quail eggs and prickly pear cactus salad.

🍷 Drinking

Posh watering holes are found in the most unlikely of spots in the Phoenix area, even amid chain stores in strip malls. Scottsdale has the greatest concentration of trendy bars and clubs as well as a convivial lineup of patios on Scottsdale Rd in Old Town; Tempe attracts the student crowd.

Phoenix

★ Postino Winecafé Arcadia   WINE BAR

(Map p116; www.postinowinecafe.com; 3939 E Campbell Ave, at 40th St; ☺11am-11pm Mon-Thu, 11am-midnight Fri, 9am-midnight Sat, 9am-10pm Sun) Your mood will improve the moment you step into this convivial, indoor-outdoor wine bar. It's a perfect gathering spot for friends ready to enjoy the good life – but solos will do fine too. Highlights include the misting patio, rave-worthy bruschetta, and more than 20 wines by the glass for $5 between 11am and 5pm. This spot used to be the home of the Arcadia Post Office.

Postino Central   WINE BAR

(Map p116; www.postinowinecafe.com; 5144 N Central Ave; ☺11am-11pm Mon-Thu, 11am-midnight Fri, 9am-midnight Sat, 9am-10pm Sun) This inviting branch of the Postino Winecafé sits in burgeoning Uptown. Offers $5 wine by the glass for listed wines from 11am to 5pm.

Vig Arcadia   BAR

(Map p116; www.thevig.us; 4041 N 40th St; ☺11am-2am Mon-Fri, 10am-2am Sat & Sun) Ignore the imposing Soviet-style exterior and step inside. The Vig is where the smart set – stylish, well-scrubbed, happy – comes to knock back a few cocktails. Sleek booths, a dark bar, bustling patio, upbeat vibe: be careful or you might find yourself tossing your hair and flashing your tan like the rest of 'em.

Complimentary valet or park in the store lot across the street, to the right of the check cashing store.

O.H.S.O. Eatery & nanoBrewery   BREWERY

(Map p116; www.ohsobrewery.com; 4900 E Indian School Rd) Small batch brews and Arizona beers are the stars at this bustling nanobrewery in Arcadia. Dog lovers can bring Fido with them to the patio. Parking is tight, so be prepared to valet (free) when it's busy. And the name? We hear it stands for Outrageous Homebrewers Social Outpost.

Lux Central Coffeebar   CAFE

(Map p116; www.luxcoffee.com; 4402 N Central Ave; ☺6am-midnight Sun-Thu, 6am-2am Fri & Sat; 🛜) Bowie's 'Rebel, Rebel' may be spilling from the speakers, but we're not convinced that the hipsters tapping away on their MacBooks in porkpie hats are breaking too many rules. But hey, the staff schmoozes just fine, the coffee is handroasted and the vibe is lively, so it's all good. A bar and cafe were added in 2011.

Edge Bar
BAR
(Map p116; 5700 E McDonald Dr, Sanctuary on Camelback Mountain, Paradise Valley) This stylish cocktail bar, perched narrowly on the side of Camelback Mountain, is an inviting place to watch the sunset. If it's full, the equally posh, big-windowed Jade Bar next door should do just fine. Both are within the plush confines of Sanctuary on Camelback Mountain. Free valet, but they'll accept a gratuity and a smile.

Alice Cooperstown
SPORTS BAR
(Map p120; www.alicecooperstown.com; 101 E Jackson St; 11am-9pm Mon-Thu, 11am-10pm Fri, noon-10pm Sat, 11am-4pm Sun) This beer hall really is the original shock rocker's (and Phoenix residents') baby. Cooperstown is both a play on Alice Cooper's name and the location of the Baseball Hall of Fame. On game days it floods with giddy sports lovers toasting their teams. For music fans, rock-and-roll memorabilia covers the walls.

Scottsdale

Rusty Spur Saloon
BAR
(480-425-7787; www.rustyspursaloon.com; 7245 E Main St; 10am-1am Sun-Thu, to 2am Fri & Sat) Nobody's putting on airs at this fun-lovin', pack-'em-in-tight country bar where the grizzled Budweiser crowd gathers for cheap drinks and twangy bands. It's in an old bank building that closed during the Depression; the vault now holds liquor instead of greenbacks – except for the dollar bills hanging from the ceiling. Pardner, we kinda like this place.

Greasewood Flat
BAR
(480-585-9430; www.greasewoodflat.net; 27375 N Alma School Pkwy; 11am-10pm Sun-Mon, until 11pm Fri & Sat) At this beer-garden-sized outdoor pub and ex-stagecoach stop, rough-and-tumble types – cowboys, bikers, preppy golfers – gather around the smoky barbecue and knock back the brewskies. The bar is cash only (an ATM is on site). Double check the address before visiting. At press time the Greasewood was considering a move.

Tempe

Four Peaks Brewing Company
BREWERY
(Map p116; 480-303-9967; www.fourpeaks.com; 1340 E 8th St; 11am-2am Mon-Sat, 10am-1am Sun) Beer lovers rejoice: you're in for a treat at this quintessential neighborhood brewpub in a cool Mission Revival–style building.

★ Entertainment

The entertainment scene in Phoenix is lively and multifaceted, if not particularly edgy. You can hobnob with high society at the opera or symphony, mingle with the moneyed at a chic nightclub or let your hair down at a punk concert in a local dive. Spectator sports are huge.

These publications will help you plug into the local scene:

Arizona Republic Calendar
MEDIA
(www.azcentral.com/thingstodo/events) The Thursday edition of this major daily newspaper includes a special section with entertainment listings.

Phoenix New Times
MEDIA
(www.phoenixnewtimes.com) This free, alternative weekly is published on Thursday and available citywide.

Performing Arts
Not much goes on during summer.

Phoenix Symphony
SYMPHONY
(Map p120; administration 602-495-1117, box office 602-495-1999; www.phoenixsymphony.org; 75 North Second St, box offices 1 North First St, 75 North Second St) Arizona's only full-time professional orchestra plays classics and pops, mostly at Symphony Hall and sometimes at other regional venues, from September to early June.

Arizona Opera
OPERA
(Map p120; 602-266-7464; www.azopera.com; 75 N 2nd St) Now in a new 28,000ft space downtown, the state ensemble produces five operas per season, usually big-ticket favorites such as Mozart's *Magic Flute* and Verdi's *La Traviata*. Performances are at Symphony Hall.

Phoenix Theatre
PERFORMING ARTS
(Map p120; 602-254-2151; www.phoenixtheatre.com; 100 E McDowell Rd) The city's main dramatic group puts on a good mix of mainstream and edgier performances. The attached Cookie Company does children's shows.

Sports
Phoenix has some of the nation's top professional teams, and tickets for the best games sell out fast.

Arizona Cardinals
FOOTBALL
(602-379-0101; www.azcardinals.com; 1 Cardinals Dr, Glendale) The Cardinals play at the architecturally distinguished University of Phoenix Stadium in the western Valley city

of Glendale, the site of Super Bowl XLIX in 2015. Check the website for information about 75-minute stadium tours (adult/child $9/7). The season runs from September through February.

Arizona Diamondbacks BASEBALL
(Map p120; ☑602-462-6500; http://arizona.diamondbacks.mlb.com; 401 E Jefferson St) The Diamondbacks won the World Series in 2001, but the real draw of attending a baseball game here is downtown **Chase Field**, which features a retractable domed roof to help keep temperatures cool.

Arizona Coyotes HOCKEY
(☑480-563-7825; http://coyotes.nhl.com; 9400 Maryland Ave, Glendale) Hosted by the **Jobing. com Arena**, the Coyotes play from October to mid-April.

Phoenix Mercury BASKETBALL
(Map p120; ☑602-252-9622; www.wnba.com/mercury; 201 E Jefferson St) The women's NBA team plays professional basketball from mid-May to mid-August at the US Airways Center; they won the national championship in 2007 and 2009.

Phoenix Suns BASKETBALL
(Map p120; ☑602-379-7867; www.nba.com/suns; 201 E Jefferson St) The Suns play at the US Airways Center from late October to mid-April.

Live Music

Char's Has the Blues BLUES
(Map p116; ☑602-230-0205; www.charshastheblues.com; 4631 N 7th Ave, Phoenix; ☺8pm-1am Sun-Wed, 7:30pm-1am Thu-Sat) Dark and intimate – but very welcoming – this blues and R&B cottage packs 'em in with solid acts most nights of the week, but somehow still manages to feel like a well-kept secret. No cover Monday through Wednesday.

> ### CACTUS LEAGUE SPRING TRAINING
> Before the start of the major league baseball season, teams spend March in Arizona (Cactus League) and Florida (Grapefruit League) trying out new players, practicing and playing games. Tickets are cheaper (from $6 to $8 depending on the venue), the seats better, the lines shorter and the games more relaxed. Check www.cactusleague.com for schedules and links to tickets.

Rhythm Room LIVE MUSIC
(Map p116; ☑602-265-4842; www.rhythmroom.com; 1019 E Indian School Rd; ☺doors usually open 7:30pm) Some of the Valley's best live acts take the stage at this small venue, where you feel like you're in the front row of every gig. It tends to attract more local and regional talent than big names, which suits us just fine. Check the calendar for show times.

Shopping

The Valley of the Sun is also the Valley of the consumer. From western wear to arts and crafts and Native Americana, it's easy to find a souvenir. Mall culture is also huge. **Old Town Scottsdale** is known for its art galleries and Southwestern crafts shops. **Mill Ave** in Tempe has a mix of indie and chain boutiques.

Phoenix

Heard Museum Shop & Bookstore ARTS & CRAFTS
(Map p120; www.heardmuseumshop.com; 2301 N Central Ave; ☺shop 9:30am-5pm, from 11am Sun, bookstore 9:30am-5:30pm Mon-Sat, to 5pm Sun) This museum store has a top notch collection of Native American original arts and crafts. The kachina collection alone is mind-boggling. Jewelry, pottery, Native American books and a broad selection of fine arts are also on offer. The bookstore sells a wide array of books about the Southwest.

Bookmans BOOKS
(Map p116; ☑602-433-0255; www.bookmans.com; 8034 N 19th Ave; ☺9am-10pm; ☎☺) The bibliophile's indie mecca, with a neighborhood vibe, events and aisle after aisle of new and used books, mags and music. Free wi-fi.

Garden Shop at the Desert Botanical Garden GARDENING
(Map p116; www.dbg.org; 1201 N Galvin Pkwy; ☺8am-8pm; ☎) Plant your own desert garden with a starter cactus from this indoor-outdoor gift shop. Southwestern cards, cactus jellies and desert-minded gardening books are also on sale.

Biltmore Fashion Park MALL
(Map p116; www.shopbiltmore.com; 2502 E Camelback Rd, at N 24th St; ☺10am-8pm Mon-Sat, noon-6pm Sun) This exclusive mall preens from her perch on Camelback just south of the Arizona Biltmore.

Scottsdale

Kierland Commons MALL
(Map p114; www.kierlandcommons.com; 15205 N Kierland Blvd; ◎10am-9pm Mon-Sat, noon-6pm Sun) This new outdoor mall in northern Scottsdale is pulling in crowds.

Scottsdale Fashion Square MALL
(www.fashionsquare.com; 7014 E Camelback, at Scottsdale Rd; ◎10am-9pm Mon-Sat, 11am-6pm Sun) From Abercrombie & Fitch to Nordstrom to Z Tejas Grill, this upscale mall has chains, department stores and restaurants.

Tempe

Changing Hands BOOKS
(✆480-730-0205; www.changinghands.com; 6428 S McClintock Dr; ◎10am-9pm Mon-Fri, 9am-9pm Sat, 10am-6pm Sun) Has used, new, hard-to-find and out-of-print books and magazines, plus lots of events.

ℹ️ Information

EMERGENCY
Police (✆emergency 911, non-emergency 602-262-6151; http://phoenix.gov/police; 620 W Washington St, Phoenix)

INTERNET ACCESS
Burton Barr Central Library (✆602-262-4636; www.phoenixpubliclibrary.org; 1221 N Central Ave; ◎9am-5pm Mon, Fri & Sat, 9am-9pm Tue-Thu, 1-5pm Sun; 🛜) Free internet; see website for additional locations.

MEDICAL SERVICES
Both hospitals have 24-hour emergency rooms.
Banner Good Samaritan Medical Center (✆602-839-2000; www.bannerhealth.com; 1111 E McDowell Rd)
St Joseph's Hospital & Medical Center (✆602-406-3000; www.stjosephs-phx.org; 350 W Thomas Rd)

POST
Downtown Post Office (Map p120; ✆602-253-9648; 522 N Central Ave; ◎9am-5pm Mon-Fri)

TELEPHONE
Greater Phoenix has three telephone area codes: 480, 602 and 623. You always need to dial the area code, regardless of where you are.

TOURIST INFORMATION
Downtown Phoenix Visitor Information Center (Map p120; ✆877-225-5749; www.visitphoenix.com; 125 N 2nd St; ◎8am-5pm Mon-Fri) The Valley's most complete source of tourist information. Located across from the Hyatt Regency.

Mesa Convention & Visitors Bureau (Map p114; ✆480-827-4700, 800-283-6372; www.visitmesa.com; 120 N Center St; ◎8am-5pm Mon-Fri)

Scottsdale Convention & Visitors Bureau (✆800-782-1117, 480-421-1004; www.experiencescottsdale.com; 4343 N Scottsdale Rd, Suite 170; ◎8am-5pm Mon-Fri) Inside the Galleria Corporate Center.

Tempe Convention & Visitors Bureau (Map p116; ✆866-914-1052, 480-894-8158; www.tempetourism.com; 51 W 3rd St, Suite 105; ◎8:30am-5pm Mon-Fri)

ℹ️ Getting There & Away

Sky Harbor International Airport (Map p116; ✆602-273-3300; http://skyharbor.com; 3400 E Sky Harbor Blvd; 🛜) Sky Harbor International Airport is 3 miles southeast of downtown Phoenix and served by 17 airlines, including United, American, Delta and British Airways. Its three terminals (Terminals 2, 3 and 4; Terminal 1 was demolished in 1990) and the parking lots are linked by the free 24-hour Airport Shuttle Bus.

Greyhound (Map p116; ✆602-389-4200; www.greyhound.com; 2115 E Buckeye Rd) Greyhound runs buses to Tucson ($18, two hours, six daily), Flagstaff ($25, three hours, five daily), Albuquerque ($70 to $87, 9½ hours, three daily) and Los Angeles ($46, 7½ hours, 7 daily). Valley Metro's No 13 buses link the airport and the Greyhound station; tell the driver your destination is the Greyhound station.

ℹ️ Getting Around

TO/FROM THE AIRPORT
All international car-rental companies have offices at the airport.

For shared rides, the citywide door-to-door shuttle service provided by **Super Shuttle** (✆602-244-9000, 800-258-3826; www.supershuttle.com) costs about $13 to downtown Phoenix, $15 to Tempe, $21 to Mesa and $17 to Old Town Scottsdale.

Three taxi companies serve the airport: **AAA/Yellow Cab** (✆480-888-8888), **Apache** (✆480-557-7000) and **Mayflower** (✆602-955-1355). The charge is $5 for the first mile and $2.30 for each additional mile; from the airport there's a $1 surcharge and $15 minimum fare. Expect to pay $16 to $19 to downtown.

The new **Phoenix Sky Train** (www.skyharbor.com/phxskytrain) runs from Terminal 4 to the METRO light-rail station at 44th St and E Washington St, via the airport's east economy parking area. Bus route 13 also connects the airport to town. Bus fare is $2 per ride.

PAYSON & MOGOLLON RIM

If you're traveling between Phoenix and Flagstaff and have extra time, consider a detour to Payson and the Mogollon Rim.

Founded by gold miners in 1882, Payson's real riches turned out to be above ground. Vast pine forests fed a booming timber industry, ranchers ran cattle along the Mogollon Rim and down to the Tonto Basin, and wild game was plentiful. Frontier life here captivated Western author Zane Grey, who kept a cabin outside town. Prime activities are hunting and fishing in the forests, lakes and streams around the Rim. The **World's Oldest Continuous Rodeo** has been held in Payson every August since 1884.

The bridge at **Tonto Natural Bridge State Park** (☑ 928-476-4202; www.azstateparks. com/parks/tona; off Hwy 87; adult/child 7-13yr $5/2; ⊙ 8am-6pm Jun-Aug, 9am-5pm Sep-May), located 11 miles north of Payson, was formed after Pine Creek, flowing downhill, ran smack into a massive dam of calcium carbonate. It gradually cut its way through, carving out the world's largest natural travertine bridge, which is 183ft high and spans a 150ft-wide canyon. You can walk over it and view it from multiple angles; there are steep trails down into the canyon for close-ups.

For more natural beauty, drive east from Payson on Hwy 260 through Tonto National Forest. This woodsy route parallels the Mogollon Rim, a 200-mile swath of forested cliffs along the edge of the towering Colorado Plateau. Thirty-two miles east, stop at the **Mogollon Rim Visitor Center** (☑ 928-535-7300; Hwy 260; ⊙ 9am-3pm Thu-Sun Jun-Aug, fall hours depend on weather) in the Apache-Sitgreaves National Forest for expansive views of lakes and forests to the south.

To continue to Flagstaff from Payson, hook northwest on Hwy 260 via Pine and Strawberry to the I-17. For more information about the region, visit www.paysonrimcountry.com or stop by the Rim Country Chamber of Commerce **Visitor Center** (☑ 928-474-4515; www.rimcountrychamber.com; 100 W Main, at Hwy 87; ⊙ 9am-5pm Mon-Fri, 9am-2pm Sat).

CAR & MOTORCYCLE
The network of freeways is starting to rival Los Angeles and so is the intensity of traffic. Always pad your sightseeing itinerary for traffic jams. The I-10 and US 60 are the main east–west thoroughfares, while the I-17 and SR 51 are the major north–south arteries. Loops 101 and 202 link most of the suburbs. Parking is plentiful outside of the downtown area.

PUBLIC TRANSPORTATION
Valley Metro (☑ 602-253-5000; www.valleymetro.org) Valley Metro operates buses all over the Valley and a 20-mile light-rail line linking north Phoenix with downtown Phoenix, Tempe/ASU and downtown Mesa. Fares for both light-rail and bus are $2 per ride (no transfers) or $4 for a day pass. Buses run daily at intermittent times.

Orbit Bus (www.tempe.gov; ⊙ 6am-10pm Mon-Fri, 8am-10pm Sat, 8am-7pm Sun) The free Orbit Mercury bus loops around downtown Tempe, along Mill Ave and University Dr.

Scottsdale Trolley (www.scottsdaleaz.gov/trolley; ⊙ 11am-6pm Fri-Wed, to 9pm Thu during Artwalk) The downtown Scottsdale Trolley loops past Old Town, the Main Street Arts District and Scottsdale Fashion.

CENTRAL ARIZONA

Much of the area north of Phoenix lies on the Colorado Plateau and is cool, wooded and mountainous. It's draped with the most diverse and scenic quilt of sites and attractions in all of Arizona. You can clamber around a volcano, channel your inner goddess on a vortex, taste wine in a former mining town, hike through sweet-smelling canyons, schuss down alpine slopes, admire 1000-year-old Native American dwellings and delve into Old West and pioneer history. The main hub, Flagstaff, is a lively and delightful college town and gateway to the Grand Canyon South Rim. Summer, spring and fall are the best times to visit.

You can make the trip between Phoenix and Flagstaff in just over two hours if you put the pedal to the metal on I-17, which provides a straight 145-mile shot between the two cities. Opt for the more leisurely Hwy 89, though, and you'll be rewarded with beautiful scenery and intriguing sites along the way.

Verde Valley & Around

These stops are listed from south to north from Phoenix along I-17. All are within a few miles of the interstate.

Rock Springs Café   AMERICAN
(☑ 623-374-5794; www.rockspringscafe.com; 35769 S Old Black Cyn Hwy; slice of pie $4.50, mains breakfast $5-12, lunch & dinner $8-20; ☉ 7am-10pm) A pit stop for pie? You betcha. Especially if it's a slice of fresh pie at Rock Springs Café in Black Canyon City. Only problem? This Old West eatery, off I-17 at exit 242, will drive you crazy with choices (apple crumble, blueberry, rhubarb, chocolate) all sitting pretty in a cooler in the dining room. Heartier grub includes burgers, steaks and pan-fried catfish. The attached farmers market sells produce, hot sauce, beef jerky and cactus arrangements. On the first Saturday of the month, roll in for **Hogs N Heat** (☉ 1-11pm) when the barbecue smokers fire up on the patio. This party draws Harley riders and, well, everybody within sniffin' distance.

Arcosanti   ARCHITECTURE
(☑ 928-632-7135; www.arcosanti.org; suggested donation for tours $10; ☉ tours 10am-4pm) Two miles east of I-17 exit 262 (Cordes Junction; 65 miles north of Phoenix), Arcosanti is an architectural experiment in urban living that's been a work in progress since 1970. The brainchild of groundbreaking architect and urban planner Paolo Soleri, who died in 2013, it is based on his concept of 'arcology,' which seeks to create communities in harmony with their natural surroundings, minimizing the use of energy, raw materials and land. If and when it is finished, Arcosanti will be a self-sufficient village with futuristic living spaces, large-scale greenhouses and solar energy. Hour-long tours explore the site and provide background about the project's history and design philosophy. A gift shop sells the famous bronze bells cast at the foundry in Cosanti, near Phoenix. Tours start on the hour beginning at 10am, with no tour at noon.

Fort Verde State Historic Park   PARK
(☑ 928-567-3275; http://azstateparks.com/Parks/FOVE; 125 E Hollamon St; adult/child 7-13yr $5/2; ☉ 9am-5pm Thu-Mon) Camp Verde was founded in 1865 as a farming settlement only to be co-opted soon after by the US Army who built a fort here to prevent Indian raids on Anglo settlers. Tonto Apache chief Chalipun surrendered here in April 1873. Today, the town's Fort Verde State Historic Park offers an authentic snapshot of frontier life in the late 19th century.

Exploring the well-preserved fort, you'll see the officer's and doctor's quarters, the parade grounds and study displays about military life and the Indian Wars. Staff occasionally dress up in period costume and conduct living history tours. To get here, take exit 287 off I-17, go south on Hwy 260, turn left at Finnie Flat Rd and left again at Hollamon St. Mediocre chain motels cluster near exit 287.

Montezuma Castle National Monument   MONUMENT
(☑ 928-567-3322; www.nps.gov/moca; adult/child 15yr & under $5/free, combination pass with Tuzigoot National Monument $8; ☉ 8am-5pm) Like nearby Tuzigoot, Montezuma Castle is a stunningly well-preserved 1000-year-old Sinagua cliff dwelling. The name refers to the splendid castlelike location high on a cliff; early explorers thought the five-story-high pueblo was Aztec and hence dubbed it Montezuma. A **museum** interprets the archaeology of the site, which can be spotted from a short self-guiding, wheelchair-accessible trail. Entrance into the 'castle' itself is prohibited, but there's a virtual tour on the website. Access the monument from I-17 exit 289, drive east for 0.5 miles, then turn left on Montezuma Castle Rd.

Montezuma Well   WELL
(☑ 928-567-4521; ☉ 8am-5pm) **FREE** Montezuma Well is a natural limestone sinkhole 470ft wide, surrounded by both Sinaguan and Hohokam dwellings. Water from the well was used for irrigation by the Native Americans and is still used today by residents of nearby Rimrock. Access is from I-17 exit 293, 4 miles north of the Montezuma Castle exit. Follow the signs for another 4 miles through McGuireville and Rimrock.

V-Bar-V Heritage Site   PETROGLYPHS
(www.redrockcountry.org/recreation/cultural/v-v; ☉ 9:30am-3pm Fri-Mon) More than 1000 petrolglyphs have been identified at this well-protected Forest Service site. Many of the etchings appear unique to the Southern Sinaguan who lived here between AD 1150 and 1400. The site was probably used by shamans, and in part as a solar calendar. And the embracing stick-figure couple? Not dancing. Red Rock pass required.

Follow Hwy 179 east about 2.5 miles from I-17, exit 298. The entrance is on your right beyond Beaver Creek Campground.

Wickenburg

POP 6532 / ELEV 2100FT

Wickenburg looks like it fell out of the sky – directly from the 1890s. Downtown streets are flanked by Old West storefronts, historic buildings and several life-size statues of the prospectors and cowboys who brought this place to life in the 1800s. In later years, once the mining and ranching played out, guest ranches began to flourish, drawing people in search of the romance of the open range. Today, the one-time 'dude ranch capital of the world' still hosts weekend wranglers, but it has also evolved (quietly and discreetly) into a 'rehab capital' for A-listers. The town, located 60 miles northwest of Phoenix via Hwy 60, is pleasant anytime but summer, when temperatures can top 110°F (43°C).

◉ Sights & Activities

The small downtown is dotted with statues of the town's founders and a few colorful characters. One of the latter was George Sayers, a 'bibulous reprobate' who was once chained to the town's **Jail Tree** on Tegner St in the late 1800s.

Desert Caballeros Western Museum
MUSEUM

(☑928-684-2272; www.westernmuseum.org; 21 N Frontier St; adult/senior/child 17yr & under $9/7/free; ⊙10am-5pm Mon-Sat, noon-4pm Sun, closed Mon Jun-Aug) Take a stroll into the early 1900s at the Desert Caballeros Western Museum, where re-created street scenes lead to an old-time saloon, the post office and the general store. Hopi kachina dolls, colorful Arizona minerals and eye-catching art by Western artists Albert Bierstadt, Thomas Moran and Frederic Remington are also highlights. The annual Cowgirl Up! exhibit and sale in March and April is a terrific tribute to an eclectic array of Western women artists; we bet you won't leave empty-handed.

Hassayampa River Preserve
NATURE RESERVE

(☑928-684-2772; www.nature.org/hassayampa; 49614 Hwy 60; adult/child 12yr & under $5/free; ⊙7-11am Fri-Sun mid-May–mid-Sep, 8am-5pm Wed-Sun mid-Sep–mid-May) The Hassayampa River normally runs underground, but just outside downtown it shows off its crystalline shimmer. Currently managed by the Nature Conservancy, this is one of the few riparian habitats remaining in Arizona and a great place for birders to look for the 280 or so feathered resident and migrating species. The 770-acre preserve is on the west side of Hwy 60, 3 miles south of town. Trails close 30 minutes before the preserve.

At press time the preserve was moving forward with plans to become part of the Vulture Mountains Recreation Area.

Vulture Mine
MINE

(www.vultureminetours.com; 36610 N 355th Ave, off Vulture Mine Rd; donation $10; ⊙tour 8:30am Sat early May–mid-Oct, 10am late Oct–early May) Town founder Henry Wickenburg discovered gold nuggets here in 1863. The mine spat out gold until 1942, then decayed into a crusty ghost town, one that spooked the hosts of the Travel Channel's *Ghost Adventures*. A mining company, Vulture Peak Gold, purchased the property in 2011. For those who want to view the site, the company offers a two-hour-guided tour on Saturday mornings. Cash only and bring water and ID. Visit the website for more details.

Head west on Hwy 60, turn left onto Vulture Mine Rd and follow it for 12 miles.

🛌 Sleeping

Dude ranches typically close for the summer in southern Arizona.

Quality Inn Wickenburg
HOTEL $

(☑928-684-5461; www.qualityinn.com; 850 E Wickenburg Way, N Tegner St; r/ste incl breakfast $77/87; ❈@🛜🏊🐾) Lost? Get your bearings with a look at the giant map painted on the lobby wall inside this welcoming two-story motel, which was recently purchased by Quality Inn. Colorful prints, comfy chairs and granite countertops add oomph to mid-size rooms. The free breakfast is extensive. Small pets OK; $15 per day per pet.

★ Flying E Ranch
DUDE RANCH $$

(☑928-684-2690; www.flyingeranch.com; 2801 W Wickenburg Way; s $200-245, d $325-365, house $265; ⊙Nov-Apr; 🛜🏊) The coolest place at this down-home working cattle ranch is the boot room, which is lined with scuffed-up cowboy boots and hats that guests can borrow on their rides. Sitting on 20,000 acres in the Hassayampa Valley, the ranch is a big hit with families and also works well for groups.

Rooms are Western-themed and rates include activities and three family-style meals daily. It's open from November to April, with two- or three-night minimum stays. Two-hour horseback rides cost $45. There's no bar; BYOB. Wi-fi available in certain areas.

VERDE VALLEY WINE TRAIL

New vineyards, wineries and tasting rooms have opened along Hwy 89A and I-17, bringing a dash of style and energy to the area. Bringing star power is Maynard James Keenan, lead singer of the band Tool and owner of Caduceus Cellars and Merkin Vineyards. His 2010 documentary *Blood into Vine* takes a no-holds-barred look at the wine industry.

In Cottonwood, drive or float to Verde River–adjacent **Alcantara Vineyards** (www.alcantaravineyard.com; 3445 S Grapevine Way; wine tasting $10-15; ⊙11am-5pm) then stroll through Old Town where two tasting rooms, **Arizona Stronghold** (www.azstronghold.com; 1023 N Main St; wine tasting $9; ⊙noon-7pm Sun-Thu, to 9pm Fri & Sat) and **Pillsbury Wine Company** (www.pillsburywine.com; 1012 N Main St; wine tasting $10; ⊙11am-5pm Mon-Thu, 11am-9pm Fri-Sun), sit across from each other on Main St.

In Jerome, start at **Cellar 433** (www.cellar433.com; 240 Hull Ave; wine tasting $10-12; ⊙11am-6pm Thu-Sun, 11am-5pm Mon-Wed) near the visitor center. From there, stroll up to Keenan's **Caduceus Cellars** (www.caduceus.org; 158 Main St; wine tasting $9-13; ⊙11am-6pm Sun-Thu, to 8pm Sun) near the Connor Hotel.

Three wineries with tasting rooms hug a scrubby stretch of Page Springs Rd east of Cornville: bistro-housing **Page Springs Cellars** (www.pagespringscellars.com; 1500 N Page Springs Rd; wine tasting $10; ⊙11am-7pm Mon-Wed, to 9pm Thu-Sun), the welcoming **Oak Creek Vineyards** (www.oakcreekvineyards.net; 1555 N Page Springs Rd; wine tasting $10; ⊙10am-6pm) and the mellow-rock-playing **Javelina Leap Vineyard** (www.javelina-leapwinery.com; 1565 Page Springs Rd; wine tasting $8; ⊙11am-5pm).

For a wine-trail map and more details about the wineries, visit www.vvwinetrail.com.

Rancho de los Caballeros DUDE RANCH $$$
(☎928-684-5484; www.ranchodeloscaballeros.com; 1551 S Vulture Mine Rd; r incl 3 meals $485-660; ⊙Oct–mid-May; ❄☷) With an 18-hole championship golf course, exclusive spa, special kids' program and fine dining, this sprawling ranch feels more *Dallas* than *Bonanza*. The lovely main lodge – with flagstone floor, brightly painted furniture and copper fireplace – gives way to cozy rooms decked out stylishly with Native American rugs and handcrafted furniture. Dinner is a dress-up affair, but afterwards you can cut loose in the saloon with nightly cowboy music. Open to guests October to early-May. Room-only rates also available.

✗ Eating

Chaparral ICE CREAM $
(www.chaparral-icecream.com; 45 N Tegner St; 1 scoop $3.50; ⊙11am-7pm Tue-Sat, noon-5pm Sun & Mon) After exploring downtown, stop by this beloved ice-cream shop for a scoop of homemade prickly pear ice cream. Or Hassayampa mud. Or boysenberry. Or chocolate. Or...you get the idea.

Horseshoe Cafe DINER $
(☎928-684-7377; 207 E Wickenburg Way; mains $5-15; ⊙5am-2pm Sep-May, shorter hours Jun-Aug) If you judge the quality of a restaurant by the number of guests wearing cowboy

hats, then this charming place has got to be the best eatery in town. It's gussied up with chaps, a saddle or two and, of course, some horseshoes. Service is super welcoming, and the biscuit with a side of gravy is lick-the-platter good.

Nana's Sandwich Saloon SANDWICHES $
(www.nanasandwichsaloon.com; 48 N Tegner St; sandwiches $7-9) Order at the counter at this busy sandwich shop near the Desert Caballeros Western Museum. The folks here load 'em up right, from the Yard Bird (grilled chicken with bacon and green chiles) to the Cowboy (roast beef, swiss and horseradish).

Screamer's Drive-In AMERICAN $
(☎928-684-9056; 1151 W Wickenburg Way; mains under $5; ⊙7am-8pm Mon-Sat, 10am-8pm Sun) If you've got a hankering for a big and juicy green chile burger with a side of crispy fries and a shake, this '50s-style diner (not really a drive-in) will steer you toward contentment. Indoor and outdoor seating.

Anita's Cocina MEXICAN $$
(☎928-684-5777; 57 N Valentine St; breakfast $3-7, lunch & dinner $7-17; ⊙7am-9pm) In the heart of downtown, this happenin' hacienda is a perfect spot for winding down south-of-the-border style. Think margaritas, fajitas, combo platters and a basket of free chips with hot or mild salsa (or both). Good for groups and

families, but solos will be just fine. Sports fans will find games on the many flat-screen TVs.

❶ Information

Chamber of Commerce (☑ 928-684-5479; www.outwickenburgway.org; 216 N Frontier St; ⊙ 9am-5pm Mon-Fri, 10am-2pm Sat & Sun) Inside an 1895 Santa Fe Railroad depot; offers local info and a walking tour of downtown.

Wickenburg Community Hospital (☑ 928-684-5421; www.wickhosp.com; 520 Rose Ln) Provides 24-hour emergency care.

❶ Getting There & Away

Wickenburg is about equidistant (60 miles) from Phoenix and Prescott off Hwy 60. There is no bus service. Coming from Kingman and the I-40 you can reach it via Hwy 93, which runs a lonely 105 miles to Wickenburg. It's dubbed Joshua Tree Forest Pkwy because pretty much the only living things growing here are those spiny bushes that are a member of the lily family – but it's a gorgeous drive nonetheless.

Prescott

POP 40,308 / ELEV 5374FT

Fire raged through Whiskey Row in downtown Prescott (press-kit) on July 14, 1900. Quick-thinking locals managed to save the town's most prized possession: the 24ft-long Brunswick Bar that anchored the Palace Saloon. After lugging the solid oak bar across the street onto Courthouse Plaza, they grabbed their drinks and continued the party.

Prescott's cooperative spirit lives on, infusing the historic downtown and mountain-flanked surroundings with a welcoming vibe. This easy-to-explore city, which served as Arizona's first territorial capital and celebrated its 150th birthday in 2014, also charms visitors with its eye-catching Victorian buildings, breezy sidewalk cafes, tree-lined central plaza and a burgeoning arts scene. But it's not all artsy gentility and Victorian airs. Whiskey Row hasn't changed much from the 1800s, and there's always a party within its scrappy saloons.

Prescott also offers some of Arizona's best outdoor scenery. Hikers, cyclists and campers in search of memorable views don't have to travel far from downtown to find them. The boulder-strewn Granite Dells rise to the north, while in the west the landmark Thumb Butte sticks out like the tall kid in your third-grade picture. To the south, the pine-draped Bradshaw Mountains form part of the Prescott National Forest.

◉ Sights

Historic Downtown NEIGHBORHOOD
Montezuma St west of Courthouse Plaza was once the infamous **Whiskey Row**, where 40 drinking establishments supplied suds to rough-hewn cowboys, miners and wastrels. A devastating 1900 fire destroyed 25 saloons, five hotels and the red-light district, but several early buildings remain. Many are still bars, mixed in with boutiques, galleries and restaurants.

Take a stroll through the infamous Palace Saloon, rebuilt in 1901. A museum's worth of photographs and artifacts (including the fire-surviving Brunswick Bar) are scattered throughout the bar and restaurant. A scene from the Steve McQueen movie *Junior Bonner* was filmed here, and a mural honoring the film covers an inside wall.

Whiskey Row has taken on a second identity as Gallery Row. Standouts include **Arts Prescott Gallery** (☑ 928-776-7717; www.artsprescott.com; 134 S Montezuma St; ⊙ 10am-6pm), a collective of 24 local artists working in all media, and **Van Gogh's Ear** (☑ 928-776-1080; www.vgegallery.com; 156 S Montezuma St; ⊙ 10am-6pm), where you can snap up metal art, fine woodwork and handmade leather shoes by nationally known artists, many making their home in the Prescott area. Sample Prescott's gallery scene during the monthly **4th Friday Art Walk** (www.artthe4th.com).

The columned County Courthouse anchoring the elm-shaded plaza dates from 1916 and is particularly pretty when sporting its lavish Christmas decorations. Cortez St, which runs east of the plaza, is a hive of antique and collectible stores, as well as home to **Ogg's Hogan** (☑ 928-443-9856; 111 N Cortez St), with its excellent selection of Native American crafts and jewelry, mostly from Arizona tribes.

Buildings east and south of the plaza escaped the 1900 fire. Some are Victorian houses built by East Coast settlers and are markedly different from adobe Southwestern buildings. Look for the fanciest digs on Union St; No 217 is the ancestral Goldwater family mansion (yes, of Barry Goldwater fame).

Sharlot Hall Museum MUSEUM
(☑ 928-445-3122; www.sharlot.org; 415 W Gurley St; adult/child 13-17yr $7/3; ⊙ 10am-5pm Mon-Sat, noon-4pm Sun May-Sep, 10am-4pm Mon-Sat, noon-4pm Sun Oct-Apr) Prescott's most important museum highlights Prescott's period as territorial capital. The museum is named for its 1928 founder, pioneer woman Sharlot

Hall (1870–1943), and a small exhibit in the lobby commemorates her legacy. The most interesting of the nine buildings here is the 1864 **Governor's Mansion**, a log cabin where Hall lived in the attic until her death. It's filled with memorabilia from guns and opium pipes to letters.

The Sharlot Hall Building next door is the main exhibit hall. Displays spotlight the region's historical highlights. Outside, the Rose Garden pays homage to Arizona's pioneer women.

Miss Hall distinguished herself first as a poet and activist before becoming Territorial Historian. In 1924, she traveled to Washington, DC, to represent Arizona in the Electoral College dressed in a copper mesh overcoat – currently in a display case in the lobby – provided by a local mine.

Phippen Museum   MUSEUM
(☑ 928-778-1385; www.phippenartmuseum.org; 4701 Hwy 89 N; adult/child 12yr & under $7/free; ☺ 10am-4pm Tue-Sat, 1-4pm Sun) The Phippen, located 7 miles north of Prescott en route to Jerome, is named after cowboy artist George Phippen. The museum hosts changing exhibits of celebrated Western artists, along with contemporary art depicting the American West. The exhibits are typically quite engaging. On Memorial Day weekend the museum hosts the Western Art Show & Sale at Courthouse Plaza, which features more than 100 artists.

Smoki Museum   MUSEUM
(☑ 928-445-1230; www.smokimuseum.org; 147 N Arizona St; adult/child/student/senior $7/free/5/6; ☺ 10am-4pm Mon-Sat, 1-4pm Sun) This pueblo-style museum displays Southwestern Native American objects – baskets, pottery, kachina dolls – dating from prehistoric times to the present. One surprising exhibit addresses the true origins of the 'Smoki' tribe. The tribe was a philanthropic society created by white Prescottonians to raise money for the city's rodeo. The group's annual Hopi Snake Dance was considered a religious mockery by local tribes and was discontinued in 1990.

Today, the museum works with area tribes to instill understanding and respect for the region's indigenous cultures. The correct pronunciation is 'smoke-eye.'

🏃 Activities

Prescott sits in the middle of the Prescott National Forest, a 1.2 million acre playground stocked with mountains, lakes and ponderosa pines. The **Prescott National Forest Office** has information about local hikes, picnic areas and campgrounds. A $5 day-use fee is required – and payable – at many area trailheads. Federal intra-agency passes, including the America the Beautiful pass, cover this fee. You can buy passes at the Forest Service office.

If you only have time for a short hike, get a moderate workout and nice views of the town and mountains on the 1.75-mile **Thumb Butte trail**. The trailhead is about 3.5 miles west of downtown Prescott on Gurley St, which changes to Thumb Butte Rd. Leashed dogs are OK.

There are five lakes within a short drive of town. The dazzling **Lynx Lake**, 4 miles east of Prescott on Hwy 69 then 3 miles south on Walker Rd, offers fishing, hiking and camping. The most scenic lake for our money is **Watson Lake**, where the eerily eroded rock piles of the Granite Dells are reflected in the crystalline stillness. About 4 miles north of town, off Hwy 89, the city-run **Watson Lake Park** is great for boating, picnicking and bouldering. The 6-mile **Peavine National Recreation Trail**, a rails-to-trails project, leads into the Granite Dells with views of Watson Lake. The trailhead is on Sun Dog Ranch Rd just off Prescott Lake Pkwy ($2 parking).

North of town, the **Granite Mountain Wilderness** attracts rock climbers in the warmer months.

✨ Festivals & Events

Prescott has a packed year-round events calendar. See www.visit-prescott.com for the full scoop.

Territorial Days Arts & Crafts Show   ART
(☑ 928-445-2000; www.prescott.org) Arts, crafts, demonstrations, performances; in June.

★ World's Oldest Rodeo   RODEO
(www.worldsoldestrodeo.com) Bronco busting (since 1888), a parade and an arts-and-crafts fair starting the week before July 4.

🛏 Sleeping

Don't expect many lodging bargains in Prescott. Check out www.prescottbb.com for links to B&Bs and inns.

Free dispersed camping is permitted at designated sites next to several fire roads in Prescott National Forest. The Forest Service manages nine campgrounds with spots available on a first-come, first-serve basis (campsites per night free to $10). See www.fs.usda.gov/prescott for details and maps. Two cabins are also available ($100 to $125 per night).

Summer tent camping (☑ 928-777-1121; www.cityofprescott.net/services/parks/rentals; camping $15, incl $2 parking fee; ⊙ Thu-Tue Apr-early Oct) is also available at 35 sites at Watson Lake Park (19 can be reserved), where you can set up your tent right beside the boulders.

Apache Lodge
MOTEL $

(☑ 928-445-1422; www.apachelodge.com; 1130 E Gurley St; r $65-99; ✳ 🐾 🛏) The well-worn Apache, around since 1946, won't impress domestic divas, but for everyone else the accommodating service and wallet-friendly price should be enough of a draw. The striking white exterior is pretty cool too. Pet fee is $10 per day.

★ Motor Lodge
BUNGALOW $$

(☑ 928-717-0157; www.themotorlodge.com; 503 S Montezuma St; r $119-139, ste $149, apt $159; ✳ 🛏) Twelve snazzy bungalows strut their stuff at the Motor Lodge, forming a bright and welcoming horseshoe around a central driveway three blocks south of Courthouse Square. Inside the rooms, whimsical prints and comfy bedding add to the overall appeal, making the Motor Lodge a top budget choice. Rooms and bathrooms can be on the small side, but many have kitchens and porches for extra space. The lime-green bungalows, built as summer cabins in the early 1900s, are within cycling distance of downtown. Just borrow one of the complimentary bicycles, and you're ready to go.

Grand Highland Hotel
BOUTIQUE HOTEL $$

(☑ 928-776-9963; www.grandhighlandhotel.com; 154 S Montezuma St; r $129-179, ste $199; ✳ 🛏) Service is king at the new Grand Highland Hotel. Or wait, maybe it's style. Or maybe it's comfort. Oh heck, all three are top notch at this new 12-room hotel perched cozily in the heart of Whiskey Row. Themed rooms, from the Rodeo Room to the Speak Easy Room, spotlight regional history.

Some are a bit snug, but the art deco and art nouveau decor, plus the exposed brick walls, keep the spaces inviting. All rooms are on the 2nd floor and accessed via a staircase; there's an elevator in the planning stages. Breakfast is included.

Hotel Vendome
HISTORIC INN $$

(☑ 928-776-0900; www.vendomehotel.com; 230 S Cortez St; r incl breakfast $129-189; ✳ 🛏) This dapper inn, dating from 1917, charms guests with lace curtains, old-fashioned quilts and a few bathrooms with clawfoot tubs. The small Fremont Bar, beside the lobby, is a fun place to sip a house-made sangria and catch up on local gossip. If you ask, the welcoming hosts might even tell you about the ghost.

Hotel St Michael
HOTEL $$

(☑ 928-776-1999; www.stmichaelhotel.com; 205 W Gurley St; r $89-119, ste $139; ✳ 🛏) Gargoyles, ghosts and a 1925 elevator keep things refreshingly offbeat at this Victorian-era, downtown hotel. The no-frills, old-fashioned rooms, which include family units, are within staggering distance of Whiskey Row. Rates include a cooked-to-order breakfast in the downstairs bistro from 7am until 9am.

Hassayampa Inn
HISTORIC HOTEL $$

(☑ 928-778-9434; www.hassayampainn.com; 122 E Gurley St; r $159-179, ste $209; ✳ 🛏) One of Arizona's most elegant hotels when it opened in 1927, today the restored inn has many original furnishings, hand-painted wall decorations and a lovely dining room. The 67 rooms vary, but all include rich linens and sturdy dark-wood furniture. It has an on-site restaurant, the Peacock Room & Bar. Pets under 45lbs are allowed for no extra charge. Breakfast included.

✕ Eating

★ Lone Spur Cafe
CAFE $

(☑ 928-445-8202; www.thelonespur.com; 106 W Gurley St; breakfast $8-18, lunch $8-11, dinner $9-24; ⊙ 8am-2pm daily, 4:30-8pm Fri) Mornin' cowboy, there's just one rule at the Lone Spur Cafe: when choosing a side at breakfast, always order the biscuit with sausage gravy. Never the toast. You can't count calories at a place this good, and the sausage gravy will knock your hat off. Even better, portions are huge and there are three bottles of hot sauce on every table. Decor includes stuffed mounts, cowboy gear and a chandelier made out of antlers. Waitstaff are super-nice.

★ Iron Springs Cafe
SOUTHWESTERN, CAJUN $$

(☑ 928-443-8848; www.ironspringscafe.com; 1501 Iron Springs Rd; brunch $9-13, lunch $9-12, dinner $9-21; ⊙ 8am-8pm Wed-Sat, 9am-2pm Sun) Cajun and Southwestern specialties are highlights inside this former train station, and the short menu is loaded with savory, often spicy, palate pleasers. From the n'awlins muffaletta with sliced ham, salami and mortadella to the black-and-blue steak with blue-cheese butter, it all sounds delicious. Train decor, colorful blankets and easy-bantering waitstaff enliven three tiny rooms.

The green chile pork stew has an addictively spicy kick. Also open for breakfast.

Raven Café CAFE $$
(☑928-717-0009; www.ravencafe.com; 142 N Cortez St; breakfast $6-7, lunch & dinner $9-11; ⊗7:30am-11pm Mon-Thu, 7:30am-midnight Fri & Sat, 8am-3pm Sun; 🕏🍴) This may be the closest you'll get to skinny jeans in Prescott: a cool, loft-like spot that changes its stripes from daytime coffee hangout to after-dark pub with live music and 22 beers on tap. The mostly organic menu offers a mix of sandwiches, burgers, salads and a few 'big plates' – and lots of vegetarian options, too.

Peacock Room & Bar FINE DINING $$
(☑928-777-9563; www.hassayampainn.com; 122 E Gurley St; breakfast $8-13, lunch $9-15, dinner $18-37; ⊗7am-2pm daily, 4:30-9pm Sun-Thu, until 9:30pm Fri & Sat) The stuffily stylish dining room at the Hassayampa Inn is famous for its classic American dinners, but we like it best before noon. Huevos rancheros (a Mexican egg dish with chile sauce and cheese) should get your day off to a scrumptious start. Unwind with after-work cocktails at the bar, which hums with live music Friday and Saturday evenings (6pm to 9pm).

Prescott Brewing Company AMERICAN $$
(www.prescottbrewingcompany.com; 130 W Gurley St; mains $9-14; ⊗11am-11pm Sun-Thu, until midnight Fri & Sat; 🍴) This popular brewpub, across from Courthouse Plaza, actually works well for families. Burgers, pizzas and fish and chips are on the menu; Lodgepole Light, Prescott Pale and Willow Wheat are among the beers on tap (the brew line-up changes weekly).

🍸 Drinking & Nightlife

Prescott likes to have a good time. Enjoy live music at clubs downtown on the weekends, while it's always fun on Whiskey Row. For the last nine years on St Patrick's Day, there's been a corporate-sponsored pub crawl downtown.

Palace Saloon BAR
(☑928-541-1996; www.historicpalace.com; 120 S Montezuma St; ⊗11am-9pm Sun-Thu, to 10pm Fri & Sat) Push open the swinging doors and time-warp to 19th-century Whiskey Row days, back when the Earp brothers would knock 'em back with Doc Holliday at the huge Brunswick Bar.

Matt's Saloon HONKY-TONK
(☑928-778-9914; www.mattssaloon.com; 112 S Montezuma St) This dark bar is similar in appearance to the Palace but has, in fact, only been around since the 1960s. Buck Owens and Waylon Jennings used to perform live back then, and today it's still Prescott's kickiest two-stepping place. There's live music on Friday and Saturday nights.

Bird Cage Saloon BAR
(www.birdcagesaloon.com; 160 S Montezuma St; ⊗9am-2am) The original Bird Cage Saloon – famous for its collection of taxidermied birds – was destroyed in a fire in 2012. A new and larger incarnation of the popular bar opened a year later just south of its old location. A few of the old birds survived, and you'll find them, together with the surviving back bar, ready for business.

According to the website they're accepting taxidermy donations – of all types.

Cupper's CAFE
(www.cupperscoffee.com; 226 S Cortez St; ⊗7am-5pm Mon-Sat, 8am-4pm Sun; 🕏) This inviting coffee shop brews up business inside a Victorian-style cottage. Surf the net while savoring a tasty scone with a Mayan mocha (dark chocolate with a spicy kick).

ⓘ Information

Police (☑928-777-1900; 222 S Marina St)

Post Office Downtown (101 W Goodwin St; ⊗9:30am-12:30pm & 1-4pm Mon-Wed & Fri, 8:30am-12:30pm & 1-4pm Thu); Miller Valley Rd (442 Miller Valley Rd; ⊗8:30am-5pm Mon-Fri, 10am-2pm Sat)

Prescott National Forest Office (☑928-443-8000; www.fs.usda.gov/prescott; 344 S Cortez St; ⊗8am-4:30pm Mon-Fri) Info on camping, hiking and more in the surrounding national forest.

Visitor Center (☑800-266-7534, 928-445-2000; www.visit-prescott.com; 117 W Goodwin St; ⊗9am-5pm Mon-Fri, 10am-2pm Sat & Sun) Information and brochures galore, including a handy walking tour pamphlet of Prescott.

Yavapai Regional Medical Center West (☑928-445-2700; www.yrmc.org; 1003 Willow Creek Rd; ⊗24hr emergency room)

ℹ Getting There & Away

Prescott's tiny **airport** (www.prcairport.com) is about 9 miles north of town on Hwy 89 and is served by Great Lakes Airlines with daily flights to and from Los Angeles, CA.

Arizona Shuttle (☑ 928-776-7433; www.prescotttransit.com; 820 E Sheldon St) Runs buses to/from Phoenix airport (one-way adult $32 to $35, child $25, 2¼ hours, 22 daily). Schedule may vary seasonally.

Jerome

POP 444 / ELEV 5000FT

It's hard to describe Jerome without using the phrase 'precariously perched.' This stubborn hamlet, which enjoys one of the most spectacular views in Arizona, is wedged into steep Cleopatra Hill. Jerome was the home of the fertile United Verde Mine, nicknamed the 'Billion Dollar Copper Camp,' as well as the copper-rich Little Daisy Mine. Dubbed the 'Wickedest Town in the West,' Jerome teemed with brothels, saloons and opium dens.

When the mines petered out in 1953, Jerome's population plummeted from 15,000 to just 50 stalwarts practically overnight. Then came the '60s, and scores of hippies with an eye for the town's latent charm. They snapped up crumbling buildings for pennies, more or less restored them and, along the way, injected a dose of artistic spirit that survives to this day inside the numerous galleries scattered across town. A groovy joie de vivre permeates the place, and at times it seems every shop and restaurant is playing a hug-your-neighbor hippy folk song.

Quaint as it is, the most memorable aspect of Jerome is its panoramic views of the Verde Valley embracing the fiery red rocks of Sedona and culminating in the snowy San Francisco Peaks. Sunsets? Ridiculously romantic, trust us.

More than 1.2 million visitors – most of them day-trippers and weekend-warrior bikers – spill into Jerome each year, but the tiny town doesn't feel like a tourist trap. It's far from over-gentrified; as one bumper sticker plastered on a downtown business put it: 'We're all here because we're not all there.'

To experience Jerome's true magic, spend the night. You might even see a ghost. This is, after all, 'Arizona's ghost capital.'

◉ Sights

If you're interested in the town's unique history, take an hour to stroll past some of Jerome's most historic buildings. Start at the corner of Main St and Jerome Ave at the **Connor Hotel**, the town's first solid stone lodging. From there, a leg-stretching climb leads to the **Jerome Grand Hotel**, the one-time home of the United Verde Hospital. This sturdy facility served miners and the community between 1927 and 1951. Known for its ghosts, it's actually a relaxing place to enjoy expansive views of the crimson-gold rocks of Sedona and the Verde Valley.

Heading back downhill, consider the fact that there are 88 miles of tunnel under your feet. Combine these tunnels with steep hills and periodic dynamiting, and it's easy to see why buildings in Jerome regularly collapsed, caught fire or migrated downhill. The **Sliding Jail**, southeast of the visitor center, has moved 225ft from its original 1927 location.

Jerome State Historic Park　　　MUSEUM
(☑ 928-634-5381; www.azstateparks.com; 100 Douglas Rd; adult/child 7-13yr $5/2; ⊙ 8:30am-5pm) This state park preserves the 1916 mansion of eccentric mining mogul Jimmy 'Rawhide' Douglas, who developed the Little Daisy Mine. An interesting variety of exhibits offer insight into the town's mining heyday. Don't miss the cool 3D model of Jerome and the mining tunnels running below it. The folksy video is worth watching before you explore the museum.

Audrey Headframe Park　　　PARK
(www.jeromehistoricalsociety.com; 55 Douglas Rd; ⊙ 8am-5pm) FREE Ready for a scare? At this small park, run by the Jerome Historical Society, bold travelers can stand on a glass platform overlooking a 1918 mining shaft. The inky black tunnel drops 1900ft, which is longer than the Empire State Building by 650ft!

Mine Museum　　　MUSEUM
(☑ 928-634-5477; www.jeromehistoricalsociety.com; 200 Main St; adult/senior/child 12yr & under $2/1/free; ⊙ 9am-5:30pm) Two halves of a 4-ton flywheel mark the entryway to this small but informative museum that highlights Jerome's hardscrabble past. Displays include a claustrophobic mining cage, a Chinese laundry machine, a story about a beloved prostitute (worth a read!) and a wall dedicated to an old-school sheriff who gunned down three vigilantes on Main St then went home and ate lunch – without mentioning to his wife what had happened. Gift shop closes at 6pm.

Jerome

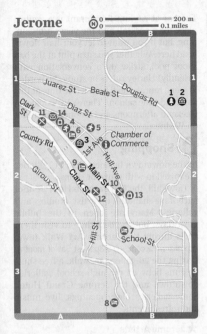

N 0 — 200 m
0 — 0.1 miles

Jerome

⊙ Sights
1	Audrey Headframe Park	B1
2	Jerome State Historic Park	B1
3	Mine Museum	A2

⊛ Activities, Courses & Tours
4	Caduceus Cellars	A2
5	Cellar 433	A2

⊟ Sleeping
6	Connor Hotel	A2
7	Ghost City B&B	B3
8	Jerome Grand Hotel	B3
9	Mile High Inn	A2

⊗ Eating
	Asylum Restaurant	(see 8)
10	Flatiron Café	B2
11	Grapes	A1
12	Haunted Hamburger	A2

⊙ Drinking & Nightlife
	Spirit Room Bar	(see 6)

⊙ Shopping
13	Jerome Artists Cooperative Gallery	B2
14	Nellie Bly	A1

🛏 Sleeping

Historic hotels, cozy inns and a few B&Bs are your choices in Jerome, and you won't find a single national chain. In fact, most accommodations are as charmingly eccentric as the town itself. (And many are home to a ghost or two.)

Ghost City B&B
B&B $$

(☏ 928-634-4678; www.ghostcityinn.com; 541 Main St; r $105-155; ❋ ☎) In an 1890s building, this B&B is owned by Jerome's police chief, Allen Muma, and his wife, Jackie. Each room has a different theme, from the cowboy-inspired Western room to the Victorian-era Verde View room with an antique brass bed and killer views.

Connor Hotel
HISTORIC HOTEL $$

(☏ 928-634-5006; www.connorhotel.com; 160 Main St; r $95-165; ❋ ☎) Jerome's past comes to life – or maybe it never left – at this rambling 1898 haunt. The 12 restored rooms convincingly capture the Victorian period, with such touches as pedestal sinks, flowery wallpaper and a pressed-tin ceiling. It's above the popular Spirit Room Bar, which has live music on weekends; rooms one to four get most of the bar noise. Enter through the gift shop.

Mile High Inn
INN $$

(☏ 928-634-5094; www.jeromemilehighinn.com; 309 Main St; r $85-130; ❋ ☎) Rooms are dapper and a bit pert at this snug B&B, which once had a stint as a bordello. The seven remodeled rooms have unusual furnishings, and the ghost of the former madam supposedly haunts the room dubbed Lariat & Lace – which is also home to a climb-up lodgepole bed. A full breakfast is served at the downstairs restaurant. Four rooms have shared bathrooms.

Jerome Grand Hotel
HOTEL $$

(☏ 928-634-8200; www.jeromegrandhotel.com; 200 Hill St; r $130-190, ste $275-460; ❋ ☎) This former hospital looks like the perfect setting for a sequel to *The Shining*. Built in 1926 for the mining community, the sturdy fortress plays up its unusual history. The halls are filled with relics of the past, from incinerator chutes to patient call lights. There's even a key-operated Otis elevator. Victorian-style rooms are more traditionally furnished. Spend an extra few dollars for a valley-side room; they're brighter and offer better views. For $20 hotel guests can join the evening ghost tour of the premises. Enjoy a fine meal and a dazzling valley panorama at the attached Asylum Restaurant.

✕ Eating

Jerome is a gourmand's delight, and you'll probably be happy at any of the restaurants in town. Enjoy!

Flatiron Café   CAFE $

(✆928-634-2733; www.theflatironjerome.com; 416 Main St; breakfast $3-11, lunch $8-10; ⊙7am-4pm Wed-Mon) This tiny cafe packs a big, delicious punch. Savor a cheesy scrambled-egg-and-salmon quesadilla at breakfast or a walnut-and-cranberry chicken salad sandwich at lunch. Order at the counter then grab an inside table, or head across the street to the small patio. The mocha latte gets rave reviews.

Grapes   AMERICAN $$

(✆928-639-8477; www.grapesjerome.com; 111 Main St; lunch & dinner $9-17; ⊙11am-9pm) Wine newbies and grape connoisseurs are equally happy at this breezy, brick-walled bistro that serves ahi tuna burgers, a Tuscan berry salad with feta, and 10 different gourmet pizzas. Wine selections come with a bin number, and these numbers are helpfully paired with food listings on the menu. From 5pm to 9pm on weekdays all wines by the glass are $5.

Haunted Hamburger   BURGERS $$

(✆928-634-0554; www.thehauntedhamburger. com; 410 Clark St; mains $5-22; ⊙11am-9pm) This beloved hamburger joint, perched high on a hill and often packed, celebrated its 20th anniversary in 2014. Come here for awesome views, solid burgers and your choice of nine margaritas. Is it haunted? They say the spirit here likes hammers.

Asylum Restaurant   AMERICAN $$$

(✆928-639-3197; www.asylumrestaurant.com; 200 Hill St; lunch $11-18, dinner $23-35; ⊙11am-9pm) Deep-red walls, lazily twirling fans, gilded artwork and views, views, views make this venerable dining room at the Jerome Grand Hotel one of the state's top picks for fine dining. Order the roasted butternut-squash soup with cinnamon-lime crème and the prickly-pear barbecue pork tenderloin, and you'll see what we mean. Superb wine list too. We've heard Senator John McCain loves it here.

🍷 Drinking

New wine-tasting rooms have opened in and around Jerome (p135), adding another level of fun.

Spirit Room Bar   BAR

(✆928-634-8809; www.spiritroom.com; 166 Main St; ⊙11am-midnight Sun-Thu, until 1am Fri & Sat)

The bar at Asylum Restaurant is a genteel place for a cocktail and the views are stunning, but if you want to let your hair down, head here. Whether you sip a pint at the bar, shoot pool, strike up a conversation with (friendly) Harley riders or study the bordello scene mural, you'll have a fine time at this dark, old-time saloon. There's live music on weekend afternoons and an open-mic night on Wednesday.

🛍 Shopping

In the downtown business district, galleries are mixed in with souvenir shops.

Downhill, the **Old Jerome High School** harbors a handful of artist studios and galleries. Many are open to the public most days, but the best time to visit them all is during the **Jerome Art Walk** (www. jeromeartwalk.com; ⊙5-8pm 1st Sat of month). During the 26-gallery art walk, a free shuttle runs between the high school, galleries downtown and the Jerome Grand Hotel. Some galleries have openings, live music and refreshments.

★ Jerome Artists
Cooperative Gallery   ARTS & CRAFTS

(✆928-639-4276; www.jeromecoop.com; 502 N Main St; ⊙10am-6pm) Need a gift? At this bright and scenic gallery more than 30 local artists work in pottery, painting, jewelry and other media, before selling their creations at very fair prices.

Nellie Bly   SPECIALTY

(✆928-634-0255; www.nellieblyscopes.com; 136 Main St; ⊙9:30am-5:30pm Sun-Thu, until 6pm Fri & Sat) This cool place is an Aladdin's cave of kaleidoscopes in all shapes and sizes. Also sells art glass.

ℹ Information

Remember the board game Chutes & Ladders? There's a similar concept at work in Jerome. The town is essentially stacked up the side of Cleopatra Hill on three distinct levels, connected by steep stairways. Hwy 89A twists tightly between the different levels and splits into two one-way streets (Hull Ave and Main St) at the Y-intersection in front of the Flatiron Café. On crowded weekends grab a parking spot as soon as you can, then walk through town.

Chamber of Commerce (✆928-634-2900; www.jeromechamber.com; Hull Ave, Hwy 89A north after the Flatiron Café split; ⊙10am-3pm) Offers tourist information.

Police (📞928-634-8992; www.jeromepd.
org; 305 Main St) Visit the website just for the
music!

Post Office (📞928-634-8241; 120 Main St;
⏱8:15am-noon & 12:30-2:45pm Mon-Fri)

❶ Getting There & Away

To reach Jerome from Prescott follow Hwy 89A
north for 34 miles. The drive is slow and windy,
and not recommended for large trailers.

Cottonwood & Around

POP 11,265 / ELEV 3300-3900FT

Cottonwood is ready for its close-up, or should
we say its selfie? For decades the city was one
of the less interesting communities in central
Arizona – simply a good place to find budget
lodging near Sedona. But today? Cottonwood,
particularly its walkable Old Town district,
is buzzing with new restaurants, stylish
wine-tasting rooms and an eclectic array of
indie shops. And, so far, it remains a cheap
and convenient base for regional exploring.
Located in the Verde Valley, it's only 16 miles
from Sedona and 9 miles from Jerome.

For information about Cottonwood, head
to the helpful **Chamber of Commerce**
(📞928-634-7593; www.cottonwoodchamberaz.
com; 1010 S Main St; ⏱9am-5pm Mon-Fri, 9am-
1pm Sat & Sun) at the intersection of Hwy 89A
and Hwy 260. For a list of shops and restaurants in Old Town, visit www.oldtown.org.

The old mining town of Clarkdale sits just
off Hwy 89A between Jerome and Cottonwood. Clarkdale was a company town built
in 1914 to process ore from the mines in
nearby Jerome.

⊙ Sights & Activities

Tuzigoot National Monument   RUINS
(📞928-634-5564; www.nps.gov/tuzi; adult/child
15yr & under $5/free, combination ticket with Mon-
tezuma Castle $8; ⏱8am-5pm) Atop a ridge
about 2 miles north of Clarkdale, Tuzigoot
National Monument, a Sinaguan pueblo like
nearby Montezuma, is believed to have been
inhabited from AD 1000 to 1400. At its peak
as many as 225 people lived in its 110 rooms.
Stop by the visitor center to examine tools,
pottery and other artifacts dug up from the
ruin, then trudge up a short, steep trail (not
suitable for wheelchairs) for memorable
views of the Verde River Valley.

Dead Horse Ranch State Park   PARK
(📞928-634-5283; www.azstateparks.com; 675
Dead Horse Ranch Rd; day-use per vehicle $7) The

Verde River runs past this 423-acre park
which offers picnicking, fishing, multi-use
trails (for bikes, horses and hikers) and
a playground. Bird-watchers will want to
make the short trek to the bird-watching
stand at **Tavasci Marsh** to train their binoculars for a sighting of the least bittern, the
Yuma clapper rail and the belted kingfisher.

For the horse-lover, **Trail Horse Adventures** (📞928-634-5276; www.trailhorseadven-
tures.com; rides $65-100) offers rides lasting
one to 2½ hours. There's also an option for a
three-hour lunch ride ($125).

Verde Canyon Railroad   SCENIC RAILROAD
(📞928-639-0010, 800-582-7245; www.verdecan-
yonrr.com; 300 N Broadway; coach adult/child/
senior $55/35/50, 1st class all passengers $80)
From Clarkdale, vintage FP7 engines pull
climate-controlled passenger cars on
leisurely four-hour narrated round-trips into
the splendid canyon north of Cottonwood
Pass, traveling through roadless wilderness
with views of red-tinged rock cliffs, riparian areas, Native American sites, wildlife
and, from December to April, bald eagles.
Views far surpass that of the Grand Canyon
Railway. Trains leave at 1pm, but days of the
week vary by month; check schedule online.
Reservations recommended.

The turnaround point is Perkinsville, a remote ranch where scenes from *How the West
Was Won* were filmed; the train returns the
way it came, over bridges and trestles.

🛏 Sleeping

Cottonwood is the land of motels, mostly of
the chain variety, but prices are as low as
you'll find in the area.

Pines Motel   MOTEL $
(📞928-634-9975; www.azpinesmotel.com; 920
S Camino Real; r $85, ste $94-135; ❄@📶❄🐾)
This two-story motel, on a hill with nice
views, offers mini-suites with kitchenettes, in
addition to standard king and queen units.
Pets are $20 the first night, then $5 each
night after that. Guest laundry available.

View Motel   MOTEL $
(📞928-634-7581; www.theviewmotel.com; 818 S
Main St; r $49-65; ❄📶❄🐾) Professionally run,
this motel delivers the views its name promises. It's an older property and the furniture is
back-to-basics, but rooms are very clean and
come with a refrigerator and microwave. A
few have kitchenette. Dogs are $10 per night.
Offers smoking and nonsmoking rooms.

Dead Horse Ranch State Park CAMPING $

(☑ 520-586-2283; www.azstateparks.com; 675 Dead Horse Ranch Rd; tent/RV/cabins from $15/25/55; ⊙ reservations 8am-5pm) Overnighters can choose between cabins or campsites, some with hookups, and enjoy hot showers. Camping reservations are now available online, as well as by phone ($5 reservation fee per site).

✗ Eating & Drinking

Old Town is packed tight with good cafes and restaurants. For more information about wine tasting rooms, see p135.

Crema Coffee & Creamery CAFE $

(www.cremacafe89a.com; 917 N Main St; breakfast $5-11, lunch $6-10; ⊙ 7am-4pm Thu-Mon; 🛜) In recent years Crema has morphed from a low-key coffee shop with pastries, sandwiches and gelato to a full-on 'craft kitchen' with an impressive line-up of gourmet breakfast and lunch sandwiches, fancy burritos (sriracha or red-chile-glazed bacon anyone?) and ingredient-packed salads. The small-batch gelato is still as delicious as ever. Beer, wine and cocktails also for sale. Grab a table inside or on one of the patios.

Bocce Pizzeria PIZZA $$

(☑ 928-202-3597; www.boccecottonwood.com; 1060 N Main St; pizzas $11-15; ⊙ 4-10pm Mon-Thu, 4-11pm Fri & Sat, 11am-3pm Sun) You don't have to be hip to enjoy this gourmet pizzeria, but it helps. Old Crow Medicine Show sings from the speakers. There's a communal fire pit on the patio. And, wait a minute – is that arugula on my pizza? With a place this delicious and welcoming, the hipsters might be on to something. If you like your food with a spicy kick, try the shrimp and hot peppers pizza. Terrific!

Blazin' M Ranch AMERICAN $$

(☑ 928-634-0334, 800-937-8643; www.blazinm. com; 1875 Mabery Ranch Rd; adult/child 3-12yr/senior $40/20/33; ⊙ Wed-Sat Feb-Nov, site opens at 5pm; 🚸) Near Dead Horse Ranch State Park, here you can yee-haw with the rest of them at chuckwagon suppers – in the dinner barn – paired with rootin' tootin' cowboy entertainment. Kids big and small love it. Opening times may vary seasonally.

Nic's Italian Steak & Crab House STEAKHOUSE, SEAFOOD $$$

(☑ 928-634-9626; www.nicsaz.com; 925 N Main St; mains $12-36; ⊙ 5-9pm Sun-Thu, until 10pm Fri & Sat) You wouldn't really expect an old Chicago vibe – dark, intimate, cozy booths – in Cottonwood, but this joint gets it right. Same goes for the grilled steaks. And did somebody say crab mac-n-cheese? This place draws a crowd.

Sedona

POP 10,037 / ELEV 4500FT

Sedona's a stunner, but it's intensely spiritual as well – some even say sacred. Nestled amid striking red sandstone formations at the south end of the 16-mile gorge that is Oak Creek Canyon, Sedona attracts spiritual seekers, artists and healers, as well as day-trippers from Phoenix trying to escape the oppressive heat. Many New Age types believe that this area is the center of vortexes (not 'vortices' here in Sedona) that radiate the Earth's power, and Sedona's combination of scenic beauty and mysticism draws throngs of tourists year-round. You'll find all sorts of alternative medicines and practices, and the surrounding canyons offer excellent hiking and mountain biking.

The town itself bustles with art galleries and expensive gourmet restaurants. In summer the traffic and the crowds can be heavy.

The town's main drag is Hwy 89A. Sedona's navigational center is the roundabout at the intersection of Hwys 89A and 179, known as the Y. Northeast of the Y is Uptown Sedona, the pedestrian center where you'll find hotels, boutiques and restaurants. Turning south at the Y will take you to Tlaquepaque Village; from here you can cross over Oak Creek and continue down to more shopping, restaurants and hotels. West of the Y is West Sedona, where strip malls line the highway and lead to Red Rock State Park.

Regionally, Oak Creek Canyon is north of Uptown Sedona. The Village of Oak Creek, however, is south of the city.

⊙ Sights

Several vortexes (swirling energy centers where the Earth's power is said to be strongly felt) are located in Sedona's Red Rock Mountains. The best-known vortexes are **Bell Rock** (near the Village of Oak Creek), **Cathedral Rock** (near Red Rock Crossing), **Airport Mesa** (Airport Rd), and **Boynton Canyon**.

Scenic Drives

The easiest scenic drive is also one of the best: the **Red Rock Scenic Byway**. This National Scenic Byway and All-American Road tracks

Hwy 179 from I-17 (exit 298) for 7.5 miles, ending just north of the Village of Oak Creek in a smash-bang, pull-over, grab-your-camera explosion of red rock impressiveness.

In Sedona, the short drive up paved **Airport Rd** opens up to panoramic views of the valley. At sunset, the rocks blaze a psychedelic red and orange. Airport Mesa is the closest vortex to town.

Any time is a good time to drive the winding 7-mile **Red Rock Loop Rd**, which is all paved except one short section and gives access to Red Rock State Park as well as **Red Rock Crossing/Crescent Moon Picnic Area** (day-use per vehicle $10). A small army of photographers usually gather at the crossing at sunset to record the dramatic light show unfolding on iconic **Cathedral Rock**, another vortex. There's also swimming in Oak Creek. Access is via Upper Red Rock Loop Rd off Hwy 89A, 4 miles west of the Y.

For a breathtaking loop, follow Dry Creek Rd to **Boynton Pass Rd**, turn left, then left again at Forest Rd 525. It's mostly paved but there are lumpy, unpaved sections. The route passes two of the most memorable rock formations, Vultee Arch and Devil's Bridge. Extend this trip by turning right on FR 525 and taking in the Palatki Heritage Site.

Red Rock State Park
PARK

(☎928-282-6907; www.azstateparks.com/Parks/rero; 4050 Red Rock Loop Rd; adult/child 7-13yr/6yr & under $5/3/free; ☺8am-5pm, visitor center 9am-4:30pm) Not to be confused with Slide Rock State Park, this low-key 286-acre park includes an environmental education center, a visitor center, picnic areas and 5 miles of well-marked, interconnecting trails in a riparian habitat amid gorgeous scenery. Ranger-led activities include nature walks and bird walks. Popular moonlight hikes are offered April though October; reservations required ($5 reservation fee).

Chapel of the Holy Cross
CHURCH

(☎928-282-4069; www.chapeloftheholycross.com; 780 Chapel Rd; ☺9am-5pm Dec-Feb, until 6pm Mar-Nov) **FREE** Situated between spectacular, statuesque red-rock columns 3 miles south of town, this modern, nondenominational chapel was built in 1956 by Marguerite Brunwig Staude in the tradition of Frank Lloyd Wright. There are no services, but even if you're not affiliated with any religion, the soaring chapel and the perch it occupies may move you as it did its architect. There are no restrooms in the chapel.

Palatki Heritage Site
RUIN

(☎reservations 928-282-3854; www.redrockcountry.org; admission free, Red Rock Pass or equivalent required; ☺9:30am-3pm) **FREE** Thousand-year-old Sinagua cliff dwellings and rock art are good-enough reasons to brave the 7 miles or so of dirt road leading to this enchantingly located archaeological site on the edge of the wilderness. There's a small visitor center and three easy trails suitable for strollers but not for wheelchairs. With limited parking and limited group sizes at the sites (maximum of 10 people at a time), reservations are required. No pets.

True ruin groupies should ask here about exploring the Honanki Ruins (9:30am-4pm), a further 3 miles north. To get to the site, follow Hwy 89A west of the Y for about 10 miles, then hook a right on FR 525 (Red Canyon Rd, a dirt road) and follow it 8 miles north to the parking lot.

Amitabha Stupa & Peace Park
BUDDHIST

(☎877-788-7229; www.stupas.org; Pueblo Dr; ☺sunrise-sunset) This consecrated Buddhist shrine and park is set quite stunningly in West Sedona amid piñon and juniper pine and the ubiquitous rocks. A few steps below the Amitabha Stupa look for the 6ft White Tara Stupa. Heading along Hwy 89A west

---

ℹ RED ROCK PASS

To park anywhere in the forest surrounding Sedona, you'll need to buy a Red Rock Pass, which is available at ranger stations, visitor centers and vending machines at some trailheads and picnic areas. Passes cost $5 per day or $15 per week and must be displayed in the windshield of your car. You don't need a pass if you're just stopping briefly for a photograph or to enjoy a viewpoint, or if you have one of the Federal Interagency Passes. With the latter, place it in the windshield with your signature facing out. You can also swing by a visitor center for a hangtag – the passes have been known to melt on dashboards! For additional details see www.redrockcountry.org. Passes are not valid at state parks, national parks and monuments, and the day-use areas of Crescent Moon, Call of the Canyon (West Fork Trail) and Grasshopper Point. The day-use areas charge $8 to $10 per vehicle. A pass for all three, called the Big 3 Pass, is $18 and valid for one week.

Sedona

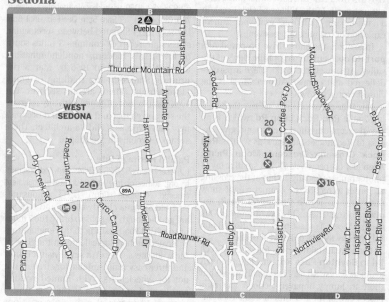

from the Y, turn right on Andante Dr, left on Pueblo Dr, then head up the gated trail on your right.

🏃 Activities

Hiking and **mountain-biking** trails crisscross the surrounding red-rock country and the woods and meadows of green Oak Creek Canyon. The free and very helpful *Recreation Guide to Your National Forest* is available at visitor centers and ranger stations. It describes hiking and biking trails for all skill levels and includes a summary of scenic drives. One deservedly popular hiking trail in Oak Creek Canyon is the 3.4-mile **West Fork Trail** (one-way) which follows the creek – the canyon walls rise more than 200ft in places. Wander up as far as you want, splash around at the numerous creek crossings and turn back when you've had enough. A sign notes the trail's official end. The trailhead lies about 3 miles north of Slide Rock, in the Call of the Canyon Recreation Area.

Rent bikes and buy coffee at **Bike & Bean** (☎ 928-284-0210; www.bike-bean.com; 75 Bell Rock Plaza; bike rental 2hr/day from $30/50) in the Village of Oak Creek, not far from the bike friendly Bell Rock Pathway.

Oak Creek holds several good swimming holes. If Slide Rock is too crowded, check out **Grasshopper Point** ($8 per car) a few miles south. Walk south to the pool. Southwest of town you can splash around and enjoy splendid views of Cathedral Rock at **Red Rock Crossing/Crescent Moon** (day-use $10 per vehicle), a USFS picnic area along a pretty stretch of Oak Creek, just off Upper Red Rock Loop Rd; look for the turnoff about 2 miles west of the hospital on Hwy 89A.

For an easy hike that leads almost immediately to gorgeous views, check out Airport Mesa. From Hwy 89A, follow Airport Dr about half a mile up the side of the mesa to a small parking turnout on your left. From here, the short **Yavapai Loop Trail** leads to an awe-inspiring view of Courthouse Butte and, after a brief scramble, a sweeping 360-degree panorama of the city and its flanking red rocks. This is one of Sedona's vortex sites. Start this hike before 8:30am, when the parking lot starts to fill. There's a Red Rock Pass machine in the parking lot. The Yavapai Loop Trail links onto the longer **Airport Loop Trail**.

Another stunningly beautiful place to hike is through the red rock of **Boynton Canyon**, an area that exudes spiritual energy and where some have reported experiencing the antics of such energetic spirits (who may not necessarily want them trek-

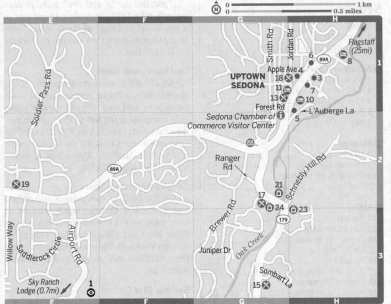

king through)! Look for the rock formation known as **Kachina Woman** and try not to be moved. Boynton Canyon is about 5 miles north of Hwy 89A up Dry Creek Rd; get an early start to avoid crowds.

Horseback Riding

M Diamond Ranch   HORSEBACK RIDING
(☎ 928-300-6466; www.sedonahorsebackrides. com; 1hr trail ride incl transportation adult/child $75/55, trail ride & cookout adult $90-120, child $75-105; ☉ Mon-Sat; ☜) This working cattle ranch takes small groups of people on trail rides through eye-catching countryside. Staff will pick you up and drop you off at your Sedona hotel.

☞ Tours

Sedona's scenery is the backdrop for many a rugged adventure, and numerous tour operators stand by to take you into the heart of it. Bumpy off-road jeep tours are popular, but it can be confusing distinguishing one company from the next. One thing to check is backcountry accessibility – the companies have permits for different routes and sites. If there's a specific rock formation or region you'd like to explore, be sure to ask. Some companies expect a minimum of four participants and charge more per person for smaller groups. Many offer discounted tour prices if you reserve online.

Two trolley companies, both with offices in Uptown, provide narrated tours of Sedona. The **Sedona Trolley** (adult/child $15/10) runs two different 55-minute tours. Tour A stops at the Chapel of the Holy Cross and Tour B heads west to Boynton and Long Canyons. The **Red Rock Magic Trolley** (adult/child $25/12) offers 85-minute tours, one heading to Boynton Canyon and another to Bell Rock. Tours are listed alphabetically.

A Day in the West   JEEP
(☎ 928-282-4320; www.adayinthewest.com; 252 N Hwy 89A; ☜) Those rootin' tootin' cowboys strolling through Uptown are most likely guides for this Western-themed jeep tour company. It offers a combo jeep tour/horseback ride with a Western-style dinner and show (adult/child $190/170). Also leads a jeep and winery trip ($99/45) and several backcountry-only trips (adult $55 to $85, child $43 to $65).

Earth Wisdom Jeep Tours   SPIRITUAL
(☎ 928-282-4714; www.earthwisdomtours.com; 293 N Hwy 89A; tours $49-98) Groovy jeep tours with a metaphysical bent and Native American focus, with journeys to vortexes and sacred Native American sites. In operation since 1989.

Sedona

Northern Light Balloon Expeditions BALLOON
(☑ 928-282-2274; www.northernlightballoon.com)
Spend about one hour floating in the air
at sunrise ($220 per person) then enjoy a
champagne picnic back on solid ground.

★ **Pink Jeep Tours** DRIVING TOUR
(☑ 928-282-5000; www.pinkjeeptours.com; 204 N
Hwy 89A; ◉) At first glance, Pink Jeep may
annoy you. It seems like the 50-year-old
company's jeeps are everywhere, buzzing
around like pink flies. But once you join
a tour, well, you just might find yourself
laughing, bumping around and having a
blast in spite of initial peevishness. We con-
cede to your domination, Pink Jeep!

The company runs 15 different thrilling
and funny, if bone-rattling, off-road and
adventure tours in Sedona, with most lasting from about two hours (adult/child from
$59/45) to four hours (from $83/110).

If you like thrills, and don't mind bounc-
ing around A LOT, the Broken Arrow tour is
a ton of fun and lives up to its hype. Tours
to the Grand Canyon are also offered (adult/
child $135/115).

Red Rock Jeep Tours JEEP
(☑ 928-282-6667; www.redrockjeep.com; 301 N
Hwy 89A; ◉) Guides in cowboy garb take you
on mild to wild jeep adventures; this is the
only company going out to the historic Soldier Pass Trail (adult/child $79/59), used by
General George Crook during his campaign
against the Apaches. Also offers a vortex
tour (adult/child $105/79).

Sedona Adventure Tours KAYAKING
(☑ 928-204-6440; www.sedonaadventuretours.
com; 57 S 10th St, Clarkdale; ◉) Specializes in
river trips, with a funyak journey down the
Verde River and a 'Water to Wine' float to Alcantara Vineyard. Water to Wine tours range
from $77.25 to $97. Funyak and inner-tube
rentals too.

Sedona Star Gazing ASTRONOMY
(☑ 928-853-9778; www.eveningskytours.com;
☉ closed mid-Jul–mid-Aug, start times vary seasonally) View planets, stars, galaxies and nebula
with the naked eye and through large Dob-
sonian telescopes. Ninety-minute tours cost
$50 to $60, depending on group size. Kids
are $35.

☆☆ Festivals & Events

Sedona International Film Festival FILM
(☑ 928-282-1177; www.sedonafilmfestival.com)
Usually takes place during the month of
February, but screenings and events occur
throughout the year.

Sedona Arts Festival ARTS & CRAFTS
(☑ 928-282-1177; www.sedonaartsfestival.org)
Fine arts, crafts and nonstop entertainment
in early October.

🛏 Sleeping

Sedona is rich with beautiful B&Bs, creekside cabins and full-service resorts. Rates at
chain motels range from $75 to $130, reasonable by Sedona standards. For lodging in
Oak Creek Canyon, see 151.

Apart from camping, tiny Sedona doesn't
have many options for the budget traveler.

Star Motel MOTEL $
(☑ 928-282-3641; www.starmotelsedona.com; 295
Jordan Rd; r $80-126, ste $176; ☎) This 10-room
motel in Uptown is one of Sedona's best

deals. Rooms are simple, with a few artsy touches, but what we like most is the hospitality. And hey, the beds in this 1950s-era motel are clean, the shower strong and the refrigerators handy for chilling those sunset beers. Shops, eateries and the visitor center are just a hop, skip and jump away.

Room 10, on the 2nd floor, has a full kitchen, sitting area and balcony ($176 per night; no kids).

La Vista Motel
MOTEL $

(☑ 928-282-7301; www.lavistamotel.com; 500 N Hwy 89A; r from $66, ste $90; ✸ ☎) Right on the side of the highway leading into Oak Creek Canyon, this basic, family-run motel has clean rooms in a variety of configurations, plus one suite. Some rooms are decked out with full kitchens, porches, tile floors, sofas, refrigerators and bathtubs.

Lantern Light Inn
INN $$

(☑ 928-282-3419; www.lanternlightinn.com; 3085 W Hwy 89A; r $159-195, guesthouse $309; @ ☎) Kris and Ed, the lovely couple running this small inn in West Sedona, put you right at ease in their comfortable antique-filled rooms. Rooms range from small and cozy, overlooking the back deck and garden, to the huge guesthouse in back; all feel comfortably overstuffed.

There's a common room (more of a family library with musical instruments) suitable for meetings. Credit cards not accepted.

Desert Quail Inn
MOTEL $$

(☑ 928-284-1433; www.desertquailinn.com; 6626 Hwy 179, Village of Oak Creek; r $99-149; ✸ ☎ ☒) Business in the front, party in the back. No, the Desert Quail Inn is not a mullet, but the ho-hum exterior is rather deceiving. Rooms inside this two-story motel are sharp, comfy and slightly modern – picture deep earth tones with pops of artsy color. Units come with microwave and mini-fridge. Some have Jacuzzis and fireplaces.

Sky Ranch Lodge
MOTEL $$

(☑ 928-282-6400; www.skyranchlodge.com; Airport Rd; r $125-180, cottages $219; ✸ ☎ ☒ ☒) At the top of Airport Rd, with spectacular views of the town and surrounding country, this lodge offers spacious motel rooms, six landscaped acres, a pool and a hot tub. Rates vary according to type of bed and your view. Decor is generally simple and low-key. Some rooms include balconies, fireplaces, kitchenettes and/or refrigerators; cottages with vaulted ceilings are also available.

★ Enchantment Resort
RESORT $$$

(☑ 800-826-4180, 928-282-2900; www.enchantmentresort.com; 525 Boynton Canyon Rd; r/studio from $425/450; ✸ @ ☎) Chic, exclusive and tucked within the beautiful Boynton Canyon, this country-club-style resort lives up to its name. Stylish Southwestern-inspired rooms, with private patios and big views, sprawl across the expansive grounds. Active travelers can hike in the canyon, splash in the pool or play tennis or golf. Or utterly unwind in Mii Amo Spa. The daily resort fee is $28.

Cozy Cactus
B&B $$$

(☑ 928-284-0082; www.cozycactus.com; 80 Canyon Circle Dr; r incl breakfast $190-340; ✸ @ ☎) This five-room B&B, run by Carrie and Mark, works well for adventure-loving types ready to enjoy the great outdoors. The Southwest-style house bumps up against a National Forest trail and is just around the bend from cyclist-friendly Bell Rock Pathway. Post-adventuring, get comfy beside the firepit on the back patio for wildlife watching and stargazing.

Breakfasts alternate between savory and sweet (huevos rancheros; apple-pie French toast) and come with fruit and Mark's famous muffins.

Orchards Inn of Sedona
MOTEL $$$

(☑ 928-282-2405; www.orchardsinn.com; 254 N Hwy 89A; r $249-259, ste $259) Smack in the middle of Uptown, but set back from the main strip, this multilevel motel is a charmer. From your private patio, enjoy views of Cleopatra Hill and the 'Snoopy' formation. Inside, framed leather headboards, hi-definition LCD televisions and crisp white bedding, plus granite counter tops in the bathrooms, will keep your aura happily aglow. Suites and deluxe rooms have fireplaces. Pet fee is $20 per night.

✗ Eating

Pick up groceries and healthy picnic components at **New Frontiers Natural Marketplace** (☑ 928-282-6311; 1420 W Hwy 89A; ⊘ 8am-9pm Mon-Sat, to 8pm Sun; ✐). Another good Arizona grocery chain is **Bashas'** (☑ 928-282-5351; 160 Coffee Pot Dr; ⊘ 6am-11pm).

Sedona Memories
DELI $

(☑ 928-282-0032; 321 Jordan Rd; sandwiches under $10; ⊘ 10am-2pm Mon-Fri) This tiny local spot assembles gigantic sandwiches on slabs of homemade bread. A great choice for a picnic, they pack 'em tight to-go, so less mess.

You can also nosh on their quiet porch. If you call in your order, they'll toss in a free cookie. Cash only.

Coffee Pot Restaurant
BREAKFAST $

(☑928-282-6626; www.coffeepotsedona.com; 2050 W Hwy 89A; breakfast $5-10, lunch $5-14; ⊙6am-2pm; ⓐ) This has been the go-to breakfast and lunch joint for decades. It's always busy and service can be slow, but it's friendly, the meals are reasonably priced and the selection is huge: 101 types of omelets for starters (peanut butter, jelly and banana perhaps?)

Red Rock Cafe
AMERICAN $

(www.facebook.com/theredrockcafe; 100 Verde Valley School Rd, Village of Oak Creek; mains $7-10; ⊙6:30am-3pm) Look for the kokopelli on the window then step inside and nab a seat quickly if it's Sunday morning – the place bustles with locals squeezing in breakfast before church. Come here for a solid, diner-style meal before hitting Bell Rock Pathway. The eatery is tucked in a strip mall behind Desert Quail Inn.

Black Cow Café
ICE CREAM $

(☑928-203-9868; 229 N Hwy 89A; scoop of ice cream $3.75; ⊙10:30am-9pm) Many claim the Black Cow has the best ice cream in town.

Picazzo's
PIZZA $$

(☑928-282-4140; www.picazzos.com; 1855 W Hwy 89A; mains $12-16, pizzas $14-18; ⊙11am-9pm Sun-Thu, until 10pm Fri & Sat; ⓐ) Pizza purists might shudder at the unorthodox toppings, but clued-in devotees gobble 'em up. If shrimp-gorgonzola or chicken-bacon-brie-mozzarella don't tickle your fancy, then design your own. Gluten-free crusts available. Lots of good pasta dishes too, including spicy Thai peanut chicken over fusilli.

Oak Creek Brewery & Grill
AMERICAN $$

(☑928-282-3300; www.oakcreekpub.com; 336 Hwy 179; mains $10-23; ⊙11:30am-8:30pm; ⓐ) Fortunately, this spacious brewery at Tlaquepaque Village will satisfy your post-hike drinking needs (although it closes ridiculously early). The menu includes upmarket pub-style dishes like a grilled mahi mahi salad and 'fire-kissed' pizza. Oak Creek also runs a low-frills brewery (p150) in West Sedona.

★Elote Cafe
MEXICAN $$$

(☑928-203-0105; www.elotecafe.com; 771 Hwy 179, King's Ransom Hotel; mains $19-26; ⊙5pm-late Tue-Sat) Some of the best, most authentic Mexican food in the region. Serves unusual traditional dishes you won't find elsewhere, like the namesake elote (fire-roasted corn with spicy mayo, lime and cotija cheese) or the tender, smoky pork cheeks.

Reservations are not accepted, unfortunately, and the line can be off-putting, but if you want to guarantee dinner, plan to queue up by 4:15pm, or resign yourself to waiting with a white sangria or a good book.

Rene at Tlaquepaque
RESTAURANT $$$

(☑928-282-9225; www.renerestaurantsedona. com; Tlaquepaque Arts & Crafts Village, Hwy 179; lunch $9-18, dinner $21-51; ⊙11:30am-2:30pm daily, 5:30-8:30pm Mon-Thu, until 9pm Fri & Sat) A sentimental favorite with locals and repeat visitors, romantic Rene infuses classic French cuisine with Southwestern touches. It does meat best (lamb is a specialty), but even lunches go well beyond the sandwich-burger-salad routine with such selections as chicken-stuffed crepes with bechamel sauce and cilantro-crusted salmon. The patio is an inviting spot for a respite after a morning of shopping.

♟ Drinking & Nightlife

For an outdoor town, Sedona is surprisingly low on pubs and breweries. For nightlife, head to Flagstaff or Prescott.

Oak Creek Brewing Company
BREWERY

(☑928-204-1300; www.oakcreekbrew.com; 2050 Yavapai Dr; ⊙4pm-close Mon-Thu, noon-close Fri-Sun) In West Sedona, this spare brewery and tap room has a bit of indoor seating and a patio. Gourmet hotdogs are for sale ($6 to $7), and there's live music most weekends.

🛍 Shopping

Shopping is a big draw in Sedona, and visitors will find everything from expensive boutiques to T-shirt shops. Uptown along Hwy 89A is the place to go souvenir hunting. For New Age shops, try **Crystal Magic** (☑928-282-1622; 2978 Hwy 89A) or **Center for the New Age** (☑928-282-7220; www.sedonanewagestore.com; 341 Hwy 179).

Tlaquepaque Village
MALL

(☑928-282-4838; www.tlaq.com; 336 Hwy 179; ⊙10am-5pm) Just south of Hwy 89A on Hwy 179, this is a series of Mexican-style interconnected plazas home to dozens of high-end art galleries, shops and restaurants.

Garland's Navajo Rugs HANDICRAFTS
(☑928-282-4070; www.garlandsrugs.com; 411 Hwy 179; ☉10am-5pm) This 38-year-old institution offers the area's best selection of rugs, and sells other Native American crafts. It's an interesting shop to visit, displaying naturally dyed yarns with their botanical sources of color, as well as descriptions of how many hours it takes to create a handwoven rug.

❶ Information

Police Station (☑emergency 911, non-emergency 928-282-3100; www.sedonaaz.gov; 100 Roadrunner Dr)

Post Office (☑928-282-3511; 190 W Hwy 89A; ☉8:45am-5pm Mon-Fri, 9am-1pm Sat)

Red Rock Visitor Contact Station (☑928-203-2900; www.redrockcountry.org; 8375 Hwy 179; ☉9am-4:30pm) Get a Red Rock Pass here, as well as hiking guides, maps and local national forest information. It's just south of the Village at Oak Creek.

Sedona Chamber of Commerce Visitor Center (☑800-288-7336, 928-282-7722; www.visitsedona.com; 331 Forest Rd, Uptown Sedona; ☉8:30am-5pm) Pick up free maps and brochures and buy a Red Rock Pass.

Verde Valley Medical Center (☑928-204-3000; www.verdevalleymedicalcenter.com; 3700 W Hwy 89A; ☉24hr) Has 24-hour emergency services.

❶ Getting There & Away

While scenic flights depart from Sedona, the closest commercial airports are Phoenix (two hours) or Flagstaff (30 minutes).

Ace Express (☑928-649-2720, 800-336-2239; www.acexshuttle.com; one way/round-trip $68/109; ☉office hours 7am-8pm Mon-Fri, 8am-8pm Sat & Sun) Door-to-door shuttle service running between Sedona and Phoenix Sky Harbor.

Amtrak (☑800-872-7245; www.amtrak.com) Stops in Flagstaff.

Greyhound (☑800-231-2222; www.greyhound.com) Stops in Flagstaff.

❶ Getting Around

Barlow Jeep Rentals (☑800-928-5337, 928-282-8700; www.barlowjeeprentals.com; 3009 W Hwy 89A; half-/full-/3-day $195/295/589; ☉8am-6pm) Great for rough road exploring. Free maps and trail information provided.

Enterprise (☑928-282-2052; www.enterprise.com; 2090 W Hwy 89A; ☉8am-6pm Mon-Fri, 9am-1pm Sat & Sun) Rental cars available here.

Oak Creek Canyon

Hwy 89A from Sedona into Oak Creek Canyon is a surreally scenic drive that won't soon be forgotten. The canyon is at its narrowest here, and the crimson, orange and golden cliffs at their most dramatic. Pine and sycamore cling to the canyon sides and the air smells sweet and romantic. Giant cottonwoods clump along the creek, providing a scenic shady backdrop for trout-fishing and swimming, and turn a dramatic golden in fall. Unfortunately, traffic can be brutal in summer.

⊙ Sights & Activities

About 2 miles into the drive north from Sedona, **Grasshopper Point** (day-use $8) is a great swimming hole. Another splash zone awaits a further 5 miles north at **Slide Rock State Park** (☑928-282-3034; www.azstateparks.com/parks/slro; 6871 N Hwy 89A; per car Memorial Day–Labor Day $20, Sep-May $10; ☉8am-7pm Jun-Aug, shorter hours rest of the year), a historic homestead and apple farm along Oak Creek. Short trails ramble past old cabins, farming equipment and an apple orchard, but the park's biggest draw is the fun rock slides. Picture people swooshing down the creek through rock-lined chutes and over water-covered rock 'slides'. It's an all-natural waterpark. Unfortunately, water quality can be an issue, but it's tested daily; call the hotline on ☑602-542-0202. This park gets jam-packed in summer, so come early or late in the day to avoid the worst congestion.

About 13 miles into the canyon, the road embarks on a dramatic zigzag climb, covering 700ft in 2.3 miles. Pull into **Oak Creek Vista** and whip out your camera to capture the canyon from a bird's-eye perspective. A small visitor center is open seasonally, and there's a year-round Native American arts and crafts market. Beyond here, the highway flattens out and reaches I-17 and Flagstaff in about 8 miles.

🛏 Sleeping

Camping

Dispersed camping is not permitted in Red Rock Canyon. The **USFS** (☑877-444-6777; www.recreation.gov; campsites $20) runs the following campgrounds along Hwy 89A in Oak Creek Canyon (none with hookups). All are nestled in woods just off the road. You don't need a Red Rock Pass. Reservations are accepted for some sites at all of the campgrounds. Cash only for first-come, first-served sites, except at Cave Springs.

Manzanita Nineteen sites; 6 miles north of town. Year-round.

Cave Springs Eighty-two sites; showers ($4 minimum); 11.5 miles north. April to early November.

Pine Flat East and Pine Flat West Fifty-nine sites; 12.5 miles north. April to October.

Lodging

Butterfly Garden Inn   CABINS $$
(☑928-203-7633; www.thebutterflygardeninn. com; 9440 N Hwy 89A; cabins $165-230; 🐾🛏) Our favorite amenity at this 26-acre retreat? The breakfast basket. Delivered early, this basket of deliciousness comes with bread, scones, fruit, granola-topped yogurt (in a Mason jar) and orange juice. The 18 cabins hit the sweet spot between rustic and stylish. Tucked amidst the pine trees 10 miles north of Sedona, Butterfly Garden is a low-key but welcoming place well-suited for relaxation.

It is also a convenient place to stay before a morning hike on the nearby West Fork Trail. No TVs, and cell phone service may be spotty. There's a $50 pet fee per stay.

Junipine Resort   LODGE $$$
(☑928-282-3375; www.junipine.com; 8351 N Hwy 89A; creekhouses from $266; @🛏) In Oak Creek Canyon 8 miles north of Sedona, this resort offers lovely, spacious one- and two-bedroom creekhouses. All have kitchens, living/dining rooms, wood-burning stoves and decks – and some have lofts. The on-site restaurant serves breakfast, lunch and dinner Wednesday through Sunday. Rooms offered at a reduced rate if booked 30 days ahead.

Eating

Indian Gardens Cafe & Market   CAFE $
(www.indiangardens.com; 3951 N Hwy 89A; breakfast $6-7, lunch $9-10.25; ⊙7am-6pm Mon-Thu, until 7pm Fri-Sun) Grab a breakfast sandwich here before heading north to the West Fork Trail or stop by for lunch while you're exploring the canyon. Lunch choices include a curried chicken salad over greens, a turkey-and-avocado sandwich and a bacon-and-brie melt. Coffee and craft beer also available. Order at the counter then relax at a table in the back garden.

Flagstaff

POP 67,468 / ELEV 7000FT

Flagstaff's laid-back charms are countless, from its pedestrian-friendly historic downtown crammed with eclectic vernacular architecture and vintage neon, to its high-altitude pursuits like skiing and hiking. Buskers play bluegrass on street corners while bike culture flourishes. Locals are a happy, athletic bunch, skewing more toward granola than gunslinger. Northern Arizona University (NAU) gives Flag its college-town flavor, while its railroad history still figures firmly in the town's identity. Throw in a healthy appreciation for craft beer, freshly roasted coffee beans and an all-around good time and you have the makings of the perfect outdoor town.

Approaching Flagstaff from the east, I-40 parallels Old Route 66. Their paths diverge at Enterprise Rd: I-40 veers southwest, while Old Route 66 curls northwest, hugging the railroad tracks, and is the main drag through the historic downtown. NAU sits between downtown and I-40. From downtown, I-17 heads south toward Phoenix, splitting off at Hwy 89A (also known as Alt 89), a spectacularly scenic road through Oak Creek Canyon to Sedona. Hwy 180 is the most direct route northwest to Tusayan and the South Rim (80 miles), while Hwy 89 beelines north to Cameron (59 miles), where it meets Hwy 64 heading west to the canyon's East Entrance.

◎ Sights

With its wonderful mix of cultural sites, historic downtown and access to outdoorsy pursuits, it's hard not to fall for Flagstaff.

Museum of Northern Arizona   MUSEUM
(☑928-774-5213; www.musnaz.org; 3101 N Fort Valley Rd; adult/child 10-17yr/senior $10/6/9; ⊙10am-5pm Mon-Sat, noon-5pm Sun) Before venturing across the Colorado Plateau, introduce yourself to the region at this small but excellent museum that spotlights local Native American archaeology, history and culture, as well as geology, biology and the arts. Don't miss the extensive collection of Hopi kachina (also spelled katsina) dolls and a wonderful variety of Native American basketry and ceramics.

Riordan Mansion State Historic Park   HISTORIC SITE
(Map p154; ☑928-779-4395; www.azstateparks. com/parks/rima; 409 W Riordan Rd; adult/child

7-13yr $10/5; ⊙9:30am-5pm May-Oct, 10:30am-5pm Nov-Apr) Having made a fortune from their Arizona Lumber Company, brothers Michael and Timothy Riordan built this sprawling duplex in 1904. The Craftsman-style design was the brainchild of architect Charles Whittlesey, who also designed El Tovar on the South Rim. The exterior features hand-split wooden shingles, log-slab siding and rustic stone. Filled with Edison, Stickley, Tiffany and Steinway furniture, the interior is a shrine to Arts and Crafts. Visitors are welcome to walk the grounds and picnic, but entrance to the house is by guided tour only. Tours leave daily and on the hour; advance reservations are accepted.

Lowell Observatory   OBSERVATORY
(Map p154; ✎main phone 928-774-3358, recorded information 928-233-3211; www.lowell.edu; 1400 W Mars Hill Rd; adult/child 5-17yr $12/6; ⊙9am-10pm Jun-Aug, shorter hours Sep-May) Sitting atop a hill just west of downtown, this national historic landmark was built by Percival Lowell in 1894. The first sighting of Pluto occurred here in 1930. Weather permitting, visitors can stargaze through on-site telescopes, including the famed Clark Telescope (closed for renovations through mid-2015). This 1896 telescope was the impetus behind the now-accepted theory of an expanding universe.

The paved Pluto Walk climbs through a scale model of our solar system. Evening programming includes a video about the making of the new, seven-story Discovery Channel Telescope, which is located 40 miles southeast of Flagstaff.

🏃 Activities

Hiking & Biking

Scores of hiking and mountain-biking trails are easily accessed in and around Flagstaff. More than 50 miles of trails crisscross the city as part of the **Flagstaff Urban Trail System** (FUTS; www.flagstaff.az.gov); trail maps are available online or at the visitor center.

Stop by the USFS Flagstaff Ranger Station (p159) for information about trails in the surrounding national forest or check www.fs.fed.us. The steep 3-mile hike (one-way) up 9299ft **Mt Elden** (Map p154) leads to a lookout at the top of the peak's tower. If it's locked when you get there, knock and if someone is there, you may be able to climb the stairs to the lookout.

Arizona Snowbowl offers several trails, including the strenuous 4.5-mile one-way

hike up 12,633ft **Humphreys Peak**, the highest point in Arizona; wear decent boots as sections of the trail cross crumbly volcanic rock. In summer, ride the **chairlift** (www.arizonasnowbowl.com; adult/child 8-12yr $15/10; ⊙10am-4pm Fri-Sun late May–mid-Oct) at Arizona Snowbowl to 11,500ft, where you can hike, attend ranger talks and take in the desert and mountain views. Children under eight ride for free.

For an inside track on the local mountain-biking scene, visit the super-friendly gearheads at **Absolute Bikes** (Map p156; ✎928-779-5969; www.absolutebikes.net; 202 E Rte 66; bike rentals per day from $39; ⊙9am-7pm Mon-Fri, 9am-6pm Sat, 10am-4pm Sun Apr-Dec, shorter hours Jan-Mar).

Other Activities

Flagstaff is full of active citizens. So there's no shortage of outdoor stores and places to buy or rent camping, cycling and skiing equipment. For ski rentals, swing by **Peace Surplus** (Map p156; ✎928-779-4521; www.peacesurplus.com; 14 W Route 66; ⊙8am-9pm Mon-Fri, to 8pm Sat, to 6pm Sun).

Arizona Snowbowl   SKIING
(✎928-779-1951; www.arizonasnowbowl.com; 9300 N Snowbowl Rd, Hwy 180 & Snowbowl Rd; lift ticket adult/youth 13-18yr/child 8-12yr $59/55/35; ⊙9am-4pm mid-Dec–mid-Apr) About 14 miles north of downtown, Arizona Snowbowl is small but lofty, with four lifts that service 32 ski runs between 9200ft and 11,500ft.

Flagstaff Nordic Center   SKIING
(✎928-220-0550; www.flagstaffnordiccenter.com; Mile Marker 232, Hwy 180; weekend/weekday from $18/12; ⊙9am-4pm Dec-Mar) 🛶 Fifteen miles north of Flagstaff, the Nordic Center offers 25 miles of groomed trails for cross-country skiing, as well as lessons and rentals. Also has snowshoe and multi-use trails. Near the Nordic Center off Hwy 180 you can ski – no permit required – across forest service land. Check with the ranger station about where to park on the fire roads.

🛏 Sleeping

If you want to walk home after visiting Flagstaff's microbreweries and its top restaurants, choose a hotel downtown. If you just want a place to crash before heading to the Grand Canyon, chain motels and hotels line S Milton Rd, Beulah Blvd and W Forest Meadows St, clustering around exit 195 off I-40.

Flagstaff

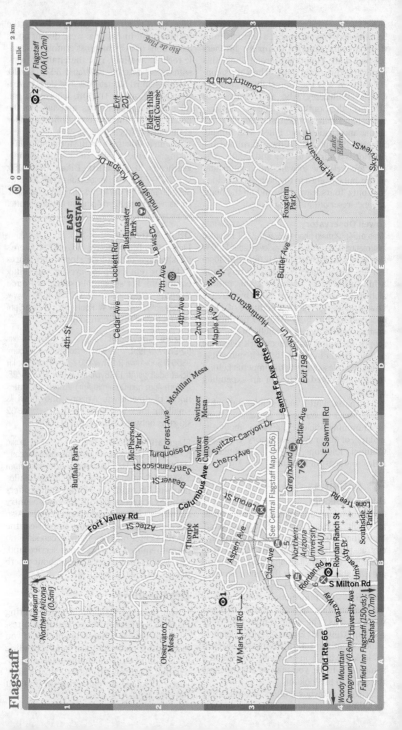

EAST FLAGSTAFF

Flagstaff KOA (0.2mi)

Exit 201

Elden Hills Golf Course

Country Club Dr

Rio de Flag

Lake Elaine

Mt Pleasant Dr

Skyview St

Foxglenn Park

Butler Ave

Kaspar Dr

Industrial Dr

Bushmaster Park

Lockett Rd

Lewis Dr

7th Ave

4th Ave

Cedar Ave

2nd Ave

Maple Ave

4th St

4th St

McMillan Mesa

4th St

Santa Fe Ave (Rte 66)

Huntington Dr

Lucky Ln

Exit 198

Butler Ave

E Sawmill Rd

Lone Tree Rd

Forest Ave

Switzer Mesa

McPherson Park

Turquoise Dr

Switzer Canyon Dr

Switzer Canyon

Cherry Ave

San Francisco St

Beaver St

Columbus Ave

Leroux St

See Central Flagstaff Map (p156)

Greyhound

Buffalo Park

Fort Valley Rd

Aztec St

Thorpe Park

Clay Ave

Aspen Ave

Northern Arizona University (NAU)

Riordan Ranch St

Riordan Rd

University Dr

S Milton Rd

Southside Park

W Old Rte 66

Woody Mountain Campground (0.6mi); University Ave

Fairfield Inn Flagstaff (150yds); Bashas' (0.7mi)

W Mars Hill Rd

Observatory Mesa

Museum of Northern Arizona (0.5mi)

0   1 mile
0   2 km

N

1   2   3   4
A   B   C   D   E   F   G

Flagstaff

Numerous nondescript and low-rate independent motels line Old Route 66 and the railroad tracks east of downtown (exit 198 off I-40). Check the room before you pay – some are much worse than others. For the money, you're better off at one of the hostels or historic hotels downtown.

Unlike in southern Arizona, summer is high season here.

Camping

Free dispersed camping is permitted in the national forest surrounding Flagstaff. USFS campgrounds in Oak Creek Canyon are 15 to 30 miles south of town.

Woody Mountain Campground CAMPGROUND $
(☎928-774-7727, 800-732-7986; www.woodymountaincampground.com; 2727 W Rte 66; tent/RV sites $20/31; ⊗Apr-Oct; @🐾🐕) Relax under the pines, play horseshoes and wash your hiking clothes at the coin laundry; off I-40 at exit 191.

Flagstaff KOA CAMPGROUND $
(☎928-526-9926, 800-562-3524; www.flagstaffkoa.com; 5803 N Hwy 89; tent sites $26-34, RV sites $34-68, cabins $65, tipis $55; ⊗year-round; 🐾🐕) This big campground lies a mile north of I-40 off exit 201, 5 miles northeast of downtown. A path leads from the campground to trails at Mt Elden. It's family friendly, with banana bike rentals, minigolf and a splash park.

Lodging

The two hostels are within a block of each other and the Amtrak station. The hostels also provide transportation to and from the Greyhound bus station. Both offer tours to the Grand Canyon and Sedona.

Dubeau Hostel HOSTEL $
(Map p156; ☎928-774-6731; www.grandcanyonhostel.com; 19 W Phoenix St; dm $24, r $60-68; P🌐@🐾) This independent hostel offers the same friendly service and clean, well-run accommodations as its sister property, Grand Canyon International Hostel. The basic rooms are like basic hotel rooms, with refrigerators and bathroom with showers, but at half the price. Breakfast is included.

Grand Canyon International Hostel HOSTEL $
(Map p156; ☎928-779-9421; www.grandcanyonhostel.com; 19½ S San Francisco St; dm $24, r with shared bath $56; 🌐@🐾) Housed in a historic building with hardwood floors and Southwestern decor, this bright, homey hostel offers private rooms or dorms with a four-person maximum. Dorms are small but clean. There's also a kitchen and laundry. This hotel gets more traffic than sister property Dubeau Hostel. Breakfast is included.

Budget Inn Flagstaff MOTEL $
(Map p154; ☎928-774-5038; www.budgetinnflagstaff.com; 913 S Milton Rd; r $96; P🌐🐾) Bland name, bland exterior, but whoa. Push open the door and you'll be pleasantly surprised by the inviting, not-so-bland style of this two-story motel. Staff is welcoming and rooms come with a microwave and refrigerator. The property is centrally located between downtown and I-40 on S Milton Rd.

★ Inn at 410 B&B $$
(Map p156; ☎928-774-0088; www.inn410.com; 410 N Leroux St; r $170-220; P🌐@🐾) This elegant and fully renovated 1894 house offers nine spacious, beautifully decorated and themed bedrooms, each with a refrigerator and private bathroom. Many rooms have four-poster beds and views of the garden or the San Francisco Peaks. A short stroll from downtown, the inn has a shady garden with fruit trees and a cozy dining room, where the full gourmet breakfast and afternoon snacks are served.

Hotel Monte Vista HOTEL $$
(Map p156; ☎928-779-6971; www.hotelmontevista.com; 100 N San Francisco St; r $70-120, ste $130-150; 🌐🐾) A huge, old-fashioned neon sign towers over this allegedly haunted 1926 hotel, hinting at what's inside: feather lampshades, vintage furniture, bold colors and eclectic decor. Rooms are named for the movie stars who slept in them, such as the Humphrey Bogart room, with dramatic black walls, yellow ceiling and gold-satin bedding.

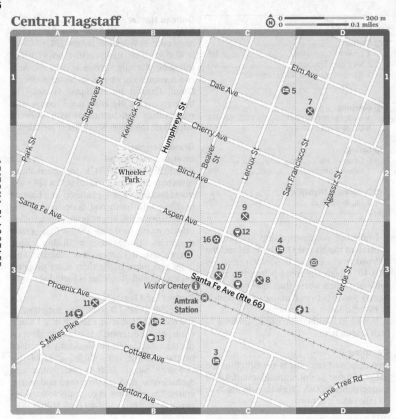

Several resident ghosts supposedly make regular appearances. The Monte Vista's appeal comes from all of its glorious funkiness, and high-maintenance travelers not enamored of funkiness may be happier elsewhere. Four rooms have shared bathrooms.

Drury Inn & Suites   HOTEL $$
(Map p154; 928-773-4900; www.druryhotels. com; 300 S Milton Rd; r $170-200, ste $215-225; P✱🕿🐾👪) The stone columns in the lobby set an adventurous mood at this six-story LEED-certified property, but the deal clincher is the Kickback happy hour which includes complimentary beer and wine (with a limit) and a hearty spread of appetizers. The free breakfast is also filling. Stylish rooms come with a microwave and refrigerator. Pets are $10 per room per day.

Comfi Cottages   BUNGALOW $$
(928-774-0731; www.comficottages.com; cottages $145-285; 🕿👪) All but one of the these bungalows are within a mile from the historic district. Most were built in the 1920s and '30s and have a homey feel, with wood floors, Craftsman-style kitchens and little lawns. Each cottage includes a TV, DVD player, cable, telephone, bicycles, tennis rackets, a BBQ grill, a picnic table and picnic baskets.

The newest cottage, which has three bedrooms, is 3 miles north of downtown on the way to the Grand Canyon. Pet fee ranges from $25 to $50 per stay, depending on number of pets. See website for specific addresses.

Fairfield Inn Flagstaff   HOTEL $$
(928-773-1300; www.fairfieldinnflagstaff.com; 2005 S Milton Rd; r include breakfast from $139; P✱🕿👪) The breakfast area has been a jam-packed affair every time we've stayed, but for some reason we keep coming back to this busy branch of the national chain. Low rates are often available through third-party websites, plus there's HBO, no-hassle wi-fi,

Central Flagstaff

and a 24-hour fitness center. Rooms are on the small side but they strut their tiny stuff with style.

✗ Eating

For groceries, **Bashas'** (☎ 928-774-3882; www.bashas.com; 2700 S Woodlands Village Blvd; ☺ 6am-11pm) is a good local chain supermarket with a respectable selection of organic foods. For health food, try the new **Whole Foods Market** (Map p154; ☎ 928-774-5747; 320 S Cambridge Lane; ☺ 8am-9pm; ⚡).

Macy's   CAFE **$**
(Map p156; www.macyscoffee.net; 14 S Beaver St; mains under $8; ☺ 6am-8pm; 🐾) The delicious house-roasted coffee at this Flagstaff institution has kept the city buzzing for more than 30 years now. The vegetarian menu includes many vegan choices, along with traditional cafe grub like pastries, steamed eggs, waffles, yogurt and granola, salads and veggie sandwiches.

★ Coppa Cafe   CAFE **$$**
(Map p154; ☎ 928-637-6813; www.coppacafe.net; 1300 S Milton Rd; lunch & brunch $9-15, dinner $21-31; ☺ 11am-7pm Wed & Thu, 11am-8pm Fri &

Sat, 10am-4pm Sun) Brian Konefal and Paola Fioravanti are the husband-and-wife team behind this inviting cafe. The couple, who met at an Italian culinary school, whip up an enticing array of European dishes and desserts that are locally sourced and, on occasion, locally 'foraged' from nearby forests. Look for salads, seasonal quiche and shepherd's pie at lunchtime and juniper-braised wild boar and pasta alla carbonara with duck egg in the evening. With its savory fare and country-bistro decor, you'll soon forget that you've just ambled in from busy S Milton Rd.

Pizzicletta   PIZZA **$$**
(Map p156; www.pizzicletta.com; 203 W Phoenix Ave; pizzas $10-15; ☺ from 5pm Tue-Sun) When the wood-fired pie is piled perfectly high – that's amore. When the crowd seems to shine like it's had too much wine – that's amore. When the train passes by like a bolt from the sky – that's amore. It's also the tiny Pizzicletta, where the thin-crusted pizzas are loaded with gourmet toppings like arugula and aged prosciutto. Ring-a-ling-a-ling, it's hard not to sing at Pizzicletta.

Beaver Street Brewery   BREWPUB **$$**
(Map p156; www.beaverstreetbrewery.com; 11 S Beaver St; lunch $8-23, dinner $13-23; ☺ 11am-11pm Sun-Thu, to midnight Fri & Sat; 🐾) Families, river guides, ski bums and businesspeople – everybody is here or on the way. The menu is typical brewpub fare, with delicious pizzas, burgers and salads, and there's usually eight hand-crafted beers on tap, like its Railhead Red Ale or R&R Oatmeal Stout, plus some seasonal brews. Serious drinkers can walk next door to play pool at the 21-and-over Brews & Cues.

Diablo Burger   BURGERS **$$**
(Map p156; www.diabloburger.com; 120 N Leroux St; mains $11-14; ☺ 11am-9pm Mon-Wed, 11am-10pm Thu-Sat) The beef maestros at this gourmet burger joint are so proud of their locally sourced creations that they sear the DB brand onto the English-muffin bun. The cheddar-topped Blake gives a nod to New Mexico with Hatch chile mayo and roasted green chiles. The place is tiny, so come early or plan to sit outside. Beer and wine are also served.

Criollo Latin Kitchen   FUSION **$$**
(Map p156; ☎ 928-774-0541; www.criollolatinkitchen.com; 16 N San Francisco St; brunch & lunch $8-18, dinner $12-23; ☺ 11am-9pm Mon-Thu, 11am-10pm Fri, 9am-10pm Sat, 9am-9pm Sun) This Latin fusion spot has a romantic, industrial setting

for cozy cocktail dates and delectable late-night small plates, but the blue-corn blueberry pancakes make a strong argument for showing up for brunch on weekends. The food is sourced locally and sustainably whenever possible, and the wine list is divine.

Karma
SUSHI, STEAK $$
(Map p156; ☑ 928-774-6100; www.karmaflagstaff.com; 6 E Route 66; mains $6-22, sushi $5-16; ⊗ 11am-10pm Mon-Sat, 4:30-10pm Sun) A trendy sushi bar with low lights and black lacquer, Karma is known for its tasty, reasonably priced rolls. And the steaks are rave-worthy, too. The 27 signature rolls include the Lucy, which comes with tuna, avocado and roasted red peppers (10% of the Lucy's sales go to animal rescue shelters). Happy hour (3pm to 6pm Mon-Sat, 4:30pm to 9pm Sun) means $2 Coronas and $5 snacks.

★Brix
AMERICAN $$$
(Map p156; ☑ 928-213-1021; www.brixflagstaff.com; 413 N San Francisco St; mains $23-34; ⊗ 5-9pm Sun-Thu, until 10pm Fri & Sat) Are you settled in at the bar? Inhale, look around, relax. This is your vacation reward. Brix brings a breath of fresh, unpretentious sophistication to Flagstaff's dining scene as well as easygoing but polished hospitality. The menu varies seasonally, regularly using what is fresh, ripe, local and organic for dishes like wild mushroom risotto with truffles and grilled ribeye with red onion jam.

Reservations are highly recommended.

Drinking & Nightlife

Craft beer fans can follow the **Flagstaff-Grand Canyon Ale Trail** (www.flagstaffaletrail.com) to sample microbrews at downtown breweries and a bar or two. Buy a trail passport at the visitor center or one of the breweries listed on the website.

For details about festivals and music programs, call the visitor center or check www.flagstaff365.com. On Saturday nights in summer, people gather on blankets for music and family movies (free) at Heritage Sq. The fun starts at 5pm.

Pick up the free *Flagstaff Live!*, published on Thursdays, or check out www.flaglive.com for current shows and happenings around town.

★Museum Club
BAR
(Map p154; ☑ 928-526-9434; www.themuseumclub.com; 3404 E Rte 66; ⊗ 11am-2am) This honky-tonk roadhouse on Route 66 has been kick-ing up its heels since 1936. Inside what looks like a huge log cabin, you'll find a large wooden dance floor, animal mounts and a sumptuous elixir-filled mahogany bar. The origins of the name? In 1931 it housed a taxidermy museum.

Charly's Pub & Grill
LIVE MUSIC
(Map p156; ☑ 928-779-1919; www.weatherfordhotel.com; 23 N Leroux St; ⊗ 8am-2am) This restaurant at the Weatherford Hotel has regular live music. Its fireplace and brick walls provide a cozy setting for the blues, jazz and folk played here. Head upstairs to stroll the wraparound veranda outside the popular 3rd-floor Zane Grey Ballroom, which overlooks the historic district.

The State Bar
BAR
(Map p156; www.facebook.com/thestatebar; 10 E Rt 66; ⊗ 11am-2am) They serve only Arizona-made beer and wines at this new bar on Route 66 downtown – and we're OK with that. Welcoming atmosphere, and solo travelers should do just fine.

Cuvee 928
WINE BAR
(Map p156; ☑ 928-214-9463; www.cuvee928winebar.com; 6 E Aspen Ave; ⊗ 11:30am-9pm Mon-Thu, to 10pm Fri & Sat, 10am-3pm Sun) This wine bar on Heritage Sq makes a pleasant venue for people-watching as well as wine tasting. It has a relaxed but upscale ambience, well-rounded menu and full bar.

Mother Road Brewing Company
BREWERY
(Map p156; www.motherroadbeer.com; 7 S Mikes Pike; ⊗ 3-8pm Mon-Thu, 3-9pm Fri, noon-9pm Sat, noon-8pm Sun) Chill out with the hoppy Roadside American and a wood-fired pizza from nearby Pizzicletta at this bare bones but popular beer-tasting room beside the old Route 66. Check the website for live music. Five to seven beers on tap but no food; it's OK to order in or bring your own. Service can be a little haphazard.

Alpine Pedaler
BAR CRAWL
(☑ 928-213-9233; www.alpinepedaler.com; per person $25) Hop on the 14-passenger bus (or is it a bicycle?) to pedal to downtown bars. Tours are two hours.

Information

Flagstaff Medical Center (☑ 928-779-3366; www.flagstaffmedicalcenter.com; 1200 N Beaver St; ⊗ emergency 24hr)

Police Station (☑ emergency 911, general information 928-556-2316, non-emergency

dispatch 928-774-1414; 911 E Sawmill Rd;
⊙ emergency 24hr)

Post Office (Map p156; ☑ 928-779-2371; 104 N
Agassiz St; ⊙ 10am-4pm Mon-Fri, 9am-1pm Sat)

USFS Flagstaff Ranger Station (☑ 928-526-
0866; 5075 N Hwy 89; ⊙ 8am-4pm Mon-Fri)
Provides information on the Mt Elden, Humphreys Peak and O'Leary Peak areas north of
Flagstaff.

Visitor Center (Map p156; ☑ 800-842-7293,
928-774-9541; www.flagstaffarizona.org; 1 E
Rte 66; ⊙ 8am-5pm Mon-Sat, 9am-4pm Sun)
Inside the Amtrak station, the visitor center
has a great Flagstaff Discovery map and tons of
information on things to do.

ⓘ Getting There & Away

Flagstaff Pulliam Airport (www.flagstaff.
az.gov) Flagstaff Pulliam Airport is 4 miles
south of town off I-17.

US Airways (☑ 800-428-4322; www.usair-
ways.com) Offers several daily flights to and
from Phoenix Sky Harbor International Airport.

Greyhound (Map p154; ☑ 928-774-4573, 800-
231-2222; www.greyhound.com; 880 E Butler
Ave) Greyhound stops in Flagstaff en route to/
from Albuquerque, Las Vegas, Los Angeles and
Phoenix.

Arizona Shuttle (☑ 800-888-2749, ext 1303,
928-226-8060; www.arizonashuttle.com) Has
shuttles that run between Flagstaff, Grand
Canyon National Park, Williams, Sedona and
Phoenix Sky Harbor Airport.

Amtrak (☑ 800-872-7245, 928-774-8679;
www.amtrak.com; 1 E Rte 66; ⊙ 3am-10:45pm)
The Southwest Chief stops at Flagstaff on its
daily run between Chicago and Los Angeles.

ⓘ Getting Around

Mountain Line Transit (☑ 928-779-6624; www.
mountainline.az.gov; adult/child $1.25/0.60)
services seven fixed bus routes daily; pick up a
user-friendly map at the visitor center. Buses
are equipped with ramps for passengers in
wheelchairs.

If you need a taxi, call **Action Cab** (☑ 928-774-
4427; www.actioncabtaxiandtours.com) or **Sun
Taxi** (☑ 928-779-1111; www.suntaxiandtours.
com). Several major car-rental agencies operate
from the airport and downtown.

Around Flagstaff

Walnut Canyon National Monument

The Sinagua cliff dwellings at **Walnut Canyon** (☑ 928-526-3367; www.nps.gov/waca; 7-day

admission adult/child $5/free; ⊙ 8am-5pm mid-
May–Oct, 9am-5pm Nov–mid-May) are set in the
nearly vertical walls of a small limestone
butte amid this forested canyon. The mile-
long **Island Trail** steeply descends 185ft
(more than 200 stairs), passing 25 rooms built
under the natural overhangs of the curva-
ceous butte. A shorter, wheelchair-accessible
Rim Trail affords several views of the cliff
dwelling from across the canyon. Even if
you're not all that interested in the Sinagua
people, who abandoned the site about 700
years ago, Walnut Canyon itself is a beautiful
place to visit, not so far from Flagstaff.

Sunset Crater Volcano National Monument

Covered by a single $5 entrance fee (valid for
seven days), both Sunset Crater Volcano and
Wupatki National Monument lie along Park
Loop Rd 545, a well-marked 36-mile loop
that heads east off Hwy 89 about 12 miles
north of Flagstaff, then rejoins the highway
26 miles north of Flagstaff.

In AD 1064 a volcano erupted on this spot,
spewing ash over 800 sq miles, spawning the
Kana-A lava flow and leaving behind 8029ft
Sunset Crater. The eruption forced farmers to vacate lands they had cultivated for
400 years; subsequent eruptions continued
for more than 200 years. The **visitor center**
(☑ 928-526-0502; www.nps.gov/sucr; adult/child
15yr & under $5/free; ⊙ visitor center 8am-5pm
mid-May–Oct, 9am-5pm Nov–mid-May) houses
a seismograph and other exhibits pertaining to volcanology, while viewpoints and a
1-mile interpretive trail through the **Bonito
lava flow** (formed c 1180) grant visitors a
firsthand look at volcanic features; a shorter 0.3-mile loop is wheelchair accessible.
You can also climb **Lenox Crater** (7024ft),
a 1-mile round-trip that climbs 300ft. More
ambitious hikers and mountain-bikers
can ascend **O'Leary Peak** (8965ft; 8 miles
round-trip) on the USFS O'Leary Peak Trail,
the only way to peer down into Sunset Crater (aside from scenic flights). Check the
website for details about evening **astronomy programs** in June and July.

Across from the visitor center, the USFS-run
Bonito Campground (☑ 928-526-0866;
www.fs.usda.gov/recmain/coconino/recreation;
tent & RV sites $20; ⊙ May–mid-Oct) provides
running water and restrooms, but no showers or hookups. No reservations.

Wupatki National Monument

The first eruptions here enriched the surrounding soil, and ancestors of today's Hopi, Zuni and Navajo people returned to farm the land in the early 1100s. By 1180 thousands were living here in advanced multistory buildings, but by 1250 their pueblos stood abandoned. About 2700 of these structures lie within **Wupatki National Monument** (☑928-679-2365; www.nps.gov/wupa; 7-day admission adult/child 15yr & under $5/free; ◉9am-5pm), though only a few are open to the public. A short self-guided tour of the largest dwelling, **Wupatki Pueblo**, begins behind the visitor center. **Lomaki, Citadel** and **Nalakihu Pueblos** sit within a half-mile of the loop road just north of the visitor center, and a 2.5-mile road veers west from the center to **Wukoki Pueblo**, the best preserved of the buildings.

On weekends in April and October rangers lead visitors on a 16-mile round-trip backpacking tour ($50; supply your own food and gear) of **Crack-in-Rock Pueblo** and nearby petroglyphs. Chosen by lottery, only 12 people may join each tour; apply two months in advance via the website or in writing.

Cameron

A tiny, windswept community 32 miles east of the Grand Canyon's East Entrance and 54 miles north of Flagstaff, Cameron sits on the western edge of the Navajo Reservation. There's not much to it; in fact, the town basically comprises just the **Cameron Trading Post & Motel** (☑gift shop 928-679-2231, motel 800-338-7385; www.camerontradingpost.com; Hwy 89; r $109, ste $179; ◉6am-9:30pm summer, 7am-9pm winter; ❄❀). In the early 1900s Hopis and Navajos came to the trading post to barter wool, blankets and livestock for flour, sugar and other goods. Today visitors can browse a large selection of quality Native American crafts, including Navajo rugs, basketry, jewelry and pottery, and plenty of kitschy knickknacks.

Spacious rooms, many with balconies, feature hand-carved furniture and a Southwestern motif. You can dine at **Cameron Trading Post Dining Room** (☑928-679-2231; www.camerontradingpost.com; breakfast $7-14, lunch $9-13, dinner $11-27; ◉6am-close), a good place to try the Navajo taco (fried dough with whole beans, ground beef, green chile and cheese).

GRAND CANYON REGION

No matter how much you read about the Grand Canyon or how many photographs you've seen, nothing really prepares you for the sight of it. One of the world's seven natural wonders, it's so startlingly familiar and iconic you can't take your eyes off it. The canyon's immensity, the sheer intensity of light and shadow at sunrise or sunset, even its very age, scream for superlatives.

At about two billion years old – half of Earth's total life span – the layer of Vishnu Schist at the bottom of the canyon is some of the oldest exposed rock on the planet. And the means by which it was exposed is of course the living, mighty Colorado River, which continues to carve its way 277 miles through the canyon as it has for the past six million years.

The three rims of the Grand Canyon – South, North and West – offer quite different experiences and, as they lie hundreds of miles and hours of driving apart, are rarely visited on the same trip. Summer is when most of the visitors arrive (4.42 million in 2012), and 90% of them only visit the South Rim, which offers easy-access viewpoints, historic buildings, Native American ruins and excellent infrastructure.

If it's solitude you seek, make a beeline for the remote North Rim. Though it has fewer and less-dramatic viewpoints, its charms are no less abundant: at 8200ft elevation (1000ft higher than the South Rim), its cooler temperatures support wildflower meadows and tall, thick stands of aspen and spruce.

Run by the Hualapai Nation and not part of Grand Canyon National Park, Grand Canyon West is famous for its Skywalk, the controversial glass bridge jutting out over the rim that debuted in 2007. Critics consider the Skywalk sacrilege and a harbinger of unwise development on the fragile West Rim, but most agree that its construction will be a much needed financial shot in the arm for the casino-less Hualapai Nation to keep their tribe afloat.

South Rim

ELEV 7000FT

Grand Canyon National Park – South Rim

If you don't mind bumping elbows with other travelers, you'll be fine on the South Rim. This is particularly true in summer when

Grand Canyon Region

UTAH

NEVADA

ARIZONA

Navajo Mtn (10,388ft)

Rainbow Bridge National Monument

Glen Canyon National Recreation Area

Page

Antelope Canyon

Navajo Reservation

Navajo Creek

Moenkopi

Hopi Reservation

Tuba City

Marble Canyon

Bitter Springs

Little Colorado River Gorge

Gray Mountain

Cameron

Navajo Bridge Interpretive Center

Lees Ferry

Paria Canyon-Vermilion Cliffs Wilderness

Paria Plateau

Jacob Lake

Kaibab Plateau

Point Imperial (8803ft)

Cape Royal (7876ft)

Bright Angel Point

North Rim

East Entrance Station

Kaibab National Forest

Grandview Lookout Tower

Valle

Kanab

Fredonia

Arizona Strip

Kaibab National Forest

North Rim Entrance Station

Grand Canyon National Park

Grand Canyon Village South Rim

Tusayan

South Entrance Station

Grand Canyon Railway

Kaibab Paiute Reservation

Pipe Spring National Monument

Kanab Creek

Supai

Havasu Canyon

Hualapai Hilltop

Coconino Plateau

Colorado City

Hurricane Cliffs

Tuweep

Toroweap Overlook

Hualapai Reservation

Grand Canyon Caverns

Peach Springs

Lake Mead National Recreation Area

Pearce Ferry

Grand Canyon West & Skywalk

Pierce Ferry Rd

Diamond Bar Rd

Hualapai Reservation

Colorado River

Music Mountains

Red Lake (dry)

Truxton

Dolan Springs

Stockton Hill Rd

Grand Canyon (South Rim)

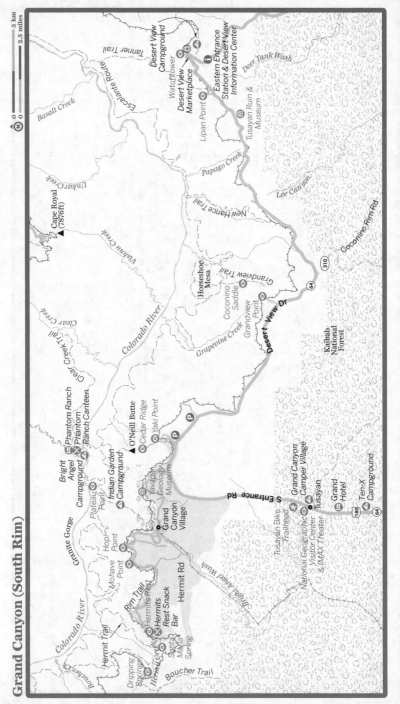

5 km
2.5 miles

Tanner Trail

Desert View Campground

Watchtower

Desert View Marketplace

Eastern Entrance Station & Desert View Information Center

Deer Tank Wash

Lipan Point

Tusayan Ruin & Museum

Escalante Route

Basalt Creek

Papago Creek

Lee Canyon

Cape Royal (7876ft)

Unkar Creek

New Hance Trail

Coconino Rim Rd

Clear Creek

Colorado River

Vishnu Creek

Horseshoe Mesa

Grandview Trail

Coconino Saddle

Grandview Point

Desert View Dr

Kaibab National Forest

Grapevine Creek

310

64

Phantom Ranch
Phantom Ranch Canteen

Clear Creek Trail

O'Neill Butte

Cedar Ridge

Yaki Point

Bright Angel Campground

Plateau Point

Indian Garden Campground

Yavapai Geology Museum

Grand Canyon Village

S Entrance Rd

Grand Canyon Camper Village

Tusayan

Grand Hotel

Ten-X Campground

180

64

Granite Gorge

Colorado River

Hopi Point

Mohave Point

Rim Trail

Hermits Rest

Hermit Rd

Tusayan Bike Trailhead

National Geographic Visitor Center & IMAX Theater

Bright Angel Wash

Hermit Trail

Hermits Rest Snack Bar

Hermit Creek

Santa Maria Spring

Boucher Trail

Dripping Springs

Boucher Trail

camera-toting day-trippers converge en masse, clogging its roads and easiest trails. Why is this rim so popular? Easy access is the most obvious reason: it's a mere 60 miles north of the I-40. Abundant infrastructure is another. This is where you'll find an entire village worth of lodging, restaurants, bookstores, libraries, a supermarket and a deli. Shuttles ply two scenic drives, and the flat and paved Rim Trail allows the mobility-impaired and stroller-pushing parents to take in the dramatic, sweeping canyon views.

If you want to venture into the inner gorge you'll have several trails to choose from – or you can just let a mule do the walking. Several museums and historic stone buildings illuminate the park's human history, and rangers lead a host of daily programs on subjects from geology to resurgent condors.

Though the accessibility of the South Rim means sharing your experience with others, there are many ways to commune with the canyon and its wildlife, and enjoy its sublime beauty, one on one. Escaping the crowds can be as easy as taking a day hike below the rim or merely tramping a hundred yards away from a scenic overlook.

Most visitors arrive via the **South Entrance**, 80 miles northwest of Flagstaff on Hwy 64/180. Avoid summer wait times of 30 minutes or more by prepaying your park ticket at the National Geographic Visitor Center in Tusayan, which allows you to cruise through in a special lane. Or arrive at the East Entrance instead. In summer, if you've bought your ticket or have a park pass, you can now hop on the park's Tusayan shuttle at the IMAX Theater in Tusayan and disembark at the Grand Canyon Visitor Center.

A few miles north of the South Entrance, **Grand Canyon Village** (or simply the Village) is the primary hub of activity. Here you'll find lodges, restaurants, two of the three developed campgrounds, a backcountry office, visitor center, medical clinic, bank, grocery store, shuttles and other services. Coin-operated showers and laundry facilities are located next to Mather Campground.

West of the Village, **Hermit Rd** follows the rim for 8 miles, ending at **Hermits Rest** (Map p162). Seven pullouts along the way offer spectacular views; from those at **Mohave** (Map p162) and **Hopi Points** (Map p162) you can spot three Colorado River rapids. Interpretive signs explain the canyon's features and geology. From March to November the road is closed to private vehicles and accessible only by tour or free shuttle bus.

In the opposite direction, **Desert View Dr** meanders 25 miles to the **East Entrance** on Hwy 64, passing some of the park's finest viewpoints, picnic areas, the Tusayan Ruin & Museum and the Watchtower. A campground, snack bar, small information center and general store are in Desert View, right by the entrance. Also here is the park's only gas station, which offers 24-hour pay-at-the-pump service from April to September. Gas stations in Tusayan are closer to the Village and open year-round.

CLIMATE

On average, temperatures are 20°F (about 11°C) cooler on the South Rim than at the bottom of the Grand Canyon. In summer, expect highs in the 80s and lows around 50°F (highs in the 30s and lows around 10°C). Weather is cooler and more changeable

---

GRAND CANYON SOUTH RIM IN...

One Day

Catch a predawn shuttle to see the sun come up at Yaki Point, then head back to the Village for coffee and pastries at the Deli at Marketplace (p172). Swing by the Grand Canyon Visitor Center (p174), stroll the Rim Trail from Mather Point to Yavapai Geology Museum (p164) and the Trail of Time exhibit, then make a beeline to El Tovar Dining Room (p173) to beat the lunchtime crowds. In the afternoon, catch the shuttle to Hermits Rest (p172) and hike about 10 minutes down the Hermit Trail to look for ancient fossil beds, then catch the sunset at Hopi Point.

Two Days

Follow the one-day itinerary, capping the day with dinner in the elegant Arizona Room (p173) and an overnight stay in the Village (book well ahead). The morning of day two, hike into the canyon on the South Kaibab Trail, stopping at Cedar Ridge for a picnic. Wrap up your Grand Canyon adventure with a drive east along Desert View Dr, stopping at viewpoints, the Tusayan Ruin & Museum (p165) and the Watchtower (p165).

TOP FIVE OVERLOOKS

➡ **Mohave Point** For a look at the river and three rapids.

➡ **Hopi Point** Catch huge sunset views.

➡ **Lipan Point** (Map p162) Creeks, palisades, rapids and sunrises.

➡ **Desert View** Climb to the top of the Watchtower and wave down at the river.

➡ **Yaki Point** (Map p162) A favorite point to watch the sunrise warm the canyon's features.

in fall, and snow and freezing overnight temperatures are likely by November. January has average overnight lows in the teens (-10°C to -7°C) and daytime highs around 40°F (4°C) Winter weather can be beautifully clear, but be prepared for snowstorms that can cause havoc.

The inner canyon is much drier, with about 8in of rain annually, around half that of the South Rim. During summer, temperatures inside the canyon soar above 100°F (38°C) almost daily, often accompanied by strong hot winds. Even in midwinter, the mercury rarely drops to freezing, with average temperatures hovering between 37°F and 58°F (3°C and 14°C).

◉ Sights

The Grand Canyon's natural splendor is the prime draw, but to enrich your trip it pays to visit the park's cultural and architectural sites. Some of the most important buildings were designed by noted architect Mary Jane Colter to complement the landscape and reflect the local culture. Unless otherwise noted, sights are in the Village and they are free.

Travelers can take a **cell-phone audio tour** at 30 sites across the north and south rims. These ranger-narrated tours last two minutes and can be accessed, at no extra charge, by dialing ☎928-225-2907 and pressing the designated stop number.

Yavapai Geology Museum　　MUSEUM
(Map p162; ⊙8am-7pm Mar-May & Sep-Nov, to 6pm Dec-Feb, to 8pm Jun-Aug) Views don't get much better than those unfolding behind the plate-glass windows of this little stone building at Yavapai Point, where handy panels identify and explain the various formations before you. There's also a helpful diorama that will get you oriented to the layout of the canyon.

The superb geology display explains the canyon's multilayered geological history.

From here, check out the **Trail of Time** (Map p168) exhibit along the Rim Trail just west of the museum. This interpretative display traces the history of the canyon's formation, and every meter equals one million years of geologic history. Rock samples from within the canyon line the trail.

Kolb Studio　　GALLERY
(Map p168; ☎928-638-2771; Grand Canyon Village; ⊙8am-7pm Mar-May & Sep-Nov, to 6pm Dec-Feb, to 8pm Jun-Aug) In 1905 photographers Ellsworth and Emery Kolb built a small studio on the edge of the rim, which has since been expanded and now holds a small bookstore and an art gallery. The brothers arrived at the canyon from Pennsylvania in 1902 and made a living photographing parties going down the Bright Angel Trail. Because there was not enough water on the rim to process the film, they had to run 4.5 miles down the trail to a spring at Indian Garden, develop the film and race back up in order to have the pictures ready when the party returned.

Lookout Studio　　HISTORIC BUILDING
(Map p168; ⊙8am-sunset mid-May–Aug, 9am-5pm Sep–mid-May) Like Mary Colter's other canyon buildings, Lookout Studio was modeled after stone dwellings of the Southwest Pueblo Native Americans. Made of rough-cut Kaibab limestone, with a roof that mirrors the lines of the rim, the studio blends into its natural surroundings. Inside, it houses a small souvenir shop and a tiny back porch that offers spectacular canyon views.

A stone stairway snakes below Lookout Studio to another terrace, which is the site of the popular ranger-led **Condor Talk**. Take a moment to look around – you might just see one of these big-winged creatures swooping past or chilling out nearby.

Hopi House　　ARCHITECTURE
(Map p168; ⊙8am-8pm mid-May–Aug, 9am-6pm Sep–mid-Oct, 9am-5pm mid-Oct–mid-May) A beautiful Colter-designed stone building, Hopi House has been offering high-quality Native American jewelry, basketwork, pottery and other crafts since its 1904 opening. The structure was built by the Hopi from native stone and wood, inspired by traditional dwellings on their reservation. Be sure to walk upstairs for the Native American Art Gallery.

Tusayan Ruin & Museum　　MUSEUM
(Map p162; ◷9am-5pm) Near the East Entrance, 22 miles east of the Village, you'll
come across what's left of the nearly
800-year-old Ancestral Puebloan settlement
of Tusayan. Only partially excavated to minimize erosion damage, it's less impressive
than other such ruins in the Southwest but
still interesting and worth a look. A small
museum displays pottery, jewelry and split-
twig animal figurines, which date back 2000
to 4000 years.

★**Watchtower**　　ARCHITECTURE
(Map p162; ◷8am-sunset mid-May–Aug, 9am-
6pm Sep–mid-Oct, 9am-5pm mid-Oct–Feb, 8am-
6pm Mar–mid-May) Scramble to the top of
Colter's stone tower at Desert View, which is
the highest spot on the rim (7522ft). Unparalleled views take in not only the canyon and
the Colorado River but also the San Francisco Peaks, the Navajo Reservation and the
Painted Desert. The Hopi Room has festive
murals depicting the snake legend, a Hopi
wedding and other scenes. The Watchtower
stairs close 30 minutes before the rest of the
building.

🏃 Activities

Hiking
To experience the full majesty of the canyon,
hit the trail. It may look daunting, but there
are options for all levels of skill and fitness.
Though summer is the most popular season for day hikes – despite oppressively hot
100°F (38°C) plus temperatures below the

rim – experienced canyon hikers know that
it's much more pleasant to hike in the spring
and fall, when there are also significantly
fewer visitors. For short, easy-to-print trail
descriptions (with mileages, turnaround
points and basic maps) check out the Plan
Your Visit section of the park website. Click
through to backcountry hiking.

The easiest and most popular is the **Rim
Trail**, which is quite literally a walk in the
park. It connects a series of scenic points
and historical sights stretching 13 miles from
the South Kaibab Trailhead west to Hermits
Rest. The section of the Rim Trail between
the South Kaibab Trailhead to Lookout Studio is paved, and mostly wheelchair accessible. It's possible to catch a shuttle bus to
a viewpoint, walk a stretch, then catch the
next shuttle back or onward. The 3 miles or
so winding through the Village are usually
packed, but crowds thin out further west.

Heading down into the canyon means ne-
gotiating supersteep switchbacks. The most
popular is the **Bright Angel Trail** (Map p168),
which is wide, well graded and easy to follow. Starting in the Village, just west of Kolb
Studio, it's a heavily trafficked route that's
equally attractive to first-time canyon hikers,
seasoned pros and mule trains. The trailhead was revamped in 2013 and is now surrounded by a small plaza with seating and
restrooms. The popularity of the trail doesn't
lessen the sheer beauty. The steep and scenic 7.8-mile descent to the Colorado River
is punctuated with four logical turnaround
spots, including two resthouses offering

ⓘ GETTING STARTED

Admission to the **park** (☎928-638-7888; www.nps.gov/grca; vehicles/cyclists & pedestrians
$25/12) is valid for seven days at both rims. Bus and train passengers may pay a lesser
fee or have it included in the tour price. Upon entering, you'll be given a map and *The
Guide*, an incredibly useful newspaper thick with additional maps, the latest park news
and information about ranger programs, hikes and park services. It also lists opening
hours of restaurants and businesses.

On the South Rim, the Grand Canyon Visitor Center (p174) should be your first stop.
Recently remodeled, it offers a number of new interpretive exhibits inside the main visitor center building. In the attached theater, the film *Grand Canyon: Journey of Wonder*
is a 20-minute introduction to the park's geology, history and plant and animal life. If you
plan to hike, look for helpful trail summaries displayed on the adjacent plaza.

If you haven't been to the park in a few years, note that you can no longer pull over on
the side of the road after entering and dash to **Mather Point** (Map p168). Traffic is now
directed away from the rim, passing several new parking lots on the way into Grand Canyon Village. Instead, follow the visitor center plaza out to Mather Point – where the views
are still as amazing.

Likewise, head to **Lonely Planet** (www.lonelyplanet.com/usa/grand-canyon-national-
park) for planning advice, author recommendations, traveler reviews and insider tips.

shade and water. The first resthouse is about 1.5 miles down the trail, the second is 3 miles. Day hikers and first-timers should strongly consider turning around at one of them or otherwise hitting the trail at dawn to safely make the longer hikes to Indian Garden or **Plateau Point** (Map p162) – 9.2 and 12.2 miles round-trip, respectively. Hiking to the Colorado River for the day is not an option.

One of the park's prettiest trails, the **South Kaibab Trail** combines stunning scenery and adventurous hiking with every step. The only corridor trail to follow a ridgeline, the red-dirt path allows for unobstructed 360-degree views. It's steep, rough and wholly exposed, which is why rangers discourage all but the shortest of day hikes during summer. A good place to turn around is **Cedar Ridge** (Map p162), reached after about an hour. It's a dazzling spot, particularly at sunrise, when the deep ruddy umbers and reds of each canyon fold seem to glow from within. During the rest of the year, the trek to Skeleton Point, 1.5 miles beyond Cedar Ridge, makes for a fine hike – though the climb back up is a beast in any season. The South Kaibab Trailhead is 4.5 miles east of the Village on Yaki Point Rd and can only be reached by shuttle or the Hikers' Express leaving from Bright Angel Lodge around dawn (stopping at the Backcountry Information Center).

One of the steepest trails in the park, dropping 1200ft in the first 0.75 miles, **Grandview Trail** is also one of the finest and most popular hikes. The payoff is an up-close look at one of the inner canyon's sagebrush-tufted mesas and a spectacular sense of solitude. While rangers don't recommend the trek to **Horseshoe Mesa** (3 miles, four to six hours)

BACKCOUNTRY ACCESS

Most overnight backpacking trips go from the South Rim to the river and then return, because South Rim-to-North Rim trips involve a tedious four- to five-hour shuttle ride. Most people spend two nights below the rim – either two nights at Bright Angel Campground or Indian Garden Campground, or one night at each. If you do arrange a shuttle you could add a night at Cottonwood Campground on the way up to the North Rim. If your time is limited, a one-night trip is also rewarding. If you prefer a bed to a sleeping bag, make reservations at the canyon-bottom Phantom Ranch at least a year in advance.

Overnight hikes require a backcountry permit. The park issued 14,201 backcountry permits in 2012, but demand far exceeds available slots. If you're caught camping in the backcountry without a permit, expect a hefty fine and possible court appearance.

Permits cost $10, plus an additional $5 per person per night, and are required for all backcountry use unless you've got a reservation at Phantom Ranch. The fee is nonrefundable and payable by check or credit card. Reservations are accepted in person or by mail or fax (☎928-638-2125) beginning the first day of the month, four months prior to the planned trip (ie on May 1, request a date in September). Permits faxed on the first day of the month before 5pm are considered first when assigning permits, though not necessarily in the order received (they are randomly assigned a computer-generated number). Be sure to list your second and third choices on the form to improve your odds of snagging a spot. Backcountry rangers read all notes on the forms and will try to meet your order of preference. Faxing your request is the best way to go. You cannot email your permit request.

For detailed instructions and to download the permit request form, go to the park's website (www.nps.gov/grca/planyourvisit/backcountry.htm) and click on the Backcountry Permit Quicklink. Alternatively, contact the Backcountry Information Center (p174) and ask them to mail you the form. If you arrive without a permit, hightail it to the center near Maswik Lodge and get on the waiting list. You must show up daily at 8am to remain on the list, but you'll likely hear your name called in one to four days, depending on the season and itinerary. For safety reasons, you will not be granted a permit for the day you show up at the office; the earliest would be for the next day. For last-minute backcountry excursions on the North Rim, you may be able to arrange to pick up your permit at Pipe Springs National Monument instead of the South Rim; call ahead.

Email backcountry questions – but not your permit request – to the office at grca_bic@nps.gov. Staff are very helpful. The backcountry office is planning to move the permit request process online in 2015, so check the website before sending your fax.

in summer – there's no water on the very exposed trail, and the climb out is a doozy – it's not overly long and certainly doable for strong hikers strapped with a hydration system and hiking early or late in the day. For a shorter but still rewarding option, hike as far as **Coconino Saddle** (Map p162). Though it's only about 2 miles round-trip, it packs a quick and precipitous punch as you plunge 1600ft in less than a mile. With the exception of a few short level sections, the Grandview is a rugged, narrow and rocky trail. The trailhead is at **Grandview Point** (Map p162), 12 miles east of the Village on Desert View Dr.

The wild **Hermit Trail** descends into pretty Hermit Canyon via a cool spring. It's a rocky trip down, but if you set out early and take it slow, it offers a wonderfully serene hike and glimpses into secluded corners. Day hikers should steer towards **Santa Maria Spring** (Map p162), a 5 mile round-trip, or to **Dripping Springs** (Map p162) via a spur trail, a 7 mile round-trip). The upper section of the Hermit is well shaded in the morning, making it a cool option in summer. The trailhead is at the end of its namesake road, 8 miles west of the Village. Although the road is only accessible via shuttle bus during the summer peak season, overnight backpackers with a Hermit Trail backcountry permit are allowed to park near the trailhead year-round.

Wildland Trekking   HIKING
(☏ 800-715-4453; www.wildlandtrekking.com; day hike per person $139, 3-/4-day camping $805/1020) Offers day hikes and camping trips from the South Rim with well-informed, experienced guides. A good choice if you don't want to pack your own gear or you simply want to learn more about the canyon. Also runs camping trips to Havasu Falls west of the park (from $850 per person).

Biking

Cyclists have limited options inside the park, as bicycles are only allowed on paved roads, dirt roads that are open to the public and the Greenway Trail. The multi-use Greenway Trail, open to cyclists as well as pedestrians and wheelchairs, stretches about 13 miles from Hermits Rest all the way to the South Kaibab Trailhead.

Hermit Rd offers a scenic ride west to Hermits Rest, about 16 miles round-trip from the village. Shuttles ply this road every 15 minutes between March and November (the rest of the year, traffic is minimal). They are not permitted to pass cyclists, so for the first 4 miles you'll have to pull over each time one drives by. However, starting from Monument Creek Vista, a completed section of the Greenway Trail diverges from the road and continues separately all the way to Hermits Rest.

Alternatively, you could ride out to the East Entrance along Desert View Dr, a 50-mile round-trip from the village. The route is largely shuttle-free but sees a lot of car traffic in summer. Just off Desert View Dr, the 1-mile dirt road to Shoshone Point is an easy, nearly level ride that ends at this secluded panoramic vista, one of the few places to escape South Rim crowds.

Bright Angel Bicycles   BICYCLE RENTAL
(Map p168; ☏ 928-638-3055; http://bikegrandcanyon.com; 10 South Entrance Rd, Visitor Center Plaza; bicycle rental full-day adult/child 16yr & under $40/30; ☺ usually Apr-Nov) Renting 'comfort cruiser' bikes on the South Rim, the friendly folks here custom-fit each bike to the individual. Rates include helmet; child trailers, strollers and wheelchairs also available. Roads bikes are $45 per day. Three-hour interpretative tours are also offered, with trips on either Hermit Rd or Yaki Rd (adult/child 15 years & under from $48/38).

Mule Rides

Visitors who want to view the canyon by mule have two choices: a three-hour day trip along the rim or a two-day trip to the bottom of the canyon, which includes a night at Phantom Ranch. Due to erosion concerns, the National Park Service (NPS) no longer allows one-day mule rides down into canyon. Both trips are run by **Xanterra** (☏ 303-287-2757, 888-297-2757; www.xanterra.com).

The three-hour Canyon Vistas Ride ($125) meets at the livery barn in Grand Canyon Village then travels by bus to the South Kaibab Trailhead, where the mules await. Guests enjoy an interpretative ride along a newly constructed 4-mile trail beside the east rim.

Overnight trips (one/two people $549/960) and two-night trips (one/two people $781/1286) still follow the Bright Angel Trail to the river, travel east on the River Trail and cross the river on the Kaibab Suspension Bridge. Riders spend the night at Phantom Ranch. It's a 5½-hour, 10.5-mile trip to Phantom Ranch, but the return trip up the 8-mile South Kaibab Trail is a half-hour shorter. Overnight trips include cabin accommodations and all meals at Phantom.

Grand Canyon Village

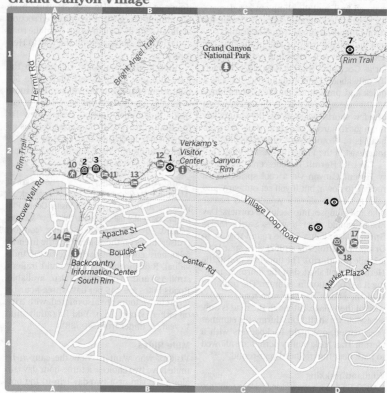

Grand Canyon Village

Riders must be at least 4ft 7in tall, speak and understand fluent English and weigh no more than 225lb (Canyon Vistas) or 200lb (Phantom Ranch) fully clothed. Personal backpacks, waist packs and purses are not allowed on the mules. Anything that could

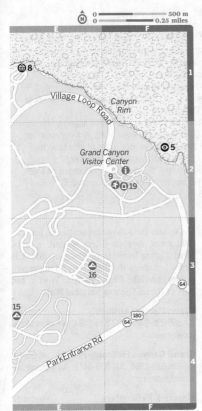

ARIZONA SOUTH RIM

possibly fall off and injure someone in the canyon below will be kept for you until you return. For complete regulations and more information, consult the Xanterra website.

Mule trips are popular and fill up quickly; to book a trip more than 24 hours and up to 13 months in advance, call Xanterra. If you arrive at the park and want to join a mule trip the following day, ask about availability at the transportation desk at Bright Angel Lodge (your chances are much better during the off season). If the trips are booked, join a waiting list, cross your fingers and show up at the lodge at 6:15am on the day of the trip and hope there's been a cancellation. Or make tracks to the other side of the canyon: mule rides on the North Rim are usually available the day before the trip.

White-Water Rafting

Rafting the Colorado – the King Kong of North American rivers – is an epic, adrenaline-pumping adventure. The biggest single drop at Lava Falls plummets 37 stomach-churning feet in just 300yd. But roller-coaster thrills are only the beginning. The canyon's true grandeur is best grasped looking up from the river, not down from the rim. Its human history comes alive in ruins, wrecks and rock art. You can hike to mystical grottoes and waterfalls, explore ethereally lit slot canyons and view wildlife.

Commercial trips vary in length from three days to three weeks and in the type of watercraft used. Motorized pontoon rafts are the most stable and generally the least scary option. The huge inflatable boats seat eight to 16 passengers and go twice as fast as oar or paddleboats. Oar boats are more common, and more exciting. Rowed by an experienced guide, they provide good stability but feel more like a raft.

A fun and intimate alternative is to float in a river dory, a small, elegant hard-shelled rowboat for four passengers that's a lot speedier than a raft. Still, if it's thrills you're after, book a trip in an inflatable raft, which has you, your raft-mates and a guide paddling all at once.

At night you'll be camping under stars on sandy beaches (gear provided). It's not as primitive as it sounds – guides are legendary not only for their white-water acumen but also for their culinary skills.

It takes about two or three weeks to run the entire 279 miles of river through the canyon. Shorter sections of around 100 miles take four to nine days. Prices listed here are just a sampling of what each company offers.

Arizona Raft Adventures   RAFTING
(☑ 800-786-7238, 928-526-8200; www.azraft.com; 6-day Upper Canyon hybrid/paddle trips $2050/2150, 10-day Full Canyon motor trips $3000) 🖋 This multigenerational family-run outfit offers paddle, oar, hybrid (with opportunities for both paddling and floating) and motor trips. Music fans can join one of the folk and bluegrass trips, with professional pickers and banjo players providing background music.

Arizona River Runners   RAFTING
(☑ 800-477-7238, 602-867-4866; www.raftarizona.com; 6-day Upper Canyon oar trip $1925, 8-day Full Canyon motor trip $2695) Have been at their game since 1970, offering oar-powered and motorized trips.

OARS   RAFTING
(☑ 209-736-4677, 800-346-6277; www.oars.com; 6-7-day Upper Canyon oar trip $2607-2787,

GRAND CANYON FOR CHILDREN

The **Junior Ranger** program for kids from four to 14 is popular. Pick up an activity book at the visitor center, fulfill the requirements and attend a ranger program – then get sworn in as a junior ranger and receive a certificate and badge. There's a separate badge for children who hike or take a mule ride to the bottom of the canyon and back.

Aspiring naturalists and their families can borrow a **Discovery Pack** containing binoculars, a magnifying glass, field guides and other tools. If you complete four or more activities in the journal you earn a Discovery Pack patch.

In summer (June to August), check *The Guide* for the South Rim for a list of Junior Ranger programs, all geared to families with children six to 14 years old. Active types can join a ranger-led **Adventure Hike** down the Hermit Trail for close-ups of fossils. In the **Kids Rock!** programs rangers use hands-on activities to teach kids about ecology and wildlife. For example, the ranger builds a forest with the children, who pretend to be trees, grasses, bees and other plants and animals. For nocturnal exploring, check out the **Twilight Zone** walk-and-talk. Bring a flashlight!

14-18-day Full Canyon dory trips $5406-5905) 🛶 One of the best outfitters out there, OARS offers oar, paddle and dory trips, and offers the option of carbon-offsetting your trip.

Ranger-Led Activities

Rangers are fonts of information, which they happily share in free programs. Their talks cover everything from condors to fire ecology, while their hikes deepen your understanding of the canyon's fossils, geology and history. *The Guide* newspaper and the displays outside Grand Canyon Visitor Center list the latest offerings.

👉 Tours

Coach Tours

First-time visitors can keep the overwhelm factor at bay by joining one of several narrated bus tours, run by Xanterra (www.grandcanyonlodges.com). Tours travel west to Hermits Rest ($29, two hours) and east to Desert View ($48, about four hours; combination tour $65), stopping at key viewpoints. Sunrise and sunset tours are also available. Stop by the transportation desk at any lodge, or ask the El Tovar concierge for the latest schedule and tickets. Kids 16 and under ride for free.

Flyovers

Helicopter and airplane flights have been restricted in number, altitude and routes to reduce noise pollution affecting the experience of other visitors and wildlife. A National Park Service proposal to further protect the Grand Canyon's soundscape, by capping the number of annual flights at 65,000, was quashed by Congress in 2012.

Contact the following companies for specific rates, as each offers several options. Most flights leave from Tusayan and Las Vegas but check the itinerary and departure points carefully; Grand Canyon West is not part of Grand Canyon National Park.

Grand Canyon Airlines   AIRPLANE
(☑866-235-9422, 702-835-8484; www.grandcanyonairlines.com)

Grand Canyon Helicopters   HELICOPTER
(☑928-638-2764, 702-835-8477; www.grandcanyonhelicopter.com)

Maverick Helicopters   HELICOPTER
(☑888-261-4414; www.maverickhelicopter.com)

Papillon Grand Canyon Helicopters   HELICOPTER
(☑888-635-7272, 702-736-7243; www.papillon.com)

Scenic Airlines   AIRPLANE
(☑855-235-9422; www.scenic.com)

🛏 Sleeping

Pitch a tent in one of three campgrounds or enjoy a solid roof in one of the six hotels ranging from no-frill motels to luxurious lodges. **Xanterra** (☑303-297-2757, 888-297-2757; www.grandcanyonlodges.com) operates all park lodges, as well as Trailer Village. Reservations are accepted up to 13 months in advance and should be made as early as possible. For same-day bookings call the **South Rim Switchboard** (☑928-638-2631). Children under 16 stay free, but cribs and cots are $10 per day.

If everything in the park is booked up, consider Tusayan (7 miles south), Valle (30 miles south) or Williams (60 miles south).

Campers can pitch a tent for free in the surrounding Kaibab National Forest.

Camping

The **National Park Service** (☎877-444-6777, international 518-885-3639; www.recreation.gov) operates Mather and Desert View Campgrounds. Reservations for Mather are accepted up to six months in advance, up until the day before your arrival.

Stays at any of the three campgrounds below the rim require a backcountry overnight permit. **Indian Garden Campground** (Map p162) has 15 sites and is 4.6 miles down the Bright Angel Trail, while **Bright Angel Campground** (Map p162) is on the canyon floor near Phantom Ranch, some 9.3 miles via the Bright Angel Trail. Both are ranger-staffed and have water and toilets. **Cottonwood Campground** is halfway up the North Kaibab Trail to the North Rim, about 16.6 miles from the South Rim.

Desert View Campground   CAMPGROUND $
(Map p162; campsites $12; ⊙May–mid-Oct) In a piñon-juniper forest near the East Entrance, this first-come, first-served campground with 50 sites is quieter than Mather Campground in the Village, with a nicely spread-out design that ensure a bit of privacy. The best time to secure a spot is mid-morning, when people are breaking camp; usually fills by mid-afternoon. Facilities include toilets and drinking water, but no showers or hookups.

Mather Campground   CAMPGROUND $
(Map p168; ☎877-444-6777; www.recreation.gov; Grand Canyon Village; campsites $18; ⊙year-round) Sites are shaded and fairly well dispersed, and the flat ground offers a comfy platform for your tent. You'll find pay showers, laundry facilities, drinking water, toilets, grills and a small general store; a full grocery store is a short walk away. Reservations are accepted from March through November; the rest of the year it's first-come, first-served. No hookups.

Trailer Village   CAMPGROUND $
(Map p168; ☎888-297-2757, same-day reservations 928-638-2631; www.grandcanyonlodges.com; Grand Canyon Village; campsites $35; ⊙year-round) This Xanterra-run campground is basically a trailer park, with RVs lined up tightly at paved pull-through sites amid a rather barren patch of ground. Check for spots with trees on the far north side. You'll find picnic tables, barbecue grills and full

hookups, but showers are a quarter-mile away at Mather Campground.

Lodges

With the exception of Phantom Ranch, which sits on the canyon floor, all of the lodges listed below are in Grand Canyon Village. All lodges are booked through Xanterra. Advance reservations are highly recommended. For same-day reservations or to reach any lodge, call the South Rim Switchboard. Pets are not allowed in any of the lodges, but there is a kennel in the village.

Phantom Ranch   CABIN $
(Map p162; ☎888-297-2757; www.grandcanyon-lodges.com; dm $48, cabin $138; ❄) Bunks at this camp-like complex are spread across cozy private cabins sleeping up to four people and single-sex dorms outfitted for 10 people. Rates include bedding, liquid soap and towels, but meals are extra and must be reserved when booking your bunk. You're free to bring your own food and stove.

Snacks, pack lunches, limited supplies, and beer and wine are sold at the canteen (p173). Without a reservation, put yourself on the waiting list at the Bright Angel Lodge transportation desk the day before you want to go (starting at 5am) then show up again at 6:15am the next morning and hope to snag a canceled bed. You can also check with Xanterra the day before about cancellations. Note that the ranch's 10-person cabins are usually booked by mule trips.

Bright Angel Lodge   LODGE $$
(Map p168; ☎888-297-2757; www.grandcanyon-lodges.com; Grand Canyon Village; r with/without private bath $94/83, ste $94-404, cabin $120-404; P❄@☎) This 1935 log-and-stone lodge on the ledge delivers historic charm by the bucketload, as well as nicely appointed rooms. Public spaces, though, are busy and less elegant. If you're economizing, get a basic double (no TV – just a bed, desk and sink) with shared bathrooms down the hall. Cabins are brighter, airier and have tasteful Western character; the most expensive have rim views.

Maswik Lodge   LODGE $$
(Map p168; ☎888-297-2757; www.grandcanyon-lodges.com; Grand Canyon Village; r south/north $92/176, cabins $94; P❄@☎) The Maswik Lodge complex includes 18 modern two-story buildings set in the woods; rooms are of the standard motel variety. Rooms at Maswik

North feature private patios, air-con, cable TV, high ceilings and forest views, while those at Maswik South are smaller, with fewer amenities, no aircon and more forgettable views.

The cramped cabins are available only in the summer and sit close to the sometimes loud staff cabins. The cabins have TVs, but no air-con.

Kachina & Thunderbird Lodges   LODGE $$

(Map p168; www.grandcanyonlodges.com; Grand Canyon Village; r streetside/rimside $194/201; ☺year-round; P❋🛜) Beside the Rim Trail between El Tovar and Bright Angel, these institutional-looking lodges, built in the late 1960s, offer standard motel-style rooms with two queen beds, full bath, flat-screen TV, Keurig coffeemaker and a refrigerator. It's worth spending up a little for the rimside rooms, some with partial canyon views.

Yavapai Lodge   LODGE $$

(Map p168; www.grandcanyonlodges.com; Grand Canyon Village; r West/East $140/174; ☺Apr–Oct; P❋🛜) The motel-style lodgings are stretched out amid a peaceful piñon and juniper forest. Rooms in Yavapai East are in six two-story buildings with air-conditioning, while rooms in Yavapai West are spread out in 10 single-story buildings, with vault ceilings but no air-conditioning. These are basic, clean motel rooms with tubs, showers and TVs.

Yavapai Lodge lies more than a mile from the chaos of the central village, but is within walking distance of the grocery store, post office and bank in Market Plaza.

★ El Tovar   LODGE $$$

(Map p168; ☎888-297-2757; www.grandcanyonlodges.com; r $187-305, ste $381-465; ☺year-round; P❋🛜) Stuffed mounts. Thick pine walls. Sturdy fireplaces. Is this the fanciest hotel on the South Rim or a backcountry hunting lodge? We'd say it's a charismatic mix of both. Despite renovations, this rambling 1905 wooden lodge hasn't lost a lick of its genteel historic patina, or its charm.

Standard rooms are on the small side, so those in need of elbow room should go for the deluxe. Even if you're not checking into one of the 78 rooms, swing by the hotel for its replica Remington bronzes, stained glass and exposed beams. Or simply to admire the stunning canyon views from its wide porches, cocktail in hand.

🍴 Eating & Drinking

Grand Canyon Village has all the eating options you need, whether it's picking up picnic sandwiches at Canyon Village Marketplace, an après-hike ice-cream cone at Bright Angel Fountain or a sit-down celebratory dinner at El Tovar Dining Room. Hours listed here are for the summer and may vary in slower seasons.

All South Rim bars close at 11pm, and drinks are prohibited along the rim itself.

Mather Point Cafe   PASTRIES, SANDWICHES $

(Map p168; www.bikegrandcanyon.com; 10 S Entrance Rd, Bright Angel Bicycles; mains under $10; ☺6am-8pm Apr-Nov, 7am-7pm Dec-Mar) If you're outside Grand Canyon Village and want a no-fuss breakfast or lunch, swing by the small cafe at Bright Angel Bicycles for a grab-and-go sandwich, wrap or salad. Also sells pastries, coffee and juices.

Maswik Cafeteria   CAFETERIA $

(Map p168; Maswik Lodge; mains $7-13; ☺6am-10pm) Though fairly predictable, the food encompasses a nice variety and isn't too greasy. The various food stations serve burgers, pasta, Mexican food, chili bowls and hot turkey sandwiches. Deli and grab-and-go sandwiches also available. The adjoining Maswik Pizza Pub serves beer and shows sporting events on TV.

Yavapai Cafeteria   CAFETERIA $

(Map p168; Yavapai Lodge; breakfast $4-8, lunch & dinner $3-8; ☺6am-9pm Mar–Sep, shorter hour srest of year) Next to Yavapai Lodge, this cafe has burgers, salads, hot dogs and pizzas. Closed November through February, except for holidays.

Canyon View Deli   CAFETERIA $

(Map p168; ☎928-638-2262; Market Plaza; mains $3-9; ☺7am-8pm late May–Aug, shorter hours rest of year) This counter in the grocery store is the best place in the village to find freshly-made sandwiches, hot dogs and grab-and-go meals.

Bright Angel Fountain   FAST FOOD $

(Map p168; ☎928-638-2631; Bright Angel Lodge; mains $3-5; ☺10am-7pm Apr-Sep, shorter hour srest of year) On the rim at Bright Angel Lodge, this cafeteria-style fountain serves hot dogs, sandwiches, ice cream and coffee. Cash only.

Hermits Rest Snack Bar   FAST FOOD $

(Map p162; ☎928-638-2351; Hermits Rest; mains $2-5; ☺8am-sunset late-May-Aug, 9am-5pm

Sep–mid-May) This walk-up window outside Hermits Rest is basically a human-powered vending machine, with cookies, chips, ice cream and hot chocolate. Cash only.

Bright Angel Restaurant AMERICAN $$

(Map p168; www.grandcanyonlodges.com; Bright Angel Lodge; breakfast $6-13, lunch $6-10.25, dinner $9-26; ☉6-10:45am, 11:15am-4pm & 4:30-10pm; ☖) Menu includes burgers, fajitas, salads and pasta. Families with small children gravitate here so it can get loud, and the harried staff provide the most perfunctory service of the three waitstaffed restaurants on the South Rim. Reservations not accepted. Breakfast hours are 6:30am-10:45am November to March.

The dark, windowless bar (appetizers $2.25 to $10; open 11am to 11pm) off the hallway doesn't offer much character, but it's a cozy spot for a beer and occasionally live music. Serves coffee, espresso and pastries in the morning.

★ El Tovar Dining Room & Lounge SOUTHWESTERN $$$

(Map p168; ☏928-638-2631, ext 6432; www.grandcanyonlodges.com; El Tovar, Grand Canyon Village; breakfast $9-13, lunch $11-16.25, dinner $17-34.25; ☉restaurant 6:30-10:45am & 11:15am-2pm & 4:30-10pm, lounge 11am-11pm) The setting and the food are equally superb. Dark-wood tables are set with china and white linen, eye-catching murals spotlight Native American tribes and huge windows frame views of the rim and canyon. The service is generally excellent, the menu creative, and the portions big. Breakfast options include El Tovar's pancake trio (buttermilk, blue cornmeal, and buckwheat pancakes with pine nut butter and prickly pear syrup) and blackened trout with two eggs. Lunch and dinner menus are equally creative. Reservations are required for dinner. To avoid lunchtime crowds, eat before the Grand Canyon Railway train arrives at 11:45am. The adjacent cocktail lounge is busy for afternoon cocktails and after-dinner drinks.

Arizona Room AMERICAN $$$

(Map p168; www.grandcanyonlodges.com; Bright Angel Lodge, Grand Canyon Village; lunch $8.25-12.25, dinner $8-29; ☉11:30am-3pm Mar-Oct, 4:30-10pm Mar-Dec) ✎ Antler chandeliers hang from the ceiling and picture windows overlook a small lawn, the rim walk and the canyon. Try to get on the waitlist when doors open at 4:30pm, because by 4:40pm you may have an hour's wait – reservations are not accepted. Mains include steak, chicken and fish dishes, while appetizers include such creative options as pulled pork quesadillas.

Phantom Ranch Canteen AMERICAN $$$

(Map p162; Phantom Ranch; mains $21-46; ☉breakfast 5am & 6:30am Apr-Oct, 5:30am & 7am Nov-Mar, dinner 5pm & 6:30pm) The communal meals at Phantom Ranch are fun – but not for the faint of heart. The hikers here are a hungry bunch, and they tend to eat fast. Grab the bacon when you can! Filling breakfasts and dinners are served, and sack lunches ($13) are prepared for the trail. You must make meal reservations before your descent, ideally when you reserve your accommodations.

The set dinner menu, served family-style, offers three choices: steaks, hearty stew and vegetarian chili, plus sides. The canteen is open to the public for cold lemonade and packaged snacks between 8am and 4pm (from 8:30am November to March), and for beer, wine and hot drinks from 8pm to 10pm.

🛍 Shopping

Books & More BOOKS

(Map p168; ☉8am-8pm Jun-Aug, varies rest of year) Located across the plaza from the Grand Canyon Visitor Center, Books & More has an extensive collection of books about the canyon. You'll also find canyon prints and T-shirts. The store is run by the Grand Canyon Association, which supports education and research at the park.

Canyon Village Marketplace MARKET

(Map p168; ☏928-631-2262; Market Plaza; ☉7am-9pm Jun-Aug, varies rest of year) The biggest source for supplies on either rim, this market offers everything you'd expect from your local grocery store, including a fair selection of organic items and over-the-counter medications. Prices and selection are better outside the park. Also sells hiking gear and apparel.

Desert View Marketplace MARKET

(Map p162; ☏928-638-2393; Desert View; ☉8am-sunset, varies rest of year) At the East Entrance of Grand Canyon National Park, this general store sells simple groceries and souvenirs. There's also a snack bar nearby.

ℹ Information

Almost all services on the South Rim are in Grand Canyon Village, easily accessible via the blue Village Route shuttles. On the east side of the village, **Market Plaza** includes the grocery/deli/outdoor shop Canyon Village Marketplace (p173), **Chase Bank** (☑ 928-638-2437; ☺ 9am-5pm Mon-Thu, 9am-6pm Fri) with a 24-hour ATM, and a **post office** (Map p168; ☑ 928-638-2512; ☺ 9am-4:30pm Mon-Fri, 11am-1pm Sat) where stamps are available via a vending machine from 5am to 10pm. You'll also find pay phones here (four minutes for $1). The main visitor center is Grand Canyon Visitor Center, just behind Mather Point.

Limited hours go into effect between October and March. If you have questions, NPS rangers and the people who staff the hotels, restaurants and services are typically helpful and friendly.

INTERNET ACCESS

Grand Canyon Community Library (☑ 928-638-2718; per 50min $3; ☺ 10:30am-5pm Mon-Fri; 🛜) This little brown building houses the community library and several terminals providing wi-fi and internet access, both free.

Park Headquarters Library (☺ 8am-4:30pm Mon-Fri; 🛜) At the back of the courtyard at Park Headquarters, the small library offers free internet access (when someone's staffing it) and free wi-fi (8am to 5pm daily).

TOURIST INFORMATION

Backcountry Information Center – South Rim (Map p168; ☑ 928-638-7875; www.nps.gov/grca; South Rim; ☺ 8am-noon & 1-5pm, phone staffed 1-5pm Mon-Fri) Located near Maswik Lodge, this is the place to get waitlisted for a backcountry permit if you haven't reserved one ahead of time. Also posts alerts and weather reports.

Bright Angel, Yavapai & Maswik Transportation Desks (☑ 928-638-2631, ext 6015; ☺ hours vary) In the lobbies of Bright Angel, Yavapai and Maswik Lodges, these service desks can book bus tours and same- or next-day mule trips. They can also answer questions about horseback rides, scenic flights and smooth-water float trips. Bright Angel can arrange last-minute lodgings at Phantom Ranch, if available.

Eastern Entrance Station & Desert View Information Center (Map p161; ☑ 928-638-7893; ☺ 8am-5pm Jun-Aug, from 9am rest of year) The staffed information center also offers books and maps.

El Tovar (☺ 8am-5pm) This hotel's helpful concierge can answer questions, sell stamps and arrange same- or next-day bus tours.

Grand Canyon Visitor Center (Map p168; ☑ 928-638-7888; www.nps.gov/grca; South Rim; ☺ 8am-5pm Mar-Nov, 9am-5pm Dec-Feb) Three hundred yards behind Mather Point, this is the South Rim's main visitor center, encompassing the theater and a bookstore. On the plaza here, bulletin boards and kiosks

display information about ranger programs, the weather, tours and hikes. Inside is a ranger-staffed information desk and a lecture hall, where rangers offer daily talks on a variety of subjects.

The theater here screens a 20-minute movie, *Grand Canyon: A Journey of Wonder*, on the hour and half-hour.

Verkamp's Visitor Center (Map p168; ☺ 8am-8pm Jun-Aug, shorter hours rest of year) Next to Hopi House, also features an exhibit highlighting the history of the Grand Canyon community.

❶ Getting Around

Though the park can seem overwhelming when you first arrive, it's actually quite easy to navigate, especially when you leave it to shuttle drivers. *The Guide* contains a color-coded shuttle-route map in the centerfold.

CAR

Grand Canyon Village is very congested in summer. Day-trippers should park in one of the four lots at the Grand Canyon Visitor Center, or ride the shuttle from Tusayan to the Visitor Center, then catch a shuttle into the village. If you do drive into the village and can't find parking near the rim, try the lot beside the Backcountry Information Center. Note that from March through November, cars are not allowed on Hermit Rd, which heads west from the village to Hermits Rest.

SHUTTLE

Free shuttle buses ply three routes along the South Rim. In the pre-dawn hours, shuttles run every half-hour or so and typically begin running about an hour before sunrise; check *The Guide* for current sunrise and sunset information. From early morning until after sunset, buses run every 15 minutes.

Hermits Rest Route (red) Runs west along Hermit Rd from March through November, during which time the road is closed to private vehicles.

Village Route (blue) Provides year-round transportation between the Grand Canyon Visitor Center, Market Plaza, the Backcountry Information Center, hotels, restaurants, campgrounds and parking lots.

Kaibab/Rim Route (orange) Provides service to and from the Yavapai Geology Museum, Mather Point, Grand Canyon Visitor Center, Pipe Creek Vista, South Kaibab Trailhead and Yaki Point. South Kaibab Trailhead and Yaki Point are on a spur road off Desert View Dr that is closed to cars year-round.

Hikers' Express This early-bird shuttle leaves daily from Bright Angel Lodge, stopping at the Backcountry Information Center and the Grand Canyon Visitor Center before heading to the

South Kaibab Trailhead. Check the guide for seasonal departure times.

Tusayan Route (purple) A summer-only shuttle; runs between Tusayan and the Grand Canyon Visitor Center. Stops include the IMAX Theater, Best Western Grand Canyon Squire Inn and the Grand Hotel. You must purchase a park permit prior to boarding. Park permits are for sale in Tusayan at the National Geographic Visitor Center next to the IMAX.

TAXI

Grand Canyon South Rim Taxi Service
(☑928-638-2822; ⊘24hr) Offers taxi service to and from Tusayan and within the park. Service is available 24 hours, but there are only a couple of taxis, so you may have to wait.

Tusayan

POP 558

The little town of Tusayan, situated 1 mile south of the park's South Entrance along Hwy 64, is basically a half-mile strip of hotels and restaurants. The National Geographic Visitor Center & IMAX Theater is a good place to regroup – and buy your park tickets – before arriving at the South Entrance. In summer, to avoid traffic jams and parking hassles inside the park, you can catch the Tusayan shuttle from here into the park.

⊙ Sights

National Geographic Visitor Center & IMAX Theater   VISITOR CENTER
(Map p162; ☑928-638-2468; www.explorethecanyon.com; 450 Hwy 64; adult/child $13.72/10.42; ⊘visitor center 8am-10pm Mar-Oct, 9am-8pm Nov-Feb, theater 8:30am-8:30pm Mar-Oct, 9:30am-6:30pm Nov-Feb) Hourly, on the half-hour, the IMAX theater here screens a terrific 34-minute film called *Grand Canyon – The Hidden Secrets*. With exhilarating river-running scenes and virtual-reality drops off canyon rims, the film plunges you into the history and geology of the canyon through the eyes of ancient Native Americans, John Wesley Powell and a soaring eagle. It is a safer, cheaper alternative to a canyon flyover.

🛏 Sleeping

Some of these motels offer a touch more character than you'd find at most other American roadside motels, but don't expect anything particularly memorable.

Ten-X Campground   CAMPGROUND $
(Map p162; ☑928-638-7851, 877-444-6777; www.recreation.gov; Hwy 64; RV & tent sites $10; ⊘May-

Sep) Woodsy and peaceful, this USFS campground 2 miles south of Tusayan has 70 sites and can fill up early in the summer. You'll find large sites, picnic tables, fire rings and BBQ grills (the campground host sells firewood), water and toilets, but no showers. Twenty sites are reservable up to six months in advance; the rest are are first-come, first-served. No hookups.

Seven Mile Lodge   MOTEL $
(☑928-638-2291; Hwy 64; r $99; ❄🐾) This simple, friendly motel doesn't take reservations, but you can show up as early as 9am to see if there are any vacancies; rooms are usually filled by early afternoon in the summer.

Grand Canyon Camper Village   CAMPGROUND $
(Map p162; ☑928-638-2887; www.grandcanyoncampervillage.com; 549 Camper Village Ln; tent sites $29, RV sites $46-56; 🐾) This private campground will never be called pretty, with many spots lacking shade or natural surroundings. On the plus side? There are a ton of sites as well as toilets and pay showers, and the campground is only 1 mile south of the park on Hwy 64. Full hookups are available.

Red Feather Lodge   MOTEL $$
(☑928-638-2414; www.redfeatherlodge.com; 300 Hwy 64; r $107-128; ❄@🐾🏊🐾) The Red Feather Lodge offers well-kept rooms in two buildings, as well as a laundry facilities and an outdoor pool. Built in 1997, the three-story hotel features elevators and interior doors, while the older two-story motor lodge offers outside entrances and stairs. Pets are $25 per stay.

Grand Hotel   HOTEL $$$
(Map p162; ☑928-638-3333, 888-634-7263; www.grandcanyongrandhotel.com; 149 Hwy 64; r from $259; ❄🐾🏊) The distinct Western motif in this hotel's open public spaces gives this modern hotel an old look, and it works. Relatively large, comfortable rooms are filled with pleasing Mission-style furniture and the ones in back face the woods. There's nightly live country-and-western music in the restaurant from 6pm to 9pm.

Best Western Grand Canyon Squire Inn   HOTEL $$$
(☑928-638-2681; www.grandcanyonsquire.com; 74 Hwy 64; r $189-351, ste $351; ❄@🐾🏊) The vibe is a little less personable here, but the rooms may win you back with their sharp Southwestern style. Rooms range from standard

ⓘ PARK PASSES

Park passes are available at the National Geographic Visitor Center when a ranger is on duty.

doubles in a two-story 1973 annex, sans elevator, to spacious interior rooms in the main hotel, with elevator. Amenities include a restaurant, popular sports bar, bowling alley, pool tables, fitness center, coin laundry and seasonal outdoor pool. Breakfast included.

 Eating

Considering the number of annual tourists that pass through Tusayan, the village manages to retain a sort of old-fashioned, roadside-hub pace. There's an OK variety of eateries to choose from, but as of yet no one has established a notable culinary presence.

RP's Stage Stop CAFE $
(www.rpsstagestop.com; 400 Hwy 64; breakfast under $5, lunch $3-11; ⊙7am-6pm; ⏶) The only place in Tusayan to grab an espresso drink and pick up a sandwich for your picnic lunch; also offers wi-fi.

Plaza Bonita MEXICAN $$
(www.casabonitaaz.com; 352 Hwy 64; mains $11-20; ⊙11am-10pm Sun-Thu, to 11pm Fri & Sat) This colorful spot beside Red Feather Lodge serves up messy plates of Mexican food, with burritos, enchiladas and combo platters on the menu.

We Cook Pizza & Pasta PIZZA $$
(☑928-638-2278; 605 Hwy 64; mains $10-29; ⊙11am-9pm; ⏶) This cavernous, busy pizza joint is the kind of place where you order, take a number and unceremoniously chow down at one of the big tables. The pizza isn't particularly compelling, but it's good and no-nonsense, just like its name.

Coronado Room AMERICAN $$$
(☑928-638-2681; mains $16-32; ⊙5-10pm; ⏶) The Best Western Grand Squire Inn serves the classiest cuisine around. Game such as elk and bison are on the menu, but tamer options like salmon and steak are also available.

Valle

POP 832

About 25 miles south of the park, Valle marks the intersection of Hwy 64 to Williams and Hwy 180 to Flagstaff. There isn't much to it

apart from a couple of curiosities, as well as a gas station, minimart and rooms at the **Grand Canyon Inn** (☑800-635-9203, 928-635-9203; www.grandcanyoninn.com; 317 S Hwy 64; r $130; ⊙closed early Jan-Feb; ❅⏶☀). This family-run motel offers standard rooms, a restaurant and a heated outdoor pool.

Flintstones Bedrock City AMUSEMENT PARK
(☑928-635-2600; admission $5; ⊙6am-8:30pm, hours vary seasonally) Kids and fans of camp (the kitsch kind) will love this slightly spooky, well-worn roadside attraction. Built in 1972, it features a constant loop of Flintstones episodes in the tiny concrete movie theater, a Flintmobile that circles a volcano and a clutch of Bedrock-style buildings.

Planes of Fame Air Museum MUSEUM
(☑928-635-1000; www.planesoffame.org; cnr Hwys 64 & 180; adult/child 5-12yr $7/2; ⊙9am-5pm) This air museum has a collection of over 150 vintage airplanes on display, most of them fully functional and in immaculate condition. Aviation enthusiasts will find it fascinating. There is also a state visitor center here.

Kaibab National Forest

No canyon views, but no crowds either. Divided by the Grand Canyon into two distinct ecosystems, this 1.6-million-acre **forest** (www.fs.usda.gov/kaibab) offers a peaceful escape from the park madness. Thick stands of ponderosa dominate the higher elevations, while piñon and juniper create a fragrant backdrop further down. Sightings of elk, mule, deer, turkeys, coyotes and even mountain lions and black bears are all possible.

Hwy 64/180 slices through 60 miles of forest between the South Rim and Williams, offering access to outdoor recreation at its finest. There's a ranger station in **Tusayan** (☑928-638-2443), but the best place to pick up maps and information is at the visitor center in Williams.

There are literally hundreds of miles of **hiking trails** to explore, and dogs are allowed off-leash as long as they don't bother anyone. **Mountain biking** is possible after the snowmelt, roughly between April and November. A popular, moderate ride is along the **Tusayan Bike Trail** (Map p162), actually an old logging road. The trailhead is 0.3 miles north of Tusayan on the west side of Hwy 64/180 (Fire Rd 605). It's 16 miles from the trailhead to the **Grandview Lookout Tower**, an 80ft-high fire tower with fabulous views. If you don't want to ride all that way, three interconnected loops offer 3-, 8- and 9-mile roundtrips. The Tusayan Bike Trail Trailhead and Grandview Lookout Tower are also access points for cycling on the Arizona Trail (www.aztrail.org), which connects the two points.

Apache Stables (☑928-638-2891; www.apachestables.com; Moqui Dr/Forest Service Rd 328; 1/2hr ride $49/89, wagon/trail ride $26/59; ⊙vary seasonally) offers horseback rides through the forest (no canyon views). You can also take a one-hour evening pony trek to a campfire and return by wagon or go both ways by wagon. Either way, you must bring your own food (think hot dogs and marshmallows) and drinks. The stables are about 1 mile north of Tusayan on Moqui Dr (Forest Service Rd 328) off Hwy 64/180.

Across the forest's three ranger districts – Tusayan, Williams and North Kaibab – there's free backcountry camping, also called dispersed camping. The forest also holds six developed campgrounds, including Ten X Campground.

Williams

POP 3023 / ELEV 6780FT

A pretty slow spot by day, Williams comes to life in the evening when the Grand Canyon Railway train returns with passengers from the South Rim...and then closes down again on the early side. It's a friendly town and caters to canyon tourists. Route 66 passes through the main historic district as a one-way street headed east; Railroad Ave parallels the tracks and Route 66, and heads one-way west. Williams is 35 miles west of Flagstaff on I-40 and 55 miles south of the park via Hwy 64.

◉ Sights & Activities

There are plenty of opportunities for hiking and biking in nearby Kaibab, Coconino and Prescott National Forests.

Grand Canyon Railway　HISTORIC RAILWAY
(☑depot 928-635-4253, reservations 800-843-8724; www.thetrain.com; Railway Depot, 233 N Grand Canyon Blvd; round-trip adult/child 2-15yr from $75/45; ⛟) Following a 9am **Wild West show** by the tracks, this historic train departs for its 2¼-hour ride to the South Rim. If you're only visiting the rim for the day, this is a fun and hassle-free way to travel. Once at the South Rim, you can explore by foot, shuttle or tour bus. Arrive back in Williams at 5:45pm.

Late March through October passengers can ride – and open the windows – in a 1923 open-air Pullman (adult/child $62/29).

Bearizona　WILDLIFE PARK
(☑928-635-2289; www.bearizona.com; 1500 E Rte 66; adult/child 4-12yr $20/10; ⊙8am-6pm Jun–Aug, hours vary rest of year) This awesomely named drive-through wildlife park is inhabited by indigenous North American fauna. Visitors drive themselves along a road that winds through various fenced enclosures over 160 acres, where they can see roaming gray wolves, bison, bighorn sheep and black bears up close.

Route 66 Zipline　ZIPLINE
(www.ziplineroute66.com; 200 N Grand Canyon Blvd; per person $15; ⊙10am-7pm, hours vary seasonally) This new zipline swooshes over the main downtown parking lot.

🛌 Sleeping

Camping

Free dispersed camping is allowed in the national forest provided you refrain from camping in meadows, within a quarter-mile of the highway or any surface water, or within a half-mile of any developed campground.

Three pleasant USFS campgrounds (Dog Town Lake, Kaibab Lake, White Horse Lake; open May to September) near Williams offer seasonal camping without hookups. Swimming is not allowed in any of the lakes. Contact the visitor center or the Williams Ranger Station for information.

Kaibab Lake Campground　CAMPGROUND $
(☑928-699-1239; www.recreation.gov; tent & RV sites $20-32; ⊙May-late Sep) Renovations in 2011 at this pleasant, woodsy campground included the addition of fire rings and picnic tables. It sits 4 miles northeast of Williams; take exit 165 off I-40 and go north 2 miles on Hwy 64. Offers both reservable and first-come, first-served campsites.

Circle Pines KOA　CAMPGROUND $
(☑928-635-2626, 800-562-9379; www.koa.com/campgrounds/williams; 1000 Circle Pines Rd; tents $33, RV sites $44-51, cabins $61-164, rental unit $214; ⊙Apr-Oct; 🛜🏊🎾) Amid 27 acres of ponderosa-pine forest, a half-mile north of I-40 (take exit 167), Circle Pines offers plenty of activities for children and adults alike.

Lodging

Grand Canyon Hotel   HOTEL $

(☎928-635-1419; www.thegrandcanyonhotel.com; 145 W Rte 66; hostel dm/private room $28/32, r with shared bath $70, r with private bath $75-125; ⊗Mar-Nov; ❋◉☎) This rambling European-style hotel first welcomed guests in 1891. Perched on the corner of Route 66 and S 2nd St downtown, the welcoming hotel struts its quirky stuff with themed rooms (Giraffe room, anyone?) and eclectic decor. Overnight options include a hostel-style dorm, rooms with shared baths, rooms with the bathroom en suite, and units in a separate carriage house ($165). There's air-con in interior rooms, but in the exterior rooms you can get a good breeze with the window open and ceiling fan whirring.

★ Lodge on Route 66   MOTEL $$

(☎877-563-4366, 928-635-4534; www.thelodgeonroute66.com; 200 E Rte 66; r incl breakfast $100-190, ste $155-190; ❋☎) This smart motel embraces its Route 66 and Southwest heritage with low-key style and loads of charm. Sturdy dark-wood furniture and wrought-iron accents give an elegant feel to this up-market lodging. Standard rooms are on the cramped side, with the big beds taking up most of the available space. Suites are roomier and most feature kitchenettes. Continental breakfast is served.

★ Red Garter Bed & Bakery   B&B $$

(☎928-635-1484; www.redgarter.com; 137 W Railroad Ave; d $135-160; ❋☎) Up until the 1940s, gambling and girls were the draw at this 1897 bordello-turned-B&B across from the tracks. Nowadays, the place trades on its historic charm and reputation for hauntings. Of the four restored rooms, the suite was once reserved for the house's 'best gals,' who would lean out the window to flag down customers. Rates include a 'continental-plus' breakfast with freshly-baked pastries from the on-site Red Garter Bakery. Sociable innkeeper John Holst knows the area well and is happy to get out a map.

Canyon Motel & RV Park   MOTEL $$

(☎928-635-9371; www.thecanyonmotel.com; 1900 E Rodeo Rd; tent $28, RV sites $36-39, cottages $79-85, train cars $85-172; ❋☎❄) Stone cottages and rooms in two railroad cabooses and a former Grand Canyon Railway coach car offer a quirky alternative to a standard motel. Kids love the cozy train cars, which come with all modern conveniences. Cottages feature wood floors, microwaves and refrigerators.

Grand Canyon Railway Hotel   HOTEL $$

(☎928-635-4010; www.thetrain.com; 235 N Grand Canyon Blvd; r $169-189, ste $249; ❋☎❄) This sprawling hotel caters primarily to Grand Canyon Railway passengers (railway packages also available). Rooms pop with monochromatic color schemes but don't include any flashy extras. A restaurant, lounge and coffeehouse cover the dining and drinking bases.

✖ Eating & Drinking

Grand Canyon Coffee & Café   DINER $

(☎928-635-4907; www.grandcanyoncoffeeandcafe.com; 125 W Route 66; breakfast $6-8, dinner $7-10; ⊗6am-3pm Sun-Wed, 6am-8pm Thu-Sat) If you have a hankering for cheese enchiladas with your eggs, grab a seat at this welcoming – and efficient – local spot. Sandwiches, burgers, Americanized Asian dishes, Mexican fare, diner standbys and children's favorites round out the eclectic menu.

Cafe 326   CAFE $

(www.facebook.com/Cafe326; 326 W Rte 66; breakfast under $5, lunch $5-7; ⊗6:30am-7pm; ☎) This extremely friendly cafe offers wi-fi access, pastries and breakfast sandwiches in the morning and a healthy array of salads and sandwiches at lunch – all from scratch. Also serves coffee and blended drinks.

Pine Country Restaurant   AMERICAN $

(☎928-635-9718; www.pinecountryrestaurant.com; 107 N Grand Canyon Blvd; breakfast $4-17, lunch $7-10, dinner $10-25; ⊗6am-9pm) This family restaurant offers reasonably priced American basics and gigantic pies. Though the menu offers few surprises, the price is right. Just across the street from the visitor center, it has wide windows and plenty of room to relax.

Dara Thai Cafe   THAI $

(☎928-635-2201; 145 W Rte 66, Suite C; mains $8-15; ⊗11am-2pm & 5-9pm Mon-Sat; ☑) Dara Thai offers a lighter alternative to meat-heavy menus elsewhere in town. Lots of choice for vegetarians and all dishes are prepared to your specified spiciness. Despite its address, the front door is found along S 2nd St.

Red Raven Restaurant   AMERICAN $$

(☎928-635-4980; www.redravenrestaurant.com; 135 W Rte 66; mains $10-22; ⊗11am-2pm & 5-9pm, hours vary seasonally) White tablecloths and candlelight set the mood at the family-run Red Raven, delivering the most upscale dining experience you'll find in Williams.

World Famous Sultana Bar   BAR
(☑928-635-2021; 301 W Rte 66; ☺10am-2am, shorter hours winter) Expect the once-over when you walk in, as this place seems to spook most tourists. But this 100-year-old bar is pretty darn cool, especially if you like the sort of place that's kitted out with dusty taxidermied animals and crusty locals. It was a speakeasy during prohibition. No food.

ⓘ Information

North Country HealthCare (☑928-635-4441; www.northcountryhealthcare.org/williams. htm; 301 S 7th St; ☺8am-8pm urgent care)

Police Station (☑928-635-4461; 501 W Rte 66)

Post Office (☑928-635-4572; 120 S 1st St; ☺9am-4:30pm Mon-Fri)

Visitor Center (☑928-635-1418, 800-863-0546; www.experiencewilliams.com; 200 Railroad Ave; ☺8am-5pm, to 6:30pm summer) Inside the historic train depot; offers a small museum and a bookstore with titles on the canyon, Kaibab National Forest and other areas of interest. USFS rangers are here, too.

Williams Ranger Station (☑928-635-5600; www.fs.usda.gov/kaibab; 742 S Clover Rd; ☺8am-4:30pm Mon-Fri) You'll find USFS rangers at both the visitor center and this office, which is just west of downtown and the Best Western Plus.

ⓘ Getting There & Around

Amtrak (☑800-872-7245; www.amtrak.com; 233 N Grand Canyon Blvd) Trains stop at Grand Canyon Railway Depot.

Arizona Shuttle (☑928-225-2290, 800-563-1980; www.arizonashuttle.com) Offers three shuttles a day to the canyon (per person $29) and to Flagstaff (per person $22). Save $4 reserving the Grand Canyon shuttle online.

Grand Canyon West

Havasupai Reservation

The blue-green waterfalls of Havasu Canyon are one of the Grand Canyon region's true treasures. Tucked in a hidden valley, the five stunning, spring-fed waterfalls here – and their inviting azure swimming holes – sit in the heart of the 185,000-acre Havasupai Reservation. Parts of the canyon floor, as well as the rock underneath the waterfalls and pools, are made up of limestone deposited by flowing water. These limestone deposits

are known as travertine, which gives the famous blue-green water its otherworldly hue.

Because the falls lie 10 miles below the rim, most trips are combined with a stay at either Havasupai Lodge in Supai or at the nearby campground. Supai is the only village within the Grand Canyon, situated 8 miles below the rim. The Havasupai Reservation lies south of the Colorado River and west of the park's South Rim – a three- to four-hour drive. From Hualapai Hilltop, a well-maintained trail leads to Supai, the waterfalls and the Colorado River. For detailed information on traveling into Havasu Canyon, see www.havasupai-nsn.gov.

Before heading down to Supai, you must have reservations to camp or stay in the lodge. Do not try to hike down and back in one day – not only is it dangerous, but it doesn't allow enough time to see the waterfalls.

About a mile beyond Supai are the newly formed (and as yet unofficially named) **New Navajo Falls** and **Rock Falls** and their blue pools below. These new falls developed above the original Navajo Falls, which were lost after a major flash flood in 2008 re-routed the water. After crossing two bridges, you will reach beautiful **Havasu Falls**; this waterfall drops 100ft into a sparkling blue pool surrounded by cottonwoods and is a popular swimming hole. Havasu Campground sits a quarter-mile beyond Havasu Falls. Just beyond the campground, the trail passes **Mooney Falls**, which tumbles 200ft down into another blue-green swimming hole. To get to the swimming hole, you must climb through two tunnels and descend a very steep trail – chains provide welcome handholds, but this trail is not for the faint of heart. Carefully pick your way down, keeping in mind that these falls were named for prospector DW James Mooney, who fell to his death here. After a picnic and a swim, continue about 2 miles to **Beaver Falls**. The Colorado River is 5 miles beyond. It's generally recommended that you don't attempt to hike to the river and, in fact, the reservation actively discourages this.

Entry requires payment of a $35 fee. A $5 environmental care fee is also applicable.

🛏 Sleeping & Eating

It is essential that you make reservations in advance; if you hike in without a reservation, you will not be allowed to stay in

Supai and will have to hike 8 miles back up to your car at Hualapai Hilltop.

In Supai, the **Havasupai Tribal Cafe** (☑ 928-448-2981; ⊙ 7am-6:15pm) serves breakfast, lunch and dinner daily, and the **Havasupai Trading Post** (☑ 928-448-2951; ⊙ 8am-5pm) sells basic but expensive groceries and snacks.

Havasu Campground CAMPGROUND **$**
(☑ 928-448-2180, 928-448-2141, 928-448-2121; www.havasupai.nsn.gov; Supai; per night per person $17) Two miles past Supai, the campground stretches three-quarters of a mile along the creek between Havasu and Mooney Falls. Sites have picnic tables and the campground features several composting toilets, as well as drinking water at Fern Spring. Fires are not permitted but gas stoves are allowed.

Havasupai Lodge LODGE **$$**
(☑ 928-448-2111; www.havasupai-nsn.gov; Supai; r $145; ❆) The only lodging in Supai offers motel rooms, all with canyon views, two double beds, air-conditioning and private showers. There are no TVs or telephones. Reservations are essential.

❶ Information

Havasupai Tourist Enterprise (☑ 928-448-2141, 928-448-2237; www.havasupai-nsn.gov; Supai; adult/child 6yr & under $35/free; ⊙ 5:30am-7pm) Visitors pay a per person entry fee and $5 environmental care fee when they arrive in Supai.

The local **post office** is the only one in the country still delivering its mail by mule, and mail sent from here bears a special postmark to prove it.

There's also a small **emergency clinic** (☑ 928-448-2641; ⊙ 8am-noon & 1-5pm Mon-Fri) in Supai.

Liquor, recreational drugs, pets and nude swimming are not allowed, nor are trail bikes allowed below Hualapai Hilltop.

❶ Getting There & Around

Seven miles east of Peach Springs on historic Route 66, a signed turnoff leads to the 62-mile paved road ending at Hualapai Hilltop. Here you'll find the parking area, stables and the trailhead into the canyon – but no services.

Don't let place names confuse you: Hualapai Hilltop is on the Havasupai Reservation, not the Hualapai Reservation, as one might think.

HELICOPTER
On Sunday, Monday, Thursday and Friday from late March through mid-October, a helicopter ($85 one way) shuttles between Hualapai Hilltop and Supai starting at 10am. It operates Sundays and Fridays the rest of the year. Advance reservations are not accepted; show up at the parking lot and sign up. However, service is prioritized for tribal members and those offering services and deliveries to the reservation. Call Havasupai Tourist Enterprise before you arrive to be sure the helicopter is running.

HORSE & MULE
If you don't want to hike to Supai, you can ride a horse (one-way/round-trip to lodge $80/135). You can also arrange for a packhorse or mule, for the same price, to carry your pack into and out of the canyon.

Horses and mules depart from Hualapai Hilltop. Call the lodge or campground (wherever you'll be staying) to arrange a ride and set a time.

Hualapai Reservation & Skywalk

Home to the much-hyped Skywalk, the Hualapai Reservation borders many miles of the Colorado River northeast of Kingman, covering the southwest rim of the canyon and bordering the Havasupai Reservation to the east and Lake Mead National Recreation Area to the west.

In 1988 the Hualapai Nation opened Grand Canyon West, which is *not* part of Grand Canyon National Park. Though the views here are lovely, they're not as sublime as those on the South Rim – but the unveiling of the glass bridge known as the Grand Canyon Skywalk in 2007 added a completely novel way to view the canyon.

◉ Sights & Activities

Grand Canyon West
Nowadays, the only way to visit **Grand Canyon West** (☑ 928-769-2636, 888-868-9378; www.grandcanyonwest.com; per person $44-81; ⊙ 7am-7pm Apr-Sep, 8am-5pm Oct-Mar), the section of the west rim overseen by the Hualapai Nation, is to purchase a package tour. These include a hop-on, hop-off shuttle ride which loops to scenic points along the rim. Tours can include lunch, cowboy activities at an ersatz Western town and informal Native American performances.

All but the cheapest package include admission to the **Grand Canyon Skywalk**, the horseshoe-shaped glass bridge cantilevered 4000ft above the canyon floor. Jutting out almost 70ft over the canyon, the Skywalk allows visitors to see the canyon through the glass walkway. Another stop, the unfortunately named **Guano Point**, is good for lunch, shopping and a bit of exploring, with fantastic canyon and river views.

Since would-be visitors to the Skywalk are required to purchase a package tour – and the extra-cost Skywalk is the primary draw – the experience can be a pricey prospect.

Peach Springs

The tribal capital of the Hualapai Reservation is tiny Peach Springs, also a jumping-off point for the only one-day rafting excursions on the Colorado River. Grand Canyon West is about 55 miles northwest of here via what locals have dubbed 'Buck-and-Doe-Rd.' It's beautiful, but don't even think about taking it without a 4WD.

If you plan to travel off Route 66 on the Hualapai Reservation, you need to buy a permit at the **Hualapai Office of Tourism** (☑ 928-769-2219; Hualapai Lodge; permits per person $25 plus tax) at the Hualapai Lodge. This is also where you arrange raft trips operated by **Hualapai River Runners** (☑ 928-769-2636, tourism office 928-769-2219; www.grandcanyonwest.com; adult/child $350/328; ☺ mid-Mar–Oct). Packages include transportation from the lodge to the river at Diamond Creek via a bone-jarring 22-mile track (the only road anywhere to the bottom of the canyon), the 40-mile motorized-raft trip to Pierce Ferry landing, a helicopter ride out of the canyon and the bus ride back to Peach Springs.

The modern **Hualapai Lodge** (☑ 928-769-2230; 900 Rte 66; r $109-119; ❄ ☎ ☎) is the only place to stay in Peach Springs and has a saltwater swimming pool and hot tub. The attached **Diamond Creek Restaurant** (mains $6-22; ☺ 6:30am-9pm) serves American standards. Lodging/rafting packages are available.

❶ Getting There & Around

For years, those driving to Grand Canyon West had to endure 9 miles of bumpy, unpaved road. In August 2014, those 9 miles – part of of the 21-mile Diamond Bar Rd – were finally paved. Drivers today can lighten their grip on the steering wheel and enjoy the desert scenery – which is quite pretty.

To get to Grand Canyon West from Kingman, fill up your gas tank and drive north on Hwy 93 for approximately 26 miles. Then head northeast along the paved Pierce Ferry Rd for about another 30 miles, before turning onto Diamond Bar Rd for the final 21-mile stretch. Directions from other towns are detailed on the Grand Canyon West website: www.grandcanyonwest.com.

North Rim

ELEV 8000FT

Grand Canyon National Park – North Rim

Solitude reigns supreme on the **Grand Canyon's North Rim** (www.nps.gov/grca; per vehicle $25, bike & pedestrian $12; ☺ mid-May–mid-Oct). There are no shuttles or bus tours, no museums, shopping centers, schools or garages. In fact, there isn't much of anything here beyond a classic rimside national park lodge, a campground, a motel, a general store and miles of trails carving through sunny meadows thick with wildflowers, willowy aspen and towering ponderosa pines. Amid these forested roads and trails, what you'll find is peace, room to breathe and a less fettered Grand Canyon experience.

At 8000ft, the North Rim is about 10°F (6°C) cooler than the south – even on summer evenings you'll need a sweater. The lodge and all services are closed from mid-October through mid-May. Rambo types can cross-country ski in and stay at the campground.

Park admission is valid for seven days at both rims. Upon entering, you'll be given a map and *The Guide*. The entrance to the North Rim is 24 miles south of Jacob Lake on Hwy 67. From here, it's another 20 miles to the Grand Canyon Lodge.

◉ Sights & Activities

Hiking & Backpacking

Your first hike? The short and easy paved trail to **Bright Angel Point** (0.3 miles one-way) provides an impressive introduction to the region. Beginning from the back porch of the Grand Canyon Lodge, it leads to a narrow finger of an overlook with unfettered views of the mesas, buttes, spires and temples of Bright Angel Canyon. That's the South Rim, 11 miles away, and beyond it the San Francisco Peaks near Flagstaff.

The 1.5-mile one-way **Transept Trail**, a rocky dirt path with moderate inclines, meanders north from the lodge through aspens to the North Rim Campground. The winding **Widforss Trail** follows the rim for 5 miles with views of canyon, meadows and woods, finishing at Widforss Point. To get to the trailhead, drive a quarter mile south of Cape Royal Rd on Hwy 67, then turn west onto the dirt road and drive 1 mile to the trailhead.

GRAND CANYON NORTH RIM IN...

One Day

Arrive at the rim as early as possible and get your first eyeful of the canyon from Bright Angel Point. If you didn't bring a picnic, grab a sandwich at Deli in the Pines (p184), then spend the rest of the morning hiking through meadows and aspen on the Widforss Trail. In the afternoon drive out to Point Imperial, soak up the view, then backtrack and head out on Cape Royal road. Return to Grand Canyon Lodge to relax in a rough-hewn rocker on the veranda before pointing the wheels back north.

Two Days

Follow the one-day itinerary, wrapping the day up with dinner and a good night's sleep at the Grand Canyon Lodge. On day two, hike down the North Kaibab Trail as far as Roaring Springs for a picnic with a side of stunning views. Chill your feet in a cool pool before making the trek back to the top. Don't have buns of steel? Let a mule do the walking.

The 2-mile one-way **Cape Final Trail** begins in a healthy grove of ponderosa pines and ends with incredible views of the canyon.

The steep and difficult **North Kaibab Trail** drops 14 miles to the river and is the only maintained rim-to-river trail on the North Rim. It connects with trails to the South Rim near Phantom Ranch. The trailhead is 2 miles north of Grand Canyon Lodge. There's a parking lot, but it's often full soon after daylight. A **hikers' shuttle** departs at 5:30am and 6am, but you need to sign up 24 hours in advance at the front desk of the lodge.

If you just want to get a taste of inner-canyon hiking, walk 0.75 miles down to **Coconino Overlook** or 2 miles to the **Supai Tunnel**. More ambitious day-hikers can continue another 2 miles or so to the waterfall at **Roaring Springs**, a good spot to enjoy a break. Take the short detour to the left, where you'll find picnic tables and a pool to cool your feet. Seasonal water is available mid-May to mid-October.

If you wish to continue to the river, plan on camping overnight (backcountry permit required) at Cottonwood Campground, some 2 miles beyond Roaring Springs. It's a beautiful spot with seasonal drinking water, pit toilets, a phone and a ranger station, but the 11 campsites are not shaded.

From the campground, it's a gentle downhill walk along Bright Angel Creek to the Colorado River. Phantom Ranch and the Bright Angel Campground are 7 and 7.5 miles respectively below Cottonwood.

Rangers suggest three nights as a minimum to enjoy a rim-to-river-to-rim hike, staying at Cottonwood on the first and third nights and Bright Angel on the second. Faster trips would be an endurance slog and not much fun. Hiking from the North Rim to the South Rim requires a ride on the Trans-Canyon Shuttle to get you back.

Mule Rides

Canyon Trail Rides GUIDED TOUR
(☑ 435-679-8665; www.canyonrides.com; North Rim; 1hr/half-day mule ride $40/80; ⊙ schedules vary mid-May–mid-Oct) You can make reservations anytime for the upcoming year but, unlike mule trips on the South Rim, you can usually book a trip upon your arrival at the park; just duck inside the lodge to the Mule Desk. Mule rides from the North Rim don't go into the canyon as far as the Colorado River, but the half-day trip gives a taste of life below the rim.

One Hour Rim of the Grand Canyon (minimum seven years old, 220lb weight limit; $40; departures between 8:30am and 1:30pm) Wooded ride to an overlook.

Half-Day Trip to Uncle Jim's Point (minimum 10 years old, 220lb weight limit; $80; 7:30am and 12:30pm) Follow the Ken Patrick Trail through the woods.

Half-Day Canyon Mule Trip to Supai Tunnel (minimum 10 years old, 200lb weight limit; $80; 7:30am and 12:30pm) Descend 2300ft into the canyon along the North Kaibab Trail.

Cross-Country Skiing

Once the first heavy snowfall closes Hwy 67 into the park (as early as late October or as late as January), you can cross-country ski the 45 miles to the rim. A backcountry permit is required for an overnight stay; request the permit at least two weeks in advance if you want to receive it by mail. For last minute trips, to avoid driving to the Backcountry Information Center on the South Rim for a permit, you may be able to pick one up at Pipe Springs National Monument.

In the park, you can camp at the campground (no water, pit toilets) or spend the night in the six-person **North Rim Yurt** ($10 for permit, per person $5; ☺Dec–mid-Apr). Check www.nps.gov/grca/planyourvisit/backcountry-permit.htm for details about at-large camping areas. You can ski any of the rim trails, though none are groomed. For more information call the Backcountry Information Center (p174) on the South Rim between 1pm and 5pm MST. The closest ski rental is in Flagstaff.

Scenic Drives
Driving on the North Rim involves miles of slow, twisty roads through dense stands of evergreens and aspen to get to the most spectacular overlooks. From Grand Canyon Lodge, drive north for about 3 miles, then take the signed turn east to Cape Royal and Point Imperial and continue for 5 miles to a fork in the road called the Y.

From the Y it's another 15 miles south to **Cape Royal** (7876ft) past overlooks, picnic tables and an Ancestral Puebloan site. A 0.6-mile paved path, lined with piñon, cliffrose and interpretive signs, leads from the parking lot to a natural arch and Cape Royal Point, arguably the best view from this side of the canyon.

Point Imperial, the park's highest overlook at 8803ft, is reached by following Point Imperial Rd from the Y for an easy 3 miles. Expansive views include Nankoweap Creek, the Vermilion Cliffs, the Painted Desert and the Little Colorado River.

The dirt roads to **Point Sublime** (34 miles round-trip; an appropriately named 270-degree overlook) and **Toroweap/Tuweep** (122 miles round-trip; a sheer-drop view of the Colorado River 3000ft below) are rough, require high-clearance vehicles and are not recommended for 2WDs. While they certainly offer amazing views, they require navigating treacherous roads and if your goal is absolute solitude, you might be disappointed. Camping at Tuweep now requires a backcountry permit. The dirt road to Point Sublime starts about 1 mile west of Hwy 67, 2.7 miles north of Grand Canyon Lodge (look for the Widforss Trail sign). It should take about two hours to drive the

17 miles each way. Toroweap is reached via BLM Rd 109, a rough dirt road heading south off Hwy 389, 8 miles west of Fredonia. The one-way trip is 61 miles and should take at least two hours. One-quarter of all visitors get a flat tire!

🛌 Sleeping

Accommodations on the North Rim are limited to one lodge and one campground.

If these two options are fully booked, try snagging a cabin at the **Kaibab Lodge** (☏928-638-2389; www.kaibablodge.com; Hwy 67; cabins $90-185; ☺mid-May–mid-Oct; 🕾🖥), on Hwy 67 about 6 miles north of the park entrance; it also has a restaurant. Nearby is **DeMotte Campground** (☏877-444-6777, visitor center 928-643-7298; www.recreation.gov; Hwy 67; campsite $18; ☺mid-May–mid-Oct; 🖥) with 38 primitive sites. Half are first-come, first-served. None have hookups. It usually fills up between noon and 3pm.

There's also free dispersed camping in the surrounding Kaibab National Forest. Otherwise, you'll find more options another 60 miles north in Kanab, Utah.

North Rim Campground CAMPGROUND $
(☏877-444-6777, 928-638-7814; www.recreation.gov; tent sites $18, RV sites $18-25; ☺mid-May–mid-Oct by reservation; 🖥) This campground, 1.5 miles north of the lodge, offers shaded sites on level ground blanketed in pine needles. Sites 11, 14, 15, 16 and 18 overlook the Transept (a side canyon) and cost $25. There's water, a store, a snack bar, coin-op showers and laundry facilities, but no hookups. Reservations are accepted up to six months in advance.

Grand Canyon Lodge LODGE $$
(☏advance reservations 877-386-4383, reservations outside USA 480-337-1320, same-day reservations 928-638-2611; www.grandcanyonlodgenorth.com; r $124, 2-person per cabin $132-199; ☺mid-May–mid-Oct; 🕾) Walk through the front door of Grand Canyon Lodge into the lofty sunroom and there, framed by picture windows, is the canyon in all its glory. Rooms are not in the lodge itself, but in rustic cabins sleeping up to five people. The nicest are the bright and spacious Western cabins, made of logs and buffered by trees and grass.

About 0.5 miles up the road are 40 simple motel rooms, each with a queen bed. Reserve far in advance. Add $10 to cabin price for each extra guest, although children under 16 sleep free.

PIPE SPRING NATIONAL MONUMENT

Fourteen miles southwest of Fredonia on Hwy 389, **Pipe Spring** (928-643-7105; www.nps.gov/pisp; adult/child $5/free; 7am-5pm Jun-Aug, 9am-4pm Sep-May) is quite literally an oasis in the desert. Visitors can experience the Old West amid cabins and corrals, an orchard, ponds and a garden. In summer, rangers and costumed volunteers re-enact various pioneer tasks. Tours (on the hour and half-hour) let you peek inside the stone **Winsor Castle** (tours 8am-4:30pm Jun-Aug, 9am-4pm Sep-May), and there's also a small **museum** (7am-5pm Jun-Aug, 8am-4pm Sep-May) that examines the turbulent history of local Paiutes and Mormon settlers.

Eating & Drinking

Visitors can contact the restaurants through the **North Rim Switchboard** (928-638-2612). With advance notice, preferably the day before, the Lodge Dining Room will prepare a sack lunch ($15), which includes a sandwich, fruit, chips, cookie and drink. Good option if you want to picnic on the trail.

Deli in the Pines CAFETERIA $
(lunch & dinner $7-15; 10:30am-9pm mid-May–mid-Aug, 11am-8pm Sep–mid-Oct) This small cafeteria adjacent to the lodge serves surprisingly good food, although the menu is limited to sandwiches, pizza and featured entrees.

Rough Rider Saloon BAR
(pastries $3, breakfast burritos $4.25-5.25, lunch $4-7; 5:30am-11pm) Early riser? Stop at this small saloon on the boardwalk beside the lodge for an espresso and a breakfast burrito. Starting at 11:30am, pizza and sandwiches are available. As for drinks, the saloon serves beer, wine and mixed drinks. Teddy Roosevelt memorabilia lines the walls, honoring his role in the history of the park.

This is the only bar in the lodge, so if you want to enjoy a cocktail on the sun porch or in your room, pick it up here.

★**Grand Canyon
Lodge Dining Room** AMERICAN $$
(928-638-2611, off-season 928-645-6865; www.grandcanyonlodgenorth.com; mains breakfast $6-13, lunch $10-15, dinner $13-33; 6:30-10am, 11:30am-2:30pm & 4:45-9:45pm mid-May–mid-Oct;) Although seats beside the window are wonderful, views from the dining room are so huge it really doesn't matter where you sit. While the solid dinner menu includes buffalo steak, western trout and several vegetarian options, don't expect culinary memories – the view is the thing. Make reservations in advance of your arrival to guarantee a spot for dinner (reservations are not accepted for breakfast or lunch).

**Grand Canyon Cookout
Experience** AMERICAN $$$
(928-638-2611; adult/child 6-15yr $30/15; 5:45pm Jun-Sep;) Chow down on barbecued meat, roasted chicken, skillet cornbread and beans served buffet style with a side of Western songs and cheesy jokes. A cute steam train will take you there.

Information

At the Lodge you'll find a restaurant, deli, saloon, postal window and gift shop, as well as the **North Rim Visitor Center** (928-638-7864; www.nps.gov/grca; North Rim; 8am-6pm mid-May–mid Oct, 9am-4pm end Oct). About a mile up the road, next to the campground, are laundry facilities, fee showers, a gas station, a **general store** (7am-8pm) and the **North Rim Backcountry Office** (928-638-7875, 928-638-2612; Administrative Building; walk-in 8am-noon & 1-5pm).

To contact the Grand Canyon Lodge front desk, saloon, gift shop, gas station or general store, call the North Rim Switchboard. An ATM can be found in the General Store and the Rough Rider saloon.

Getting There & Around

The only access road to the Grand Canyon North Rim is Hwy 67, which closes with the first snowfall and reopens in spring after the snowmelt (exact dates vary).

Although only 11 miles from the South Rim as the crow flies, it's a grueling 215-mile, four- to five-hour drive on winding desert roads between here and Grand Canyon Village. You can drive yourself or take the **Trans-Canyon Shuttle** (877-638-2820, 928-638-2820; www.trans-canyonshuttle.com; one-way/round-trip $85/160; mid-May–Oct), which departs from Grand Canyon Lodge at 7am daily to arrive at the South Rim at 11:30am. Reserve at least two weeks in advance.

Arizona Strip

Wedged between the Grand Canyon and Utah, the vast Arizona Strip is one of the state's most remote and sparsely populated regions. Only about 6000 people live here, in relative isolation, many of them members of the Fundamentalist Church of Latter-Day Saints (FLDS), who defy US law by practicing polygamy.

At 14,000 square miles, the region is larger than the state of Vermont. Only one major paved road – Hwy 89A – traverses the Arizona Strip. It crosses the Colorado River at Marble Canyon before getting sandwiched by the crimson-hued Vermilion Cliffs to the north and House Rock Valley to the south. Scan the skies for California condors, an endangered species reintroduced to the area. Desert scrub gives way to piñon and juniper as the highway climbs up the Kaibab Plateau to enter the Kaibab National Forest. At Jacob Lake, it meets with Hwy 67 to the Grand Canyon North Rim. Past Jacob Lake, as the road drops back down, you get stupendous views across southern Utah.

Marble Canyon & Lees Ferry

About 14 miles past the Hwy 89/89A fork, Hwy 89A crosses the Navajo Bridge over the Colorado River at Marble Canyon. Actually, there are two bridges: a modern one for motorists that opened in 1995 and a historical one from 1929. Walking across the latter, you'll enjoy fabulous views down Marble Canyon to the northeast lip of the Grand Canyon. The Navajo Bridge Interpretive Center (✆ 928-355-2319; www.nps.gov/glca; Hwy 89A; ☉ 9am-5pm late Apr-Oct) on the west bank has good background info about the bridges, as well as the area and its natural wonders. Keep an eye out for California condors!

Just past the bridge, a paved 6-mile road – and a stunning drive – veers off to the fly-fishing mecca of Lees Ferry. Sitting on a sweeping bend of the Colorado River, it's in the far southwestern corner of Glen Canyon National Recreation Area and a premier put-in spot for Grand Canyon rafters. Fishing here requires an Arizona fishing license, available at local fly shops and outfitters such as Marble Canyon Outfitters (✆ 928-645-2781; www.leesferryflyfishing.com; inside Marble Canyon Lodge, Alt 89).

Lees Ferry was named for John D Lee, the leader of the 1857 Mountain Meadows Mas-

sacre, in which 120 emigrants from Arkansas were brutally murdered by Mormon and Paiute forces. To escape prosecution, Lee moved his wives and children to this remote outpost, where they lived at the Lonely Dell Ranch and operated the only ferry service for many miles around. Lee was tracked down and executed in 1877, but the ferry service continued until the Navajo Bridge opened in 1929. You can walk around Lonely Dell Ranch and have a picnic amid the stone house and the log cabins.

On a small hill, Lees Ferry Campground (www.nps.gov/glca; tent & RV sites $12) has 54 riverview sites along with drinking water and toilets, but no hookups. With views of towering red rocks and the river, it's a strikingly pretty spot to camp. Public coin showers and a laundry are available at Marble Canyon Lodge (✆ 928-355-2225; www.marblecanyoncompany.com; Alt 89, Marble Canyon, 0.4 miles west of Navajo Bridge; s/d/apt $75/80/140; ☏), which has simple rooms.

Another option is the rustic but comfortable Lees Ferry Lodge (✆ 928-355-2231; www.vermilioncliffs.com; Hwy 89A; r $64-74, apt $90-125; P ✻ ☏), which has 10 rooms plus a restaurant and bar with 95 international beers (unless somebody finished off a few brands the night before). It's one of those bars where you're never quite sure who's going to roar off the highway and stomp through the door – but they'll surely have an interesting story.

Jacob Lake

From Marble Canyon, Hwy 89A climbs 5000ft over 40 miles to the Kaibab National Forest and the oddly lakeless outpost of Jacob Lake. All you find is a motel with a restaurant, a gas station and the USFS Kaibab

---

ℹ **NEED A LIFT?**

The main town in the Arizona Strip is postage-stamp-sized Fredonia, some 30 miles northwest of Jacob Lake. Fredonia has the Kaibab National Forest District Headquarters (✆ 928-643-7395; 430 S Main St; ☉ 8am-4:30pm Mon-Fri), where you can pick up info on hiking and camping in the forest. Fredonia also has a service station, Judd Auto Service (✆ 928-643-7726; 623 S Main St), which provides towing as well as tire repair and simple mechanical work.

Plateau Visitor Center (☎928-643-7298; cnr Hwys 89A & 67; ☺8am-4pm, mid-May–mid-Oct). From here Hwy 67 runs south for 44 miles past meadows, aspen and ponderosa pine to the Grand Canyon North Rim. The only facilities between Jacob Lake and the rim are the Kaibab Lodge, North Rim Country Store and DeMotte Campground, about 18 miles south.

Camping is free in the national forest or you can try **Jacob Lake Inn** (☎928-643-7232; www.jacoblake.com; intersection of Hwys 89A & 67, 44 miles north of North Rim; r $126-144, cabins $94-144; ☺6:30am-9pm mid-May–mid-Oct, 8am-8pm mid-Oct–mid-May; 🐾), a year-round lodging which has a range of options: no-frills cabins with tiny bathrooms (summer only), and well-worn motel rooms and spacious doubles in the modern hotel-style building. There's also a **restaurant** with an ice-cream counter and a great bakery, famed for its cookies. Try the Cookie in a Cloud, a cakey cookie topped with marshmallow and chocolate.

Kaibab Lodge Camper Village (☎928-643-7804; www.kaibabcampervillage.com; tent/RV sites $18/36; ☺mid-May–mid-Oct), a mile south of Jacob's Lake, has more than 100 sites for tents and RVs, plus one cabin-style room ($85).

Page & Glen Canyon National Recreation Area

POP 7316 / ELEV 4300FT

An enormous lake tucked into a landlocked swath of desert? You can guess how popular it is to play in the spangly waters of **Lake Powell**. Part of the **Glen Canyon National Recreation Area** (Map p420; ☎928-608-6200; www.nps.gov/glca; 7-day pass per vehicle $15, per pedestrian or cyclist $7), the country's second-largest reservoir was created by the construction of Glen Canyon Dam in 1963. To house the scores of workers an entire town was built from scratch near the dam. Now a modern town with hotels, restaurants and supermarkets, Page is a handy base for lake visitors.

Straddling the Utah–Arizona border, the 186-mile-long lake has 1960 miles of empty shoreline set amid striking red-rock formations, sharply cut canyons and dramatic desert scenery. Lake Powell is famous for its houseboating, which appeals to families and college students alike. Though hundreds of houseboats ply its waters at any given time, it's possible to explore its secluded inlets, bays, coves and beaches for days while hardly seeing anyone at all.

The gateway to Lake Powell is the small town of Page, which sits right next to Glen Canyon Dam in the far southwest corner of the recreation area. Hwy 89 (called N Lake Powell Blvd in town) forms the main strip.

Aramark (☎888-896-3829; www.lakepowell.com) runs five of the lake's six marinas, including the often frenetic **Wahweap Marina** (☎928-645-2433), 6 miles north of Page. The only other marina on the Arizona side is the much more peaceful **Antelope Point Marina** (☎928-645-5900, ext 5), which opened in 2007 on the Navajo Reservation about 8 miles east of Page. Amenities and services vary by marina. Check www.lakepowell.com for specifics. You'll find a restaurant, gift shop and water-sport rentals, from boats to water skis to kayaks, at both Wahweap and Bullfrog marinas.

◉ Sights

Antelope Canyon   CANYON
(www.navajonationparks.org) Unearthly in its beauty, Antelope Canyon is a popular slot canyon on the Navajo Reservation a few miles east of Page and open to tourists by Navajo-led tour only. Wind and water have carved sandstone into an astonishingly sensuous temple of nature where light and shadow play hide and seek. Less than a city block long (about a quarter-mile), its symphony of shapes and textures are a photographer's dream.

Lighting conditions are best around mid-morning between April and September, but the other months bring smaller crowds and a more intimate experience. Four tour companies offer trips into upper Antelope Canyon. These tours can feel a bit like a cattle call, but the uniqueness of the experience makes a visit worthwhile. The guides at **Roger Ekis' Antelope Canyon Tours** (☎928-645-9102; www.antelopecanyon.com; 22 S Lake Powell Blvd; adult/child 5-12yr from $37/27) will help you find the best photo angles during the 90-minute Sightseer's Tour. Price includes $6 tribal fee.

John Wesley Powell Museum   MUSEUM
(☎928-645-9496; www.powellmuseum.org; 64 N Lake Powell Blvd; adult/child 5-15yr $5/1; ☺9am-5pm Mon-Fri year-round, also 9am-5pm Sat Apr-Oct) In 1869, one-armed John Wesley Powell led the first Colorado River expedition through the Grand Canyon. This small museum displays memorabilia of early river runners, including a model of Powell's boat, with photos and illustrations of his excursions. Also houses the regional visitor center.

Glen Canyon Dam DAM

(☎928-608-6072; www.glencanyonnha.org; tour adult/child 7-16yr $5/2.50; ◷tours 8:30am-4pm mid-May–mid-Sep, varies rest of year) At 710ft tall, Glen Canyon Dam is the nation's second-highest concrete arch dam – Hoover Dam is only 16ft taller. Construction lasted from 1956 through 1964. From April through October, 45-minute guided tours depart from the Carl Hayden Visitor Center (p189) and descend deep inside the dam in elevators. Exhibits tell the story of the dam's construction, complete with all kinds of astounding technical facts. Three different videos spotlight various aspects of the region.

The well-stocked bookstore carries a wide range of books about the region – although you won't find Edward Abbey's dam-busting call-to-arms *The Monkey Wrench Gang*.

Rainbow Bridge National Monument PARK

(☎928-608-6200, tours 928-645-2433; www.nps.gov/rabr) On the south shore of Lake Powell, about 50 miles by water from Wahweap Marina, Rainbow Bridge is the largest natural bridge in the world, at 290ft high and 275ft wide. A sacred Navajo site, it resembles the graceful arc of a rainbow. Most visitors arrive by boat (www.lakepowell.com), with a 2-mile round-trip hike. From April through October, a 7½-hour tour departs from Wahweap Marina at 7:30am.

Experienced backpackers can drive on dirt roads to access two unmaintained trails (each 28 miles round-trip) on the Navajo Reservation. Tribal permits are required. Check with the Navajo Parks & Recreation Department (p189) for details.

🏃 Activities

Boating & Cruises

At Wahweap and Bullfrog marinas you can rent kayaks (per day $45), 19ft powerboats ($400), wakeboards ($45), water skis ($40) and other toys. Stand-Up paddleboards are available at Wahweap for $90 per day. From Wahweap Marina, Aramark runs boat cruises to Rainbow Bridge. Canyons cruises and a dinner cruise are also offered.

Hiking & Mountain Biking

If you only have time for one activity in the region, make sure it's the 1.5-mile round-trip hike to the overlook at **Horseshoe Bend**, where the river wraps around a monolithic outcropping to form a perfect U. Calling the view dramatic is an understatement – the overlook sits on sheer cliffs that drop 1000ft to the river below. Though it's short, the sandy, shadeless trail and moderate incline can be a slog. Toddlers should be secured safely in a backpack, as there are no guardrails at the viewpoint. Those with a fear of heights may want to stop at the shady overlook at the top of the hill beside the parking lot. The trailhead is south of Page off Hwy 89, just past mile marker 545.

The 8-mile **Rimview Trail**, a mix of sand, slickrock and other terrain, bypasses the town and offers views of the surrounding desert and Lake Powell. A popular starting point is behind Lake View School at the end of N Navajo Dr. It's open for hiking and bicycling; pick up a brochure at the Powell Museum.

Ask at the Carl Hayden Visitor Center at Glen Canyon Dam for information about the area's many hiking and mountain-biking trails.

🛌 Sleeping

You can camp anywhere along the Lake Powell shoreline for free, as long as you have a portable toilet or toilet facilities on your boat. There are several good mom-and-pop motels along the Avenue of Little Motels in downtown Page.

Lone Rock Beach CAMPGROUND $

(per vehicle $10; 🐾) Everyone pulls up next to the water and sets up house. This first-come, first-served campground is a popular spot with college revelers, and can be busy and loud late into the night on weekends. Escape to the dunes or the far edges of the lot if you're looking for quiet. There are bathrooms and outdoor cold showers. In Utah, just north of the state line.

Lake Powell Motel MOTEL $$

(☎928-645-3919; www.powellmotel.com; 750 S Navajo Dr; r $69-159; ◷Apr-Oct; ❉🐾) Formerly Bashful Bob's, this revamped motel was originally constructed to house Glen Canyon Dam builders. Four units have kitchens and book up quickly. A fifth smaller room is typically held for walk-ups unless specifically requested.

Comfort Inn & Suites HOTEL $$

(☎928-645-6931; www.comfortinn.com; 890 Haul Rd; r incl breakfast $180-309, ste $185-190; ❉@🌐🐾) If you're in the mood for the no-surprise conformity of a national chain hotel, this new and pleasant Comfort Inn should do just fine.

❶ HIGHWAY 89

Travelers should note that the 24-mile stretch of Hwy 89 between Page and Bitter Springs, which is just south of Lees Ferry, closed in February 2013 after a landslide buckled the road. Since August 2013, drivers headed from Page to Lees Ferry and the North Rim have been rerouted to Navajo Route 20/Coppermine Rd, which has been paved and temporarily renamed Hwy 89T. It is the most direct route to Lees Ferry until Hwy 89 is re-opened. At press time it was scheduled re-open by the summer of 2015. Visit www.azdot.gov/us89/ for the latest status.

Rooms have a low-key modern style and feel spacious, and they come with a microwave and refrigerator. On-site guest laundry.

Lake Powell Resort　　　　　RESORT $$$
(☎888-896-3829; www.lakepowell.com; 100 Lakeshore Dr; r/ste from $260/345, child under 18yr free; ❋ ❧ ≋) This bustling resort on the shores of Lake Powell offers beautiful views and a lovely little pool perched in the rocks above the lake, but it is impersonal and frenetic. Rates for lake-view rooms with tiny patios are well worth the extra money. In the lobby you can book boat tours. Wi-fi is available in the lobby and lounge only.

Pets require $20 non-refundable deposit.

✕ Eating & Drinking

Starbucks is inside the Safeway (650 Elm St).

Blue Buddha Sushi Lounge　　　SUSHI $$
(☎648-645-0007; www.bluebuddhasushi.com; 644 N Navajo; sushi $6.50-12, mains $12-33; ❧5-9pm Tue-Sat) Darn good sushi for the desert we say, and the food and drinks at this blue-hued, ultra-cool hideaway hit the spot after a hot and dusty day of exploring. Beyond sushi, there's a limited menu including teriyaki chicken and blackened tuna.

Bonkers　　　　　　　　AMERICAN $$
(☎928-645-2706; www.bonkerspageaz.com; 810 N Navajo Dr; mains $9-23; ❧4pm-close Mar-Oct) Impressive murals of local landscapes cover the walls inside this unfortunately named dinner restaurant, which serves satisfying steaks, seafood and pasta dishes. Burgers and sandwiches come with fries and a soup or salad.

Ranch House Grille　　　　　DINER $$
(www.ranchhousegrille.com; 819 N Navajo Dr; mains $7-16; ❧6am-3pm) There's not much ambience but the food is good, the portions huge and the service is fast. This is your best bet for breakfast. For lunch, get a bowl of the tasty pork chile verde. To get here from the dam, turn left off of N Lake Powell Blvd onto N Navajo Dr.

Rainbow Room　　　　　　　BAR
(☎928-645-2433; Lake Powell Resort, 100 Lake Shore Dr; ❧6-10am, 11am-2pm & 5-11pm) Perched above Lake Powell, picture windows frame dramatic red-rock formations against blue water. Your best bet is to eat elsewhere and come to the bar here for a beautiful sunset drink.

❶ Information

The Glen Canyon National Recreation Area entrance fee, good for up to seven days, is $15 per vehicle or $7 per individual entering on foot or bicycle.

EMERGENCY

National Park Service 24-Hour Dispatch Center (☎800-582-4351, 928-608-6300) On the water, use Marine Band Channel 16.

Police Station (☎928-645-2462; 808 Coppermine Rd)

MARINAS

All the marinas except Antelope Point have rangers stations, and Wahweap and Bullfrog rent boats. Check the Glen Canyon National Recreation Area newspaper for additional services at each marina. Aramark (p186) runs all the marinas except for Antelope Point, which is on Navajo land.

Antelope Point (☎928-645-5900; www.antelopepointlakepowell.com; 537 Marina Pwy) Peaceful Navajo-owned marina, 8 miles northeast of Page.

Wahweap (☎928-645-2433; www.nps.gov/glca) Frenetic place popular with shops, food, fuel, lodging and campgrounds. Offers boat and water-sport rentals, as well as tours. Six miles northwest of Page.

MEDICAL SERVICES

Page Hospital (☎928-645-2424; 501 N Navajo Dr) 24-hour emergency services.

Pharmacy (☎928-645-5714; 650 Elm St; ❧9am-8pm Mon-Fri, 9am-6pm Sat, 10am-4pm Sun) Inside the Safeway.

POST

Post Office (☎928-645-2571; 44 6th Ave; ❧7:30am-4pm Mon-Fri)

TOURIST INFORMATION

For regional information, stop by the Powell Museum (p186). In addition to the Bullfrog Visitor Center and Carl Hayden Visitor Center, there is a third GCNRA Visitor Center 39 miles southwest of Page at Navajo Bridge (p185) in Marble Canyon.

Bullfrog Visitor Center (☑435-684-7423; ⊗9am-1pm Thu-Sun Jun-Aug) On the lake's north shore, this is a drive of more than 200 miles from Page. Opening hours may vary based on personnel availability.

Carl Hayden Visitor Center (☑928-608-6404; www.nps.gov/glca; Hwy 89; ⊗8am-6pm mid-May–mid-Sep, shorter hours rest of year) A well-stocked bookstore and the best source of regional information in Page. It's located at Glen Canyon Dam on Hwy 89, 2 miles north of Page.

ⓘ Getting There & Away

Great Lakes Airlines (☑928-645-1355, 800-554-5111; www.flygreatlakes.com) offers flights between **Page Municipal Airport** (www.cityofpage.org/airport.html) and Phoenix. Page sits 125 miles northwest of the North Rim.

Car rental is available at the airport through **Avis** (☑928-645-2024, 800-331-1212; www.avis.com).

NAVAJO RESERVATION

POP 287,600

A famous Navajo poem ends with the phrase 'May I walk in beauty.' This request is easily granted at many spots on the Navajo Reservation in northeastern Arizona. At 27,000 sq miles the reservation is the country's largest, spilling over into the neighboring states of Utah, Colorado and New Mexico. Most of this land is as flat as a calm sea and just as barren, until – all of a sudden – Monument Valley's crimson red buttes rise before you or you come face-to-face with ancient history at the cliff dwellings at Canyon de Chelly and Navajo National Monuments. Elsewhere, you can walk in dinosaur tracks or gaze at the shifting light of hauntingly beautiful Antelope Canyon (p186).

While it's true that this remote northeastern corner of the state embraces some of Arizona's most photogenic and iconic landscapes, there's also evidence of the poverty, depression and alcoholism that affect Native American communities. You'll see it in rusting, ramshackle trailers, or in crumbling social services buildings in small towns, or in the paucity of stores and businesses.

Many Navajo rely on the tourist economy for survival. You can help keep their heritage alive by staying on reservation land, purchasing their crafts and trying their foods, such as the ubiquitous Navajo taco.

ⓘ Information

Unlike Arizona, the Navajo Reservation observes daylight saving time. The single best source of information for the entire reservation is the **Navajo Tourism Office** (☑928-871-6436; www.discovernavajo.com). Contact the **Navajo Parks & Recreation Department** (☑Central Office 928-871-6647, Lake Powell 928-698-2808; www.navajonationparks.org; hiking & backcountry permit $5; ⊗8am-5pm) for general information about permits for hiking ($5 per day) and camping ($5 to $15), which are required. For a list of park offices selling permits, visit www.navajonationparks.org/permits.htm.

Pick up a copy of the **Navajo Times** (www.navajotimes.com) for the latest Navajo news. Tune your radio to AM 660 KTNN for a mix of news and Native American music.

Keep in mind that due to historical and present-day problems, alcohol is illegal here.

ⓘ Getting There & Around

You really need your own wheels to properly explore this sprawling land. Gas stations are scarce and fuel prices are higher than outside the reservation.

The only public transportation is provided by the Navajo Transit System (p196), but services are geared towards local, not tourist, needs. There are currently 17 listed routes, with destinations within and outside the reservations, but not all of them are daily and some were out of service at press time. Route 1 currently runs Monday through Thursday from Tuba City to Window Rock and Fort Defiance via the Hopi Reservation.

Tuba City & Moenkopi

TUBA CITY POP 8611 / ELEV 4936FT

Hwy 160 splits these contiguous towns in two: to the northwest, Tuba City is the largest single community in the Navajo Nation, with a handful more folks than Shiprock, New Mexico. To the southeast is the village of Moenkopi, a small Hopi island surrounded by Navajo land. Moenkopi has a gas station, a new 24-hour Denny's and one of the best hotels on either reservation – but doesn't have much else.

Tuba City is named for 19th-century Hopi chief Tuve (or Toova), who welcomed a group of Mormons down from Utah to build a village of their own next to Moenkopi. The best reason to stop on this side of Hwy 160 is the Navajo cultural museum.

◉ Sights

Explore Navajo Interactive Museum
MUSEUM

(928-640-0684; www.explorenavajo.com; 10 N Main St, cnr Main St & Moenave Rd; adult/child 7-12yr/senior $9/6/7; 8am-6pm Mon-Sat, noon-6pm Sun) The Explore Navajo Interactive Museum is a perfect introductory stop for your reservation explorations and will deepen your understanding of the land, its people and their traditions. In this small museum, you'll learn why the Navajo call themselves the 'People of the Fourth World,' details about the Long Walk and aspects of contemporary life. Next door, and included in your entry fee, is a small feature about the Navajo Code Talkers, with a display explaining how the famously uncrackable code was designed.

Visits wrap up in the historic **Tuba Trading Post**, which dates to the 1880s and sells authentic Native American arts and crafts.

🛏 Sleeping & Eating

Tuba City/Moenkopi is a convenient place to stay before or after a trip through the Hopi Reservation to the east.

For a latte and wi-fi (for customers), swing by **Hogan Espresso & More** (10 Main St, cnr Main St & Moenave Rd; 7am-7pm Mon-Fri, 9am-7pm Sat & Sun;).

Moenkopi Legacy Inn & Suites HOTEL $$
(928-283-4500; www.experiencehopi.com; cnr Hwys 160 & 264; r incl breakfast $165, ste $185-205;) Open since 2010, this hotel brings a new level of luxury to town. The exterior is a stylized version of traditional Hopi village architecture, and the lobby, with a soaring ceiling supported by pine pillars, is stunning. Rooms have marble and granite baths and reproductions of historic photographs from the Hopi archives at Northern Arizona University. Ask for a room with a balcony facing the inner courtyard. The continental breakfast is hearty, with eggs, potatoes and sausage as well as oatmeal and cereal.

Quality Inn HOTEL $$
(928-283-4545; www.explorenavajo.com; 10 N Main St, at Moenave Rd; r $130-140, ste $173;) Comfortable, modern and well maintained, the Quality Inn has been a long-time stand-by, and it still holds up. Room rates include breakfast at the popular **Hogan Restaurant** (cnr Main St & Moenave Rd; mains $8-23; 6am-9pm) next door, which has an extensive menu of Southwestern, Navajo and American dishes. Smoking rooms available. Pets $10 per night.

Tuuvi Cafe NATIVE AMERICAN, AMERICAN $
(www.experiencehopi.com; junction Hwys 160 & 264, Tuuvi Travel Center; breakfast $7-8, lunch & dinner $7-13; 7am-9pm) Inside the travel center across the street from the Moenkopi Inn, this casual, welcoming Hopi eatery is a good place to refuel after a day of exploring. Look for omelets at breakfast, and burgers, fry-bread tacos and daily stews for lunch and dinner.

Navajo National Monument

The sublimely well-preserved Ancestral Puebloan cliff dwellings of Betatkin and Keet Seel are protected as the **Navajo National Monument** (928-672-2700; www.nps.gov/nava; Hwy 564; visitor center 8am-5:30pm Jun–early-Sep, 9am-5pm early-Sep–May) FREE and can only be reached on foot. It's no walk in the park, but there's truly something magical about approaching these ancient stone villages in relative solitude. The site is administered by the National Park Service, which controls access and maintains a visitor center 9 miles north of Hwy 160 at the end of paved Hwy 564. For a distant glimpse of Betatkin, follow the easy Sandal Trail about half a mile from the center. There's a free year-round campground, **Sunset View**, with 31 first-come, first-served sites and water nearby. Also free, **Canyon View** campground is open during the summer, with 17 sites.

Betatkin, which translates as 'ledge house,' is reached on one of two ranger-led hikes between June and early September: a strenuous 2.5-mile hike (one-way) departing from the visitor center daily at 8:15am or a 1.5-mile hike (one-way) on a shorter and even more strenuous trail at 10am. Carry plenty of water; it's a tough slog back up to the canyon rim.

The 8.5-mile trail (one-way) to the astonishingly beautiful **Keet Seel** is steep, strenuous and involves crossing sand gullies and shallow streams, but it's well worth the effort. The trail is open from late May to early September and requires a backcountry permit reservable beginning in early February. Call early since daily access is limited to 20 people; alternatively show up early on the day

WINDOW ROCK

The tribal capital of Window Rock sits at the intersection of Hwys 264 and 12, near the New Mexico border. The namesake rock is a nearly circular arch high up on a red sandstone cliff in the northern part of town. At its base is the **Navajo Veterans Memorial Park** (📞928-871-6647; www.navajonationparks.org/htm/veterans.htm; ⊙8am-7pm) **FREE**, whose layout is patterned after a medicine wheel. A statue memorializes the Navajo Code Talkers, and 16 steel bayonets honor soldiers killed in action.

The sleek and modern **Navajo Nation Museum** (📞928-871-7941; cnr Hwy 264 & Loop Rd; admission by donation; ⊙8am-5pm Mon, 8am-6pm Tue-Fri, 9am-5pm Sat) looks more imposing and interesting than it really is, with temporary shows that are hit or miss. For an unusual experience, step into the small outdoor amphitheater beside the entrance and plant yourself at the intersection of the two indented lines on the central platform. Then speak aloud. As noted in Sam Lowe's *Arizona Curiosities*, it will sound like your voice is echoing just outside your head. Step away, and the effect disappears. How to explain it? We don't know, but this **audible vortex** is kind of cool.

For a superb selection of Navajo jewelry and crafts, swing by **Navajo Arts & Crafts Enterprise** (NACE; 📞928-871-4090; Hwy 264 at Rte 12; ⊙9am-8pm Mon-Sat, noon-6pm Sun) next to the Quality Inn. Established in 1941, NACE is wholly Navajo operated and guarantees the authenticity and quality of its products.

The **Navajo Nation Fair** (www.navajonationfair.com) held in early September is a week-long blowout with rodeos, the Miss Navajo Nation pageant, song and dance, horticulture shows, horse races, a fry bread contest and lots of other events.

Rooms at the **Quality Inn Navajo Nation Capital** (📞928-871-4108; www.qualityinn.com; 48 W Hwy 264; r incl breakfast $89-99; ❄@🛜🐾) are nothing fancy, but we liked the Southwestern motif. The hotel's biggest asset, though, is the falling-over-backwards staff. Rates include a filling breakfast in the reasonably priced restaurant serving Navajo, American and Mexican fare all day long.

and hope for cancellations. You hike on your own but are met at the pueblo by a ranger who will take you on a tour. Because the hike is strenuous, most visitors stay at the primitive campground down in the canyon, which has composting toilets but no drinking water. Check the park website for more details.

During summer months the park observes daylight saving time.

Kayenta

POP 5132 / ELEV 5641FT

A top contender for stray-dog capital of Arizona, Kayenta is a cluster of businesses and mobile homes around the junction of Hwys 160 and 163. It's only draw is being the closest town to Monument Valley, some 20 miles away. It has gas stations, motels, restaurants, a supermarket and an ATM.

The Burger King near the junction has a well-meaning but minimal exhibit on the Navajo Code Talkers. **Roland's Navajoland Tours** (📞928-697-3524) and **Sacred Monument Tours** (📞435-727-3218; www.monumentvalley.net) offer vehicle, hiking and

horseback-riding tours through Monument Valley.

🛏 Sleeping

A dearth of options sends prices sky-high in summer when demand at the three main motels exceeds capacity. Rates drop by nearly half in the slower seasons. Several fast food restaurants line Hwy 160.

Hampton Inn   HOTEL **$$**
(📞928-697-3170; www.hamptoninn.com; Hwy 160; r incl breakfast from $199; ❄🛜🐾) The decor is Native American, and there's an outdoor pool perfect for chilling out in after a day on the dusty roads. For weekends in summer, book well in advance. Kids under 18 stay free and pets are $20 per night.

Wetherill Inn   MOTEL **$$**
(📞928-697-3231; www.wetherill-inn.com; 1000 Main St/Hwy 163; r incl breakfast $140; ❄@🛜) This motel has 54 standard-issue rooms hued in appealing earth tones. All have refrigerators and flat-screen TVs. Other amenities include an indoor pool and a laundry.

Monument Valley Navajo Tribal Park

Like a classic movie star, Monument Valley has a face known around the world. Her fiery red spindles, sheer-walled mesas and grand buttes have starred in films and commercials, and have been featured in magazine ads. Monument Valley's epic beauty is heightened by the drab landscape surrounding it. One minute you're in the middle of sand, rocks and infinite sky, then suddenly you're transported to a fantasyland of crimson sandstone towers soaring up to 1200ft skyward.

Long before the land became part of the Navajo Reservation, the valley was home to Ancestral Puebloans, who abruptly abandoned the site some 700 years ago. When the Navajo arrived a few centuries ago, they called it Valley Between the Rocks. Today, Monument Valley straddles the Arizona-Utah border and is traversed by Hwy 163.

The most famous formations are conveniently visible from the rough 17-mile dirt road looping through **Monument Valley Navajo Tribal Park** (☑ 435-727-5874; www. navajonationparks.org; per 4-person vehicle $20; ☺ drive 6am-8:30pm May-Sep, 8am-4:30pm Oct-Apr; visitor center 6am-8pm May-Sep, 8am-5pm Oct-Apr). It's usually possible to drive the loop in your own vehicle, even standard passenger cars, but expect a dusty, bumpy ride. There are multiple overlooks where you can get out and snap away or browse for trinkets and jewelry offered by Navajo vendors. Most of the formations were named for what they look like: the Mittens, Eagle Rock, Bear and Rabbit, and Elephant Butte.

Budget at least 1½ hours for the drive, which starts from the visitor center parking lot at the end of a 4-mile paved road off Hwy 163. There's also a restaurant, gift shop, small museum, tour desk and the View Hotel. National Park passes are not accepted for admission into the park.

The only way to get off the road and into the backcountry is by taking a Navajo-led tour on foot, on horseback or by vehicle. You'll see rock art, natural arches, and coves such as the otherworldly Ear of the Wind, a bowl-shaped wall with a nearly circular opening at the top. Guides shower you with details about life on the reservation, movie trivia and whatever else comes to mind. Guides have booths set up in the parking lot at the visitor center; they're pretty easygoing, so don't worry about high-pressure sales. Tours leave frequently in summer, less so in winter, with rates from $55 for a 90-minute motorized trip. Outfitters in Kayenta and at Goulding's Lodge also offer tours. If you want to set things up in advance, check out the list of guides on the tribal park's website (www.navajonationparks.org).

The only hiking trail you are allowed to take without a guide is the **Wildcat Trail**, a 3.2-mile loop trail around the West Mitten formation. The trailhead is at the picnic area, about a half-mile north of the visitor center.

🛏 Sleeping & Eating

Goulding's Camp Park   CAMPGROUND **$**
(☑ 435-727-3235; www.gouldings.com; tent sites $26, RV sites $26-45, cabins $92; ☉ ☒) Tucked snugly between red sandstone walls with a shot of the Mittens from the mouth of the canyon, this is a scenic full-service campground that includes a store, pool and hot showers. The three pre-fab cabins have air conditioning, wi-fi and bathrooms and can sleep up to six people (if some of them are small).

Monument Valley Campground   CAMPGROUND **$**
(☑ 435-727-5802; www.monumentvalleyview.com/campground; tent/RV sites $20/40) This new campground on the Navajo Reservation is located about ¼ mile southwest of the View Hotel. Restrooms and showers are available. Cabins with bathrooms can also be rented (from $175 per night). At press time the campground had just re-opened. Prices may change.

★ View Hotel   HOTEL **$$$**
(☑ 435-727-5555; www.monumentvalleyview.com; Hwy 163; r/ste from $209/299; ☒ @ ☉) You'll never turn-on the TV, at least not during the day, at this aptly named hotel. The Southwestern-themed rooms are nice but nothing compared to the show you can see from the balconies. Rooms that end in numbers higher than 15 (eg 216) have unobstructed panoramas of the valley below; the best are on the 3rd floor (these cost $20 more).

The restaurant (mains $9 to $14) serves three OK meals a day in a dining room with floor-to-ceiling windows and an outdoor patio. Wi-fi available in the lobby only.

Goulding's Lodge   MOTEL **$$$**
(☑435-727-3231; www.gouldings.com; r $205-242; ❄️📶💺🐾) This historic hotel a few miles west of Monument Valley has 62 modern rooms, most with views of the megaliths in the distance. The style is standard Southwestern, and each has a DVD player so you can watch one of the movies shot here, available for rent ($5) in the lobby. Rooms also have a refrigerator. Pets cost $20 per pet per night.

The hotel's Stagecoach Dining Room (mains $9 to $27) is a replica of a film set built for John Ford's 1949 Western *She Wore a Yellow Ribbon*. Get some roughage from the salad bar before cutting into the steaks or popular Navajo tacos.

Canyon de Chelly National Monument

Beautiful and noticeably quiet, the remote and multipronged Canyon de Chelly (pronounced d-*shay*) feels far removed from time and space. Inhabited for 5000 years, it shelters prehistoric rock art and 1000-year-old Ancestral Puebloan dwellings built into alcoves.

Today, **Canyon de Chelly** (☑928-674-5500; www.nps.gov/cach; Chinle; ⊙visitor center 8am-5pm) **FREE** is private Navajo land administered by the NPS. The name itself is a corruption of the Navajo word *tsegi*, which means 'rock canyon.' The Navajo arrived in the canyon in the 1700s, using it for farming and as a stronghold and retreat for their raids on other tribes and Spanish settlers. But if these cliffs could talk, they'd also tell stories of great violence and tragedy. In 1805, Spanish soldiers killed scores of Navajo hiding deep in the canyon in what is now called Massacre Cave. In 1864, the US Army – led by Kit Carson – drove thousands of Navajos into the canyon and starved them into surrendering, then forced the survivors to march 300 miles – the Long Walk – to Fort Sumner in New Mexico. Four years later, the Navajos were allowed to return.

Today about 40 to 50 large Navajo families still raise animals and grow corn, squash and beans on the land, allowing a glimpse of traditional life. While visiting, you may see a small structure made of logs, with a door facing east. Called hogans, these are Navajo dwellings. Only enter hogans with a guide. Don't take photographs of people, their homes or property without permission.

The visitor center is about 3 miles east of Chinle, where services include a gas station, supermarket, bank with ATM, motels and fast-food outlets.

◎ Sights & Activities

If you only have time for one trip, make it the **South Rim Drive**, which runs along the main canyon and has the most dramatic vistas. The 16-mile road passes six viewpoints before dead-ending at the spectacular **Spider Rock Overlook**, with views of the 800ft freestanding tower atop of which lives Spider Woman, an important Navajo god. Start early so that you have Spider Woman all to yourself; the silence here is strangely invigorating as you watch birds soaring between you and the majestic spire. It's easy to see why this is a sacred spot for the Navajo. Budget about two hours for the round-trip, including stops.

For the most part, **North Rim Drive** follows a side canyon called Canyon del Muerto, which has four overlooks. At the first one, **Antelope House Overlook**, you'll have stunning cliff-top views of a natural rock fortress and cliff dwellings. To see the latter, walk to your right from the walled Navajo fortress viewpoint to a second walled overlook. With few walls and no railings, this stop may not be suited for small children or pets. The North Rim Drive ends at the Massacre Cave Overlook, 15 miles from the visitor center. The road continues 13 miles to the town of **Tsaile** (say-*lee*), where Diné College has an excellent museum, as well as a library and bookstore with a vast selection of books about the Navajo.

Bring binoculars and water, lock your car and don't leave valuables in sight when taking the short walks at each scenic point. The lighting for photography on the North Rim is best in early morning and on the South Rim in late afternoon.

☞ Tours

Entering the canyon maze is an amazing experience, as walls start at just a few feet but rise dramatically, topping out at about 1000ft. At many stops, Navajo vendors sell jewelry and crafts, usually at prices much lower than at the trading posts. Summer tours can get stifling hot and mosquitoes are plentiful, so bring a hat, sunscreen, water and insect repellent. Tour guides offer vehicle, hiking and horseback tours into the canyon. For a list of approved guides, stop by the visitor center or check the park's website at www.nps.gov/cach/planyourvisit.

For a vehicle tour, expect to pay $175 to $200 for a three-hour trip for between one and three people.

Hiking

With one exception, you need a guide in order to hike anywhere in the canyon. A link to authorized guides can be found on the park website. You can also pick up the list at the park visitor center. A backcountry permit (free) is required. Expect to pay a guide about $25 to $40 per hour with a three-hour minimum. Rangers sometimes lead hikes in summer.

Otherwise, the steep and stunning White House Trail is your only option. Narrow switchbacks drop 550ft down from the White House Overlook on the South Rim Drive, about 6 miles east of the visitor center. It's only 1.25 miles to the stupendous White House Ruin, but coming back up is strenuous, so carry plenty of water and allow at least two hours. In summer, start out early or late in the day to avoid the worst of the heat.

🛏 Sleeping & Eating

Lodging near the canyon is limited and often booked solid in summer, so plan ahead.

Hotels & Motels

Best Western Canyon de Chelly Inn MOTEL $
(📞928-674-5874; www.bestwestern.com; 100 Main St, Chinle; r $90-100; ✳@🛜✳) In Chinle but still close to the canyon, this two-story property has an indoor pool and sauna. Rooms are slightly larger than average, if a bit uninspired and dark. The on-site Junction Restaurant serves mediocre Native American and American dishes. The restaurant also shares its menu and dining room with a Pizza Hut.

Sacred Canyon Lodge MOTEL $$
(📞800-679-2473; www.sacredcanyonlodge.com; r $99-109, ste $169; ✳@🛜✳) Formerly Thunderbird Lodge, this Navajo-owned property is the only lodging in the park. The ranch-style buildings house 70 comfortable rooms, with wood beams and chunky wood furniture. An inexpensive cafeteria serves Navajo and American meals ($5 to $17). Wi-fi is best in the rooms near the lobby.

Campgrounds

Cottonwood Campground CAMPGROUND $
(📞928-674-2106; campsite $14; ✳) Near the visitor center, this Navajo-run campground has 93 primitive sites on a first-come, first-served basis. Water is available from April to October, and there are restrooms but no hookups or showers. Fewer sites available November to March. Grills and picnic table available; no hookups. Cash only.

Spider Rock Campground CAMPGROUND $
(📞928-781-2016, 928-674-8261; www.spiderrock-campground.com; tent/RV sites $11/16, hogans $31-47; ✳) This Navajo-run campground 12 miles from the visitor center on South Rim Dr is surrounded by piñon and juniper trees. No tent? Rent one for $9 or spend the night in a hogan. Solar-heated showers $3. No credit cards.

ℹ Information

En route to the canyon you'll pass the **visitor center** (📞928-674-5500; www.nps.gov/cach; ⏰8am-5pm), which has information about guides and tours. Scenic drives skirting the canyon's northern and southern rim start nearby. Both are open year-round and, aside from one hiking trail, they are the only way to see the canyon without joining a guided tour.

Ganado & Hubbell Trading Post

Widely respected merchant John Lorenzo Hubbell established this **trading post** (📞928-755-3475; www.nps.gov/hutr; ⏰visitor center 8am-5pm, trading post 8am-8pm late Apr-Oct) FREE in 1878 to supply Navajos returning from Fort Sumner with dry goods and groceries. Now run by the NPS, it still sells food, souvenirs and local crafts. Navajo women often give weaving demonstrations inside the visitor center. Hubbell himself was an avid collector of these woolen artworks as you'll discover on a tour of his house (adult/child $2/free), given at 10am, 11am, 1pm, 2pm and 3pm.

The post is in the village of Ganado, about 30 miles south of Chinle/Canyon de Chelly and 40 miles north of the I-40.

HOPI RESERVATION

POP 9500

Scattered across the tops of three rocky, buff-colored mesas and along the valleys below are the villages of the Peaceful Ones, which is what the Hopi call themselves. Their reservation – at the heart of their ancestral territory, though only containing a scant fraction of it – is like a 2410-sq-mile island floating in the Navajo Reservation. To the Hopi, Arizona's oldest and most traditional tribe, this remote terrain is not merely their homeland but also the hub of their spiritual world.

Deeply ingrained in the Hopi way is an ethic of welcoming strangers – they were even nice (for a long time, anyway) to Spanish conquistadors and missionaries. But decades of cultural abuses by visitors, even well-intentioned ones, have led Hopi villages to issue strict guidelines to protect their world. This is not just a matter of cultural survival, it's also about defending what is most deeply sacred to them.

Because of their isolated location, the Hopi have received less outside influence than other tribes and have limited tourist facilities. Aside from ancient Walpi on First Mesa, villages don't hold much intrinsic appeal for visitors. But a tour of the mesas with a knowledgeable guide can open the door to what's truly fascinating about this place: the people, their history and their traditions, which still thrive today. The Hopi are also extremely accomplished artists and craftspeople and it's well worth stopping at several shops along the main highway to peruse handmade baskets, kachina dolls, overlay silver jewelry and pottery. The new **Hopi Arts Trail** (www.hopiartstrail.com) introduces visitors to Hopi arts and crafts, and a list of artists and galleries can be found on its website.

Eleven of the 12 Hopi villages lie at the base or on the top of three mesas named by early European explorers, rather prosaically, First Mesa, Second Mesa and Third Mesa. They are linked by Hwy 264 along with the non-Hopi village of Keams Canyon. Narrow and often steep roads lead off the highway to the mesa tops. The 12th village is Moenkopi, about 45 miles to the west, near Tuba City.

For an eclectically refreshing mix of background music, from Native American music to Cajun to blues to honky-tonk, turn your radio dial to KUYI 88.1, Hopi's radio station.

For more details about the villages and tourism on the reservation, visit www.experiencehopi.com. If you're the type of traveler that likes to barge around discovering things on your own, dial it down a notch here, and please join a tour if you want to explore beyond the highway and the Hopi Arts Trail. Sketching, videotaping, photography and audio recording are not permitted.

◉ Sights

◉ First Mesa

Three villages sit atop this mesa and another village, nontraditional Polacca, hugs its base. To explore the mesa-top villages, stop by the **First Mesa Consolidated Visitor Center** (☏ 928-737-2670; www.experiencehopi.com; Polacca; tour adult/child 17yr & under $20/15; ⊗ 8-11am & 1-4pm Mon-Sat Jun-Aug, 9-11am & 1-3pm Mon-Sat Sep-May) in Polacca to join a tour. Once on the mesa, the first village is **Hano**, which blends imperceptibly into **Sichomovi**. The most dramatic of the the three Hopi enclaves is **Walpi**, which dates back to AD 900 and clings like an aerie onto the mesa's narrow end. Sandstone-colored stone houses seem to sprout organically from the cliffs. The last inhabitants, a few older ladies who lived without plumbing or electricity, have left but the homes are still used by families during ceremonies atop the mesa. Arts and crafts sold by local artisans may be available for purchase during your tour.

It's best to call before visiting to confirm timing and availability of tours, which may not run if there are private rituals scheduled on a particular day. First Mesa ceremonial dances are not open to the public. Driving west on Hwy 264, turn right at the stop sign at mile marker 390.8 and drive a quarter mile. The visitor center is just left of the post office.

◉ Second Mesa

On Second Mesa, some 10 miles west of First Mesa, the **Hopi Cultural Center Restaurant & Inn** (☏ 928-734-2401; www.hopiculturalcenter.com; Hwy 264; r $95-105, meals $7-16; ⊗ restaurant 7am-9pm summer, until 8pm winter) is the most developed visitor area, providing food and lodging. There's also the small **Hopi Museum** (☏ 928-734-6650; adult/child 12yr & under $3/1; ⊗ 8am-5pm Mon-Fri, 9am-3pm Sat), with walls full of historic photographs and simple exhibits that share just enough about the Hopi world to allow you to understand that it's something altogether different from the one you likely inhabit. The diorama of Walpi is also interesting.

Second Mesa has three villages; the oldest, **Shungopavi**, is famous for its Snake dances, when dancers carry live rattlesnakes in their mouths. **Mishongnovi** and **Sipaulovi** sometimes have Social or Butterfly dances open to the public. Call the cultural center to check dates.

Third Mesa

The tribal capital of **Kykotsmovi** sits below Third Mesa with **Batavi**, **Hotevila** and **Old Oraibi** up on top. Old Oraibi was established around AD 1200 and vies with Acoma Pueblo in New Mexico for the title of the USA's oldest continuously inhabited village. To visit Old Oraibi, park next to **Hamana So-O's Arts and Crafts** (☑ 928-734-9375) and stick your head inside to say hi and let someone know you're going to walk around. The shop itself has some great locally carved kachinas. Visitors may check out the other villages on their own, but this is not encouraged by the tribe. Use a certified guide if you want to explore beyond the galleries and shops on the Hopi Arts Trail.

☞ Tours

When visiting Hopi country, the tour is the thing. So little about the place or the culture is obvious, even to the most astute outside eye, that visiting the villages with a knowledgeable local guide is really the only way to get a glimpse inside. There is a list of authorized guides at www.experiencehopi.com. Some guides include a trip to nearby Dawa Park, where thousands of ancient petroglyphs are etched into the rocks. **Hopi Tours** (☑ 928-206-7433; www.hopitours.com) are led by Micah Loma'omvaya, a member of the Bear Clan from Shungopavi and an experienced anthropologist and former tribal archaeologist. His engaging tours blend a trove of historical fact with the personal understanding of the Hopi world that comes from living in it. Bertram Tsavadawa of **Ancient Pathways** (☑ 928-797-8145; www.experiencehopi.com) and Gary Tso of **Left-Handed Hunter Tour Company** (☑ 928-734-2567; www.experiencehopi.com) are also recommended. Prices depend on tour length and group size.

✿ Festivals & Events

Each village decides whether to allow non-Hopis at ceremonial dances. Some of the kachina dances, held between January and July, are closed affairs, as are the famous Snake or Flute dances in August. It's much easier to attend Social dances and Butterfly dances, held late August through November. For upcoming festivities, call the visitor center at the Hopi Cultural Center atop Second Mesa a few days before your visit or ask when you are visiting. Not all public ceremonies are scheduled on a long-term calendar, and you may only hear about one by word of mouth.

🛏 Sleeping & Eating

The only hotel on the mesas is part of the Hopi Cultural Center (p195). Reservations are essential, especially in summer when its 33 modern, if bland, rooms usually book out. The Moenkopi Inn (p190) is about 60 miles west in Moenkopi, beside Tuba City. The Hopi Cultural Center restaurant is your chance to taste Hopi treats like *noqkwivi* (lamb and hominy stew) served with blue-corn fry bread. Less adventurous palates will find the usual American fare – burgers and grilled chicken.

ℹ Information

Make your first stop the Hopi Cultural Center on Second Mesa to pick up information and get oriented. Each village has its own rules for visitors, which are usually posted along the highways, but generally speaking any form of recording, be it camera, video or audiotape, or even sketching, is strictly forbidden. This is partly for religious reasons but also to prevent commercial exploitation by non-Hopis. Alcohol and other drug use is also prohibited.

As with the rest of Arizona (but different from the surrounding Navajo Reservation), the Hopi Reservation does not observe daylight saving time in summer. The climate is harsh – ungodly hot in summer and freezing cold in winter – so come prepared either way.

Hopi prefer cash for most transactions. There's an ATM outside the one store in Polacca. There's a **hospital** (☑ 928-737-6000; Hwy 264, mile marker 388, Polacca) with 24-hour emergency care in Polacca. For emergencies or police issues call the **BIA police** (☑ 928-738-2236, 928-738-2233).

ℹ Getting There & Away

The Hopi mesas are about 50 miles east of Tuba City and 85 miles west of Window Rock via flat and largely uneventful Hwy 264. Three roads enter the reservation from I-40 in the south. Coming from Flagstaff, the closest approach is by heading east on I-10 to Winslow, then cutting north on Hwy 87 (130 miles). From Winslow it's 70 miles via Hwy 87, and from Holbrook 80 miles on Hwy 77. Buses operated by **Navajo Transit System** (☑ 928-729-4002, 866-243-6260; www.navajotransit.com; fare $2) pass through Monday through Thursday between Tuba City and Window Rock.

WESTERN ARIZONA

The western border of Arizona lies along the Colorado River, which stretches south from the Hoover Dam all the way to Yuma and Mexico. Savvy marketers have dubbed this region the 'West Coast.' The famous Hoover Dam is one of a series of mega-dams that regulate the flow of the river after it emerges from the Grand Canyon. In winter, migratory flocks of birds arrive from frigid northern climes seeking out riverside wildlife refuges. At the same time, two-legged 'snowbirds' pack dozens of dusty RV parks, especially in Yuma. Although summers are hellishly hot, the cool Colorado brings in scores of water rats and boaters seeking relief from the heat in such places as Lake Havasu and Laughlin.

Bullhead City & Laughlin

BULLHEAD CITY POP 39,571 / ELEV 554FT

Named for a rock that resembled the head of a snoozing bull, Bullhead City began as a construction camp for Davis Dam, built in the 1940s. The rock was eventually submerged by Lake Mojave, but the town stuck around and survives today, primarily because of the casinos across the Colorado River in Laughlin, Nevada.

And location makes all the difference. Laughlin has more sizzle than Bullhead City and is known by a number of nicknames: 'Vegas on the cheap,' the 'un-Vegas,' the 'anti-Sin City.' It's all just fine by this gambling town, founded in 1964 by gaming impresario Don Laughlin, a high-school dropout from Minnesota. The image of good, clean fun (no leggy showgirls, no sleazy types touting escort services) is a winner with the blue-haired set and, increasingly, families looking for an inexpensive getaway.

If casinos aren't your thing, check out the hiking and biking trails in the brand-new **Colorado River Heritage Greenway Park & Trails** (www.clarkcountynv.gov; ☉6am-11pm) in Laughlin. You'll find parking and an information kiosk at the Bridge Trailhead, which is on the west side of Casino Dr, just north of Riverside Resort. This recreation area is also known as North Reach.

Skip either town in summer when temperatures often soar to a merciless 120°F (almost 50°C).

🛏 Sleeping

Laughlin's big hotel-casinos are a fantastic value, with spacious doubles starting around $40 during midweek and $70 on weekends. Some may charge for wi-fi since they'd rather have you downstairs pulling slots. All are on Casino Dr, which parallels the river.

Golden Nugget HOTEL $
(☎702-298-7111; www.goldennugget.com/laughlin; 2300 S Casino Dr; r $80-90; 🅿@🛜🏊) This cool and inviting place is the casino on which Vegas mogul Steve Wynn cut his teeth back in 1989. The latest owners of this 300-room 'boutique casino' have sunk big bucks into creating an intimate but classy experience with tropical-themed rooms, a palm-tree-flanked riverfront pool and above-average eateries. Rooms can drop as low as $37 during the week.

Davis Camp Park CAMPGROUND $
(☎928-754-7250; www.mcparks.com; 2251 Hwy 68; tent $17, RV site $25-30, vacation home from $80; 🛜🏊) If you're traveling with kids and don't want to stay in a Laughlin casino, give serious consideration to this Mojave County Park, which sits on a pretty stretch of the Colorado River not far from the action. You can camp right beside the river or rent a small vacation home. Restrooms, showers, laundry and full hookups are also available. It's $2 per pet per night. Wi-fi is $5 per day.

Aquarius Casino Resort HOTEL $$
(☎702-298-5111; www.aquariuscasinoresort.com; 1900 S Casino Dr, Laughlin; r $75-120, ste $215-335; 🅿@🛜🏊) The Aquarius hits the jackpot: chic, welcoming and budget friendly. The lobby has art deco touches, while rooms are modern with big windows and flat-screen TVs. The Splash Cabaret has free entertainment on Friday and Saturday nights, and the pool and tennis court area is up on a rooftop mezzanine. Wi-fi is $12 per day or free at the coffee shop.

🍴 Eating & Drinking

All casinos feature multiple restaurants, usually including a buffet, a 24-hour cafe and an upscale steak house, along with bars and lounges. The weekly *Entertainer* magazine lists upcoming concerts and shows.

Earl's Home Cookin' at the Castle AMERICAN $
(☎928-754-1118; 491 Long Ave, Bullhead City; $3.25-12; ☉7am-9pm) Folks are friendly inside this turreted mock-castle in Old Bullhead, where the food sure tastes good and the $5.49 breakfast specials are a deal. Children's menu options under $6.

Saltgrass Steakhouse
STEAK $$$

(☎702-298-7153; www.saltgrass.com; 2300 S Casino Dr, Laughlin; mains $11-35; ☺4-10pm Mon-Thu, 4-11pm Fri, noon-11pm Sat, noon-10pm Sun) Feeling carnivorous? Succumb to your cravings at this river-view, Wild West–themed restaurant at the Golden Nugget. The savory cuts of Angus beef are the way to go, but chargrilled chicken and fish also put in menu appearances.

Loser's Lounge
BAR

(☎702-298-2535; 1650 S Casino Dr, Laughlin; ☺7pm-late) Pictures of General Custer, Robert E Lee and other famous 'losers' decorate the walls at this bar and dance-club fixture at the Riverside Resort. Live bands play Top 40 music nightly starting at 9pm.

The Hideout
BAR

(www.hideoutlaughlin.com; 2311 S Casino Dr, Laughlin; ☺24hr) The bar is always open at the Hideout, a convenient place to escape the bling and glitz of the casinos. You can also catch a game on one of eight TV screens. The bar is on the 2nd floor of a small strip mall across from the Pioneer Hotel & Casino.

ℹ Information

Remember, Nevada time is one hour behind Arizona in winter, but in the same time zone in summer (Arizona doesn't observe daylight saving time). Pick up copies of the *Entertainer*, a weekly guide to the Laughlin casino scene, at the visitor centers.

Bullhead Area Chamber of Commerce
(☎928-754-4121; www.bullheadareachamber. com; 1251 Hwy 95; ☺9am-5pm Mon-Fri) Has area info.

Laughlin Visitor Center (☎702-298-3321; www.visitlaughlin.com; 1555 S Casino Dr; ☺8am-4:30pm Mon-Fri) Has area info and a basic map for the Colorado River Heritage Greenway Park & Trails.

Post Office (990 Hwy 95, cnr 7th St, Bullhead City; ☺10am-2pm Mon-Fri)

ℹ Getting There & Away

At press time there were no commercial flights into Bullhead City/Laughlin International Airport. Riverside and Harrah's casinos offer charter flights. Las Vegas' McCarran International Airport (www.mccarran.com) is about 100 miles north of town. Check the McCarran website for a list of commercial shuttles running between Las Vegas and Laughlin. Water taxis (www.riverpassagewatertaxi.com; one-way $4) travel back and forth along the river between the nine casinos. Buy tickets at the casino docks.

Route 66: Topock To Kingman

Topock Gorge to Oatman

Coming from California, Route 66 enters Arizona at Topock, near the 20-mile **Topock Gorge**, a dramatic walled canyon that's one of the prettiest sections of the Colorado River. It's part of the **Havasu National Wildlife Refuge** (☎760-326-3853; www.fws.gov/refuge/ havasu), a major habitat for migratory and water birds. Look for herons, ducks, geese, blackbirds and other winged creatures as you raft or canoe through the gorge. There are plenty of coves and sandy beaches for picnics and sunning. Companies renting boats include **Jerkwater Canoe & Kayak** (☎928-768-7753; www.jerkwatercanoe.com; tours $46; ☺launch at 7:30am PCT) which launches day trips from Park Moabi in Needles, CA, just west of the state line. Rates include canoe rental for the 17-mile float from the park to Castle Rock and the return shuttle.

North of here, in **Golden Shores**, you can refuel on gas and grub before embarking on a rugged 20-mile trip to the terrifically crusty former gold-mining town of **Oatman**, cupped by pinnacles and craggy hills. Since the veins of ore ran dry in 1942, the little settlement has reinvented itself as a movie set and unapologetic Wild West tourist trap, complete with staged gunfights (daily at noon, 1:30pm and sometimes 3:30pm) and gift stores named Fast Fanny's Place and the Classy Ass. And speaking of asses, there are plenty of them (the four-legged kind, that is) roaming the streets and shamelessly begging for food. You can buy hay squares in town. Stupid and endearing, they're descendents from pack animals left behind by the early miners.

Squeezed among the shops is the 1902 **Oatman Hotel**, a surprisingly modest shack (no longer renting rooms) where Clark Gable and Carole Lombard first shagged, presumably, on their wedding night in 1939. Clark apparently returned quite frequently to play cards with the miners in the downstairs saloon, which is awash in one-dollar bills (some $40,000 worth by the barmaid's estimate). At the time of research, the upstairs, where visitors used to be able to peek into the old guest rooms, was closed for renovations. Beyond Oatman, keep your wits about you as the road twists and turns past tumbleweeds, saguaro cacti and falling rocks as it travels over **Sitgreaves Pass** (3523ft) and corkscrews into the rugged Black Mountains before arriving in Kingman.

Kingman

POP 28,336 / ELEV 3300FT

Among Route 66 aficionados, Kingman is known as the main hub of the longest uninterrupted stretch of the historic highway, running from Topock to Seligman. Among its early 20th-century buildings is the former Methodist church at 5th and Spring St where Clark Gable and Carole Lombard wed in 1939. Hometown hero Andy Devine had his Hollywood breakthrough as the perpetually befuddled driver of the eponymous *Stagecoach* in John Ford's Oscar-winning 1939 movie.

These days, Kingman feels like a place waking up from a long nap. New eateries, watering holes and galleries have been opening on Beale St, the axis of historic downtown, adding some foot traffic and modern verve.

Route 66 barrels through town as Andy Devine Ave. It runs parallel to the up-and-coming Beale St. Supermarkets, gas stations and other businesses line up along northbound Stockton Hill Rd, which is also the road to take for Grand Canyon West.

◉ Sights & Activities

Route 66 Museum MUSEUM
(☑ 928-753-9889; www.gokingman.com; 120 W Andy Devine Ave; adult/senior/child 12yr & under $4/3/free; ☉ 9am-5pm) On the 2nd floor of the 1907 powerhouse, which also holds the visitor center, this small but engaging museum has an informative historical overview of the Mother Road. Check out that crazy air conditioner on the 1950 Studebaker Champion! Ticket allows entry into the nearby Mohave Museum.

Mohave Museum of History & Arts MUSEUM
(☑ 928-753-3195; www.mohavemuseum.org; 400 W Beale St; adult/senior/child 12yr & under $4/3/free; ☉ 9am-5pm Mon-Fri, 1-5pm Sat) Admission to the Route 66 Museum also gets you into the Mohave Museum, a warren of rooms filled with extraordinarily eclectic stuff. All sorts of regional topics are dealt with, from mining towns to Andy Devine. There's also an entire wall of oil portraits of American first ladies – all painted by the same artist! And check out the piece of petrified light-

ning. Tickets can also be used at the Route 66 Museum in the Powerhouse.

Hualapai Mountain Park PARK
(☑ 928-681-5700; www.mcparks.com; 6250 Hualapai Mountain Rd; day use $7) In summer locals climb this nearby mountain for picnics, hiking, mountain biking and wildlife-watching amid cool ponderosa pine and aspen.

⚑ Festivals & Events

Historic Route 66 Fun Run CAR SHOW
(☑ 928-753-5001; www.azrt66.com) Vintage car rally from Seligman to Topock on the first weekend in May.

Andy Devine Days Parade PARADE
(☑ 928-757-7919; www.gokingman.com) Floats followed by a rodeo in late September.

🛏 Sleeping

Kingman has plenty of motels along Route 66/Andy Devine Ave north and south of the I-40. The cheapest places are dingy and popular with down-on-their-luck, long-term residents. Inspect before committing.

Hualapai Mountain Park CAMPGROUND $
(☑ 928-681-5700, 877-757-0915; www.mcparks. com; Hualapai Mountain Rd; tent/RV sites $17/30, tipis $35, cabins $65-135; ☀) Camp among granite rock formations and ponderosa pine at this pretty county park, some 15 miles south of town. The tipis are cool, but we hear they stay rather chilly in cold weather. Some cabins have restrooms and showers. Tent sites are first-come, first-served but RV sites can be reserved. Pets are $2 per pet per day; $5 reservation fee.

Hualapai Mountain Resort LODGE $
(☑ 928-757-3545; www.hmresort.net; 4525 Hualapai Mountain Rd; r $79-99, ste $159; ☀) Think mountain-man chic: chunky wood furniture, bold paintings of wild game and a front porch that's made for wildlife-watching among the towering pines. The lodge advertises wi-fi, but we were not able to get it to work. The good on-site **restaurant** serves breakfast, lunch and dinner Wednesday through Sunday. Try to get a table near the window to scan for elk.

Travelodge MOTEL $
(☑ 928-757-1188; www.travelodge.com; 3275 E Andy Devine Ave; r incl breakfast $61-81; ❋ ☎ ☀ ☀) Budget travelers, rejoice. This two-story motel provides everything you need for a satisfying overnight stay in

Kingman: a Route 66–adjacent location, helpful staff, continental breakfast, refrigerator and microwaves in the room, a laundry and free wi-fi. Pet fee is $10 per pet per day.

Hilltop Motel MOTEL $
(☎928-753-2198; www.hilltopmotelaz.com; 1901 E Andy Devine Ave; r from $44; 🅿@🛜🐾🏊) Rooms here are a bit of a throwback, but well kept. On Route 66, with nice views and a cool neon sign. Pets are $5 per day.

✖ Eating & Drinking

Sirens Cafe SANDWICHES $
(www.sirensinkingman.com; 419 E Beale St; sandwiches $7; ⊙10am-4pm Mon-Fri) A mother-daughter team runs this welcoming cafe, which serves gourmet sandwiches and paninis. Desserts look nothing less than decadent.

Redneck's Southern Pit BBQ BARBECUE $$
(www.redneckssouthernpitbbq.com; 420 E Beale St; mains $5.25-24; ⊙11am-8pm Tue-Sat; 🖭) As rednecks, we can confirm that the pork is darn tasty at this Beale St BBQ joint, but we're not too keen on the word 'sammiches,' which appears on the menu. 'Big old tater,' however, is fine. Also serves rib platters. Order at the counter then grab a seat. Good option for families.

Cellar Door WINE BAR
(☎928-753-3885; www.the-cellar-door.com; 414 E Beale St; appetizers under $8; ⊙4-10pm Wed & Thu, 4pm-midnight Fri & Sat) This downtown wine bar offers about 140 wines by the bottle, 30 by the glass, an international selection of beers and tasty appetizer plates. It's a hot little spot that embodies the spirit of revival in Kingman.

Beale Street Brews COFFEE SHOP
(www.bealestreetbrews.net; 418 E Beale St; ⊙7am-3pm Mon-Thu, until 7pm Thu, until 10pm Fri & Sat; 🛜) This cute indie coffee shop draws local java cognoscenti with its lattes and gallery.

ℹ Information

Kingman Regional Medical Center (☎928-757-2101; www.azkrmc.com; 3269 Stockton Hill Rd) 24-hour emergency room.
Police (☎928-753-2191; 2730 E Andy Devine Ave)
Powerhouse Visitor Center (☎866-427-7866, 928-753-6106; www.gokingman.com; 120 W Andy Devine Ave; ⊙8am-5pm) Lots of information about Route 66 attractions.

ℹ Getting There & Away

Great Lakes Airlines (☎800-554-5111; www.flygreatlakes.com) Provides the only commercial flights in and out of Kingman Airport, with flights to and from Los Angeles.
Greyhound (☎928-753-1818; www.greyhound.com; 953 W Beale St) Runs several buses daily to Phoenix ($53 to $59, 5½ hours), Las Vegas ($70 to $77, three hours) and Los Angeles ($90 to $98, 10 to 12 hours).
Amtrak (☎800-872-7245; www.amtrak.com) The westbound Southwest Chief stops at 11:46pm, the eastbound at 2:33am. There's a train waiting room at the corner of Andy Devine Ave (Route 66) and 4th St. It's not a full station and you cannot buy a ticket here, so book ahead.

Route 66: Kingman To Williams

Past Kingman, Route 66 arcs north away from the I-40 for 115 dusty miles of original Mother Road through scrubby, lonely landscape. It merges with the I-40 near Seligman, then reappears briefly as Main St in Williams. Gas stations are rare, so make sure you've got enough fuel. The total distance to Williams is 130 miles.

Kingman to Peach Springs

It's tempting to try to race the train on this lonely stretch of Mother Road where your only other friend is the pavement unfurling for miles ahead. The first opportunity for socializing arises in tiny **Hackberry**, where highway memorialist Robert Waldmire lures passersby with his much loved **Old Route 66 Visitor Center** (☎928-769-2605; www.hackberrygeneralstore.com; 11255 E Rte 66; ⊙typically 8am-6pm) **FREE** inside an eccentrically decorated gas station. It's a refreshing spot for a cold drink and souvenirs. Keep going and you'll pass through the blink-and-you'll-miss-them towns of Valentine and Truxton.

Grand Canyon Caverns

Nine miles past Peach Springs, a plaster dinosaur welcomes you to the **Grand Canyon Caverns & Inn** (☎928-422-3223; www.gccaverns.com; Rte 66, mile 115; 45min tour adult/child $20/13; ⊙9am-5pm Jun-Sep, 10am-5pm Oct-May; 🖭), a cool subterranean retreat from the summer heat. An elevator drops 21 stories underground to limestone caverns and the skeletal remains of a prehistoric ground sloth. If you've seen other caverns these might not be as impressive, but kids get a kick out of a visit. The 25-minute short tour is wheelchair accessible (adult/child $16/11). The Cavern Suite ($800), which opened in 2010, is an underground 'room' in the cavern with two double beds, a sitting area and multicolored lamps. If you ever wanted to live in one of those postapocalyptic sci-fi movies, here's your chance! One of the DVDs on offer is underground horror flick *The Cave* – watch it here only if you're especially twisted.

The **restaurant** (☺8am-6pm Jun-Oct, varies rest of year) is nice if you already happen to be here; it has a small playground and serves simple American fare. The bar opens at 3pm on Fridays and Saturdays and closes at 10pm or later depending on crowd-size. The **campground** (tent/RV sites $15/30) here has over 50 sites carved out of the juniper forest, plus new open-air, roof-free rooms (from $60) on raised platforms for star-gazers. The **Caverns Inn** (r $90; ✦✦) has rooms that are basic but well kept. There's wi-fi in the lobby. Pets are $5 per day with a refundable $50 deposit.

Seligman

POP 469 / ELEV 5240FT

Look out for red-and-white Burma Shave signs on the 23 miles of road slicing through rolling hills to Seligman. This tiny town embraces its Route 66 heritage with verve, thanks to the Delgadillo brothers, who for decades were the Mother Road's biggest boosters. Juan passed away in 2004, but nonagenarian Angel and his wife Vilma still run **Angel's Barbershop** (☎928-422-3352; www.route66giftshop.com; 217 E Rte 66). OK, so he doesn't cut hair anymore, but the barber's chair is still there and you can poke around for souvenirs and admire license plates sent in by fans from all over the world. If Angel is around, he's usually happy to regale you with stories about the Dust Bowl era. He's seen it all.

Angel's madcap brother Juan used to rule prankishly supreme over the **Snow Cap Drive-In** (☎928-422-3291; 301 E Rte 66; mains $3.25-6.25; ☺10am-6pm mid-Mar–Nov), a Route 66 institution now kept going by his sons Bob and John. The crazy decor is only the beginning. Wait until you see the menu featuring cheeseburgers with cheese and 'dead chick-

en!' Beware the fake mustard bottle... They sometimes open at 9am in mid-summer.

Two good restaurants stare each other down from opposite sides of Route 66. For friendly service and good American and German grub, try **Westside Lilo's Cafe** (415 W Rte 66; breakfast & lunch $5-14, dinner $13-21; ☺6am-9pm), which also has an outdoor patio. For beer and a few tongue-in-cheek menu items, try the **Roadkill Café & OK Saloon** (502 W Rte 66; breakfast $7-12, lunch & dinner $7-22; ☺7am-9pm) across the street, which has an all-you-can-eat salad bar, juicy steaks and burgers and, of course, the 'splatter platter.'

For welcoming hosts and the town's best neon sign, look no further than the **Supai Motel** (☎928-422-4153; www.supaimotel.com; 134 W Chino Ave; s/d $60/72; ✦✦), a classic courtyard motel offering simple but perfectly fine rooms with refrigerators and microwaves. The Havasu Falls mural is an inspiring way to start the morning.

Lake Havasu City

POP 52,819 / ELEV 450FT-1500FT

This manufactured city on the banks of Lake Havasu lacks a soul, not to mention charm. But hey, it does have London Bridge. Yes, that would be the original gracefully arched bridge that spanned the Thames from 1831 until 1967, when it was quite literally falling down (as predicted in the old nursery rhyme) and put up for sale. Robert McCulloch was busy developing a master-planned community on Lake Havasu and badly in need of some gimmick to drum up attention for his project. Bingo! McCulloch snapped up London Bridge for a cool $2.46 million, dismantled it into 10,276 slabs and reassembled it in the Arizona desert. The first car rolled across in 1971.

Listed in the *Guinness World Records* as the world's largest antique, London Bridge may be one of Arizona's most incongruous tourist sites, but it's also among its most popular. Day-trippers come by the busload to walk across it and soak up faux British heritage in the kitschy-quaint English Village. The lake itself – which can be very pretty – is the other major draw. Formed in 1938 by the construction of Parker Dam, it's much beloved by water rats, especially students on spring break (roughly March to May) and summer-heat refugees from Phoenix and beyond.

Lake Havasu City

◉ Sights & Activities

Once you've snapped pics of **London Bridge**, you'll find that most of your options are water related. Several companies offer boat tours (from around $20) from English Village. Options include one-hour narrated jaunts, half-day and full-day trips, and sunset tours, which can usually be booked on the spot. Several companies along the waterfront in English Village rent jet skis and other watercraft.

London Bridge Beach   BEACH
(1340 McCulloch Blvd; ☺ sunrise-10:30pm; 👶) This sandy strip has palm trees, a sandy beach, playgrounds, ramadas and a fenced dog park with faux fire hydrant in the middle. It's also offers a pretty, palm-framed view of the lake and distant peaks. The beach is off W McCulloch Blvd, behind Island Inn hotel. Nearby is the **Lake Havasu Marina** (☎ 928-855-2159; www.lakehavasumarina.com; 1100 McCulloch Blvd), which has boat ramps but no rentals.

🛏 Sleeping

Rates fluctuate tremendously from summer weekends to winter weekdays. Local budget and national chain hotels line London Bridge Rd.

Windsor Beach Campground   CAMPGROUND $
(☎ 928-855-2784, reservations 520-586-2283; www.azstateparks.com; 699 London Bridge Rd, Lake Havasu State Park; campsite $30-35) Sleep just steps from the water at this scenic beach and camping area at Lake Havasu State Park. Amenities include showers, boat-launch facilities and new hookups. The 1.75-mile Mohave Sunset Trail runs almost the full-length of the park. Day use is $15 per vehicle Friday through Sunday, and $10 the rest of the week. Sites available by reservation.

Travelodge   HOTEL $
(☎ 928-680-9202; www.travelodge.com; 480 London Bridge Rd; r incl $94; ❋@🐾) For a low-cost, welcoming place that's only a short drive from the London Bridge action, try this Travelodge. Decor isn't particularly compelling, but you should get a good night's sleep. Pets under 40lb allowed (call to confirm permitted breeds) for $10 per pet per night.

Heat   BOUTIQUE HOTEL $$$
(☎ 928-854-2833; www.heathotel.com; 1420 N McCulloch Blvd; r $209-299, ste $249-439; ❋🐾) Rooms are hip and contemporary at Heat, the slickest hotel on Arizona's West Coast. Most rooms also come with private patios with views of London Bridge. In the 'inferno'

rooms, bathtubs fill from the ceiling. An outdoor cocktail lounge overlooking the bridge and the lake feels almost like the deck of a cruise ship.

London Bridge Resort HOTEL $$$
(☏928-855-0888; www.londonbridgeresort.com; 1477 Queens Bay Rd; ste $164-329; ✳@🔊🏊) Enjoy flat-screen TVs, new mattresses, kitchenettes and rooms with views of London Bridge (of course) at this popular all-suite property, where a replica of a 1762 royal coach greets guest in the lobby. It can feel a little impersonal, but it's a good choice if you want pools, nightclubs, bars and restaurants in one place.

✗ Eating & Drinking

There's no shortage of places to eat and drink in Havasu, but quantity may win out over quality.

Red Onion AMERICAN $
(☏928-505-0302; www.redonionhavasu.com; 2013 N McCulloch Blvd; breakfast & lunch $6.25-12, dinner $10-15; ◷7am-8pm Mon-Thu, 7am-9pm Fri & Sat, 7am-2pm Sun) The dining room here opens up onto Havasu's 'uptown district.' Try the omelets for a hearty start to your day. Look for salads, sandwiches and burgers at lunch, with a few heartier dishes, like steaks, at dinner. Service is friendly, if disorganized.

Angelina's Italian Kitchen ITALIAN $$
(☏928-680-3868; 1530 El Camino Dr; mains $12-28; ◷4-10pm Sun & Tue-Thu, until 10:30pm Fri & Sat) If you like your Italian food cooked as if mama was behind the stove, you'll like this popular restaurant, now in a new location

closer to London Bridge Rd and Lake Havasu State Park. The home-cooked Italian dishes weave together pungent flavors like fine tapestry.

Barley Brothers PUB FOOD $$
(☏928-505-7837; www.barleybrothers.com; 1425 N McCulloch Blvd; mains $9-24; ◷11am-9pm Sun-Thu, to 10pm Fri & Sat) It's brews and views at this busy microbrewery overlooking London Bridge. Steaks, burgers and salads are on the menu, but the place is known for its wood-fired pizzas. Lots of flat-screen TVs for sports fans, and beer drinkers can choose from one of six different microbrews. Biggest drawback? No outdoor patio.

BJ's Tavern BAR
(2122 N McCulloch Blvd; ◷6am-2am) Not stylish. Not contemporary. Not hip. And depending on your personality, that may be a good thing. Inside there's a jukebox, pool tables and karaoke. Outside is a misted smoking patio.

ℹ Information

Lake Havasu Post Office (☏928-855-2361; 1750 N McCulloch Blvd; ◷8:30am-5pm Mon-Fri, 9am-1pm Sat)
Visitor Center (☏928-855-5655; www.golakhavasu.com; 422 English Village; ◷9am-5pm) Has all the need-to-know info.

ℹ Getting There & Away

Lake Havasu is on Hwy 95, about 20 miles south of the I-40. Several commercial shuttles run between Las Vegas' McCarran International Airport and Lake Havasu, and a one-way trip takes three to 3½ hours. See www.mccarran.com for a list of companies.

Parker

POP 3073 / ELEV 420FT
Hugging a 16-mile stretch of the Colorado River known as the Parker Strip, this tiny town south of Lake Havasu is a convenient stop for those wanting to explore the region's unique riparian parks and preserves. All hell breaks loose in late January/early February when the engines are revved up for the **Best in the Desert Parker 425** (www.bitd.com), an off-road race that lures up to 100,000 speed freaks. If you're here in early June, buy an inner tube and register to join the **Parker Tube Float** ($10), which celebrates its 38th anniversary in 2015. Contact the **Chamber of Commerce**

(☑928-669-6511; www.parkerareatourism.com; 1217 California Ave; ☉8am-5pm Mon-Fri) for the lowdown on it all.

Parker is 35 miles south of Lake Havasu via Hwy 95.

◉ Sights & Activities

Water-skiing, jet-skiing, fishing, boating and tubing are popular here, and there are plenty of concessionaires along the Parker Strip.

Parker Dam   DAM
Finished in 1938, this mighty dam formed Lake Havasu 15 miles north of town. It may not look like it, but it is the world's deepest dam, with 73% of its structural height of 320ft buried beneath the original riverbed. The interior of the dam has been off limits to tourists since September 11, 2001, but you can drive over it between 5am and 11pm (the road is too narrow for large RVs).

Enjoy nice views of the dam from pull-offs on the California side. For a pleasant scenic drive along the river, continue south on the 11-mile Parker Dam Backcountry Byway, which tracks the Parker Strip in California. Drive slowly, resident burros walk on the road – we saw 'em! You can cross back over to Parker at Earp, CA.

Buckskin Mountain State Park   PARK
(☑928-667-3231; www.azstateparks.com; 5476 N Hwy 95; admission per vehicle $10; 👪🐕) Tucked along a mountain-flanked bend in the Colorado River about 11 miles north of Parker, this park has great family-friendly infrastructure with a playground, swimming beach, basketball court, cafe and grocery store (summer only). Wi-fi is available at the group ramada at no charge. Campsites are available by reservation online or by phone.

**Bill Williams National
Wildlife Refuge**   PRESERVE
(☑928-667-4144; www.fws.gov/refuge/Bill_Williams_River; 60911 Hwy 95; ☉visitor center 8am-4pm Mon-Fri, 10am-2pm Sat & Sun) 🅿FREE Abutting Cattail Cove, where the Bill Williams River meets Lake Havasu, is this calm wildlife refuge, which helps protect the unique transition zone between Mohave and Sonoran desert ecosystems. On a finger of land pointing into the lake, there's a 1.4-mile interpretive trail through a botanic garden of native flora, with shaded benches and access to fishing platforms.

Endangered birds like to roost in the largest cottonwood/willow grove along the en-

tire length of the Colorado River. Entrance is between mile markers 161 and 162.

🛌 Sleeping & Eating

There aren't really any great properties in town, but if you must spend the night, try the Best Western.

Buckskin Mountain State Park   CAMPING $
(☑520-586-2283, River Island State Park 928-667-3386; www.azstateparks.com; 5476 N Hwy 95; tent & RV sites $30) Tent campers who want to be close to the water should opt for a covered waterside cabana; those looking for quieter, more scenic desert camping can drive another mile north to River Island State Park (sites $25).

Bobby D's Diner   DINER $
(mains $5-15; ☉8am-9pm Thu-Tue; 👪) Twist back in time at family friendly Bobby D's Diner, a '50s-themed place north of town. Settle into a red booth for burgers, shakes and classic oldies.

Yuma
POP 95,429 / ELEV 141FT

This sprawling city at the confluence of the Gila and Colorado Rivers celebrated its 100th birthday in 2014. That anniversary coincided with a new emphasis on the city's future, not just its storied past. A revitalized downtown welcomes visitors to Gateway Park and its new plaza as well as a growing trail system that stretches from the park into restored wetlands beside the Colorado. But the past hasn't completely gone away. The infamous territorial prison here, which was nicknamed the Hellhole of the West, still draws tourists to its sun-baked yard. Yuma is also the birthplace of farmworker organizer César Chávez and the winter camp of some 80,000 snowbirds craving Yuma's sunny skies, mild temperatures and cheap RV park living.

◉ Sights & Activities

To get a better feel for the city and a chance for some exercise, park downtown and walk to the sites (unless it's 100 degrees). From Gateway Park, a stroll upstream along the Colorado River leads to the prison and the east wetlands trails; a short walk downstream leads to the Quartermaster Depot. On Main St you'll find restaurants and the inviting **Yuma Art Center** (www.yumafinearts.org; 254 S Main St) which sells contemporary art.

Yuma Territorial Prison State Historic Park
HISTORIC SITE

(☑ 928-783-4771; www.azstateparks.com; 1 Prison Hill Rd; adult/child 7-13yr $6/$3; ☺ 9am-5pm daily, closed Tue & Wed Jun-Sep) Hunkered on a bluff overlooking the Colorado River, this infamous prison is Yuma's star attraction. Between 1876 and 1909, 3069 convicts were incarcerated here for crimes ranging from murder to 'seduction under the promise of marriage.' The small museum is fascinating, with photos and descriptions of individual inmates and their offenses, including a display devoted to the 29 women jailed here. Walking around the yard, behind iron-grille doors and into cells crowded with stacked bunks, you might get retroactively scared straight. Don't miss the Dark Cell, a cave-like room where troublesome prisoners were locked together in a 5ft-high metal cage.

Yuma Quartermaster Depot State Park
HISTORIC SITE

(☑ 928-783-0071; www.azstateparks.com; 201 N 4th Ave; adult/child 7-13yr $4/2; ☺ 9am-5pm) Decades before the jail was built, Yuma became a crucial junction in the military supply lines through the West. Its role in getting gear and victuals to the troops is commemorated at the low-key quartermaster depot, set around a manicured green lawn. New exhibits in the Corral House spotlight the Yuma East Wetlands Restoration Project and the Yuma Siphon – a massive 1912 irrigation tunnel that runs beneath the Colorado River and is still in use today.

Pause-Rest-Worship Church
CHURCH

(Hwy 95) Fourteen miles north of Yuma, a tiny white-and-blue chapel sits on a patch of farmland on the west side of Hwy 95. A local farmer built the original in 1995 as a memorial to his deceased wife. A freak storm destroyed the structure in 2011, but the community helped rebuild it. The 8ft-by-12ft church seats about 12 and has stained glass windows. Feeling contemplative? Pull over and step inside.

🛏 Sleeping & Eating

Yuma has plenty of chain hotels, mostly around exit 2 off the I-8.

La Fuente Inn & Suites
INN $

(☑ 928-329-1814, 800-841-1814; www.lafuenteinn.com; 1513 E 16th St; r incl breakfast $69-89; ▣ ❋ 🛜 ⛱ 🐕) At this happy-to-help place, pretty gardens wrap around a modern, Spanish Colonial–style building. The evening social hour is great for mingling with fellow guests over free wine. Enjoy an extensive complimentary breakfast spread in the morning.

Best Western Coronado Motor Hotel
MOTEL $$

(☑ 928-783-4453; www.bestwestern.com; 233 4th Ave; r incl breakfast $90-110; ❋ @ 🛜 ⛱ 🐕) Red-tile roof, bright turquoise doors and newly upgraded rooms with flat-screen TVs – the oldest Best Western in the world doesn't feel old at all. At this sprawling downtown complex you also get two swimming pools and a sit-down breakfast. Some rooms have kitchenettes, there are three laundry rooms and kids under 13 stay free.

Lutes Casino
AMERICAN $

(☑ 928-782-2192; www.lutescasino.com; 221 S Main St; mains under $8; ☺ 10am-8pm Mon-Fri, to 9pm Sat, to 6pm Sun) Lutes is awesome! If you're in town to see the prison, stop here for lunch afterwards. And note that the word casino is misleading – you won't find slots at this 1940s-era hang-out, just a warehouse-big gathering spot. What's here? Attic-like treasures hanging from the ceiling, movie memorabilia, maybe a dude playing the piano and a true cross-section of the town.

Expect diner-style, nuthin' fancy fare. The 'especial' is a burger topped with a sliced hot dog. Antacid not included.

River City Grill
FUSION $$

(☑ 928-782-7988; www.rivercitygrillyuma.com; 600 W 3rd St; lunch $9-12, dinner $17-36; ☺ 11am-2pm Mon-Fri, dinner 5-10pm daily; ☑) Chic, funky and gourmet, with a shaded outdoor patio in back, the River has scrumptious crab cakes and brie-stuffed chicken, as well as mouthwatering vegetarian mains. Come here for a snappy weekday lunch or romantic dinner for two.

Da Boyz Italian Cuisine
ITALIAN $$

(☑ 928-783-8383; www.daboyzyuma.com; 284 S Main St; dishes $9-19; ☺ 11am-9pm Sun-Thu, until 10pm Fri & Sat; 🍴) This stylish downtown Italian eatery with big burgundy booths works well for a variety of travelers: solos, couples and girlfriends on getaways. It's also good family value. Look for filling gourmet pizzas and platters of pasta, plus a decent wine list.

❶ Information

Visitor Center (☑ 928-783-0071; www.visityuma.com; 201 N 4th Ave; ☺ 9am-5pm daily Oct-May, closed Mon Jun-Sep) For maps and information, stop by the visitor center, which sits beside Yuma Quartermaster Depot State Park.

ⓘ Getting There & Away

Yuma Airport (☑ 928-726-5882; www.yuma airport.com; 2191 32nd St) Has daily flights to Phoenix and Los Angeles.

Greyhound (☑ 928-783-4403; 1245 Castle Dome Ave) Runs two buses daily to Phoenix ($46 to $51, four hours). Currently, tickets are purchased at 2115 E 14th St, not the bus stop.

Amtrak (www.amtrak.com; 281 S Gila St) The Sunset Limited stops briefly at Yuma station thrice weekly on its run between Los Angeles ($83, six hours) and New Orleans ($317, 41 hours).

SOUTHERN ARIZONA

This is a land of Stetsons and spurs, where cowboy ballads are sung around the campfire under starry, black-velvet skies and thick steaks sizzle on the grill. Anchored by the bustling college-town of Tucson, it's a vast region, where long, dusty highways slide past rolling vistas and steep, pointy mountain ranges. Majestic saguaro cacti, the symbol of the region, stretch out as far as the eye can see. Some of the Wild West's most classic tales were begot in small towns like Tombstone and Bisbee, which still attract tourists by the thousands for their Old West vibe. The desert air is hot, sweet and dry by day, cool and crisp at night. And the sunsets? Stupendous.

Tucson

POP 524,295 / ELEV 2643FT

An energetic college town, Tucson (*too-sawn*) is attractive, fun-loving and one of the most culturally invigorating places in the Southwest. Set in a flat valley hemmed in by craggy, odd-shaped mountains, Arizona's second-largest city smoothly blends Native American, Spanish, Mexican and Anglo traditions. Distinct neighborhoods and 19th-century buildings give a rich sense of community and history not found in the more modern and sprawling Phoenix. This is a town rich in Hispanic heritage (more than 40% of the population is Hispanic), so Spanish slides easily off most tongues and high-quality Mexican restaurants abound. The eclectic shops toting vintage garb, scores of funky restaurants and dive bars don't let you forget Tucson is a college town at heart, home turf to the 40,000-strong University of Arizona (UA).

Although it's fun to wander around the colorful historic buildings and peruse the shops, Tucson's best perks are found outside town. Whether you yearn to hike past giant cacti in the beautiful Saguaro National Park, watch the sun set over the rugged Santa Catalina Mountains or check out the world-class Arizona-Sonora Desert Museum, straying beyond the city limits is worth it.

Tucson lies mainly to the north and east of I-10 at its intersection with I-19, which runs to the Mexican border at Nogales. Downtown Tucson and the main historic districts are east of I-10 exit 258 at Congress St/Broadway Blvd, a major west–east thoroughfare. Most west–east thoroughfares are called streets, while most north–south thoroughfares are called avenues (with a sprinkling of roads and boulevards). Stone Ave, at its intersection with Congress, forms the zero point for Tucson addresses. Streets are designated west and east, and avenues north and south, from this point.

A new street car (ticket/day pass $1.50/4), linking downtown and the university opened in 2014. Bikes are permitted on board.

◉ Sights & Activities

Most of Tucson's blockbuster sights, including the Saguaro National Park and the Arizona-Sonora Desert Museum, are on the city outskirts. The downtown area and 4th Ave near the university are compact enough for walking. Opening hours for outdoor attractions may change seasonally, typically opening at an earlier hour during the hot summer.

For avid explorers, the Tucson Attractions Passport ($18) may be a ticket to savings. It's available through www.visittucson.org or at the visitor center and entitles you to two-for-one tickets and other discounts at major museums, attractions, tours and parks throughout southern Arizona.

◉ Downtown Tucson

Downtown Tucson has a valid claim to being the oldest urban space in Arizona. Although spates of construction have marred the historical facade, this is still a reasonably walkable city center. The long-delayed streetcars, connecting downtown, 4th Ave and the University, began running in July 2014.

Tucson Museum of Art &
Historic Block MUSEUM
(Map p212; ✆520-624-2333; www.tucsonmuseum
ofart.org; 140 N Main Ave; adult/student/senior/
child 18yr & under $10/5/8/free; ☉10am-5pm Tue-
Wed & Fri-Sat, to 8pm Thu, noon-5pm Sun) For a
small city, Tucson boasts an impressive art
museum. There's a respectable collection
of Western and contemporary art, and the
permanent exhibition of pre-Columbian
artifacts will awaken your inner Indiana
Jones. The special exhibits are varied and
interesting. A superb gift shop rounds out
the works. First Sunday of the month is free.

Presidio Historic District NEIGHBORHOOD
(Map p212; www.nps.gov/nr/travel/amsw/sw7.htm)
The Tucson Museum of Art is part of this low-
key neighborhood, which embraces the site
of the original Spanish fort and a ritzy residential area once nicknamed 'Snob Hollow.'
This is (per current historical knowledge) one
of the oldest inhabited places in North America. The Spanish **Presidio de San Agustín
del Tucson** dates back to 1775, but the fort
itself was built over a Hohokam site that has
been dated to AD 700–900. The original fort
is completely gone, although there's a short
reconstructed section at the corner of Church
Ave and Washington St. The historical district teems with adobe townhouses and restored 19th-century mansions.

Shoppers should steer towards Old Town
Artisans (p217), a block-long warren of adobe apartments filled with galleries and crafts
stores set around a lush and lovely courtyard
(this use of an enclosed courtyard comes
from Andalucia in southern Spain by way
of North Africa). The popular **La Cocina**
(Map p212; www.lacocinatuson.com; ☉10am-4pm
Sun, 11am-3pm Mon, 11am-10pm Tue, 11am-2am
Wed-Sat), also within the complex, serves
Southwestern fare, Arizona beers and cool
live music (generally Thursday to Saturday).

The area is bounded by W 6th St, W
Alameda St, N Stone Ave and Granada Ave.

**Barrio Histórico
District/Barrio Viejo** NEIGHBORHOOD
(Map p210) This compact neighborhood was
an important business district in the late
19th century. Today it's home to funky shops
and galleries in brightly painted adobe
houses. The Barrio is bordered by I-10, Stone
Ave and Cushing and 17th Sts.

4th Avenue NEIGHBORHOOD
(Map p212; www.fourthavenue.org) Linking historic downtown and the university, lively
4th Ave is a rare breed: a hip yet alt-flavored
strip with a neighborhood feel and not a single chain store or restaurant (oops, except
for Dairy Queen). The stretch between 9th
St and University Blvd is lined with buzzy
restaurants, coffee houses, bars, book stores,
galleries, indie boutiques and vintage shops.

Under the overpass that crosses 4th Ave
and Broadway is the **Tucson Portrait Project** (Map p212; www.tucsonportraitproject.com),
one of our favorite public art projects anywhere. This wall-to-wall mosaic of about
7000 Tucsonian faces is a simple yet powerful testament to the diversity of the city's
population.

Metered parking is free on weekends.
The best time to visit 4th Ave is during the
two annual street fairs held for three days
in mid-December and late March or early
April. See the 4th Ave website for details.

◉ **University of Arizona**

Rather than being a collection of public
greens, the UA campus seamlessly integrates
the desert into its learning space – although
there are some soft lawns for the students to
lounge around on. There are several excellent museums on campus.

WHEN YOU WISH UPON A LOVE TRIANGLE

In Barrio Histórico look for **El Tiradito** (Map p212; 356 S Main Ave), a 'wishing shrine' with
a tale of passion and murder behind it. Locals say that in the 19th century a young man
fell for his wife's mother. Her husband – his father-in-law – killed the young man. The
dead lover was never absolved of his sins, and was thus turned away from the consecrated ground at the nearby Roman Catholic church, so he was buried under the front porch
of the house that marks the spot of El Tiradito. Locals took pity on the young man and
began offering prayers and burning candles at the site; over time, El Tiradito became a
shrine for anyone commemorating a lost loved one. The *Phoenix New Times* ran a story
that claimed El Tiradito was the only Catholic shrine in the country dedicated to a sinner
buried in unconsecrated ground.

Metropolitan Tucson

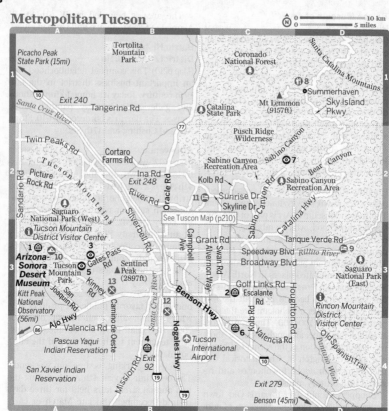

Arizona State Museum
MUSEUM

(Map p210; ☏520-621-6302; www.statemuseum. arizona.edu; 1013 E University Blvd; adult/child 17yr & under $5/free; ☻10am-5pm Mon-Sat) To learn more about the history and culture of the region's Native American tribes, spend an hour or two exploring the Arizona State Museum, the oldest and largest anthropology museum in the Southwest. The exhibit covering the tribes' cultural history is extensive, but easy to navigate and should appeal to newbies and history buffs alike. These galleries are complemented by much-envied collections of minerals and Navajo textiles.

Don't miss the impressive Wall of Pots and take a peek into the climate-controlled Pottery Vault (the museum has more than 20,000 whole vessels).

Center for Creative Photography
MUSEUM

(CCP; Map p210; ☏520-621-7968; www.creative photography.org; 1030 N Olive Rd; donations appreciated; ☻9am-5pm Mon-Fri, 1-4pm Sat & Sun)

FREE CCP is known for its ever-changing, high-caliber exhibits. It also administers the archives of Ansel Adams, perhaps the best-regarded landscape photographer in US history, and occasionally displays his works.

University of Arizona Museum of Art
MUSEUM

(Map p210; ☏520-621-7567; www.artmuseum. arizona.edu; 1031 Olive Rd; adult/child 18yr & under $5/free; ☻9am-5pm Tue-Fri, noon-4pm Sat & Sun) Peruse 500 years of European and American paintings and sculpture. The permanent collection features Rodin, Matisse, Picasso and Pollock.

Arizona History Museum
MUSEUM

(Map p210; ☏520-628-5774; www.arizonahistorical society.org; 949 E 2nd St; adult/child 12-16yr $5/4; ☻10am-4pm Mon-Sat; ⊕) For an engaging, succinct look at highlights from Arizona's past, spend an hour at this family-friendly museum near the University of Ar-

Metropolitan Tucson

izona. Here you can walk though a replica of an old copper mine and take a look at Geronimo's rifle.

◉ Metropolitan Tucson East of Downtown

★ **Mini Time Machine Museum of Miniatures** MUSEUM
(Map p210; www.theminitimemachine.org; 4455 E Camp Lowell Dr; adult/child 4-17yr $9/6; ⊙9am-4pm Tue-Sat, noon-4pm Sun; ⊕) 'Meddle not in the affairs of Dragons, for ye are crunchy and tasteth good with condiments,' reads the sign beside a collection of Pocket Dragons, one of several intricate scenes in the Enchanted Realm gallery at this fun museum of miniatures. Here you can walk over a snow-globe-y Christmas village, peer into tiny homes constructed in the 1700s and 1800s, and search for the little inhabitants of a magical tree. Parents may find themselves having more fun than their kids.

◉ Around Tucson

Several of Tucson's best attractions are about 15 miles west of the University. For a scenic, saguaro-dotted drive, follow Speedway Blvd west until it turns into W Gate Pass Rd. As you approach the top of Gates Pass, look for

the one-way sign on the right. Follow it into **Gates Pass Scenic Overlook** (Map p208) where you'll have a sweeping view of the west that is especially nice at sunset. If you miss the turn, you can turn around at the parking lot below the pass.

★ **Arizona-Sonora Desert Museum** MUSEUM
(Map p208; ☑520-883-2702; www.desert museum.org; 2021 N Kinney Rd; adult/child 13-17yr $19.50/15.50; ⊙8:30am-5pm Oct-Feb, 7:30am-5pm Mar-Sep, to 10pm Sat Jun-Aug) Home to cacti, coyotes and palm-sized hummingbirds, this ode to the Sonoran desert is one part zoo, one part botanical garden and one part museum – a trifecta that'll entertain young and old for easily half a day. Desert denizens, from precocious coatis to playful prairie dogs, inhabit natural enclosures. The grounds are thick with desert plants, and docents give demonstrations.

There are two walk-through aviaries, a mineral exhibit inside a cave, a half-mile desert trail and an underground exhibit with windows into ponds where beavers and otters frolic. Strollers and wheelchairs are available, and there's a gift shop, art gallery, restaurant and cafe. A tip: wear a hat and walking shoes, and remember that the big cats are most active in the morning. The museum is off Hwy 86, about 12 miles west of Tucson, near the western section of Saguaro National Park.

TUCSON FOR CHILDREN

Reid Park Zoo (Map p210; ☑520-791-4022; www.tucsonzoo.org; 1100 S Randolph Way; adult/child 2-14yr/senior $9/5/7; ⊙9am-4pm Oct-May, 8am-3pm Jun-Sep; ⊕) A global menagerie including giant anteaters and pygmy hippos delights young and old at the small and compact Reid Park Zoo. Cap a visit with a picnic in the surrounding park, which also has playgrounds and a pond with paddleboat rentals.

Tucson Children's Museum (Map p212; ☑520-792-9985; www.childrensmuseumtucson.org; 200 S 6th Ave; admission $8; ⊙9am-5pm Mon-Fri, 10am-5pm Sat & Sun; ⊕) Parents sing the praises of the Tucson Children's Museum, which has plenty of engaging, hands-on exhibits – from Dinosaur World to an aquarium.

Tucson

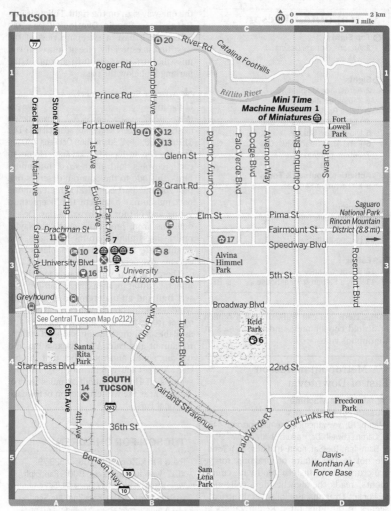

Saguaro National Park PARK
(☑Rincon 520-733-5153, Tucson 520-733-5158, park information 520-733-5100; www.nps.gov/sagu; 7-day pass per vehicle/bicycle $10/5; ☺sunrise to sunset) Saguaros are the most iconic symbol of the American Southwest, and an entire army of these majestic ribbed sentinels is protected in this desert playground. Or, more precisely, playgrounds. The park is divided into two units separated by 30 miles and the city of Tucson. Both sections – the Rincon Mountain District in the east and Tucson Mountain District in the west – are filled with trails and desert flora; it's not necessary to visit them both.

The larger section is the **Rincon Mountain District**, about 15 miles east of downtown. The **visitor center** (Map p208; ☑520-733-5153; 3693 S Old Spanish Trail; ☺9am-5pm) has information on day hikes, horseback riding and backcountry camping. The latter requires a permit ($6 per site per day) and must be obtained by noon on the day of your hike. The meandering 8-mile **Cactus Forest Scenic Loop Drive**, a paved road open to cars and bicycles, provides access to picnic areas, trailheads and viewpoints.

Two quick, easy and rewarding hikes are the 0.8-mile **Valley View Overlook** (awesome at sunset) and the half-mile **Signal Hill Trail** to scores of ancient petroglyphs. For a more strenuous trek we recommend the 7-mile **King Canyon Trail**, which starts 2 miles south of the visitor center near the Arizona-Sonora Desert Museum. The 0.5-mile informative **Desert Discovery Trail**, which is 1 mile northwest of the visitor center, is wheelchair accessible. Distances for all four hikes are round-trip.

As for the park's namesake cactus, don't refer to the limbs of the saguaro (sah-wah-ro) as branches. As park docents will quickly tell you, the mighty saguaro grows arms, not lowly branches – a distinction that makes sense when you consider their human-like features.

Saguaros grow slowly, taking about 15 years to reach 1ft in height, 50 years to reach 7ft and almost a century before they begin to take on their typical many-armed appearance. The best time to visit is April, when the saguaros begin blossoming with lovely white blooms – Arizona's state flower. By June and July, the flowers give way to ripe red fruit that local Native Americans use for food. Their foot soldiers are the spidery ocotillo, the fluffy teddy bear cactus, the green-bean-like pencil cholla and hundreds of other plant species. It is illegal to damage or remove saguaros.

Note that trailers longer than 35ft and vehicles wider than 8ft are not permitted on the park's narrow scenic loop roads.

Hikers pressed for time should follow the 1-mile round-trip **Freeman Homestead Trail** to a grove of massive saguaro. For a full-fledged desert adventure, head out on the steep and rocky **Tanque Verde Ridge Trail**, which climbs to the summit of Mica Mountain at 8666ft and back in 18 miles (backcountry camping permit required for overnight use). Family-run outfitter **Houston's Horseback Riding** (☑520-298-7450; www.tucsonhorsebackriding.com; 2hr tour per person $60) offers a two-hour trail ride into the park (per person $60), as well as sunset tours in the park with a steak dinner (per person $90).

West of town, the **Tucson Mountain District** has its own **visitor center** (Map p208; ☑520-733-5158; 2700 N Kinney Rd; ⊙9am-5pm). The Scenic Bajada Loop Drive is a 6-mile graded dirt road through cactus forest that begins 1.5 miles north of the visitor center.

Old Tucson Studios FILM LOCATION
(Map p208; ☑520-883-0100; www.oldtucson.com; 201 S Kinney Rd; adult/child 4-11yr $18/11; ⊙Oct–late-May, hours vary; ⛟) Nicknamed 'Hollywood in the Desert,' this old movie set of Tucson in the 1860s was built in 1939 for the filming of *Arizona*. Hundreds of flicks followed, bringing in movie stars from Clint Eastwood to Leonardo DiCaprio. Now a Wild West theme park, it's all about shootouts, stagecoach rides, stunt shows and dancing saloon girls. The studios are a few miles southeast of the Arizona-Sonora Desert Museum off Hwy 86.

Pima Air & Space Museum MUSEUM
(Map p208; ☑520-574-0462; www.pimaair.org; 6000 E Valencia Rd; adult/child 7-12yr/senior & military $16/9/13 Nov-May, $14/8/12 Jun-Oct; ⊙9am-5pm, last admission 4pm; ⛟) An SR-71 Blackbird spy plane and a massive B-52 bomber are among the stars of this extraordinary

Central Tucson

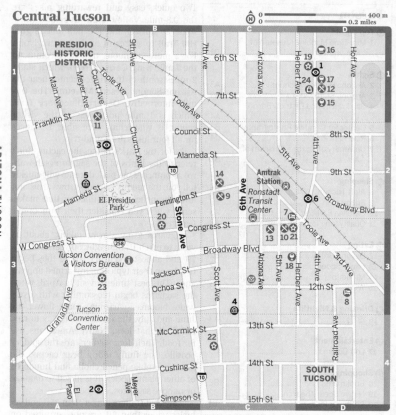

private aircraft museum. Allow at least two hours to wander through hangars and around the airfield where more than 300 'birds' trace the evolution of civilian and military aviation. A free 50-minute walking tour is offered at 10:30am and 11:30am daily (plus 1:30pm and 2:30pm December through April).

Alternatively, shell out an extra $6 for the one-hour tram tour departing at 10am, 11:30am and 1:30pm (plus 3pm December through April).

Hardcore plane-spotters should call ahead to book space on the 90-minute bus tour of the nearby 309th **Aerospace Maintenance & Regeneration Center** (AMARG; Map p208; adult/child $9/4; ⊙ Mon-Fri, departures vary) – aka the boneyard – where 4000 or so aircraft are mothballed in the dry desert air. You don't need to pay museum admission to join this tour.

◉ Santa Catalina Mountains

The Santa Catalinas northeast of Tucson are the best-loved and most visited among the region's mountain ranges. You need a Coronado Forest Recreation Pass ($5 per vehicle per day) to park anywhere in the mountain area. One pass covers Sabino Canyon and Mt Lemmon. It's available at the USFS **Santa Catalina Ranger Station** (☑520-749-8700; www.fs.usda.gov/coronado; 5700 N Sabino Canyon Rd; ⊙8am-4:30pm) at the mouth of Sabino Canyon, which also has maps, hiking guides and camping information.

Sabino Canyon (Map p208; www.sabino canyon.com; 5900 N Sabino Canyon Rd), a lush, pretty and shaded mini-gorge, is a favorite year-round destination for both locals and visitors. Narrated hop-on, hop-off tram tours along the **Sabino Canyon Trail** (☑520-749-2861; www.sabinocanyon.com; adult/child $8/4) depart every half hour for

Central Tucson

a 45-minute, nine-stop loop with access to trailheads and riverside picnic areas. It's nicest in the afternoon, when the sun plays hide and seek against the canyon walls. The last stop is only 3.8 miles from the visitor center, so hikers can listen to the tram driver's narration on the way up then hike back to the visitor center, either on the road or on the lofty but exposed **Telephone Line Trail**. There is no fee, beyond the recreation pass, if you want to hike into the canyon without riding the tram. A non-narrated shuttle (adult/child $3/1) provides access to Bear Canyon and the trailhead to Seven Falls, which has picnic sites and swimming but no facilities. From the falls, the trail continues up as high as you want to go. Parking at Sabino Canyon is $5.

A great way to escape the summer heat is by following the super-scenic **Sky Island Parkway** (officially called Catalina Hwy), which meanders 27 miles from saguaro-dappled desert to pine-covered forest near the top of Mt Lemmon (9157ft), passing through ecosystems equivalent to a journey from Mexico to Canada. Budget at least three hours round-trip. Of the vista points, Babad Do'ag, Windy Point and Aspen are the most rewarding. Get your camera ready for the sweeping views at Windy Point. There is no cost for the drive or stopping at the vista points, but if you plan to explore the forest you must pay for the aforementioned $5 day-use permit, which can be purchased at the Palisades Visitor Center.

In winter, Mt Lemmon has the southernmost **ski area** (Map p208; ☎520-576-1321; www.skithelemmon.com; 10300 Ski Run Rd; adult/child $40/20; ⊙late Dec-Mar) in the USA. With snow levels rather unpredictable, it's more about the novelty of schussing down the slopes with views of Mexico than having a world-class alpine experience. Rentals, lessons and food are available on the mountain.

And talk about crazy, skateboarders have been known to zoom down the highway on their boards. Do not do this.

🎊 Festivals & Events

Tucson knows how to party and keeps a year-round schedule of events. For details check out www.visittucson.org.

Tucson Gem and Mineral Show
MINERAL SHOW
(☎520-332-5773; www.tgms.org) This is the most famous event on the city's calendar, held on the second full weekend in February. It's the largest of its kind in the world, and an estimated 250 retail dealers who trade in minerals, crafts and fossils take over the Tucson Convention Center.

Fiesta de los Vaqueros
RODEO
(Rodeo Week; ☎520-741-2233; www.tucsonrodeo. com; ⊙last week of Feb) Held the last week of February for 90 years, the Fiesta brings world-famous cowboys to town and features a spectacular parade with Western-themed floats and buggies, historic horse-drawn coaches, folk dancers and marching bands.

Tucson Folk Festival MUSIC
(www.tkma.org) Held in early May, this music festival with more than 120 local, regional and national performers is put on by the Tucson Kitchen Musicians Association.

🛏 Sleeping

Tucson's gamut of lodging options rivals Phoenix for beauty, comfort and location. Rates plummet as much as 50% between June and September, making what would otherwise be a five-star megasplurge an affordable getaway. Chains are abundant along the I-10 and around the airport.

🛏 Downtown Tucson

Roadrunner Hostel & Inn HOSTEL $
(Map p212; ☑520-940-7280; www.roadrunner hostelinn.com; 346 E 12th St; dm/r incl breakfast $22/45; ❄@🛜🐾) Cultural and language barriers melt faster than snow in the desert at this small and friendly hostel within walking distance of 4th Ave. The guest kitchen and TV lounge are convivial spaces, and freebies include coffee, tea and a waffle breakfast. The 1900 adobe building once belonged to the sheriff involved in capturing the Dillinger gang at the Hotel Congress in 1934.

Closed between noon and 3pm. No credit cards. Pets OK in private room.

Hotel Congress HISTORIC HOTEL $$
(Map p212; ☑520-622-8848; www.hotelcongress. com; 311 E Congress St; r $89-149; P❄@🛜🐾) Charming, confident and occasionally a pain in the ass? Yes. But rest assured, downtown Tucson's most famous lodging is never, ever boring. Beautifully restored, this 1919 hotel feels very modern, mostly because of its popular cafe, bar and club. Many rooms have period furnishings, rotary phones and wooden radios – but no TVs.

Infamous bank robber John Dillinger and his gang were captured here during their 1934 stay when a fire broke out at the hotel. Avoid the Club Rooms (above the club) if you're noise-sensitive. Pets are $10 per night.

🛏 University of Arizona

Quality Inn Flamingo Downtown MOTEL $
(Map p210; ☑520-770-1910; www.flamingohotel tucson.com; 1300 N Stone Ave; r incl breakfast $65-80; ❄@🛜🐾) Though recently purchased by the Quality Inn chain, the former Flamingo Hotel retains a bit of its great 1950s Rat Pack vibe, and the fact that Elvis slept

here doesn't hurt (although the rooms were renumbered and now no one is sure which room he slept in. Sad face.). Rooms come with chic striped bedding, flat-screen plasma TVs, a good-sized desk and comfy beds.

Pets are $25 per day. Wi-fi can be a bit unreliable in the rooms.

★ Catalina Park Inn B&B $$
(Map p210; ☑520-792-4541; www.catalinaparkinn. com; 309 E 1st St; r $145-189; ⊙ closed Jul & Aug; ❄@🛜🐾) Style, hospitality and comfort merge seamlessly at this inviting B&B just west of the University of Arizona and 4th Ave. Hosts Mark Hall and Paul Richard have poured their hearts into restoring this 1927 Mediterranean-style villa, and their efforts are on display in each of the six rooms, which vary in style.

The East and West Rooms have balcony porches perfect for sipping early morning coffee. Don't miss the delicious breakfast.

The cacti-and-desert garden has lots of little corners for lazy afternoon cat naps. Small pets OK in the Cottage Room.

Aloft Tucson HOTEL $$
(Map p210; ☑520-908-6800; www.starwood hotels.com; 1900 E Speedway Blvd; r $169; ❄🛜) Tucson is surprisingly light on trendy boutique hotels. The new Aloft, near the university, isn't an indie property, but it does project a cool, modern vibe that caters to tech-minded, style-conscious travelers. Rooms and common areas pop with bright but spare decor that manages to feel inviting. Beer and cocktails served at the on-site bar, and there's 24-hour grab-n-go food beside the lobby.

🛏 Metropolitan Tucson

Desert Trails B&B B&B $$
(Map p208; ☑520-885-7295; www.deserttrails. com; 12851 E Speedway Blvd; r incl breakfast $140-170, guesthouse $175; ❄🛜🐾) Outdoorsy types who want a personable B&B close to Saguaro National Park (Rincon Mountain District) have their answer at Desert Trails on the far eastern fringe of Speedway Blvd. Rooms are comfy with all the latest amenities. John Higgins, an avid backpacker, was a fireman for Saguaro National Park for six years and is glad to share his knowledge about the park's trails.

Houston's Horseback Riding (p211), which leads equestrian tours into the park, is next door.

Arizona Inn
RESORT **$$$**

(Map p210; ☑ 800-933-1093, 520-325-1541; www.arizonainn.com; 2200 E Elm St; r $199-259, ste $299-379; ❋@☎☒) Our favorite part? High tea in the library, complete with scones and finger sandwiches. Croquet might be a highlight too, if only we could find a teammate. Historic and aristocratic touches such as these provide a definite sense of privilege – and we like it. Mature gardens and old Arizona grace also provide a respite from city life and the 21st century. Rooms are furnished with antiques. Be sure to pop into the country-clubbish Audubon Bar.

Hacienda del Sol
HISTORIC INN **$$$**

(Map p208; ☑ 520-299-1501; www.haciendadelsol.com; 5501 N Hacienda del Sol Rd; r $178-295, ste $358, casitas $412; ❋@☎☒) An elite, hilltop girls' school built in the 1920s, this relaxing refuge has artist-designed, Southwest-style rooms and teems with unique touches like carved ceiling beams and louvered exterior doors to catch the courtyard breeze. Having been on the radar of Spencer Tracy, Katharine Hepburn and other legends, you'll be sleeping with history. Fabulous restaurant, too.

🛏 Around Tucson

Gilbert Ray Campground
CAMPGROUND **$**

(Map p208; ☑ 520-883-4200; www.pima.gov; Kinney Rd; tent/RV sites $10/20; ☒) Camp among the saguaros at this Pima County campground 13 miles west of downtown. It has 130 first-come, first-served sites along with water and rest rooms, but no showers. There are five tent-only sites but tenters can camp at RV sites. No credit cards. Located near the Arizona-Sonora Desert Museum.

🍴 Eating

Tucson's culinary scene delivers a flavor-packed punch, from family-run 'nosherias' to five-star dining rooms. Intricately spiced and authentic Mexican and Southwestern fare is king here, and much of it is prepared fresh with regional ingredients. Lots of new restaurants have opened downtown, including a satellite of Flagstaff's popular **Diablo Burger** (Map p212; www.diabloburger.com; 312 E Congress St), all just ahead of the arrival of the new streetcar.

Food Conspiracy Cooperative (Map p212; 412 4th Ave; sandwiches under $7; ☺ 8am-10pm) is great for stocking up on organic produce and products, plus tasty to-go sandwiches.

Mi Nidito
MEXICAN **$**

(Map p210; ☑ 520-622-5081; www.minidito.net; 1813 S 4th Ave; mains $6-13; ☺ from 11am Wed-Sun) Former president Bill Clinton's order (pre-quadruple bypass) at 'My Little Nest' has become the signature president's plate, a heaping mound of Mexican favorites – tacos, tostadas, burritos, enchiladas and more – groaning under melted cheese. Give the prickly pear cactus chili or the *birria* (spicy, shredded beef) a whirl.

Solo diners beware – the loudspeaker will boldly announce your name followed by 'party of one' when they're ready for you.

Lovin' Spoonfuls
VEGAN **$**

(Map p210; ☑ 520-325-7766; 2990 N Campbell Ave; breakfast $6-9, lunch $5.25-8, dinner $7.25-11.25; ☺ 9:30am-9pm Mon-Sat, 10am-3pm Sun; ☑) Burgers, country-fried chicken and club sandwiches – the menu reads like those at your typical diner but there's one big difference: no animal products will ever find their way into this vegan haven. Outstandingly creative choices include the cashew-mushroom pâté and the adzuki-bean burger.

Beyond Bread
SANDWICHES **$**

(Map p210; www.beyondbread.com; 3026 N Campbell Ave; sandwiches $7-11; ☺ 6:30am-8pm Mon-Fri, 7am-8pm Sat, 7am-6pm Sun) Free chunks of homemade bread are perched temptingly between the door and the front counter at this busy cafe and bakery, which has a handful of locations across town. Their specialties? Daily breads and a mouthwatering array of sandwiches – with several veggie options. Soups and salads too.

★ Cafe Poca Cosa
SOUTH AMERICAN **$$**

(Map p212; ☑ 520-622-6400; www.cafepocacosatucson.com; 110 E Pennington St; lunch $12-15, dinner $18-26; ☺ 11am-9pm Tue-Thu, to 10pm Fri & Sat) At this award-winning nuevo-Mexican bistro a Spanish-English blackboard menu circulates between tables because dishes change twice daily. It's all freshly prepared, innovative and beautifully presented. The undecided can't go wrong by ordering the Plato Poca Cosa and letting chef Suzana Davila decide. Great margaritas, too.

Cup Cafe
AMERICAN, GLOBAL **$$**

(Map p212; ☑ 520-798-1618; www.hotelcongress.com/food; 311 E Congress St; breakfast $7-12, lunch $10-12, dinner $13-25; ☺ 7am-10pm Sun-Thu, to 11pm Fri & Sat; ☑) Cup Cafe, we like your style. Wine-bottle chandeliers. A penny-tiled floor. And 'Up on Cripple Creek' on the speakers.

HOT DIGGETY DOG

Tucson's signature dish is the Sonoran hotdog, a tasty example of what happens when Mexican ingredients meet American processed meat and penchant for excess. So what is it? A bacon-wrapped hotdog layered with tomatillo salsa, pinto beans, shredded cheese, mayo, ketchup, mustard, chopped tomatoes and onions. We like 'em at **El Guero Canelo** (Map p208; www.elguerocanelo.com; 5201 S 12th Ave; mains $3-8.29; ☺10am-11pm Mon-Thu, 8am-midnight Fri & Sat, 9am-11pm Sun), which has another location at 2480 N Oracle Rd.

In the morning, choices include a Creole dish with andouille sausage, eggs, potatoes, buttermilk biscuits and sausage gravy, and cast-iron baked eggs with Gruyère cheese. And the coffee is excellent. There's a global mix of dishes, with a decent selection of vegetarian options.

Hub Restaurant & Creamery AMERICAN $$
(Map p212; ☏520-207-8201; www.hubdowntown.com; 266 E Congress Ave; lunch $10-16, dinner $10-24; ☺11am-2am; ✎) Exposed brick walls, a lofty ceiling, sleek booths and, surprisingly, a walk-up ice-cream stand beside the hostess desk – industrial chic takes a Mayberry spin. Upscale comfort food is the name of the game here, from lobster mac 'n' cheese to chicken pot pie, plus a few sandwiches and salads.

Even if you don't want a meal, you can pop in for a scoop of salted caramel.

Reilly Craft Pizza & Drink PIZZA $$
(Map p212; www.reillypizza.com; 101 E Pennington St; mains $12-15; ☺11am-10pm Mon-Thu, 11am-midnight Fri, noon-midnight Sat, noon-9pm Sun) The prosciutto and arugula pizza here is so darn good it might just wake the dead. Oh, sorry, too soon? We jest, but this trendy gourmet pizza joint *is* housed inside a former funeral home, which might explain the chapel-like arches in the airy dining room. The selection of craft beers is fairly extensive, and they're all $5. Heavenly.

Wilko GASTROPUB $$
(Map p210; www.barwilko.com; 943 E University Blvd, cnr N Park & University; breakfast $7-9, lunch & dinner $9-14) For a pleasant lunch near the University of Arizona, tuck in at this stylish new gastropub across the street from campus. Look for savory sandwiches and pizzas on the menu, plus a few 'tasty misfits.' As for sandwiches, try the unfortunately named Jerk, with marinated, dry-rubbed chicken, coleslaw and curry aioli. At the bar, the beers are microbrewed and the cocktails crafted.

Tiny's Saloon & Steakhouse AMERICAN $$
(Map p208; ☏520-578-7700; 4900 W Ajo Hwy; mains $7-21; ☺11am-10pm Mon-Thu & Sat-Sun, until midnight Fri; ✎) Motorcycles are lined up like horses in front of Tiny's, a well-worn watering hole just west of the city. Inside, once your eyes adjust, slide into a booth, nod at the barflies then order a steerburger with a cold beer. A docent at the Pima Air & Space Museum told us that Tiny's has the best burgers in town, and we think he might be right.

For a saloon, Tiny's is family friendly – at least during the day – and makes a nice stop after a day at the Arizona-Sonora Desert Museum or Saguaro National Park. Cash only, but ATM on-site.

El Charro Café MEXICAN $$
(Map p212; ☏520-622-1922; www.elcharrocafe.com; 311 N Court Ave; lunch $6-11, dinner $7-18; ☺11am-9pm Mon-Thu, 11am-10pm Fri & Sat, 10am-10pm Sun; ✎) In this rambling, buzzing hacienda the Flin family has been making innovative Mexican food since 1922. They're particularly famous for the *carne seca,* sundried lean beef that's been reconstituted, shredded and grilled with green chile and onions. The food may have lost of little of its wow over the years, but it's good for families exploring downtown.

The fabulous margaritas pack a Pancho Villa punch.

 **Drinking & Nightlife**

Congress St in downtown and 4th Ave near the University are both busy party strips.

Che's Lounge BAR
(Map p212; ☏520-623-2088; 350 N 4th Ave; ☺noon-2am) Drinkers unite! If everyone's favorite revolutionary heartthrob was still in our midst, he wouldn't have charged a cover either. A slightly skanky but hugely popular watering hole with $1.50 drafts, a huge wraparound bar and local art gracing the walls, this college hangout rocks with live music most Saturday nights and on the patio on Sunday afternoons (4pm to 7pm) in the summer.

Surly Wench
BAR

(Map p212; ☑520-882-0009; www.surlywench pub.com; 424 4th Ave; ☺2pm-2am Mon-Fri, 11am-2am Sat & Sun) This bat cave of a watering hole is generally packed with pierced pals soaking up $2 beer, giving the pinball machine a workout or head-banging to deafening bands, from punkgrass to alt-rock. There's a burlesque show the first Friday of the month. See the website for dates and times.

Thunder Canyon Brewery
MICROBREWERY

(Map p212; www.thundercanyonbrewery.com; 220 E Broadway Blvd; ☺11am-11pm Sun-Thu, to 2am Fri & Sat) This cavernous microbrewery, within walking distance of Hotel Congress, has more than 40 beers on tap, serving up its own creations as well as handcrafted beers from across the US.

Chocolate Iguana
COFFEE SHOP

(Map p212; www.chocolateiguanaon4th.com; 500 N 4th Ave; ☺7am-8pm Mon-Thu, 7am-10pm Fri, 8am-10pm Sat, 9am-6pm Sun) Chocoholics have their pick of sweets and pastries inside this green-and-purple cottage, while coffee lovers can choose from numerous coffee brews and a long list of specialty drinks. Watching your diet? The delicious Frozen Explosion is a fat-free mocha. Also sells sandwiches ($6 to $7) and gifts.

IBT's
GAY CLUB

(Map p210; ☑520-882-3053; 616 N 4th Ave; ☺noon-2am) At Tucson's most sizzling gay fun house, the theme changes nightly – from drag shows to karaoke, plus the monthly Sunday gospel brunch. Chill on the patio, check out the bods or sweat it out on the dance floor.

☆ Entertainment

The free *Tucson Weekly* (www.tucsonweekly. com) has comprehensive entertainment listings.

Live Music

Club Congress
LIVE MUSIC

(Map p212; ☑520-622-8848; www.hotelcongress. com; 311 E Congress St) Skinny jeansters, tousled hipsters, aging folkies, dressed-up hotties – the crowd at Tucson's most-happening club inside the grandly aging Hotel Congress defines the word eclectic. And so does the musical line-up, which usually features the finest local and regional talent. Wanna sit and just drink at a no-fuss bar? Step inside the adjacent **Tap Room**, open since 1919.

Try the **Lobby Bar** for fancy cocktails.

Rialto Theatre
LIVE MUSIC

(Map p212; ☑520-740-1000; www.rialtotheatre. com; 318 E Congress St) This gorgeous 1920 vaudeville and movie theater has been reborn as a top venue for live touring acts. Featuring everything from alt-pop to reggae, Latin dance to swing, plus the odd comedian; basically anyone too big to play at Club Congress across the street.

Flycatcher
LIVE MUSIC

(Map p212; ☑520-207-9251; www.theflycatcher tucson.com; 340 E 6th St) Formerly known as Plush, Flycatcher is a club to watch when it comes to catching cool regional bands.

Cinema & Performing Arts

Fox Theatre
THEATER

(Map p212; ☑520-547-3040; www.foxtucsont heatre.org; 17 W Congress St) It's always worth checking out what's on at the deco Fox Theatre, a gloriously glittery venue for classic and modern movies, music, theater and dance.

Loft Cinema
MOVIE THEATER

(Map p210; ☑520-795-0844; www.loftcinema. com; 3233 E Speedway Blvd) For indie, art-house and foreign movies head to Loft Cinema.

Tucson Music Hall
CLASSICAL

(Map p212; 260 S Church Ave) The **Arizona Opera** (☑520-293-4336; www.azopera.org; ☺Oct-Apr) and **Tucson Symphony Orchestra** (☑520-792-9155; www.tucsonsymphony.org; ☺Sep-May) perform here between October and April.

Temple of Music & Art
THEATER

(Map p212; 330 S Scott Ave) The **Arizona Theatre Company** (☑520-622-2823; www.arizona theatre.org; ☺Sep-Apr) stages shows at this renovated 1920s building.

🛍 Shopping

Old Town Artisans (Map p212; www.oldtown artisans.com; 201 N Court Ave; ☺10am-5:30pm Mon-Sat, 11am-5pm Sun Sep-May, until 4pm Jun-Aug) in the Presidio Historic District is a good destination for quality arts and crafts produced in the Southwest and Mexico. For fun, eclectic shopping you can't beat 4th Ave, where there's a great cluster of vintage stores between 8th and 7th Sts. The Chocolate Iguana has an impressive array of chocolate candy, as well as cute gifts.

Native Seeds/Search
AGRICULTURAL

(Map p210; www.nativeseeds.org; 3061 N Campbell Ave; ☺10am-5pm) The special Native Seeds/

Search sells rare seeds of crops traditionally grown by Native Americans, along with quality books and crafts.

Antigone Books   BOOKS
(Map p212; www.antigonebooks.com; 411 N 4th Ave; ☺10am-7pm Mon-Thu, 10am-9pm Fri & Sat, 11am-5pm Sun) Great indie bookstore with a fun, girl-power focus.

Bookmans   BOOKS
(Map p210; www.bookmans.com; 1930 E Grant Rd; ☺9am-10pm; ☏) Well-stocked Arizona indie chain and locals' hangout.

St Philips Plaza   OUTDOOR MALL
(Map p210; www.stphilipsplaza.com; 4280 N Campbell Ave) Stop by **Bahti Indian Arts** (www.bahti.com) for Native American wares.

❶ Information

EMERGENCY
Police (☏520-791-4444; www.police.tucsonaz.gov/police; 270 S Stone Ave)

MEDIA
The local mainstream newspapers include the morning **Arizona Daily Star** (http://azstarnet.com). The free **Tucson Weekly** (www.tucsonweekly.com) is chock-full of great entertainment and restaurant listings. **Tucson Lifestyle** (www.tucsonlifestyle.com) is a glossy monthly mag. Catch National Public Radio (NPR) on 89.1.

MEDICAL SERVICES
Tucson Medical Center (☏520-327-5461; www.tmcaz.com/TucsonMedicalCenter; 5301 E Grant Rd) Has 24-hour emergency services.

POST
Post Office (☏520-903-1958; 141 S 6th Ave; ☺9am-5pm)

TOURIST INFORMATION
Coronado National Forest Supervisor's Office (☏520-388-8300; www.fs.usda.gov/coronado; Federal Bldg, 300 W Congress St; ☺8am-4:30pm Mon-Fri) Provides information on trekking and camping in Coronado National Forest.

Tucson Convention & Visitors Bureau (Map p212; ☏800-638-8350, 520-624-1817; www.visittucson.org; 100 S Church Ave; ☺9am-5pm Mon-Fri, to 4pm Sat & Sun) Ask for its free Tucson travel guide.

❶ Getting There & Away

Tucson International Airport (Map p208; ☏520-573-8100; www.flytucson.com; 7250 S Tucson Blvd) Fifteen miles south of downtown and served by six airlines, with nonstop flights to more than 15 destinations including Atlanta, Denver, Las Vegas, Los Angeles and San Francisco.

Greyhound (Map p210; ☏520-792-3475; www.greyhound.com; 471 W Congress St) Runs six buses to Phoenix ($18, two hours), among other destinations.

Amtrak (☏800-872-7245, 520-623-4442; www.amtrak.com; 400 E Toole Ave) The *Sunset Limited* train comes through on its way west to Los Angeles ($89, 10 hours, three weekly) and east to New Orleans ($285, 36 hours, three weekly).

❶ Getting Around

All major car-rental agencies have offices at the airport. **Arizona Stagecoach** (☏520-889-1000; www.azstagecoach.com) runs shared-ride vans into downtown for about $25 per person. A taxi from the airport to downtown costs around $25. One taxi company is **Yellow Cab** (☏520-624-6611; www.aaayellowaz.com).

The **Ronstadt Transit Center** (Map p212; 215 E Congress St, cnr Congress St & 6th Ave) is the main hub for the public **Sun Tran** (☏520-792-9222; www.suntran.com) buses serving the entire metro area. Fares are $1.50 one-way.

Tucson to Phoenix

If you just want to travel between Arizona's two biggest cities quickly, it's a straight 120-mile shot on a not terribly inspiring stretch of the I-10. However, a couple of rewarding side trips await those with curiosity and a little more time on their hands.

Picacho Peak State Park   STATE PARK
(☏520-466-3183, camping reservations 520-586-2283; http://azstateparks.com; I-10, exit 219; per vehicle $7, campsites $25; ☺5am-9pm, visitor center 8am-5pm, park closed late-May–mid-Sep) The westernmost battle of the American Civil War was fought near this distinctive peak (3374ft) in 1862. Here, a small band of Confederate Arizona Rangers killed three Union cavalrymen. After the skirmish, Confederate soldiers retreated to Tucson and dispersed, knowing full well that they would soon be greatly outnumbered. The battle is reenacted every March with much pomp, circumstance and period costumes. The pretty state park has a visitor center that acts as a jump-off point for trails onto the mountain.

If you're fit, you can walk to the peak of the mountain via a rugged trail that includes cables and catwalks. Camping is available at 85 electric, first-come, first-served sites; they're suitable for tents or RVs. No hookups. Wi-fi is available for a fee. The park is 40 miles northwest of Tucson.

Biosphere 2 BIOSPHERE

(📞520-838-6200; www.b2science.org; 32540 S Biosphere Rd, Oracle; adult/child 6-12yr/senior $20/13/18; ⊙9am-4pm) Built to be completely sealed off from Biosphere 1 (that would be Earth), Biosphere 2 is a 3-acre campus of glass domes and pyramids containing five ecosystems: tropical ocean, mangrove wetlands, tropical rain forest, savanna and coastal fog desert. In 1991, eight biospherians were sealed inside for a two-year tour of duty from which they emerged thinner but in fair shape. Tours take in the biospherians' apartments, farm area and kitchen, the one-million gallon 'tropical ocean' and the 'technosphere' that made it all possible.

Although this experiment was ostensibly a prototype for self-sustaining space colonies, the privately funded endeavor was engulfed in controversy. Heavy criticism came after the dome leaked gases and was opened to allow a biospherian to emerge for medical treatment. After several changes in ownership, the sci-fi-esque site is now a University of Arizona–run earth science research institute.

Biosphere 2 is near Oracle, about 30 miles north of Tucson via Hwy 77 (Oracle Rd) or 30 miles east of the I-10 (exit 240, east on Tangerine Rd, then north on Hwy 77). No pets.

Casa Grande Ruins National
Monument NATIONAL MONUMENT

(📞520-723-3172; www.nps.gov/cagr; 1100 W Ruins Dr, Coolidge; adult/child 15yr & under $5/free; ⊙9am-5pm) Built around AD 1350, Casa Grande (Big House) is the country's largest Hohokam structure still standing, with 11 rooms spread across four floors and mud walls several feet thick. It's in reasonably good shape, partly because of the metal awning that's been canopying it since 1932. Although you can't walk inside the crumbling structure, you can peer into its rooms. A few strategically placed windows and doors suggest that the structure may have served as an astronomical observatory.

Experts aren't 100% sure of the purpose of the oval ball pit, one of about 200 found regionally in Hohokam villages, but it may be linked to similar courts used for ball games by the Aztecs.

The visitor center has exhibits about the Hohokam society and Casa Grande itself, including a model of what the place may have originally looked like. Guided tours are offered from late November through mid-April. Call for times. Tours may be offered the rest of the year depending on staffing, weather and group size.

The ruins are about 70 miles northwest of Tucson. Leave the I-10 at exit 211 and head north on Hwy 87 towards Coolidge and follow the signs. Don't confuse the monument with the modern town of Casa Grande, west of the I-10.

West of Tucson

West of Tucson, Hwy 86 cuts through the Tohono O'odham Indian Reservation, the second largest in the country. Although this is one of the driest areas in the Sonora Desert, it's an appealing drive for anyone craving the lonely highway – however, you can expect to see a number of green-and-white border patrol SUVs cruising past. Listen for the sounds of the desert: the howl of a coyote, the rattle of a snake. The skies are big, the land vast and barren. Gas stations, grocery marts and motels are sparse, so plan ahead and carry plenty of water and other necessities.

Kitt Peak National Observatory

Dark and clear night skies make remote **Kitt Peak** (📞520-318-8726; www.noao.edu/kpno; Hwy 86; admission by donation; ⊙9am-4pm) a perfect site for one of the world's largest observatories. Just west of Sells, 56 miles southwest of Tucson, this 6875ft-high mountaintop is stacked with two radio and 23 optical telescopes, including one boasting a staggering diameter of 12ft.

There's a visitor center with exhibits and a gift shop, but no food. Guided one-hour **tours** (adult/child $7.75/4 Nov-May, $5.75/3 Jun-Oct; ⊙10am, 11:30am & 1:30pm) take you inside the building housing the telescopes, but alas you don't get to peer through any of them. To catch a glimpse of the universe, sign up for the **Nightly Observing Program** (adult/student/senior $48/44/44; ⊙closed mid-Jul–Aug), a three to 3½ hour stargazing session starting at sunset and limited to 46 people. This program books up weeks in advance but you can always check for cancellations when visiting. Dress warmly! It gets cold up there. Light dinner included. For this program, children must be at last eight years old.

There is no public transportation to the observatory, but **Adobe Shuttle**

(☎520-609-0593) runs vans out here from Tucson for $275 for one to three people; if four to six people then $75 per person.

Organ Pipe Cactus National Monument

You can't get much further off the grid than this huge and exotic **park** (☎520-387-6849; www.nps.gov/orpi; Hwy 85; per vehicle $8; ☺visitor center 8:30am-4:30pm) along the Mexican border. It's a gorgeous, forbidding land that supports an astonishing number of animals and plants, including 28 species of cacti, first and foremost its namesake organ-pipe. A giant columnar cactus, it differs from the more prevalent saguaro in that its branches radiate from the base. Organ-pipes are common in Mexico but very rare north of the border. The monument is also the only place in the USA to see the senita cactus. Its branches are topped by hairy white tufts, which give it the nickname 'old man's beard.' Animals that have adapted to this arid climate include bighorn sheep, coyotes, kangaroo rats, mountain lions and the piglike javelina. Your best chance of encountering wildlife is in the early morning or evening. Walking around the desert by full moon or flashlight is another good way to catch things on the prowl, but wear boots and watch where you step.

Winter and early spring, when Mexican gold poppies and purple lupine blanket the barren ground, are the most pleasant seasons to visit. Summers are shimmering hot (above 100°F, or 38°C) and bring monsoon rains between July and September.

The only paved road to and within the monument is Hwy 85, which travels 26 miles south from the hamlet of Why to Lukeville, near the Mexican border. After 22 miles you reach the **Kris Eggle Visitor Center** (☺8am-5pm Jan-Mar, 8:30am-4:30pm Apr-Dec), which has information, drinking water, books and exhibits. Ranger-led programs run from January to March.

◎ Sights & Activities

Two scenic drives are currently open to vehicles and bicycles, both starting near the visitor center. The 21-mile **Ajo Mountain Drive** takes you through a spectacular landscape of steep-sided, jagged cliffs and rock tinged a faintly hellish red. It's a well-maintained but winding and steep gravel road navigable by regular passenger cars (not recommend-

ed for RVs over 24ft long). The other route is **Puerto Blanco Drive**, of which only the first 5 miles are open, leading to a picnic area and overviews. Ranger-led van tours available from January to March.

Unless it's too hot, the best way to experience this martian scenery is on foot. There are several **hiking trails**, ranging from a 200yd paved nature trail to strenuous climbs of over 4 miles. Cross-country hiking is also possible, but bring a topographical map and a compass and know how to use them – a mistake out here can be deadly. Always carry plenty of water, wear a hat and slather yourself in sunscreen.

🛏 Sleeping & Eating

There are 208 first-come, first-served sites at **Twin Peaks Campground** (www.nps.gov/orpi; tent & RV sites $12) by the visitor center. You can probably find a site here, even in high season. The campground has drinking water and toilets, but no showers or hookups. Tenters might prefer the scenic, if primitive, **Alamo Canyon Campground** (campsites $8), which requires reservations at the visitor center. There's no backcountry camping because of illegal border crossings.

No food is available at the monument, but there's a cafe in Lukeville 5 miles south. You'll find a gas station and convenience store in Why, which is 22 miles north of the visitor center. The closest lodging is in **Ajo**, about 11 miles north of Why, on Hwy 85.

Dangers & Annoyances

Rubbing up against the Mexican border, this remote monument is a popular crossing for undocumented immigrants and drug smugglers, and large sections are closed to the public. A steel fence intended to stop illegal off-road car crossings marks its southern boundary. In 2002, 28-year-old ranger Kris Eggle, for whom the visitor center is named, was killed by drug traffickers while on patrol in the park. Call ahead or check the website for current accessibility.

South of Tucson

From Tucson, the I-19 is a straight 60-mile shot south through the Santa Cruz River Valley to Nogales on the Mexican border. A historical trading route since pre-Hispanic times, the highway is unique in the US because distances are posted in kilometers – when it was built there was a strong push to go metric. Speed limits, however, are posted in miles!

Though not terribly scenic, I-19 is a ribbon of superb cultural sights with a bit of shopping thrown in the mix. It makes an excellent day trip from Tucson. If you don't want to backtrack, follow the prettier Hwys 82 and 83 to the I-10 for a 150-mile loop.

◉ Sights & Activities

Mission San Xavier del Bac HISTORIC BUILDING
(Map p208; ☑ 520-294-2624; www.patronato sanxavier.org; 1950 W San Xavier Rd; donations appreciated; ⊘ museum 8:30am-5pm, church 7am-5pm) The dazzling white towers of this mission rise from the dusty desert floor 8 miles south of Tucson – a mesmerizing mirage just off I-19 that brings an otherworldly glow to the scrubby landscape surrounding it. Nicknamed 'White Dove of the Desert,' the original mission was founded by Jesuit missionary Father Eusebio Kino in 1700 but was mostly destroyed in the Pima uprising of 1751.

Its successor was gracefully rebuilt in the late 1700s in a harmonious blend of Moorish, Byzantine and Mexican Renaissance styles. Carefully restored in the 1990s with the help of experts from the Vatican and still religiously active, it's one of the best-preserved and most beautiful Spanish missions in the country.

The extraordinary splendor behind its thick walls begs for a closer look. Your eyes are instantly drawn to the wall-sized carved, painted and gilded retable behind the altar, which tells the story of creation in dizzying detail. In the left transept the faithful line up to caress and pray to a reclining wooden figure of St Francis, the mission's patron saint. Metal votive pins shaped like body parts have been affixed to his blanket, offered in the hope of healing.

A small museum explains the history of the mission and its construction. Free 45-minute docent tours add helpful context. Visit the website for daily tour times. Native Americans sell fry bread, jewelry and crafts in the parking lot.

From I-19, take exit 92.

Titan Missile Museum MUSEUM
(☑ 520-625-7736; www.titanmissilemuseum. org; 1580 W Duval Mine Rd, Sahuarita; adult/child 7-12yr/senior $9.50/6/8.50; ⊘ 8:45am-5pm, last tour at 4pm) At this original Titan II missile site, a crew stood ready 24/7 to launch a nuclear warhead within seconds of receiving a presidential order. The Titan II was the first liquid-propelled Intercontinental Ballistic Missile (ICBM) that could be fired from below ground and could reach its target – halfway around the world or wherever – in 30 minutes or less. On alert from 1963 to 1986, this is the only one of 54 Titan II missile sites nationwide that has been preserved as a museum.

The one-hour tours, which are usually led by retired military types, are both frightening and fascinating. After descending 35ft and walking through several 3-ton blast doors, you enter the control room where you experience a simulated launch before seeing the actual (deactivated, of course) 103ft-tall missile still in its launch duct.

The tour is wheelchair accessible. Exhibits in the small museum trace the history of the Cold War and related topics.

The museum is 24 miles south of Tucson, off I-19 exit 69.

Tubac VILLAGE
(www.tubacaz.com) Tubac, about 45 miles south of Tucson, started as a Spanish fort set up in 1752 to stave off Pima attacks. These days, the tiny village depends entirely on tourists dropping money for crafts, gifts, jewelry, souvenirs, pottery and paintings peddled in its more than 100 galleries, studios and shops. Compact and lined with pre-fab, adobe-style buildings, it's attractive but somewhat sterile.

Tumacácori National Historic Park MUSEUM
(☑ 520-398-2341; www.nps.gov/tuma; I-19 exit 29; adult/child 15yr & under $3/free; ⊘ 9am-5pm) Three miles south of Tubac, this pink-and-cream edifice shimmers in the desert like a conquistador's dream. In 1691 Father Eusebio Kino and his cohorts arrived at the Tumacácori settlement and quickly founded a mission to convert the local Native Americans. However, repeated Apache raids and the harsh winter of 1848 drove the priests out, leaving the complex to crumble for decades. For self-guided tours of the hauntingly beautiful ruins (ask for the free booklet) start at the visitor center, which also has a few exhibits.

Wander through the cool church and its alcoves and the thorny gravesites. An impressive mass is held here on Christmas Eve. Check the website for dates and times for river walks (January to March) and bird walks (February to March).

Santa Cruz Chili & Spice SPICES
(☑ 520-398-2591; www.santacruzchili.com; 1868 E Frontage Rd; ☉ 8am-5pm Mon-Fri, 10am-5pm Sat, to 3pm Sat summer) Warning: if you sample the salsa, you won't be able to resist purchasing a bottle for later consumption. Yep, this spice factory south of the mission has been in business for more than 60 years for a reason. And it sells just about every seasoning under the sun. In addition to salsa, the stuff to buy is its homemade chile pastes.

Tubac Presidio State Historic Park & Museum MUSEUM
(☑ 520-398-2252; http://azstateparks.com; 1 Burruel St; adult/child 7-13yr $5/2; ☉ 9am-5pm) The foundation of the fort is all that's left at this state park, which is within walking distance of Tubac's shops and galleries. The attached museum has some worthwhile exhibits, including Arizona's oldest newspaper-printing press from 1859. The presidio was the staging point for de Anza's expedition to California in the 1770s, and today the site is also trailhead for a 4.5-mile section of the Juan Baptista de Anza National Historic Trail linking the park and Tumacacori National Historic Park.

✺ Festivals & Events

The Tubac Festival of the Arts is held in early February; Taste of Tubac showcases local culinary flair in early April; Anza Days, on the third weekend in October, are marked by historical reenactments, including some pretty cool parade ground maneuvers by faux-Spanish mounted lancers; and in early December the streets light up during Luminaria Nights, a Mexican-influenced Christmas tradition. Check the town's website for exact dates (wwwtubacaz.com).

🛏 Sleeping & Eating

Tubac Country Inn B&B $$
(☑ 520-398-3178; www.tubaccountryinn.com; 13 Burruel St; r $130-165; ❋ 🎧) The decor at this charming five-room inn is best described as Southwest-lite: Navajo prints, Native American baskets and chunky wood furniture. A breakfast basket is delivered to your door in the morning.

Shelby's Bistro CAFE $$
(☑ 520-398-8075; www.shelbysbistro.com; 19 Tubac Rd; lunch $11-17, dinner $12-26; ☉ 11am-4pm daily, 5-8:30pm Wed-Sat) The patio at Shelby's is a friendly place to relax after a hard day of shopping and museum hopping. Serving mainly salads, wraps and gourmet pizzas, it's also a good place to enjoy a lighter lunch. The Wine Country Salad with pecans, sweet dried cherries, grilled portabella and gorgonzola is particularly delicious.

Wisdoms Café MEXICAN $$
(☑ 520-398-2397; www.wisdomscafe.com; 1931 E Frontage Rd; mains $6-18; ☉ 11am-3pm Mon-Sat & 5-8pm Mon-Thu, 5-9pm Fri & Sat) Locally beloved, this institution has been luring 'em in since 1944. The Mexican-themed menu touts the signature 'fruit burros' (a fruit-filled crispy tortilla rolled in cinnamon and sugar). We think it executes an excellent take on the enchilada. Located 2 miles south of Tubac. A sister restaurant, DOS, serving burritos and street tacos, recently opened in the village of Tubac (4 Plaza Rd).

❶ Information

There are approximately 100 galleries, art studios and crafts stores in town. As exhibitions and artists constantly rotate it's hard to recommend any one place over the next, but seeing as Tubac is a small village, you can wander all it has to offer very easily on foot.

For more information stop by the **Tubac Chamber of Commerce** (☑ 520-398-2704; www.tubacaz.com; 12B Tubac Rd; ☉ 10am-5pm Mon-Fri).

❶ Getting There & Away

Tubac is 50 miles south of Tucson off I-19; the main exit into town is exit 34.

Patagonia & the Mountain Empire

Sandwiched between the Santa Rita Mountains and the Patagonia Mountains, just north of the Mexican border, this region is one of the shiniest gems in Arizona. In a valley by the small town of Patagonia are long vistas of lush, windswept upland grassland; dark, knobby forest mountains; and a crinkle of slow streams. The valleys that furrow across the landscape occupy a special microclimate that is amenable to wine grapes. It may not be the Napa Valley, but who needs 20 chardonnay varietals when you boast hard-bitten cowboys, artistic refugees and an amazing array of migratory birds?

Patagonia and smaller Sonoita (and tiny Elgin) sit almost 5000ft above sea level, so the land here is cool and breezy. The first two towns were once important railway stops, but since the line closed in 1962 tourism and the arts have been their bread and butter. The beauty of the montane grasslands was not lost on film scouts; the musical *Oklahoma* and John Wayne's *Red River* were both filmed here.

◉ Sights & Activities

Patagonia Lake State Park   PARK

(📞520-287-6965;   http://azstateparks.com; 400 Patagonia Lake Rd; vehicle $10-15, bike $3; ⊙park 4am-10pm, visitor center 8:30am-5pm) A brilliant blue blip dolloped into the mountains, 2.5-mile-long Patagonia Lake was formed by the damming of Sonoita Creek. About 7 miles southwest of Patagonia, the lake is open year-round. At 4050ft above sea level, buffeted by lake and mountain breezes, the air is cool – making this a perfect spot for camping, picnicking, walking, bird-watching, fishing, boating and swimming. The **campground** (📞520-586-2283; http://azstateparks.com; 400 Patagonia Lake Rd; campsite $17, with hookups $25-28) makes a fine base for exploring the region.

The visitor center is open 7am-10pm on Fridays April through October.

Patagonia-Sonoita
Creek Preserve   NATURE RESERVE

(📞520-394-2400; www.nature.org/arizona; 150 Blue Heaven Rd; admission $6; ⊙6:30am-4pm Wed-Sun Apr-Sep, 7:30am-4pm Wed-Sun Oct-Mar) A few gentle trails meander through this enchanting riparian willow forest. Managed by the Nature Conservancy, the preserve supports seven distinct vegetative ecosystems, four endangered species of native fish and more than 300 species of birds, including rarities from Mexico. For bird-watchers, the peak migratory season is April and May, and late August to September. There are guided nature walks on Saturday morning at 9am.

Reach the preserve by going northwest on N 4th Ave in Patagonia, then south on Pennsylvania Ave, driving across a small creek and continuing another mile.

Wineries

The Arizona wine industry is attracting notice in the viticulture world. A map and listing of wineries on the **Sonoita/Elgin Wine Trail** can be found at www.arizonawine.org/sonoitawinetrail.html. This beautiful, sun-kissed hill country is a pleasant place to get tipsy.

Callaghan Vineyards   WINERY

(📞520-455-5322; www.callaghanvineyards.com; 336 Elgin Rd; tasting $10; ⊙11am-4pm Thu-Sun) About 20 miles east of Patagonia, Callaghan has traditionally been one of the most highly regarded wineries in the state. To get here, head south on Hwy 83 at the village of Sonoita, then east on Elgin Rd.

Flying Leap Vineyards   WINERY

(📞520-455-5499; www.flyingleapvineyards.com; 342 Elgin Rd; tasting $10; ⊙11am-4pm) In 2013 Flying Leap took over the Canelo Hills Vineyard & Winery, next door to Callaghan Vineyards in Elgin. With small batch wines, an inviting tasting room and a gorgeous view of distant-sky islands, go ahead and give 'em a sip.

Dos Cabezas Wineworks   WINERY

(📞520-455-5141; www.doscabezaswineworks.com; 3248 Hwy 82; tasting $15; ⊙10:30am-4:30pm Thu-Sun) This rustically pretty and well-regarded family-run operation is in Sonoita, near the crossroads of Hwys 82 and 83.

🛏 Sleeping

The only really cheap sleeping option is camping at Patagonia Lake State Park.

Stage Stop Inn   INN $

(📞520-394-2211; www.stagestophotelpatagonia. com; 303 McKeown, Patagonia; s $79, d $89-109, ste $139; 🛜🐾🏊) Salute the Old West and its simple charms at this two-story inn, once a stagecoach stop on the Butterfield Trail. Rooms surround a central courtyard and pool. Some have kitchenettes. Pets are allowed in 1st floor rooms ($10 per pet per night).

Duquesne House   B&B $$

(📞520-394-2732; www.theduquesnehouse.com; 357 Duquesne Ave, Patagonia; r $130 Fri-Sun, $105 Mon-Thu; @) This photogenic, ranch-style B&B was once a boarding house for miners. Today there are three spacious, eclectically appointed suites with their own distinct garden areas where you can watch the sun set, listen to the birds chirp, smell the rosemary and generally bliss out. Mondays through Thursdays the B&B offers a 'Bed, No Bread' special – $105 per night with no breakfast.

✗ Eating & Drinking

Velvet Elvis   PIZZA $$

(📞520-394-2102; www.velvetelvispizza.com; 292 Naugle Ave, Patagonia; mains $8-24; ⊙11:30am-8:30pm Thu-Sat, to 7:30pm Sun) Yes, a velvet

BIRDING IN SOUTHERN ARIZONA

Dedicated birders flock to Patagonia and nearby Sierra Vista to scout for migratory birds along the San Pedro River and in the mountains. Most reserves and conservation areas are also good spots for hiking, especially for ramblers in search of greenery and wildlife.

In Patagonia, in addition to the Patagonia-Sonoita Creek Preserve, birders should stop by the **Paton House** (Blue Heaven Rd), which is on Pennsylvania Ave on the way to the preserve. A chain-link fence surrounds the property, and you'll likely see several cars parked outside. The backyard of the house is decked out with binoculars, birding books and sugar feeders that attract rare hummingbirds. It's free and there are no official hours (enter only if the gate is open), but donations for the feeders are appreciated. The famed **Roadside Rest Area** is in a scenic canyon 4.2 miles southwest of Patagonia. A simple-looking pullout beside Hwy 82, it also happens to be one of the most famous birding spots in the state. This is a relatively reliable place to catch the rare rose-throated bectard, as well as the more-common canyon wren. Be careful, as cars may pull over to park at any time.

A sycamore- and yucca-weaved dome some 5500ft in the sky marks where the Huachuca Mountains meet the Rockies, the Sierra Madres and the Sonoran Desert. The area is also home to **Ramsey Canyon Preserve** (☏520-378-2785; www.nature.org; 27 E Ramsey Canyon Rd; adult/child $6/free, 1st Sat of month free; ⏱8am-5pm Thu-Mon), south of Sierra Vista. This beautiful Nature Conservancy–owned preserve is one of the best hummingbird bagging spots in the USA. The little birds flit over the igneous outcrops and a wiry carpeting of trees throughout the year, with heavy sightings from April to September. At lower altitudes an incredible diversity of wildlife stalks through the river canyon, including coatis, cougars and javelinas. Also here is the critically endangered Ramsey Canyon leopard frog, found nowhere else in the world.

A very easy 0.7-mile nature-loop trail leaves from here, as well as guided walks on Monday, Thursday and Saturday at 9am, March through October. The reserve is about 11 miles south of Sierra Vista off Hwy 92. Drive to the very end of Ramsey Canyon Rd, bearing left onto the driveway at the final cul-de-sac. Visitation is limited to the 23 parking spots beside the visitor center – do not park on the road.

About 95% of Arizona's riparian habitat has become victim to overgrazing, logging and development, so what little riverfront ecosystem remains is incredibly important to the state's ecological health. Some 350 bird species (many endangered), more than 80 mammal species and more than 40 species of reptiles and amphibians have been recorded along the 40-mile stretch of the San Pedro River within the **San Pedro Riparian National Conservation Area** (☏520-439-6400; www.blm.gov/az/st/en.html; Fry Blvd/Hwy 90; ⏱visitor center 9:30am-4:30pm), a vital riparian ecosystem that has, unfortunately, become a corridor for drug smuggling from Mexico, so suspicious activity should be reported.

The visitor center, in the 1930s San Pedro House, is 6 miles east of Sierra Vista on Fry Blvd. From here you can access several hiking trails.

For lodging near the San Pedro conservation area, try the stylish **Casa de San Pedro B&B** (☏520-366-1300; www.bedandbirds.com; 8033 S Yell Lane; r/ste $169/250; ❄@), with ten comfy rooms and a lovely courtyard. Close to Ramsay Canyon is **Battiste's B&B** (☏520-803-6908; www.battistebedandbirds.com; 4700 E Robert Smith Lane, Hereford; r $155; ☎) which is oriented toward bird-watching and features cozy rooms arrayed in colorful, Southwestern decor. The owners have counted scores of bird species in their backyard. A popular pair of nesting elf owls appears in spring.

Elvis does indeed hang on the wall at this gourmet pizza joint in Patagonia. Motorcyclists, foreign visitors, date-night couples – everybody visiting the area – rolls in at some point for one of the 14 designer pies. These diet-spoilers will make you feel like Elvis in Vegas: fat and happy.

Gathering Grounds Cafe   COFFEE SHOP **$$**
(☏520-394-2009; www.patagoniasbuzz.com; 319 McKeown Ave, Patagonia; breakfast $6-9, lunch $7-11, dinner $10-14; ⏱7am-4pm Sun-Wed, until 8pm Thu-Sat; ☎) Did somebody say breakfast bowl? This baby comes with green chile, cheddar and two eggs atop grilled potatoes,

plus meat if ya' want it. Look for wraps and sandwiches at lunch, plus a few heartier entrees, like steak and spaghetti, added at dinner. It's also OK to pop in for pastries and a civilized cup o' Joe.

The Cafe
CAFE $$

(☎520-455-5044; www.cafesonoita.com; 3280 Hwy 82; lunch $7-12, dinner $8-20; ⊗11am-2pm daily, 5-8pm Thu-Sat) This cafe at the crossroads of Hwys 82 and 83 is a breezy place to nosh after day of wine tasting, bird watching or scenic driving. Salads, sandwiches and burgers are on the menu at lunch, with steak and pasta stepping it up at dinner. The black-and-blue salad with steak, blue cheese, baby greens and balsamic is superb.

Wagon Wheel Saloon
BAR

(www.wagonwheelpatagonia.com; 400 Naugle Ave, Patagonia; ⊗noon-8pm Mon-Sat, 11am-8pm Sun, bar until 10pm or so) Kick it cowboy-style at the Wagon Wheel, where the bar is big, the 'art' is taxidermied and the pool table is ready for action. Burger and Mexican dishes on the menu.

🛈 Information

The main road is Hwy 82, the Patagonia Hwy. Patagonia, with about 800 people, is the local center of activity (we use the term loosely). The folks in the **visitor center** (☎888-794-0060; www.patagoniaaz.com; 307 McKeown Ave, Patagonia; ⊗10am-4pm Mon-Sat) are helpful, and the place also rents bikes ($35 to $45 per day). Sonoita isn't much more than an intersection, and Elgin is just the name for a swath of unincorporated land 20 minutes east of Sonoita. Keep your dial tuned to KPUP 100.5 FM, the awesome local radio station.

🛈 Getting There & Away

Patagonia and the Mountain Empire are connected to the rest of the state by Hwys 82 and 83; the closest major town is Nogales, 20 miles to the southwest.

Tombstone

POP 1595 / ELEV 4540FT

The epitaphs on the grave markers at Boothill Cemetery typically include the cause of death: Murdered. Shot. Suicide. Killed by Indians. One quick stroll around the place tells you everything you need to know about living – and dying – in Tombstone in the late 1800s. How did this godforsaken place come to be? In 1877, despite friends' warnings that all he would find was his own tombstone, prospector Ed Schieffelin braved the dangers of Apache attack in the region and struck it rich. He named the strike Tombstone, and a legend was born. This is the town of the infamous 1881 shootout at the OK Corral, when Wyatt Earp, his brothers Virgil and Morgan and their friend Doc Holliday gunned down outlaws Billy Clanton and Tom and Frank McLaury. The fight so caught people's imaginations, it not only made it into the history books but also onto the silver screen – many times. Watch the 1993 *Tombstone,* starring Kurt Russell and Val Kilmer, to get you in the mood.

Most boomtowns went bust, but Tombstone declared itself 'Too Tough to Die.' Tourism was the new silver and as the Old West became en vogue, Tombstone didn't even have to reconstruct its past – by 1962 the entire town was a National Historic Landmark. Yes, it's a tourist trap; but a delightful one and a fun place to find out how the West was truly won.

◉ Sights

Walking around town is free, but you'll pay to visit most attractions.

OK Corral
HISTORIC SITE

(☎520-457-3456; www.ok-corral.com; Allen St btwn 3rd & 4th Sts; admission $10, without gunfight $6; ⊗9am-5pm) Site of the famous gunfight on October 26, 1881, the OK Corral is the heart of both historic and touristic Tombstone. It has models of the gunfighters and other exhibits, including CS Fly's early photography studio and a recreated 'crib,' the kind of room where local prostitutes would service up to 80 guys daily for as little as 25¢ a pop. Fights are reenacted at 2pm, with additional shows on busy days.

Tickets are also good next door at the kitschy **Tombstone Historama**, a 25-minute presentation of the town's history using animated figures, movies and narration (by Vincent Price). Pick up your free copy of the Tombstone Epitaph reporting on the infamous shootout at the historic newspaper office, now the **Tombstone Epitaph Museum** (☎520-457-2211; near cnr 5th & Fremont Sts; ⊗9:30am-5pm) FREE. And the name Epitaph? According to the newspaper's first editor, every Tombstone should have one.

The losers of the OK Corral – Billy Clanton and the McLaury brothers – are buried (in row 2), along with other desperados, at **Boothill Graveyard** (www.boothillgiftshop.com;

Hwy 80; ⊙ 7:30am-6pm) **FREE** about a quarter-mile north of town. The entrance is via a gift shop, but admission is free ($3 for list of specific graves, with location and short bios). Some headstones are twistedly poetic. The oft-quoted epitaph for Lester Moore, a Wells Fargo agent, reads: Here lies Lester Moore / Four slugs from a 44 / No les, no more.

Tombstone Courthouse
State Historic Park   MUSEUM
(☑ 520-457-3311; http://azstateparks.com/parks/toco; 223 Toughnut St; adult/child 7-13yr $5/2; ⊙ 9am-5pm) Tombstone's history isn't limited to the shoot-out at the OK Corral, and exhibits at this informative museum spotlight various aspects of the town's colorful past. On the 1st floor, check out town founder Ed Shiefflin's .44 caliber Henry and the local doctor's old-timey bullet-removal kit. Upstairs, you can read about some of the town's most interesting former residents. Seven men were hanged in the courthouse courtyard, and today a couple of nooses dangle ominously from the recreated gallows.

Bird Cage Theater   HISTORIC SITE
(☑ 520-457-3421; www.tombstonebirdcage.com; 517 E Allen St; adult/child 8-18yr/senior $10/8/9; ⊙ 8am-6pm) In the 1880s the Bird Cage was a one-stop sin-o-rama. Besides onstage shows, it was a saloon, dance hall, gambling parlor and a home for 'negotiable affections.' The very name derives from the 14 compartments lining the upper floor of the auditorium – like boxes at the opera – where the 'soiled doves' entertained their customers.

The entire place is stuffed with dusty old artifacts that bring the period to life, including a faro gambling table used by Doc Holliday, a big black hearse, a fully furnished 'crib' and a creepy 'merman.' And, of course, the theater is haunted.

Rose Tree Museum   MUSEUM
(☑ 520-457-3326; cnr 4th & Toughnut Sts; adult/child 13yr & under $5/free; ⊙ 9am-5pm, shorter hours Jun-Aug) In April the world's largest rosebush – planted in 1886 – puts on an intoxicating show in the courtyard of this museum, a beautifully restored Victorian home still owned by the Macia family. The inside is brimming with family and town memorabilia, including a 1960 photograph showing the matriarch with Robert Geronimo, son of the Apache chief.

Fairbank Historic Site   GHOST TOWN
(www.sanpedroriver.org/fairbank; Hwy 82, just east of San Pedro River; ⊙ dawn-dusk) It's the silence that grabs you on a stroll through Fairbank, 10 miles west of Tombstone. Established in 1881 to serve the New Mexico & Arizona Railroad, Fairbank was a transportation hub for nearby mining towns. The last residents left in the 1970s. There's a visitor center in the restored 1920s school house (9:30am to 4:30pm Friday to Sunday). If it's closed, look for a walking tour brochure in the kiosk then loop past houses, a stable and an 1882 mercantile building.

✪✰ Festivals & Events

Tombstone events revolve around weekends of Western hoo-ha with shootouts (of course!), stagecoach rides, mock hangings and costume contests. The biggest event is **Helldorado Days** (www.helldoradodays.com; ⊙ 3rd weekend in Oct). See the Chamber of Commerce website for details about other events, which include **Wyatt Earp Days** and **Vigilante Days** (⊙ 2nd weekend in Aug).

🛏 Sleeping

Properties increase their rates during special events; reservations are recommended at these times.

★ Larian Motel   MOTEL $
(☑ 520-457-2272; www.tombstonemotels.com; 410 E Fremont St; r $69-79; ❄ 🤖) This one's a rare breed: a motel with soul, thanks to the personalized attention from the proprietor, cute retro rooms named for historical characters (Doc Holliday, Curly Bill, Wyatt Earp) and a high standard of cleanliness. It's also close to the downtown action. Children 12 and under stay free.

Tombstone Bordello B&B   B&B $
(☑ 520-457-2394; www.tombstonebordello.com; 107 W Allen St; r $89-99; ❄ @ 🤖) This fascinating place used to be a house of ill-repute, and the names of the rooms – Shady Lady, Fallen Angel – embrace its colorful past. The 10-room B&B, built in 1881, was once owned by Big Nose Kate (Doc Holiday's lady friend).

The Victorian-style bedrooms, which held up to four working girls, feel very much of the era, so much so that some of the former residents are said to haunt the building.

Lookout Lodge   MOTEL $$
(☑ 520-457-2223; www.lookoutlodgeaz.com; 781 N Hwy 80; r incl breakfast $89; ❄ @ 🤖 🐾)

Formerly the Best Western, this property perched on a hill on the outskirts of town gets high marks for its spacious rooms overlooking the Dragoon Mountains. Pretty gardens, outdoor firepits and its Ranch 22 restaurant, cooked breakfast included, are also a draw. Pets are $10 per night, per pet.

🍴 Eating & Drinking

It's a tourist town, so don't expect any culinary flights of fancy. In keeping with its Old West theme, the food is mostly standard American and Mexican. Most of the saloons have decent grub. There's little more to do in the evening than to go on a pub crawl – or make that a saloon stagger.

Crystal Palace Saloon
AMERICAN $$

(www.crystalpalacesaloon.com; 436 E Allen St, at 5th St; mains $7-29; ⊙ restaurant 11am-8pm, bar open later) This lively saloon was built in 1879 and has been restored. It's a favorite end-of-the-day watering hole with Tombstone's costumed actors or anyone wanting to play outlaw for a night. With its long bar, stuffed elk mount and Old West paintings, it just feels... Tombstone-y. They say there are bullet holes in the ceiling and blood stains on the floor.

Look for burgers, sandwiches and steaks on the menu.

Café Margarita
MEXICAN $$

(☎ 520-457-2277; www.cafe-margarita.com; 131 S 5th St; mains $7-12; ⊙ 11am-7pm Thu & Sun, until 8pm Fri & Sat) Formerly Nellie Cashman's in the Russ House, this eatery serves Mexican fare as well as a few Italian dishes. Eat inside or on the patio. Prickly pear margaritas also served. Enjoy live music on Friday and Saturday nights.

Big Nose Kate's
BAR

(www.bignosekates.info; 417 E Allen St; ⊙ 10am-midnight) Full of Wild West character, Doc Holliday's girlfriend's bar is a fun place for drinking, featuring great painted glass, historical photographs and live music in the afternoons. Down in the basement is the room of the Swamper, a janitor who dug a tunnel into the silver mine shaft that ran below the building and helped himself to buckets of nuggets. Or so the story goes...

ℹ Information

Police (☎ 520-457-2244; 315 E Fremont St)
Post Office (☎ 520-457-3479; 100 Haskell St; ⊙ 8:30am-4:30pm Mon-Fri)

Tombstone Chamber of Commerce (☎ 520-457-3929, 888-457-3929; www.tombstonechamber.com; 395 E Allen St, at cnr of 4th St; ⊙ 9am-4pm Mon-Thu, 9am-5pm Fri-Sun)

ℹ Getting There & Away

Tombstone is 24 miles south of the I-10 via Hwy 80 (exit 303 towards Benson/Douglas). The Patagonia Hwy (Hwy 82) links up with Hwy 80 about 3 miles north of Tombstone. There is no public transport into town.

Bisbee

POP 5498 / ELEV 4540FT

At first glance, Bisbee isn't that attractive. Wedged between the steep walls of Tombstone Canyon, its roads are narrow and twisty, the buildings old and fragile, and there's a monstrous open-pit mine gaping toward the heavens at the east end of town. You drove all the way here for this? But then you take a closer look. Those 19th-century buildings are packed tight with interesting galleries, splendid restaurants and charming hotels. As for the citizens, well, just settle onto a bar stool at a local watering hole and a chatty local will likely share all of the town's gossip before you order your second drink.

Bisbee built its fortune on ore found in the surrounding Mule Mountains. Between 1880 and 1975, underground and open-pit mines coughed up copper in sumptuous proportions, generating more than $6 billion worth of metals. Business really took off in 1892 when the Phelps Dodge Corporation, which would soon hold a local monopoly, brought in the railroad. By 1910 the population was 25,000, and with nearly 50 saloons and bordellos crammed along Brewery Gulch, Bisbee gained a reputation as the liveliest city between El Paso and San Francisco.

As the local copper mines began to fizzle in the 1970s, Bisbee began converting itself into a tourist destination. At the same time hippies, artists and counterculture types migrated here and stayed. The interweaving of the new creative types and the old miners has produced a welcoming bunch of eccentrics clinging to the mountainside. It's one of the coolest places (weather and attitude) in southern Arizona – and definitely worth the drive.

Hwy 80 runs through the center of town. Most businesses are found in the Historic District (Old Bisbee), along Main St and

Bisbee

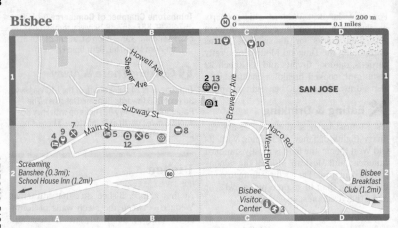

SAN JOSE

Screaming
Banshee (0.3mi);
School House Inn (1.2mi)

Bisbee
Breakfast
Club (1.2mi)

Bisbee
Visitor
Center

near the intersection of Howell and Brewery
Aves. Many businesses and restaurants close
from Monday to Wednesday, so plan your
visit for later in the week.

◎ Sights & Activities

Walking through Old Bisbee – up winding
back alleys, steep staircases and cafe- and
shop-lined Main St – is a delight in itself.
For sweeping views, walk up OK St above
the southern edge of town. A path at the
top leads to a hill where locals have built
colorful shrines filled with candles, plastic
flowers and pictures of the Virgin Mary.

**Bisbee Mining &
Historical Museum**   MUSEUM
(☎520-432-7071; www.bisbeemuseum.org; 5
Copper Queen Plaza; adult/child 15yr & under/
senior $7.50/3/6.50; ⏱10am-4pm)   This
two-story museum is affiliated with the
Smithsonian Institution, and it shows. Located in the 1897 former headquarters of
the Phelps Dodge Corporation, it does an
excellent job delineating the town's past,
the changing face of mining and the use
of copper in our daily lives. You even get
to 'drive' a shovel with a dipper larger than
most living rooms.

Queen Mine   MINE TOUR
(☎520-432-2071; www.queenminetour.com; 478
Dart Rd, off Hwy 80; adult/child 4-12yr $13/5.50;
🚼) Don miners' garb, grab a lantern and
ride a mine train 1500ft into one of Bisbee's
famous copper mines. In the early 20th century this was the most productive mine in
Arizona, famous for producing particularly deep-shaded turquoise rocks known as
Bisbee Blue. The tour, which lasts about an
hour, is good fun for the kids, but maybe not
so much for the claustrophobic. Call for tour
times, which vary. To see the aftermath of
open-pit mining, drive a half-mile south on
Hwy 80 to the not-so-truthful 'Scenic View'
sign. It's pointing toward the **Lavender
Pit**, an immense stair-stepped gash in the
ground that produced about 600,000 tons
of copper between 1950 and 1974. It's ugly,
but it's impressive.

☞ Tours

Stop by the visitor center for information about jeep and other tours. Visit the Sweet Midnight (p230) store beside the Copper Hotel for tickets for a **ghost tour** (🕿520-432-3308; www.oldbisbeeghosttour; adult/child 11yr & under from $13/11). Tour choices include an evening walking tour through town, a hearse tour and a haunted pub crawl.

🛏 Sleeping

Bisbee is refreshingly devoid of chain hotels, with most lodging in historic hotels or B&Bs. Weekends often fill early, so come midweek if you don't have a reservation.

★Shady Dell   CAMPGROUND $$
(🕿520-432-3567; www.theshadydell.com; 1 Douglas Rd; rates $87-145, closed early Jul–mid-Sep; ❄) This fun-loving trailer park has a deliciously retro twist: each 'unit' is an original 1950s-era travel trailer, meticulously restored and outfitted with period accoutrements such as vintage radios (playing '50s songs upon arrival) and record players. All have tiny kitchens, some have toilets, but showers are in the bathhouse. A 1947 Chris Craft yacht and a tiki-themed bus are also available. Units use swamp coolers for cold air.

Bisbee Grand Hotel   HOTEL $$
(🕿520-432-5900; www.bisbeegrandhotel.com; 61 Main St; r incl breakfast $79-179; ❄🕸) You can sleep inside a covered wagon at this quirky but fun two-story hotel where the Old West comes to life (or maybe it never died). The 14 themed rooms and suites feature Victorian-era decor. Check-in at the kick-up-your-heels saloon.

Letson Loft Hotel   HOTEL $$
(🕿520-432-3210; www.letsonlofthotel.com; 26 Main St; r $130-175) Urban sophistication meets Victorian quaintness at this sweet eight-room boutique inn in a sensitively restored 19th-century building. Original touches like exposed adobe and brick walls add character to high-ceilinged rooms with flat-screen TV but no phones. Pastries and coffee available in the morning. A little more impersonal compared to other Bisbee lodgings.

School House Inn   B&B $$
(🕿520-432-2996; www.schoolhouseinnbb.com; 818 Tombstone Canyon; r $89-149; 🕸) Report to the Principal's Office or get creative in the Art Room. No matter which of the nine darling rooms in this converted 1918 school you choose, you'll be charmed by the detailed decor, the homey comforts, and John (the proprietor). Relax below the 160-year-old live oak in the patio. Rates include a delicious full breakfast.

🍴 Eating

★Cafe Cornucopia   CAFE $
(www.facebook.com/cafecornucopia; 14 Main St; mains $5-10; ⊙11am-4pm Fri-Tue) Local art hangs from the exposed brick walls at this small cafe, a welcoming place that feels like home – in a good way. Order homemade soup, quiche, sandwiches and desserts at the counter then settle in for a delicious lunch. If you listen close (and it's hard not to), the local chitchat here can be downright, well, personal. The green chile quiche is quite good.

Bisbee Breakfast Club   BREAKFAST $
(www.bisbeebreakfastclub.com; 75a Erie St; breakfast $6-9, lunch $8-9; ⊙7am-3pm) The breakfasts at this longtime favorite seem to have have lost a touch of their wow factor. That being said, this bustling eatery is still the see-and-be-seen spot in town, and the food remains pretty darn yummy.

★Cafe Roka   NEW AMERICAN $$
(🕿520-432-5153; www.caferoka.com; 35 Main St; dinner $17-24; ⊙5-9pm Wed-Sat) Past the art-nouveau steel door awaits this sensuously lit grown-up spot with innovative American cuisine that is at once smart and satisfying. The four-course dinners include salad, soup, sorbet and a rotating choice of mains. The welcoming central bar is great for solo diners, and if you chat with your neighbors you might just hear some juicy town gossip. Reservations recommended.

WHAT THE...?

Bisbee Museum of the Bizarre
(🕿520-432-3308; www.bizarrebisbee.com; 7 Howell Ave; admission $3; ⊙11am-5pm Thu-Mon) This fantastical museum displays the death mask of John Dillinger, Bigfoot's footprint, a two-headed squirrel, a mummified cat, a Fiji mermaid and two shrunken heads – the sort of kitschy crap that makes you proud to be an American, dammit. It's in the back of the Sweet Midnight store.

Screaming Banshee
PIZZA **$$**

(☑ 520-432-1300; www.screamingbansheepizza.net; 200 Tombstone Canyon Rd; mains $7-15; ☺ 4-9pm Tue & Wed, 11am-10pm Thu-Sat, 11am-9pm Sun) The ingredients are fresh, the crust is charred over a wood fire and the end result is tasty. There's a good array of toppings too, from gorgonzola cheese to house-made fennel sausage. The decor is punk rock meets Mardi Gras. It's across from the Iron Man, a 1935 socialist-aesthetic statue of a manly, bare-chested miner.

 Drinking
===

Old Bisbee Brewing Company
BREWERY

(www.oldbisbeebrewingcompany.com; 200 Review Alley; ☺ noon-10:30pm Sun-Thu, noon-11:30pm Fri & Sat) This new brewery serves a half-dozen or so lip-smacking brews (plus root beer) in its simple tap room. Brats and free popcorn available, but it's OK to bring in food from elsewhere.

St Elmo's
BAR

(36 Brewery Ave) This 100-year-old dive is Arizona's oldest bar. Today, a boisterous mix of thirsty locals and tourists keep things hoppin'. The signed beer mugs behind the cash register belong to regulars.

Bisbee Grand Hotel
BAR

(www.bisbeegrandhotel.com; 61 Main St) The bar in the Grand Hotel has a cool punk rock meets Old West vibe. In fact, we saw a young buck with a handlebar moustache more kick-ass than Wyatt Earp's. Hipster or cowboy? We weren't 100% sure, but no one seemed to mind either way.

Bisbee Coffee Co
COFFEE SHOP

(www.bisbeecoffee.com; 2 Copper Queen Plaza; ☺ 6:30am-9pm; ☎) This easy-going shop near the post office serves java strong enough to get you through a double shift on the tourist track.

 Shopping
===

You can't walk in Bisbee without tripping on an art gallery. There's a wide range of styles and quality; have a wander up Main St to get a feel for what's out there.

Atalanta Music & Books
BOOKS

(☑ 520-432-9976; 38 Main St; ☺ 10am-6pm) A chaotic whirlwind of used books, art and music supplies and cool hats.

Sweet Midnight
ECLECTIC

(☑ 520-432-3308; www.sweetmidnight.com; 7 Howell Ave; ☺ 11am-8:30pm) Looking for something a little macabre? Pop in here for coffin purses and Day of the Dead mugs. As its brochure says, the store sells 'the darker side of cute.' The owner lives nearby and can open the store if it's closed when you stop by. Just call the number posted on the door.

ℹ️ **Information**
===

Bisbee Visitor Center (☑ 866-224-7233, 520-432-3554; www.discoverbisbee.com; 478 Dart Rd; ☺ 8am-5pm Mon-Fri, 10am-4pm Sat & Sun) The visitor center is located in the Queen Mine Tour Building south of downtown.

Copper Queen Hospital (☑ 520-432-5383; www.cqch.org; 101 Cole Ave) Has 24-hour emergency services.

Police (☑ 520-432-2261; 1 Hwy 92)

Post Office (☑ 520-432-2052; 6 Main St; ☺ 7:30am-noon & 1-4pm Mon-Fri, 9am-noon Sat)

ℹ️ **Getting There & Away**
===

Bisbee is about 50 miles south of the I-10 (exit 303 towards Benson/Douglas), 25 miles south of Tombstone and only about 10 miles north of the Mexican border.

Chiricahua National Monument
===

A wonderfully rugged yet whimsical wonderland, **Chiricahua National Monument** (☑ 520-824-3560; www.nps.gov/chir; Hwy 181; adult/child $5/free) is one of Arizona's most unique and evocative landscapes. Rain, thunder and wind have chiseled volcanic rocks into fluted pinnacles, natural bridges, gravity-defying balancing boulders and soaring spires reaching skyward like totem poles carved in stone. The remoteness made Chiricahua, which is pronounced 'cheery-cow-wha,' a favorite hiding place of Apache warrior Cochise and his men. Today it's attractive to birds and wildlife, including bobcats, bears, deer, coatis and javelinas.

Past the entrance, the paved **Bonita Canyon Scenic Drive** climbs 8 miles to Massai Point at 6870ft, passing several scenic pullouts and trailheads along the way. RVs longer than 29ft are not allowed beyond the **visitor center** (☺ visitor center 8:30am-4pm May–mid-Oct, 8am-4:30pm rest of year), which is about 2 miles along the road.

To explore in greater depth, lace up your boots and hit the trails. Eighteen miles of hiking trails range from easy, flat 0.2-mile loops to strenuous 7-mile climbs. If you're

FORT BOWIE NATIONAL HISTORIC SITE

Somewhere between the abandoned stagecoach stop and the sun-bleached cemetery, it hits you: this hike is a little spooky. Why? Because the 1.5-mile trail to **Fort Bowie** (☎520-847-2500; www.nps.gov/fobo; Old Fort Bowie Rd, off Hwy 186; ⊙trail sunrise to sunset; visitor center Sat & Sun 8am-4pm May–mid-Oct, varies seasonally) **FREE** is the closest you'll come to time travel in the Southwest. The fort was established in 1862 in response to raids by the Chiricahua Apache, and the interpretive trail through this lonely place passes violent skirmish sites. As you walk, you can easily imagine Apache warriors watching your every move from hiding places on the rocky hills that flank the trail. To flip the picture, the trail returns to the parking lot along the ridge of one of those very hills, offering the Apache perspective of the activity below. In the 1880s and 1890s, that activity would have been pioneers and soldiers invading your turf.

The fort itself is mostly in ruins, but black-and-white photos beside various buildings illuminate the 19th-century scene. The fort's location was strategic: it's close to the regionally important Apache Spring, which sits beside the trail. Inside the visitor center, check out the heliograph. This mirrored device was placed on a nearby hilltop to send messages to other heliographs along a series of lofty military outposts.

Follow Hwy 186 south from Willcox and the I-10 for 22 miles to the turnoff. Here, an unpaved but graded road, with mileage signs, runs 8 miles east to the trailhead.

short on time, hike the **Echo Canyon Trail** at least half a mile to the Grottoes, an amazing 'cathedral' of giant boulders where you can lie still and enjoy the wind-caressed silence. The most stupendous views are from **Massai Point**, where you'll see thousands of spires positioned on the slopes like some petrified army.

A free hikers' shuttle bus leaves daily from the visitor center at 9am (8:30am mid-October to April) going up to the trailheads at Massai Point or Eagle Canyon. Hikers return by hiking downhill. Registration for the shuttle is required at the visitor center.

Bonita Campground (campsites $12), near the visitor center, has 22 first-come, first-served sites that often fill by noon. There's water, but no hookups or showers. Wilderness camping is not permitted inside the monument, but there is a free, dispersed USFS **camping** (www.fs.fed.us/r3/coronado) at Pinery Canyon Campground about 5 miles up Pinery Rd (Forest Rd 42), which is near the park entrance station.

The monument is about 37 miles off I-10 at Willcox.

Benson & Around

POP 5090 / ELEV 3576FT

A railway stop since the late 1800s, Benson is best known as the gateway to the famous Kartchner Caverns, among the largest and most spectacular caves in the USA. This wonderland of spires, shields, pipes, columns, soda straws and other ethereal formations has been five million years in the making, but miraculously wasn't discovered until 1974. In fact, its very location was kept secret for another 25 years in order to prepare for its opening as **Kartchner Caverns State Park** (☎information 520-586-4100, reservations 520-586-2283; http://azstateparks.com; Hwy 90; park entrance per vehicle/bicycle $6/3, Rotunda Tour adult/child 7-13yr $23/13, Big Room Tour mid-Oct–mid-Apr $23/13; ⊙park 7am-6pm, visitor center 8am-6pm Nov-May, shorter hours rest of year). Two tours are available, both about 90 minutes long and equally impressive. The Big Room tour closes to the public around mid-April, when a colony of migrating female cave myotis bats starts arriving from Mexico to roost and give birth to pups in late June. Moms and baby bats hang out until mid-September before flying off to their wintering spot. While a bat nursery, the cave is closed to the public.

The focus here is on education, so there are a number of rules – no purses, no water, no cameras, no touching the walls – to protect the delicate ecosystem. Tours often sell-out far in advance, so make reservations – online or by phone – early. The entrance is 9 miles south of I-10, off Hwy 90, exit 302.

About 15 miles east of Benson, in Dragoon, the private, nonprofit **Amerind Foundation** (☎520-586-3666; www.amerind. org; 2100 N Amerind Rd; adult/child 12-18yr/senior $8/5/7; ⊙10am-4pm Tue-Sun) exhibits Native American artifacts, history and culture from tribes from Alaska to Argentina, from the Ice Age to today. On the 2nd floor look for Native American arts and crafts, including kachina dolls, fetishes, Mata Ortiz pottery and Navajo pipes. The Western gallery has rotating exhibits of Native American art and permanent works with a Western or Southwestern theme. It's right off I-10 exit 318.

The complex is near Texas Canyon in the **Little Dragoon Mountains**, which is known for its clumps of giant and photogenic granite boulders. For a closer look, swing by the historic **Triangle T Guest Ranch** (✆520-586-7533; www.azretreatcenter.com; 4190 Dragoon Rd; casitas $159-249, cabins/bunkhouses $219/459; ◎), which got a professional revamp on the reality show Hotel Impossible. Here you can arrange horseback rides ($45 per hour), enjoy refreshments in the saloon or spend the night in inviting casitas. Campers ($23) and RVers ($28 to $33) can set up among the rocks. The saloon is open to the public for lunch and dinner Friday and Saturday, and lunch Sunday, with a Western band on Saturday nights. High season is September to May.

If you're a bibliophile and driving near Benson, the **Singing Wind Bookshop** (✆520-586-2425; www.bensonvisitorcenter. com; 700 W Singing Wind Rd; ◎9am-5pm) is a must-visit. One of the Southwest's great indie book stores, this inviting place is run by the wonderful Winnifred 'Winn' Bundy on her ranch. Visit the website for directions. Lodging in Benson is mostly about chain motels, which cluster off I-10 exits 302 and 304. One appealing option is the friendly **Comfort Inn** (✆520-586-8800; www.comfortinn.com; 630 S Village La; r $99-119), which is just off I-10 and almost a straight shot north from Kartchner Caverns via Hwy 90.

Benson isn't exactly a culinary hotspot, with the exception of **Mi Casa** (✆520-245-0343; mains $8-17; ◎11am-7pm Mon-Fri), a tiny mustard-yellow hacienda with blue trim that serves very good Mexican food. For quick-and-easy coffee before your next adventure, drive through **Old Benson Ice Cream Stop** (✆520-586-2050; 102 W 4th St; ◎10am-8pm Sun-Thu, to 9:30pm Fri & Sat, varies seasonally) beside the railroad tracks. It also sells 44 flavors of soft serve.

Benson is about 50 miles southeast of Tucson and 65 miles northeast of Patagonia. If you're approaching from any direction but the south you'll get here via I-10; if coming from the south, use Hwy 90 or Hwy 80. The main exit into town is exit 303 off I-10. Amtrak's *Sunset Limited* comes through thrice weekly on its run between Los Angeles and New Orleans.

EASTERN ARIZONA

From Flagstaff east to the New Mexico line, the most dominant scenic feature often seems to be the Burlington Northern-Santa Fe Railway freights that run alongside the interstate. But there are some iconic Route 66 sites along here, and a few spots that will surprise you just off the road.

Meteor Crater

The wooly mammoths and ground sloths that slouched around northern Arizona 50,000 years ago must have got quite a nasty surprise when a fiery meteor crashed into their neighborhood, blasting a hole some 550ft deep and nearly 1 mile across. Today the privately owned **crater** (✆928-289-5898; www.meteorcrater.com; adult/child 6-17yr/senior $18/9/16; ◎7am-7pm Jun–mid-Sep, 8am-5pm mid-Sep–May) is a major tourist attraction with exhibits about meteorites, crater geology and the Apollo astronauts who used its lunar-like surface to train for their moon missions. You're not allowed to go down into the crater, but there are guided walking tours beginning at 9:15am (free with admission). The crater is about 6 miles off I-40 exit 233, 35 miles east of Flagstaff and 20 miles west of Winslow.

Winslow

POP 9409 / ELEV 4880FT

'Standing on a corner in Winslow, Arizona...' Sound familiar? Thanks to the Eagles' catchy '70s tune 'Take It Easy,' lonesome little Winslow is now a popular stop on the tourist track. In a small **park** (www.standinonthecorner. com; 2nd St & Kinsley Ave) on Route 66 you can pose with a life-size bronze statue of a hitchhiker backed by a charmingly hokey trompe l'oeil mural of that famous girl – my Lord! – in a flatbed Ford. Above, a painted eagle keeps an eye on the action, and sometimes a red antique Ford parks next to the scene. In 2005 a fire gutted the building behind the mural, which was miraculously saved.

⊙ Sights & Activities

Homolovi State Park PARK
(☑ 928-289-4106; http://azstateparks.com; per vehicle $7; ⊙ visitor center 8am-5pm) Closed in 2010 during the state budget crisis, this grasslands park beside the Little Colorado River re-opened in 2011 with a renewed commitment to protect the artifacts and structures within this sacred Hopi ancestral homeland. Before the area was converted into a park in 1993, bold thieves used backhoes to remove artifacts. Today, short hikes lead to petroglyphs and partly excavated ancient Native American sites.

The park is 3 miles northeast of Winslow via Hwy 87 (exit 257).

🛏 Sleeping & Eating

Winslow is a handy base for the Hopi Reservation, some 60 miles northeast of here. There are plenty of chain hotels and restaurants off I-40 at exit 253.

Homolovi State Park Campground CAMPING $
(☑ 520-586-2283; http://azstateparks.com; tent & RV sites $15-25) There's a campground with electric hookups, water and showers near the Homolovi ruins. Reserve a campsite online or by phone.

La Posada HISTORIC HOTEL $$
(☑ 928-289-4366; www.laposada.org; 303 E 2nd St; r $139-169; ❋ 🐾 🖥) An impressively restored 1930 hacienda designed by star architect du jour Mary Jane Colter, this was the last great railroad hotel built for the Fred Harvey Company along the Santa Fe Railroad. Elaborate tilework, glass-and-tin chandeliers, Navajo rugs and other details accent its palatial Western-style elegance.

They go surprisingly well with the splashy canvases of Tina Mion, one of the three preservation-minded artists who bought the rundown place in 1997. The period-styled rooms are named for illustrious former guests, including Albert Einstein, Gary Cooper and Diane Keaton. Pet fee is $10 per visit.

★ Turquoise Room SOUTHWESTERN $$$
(www.theturquoiseroom.net; La Posada; breakfast $8-12, lunch $10-13, dinner $19-42; ⊙ 7am-4pm & 5-9pm) Even if you're not staying at La Posada, treat yourself to the best meal between Flagstaff and Albuquerque at this unique restaurant. Dishes have a neo-Southwestern flair, the placemats are handpainted works of art and there's a children's menu as well.

If the fried squash blossoms are on the appetizer menu, toast your good fortune and order up.

❶ Information

The **visitor center** (☑ 928-289-2434; www.winslowarizona.org; 523 W 2nd St; ⊙ 9am-5pm Mon-Fri, 9am-3pm Sat) can be found inside the recently renovated Lorenzo Hubbell Trading Post.

❶ Getting There & Away

The *Southwest Chief* stops daily (westbound at 7:50pm, eastbound at 5:39am) at La Posada (303 E 2nd St), which serves as the Winslow Amtrak station. It is not staffed. You may be able to purchase tickets aboard, call ahead to check (☑ 800-872-7245), but you will be paying the full, undiscounted fare.

Holbrook & Around

POP 5800 / ELEV 5080FT

In the 1880s Holbrook may have been one of the wickedest towns in the Old West ('too tough for women and churches'), but today this collection of rock shops and gas stations is better known as the Route 66 town with the wacky Wigwam Motel. It's also a convenient base for exploring Petrified Forest National Park and its fossilized wood.

East of Holbrook, Route 66 barrels on as I-40 for 70 miles before entering New Mexico just beyond Lupton. The only attraction to break the monotony of the road is the section cutting through the Painted Desert in Petrified Forest National Park.

The most interesting attraction in Holbrook is the **Wigwam Motel** (☑ 928-524-3048; www.galerie-kokopelli.com/wigwam; 811 W Hopi Dr; r $56-62; ❋) on Route 66, where each room is its own concrete tipi. Rooms are outfitted with restored 1950s hickory logpole furniture and retro TVs. It's a fun place to stay or snap a photo. The 1898 county courthouse is home to Holbrook's chamber of commerce and visitor center as well as the **Navajo County Historical Museum** (☑ 928-524-6558; 100 E Arizona St; donations appreciated; ⊙ 8am-5pm Mon-Fri, 8am-4pm Sat & Sun), an eclectic assortment of historic local exhibits, including a creepy old jail. If you want to buy petrified wood or other rocks and minerals, visit **Jim Gray's Petrified Wood Co** (☑ 928-524-1842; www.petrifiedwoodco.com; cnr Hwys 77 & 180; ⊙ 7am-7pm), an expansive complex about a mile south of town.

Chain hotels are spaced along the northern part of Navajo Blvd. Along the same strip is **Mesa Italiana** (☑ 928-524-6696; 2318 E Navajo Blvd; mains $12-19; ⊘ 11am-2pm Mon-Fri, 4-9pm daily), a busy Italian place serving pasta and pizzas.

Petrified Forest National Park

The 'trees' of the Petrified Forest are fragmented, fossilized logs scattered over a vast area of semidesert grassland. Sounds boring? Not so! First, many are huge – up to 6ft in diameter – and at least one spans a ravine to form a natural bridge. Second, they're beautiful up close, with extravagantly patterned cross-sections of wood shimmering in ethereal pinks, blues and greens. And finally, they're ancient: 225 million years old, making them contemporaries of the first dinosaurs that leapt onto the scene in the Late Triassic period.

The trees arrived via major floods, only to be buried beneath silica-rich volcanic ash before they could decompose. Groundwater dissolved the silica, carried it through the logs and then crystallized into solid, sparkly quartz mashed up with iron, carbon, manganese and other minerals. Uplift and erosion eventually exposed the logs. Souvenir hunters filched thousands of tons of petrified wood before Teddy Roosevelt made the forest a national monument in 1906 (it became a national park in 1962). Scavenge today and you'll be looking at fines and even jail time.

Aside from the logs, the park also encompasses Native American ruins and petroglyphs, plus an especially spectacular section of the Painted Desert north of the I-40. **Petrified Forest National Park** (☑ 928-524-6228; www.nps.gov/pefo; vehicle/walk-in, bicycle & motorcycle $10/5; ⊘ scenic drive 7am-8pm Jun & Jul, shorter hours Aug-May), which straddles the I-40, has an entrance at exit 311 off I-40 in the north and another off Hwy 180 in the south. A 28-mile paved scenic road links the two. To avoid backtracking, westbound travelers should start in the north, eastbound ones in the south.

A video describing how the logs were fossilized runs regularly at the **Painted Desert Visitor Center** (⊘ 8am-5pm) near the north entrance, and the **Rainbow Forest Museum** (⊘ 8am-7pm) near the South Entrance. Both have bookstores, park exhibits and rangers that hand out free maps and information pamphlets.

The scenic drive has about 15 pullouts with interpretive signs and some short trails. Two trails near the southern entrance provide the best access for close-ups of the petrified logs: the 0.6-mile **Long Logs Trail**, which has the largest concentration, and the 0.4-mile **Giant Logs Trail**, which is entered through the Rainbow Forest Museum and sports the park's largest log.

A highlight in the center section is the 3-mile loop drive out to **Blue Mesa**, where you'll be treated to 360-degree views of spectacular badlands, log falls and logs balancing atop hills with the leathery texture of elephant skin. The short **Blue Mesa Trail** leads scenically into the badlands. Nearby, at the bottom of a ravine, hundreds of well-preserved petroglyphs are splashed across **Newspaper Rock** like some prehistoric bulletin board. Hiking down is verboten, but free spotting scopes are set up at the overlook.

There's more rock art at **Puerco Pueblo**, but the real attraction here is the partly excavated 100-room ruins that may have been home to as many as 1200 people in the 13th century.

Just north of I-40 is a **Route 66 interpretative marker**, where you'll find a map of the whole Mother Road. Further north you'll have sweeping views of the **Painted Desert**, where nature presents a hauntingly beautiful palette, especially at sunset. The most mesmerizing views are from **Kachina Point** behind the **Painted Desert Inn** (admission free; ⊘ 9am-5pm year-round) **FREE**, an old adobe turned museum adorned with impressive Hopi murals.

Kachina Point is also the trailhead for wilderness hiking and camping. There are no developed trails, water sources or food, so come prepared. Overnight camping requires a free permit available at the visitor centers.

There are no accommodations within the park and food service is limited to snacks available at the visitor centers. The closest lodging is in Holbrook.

New Mexico

Best Places to Eat

➡ Adobe Deli (p333)

➡ The Curious Kumquat (p331)

➡ Love Apple (p300)

➡ Pie-O-Neer Cafe (p325)

Best Places to Stay

➡ Ellis Store Country Inn (p344)

➡ Riverbend Hot Springs (p328)

➡ Inn at Halona (p322)

➡ Los Poblanos (p248)

➡ La Fonda (p272)

Why Go?

They call this the 'Land of Enchantment' for a reason. Maybe it's the drama of sunlight and shadow playing out across juniper-speckled hills; or the traditional mountain villages of horse pastures and adobe homes; or the centuries-old towns on the northern plateaus, overlooked by the magnificent Sangre de Cristos Mountains; or the volcanoes, canyons and vast desert plains spread beneath an even vaster sky. The beauty casts a powerful spell. Mud-brick churches filled with sacred art; ancient Indian pueblos; real-life cowboys and legendary outlaws; chile-smothered enchiladas – all add to the pervasive sense of otherness that often makes New Mexico feel like a foreign country.

Maybe the state's all-but-indescribable charm is best expressed in the iconic paintings of Georgia O'Keeffe. The artist herself exclaimed, on her very first visit: 'Well! Well! Well!...This is wonderful! No one told me it was like this.'

But seriously, how could they?

When to Go
Santa Fe

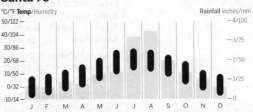

Mid-Aug–mid-Oct New Mexico at its best: gorgeous weather, wild sunflowers, chiles, fiestas.

Christmas Ski the Sangres, walk Canyon Rd on Christmas Eve, join in local traditions.

Jun–mid-Aug Prime time for outdoor activities – but beware monsoon storms.

NEW MEXICO

Fast Facts

→ **Area** 121,599 sq miles

→ **Population** 2.1 million

→ **Sales Tax** 5–9%

→ **Albuquerque to Las Cruces** 223 miles, 3½ hours

→ **Gallup to Tucumcari** 311 miles, 4½ hours

→ **Santa Fe to Taos** 70 miles, 1½ hours

State Bird

The roadrunner can run nearly 20mph. It kills and eats rattlesnakes.

Resources

→ **New Mexico Department of Tourism** (www.newmexico.org)

New Mexico Planning

Thanks to major differences in altitude, when it's comfy in the lower, southern part of the state, it may well be freezing in the northern mountains. Likewise, when the weather's perfect in Santa Fe, it's scorching in Carlsbad. If traveling around the state, bring a versatile wardrobe. With rare exception, casual dress is the way to go in New Mexico.

If you're afraid of spicy foods, order your chile (green, red or 'Christmas') on the side – but do try it. If you enjoy hot foods, look out: New Mexican chile has addictive properties.

DON'T MISS

Steeped in Native American and Hispanic cultures, soulful **Santa Fe** has world-class art, gourmet restaurants and great local food, adobe architecture and famous festivals. An hour-and-a-half north is **Taos**, art colony and alternative haven, known for its historic Pueblo and world-class ski area. These two towns feel like nowhere else in the USA. Both sit beneath the **Sangre de Cristo Mountains**, laced with hiking/mountain biking trails and wilderness backpacking routes. Further south, tiny **Lincoln**, set in a scenic valley along the meandering Rio Bonito, oozes Wild West history as the former stomping ground of Billy the Kid.

Among the state's most fantastic natural features are **White Sands National Monument**, a playground where gleaming white dunes ripple, swell and curl through the Tularosa Basin; and **Carlsbad Caverns National Park**, a colossal subterranean fantasyland of stalagmites and stalactites. Most beautiful of all might be the **Ghost Ranch** area, where you can explore the landscape that inspired Georgia O'Keeffe.

Tips for Drivers

→ New Mexico's main arteries are I-40, which cuts east–west from Texas to Arizona via Albuquerque; and I-25, running north–south from Colorado, via Santa Fe and Albuquerque, to Las Cruces. I-40 is sometimes closed by windstorms in spring; heavy blizzards may close both interstates in winter.

→ Along highways in the south, you'll hit Border Patrol checkpoints with dogs (think twice before bringing your cannabis prescription down from Denver).

→ Interstate speed limits are 75mph, while state highways may go to 70mph.

→ For road conditions, call ☏ 800-432-4269 or visit www.nmroads.com.

History

People have roamed this land for at least 12,000 years but, by the time Francisco Vasquez de Coronado got here in the 16th century, Pueblo Indians were the dominant presence. After Santa Fe was established as the Spanish Colonial capital in around 1610, Spanish settlers and farmers fanned out across northern New Mexico and Catholic missionaries began their often violent efforts to convert the Puebloans. Following the Pueblo Revolt of 1680, Native Americans occupied Santa Fe until 1692, when Don Diego de Vargas recaptured the city.

New Mexico became a US Territory in 1850. Native American wars, settlement by cowboys and miners, and trade along the Santa Fe Trail further transformed the region, and the arrival of the railroad in the 1870s prompted an economic boom.

Painters and writers set up art colonies in Santa Fe and Taos in the early 20th century, and New Mexico became the 47th state in 1912. A top-secret scientific community descended on Los Alamos in 1943 and developed the atomic bomb. Some say that aliens crashed outside of Roswell four years later. Maybe that's why New Mexico is now a leader in space tourism and commercial space flights.

New Mexico Scenic Routes

One of the best ways to explore New Mexico is to travel its scenic highways. Eight have been selected as **National Scenic Byways** (www.byways.org), but the state holds plenty of other striking stretches of pavement. Here are a few of its most rewarding roads:

Billy the Kid Scenic Byway (www.billyby-way.com) This mountain-and-valley loop in southeastern New Mexico swoops past Billy the Kid's stomping grounds, Smokey Bear's gravesite and the orchard-lined Hondo Valley. From Roswell, take Hwy 380 west.

High Road to Taos The back road between Santa Fe and Taos passes through sculpted sandstone desert, fresh pine forests and rural villages with adobe churches and horse-filled pastures. The 13,000ft Truchas Peaks soar above. To reach it from Santa Fe, take Hwy 84/285 to Hwy 513.

NM Hwy 96 From Abiquiú Lake to Cuba, this little road wends through the heart of Georgia O'Keeffe country, beneath the distinct profile of Cerro Pedernal, then past Martian-red buttes and sandstone cliffs striped purple, yellow and ivory.

NM Hwy 52 Head west from Truth or Consequences into the dramatic foothills of the Black Range, stopping off in the old mining towns of Winston and Chloride. Continue north, emerging onto the sweeping Plains of San Agustin before reaching the bizarre Very Large Array.

ℹ Dangers & Annoyances

Albuquerque sits over 5000ft above sea level, Santa Fe and Taos are at 7000ft and the mountains top 13,000ft – so if you're arriving from sea level, you may feel the altitude. Take it easy for the first day or two, and be sure to drink plenty of water – a good idea, anyway, considering how arid the state is. Combined with altitude, the 300-plus days of sunshine also make this an easy place to get sunburned. And New Mexico leads the nation in lightning-strike deaths per capita, so be cautious if hiking in exposed areas during monsoon thunderstorms, which can be downright apocalyptic.

If you're into outdoor adventures, your New Mexico plans may hinge on how wet or dry the year has been. Ski areas may have some of the best or worst conditions in the West depending on snowfall; national forests sometimes close completely during severe summer drought.

As Territorial Governor Lew Wallace put it back in 1880: 'Every calculation based on experience elsewhere fails in New Mexico.' Things here just don't work the way you might expect. That, paired with the *mañana* (tomorrow) mindset, may create some baffling moments. Our advice: just roll with it.

ℹ Getting There & Around

Most travelers fly into Albuquerque International Sunport (ABQ), but a few flights also land in Santa Fe (SAF).

Amtrak offers passenger train service on the *Southwest Chief*, which runs between Chicago and Los Angeles, stopping in Raton, Las Vegas, Lamy (for Santa Fe), Albuquerque and Gallup. A Native American guide hops aboard between Albuquerque and Gallup to provide insightful commentary. The *Sunset Limited* stops in Deming on its way from Florida to Los Angeles.

A fast and amazingly inexpensive light-rail system, the Rail Runner, now connects Albuquerque and Santa Fe. Otherwise, a dwindling network of Greyhound buses links certain New Mexico towns, and northern New Mexico in particular holds some cheap or free regional bus routes. On the whole, though, limited public transportation options and long distances make renting a car the best choice for most visitors.

New Mexico Highlights

1 Immersing yourself in art and culture in the iconic state capital, **Santa Fe** (p257).

2 Visiting the famous Pueblo, skiing fluffy powder and getting your mellow on in groovy **Taos** (p291).

3 Hiking into the mighty Rio Grande Gorge in the new **Río Grande del Norte National Monument** (p289).

4 Walking in the bootprints of Billy the Kid in historic **Lincoln** (p344).

5 Venturing into the underground extravaganza that is **Carlsbad Caverns National Park** (p349).

6 Sliding down the mesmerizing dunes at **White Sands National Monument** (p337)

7 Getting healed at the 'Lourdes of America' – the **Santuario de Chimayó** (p287).

8 Wondering at the mystery of ancient civilization at **Chaco Culture National Historical Park** (p318).

9 Trekking through rugged wilderness and climbing into cliff dwellings in **Gila National Forest** (p331).

ALBUQUERQUE

POP 550,000 / ELEV 5312FT

This bustling desert crossroads has an understated charm, one based more on its locals than on any kind of urban sparkle. In New Mexico's largest city, immediately west of the Sandia mountains at the point where the east–west Route 66 bridges the north–south Rio Grande, folks are more than happy to share history, highlights and must-try restaurants.

Centuries-old adobes pepper the lively Old Town area, and the shops, restaurants and bars in the hip Nob Hill zone are all within easy walking distance. Good hiking trails abound just outside of town, through evergreen forests or among panels of ancient petroglyphs, while the city's modern museums explore space and nuclear energy. There's a vibrant mix of university students, Native Americans, Hispanics and gays and lesbians. You'll find fliers for square dances and yoga classes distributed with equal enthusiasm, and see ranch hands and real-estate brokers chowing down beside each other at hole-in-the-wall *taquerías* (Mexican fast-food restaurants) and retro cafes.

◉ Sights

Central Ave, the former Route 66, is still Albuquerque's main street, passing from east to west through the state fairground, Nob Hill, the University of New Mexico (UNM), downtown and Old Town before crossing the Rio Grande. Street addresses often conclude with a directional designation, such as Wyoming NE, that specifies one of the city's four quadrants: the center point is where Central Ave crosses the railroad tracks, just east of downtown.

Albuquerque's top sights are largely concentrated in and around Old Town and beside the river, but several interesting attractions – including the Indian Pueblo Cultural Center, Petroglyph National Monument and Sandia Peak Tramway – lie further afield, and are only readily accessible by car.

◉ Old Town

Some of the quaint adobe buildings that line the alleyways of Old Town began life as private residences in 1706, when the first 15 Spanish families called the newly named 'Alburquerque' their home (yes, it originally had

---

NEW MEXICO'S PUEBLOS

New Mexico is home to 19 Native American Pueblos, concentrated especially in the vicinity of Santa Fe. The word 'pueblo' comes from the Spanish for 'village', and that's exactly what they are – small clusters of adobe houses, which in many cases are still standing right where the conquistadors found them five centuries ago. The Native American experience here is thus very different from Indian reservations in the rest of the country. While some of today's Pueblos are populated by the descendants of refugees whose homes were destroyed by the Spanish, most Pueblo Indians were not radically displaced and have long and deep ties to their lands.

For a compelling overview of these communities, stop by Albuquerque's Indian Pueblo Cultural Center (p244). Operated by the Puebloans themselves, the museum traces the development of Pueblo cultures, including Spanish influence, and features exhibits of the arts and crafts created in each Pueblo.

Don't expect all Pueblos to be tourist attractions. Most are simply communities where people live, and offer little for visitors outside of festival weekends. Those that do welcome visitors usually charge admission fees, and either forbid photography or charge additional fees; always check before you take any pictures. As gambling is only legal in New Mexico on Indian reservations, many Pueblos run their own casinos, usually well away from the Pueblo proper.

Our pick of the top three Pueblos for visitors:

Taos Pueblo (p303) The most famous Pueblo in New Mexico, in a gorgeous spot below Pueblo Peak.

Zuni Pueblo (p321) Less touristy than other Pueblos, with creative jewelry and wild scenery; it's 35 miles south of Gallup.

Acoma Pueblo (p324) The dramatic mesa-top 'Sky City' is, along with Taos Pueblo and Arizona's Hopi villages, one of the oldest continually inhabited spots in the US.

ALBUQUERQUE IN...

One Day

Jump-start your belly with a plate of *huevos rancheros* (fried eggs in a spicy tomato sauce, served atop tortillas) from Frontier (p250), before heading to the Indian Pueblo Cultural Center (p244), for a heads-up introduction to Pueblo traditions and culture.

Next up visit the BioPark (p242), which has a zoo, aquarium, botanical gardens and nature trails along the bosk. Head back into town for a bite at Golden Crown Panaderia (p249), then wander over to Old Town (p240) for the afternoon. Walk off lunch admiring the San Felipe de Neri Church (p241), browsing the galleries around the plaza and catching up on your snake trivia at the American International Rattlesnake Museum (p241). Dine outdoors in Nob Hill (p250); Albuquerque's grooviest neighborhood is thick with restaurants.

Two Days

Wander around the Petroglyph National Monument (p244), then head over to Loyola's (p250) for lunch before blowing your mind at the National Museum of Nuclear Science & History (p244). Reach the top of Sandia Crest (p247) before sunset, either by Tramway or by scenic road, for expansive views of the Rio Grande Valley. When you come back down, linger over delicious food and wine at the Slate Street Cafe & Wine Loft (p249).

an extra 'r', which somehow got lost after the Americans took over). Until the arrival of the railroad in 1880, Old Town Plaza was the hub of daily life. With many museums, galleries and original buildings within walking distance, this is the city's most popular tourist area. As you walk around, keep your mind's eye trained partly on the past. Imagine this area as it began, with a handful of hopeful families grateful to have survived a trek across hundreds of miles of desert wilderness.

★ **New Mexico Museum of Natural History & Science**　　MUSEUM
(Map p244; www.nmnaturalhistory.org; 1801 Mountain Rd NW; adult/child $7/4; ⊙9am-5pm; ⏩) Dinosaur-mad kids are certain to love this huge modern museum, on the northeastern fringes of Old Town. From the T Rex in the main atrium onwards, it's crammed with ferocious ancient beasts. The emphasis throughout is on New Mexico, with dramatic displays on the state's geological origins, details of the impact of climate change, and also an exhibit on Albuquerque's role in computer history – did you know this is where Microsoft first started out?

★ **American International Rattlesnake Museum**　　MUSEUM
(Map p244; www.rattlesnakes.com; 202 San Felipe St NW; adult/child $5/3; ⊙10am-6pm Mon-Sat, 1-5pm Sun Jun-Aug, 11:30am-5:30pm Mon-Fri, 10am-6pm Sat, 1-5pm Sun Sep-May) Anyone charmed by snakes and all things slithery will find this museum fascinating; for ophidiaphobes, it's

a complete nightmare, filled with the world's largest collection of different rattlesnake species. You'll also find snake-themed beer bottles and postmarks from every town named 'Rattlesnake' in the US.

Albuquerque Museum of Art & History　　MUSEUM
(Map p244; ☎505-242-4600; www.cabq.gov/museum; 2000 Mountain Rd NW; adult/child $4/1; ⊙9am-5pm Tue-Sun, Old Town walking tours 11am Tue-Sun Mar–mid-Dec) With revamped history galleries exploring the city's past from Spanish days onward, and a permanent art collection that extends to outsider and vernacular work as well as 20th-century masterpieces from the Taos School, this showpiece museum should not be missed. There's free admission on the first Wednesday of the month and on Sunday until 1pm, and free guided walking tours of Old Town.

San Felipe de Neri Church　　CHURCH
(Map p244; www.sanfelipedeneri.org; Old Town Plaza; ⊙7am-5:30pm daily, museum 9:30am-5pm Mon-Sat) Dating in its present incarnation from 1793, the façade of this adobe church now provides Old Town's most famous photo to op. Mass is celebrated Monday, Tuesday, Wednesday and Friday at 7am, with Sunday Mass at 7am, 10:15am and noon.

Turquoise Museum　　MUSEUM
(Map p244; ☎505-247-8650; www.turquoisemuseum.com; 2107 Central Ave NW; adult/child $10/5; ⊙11am & 1pm Mon-Sat) Reserve ahead to join owner Joe Dan Lowry on one of his

Greater Albuquerque

See Old Town Albuquerque (p244)

two daily tours, and get an enlightening crash course in determining the value of turquoise – from high quality to fakes. He's as opinionated as he is knowledgeable, so you're in for an interesting time.

¡Explora!   MUSEUM

(Map p244; www.explora.us; 1701 Mountain Rd NW; adult/child $8/4; 10am-6pm Mon-Sat, noon-6pm Sun;) From the lofty high-wire bike to the mind-boggling Light, Shadow, Color area, this gung-ho museum holds a hands-on exhibit for every type of child (don't miss the elevator). Not traveling with kids? Check the website to see if you're around for the bi-monthly 'Adult Night.' Hosted by an acclaimed local scientist, it's one of the hottest tickets in town.

Albuquerque BioPark

Especially for anyone traveling with kids, the riverside Albuquerque BioPark makes a wonderful escape from the city's summer heat. A combo ticket, sold until noon daily, covers its three main attractions: an aquarium and botanic garden just west of Old Town, and a zoo further south. The park also includes the open space of Tingley Beach – in truth, more of a fishing lake than a beach – to which access is free.

Albuquerque Aquarium   AQUARIUM

(Map p242; 505-764-6200; www.cabq.gov/biopark; 2601 Central Ave NW; adult/child $12.50/4, combo ticket for 3 sites $20/6; 9am-5pm, to 6pm Sat & Sun Jun-Aug;) The Albuquerque Aquarium, a few blocks west of Old Town and the centerpiece of the northern segment of the Albuquerque BioPark, holds a 285,000-gallon tank where colossal rays and turtles live side by side with razor-toothed sharks. Human divers literally drop in at feeding time.

Botanic Garden   GARDENS

(Map p242; www.cabq.gov/biopark; 2601 Central Ave NW; adult/child $12.50/4; combo ticket for 3 sites $20/6; 9am-5pm, until 6pm Sat & Sun Jun-Aug) The twin highlights in this peaceful park are the two large conservatories of Mediterranean and desert plants. You'll also find formal Japanese gardens, an elaborate model-train layout and a fantasy playground for kids. The Butterfly Pavilion is open from May until September, while special events take place throughout the year.

Rio Grande Zoo   ZOO

(Map p242; 505-768-2000; www.cabq.gov/biopark; 903 10th St SW; adult/child $12.50/4, combo ticket for 3 sites $20/6; 9am-5pm, to 6pm Sat & Sun Jun-Aug) Set on 60 shady acres beside the Rio Grande, this zoo is home to more than

Greater Albuquerque

NEW MEXICO ALBUQUERQUE

250 species and puts on a busy rota of events and activities, including daily sea-lion feedings at 10:30am and 3:30pm. Every day except Monday, a half-hourly **miniature train** connects the zoo with the aquarium and botanic gardens 2 miles northwest.

◎ Downtown

Albuquerque's small downtown is no longer the epicenter for action it used to be, back when Route 66 was a novelty and reason enough to set out from either coast in a big '55 Chevy. City planners and business owners have tried in recent years to restore some of that fab '50s neon while encouraging trendy restaurants, galleries and clubs, but few people actually live here, and the office-dominated central blocks are busiest during the working week. On Saturday night, however, Central Ave is jammed with 20-somethings cruising in low riders to see and be seen. Note: the area around the Alvarado Transportation Center has a particularly sketchy vibe.

◎ Nob Hill & UNM Area

A fun and funky place to shop, eat, see art films or get a haircut at a cigar/wine bar, the stretch of Central Ave known as Nob Hill starts at UNM and runs east to about Carlisle Blvd.

Fashion-lovers can browse colorful shops for that unique outfit or accessory; artists will find inspiration and supplies. Even those not looking for anything in particular should find something of interest to muse over.

University of New Mexico MUSEUM
(UNM; Map p242; www.unm.edu; Central Ave NE) There are eight museums and galleries packed into the small but peaceful campus of UNM, along with abundant public art and a performing arts center. The **Tamarind Institute** (☑505-277-3901; http://tamarind.unm.edu; 2500 Central Ave SE; ◎9am-5pm Mon-Fri) FREE helped to save the art of lithography from extinction in the 1960s and '70s, while the **Maxwell Museum of Anthropology** (Map p242; ☑505-277-4405; www.unm.edu/~maxwell; ◎10am-4pm Mon-Fri) FREE has a wonderful collection of ancient Mimbres ceramics. Visit the **UNM Welcome Center** (Map p242; ☑505-277-1989; 2401 Redondo Dr; ◎8am-5pm Mon-Fri) for information and maps.

◎ Metropolitan Albuquerque

Try joining the locals by walking the *acequias*; early risers who value cool temperatures consider the footpaths that border these long-established irrigation channels a real gift in summer. Get hold of a decent city

Old Town Albuquerque

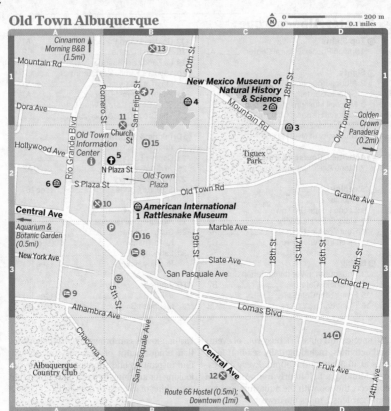

map and find the thin blue lines branching out in North Valley from the Rio Grande between Montaño Rd and Paseo del Norte and around Rio Grande Blvd.

★ Indian Pueblo Cultural Center

MUSEUM

(IPCC; Map p242; ☑ 505-843-7270; www.indian pueblo.org; 2401 12th St NW; adult/child $6/3; ⊘ 9am-5pm) Collectively run by New Mexico's 19 Pueblos, this cultural center makes an essential stop-off during even the shortest Albuquerque visit. The museum downstairs holds fascinating displays on the Pueblos' collective history and individual artistic traditions, while the galleries above offer changing temporary exhibitions. They're arrayed in a crescent around a plaza that's regularly used for dances and crafts demonstrations, and as well as the recommended Pueblo Harvest Cafe (p250) there's also a large gift shop and retail gallery.

National Museum of Nuclear Science & History

MUSEUM

(☑ 505-245-2137; www.nuclearmuseum.org; 601 Eubank Blvd SE; adult/child & senior $8/7; ⊘ 9am-5pm; ⊡) Located at the edge of the massive Kirtland Air Force Base in Albuquerque's southeast corner, and surrounded by an outdoor Heritage Park holding discarded missiles and fighter planes, this lively museum explores the history of nuclear energy in war and peace, from the Manhattan Project and the Cold War up to today. Retired military personnel serve as docents.

Petroglyph National Monument

ARCHAEOLOGICAL SITE

(☑ 505-899-0205; www.nps.gov/petr; 6001 Unser Blvd NW; ⊘ visitor center 8am-5pm) ✐ The lava field preserved in this large desert park, west of the Rio Grande, is adorned with more than 20,000 ancient petroglyphs. Take exit 154 off I-40 to reach the visitor center, 5.5 miles northwest of Old Town, and choose a hik-

Old Town Albuquerque

ing trail. Boca Negra Canyon is the busiest; Rinconada Canyon – the longest at 2.2 miles round-trip – offers the most solitude; and Piedras Marcadas holds 300 petroglyphs. Smash-and-grab thefts have been reported, so don't leave valuables in your vehicle.

Sandia Peak Tramway CABLE CAR
(☑505-856-7325; www.sandiapeak.com; 30 Tramway Rd NE; parking $1; adult/youth 13-20yr/child $20/17/12; ⊗9am-9pm Jun-Aug, 9am-8pm Wed-Mon Sep-May, from 5pm Tue) The world's longest aerial tram climbs 2.7 miles from the desert floor in the northeast corner of the city to the summit of 10,378ft Sandia Crest. The views are spectacular at any time, though sunsets are particularly brilliant. The complex at the top holds gift shops and restaurants, while hiking trails lead off through the woods, and there's also a small ski area.

National Hispanic Cultural Center CULTURAL BUILDING
(Map p242; www.nhccnm.org; 1701 4th St SW; adult/child $3/free, Sun free; ⊗10am-5pm Tue-Sun) In the historic Barelas neighborhood, near the river a mile south of downtown, this modern, architecturally imaginative center for Hispanic visual, performing and literary arts holds three galleries used for temporary exhibitions, recommended cafe Fonda del Bosque (p250) and the nation's premier Hispanic genealogy library. Each June it hosts the Festival Flamenco.

South Valley & North Valley NEIGHBORHOODS
Both these traditional agricultural areas near the Rio Grande are characterized by open spaces, small ranches, farms, and *acequias* (irrigation ditches paralleled by footpaths). Chickens and horses roam fields

between historical adobe and wood-frame houses and newer developments. Of the two, the larger North Valley is more mixed and upscale, with a reputation as affluent, pastoral, quiet and determined to stay that way. Even though it's just 7 miles north of downtown Albuquerque, it feels a world away.

Corrales NEIGHBORHOOD
When Spanish settlers established this village in 1710, Tewa Indians had already been growing crops here for a thousand years. These days, the hills produce surprising quantities of fine wine. Even more rural than North Valley, immediately south, Corrales offers splendid strolling through the bosk (riparian woods) and along *acequias*. Drive or walk along the unpaved side roads off Hwy 448 to find rabbits and quail crisscrossing your path among 200-year-old adobes and modern replicas.

Casa Rondeña WINERY
(☑505-604-5573; www.casarondena.com; 733 Chavez Rd NW; ⊗noon-7pm) This winery in the Los Ranchos area of the North Valley often serves as a wedding venue. At any other time, you can drop in for a $5 wine tasting, and they also offer tours during the area's summer Lavender Festival.

🏃 Activities

The ideal way to get out into the fresh air in Albuquerque, and explore the city under your own steam, is to explore the city by bike. Cycling is a big deal here, for commuting locals and national-level competitors alike. For details of the excellent network of cycling lanes, which include the stretch of Central Ave between Old Town and downtown as well as dedicated off-road tracks along arroyos, download the city map at www.cabq.gov/bike.

Elena Gallegos Open Space   HIKING

(www.cabq.gov; Simms Park Rd; weekday/weekend parking $1/2; ⊘ 7am– 9pm Apr-Oct, closes 7pm Nov-Mar) Sandia Crest is Albuquerque's outdoor playground, popular for skiing and hiking. As well as several picnic areas, this foothills park holds trailheads for hiking, running and mountain-biking; some routes are wheelchair-accessible. Come early, before the sun gets too hot, or late, to enjoy the panoramic views at sunset, as the city lights start to twinkle below. Time evening walks carefully, though; darkness falls quickly and howling coyotes ring the park. They won't bother you, but it can be unnerving.

Routes Rentals   CYCLING

(Map p244; ☑ 505-933-5667; www.routesrentals.com; 404 San Felipe St NW; tours incl rental from $30; ⊘ 8am-7pm Mon-Fri, 7am-7pm Sat & Sun) This friendly Old Town cycle shop rents out all kinds of bikes from $20 for a half-day, and also runs a great program of guided cycling tours, including a daily riverside trip and several routes focused on hit TV series *Breaking Bad*.

Stone Age Climbing Gym   ROCK CLIMBING

(Map p242; ☑ 505-341-2016; www.climbstoneage.com; 4130 Cutler Ave NE; day pass $16; ⊘ noon-11pm Mon-Fri, 10am-9pm Sat & Sun) While there are lots of great climbing routes in the Sandias, rock climbers itching to hit the wall will also dig this gym, offering 21,000 sq ft of climbing terrain simulating a wide range of rock features. Classes are offered and you can rent gear. To get here, take the Carlisle exit off I-40.

☞ Tours

Story of New Mexico Program   TOURS

(☑ 505-277-0077; www.dcereg.com) The UNM Department of Continuing Education offers excellent lectures on all things New Mexico, as well as tours to Santa Fe, Taos and sites throughout the state, including visits to Pueblo feast days and trips to the otherwise inaccessible Lawrence Ranch, home to the ashes of novelist DH Lawrence. Advance registration is required.

✯✯ Festivals & Events

Friday's *Albuquerque Journal* (www.abqjournal.com) includes exhaustive listings of festivals and activities.

Gathering of Nations Powwow   CULTURAL

(www.gatheringofnations.com; ⊘ Apr) Dance competitions, displays of Native American arts and crafts, and the 'Miss Indian World' contest. Held in late April.

New Mexico Wine
Festival at Bernalillo   WINE

(www.newmexicowinefestival.com; admission $15; ⊘ early Sep) Locally produced wine, and live music too, staged about 15 minutes' drive north of Albuquerque, and also accessible using the Rail Runner – a real treat if you're in town over the Labor Day weekend.

New Mexico State Fair   RODEO

(www.exponm.com; adult/child $10/7; ⊘ Sep) New Mexico's biggest jamboree, with rodeo, live music, games and rides as well as livestock shows, runs for 12 days in September.

International Balloon Fiesta   BALLOON

(www.balloonfiesta.com; ⊘ early Oct) The largest balloon festival in the world. You simply haven't lived until you've seen a three-story-tall Tony the Tiger land in your hotel courtyard, and that's exactly the sort of thing that happens during the festival, which features mass dawn take-offs on each of its nine days, overlapping the first and second weekends in October.

🛌 Sleeping

Although Albuquerque holds about 150 hotels – all of which fill during the International Balloon Fiesta and the Gathering of Nations – few are in any way exceptional. If you're looking for character or charm, a B&B makes a better option.

The cheapest motels of all line Central Ave, especially around the I-25 on-ramp and east of Nob Hill. You can usually score a room for under $50, but some can be pretty sleazy. Smarter chain hotels gather a little further south, close to the airport and UNM.

🛏 Old Town

Econo Lodge Old Town   MOTEL $

(Map p242; ☑ 505-243-8475; www.econolodge.com; 2321 Central Ave NW; r incl breakfast $69; P ✲ @ 🛜 🛋) Just five minutes' walk west of the plaza, this bright, clean motel makes a great deal for anyone planning to explore the Old Town or the BioPark, with spacious and well-equipped modern rooms, an indoor pool and free hot breakfasts.

Böttger Mansion   B&B $$

(Map p244; ☑ 505-243-3639; www.bottger.com; 110 San Felipe St NW; r incl breakfast $104-179; P ✲ @ 🛜 🛋) The friendly proprietor gives

ALBUQUERQUE'S MOUNTAIN: SANDIA CREST

Albuquerqueans always know which way is east thanks to 10,378ft **Sandia Crest**, sacred to Sandia Pueblo and well named for both its wavelike silhouette and the glorious pink (*sandia* is Spanish for 'watermelon') its granite cliffs glow at sunset. There are three ways to the top.

➡ Beautiful 8-mile (one-way) **La Luz Trail** (FR 444; parking $3) is the most rewarding, rising 3800ft from the desert, past a small waterfall to pine forests and spectacular views. It gets hot, so start early. Take Tramway Blvd east from I-25, then turn left on FR 333 to the trailhead.

➡ Sandia Peak Tramway (p245) is the most extravagant route to the summit; ride round-trip or take the tram up and then hike down La Luz, walking 2 miles more on Tramway Trail to your car.

➡ Finally you can drive, via Hwy 14, making a left onto Sandia Crest Rd (Hwy 165). The road is lined with trailheads and picnic spots (a daily $3 parking fee covers all of them), and low-impact camping ($3) is allowed by permit throughout Cibola National Forest. The choices are endless, but don't skip the easy mile round-trip to **Sandia Man Cave**, where one of the earliest known human encampments in North America was discovered in 1936; bring a flashlight. The trailhead is along Hwy 165, north of the spur road to Sandia Crest.

At the top, the **Sandia Crest Visitor Center** (☏505-248-0190; Hwy 165; ☉10am-sunset in winter, to 7pm in summer) offers nature programs daily; **Sandia Crest House** (☏505-243-0605; www.sandiacresthouse.com; dishes $4-9; ☉10am-5pm), in the same building, serves burgers and snacks. This is the jumping-off point for the exquisite **Sandia Crest Trail**. With incredible views either way you go, paths lead north along the ridgeline for 11 miles and south along the ridge for 16 miles.

Take the trail 2 miles south, past **Kiwanis Cabin** rock house, to the tram terminal and **High Finance** (☏505-243-9742; www.sandiapeakrestaurants.com; lunch mains $7-15, dinner mains $20-38; ☉11am-3pm Wed-Sun, 4:30-9pm daily), where the food is nothing special but the views are fabulous.

This is also the site of **Sandia Peak Ski Park** (☏505-242-9052; www.sandiapeak.com; lift tickets adult/child $50/40; ☉9am-4pm Dec-Mar & Jun-Sep), a smallish but scenic ski area. In summer, the park has a bike-and-lift combo for $58 (with $650 deposit) – you get a bike and lift pass to blaze those downhill runs all day long (note that bikes aren't allowed on the tram).

---

this well-appointed B&B, built in 1912 and one minute's walk from the plaza, an edge over tough competition. Three of its seven themed, antique-furnished rooms have pressed-tin ceilings, one has a Jacuzzi tub, and sumptuous breakfasts are served in a honeysuckle-lined courtyard loved by bird-watchers. Past guests include Elvis, Janis Joplin and Machine Gun Kelly.

Casas de Sueños　　　　　　B&B $$
(Map p244; ☏505-247-4560; www.casasdesuenos.com; 310 Rio Grande Blvd SW; r incl breakfast from $149; P ✳ @ ☎) Set in luscious gardens a short walk from Old Town, this lovely and peaceful place holds 21 adobe casitas (small cottages). All feature handcrafted furniture and original artwork, while some have kitchenettes, fireplaces and/or private hot tubs. Full breakfasts are cooked to order.

🛏 Downtown

Route 66 Hostel　　　　　　HOSTEL $
(Map p242; ☏505-247-1813; www.rt66hostel.com; 1012 Central Ave SW; dm $20, r from $25; P @ ☎) This pastel-lemon hostel, in a former residence a few blocks west of downtown, holds male and female dorms plus simple private rooms, some of which share bathrooms. The beds are aging, but there's a welcoming atmosphere, with common facilities including a library and a kitchen offering free self-serve breakfasts. Voluntary chores; no check-ins between 1:30pm and 4:30pm.

★ Andaluz　　　　　BOUTIQUE HOTEL $$
(Map p242; ☏505-242-9090; www.hotelandaluz.com; 125 2nd St NW; r $112-279; P ✳ @ ☎) Albuquerque's finest historic hotel, built in the heart of downtown in 1939, has been

BREAKING BAD IN ALBUQUERQUE

TV viewers captivated by the epic five-season run of *Breaking Bad*, in which unassuming high-school chemistry teacher Walter White transformed himself into death-dealing drugs overlord Heisenberg, have been flocking to Albuquerque to follow in his blood-stained footsteps.

Although the raw New Mexican landscape provided an unforgettable backdrop for the action, relatively few of the city's real-life landmarks actually turned up on screen; you may remember the Octopus Car Wash just off Menaul Blvd at Snow Heights Circle, or fleeting glimpses of Route 66 icons like the Dog House diner at 1216 Central Ave NW. Perhaps the most accessible of all is the excellent downtown coffee bar **Java Joe's**, instantly recognizable as the mural-marked headquarters of Tuco the gangster, blown up by Walter White when he first displays his true mettle.

Various *Breaking Bad* tours explore further afield, delving into the lesser-known corners of Albuquerque, where crossing some humdrum intersection may suddenly confront you with the home or workplace of a favorite character, or the scene of a memorable shootout. Our pick of the bunch is the Biking Bad cycle tour by Routes Rentals (p246), which lets customers choose from five *Breaking Bad*–themed tours, each costing $50 to $65 including bike rental.

modernized while retaining period details like its stunning central atrium, where cozy arched nooks hold tables and couches. Rooms feature hypoallergenic bedding and carpets, the Más Tapas Y Vino (p250) restaurant is excellent, and there's a rooftop bar. Reserve 30 days in advance for the best rates.

Mauger Estate B&B　　　　　B&B $$
(Map p242; ☑505-242-8755; www.maugerbb.com; 701 Roma Ave NW, cnr 7th St NW; r incl breakfast from $129, townhouse from $169; P 🕸 🛎) This restored Queen Anne mansion holds comfortable rooms of varying sizes, with down comforters, stocked refrigerators and freshly cut flowers. Kids are welcome, and there are also a couple of great-value, two-bedroom townhouses, complete with Wild West decor, which accept dogs for a $20 extra fee. Mauger, incidentally, is pronounced 'major.'

🛏 Metropolitan Albuquerque

Sandia Peak Inn Motel　　　　MOTEL $
(☑505-831-5036; www.sandiapeakinnmotel.com; 4614 Central Ave SW; r $65; P 🕸 🛎)Old-fashioned, family-run and utterly exemplary Route 66 motel, across the Rio Grande a mile west of Old Town (and thus, despite the name, nowhere near Sandia Peak), with two floors of decently upgraded rooms plus an indoor swimming pool and free continental breakfasts.

Sleep Inn Albuquerque　　　　HOTEL $
(Map p242; ☑505-244-3325; www.sleepinnalbu querque.com; 2300 International Ave SE; r $64;

P 🕸 @ 🕸 🛎) Of the dozen or so large chain hotels that congregate immediately north of the airport, along Yale Blvd a couple of miles south of Nob Hill, this offers the best bang for your buck, with large, modern, earth-toned rooms, indoor heated pool and free airport shuttles. For the lowest rates, look for motel-coupon magazines.

Albuquerque North

Bernalillo KOA　　　　　　CAMPGROUND $
(☑505-867-5227; www.koa.com; 555 S Hill Rd, Bernalillo; tent sites from $25, RV sites from $40, cabins $39; 🕸 🛎 🛎) About 15 miles north of the city limits, a mile from the nearest Rail Runner station, the better of Albuquerque's two KOA franchises has rental cabins as well as spaces for tents and RVs, and stands within easy exploring distance of city attractions. Use exit 240 off I-25.

Cinnamon Morning B&B　　　　B&B $$
(☑800-214-9481; www.cinnamonmorning.com; 2700 Rio Grande Blvd NW; r from $115, casita from $149, guesthouse $239; P 🕸 🛎) This friendly B&B, not far north of Old Town, has three guest rooms in the main house, two casitas with kitchenettes and private patios, and a two-bedroom guesthouse. Lots of Southwest charm and common areas make it a relaxing and homey place to slumber.

★**Los Poblanos**　　　　　　B&B $$$
(☑505-344-9297; www.lospoblanos.com; 4803 Rio Grande Blvd NW; r $180-330; P 🕸 @ 🕸) This amazing 20-room B&B, on a 1930s rural ranch that's a National Historic Place, is five

minutes' drive north of Old Town. Close to the Rio Grande, it's set amid 25 acres of gardens, lavender fields (blooming mid-June through July) and an organic farm. The gorgeous rooms feature kiva fireplaces, while produce from the farm is served for breakfast.

✖ Eating

Albuquerque offers plenty of definitive down-home New Mexican grub, plus the region's widest variety of international cuisines. It's not a foodie destination like Santa Fe, and restaurants geared towards tourists tend to be less than outstanding. To browse options from hip to homey, budget to blowout, the Nob Hill district, around the University, is by far the best bet.

✖ Old Town

The Plaza is surrounded by average eateries that serve average food at premium prices. To find a better selection, consider walking a block or two away.

★ Golden Crown Panaderia   BAKERY $

(Map p242; ✆ 505-243-2424; www.goldencrown. biz; 1103 Mountain Rd NW; mains $7-20; ⊗ 7am-8pm Tue-Sat, 10am-8pm Sun) Who doesn't love a friendly neighborhood cafe-bakery? Especially one in a cozy old adobe, with gracious staff, oven-fresh bread and pizza, fruity empanadas, smooth espresso coffees and free cookies all round? Call ahead to reserve a loaf of quick-selling green chile bread – then eat it hot, out on the patio.

Garcia's Kitchen   NEW MEXICAN $

(Map p244; ✆ 505-842-0071; www.garciaskitchen. com; 1736 Central Ave SW; mains $5-10; ⊗ 7am-9pm Sun-Thu, to 10pm Fri & Sat) Part of a small local chain, this Route 66–style diner just east of Old Town serves some of the best New Mexican food in Albuquerque, making it a great spot for breakfast. The red vinyl booths and eclectic crowd give it a pure local feel.

Church St Cafe   NEW MEXICAN $$

(Map p244; ✆ 505-247-8522; www.church streetcafe.com; 2111 Church St NW; mains $9-17; ⊗ 8am-9pm Mon–Sat, to 4pm Sun) This 18th-century adobe complex makes the nicest setting for a meal near the Plaza, and it has a well-shaded patio. Besides New Mexican favorites like the hot chile dip and veggie burritos, the menu includes salads and sandwiches.

Seasons Rotisserie & Grill   MODERN AMERICAN $$$

(Map p244; ✆ 505-766-5100; www.seasonsabq. com; 2031 Mountain Rd NW; lunch $10-16, dinner $21-42; ⊗ 11:30am-2pm & 4-10pm Mon-Fri, 4-11pm Sat, 4-10pm Sun) With bright-yellow walls, high ceilings, fresh flowers and a creative menu, this contemporary restaurant provides welcome relief from the usual Old Town atmosphere, and its rooftop terrace is a gem. Try the house-made raviolis or fresh grilled fish and meats.

Antiquity   STEAKHOUSE $$$

(Map p244; ✆ 505-247-3545; www.antiquity restaurant.com; 112 Romero St NW; mains $22-34; ⊗ 5-9pm) With just 14 tables in an atmosphere of rustic elegance, Antiquity specializes in steak, seafood and fine wine. The desserts list isn't long, but it doesn't need to be. A favorite of locals and visitors alike.

✖ Downtown

The Grove Cafe & Market   MODERN AMERICAN $

(Map p242; ✆ 505-248-9800; www.thegrovecafe-market.com; 600 Central Ave SE; ⊗ 7am-4pm Tue-Sat, 8am-3pm Sun) Much more cafe than market, this light, bright 'EDo' (east downtown) bistro is renowned for healthy, all-day organic breakfasts, and does a brisk trade in salads and sandwiches for the office crowd. There's no wi-fi, on principle.

★ Slate Street Cafe & Wine Loft   MODERN AMERICAN $$

(Map p242; ✆ 505-243-2210; www.slatestreetcafe. com; 515 Slate St; breakfast $6-12, lunch $9-16, dinner $12-28; ⊗ 7:30am-3pm Mon-Fri, 9am-2pm Sat & Sun, 5-9pm Tue-Thu, 5-10pm Fri & Sat) Popular downtown rendezvous, off 6th St NW, just north of Lomas Blvd. The cafe downstairs is usually packed with people enjoying imaginative Southwestern/American comfort food, from peanut butter and jelly sandwiches to herb-crusted pork chops, while the upstairs wine loft serves 25 wines by the glass and offers regular tasting sessions.

DID YOU KNOW?

New Mexico is the only state with an official state question: 'red or green?' – referring to chile, of course. You'll hear it every time you order New Mexican food. Feeling ambivalent? Ask for 'Christmas' to get both.

Más Tapas Y Vino
MEDITERRANEAN,TAPAS $$$

(Map p242; ☑505-923-9080; www.hotelandaluz.com; 125 2nd St NW; ⊗7am-2pm & 5-9:30pm) This smart, see-and-be-seen hotel restaurant serves a fabulous array of tapas-style small plates, including Spanish ham and cheeses, plus substantial mains like delicious lamb chops or duck breast with couscous and Moroccan carrot sauce.

Artichoke Cafe
MODERN AMERICAN $$$

(Map p242; ☑505-243-0200; www.artichokecafe.com; 424 Central Ave SE; lunch mains $10-16, dinner mains $19-39; ⊗11am-2:30pm & 5-9pm Mon-Fri, 5-10pm Sat) Elegant and unpretentious, this popular bistro prepares creative gourmet cuisine with panache and is always high on foodies' lists of Albuquerque's best. It's on the eastern edge of downtown, between the bus station and I-40.

✖ Nob Hill & UNM Area

In the tradition of university neighborhoods, Nob Hill offers a fine selection of cheap, healthy and vegetarian places to eat, though also has its fair share of swanky options.

★ Frontier
NEW MEXICAN $

(Map p242; ☑505-266-0550; www.frontierrestaurant.com; 2400 Central Ave SE; mains $3-12; ⊗5am-1am; 🖉🐕) Get in line for enormous cinnamon rolls (made with lots of butter) and some of the best *huevos rancheros* (fried eggs in a spicy tomato sauce, served atop tortillas) in town. The food, people-watching and Western art are all outstanding.

Annapurna's World Vegetarian Cafe
INDIAN $

(Map p242; ☑505-262-2424; www.chaishoppe.com; 2201 Silver Ave SE; mains $7-11; ⊗7am-9pm Mon-Fri, 8am-9pm Sat, 10am-8pm Sun) This awesome vegetarian and vegan cafe, one block south of Route 66 and part of a small local chain, serves fresh, tasty Indian specialties, including delicately spiced Ayurvedic delights that even carnivores love. Dishes are complemented by authentic chai.

Il Vicino Pizzeria
ITALIAN $

(Map p242; ☑505-266-7855; www.ilvicino.com; 3403 Central Ave NE; mains $7-11; ⊗11am-11pm, to midnight Fri & Sat) Line up at the counter to order simple Italian meals like wood-fired pizza, salads and pasta, but don't forget the real star attraction – spectacular, award-winning microbrewed beer, including Wet Mountain IPA and Slow Down Brown.

Flying Star Cafe
AMERICAN $$

(Map p242; ☑505-255-6633; www.flyingstarcafe.com; 3416 Central Ave SE; mains $8-13; ⊗6am-11pm, to midnight Fri & Sat; 🖰🖉🐕) For visitors, the Nob Hill location of this deservedly popular local chain is the most convenient of outlets throughout Albuquerque and beyond. Locals flock here from early morning onwards, to enjoy an extensive breakfast menu and innovative main courses later on, amid creative, colorful decor. The whole experience is enhanced by the use of organic, free-range and antibiotic-free ingredients.

✖ Metropolitan Albuquerque

Loyola's Family Restaurant
NEW MEXICAN $

(Map p242; ☑505-268-6478; 4500 Central Ave SE; mains $6-9; ⊗6am-2pm Tue-Fri, 6am-1pm Sat, 7am-1pm Sun) Pure Route 66 style, baby. Set a quarter-mile east of Nob Hill, Loyola's has been serving no-frills New Mexican staples, including hands-down the best chile in town, since before there was even a song about the Mother Road.

La Fonda del Bosque
LATIN AMERICAN $$

(Map p242; ☑505-247-9480; www.lafondadelbosque.com; 1701 4th St SW; ⊗11am-2pm Tue-Sat, 9am-2pm Sun) The bright, friendly dining room at the National Hispanic Cultural Center is a perfect lunch option; its three-course, $15 prix-fixe deal is a real bargain, or you can simply order mains such as avocado crab quesadillas or the Cuban sandwich.

Pueblo Harvest Cafe
NATIVE AMERICAN $$$

(Map p242; ☑505-724-3510; www.indianpueblo.org; 2401 12th St NW; lunch $9-11, dinner $9-28; ⊗8am-8:30pm Mon-Sat, 8am-4pm Sun; 🖉🐕) A rare chance to sample the *real* local cuisine, with dishes like blue corn porridge for breakfast, Tewa tacos for lunch – the Pueblo take on Indian fry bread – and rack of lamb crusted with sunflower seeds for dinner. On summer weekends, it hosts an early evening pizza-and-music 'Party on the Patio'.

🍷 Drinking

Albuquerque's bar scene, which has long focused on downtown and Nob Hill, has been enlivened in recent years by the emergence of a new breed of brewpubs scattered across the city.

Satellite Coffee
CAFE

(Map p242; www.satellitecoffee.com; 2300 Central Ave SE; ⊗6am-11pm Mon-Fri, from 7am Sat & Sun; 🖰) Albuquerque's answer to Starbucks lies in these hip coffee shops – look for the other eight locations around town – luring lots of laptop-toting regulars. Set up and still owned by the same brilliant folks responsible for the Flying Star chain.

Anodyne BAR
(Map p242; ☑505-244-1820; www.theanodyne.com; 409 Central Ave NW; ☺4pm-1:30am Mon-Sat, 7-11:30pm Sun) An excellent spot for a game of pool, Anodyne is a huge space with book-lined walls, wood ceilings, plenty of over-stuffed chairs, more than 100 bottled beers and great people-watching on Central Ave.

Marble Brewery BREWERY
(Map p242; ☑505-243-2739; www.marble brewery.com; 111 Marble Ave NW; ☺noon-midnight, to 10:30pm Sun) Popular downtown brewpub, attached to its namesake brewery, with a snug interior for winter nights and a beer garden where local bands play early-evening gigs in summer. Be sure to try their 11%-strength Imperial Stout.

Java Joe's CAFE
(Map p242; ☑505-765-1514; www.downtownjava joes.com; 906 Park Ave SW; mains $5-9; ☺6:30am-3:30pm; ♿☺) Best known these days for its explosive cameo role in *Breaking Bad*, this comfy coffee shop still makes a great stop-off for a java jolt or a bowl of the hottest chile in town.

Copper Lounge LOUNGE
(Map p242; ☑505-242-7490; www.thecopper lounge.com; 1504 Central Ave SE; ☺11am-2am Mon-Sat) Just west of the UNM campus, you'll find a friendly, mixed crowd and daily drink specials at this place, which has a casual patio and a dark lounge area.

☆ Entertainment

For comprehensive listings of Albuquerque's many nightspots and a calendar of upcoming events, pick up the free weekly *Alibi* (www.alibi.com), published every Tuesday. Friday's *Albuquerque Journal* is helpful, too. Downtown has a great nightlife scene, while the proximity of UNM makes Nob Hill pretty lively too. The **UNM Lobos** (www.go lobos.com) have a full roster of sports teams, but are best known for basketball (men's and women's) and women's volleyball.

Launch Pad LIVE MUSIC
(Map p242; ☑505-764-8887; www.launchpadrocks.com; 618 Central Ave SW) This retro-modern place is the hottest stage for local live music.

Caravan East LIVE MUSIC
(☑505-980-5466; www.caravaneast.com; 7605 Central Ave NE) Put on your cowboy boots and 10-gallon hat and hit the dancefloor to practice your line dancing and two-stepping at this classic Albuquerque music club. Live country and/or Latin bands perform and the ambience is friendly.

Guild Cinema CINEMA
(Map p242; ☑505-255-1848; www.guildcinema.com; 3405 Central Ave NE; admission $8) The only independently owned, single-screen theater in town programs great indie, avant-garde, Hollywood fringe, political and international features. Stick around for discussions following select films.

Albuquerque Isotopes BASEBALL
(Map p242; www.albuquerquebaseball.com; Ave Cesar Chavez, Isotopes Park, University SE) First of all: yes, the city's baseball team really was named for the episode of *The Simpsons*, 'Hungry, Hungry Homer,' when America's favorite TV dad tried to keep his beloved Springfield Isotopes from moving to Albuquerque. The 'topes sell more merchandise than any other minor (and most major) league team. They sometimes win, too.

🔒 Shopping

Albuquerque's most interesting shops are in Old Town and Nob Hill.

Mariposa Gallery ARTS & CRAFTS
(Map p242; ☑505-268-6828; www.mariposa-gallery.com; 3500 Central Ave SE) Beautiful, funky arts, crafts and jewelry, by regional artists.

Palms Trading Post
ARTS & CRAFTS

(Map p244; www.palmstrading.com; 1504 Lomas Blvd NW; ⊙9am-5:30pm Mon-Fri, 10am-5:30pm Sat) Large gallery where knowledgeable salespeople sell Native American pottery, jewelry, rugs and crafts.

Santisima
ARTS & CRAFTS

(Map p244; ☑505-246-2611; 328 San Felipe NW; ⊙Wed-Mon 11:30am-8:30pm) Interesting folk-art gallery selling Day of the Dead artifacts and images, some imported from Mexico and some quirky variations by artists including owner Johnny Salas.

Silver Sun
JEWELRY

(Map p244; ☑505-246-9692; www.silversunalbuquerque.com; 116 San Felipe St NW; ⊙9am-4pm) A reputable Old Town store specializing in natural American turquoise, as stones as well as finished jewelry.

IMEC
JEWELRY

(International Metalsmith Exhibition Center; Map p242; ☑505-265-8352; 101 Amherst SE; ⊙noon-6pm Tue-Sat) Just off Central Ave, IMEC displays and sells intriguing jewelry by local craftspeople.

Page One
BOOKS

(www.page1book.com; 5850 Eubank Blvd NE; ⊙9am-7pm Mon-Thu, 9am-8pm Fri & Sat, 10am-6pm Sun) A huge and comprehensive selection of books, some secondhand, in the northeast quadrant of the city.

OFF THE BEATEN TRACK

WEIRD, WILD & WONDERFUL

Aztec's Sandstone Arches (p316) Hundreds of little-known natural arches lie waiting to be found in the desert canyons that surround sleepy little Aztec.

The Very Large Array (p325) These vast, white, deep-space listening devices make a memorable sight, maneuvering across an all-but-empty high-desert plain.

Simon Canyon Recreation Area (p315) A short hike into this remote corner of northwest New Mexico leads to a solitary, time-forgotten Navajo ruin.

Chloride (p329) Definitive Wild West ghost town, reached by a dramatic dead-end drive into the Black Range.

Puyé Cliff Dwellings (p282) A real rarity: modern Pueblo guides lead you through the spectacular cliffside village that was home to their ancestors.

---

❶ Information

EMERGENCY
Police (☑505-242-2677; 400 Roma Ave NW)

INTERNET ACCESS
Albuquerque is wired. The Old Town Plaza, Sunport, downtown Civic Plaza, Aquarium and Botanic Garden have free wi-fi, as do Rapid Ride buses.

INTERNET RESOURCES
Albuquerque Online (www.abqonline.com) Exhaustive listings and links for local businesses.

Albuquerque.com (www.albuquerque.com) Information on attractions, hotels and restaurants.

City of Albuquerque (www.cabq.gov) Public transportation, area attractions and more.

MEDICAL SERVICES
Presbyterian Hospital (☑505-841-1234; www.phs.org; 1100 Central Ave SE; ⊙24hr emergency)

UNM Hospital (☑505-272-2411; 2211 Lomas Blvd NE; ⊙24hr emergency) Head here if you don't have insurance.

POST
Post office (Map p242; 201 5th St SW; ⊙9am-4:30pm Mon-Fri)

TOURIST INFORMATION
Albuquerque Convention & Visitors Bureau (☑505-842-9918; www.itsatrip.org; 20 First Plaza NW, cnr 2nd St & Copper Ave; ⊙9am-4pm Mon-Fri)

Old Town Information Center (Map p244; ☑505-243-3215; www.itsatrip.org; 303 Romero Ave NW; ⊙10am-5pm Oct-May, to 6pm Jun-Sep)

❶ Getting There & Away

AIR
New Mexico's largest airport, the **Albuquerque International Sunport** (Map p242; ☑505-244-7700; www.cabq.gov/airport; 2200 Sunport Blvd SE; ☎), 5 miles southeast of downtown, is served by multiple airlines. Free shuttles connect the terminal building with the Sunport Car Rental Center at 3400 University Blvd SE, home to all the airport's car-rental facilities.

BUS
The **Alvarado Transportation Center** (Map p242; 100 1st St SW, cnr Central Ave) is home to **Greyhound** (☑800-231-2222, 505-243-4435; www.greyhound.com; 320 1st St SW), which serves destinations throughout the state and beyond, though not Santa Fe or Taos.

TRAIN

Amtrak's *Southwest Chief* stops at Albuquerque's **Amtrak Station** (☑ 800-872-7245, 505-842-9650; www.amtrak.com; 320 1st St SW; ☺ 9:45am-5pm), which forms part of the Alvarado Transportation Center. Trains head east to Chicago (from $140, 26 hours) or west to Los Angeles (from $100, 16½ hours), once daily in each direction.

A commuter lightrail line, the **New Mexico Rail Runner Express** (www.nmrailrunner.com), shares the station. It makes several stops in the Albuquerque metropolitan area, but more importantly for visitors it runs all the way north to Santa Fe (one-way/day pass $9/10, 1¾ hours), with eight departures on weekdays, four on Saturday and three on Sunday.

❶ Getting Around

TO/FROM THE AIRPORT

ABQ Ride bus 250 provides free service between the Sunport and the downtown Rail Runner station, four times a day, weekdays only; each bus coincides with a train to Santa Fe. The **Sunport Shuttle** (☑ 505-883-4966; www.sunportshuttle.com) runs to local hotels and other destinations; the **Sandia Shuttle** (☑ 888-775-5696; www.sandiashuttle.com; 1-way/round-trip $28/48; ☺ 8:45am-11:45pm) runs to Santa Fe (one-way/round-trip $28/48) hourly between 8:45am and 11:45pm.

BICYCLE

Contact **Parks & Recreation** (☑ 505-768-2680; www.cabq.gov/bike) or visit the website for a free map of the city's elaborate system of bike trails. All ABQ Ride buses are equipped with front-loading bicycle racks.

BUS

ABQ Ride (☑ 505-243-7433; www.cabq.gov/transit; 100 1st St SW; adult/child $1/0.35; day pass $2) is a public bus system covering most of Albuquerque on weekdays and major tourist spots daily. Maps and schedules are available on the website; most lines run till 6pm. **Rapid Ride** buses serve the BioPark, Old Town, downtown, Nob Hill and the fairgrounds; bus 66 runs up and down Central Ave.

CAR & MOTORCYCLE

Albuquerque is an easy city to drive around. Streets are wide and there's usually metered or even free parking within blocks from wherever you want to stop.

New Mexico's largest city is also motorcycle friendly: the town has its share of biker bars and you're always likely to be within earshot of a 'hog' thundering down the street.

TAXI

In general you have to call for a taxi, though they do patrol the Sunport, and the rail and bus stations.

Albuquerque Cab (☑ 505-883-4888; www.albuquerquecab.com)

Albuquerque Area Pueblos

Several Pueblos continue to occupy their ancestral lands in the vicinity of Albuquerque, especially north toward Santa Fe.

Isleta Pueblo

POP 3000 / ELEV 4887FT

Isleta Pueblo (www.isletapueblo.com), 16 miles south of Albuquerque at I-25 exit 215, is best known for its church. Built in 1613, the San Augustin Mission has been in constant use since 1692. A few plaza shops sell local pottery, and there's gambling at the flash **Isleta Resort & Casino** (www.isleta.com; ☺ 8am-4am Mon-Thu, 24hr Fri-Sun). Visitors are welcome to the ceremonial dances on **Saint Augustine's Day** (September 4).

Sandia Pueblo

POP 400 / ELEV 5039FT

About 13 miles north of Albuquerque, and served by its own Rail Runner station, **Sandia Pueblo** (www.sandiapueblo.nsn.us; I-25, exit 234) was established around 1300 AD. Thanks to the wealth generated by Sandia Casino, it has successfully lobbied to prevent further development of Sandia Crest, which its people have long held sacred. The tribe welcome visitors to corn dances on its **Feast Day** (June 13).

Sandia Casino CASINO
(☑ 505-796-7500; www.sandiacasino.com; 30 Rainbow Road NE; ☺ 8am-4am Mon-Thu, 24hr Fri-Sun) One of the first casinos to open in New Mexico, this lavish property is best known for its elegant outdoor amphitheater, which has become Albuquerque's premier live entertainment venue, hosting everything from symphony orchestras to Ringo Starr.

Bien Mur Indian Market ARTS & CRAFTS
(☑ 505-821-5400; 100 Bien Mur Dr NE; ☺ 9am-5:30pm Mon-Sat, 11am-5:30pm Sun) The largest Native American–owned trading post in the Southwest, across from the casino, sells crafts from all the region's native peoples, and has its own showpiece **buffalo herd**.

Santa Ana Pueblo

POP 600 / ELEV 5248FT

Across the Rio Grande 30 miles north of Albuquerque, **Santa Ana Pueblo** (www.santa ana.org) is posh. Really posh. Nonetheless, ancient tradition has survived the modern glitz of its upscale resort and casino, and it continues to celebrate Corn Dances on June 24 and July 26.

Stables at Tamaya HORSEBACK RIDING
(⏹505-771-6060; 2hr trail ride $75) Santa Ana Pueblo's own riding stables offer trail rides and lessons through the reservation's woodlands, which have recently benefited from a million-dollar clean-up and restoration program, and also host Friday-night rodeos in summer.

Santa Ana Star Casino CASINO
(⏹505-867-0000; www.santaanastar.com; US 150; ◷8am-4am Sun-Wed, 24hr Thu-Sat) The Pueblo's casino offers a staggering buffet, 36 lanes of bowling and live entertainment ranging from Michael Jackson impersonators to the real Bob Dylan.

Hyatt Tamaya HOTEL
(⏹505-867-1234; www.tamaya.hyatt.com; 1300 Tuyuna Trail; r from $189; P@☎☲) This luxury resort, a low-slung adobe complex tucked unobtrusively into the desert landscape while enjoying expansive views, has three pools, three restaurants and a small spa, as well as two great **golf courses** (⏹505-867-9464, 800-851-9469; www.santaanagolf.com;

green fees $45-80): the Santa Ana Golf Club, a 27-hole links-style course, and the extravagant Twin Warriors Golf Club, with 18 holes amid desert and waterfalls.

ALBUQUERQUE TO SANTA FE

Two alternative routes connect New Mexico's two major cities. It takes a speedy hour to drive from Albuquerque to Santa Fe along the semiscenic I-25, or about 90 minutes on the lovelier NM 14, known as the Turquoise Trail.

Along I-25

Potential distractions on the Pueblo lands that lie just off the interstate include the intriguing Kasha-Katuwe National Monument, which offers some fantastic hiking.

Coronado Historic Site

Across the Rio Grande from Bernalillo, **Coronado Historic Site** (www.nmmonuments.org; US 550, 1.7 miles west of I-25 exit 242; adult/under 17yr $3/free; ◷8:30am-5pm Wed-Mon) preserves the ruins of **Kuaua Pueblo**, abandoned shortly after the Spaniards first reached New Mexico. While it's no Chaco Canyon, the murals from its ancient underground kiva (religious chamber) are considered prime examples of precontact mural art. Now displayed under glass in the visitor center, with replicas in the kiva itself, the

---

WORTH A TRIP

SALINAS PUEBLO MISSIONS

Smack in the center of New Mexico you'll find a mostly empty region of hills and plains. But 350 years ago, the Salinas Valley was one of the busiest places in the Pueblo Indian world. Some 10,000 people lived there, and it bustled with trade between local Pueblos, the Rio Grande Valley, Acoma, Zuni, the Spaniards and the Apaches.

The Spaniards who arrived at the end of the 16th century valued the Salinas region for the vast quantities of salt nearby, as well as the prospect of converting so many Native Americans to Christianity. Impressive churches were built of stone and wood, and what remains of them and the pueblos are preserved within **Salinas Pueblo Missions National Monument** (www.nps.gov/sapu; ◷visitor center 8am-5pm; sites 9am-5pm, to 6pm in summer) FREE. While the **visitor center** is in the town of Mountainair, about 1½ hours by car from Albuquerque, the monument itself consists of three separate sites, each with interpretive trails. **Abó**, off of Hwy 60, 9 miles west of Mountainair, is known for the unusual buttressing of its church, rarely seen in buildings of that era. **Quarai**, 8 miles north of Mountainair along Hwy 55, features the most intact church within the monument. **Gran Quivira**, 25 miles south of Mountainair along Hwy 55, has the most extensively excavated Indian ruins, along with exhibits about Salinas Pueblo life. The most scenic way to reach the area from Albuquerque is to take Hwys 337 and 55 south along the eastern side of the Manzano Mountains.

paintings depict various kachinas (spirit messengers) as personifications of nature; images include the Corn Mother, who gave the Pueblo people corn. There's also a campground (☏505-980-8256; tent/RV sites $14/18) with shade shelters and showers.

San Felipe Pueblo

POP 2700 / ELEV 5130FT

Although the conservative Keres-speaking **San Felipe Pueblo** (Map p521; I-25 exit 252) does not encourage visitors for most of the year, outsiders are welcome at the spectacular **San Felipe Feast Green Corn Dances** in its sunken central plaza on May 1, as well as the **San Pedro Feast Day** (June 29). The tribe also runs the large **Casino Hollywood** (www. sanfelipecasino.com; I-25 exit 252; ⊙8am-4am Sun-Wed, 24hr Thu-Sat), beside the interstate.

Kewa Pueblo

POP 2500 / ELEV 5185FT

Long known as Santo Domingo Pueblo, but now officially called **Kewa Pueblo** (www.santo domingotribe.com; Hwy 22 , 6 miles northwest of I-25 exit 259), this conservative, nongaming community, poised halfway between Albuquerque and Santa Fe, has traditionally played a prominent role in inter-Pueblo affairs. Several galleries and studios abut the plaza in front of the pretty 1886 **Santo Domingo Church**, with murals and frescoes by local artists. The tribe is most famous for *heishi* (shell bead) jewelry, as well as huge **Corn Dances** (August 4) and a popular **Arts & Crafts Fair** in early September.

Cochiti Pueblo

POP 520 / ELEV 5276FT

Tucked away well west of the interstate, **Cochiti Pueblo** (Map p521; www.pueblodecochiti. org; Hwy 22, 14 miles northwest of I-25 exit 259) is famed for its arts and crafts, particularly ceremonial bass drums and storyteller dolls. Come in summer and you should find stands and shops in action around the plaza and 1628 mission church; public dances are held on the **Feast Day of San Buenaventura** (July 14) and various other occasions. A colossal earthen dam north of the Pueblo bottles the waters of the Rio Grande into **Cochiti Lake**, favored by swimmers and boaters (no motors allowed), and there's also a challenging **golf course** (Pueblo de Cochiti Golf Course; ☏505-465-2239; www.cochitigolfclub.com; 5200 Cochiti Hwy; 9/18 holes $24/38) nearby.

Kasha-Katuwe Tent Rocks National Monument

The bizarre and beautiful **Kasha-Katuwe Tent Rocks National Monument** (www. blm.gov/nm/tentrocks; per vehicle $5; ⊙8am-7pm mid-Mar–Oct, to 5pm Nov–mid-Mar), 5 miles west of Cochiti Pueblo, is a favorite hiking spot for Santa Fe and Albuquerque residents. At this surreal geologic enclave, volcanic ash from the ancient Jemez Mountain volcanoes has been sculpted into tipi-like formations and slender, steep-sided canyons that glow a strange light orange.

The 1.2-mile **Cave Loop Trail** only scrapes the surface of this extraordinary terrain. So long as you have time for at least an hour's hiking, head instead along the more demanding **Canyon Trail**, a 3-mile round-trip on which you'll climb up a slot canyon that narrows to the width of a single foot, to reach the uplands and enjoy fantastic views over and beyond the towering tent rocks.

Note that dogs are not permitted in the monument.

The Turquoise Trail

The Turquoise Trail was already a major trading route 2000 years ago, when turquoise mined in Cerrillos first found its way south to burgeoning civilizations in what's now Mexico. Today, as NM 14, it's a National Scenic Backway, lined with quirky communities and other diversions, which makes an attractive back road between Albuquerque and Santa Fe. See www.turquoisetrail.org.

Cedar Crest

POP 1200 / ELEV 6578FT

The first town you come to on the Turquoise Trail, immediately after you turn north off I-40, 20 miles east of Albuquerque, is the little hillside community of Cedar Crest, on the eastern flank of the Sandia Mountains.

◎ Sights

Tinkertown Museum MUSEUM
(☏505-281-5233; www.tinkertown.com; 121 Sandia Crest Rd; adult/child $3.50/1; ⊙9am-6pm Apr-Oct;) A folk-art classic, the Tinkertown Museum stands just up Sandia Crest Rd (NM 165), west of Cedar Crest. Huge, detailed handcarved dioramas of Western towns, circuses and other scenes come alive with a quarter. Woodcarver and wisdom collector

Ross J Ward, who passed away in 2002, built it and surrounded it with antique toys, 'junque' (fancy junk) and suggestions that you eat more mangoes naked.

🛏 Sleeping

Turquoise Trail Campground　CAMPGROUND $
(☑505-281-2005; www.turquoisetrailcampground.
com; 22 Calvary Rd; tent/RV sites $17.50/27, cabins $36-58) Camp in a meadow, just off NM 14 near the Tinkertown Museum, with hot showers and cool shade, or rent a simple cabin. In theory, the owners also operate an outdoor 'archaeological site' and museum, but it's seldom open these days.

★ **Elaine's**　B&B $$
(☑505-281-2467; www.elainesbnb.com; 72 Snowline Rd; r from $105; 🅿 ❂ 🛜) This beautifully decorated lodge, nestled up in the woods with superb views, holds five antique-furnished B&B rooms, each with private bath. The lovely Unicorn room has its own Jacuzzi, while the Sangre de Cristo room has a private balcony, and Elaine herself is a wonderful hostess.

Madrid

POP 200 / ELEV 6020FT

Madrid (pronounced '*maa*-drid'), 30 miles south of Santa Fe on Hwy 14, was a bustling company coal-mining town in the 1920s and '30s. After WWII it was all but abandoned. Tie-dyed wanderers bought up cheap lots during the mid-1970s, and their spiritual descendants are still here, having built a thriving arts community. Madrid has become a lot more touristy over the years, but beneath the surface its outlaw heart still beats, and it remains a favorite stop on Harley rallies.

◉ Sights

Madrid Old Coal Town Museum　MUSEUM
(☑505-438-3780; www.themineshafttavern.com; 2846 Hwy 14; adult/child $5/3; ⊙11am-5pm Apr-Sep, 11am-5pm Sat & Sun Oct-Mar) A gleeful and exhaustive celebration of every last detail of mining-town life, holding everything from hospital equipment to old shop fittings, an impressive array of old digging and tunneling equipment and even a steam locomotive.

🛏 Sleeping & Eating

Java Junction B&B　B&B $$
(☑505-438-2772; www.java-junction.com; 2855 Hwy 14; ste $129; 🛜) Conveniently located above a cafe where they take their brew very seriously, this friendly B&B consists of just

one bright, light kitchenette suite, complete with claw-foot tub and roof terrace.

Mine Shaft Tavern　TAVERN $$
(☑505-438-3780; www.themineshafttavern.com; 2846 Hwy 14; mains $11-28; ⊙11:30am-7:30pm Sun-Thu, to 9pm Fri & Sat, bar open late daily; 🎵) Attached to the town museum, this 1919 tavern is a great spot to meet locals, eat burgers and steaks, and enjoy live music on weekends. It's also home to the 'longest stand-up bar in New Mexico,' built in 1946 and Madrid's favorite attraction ever since. As the sign inside puts it: 'Madrid has no town drunk; we all take turns.'

Mama Lisa's Ghost Town Kitchen　CAFE $$
(☑505-471-5769; 2859 Hwy 14; daily specials $9-12; ⊙11:30am-2:30pm & 5:30-9pm Wed-Mon, weekends only in winter) Also known as the No Pity Cafe, this obliging little place offers indoor and outdoor seating, and serves everything from breakfast burritos to gourmet hamburgers and mixed vegetarian plates – not to mention the irresistible red-chile chocolate cake.

☆ Entertainment

Engine House Theatre　THEATER
(☑505-473-0743; www.themineshafttavern.com; 2846 Hwy 14; adult/child $10/4; ⊙3pm Sat & Sun May-Oct) Spectacular summer-weekend melodramas in the Mineshaft Tavern's cozy, old-fashioned theater space abound in Wild West desperadoes, scoundrels and vixens. What's more, there's still a steam train right on the stage. Admission includes a six-shooter loaded with marshmallows to unload at the villains.

🛍 Shopping

With dozens of galleries and wacky shops scattered through this one-horse town, it's easy to spend half a day browsing.

Weasel and Fitz　ARTS & CRAFTS
(www.weaselandfitz.com; 2878 Hwy 14; ⊙Thu-Tue 10am-6pm) Quirky sculptures and ornaments made from recycled household items; look especially for the customized vintage plates, featuring portraits transmogrified into animal heads.

**Seppanen & Daughters
Fine Textiles**　ARTS & CRAFTS
(☑505-424-7470; www.finetextiles.com; 2879 Hwy 14) Colorful and irresistibly tactile Oaxacan, Navajo and Tibetan rugs.

Range West ARTS & CRAFTS

(☎505-474-0925; www.rangewest.com; 2861 Hwy 14; ☺10am-5pm, closed Tue & Wed in winter) Shoplifters be warned: these elegant water fountains, carved from monolithic granite chunks, are not the easiest items in the world to carry.

Cerrillos

POP 320 / ELEV 5687FT

A few miles north of Madrid on Hwy 14, Cerrillos still has one foot in the Old West. With unpaved streets threading through an adobe town relatively unchanged since the 1880s, it's home to what may have been the first mine in North America, which started extracting turquoise around AD 100, and reached its peak – under different management – in the 19th century.

◉ Sights & Activities

**Casa Grande Trading
Post & Petting Zoo** MUSEUM

(☎505-438-3008; www.casagrandetradingpost. com; 17 Waldo St; admission $3; ☺9am-5pm Apr-Sep) This top-drawer roadside attraction packs five rooms with Chinese art, pioneer-era tools, prehistoric mining gear, bottles excavated from an abandoned hotel, and anything else the owners feel like displaying. Pay $2 extra to feed the goats, llamas and exotic chickens.

Broken Saddle Riding Co HORSEBACK RIDING

(☎505-424-7774; www.brokensaddle.com; off County Rd 57; rides $65-115) One- to three-hour horseback rides through juniper-dotted hills and abandoned mines, including a special sunset/moonlight ride. Along the way, you'll learn about local history and geology.

Cerrillos Hills State Park PARK

(☎505-474-0196; www.nmparks.com; per vehicle $5; ☺sunrise-sunset; visitor center 2-4pm) A mile north of Cerrillos, amid scrubby desert hills pockmarked with historic mining sites, this park holds 5 miles of well-marked hiking and biking trails.

SANTA FE

POP 69,000 / ELEV 7260FT

Welcome to 'the city different,' a place that makes its own rules without ever forgetting its long and storied past. Walking through its historic neighborhoods, or around the busy Plaza that remains its core, there's no denying that Santa Fe has a timeless, earthy soul. Founded around 1610, Santa Fe is the second-oldest city and the oldest state capital in the US, and is all but unique in having not only preserved many of its seductive original adobe buildings, but also insisted that all new downtown structures follow the same architectural style. And yet, despite being home to the country's oldest public building and throwing its oldest annual party, Fiesta, Santa Fe is also synonymous with contemporary chic, thanks to its thriving art market, gourmet restaurants, great museums, upscale spas and world-class opera.

At over 7000ft above sea level, Santa Fe is also the nation's highest state capital. Sitting at the foot of the glowing Sangre de Cristo range, it makes a fantastic base for hiking, mountain biking, backpacking and skiing. When you come off the trails, you can indulge in chile-smothered local cuisine, buy turquoise and silver directly from Native American jewelers in the Plaza, visit remarkable churches, or simply wander along centuries-old, cottonwood-shaded lanes and daydream about some day moving here.

Santa Fe's mind-boggling assortment of characters include traditional and avant-garde artists, New Age hippy transplants, Spanish families have called the city home for centuries, Mexican immigrants, retirees from both coasts, and more than a few Hollywood producers and movie stars. Most are drawn above all by the relaxed attitude, the sense of space, the unbeatable climate and that certain something that gives Santa Fe a singularly alluring essence.

◉ Sights

For a city of its size, Santa Fe punches way above its weight. Not only is its small downtown core still filled with Colonial-era adobe homes and churches, with the region's Native American heritage everywhere apparent, but they've been joined by an array of world-class museums and art galleries. There's also a separate cluster of wonderful museums on Museum Hill, a short drive southeast.

◉ Downtown

Downtown Santa Fe still centers on its historic Plaza and the grid of streets that surrounds it. It's easy to while away a full day within these few blocks, punctuating visits to the art and history museums with downtime in the countless cafes, restaurants and shops.

NEW MEXICO SANTA FE

Greater Santa Fe

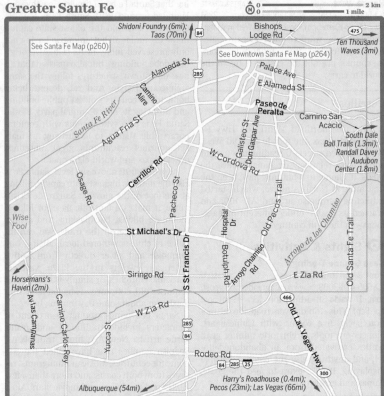

Across the Santa Fe River – dry for much of the year, but lined by verdant footpaths – lie the official buildings of New Mexico's state government. The Guadalupe and Railyard districts, home to lively bars and restaurants, are immediately west, while gallery-lined Canyon Rd stretches away east.

★ **The Plaza** PLAZA
(Map p264) For over 400 years, the Plaza has stood at the heart of Santa Fe. Originally it marked the far northern end of the Camino Real from Mexico; later, it was the goal for wagons heading west along the Santa Fe Trail. Today, this grassy square is peopled by tourists, wandering from museum to margarita; food vendors; skateboarding kids; and street musicians. Beneath the portico of the Palace of the Governors, along its northern side, Pueblo Indians sell jewelry and pottery.

★ **Palace of the Governors** HISTORIC BUILDING
(Map p264; ☎505-476-5100; www.palaceofthe governors.org; 105 W Palace Ave; adult/child $9/ free; ☉10am-5pm, closed Mon Oct-May) The oldest public building in the US, this low-slung adobe complex started out as home to New Mexico's first Spanish governor in 1610; was occupied by Pueblo Indians following their Revolt in 1680; and after 1846 became the seat of the US Territory's earliest governors. It now holds fascinating displays on Santa Fe's multi-faceted past, and some superb Hispanic religious artworks, while its modern adjunct alongside, the **New Mexico History Museum**, tells the story of the state as a whole.

★ **Georgia O'Keeffe Museum** MUSEUM
(Map p264; ☎505-946-1000; www.okeeffemuseum. org; 217 Johnson St; adult/child $12/free; ☉10am-5pm, to 7pm Fri) With 10 beautifully lit galleries in a rambling 20th-century adobe, this museum boasts the world's largest collection

of O'Keeffe's work. She's best known for her luminous New Mexican landscapes, but the changing exhibitions here range through her entire career, focusing for example on her years in New York. Major museums worldwide own her most famous canvases, so you may not see familiar paintings, but you're sure to be bowled over by the thick brushwork and transcendent colors on show.

Visit the museum website to reserve a tour of O'Keeffe's former home, in the village of Abiquiú, 50 miles northwest of Santa Fe.

New Mexico Museum of Art · MUSEUM
(Map p264; ☏ 505-476-5072; www.museumofnewmexico.org; 107 W Palace Ave; adult/child $9/free; ☺10am-5pm Tue-Sun, tours 1:30pm) Built in 1917, and a prime early example of Santa Fe's Pueblo Revival architecture, the New Mexico Museum of Art has spent a century collecting and displaying works by regional artists. A treasure trove of works by the great names who put New Mexico on the cultural map, from Georgia O'Keeffe to printmaker Gustave Baumann, it's also a lovely building in which to stroll around, with a cool garden courtyard. Constantly changing temporary exhibitions ensure its continuing relevance.

Museum of Contemporary Native Arts · MUSEUM
(Map p264; ☏ 505-983-8900; www.iaia.edu/museum; 108 Cathedral Pl; adult/child $10/free; ☺10am-5pm Mon & Wed-Sat, noon-5pm Sun) Primarily showing work by the students and faculty of the esteemed Institute of American Indian Arts, this museum also has the finest contemporary offerings of Native American artists from tribes across the US. It's an excellent place to see cutting-edge art and understand its role in modern Native American culture.

St Francis Cathedral · CHURCH
(Map p264; www.cbsfa.org; 131 Cathedral Pl; ☺8:30am-4:30pm) Santa Fe's French-born bishop Jean-Baptiste Lamy – hero of Willa Cather's *Death Comes for the Archbishop* – set about building this cathedral in 1869. Its Romanesque exterior might seem more suited to Europe than the Wild West, but the Hispanic altarpiece inside lends a real New Mexican flavor. A side chapel holds a diminutive Madonna statue that was taken into exile following the Pueblo Revolt, and has been known since the Spaniards' triumphant return in 1692 as *La Conquistadora*.

Loretto Chapel · HISTORIC BUILDING
(Map p264; ☏ 505-982-0092; www.lorettochapel.com; 207 Old Santa Fe Trail; adult/child $3/2.50; ☺9am-5pm Mon-Sat, 10:30am-5pm Sun) Built in 1878 for the Sisters of Loretto, this tiny Gothic chapel is famous as the site of St Joseph's Miraculous Staircase, a spiraling and apparently unsupported wooden staircase added by a mysterious young carpenter who vanished without giving the astonished nuns his name. The chapel is no

NEW MEXICO SANTA FE

SANTA FE IN...

Two Days
After breakfast at Cafe Pasqual's (p274), art up at the Georgia O'Keeffe Museum (p258). Stroll around the Plaza, checking out the Native American jewelry being sold on the sidewalk, then pop into the historic Palace of the Governors (p258). Have a classic (and cheap) New Mexican lunch at Tia Sophia's (p273) before heading over to check out the galleries along Canyon Rd (p278). For dinner, hit the Tune-Up Cafe (p275) for casual local dining.

The next morning, chow down at the Santa Fe Baking Co (p275). Head over to Museum Hill, prioritizing the fabulous Museum of International Folk Art (p261). Pop into Harry's Roadhouse (p275) for lunch, then take a scenic drive up Ski Basin Rd, where there are loads of hiking and biking trails (p267). Have dinner and catch some live music at the city's oldest tavern, El Farol (p274). Olé!

Three Days
After two days in town, grab breakfast at the Tesuque Village Market (p275), then head on up to Bandelier National Monument (p284) to hike through the canyon and climb ladders to reach ancient cliffside kivas. Then it's back to Santa Fe for a dinner of barbecue brisket quesadillas and a Mescal margarita or two at the Cowgirl Hall of Fame (p274).

Santa Fe

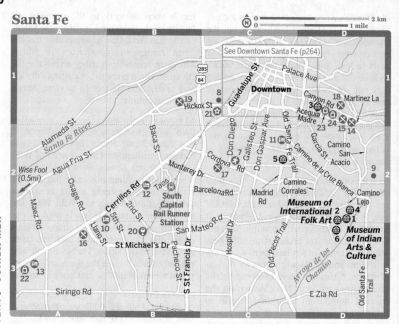

See Downtown Santa Fe (p264)

longer consecrated, and can be rented for (nondenominational) weddings.

San Miguel Mission
CHURCH

(Map p264; 401 Old Santa Fe Trail; admission $1; ⊙10am-4pm Mon-Sat, Mass 2pm (Latin) & 5pm Sun) Erected from 1610 onwards, by and for the Tlaxcalan Indians who arrived from Mexico with Santa Fe's first Spanish settlers, this is considered to be the oldest church in the US. Much of the original building was destroyed during the Pueblo Revolt of 1680, so it was rebuilt with new walls in 1710. Holes in the floor reveal the foundations of an ancient pueblo beneath, while the high viga beams and devotional artwork inside are well worth a peek.

DISCOUNT MUSEUM PASSES

The Palace of the Governors (p258) and the New Mexico Museum of Art (p259) downtown, and the museums of International Folk Art (p261) and Indian Arts & Culture (p261) on Museum Hill, all charge adults $9 to enter. Cut the cost by buying either a $15 one-day pass, covering any two, or a $20 four-day pass to see all four.

Santuario de Guadalupe
CHURCH

(Map p264; www.ologsf.com; 100 Guadalupe St; ⊙9am-noon & 1-4pm Mon-Sat, Mass noon Sun) **FREE** The oldest shrine in the US to Our Lady of Guadalupe, the patroness of Mexico, this adobe church was constructed between 1776 and 1796, though there have been several additions and renovations since then. The Spanish baroque *retablo* (altar painting) inside was painted in Mexico in 1783, then taken apart and transported up the Camino Real on mule back. Other cultural treasures here include a fine collection of *santos,* wood-carved portraits of saints.

State Capitol
HISTORIC BUILDING

(Map p264; ☑505-986-4589; cnr Paseo de Peralta & Old Santa Fe Trail; ⊙7am-6pm Mon-Fri, plus 9am-5pm Sat in summer) **FREE** New Mexico's State Capitol, informally known as the Roundhouse, was laid out in the shape of the state symbol – also the emblem of Zia Pueblo – in 1966. Home to the state legislature, which sits for 60 days in even-numbered years and just 30 in odd years, it holds one of the finest (free) art collections in New Mexico. Visitors can simply wander in and stroll around.

SITE Santa Fe   GALLERY
(Map p264; ☎505-989-1199; www.sitesantafe.org; 1606 Paseo de Peralta; adult/child $10/free, free Fri & 10am-noon Sat; ◷10am-5pm Thu & Sat, 10am-7pm Fri, noon-5pm Sun, also 10am-5pm Wed Jul & Aug) Looming over the Railyard District, the enormous, whitewashed SITE Santa Fe is a nonprofit art gallery/museum dedicated to presenting world-class contemporary art to the local community. Besides radical installation pieces and cutting-edge multimedia exhibitions, it also hosts wine-splashed openings, artist talks, movie screenings and performances of all kinds.

⊙ Museum Hill

Four of Santa Fe's finest museums stand together on Museum Hill, 2 miles southwest of the Plaza. This low but beautifully situated mountain-view hillock is not a neighborhood in any sense – all the museums hold superb gift shops, but there's nothing else here, apart from a research library and a recommended cafe. Neither is it a good walking destination; if you can't drive or cycle, use the Santa Fe Trails bus network, catching either the M Line, or, between May and mid-October, the free Pick-Up.

★ Museum of International Folk Art   MUSEUM
(Map p260; ☎505-827-6344; www.internationalfolkart.org; 706 Camino Lejo; adult/child $9/free; ◷10am-5pm, closed Mon Sep-May) Santa Fe's most unusual and exhilarating museum centers on the world's largest collection of folk art. Its huge main gallery displays whimsical and mind-blowing objects from more than 100 different countries. Tiny human figures go about their business in fully realized village and city scenes, while dolls, masks, toys and garments spill across the walls. Changing exhibitions in other wings explore vernacular art and culture worldwide. Try to hit the incredible **International Folk Art Market**, held here in mid-July.

★ Museum of Indian Arts & Culture   MUSEUM
(Map p260; www.indianartsandculture.org; 710 Camino Lejo; adult/child $9/free; ◷10am-5pm, closed Mon Sep-May) This top-quality museum sets out to trace the origins and history of the various Native American peoples of the entire desert Southwest, and explain and illuminate their widely differing cultural traditions. Pueblo, Navajo and Apache interviewees describe the contemporary realities each group now faces, while a truly superb collection of ceramics, modern and ancient, is complemented by stimulating temporary displays.

Wheelwright Museum of the American Indian   MUSEUM
(Map p260; ☎505-982-4636; www.wheelwright.org; 704 Camino Lejo; ◷10am-5pm) **FREE** Mary Cabot established this museum in 1937 to showcase Navajo ceremonial art, and its

major strength continues to be exquisite Navajo textiles, displayed under dim lighting to protect the natural dyes. Recent expansion work has added extra space for contemporary Native American art and historical artifacts. The gift store, known as the Case Trading Post, sells museum-quality rugs, vintage jewelry, kachinas and crafts.

Museum of Spanish Colonial Art   MUSEUM
(Map p260; ☑505-982-2226; www.spanish colonial.org; 750 Camino Lejo; adult/child $5/free; ⊙10am-5pm, closed Mon Sep-May) Celebrating the long history of Hispanic culture in New Mexico, this museum places the religious and domestic art of the region in the context of the Spanish Colonial experience worldwide. The carved statues and paintings of saints familiar from churches throughout the state are displayed alongside the personal possessions treasured by colonists as reminders of their original homeland.

◉ Around Santa Fe

Rancho de las Golondrinas   MUSEUM
(Map p270; ☑505-473-4169; www.golondrinas.org; 334 Los Pinos Rd, La Cienega; adult/child $6/free; ⊙10am-4pm Wed-Sun Jun-Sep, tours by reservation only in Apr, May & Oct; ⊛) ⬤ Built as a fortified residence along the Camino Real, the 'Ranch of the Swallows' is nearly as old as Santa Fe itself. Now it's a 200-acre living museum,

reconstructed and populated with historical re-enactors, amid orchards, vineyards and livestock (no pets). Kids will love watching bread being baked in a traditional adobe oven, and visiting the blacksmith, the molasses mill and crafts workshops. Assorted themed festivals are held throughout the summer. To find it, follow signs from I-25 exit 276.

Shidoni Foundry   GARDENS, GALLERY
(Map p270; ☑505-988-8001; www.shidoni.com; 1508 Bishop's Lodge Rd, Tesuque; ⊙9am-5pm Mon-Sat; ⊛) FREE Five miles north of Santa Fe, the grassy sculpture garden at Shidoni is a great place for a picnic, or for kids to run around the funky artwork. There's also an indoor gallery and a glass-blowing studio. Take a self-guided foundry tour (noon to 1pm Monday to Friday; $3), or come on Saturday to watch 2000°F (1093°C) molten bronze being poured into ceramic shell molds, in the complex, age-old casting technique (call for schedule; $5).

🏃 Activities

Santa Fe's cultural attractions may be second to none, but visitors do not live by art appreciation alone. Get thee to the great outdoors. The best one-stop spot to peruse your options is the Public Lands Information Center (p280), inconveniently located south of town off of Hwy 14.

SANTA FE FOR CHILDREN

Check out Friday's 'Pasatiempo' arts and entertainment section in the *Santa Fe New Mexican* (www.santafenewmexican.com) or the free local magazine *New Mexico Kids* (www.newmexico-kids.com), published every two months, for a rundown on kids' events.

➡ The **Santa Fe Children's Museum** (Map p260; ☑505-989-8359; www.santafechildrensmuseum.org; 1050 Old Pecos Trail; $7.50, kids free Mon in summer only; ⊙noon-5pm Sun & Mon, 10am-5pm Tue-Sat, closed Mon & Tue Sep-May; ⊛) features hands-on science and art exhibits for young children, but adults will enjoy it as well. Daily two-hour programs tackle subjects such as solar energy and printmaking.

➡ The amazing Museum of International Folk Art (p261) has a big indoor play area with books, Lego and other toys that offers fantastic rainy-day entertainment.

➡ If you're traveling with a budding thespian, check out the backstage tours of the Santa Fe Opera (p276) during opera season. They're interesting and free for anyone under 23.

➡ Most restaurants, except those that are seriously upscale, are happy to host your kids, and most have special menus – but only the Cowgirl Hall of Fame (p274) has a playground *and* a full bar. One of Santa Fe's top breakfast spots, Cafe Pasqual's (p274), is also very child-friendly.

➡ If you want to get out on your own, **Magical Happenings Babysitting** (☑505-982-9327) can have sitters stay with your kids in your hotel room; it's $20 an hour for one child or $22 an hour for two, with a four-hour minimum and an additional $7 transportation charge. Reserve well in advance.

Before heading out for any strenuous activities, remember the elevations here abouts; take time to acclimatize, and watch for signs of altitude sickness if you're going high. Weather changes rapidly in the mountains, and summer storms are frequent, especially in the afternoons, so keep an eye on the sky and hike prepared. Most trails are usually closed by snow in winter, and higher trails may be closed through May.

The best local map for trails and outdoor action is the *Santa Fe/Bandelier/Los Alamos* map published by Sky Terrain.

Skiing

Downhill gets most of the attention in these parts, but both the Sangre de Cristo and Jemez Mountains have numerous cross-country ski trails.

Ski Santa Fe   SKIING
(Map p270; ☎505-982-4429, snow report 505-983-9155; www.skisantafe.com; lift ticket adult/child $69/49; ⏰9am-4pm late Nov-early Apr) Often overlooked for its more famous cousin outside Taos, the Santa Fe ski area boasts the same fluffy powder (though usually a little less), with a higher base elevation (10,350ft) and higher chairlift service (12,075ft). It caters to families and expert skiers, who fly down powder glade shoots, steep bump runs or long groomers, though the length and quality of the season varies wildly from year to year.

On autumn weekends, the chairlift takes passengers up through the shimmering golden foliage of the aspen forest (one-way/round-trip $8/12, small children free); there's also an extensive system of hiking trails.

Cottam's   OUTDOORS
(Map p270; ☎505-982-0495; www.cottamsskishops.com; 740 Hyde Park Rd; adult/child ski-gear rental from $25/20; ⏰7:30am-6pm) Though the ski area rents gear, many people prefer to pick up skis, poles, boots and boards here, on the way to the slopes.

Mountain Biking

Dale Ball Trails   MOUNTAIN BIKING
(www.santafenm.gov/trails_1) Over 20 miles of paved and unpaved bike and hiking trails, with fabulous desert and mountain views. The challenging **South Dale Ball Trails** start with a super-long, hard and rocky single-track climb, followed by harrowing switchbacks, while the intermediate **Winsor Trail** (No 254) leads through breathtaking scenery in Hyde State Park and Santa Fe National Forest.

Mellow Velo   MOUNTAIN BIKING
(Map p264; ☎505-995-8356; www.mellowvelo.com; 132 E Marcy St; rentals per day from $35; ⏰10am-6pm Mon-Sat) The kind gentlefolk at this downtown bike shop offer rental and repair, and provide information on regional trails. Their website holds some really useful trail maps.

Rafting

The two rivers worth running in the vicinity of Santa Fe are the **Rio Grande** – for white-water thrills – and the **Rio Chama** – mellower but better for multiday trips and arguably more scenic. Outfitters offer all sorts of variations on the basic themes, so check which options are available.

As soon as it's marginally warm enough, rafting outfits head to the Rio Grande north of Taos to crash through rapids on the renowned Class V **Taos Box**, which traverses 16 miles of spectacular wilderness gorge. It's fantastic fun but not for the faint of heart, and commercial companies require passengers to be at least 12 years old. Flows in this stretch are usually too low to boat beyond early July.

Less extreme but still exciting is the Class III **Racecourse**, also on the Rio Grande, south of Taos. It's fine for kids over six or seven (depending on the company), and the put-in is closer to Santa Fe than for the Box. The season here usually runs from May to October, depending on water levels. This is also a classic playground for kayakers.

The Rio Chama has a few Class III rapids, but most of it is fairly flat, making it a great choice for families.

Downtown Santa Fe

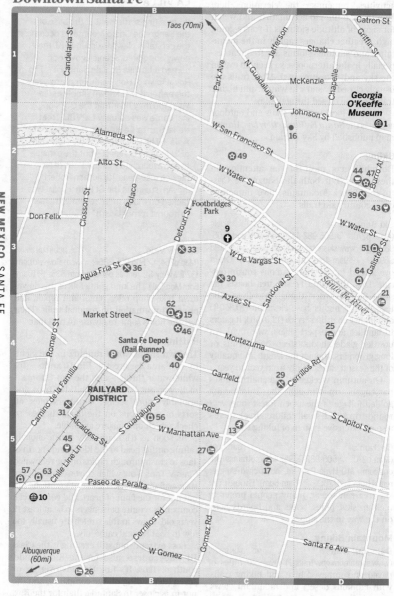

★ **New Wave Rafting Co** RAFTING
(☎800-984-1444; www.newwaverafting.com; per person Taos Box $110; Racecourse adult/child $55/47; 3-day Chama $400) Rio Grande trips meet at the Rio Grande Gorge Visitor Center in Pilar; Rio Chama trips meet in Abiquiú.

Santa Fe Rafting Co RAFTING
(☎888-988-4914; www.santaferafting.com; per person Taos Box $110-120; Racecourse $65; 3-day Chama $595) Pickup from Santa Fe or meet at the river.

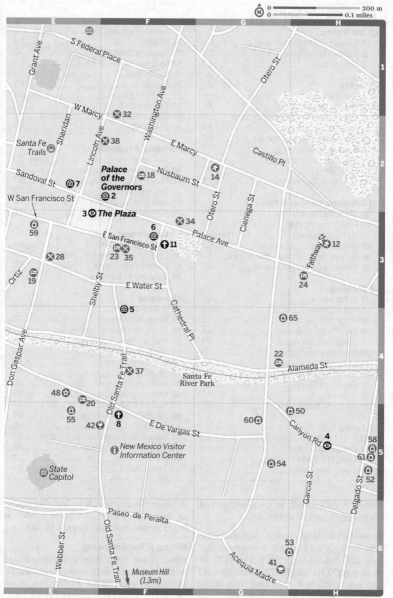

Kokopelli Rafting Adventures RAFTING
(☏800-879-9035; www.kokopelliraft.com; per person Taos Box $110-125; Racecourse adult/child $58/45; 2-day Chama $359) Pickup from Santa Fe or meet near the river.

Horseback Riding

No Western fantasy is complete without hopping into a saddle. There's some great riding to be done around Santa Fe itself, as well as further afield, for example with

Downtown Santa Fe

Broken Saddle (p257) in Cerrillos, and at Ghost Ranch (p286), near Abiquiú.

Stables at Bishop's Lodge HORSEBACK RIDING
(Map p270; ☑505-819-4013; www.bishopslodge. com; 1297 Bishop's Lodge Rd; kids ride $20, 1hr sunset ride $79, 2hr ride $90-120; ⊗8am-5pm; ⊕) The long menu of themed trail rides at the Stables at Bishop's Lodge includes 15-minute kids introductory rides, and a sunset ride on Tuesday and Thursday.

Roy-El Morgan Farm HORSEBACK RIDING
(☑505-603-6016; www.roy-elmorgans.com; 1302 McCurdy Rd, Española; lessons from $50; ⊕) If you're looking for riding lessons – Western or English – head a half-hour north to Españo-

la, where the affable Erlene Seybold-Smythe, an expert instructor and horse trainer, is based at this champion Morgan facility.

Hiking & Backpacking
Some of the best hiking and backpacking in New Mexico is right outside of Santa Fe. The undeveloped **Pecos Wilderness**, in the heart of the **Santa Fe National Forest**, holds almost 1000 miles of trails that lead through spruce and aspen forest, across grassy alpine meadows, and up to several peaks surpassing 12,000ft. The quickest way to get above the treeline is to drive to the ski basin, hop on the **Winsor Trail** (Map p270), and trudge up the switchbacks. The most immediately

accessible hiking trails are on the **Dale Ball Trail System**, 3 miles east of downtown.

Randall Davey Audubon Center OUTDOORS
(☎ 505-983-4609; http://nm.audubon.org; 1800 Upper Canyon Rd; trail use $2; ⏱ 8am-4pm Mon-Sat) Protecting 135 acres along the acequia of Santa Fe Canyon, near the Dale Ball Trails, this center provides information on the coyotes, bobcats and wildlife of the juniper and piñon forest. The **Bear Canyon Trail**, a 3-mile round-trip, leads into the steep-sided canyon. Free walks take place Saturday at 8am.

Sangre de Cristo Mountain Works OUTDOORS
(Map p264; ☎ 505-984-8221; www.sdcmountainworks.com; 328 S Guadalupe St; ⏱ 10am-7pm Mon-Fri, 10am-6pm Sat, noon-5pm Sun) Shop here for anything high-end outdoorsy, from a GPS unit to a fleece. It's also a good place to pick up information, and has a website packed with details about where to hike, climb, bike and camp.

Fishing
New Mexico's most outstanding fishing holes are better accessed from Taos and the Enchanted Circle, but abundant opportunities out of Santa Fe include Abiquiú and Nambé Lakes. You'll need a license (one-day/five-day $12/24).

High Desert Angler FISHING
(Map p264; ☎ 505-988-7688; www.highdesertangler.com; 460 Cerrillos Rd; ⏱ 10am-6pm Mon-Sat, 11am-4pm Sun) Friendly store a short walk south of downtown, which sells licenses and a large array of gear, and offers fly-fishing lessons plus guided fishing excursions (one/two people from $300/350).

⛵ Courses

Santa Fe School of Cooking COOKING
(Map p264; ☎ 505-983-4511; www.santafeschoolofcooking.com; 125 N Guadalupe St; 2/3hr class $75/98; ⏱ 9:30am-5pm Mon-Sat, noon-4pm Sun) If your love for New Mexican cuisine knows no bounds, take a lesson at this Southwestern-style cooking school, where the cost includes the meal at the end.

Santa Fe Workshops PHOTOGRAPHY
(Map p260; ☎ 505-983-1400; www.santafeworkshops.com; 50 Mt Carmel Rd; courses $1075-1700)

TOP FIVE SANTA FE DAY HIKES

There are a ton of trails around Santa Fe. Whether you're looking for all-day adventure or a relaxing stroll through a special landscape, you'll find it. Trailheads for all the hikes below are within an hour's drive from the Plaza.

Raven's Ridge (Map p270) Starting along the Upper Winsor Trail from the ski basin parking lot, Raven's Ridge cuts east after the first steep mile of switchbacks to follow the Pecos Wilderness boundary high above the treeline to the top of Lake Peak (12,409ft). A strenuous hike at substantial elevation, it's well worth it if your body can take it. No trail has better views; you can see forever from up here. Loop back by hiking down the ski slopes to complete a round-trip of about 4 miles.

Upper Winsor (Map p270) After its steep first mile from the ski basin, the Upper Winsor Trail mellows out, contouring around forested slopes with a moderate uphill section toward the end. Puerto Nambé (11,050ft), a huge and beautiful meadow in the saddle between Santa Fe Baldy (12,622ft) to the north and Penitente Peak (12,249ft) to the south, is a great place for a picnic. The round-trip is about 10 miles.

Aspen Vista The premier path for immersing yourself in the magical fall foliage, this trail lives up to its name. The first mile or so is supereasy, gaining little elevation and following an old dirt road. It gets a little more difficult the further you go; just turn back when you've had enough. The trailhead is at about 10,000ft, along the road to the ski basin; it's marked 'Trail No 150.' Mountain bikers love this one, too.

La Cieneguilla Petroglyph Site Half a mile along a dirt track from a clearly marked trailhead on Airport Rd, 12 miles southwest of downtown, this trail climbs the low hillside to reach a rocky bluff that's covered with ancient Keresan petroglyphs, including images of the flute player Kokopelli. Allow an hour's hiking time in total.

Tent Rocks There's truly surreal hiking at Kasha-Katuwe Tent Rocks National Monument (p255), near Cochiti Pueblo 40 miles southwest of Santa Fe, where short trails meander through a geologic wonderland.

Develop your inner Ansel Adams awareness at these legendary worshops, covering all aspects of traditional photography and digital imagery, and lasting from two to five days. Course fees do not include meals and lodging.

Santa Fe Clay CERAMICS
(Map p260; 505-984-1122; www.santafeclay.com; 1615 Paseo de Peralta; week-long workshop $768; 9am-5pm Mon-Sat) This ceramics gallery offers week-long workshops taught by master potters during the summer, plus occasional weekend workshops in winter and spring. Most are open to aspiring ceramicists of all levels.

Wise Fool CIRCUS
(Map p258; 505-992-2588; www.wisefoolnewmexico.org; 2778d Agua Fria St; drop-in class $25) Ever want to learn the arts of trapeze, juggling, or just plain clowning around? As well as drop-in classes, Wise Fool has multi-day intensives for adults ($175) and week-long summer day camps for kids ($100).

Tours

Several companies offer walking and bus tours of Santa Fe and northern New Mexico. Others organize guided trips to the Pueblos, as well as air tours and biking, hiking, rafting and horseback-riding trips.

Santa Fe Walkabouts ADVENTURE
(505-216-9161; www.santafewalkabouts.com; half-day per person around $80) Enthusiastic company offering private, customized hiking, biking, sightseeing and jeep tours all over northern New Mexico. Rates depend on the activity and the size of your party.

A Well-Born Guide/Have PhD, Will Travel WALKING
(505-988-8022; www.swguides.com; tours from $20) If the name doesn't lure you in, the tours will. Stefanie Beninato, an informative local historian with a knack for good storytelling, offers lively themed walks around Santa Fe that focus on everything from bars and former brothels to ghosts, architecture and, of course, art, as well as multiday trips around New Mexico.

Seven Directions CULTURAL
(877-992-6128; www.sevendirections.net; full-day tour per person around $260) Sightseeing and cultural tours of the city and the state, available in French, Italian and Spanish as well as English.

Pink Lady Tours WALKING
(505-699-4147; www.pinkladytours.com; 311 Old Santa Fe Trail; tours from $14; 10am Mon-Sat) Walking tours of Santa Fe, with the guide who strives for the most laughs per minute.

Loretto Line HISTORICAL
(505-982-0092; www.toursofsantafe.com; adults/children $15/12; 10am, noon & 2pm mid-Mar–Oct) Cruise around Santa Fe in an open-sided tram and learn about its history and culture from experienced guides.

Festivals & Events

The **Santa Fe Visitors Bureau** (www.santafe.org) maintains an excellent calendar of events, musical and theatrical productions and museum shows. Some of the biggies:

ARTfeast ART
(www.artfeast.com; late Feb) Eat your way around Santa Fe's galleries during this weekend festival in late February, which incorporates art, food, wine and fashion, and benefits art programs for local children.

Rodeo de Santa Fe CULTURAL
(505-471-4300; www.rodeodesantafe.org; adult/child from $17/10; Jun) For more than half a century, wranglers, ranchers and cowpokes, along with plenty of rhinestone cowpersons, have been gathering to watch bucking broncos, clowns in barrels, lasso tricks and fancy shooting. A pre-rodeo parade takes it all downtown. Held on the midsummer weekend in June.

Pride on the Plaza GAY PRIDE
(www.santafehra.org; Jun) Drag queens, parades and floats celebrate this annual party, held on the last Saturday of June in the city ranked 'second gayest in America' by the *Advocate* magazine. The preceding week usually sees all sorts of associated events.

★ International Folk Art Market CULTURAL
(505-992-7600; www.folkartalliance.org; Jul) The world's largest folk art market draws around 150 artists from 50 countries to the Folk Art Museum for a festive weekend of craft shopping and cultural events in July. Things get off to a fun start with Thursday's free World Music concert at the Railyard.

★ Spanish Market CULTURAL
(www.spanishcolonial.org; late Jul) Traditional Spanish Colonial arts, from *retablos* and *bultos* (carved wooden religious statues) to handcrafted furniture and metalwork, make

LOCAL MAGIC: CHRISTMAS EVE ON CANYON ROAD

On the night before Christmas, Santa Fe is an ethereal spectacle. A thousand adobe buildings glow warm yellow in the lights of the thousands of *farolitos* – real candles nestled in greased brown paper bags – arrayed along its streets, entranceways and even the roofs of its homes and shops.

Walking down gallery-lined Canyon Rd on Christmas Eve is a uniquely Santa Fe experience, and in our book a magical must. There's something overwhelmingly graceful and elegant about the taste of the frosty air, the look of miles of glowing pathways of tiny candles and comradely quiet, the way the night sky meets softly lit windows filled with fine art.

The magic comes partly from the intoxicating sights and scents of the small roadside piñon and cedarwood bonfires that offer guiding light and unforgettable memories. Partly it's a few equestrians prancing on horseback, jingle bells jangling, clickity-clacking along the narrow street, evoking memories of early Santa Feans who led their burros up the 'Road of the Canyon' to gather firewood in mountain forests. Partly it's the shimmering silhouettes of 250-year-old adobes picked out by rows of twinkling *farolitos*.

Dress warmly and arrive early – say, by 6pm – if you want to beat the crowds. As night falls, the streets fill with human revelers and their canine friends, all giddy with the Christmas spirit. Small groups of carolers sing remarkably in tune. Join them, then pop into a gallery for a cup of spiced cider and a quick perusal of post-Leninist Russian art to warm up.

this juried show in late July an artistic extravaganza, second only to Indian Market.

Zia Regional Rodeo RODEO
(www.nmgra.org; 3237 Rodeo Rd; ☉ late Jul) Three days of riding and roping, sponsored by the NM Gay Rodeo Association.

★ Santa Fe Indian Market CULTURAL
(☑ 505-983-5220; www.swaia.org; ☉ Aug) Over a thousand artists from 100 tribes and Pueblos show work at this world-famous juried show, held the weekend after the third Thursday in August. One hundred thousand visitors converge on the Plaza, at open studios, gallery shows and the Native Cinema Showcase. Come Friday or Saturday to see pieces competing for the top prizes; wait until Sunday before trying to bargain.

★ Santa Fe Fiesta CULTURAL
(☑ 505-913-1517; www.santafefiesta.org; ☉ early Sep) This two-week celebration of the September 4, 1692, resettlement of Santa Fe after the Pueblo Revolt, from Labor Day through early September, includes concerts, a candlelit procession and the much-loved Pet Parade. Everything kicks off with the bizarrely pagan Friday-night torching of Zozobra before a baying mob in Fort Marcy Park.

Wine & Chile Fiesta FOOD
(☑ 505-438-8060; www.santafewineandchile.org; ☉ late Sep) A gourmet's fantasy fiesta, with wine tastings and fine cuisine; dinner events sell out early.

🛏 Sleeping

When it comes to luxury accommodations, Santa Fe boasts more than its share of opulent hotels and posh B&Bs, with some unforgettable historic options within a block of the Plaza. Rates steadily diminish the further you go from downtown, with low-budget and national chain options strung out along Cerrillos Rd toward I-25.

Santa Fe has two peak seasons, when you should book well in advance and can expect to pay premium prices: summer, particularly during Indian Market in August and on opera nights, and also December. January and February are the cheapest months. Room rates shown here do not include taxes and other add-ons, which can total 11% to 15%.

Santa Fe National Forest and Hyde State Park are the best nearby locations for car camping. Stop by the Public Lands Information Center (p280) for maps and detailed information.

🛏 Downtown Santa Fe

★ El Paradero B&B $$
(Map p264; ☑ 505-988-1177; www.elparadero.com; 220 W Manhattan Ave; r from $130; 🅿 ❄ @ 🛜) Each room in this 200-year-old adobe B&B, south of the river, is unique and loaded with character. Two have their own bathrooms across the hall, the rest are en suite; our favorites are rooms 6 and 12. The full breakfasts satisfy, and rates also include afternoon

Santa Fe & Around

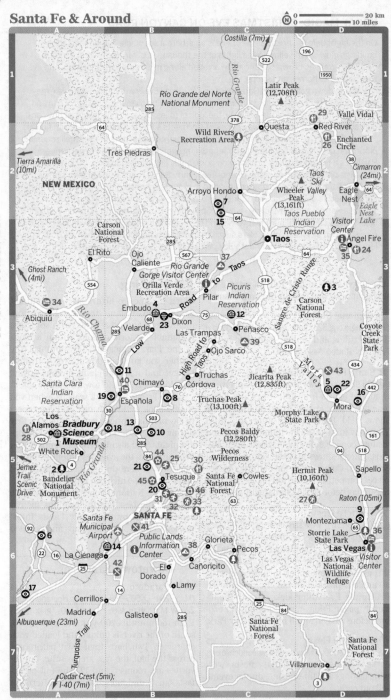

Santa Fe & Around

NEW MEXICO SANTA FE

tea. A separate casita holds two kitchenette suites that can be combined into one ($350).

Santa Fe Motel & Inn HOTEL $$
(Map p264; ☏505-982-1039; www.santafemotel. com; 510 Cerrillos Rd; r from $149, casitas from $169; P❋@☞❀) Even the motel rooms in this downtown option, close to the Railyard and a real bargain in low season, have the flavor of a Southwestern B&B, with colorful tiles, clay sunbursts and tin mirrors. The courtyard casitas cost a little more and come with kiva fireplaces and little patios. Rates include a full hot breakfast, served outdoors in summer.

Old Santa Fe Inn INN $$
(Map p264; ☏800-734-9910; www.oldsantafeinn. com; 320 Galisteo St; r from $189; P@☞) Harking back to the heyday of Route 66, this up-

dated motel, in a surprisingly quiet location a few blocks south of the Plaza, offers light, bright rooms, some with kiva-style gas fireplaces, at rates that vary widely with season and occupancy. Tuck into the fabulous breakfast burrito buffet each morning.

Inn on the Alameda HOTEL $$
(Map p264; ☏888-984-2121; www.innonthealameda. com; 303 E Alameda St; r from $195; P❋@☞❀❀) Handmade furniture, kiva fireplaces, luxe linens, elegant breakfasts and afternoon wine-and-cheese receptions bring B&B-style elegance to a pleasantly efficient hotel. The staff can arrange cooking classes, outdoor adventures and more, with local experts. Small dogs welcome for $50 extra per night.

Hotel Chimayo
HOTEL **$$**

(Map p264; ☑505-992-5861; www.hotelchimayo. com; 125 Washington Ave; r from $186) Decor in this welcoming hotel draws on New Mexico's Hispanic traditions, with abundant attractive carvings and wall hangings, while the Low'n'Slow bar is adorned with gleaming hubcaps and images of low riders. Guest rooms have a warm, comfortable feel, and either share or have their own balconies.

Hotel St Francis
HISTORIC HOTEL **$$**

(Map p264; ☑505-983-5700; www.hotelstfrancis. com; 210 Don Gaspar Ave; r from $177; P ✷ @ 🛜 🏊) Large hotel, just south of the Plaza, that has benefitted from recent modernization while retaining enough hand-crafted furniture and woolen rugs to evoke the city's mission-era heritage. There's good food at the in-house Tabla de los Santos restaurant, though the setting lacks atmosphere. Reserve well ahead for the best rates.

★La Fonda
HISTORIC HOTEL **$$$**

(Map p264; ☑800-523-5002; www.lafondasantafe. com; 100 E San Francisco St; r/ste from $219/309; P ✷ @ 🛜 🏊) Long renowned as the 'Inn at the end of the Santa Fe Trail,' Santa Fe's loveliest historic hotel sprawls through an old adobe just off the Plaza. Recently upgraded while retaining its beautiful folk-art windows and murals, it's both classy and cozy, with some wonderful top-floor luxury suites, and superb sunset views from the rooftop Bell Tower Bar.

★Inn of the Five Graces
BOUTIQUE HOTEL **$$$**

(Map p264; ☑505-992-0957; www.fivegraces. com; 150 E DeVargas St; ste $450-800; P ✷ 🛜) Much more than just another luxury getaway, this exquisite, one-of-a-kind gem offers an upscale gypsy-style escape. Sumptuous suites are decorated in a lavish Persian/Indian/Asian fusion theme, with fireplaces, beautifully tiled kitchenettes and a courtyard behind river-rock walls. The Luminaria House ($2500 per night) has two master bedrooms, five fireplaces and all the opulence you'd expect for the price.

La Posada de Santa Fe
LUXURY HOTEL **$$$**

(Map p264; ☑505-986-0000; www.laposadade santafe.com; 330 E Palace Ave; r from $250; P ✷ @ 🛜 🏊) This beautiful, low-slung property, set amid quiet gardens a few blocks east of the Plaza, caters to its guests' every need, with elegantly furnished adobe casitas outfitted with gas fireplaces, as well as smaller, more historical rooms. There's a fabulous spa, while the cigar-friendly Staab House cocktail bar (open from 11:30am to 11pm) is a local favorite for its leather-chaired ambience and single-malt scotch.

Inn of the Governors
HOTEL **$$$**

(Map p264; ☑505-982-4333; www.innofthe governors.com; 101 W Alameda St; r from $209; P ✷ @ 🛜 🏊) An intimate place to slumber, in a hard-to-beat location two blocks from the Plaza. Rooms are elegantly decorated with kiva fireplaces, warm-hued bedspreads and Southwestern-style doors and windows. Book direct for daily credits in the Del Charro Saloon, offering some of downtown's cheapest eats.

🛏 Cerrillos Road & Metro Santa Fe

★Silver Saddle Motel
MOTEL **$**

(Map p260; ☑505-471-7663; www.santafesilver saddlemotel.com; 2810 Cerrillos Rd; r from $62; P ✷ @ 🛜 🏊) This old-fashioned, even kitschy Route 66 motel compound, 3 miles southwest of the Plaza, offers the best budget value in town. Some rooms have pleasant tiled kitchenettes, while all have shady wooden arcades outside and comfortable cowboy-inspired decor inside – get the Kenny Rogers or Wyatt Earp rooms if you can. Rates include continental breakfast.

Santa Fe International Hostel
HOSTEL **$**

(Map p260; ☑505-988-1153; www.hostelsantafe. com; 1412 Cerrillos Rd; dm $18, r $25-35; P @ 🛜) This not-for-profit hostel, in a disheveled former motel, is in reach of South Capitol Rail Runner station. Three bare-bones rooms hold six-bed dorms, the rest have private or shared bathrooms. The communal lounge and kitchen make it easy to meet other travelers and get travel tips from staff, and there's a weekly donation of free food. Cash only, short daily chores required.

Rancheros de Santa Fe Campground
CAMPGROUND **$**

(Map p270; ☑505-466-3482; www.rancheros. com; 736 Old Las Vegas Hwy; tent/RV sites/cabins $25/42/49; ☺mid-Mar–Oct; 🛜 🏊 🐾) Eight miles southeast of the Plaza, off I-25 exit 290, Rancheros has shady, spacious sites for tents and RVs, plus simple forest cabins, nice views, a convenience store and free wi-fi. Enjoy hot showers, cheap morning coffee and evening movies.

El Rey Inn
HOTEL **$$**

(Map p260; ☑505-982-1931; www.elreyinnsantafe.
com; 1862 Cerrillos Rd; r from $105; P❋@🐾📶)
This classic courtyard hotel is highly recommended, thanks to its super, Southwestern-themed rooms and suites, scattered through 5 acres of landscaped gardens. Some rooms have kitchenettes, and the sizable outdoor pool has a hot tub alongside.

Inn of the Turquoise Bear
B&B **$$**

(Map p260; ☑800-396-4104; www.turquoisebear.
com; 342 E Buena Vista St; r from $150; P❋📶🐾)
Visitors enjoy the quiet now, but this expansive adobe B&B, built by local legend Witter Bynner and partner Robert Hunt, was once home to parties hosting Thornton Wilder, Robert Oppenheimer, Edna St Vincent Millay, Robert Frost and many others. Surrounded by sculpted gardens, its 11 rooms are named for former house guests, and combine authentic ambience with modern amenities.

Sage Inn
HOTEL **$$**

(Map p264; ☑505-982-5952; www.santafesage
inn.com; 725 Cerrillos Rd; r from $119; P❋@
📶🐾) While not exactly boutique accommodations, the 155 well-sized rooms here have appealing Southwestern touches, making the Sage Inn a step up from typical chain hotels, within reasonable walking distance of downtown (and right next to Whole Foods). Modern and clean, it's a good option for budget-minded families. Pets are OK (for an additional $15).

★ Ten Thousand Waves
RESORT **$$$**

(Map p270; ☑505-982-9304; www.tenthousand
waves.com; 3451 Hyde Park Rd; r from $239;
P❋📶🐾) This Japanese spa resort, 4 miles northeast of the Plaza, features 13 gorgeous, Zen-inspired freestanding guesthouses. Most come with fireplaces and either a deck or courtyard, and all are within walking distance of the mountainside hot tubs and massage cabins. Pets are welcomed – for $20 extra – with custom-size beds, bones and treats.

✕ Eating

Food is another art form in Santa Fe, and some restaurants are as world-class as the galleries. From spicy, traditional Southwest favorites to cutting-edge cuisine, it's all here. Reservations are always recommended for the more expensive venues, especially during summer and ski season.

✕ The Plaza & Canyon Road

French Pastry Shop
CREPERIE **$**

(Map p264; ☑505-983-6697; www.thefrench
pastryshop.com; 100 E San Francisco St; mains $6-10; ☺6:30am-5pm) Charming cafe serving delicious French bistro food inside La Fonda Hotel, including crepes filled with everything from ham and cheese to strawberries and cream – along with a host of quiches, sandwiches, cappuccinos and, of course, pastries.

Tia Sophia's
NEW MEXICAN **$**

(Map p264; ☑505-983-9880; 210 W San Francisco St; mains $7-10; ☺7am-2pm Mon-Sat, 8am-1pm Sun; ☑♿) Local artists and visiting celebrities outnumber tourists at this longstanding and always packed Santa Fe favorite. Breakfast is the meal of choice, with fantastic burritos and other Southwestern dishes, but lunch is pretty damn tasty too; try the perfectly prepared *chile rellenos* (stuffed chile peppers), or the rota of daily specials. The shelf of kids' books helps little ones pass the time.

Taberna La Boca
TAPAS **$$**

(Map p264; ☑505-988-7102; www.tabernasf.com; 125 Lincoln Ave; tapas $7-15; ☺11:30am-2pm & 5-10pm) A casual offshoot of the all-but-identical La Boca restaurant nearby, this relaxed central tavern-wine bar offers a changing but consistently tasty selection of Spanish tapas, from paella to crab salad. Prices are slashed in the early evening happy hour, and there's a $17 set menu for lunch.

Santa Fe Bite
BURGERS **$$**

(Map p264; ☑505-982-0544; www.santafebite.
com; 311 Old Santa Fe Trail; mains $9-21; ☺11am-8pm Tue-Thu, 11am-9pm Fri, 8am-9pm Sat, 8am-5pm Sun) Repeatedly hailed by locals as serving the best burger in Santa Fe, this souped-up classic-style diner, now in a new location at Gerrett's Desert Inn, really does make an outstanding green chile cheeseburger ($11) – but the steaks are pretty darn good too.

Il Piatto
ITALIAN **$$**

(Map p264; ☑505-984-1091; www.ilpiattosantafe.
com; 95 W Marcy St; lunch $11, dinner $16-30; ☺11:30am-10:30pm Mon-Sat, 4:30-10:30pm Sun) This classy but welcoming Italian place, on the sleepier blocks north of the Plaza, is a good spot for a romantic dinner, while its light zestful flavors are showcased on the good-value prix-fixe lunch menu ($17).

★ **La Plazuela** NEW MEXICAN $$$

(Map p264; ☎ 505-982-5511; www.lafondasantafe.com; 100 E San Francisco St, La Fonda de Santa Fe; lunch $11-18, dinner $14-32; ⏱ 7am-2pm & 5-10pm Mon-Fri, 7am-3pm & 5-10pm Sat & Sun) One of Santa Fe's greatest pleasures is a meal in the Fonda's irresistible see-and-be-seen central atrium, with its excited bustle, colorful decor and high-class New Mexican food, with contemporary dishes sharing menu space with standards like fajitas and tamales.

★ **El Farol** TAPAS, SPANISH $$$

(Map p260; ☎ 505-983-9912; www.elfarolsf.com; 808 Canyon Rd; lunch $8-18, dinner $25-35; ⏱ 11:30am-late; ⌨ ♿) This popular restaurant and bar, set in a rustically authentic adobe, has live music nightly. Although El Farol serves excellent steaks, most people come to sample the extensive list of tapas (three for $25). The weekly $25 flamenco dinner show and other entertainment (usually starting at 8pm) is perfect for special occasions. Kids will also dig it.

★ **Cafe Pasqual's** INTERNATIONAL $$$

(Map p264; ☎ 505-983-9340; www.pasquals.com; 121 Don Gaspar Ave; breakfast & lunch $9-16, dinner $24-43; ⏱ 8am-3pm & 5:30-9:30pm Sun-Thu, to 10pm Fri & Sat; ⌨ ♿) Whatever time you visit this exuberantly colorful, utterly unpretentious place, the food, most of which has a definite south-of-the-border flavor, is worth every penny of the high prices. The breakfast menu is famous for dishes like *huevos motuleños,* made with sautéed bananas, feta cheese and more; later on, the meat and fish mains are superb. Reservations taken for dinner only.

La Casa Sena NEW MEXICAN $$$

(Map p264; ☎ 505-988-9232; www.lacasasena.com; 125 E Palace Ave; lunch $12-20, dinner $16-36; ⏱ 11am-9pm Sun-Wed, to 10pm Thu-Sat) Several downtown restaurants have outdoor seating but this is the prettiest, in the flower-filled garden of an old adobe that also has a snug interior. The New Mexican food's good too, with green chile cheeseburgers available all day, and fancier dinner dishes like pan-seared scallops. Sit in the cantina section to be serenaded by singing waitstaff from 6pm onwards.

Geronimo MODERN AMERICAN $$$

(Map p260; ☎ 505-982-1500; www.geronimorestaurant.com; 724 Canyon Rd; mains $30-45; ⏱ 5:45-10pm Sun-Thu, to 11pm Fri & Sat) Housed in a 1756 adobe, Geronimo is among the finest and most romantic restaurants in town. Highlights on the short but diverse menu include honey-grilled white prawns with fiery sweet chile and peppery elk tenderloin with apple-wood smoked bacon.

The Compound MODERN AMERICAN $$$

(Map p260; ☎ 505-982-4353; www.compoundrestaurant.com; 635 Canyon Rd; lunch $12-20, dinner $28-44; ⏱ noon-2pm & 6-9pm Mon-Sat, 6-9pm Sun) A longtime foodie favorite, featuring the contemporary American creations of much-lauded chef and owner Mark Kiffin. Ingredients are always fresh, and presentation perfect, while the menu ranges through elegant Southwestern and Mediterranean flavors. Come to celebrate: the wine list includes top-notch champagnes.

✕ Guadalupe Street & the Railyard

This lively neighborhood, 10 minutes' walk southwest of the Plaza and boosted since the arrival of the Rail Runner line, is home to several distinctive dining and drinking options frequented by younger locals.

Cleopatra's Cafe MIDDLE EASTERN $

(Map p264; ☎ 505-820-7381; www.cleopatrasantafe.com; 418 Cerrillos Rd, Design Center; mains $7-17; ⏱ 11am-8pm Mon-Sat; 🕾 ⌨) This simple cafe makes up for a slight deficit in ambience with taste and value: big platters of delicious kabobs, hummus, falafel and other Greek and Middle Eastern favorites.

Flying Star Cafe AMERICAN $

(Map p264; ☎ 505-216-3939; www.flyingstarcafe.com; 500 Market St; mains $8-13; ⏱ 7am-9:30pm Sun-Thu, to 10:30pm Fri & Sat; 🕾 ♿) Santa Fe's Railyard branch of this casual, Albuquerque-based chain, known for its healthy breakfast offerings, is a firm local favorite, especially among families with kids.

Raaga INDIAN $$

(Map p264; ☎ 505-820-6440; www.raagacuisine.com; 544 Agua Fria St; mains $13-18; ⏱ 11am-2:30pm & 5-9:30pm Mon-Sat; ⌨) Santa Fe's best Indian restaurant prepares delicious curries, biryanis and tandoori specialties with a refreshingly light touch. One flaw: the chai is lame.

Cowgirl Hall of Fame BARBECUE $$

(Map p264; ☎ 505-982-2565; www.cowgirlsantafe.com; 319 S Guadalupe St; mains $8-23; ⏱ 11:30am-midnight Mon-Thu, 11am-1am Fri & Sat, 11am-11:30pm Sun; ♿) With its juicy barbecue, awesome margaritas, outside patio, billiard room and live music – and its exuberant celebration of the women who made the West –

this restaurant-bar is a fun place for all ages; there's even a kids' playground out back. Be sure to try the barbecue brisket, say in a quesadilla with red chile.

Tomasita's NEW MEXICAN **$$**
(Map p264; ☎505-983-5721; www.tomasitas. com; 500 S Guadalupe St; mains $9-20; ☺11am-9pm Mon-Thu, to 10pm Fri & Sat; ☻) Sure this raucous, cavernous, Railyard landmark is always packed with tourists, and most likely you'll have to wait, but it's good – even great – for families hauling exuberant kids. Traditional New Mexican dishes here include burritos and enchiladas, and there are huge blue-plate specials.

★**Joseph's Culinary Pub** MEDITERRANEAN **$$$**
(Map p264; ☎505-982-1272; www.josephsofsan tafe.com; 428 Agua Fria St; ☺5:30-10pm Sun-Thu, to 11pm Fri & Sat) This romantic old adobe, open for dinner only, is best seen as a fine-dining restaurant rather than a pub. Order from the shorter, cheaper bar menu if you'd rather, but it's worth lingering in the warm-hued dining room to savor rich, modern Mediterranean dishes like crispy duck with French lentils, or rabbit lasagna with mascarpone cheese.

✗ Metro Santa Fe

★**San Marcos Cafe** NEW MEXICAN **$**
(Map p270; ☎505-471-9298; www.sanmarcosfeed. com; 3877 Hwy 14; mains $7-10; ☺8am-2pm; ☻) Down-home, country-style cafe that's well worth the 10-minute drive south, halfway to Cerrillos on Hwy 14. Aside from the best red chile you'll ever taste, and desserts like bourbon apple pie to sate that sweet tooth, turkeys and peacocks strut and squabble outside and the attached feed store adds some genuine Western soul. Reserve on weekends.

Horseman's Haven NEW MEXICAN **$**
(Map p270; ☎505-471-5420; 4354 Cerrillos Rd; mains $8-12; ☺8am-8pm Mon-Sat, 8:30am-2pm Sun; ☻) Hands down, this diner has the hottest green chile in town – faint-hearts, order it on the side. Service is friendly and fast, and the enormous 3D burrito – a mighty pile incorporating beans, rice and potatoes – might be the only thing you need to eat all day.

Santa Fe Baking Company AMERICAN **$**
(Map p260; ☎505-988-4292; www.santafebaking companycafe.com; 504 W Cordova Rd; mains $6-12; ☺6am-8pm Mon-Sat, to 6pm Sun; ☻☻☻) This bustling cafe, serving burgers, sandwiches

and big breakfast platters – and smoothies – all day, epitomizes the human melting pot that is Santa Fe. Need proof? Local radio station KSFR broadcasts a talk show from here at 8am on weekdays.

★**Jambo Cafe** AFRICAN **$$**
(Map p260; ☎505-473-1269; www.jambocafe.net; 2010 Cerrillos Rd; mains $9-16; ☺11am-9pm Mon-Sat) Despite expanding year on year, this African-flavored cafe is hard to spot from the highway; once inside, though, it's a lovely spot, always busy with locals who love its distinctive goat, chicken and lentil curries, veggie sandwiches and roti flatbreads, not to mention the reggae soundtrack.

Harry's Roadhouse AMERICAN, NEW MEXICAN **$$**
(☎505-989-4629; www.harrysroadhousesantafe. com; 96 Old Las Vegas Hwy; breakfast $6-10, lunch $8-11, dinner $8-22; ☺7am-9:30pm; ☻) This casual longtime favorite on the southern edge of town feels like a rambling cottage with its various rooms and patio garden – and there's also a full bar. And, seriously, *everything* here is good. Especially the desserts.

Tune-Up Cafe INTERNATIONAL **$$**
(Map p260; ☎505-983-7060; www.tuneupsantafe. com; 1115 Hickox St; mains $8-15; ☺7am-10pm Mon-Fri, from 8am Sat & Sun; ☻) Casual neighborhood hangout, west of the Railyard, where the chef, from El Salvador, adds his own twists to classic New Mexican and American brunch favorites while also serving fantastic Salvadoran *pupusas* (stuffed corn tortillas), *molé colorado* enchiladas and fish tacos.

Tesuque Village Market CAFE **$$**
(Map p270; ☎505-988-8848; www.tesuquevillage market.com; 138 Tesuque Village Rd, Tesuque; mains $9-24; ☺7am-9pm) Hole-in-the-wall turned country-hip, this is a weekend hotspot for folks heading to or from Tesuque Flea Market. If you're hungry and in a hurry, grab a handheld burrito – the breakfast burritos will start your day right, and the *carne adovada* (stewed pork with red chile) is among the best anywhere. Take Bishops Lodge Rd or Hwy 285 north to exit 168.

♀ Drinking

Talk to 10 residents and you'll get 10 different opinions about where to find the best margarita. You may have to sample the lot to decide for yourself. Similarly, Santa Feans take their tea and coffee seriously too; the cafes that last here know what they're brewing.

★ **The Teahouse** CAFE

(Map p260; ☑505-992-0972; www.teahousesan
tafe.com; 821 Canyon Rd; ⊘9am-9pm; 🛜) This
spacious, relaxed indoor/outdoor cafe at the
eastern end of Canyon Rd makes the perfect
break while gallery hopping. One hundred
and sixty teas from all over the world – with
scones – plus a full menu (mains $11 to $16)
of eggy brunch items, paninis and salads.

Evangelo's BAR

(Map p264; 200 W San Francisco St; ⊘noon-
1:30am Mon-Sat, to midnight Sun) Everyone is
welcome in this casual, rowdy, cash-only
joint, owned by the Klonis family since 1971
(ask owner-bartender Nick about his father's
unusual fame). Drop in, put on some Patsy
Cline and grab a draft beer – it's the perfect
escape from Plaza culture. Live Goth and alternative bands perform downstairs in the
appropriately named Underground.

Bell Tower Bar BAR

(Map p264; 100 E San Francisco St; ⊘ 3pm-sunset
Mon-Thu, 2pm-sunset Fri-Sun May-Oct, closed Nov-
Apr) In summer this bar atop La Fonda hotel
is the premier spot to catch one of those pat-
ented New Mexican sunsets while sipping
a killer margarita. After dark, retire to the
hotel's lobby Fiesta Bar for live country or
folk music.

GAME OF SCREENS

Like many a local resident, *Game of
Thrones* author George RR Martin felt
a definite tinge of regret each time he
walked past Santa Fe's much missed
Jean Cocteau Cinema (Map p264;
☑505-466-5528; www.jeancocteaucinema.
com; 418 Montezuma Ave), which closed
its doors in 2006. Unlike his neighbors,
however, Martin was in a position to do
something about it. He bought the place
and reopened it in 2013.

The Cocteau is now once more programming art-house and new-release
movies, with the same bent it always had
toward sci-fi and fantasy, and with Martin's reputation helping to draw in writers
and performers for special events. Best of
all, it's become a tradition for the cinema
to hail each new season of the *Game of
Thrones* series with free advance screenings. Costumed fans wait overnight on
the sidewalk outside for Q&A sessions
with Martin and the various actors.

Holy Spirit Espresso CAFE

(Map p264; 225 W San Francisco St; ⊘7am-4pm
Tue-Sat, 7am-2pm Sun) With just enough room
for a counter, an espresso machine and two
or three customers, plus two tables somehow squeezed onto the sidewalk, there's not
really a lot to this tiny hole-in-the-wall cafe –
but for a friendly morning pick-me-up, what
little there is, is absolutely perfect.

Second Street Brewery PUB

(Map p264; ☑505-989-3278; www.secondstreet
brewery.com; 1607 Paseo de Peralta, Railyard;
⊘11am-10pm Mon-Thu, 11am-11pm Fri & Sat, noon-
9pm Sun) Both pubs run by Santa Fe's favorite
brewery make great places for a pint after
a long hike, serving their own handcrafted
English-style beers plus a hearty selection of
better-than-average pub grub, and putting
on regular live music. We prefer this newer
Railyard location to the **original** (Map p260;
☑505-982-3030; www.secondstreetbrewery.com;
1814 2nd St).

Downtown Subscription CAFE

(Map p264; ☑505-983-3085; 376 Garcia St;
⊘7am-7pm) The coffee shop of choice for
Santa Fe's artists and writers, a block off
Canyon Rd, serves 31 types of tea, plus espresso, pastries and savory offerings, all
complemented by a truly spectacular newsstand and flagstone patio.

Dragon Room Bar BAR

(Map p264; ☑505-983-7712; 406 Old Santa Fe
Trail; ⊘4pm-midnight Tue-Sun) This 300-year-
old adobe is a consistent top fave for locals
and Hollywood-famous visitors alike. Drop
by for a signature Black Dragon margarita.
Visit after 9pm on Tuesday, Thursday or Saturday if you want it served with live music
(flamenco guitar, Latin jazz and the like).

☆ Entertainment
Performing Arts

Opera, chamber music, performance and
visual arts draw patrons from the world's
most glittering cities to Santa Fe in July and
August. The opera may be the belle of the
ball – clad in sparkling denim – but there
are lots of other highbrow and lowbrow
happenings every week. Let the exhaustive
online **Event Calendar** (www.santafe.com/
calendar) become your new best friend.

★ **Santa Fe Opera** OPERA

(Map p270; ☑505-986-5900; www.santafeopera.
org; Hwy 84/285, Tesuque; tickets $32-254; back-
stage tours adult/child $5/free; ⊘Jun-Aug, backstage

tours 9am Mon-Fri Jun-Aug) Many visitors flock to Santa Fe for the opera alone: the theater is a marvel, with 360-degree views of sandstone wilderness crowned with sunsets and moon-rises, while at center stage the world's finest talent performs magnificent masterworks. It's still the Wild West, though; you can even wear jeans. Shuttles run to and from Santa Fe and Albuquerque; reserve online.

Gala festivities begin two hours before the curtain rises, when the ritual tailgate party is rendered glamorous in true Santa Fe style right in the parking lot. Bring your own cav-iar and brie, make reservations for the buffet dinner and lecture or a picnic dinner, or have your own private caterer pour the champagne (several customize their menu to the opera's theme). **Prelude Talks**, free to all ticket hold-ers, are offered in Stieren Orchestra Hall one and two hours before curtain.

Youth Night at the Opera offers family tickets for dress rehearsals for bargain rates; one precedes the run of each of the season's operas – with brief talks aimed at ages six to 22. Backstage tours offer opportunities to poke around the sets, costume and storage areas.

Lensic Performing
Arts Center PERFORMING ARTS
(Map p264; ☑ 505-988-7050; www.lensic.com; 211 W San Francisco St) A beautifully renovated 1930 movie house, the theater hosts touring productions and classic films as well as sev-en different performance groups, including the Santa Fe Symphony Orchestra & Chorus.

Santa Fe Playhouse THEATER
(Map p264; ☑ 505-988-4262; www.santafeplay house.org; 142 E De Vargas St; ⊙ Thu-Sun) The state's oldest theater company performs avant-garde and traditional theater and mu-sical comedy, typically with evening programs Thursday to Saturday plus a Sunday matinee.

Santa Fe Chamber
Music Festival CLASSICAL MUSIC
(☑ 505-982-1890; www.santafechambermusic.com; ⊙ Jul-Aug) Santa Fe's *other* major annual cul-tural event – apart from the opera – fills elegant venues like the Lensic to hear Brahms, Mozart and other masters performed by world-class virtuosos like violinist Pinchas Zukerman and pianist Yuja Wang.

Santa Fe Desert Chorale LIVE MUSIC
(☑ 505-988-2282; www.desertchorale.org; ⊙ Jul & Aug) Twenty-four lauded professional sing-ers from around the country come together

each summer to perform everything from Gregorian chants and gospel to Renaissance madrigals and modern love songs at venues like St Francis Cathedral, Loretto Chapel and Warehouse 21.

Live Music & Dance Clubs

Many of the hotel bars in Santa Fe offer live music on one or more nights of the week. Check the *Santa Fe Reporter* and Friday's *New Mexican* for a thorough listing of what's going on – clubs here change faster than the seasons.

★ **El Farol** DINNER SHOW
(Map p260; ☑ 505-983-9912; www.elfarolsf.com; 808 Canyon Rd; dinner shows $25; ⊙ 11am-midnight Mon-Sat, 11am-11pm Sun) Aside from its weekly fla-menco dinner shows, this popular restaurant/bar programs live entertainment every night, including regular Latin soul shows.

Vanessie of Santa Fe CABARET
(Map p264; ☑ 505-982-9966; 427 W Water St) You don't really come to Vanessie for the food, though there's nothing wrong with it. No, the attraction here is the piano bar, featur-ing blow-dried lounge singers who bring Neil Diamond and Barry Manilow classics to life in their own special way.

Warehouse 21 LIVE MUSIC
(Map p260; ☑ 505-989-4423; www.warehouse21. org; 1614 Paseo de Peralta) This all-ages club and arts center in a 3500-sq-ft warehouse by the Railyard is the perfect alcohol-free venue for edgy local bands, plus a fair number of nationally known acts, or for just showing off the latest in multihued hairstyles.

🛍 Shopping

Besides the Native American jewelry sold directly by the artists under the Plaza *por-tales,* Santa Fe holds enough shops for you to spend weeks browsing and buying. Many venues combine both gallery and shop. The focus is mainly on art, from jewelry to wild contemporary paintings.

★ **Seret & Sons** HANDICRAFTS
(Map p264; ☑ 505-988-9151; www.seretandsons. com; 224 Galisteo St) Feel like you've stepped into an Arabian bazaar at this emporium of art and sculpture, overflowing with gor-geous Afghan rugs, Tibetan furniture, giant stone elephants and solid teak doors. Get-ting such treasures home is easier said than done, but it's fun just to browse too.

SANTA FE GALLERY-HOPPING

Originally a Pueblo Indian footpath, later the main street through a Spanish farming community, Santa Fe's most famous art avenue, **Canyon Road** (Map p264; www.canyon roadarts.com), embarked on its current incarnation in the 1920s, when artists led by Los Cinco Pintores (five painters who fell in love with New Mexico's landscape) moved in to take advantage of the cheap rent.

Today Canyon Rd is a must-see attraction, holding more than a hundred of Santa Fe's 300-plus galleries. The epicenter of the city's vibrant art scene, it offers everything from rare Native American antiquities to Santa Fe School masterpieces and in-your-face modern work. If gallery-hopping seems a bit overwhelming, don't worry, just wander.

Friday nights are particularly fun: that's when the galleries put on glittering openings, starting around 5pm. Not only are these great social events, but you can also browse while nibbling on cheese, sipping Chardonnay or sparkling cider, and chatting with the artists.

Below is just a sampling of our Canyon Rd (and around) favorites. For more, pick up the handy, free *Collector's Guide* map, or check out www.santafegalleries.net. Further galleries are concentrated around the Railyard, and along Lincoln Ave just north of the Plaza.

★**LoneDog NoiseCat** (Map p264; ☑ 505-412-1797; www.lonedognoisecat.com; 241 Delgado St; ⊙ 10am-4pm) Exactly the kind of gallery first-timers hope to find along Canyon Rd, and until now seldom did – a provocative and stimulating array of proudly contemporary Native American (or 'Neo-Aboriginal') art, eschewing stereotypes in favor of confronting modern realities, and curated by artists Ed Archie NoiseCat and Todd LoneDog Bordeaux.

Adobe Gallery (Map p264; ☑ 505-955-0550; www.adobegallery.com; 221 Canyon Rd; ⊙ 10am-5pm Mon-Sat) This gallery specializes in exquisite 20th-century ceramic pieces from the Pueblo pottery renaissance, and also sells rugs, kachinas and other artifacts produced by Southwestern Indian artisans.

Economos/Hampton Galleries (Map p264; ☑ 505-982-6347; 500 Canyon Rd; ⊙ 10am-5pm Mon-Sat) Museums come here to purchase superlative ancient Native American art, pre–Columbian Mexican pieces and much, much more, crammed into two huge floors swirling with history.

GF Contemporary (Map p264; ☑ 505-983-3707; www.gfcontemporary.com; 707 Canyon Rd; ⊙ 10am-5pm) An eclectic and well displayed assortment of modern paintings and sculpture, few of which have any overt Southwestern connection.

Marc Navarro Gallery (Map p260; ☑ 505-986-8191; www.marcnavarrogallery.com; 520 Canyon Rd; ⊙ 11am-4pm) Collectors come here to find antique Spanish and Mexican silver jewelry, including pieces studded with onyx and amethysts, as well as contemporary paintings.

Morning Star Gallery (Map p260; ☑ 505-982-8187; www.morningstargallery.com; 513 Canyon Rd; ⊙ 9am-5pm Mon-Sat) This stunning gallery focuses on historic Plains Indian ephemera, with weavings, jewelry, beadwork, kachina dolls and even original ledger drawings just some of the stars among artifacts that in many cases are finer than those in museums. A 1775 Powhoge ceramic storage jar sold for $225,000, and an 1860 Nez Perce war shirt for $220,000.

Pushkin Gallery (Map p260; ☑ 505-982-1990; www.pushkingallery.com; 550 Canyon Rd; ⊙ 10am-5pm Mon-Sat) Owned by descendants of poet Alexander Pushkin, this gallery showcases modern Russian masters including Nikolai Timkov and Boris Chetkov.

★**Santa Fe Farmers Market** MARKET (Map p264; ☑ 505-983-4098; www.santafefarmers market.com; Paseo de Peralta & Guadalupe St, Railyard; ⊙ 8am-1pm Sat, plus Tue May-Nov; ☒) Local produce, much of it heirloom and organic, is on sale at this spacious indoor/outdoor market, alongside homemade goodies, inexpensive food, natural body products and arts and crafts.

Pueblo of Tesuque Flea Market MARKET
(Map p270; ☑505-670-2599; www.pueblof
tesuquefleamarket.com; 15 Flea Market Rd; ⊘8am-
4pm Fri-Sun Mar-Dec) Vendors at this outdoor
market, beside the Santa Fe Opera 7 miles
north of Santa Fe, sell everything from
high-quality rugs, turquoise rings and
clothing to the best used (read: broken-in)
cowboy boots in the state. Nowadays, most
booths are like small shops; a few individuals still turn up to sell funky junk.

Kowboyz CLOTHING
(Map p264; ☑505-984-1256; www.kowboyz.com;
345 W Manhattan Ave; ⊘10am-5:30pm) Secondhand shop selling everything you need to
cowboy up. Shirts are a great deal at $12 each;
the amazing selection of boots, however, de-
mands top dollar. Movie costumers in search
of authentic Western wear often come here.

Nambé Foundry Outlet HOMEWARES
(Map p264; ☑505-988-3574; www.nambe.com;
104 W San Francisco St) Nambéware, a unique
metal alloy that looks like silver without
containing silver, lead or pewter, was developed near Nambé, north of Santa Fe, in 1951.
Gleaming, elegant bowls, plates and vases,
individually sand-cast, are now an essential
component of Santa Fe style. There's another,
larger **outlet** (Map p264; ☑505-988-5528; 924
Paseo de Peralta) facing the start of Canyon Rd.

Nathalie CLOTHING
(Map p264; ☑505-982-1021; www.nathaliesan
tafe.com; 503 Canyon Rd; ⊘10am-6pm Mon-Sat)
Come here for exquisite cowboy and cowgirl
gear, including gemstone-studded gun hol-
sters, handmade leather, denim couture and
lingerie for that saloon girl with a heart of
gold. Stunning Spanish Colonial antiques.

Gerald Peters Gallery ARTWORKS
(Map p264; ☑505-954-5700; www.gpgallery.com;
1011 Paseo de Peralta; ⊘10am-5pm Mon-Sat)
Owned by a local restaurant and real-estate
tycoon, this gallery, two blocks from Canyon
Rd, carries fine art by Southwestern masters
including Nicolai Fechin, Charles Russell
and Edward Borein.

LewAllen Galleries ARTWORKS
(Map p264; ☑505-988-3250; www.lewallengaller-
ies.com; 1613 Paseo de Peralta; ⊘10am-6pm Mon-
Fri, to 5pm Sat) The most prominent modern
contemporary art gallery in town, occupying three stories in the Railyard district,
LewAllen also shows modernist masters.

Jackalope HANDICRAFTS
(Map p260; ☑505-471-8539; www.jackalope.com;
2820 Cerrillos Rd; ⊘10am-6pm) Essential pieces
of Southwest decor – albeit largely imported
from Mexico – can be yours for a song. Start
with a cow skull like the ones Georgia O'Keeffe
made famous, snap up a kiva ladder, add
some colorful pottery and Navajo pot holders
and you'll be set. Don't leave without watching live prairie dogs frolic in their 'village'.

Travel Bug BOOKS
(Map p264; ☑505-992-0418; www.mapsof
newmexico.com; 839 Paseo de Peralta; ⊘7:30am-
5:30pm Mon-Sat, 11am-4pm Sun; 🔊) One of the
largest selections of travel books and maps
you'll ever find; you can even print topo
maps on demand, on waterproof paper. Local travelers, authors and photographers give
free talks about their adventures Saturday at
5pm. There's also a coffee bar with wi-fi.

Collected Works BOOKS
(Map p264; ☑505-988-4226; www.collectedworks
bookstore.com; 202 Galisteo St; ⊘8am-8pm Mon-
Sat, to 6pm Sun) Large bookstore close to the

SHOPPING FOR NATIVE AMERICAN ART

Santa Fe's best shopping is beneath the
portales (overhanging arcades) in front
of the **Palace of the Governors**, to
which Pueblo Indians travel as far as 200
miles to sell gorgeous handmade jewelry.
The tradition started in the 1880s, when
Tesuque artisans first greeted arriving
trains with all manner of wares. Today up
to 1200 members, representing almost
every New Mexican tribe, draw lots for
the 76 spaces under the vigas each
morning. Those lucky enough to procure
the desirable spots display bracelets,
pendants, fetishes (small carved images)
and thick engraved silver wedding bands
on bright blankets. Classic turquoise and
silver jewelry is the most popular, but
you'll find many other regional stones
in a rainbow of colors. Most artists are
happy to tell you the story behind each
piece in his or her open-air gallery – and
most are one-of-a-kinds. Not only are the
prices better here than in a store but the
money goes directly back to the source:
the artist. Only attempt to bargain if
it's suggested; the vendors may find it
insulting.

Plaza, with a good selection of regional fiction and nonfiction and a spacious coffee bar.

Garcia Street Books BOOKS
(Map p264; ☎505-986-0151; www.garciastreetbooks.com; 376 Garcia St; ☉9am-6pm Mon-Sat, to 5pm Sun) Scavengers are rewarded with excellent bargains as well as the town's best selection of art books, and rarities like the woodblock prints of Willard Clark.

ℹ Information

EMERGENCY

Police (☎505-428-3710; 2515 Camino Entrada)

MEDICAL SERVICES

St Vincent's Hospital (☎505-983-3361; www.stvin.org; 455 St Michael's Dr; ☉24hr emergency)

Walgreens (☎505-982-9811; 1096 S St Francis Dr; ☉24hr)

POST

Post office (Map p264; 120 S Federal Pl; ☉8am-5:30pm Mon-Fri, 9am-4pm Sat)

TOURIST INFORMATION

New Mexico Visitor Information Center (Map p264; ☎505-827-7336; www.newmexico.org; 491 Old Santa Fe Trail; ☉8am-5pm Mon-Fri, 8am-4pm Sat & Sun) Housed in the historic 1878 Lamy Building, this friendly place offers helpful advice – and free coffee.

Public Lands Information Center (Map p270; ☎505-954-2002; www.publiclands.org; 301 Dinosaur Trail; ☉8:30am-4pm Mon-Fri) Staff at this hugely helpful office have maps and information on public lands throughout New Mexico, and can talk you through hiking options.

Santa Fe CVB (☎505-955-6200; www.santafe.org; 201 W Marcy St; ☉8am-5pm Mon-Fri) The bricks-and-mortar office, at the Sweeny Convention Center, offers little you won't find on the website.

ℹ Getting There & Around

The great majority of visitors reach and explore Santa Fe by car, but the city does have good transport connections with Albuquerque.

AIR

Daily flights to/from Denver, Dallas and Los Angeles serve the small **Santa Fe Municipal Airport** (SAF; Map p270; ☎505-955-2900; www.santafenm.gov/airport; 121 Aviation Dr), 10 miles southwest of downtown.

BUS

The free **Santa Fe Pick-Up** meets arriving Rail-Runner trains, looping around downtown and also heading out to Museum Hill between May and mid-October, while **Santa Fe Trails** (Map p264; ☎505-955-2001; www.santafenm.gov; 1-way adult/child $1/free, day pass $2) operates buses ($1) from the Downtown Transit Center, with routes M, to Museum Hill, and 2 along Cerrillos Rd, being the most useful for visitors.

The **Sandia Shuttle Express** (☎888-775-5696; www.sandiashuttle.com) connects Santa Fe with the Albuquerque Sunport ($28; book in advance), while **North Central Regional Transit** (☎505-629-4725; www.ncrtd.org) provides free shuttle bus service from downtown Santa Fe to Española on weekdays, where you can transfer to shuttles to Taos, Los Alamos, Ojo Caliente and other northern destinations. Downtown pick-up/drop-off is by the Santa Fe Trails bus stop on Sheridan St, a block northwest of the Plaza. Friday to Sunday, the **Taos Express** (☎575-751-4459; www.taosexpress.com; one-way $10; ☉Fri-Sun) runs north to Taos from the corner of Guadalupe and Montezuma Sts, by the Railyard.

TRAIN

The **Rail Runner** (www.nmrailrunner.com) commuter train offers multiple daily connections with Albuquerque from its terminus in the Railyard and the South Capitol Station, a mile southwest. The trip takes about 1½ hours. Arriving passengers can make free use of the Santa Fe Trails bus network. **Amtrak** (☎800-872-7245; www.amtrak.com) serves Lamy station, 17 miles southeast, with bus connections to Santa Fe.

AROUND SANTA FE

Don't get too comfortable in Santa Fe, because there's plenty to explore nearby. Whichever direction you head in, you'll enjoy some of New Mexico's finest scenery, from pine forests to rainbow-colored canyons, mesa lands to mountain views. This area also offers the state's best hot-spring resort, streams made for fly-fishing, endless hiking trails, and museums celebrating everything from Pueblo crafts to the building of the atom bomb. Small towns reveal unexpected treasures – from beautiful adobe churches to fabulous local restaurants to studios where artists and artisans create and sell their work.

Pecos National Historic Park

When the Spanish first reached **Pecos Pueblo**, they found a five-story, 700-room structure that was a major center for trade between the Pueblo peoples and the Plains Indians to the east. The Spaniards completed a church in 1625, but it was destroyed during the 1680 Pueblo Revolt. Subsequently the Pueblo itself declined, and in 1838 its 17 remaining inhabitants moved to Jemez Pueblo. The sturdy remains of the mission church, rebuilt in 1717, are now the major attraction at **Pecos National Historical Park** (Map p270; ☑ 505-757-7241; www.nps.gov/peco; adult/child $3/free; ☺ 8am-6pm May-Sep, until 4:30pm Oct-Apr), 30 miles southwest of Santa Fe via I-25 (toward Las Vegas). It takes around an hour to explore the site thoroughly.

Tesuque Pueblo

POP 500 / ELEV 6759FT

Nine miles north of Santa Fe along Hwy 84/285 is **Tesuque Pueblo** (Map p270; ☑ 505-983-2667), whose members played an important role in the Pueblo Revolt of 1680, and later suffered as a result. Today, the reservation encompasses more than 17,000 acres of spectacular landscape, including sections of the Santa Fe National Forest. San Diego Feast Day (November 12) features dancing; the Deer and Buffalo dances in December are known for their costumes and attention to ritual detail. The flea market held here is well worth checking out. Look for the aptly named Camel Rock on the west side of the highway, more or less opposite **Camel Rock Casino** (Map p270; www.camelrockcasino.com; ☺ 8am-2am Mon-Thu, 24hr Fri-Sun).

Pojoaque Pueblo

POP 1300 / ELEV 5853FT

Although the history of **Pojoaque Pueblo** (Map p521; ☑ 505-455-4500; www.pojoaque.org) predates the Spaniards, a smallpox epidemic in the late 19th century killed most of its inhabitants, and forced the rest to evacuate. No old buildings remain. The few survivors intermarried with other Pueblo people and Hispanics, and a handful returned to the Pueblo in 1932, working to rebuild its traditions, crafts and culture. Their descendants now number about 300 – most of those who live on the Pueblo's land are not Native American. The annual **Virgin de Guadalupe Feast Day** on December 12 is celebrated with ceremonial dancing.

A modern complex on the east side of Hwy 84/285, 16 miles north of Santa Fe and just south of the point where the High Rd branches off to Taos, holds the Pueblo's public buildings.

Poeh Cultural Center & Museum MUSEUM (☑ 505-455-5041; www.poehcenter.com; Hwy 84/285; ☺ 10am-4pm Mon-Sat) This ambitious project, set up by the Pueblo's current governor, artist George Rivera, features superb displays on the history and culture of the Pueblo, tracing the story of the Tewa-speaking people from their emergence into this earth. The museum shop sells top-quality crafts.

Buffalo Thunder Resort HOTEL (☑ 877-848-6337; www.buffalothunderresort.com; 20 Buffalo Thunder Trail; r from $129; ❄ @ 🎧 🐾) As well as offering luxurious rooms and suites at reasonable rates, this enormous Pueblo-run resort also holds three nine-hole golf courses, a spa, and, of course, a casino.

San Ildefonso Pueblo

POP 750 / ELEV 5550FT

Eight miles west of Pojoaque along Hwy 502, this ancient **Pueblo** (Map p521; ☑ 505-455-2273; www.sanipueblo.org; per vehicle $10, camera/video/sketching permits $10/20/25; ☺ 8am-5pm) traces its origins back to Bandelier and Mesa Verde. It's best known now as the birthplace of Maria Martínez, who in 1919, along with her husband, Julian, revived a distinctive traditional black-on-black pottery style. Her work, now valued at tens of thousands of dollars, has become world famous and is ranked by collectors among the finest pottery ever produced.

Several exceptional potters (including Maria's direct descendants) work in the Pueblo, and many different styles are produced, but black-on-black remains San Ildefonso's hallmark. Studios and private homes around its two plazas sell prime examples. The **Pueblo Museum**, with exhibits on the Pueblo's history and culture and a small store, is next to the visitor center.

Visitors are welcome to **Feast Day** (January 23) and **corn dances**, held throughout the summer.

Santa Clara Pueblo

POP 1000 / ELEV 5605FT

Santa Clara Pueblo (Map p521; ☑ 505-753-7330) itself, just a mile southwest of Española along Hwy 30, springs to life in summer for the Harvest and Blue Corn Dances on **Santa Clara Feast Day** (August 12) and

St Anthony's Feast Day (June 13). During the rest of the year, various galleries and private homes sell intricately patterned black pottery, but the main reason visitors come here is to see the nearby Puyé Cliff Dwellings.

Puyé Cliff Dwellings　　ARCHAEOLOGICAL SITE
(☑888-320-5008; www.puyecliffs.com; 300 Hwy 30; tour adult/child $20/18, 2 tours $35/33; ☺hourly tours 9am-5pm May-Sep, 10am-2pm Oct-Apr) Two separate hour-long tours explore these ancient ruins, 5 miles west of the Pueblo at the entrance to Santa Clara Canyon. Abandoned around 1500, they're similar in style to those at Bandelier National Monument. The most impressive are sculpted into the cliffside, with the rest freestanding on the mesa-top above. The big appeal is that the Pueblo guides who show you around are directly descended from the original inhabitants, and thus provide an electrifying connection with the vanished past.

Los Alamos

POP 17,000 / ELEV 7355FT

When the top-secret Manhattan Project sprang to life in 1943, it turned the sleepy mesa-top village of Los Alamos into a busy laboratory of secluded brainiacs. Here, in the 'town that didn't exist,' the atomic bomb was developed in almost total secrecy. Humanity can trace some of its greatest achievements and darkest fears directly to this little town. Los Alamos National Laboratory still develops weapons, but it's also at the cutting edge of other scientific discoveries, including mapping the human genome and making mind-boggling supercomputing advances.

Los Alamos remains a place unto itself, where the Lab dominates everything; it has the highest concentration of PhDs per capita in the US, along with the highest per-capita income in New Mexico. In principle, the setting is beautiful, amid the national forest, but successive disastrous fires, including the colossal Las Conchas blaze of 2011, have left the surrounding hillsides eerily barren.

◎ Sights & Activities

One reason Los Alamos makes such a perfect spot for a top-secret base is its extraordinary geography. The town stretches along a sequence of finger-thin, high-sided mesas, which makes it easy to restrict access to un-wanted visitors. It also makes it a baffling place to drive around; follow signs to access the small town center, where Central Ave is the main axis, and don't try to explore further afield. If you do, you will in any case soon come up against security roadblocks.

Most of the local sights are related to the A-bomb project. Outside of town, there's some good rock climbing (with plenty of top-roping), including the **Overlook** and the **Playground** in the basalt cliffs east of Los Alamos.

★**Bradbury Science Museum**　　MUSEUM
(Map p270; ☑505-667-4444; www.lanl.gov/museum; 1350 Central Ave; ☺10am-5pm Tue-Sat, 1-5pm Sun & Mon) FREE You can't actually visit the Los Alamos National Laboratory, where the first atomic bomb was conceived, but the Bradbury Science Museum has compelling displays on bomb development and atomic history, along with medical and computer sciences. There's even a room where you can twist your brain into a pretzel with hands-on problem-solving games.

Los Alamos Historical Museum　　MUSEUM
(Map p270; ☑505-662-6272; www.losalamoshistory.org; 1050 Bathtub Row; ☺9:30am-4:30pm Mon-Fri, 11am-4pm Sat & Sun) FREE Housed in a former school building, this interesting museum displays pop-culture artifacts from the atomic age and details the everyday social history of life 'on the hill' during the secret project. Pick up one of the self-guided downtown walking-tour pamphlets.

Art Center at Fuller Lodge　　MUSEUM
(www.fullerlodgeartcenter.org; 2132 Central Ave; ☺10am-4pm Mon-Sat) FREE Built in 1928 to serve as the dining hall for the local boys school, Fuller Lodge, alongside the historical museum, was purchased by the US government for the Manhattan Project. Its Art Center mounts mixed-media shows of local and national artists.

Pajarito Mountain
Ski Area　　SKIING, MOUNTAIN BIKING
(Map p270; ☑505-662-5725; www.skipajarito.com; lift tickets adult/child $62/35; ☺Fri-Sun Dec-Mar) Ever wanted to ski down the rim of a volcano? This ski area, 7 miles west of downtown, has 40 runs – from easy groomers to challenging mogul steeps – plus a terrain park for snowboarders. In summer, lifts run on weekends ($26) for some serious mountain-biking action, including courses with jump ramps and log rides.

SCENIC DRIVE: JEMEZ MOUNTAIN TRAIL

West of Los Alamos, Hwy 4 twists and curves through the heart of the Jemez Mountains, on a sublime scenic drive that's made even better by all the places to stop.

The **Las Conchas Trail**, which starts between mile markers 36 and 37, is the first temptation en route. It's a lovely place to hike, following the east fork of the Jemez River for its first 2 miles before climbing out of the canyon via steep switchbacks. That's the obvious point at which to head back to your car, though there's some great rock climbing if you have time to linger.

A few miles further along, you'll enter the **Valles Caldera National Preserve** (☑ 866-382-5537; www.vallescaldera.gov; permits adult/child $10/5), which is basically what the crater of a dormant supervolcano looks like 1,250,000 years after it first blows. (The explosion was so massive chunks were thrown as far away as Kansas.) The 140-sq-mile bowl – home to New Mexico's largest elk herd – is simply breathtaking, with vast meadows from which hills rise like pine-covered islands. Two trails on the edge of the preserve offer free, open hiking, but you need to reserve in advance, as only a few permits are given out to hike within the caldera on any given day, and you can only access the trailheads via shuttle buses from the **Staging Area** (Mile 39.2, Hwy 4; ☺ 8am-6pm mid-May–mid-Oct, 9am-5pm Fri-Sun mid-Oct–mid-May). It's also possible to mountain bike, ride horseback, fish, hunt, and cross-country ski here.

As you continue along Hwy 4, you can hike into a number of natural hot springs. One of the most accessible is **Spence Hot Springs**, between miles 24 and 25. The temperature's about perfect, and the inevitable weird naked guy adds authenticity to the experience.

The pretty village of **Jemez Springs** (www.jemezsprings.org) was built around a cluster of springs, as was the ruined pueblo at the small **Jemez Historic Site** (www.nmmonuments.org; Hwy 4; adult/child $3/free; ☺ 8:30am-5pm Wed-Sun). You can experience the waters yourself at rustic **Jemez Springs Bath House** (☑ 575-829-3303; 62 Jemez Springs Plaza; per hr $18; ☺ 10am-7pm), which has private tubs, massages and more.

Eat at the cavernous **Los Ojos Restaurant & Saloon** (☑ 575-829-3547; www.losojos saloon.com; Hwy 4; mains $5-17; ☺ 11am-9:30pm Mon-Fri, from 8am Sat & Sun, bar open late; ☑), usually peopled by some real Wild West characters, where the largely Mexican menu holds a surprising range of vegetarian dishes considering the number of animal heads on the walls, and there's also a pool table. And if you're not traveling with kids or pets, stay at **Cañon del Rio B&B** (☑ 575-829-4377; www.canondelrio.com; r from $129; ☜ ☒), which has gorgeous canyon views, a pool, hot tub and day spa, killer breakfasts and terrific hosts.

At **Jemez Pueblo**, 20 miles south of Jemez Springs, the **Walatowa Visitor Center** (☑ 575-834-7235; www.jemezpueblo.com; 7413 Hwy 4; ☺ 8am-5pm Apr-Oct, 10am-4pm Wed-Sun Nov-Mar) houses an excellent museum of Pueblo culture and history. If you're into wine, take a little detour to **Ponderosa Valley Winery** (www.ponderosawinery.com; 3171 Hwy 290; ☺ 10am-5pm Tue-Sat, noon-5pm Sun) for a bottle of late-harvest riesling or pinot noir, before emerging onto Hwy 550, between Bernalillo and Cuba. From there, continue on to Albuquerque, back to Santa Fe, or up toward Chaco Canyon and the Four Corners.

🛌 Sleeping

Los Alamos is not a place where many tourists choose to spend the night, but a handful of chain hotels cater to visiting scientists.

Canyon Inn   B&B $
(Map p270; ☑ 505-662-9595; www.canyoninnbnb. com; 80 Canyon Rd; r $97) This welcoming, single-story family home, a short walk from downtown, offers four spacious en suite rooms with full breakfast; guests are free to use the fully equipped kitchen.

🍴 Eating

Blue Window Bistro   AMERICAN $$
(Map p270; ☑ 505-662-6305; www.labluewindow bistro.com; 813 Central Ave; lunch $10-12, dinner $10-27; ☺ 11am-2:30pm & 5-8:30pm Mon-Fri, 5-9pm Sat) On the north side of the shopping center, this brightly colored cafe offers lunchtime gyros and poached salmon, and dinners like Southwestern chicken and double-cut pork chops.

Pyramid Cafe   MIDDLE EASTERN $$
(Map p270; ☑ 505-661-1717; www.pyramidcafesf. com; 751 Central Ave; mains $12-22; ☺ 11am-2:30pm

& 4:30-8pm, from noon Sat & Sun) Middle Eastern food is the name of the game at this offshoot of a popular Santa Fe restaurant. Gyros, felafel, shawarma, and moussaka bring in the crowds – or maybe it's the Turkish coffee.

❶ Information

Los Alamos Visitor Center (☑ 505-662-8105; www.visitlosalamos.org; 109 Central Park Sq; ⊙ 9am-5pm Mon-Fri, 9am-4pm Sat, 10am-3pm Sun)

Bandelier National Monument

The sublime, peach-colored cliffs of Frijoles Canyon, pocked with caves and alcoves that were home to Ancestral Puebloans until the mid-1500s, are the main attraction at **Bandelier National Monument** (Map p270; www.nps.gov/band; per vehicle $12; ⊙ dawn-dusk; ▣), 12 miles south of Los Alamos and an hour's drive from Santa Fe. A popular day trip from the city, it's rewarding whether you're interested in ancient Southwestern cultures or just want to walk among pines and watch the light glowing off the canyon walls.

An easy trail leads from the **Visitor Center** (⊙ 8am-6pm Jun-Sep, 9am-4:30pm Oct-May) in Frijoles Canyon to the main ruins, carved into the soft volcanic rock like a prehistoric apartment complex. Short ladders enable you to clamber into the individual homes. Continue along the canyon floor for a further mile to reach the remarkable **Ceremonial Cave**, poised 140ft above the ground and reached by climbing four much longer ladders.

Sadly, though, Frijoles Canyon has suffered severe environmental damage in recent years, making it less appealing as a backcountry hiking destination. The ruins remain intact, but fires have not only devastated its trees, but allowed torrential floods to sweep along the riverbed.

Between late May and late October, visitors can only drive all the way to the canyon before 9am or after 3pm. For most of the day, you have to park 11 miles north at the **White Rock Visitor Center** (⊙ 8am-6pm May-Sep, 10am-2pm Oct-Apr), on Hwy 4 south of Los Alamos, and ride a free shuttle bus from there, which adds considerable time to a visit.

Bandelier also has a satellite section, **Tsankawi**, north of White Rock near the intersection of Hwy 502 and Hwy 4, where a 1.5-mile loop trail follows an ancient footpath to cut across a mesa top and wind down a cliffside passing a few small caves.

Set among the pines near the monument entrance, the park's **Juniper Campground** (☑ 877-444-6777; www.recreation.gov; campsites $12) holds about 100 campsites, drinking water, toilets, picnic tables and fire grates, but no showers or hookups. Free backcountry camping is allowed but permits must be obtained in person from the visitor center.

Española

POP 10,500 / ELEV 5595FT

Founded by conquistador Don Juan de Oñate in 1598, **Española** (www.espanola online.com) sits at a major fork in the road between Santa Fe and points north, including Taos, Ojo Caliente and Abiquiú. There's not much to appeal to visitors here, unless you're in search of a Super Wal-Mart or the best chicken-guacamole tacos on the planet.

Española is known as the 'Low Rider Capital of the World.' You're still likely to see some seriously pimped-up rides cruising through town on summer weekend nights, though there are far fewer around now than in its heyday. For some of the craziest stories you'll ever read, check out the police blotter in the local paper, the *Rio Grande Sun* (www.riograndesun.com).

▣ Sleeping & Eating

Santa Claran   CASINO HOTEL **$$**
(Map p270; ☑ 877-505-4949; www.santaclaran. com; 460 N Riverside Dr; r from $100; ▣@⊛) Run by Santa Clara Pueblo, this upscale, earth-toned hotel is Española's nicest and most reliable option. The pueblo theme throughout adds some character. Even better than the casino is the 24-lane bowling center on the ground floor.

★ **El Parasol**   NEW MEXICAN **$**
(Map p270; ☑ 505-753-8852; www.elparasol.com; 603 Santa Cruz Rd; mains $3-6; ⊙ 7am-9pm) This tiny trailer, the somehow more delicious offspring of the fancy-ish *El Paragua* next door, is as local as it gets. Order at least two chicken-guacamole tacos – handfuls of greasy goodness – or the succulent *carne adovada* (pork in red chile), then eat in the shaded parking lot alongside. They've opened other branches, but this is still the best.

Ohkay Owingeh Pueblo

POP 6700 / ELEV 5660FT

Ohkay Owingeh Pueblo (Map p270; ☑505-852-4400), 5 miles north of Española, was visited in 1598 by Juan de Oñate, who named it San Juan and briefly designated it as the first capital of New Mexico. When it reverted to its original Tewa name in 2005, statues of Popé, who was born here and became the prime instigator of the 1680 Pueblo Revolt, were erected both here in the Pueblo plaza and in Statuary Hall in the US Congress in Washington DC.

Public events include the **Basket Dance** (January), **Deer Dance** (January or February), **Corn Dance** (June 13), **San Juan Feast Day** (June 23–24) and a series of Catholic and traditional dances and ceremonies (December 24–26).

The Pubelo-run **Oke Oweenge Crafts Cooperative** (☑505-852-2372; Hwy 74; ☺9am-4:30pm Mon-Sat) stocks a good selection of traditional red pottery, seed jewelry, weavings and drums.

Abiquiú

POP 230 / ELEV 6063FT

The tiny village of Abiquiú (sounds like 'barbeque'), on Hwy 84 about an hour's drive northwest of Santa Fe, is primarily famous thanks to Georgia O'Keeffe, who lived and painted here. With the Rio Chama flowing through farmland, and spectacular rock formations, the ethereal landscape continues to lure artists.

☉ Sights & Activities

Surrounded by red rock and high-desert terrain, **Abiquiú Lake & Dam** (Hwy 84; ☺dawn-dusk) is a beautiful swimming spot.

Georgia O'Keeffe Home   HOUSE

(☑505-685-4539; www.okeeffemuseum.org; tours $35-65; ☺Tue-Sat Jun-Oct, Tue & Thu-Fri mid-Mar–May & Nov, by private arrangement any other time) Georgia O'Keeffe died in 1986, at age 98. The Spanish Colonial adobe house she restored is open for guided visits, run by the Georgia O'Keeffe Museum in Santa Fe. Standard tours last one hour, while 'Behind the Scenes' tours are significantly longer. All tend to be booked months in advance, so plan ahead.

Dar Al Islam Mosque   MOSQUE

(www.daralislam.org) Muslims worship at this adobe mosque that welcomes visitors. From Hwy 84, take Hwy 554 (southeast of Abiquiú) toward El Rito, cross the Rio Chama, take your first left on to County Rd 155 and follow it for 3 miles. The mosque is up a dirt road on the right.

☰ Sleeping & Eating

★ **Abiquiú Inn**   HOTEL $$

(Map p270; ☑505-685-4378; www.abiquiuinn.com; US Hwy 84; r from $120, casitas from $220; ⓟ🛜)

GEORGIA O'KEEFFE

Although classically trained as a painter at art institutes in Chicago and New York, Georgia O'Keeffe was always uncomfortable with traditional European style. For four years after finishing school, she did not paint, and instead taught drawing and did graphic design.

After studying with Arthur Wesley Dow, who shared her distaste for the provincial, O'Keeffe began to develop her own style. She drew abstract shapes with charcoal, representing dreams and visions, and eventually returned to oils and watercolors. These first works caught the eye of her future husband and patron, photographer Alfred Stieglitz, in 1916.

In 1929 O'Keeffe visited Taos' Mabel Dodge Luhan Ranch and returned to paint *The Lawrence Tree*; the tree still presides over the **DH Lawrence Ranch** in northern New Mexico, which is no longer open to visitors. O'Keeffe tackled the San Francisco de Asis Church in Ranchos de Taos, painted by so many artists before her, in a way that had never been considered: only a fragment of the mission wall, contrasted against the blue of the sky.

It was no wonder O'Keeffe loved New Mexico's expansive skies, so similar to her paintings' negative spaces. As she spent more time here, landscapes and fields of blue permeated her work. During desert treks, she collected the smooth white bones of animals, subjects she placed against that sky in some of her most identifiable New Mexico pieces.

Telltale scrub marks and bristle impressions reveal how O'Keeffe blended and mixed her vibrant colors on the canvas itself – you'd never know that from photographs, which convey a false, airbrush-like smoothness. You can experience her work firsthand at Santa Fe's Georgia O'Keeffe Museum (p258).

This sprawling riverside collection of shaded faux-dobes is peaceful and lovely; some of the spacious rooms have kitchenettes.

Cafe Abiquiú NEW MEXICAN **$$**
(☎505-685-4378; www.abiquiuinn.com; Abiquiú Inn; breakfast $11, lunch & dinner $12-28; ☺7am-9pm) The restaurant in the main lodge building at the Abiquiú Inn is the best place to eat for miles around. Specialties include pistachio-crusted salmon and fresh trout tacos.

Bode's General Store DELI **$**
(www.bodes.com; US Hwy 84; mains $5-12; ☺6:30am-7pm Mon-Sat, to 6pm Sun; ☜) The hub of Abiquiú, Bode's (pronounced *boh-dees*) has been here ever since 1919. This is the place to buy everything from artsy postcards to fishing lures to saddle blankets. Grab a sandwich or tamale at the deli and hang out with the locals.

Ghost Ranch

From 1934 onwards, before she made her home in Abiquiú, Georgia O'Keeffe lived and worked for extended periods on a dude ranch amid the colorful canyonlands 15 miles northwest. Now a retreat center run by the Presbyterian Church, **Ghost Ranch** (☎505-685-1000; www.ghostranch.org; US Hwy 84; suggested donation $3; Day Pass adult/child $29/14.50; ♿) welcomes visitors and **overnight guests** (☎505-685-4333; www.ghostranch.org; US Hwy 84; tent/RV sites $23/27, dm incl board $53, r with shared/private bath incl breakfast $118/131; P).

Buying a day pass entitles you to visit the **Ruth Hall Museum of Paleontology** (adult/child $4/2; ☺9am-5pm Mon-Sat, 1-5pm Sun), which holds exhibits on a trove of dinosaurs found on this very spot; join a historical walking tour of the site; have lunch; and take part in an activity such as archery or climbing. Ghost Ranch also offers an additional program of guided tours covering themes such as Georgia O'Keeffe or the various movies (such as *City Slickers*) that have been filmed here, as well as **horseback riding** for riders of all levels, and for kids as young as four (trail rides $80, beginners' pony rides $20).

You don't need a day pass if you simply want to hike along the magnificent trails here, of which the best is the 3-mile round-trip trek to **Chimney Rock**. This distinctive landmark is visible from the highway, but the steep hike up to reach it, which takes around 40 minutes each way, is truly superb.

Stupendous views unfold the higher you climb, while Chimney Rock itself, an enormous pillar breaking off from the mesa-top, is breathtaking.

Monastery of Christ in the Desert

Day visitors are welcome at this ecosustainable **Benedictine monastery** (☎505-990-8581; www.christdesert.org; off Hwy 84; ☺9:15am-5pm), in a secluded geological wonderland, for a unique spiritual-architectural experience. So long as conditions aren't muddy, simply follow Forest Service Rd 151, a dirt road that leaves Hwy 84 5 miles north of Ghost Ranch, for 13 beautiful miles.

If you want to get away from it all for a while, you can also stay at the monastery (two-night minimum). Rates for the simple rooms (single/double $70/100), most of which are single and share bathrooms, include vegetarian meals served without conversation, plus outrageous trails and peace and quiet. Requested – not required – chores include minding the gift shop or tending the garden.

Ojo Caliente

At 140 years old, Ojo Caliente, 50 miles north of Santa Fe on Hwy 285, is one of the oldest health resorts in the US – and Pueblo Indians were using the hot springs long before that. The resort itself holds **soaking pools** (shared/private pools from $12/30) with various combinations of minerals, as well as a glorious mud bath. Hit the sauna and steam room before indulging in a superpampering **spa treatment** (massages $89-149, wraps $12-89, facials from $59, luxury packages from $124), a yoga class in a yurt, or hiking one of the trails. Admission to the pools is free for resort guests.

🛏 Sleeping & Eating

Ojo Caliente Mineral Springs Resort & Spa RESORT **$$**
(☎505-583-2233; www.ojospa.com; 50 Los Baños Rd; r $139-169, cottages $179-209, ste $229-349; ❄☜) In addition to pleasant, if nothing-special, historic hotel rooms, the resort has added some plush, boldly colored suites with kiva fireplaces and private soaking tubs, and New Mexican–style cottages.

Inn at Ojo B&B **$$**
(☎505-583-9131; www.ojocaliente.com; 11 Los Baños Dr; r $130; ❄☜) This friendly small-

scale alternative to the resort hotel, on the main approach road a short walk from the springs, offers bright, tastefully decorated rooms above a mercantile store, plus full breakfasts, with gluten-free options available.

Mesa Vista Cafe NEW MEXICAN $
(📞505-583-2245; Hwy 285; dishes $5-9; ⊙8am-9pm; 🍴) Simple diner on the highway near the resort, serving New Mexican favorites with plenty of veggie options as well as a recommended red chile cheeseburger.

Artesian Restaurant ORGANIC $$
(www.ojospa.com; breakfast $7-10, lunch $9-13, dinner $16-29; ⊙7:30am-11am, 11:30am-2:30pm & 5-9pm) The smart but relaxed dining room at the resort is open for all meals, and prepares organic and local ingredients with aplomb.

High Road to Taos

Go on, take the high road. Of the two routes between Santa Fe and Taos, the famous High Rd isn't necessarily any prettier than the faster Low Rd – beauty is relative here; both are gorgeous – but it has a special rural mountain feeling that is classic northern New Mexico. The road winds through river valleys, skirts sandstone cliffs and traverses high pine forests, all beneath the gaze of the 13,000ft Truchas Peaks. Villages enroute are filled with old adobe houses with pitched tin roofs. Massive firewood piles rise next to rusting, disassembled pickup trucks in yards surrounded by grassy horse pastures. Many of these towns are home to art studios and traditional handicraft workshops.

We've presented both High and Low routes from south to north. Many people drive the High Rd north from Santa Fe to Taos and take the Low Rd back, but actually you get more impressive vistas in both directions by taking the Low Rd north and the High Rd south.

To follow the High Rd from Santa Fe to Taos, take Hwy 84/285 to Pojoaque; turn right on Hwy 503, continue beyond Nambé, then take Hwy 76 to Hwy 75 to Hwy 518.

Nambé Pueblo

POP 1100 / ELEV 6079FT

Thanks perhaps to its isolated location (or inspirational geology), **Nambé Pueblo** (Map p270; 📞505-455-2036; www.nambepueblo. org) has long been a spiritual center for the Tewa-speaking tribes, a distinction that attracted the cruel attentions of Spanish priests intent on conversion by any means necessary. After the Pueblo Revolt and Reconquista wound down, Spanish settlers annexed much of their land.

Public events include **dances** at Nambé Falls on July 4, **San Francisco de Asis Feast Day** (October 4) and the **Buffalo Dance** (December 24).

Two lovely 20-minute hikes, starting from the Ramada Area 5 miles off Hwy 503, lead to the biggest attraction on Nambé lands, **Nambé Falls** (📞505-455-4400; nambepueblo. org; day-use per vehicle $10, camping $15 extra). The steep upper hike has a photogenic overlook of the falls, while the easier, lower hike along the river takes in ancient petroglyphs. The nearby Lake Nambé, created by the federal damming of the Rio Nambé in 1974, has been closed to visitors since its fish were killed by contaminated run-off following a 2011 forest fire.

Chimayó

POP 3200 / ELEV 6075FT

Even though by this point, 28 miles north of Santa Fe, the High Rd to Taos has barely climbed out of the valley, the Hispanic village of Chimayó is generally regarded as the single biggest attraction on the entire route. It's home to a little twin-towered adobe chapel, **El Santuario de Chimayó** (Map p270; 📞505-351-9961; www.elsantuariodechimayo.us; ⊙9am-5pm Oct-Apr, to 6pm May-Sep), which is not only extraordinarily pretty, but also ranks as perhaps the most important religious site in New Mexico. Often called the 'Lourdes of America,' the chapel was built in 1816, over a spot of earth said to have miraculous healing properties. The faithful come to rub the *tierra bendita* – holy dirt – from a small pit inside the church on whatever hurts; some mix it with water and drink it. The walls of the dirt room are covered with *milagros,* small tokens left by those who have been healed.

During Holy Week, around 30,000 pilgrims walk to Chimayó from Santa Fe, Albuquerque and beyond in the largest Catholic pilgrimage in the US, and the church now stands at the center of an ever-growing complex of gift shops, visitor centers and riverside gardens.

Chimayó is also famous for its arts and crafts, and has a centuries-old tradition of producing superb weaving. Family-run galleries sell magnificent creations.

🛏 Sleeping & Eating

Casa Escondida   B&B
(☎505-351-4805; www.casaescondida.com; 64
County Rd 100; r from $115; 🌐🐾) Set on 6 acres,
a mile or so north of Chimayó, this unpretentious and highly recommended B&B features eight beautiful rooms, all en suite and
furnished in Southwestern style. Some have
outdoor decks, all share use of a communal
covered porch and a hot tub.

Rancho de Chimayó   NEW MEXICAN $$
(☎505-984-2100; www.ranchodechimayo.com;
County Rd 98; mains $8-21; ⊙11:30am-9pm, closed
Mon Nov-Apr) Half a mile north of the Santuario, this bright, spacious garden-set restaurant
serves classic New Mexican cuisine, courtesy of the Jaramillo family's famed recipes.
Best of all is the basket of warm, fluffy
sopaipillas (puffed-up pastries) that comes
with each dish. The same management offers
cozy B&B rooms (from $79) across the street.

🛍 Shopping

★Centinela Traditional Arts   ARTS & CRAFTS
(☎505-351-2180; www.chimayoweavers.com; Hwy
76; ⊙9am-6pm Mon-Sat, 10am-5pm Sun) This
part studio, part cooperative gallery is run by
seventh-generation weaver Irvin Trujillo and
his wife Lisa. Irvin's work is displayed at the
Smithsonian in Washington DC and the Museum of Art in Santa Fe. Naturally dyed blankets, vests and pillows are sold, and you can
watch the couple weaving on handlooms.

Oviedo Gallery   ARTS & CRAFTS
(☎505-351-2280; www.oviedoart.com; Hwy 76;
⊙10am-6pm) The Oviedo family has been
carving native woods since 1739. Today the
Oviedo Gallery is housed in the centuries-
old family farm, and also displays and sells
a wide range of bronze sculptures, made in
the on-site foundry.

Truchas

POP 1200 / ELEV 8051FT

Rural New Mexico at its most sincere is
showcased in Truchas, originally settled by
the Spaniards in the 18th century. Robert
Redford's *The Milagro Beanfield War* was
filmed here (but don't bother with the movie –
the book it's based on, by John Nichols, is
waaay better).

To see the village itself, don't follow the
main road as it turns left toward Taos, but
head straight on uphill toward the Truchas
Peaks. Narrow roads, many unpaved, wend

between century-old adobes. Fields of grass
and alfalfa spread toward the sheer walls
and plunging ridges of the mountains. Between the run-down homes, some wonderful
galleries double as workshops for local weavers, painters, sculptors and other artists.

🛏 Sleeping

Rancho Arriba   B&B
(☎505-689-2374; www.ranchoarriba.com; Main Truchas Rd; r with shared/private bath $90/120; 🖳🐾)
High up at the far end of Truchas village, near
the point where trails head off into the Pecos
Wilderness, this sprawling old ranch complex
offers three B&B rooms in an adobe farmhouse. They have horses and wood stoves,
and serve dinner given advance notice.

🛍 Shopping

Cordovas Handweaving
Workshop   ARTS & CRAFTS
(☎505-689-1124; Main Truchas Rd; ⊙irregu-
lar hours) Watch Harry, a friendly fourth-
generation weaver, at work, in between
browsing his beautiful blankets, placemats
and rugs.

High Road Marketplace   ARTS & CRAFTS
(☎505-689-2689; www.highroadmarketplace.com;
1642 Hwy 76; ⊙10am-5pm, to 4pm winter) This
cooperative art gallery displays a huge range
of work by regional artists, from potters and
painters to quilters and metalworkers.

Ojo Sarco Pottery   ARTS & CRAFTS
(☎505-689-2354; www.ojosarco.com; County Rd
73; ⊙10am-5pm May-Dec, closed Jan-Apr) Turn
left 6 miles north of Truchas, onto County
Rd 73, then follow signs to find this gallery
and check out the fine clay creations of master potters Kathy Riggs and Jake Willson,
as well as work by other local artists, from
glass-crafters to bell-makers.

Las Trampas

POP 250 / ELEV 7802FT

Completed in 1780 and constantly defend-
ed against Apache raids, the sturdy adobe
Church of San José de Gracia (☎505-351-
4360; Hwy 76; ⊙by appointment, call ahead) in tiny
Las Trampas is considered one of the finest
surviving 18th-century churches in the US
and is a National Historic Landmark. It's still
surrounded by a low adobe wall, while the
paintings and carvings inside remain in excellent condition. Self-flagellation bloodstains
from the Penitentes, a 19th-century religious

RÍO GRANDE DEL NORTE NATIONAL MONUMENT

A vast wedge of northern New Mexico, covering 380 sq miles, was designated in 2013 as **Río Grande del Norte National Monument** (☎575-758-8851; www.blm.gov/nm/riograndedelnorte). From its southernmost tip, near Pilar 20 miles south of Taos, it stretches north along the Rio Grande as far as the Colorado state line, and also fans into the roadless wilderness to the west. Administered by the Bureau of Land Management (BLM), it was created to protect vital wildlife habitat, including a corridor used by migratory birds, and to guard against mining and mineral exploitation.

As far as most visitors are concerned, the monument consists of three major components. The first is the **Rio Grande** itself, and in particular the mighty gorge west of Taos, a prime white-water rafting destination. The other two are the Lower and Upper Gorge areas, south and north of Taos. Each offers scenic driving, camping, and, above all, superb hiking.

For information on the **Lower Gorge**, call in at the **Rio Grande Gorge Visitor Center** (Map p270; ☎575-751-4899; Hwy 68; ☺8am-4:30pm May-Oct, 10am-2pm Sep-Apr), where Hwy 68 meets Hwy 570. This popular stretch of river, also known as the **Orilla Verde Recreation Area** (Map p270; day-use $3, tent/RV sites $7/15), features flat water appreciated by fishers and inner-tubers, as well as waterside picnic tables and campgrounds. Six miles along from Hwy 68, Hwy 570 crosses the Rio Grande to reach the **Taos Junction Campground**, and then its surface turns to dirt. You can't drive beside the river all the way to Taos, but hiking trails climb either side of the gorge. We like the 1.3-mile **Slide**, which heads east up a dirt road blocked by a landslide, to give expansive vistas of the Taos Plateau and the Sangre de Cristo Mountains. Alternatively, the 9-mile **West Rim Trail** heads all the way north to the Rio Grande Gorge Bridge northwest of Taos. The walking itself is easy, but you'll need a vehicle pickup at the far end; it also makes a great biking route.

To reach the **Upper Gorge**, drive north of Taos on Hwy 522 for 27 miles, then turn west beyond Questa to follow the spectacular 13-mile Wild Rivers Backcountry Byway, beside one of the most impressive stretches of the Rio Grande Gorge, into the **Wild Rivers Recreation Area** (day use $3, campsite $5-7). Several vantage points offer stupendous views – be sure not to miss the Chawalauna Overlook – while a **visitor center** (Map p270; ☎575-586-1150; ☺9am-6pm May-Sep) has details on hiking and camping; five semideveloped tent campgrounds are accessible by car, while hikers can also reach riverside campsites down in the canyon. The **La Junta Trail** plunges 800ft down into the canyon to access the confluence of the Rio Grande and the Red River. It's only 1.3 miles one-way, but the trek back up again is so steep that you'd do better to stay down beside the Rio Grande and hike to the **Little Arsenic Campground**. Climb the gentler (but still demanding) trail to the rim from there to complete a 5-mile loop that takes around three hours.

order with a strong following in the northern mountains of New Mexico, remain visible.

Picuris Pueblo

POP 200 / ELEV 5852FT

Tucked away inconspicuously below the High Rd, just west of the junction of Hwy 76 and Hwy 75, **Picuris Pueblo** (☎575-587-2519; photo/video permits $5/10; ☺8am-5pm Mon-Fri) was once among the largest and most powerful Pueblos in New Mexico. The Picuris built adobe cities at least seven stories tall and boasted a population approaching 3000. After the Pueblo Revolt and Reconquista, when many retreated to Kansas rather than face De Vargas' wrath, only 500 returned. Between raids by the Spanish and Comanches, their numbers continued to dwindle.

Call well in advance to arrange a guided Pueblo tour, taking in their small buffalo herd, organic gardens, ruins from the old Pueblo site and the exquisite 1770 **San Lorenzo de Picuris Church**. The unique tower kiva is off-limits to visitors but makes an impression even from the outside. The small **Picuris Pueblo Museum** (Map p521; ☎505-587-1099; ☺irregular hours) displays artifacts and artworks. The best time to visit is during the popular **San Lorenzo Feast Days** (August 9 and 10), which sees food and craft booths, dances, races and pole climbs.

Peñasco

POP 600 / ELEV 7685FT

This scenic village along the Rio Santa Barbara and beneath **Jicarita Peak** (12,835ft) is the gateway to the less crowded northern side of the **Pecos Wilderness**. You'll find trailheads at nearby **Santa Barbara Campground** (Map p270; tent & RV sites $16), which has 22 RV/ tent sites. From there, it's possible to access the **Skyline Trail**, a multiday backpacking loop that traverses above-treeline ridges and can easily include ascents of **Truchas Peak** (13,102ft), New Mexico's second-highest, and Jicarita; both are nontechnical walk-ups.

🏃 Activities

Sipapu Ski Resort   SKIING

(☏800-587-2240; www.sipapunm.com; lift tickets adult/13-20yr/7-12 yr $44/37/29; 🚗) The snow and terrain at this small, family-oriented ski resort on Hwy 518, 10 miles east of Peñasco toward Mora, can't compare to Taos Ski Valley, but lift tickets are cheap and special deals make it a reasonable place to bring the kids. In summer, Sipapu has one of the country's top-ranked disc (Frisbee) golf courses.

🍴 Eating

Sugar Nymphs Bistro   CAFE **$$**

(☏575-587-0311; www.sugarnymphs.com; 15046 Hwy 75; mains $10-15; ⊙11:30am-2:30pm Mon-Wed, 11:30am-2:30pm & 5-7:30pm Thu-Sat, 11am-2:30pm Sun) Alongside the Peñasco Theatre and part of the same operation, this homespun little bistro serves gourmet comfort food using local produce, including a great goat's cheese salad and desserts that often sell out.

☆ Entertainment

Peñasco Theatre   THEATER

(☏575-587-2726; www.penascotheatre.org; 15046 Hwy 75) Historic theater that offers myriad programs, concerts, movies and classes throughout the year, including weeklong youth circus camps in summer, thanks to its close connection with Wise Fool, a collective of performance artists who blend clowning, trapeze, puppetry, music and other forms of storytelling.

Low Road to Taos

Don't let the fact that it starts from unpromising Española – take Hwy 84/285 from Santa Fe to Hwy 68 – put you off driving the Low Rd to Taos. It's a spectacular route, heading north through the Rio Grande Gorge, between towering walls of granite, sculpted volcanic tuff and black basalt. The river tumbles by on your left, carrying tourist-packed white-water rafts downstream, with numerous waterfront pull-off and picnic spots.

Ultimately, the road climbs steeply out of the gorge to emerge onto the Taos Plateau. The first vista is truly awesome, with both the Sangre de Cristo Mountains straight ahead, and the awesome river canyon to your left, coming suddenly and simultaneously into view.

Embudo

POP 300 / ELEV 5880FT

Tiny Embudo, 18 miles north of Española, is no more than a cluster of low-slung homes and ranches on the east side of the highway.

As you drive through Embudo, your eye will inevitably be caught by the array of ancient gas pumps and Route 66 paraphernalia outside **Classical Gas** (Map p270; ☏505-852-2995; Mile 18, Hwy 68; ⊙9am-5pm). What's inside is even better: a dazzling array of historic neon signs, put together as a true labor of love by retiree Johnnie Meier.

On the east side of the highway a short way south of Classical Gas, tin-clad trailer **Sugar's BBQ** (Map p270; ☏505-852-0604; 1799 Hwy 68; mains $5-12; ⊙11am-6pm Thu-Sun) has, thanks to its sublimely juicy barbecue, been hailed one of the top 10 roadside joints in America by *Gourmet* magazine. Brisket burritos = genius.

Dixon

POP 800 / ELEV 6080FT

As you drive through the Rio Grande Gorge, it's well worth taking a slight detour east on Hwy 75, just north of Embudo, to reach this small farming and artist community, a couple of miles off the main road in the gorgeous Rio Embudo Valley. Dixon is famous for its apple orchards, but other crops are grown here too; try to catch the local **farmers market** on Wednesday afternoon in summer and fall, with food fresh from the fields. By the way if you ask at the local food co-op, some kind soul might point you to the **waterfalls**, which are up a nearby dirt road. New Mexico's original **studio tour** (www.dixonarts.org) is still going strong in Dixon; it's held the first full weekend in November.

Sights

Vivac Winery WINERY

(Map p270; 505-579-4441; www.vivacwinery. com; 2075 Hwy 68; tasting $6; 10am-6pm Mon-Sat, from 11am Sun) Right where Hwy 68 meets Hwy 75, this winery is run by the genial Padberg brothers, born and raised in Dixon. Vintages in their tasting room include a highly rated Syrah – and be sure to sample the handmade chocolates.

La Chiripada Winery WINERY

(Map p270; 505-579-4437; www.lachiripada. com; Hwy 75; 11am-6pm Mon-Sat, from noon Sun) Award-winning vintner, 2.5 miles east of Hwy 68 along Hwy 75, that only uses New Mexican grapes. Excellent and relatively inexpensive white wines include a fine riesling at $20 a bottle. As well as offering tastings here, they also run a tasting room in Taos, at 103 Bent St.

Sleeping & Eating

For such a small village, there are plenty of great guesthouses, including the charming adobe **La Casita** (505-579-4297; www.vrbo. com/79296; casita $95;); **Rock Pool Gardens** (505-579-4602; www.vrbo.com/107806; ste $95;), with an indoor heated pool; and **Tower Guest House** (505-579-4288; www.vrbo.com/118083; cottage $95;) on a working garlic farm beside the Rio Embudo. Book rooms well in advance during November's studio tour.

Zuly's Cafe CAFE $

(Map p270; 505-579-4001; 234 Hwy 75; mains $6-14; 7:30am-3pm Tue-Thu, 7:30am-8pm Fri, 9am-8pm Sat) This superfriendly place, run by Dixon native Chalako Chilton, serves some of the best green chile you'll find anywhere, plus espresso coffees.

Rinconada & Pilar

The small community of Rinconada, just north of Dixon on Hwy 68, is home to an appealing little pub as well as a few galleries. Seven miles further north, immediately before Hwy 68 starts its climb toward Taos, tiny Pilar serves as access point for the southernmost portion of the new Río Grande del Norte National Monument. To reach the river, branch off the main road onto Hwy 570.

Drinking

Blue Heron Brewing Co BREWERY

(505-579-9188; www.blueheronbrews.com; 2214 Hwy 68, Rinconada; noon-6pm Sun-Tue, 10am-8pm Wed-Sat) Funky little adobe, formerly a veterinarian's office, where local brewmasters pour handcrafted ales in an arty cafe space – it's a great spot to grab a pint or a jug.

Shopping

Rift Gallery ARTS & CRAFTS

(505-579-9179; www.saxstonecarving.com; 2249 Hwy 68, Rinconada; 10am-5pm Wed-Sun) Just up the road from the Blue Heron, this gallery showcases the work of sculptor Mark Saxe and Betsy Williams, a potter specializing in the Japanese Karatsu tradition. Each summer, they host highly regarded weeklong stone-carving workshops.

Stephen Kilborn's Studio ARTS & CRAFTS

(575-758-0135; www.stephenkilborn.com; Hwy 68, Pilar; 10am-5pm Mon-Sat, from 11am Sun) The whimsically painted Southwestern-style pottery here puts the 'fun' into functional; sometimes there are great deals on 'factory' seconds.

TAOS

POP 5700 / ELEV 6960FT

A magical spot even by the standards of this land of enchantment, Taos remains forever under the spell of the powerful landscape that surrounds it: 12,300ft snowcapped peaks rise behind town, while a sage-speckled plateau unrolls to the west before plunging 800ft straight down into the Rio Grande Gorge. The sky can be a searing sapphire blue or an ominous parade of rumbling thunderheads so big they dwarf the mountains. And then there are the sunsets...

Taos Pueblo, a marvel of adobe architecture, ranks among the oldest continuously inhabited communities in the US, and stands at the root of a long history that also extends from conquistadors to cowboys. Kit Carson – legendary mountain man, soldier and Indian enemy turned Indian advocate – settled here in 1842. His name is still found everywhere, from the main street in the historic district to the surrounding national forest to the local electric company.

A broken wagon wheel stranded artists Bert Phillips and Ernest Blumenschein in Taos in 1898. They stayed, and their reasons

NEW MEXICO TAOS

Taos Area

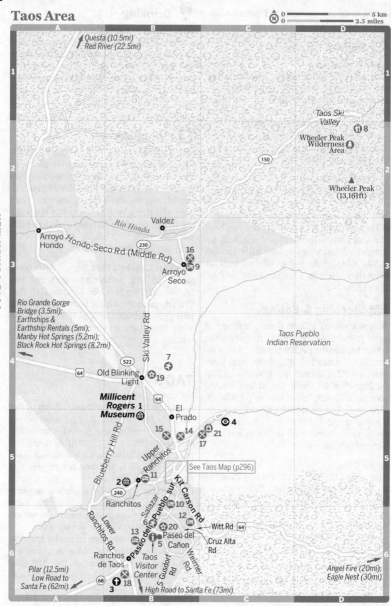

N

0 ——— 5 km
0 ——— 2.5 miles

Questa (10.5mi);
Red River (22.5mi)

Taos Ski
Valley

8

Wheeler Peak
Wilderness
Area

150

Wheeler Peak
(13,161ft)

Rio Honda

Valdez

Arroyo
Hondo

Hondo-Seco Rd (Middle Rd)

230

16
9

Arroyo
Seco

Rio Grande Gorge
Bridge (3.5mi);
Earthships &
Earthship Rentals (5mi);
Manby Hot Springs (5.2mi);
Black Rock Hot Springs (8.2mi)

Taos Pueblo
Indian Reservation

Ski Valley Rd

522

64

Old Blinking
Light

19

7

Millicent
Rogers 1
Museum

64

El
Prado

4

15
14

21

17

Blueberry Hill Rd

Upper
Ranchitos

See Taos Map (p296)

Kit Carson Rd

2
11

240

Ranchitos

10

Salazar

Paseo del Pueblo Sur

12

Witt Rd
64

Lower Ranchitos Rd

13

6

20

Cruz Alta
Rd

Weimer Rd

Paseo del Pueblo Sur

S Gusdorf Rd

5
Paseo del
Cañon

i

Ranchos
de Taos

Taos
Visitor
Center

Pilar (12.5mi)
Low Road to
Santa Fe (62mi)

68

3

18

Angel Fire (20mi);
Eagle Nest (30mi)

High Road to Santa Fe (73mi)

NEW MEXICO TAOS

for staying soon got out; before too long an artists' enclave, drawn by light unencumbered by the weight of atmosphere, by colors at once subtle and brilliant, was formed. Today Taos is home to around 100 galleries, and about 30% of locals call themselves artists.

This little town also became a magnet for writers and creative thinkers. DH Lawrence dreamed of building a utopia here; Carl Jung was deeply affected by his visit to Taos Pueblo, and Aldous Huxley found some of his inspiration for *Brave New World* there; Dennis Hop-

Taos Area

per shot key scenes from *Easy Rider* around Taos, and was so enchanted he moved here.

Taos remains a relaxed and eccentric place, with classic mud-brick buildings, fabulous museums, quirky cafes and excellent restaurants. Its 5700 residents include bohemians, hippies, alternative-energy aficionados and old-time Hispanic families. It's both rural and worldly, and a little bit otherworldly.

◎ Sights

The most compelling attraction in the Taos area is unquestionably Taos Pueblo (p303), the largest surviving multistoried Pueblo, built around 1450. Taos itself is surprisingly small – once you've strolled beneath the verandahs of the old adobes that surround picturesque **Taos Plaza**, and explored the shops along Bent St to the north and Kit Carson Lane to the east, you've pretty much seen the entire downtown core – but it boasts a phenomenal crop of top-quality museums, galleries and attractions.

The Museum Association of Taos sells a $25 pass, valid for a year, that covers admission to the five most important museums – the Millicent Rogers, Harwood Foundation and Taos Art museums, plus the Blumenschein Home and Martínez Hacienda. Visit them all, and you'll save $19.

⭐ **Millicent Rogers Museum**　　MUSEUM
(Map p292; ☎575-758-2462; www.millicentrogers. org; 1504 Millicent Rogers Rd; adult/child $10/2; ⊙10:10am-5pm Apr-Oct, closed Mon Nov-Mar) Rooted in the private collection of model

and oil heiress Millicent Rogers, who moved to Taos in 1947, this superb museum, 4 miles northwest of the Plaza, ranges from Hispanic folk art to Navajo weaving, and even modernist jewelry designed by Rogers herself. The principal focus is on Native American ceramics, and especially the beautiful black-on-black pottery created during the 20th century by Maria Martínez from San Ildefonso Pueblo.

Martínez Hacienda　　MUSEUM
(Map p292; ☎575-758-1000; www.taoshistoric museums.org; 708 Hacienda Way, off Lower Ranchitos Rd; adult/child $8/4; ⊙10am-5pm Mon-Sat, noon-5pm Sun Apr-Oct, Mon-Tue & Thu-Sat 10am-4pm Nov-Mar) Set amid the fields 2 miles southwest of the Plaza, this fortified adobe homestead was built in 1804. It served as a trading post, first for merchants venturing north from Mexico City along the Camino Real, and then west along the Santa Fe Trail. Its 21 rooms, arranged around a courtyard, are furnished with the few possessions that even a wealthy family of the era would have been able to afford. Cultural events are held here regularly.

Harwood Foundation Museum　　MUSEUM
(Map p296; ☎575-758-9826; www.harwood museum.org; 238 Ledoux St; adult/child $10/free; ⊙10am-5pm Mon-Sat, noon-5pm Sun Apr-Oct, closed Mon Nov-Mar) Attractively displayed in a gorgeous and very spacious mid-19th-century adobe compound, the paintings, drawings, prints, sculpture and photographs here are predominantly the work of northern New

TOP 10 TAOS

Taos Pueblo (p303) For breathtaking architecture, Native American history and delicious fry bread.

Taos Ski Valley (p304) For champagne powder, tree glades and snowboarding.

Mabel Dodge Luhan House (p298) For a night's sleep evoking Taos' bohemian heyday.

Millicent Rogers Museum (p293) For a look at one of the finest collections of Southwestern jewelry and art anywhere.

Adobe Bar (p301) For a potent margarita and live music.

Martínez Hacienda (p293) For a flavor of life in a Hispanic frontier town.

Earthship Rentals (p298) For sleeping off the grid.

Rafting the Taos Box (p297) For sheer white-water thrills.

Rio Grande Gorge Bridge (p294) For the view.

Taos Plaza (p293) For wandering.

Mexican artists, both historical and contemporary. Founded in 1923, the Harwood is the second-oldest museum in New Mexico, and is as strong on local Hispanic traditions as it is on Taos' 20th-century school.

Blumenschein Home & Museum   MUSEUM
(Map p296; ☎ 575-758-0505; www.taoshistoric museums.org; 222 Ledoux St; adult/child $8/4; ⊙10am-5pm Mon-Sat, noon-5pm Sun Apr-Oct, Mon-Tue & Thu-Sat 10am-4pm Nov-Mar) Wonderfully preserved adobe residence, dating originally from 1797, which provides a vivid glimpse of life in Taos' artistic community during the 1920s. Ernest L Blumenschein, founding member of the Taos Society of Artists, lived here with his wife and daughter, Mary and Helen Greene Blumenschein, both also artists, and every room remains alive with their artworks and personal possessions.

Taos Art Museum & Fechin Institute   MUSEUM
(Map p296; ☎ 575-758-2690; www.taosartmuseum. org; 227 Paseo del Pueblo Norte; adult/child $8/free; ⊙10am-5pm Tue-Sun May-Oct, to 4pm Nov-Apr) Russian artist Nicolai Fechin moved to Taos in 1926, aged 46, and adorned the interior of this adobe home with his own distinctly Russian woodcarvings between 1928 and 1933. Now a museum, it displays Fechin's paintings and sketches along with his private collection and choice works by members of the Taos Society of Artists, and also hosts occasional chamber music performances in summer.

Earthships   ARCHITECTURE
(Map p270; ☎ 575-613-4409; www.earthship.com; US Hwy 64; self-guided tours $7; ⊙9am-6pm Apr-Oct, 10am-4pm Nov-Mar) 🌱 Numbering 70 Earthships, with capacity for 60 more, Taos' pioneering community was the brainchild of architect Michael Reynolds. Built with recycled materials like used automobile tires and cans, and buried on three sides, Earthships heat and cool themselves, make their own electricity and catch their own water; dwellers grow their own food. Stay overnight (p298) if possible; the 'tour' is a little disappointing. The visitor center is 1.5 miles west of the Rio Grande Gorge Bridge on US Hwy 64.

San Francisco de Asís Church   CHURCH
(Map p292; ☎ 575-751-0518; St Francis Plaza, Ranchos de Taos; ⊙9am-4pm Mon-Fri) Just off Hwy 68 in Ranchos de Taos, 4 miles south of Taos Plaza, this iconic church was completed in 1815. Famed for the rounded curves and stark angles of its sturdy adobe walls, it was repeatedly memorialized by Georgia O'Keeffe in paint, and Ansel Adams with his camera. Mass is celebrated at 6pm the first Saturday of the month, and usually at 7am, 9am and 11:30am every Sunday.

Rio Grande Gorge Bridge   BRIDGE, CANYON
(Map p270) Constructed in 1965, this vertigo-inducing steel bridge carries Hwy 64 across the Rio Grande about 12 miles northwest of Taos. It's the seventh-highest bridge in the US, 650ft above the river and measuring 500ft wide. The views from the pedestrian walkway, west over the empty Taos Plateau as well as down the jagged walls of the gorge, will surely make you gulp as you gape. Vendors selling jewelry, sage sticks and other souvenirs congregate on the eastern side.

Kit Carson Home & Museum   MUSEUM
(Map p296; ☎ 575-758-4945; www.kitcarsonhome andmuseum.com; 113 Kit Carson Rd; adult/child $7/5; ⊙10am-5pm) A short walk east of the Plaza, the little-changed former home of Kit Carson (1809–68) – perhaps the Southwest's most famous mountain man, guide,

trapper, soldier and scout – is now a monument to his memory. Only five of its 12 rooms, built in 1825 with 30in adobe walls, are open to visitors. Furnished as Carson might have known them, they hold artifacts including his rifles, telescope, walking cane and saber.

 Activities

Hike, bike, raft, ski, fish… the sheer range of outdoor activities in the Taos area is exhaustive. Local outfitters can help you plan and execute your outdoor excursions.

Winter Sports

In winter it's all about skiing. Most of the action takes place at the Taos Ski Valley (p304), a ski and snowboard resort located 20 miles northeast of the town itself, which holds a slew of lodging and eating options.

The best cross-country skiing hereabouts is at the Enchanted Forest up by Red River (p306), a 40-mile drive northeast, but there's also a great little area in Carson National Forest at **Amole Canyon**, 15 miles south of Taos on Hwy 518.

Just north of Amole Canyon along Hwy 518, **US Hill** – the primo sledding spot in the area – is the most popular place around for kids to get frostbitten and bruised and love every minute of it.

Cottam's Ski & Outdoor   OUTDOORS
(Map p296; ☑800-322-8267; www.cottamski shops.com; 207a Paseo del Pueblo Sur; ⊙7am-8pm in season) A reliable place to rent or buy whatever winter gear you need, with another location at the Tao Ski Valley.

Mountain Biking

Where else are you going to find mountain biking this good, this close to the sky? Why bother looking elsewhere when an enormous network of mountain-bike and multi-use trails cover the region of the **Carson National Forest** (Map p270) between Taos, Angel Fire and Picuris Peak.

The Taos Visitor Center (p302) stocks a surprising amount of information on mountain biking. Standouts include the 9-mile **West Rim Trail** in the Orilla Verde section of Río Grande del Norte National Monument, which enables strong beginners and intermediate cyclists to enjoy views of the Rio Grande Gorge. Considered one of the nation's best mountain-bike trails, the storied **South Boundary Trail** is a 28-mile ride for experienced cyclists.

If you really want to challenge yourself, try the 84-mile **Enchanted Circle** loop. It makes a fine regional road-bike circuit once you've acclimatized to the altitude.

Gearing Up Bicycle Shop   MOUNTAIN BIKING
(Map p296; ☑575-751-0365; www.gearingup-bikes.com; 129 Paseo del Pueblo Sur; bikes per day from $50; ⊙9:30am-6pm Mon-Sat, noon-5pm Sun Jun-Sep, shorter hours rest of year) For mountain-biking info, trail maps, spares and equipment – not to mention bikes – drop in at this friendly central shop, which also rents full-suspension bikes.

Hiking & Hot Springs

While there are several day-use trails just outside of Taos, particularly on the south side of Hwy 64 east of town, the best day hiking and backpacking is a little further afield, up in the Wild Rivers area of Río Grande del Norte National Monument, and in the Latir Peak and Pecos wildernesses.

A couple of fabulous hot springs close to the Rio Grand Gorge – and now incorporated into the new national monument – can be reached by hiking from dirt roads west of Arroyo Hondo, some 9 miles north of Taos. The more readily accessible is **Black Rock Hot Springs** near the John Dunn Bridge. **Manby Hot Springs** (aka Stagecoach Hot Springs) is harder to find, but it's a worthy place of pilgrimage – this is where the hot-springs scenes were shot in *Easy Rider*.

NEW MEXICO TAOS

ANDEAN-ESQUE ADVENTURE

Not everyone who loves to hike and camp has the stamina – or desire – to haul a pack around at 11,000ft above sea level. Around Taos, you don't need to – that's what the llamas are for. **Wild Earth Llama Adventures** (☑800-758-5262; www.llamaadventures.com) runs day hikes and multiday treks in the sweetest spots in the Sangres. They're experts at getting even young kids out into the backcountry, and their lead guide also happens to be a chef. No, no llama riding, but you'll be too busy doing your 'Julie Andrews in an alpine meadow' impersonation to care.

Day trips (adult/child $99/69) run year-round; multiday trips (adult/child from $375/125 for two days, one night) run from March to November and can be customized to your needs.

NEW MEXICO TAOS

Taos

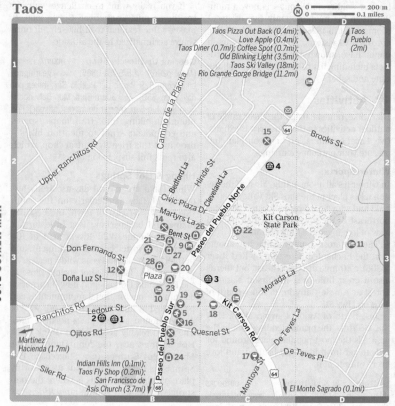

Mudd-n-Flood
OUTDOORS

(Map p296; ☑575-751-9100; www.muddnflood.com; 103a Bent St; ⊙10am-6pm) This evocatively named store, just north of the Plaza, is well stocked with outdoor supplies, and usually has a substantial sale rack. The folk behind the counter know what they're talking about.

Taos Mountain Outfitters
OUTDOORS

(Map p296; ☑575-758-9292; www.taosmountain outfitters.com; 113 N Plaza; ⊙10am-6pm) Huge store on the Plaza, selling or renting everything you need to get out and play. The helpful staff can supply hiking info and maps.

Rafting

Poised between the Box and Racecourse sections of the Rio Grande, Taos is in an ideal position for seeking white-water satisfaction. Rafting companies run trips to the frothy Taos Box, north of town, when there's enough water to boat it – usually in late spring and early summer. This stretch of river is not for the easily panicked; the rapids can hit Class V (most difficult but still possible, with Class VI being something like 'certain death'), and the remote feeling of the canyon makes it all that much more intense. From spring to fall, the Racecourse – downriver at Pilar – is perpetually popular; it's exciting, but rarely feels death-defying.

Los Rios River Runners
RAFTING

(Map p292; ☑575-776-8854; www.losriosriver runners.com; 1033 Paseo Del Pueblo Sur; Box trips $105-125, Racecourse trips adult/child $54/44, 3-day Chama trips adult/child $495/375; ⊙8am-6pm) Half-day trips on the Racecourse – in one- and two-person kayaks if you prefer – full-day trips on the Box (minimum age 12), and multinight expeditions on the scenic Chama. On the 'Native Cultures Feast and Float' ($85) you're accompanied by a Native American guide and have lunch homemade by a local Pueblo family. Rates rise slightly at weekends.

Fishing

The creeks, rivers and lakes around Taos hold enough variety to please experts and beginners alike, and scenery ranging from deep rocky canyons to high alpine meadows. Teach the kids at Eagle Nest Lake (p307) or the Orilla Verde (p289) section of Río Grande del Norte National Monument, take your fly rod up to the Red River (p306) or down to the Rio Santa Barbara. Don't forget to pick up a one-/five-day license for $12/24.

Taos Fly Shop
FISHING

(☑575-751-1312; www.taosflyshop.com; 308c Paseo del Pueblo Sur; ⊙8am-6pm, shorter hours in winter) If you're looking for the right flies for the waters around Taos, stop by this helpful shop and find out what's hatching where. They have expert guides (half-/full day from $250/350) and offer fly-fishing instruction.

Horseback Riding

Rio Grande Stables
HORSEBACK RIDING

(Map p292; ☑575-776-5913; www.lajitasstables. com/taos.htm; ⊙mid-May–mid-Sep) Based up by the Taos Ski Valley, this recommended company offers rides from one to four hours ($50 to $105), all-day rides (including a $175 trip to the top of Wheeler Peak) and combination horseback/rafting/camping treks they'll customize just for you. Call in advance.

☞ Tours

Historic Taos Trolley Tours
HISTORICAL

(Map p292; ☑505-550-5612; www.taostrolley tours.com; cnr Paseo del Pueblo Sur & Paseo del Cañon; adult/child $33/10; ⊙10:30am & 2pm May-Oct) Two different tours aboard red trolleys, with pick-ups at the visitor center and the Plaza. Both include the Plaza and San Francisco de Asís church, but Tuesday to Saturday they go to Taos Pueblo, while Sunday and Monday they take in Millicent Rogers Museum and the Martínez Hacienda. Fares might sound steep, but they include the relevant admissions.

★ Festivals & Events

Taos sees numerous athletic and cultural events all year, as well as visual arts workshops; the visitor center (p302) has details. Some of the most memorable and unique are held at Taos Pueblo. In theory the green Solar Music Festival (www.solarmusicfest.com) takes place in June, though it's recently been in a state of flux; check the website for the latest news. The Fiestas de Taos (www.fiestas detaos) in mid-July rock with New Mexican music and dance, and fill the streets with parades. Christmas holiday celebrations include mass at San Francisco de Asís Church, while carolers and *farolitos* (little candles in paper bags) everywhere help keep spirits bright.

🛏 Sleeping

Accommodation options in Taos range from free camping in national forests to gourmet B&Bs in historic adobes. Rates fluctuate week to week, but it's not a place where you can expect to find a decent room in summer for much under $100. June to September and December to February are usually considered high season, with a major spike around Christmas. Reservation services include the **Taos Association of Bed & Breakfast Inns** (www.taos-bandb-inns.com).

★ **Doña Luz Inn** B&B $

(Map p296; ☑ 575-758-9000; www.stayintaos.com; 114 Kit Carson Rd; r $94-229; ✳@🛜) Funky and fun, this central B&B is a labor of love by owner Paul Castillo. Rooms are decorated in colorful themes from Spanish Colonial to Native American, with abundant art, murals and artifacts plus adobe fireplaces, kitchenettes and hot tubs. The cozy La Luz room is the best deal in town, and there are also sumptuous larger suites.

Sagebrush Inn HOTEL $

(Map p292; ☑ 505-758-2254; 1508 Paseo del Pueblo Sur; r from $89; ✳🐾) Parts of this lawn-set adobe hotel, 3 miles south of the Plaza, date back to 1929; you can even stay in Georgia O'Keeffe's old room. The public spaces share an appealing Southwestern-theme decor, and there are two pools and three hot tubs. The fancier suites are nice, the standard rooms more ordinary, though the good-value rates include cooked breakfast.

Indian Hills Inn HOTEL $

(☑ 575-758-4293; www.indianhillsinntaosplaza. com; 233 Paseo del Pueblo Sur; r from $89; ✳@🛜🐾) The Indian Hills Inn is really nothing special, but if you want a budget hotel near the Plaza, you won't find anything cheaper, and at least there's a swimming pool and sociable barbecue area. The Deluxe King rooms are noticeably nicer than the Double Queen family rooms.

★ **Earthship Rentals** BOUTIQUE HOTEL $$

(Map p270; ☑ 575-751-0462; www.earthship.com; US Hwy 64; Earthship $145-350; 🛜🐾) 🖋 How about an off-grid night in a boutique-chic, solar-powered dwelling? Part Gaudí-esque visions, part space-age fantasy, these futuristic structures are built using recycled tires and aluminum cans, not that those components are visible. Set on a beautiful mesa across the river 14 miles northwest, they offer a unique experience, albeit rather different to staying in Taos itself. Drop-ins welcome.

★ **Mabel Dodge Luhan House** HISTORIC HOTEL $$

(Map p296; ☑ 505-751-9686; www.mabeldodgeluhan.com; 240 Morada Lane; r from $105; 🅿) Every inch of this rambling compound, once home to Mabel Dodge Luhan, the so-called 'Patroness of Taos,' exudes elegant-meets-earthy beauty. Sleep where Georgia O'Keeffe, Willa

TAOS SOCIETY OF ARTISTS

In 1893, artist Joseph Henry Sharp visited Taos to prepare a set of illustrations depicting the Pueblo for publication. Smitten with the scene, Sharp spread the word among his colleagues about his 'discovery,' and shortly afterward relocated here permanently.

Ernest Blumenschein, Bert Phillips and many more of his contemporaries followed, and in 1912 they, along with Oscar Berninghaus, Eanger Irving Couse and Herbert Dunton, established the Taos Society of Artists (TSA). The original six were later joined by other prominent painters, including Lucy Harwood, the only female member, and Juan Mirabol from Taos Pueblo.

Early TSA paintings were inspired by the backdrop of the Sangre de Cristo Mountains as well as the buildings and people of Taos Pueblo. Set against the tonal shapes and neutral colors of earth, human figures act as flashes of color seen nowhere else in the desert. Pueblo architecture, with clusters of organic and sculptural block shapes reflecting the high desert light, also appealed to the Taos painters' artistic sensibilities.

The artists' styles were as diverse and experimental as the many philosophies of painting that defined the first half of the 20th century. From Sharp's illustrative and realistic approach and Blumenschein's impressionistic treatment of Southwestern themes to the moody art-deco spirit of Dunton's landscapes, the TSA portrayed the same subjects in myriad ways.

Only in later years would the TSA's contribution to contemporary art be fully recognized. Historically the paintings of the TSA are seen as a visual documentary of the cultures of northern New Mexico, which had yet to be dramatically influenced by the industrial age.

Cather or Dennis Hopper once laid their heads, or even use a bathroom decorated by DH Lawrence. It also runs arts, crafts, spiritual and creative workshops. Rates include buffet breakfast.

★ Historic Taos Inn
HISTORIC HOTEL $$

(Map p296; ☑ 575-758-2233; www.taosinn.com; 125 Paseo del Pueblo Norte; r from $105; P ❄ 🛜) Lovely and always lively old inn, where the 45 characterful rooms have Southwest trimmings like heavy-duty wooden furnishings and adobe fireplaces (some functioning, some for show). The famed Adobe Bar spills into the cozy central atrium, and features live music every night – for a quieter stay, opt for one of the detached separate wings – and there's also a good restaurant.

American Artists Gallery House B&B
B&B $$

(Map p292; ☑ 800-532-2041; www.taosbedandbreakfast.com; 132 Frontier Lane; casitas/r from $109/119; ❄ @ 🛜 🐾) This quiet garden complex, a mile south of the Plaza, holds tasteful rooms and casitas, all with wood-burning fireplaces. The smallest casita is little more than a shed, albeit a very nice one, while the Jacuzzi suites will blow your mind. George the peacock regularly drops in during the sumptuous breakfasts, while changing art displays come from local galleries.

Casa Benavides Bed & Breakfast
B&B $$

(Map p296; ☑ 575-758-1772; www.taos-casabenavides.com; 137 Kit Carson Rd; r $105-300; ❄ @ 🛜) Spreading through five garden-set buildings a block east of the Plaza, this romantic B&B abounds in fireplaces, patios and balconies. Furniture is mostly antique and handmade, and shares space with artful treasures. A couple of rooms are on the small and dark side, but most are big and bright – check the website. Breakfasts are full and made from scratch.

Old Taos Guesthouse
B&B $$

(Map p292; ☑ 575-758-5448; www.oldtaos.com; 1028 Witt Rd; r from $125; ❄ @ 🛜) Hidden away in a quiet residential neighborhood, this atmospheric treasure has spacious, old-world adobe rooms with undulating walls (just try to find a right angle) and handcarved wood furnishings and doors; the older rooms are nicest. The shady lawn and gardens beckon, with inviting hammocks and 60-mile sunset views. Seasoned adventurers both, the proprietors can point you toward great excursions.

Casa Europa
B&B $$

(Map p292; ☑ 575-758-9798; www.casaeuropanm.com; 840 Upper Ranchitos Rd; r from $115; 🛜) Cool breezes provide the air-conditioning at this stunning and very welcoming 18th-century estate, enjoying sublime meadow and mountain views. In the light, comfortable guest rooms, Euro-style antiques mix artfully with Southwestern-style pieces. Elaborate breakfast and afternoon treats are offered in summer, evening hors d'oeuvres in winter. two-night minimum stay.

El Pueblo Lodge
HOTEL $$

(Map p296; ☑ 575-758-8700; www.elpueblolodge.com; 412 Paseo del Pueblo Norte; r from $110; ❄ 🛜 🐾) Old-fashioned hotel at the northern edge of downtown, where the fake adobe style extends to a spectacular mock-up of nearby Taos Pueblo. Large, clean rooms, some with kitchenettes and/or fireplaces, plus a pool, hot tub, outdoor seating and barbecue grills, and fresh pastries in the morning.

La Fonda de Taos
HISTORIC HOTEL $$

(Map p296; ☑ 575-758-2211; www.lafondataos.com; 108 S Plaza; r from $149; @ 🛜) This venerable inn, the only lodging on the Plaza, is not quite as upscale as you might expect – well, apart from the penthouse suite – but it certainly has charm, and the smallish, antique-furnished rooms come with kiva gas fireplaces. There's also a unique claim to fame – the 'Forbidden Art' paintings by DH Lawrence, banned in 1929 Europe.

El Monte Sagrado
LUXURY HOTEL $$$

(☑ 575-758-3502; www.elmontesagrado.com; 317 Kit Carson Rd; r from $209; ❄ @ 🛜 🐾) 🐾 A lush oasis in the high desert, this lavishly decorated ecoresort holds bright, luxurious suites arranged around a flourishing courtyard and whimsically decorated with Native American, Mexican, Moroccan and Egyptian notes. There's also a full-service on-site spa, plus a good restaurant and the attractive Anaconda Bar. Look out for ski deals in winter.

✕ Eating

Taos rates second only to Santa Fe among New Mexico's culinary hotspots. There are some great options here at both ends of the price spectrum, with plenty of good places within easy walking distance of the Plaza.

Michael's Kitchen
NEW MEXICAN $

(Map p296; ☑ 575-758-4178; www.michaelskitchen.com; 304c Paseo del Pueblo Norte; mains $7-16; ⏱ 7am-2:30pm Mon-Thu, to 8pm Fri-Sun; 🚸)

Locals and tourists alike converge on this old favorite because the menu is long, the food's reliably good, it's an easy place for kids, and the in-house bakery produces goodies that fly out the door. Plus, it serves the best damn breakfast in town. You just may spot a Hollywood celebrity or two digging into a chile-smothered breakfast burrito.

La Cueva Cafe
MEXICAN $

(Map p296; ☎ 575-758-7001; www.lacuevacafe.com; 135 Paseo del Pueblo Sur; mains $6-14; ☺10am-9pm) This little Mexican cafe on downtown's southeastern edge has rapidly established itself as a local classic. Satisfaction is guaranteed, whether you drop in for a morning blast of *huevos rancheros*, come for dinner to savor the garlic salmon or *cochinita pibil* (shredded citrus-marinated pork, wrapped in a banana leaf), or indulge in a slice of coconut Key lime pie.

El Gamal
MIDDLE EASTERN $

(Map p296; ☎ 575-613-0311; 12 Doña Luz St; mains $7-12; ☺9am-5pm Mon-Wed, 9am-9pm Thu-Sat, 11am-3pm Sun; 🐾🖊🖨) Vegetarians rejoice – at this casual Middle Eastern place, there's no meat anywhere. Even if the falafel doesn't quite achieve the stated aim to promote peace through 'evolving people's consciousness and taste buds,' it certainly tastes good. There's a kids playroom in the back with tons of toys, plus a pool table and free wi-fi.

Taos Diner
DINER $

(☎ 575-758-2374; www.taosdiner.com; 908 Paseo del Pueblo Norte; mains $4-14; ☺7:30am-2:30pm; 🖨) Diner grub at its finest, prepared with a Southwestern, organic spin. Mountain men, scruffy jocks, solo diners and happy tourists – everyone's welcome here. The breakfast burritos rock. There's another branch, open the same hours, at 216b Paseo del Pueblo Sur.

Raw To Go
VEGETARIAN $

(Map p296; ☎ 575-613-0893; 105b Quesnel St; mains $6-12; ☺11am-7pm Thu-Sat, 2-7pm Sun; 🖊) Expect the unexpected at this pocket-size little vegan restaurant; there's no fixed menu, they simply prepare whatever's freshly available on the day. It's all organic and, yes, pretty much all of it is entirely raw. Tasty possibilities include shiitake seaweed soup, bountiful hummus or raw pizza, plus smoothies and homemade kombucha.

★ Love Apple
NEW MEXICAN $$

(☎ 575-751-0050; www.theloveapple.net; 803 Paseo del Pueblo Norte; mains $14-25; ☺5-9pm Tue-Sun) A real 'only in New Mexico' find, from the setting in the converted 19th-century adobe Placitas Chapel, to the delicious, locally sourced and largely organic food. Everything – from the local beefburger with red chile and blue cheese, via the tamales with mole sauce, to the wild boat tenderloin – is imbued with regional flavors, and the understated rustic-sacred atmosphere enhances the experience. Make reservations.

Doc Martin's
NEW MEXICAN $$

(Map p296; ☎ 575-758-2233; www.taosinn.com; 125 Paseo del Pueblo Norte, Historic Taos Inn; breakfast & lunch $7-15, dinner $12-34; ☺7:30am-3pm & 5-9:30pm) Hang out where Bert Philips (the original Doc Martin's bro-in-law) and Ernest Blumenschein cooked up the idea of the Taos Society of Artists. Sit by the kiva fireplace, pop a cork on an award-winning wine, dive into the *chile rellenos*, sautéed shrimp with polenta or braised lamb shank, and maybe you'll be inspired to great things as well.

Orlando's
NEW MEXICAN $$

(Map p292; ☎ 575-751-1450; www.orlandostaos.com; 1114 Don Juan Valdez Lane; mains $8-12; ☺10:30am-9pm; 🖨) Renowned for serving what's hands-down the best New Mexican food in Taos – be sure to try the blue corn chicken enchiladas – this inconspicuous little cafe, just left of the highway as you head north of town, gets really busy in high season.

Taos Pizza Out Back
PIZZA $$

(☎ 575-758-3112; 712 Paseo del Pueblo Norte; slices $4-10, whole pies $13-29; ☺11am-10pm May-Sep, to 9pm Oct-Apr; 🖊🖨) Pizza dreams come true with every possible ingredient under the sun at Taos' top pizza palace; for example, the recommended Vera Cruz has chicken breast and veggies marinated in a honey-chipotle sauce. Slices are enormous, and crusts are made with organic flour (or gluten-free for $3 extra). Out Back also has a great back patio.

★ Lambert's
MODERN AMERICAN $$$

(Map p296; ☎ 505-758-1009; www.lambertsoftaos.com; 123 Bent St; lunch $9-19, dinner $18-39; ☺noon-2pm & 5:30-9pm mid-May–mid-Sep, 5:30-9pm Mon-Sat, 10am-2pm Sun mid-Sep–mid-May; 🖊🖨) Consistently hailed as the 'Best of Taos,' and now relocated into a charming old adobe just north of the Plaza, Lambert's remains what it's always been – a cozy, romantic local hangout where patrons relax and enjoy sumptuous contemporary cuisine, with mains ranging from lunchtime's barbecue pork sliders to dinner dishes like chicken mango enchiladas or Colorado rack of lamb.

Trading Post Cafe
ITALIAN $$$

(Map p292; ☑575-758-5089; www.tradingpostcafe.com; 4179 Hwy 68, Ranchos de Taos; lunch mains $8-14, dinner mains $15-32; ⊙11am-9pm Tue-Sat) This longtime favorite strikes a perfect balance of relaxed and refined. Everything on the largely Italian menu, from pasta specials to rosemary chicken, tastes good. Portions tend to be large, so think about splitting a dish – or, if you want to eat cheap but well, get a small salad and small soup. It'll be plenty.

El Meze
NEW MEXICAN $$$

(Map p292; ☑575-751-3337; www.elmeze.com; 1017 Paseo del Pueblo Norte; sharing plates $8-14, mains $16-42; ⊙5:30-9:30pm Mon-Sat) Attractive, intimate but often rather hectic little restaurant that serves Spanish-style sharing plates such as pork rinds or roasted peppers as well as more substantial mains including lemon-and-rosemary roasted chicken, buffalo tamales with green chiles, and a fabulous vegetarian pasta with mushrooms and asparagus.

 Drinking

Adobe Bar
BAR

(Map p296; ☑575-758-2233; Historic Taos Inn, 125 Paseo del Pueblo Norte; ⊙11am-11pm, music 7-10pm) There's something about the Adobe Bar. All Taos seems to turn up at some point each evening, to kick back in the comfy covered atrium, enjoying no-cover live music from bluegrass to jazz, and drinking the famed 'Cowboy Buddha' margaritas. If you decide to stick around, you can always order food off the well-priced bar menu.

Coffee Spot
CAFE

(☑575-758-8556; 900 Paseo del Pueblo Norte; ⊙7am-5pm; 🛜) Large, ramshackle and popular coffeehouse and bakery, serving all-day breakfasts – try the chile-smothered Taos Benedict – plus espresso, juices, smoothies and salads, and plentiful gluten-free options. Locals lured by the free wi-fi spread out through the copious indoor space and sunny patio.

Eske's Brew Pub & Eatery
BREWERY

(Map p296; ☑575-758-1517; www.eskesbrewpub.com; 106 Des Georges Lane; ⊙noon-10pm Mon-Sat, to 9pm Sun) This crowded hangout, set well back from the highway and extending into a beer garden, rotates more than 25 microbrewed ales, from Taos Green Chile to Doobie Rock Heller Bock, to complement hearty bowls of Wanda's green chile stew

and sushi on Tuesday. Live local music, from acoustic guitar to jazz, is usually free.

Anaconda Bar
BAR

(Map p296; ☑575-737-9855; 317 Kit Carson Rd, El Monte Sagrado; ⊙3-11pm) The Anaconda is a work of art, a real feast for the eyes. The bartenders and chefs take care of the other senses, with perfectly made drinks and gourmet pub grub. It is pricey, but it's unique.

World Cup
COFFEE SHOP

(Map p296; ☑575-737-5299; 102 Paseo del Pueblo Norte; ⊙7am-7pm) The little World Cup coffeehouse is one of those places that looks too obvious, perfectly poised between the Plaza and the highway, to be any good. Or maybe you don't have that problem? Anyway, if you fancy a quick well-made espresso or succulent pastry, with some good old-fashioned counter-cultural edge, it's actually ideal, albeit short of seating room.

Caffe Tazza
CAFE

(Map p296; ☑575-758-8706; 122 Kit Carson Rd; ⊙7am-10pm) For a taste of how Taos used to be, back when hippies stalked the earth – or just to enjoy some great coffee – call in at Tazza, which now caters mostly to the crunchy-hipster-tattooed crowd. It's not everyone's cup of tea, but there's plenty of space to kick back, and most evenings see open mics or live music.

☆ **Entertainment**

KTAO Solar Center
LIVE MUSIC

(Map p292; ☑575-758-5826; www.ktao.com; 9 Ski Valley Rd; ⊙bar 4-9pm Sun-Thu, to 11pm Fri & Sat) Taos' best live-music venue, at the start of Ski Valley Rd, shares its space with much-loved radio station KTAO 101.9FM. Local and touring acts stop by to rock the house; when there's no show, watch the DJs in the booth at the 'world's most powerful solar radio station' while hitting happy hour at the bar.

Taos Chamber Music Group
CLASSICAL MUSIC

(www.taoschambermusicgroup.org) As well as classical music from baroque to contemporary, this ensemble also performs folk- and jazz-flavored compositions from all over the world, with concerts at venues throughout New Mexico. Schedules are on the website.

Taos Center for the Arts
PERFORMING ARTS

(TCA; Map p296; ☑575-758-2052; www.tcataos.org; 133 Paseo del Pueblo Norte) In a remodeled 1890s adobe mansion, the TCA programs local and international performances of everything from chamber music to belly dancing to theater, as well as readings and movie screenings.

Alley Cantina
LIVE MUSIC

(Map p296; ☑575-758-2121; www.alleycantina. com; 121 Teresina Lane; ☺11:30am-11pm) It figures that the oldest building in Taos is a comfy bar. Built almost four centuries ago by Pueblo Indians, and briefly the office of New Mexico's first US Territorial Governor, it's now a rambling, friendly place with a poolroom, a full pub-grub menu, and live music from zydeco to rock and jazz almost nightly.

Storyteller Cinema
CINEMA

(Map p292; ☑505-751-4245; http://storyteller7. com; 110 Old Talpa Cañon Rd; tickets adult/child $8/6) Catch mainstream flicks at Taos' only movie house, a seven-screen theater right off Paseo del Pueblo Sur.

🛍 Shopping

Galleries and studios in and around Taos testify to the town's ongoing appeal for artists and craftsworkers.

Taos Drums
MUSIC

(☑800-424-3786; www.taosdrums.com; 3956 Hwy 68, Ranchos de Taos; ☺10am-5pm) Touted as the world's largest selection of Native American drums, just south of town. All are handmade by masters from Taos Pueblo and covered with real hide. Choose from hand drums, log drums, natural-looking drums or those painted with wildlife or Pueblo motifs.

El Rincón Trading Post
VINTAGE

(Map p296; ☑575-758-9188; 114 Kit Carson Rd; ☺10am-5pm) This shop dates back to the arrival of German trader Ralph Meyers in 1909. Even if you're not looking to buy anything, step into the dusty museum-like backroom devoted to artifacts including Indian crafts, jewelry and Old West memorabilia.

Moby Dickens
BOOKS

(Map p296; ☑575-758-3050; www.mobydickens. com; 124a Bent St; ☺10am-5pm Mon-Wed, 10am-6pm Thu-Sat, noon-5pm Sun) Great name, great shop. Taos' best bookstore carries a fine stock of regional fiction and nonfiction, plus maps and guides, and the friendly staff are always happy to advise.

Buffalo Dancer
JEWELRY

(Map p296; ☑575-758-8718; www.buffalodancer. com; 103a East Plaza) One of the older outlets for Native American jewelry on the Plaza, carrying Rodney Concha's fine pieces plus other work in silver and semiprecious stones.

Seconds Ecostore
ARTS & CRAFTS

(Map p296; ☑575-751-4500; www.secondsecostore. com; 120 Bent St; ☺10am-6pm) The pick of several artsy little boutiques in the John Dunn Shops, just north of the Plaza, this quirky store sells all kinds of cool recycled gifts, from solar-powered crickets to purses made from tins and miniature cardboard animal heads.

ℹ Information

Holy Cross Hospital (☑575-751-5835; http://taoshospital.org; 1397 Weimer Rd; ☺24hr emergency)

Police (☑575-758-4656; 400 Camino de la Placita)

Post Office (Map p296; 318 Paseo del Pueblo Norte, at Brooks St)

Taos Visitor Center (Map p292; ☑575-758-3873; http://taos.org; 1139 Paseo del Pueblo Sur; ☺9am-5pm; 🛜) This excellent visitor center stocks information of all kinds on northern New Mexico and doles out free coffee; everything, including the comprehensive *Taos Vacation Guide,* is also available online.

ℹ Getting There & Around

BUS

Greyhound buses do not serve Taos, but on weekdays, **North Central Regional Transit** (☑866-206-0754; www.ncrtd.org) provides free shuttle service to Española, where you can transfer to Santa Fe and elsewhere; pick-up/drop-off is at the Taos County offices off Paseo del Pueblo Sur, a mile south of the Plaza.

Taos Express (☑575-751-4459; www.taos express.com) has shuttle service to Santa Fe Friday through Sunday (round-trip adult/child $10/free), connecting with Rail Runner trains to and from Albuquerque, and also serves the Ski Valley in winter ($1).

On weekdays only, the **Chile Line** (www.taosgov. com; one-way 50¢; ☺7am-5:30pm Mon-Fri) runs north–south along Hwy 68 between the Rancho de Taos post office and Taos Pueblo every 30 minutes. It also serves the Ski Valley and Arroyo Seco in winter. All buses are wheelchair accessible.

CAR

Half a mile north of town, Paseo del Pueblo Norte forks: to the northeast it becomes Camino del Pueblo and heads toward Taos Pueblo, and to the northwest it becomes Hwy 64. The crossroads 4 miles north of town, still known as the 'old blinking light' though it's long been a regular traffic light, is a major landmark. From here, Hwy

64 heads west to the Rio Grande Gorge Bridge, Hwy 522 heads northwest to Questa and the Enchanted Circle, and Hwy 150 heads northeast to Arroyo Seco and the Taos Ski Valley.

AROUND TAOS

Besides Taos Pueblo, the area around Taos has fabulous skiing, cool little towns and spectacular scenery. Driving the Enchanted Circle makes a fantastic day trip from Taos, while a night in little Arroyo Seco delivers rural New Mexican flavor and crisp high desert air. The northern segment of Río Grande del Norte National Monument offers dramatic views and great hiking, and there's good fly-fishing and cross-country skiing around Red River.

Taos Pueblo

POP 1950 / ELEV 7112FT

New Mexico's most extraordinary – and most beautiful – Native American site stands 3 miles northeast of Taos Plaza. An absolute must-see for anyone interested in Pueblo Indian life, history and culture, Taos Pueblo (Map p521; ☑ 575-758-1028; www.taospueblo.com; Taos Pueblo Rd; adult/child $16/free; ⊙ 8am-4pm Mon-Sat, 8:30am-4pm Sun, closed mid-Feb–mid-Apr) has been continuously inhabited for almost a thousand years, making it a strong contender to be the oldest community in the entire US. It's also the only living Native American community to be designated both a World Heritage Site by Unesco and a National Historic Landmark.

While reservation lands also extend west from the town of Taos toward the Rio Grande, the Pueblo itself focuses on twin five-story adobe complexes, set either side of the Río Pueblo de Taos, against the stunning backdrop of the Sangre de Cristo Mountains. The quintessential example of ancient Pueblo architecture, they're thought to have been completed by around 1450 AD. Modern visitors are thus confronted by the same staggering spectacle as New Mexico's earliest Spanish explorers, albeit with a small and very picturesque Catholic mission church now standing nearby.

Guided walking tours of the Pueblo, led by residents, explain its history and provide a chance to buy fine jewelry, pottery and other arts and crafts, and sample flatbread baked in traditional beehive-shaped adobe ovens.

Note that the Pueblo closes for 10 weeks around February to April, and at other times for ceremonies and events; call ahead, or check its website for dates.

🏃 Activities

Taos Indian Horse Ranch HORSEBACK RIDING
(Map p292; ☑ 575-758-3212; Piñon Rd; 1hr/2hr easy ride $55/95, 2hr experienced ride $125) This Native American–owned stables offers guided riding trips through Indian land – experienced riders can go fast. It also arranges an overnight rafting/riding/camping trip; call for details.

🎎 Festivals & Events

Of all the Pueblos in northern New Mexico, Taos Pueblo has the most events and celebrations open to the public. Plains and Pueblo Indians gather for dances and workshops during the huge **Taos Pueblo Pow-Wow** (☑ 575-741-0974; www.taospueblopowwow.com; adult/child $15/free) in the second week of July, continuing a centuries-old tradition, while **San Geronimo Day** (September 29–30) is another massive feast, with dancing and food.

🍴 Eating

Tiwa Kitchen NATIVE AMERICAN $$
(Map p292; ☑ 575-751-1020; 328 Veterans Hwy; mains $7-15; ⊙ 8am-4pm Wed-Mon) Pueblo residents and visitors alike flock to one of the few places in the state where you can sit down to a plate of Native American treats like *phien-ty* (blue-corn fry bread stuffed with buffalo meat), *twa chull* (grilled buffalo) or a bowl of heirloom green chile grown on Pueblo grounds.

🛍 Shopping

Tony Reyna Indian Shop ARTS & CRAFTS
(Map p292; ☑ 575-758-3835; 915 Veterans Hwy; ⊙ 8am-noon & 1-6pm) In business since 1950 and now run by Tony's son Phillip, this simple adobe shop continues to sell a fine assortment of arts and crafts from Taos and neighboring Pueblos.

Arroyo Seco

POP 1450 / ELEV 7634FT

For some unprocessed local flavor, a groovy plaza and a growing art scene, Arroyo Seco is the place to be. It's just 10 minutes north of Taos, halfway to Taos Ski Valley; there's not much to do, but you'll find plenty of ways to do nothing.

✕ Eating & Sleeping

Abominable Snowmansion   HOSTEL $
(Map p292; ☎575-776-8298; www.snowmansion.
com; 476 Hwy 150; tent sites/dm/tipi $22/27/55,
r without/with bath $50/55; ⓟ@☎☀) Popular
and affordable hostel in the heart of Arroyo
Seco, which makes a cozy high-country alternative to paying Taos prices. A big round fireplace in the central lodge warms guests in
winter, there's a shared kitchen, and you can
choose between clean (if a tad threadbare)
private rooms, simple dorms, a wonderful
campground, and even, in summer, a tipi.

★ Taos Cow   ICE CREAM $
(Map p292; ☎575-776-5640; www.taoscow.com;
485 Hwy 150; mains $5-9; ⓧ7am-7pm, to 6pm
in winter; ☎) The social center of Arroyo
Seco makes a great stop-off en route to or
from Taos Ski Valley. It's famous above all
for its tasty, rich all-natural ice cream, but
the espresso coffees, baked goods and deli
sandwiches are all good. Cooked breakfasts
include green eggs and ham – the green in
question being green chile, naturally.

Taos Ski Valley

Some people move to New Mexico just to
'ski bum' for a couple of years at **Taos Ski
Valley** (Map p292; www.skitaos.org; half-/full-day
lift ticket $64/77; ⓧ9am-4pm), 20 miles north-
east of Taos proper; some end up staying
longer than they planned. There's just something about the snow, challenging terrain
and laid-back atmosphere that makes this
mountain a wintry heaven on earth – that is,
if heaven has a 3274ft vertical drop.

Some of the country's most difficult skiing and snowboarding terrain makes the Ski
Valley a great place to zip down steep tree
glades and jump cliffs into untouched powder bowls. Seasoned skiers luck out, with
more than half of the 100-plus trails ranked
as expert. The valley has a peak elevation
of 11,819ft and gets an average of more
than 300in of all-natural powder annually,
though some seasons are better than others.
The resort has recently added a skier-cross
obstacle course to its popular terrain park.

Summer visitors to the village, which was
once the rough-and-tumble gold-mining
town of Twining, find an alpine wilderness
with great hiking and cheap lodging. Several trailheads are located along Hwy 150 to
Taos Ski Valley and at the northern end of
the Ski Valley parking lot. One leads to the
top of **Wheeler Peak**, New Mexico's highest
summit at 13,161ft.

To reach the valley, follow Hwy 64 for 4
miles north of Taos, then head right on Hwy
150 toward Arroyo Seco. The 20-mile drive
winds along a beautiful mountain stream. In
winter, the Chile Line runs several times a
day from downtown Taos.

✕ Eating & Sleeping

When it comes to Ski Valley lodging, high
season typically runs from mid-December
to April, dipping in March and peaking during the holidays. From March to November,
many lodges are closed, while those that are
open offer excellent discounts. Check the Ski
Valley website for ski-and-stay deals, including weeklong packages with room, board,
lessons and lift tickets; bargain specials are
often available early in the season.

**Snakedance
Condominiums & Spa**   RESORT $$$
(Map p292; ☎575-776-2277; www.snakedance
condos.com; 110 Sutton Pl; r $275-575; ❋@☎)
This giant complex, which offers ski-lodge
condo-style digs at the foot of the lifts, is
probably the Ski Valley's best all-round op-
tion, and has the best specials. It also holds
a restaurant, a bar, in-room massages and
lots of other amenities, including a hot tub,
a sauna and in-room kitchens.

Tim's Stray Dog Cantina   MEXICAN $$
(Map p292; ☎505-776-2894; http://straydogtsv.com;
105 Sutton Pl; mains $8-15; ⓧ8am-9pm Dec-May,
11am-9pm Jun-Nov) Famous for its flame-roast-
ed red and green chile, this Ski Valley institution serves fabulous northern New Mexican
cuisine – the breakfast burritos make great fu-
el-up food – along with fresh margaritas and
a big selection of bottled brews. The perfect
après-ski or hiking hangout.

Enchanted Circle

Unplug, sit back, unwind and absorb the
beauty. Comprising Hwys 522, 38 and 64, this
scenic, looping 84-mile byway is generous
with its views – crystalline lakes, pine forests
draped with feldspar, alpine highlands rising
to Wheeler Peak, and rolling steppes carpeted
with windswept meadows. You'll understand
why they call it the Enchanted Circle as soon
as you start driving. To fully experience its
sublime natural nuances, though, ride it on
a mountain bike. In warm weather, the heady
combination of spectacular scenery and chal-

lenging altitude and terrain entices cyclists from all over the world.

Most towns on the circuit (with the notable exception of Questa) are relatively young by New Mexico standards, founded during the 1880s gold rush by predominantly Anglo settlers looking for the motherlode. That never quite panned out, and the abandoned mines and ghost towns are highlights of the trip.

Those pioneers who remained turned to tourism, opening ski resorts at Red River and Angel Fire. Just driving through is a pleasant skim of the surface, but take a little time to explore and who knows what you may discover.

The site www.enchantedcircle.org has information about events along the route. Fill your gas tank in Taos, where it's cheaper, and allow at least a full day to make the journey.

Questa

POP 1780 / ELEV 7450FT

Four centuries ago, when Spain held sway in these parts, little Questa, 24 miles north of Taos, was the northernmost settlement in the Americas. Historically a mining town (the nearby molybdenum mine finally closed down in 2014), Questa has recently acquired a new identity as an enclave for artists, subsistence farmers and other organic types who choose to move off the grid.

The curious name comes courtesy of a typo when the modern township was founded in 1842: it was meant to be called 'Cuesta,' the Spanish for cliff or large hill, which would fit its looks perfectly.

Just northeast of town, the **Latir Peak Wilderness** is one of the sweetest spots around, perfect for a rewarding night or two of backpacking, or an intense day hike. Scenic alpine trails that climb high above the treeline include a loop that ascends 12,708ft Latir Peak.

✖ Eating

Wildcat's Den DINER $
(☎575-586-1119; 2457 Hwy 522; mains $5-9; ⊙11am-7pm Tue-Sat) Burger joint that also serves Mexican-style fast food, featuring its renowned homemade salsa.

🛍 Shopping

Artesanos Cultural Center ARTS & CRAFTS
(☎575-586-0443; 41 Hwy 38; ⊙11am-4pm Mon & Thu-Sat) A short way east of the center of Questa, this cooperative gallery sells work by local artists, and can point you toward artists' studios.

Red River

POP 500 / ELEV 8650FT

The cusp of the 19th and 20th centuries saw a pretty wild populace of gold miners and mountain men up in Red River, with saloons and brothels lining its muddy thoroughfares. In the early years of the 21st century, you'll still encounter mountain men, and women as well, but this time around they're tricked out in Gore-Tex instead of skins, and looking for a whole different kind of extracurricular activity – for the most part. When the hard-drinking

NEW MEXICO ENCHANTED CIRCLE

SCENIC DRIVE: VALLE VIDAL LOOP

In the mood for a longer drive through the highlands? Try the 173-mile **Valle Vidal Loop**, which departs the Enchanted Circle in Questa, heading north past the Wild Rivers Recreation Area on Hwy 522 and rejoining the road more traveled in Eagle Nest via Hwy 64.

The bulk of the route is impassable during winter, and the washboard gravel road of FR 1950 is no picnic at the best of times – bring a spare tire. The northern gate to FR 1950 is closed April 1 to early June for elk calving season, while the southern gate closes January through March to let them winter in peace. Best seen in the morning and evening, the estimated 1500 elk are a major attraction the rest of the year.

From the small town of **Costilla**, just below the Colorado border, take Hwy 196 east. Before long, the road turns to dirt and heads into a wilderness – where elk, wildcats and bears roam – that's sometimes called 'New Mexico's Yellowstone.'

FR 1950 follows stocked Rio Costilla – a fly-fisher's paradise – and opens on to national forest with unlimited access to multiday backpacking adventures. The road wends through meadows and forest, with outstanding views of granite peaks. Though it's possible to make this drive in a long day trip from Taos, it's much better to stay overnight, either in one of the four developed campgrounds or in the backcountry.

The route becomes blessedly paved again when you make a left onto Hwy 64 for the drive back to Eagle Nest, where you meet the Enchanted Circle once more.

miners' hopes were crushed by the difficulty of processing the ore, those who stayed realized that their outdoor paradise might appeal to flatlanders with income. Indeed.

Red River now appears as a cluster of cheerfully painted shops and chalets, gleaming in the high desert sun, and decked out in German-peasant style with an Old West theme – you'd think it wouldn't work, but it does. The historic buildings at its core, and the dilapidated mines scattered around the edges, have been joined by a ski resort, adventure outfitters, ticky-tacky shops galore and, this being New Mexico, art galleries.

Just be warned that the whole place pretty much shuts down during the off-season, from mid-March to mid-May.

Activities

Take Hwy 578 to the edge of the **Wheeler Peak Wilderness** (Map p292) for challenging but oh-so-worth-it hikes. **Horseshoe Lake Trail** leaves the Ditch Cabin Site for a 12-mile round-trip to the 11,950ft-high lake with good camping and fishing. The trailhead is on FR 58A, off Hwy 578, about 8 miles from Red River.

★**Enchanted Forest**   SKIING
(Map p270; ☑575-754-6112; www.enchantedfor-estxc.com; Hwy 38; adult/teen/child $18/15/9; ☺9am-4:30pm Nov-Mar) At New Mexico's premier Nordic ski area, 23 miles of groomed cross-country ski trails and 12 miles of snowshoe trails wend though aspen and fir forests, leading to scenic viewpoints. You can even stay overnight in a backcountry yurt (winter/summer $85/50). Don't miss February's **Just Desserts**, when area restaurants set up stands to showcase their sweet stuff.

Red River Ski Area   SKIING
(Map p270; ☑575-754-2223; www.redriverskiarea. com; full-/half-day lift ticket $66/51) Red River gets most of its tourism in winter, when folks flock to this ski area catering to families and newbies with packages that include lessons and equipment or half-price early-season weekends. Snowboarders and skiers alike should check out the terrain park complete with boxes and rails, specifically designed to lure you east from Angel Fire.

Frye's Old Town Shootout   WILD WEST
(☑575-754-3028; 100 W Main St; ☺4pm Tue, Thu & Sat Jun-Sep; ⊛) FREE In summer, the kids won't want to miss downtown Frye's Old Town Shootout. It celebrates the Second Amendment in all its ten-gallon hat, buckskin-jacket glory, as good guys try to stop the bad guys from robbing a bank and end up in a faux showdown right in the center of town.

Sleeping

Many of Red River's 50-plus RV parks, lodges, B&Bs and hotels offer package deals with local outfitters and the ski area, plus healthy discounts on off-season room rates. Attractive USFS campgrounds line the road between Questa and Red River, open from the end of May until some time in September.

Copper King Lodge   LODGE $$
(☑800-727-6210; www.copperkinglodge.com; 307 E River St; r $79-200; ⊛⟨) Rough-hewn wood, rustic furnishings and a great backyard make these cabin-style apartments and condos with kitchenettes, stretching beside the river close to the ski lifts, great value. But it's the riverfront hot tub that seals the deal. Rates vary wildly throughout the year.

Texas Red's Steakhouse   INN $$
(☑575-754-2922; www.texasredssteakhouse.com; 400 E Main St; r from $84; ⊛⟨) Dating from the 1940s, this downtown joint feels historic and quaint but not old. Rooms are small but comfy, and an upstairs lounge holds couches and books. Formerly known as the Lodge at Red River, it now takes its identity from Red River's best beef house, downstairs, which also serves seafood, lamb, chicken and elk.

Eating & Drinking

If you prefer a little line dancing with your barbecue, Red River is a favorite stop on the country music circuit. Catch live acts on weekends at venues around town, including the **Motherlode Saloon** next to Texas Red's Steakhouse.

Shotgun Willie's   DINER $
(☑575-754-6505; 403 W Main St; mains $6-12; ☺7am-2pm) Locals love this tiny place, serving the ultimate hangover sop-up, artery-clogging breakfast specials of fried eggs, meats and potatoes. The true house specialty is barbecue, served by the pound. Order the brisket combo.

Information

The local chamber of commerce runs a helpful **visitor center** (☑575-754-3030; www.re-drivernewmex.com; River St; ☺8am-5pm), and publishes a comprehensive guide with details of the surrounding wilderness.

Eagle Nest

POP 290 / ELEV 8200FT

This windswept high-meadow hamlet is a better place to explore the great outdoors if you can't take the tourist overkill of Red River. In winter, it's home to roughly five times as many elk as people; the 1500-strong local herd can frequently be seen browsing on the slopes above the highway.

◉ Sights

Eagle Nest Lake State Park LAKE
(☎575-377-1594; www.nmparks.com; day-use per vehicle $5; tent/RV sites $8/14) The community of Eagle Nest sits at the edge of a 2400-acre lake that's filled with trout and kokanee salmon. Boat rentals are available at **Eagle Nest Marina** (☎575-377-6941; www.cti-excursions.com; 28386 Hwy 64; half-day rentals $80).

Cimarron Canyon State Park PARK
(☎575-377-6271; www.nmparks.com; day-use per vehicle $5; tent/RV sites $8/14) Seven miles east of Eagle Nest on US 64, Cimarron Canyon State Park runs alongside a dramatic 8-mile stretch of the scenic Cimarron River, hued in pine greens and volcanic grays. It also encompasses Horseshoe Mine, beaver ponds, lots of wildlife and fishing, and several hiking trails.

🛏 Sleeping

Laguna Vista Lodge HISTORIC HOTEL $
(☎505-377-6522; www.lagunavistalodge.com; 51 Therma Dr; r $85; ❄🐾) This in-town lodge doesn't look that promising from outside, but its rooms and cabins are spacious and comfortable – some beside the lake have full kitchens – and it's all part of an Old West complex that includes **Calamity Jane's Restaurant** (mains $7 to $20; h dinner only) and the old-timey **Laguna Vista Saloon**.

Angel Fire

POP 1200 / ELEV 8400FT

Some love it, others hate it. **Angel Fire** (Map p270; ☎800-633-7463; www.angelfireresort.com; Hwy 434; half-/full-day lift ticket $49/66; 🎿) remains one of New Mexico's most popular ski resorts. Even if the town itself looks pretty much like time-share condo-land, no one can question the beauty of the surrounding mountains and valleys, and that famous northern New Mexico light.

As if its 2077ft vertical drop and 450 acres of trails weren't enough, the ski resort allows snowbiking (on bikes with skis) and snowskating (on skateboards without wheels), along with snowshoeing. There's also a 400ft-long, competition-quality half-pipe with a wicked 26% grade, plus terrain parks and a kids' ski park. Six zip lines at the summit entertain summer visitors.

🛏 Sleeping & Eating

Hwy 434, or Mountain View Blvd as it is known in town, is the main drag through Angel Fire and has a couple of places to stay.

Lodge at Angel Fire LODGE $$
(☎800-633-7463; www.angelfireresort.com; Hwy 434; r from $124; ❄@🐾🏊) Families will dig the ski resort's ski-chalet-style lodging option, which offers family-oriented packages and organizes children's activities, especially in summer. If you're not traveling with children, it's big enough to not feel like kid central. Three on-site restaurants mean you won't go hungry. Multinight stays are often required.

Elkhorn Lodge LODGE $$
(Map p270; ☎575-377-2811; www.elkhornlodgenm.com; 3377 Hwy 434; r $100-250; ❄🐾) This central lodge features decks off all rooms, and suites that sleep six and have kitchenettes. Its Campfire Cafe is open for all meals, while the Equestrian Center offers lessons and trail rides.

Pub'n'Grub PUB FOOD $$
(Map p270; ☎505-615-5446; www.thepubngrubangelfire.com; 52 North Angel Fire Rd; mains $7-29; ⊙5-9pm, closed mid-Mar–May & mid-Oct–late Nov) Who needs restaurant reviews when you've got a name like that? In fact, the food is a bit more than just grub, with steaks and flatbreads as well as burgers and green chile. It's all especially cozy on a winter's night.

Elements AMERICAN $$$
(Map p270; ☎575-377-3055; www.angelfireresort.com; 10 Miller Lane, Angel Fire Resort Country Club; mains $26-36; ⊙5-9pm Tue-Sat) This elegant, opulent mountain-view restaurant is very much Angel Fire's fine-dining option, serving hearty alpine food like organic elk loin and Vienna-style veal cutlets – vegetarians are advised to seek their pleasures elsewhere.

❶ Information

Visitor center (Map p270; ☎575-377-6555; www.angelfirefun.com; 3365 Mountain View Blvd; ⊙9am-5pm) To call on local expertise and pick up information, be sure to drop in at Angel Fire's excellent new visitor center.

ℹ️ Getting There & Around

Angel Fire is strung out along the northern terminus of Hwy 434, just south of the intersection with Hwy 64. Continue west on Hwy 64 through the Carson National Forest back to Taos.

MORA VALLEY & NORTHEASTERN NEW MEXICO

East of Santa Fe, the lush Sangre de Cristo Mountains give way to high and vast rolling plains. Dusty grasslands stretch to infinity and beyond – or at least to Texas. Cattle and dinosaur prints dot a landscape punctuated by volcanic cones. Ranching is an economic mainstay, and on many stretches of road you'll see more cattle than cars – and quite possibly herds of bison too.

The Santa Fe Trail, along which pioneer settlers rolled in wagon trains, ran from Missouri to New Mexico. You can still see the wagon ruts in some places off I-25 between Santa Fe and Raton. For a bit of the Old West without a patina of consumer hype, this is the place.

Raton & Around

POP 6900 / ELEV 6700FT

Raton may not be a big tourist destination, but this well-preserved town will hold your attention for a short stroll. Founded when the railroad arrived in 1879, it quickly grew into an important railway stop and mining and ranching center. The small **historic district** along 1st, 2nd and 3rd Sts (between Clark and Rio Grande Aves) harbors over two dozen buildings.

◎ Sights

Raton Museum   MUSEUM
(www.theratonmuseum.org; 108 S 2nd St) FREE
Housed in the 1906 Coors Building, the great little Raton Museum was being restored at the time of research. Hopefully it will have reopened by the time you read this, with similar displays of fading photos, artifacts from Raton's mining days, and historical accounts of the Santa Fe Trail.

Shuler Theater   THEATER
(www.shulertheater.com; 131 N 2nd St) Still used for performances, this downtown theater dates from 1915, and has an elaborate European rococo interior. The murals gracing its foyer, depicting regional history from 1845 to 1895, were painted in the 1930s by Manville Chapman.

International Bank   ARCHITECTURE
(200 S 2nd St) Now a bank, this downtown landmark was originally built in 1929 as the Swastika Hotel. Note the reversed swastika signs (a Hindu symbol of good luck) on top. During WWII they were covered with tarp and the hotel changed its name in 1943.

🛏️ Sleeping & Eating

Mom-and-pop motels line 2nd St south of downtown, while the national chain hotels gather on Hwy 64 to the west.

Sugarite Canyon State Park   CAMPGROUND $
(☑ 575-445-5607; www.nmparks.com; Hwy 526; tent/RV sites $8/14) Much the nicest place to stay near Raton, in the pretty meadows and forests of the Rocky Mountain foothills 10 miles northeast of town via Hwy 72 and Hwy 526. In summer, 15 miles of hiking trails branch off a half-mile nature trail, while in winter the 7800ft elevation is perfect for cross-country skiing.

Vermejo Park Ranch   RANCH
(☑ 575-445-3097; www.vermejoparkranch.com; Hwy 555; r per person incl meals & outdoor guide $375; @ 🛜) Maintained by Ted Turner as a luxury fishing and hunting lodge, this beautifully situated ranch sprawls splendidly across 920 sq miles of forests, meadows and mesas 40 miles west of Raton. Besides killing things, guests can take wildlife-watching and photography tours, or ride horses through classic Western terrain.

Oasis Restaurant   DINER $
(☑ 575-445-2221; 1445 S 2nd St; mains $7-19; ⊙ 6am-8pm) This bustling and efficient restaurant, on the forecourt of one of the many homey motels hereabouts, serves decent diner food. Whatever you opt for, from a megacheeseburger with fries to a Mexican combination plate, it will almost certainly cost under $10.

Enchanted Grounds   CAFE $
(☑ 575-445-2219; www.egespressobar.com; 111 Park Ave; ⊙ 7am-2pm Mon, 7am-4:30pm Tue-Fri, 7:30am-4:30pm Sat; 🛜) Downtown Raton is surprisingly short of eating options, but you can pick up good coffee and snacks at this

SCENIC DRIVE: CAPULIN VOLCANO & FOLSOM MAN TERRITORY

A 50-mile loop through the high mountain plains above Raton, **Capulin Volcano & Folsom Man Territory** isn't just another stretch of pavement – it's also a history lesson (with volcanoes, which alone should be enticement enough for the kids).

In 1908, local cowboy George McJunkin, a former slave, made one of the most important archaeological discoveries in US history, near the tiny town of Folsom, 40 miles east of Raton. Spotting some strange bones in Wild Horse Arroyo, he realised that these were no ordinary cattle bones. And so he kept them, suspecting correctly that they came from an extinct species of bison. McJunkin mentioned his find to various people, but not until 1926–28 was the site properly excavated.

Until then, scientists thought that humans had inhabited North America for, at most, 4000 years. With this single find, the facts about the continent's ancient inhabitants had to be completely revised. Subsequent excavations found stone arrowheads in association with extinct bison bones thought to date from 8000 BC. These Paleo-Indians became known as **Folsom Man**. Recent dating techniques suggest that these artifacts are in fact 10,800 years old, among the oldest discovered on the continent, although it's now clear that people have lived in the Americas for even longer.

The area is also renowned for its volcanoes. Rising 1300ft above the surrounding plains, **Capulin Volcano National Monument** (☑575-278-2201; www.nps.gov/cavo; vehicle $5; ☺8am-5pm Jun-Aug, to 4:30pm Sep-May) is the easiest to visit. From the visitor center, a 2-mile road winds precariously up the mountain to a parking lot just below the crater rim. A quarter-mile trail drops into the crater, created by an eruption 60,000 years ago and now partly covered by ponderosa pine forest, while a more demanding mile-long trail undulates around the rim, which at its highest point is 8182ft above sea level. The entrance is 3 miles north of Capulin, which is 30 miles east of Raton on Hwy 87.

small cafe, a lively morning meeting place for locals close to the railroad station.

❶ Information

Raton's helpful **visitor center** (☑575-445-9551; www.exploreraton.com; 100 Clayton Rd; ☺8am-5pm) has statewide information.

❶ Getting There & Away

Raton stands beside I-25, 8 miles south of the Colorado border. Amtrak's *Southwest Chief* stops here, but almost all visitors come in private vehicles. Note that winter snowstorms sometimes close Raton Pass, just north of town, potentially stranding drivers heading to Colorado.

Clayton & Around

POP 3000 / ELEV 5050FT

Ranches and prairie grasses surround Clayton, a quiet town with a sleepy Western feel, close to the Bravo Dome Field – the world's largest natural deposit of carbon dioxide gas – and the Texas state line.

Sometimes when you're in the mood for a detour to nowhere, there's nowhere to go. Not true here. Southwest of Clayton, extending from New Mexico's least populated county into Texas and Oklahoma, the **Kiowa National Grasslands** consist of high-plains ranchland – endless, vast and lonely. Farmed throughout the early 20th century, the soil suffered from poor agricultural techniques and essentially blew away during the dust-bowl years of the 1930s. The most visited section (though visitors are scarce) is **Mills Canyon**, north of Roy (with only a gas station and grocery store).

❂ Sights

Herzstein Memorial Museum   MUSEUM
(☑575-374-2977; www.herzsteinmuseum.com; 22 S 2nd St; ☺10am-5pm Tue-Sat May-Aug, to 4pm Sep-Apr) **FREE** The chief focus here is the story of the biggest event in Clayton's history – the 1901 arrest and hanging of infamous train robber Black Jack Ketchum.

Clayton Lake State Park   LAKE
(☑575-374-8808; www.nmparks.com; Hwy 370; day-use per vehicle $5, tent/RV sites $8/14) This pretty lake 12 miles northwest of Clayton makes a good spot for swimming and camping, and also holds over 500 dinosaur footprints left by eight different species.

🛏 Sleeping

Hotel Eklund HISTORIC HOTEL $
(🖉575-446-1939; www.hoteleklund.com; 15 Main St;
r from $85, ste $135; ❉ 🕾) For a meal, a drink, or
a good night's sleep you can't do better than
this historic 1890 hotel, which has been extensively renovated while retaining the original
feel of its elegant dining room and Old West
saloon, home to a beautifully carved bar.

Cimarron

POP 900 / ELEV 6430FT

Even for this wild part of the world, Cimarron has a wild past. Right at the far western
edge of the plains, just as the mountains
begin to swell, it long served as a stop on
the Santa Fe Trail, a hangout for gunslingers,
train robbers, desperadoes, lawmen and other Wild West figures like Kit Carson, Buffalo
Bill Cody, Annie Oakley, Wyatt Earp, Jesse
James and Doc Holliday.

Today, though, Cimarron is a peaceful and
serene village on Hwy 64, 41 miles southwest
of Raton and 54 winding miles east of Taos.
Most of its historic buildings are tucked away
out of sight south of the Cimarron River on
Hwy 21, including the old town plaza, Dold
Trading Post, the Santa Fe Trail Inn (which
dates to 1854), Schwenk's Gambling Hall, a
Wells Fargo Station and the old jail (1872).

◉ Sights

St James Hotel HISTORIC BUILDING
(www.exstjames.com; 617 Collison St) Even if
you don't plan to spend the night, be sure
to sneak a peek behind the Territorial-style
adobe exterior of the old St James Hotel,
which started life as a saloon in 1873, and
whose venerable walls – sadly, they can't
speak – are said to have witnessed the deaths
of 26 men. Not surprisingly, it's said to be so
haunted that one room is never rented out.

Philmont Scout Ranch RANCH
(🖉575-376-2281; www.philmontscoutranch.org;
47 Caballo Rd) South of Cimarron on Hwy 21,
the country's largest Boy Scout camp spreads
over 214 sq miles along the breathtaking eastern slope of the Sangre de Cristo Mountains.
Only scouts can trek the trails, but anyone
can drop into the **Philmont Museum** (🖉575-
376-1136; 17 Deer Run Rd; ⊙8am-5:30pm Jun-Aug;
8am-5pm Mon-Fri Sep-May) **FREE**, which offers
tours by arrangement of Villa Philmonte, the
Spanish Mediterranean mansion of oil baron
Waite Phillips, Philmont's original benefactor.

🛏 Sleeping

St James Hotel HISTORIC HOTEL $$
(🖉575-376-2664; www.exstjames.com; 617 Col-
lison St; r $85-135; ❉🕾) The public spaces
here, including a decent midrange restau-
rant and a bar with pool table, are pure Vic-
toriana, all dark wood and animal heads. To
lighten things up, there's a pleasant court-
yard, known as the Pizza Patio and yes,
serving pizzas. The 12 historic rooms in the
main building have a genuine period feel; an
annex holds 10 modern rooms.

Casa del Gavilan B&B
(🖉575-376-2246; www.casadelgavilan.com; Hwy 21;
r from $114; 🕾) Set on 225 acres, surrounded by
the Philmont Ranch 6 miles south of Cimar-
ron, this magnificent Pueblo Revival house
was built around 1908. The four double rooms
are decorated with Southwestern antiques
and art and come complete with high ceil-
ings, vigas and thick adobe walls. A two-room
guesthouse sleeps up to four people.

Las Vegas & Around

POP 13,500 / ELEV 6430FT

The bordellos of America's original sin city,
Las Vegas, NM, were dishing out carnal
pleasures when Las Vegas, NV, was still just
a meadow in the wilderness. On a site that
had been home to generations of Comanche,
the city was established by the Mexican gov-
ernment in 1835, in time to serve as a stop
along the Santa Fe Trail and later the Santa
Fe Railroad. It quickly grew into one of the
biggest, baddest boomtowns in the West,
and in 1846 the United States took posses-
sion. Nineteenth-century Las Vegas was a
true-blue outlaw town, a place where Billy
the Kid held court with his pal Vicente Sil-
va (leader of the Society of Bandits – New
Mexico's roughest, toughest gang), and Doc
Holliday owned a saloon (his business ulti-
mately failed because he kept shooting at
the customers).

A century and a half later, there's still the
occasional shoot-out, but Las Vegas these days
is something of a backwater, a place of faded
charm that thanks to its two small universi-
ties nonetheless has a lively social swirl. Hun-
dreds of historic buildings grace its quaint
downtown, which has repeatedly served Hol-
lywood as a Western backdrop; *Wyatt Earp*
and Oscar-winner *No Country for Old Men*
are just a couple of the movies filmed here.
Las Vegas also acts as gateway to the south-

MORA VALLEY

Traditional Hispanic ways remain strong in this scenic agricultural valley. The real-life model for Frank Waters' novel *People of the Valley*, it's also one of the poorest nooks in New Mexico, where more than a quarter of families live below the poverty line. The town of Mora is the hub of the valley, with small communities strung out east and west along Hwy 518.

On Mora's main drag, stop into **Tapetes de Lana Weaving Center** (Map p270; ☑ 575-387-2247; www.moravalleyspinningmill.com; Hwy 518, at Hwy 434; ⊘ 7:30am-4pm Mon-Sat, from 10am Sun), where you can see handlooms in action, browse for handmade rugs and buy yarns that are spun and dyed on site. In back, one of the few active wool mills in the US offers **tours** (admission $5; ⊘ 7am-3pm Mon-Thu), while out front they run a little espresso cafe.

Getting hungry? Hit **Little Alaska** (☑ 575-387-5066; 346 Hwy 518; mains $5-7; ⊘ 11am-6pm Sun-Thu) in Mora, specializing in barbecue, enchiladas and ice cream. For some of the best tamales ever (plus burgers, burritos and more), served in a friendly local joint, head 6 miles west to the village of Holman, where you'll find **Teresa's Tamales** (Map p270; Hwy 518; mains $5-7; ⊘ 8am-5pm, closed Sun in winter).

Kids love visiting the **Victory Ranch** (Map p270; ☑ 575-387-2254; www.victoryranch.com; Hwy 434; adult/child $5/3; ⊘ 10am-4pm May-Aug, 10am-4pm Fri-Sun Sep-Dec & Apr, closed Jan–mid-Mar; ⚐), a mile north of Mora, where you can hand-feed the herds of cute and fluffy alpacas, shop for alpaca wool gifts and even watch a shearing if you're here in early June.

Three miles west of Mora on Hwy 518 is the **Cleveland Roller Mill Historical Museum** (Map p270; www.clevelandrollermillmuseum.com; ⊘ 10am-3pm Sat & Sun in summer) **FREE**, housed in a functional 19th-century flour mill – a beautiful old adobe and stone structure with gears and cogs and pulleys inside.

Six miles east of Mora, the **Salman Ranch** (Map p270; ☑ 866-281-1515; www.salmanraspberryranch.com; Hwy 518 , at Hwy 442; ⊘ 10am-4pm Tue-Sun in season; ⚐) at **La Cueva** is famous for its pesticide-free raspberry fields, where between mid-August and mid-October – weather permitting – you can pick your own fruit for $6 a pound. If you're passing by in off-season, stop by the ranch store and take a look at **La Cueva Mill** (Map p270; ⊘ 9am-5pm Jun-Dec, to 4pm Thu-Mon Jan-May), where the superbly preserved 19th-century industrial adobe buildings are a National Historic Site.

Heading to or from Las Vegas, consider taking Hwy 94, a ridiculously scenic stretch of road, which passes old adobe farmhouses and **Morphy Lake State Park** (Map p270; ☑ 575-387-2328; www.nmparks.com; per vehicle $5, tent/RV sites $8/14), with picnic tables, trout fishing and camping, but no drinking water.

eastern corner of the Pecos Wilderness and to Las Vegas National Wildlife Refuge.

⊙ Sights & Activities

Hwy 85, or Grand Ave, which runs north–south parallel to the interstate, is the main thoroughfare; the historic district centers on the Old Town Plaza, a few blocks west. Beautiful neighborhoods surround the Plaza and Bridge St; note especially the lovely Plaza Hotel in the plaza itself, which dates from 1882 and is still in use. Pick up a walking tour map from the visitor center (p313) if you want to explore.

City of Las Vegas Museum & Rough Rider Memorial Collection MUSEUM
(www.lasvegasmuseum.org; 727 Grand Ave; suggested donation $2; ⊘ 10am-4pm Tue-Sat) This small but informative museum chronicles the fabled cavalry unit led by future US president Theodore Roosevelt in the 1898 fight for Cuba. More than one third of the volunteers came from New Mexico, and the museum displays their furniture, clothes and military regalia.

Santa Fe Trail Interpretive Center MUSEUM
(www.santafetrailnm.org; 116 Bridge St; ⊘ 10am-3pm Mon-Sat) **FREE** Enthusiastic local historians curate an impressive collection of old photos and artifacts from Las Vegas' heyday as a rough-and-tumble trading post on the Santa Fe Trail. Guided tours available.

Montezuma HOT SPRING
(Map p270) Five miles northwest of Las Vegas on Hwy 65, this little area is dominated by Montezuma Castle, built in 1886 as a luxury

hotel and now the United World College of the West. If open (closed at time of writing due to flood damage), don't miss the **Dwan Light Sanctuary** (☉6am-10pm) `FREE` on campus, a meditation chamber where prisms in the walls cast rainbows inside. Along the road there, you can soak in a series of natural **hot spring pools**. Bring a swimsuit and test the water – some are scalding hot.

Santa Fe National Forest   OUTDOORS

(www.fs.fed.us/r3/sfe) Beyond Montezuma, Hwy 65 leads to the eastern edge of the forest, where trails head off into the Pecos Wilderness. The most popular day hike, a 10-mile round-trip starting at **El Porvenir campground** (tent & RV sites $8, no hookups), follows **trail 223** (Map p270) to the flat summit of **Hermit Peak** (10,160ft), with amazing views. Some sections switchback steeply and might be a little unnerving if you're prone to vertigo. To pick up topo maps and free trail guides, stop into the ranger station.

Las Vegas National Wildlife Refuge   WILDLIFE RESERVE

(☉dawn-dusk) `FREE` Five miles southeast of Las Vegas via Hwys 104 and 281, this 14-sq-mile refuge has marshes, woodlands and grasslands to which upwards of 250 bird species have found their way. Visitors can follow a 7-mile drive and walking trails.

Villanueva State Park   PARK

(Map p270; ☎575-421-2957; www.nmparks.com; day-use per vehicle $5) This pretty state park, about 35 miles south of Las Vegas via I-25 and Hwy 3, lies in a red rock canyon on the Rio Pecos valley. A small visitor center and self-guided trails explain the area's history: this was once a main travel route for Native Americans and, in the 1500s, for the Spanish conquistadors. A **campground** (tent/RV sites $8/14) is open April to October.

Villanueva & San Miguel   HISTORIC SITE

Along Hwy 3, the Spanish colonial villages of Villanueva and San Miguel (which has a fine church built in 1805), stand amid vineyards belonging to the **Madison Winery** (☎575-421-8028; www.madison-winery.com; Hwy 3; ☉call to arrange tastings), which has a tasting room. Don't miss **La Risa** (www.thelarisacafe.com; Hwy 3; mains $8-14; ☉11am-8pm Thu-Sat, 8am-6pm Sun; 🛜), a gourmet anomaly in the middle of nowhere, with homemade breads, pastries and desserts.

✨ Festivals & Events

The four-day party surrounding the **Fourth of July** is a colorful mix of festivities that includes Mexican folk music, dancing and mariachi bands. Other events include the **San Miguel/More County Fair** in August and a **Harvest Festival** on the third Saturday of September, with music and food.

🛏 Sleeping

Plaza Hotel   HISTORIC HOTEL $

(☎505-425-3591; www.plazahotel-nm.com; 230 Old Town Plaza; r incl breakfast from $54; P❄@🛜🐾) This historic hotel, opened in 1882, currently offers bargain rates for its 72 spacious, high-ceilinged rooms, of which half are in the adjoining Ilfeld Building. Rates include breakfast in the unremarkable restaurant; there's also a lively bar. The whole place has an appealing Wild West flavor, but new owner Alan Affeldt will need to upgrade extensively to restore its iconic status.

Knight's Inn   MOTEL $

(Map p270; ☎505-425-5994; www.knightsinn.com; 1152 N Grand Ave; r $51) The pick of the many budget motels along Grand Ave through town, with clean, large rooms that have been nicely spruced up. Rates include a simple breakfast.

THE RETURN OF THE CASTAÑEDA

Las Vegas was thrilled in 2014 to hear that downtown's landmark Hotel Castañeda is to reopen. Built alongside the railroad station in 1898, as the first in legendary entrepreneur Fred Harvey's chain of Western hotels, the Castañeda only lasted 50 years before closing its doors in 1948.

Now, this Mission Revival gem has been bought – reportedly for a mere $400,000 – by Alan Affeldt, the man responsible for the hugely successful restoration of the extraordinary La Posada hotel in Winslow, Arizona. Affeldt has also acquired the Plaza Hotel up in the Old Town, which he plans to keep open while the Castañeda is being re-modelled. Both will be refurbished with historic furniture transplanted from the Fonda hotel in Santa Fe, and then run in conjunction. If Affeldt can match his previous triumph with La Posada, Las Vegas may soon resume its rightful place on every tourist's must-see list.

Eating

Charlie's Spic & Span Bakery & Cafe   DINER $
(☑505-426-1921; 715 Douglas Ave; mains $8-13; ☉6:30am-6pm Mon-Sat, 7am-3pm Sun; ☎) This Las Vegas institution has listened to the town's gossip for more than half a century, and is still the place for locals to hang out and catch up over a cup of coffee (or vanilla latte) and New Mexican diner fare. Think bean-and-cheese-stuffed *sopaipillas* (fried dough), pancake sandwiches and good old-fashioned hamburgers. Save room for dessert.

El Rialto   MEXICAN $
(☑505-454-0037; 141 Bridge St; mains $7-11; ☉10:30am-8:30pm Tue-Thu, to 9pm Fri & Sat, closed Sun & Mon) Family-run Mexican restaurant; enter through the swinging saloon doors, and you'll doubtless find local families chowing down on huge, great-value plates of cheese-smothered burritos, tacos and fajitas.

World Treasures Traveler's Cafe   CAFE $
(☑505-426-8638; 1814 Plaza St; snacks $3-6; ☉7am-7pm Mon-Sat; ☎) With no sign of its presence outside, this plaza coffee-and-sandwich shop is not easy to spot. Once inside, though, it's enormous, housed in a weaving gallery and filled with in-the-know locals enjoying espressos, breakfast waffles and deli sandwiches, plus a book exchange, board games and couches.

Drinking & Entertainment

Byron T's Saloon   BAR
(230 Old Town Plaza, Plaza Hotel) Within the Plaza Hotel, and named for its resident ghost, this Wild West bar hosts live jazz, blues and country music on weekends.

Fort Union Drive-In   CINEMA
(☑505-425-9934; 3300 7th St; per car $7; ☉Fri-Sun May-Sep) One of New Mexico's few remaining drive-in movie theaters lies just north of town and has great views of the surrounding high desert. Call for showtimes.

Information

Alta Vista Regional Hospital (☑505-426-3500; 104 Legion Dr; ☉24hr emergency)
Police (☑505-425-7504; 318 Moreno St)
Santa Fe National Forest Ranger Station (☑505-425-3534; 1926 N 7th St; ☉8am-5pm Mon-Fri)
Visitor center (Map p270; ☑505-425-3707; www.visitlasvegasnm.com; 500 Railroad Ave; ☉9am-5pm)

Getting There & Around

Las Vegas is located on I-25, 65 miles east of Santa Fe. The **Amtrak** (www.amtrak.com) *Southwest Chief* train between Chicago and Los Angeles stops in Las Vegas daily at 12:38pm westbound, 3:03pm eastbound.

CHACO CANYON & NORTHWESTERN NEW MEXICO

New Mexico's wild northwest is home to wide-open, empty spaces. It is still dubbed 'Indian Country,' and for good reason: huge swaths of land fall under the aegis of the Navajo, Zuni, Acoma, Apache and Laguna tribes. This portion of New Mexico showcases remarkable ancient sites alongside modern, solitary Native American settlements. And when you've had your fill of culture, you can ride a historic narrow-gauge railroad through the mountains, hike around some trippy badlands, or cast for huge trout.

Chama

POP 1000 / ELEV 7875FT

Eight miles south of the Colorado border, little Chama is tucked into a lush valley that's carved into Rocky Mountain foothills. Native Americans lived and hunted here for centuries, and Spanish farmers settled the Chama River Valley in the mid-1700s, but it was the arrival of the Denver & Rio Grande Railroad in 1880 that really put Chama on the map. Although the railroad closed, the prettiest part still operates as one of the West's most scenic train trips.

Activities

★ Cumbres & Toltec Scenic Railway   TRAIN RIDE
(☑888-286-2737; www.cumbrestoltec.com; adult/child from $95/49; ☉late May–mid-Oct) The longest and highest narrow-gauge steam railroad in the US runs for 64 miles between Chama and Antonito, CO, over the 10,015ft-high Cumbres Pass. A beautiful trip, through mountains, canyons and high desert, it's at its finest in September and October, when the aspens shimmer with golden leaves. Some carriages are fully enclosed, but none are heated, so dress warmly. You can buy snacks on board, and there's a lunch stop in Osier. Reservations essential, two weeks in advance.

WORTH A TRIP

SCENIC DRIVE: CHAMA TO TAOS

This nearly 100-mile route makes a fabulous scenic way to get between Chama and Taos from late May through the first snows in mid-October. The best time for the drive is late September or early October, when the leaves are turning.

From Chama, start by taking Hwy 84/64 about 11 miles south to tiny Tierra Amarilla ('yellow earth,' known locally as TA), then head east on scenic Hwy 64. As the road climbs out of the Chama Valley, toward a 10,000ft pass through the Tusas Mountains, you're rewarded by spectacular views of the furrowed cliffs of **Brazos Canyon**.

Before you leave the valley, though, don't miss a visit to **Tierra Wools** (☑ 575-588-7231; www.handweavers.com; 91 Main St; r $75-90; ⊙ 9am-6pm Mon-Sat & 11am-4pm Sun Apr-late Oct, 10am-5pm Mon-Sat late Oct-Mar), a famous century-old cooperative in a rustic, century-old building in Los Ojos, south of Los Brazos, where artisans carry on the Hispanic traditions of hand-spinning, dyeing and weaving. Tierra Wools also offers a two-bedroom guesthouse, and weaving classes in summer.

Cumbres Nordic Adventures   SKIING
(☑ 575-756-2746; www.yurtsogood.com) Back-country ski tours in the snowy San Juan Mountains and deluxe backcountry yurt rentals for $115 to $145 per night.

Cumbres Adventure Tours   OUTDOORS
(☑ 719-376-2161; www.cumbresadventuretours.com) All-seasons adventure company, arranging snowmobile and cross-country ski trips in winter, and ATV rentals and mountain-bike tours in summer.

🎊 Festivals & Events

Chama has a few events worth dropping in for, including the **Chama Chile Ski Classic** (www.chamaski.com; ⊙ Jan), a cross-country race that attracts hundreds of competitors to 3.1-mile and 6.2-mile races, and **Chama Days** (⊙ early Aug), which features a rodeo, firefighters' water fight and chile cook-off.

🛏 Sleeping & Eating

Chama Trails Inn   MOTEL $
(☑ 575-756-2156; www.chamatrailsinn.com; 2362 Hwy 17; r from $79; ❄🖥) More than another roadside motel, with 16 character-packed rooms with abundant Southwestern furniture, local artwork and hand-painted tiles. A few rooms are further warmed by gas fireplaces. A communal hot tub and sauna come in handy after hiking.

Foster Hotel   HISTORIC HOTEL $
(☑ 575-756-2296; www.fosters1881.com; 393 S Terrace Ave; $58) If you're in search of local culture, look no further. Built in 1881 as a bordello, it's the only building in Chama that survived a massive fire in the 1920s. A few rooms are said to be so haunted they're kept locked

shut. The others are a bit rough around the edges; stay for the experience, not for luxury.

Elkhorn Lodge & Cafe   CABINS $$
(☑ 575-756-2105; www.elkhornlodge.net; Hwy 84; r/cabin from $79/89; ❄) On the banks of the Rio Chama, Elkhorn offers blue-ribbon fly-fishing spots, chuckwagon barbecue dinners and old-time cowboy dances. Choose a simple but spacious motel room in the main log cabin or a freestanding cabin with kitchenette (great for families).

★ **High Country**
Restaurant & Saloon   STEAK $$
(☑ 575-756-2384; www.thehighcountrychama.com; 2289 S Hwy 17; mains $7-28; ⊙ 11am-10pm) The round-the-clock throng of diners tell you this Wild West diner, at the Y-junction south of town, is something out of the ordinary. Whether you order a simple chile burger, a Mexican staple or one of the pricier daily grilled fish or meat specials, you can bet good money it'll be both substantial and delicious.

ℹ Getting There & Away

Chama's old downtown is 1.5 miles north of the so-called Y-junction where Hwy 84/64 turns west toward Farmington and Pagosa Springs, CO, while Hwy 17 heads north toward Antonito, CO.

Jicarilla Apache Indian Reservation

POP 3000

The Apache were relatively late arrivals in the Southwest, migrating in small bands from the north to reach the region around the 14th century, at much the same time as the related Navajo. Centuries of alternating conflict and cooperation with the Pueblo peoples already living here ensued. Indeed, the very name 'Apache' comes from the Zuni word for enemy, '*apachu*.' The current name of the Jicarilla people (pronounced hic-a-*ree*-ya) means 'little basket' in Spanish reflecting their great skill in basket weaving. Apache crafts generally draw visitors to the 1360-sq-mile **reservation** (www.jicarillaonline.com).

Tiny **Dulce**, on Hwy 64 in the northern part of the reservation, is the tribal capital. Unlike most reservations, alcohol is available. No permits or fees are needed to drive through, and photography is permitted. The **Little Beaver Celebration**, which includes a rodeo, powwow and pony race, is held the third weekend of July.

Cuba

POP 750 / ELEV 6906FT

Attractively overlooked by the Nacimiento Mountains, the village of Cuba marks the point where the broad, fast Hwy 550 crosses the Rio Puerco, roughly halfway between the I-25 interstate and the turnoff for Chaco Canyon – Bernalillo is 65 miles southeast, and Nageezi 50 miles northwest.

Sleeping & Eating

★ **Circle A Ranch** RANCH
(☑575-289-3350; www.circlearanchnm.com; 510 Los Pinos Rd; r/apt $89/250) Set on 360 beautiful riverside acres, 5 miles north of Cuba, this lovely old adobe lodge has exposed beams, peaceful grounds, hiking trails and a classic kitchen. It's an ideal overnight stop for Chaco visitors, a site the proprietor is passionate about – if you mention your intention to visit Chaco when booking you'll get the discounted rate quoted here. They have comfortable refurbished rooms and private apartments, but no hostel-style accommodations.

El Bruno's MEXICAN
(☑575-289-9429; www.elbrunos.com; Hwy 550; mains $8-25; ⊙11am-10pm) The best place to eat for many miles, this riverside restaurant, close to the bridge, serves high-class Mexican specialties from *carne asada* (spicy marinated steak strips in a burrito or taco) to steak, and has a shaded outdoor patio.

Navajo Dam

Trout are jumpin' and visitors are floatin'. Navajo Lake, which stretches over 30 miles

northeast and across into Colorado, was created by damming the San Juan River. At the base of the dam, there's world-class **trout fishing**. You can fish year-round, but a series of designated zones, each with different regulations, protect the stocks.

Activities

Simon Canyon Recreation Area HIKING
(www.blm.gov; County Rd 4280; ⊙24hr) FREE For a superb short hike, follow County Rd 4280 a mile east of Cottonwood Campground, then walk north into the Simon Canyon Recreation Area. A round-trip hike of 40 minutes leads onto the rim of this small side canyon, and then to an amazing single-room round tower, somehow built atop a solitary boulder by the Navajo 300 years ago.

Born-n-Raised on the San Juan River FISHING
(☑505-632-2194; www.sanjuanriver.com; 1791 Hwy 173; half-/full-day trip from $255/325) Based at Abe's Motel & Fly Shop, this is the best of several outfitters in the tiny community of Navajo Dam who provide equipment, information and guided trips. The more people in your group, the cheaper the trip.

Navajo Lake Marina BOATING
(☑505-632-3245; www.navajomarina.com; 1448 Hwy 511; half-day rental from $150) River floating is popular downstream from Navajo Lake. Rent boats here and put in at the Texas Hole parking lot at Mile 12 on Hwy 511. Then lazily float 2.5 miles to Crusher Hole. Ahhh.

Sleeping & Eating

Pine Campground CAMPGROUND
(☑505-632-2278; www.nmparks.com; Hwy 511; tent/RV sites $8/14) The largest of several campgrounds beside the lake, a couple of miles north of the dam, also holds a visitor center and marina.

Cottonwood Campground CAMPGROUND
(☑505-632-2278; www.nmparks.com; Hwy 511; tent/RV sites $8/14) Smaller-scale campground, occupying a lovely spot under the cottonwoods on the San Juan River, 8 miles west of Navajo Lake. It has drinking water and toilets but no showers.

Enchanted Hideaway Lodge LODGE $
(☑505-632-2634; www.enchantedhideawaylodge.com; Hwy 173; ste/house from $65/200; ❋ 🕾) The Enchanted Hideaway Lodge, 8 miles west of the dam, is a friendly and low-key place to spend a night or two, with several pleasant

suites. Fisherfolk on a budget can stay in the good-value Fly Room, while the spacious Stone House can sleep up to 8 people.

Soaring Eagle Lodge   LODGE $$$

(☑505-632-3721;   www.soaringeaglelodge.net; Hwy 173; r incl breakfast from $370; ❄️ 🛜) For anglers especially, this peaceful riverside lodge offers multinight guided fishing tours and half- and full-board options (perfect for those wanting to devote all their waking hours to fishing). Its kitchenette suites are beautifully sited beneath the cliffs; try to get one right on the river.

El Pescador   MEXICAN $

(☑505-632-5129; 1794 Hwy 173; mains $6-12; ⏱11am-8pm) Standard, but decent, Mexican and American meals, 6 miles west of the dam.

Aztec

POP 6700 / ELEV 5623FT

Little Aztec, a sleepy old-fashioned counterpoint to hyperactive Farmington a dozen miles southwest, is best known as the site of the ancient Pueblo now preserved at Aztec Ruins National Monument. Its quaint downtown area along Main St holds some interesting century-old architecture. The annual **Aztec Fiesta Days** (first weekend in June) has arts and crafts, food booths and a bonfire during which 'Old Man Gloom' is burned to celebrate the start of summer.

💿 Sights

Aztec Ruins National Monument   ARCHAEOLOGICAL SITE

(☑505-334-6174; www.nps.gov/azru; 84 Ruins Rd; adult/child $5/free; ⏱8am-5pm Sep-May, to 6pm Jun-Aug) This prehistoric Pueblo was built around AD 1100, and connected with the larger settlement at Chaco – literally so, by a 'road' that ran due south. Its central feature, a huge Great Kiva of the kind seen in ruins at Chaco, has been reconstructed to give an eerie impression of how such places must have looked in use a thousand years ago. Rangers give early afternoon talks about ancient architecture, trade routes and astronomy in summer.

Aztec Museum & Pioneer Village   MUSEUM

(☑505-334-9829; www.aztecmuseum.org; 125 N Main Ave; adult/child $3/1; ⏱10am-4pm Tue-Sat May-Sep) Small but excellent history museum, with an eclectic collection of historical objects, including telephones, barbershop chairs and a great display Victorian-era photographs, as well as original and replica early buildings, such as a church, jail and bank.

🛏️ Sleeping & Eating

Step Back Inn   HOTEL $

(☑505-334-1200; www.stepbackinn.com; 123 W Aztec Blvd; r from $72; ❄️ 🛜) Much the best place to stay in Aztec, this friendly and unexpectedly smart little motel, on the highway across from Main St and looking more like something you'd expect to find in New England than New Mexico, offers tasteful antique-furnished rooms.

Wonderful House   CHINESE $$

(☑505-334-1832; 115 W Aztec Blvd; mains $9-16; ⏱11am-9pm Tue-Sun) The dynamic young staff here, on the main highway next to the Step Back Inn, work hard to live up to its far-from-bashful name, serving up quick-fire platefuls of tasty Chinese food.

HIKING AZTEC'S GOLDEN ARCHES

The great little *Aztec Arches* brochure, available at Aztec's helpful **visitor center** (☑505-334-9551; www.aztecnm.com; 110 N Ash St; ⏱8am-5pm Mon-Fri), provides driving directions to 16 of what it claims are 220 natural sandstone arches hidden away nearby.

Several of the most accessible lie just off Hwy 173, which branches east toward Navajo Dam from US 550, 1 mile north of Aztec. Exactly 5.6 miles along Hwy 173, head south into **Potter Canyon** for half a mile on a dirt road, and park at a little gas well. Three distinct arches loom within a few hundred yards' walk in different directions from here – Pillar Arch directly above the lot, and Outcrop and Alien arches silhouetted to the south and west.

Another group can be found in **Pilares Canyon**, 10.9 miles east of US 550 on Hwy 173. This time you turn left for 0.2 miles, and then left again, driving 0.4 miles to reach Peephole Arch. Be careful if you're in an ordinary vehicle; the road here is very sandy, so it may well be safer to walk from this point to reach Petroglyph, Rooftop and Two Cracks Arches.

WORTH A TRIP

FINDING NAVAJO RUGS

Sure, galleries in cities and towns throughout New Mexico sell Navajo rugs, but why not have a little adventure and seek them out close to the homes of the finest weavers? The villages of **Two Grey Hills** and **Toadlena**, tucked into the eastern flank of the Chuska Mountains 35 miles south of Shiprock, are famous as the sources of the finest rugs in Navajo country. Local weavers largely reject commercially produced wool and synthetic dyes, preferring the wool of their own sheep in its natural hues. They card white, brown, gray and black hairs together, blending the colors to the desired effect, then spin and weave the wool – tight – into mesmerizing geometric patterns. Many of these world-class artisans sell their work at the **Toadlena Trading Post** (☑505-984-0005; www.toadlenatradingpost.com), just off Hwy 491 in **Newcomb**. Prices range from $125 to $7000 or more.

Another off-the-beaten-path spot to check out Native American textiles is at the monthly **Crownpoint Navajo Rug Auction** (☑505-730-9689; www.crownpointrugauction.com), where you can talk to and buy from the weavers directly. Check the website for dates and driving directions.

☆ Entertainment

Historic Aztec Theater   LIVE MUSIC
(☑505-427-6748; www.crashmusicaztec.com; 104 N Main St) Great things are afoot in this venerable theater, across from the local museum. It's being brought back to life by a dynamic husband-and-wife duo who run it as a cafe and music workshop, and bring in rockabilly, blues, and Americana acts to play riproaring live gigs on alternate Saturday nights. Be sure to check it out if you're in town.

Farmington & Around

POP 46,000 / ELEV 5395FT

The region's largest town is a modern oil- and gas-industry center that makes a decent overnight base. Farmington itself has some nice parkland on the San Juan River, but most visitors are simply passing through en route to Monument Valley or the remote and beautiful Chaco Culture National Historical Park, two hours' drive south.

◉ Sights & Activities

Farmington Museum at
Gateway Park   MUSEUM
(www.farmingtonmuseum.org; 3041 E Main St; suggested donation $3; ⊙8am-5pm Mon-Sat) Farmington's one significant visitor attraction, this large modern museum traces the town's history and growth, with a reconstruction of its first trading post, and also mounts changing art shows. Its new Energy Wing covers the local gas and oil industry.

Shiprock   MOUNTAIN
By far the coolest sight around these parts, Shiprock looms eerily over the landscape 40 miles west of Farmington. A 1700ft-high volcanic plug and a lofty landmark for Anglo pioneers, it's also a sacred site to the Navajo. While it's visible from Hwy 64, you'll get better views from Hwy 491 (which when known as Hwy 666 had a starring role in Oliver Stone's *Natural Born Killers*). Indian Hwy 13, which almost skirts its base, is another good photo-op area.

Salmon Ruins   ARCHAEOLOGICAL SITE
(☑505-632-2013; www.salmonruins.com; adult/child $3/1; ⊙8am-5pm Mon-Fri, 9am-5pm Sat & Sun, from noon Sun Nov-Apr) The ancient Pueblo preserved here was built in the early 1100s by the Chaco people. Abandoned, resettled by refugees from Mesa Verde and again abandoned before 1300, the site also includes the remains of a homestead, petroglyphs, a Navajo hogan and a wickiup (a rough brushwood shelter). To reach it, follow Hwy 64 11 miles east of Farmington toward Bloomfield.

Bisti Badlands   HIKING
This undeveloped realm of multicolored hoodoos, sculpted cliffs and balancing rocks is 38 miles south of Farmington, off Hwy 371. Follow the well-worn (but unmaintained) path from the parking area for a mile to reach the heart of the formations, then wander as you will, taking care not to damage the fragile geology. Overnight camping is allowed – dawn and dusk are the most spectacular times – but you have to haul in all your water. Farmington's Bureau of Land Management (BLM) office has information.

DON'T MISS

CHACO CULTURE NATIONAL HISTORICAL PARK

A thousand years ago, **Chaco Canyon** (www.nps.gov/chcu; per vehicle $8; ⊙ 7am–sunset) – set in the high, arid desert in what's now a remote corner of northwestern New Mexico and a National Historical Park – stood at the center of a highly organized and integrated culture that extended far beyond the immediate area. Thought to have been primarily religious rather than residential, attracting pilgrims from across the region, it was also a trading center. Turquoise from Chaco found its way south to the great civilizations of Mexico. A carefully engineered network of 30ft-wide roads radiated out from the canyon; few are visible to the naked eye, but 450 miles have been identified from aerial photos and ground surveys.

The canyon floor is scattered with the remarkably preserved remains of 'Great Houses,' each a vast semicircular Pueblo in its own right. The largest of them all, **Pueblo Bonito**, towers four stories tall. Built from around AD 850 onwards, it held 600 to 800 rooms and kivas. None of the ruins have been reconstructed, but their intricate masonry remains astonishingly intact. If you relish isolation and using your imagination, few places compare.

The park can only be accessed along rough and unpaved dirt roads, which can become impassable after heavy rains or snow. Park rangers prefer visitors to enter from the northeast, by turning south onto County Rd 7900 at mile marker 112.5 on Hwy 44/550, 3 miles south of the Nageezi Trading Post. The first 5-mile stretch from there is paved; you then turn right onto County Rd 7950, with only 3 miles of the remaining 16 to the park entrance being paved. You can also reach the park from the south, however, by following Hwy 9 and Hwy 14 northeast from Crownpoint.

Bring food and plenty of gas; none is available at the park itself, where facilities are minimal. There is a good **visitor center** (☎ 505-786-7014; ⊙ 8am–5pm), though, which is the only place you can get water, and also runs evening astronomy programs in summer, and issues free backcountry hiking permits. The only permitted camping is 1 mile east. The **Gallo Campground** (☎ 877-444-6777; www.recreation.gov; sites $15) has toilets, picnic tables, and grills – you'll need your own wood or charcoal – but no hookups.

✸ Festivals & Events

Riverfest FESTIVAL
(⊙ late May) Music, arts and crafts, and food.

Totah Festival CULTURAL
(www.totahfestival.farmingtonnm.org; ⊙ early Sep) Labor Day weekend, with juried Native American arts and crafts and a Navajo rug auction.

Northern Navajo Nation Fair CULTURAL
(www.northernnavajonationfair.org; ⊙ early Oct) Held in Shiprock and featuring a rodeo, powwow and traditional dancing, this fair is perhaps the most traditional of the large Native American gatherings. It begins with the Night Way, a complex Navajo healing ceremony, and the Yei Bei Chei chant, which lasts for several days.

🛏 Sleeping & Eating

You can find every chain hotel imaginable around the intersection of Broadway and Scott Ave.

Silver River Adobe Inn B&B B&B $$
(☎ 575-325-8219; www.silveradobe.com; 3151 W Main St; r $115-175; ❄ 🛜) Three miles from downtown, this lovely two-room place offers a peaceful respite among the trees on the San Juan River. Fall asleep to the sound of the river, wake to organic blueberry juice and enjoy a morning walk to the prairie-dog village. There's also an attractive adobe-and-wood guesthouse. Advance reservations required.

★ Kokopelli's Cave QUIRKY $$$
(☎ 505-860-3812; www.bbonline.com/nm/kokopelli; cave $280) For something truly unique, sleep 70ft underground in this incredible 1650-sq-ft cave dwelling, carved from La Plata River sandstone. Equipped with a kitchen stocked for breakfast, DVD player and hot tub, it offers magnificent views over the desert and river, in astonishing isolation. A 3-mile drive on dirt roads and a short hike is required to reach it.

Three Rivers Eatery & Brewhouse
AMERICAN $$

(☑505-324-2187; www.threeriversbrewery.com; 101 E Main St; mains $9-32; ☺11am-9pm; ⊕)
Managing to be both trendy *and* kid-friendly, this hip spot spreads through an entire block, serving good food and its own microbrews. Try the homemade potato skins or artichoke and spinach dip, but remember the steaks are substantial. Spiffy sandwiches (like a Thai turkey wrap) and soups (broccoli cheddar) are served at lunchtime.

❶ Information

Bureau of Land Management (BLM; ☑505-564-7600; www.nm.blm.gov; 6251 College Blvd; ☺7:45am-4:30pm Mon-Fri)

San Juan Regional Medical Center Hospital (☑505-609-2000; www.sanjuanregional.com; 801 W Maple St) Has a 24hr emergency department.

Visitors Bureau (☑505-326-7602; www.farmingtonnm.org; 3041 E Main St; ☺8am-5pm Mon-Sat) Useful information desk in the Farmington Museum.

❶ Getting There & Away

Greyhound buses no longer serve Farmington, but **Great Lakes Airlines** (www.flygreatlakes.com) offers daily connections between the **Four Corners Regional Airport** (☑505-599-1395), a mile northwest of Farmington, and the cities of Denver and Phoenix.

Gallup

POP 21,700 / ELEV 6468FT

The mother town on New Mexico's Mother Road seems stuck in time. Settled in 1881, when the railroad came to town, Gallup had its heyday during the 1950s, and many of its dilapidated old motels, pawn shops and billboards have barely changed since the Eisenhower administration.

Just outside the Navajo reservation, modern-day Gallup is an interesting mix of Anglos and Native Americans. Tourism is limited mostly to Route 66 road-trippers and those in search of Native American history. Even with visitors, it's not exactly crowded, and at night it turns downright quiet.

Gallup has started to capitalize on its outdoor attractions, and a growing number of rock climbers and mountain bikers come to challenge their bodies on surrounding sandstone buttes and red mesa tops.

◉ Sights

Local Native Americans perform social **Indian dances** at 7pm nightly from late June to early September at the McKinley County Courthouse (p320).

Historic District
NEIGHBORHOOD

Route 66, the 'main street of America,' runs straight through downtown Gallup's historic district, lined with pretty, renovated light-red sandstone buildings housing kitschy souvenir shops and galleries selling Native American arts and crafts. A brochure available at the visitor center details around 20 noteworthy structures, built along 1st, 2nd and 3rd Sts between 1895 and 1938. They include the small **Rex Museum** (☑505-863-1363; 300 W Rte 66; admission by donation; ☺8:30am-3:30pm Mon-Fri), displaying historical artifacts in a former hotel.

El Morro Theatre
THEATER

(☑505-726-0050; www.elmorrotheatre.com; 207 W Coal Ave) Downtown Gallup's centerpiece is this beautifully restored Spanish Colonial-style theater, which originally opened in 1928. As well as live theater, music and dance, it hosts movies and children's programs.

Gallup Cultural Center
CULTURAL BUILDING

(www.southwestindian.com; 218 E Rte 66; ☺8am-5pm) This cultural center houses a good little museum of Indian art, including excellent collections of kachina dolls both new and old, plus pottery, sand painting and weaving. A 10ft-tall bronze sculpture of a Navajo code-talker honors the sacrifices made by Navajo men in WWII. A tiny theater screens films about Chaco and the Four Corners region. In summer, traditional dances are held nightly at 7pm.

🏃 Activities

Red Rock Park
OUTDOORS

(☑505-722-3839; ☺park 24hr, museum 8am-4pm Mon-Fri) Gallup is becoming known as the kind of outdoors town where those who wish to can still get lost on the bike trails. Hikers should head 6 miles east to this beautiful park, which holds a little museum and trading post with modern and traditional Indian crafts, a campground and hiking trails. The 3-mile round-trip **Pyramid Rock** trail leads past amazing rock formations, with 50-mile views – on clear days – from the 7487ft summit.

STRETCH YOUR LEGS: GALLUP MURAL WALK

Outdoor murals all over downtown, portraying local life over the centuries, showcase Gallup's tricultural and distinctly Southwestern soul.

The oldest, like those in the **McKinley County Courthouse** (213 W Coal Ave), were created during the Depression, when President Franklin D Roosevelt's 1930s WPA program set unemployed men to work building and beautifying towns and parks across the country.

Eleven new murals by local artists can be viewed on a 10-block walk. Ranging from abstract to realist, they depict tales of peace and turmoil throughout Gallup's history. Although the murals are large, they don't detract from the overall historic aesthetic; rather, they lend a different look to another small, struggling Western town.

Start at the corner of W Aztec Ave and S 2nd St. The first mural, **Great Gallup** by Paul Newman and Steve Heil, is on the west-facing wall of City Hall and uses assorted media to create a graphic narrative of life in Gallup in panels. Look for locals on horseback in one, and a blue pickup truck, so laboriously detailed it resembles an old photograph, in another. Our other favorite is the last mural on the walk, Irving Bahl's **Gallup Inter-Tribal Indian Ceremonial Mural** on the Ceremonial Building between 2nd and 3rd Sts on Coal Ave, illustrating Native American traditions and sacred Navajo symbols.

High Desert Trail System   MOUNTAIN BIKING
(www.galluptrails2010.com) Mountain bikers can test their skills 3 miles north of Gallup on Hwy 491, off the Chico/Gamerco Rd. Terrain to suit all skill levels includes plenty of sick, slick rock – try the loops off the main trail for the most challenging rides. Pick up maps at the tourist office.

Mentmore Rock Climbing Area   ROCK CLIMBING
This climbing area lets you challenge yourself with 50 different bolted toprope climbs and some free-climbing areas. Difficulty levels range from 5.0 to 5.13 – grab maps and info at the visitor center. You'll need your own gear and to know what you are doing. Reach the park via Exit 16 off I-40; head north on County Rd 1.

✪ Festivals & Events

Book accommodations as far ahead as possible during these annual events.

Lions Club Rodeo   CULTURAL
(www.galluplionsclubrodeo.com; ☉ Jun) The most professional and prestigious of several area rodeos, held in the third week in June.

Gallup Inter-Tribal Indian Ceremonial   CULTURAL
(☉ early Aug) Thousands of Native Americans and non-Indian tourists throng the streets of Gallup and the huge amphitheater at Red Rock State Park in early August for the Gallup Inter-Tribal Indian Ceremonial. Instigated almost a century ago, it features a professional all-Indian rodeo, beautifully bedecked ceremonial dancers from many tribes and a powwow with competitive dancing.

Navajo Nation Fair   CULTURAL
(www.navajonationfair.com; ☉ early Sep) While this huge fair, on the first weekend in September, actually takes place in nearby Window Rock, just across the Arizona state line, it effectively spills over into Gallup, which is in any case a better place to stay.

Red Rock Balloon Rally   BALLOON
(www.redrockballoonrally.com; ☉ early Dec) Almost 200 hot-air balloons take part in demonstrations and competitions at Red Rock State Park, on the first weekend in December.

🛏 Sleeping

Chain and independent motels cluster just off I-40 at the edge of Gallup. Only a few of the 1950s motor lodges in town are still open, and most of those are pretty dodgy. Room rates double during Ceremonial week and other big events.

Red Rock Park Campground   CAMPGROUND $
(☎ 505-722-3839; Churchrock, off Hwy 66; tent/RV sites $17/20; ☒) Pop your tent up in this beautiful setting with easy access to tons of hiking trails. Six miles east of town, it has showers, flush toilets, drinking water and a grocery store.

★ **El Rancho**   HISTORIC HOTEL $$
(☎ 505-863-9311; www.elranchohotel.com; 1000 E Hwy 66; r from $102; ▣❀❈☒) Opened in 1937, with a superb lobby resembling a rus-

tic hunting lodge, Gallup's finest historic hotel quickly became known as the 'home of the movie stars.' Big, bright and decorated with eclectic Old West fashions, rooms are named after former guests like Humphrey Bogart and John Wayne. There's also a good restaurant and bar, plus a cheaper, modern motel wing.

✖ Eating & Drinking

Many restaurants in Gallup do not serve liquor, so choose carefully if you want to have beer with dinner.

Coffee House CAFE $
(☑505-726-0291; 203 W Coal Ave; mains $4-10; ☺7am-8:30pm Mon-Sat) With local art on the walls and casual simplicity infusing the space, this is Gallup's quintessential coffee shop. Soups, sandwiches, pastries – all good.

Genaro's Cafe MEXICAN $
(☑505-863-6761; www.genarosrestaurant.com; 600 W Hill Ave; mains $7-15; ☺10:30am-7:30pm Tue-Sat) Smart Mexican restaurant, three blocks up from Route 66, serving large portions of food but no alcohol. If you like your chile hot, you'll feel right at home here, just like the rest of Gallup – this place can get crowded.

El Rancho Restaurant AMERICAN $$
(☑505-863-9311; 1000 E Hwy 66; breakfast & lunch $6-14, dinner $9-24; ☺6:30am-10pm; ⊛) Western-themed restaurant, serving good steaks, burgers and salads. Dishes are named for movie stars, on a decidedly pre-feminist menu where 'leading ladies' like Lucille Ball are assigned fruit and cottage cheese while the boys get to sink their teeth into hunks of beef. The adjoining 49ers Lounge offers drinks in an Old West setting and live music once a month.

Earl's Family Restaurant DINER $$
(☑505-863-4201; 1400 E Hwy 66; mains $8-17; ☺6am-9pm Mon-Sat, from 7am Sun; ⊛) The name says it all – Earl's is a great place to bring the kids. Fast food and dinerlike, it has been serving great green chile and fried chicken (but no alcohol) since the late 1940s, and is always packed on weekends. You may even get some shopping done: Navajo vendors sell goods to passing tourists.

🔒 Shopping

Gallup serves as the Navajo and Zuni peoples' major trading center, and is arguably the best place in New Mexico to buy top-quality

goods at fair prices. Many trading posts are located in the historic downtown.

Ellis Tanner Trading Company ARTS & CRAFTS
(☑505-863-4434; www.etanner.com; 1980 Hwy 602; ☺8am-7pm Mon-Sat) Just south of town toward Zuni, this long-established store, run by a fourth-generation trader, sells everything from rugs and jewelry to hardware and groceries. Be sure to check out the pawn shop.

ℹ Information

Gallup Visitor Information Center (☑505-727-4440; www.gallupnm.org; 201 E Rte 66; ☺8:30am-5pm Mon-Fri) Grab a copy of the annual, full-color Gallup visitors guide.
Police (☑505-863-9365; 451 S Boardman Ave)
Post Office (950 W Aztec Ave)
Rehoboth McKinley Christian Hospital (☑505-863-7000; www.rmch.org; 1901 Red Rock Dr; ☺24hr emergency)

ℹ Getting There & Around

From the **Amtrak** (www.amtrak.com; 201 E Hwy 66) station downtown, one daily train runs west to Flagstaff, AZ ($45, 2½ hours), and one heads west to Albuquerque ($24, 3½ hours), complete with informative narration from an 'Indian Country Guide.'

Greyhound (☑505-863-9078; 3060 W Hwy 66) buses stop at the Route 66 Minimart, inconveniently located 4 miles east of downtown. Three daily services go to both Flagstaff ($26, three hours) and Albuquerque ($22, 2½ hours).

Zuni Pueblo

POP 10,000 / ELEV 6293FT

Zuni Pueblo (☑505-782-7238; www.zuni tourism.com; 1239 Hwy 53; tours $10; ☺8:30am-5:30pm Mon-Fri, 10:30am-4pm Sat, noon-4pm Sun), 35 miles south of Gallup and the largest in New Mexico, was the first to be encountered by Coronado's Spanish expedition in 1540. It's now famous for its jewelry and fetishes (small stone animal carvings). Small shops and galleries along Hwy 53 at the edge of town sell beautiful pieces; whether or not you buy, it's still worth driving through for the sublime sandstone scenery.

At the heart of the Pueblo, beyond stone houses and beehive-shaped mud-brick ovens, the massive **Our Lady of Guadalupe Mission**, originally dating from 1629, features impressive murals of about 30 kachinas (ancestral spirits).

The most famous ceremony at Zuni is the all-night **Shalak'o** ceremonial dance, held on the last weekend in December. The **Zuni Tribal Fair** (late August) features a powwow, local food, and arts-and-crafts stalls. To participate in any ceremony hosted by the Zuni community, you must attend an orientation; call the tourist office for more information.

⊙ Sights

Ashiwi Awan Museum & Heritage Center   MUSEUM
(☑ 505-782-4403; www.ashiwi-museum.org; Ojo Caliente Rd; admission by donation; ⊙ 9am-5pm Mon-Fri) The Pueblo's museum holds imaginative and highly informative displays of tribal artifacts and historic photos. They'll also cook traditional meals for groups of 10 or more ($10 per person) with advance reservations.

Sleeping

★ **Inn at Halona**   INN $
(☑ 505-782-4547; www.halona.com; 23b Pia Mesa Rd; r from $75; P 🐾) This exceptionally friendly inn, across from the museum behind the Halona Plaza food store, is the only place in New Mexico where visitors can stay in the middle of a Pueblo. Check out which of its eight pleasant and very different rooms, decorated with Zuni arts and crafts, fits your fancy. Breakfast is served in the flagstone courtyard in summer.

❶ Information

Zuni Tourism Office   VISITOR CENTER
(☑ 505-782-7238; www.zunitourism.com; 1239 Hwy 53; ⊙ 8am-5:30pm Mon-Fri, 10am-4pm Sat, noon-4pm Sun) Extremely helpful information center, which sells photography permits and offers daily tours.

SCENIC ROUTE 53

A great alternative way to reach Grants from Gallup is via Scenic Route 53, which runs parallel to, and south of, I-40. It takes a full day to really experience this out-of-this-world landscape of lava tubes and red arches, volcanic craters and ice caves, as well as unique historical attractions and traditional New Mexican towns.

Start your day by heading a half-hour south of Gallup on Hwy 602, then turn east on Hwy 53 to begin. **El Morro National Monument** (☑ 505-783-4226; www.nps.gov/elmo; ⊙ 9am-6pm Jun-Aug, to 5pm Sep-May) **FREE**, 52 miles southeast of Gallup, is home to the extraordinary **Inscription Rock**. For many centuries, travelers have left their mark on this 200ft outcrop, making it something like a sandstone guestbook, covered with carvings from Pueblo petroglyphs at the top (c 1250) to inscriptions by Spaniard conquistadors and Anglo pioneers. Of the two trails from the visitor center, the paved, half-mile loop to Inscription Rock itself is wheelchair accessible; the more demanding, 2-mile **Mesa Top loop trail** is unpaved, and requires a steep climb to reach ancient pueblo sites. Trail access ends one hour before closing.

To camp, visit **El Morro RV Park & Cabins** (☑ 505-783-4612; www.elmorro-nm.com; Hwy 53; tent/RV sites $15/25, cabins $79-94; 🐾) a mile east of the visitor center with 26 sites and six cabins. The on-site **Ancient Way Cafe** (mains $6-12; ⊙ 9am-5pm Sun-Thu, 9am-8pm Fri & Sat; 🍴) serves home-cooked American, New Mexican and veggie specialties in a rustic dining room. You can wake up in the morning with an espresso and eggs. Before you reach El Morro, you'll pass through the small town of **Ramah**. Some of Ramah's Navajo population still practice sheep raising, weaving and other land-based traditions. Most non-Indians are descendents of Mormon settlers. The **Stage Coach Cafe** (☑ 505-783-4288; 3370 Bond St/Hwy 53; mains $6-16; ⊙ 7am-9pm Mon-Sat) is a worthy place to eat, with friendly service, great steaks and Mexican food, and a giant selection of pies.

Animal-lovers won't want to miss the **Wild Spirit Wolf Sanctuary** (☑ 505-775-3304; www.wildspiritwolfsanctuary.org; 378 Candy Kitchen Rd; tours adult/child $7/4, tent $15, cabin $85; ⊙ tours 11am, 12:30pm, 2pm & 3:30pm Tue-Sun; 🐾), a 20-mile detour off Hwy 53, southeast of Ramah. Home to rescued captive-born wolves and wolf-dog mixes, the sanctuary offers four quarter-mile walking tours per day, where you walk with the wolves that roam the large natural-habitat enclosures. If you want to stay overnight, you can choose between primitive camping or a guest cabin with two bedrooms, a big loft and full kitchen; both include all the wolf howling you ever wanted to hear.

Grants

POP 9200 / ELEV 6460FT

Having boomed first as a railroad stop, and then as a mining town, Grants today seems to be an ever-dwindling strip along Route 66, largely relying on jobs at state prison facilities nearby.

About 16 miles northeast of Grants looms **Mt Taylor** (11,301ft), sacred to the Navajo. Follow Hwy 547 to USFS (US Forestry Service) Rd 239, then USFS Rd 453 to **La Mosca Lookout** (11,000ft) for views. There are a couple of USFS campgrounds along the way, and chain hotels around exit 85 off I-40.

Sights

New Mexico Mining Museum MUSEUM
(☑505-287-4802; 100 N Iron Ave; adult/child $3/2; ☺9am-4pm Mon-Sat;) What claims to be the world's only uranium-mining museum also doubles as the local visitor center. Hands-on exhibits are made for kids, who will dig descending the 'mine shaft' into the underground mine – it's a mock-up of course, with a distinct resemblance to a fairground ghost train, but it's fun and informative.

Eating

Coco Bean Cafe CAFE $
(☑505-285-4143; 333 Nimitz Dr; mains $5-7; ☺7am-7pm Mon-Fri, 8am-4:30pm Sat, 9am-2pm Sun) Large and very local coffee bar, a few blocks north of the main drag, serving good-value sandwiches and salads along with its espresso drinks.

La Bella Vita ITALIAN $$
(☑505-287-4200; 319 W Santa Fe Ave; mains $11-19; ☺11am-8:30pm) Colorful, cheerful Italian cafe and take-out in a central old adobe, serving an excellent range of meat, seafood

For a few more comforts, head back to Hwy 53 and continue east to find **Cimarron Rose** (☑800-856-5776; www.cimarronrose.com; 689 Oso Ridge Rd; ste $145-210), an ecofriendly B&B between Miles 56 and 57. There are three Southwestern-style suites (two have kitchens), plus a charming common room. Two goats and a horse fertilize Cimarron's perennial gardens, which provide food and shelter for more than 80 bird species.

Next up is **El Malpais National Monument** (www.nps.gov/elma). Pronounced 'el-mahl-pie-ees', and meaning 'bad land' in Spanish, it consists of almost 200 sq miles of lava flows abutting adjacent sandstone. Five major flows have been identified, the most recent pegged at 2000 to 3000 years old. Prehistoric Native Americans may have witnessed the final eruptions: local legends refer to 'rivers of fire.' Scenic Hwy 117 leads modern-day explorers past cinder cones and spatter cones, smooth pahoehoe lava and jagged a'a lava, ice caves and a 17-mile-long lava tube system.

El Malpais is a hodgepodge of National Park Service (NPS) land, private land, conservation areas and wilderness areas administered by the Bureau of Land Management (BLM); each area has different regulations. The **BLM Ranger Station** (☑505-280-2918; Hwy 117; ☺8:30am-4:30pm), 9 miles south of I-40, has permits and information for the Cibola National Forest, while the **El Malpais Information Center** (☑505-783-4774; Hwy 53; ☺8:30am-4:30pm), 22 miles southwest of Grants, has permits and information for the lava flows and NPS land. Backcountry camping is allowed, but free permits are required. Though the terrain can be difficult, there are several opportunities for hiking. One interesting but rough hike (wear sturdy footwear), the 7.5-mile (one-way) **Zuni-Acoma Trail**, leaves Hwy 117 about 4 miles south of the ranger station, and crosses several lava flows to end at Hwy 53 on the west side of the monument. Just beyond **La Ventana Natural Arch**, a mighty hold in a sandstone cliff that's visible from Hwy 117 and is 17 miles south of I-40, is the **Narrows Trail**, about 4 miles (one-way). Thirty miles south of I-40, **Lava Falls** is a 1-mile loop.

If you have a high-clearance 4WD, set off along the unpaved County Rd 42, which leaves Hwy 117 about 34 miles south of I-40 and meanders for 40 miles through the BLM country on the west side of El Malpais. It passes several craters, caves and lava tubes (reached by signed trails) and emerges at Hwy 53 near Bandera Crater. Be prepared for poor signage at the many forks en route, so drive during daylight, when you can (hopefully) intuit which turns to make. If you go spelunking, the park service requires each person to carry two sources of light and to wear a hard hat. Take a companion – this is an isolated area.

and vegetarian pasta dishes, from eggplant parmesan to shrimp scampi.

❶ Information

Cibola National Forest Mount Taylor Ranger Station (📞 505-287-8833; www.fs.usda.gov/cibola; 1800 Lobo Canyon Rd; ⏰ 8am-noon & 1-5pm Mon-Fri)

Northwest New Mexico Visitor Center (📞 505-876-2783; south side of I-40 exit 85; ⏰ 8am-5pm) Run by the National Park Service, this large modern Pueblo-style building is an invaluable resource for anyone visiting nearby public lands, and especially the El Morro and El Malpais national monuments southwest of Grants.

❶ Getting There & Away

Greyhound (www.greyhound.com) Greyhound stops at the Historic Route 66 Motel, 1150 E Santa Fe Ave, with two daily buses to Albuquerque ($13.50, 1¼ hours), Flagstaff, Arizona ($32, 4½ hours), and beyond. Book online for the best rates, or pay the driver in cash.

Acoma Pueblo

POP 5000 / ELEV 6460FT

The modern Indian reservation of **Acoma Pueblo** (📞 800-747-0181; www.acomaskycity.org) straddles the I-40 interstate 20 miles east of Grants and 60 miles west of Albuquerque. As well as three separate small communities here – Acomita, Anzac and McCartys – you'll no doubt spot the **Sky City Casino** (📞 877-552-6123; www.skycity.com; I-40, exit 102; r from $89; ❄ 🛜 🏊) beside the interstate, which offers 132 motel-style rooms, plus live entertainment. Dining options include an all-you-can-eat buffet ($8) that's a real bargain so long as you resist the urge to gamble as well.

The compelling reason to visit Acoma, however, is to see the extraordinary ancient Pueblo, 13 miles south of the interstate, and known as 'Sky City.'

Sky City

Journeying to the mesa-top village at Acoma Pueblo, famous as 'Sky City,' is like venturing into another world. There can be few more dramatic locations – it's set atop an isolated outcrop, 367ft above the surrounding plateau and 7000ft above sea level. People have lived here since the 11th century, making Acoma one of the oldest continuously inhabited locations in North America. In addition to its singular history and stunning setting, it's also justly famous for its pottery, sold by individual artists on the mesa. There is a distinction between 'traditional' pottery (made with clay dug on the reservation) and 'ceramic' pottery (made elsewhere with inferior clay and simply painted by the artist), so ask the vendor.

Visitors can only see the village on guided tours, which leave from the **Sky City Cultural Center** (📞 800-747-0181; www.acomaskycity.org; adult/child/camera $23/15/13; ⏰ tours 9:30am-3:30pm Mar-Nov) at the foot of the mesa. To avoid potential long waits here – though the building also holds the excellent **Haak'u Museum** (adult/child $4/2; ⏰ 9am-5pm Mar-Nov) of Pueblo history, a good shop, and a decent cafe – it's best to call in advance to reserve a specific time. Highlight of the tour itself is the mission church of San Esteban del Rey, decorated with Pueblo motifs. All visitors ride a shuttle van to the top of the mesa, but you can choose to return to the visitor center by walking down a rock footpath on your own. It's definitely worth doing this.

Festivals and events include the **Governor's Feast** (February), a harvest dance on **San Esteban Day** (September 2) and festivities at the **San Esteban Mission** (December 25–28). Note that the Pueblo is closed to visitors in winter (though check online for occasional weekend openings), and also June 24, June 29, July 9–14, July 25, and either the first or second weekend in October.

The Sky City Cultural Center stands around 13 miles south of either exit 96 or exit 108 off I-40.

Laguna Pueblo

POP 1250 / ELEV 5807FT

Laguna Pueblo (📞 505-552-6654; www.lagunapueblo-nsn.gov), 40 miles west of Albuquerque or 30 miles east of Grants, is New Mexico's youngest Pueblo. Founded in 1699 by a mixed group of settlers fleeing the Spaniards in the aftermath of the Pueblo Revolt, it consists of six small villages, each of which celebrates its own annual feast day, with the largest events on March 19, July 26, August 15 and September 19.

The imposing stone and adobe **San José Mission** (📞 505-552-9330; ⏰ 9am-3pm Mon-Fri) church, visible from I-40, was completed in 1705 and houses fine examples of early Spanish-influenced religious art.

SILVER CITY & SOUTHWESTERN NEW MEXICO

The Rio Grande Valley unfurls from Albuquerque down to the bubbling hot springs of funky Truth or Consequences and on toward Texas. En route, it feeds one of New Mexico's agricultural treasures: Hatch, the so-called 'chile capital of the world.' East of the river, the desert is so dry it's been known since Spanish times as the Jornada del Muerto, which literally translates as the 'day-long journey of the dead man.' Pretty appropriate that this area was chosen for the detonation of the first atomic bomb, at what's now Trinity Site.

Away from Las Cruces, the state's second-largest city, residents in these parts are few and far between. To the west, the rugged Gila National Forest is wild with backcountry adventure, while the Mimbres Valley is rich with archaeological treasures.

Be open to surprises: one of the state's most unique museums is in little Deming, and there are plenty more unexpected finds if you look around.

Socorro

POP 8900 / ELEV 4579FT

A quiet and amiable layover, Socorro has a good mix of buildings in its downtown, mostly dating from the late 19th century. Its name – *socorro* means 'help' in Spanish – supposedly dates to 1598, when Juan de Onate's expedition received help from Pilabo Pueblo (now defunct).

With the introduction of the railroad in 1880 and the discovery of gold and silver, Socorro became a major mining center. Until the mining boom went bust in 1893, it was

---

ONLY IN NEW MEXICO: SCENIC ROUTE 60

Highway 60 runs west from Socorro to the Arizona border, cutting past the surreal Sawtooth Mountains, across the vast, flat Plains of San Agustin, and through endless juniper hills. A few spots along the way are well worth a detour if you have the time.

Out on the plains, 40 miles west of Socorro, 27 huge antenna dishes (each weighing 230 tons) together comprise a single superpowered telescope – the **Very Large Array Radio Telescope** (VLA; ☑ 505-835-7243; www.nrao.edu; off Hwy 52; ☉ 8:30am-sunset) **FREE**, run by the National Radio Astronomy Observatory. Four miles south of the highway, they move along railroad tracks, reconfiguring the layout as needed to study the outer limits of the universe. To match this resolution, a regular telescope would have to be 22 miles wide. Not only has the VLA increased our understanding of such celestial phenomena as black holes, space gases and radio emissions, but it's appeared in movies including *Contact, Armageddon* and *Independence Day*. They're also unbelievably cool. From the small museum at the visitor center, you can take a free, self-guided tour.

Further west on Hwy 60, you'll pass through tiny **Pie Town**. Yes, seriously, a town named after pie. And for good reason. They say you can find the best pies in the universe here (which makes you wonder what they've *really* been doing at the VLA). The **Pie-O-Neer Cafe** (☑ 575-772-2711; www.pie-o-neer.com; Hwy 60; slices $4.95; ☉ 11am-4pm Thu-Sun) just might prove their case. The pies are dee-lish, the soups and stews they serve are homemade, and you'll be hard pressed to find another host as welcoming as Kathy Knapp – who suggests you call ahead to check someone hasn't eaten all the pie. On the second Saturday of September, Pie Town's **Pie Festival** (www.pietownfestival.com) features baking and eating contests, the coronation of a Pie Queen, Wild West gunfights and horned toad races.

Heading on toward Arizona, out in the high plains around Quemado, gleams the **Lightning Field** (☑ 505-898-3335; www.diaart.org/sites/main/lightningfield; adult/child $250/100 Jul-Aug, $150/100 May-Jun & Sep-Oct), an art installation created by Walter de Maria in 1977. Four hundred polished steel poles stand in a giant grid; each stainless rod is about 20ft tall, but the precise lengths vary so the tips are all level with each other. During summer monsoons, the poles seem to draw lightning out of hovering thunderheads. The effect is truly electrifying. You can only visit if you stay overnight in the simple on-site cabin, with only six visitors allowed per night. Advance reservations are required.

You can also reach Hwy 60 by heading south along back roads from Zuni Pueblo, Scenic Rte 53 and El Malpais.

EL CAMINO REAL

El Camino Real de Tierra Adentro – the Royal Road of the Interior Lands – was the Spanish colonial version of an interstate highway, linking Mexico City to the original capital of New Mexico at Ohkay Owingeh Pueblo. Later, the trail was extended to Taos. By 1600, two decades before the *Mayflower* hit Plymouth Rock, the route up the Rio Grande Valley was already heavily traveled by Europeans. The first horses, sheep, chickens and cows to reach what became the western US arrived this way. Merchants, soldiers, missionaries and immigrants usually covered about 20 miles a day, spending each night in a *paraje* (inn or campsite). For over 200 years, until the Santa Fe Trail reached the area in 1821, the Camino Real was the only road into New Mexico, the one economic and cultural artery that connected it to Colonial Spain.

Thirty miles south of Socorro, close to I-25 exit 115, an impressive modern museum, the **El Camino Real Historic Trail Site** (www.caminorealheritage.org; adult/child $5/free; ⊙ 8:30am-5pm Wed-Sun), explores the history of the Royal Road with artifacts, bilingual visual displays and special events. Panoramic windows overlook a particularly bleak portion of desert, right outside. The original trail, however, ran along the other side of the Rio Grande at this point, paralleling the eastern flank of the Fra Cristobal mountains that line the river's east bank. It followed a waterless 90-mile cut-off known as the **Jornada del Muerto**, in part to avoid potential Native American attacks along the river itself. Although that name literally translates as the 'day-long journey of the dead man,' it could take weeks for wagons to get through this desolate and still uninhabited region. It's possible to drive very close to this portion of the trail by leaving I-25 at exit 139 or 124 if you're coming from the north, or exit 32 if you're coming from the south. Only the sections closest to Truth or Consequences are paved; the route passes near Spaceport America (p328), but you can't see anything from the road.

briefly New Mexico's largest town. The New Mexico Institute of Mining and Technology (locally called Tech) offers postgraduate education and advanced research facilities here, and runs a mineral museum. Most visitors are birders drawn to the nearby Bosque del Apache refuge.

◉ Sights & Activities

San Miguel Mission   CHURCH
(www.sdc.org/~smiguel; 403 San Miguel Rd) The small church built by Socorro's earliest Spanish settlers expanded to become the San Miguel Mission in the 1620s. You'll find it three blocks north of the Plaza. While much altered, the mission still retains its colonial feel, and parts of the walls date back to the original building.

★ Bosque Del Apache
National Wildlife Refuge   WILDLIFE RESERVE
(www.fws.gov/refuge/bosque_del_apache; per vehicle $5; ⊙ dawn-dusk) These fields and marshes, 8 miles south of Socorro, are the wintering ground for migratory birds including snow geese, sandhill cranes and bald eagles, though sadly no longer the whooping crane. The season lasts from late October to March, and peaks in December and January. Upwards of

325 bird species and 135 mammal, reptile and amphibian species have been sighted. From the **visitor center** (📞 575-835-1828; ⊙ 7:30am-4pm Mon-Fri, 8am-4:30pm Sat & Sun), a 15-mile loop circles the refuge; hiking trails and viewing platforms are easily accessible.

★ Festivals & Events

All Socorro turns out for mid-October's annual **49ers Festival**, with parades, dancing and gambling, while the **Festival of the Cranes** (www.festivalofthecranes.com; ⊙ Nov) on the third weekend of November features special tours of Bosque del Apache, wildlife workshops and arts and crafts.

⌂ Sleeping & Eating

California St holds budget motels and a few national chains.

Socorro Old Town B&B   B&B $$
(📞 575-418-9454; www.socorrobandb.qwestoffice.net; 114 W Baca St; r $125; ❈ 🐾) Across from San Miguel Mission in the Old Town neighborhood, and housed in an extensively restored old adobe, this B&B has the feeling of a family home, with easygoing hosts and two clean, comfortable rooms.

Owl Bar Cafe
BURGERS $

(📞575-835-9946; 79 Main St, San Antonio; mains $6-15; ⏰8am-8:30pm Mon-Sat) Leave I-25 at Exit 139, 10 miles south of Socorro, to sample the finest green chile cheeseburgers this side of Hatch. The potent mix of greasy beef, soft bun, sticky cheese, tangy chile, lettuce and tomato drips onto the plate in perfect burger fashion.

Manzanares Street Coffeehouse
CAFE $

(📞575-838-0809; 110 Manzanares St; mains $6-8; ⏰7am-8pm) This large and lively central rendezvous, a block from both the plaza and the highway, serves soup and sandwiches as well as espressos and pastries. You've got to love a place that posts advice on 'How to Use a Semicolon' in its rest room.

Socorro Springs Brewing Co
ITALIAN $$

(📞575-838-0650; www.socorrosprings.com; 1012 N California St; mains $9-23; ⏰11am-10pm) In the mood for a relatively sophisticated experience? Come to this busy brewpub-restaurant for a really good clay-oven pizza, big calzones, decent pasta dishes, lots of salads and homemade soups. At times, the selection of brews in the pub section at the front can be limited, but they're alway smooth and tasty.

ℹ️ Information

The **Socorro Heritage and Visitors Center** (📞575-835-8927; www.socorronm.org; 217 Fisher Ave; ⏰9am-5pm Mon-Fri), just west of the plaza, hands out a good Old Town walking map.

Truth or Consequences & Around

POP 7000 / ELEV 4242FT

Home to New Age devotees, off-the-grid artists and ecowarriors, kooky Truth or Consequences (T or C) vies for the title of quirkiest little town in New Mexico. This high-desert oasis was originally called Hot Springs, for the cluster of mineral-rich springs that line the banks of the Rio Grande hereabouts. It changed its name to match a popular radio game show in 1950, hoping to increase tourism. The geothermal energy in the vicinity is supposedly similar to Sedona's, and T or C's shabby-chic double main drag – split into two one-way sections downtown, Main St and Broadway – is filled with crystal shops, herbalist offices, yoga studios, eclectic art galleries and off-the-wall boutiques.

T or C's latest publicity stunt? It's about to become the world's first commercial space-flight launch pad. Yup, you heard us, at some point in the near future Richard Branson's Virgin Galactic will start blasting tourists off the planet from the nearby spaceport.

◉ Sights & Activities

It won't take you more than an hour to get your bearings in tiny T or C by strolling down Main St and Broadway. Each day it seems another art gallery or new herbal-remedy shop opens, and it's fun to just walk and window-shop.

Geronimo Springs Museum
MUSEUM

(www.geronimospringsmuseum.com; 211 Main St; adult/student $6/3; ⏰9am-5pm Mon-Sat, noon-5pm Sun) This engaging mishmash features a mastodon skull, minerals and artifacts ranging from Mimbres pottery to beautifully worked cowboy saddles, plus sections on the Truth or Consequences radio show and Apache leader Geronimo.

Elephant Butte Lake State Park
LAKE

(📞575-744-5923; www.nmparks.com; Hwy 195; vehicle per day $5, tent/RV sites $8/14) Just 5 miles north of T or C, New Mexico's largest artificial lake (60 sq miles) is much loved by local anglers, waterskiers and windsurfers. The **marina** (📞575-744-5567; www.marinadelsur.info) rents tackle and boats (for fishing, pontoon and skiing). Spring and fall are best for fishing; guides for one to four anglers cost around $225 to $350 per day; contact **Fishing Adventures** (📞575-740-4710; www.stripersnewmexico.com) to make sure you take home your fill of striped bass.

Hot Springs

For centuries people from these parts, including Geronimo, have bathed in the area's mineral-laden hot springs. Long said to have therapeutic properties, the waters range from 98°F to 115°F (36°C to 46°C). Since the damming of the Rio Grande upstream, T or C's springs no longer flow naturally, but anyone can still tap into the underlying hot water by digging on their own property.

Most of T or C's hotels and motels double as spas. Guests soak free, and massages and other treatments are usually available. For sheer open-air enjoyment, head for the outdoor tubs at **Riverbend Hot Springs** (www.riverbendhotsprings.com; 100 Austin St; shared/private per hr $10/15; ⏰8am-10pm). The swankier **Sierra Grande Lodge & Spa** (📞575-894-6976;

SPACEPORT AMERICA: THE ULTIMATE SIDETRIP

New Mexico has been hurling objects out beyond the stratosphere since 1947, when the first missile was launched from the rolling dunes of White Sands, courtesy of NASA's Werner von Braun. Now, thanks to Sir Richard Branson, the CEO of **Virgin Galactic** (www.virgingalactic.com), along with former Governor Bill Richardson and lots of other pie-in-the-sky visionaries (not to mention state taxpayers who may foot most of the projected $225 million bill), **Spaceport America** (www.spaceportamerica.com), the world's first private spaceport has opened 25 miles southeast of Truth or Consequences.

Space tourism will consist of a simple 62-mile (straight up) add-on to your New Mexico vacation package. For a mere $250,000 you can join the likes of Brad Pitt and Katy Perry by booking a two-hour flight that will include six minutes of weightlessness. The vessel, *SpaceShipTwo*, is a plush, six-passenger cruiser with reclining seats, big windows and a pressurized cabin so you won't need space suits. It's designed by legendary aerospace engineer Bob Rutan, whose *SpaceShipOne* was the first privately funded (by Microsoft cofounder Paul Allen), manned vehicle to reach outer space twice in a row, winning him the $10 million 2004 Ansari X-Prize.

State officials hope Spaceport America will pump hundreds of millions of dollars annually into the local economy, particularly in Alamogordo and Truth or Consequences, and also raise international awareness of New Mexico as a serious high-tech center. Authorized half-day **bus tours** (☎505-897-2886; www.ftstours.com) to Spaceport America in recent years have run from T or C and Elephant Butte; they weren't operating at research time, but check to see whether they've resumed.

www.sierragrandelodge.com; 501 McAdoo St) holds mineral baths (nonguests $25 for first person, $5 for each additional person) plus a holistic spa with massage and aromatherapy.

Festivals & Events

The **T or C Fiesta**, held the first weekend in May, celebrates the town's 1950 name change with a rodeo, barbecue, parade and other events, while the **Old Time Fiddlers State Championship** (early October) features country-and-western, bluegrass and mariachi music.

Sleeping & Eating

★ **Riverbend Hot Springs**   BOUTIQUE HOTEL **$**
(☎575-894-7625; www.riverbendhotsprings.com; 100 Austin St; r/ste from $70/105; ❄☎) This delightful place, occupying a fantastic perch beside the Rio Grande, is the only T or C hotel to feature outdoor, riverside hot tubs – tiled, decked and totally irresistible. Accommodation, colorfully decorated by local artists, ranges from motel-style rooms to a three-bedroom suite. Guests can use the public pools for free, and private tubs for $10.

Blackstone Hotsprings   BOUTIQUE HOTEL **$**
(☎575-894-0894; www.blackstonehotsprings.com; 410 Austin St; r $75-135; ℗❄☎) Blackstone embraces the T or C spirit with an upscale wink, decorating each of its seven rooms in the style

of a classic TV show, from *The Jetsons* to *The Golden Girls* to *I Love Lucy*. Best part? Each room comes with its own oversized tub or waterfall fed from the hot springs.

Passion Pie Cafe   CAFE **$**
(☎575-894-0008; deepwaterfarm.com; 406 Main St; breakfast & lunch mains $5-10, pizzas $13-18; ⏰7am-3pm daily, plus 4-9:30pm Fri & Sat) Watch T or C get its morning groove on through the windows of this espresso cafe, and set yourself up with a breakfast waffle; the Elvis (with peanut butter) or the Fat Elvis (with bacon too) should do the job. Later on there are plenty of healthy salads and sandwiches, plus pizza on Friday and Saturday nights.

Latitude 33   FUSION **$$**
(☎575-740-7804; 334 S Pershing St; mains $8-16; ⏰11am-8pm Mon-Sat) Relaxed, friendly bistro, tucked away downtown between the two main drags, which serves excellent pan-Asian dishes at good prices. Spicy peanut noodles cost $8 at lunch, $10 for dinner.

Cafe Bellaluca   ITALIAN **$$**
(☎575-894-9866; www.cafebellaluca.com; 303 Jones St; lunch $8-15, dinner $10-38; ⏰11am-9pm Mon & Wed-Thu, to 10pm Fri & Sat, to 8pm Sun) Deservedly popular for its Italian specialties; the pizzas are amazing, while the spacious dining room is a pitch-perfect blend of classy and funky.

ℹ Information

The **Geronimo Trail Scenic Byway Visitor Center** (☑ 575-894-1968; www.geronimotrail.com; 529 N Broadway; ☉9am-4:30pm Mon-Fri, 9am-5pm Sat, noon-5pm Sun) and Gila National Forest Ranger Station provide detailed information.

Silver City & Around

POP 10,300 / ELEV 5938FT

Once a rough-and-ready silver hub, and still at heart a copper-mining town, Silver City has been attracting national attention of late, deservedly acclaimed as one of America's nicest small towns and, especially, as an up-and-coming destination for everything from outdoor thrills to fine dining and historic hotels. The streets of its pretty downtown hold a lovely mishmash of old brick and cast-iron Victorian and thick-walled red adobe buildings, and the whole place still reeks of the Wild West. Billy the Kid spent some of his childhood here, and a few of his haunts still lurk amid the new gourmet coffee shops, quirky galleries and Italian ice-cream parlors.

A growing number of adventure addicts are coming to Silver City to work and play in its surrounding great outdoors, with some 15 mountain ranges, four rivers, the cartoonish rock formations in City of Rocks State Park and the action-packed Gila National Forest all in the vicinity. Plus, as home to Western New Mexico University, Silver City is infused with a healthy dose of youthful energy.

◉ Sights & Activities

The heart of this gallery-packed Victorian town is encompassed by Bullard, Texas and Arizona Sts between Broadway and 6th St. The former Main St, one block east of Bullard, was washed out by massive floods between 1895 and 1902. Caused by runoff from logged and overgrazed areas north of town, the floods eventually cut 55ft down below the original height of the street. In a stroke of marketing genius, it's now called **Big Ditch Park**.

Western New Mexico University Museum MUSEUM
(www.wnmu.edu/univ/museum.shtml; 1000 W College Ave; ☉9am-4:30pm Mon-Fri, 10am-4pm Sat & Sun) **FREE** This excellent, if musty, museum already boasted the world's largest collection of ancient Mimbres ceramics, even before it was augmented by a further treasure trove unearthed at New Mexico's NAN Ranch. Renowned for their vibrant decoration, most Mimbres pots were 'terminated' by their prehistoric owners, by being deliberately punctured with a 'kill hole'. The gift shop specializes in Mimbres motifs.

Silver City Museum MUSEUM
(www.silvercitymuseum.org; 312 W Broadway; suggested donation $3; ☉9am-4:30pm Tue-Fri, 10am-4pm Sat & Sun) Ensconced in an elegant 1881 Victorian house, the local history museum displays Mimbres pottery, as well as mining and household artifacts from Silver City's heyday and an exhibit on the Gila wilderness.

NEW MEXICO SILVER CITY & AROUND

WORTH A TRIP

CHLORIDE

At the end of the 19th century, tiny Chloride (population 11), in the foothills of the Black Range 40 miles northeast of T or C, was abustle with enough silver miners to support eight saloons. A century later, its historic buildings were on the verge of disintegration, until Don and Dona Edmund began renovating the old **Pioneer Store** (☑575-743-2736; www.pioneerstoremuseum.com; ☉10am-4pm) in 1994. Today, this 1880 general store holds a rich collection of miscellany from Chloride's heyday. Immediately behind it, the Edmunds have restored the two-bedroom **Harry Pye Cabin** ($125) – Chloride's first building – to hold overnight guests.

When Chloride was first founded, everything had to be hauled 60 miles by wagon to get here. It's hardly surprising, therefore, that it's pretty much all still here, including wooden dynamite detonators, farm implements, children's coffins, saddles and explosion-proof telephones used in mines. Landmarks include the **Hanging Tree**, to which rowdy drunks were tied until they sobered up, the **Monte Cristo Saloon** (now an artist co-op/gift shop) and a few other buildings in various stages of rehabilitation.

On a typical summer's day, around 10 visitors find their way to Chloride. It's a glorious drive, crossing successive ridges west of the Rio Grande to reach unspoiled little agricultural valleys. Coming from T or C, take I-25 north to exit 83, then Hwy 52 west.

SCENIC ROUTE 152

South of T or C, Hwy 152 west leads into mining country and twists over the Black Range to Silver City.

The first community you'll drive through is charming **Hillsboro**, which was revived by local agriculture after mining went bust. Today it's known for its Apple Festival on Labor Day, when fresh-baked apple pies, delicious cider, street musicians and arts-and-crafts stalls attract visitors. Grab anything from a burrito to the 12-oz 'slab o'beef' at the charming **Hillsboro General Store Cafe** (575-895-5306; www.hillsborogeneralstore. com; 100 Main St; mains $8-18; 8am-3pm Fri-Wed), which was orginally the town's dry-goods shop. You can stay at the homey **Enchanted Villa B&B** (575-895-5686; http:// enchanted-villa.com; r from $84;) just up the street.

Continuing west on Hwy 152, you'll pass the town of **Kingston**, which held 7000 residents during the silver rush of the 1880s, but is today home to just a handful. The road then starts to snake around a series of hairpin curves – it's slow going up to **Emory Pass** (8228ft), where a lookout gives expansive views of the Rio Grande basin to the east. Heading down the other side, you'll pass a number of USFS campgrounds.

At **San Lorenzo**, either turn north on Hwy 35 and head up the Mimbres Valley toward the Gila Cliff Dwellings, or continue west toward Silver City, passing the impossible-to-miss **Santa Rita Chino Open Pit Copper Mine**, which has an observation point on Hwy 152 about 6 miles before it hits Hwy 180. Successively worked by Indians and Spanish and Anglo settlers, it was once the largest in the world. Now reopened after a brief hiatus, it's the oldest active mine in the Southwest. A staggering 1.5 miles wide, the gaping hole is 1800ft deep and produces 250 million pounds of copper annually.

Climb to its 3rd-floor cupola for panoramic views of downtown.

Pinos Altos
HISTORIC SITE

(www.pinosaltos.org) Established in 1859 as a gold-mining town, Pinos Altos, 7 miles north of Silver City along Hwy 15, is almost a ghost town these days, though its few residents strive to retain its 19th-century flavor. Cruise Main St to see its log-cabin 1866 schoolhouse, an opera house, a reconstructed fort and an 1870s courthouse. The Buckhorn Saloon is a great spot for dinner or a beer.

City of Rocks State Park
PARK

(575-536-2800; www.nmparks.com; Hwy 61; day-use $5, tent/RV sites $8/14) This state park, 33 miles southeast of Silver City via Hwy 180 and Hwy 61, has a quirky, cartoonish beauty. More village than 'city,' it's a bit too pocket-sized to count as a hiking destination, but kids will love exploring the pathways between its rounded volcanic towers, and secluded sites with tables and fire pits make it a memorable camping spot.

Gila Hike and Bike
MOUNTAIN BIKING

(575-388-3222; www.gilahikeandbike.com; 103 E College Ave; in-town bikes per day from $20, mountain bikes from $40; 9am-5:30pm Mon-Fri, 9am-5pm Sat, 10am-4pm Sun) Drop into this friendly shop, on downtown's northern edge, to rent a bike or learn about regional single-track routes like the gorgeous trail through the oaks and ponderosas of Signal Peak just above town, with views right to Mexico. It's also the HQ for May's Tour of the Gila race.

Festivals & Events

The two biggest events in Silver City's annual calendar, during both of which the town's hotels and restaurants fill to bursting, are either end of May. The five-day **Tour of the Gila** (www.touroftthegila.com; early May) bike race culminates with a grueling tour of the mountains on the first Sunday of the month, while the free **Silver City Blues Festival** (http://mimbresarts.org; late May), on the last full weekend in May, attracts big-name performers from all over the country.

Sleeping

Palace Hotel
HISTORIC HOTEL $

(575-388-1811; www.silvercitypalacehotel.com; 106 W Broadway; r from $51;) A restored 1882 hotel, exuding a low-key, turn-of-the-20th-century charm, it makes an atmospheric historical stopover. All rooms feature old-fashioned Territorial-style decor; they vary from small (with a double bed) to two-room suites (king- or queen-size beds) outfitted with refrigerators, microwaves, phones and TVs.

Murray Hotel　　　　　HISTORIC HOTEL **$$**
(☑575-956-9400; www.murray-hotel.com; 200 W
Broadway; r from $109) Built in 1938, this re-
cently reopened downtown hotel is more
about art-deco panache than Wild West
history; it's a classy spot, with five stories of
tastefully retro-furnished rooms. It doesn't
serve breakfast, but each guest gets a $5
voucher for the recommended Millie's Bake
House nearby.

The 400　　　　　　　　　　B&B **$$**
(☑575-313-7015; www.gilahouse.com; 400 N Ari-
zona St; r from $90; ❄🐾) Housed in an ado-
be that's over 100 years old, this B&B has
preserved its character while upgrading to
21st-century comforts. The common area
doubles as a well-regarded art gallery.

🍴 Eating & Drinking

Javalina　　　　　　　　　　　CAFE **$**
(☑575-388-1350; 201 N Bullard St; pastries from
$2; ⏰6am-6pm Sun-Thu, to 9pm Fri & Sat; 🐾)
A great coffee shop, with seating of all sizes and styles, from couches to love seats to
wooden chairs, along with board games,
reading material and a few computers.

★ Buckhorn Saloon　　　　　STEAK **$$**
(☑575-538-9911; www.buckhornsaloonandopera
house.com; 32 Main St, Pinos Altos; mains $10-39;
⏰3-11pm Mon-Sat) Once an opera house, this
venerable adobe, 7 miles north of Silver City,
offers serious steaks and seafood amid 1860s
Wild West decor – try the fresh and tasty
buffalo burgers. Live country music livens
things up most nights.

Diane's Restaurant & Bakery　　AMERICAN **$$**
(☑575-538-8722; www.dianesrestaurant.com; 510
N Bullard St; lunch $7-9, dinner $15-28; ⏰10am-
2pm & 5-9pm Tue-Sat, 10am-4pm Sun) Diane's is
the local restaurant of choice, especially for
weekend breakfasts. If you visit then, order
the Hatch Benedict eggs, doused with chile.
There's a busy lunch trade during the week,
while the romantic appeal is upped with
dim lighting and white linen at dinner.

**★ The Curious
Kumquat**　　　　　　　MODERN AMERICAN **$$$**
(☑575-534-0337; curiouskumquat.com; 111 E Col-
lege Ave; lunch mains $7-8, dinner mains $17-23;
⏰11am-4:30pm & 5:30-8:30pm Tue-Sat) Silver
City has become a gourmet dining destina-
tion, and this culinary hotspot, deceptive-
ly housed in a Victorian garden cottage,
epitomizes the local scene at its best. It's
a one-man show by chef Rob Connoley, a

devotee of new-fangled molecular gastron-
omy; many of his signature creations, best
sampled on the $44 tasting menu, use ingre-
dients foraged in the Gila Forest nearby.

Shevek & Co　　　　　　INTERNATIONAL **$$$**
(☑575-534-9168; www.silver-eats.com; 602 N
Bullard St; mains $20-30; ⏰5-9pm Sun-Tue, to
9:30pm Fri & Sat) Depending on which room
you choose, this delightful place is at turns
formal, bistro-like and patio-casual. Sunday
brunch is decidedly New York, à la Upper
West Side; dinners range from Moroccan
to Spanish to Italian, and everything can be
ordered tapas-size. Enjoy the excellent beer
and wine list.

🛈 Information

Gila National Forest Ranger Station (☑575-
388-8201; www.fs.fed.us/r3/gila; 3005 E
Camino Del Bosque; ⏰8am-4:30pm Mon-Fri)
Gila Regional Medical Center (☑575-538-
4000; www.grmc.org; 1313 E 32nd)
Post office (500 N Hudson St)
Visitor center (☑575-538-5555; www.silver-
citytourism.org; 201 N Hudson St; ⏰9am-5pm
Mon-Sat, 10am-4pm Sun) This extremely
helpful office can provide everything you need
to make the most of Silver City.

🛈 Getting There & Around

Silver City sits just south of the junction of Hwy
180 and Rte 90 and is best reached by private
transportation. From Las Cruces, the closest
sizeable junction town, the 115-mile drive heads
west on US 10, then follows Hwy 180 north.

Downtown Silver City is small and walkable
and street parking is plentiful.

Gila National Forest

For anyone in search of the isolated and the
undiscovered, and a real sense of wildness,
'The Gila' has it in spades. Its 5156 sq miles
cover eight mountain ranges, including the
Mogollon, Tularosa, Blue and Black. It was
here that legendary conservationist Aldo
Leopold spearheaded a movement to estab-
lish the world's first designated wilderness
area, resulting in the creation of the **Gila
Wilderness** in 1924; in 1980, the adjacent
terrain to the east was also designated as
wilderness and named after Leopold.

This is some rugged country, just right for
black bears, mountain lions and the reintroduced Mexican gray wolves. Trickling creeks
are home to four species of endangered fish,

SHAKESPEARE'S GHOSTS

As far as we know, the dusty south-western corner of New Mexico isn't haunted by spirits speaking in iambic pentameter, but it is where you'll find **Shakespeare** (⏵575-542-9034; www.shakespeareghosttown.com; Hwy 494; 1hr tours adult/child $4/3), 2.5 miles south of Lordsburg. Among the best-preserved ghost towns in the Old West, it was first established as a stop on the Southern Pacific Mail Line, then grew into a silver-mining boom town. Plenty of the West's famous outlaws roosted here at one time or another: 'Curly' Bill Brocius, the killer and rustler, called this home; a young Billy the Kid washed dishes at the still-standing Stratford Hotel; and Black Jack Ketchum's gang used to come into town to buy supplies.

Shakespeare is open to visitors one weekend each month between June and December, with occasional historical reenactments. Check the website for dates.

including the Gila trout. In other words, it's ideal for remote and primitive hiking and backpacking. Silver City is the main base for accessing the Gila Wilderness and the interior of the forest, while T or C or Hillsboro are more convenient for reaching the eastern slope of the Black Range.

If you're only up for a day trip, the Gila has a few gems. On the western side of the forest, 65 miles northwest of Silver City off Hwy 180, the summer-only **Catwalk** trail, wheelchair-accessible and great for kids, follows a suspended metal walkway through narrow Whitewater Canyon. You can see the creek rushing beneath your feet. While some find it disappointingly short, it offers a painless way to experience the Gila – and from the far end you can continue forever into the mountains on dirt trails, should you choose. To get here, turn east onto Hwy 174 at Glenwood, where the forest service maintains **Bighorn Campground** (⏵575-539-2481; ☉year-round) **FREE**, with no drinking water or fee.

Just north of Glenwood, Hwy 159 twists its way off Hwy 180 for 9 vertiginous miles on the slowgoing route to **Mogollon**, a semi–ghost town (inaccessible during the winter). Once an important mining com-munity, it now holds just a few antique and knickknack shops and, as is typical for mid-dle-of-nowhere New Mexico, one proud little restaurant. This one is called the **Purple Onion** (Main St; mains $5-10; ☉9am-5pm Fri-Sun May-Oct), and it's as good as you'd hope after making the trip.

If you've a high-clearance 4WD and a little extra time, you can follow a sce-nic road from the Silver City area right through the heart of the Gila. From Hwy 35 north of Mimbres, **Forest Road 150** wends through the forest for 60 miles be-fore emerging onto the sweeping Plains of San Agustin. Another option off Hwy 35 is to drive the rough **Forest Road 151** to the Aldo Leopold Wilderness boundary, then hike a few miles up to the top of **McKnight Mountain**, the highest summit in the Black Range at 10,165ft.

For serene forest slumbers, rent one of the stunningly situated **Casitas de Gila** (⏵575-535-4455; www.casitasdegila.com; off Hwy 180, near Cliff; $160-225; ☎), five one- or two-bedroom adobe-style cottages set on 265 beautiful acres. Rates drop for longer stays. There are telescopes, an outdoor hot tub and grills to keep you occupied.

In addition to the Gila National Forest offices in Silver City and T or C, Mimbres' wilderness **ranger station** (⏵575-536-2250; Hwy 35; ☉8am-4:30pm Mon-Fri) is particularly useful.

Gila Cliff Dwellings National Monument

Mysterious, isolated and yet readily accessi-ble by car, these remarkable cliff dwellings were constructed by the Mogollon people, in rocky alcoves overlooking the Gila river, toward the end of the 13th century. A mile round-trip self-guided trail climbs 180ft to the well-preserved ruins, above a lovely for-ested canyon; it's quite a steep hike, involv-ing the use of ladders. The trail begins at the end of Hwy 15, 2 miles beyond the **visi-tor center** (⏵575-536-9461; www.nps.gov/gicl; adult/child $3/free; ☉8am-4:30pm, trail access 9am-4pm), which is itself a two-hour drive north from Silver City. Two small **camp-grounds** just back from the trailhead have drinking water, picnic areas and toilets; free on a first-come, first-served basis, they of-ten fill on summer weekends. A short trail behind the Lower Scorpion Campground leads to pictographs.

Gila Hot Springs

Used by Native Americans since ancient times, these **hot pools** (day use $3) are 39 miles north of Silver City, within the **Gila Hot Springs Ranch** (☑575-536-9551; www.gilahotspringsranch.com; Hwy 15; tent/RV sites $15/20, r from $76; 🐾), a pet-friendly resort – dogs can stay for an extra $5 per night – which holds simple rooms with kitchenettes in a giant red barnlike structure, along with campsites and an RV park with a spa and showers fed by the hot springs. There's also primitive **camping** ($4) alongside the hot springs. Horseback rides, guided fishing and wilderness pack trips, and other outfitting services can be arranged in advance, via the ranch.

Deming & Around

POP 14,800 / ELEV 4337FT

Founded in 1881 as a railway junction, Deming stands in New Mexico's least populous quadrant, surrounded by cotton fields on the northern edge of the Chihuahuan Desert. But if this is a desert, where does all the water come from for the family ranches? It's tapped from the invisible Mimbres River, which disappears underground about 20 miles north of town and re-emerges in Mexico.

◉ Sights

★ **Deming Luna Mimbres Museum**   MUSEUM
(☑505-546-2382; www.lunacountyhistoricalsociety.com; 301 S Silver Ave; ◷9am-4pm daily, closed Sun in summer) **FREE** One of New Mexico's best regional museums, a sprawling, enormous affair that holds a superb display of Mimbres pottery, and a great doll collection, including one rescued from the rubble of Hiroshima. A re-created Victorian street includes the actual contents of many long-lost local shops, while another room is devoted to fading snapshots of local families. You can see an actual iron lung and, get this, a braille edition of *Playboy* (maybe someone *was* reading it for the articles).

Rockhound State Park   PARK
(☑575-546-6182; www.nmparks.com; 9880 Stirrup Rd SE; per car $5, tent/RV sites $8/14; ◷7am-dusk) Rockhound State Park, 14 miles southeast of Deming via Hwys 11 and 141, gives visitors the chance to collect all sorts of semiprecious or just plain pretty rocks, including jasper, geodes and thunder eggs.

You'll need a shovel and some rockhounding experience to uncover anything special; local experts suggest walking into the Little Florida Mountains for a while before you start searching. The park's Spring Canyon section holds shaded picnic tables and the half-mile Lovers Leap trail.

St Clair Winery   WINERY
(☑575-546-1179; www.stclairwinery.com; 1325 De Baca Rd; ◷9am-6pm Mon-Sat, noon-6pm Sun) The tasting room for New Mexico's largest vintner is located beside Hwy 549, 3 miles east of Deming.

✯ Festivals & Events

Great American Duck Race   FESTIVAL
(www.demingduckrace.com; ◷Aug) Deming's biggest annual draw occurs on the fourth weekend in August. Anyone can enter the races for a $10 fee (kids $5), which includes 'duck rental,' to compete for thousands of dollars. Other wacky events include the Tortilla Toss, Outhouse Races and a Duckling Contest. Entertainment ranges from cowboy poets to musicians, and there's a parade, hot-air balloons and food.

🛏 Sleeping & Eating

You'll find chain hotels around the interstate exits, and plenty of Mexican-American restaurants downtown.

Grand Motor Inn   MOTEL $
(☑575-546-2632; www.grandhoteldeming.com; 1721 E Pine St; r from $47; 🅿❄🐾) Red-brick motel, on the main road just east of downtown, which makes a decent spot to sleep, with a grassy inner courtyard and a busy restaurant.

★ **Adobe Deli**   STEAKHOUSE $$
(☑575-546-0361; www.adobedeli.com; 3970 Lewis Flats Rd SE; mains $7-27; ◷11am-5pm & 6-10pm Mon-Sat, 11am-9pm Sun) This amazing, cavernous barnlike structure, on a rundown farm 12 miles east via US 549 (follow Pine St), is filled with stuffed animals from mouflon to marlin and even a mermaid. Food ranges from excellent sandwiches or the specialty onion soup to ribs and giant steaks, while there's often live music, or sports events on a giant TV.

🔒 Shopping

Readers' Cove   BOOKS
(☑575-544-2512; 200 S Copper St; ◷10am-5pm) If you just finished your book, trade it in at this fantastic used-book store, in a 19th-century

adobe house where the shelves are groaning with everything from literature to history to pulp.

ℹ️ Information

The helpful **visitor center** (📞 575-567-1962; www.demingvisitorcenter.webs.com; 800 Pine St; ⏰ 9am-5pm Mon-Fri, to noon Sat; 📶) has masses of local information, and staff are happy to give candid advice.

ℹ️ Getting There & Away

Greyhound (📞 575-546-3881; www.greyhound. com; 420 E Cedar St) runs daily buses to El Paso, TX ($32, two hours), Phoenix, AZ ($64, six hours), and Las Cruces ($17, one hour), along the I-10 corridor.

Las Cruces & Around

POP 94,000 / ELEV 3908FT

Las Cruces and her older and smaller sister city, Mesilla, sit at the edge of a broad basin beneath the fluted Organ Mountains, at the crossroads of two major highways, I-10 and I-25. There's something special about the combination of bright white sunlight, glassy blue skies, flowering cacti, rippling red mountains and desert lowland landscape found here. The city itself, however, is less than a dream town: sprawling, and beastly hot for much of the year.

An eclectic mix of old and young, Las Cruces is home to New Mexico State University (NMSU), whose 18,000 students infuse it with a healthy dose of youthful liveliness, while at the same time its 350 days of sunshine and numerous golf courses are turning it into a popular retirement destination.

👁 Sights

⭐ **Mesilla**   NEIGHBORHOOD
(www.oldmesilla.org) Dating back 150 years and little changed since, Mesilla is a charming old adobe town. Despite the souvenir shops and touristy restaurants, its beautiful historic Plaza, 4 miles south of Las Cruces, provides a perfect opportunity to lose track of time. The 1855 San Albino Church here offers Mass in English and Spanish. Wander a few blocks in any direction to garner the essence of a mid-19th-century Southwestern border town.

⭐ **New Mexico Farm & Ranch
Heritage Museum**   MUSEUM
(📞 575-522-4100; www.nmfarmandranchmuseum. org; 4100 Dripping Springs Rd; adult/child $5/2;

⏰ 9am-5pm Mon-Sat, noon-5pm Sun; �) This terrific museum doesn't just hold engaging exhibits on the state's agricultural history – it's got livestock too. Enclosures on the working farm alongside hold assorted breeds of cattle, along with horses, donkeys, sheep and goats. The taciturn cowboys who tend the animals proffer little extra information, but they add color, and you can even buy a pony if you have $450 to spare. There are daily milking demonstrations plus weekly displays of blacksmithing, spinning and weaving, and heritage cooking.

**White Sands Missile Test
Center Museum**   MUSEUM
(📞 575-678-8800; www.wsmr-history.org; ⏰ 8am-4pm Mon-Fri, 10am-3pm Sat) **FREE** Explore New Mexico's military technology history with a visit to this museum, 25 miles east of Las Cruces along Hwy 70. It represents the heart of the White Sands Missile Range, a major testing site since 1945. There's a missile garden, a real V-2 rocket and a museum with lots of defense-related artifacts. Visitors have to park outside the Test Center gate and check in at the office before walking in.

🎉 Festivals & Events

Whole Enchilada Fiesta   FOOD
(www.enchiladafiesta.com; ⏰ Sep) Held in late September, the city's best-known event features live music, food booths, arts and crafts, sporting events, a chile cook-off, carnival rides and a parade. It culminates in the cooking of the world's biggest enchilada on Sunday morning.

**Southern New Mexico
State Fair & Rodeo**   CULTURAL
(www.snmstatefairgrounds.net; adult/child $15/10; ⏰ Oct) At the start of October, and featuring a livestock show, auction, daredevil rodeo and live country music.

International Mariachi Conference   MUSIC
(www.lascrucesmariachi.org; ⏰ Nov) In late November, Las Cruces celebrates all things mariachi with educational workshops and big-name performances.

**Fiesta of Our Lady of
Guadalupe**   RELIGIOUS
(⏰ Dec 10-12) Held in December in the Native American village of Tortugas, between Las Cruces and Mesilla. Late into the first night, drummers and masked dancers accompany a statue of Mary in a procession. On the following day, participants climb several miles

ORGAN MOUNTAINS-DESERT PEAKS NATIONAL MONUMENT

New Mexico acquired its latest federal park in May 2014. The **Organ Mountains-Desert Peaks National Monument** (☏575-525-4300; www.blm.gov/nm/omdp) consists of several separate components, totaling almost 780 sq miles,000 acres and all lying within a 50-mile radius of Las Cruces. None is especially developed for visitors, however, and that's not likely to change in the immediate future.

The most accessible region is the 9000ft **Organ Mountains**, east of the city, which you'll cross if you drive to or from White Sands on US 70. The area incorporated into the new monument extends for 20 miles south of the highway, and offers a network of hiking and biking trails. The **Dripping Springs Natural Area** here holds the monument's **visitor center** (☏575-522-1219; day use $5 per vehicle; ⊗8am-5pm), while its only campground is at **Aguirre Spring** (day use per vehicle $5, campsite $7).

The **Desert Peaks** segment of the park encompasses the **Doña Ana Mountains**, across the river northeast of Las Cruces, and the **Robledo Mountains** and the **Sierra de las Uvas**, stretching northwest along the western edge of the Rio Grande Valley as far as Hatch. It adjoins the tiny **Prehistoric Trackways National Monument**, created in 2009 to protect a treasure trove of dinosaur footprints, but not at all geared up for casual sightseers.

Finally, the monument also includes the **Potrillo Mountains**, an expanse of cinder cones and volcanic craters scattered through the desert southwest of Las Cruces.

to Tortugas Mountain for Mass; dancing and ceremonies continue into the night in the village.

🛌 Sleeping

Thanks to NMSU, Las Cruces holds a plentiful supply of chain hotels and motels, as well as a scattering of more idiosyncratic options.

★ Best Western Mission Inn　　　MOTEL $
(☏575-524-8591; www.bwmissioninn.com; 1765 S Main St; r from $69) A truly out-of-the-ordinary accommodation option; yes it's a roadside chain motel, but the rooms are beautifully kitted out with attractive tiling, stonework and colorful stenciled designs; they're sizeable and comfortable; and the rates are great.

Royal Host Motel　　　MOTEL $
(☏575-524-8536; 2146 W Picacho Ave, Las Cruces; r from $59; ❄ 🐾 ☎ 🏊) This basic budget motel downtown is clean and friendly, and has 26 spacious rooms. An on-site restaurant and swimming pool win points. Pets are welcome for an extra $10.

★ Lundeen Inn of the Arts　　　B&B $$
(☏505-526-3326; www.innofthearts.com; 618 S Alameda Blvd, Las Cruces; r incl breakfast from $82, ste from $99; 🅿 ❄ ☎ 🏊) Each of the 20 guest rooms in this large and very lovely century-old Mexican Territorial–style inn is unique and named for – and decorated in the style of – a New Mexico artist. Check out the soaring pressed-tin ceilings in the great room. Owners Linda and Jerry offer the kind of genteel hospitality you seldom find these days.

Hotel Encanto de Las Cruces　　　HOTEL $$
(☏505-522-4300; www.hotelencanto.com; 705 S Telshor Blvd, Las Cruces; r from $118; ❄ @ ☎ 🏊) The pick of the city's larger hotels, this Spanish Colonial resort property holds 200 spacious rooms, decorated in warm Southwestern tones, plus a palm-fringed outdoor pool, an exercise room, restaurant and lounge with patio.

🍴 Eating

Located in the heart of the world chile capital, both Las Cruces and Mesilla serve up some of the spiciest Mexican food in the state. Yum.

🍴 Las Cruces

Nellie's Cafe　　　MEXICAN $
(☏575-524-9982; 1226 W Hadley Ave; mains $5-9; ⊗8am-2pm Tue-Sat) Cherished by locals, Nellie's has been serving homemade burritos, *chile rellenos* and tamales for decades now, under the slogan 'Chile with an Attitude.' It's small and humble in decor but big in taste, with deliciously spicy food.

Spirit Winds Coffee Bar　　　CAFE $
(☏575-521-1222; 2260 S Locust; mains $5-15; ⊗7am-7pm Mon-Fri, 7:30am-7pm Sat, 8am-6pm Sun; ☎) Join the university crowd for excellent cappuccino and gourmet tea, plus good

HATCH

The town of Hatch sits at the heart of New Mexico's chile-growing country 40 miles north of Las Cruces, up I-25. New Mexican chiles didn't originate here – most local varieties have centuries-old roots in the northern farming villages around Chimayó and Española – but the soil and irrigation in these parts proved perfect for mass production. Although recent harvests have declined sharply, as imported chile takes over the market, the town still clings to its title as 'Chile Capital of the World.' Even if you miss the annual Labor Day Weekend **Chile Festival** (www.hatchchilefest.com; per vehicle $5; ☉ Sep), just pull off the interstate at Exit 41 and pop into **Sparky's Burgers** (☎575-267-4222; www.sparkysburgers.com; 115 Franklin St; mains $4-10; ☉10:30am-7pm Thu-Fri & Sun, to 7:30pm Sat) for what might be the best green chile cheeseburger in the state (*New Mexico Magazine* thinks so), served with casual pride.

sandwiches, salads, soups and pastries, and more substantial dinner dishes. A gift and card shop and occasional live entertainment keep the students, artsy types and business folks coming back.

Mesilla

Chope's Bar & Cafe　　　　NEW MEXICAN $
(☎575-233-3420; 16145 S Hwy 28, La Mesa; mains $5-10; ☉11:30am-8:30pm Tue-Sat) Worth every second of the 15-mile drive south of town, Chope's may not be much to look at, but the hot chile will turn you into an addict within minutes. From *chile rellenos* to burritos, you've seen the menu before; you just haven't had it this good. The adjacent bar is loads of fun.

La Posta　　　　　　　　　MEXICAN $$
(☎575-524-3524; www.laposta-de-mesilla.com; 2410 Calle de San Albino; mains $8-16; ☉11am-9pm) Mexican restaurant that's a local legend. This rambling old adobe was here before Mesilla itself, and became a Butterfield stagecoach stop in the 1850s. Now standing at the corner of the Plaza, it's entered from the next block. Don't miss the parrots in its covered central courtyard. Besides tasty enchiladas and fajitas, it stocks almost 100 varieties of tequila.

Savoy de Mesilla　　　　　FUSION $$
(☎575-527-2869; www.savoydemesilla.com; 1800 Av de Mesilla; mains $12-28; ☉11am-2pm & 5-9pm Mon-Fri, 8am-9pm Sat, 8am-8pm Sun) The setting may be humdrum, beside the highway between Las Cruces and Mesilla, but this modern bistro serves a distinctive take on contemporary international cuisine, like the salmon garlic naan-bread 'sandwich' or the Korean-style bulgogi pork ribs, and throws in gimmicks like using liquid nitrogen to prepare ice cream at your table, or the hilariously over-the-top waterfalls in the restrooms.

★**Double Eagle Restaurant**　STEAKHOUSE $$$
(☎575-523-6700; www.double-eagle-mesilla.com; 308 Calle de Guadalupe; mains $23-49; ☉11am-10pm Mon-Sat, noon-9pm Sun) A glorious melange of Wild West opulence, all dark wood and velvet hangings, and featuring a fabulous old bar, this Plaza restaurant is on the National Register of Historic Places. The main dining room offers delicious continental and Southwestern cuisine, especially steaks, while the less formal **Peppers** in the courtyard claims to serve the world's largest green chile cheeseburger ($25).

🍷 Drinking & Entertainment

Both Mesilla and Las Cruces hold thriving fine-arts and performing-arts communities, with 40 galleries as well as theatrical and musical companies scattered around the valley. Many galleries double as artists' studios and most are happy to chat with visitors. The *Bulletin,* a free weekly published on Thursday, has up-to-the-minute entertainment information, while you can find out more about arts, theater and dance at the **Branigan Cultural Center** (☎575-541-2154; 501 N Main St; ☉9am-4:30pm Tue-Sat) FREE.

The American Southwest Theater Company presents plays at the **Center for the Arts** (☎575-646-4515; http://panam.nmsu.edu/astc; 1810 E University Ave, Pan Am Center) on the NMSU campus, while the **Las Cruces Symphony** (☎575-646-3709; www.lascrucessymphony.com) performs at the NMSU Music Center Recital Hall.

El Patio　　　　　　　　　　　　BAR
(☎575-526-9943; 2171 Calle de Parian, Mesilla Plaza; ☉2-11pm Sun-Wed, until 2am Thu-Sat) In an old adobe building, this historic bar has been rocking Mesilla since the 1930s. It serves cocktails along with live rock and jazz.

Graham Central Station CLUB
(☑575-524-9131; www.grahamcentralstationlas-
cruces.com; 505 S Main St, Las Cruces; cover $2-20;
☺9pm-2am Wed, 7pm-2am Thu & Sat, 6pm-2am
Fri) Join the university students for a night of
revelry at this four-in-one club buffet. Listen
to big-name country and Latin artists, enter
a shot-taking contest or dance like you're in
Miami at a South Beach–themed lounge. It's
a bit of a meat market – college kids come
here to hook up.

Fountain Theater CINEMA
(☑575-524-8287; www.mesillavalleyfilm.org; 2469
Calle de Guadalupe, Mesilla; adult/student $7/6)
Home of the nonprofit Mesilla Valley Film
Society, this splendid old adobe theater
screens foreign and art films.

ℹ Information

Las Cruces CVB (☑575-541-2444; www.
lascrucescvb.org; 211 N Water St) Helpful office
with all sorts of visitor information.

Memorial Medical Center (☑575-522-8641;
www.mmclc.org; 2450 S Telshor Blvd, Las
Cruces; ☺24hr emergency)

Mesilla Visitor Center (☑575-524-3262; www.
oldmesilla.org; 2231 Ave de Mesilla; ☺9:30am-
4:30pm Mon-Sat, 11am-3pm Sun) Staffed by
eager local volunteers, Mesilla's visitor center
holds interesting displays on the town's past.

Police (☑505-526-0795; 217 E Picacho Ave,
Las Cruces)

Post office (201 E Las Cruces Ave, Las Cruces)

ℹ Getting There & Away

Greyhound (☑575-524-8518; www.greyhound.
com; 800 E Thorpe Rd, Chucky's Convenience
Store) buses run along the east–west interstate
corridor, I-10.

Las Cruces Shuttle Service (☑575-525-1784;
www.lascrucesshuttle.com) runs 12 vans daily to
the El Paso International Airport ($45 one-way,
$25 each additional person), and to Deming,
Silver City and other destinations on request.

CARLSBAD CAVERNS & SOUTHEASTERN NEW MEXICO

Two extraordinary natural wonders are
tucked away in New Mexico's arid southeast:
mesmerizing White Sands National Monument and magnificent Carlsbad Caverns
National Park. This region also swirls with
some of the state's most enduring legends:
aliens in Roswell, Billy the Kid in Lincoln,
and Smokey Bear in Capitan. Most of the
lowlands are covered by hot, rugged Chihuahuan Desert – once submerged under
the ocean – but you can always escape to the
cooler climes around the popular forest resorts of Cloudcroft or Ruidoso.

White Sands National Monument

Undulating through the Tularosa Basin like
something out of a dream, these ethereal
dunes are a highlight of any trip to New
Mexico, and a must on every landscape photographer's itinerary. Try to time a visit to
White Sands (☑575-479-6124; www.nps.gov/
whsa; adult/under 16yr $3/free; ☺7am-9pm Jun-
Aug, to sunset Sep-May) with sunrise or sunset
(or both), when the dazzlingly white sea of
sand is at its most magical. From the **visitor**

WORTH A TRIP

THREE RIVERS PETROGLYPH NATIONAL RECREATION AREA

The remote **Three Rivers Petroglyph NRA** (☑575-525-4300; www.blm.gov/nm/three
rivers; County Rd B30, off Hwy 54; per car $5, tent/RV sites $7/18; ☺8am-7pm Apr-Oct, to 5pm
Nov-Mar) showcases over 21,000 petroglyphs, incised six centuries ago by the Jornada
Mogollon people onto the flat surfaces of boulders atop a low ridge at the eastern edge
of the Tularosa. The images include birds, animals, masks and human figures, and can be
seen on an easy mile hike that leads through mesquite and cacti, with good views of the
Sacramento Mountains to the east and White Sands on the western horizon. There are
six camping shelters at the parking lot, along with barbecue grills (free), restrooms, water and two hookups for RVs. Pets are allowed in the campground but not on the trails.

The site is 27 miles north of Alamogordo on Hwy 54, and then 5 miles east on a signed
road. If you fancy roughing it for the night, a dirt road continues beyond the petroglyphs
for about 10 miles to the Lincoln National Forest, where you'll find **Three Rivers Campground** (☑575-434-7200; www.fs.usda.gov; per vehicle $6).

center drive the 16-mile scenic drive, which loops into the heart of the world's largest gypsum dune field, covering 275 sq miles. Along the way, get out of the car and romp around, or escape the crowds by hiking either the **Alkali Flat**, a 4.5-mile (round-trip) backcountry trail through the heart of the dunes, or the simple mile loop **nature trail**. Don't forget your sunglasses – the sand's as bright as snow.

It's a long, long way to the ocean from here, so don't be surprised to find locals picnicking, playing, sunbathing and generally enjoying the full-on beach experience. Join them by springing for a $15 plastic saucer at the visitor center gift shop, and sledding the back dunes; you can sell it back for $5 at day's end (no rentals to avoid liability). Check the park calendar for sunset strolls and occasional moonlight bicycle rides (adult/child $5/2.50).

Backcountry campsites, with no water or toilet facilities, stand a mile from the scenic drive. Pick up a permit ($3; first-come, first-served) in person at the visitor center at least one hour before sunset.

To reach the park, drive Hwy 70 either 50 miles northeast of Las Cruces or 15 miles southwest of Alamogordo – and bear in mind that the road occasionally closes at very short notice for up to three hours, during missile tests.

Alamogordo & Around

POP 31,500 / ELEV 4334FT

Despite a dearth of amenities, Alamogordo (Spanish for 'fat cottonwood tree') is the center of an important space and atomic research program. Most of its sights are child-oriented, but any adult who's young at heart will enjoy them too. You can also check out two tiny towns nearby, the art outpost of La Luz and pretty little Tularosa.

⦿ Sights & Activities

New Mexico Museum of Space History   MUSEUM
(📞575-437-2840; www.nmspacemuseum.org; 3198 Hwy 2001; adult/child $6/4; ⦿9am-5pm; 👶) Looming over the northeast corner of town and nicknamed 'the golden cube,' this four-story museum is surrounded by historic missiles, and holds excellent exhibits on space exploration. A Hall of Fame hails pioneers from William Congreve, whose rockets were fired at the Battle of Waterloo, to Neil Armstrong, while other displays cover New Mexico's potential role in commercial space flight. The adjoining **Tombaugh IMAX Theater & Planetarium** (adult/child $6/4.50; 👶) shows giant-screen movies.

Toy Train Depot   MUSEUM
(📞888-207-3564; www.toytraindepot.homestead. com; 1991 N White Sands Blvd; admission $4; ⦿noon-4:30pm Wed-Sun; 👶) Railroad buffs and kids flock to this 1898 railway depot, for five rooms of train memorabilia and toy trains, and a 2.5-mile narrow-gauge minitrain you can ride through Alameda Park.

Alameda Park & Zoo   ZOO
(📞575-439-4290; 1321 N White Sands Blvd; adult/3-11yr $2.50/1.50; ⦿9am-5pm; 👶) Said to be the oldest zoo west of the Mississippi, established in 1898, this small but well-run place features exotics from around the world. Assuming both you and they are in the mood to brave the heat, you may see bears, bald eagles, alligators or the endangered Mexican gray wolf.

Alamogordo Museum of History   MUSEUM
(📞575-434-4438; www.alamogordohistory.com; 1301 N White Sands Blvd; ⦿10am-4pm Mon-Fri, 10am-3pm Sat) **FREE** Thoroughly local little museum, focusing on the Mescalero Indians and the mining, railroad and logging industries. Its most cherished holding is a 47-star US flag, ultra-rare because Arizona joined the Union just six weeks after New Mexico.

La Luz & Tularosa   NEIGHBORHOODS
The painters, writers and craftspeople who live in the tiny enclave of **La Luz**, 4 miles north of Alamogordo, share a passion for creating artwork and living off the land; a wild outpost, it's well worth a browse. Another 10 miles north, the attractive village of **Tularosa** is dominated by the 1869 St Francis de Paula Church, built in a simple New Mexican style.

🛏 Sleeping & Eating

Oliver Lee Memorial State Park   CAMPGROUND $
(📞575-437-8284; www.nmparks.com; 409 Dog Canyon Rd; day-use $5, tent/RV sites $8/14) Spending a night or two in the fully equipped campground in this spring-fed canyon, 12 miles south of Alamogordo, will give you the chance to see ferns and flowers growing in the desert. The 5.5-mile Dog Canyon National Recreational Trail climbs 2000ft over 5.5 miles, for terrific views of the Tularosa Basin.

Best Western Desert Aire Hotel
HOTEL $

(☑575-437-2110; www.bestwestern.com; 1021 S White Sands Blvd; r from $79; ❋@☎☀) This large and well-maintained chain hotel has standard-issue rooms and suites (some with kitchenettes), along with a sauna and whirlpool. In summer, the swimming pool makes a cool sanctuary.

Margo's
NEW MEXICAN $

(☑575-434-0689; www.margosmexicanfood.com; 504 E 1st St; mains $7-15; ☉10:30am-9pm Mon-Sat, 11am-8:30pm Sun) There's not much to look at inside, but the New Mexican cuisine is solid and the prices are fair. Family-owned since the early 1980s, Margo's has a robust and tasty combo plate.

Pizza Patio & Pub
ITALIAN $$

(☑575-434-9633; 2203 E 1st St; mains $7-16; ☉11am-8pm Mon-Thu & Sat, to 9pm Fri; ⊛) The best something-for-everyone place in Alamogordo, with an outdoor patio and casual indoor dining room. Pizzas and pastas are good, salads are big, and pitchers or pints of beer are on tap.

Stella Vita
AMERICAN $$$

(☑575-434-4444; www.stellavitarestaurant. com; 902 New York St; lunch $8-12, dinner $16-29; ☉11am-2pm Mon-Wed, 11am-9pm Thu & Fri, 5-9pm Sat) Alamogordo's most upscale dining, a block off the highway in the sleepy old downtown. Choose from a meaty menu in an atmosphere of faux elegance under the gaze of a large cow skull; staff is very friendly, but the light jazz soundtrack can be irritating.

ⓘ Information

Gerald Champion Regional Medical Center (☑575-439-6100; www.gcrmc.org; 2669 N Scenic Dr; ☉24hr emergency)

Lincoln USFS National Forest Ranger Station (☑575-434-7200; www.fs.usda.gov/lincoln; 3463 Las Palomas Rd; ☉8am-4:30pm Mon-Fri)

Police (☑575-439-4300; 700 Virginia Ave)

Post office (930 E 12th St)

Visitor center (☑575-437-6120; www. alamogordo.com; 1301 N White Sands Blvd; ☉8am-5pm Mon-Fri, 9am-4pm Sat, 10am-3pm Sun; ☎)

ⓘ Getting There & Around

Greyhound (☑575-437-3050; www.greyhound. com; 3500 N White Sands Blvd) has daily buses to Albuquerque ($29, 4½ hours), Roswell ($20, 2½ hours) and El Paso, TX ($15, 2½ hours). The **Alamo El Paso Shuttle** (☑575-437-1472) has four buses daily to the El Paso International Airport ($50, 1½ hours) in Texas.

Cloudcroft & Around

POP 9700 / ELEV 8600FT

Nestled almost 2 miles up in the mountains east of Alamogordo, Cloudcroft makes a pleasant escape year-round. In winter there's snow tubing and snowmobiling across powder-soaked meadows. In summer, Cloudcroft offers refreshing respite from the desert heat, plus awesome hiking and biking. The town itself is a quaint place to wander, with some early-19th-century buildings, a low-key

---

THE BLAST HEARD 'ROUND THE WORLD

On just one day each year, the first Saturday in April, the public is permitted to visit the **Trinity Site** (per car $25), out on the White Sands Missile Range 35 miles west of Carrizozo, where the first atomic bomb was detonated on July 16, 1945. This eerie tour includes the base camp, the McDonald Ranch house where the plutonium core for the bomb was assembled, and ground zero itself. Carried out above ground, the test created a quarter-mile-wide crater and an 8-mile-high mushroom cloud above the desert. The radiation level is 'only' 10 times greater than the region's background level; a one-hour visit to ground zero will result in an exposure of one-half to one milliroentgen (mrem) – two to four times the estimated exposure of a typical adult on an average day in the US. Trinitite, a green, glassy substance resulting from the blast, is still radioactive, still scattered around and still must not be touched. Resist the urge to add it to your road-trip rock collection.

Two different access routes are open to visitors, for that one day only. A 'caravan' of vehicles leaves Alamogordo at 8am, drives the 85 miles to Trinity Site in convoy, and returns in the afternoon; for details, contact the **Alamogordo Chamber of Commerce** (☑505-437-6120; www.alamogordo.com). Alternatively, you can drive to the spot on your own by leaving I-25 at the San Antonio exit, 12 miles south of Socorro, heading 7 miles east on Hwy 380, and then another 5 miles southeast on a dirt road to the Stallion Gate. Once you've been cleared by security, you can then drive the remaining 17 miles to Trinity.

mountain vibe and a historic resort hotel, but most visitors are here to play in the surrounding peaks and forests.

⊙ Sights & Activities

Hiking is popular here from April to November; options range from short hikes close to town to overnight backpacking trips. Although trails are often fairly flat, the 9000ft elevation can make for some strenuous hiking if you are not acclimatized. The most popular day hike is the 2.2-mile **Cloud Climbing Rail Trail**, which leaves from the edge of town and ventures out to an amazing old railroad trestle bridge that you may have glimpsed from Hwy 82 as you drove up. The **Willie White/Wills Canyon Trails** loop through open meadows, with a good chance of seeing elk. The ranger station has free trail maps and detailed topo maps for sale.

Sacramento Peak Observatory   OBSERVATORY
(☑575-434-7000; http://nsosp.nso.edu; guided tours adult/child $3/free; ⊙visitor center 9am-5pm, closed Feb, self-guided tours dawn-dusk year-round, guided tours 2pm summer only) One of the world's largest solar observatories is near Sunspot, 20 miles south of Cloudcroft. Though it's primarily for scientists, tourists can take self-guided or guided tours. The high and beautiful Sunspot Scenic Byway leads to the site, with the mountains to the east and White Sands to the west. From Cloudcroft, take Hwy 130 to Hwy 6563 – and fill your tank before you set off.

High Altitude   MOUNTAIN BIKING
(☑575-682-1229; www.highaltitude.org; 310 Burro Ave; rentals per day from $30; ⊙10am-5:30pm Mon-Thu, to 6pm Fri & Sat, to 5pm Sun) Trails in the Sacramento Mountains offer great mountain biking. High Altitude rents bikes and will point you in the right direction.

Ski Cloudcroft   SKIING
(☑575-682-2333; www.skicloudcroft.net; 1920 Hwy 82; all-day ski/tube $35/20; ⊙9am-4pm Nov-Mar) Family-oriented ski resort with the southernmost run in the US. In winter, grab the lift up and ski, snowboard or race an inner tube (weekends only) down the hill.

Lodge Resort Golf Course   GOLF
(☑575-682-2098; 9/18 holes from $26/46) The Lodge Resort has a beautiful 18-hole golf course that's among the highest and oldest in the country and is groomed for cross-country skiing In winter.

✾ Festivals & Events

Cloudcroft celebrates midsummer with both the annual **Cherry Festival**, on the third Sunday of June – the nearby hills are rife with cherry orchards – and the **Bad Ass Mountain Music Festival** at Ski Cloudcroft in the middle of the month.

🛏 Sleeping & Eating

Cloudcroft is blessed with some heavenly choices. There are several summer-only USFS campgrounds nearby.

★**Cloudcroft Mountain Park Hostel**   HOSTEL $
(☑575-682-0555; www.cloudcrofthostel.com; 1049 Hwy 82; dm $17, r with shared bath $30-50; ☞) Situated on 28 wooded acres, down the highway 6 miles west of Cloudcroft, this lurid blue hostel is the best lodging deal around. Entire families can fit in the large rooms, which are simple but tidy. Shared bathrooms are clean, and there's a fully equipped kitchen with coffee and tea. The common area is a great place to swap stories.

★**Lodge Resort & Spa**   HISTORIC HOTEL $$
(☑800-395-6343; www.thelodgeresort.com; 601 Corona Pl; r from $141; @☞☒) Built in 1899 as a getaway for railroad employees, this historic hilltop lodge is now a full-scale resort, with a wonderful restaurant, golf course, beautiful grounds and pampering spa. Period-furnished rooms in the main Bavarian-style building can be a bit small but they're cozy, with high beds and showers not baths; less attractive Pavilion rooms are a few blocks away.

Rebecca's   AMERICAN $$
(☑575-682-3131; Lodge Resort, 601 Corona Pl; mains $8-38; ⊙7-10am, 11:30am-2pm & 5:30-9pm) Up at the Lodge, Rebecca's serves by far the best food in Cloudcroft, with rich, meaty dishes like chile-crusted rack of lamb to match the opulent Victorian setting. The Sunday brunch is a long-standing local favorite. Kick back on the outside deck, have a beer and check out the spectacular views, before you head back into the elegant dining room.

❶ Information

Visit Cloudcroft's online-only **E-Visitor Center** (☑575-682-2733; www.cloudcroft.net) – '9000 Feet above Stress Level' – or **Sacramento Ranger Station** (☑575-682-2551; 4 Lost Lodge Rd; ⊙8am-4:30pm Mon-Fri) for local info.

Ruidoso & Around

POP 9500 / ELEV 6920FT

Perched on the eastern slopes of the Sierra Blanca (11,981ft), Ruidoso is a year-round resort town that's downright bustling in the summer, attracts skiers in winter, has a lively arts scene, and is also home to a renowned racetrack. Neighboring Texans and locals escaping the summer heat of Alamogordo (46 miles southwest) and Roswell (71 miles east) are happy campers here (or more precisely, happy cabiners). The lovely Rio Ruidoso, a small creek with good fishing, runs through town.

⊙ Sights & Activities

Hwy 48, the main drag through town, is called Mechem Dr as it approaches Ruidoso from the north, then becomes Sudderth Dr in the small downtown area, and heads east to the Y-intersection with Hwy 70. The community of Alto, 6 miles north on Mechem Dr, holds more accommodations.

Hiking is popular in warmer months. If you're out for a day, try the 4.6-mile hike from Ski Apache to **Sierra Blanca Peak** itself, an ascent of 2000ft. Take Trail 15 from the small parking area just before the main lot and follow signs west and south along Trails 25 and 78 to Lookout Mountain (11,580ft). An obvious trail continues due south for 1.25 miles to Sierra Blanca Peak. For multiday trips, head into the **White Mountains Wilderness**, where 50 miles of trails crisscross 75 scenic sq miles. Ruidoso's ranger station has maps and information.

Hubbard Museum of the American West   MUSEUM
(☑575-378-4142; www.hubbardmuseum.org; 26301 Hwy 70; adult/child $7/2; ⊙9am-5pm; 🖐) This town-run museum focuses on local history, with a wonderful gallery of old photos, and also displays Native American kachinas, war bonnets, weapons and pottery. Traces of its original incarnation as the Museum of the Horse linger in various horse-related exhibits – and be sure to check out the fascinating, if completely irrelevant, history of toilets in the restrooms.

Ruidoso Downs Racetrack   HORSE RACING
(☑575-378-4431; www.raceruidoso.com; Hwy 70; grandstand seats free; ⊙Fri-Mon late May-early Sep) National attention focuses on the Ruidoso Downs racetrack on Labor Day for the world's richest quarter-horse race, the All American Futurity, which has a purse of $2.4 million. The course is also home to the Racehorse Hall of Fame, and the small Billy the Kid Casino.

Mescalero Apache Indian Reservation   INDIAN RESERVATION
Around 4000 Apache – not only Mescalero, but also Chiricahua and Lipan – live on this 720-sq-mile reservation, stretching south and west of Ruidoso on the flanks of the magnificent Sierra Blanca Peak. These nomadic peoples reached the area eight centuries ago; with their mobility increased by the acquisition of the horse, they later became much-feared raiders. They now own a casino hotel (p342), a **golf course** (guest/nonguest from $60/75) and a ski area (p341).

Ski Apache   SKIING
(www.skiapache.com; lift ticket adult/child $51/33) Unlikely as it sounds, Ski Apache, 18 miles northwest of Ruidoso on the slopes of Sierra Blanca Peak, really is owned by the Apache. Potentially it's the finest ski area south of Albuquerque, a good choice for affordability and fun – and it's also home to New Mexico's only gondola. Recent seasons, however, have seen poor snowfall – check ahead.

✯ Festivals & Events

Apache Maidens' Puberty Ceremony   CULTURAL
(⊙Jul) Takes over the July 4 weekend, and features a powwow, rodeo and arts-and-crafts demonstrations.

Ruidoso Art Festival   ART
(⊙Jul) This juried art show, on the last weekend of July, attracts artists, browsers and buyers from all over the Southwest.

Golden Aspen Motorcycle   MOTORCYCLE RALLY
(www.motorcyclerally.com; ⊙Sep) Thirty thousand motorcycle-riders flock to Ruidoso on the third weekend of September.

Aspenfest   STREET
(⊙Oct) Held on the first weekend in October, Aspenfest features a golf tournament, chile cook-off and street festival.

Lincoln County Cowboy Symposium   CULTURAL
(www.cowboysymposium.org; ⊙Oct) Held at Ruidoso Downs on the second weekend in October, with cowboy poetry, chuckwagon cooking and horsebreaking.

Oktoberfest CULTURAL
(www.trekwest.com/oktoberfest; ⊙Oct) Bavarian-themed, with German food and beer, along with professional polka dancing and oompah bands. Held the third weekend in October.

🛏 Sleeping

Rental cabins are a big deal in Ruidoso. Most have kitchens and grills, and often fireplaces and decks. Some cabins in town are cramped, while newer ones are concentrated in the Upper Canyon. The team at **4 Seasons Real Estate** (☏575-257-7577; www.casasderuidoso.com; 712 Mechem Dr; ⊙8am-5pm) arranges condominium, cabin and lodge rentals. There's also plenty of free primitive camping along the forest roads on the way to the ski area.

Sitzmark Chalet HOTEL $
(☏575-257-4140; www.sitzmark-chalet.com; 627 Sudderth Dr; r from $59; ❄🐾) This ski-themed chalet offers 17 simple but nice rooms. Picnic tables, grills and an eight-person hot tub are welcome perks.

Bonito Hollow Campground CAMPGROUND $
(☏575-336-4325; www.bonitohollow.com; 221 Hwy 37, Alto; tent/RV sites $19/36, cabin $90; ⊙Apr-Nov; ❄) Private campground in peaceful wooded surroundings, adjoining Lincoln National Forest. Decent spaces for tents and RVs, and progressively replacing the log cabins lost in a 2012 wildfire.

Shadow Mountain Lodge LODGE $$
(☏575-257-4886; www.smlruidoso.com; 107 Main St; r & cabins from $125; 🐾) Geared toward couples, the immaculate, romantic rooms in the lodge feature fireplaces, while a wraparound balcony overlooks the landscaped grounds; the hot tub is tucked away in a gazebo. Individual cabins have Jacuzzi tubs and giant TVs.

Upper Canyon Inn LODGE $$
(☏575-257-3005; www.uppercanyoninn.com; 215 Main Rd; r/cabins from $89/129; 🐾) Rooms and cabins here range from simple good values to rustic-chic luxury. Bigger doesn't necessarily mean more expensive, so look at a few options. The pricier cabins have some fine interior woodwork and Jacuzzi tubs.

Inn of the Mountain Gods HOTEL $$
(☏575-464-7059; www.innofthemountaingods.com; 287 Carrizo Canyon Rd; r from $110; ❄🐾🏊) This luxury, lakeside casino-resort on the Mescalero Apache reservation offers surprisingly low online rates. Gamblers can feed

THE LEGEND OF BILLY THE KID

Even the most basic information about Billy the Kid tends to cast a shadow larger than the outlaw himself. Here's what we know, or don't. Most historians agree that he was born sometime in 1859, most likely in New York City (or Indiana or Missouri). He may be buried in Old Fort Sumner, where his skull may have been stolen and possibly recovered) – that is, unless he colluded with his presumed assassin, Sheriff Pat Garrett, and lived to a ripe old age...somewhere.

The Kid didn't start out as a murderer. His first known childhood crimes included stealing laundry and fencing butter. In the mid-1870s, about the time the teenage Billy arrived in New Mexico, the 400 residents of Lincoln shopped at 'Murphy's,' the only general store in the region. In 1877, though, Englishman John Tunstall arrived and built a competing general store.

Within a year, Tunstall was dead, allegedly shot by Murphy and his boys. The entire region erupted in what became known as the Lincoln County War. Tunstall's most famous follower was a wild teenager named Henry McCarty, alias William Bonney, aka Billy the Kid, who was on the run from his previous home in Silver City. Over the next several months the Kid and his gang gunned down any members of the Murphy faction they could find. Repeatedly captured or cornered, the Kid managed brazen and lucky escapes before finally being shot by Sheriff Pat Garrett near Fort Sumner in 1881, where he lies in a grave in a barren yard. Maybe.

Near the end of his term as governor in 2010, Bill Richardson considered granting the Kid a posthumous pardon, based on historical evidence that he'd been promised one by territorial governor Lew Wallace if he'd give testimony about the murder of Lincoln County Sherriff William Brady in 1878. The Kid testified but, rather than being pardoned, was sentenced to death. After much deliberation, and partly due to protests raised by descendants of Pat Garrett and Lew Wallace, the pardon was declined.

slots, while guided fishing, paddleboat rentals, a championship golf course and horseback riding are just a concierge call away. Several restaurants, a nightclub, and a sports bar are also on-site. It's fun for a night or two.

High Country Lodge LODGE $$
(☎575-336-4321; www.highcountrylodge.net; 859 N Hwy 48, Alto; r from $129; ▣) This funky older place welcomes you with three friendly (wooden) bears. It offers a comfortable selection of rustic and basic two-bedroom cabins, each with kitchen, fireplace and porch, plus an indoor pool and hot tub.

✗ Eating

★**Cornerstone Bakery** CAFE $
(☎575-257-1842; www.cornerstonebakerycafe. com; 359 Sudderth Dr; mains under $10; ☉7am-2pm; ☑) Totally irresistible, hugely popular local bakery-cafe, where everything, from the breads, pastries and espresso to the omelets and croissant sandwiches, is just the way it should be. Stick around long enough and the Cornerstone may become your morning touchstone.

Cafe Rio PIZZA $
(☎575-257-7746; http://caferiopizza.com; 2547 Sudderth Dr; mains $5-24; ☉11:30am-8pm, closed Wed off-season; ☑☑) Locals come here for the New York–style thick-crust pizza – there's no connection with the regional Mexican chain of the same name – but the stuffed calzones and Greek offerings are also decent for a small-town restaurant. Wash it down with a big selection of international and seasonal beer. Cash only.

★**Michael J's** ITALIAN $$
(☎575-257-9559; www.michaeljsrestaurant.com; 601 Mechem Dr; mains $13-29; ☉5-9pm Tue-Sat) Excellent and very convivial Italian restaurant, cozy and romantic in winter and offering outdoor patio seating in summer. The delicious pasta dishes concentrate on seafood like clams and shrimp, but it also serves meaty Italian classics using steak and veal.

Casa Blanca MEXICAN $$
(☎575-257-2495; 501 Mechem Dr; mains $10-20; ☉11am-9pm Mon-Thu, to 10pm Fri & Sat, to 8pm Sun) Dine on Southwestern cuisine in a renovated Spanish-style house or on the pleasant patio in the summer. It's hard to go wrong with the New Mexican plates, but it also has big burgers and chicken-fried steak.

☆ Entertainment

Quarters Lounge BAR
(☎575-257-9535; 2535 Sudderth Dr; ☉11am-2am Mon-Sat, noon-midnight Sun) Dance the night away to live blues and rock on the big dancefloor, or listen from a barstool or at one of the comfortable tables.

Spencer Theater for the Performing Arts THEATER
(☎575-336-4800; www.spencertheater.com; 108 Spencer Rd, Alto) Larger than you'd expect in small-town New Mexico, and enjoying a stunning mountain setting in Alto, this community theater hosts drama, music and dance performances.

Flying J Ranch DINNER SHOW
(☎575-336-4330; www.flyingjranch.com; 1028 Hwy 48; adult/child $27/15; ☉from 5:30pm Mon-Sat late May-early Sep, Sat only early Sep–mid-Oct; ☑) Families with little ones will love this 'Western village,' 1.5 miles north of Alto, as it delivers a full night of entertainment, with gunfights, pony rides and Western music, to go with its cowboy-style chuckwagon dinner.

ℹ Information

Both the **chamber of commerce** (☎575-257-7395; www.ruidosonow.com; 720 Sudderth Dr; ☉8am-5pm Mon-Fri, 9am-3pm Sat) and the **Smokey Bear Ranger Station** (☎575-257-4095; www.fs.usda.gov/lincoln; 901 Mechem Dr; ☉7:30am-4:30pm Mon-Fri, plus Sat in summer) are helpful. The chamber's website has Spanish, Italian, German and French translations.

ℹ Getting There & Around

Greyhound (☎575-257-2660; www.greyhound. com; 138 Service Rd) operates daily service to Alamogordo ($15, one hour), Roswell ($22, 1½ hours), and El Paso, TX ($32, 3½ hours).

Carrizozo

POP 1100 / ELEV 5425FT

The little town of Carrizozo sits where the Sacramento Mountains hit the Tularosa Basin. Art galleries and antiques shops line historic 12th St, downtown's main axis, a block east of modern Hwy 54. Unfortunately, though, cafes open and close here with a sad inevitability; at the time of research, there was nowhere to recommend either to eat or stay.

NEW MEXICO CARRIZOZO

⊙ Sights

Valley of Fires Recreation Area   PARK
(🖉575-648-2241; Hwy 380; 1-person-/2-or-more-people vehicle $3/5, tent/RV sites $7/12) At the Valley of Fires Recreation Area, 4 miles west of Carrizozo, you can explore the rocky blackness of a 125-sq-mile lava flow that's 160ft deep in the middle. The paved 0.6-mile nature trail is easy for kids and holds informative signs describing the geology and biology of this volcanic wasteland, or simply hike off-trail, cutting cross-country over the flow. You'll find campsites and shaded picnic tables near the visitor center.

🛍 Shopping

Gallery 408   ARTS & CRAFTS
(🖉575-648-598; www.gallery408.com; 408 12th St; ⊙10am-5pm Mon, Fri & Sat, noon-5pm Sun) Friendly little gallery that sells work by regional artists, and still holds a few of Carrizozo's herd of Painted Burros (if you ever saw the Cow Parades of Chicago and New York, you'll know what to expect).

Lincoln

POP 50 / ELEV 5702FT

Fans of Western history won't want to miss little Lincoln. Twelve miles east of Capitan along the **Billy the Kid National Scenic Byway** (www.billybyway.com), this is where the gun battle that turned Billy the Kid into a legend took place.

It's hard to believe that in Billy the Kid's era Lincoln was home to a bustling population of nearly 900. Today it is essentially a ghost town, with only about 50 people living here. Those who do, however, are dedicated to preserving its 1880s buildings. Modern influences, such as souvenir stands, are not allowed, and New Mexico has designated the entire town as the **Lincoln Historic Site** (🖉575-653-4372; www.nmmonuments.org/lincoln; adult/child $5/free; ⊙hours vary for individual sites). It's a pretty cool place to get away from this century for a night.

Visits consist of strolling the half-mile length of Lincoln's one street. Start at the east end, where exhibits in the **Anderson-Freeman Visitors Center** (⊙8:30am-5pm), on the Buffalo soldiers, Apaches, and the Lincoln County War, explain the town's history. The admission price includes entry to the **Tunstall Store** (with a remarkable display of late-19th-century merchandise), the **Courthouse** from which the Kid famously shot his way to freedom, killing two deputies, and **Dr Wood's House**, an intact 19th-century doctor's home and office.

During **Old Lincoln Days**, over the first full weekend in August, musicians and mountain men, doctors and desperadoes wander the streets in period costume, and there are demonstrations of spinning, blacksmithing and other frontier skills. The evening sees the folk pageant, 'The Last Escape of Billy the Kid.'

🛏 Sleeping & Eating

★**Ellis Store Country Inn**   B&B $$
(🖉800-653-6460; www.ellisstore.com; Hwy 380; r incl breakfast $89-129) This fabulous 19th-century adobe farmhouse at Lincoln's east end offers three antiques-filled ensuite rooms (with stoves) in the main building, and five more, some sharing bathrooms, in a historic mill behind. The host – a former New Mexico Chef of the Year – offers a six-course dinner in the cozy dining room (daily except Sun; $75 per person; nonguests welcome by reservation).

Hurd Ranch Guest Homes   GUESTHOUSE $$
(🖉800-658-6912; www.wyethartists.com; 105 La Rinconada, San Patricio; casitas $140-250; 🐾) Huge rural property, 14 miles south of Lincoln, holding six lovely rental casitas beside an apple orchard, furnished with style, grace, and lots of original art, and sleeping up to six people. Owner and artist Peter Hurd shows his own work and that of his relatives NC and Andrew Wyeth, his mother Henriette Wyeth and his father Michael Hurd.

Roswell

That Roswell has become a phenomenon in its own right, and a byword for kookiness of all kinds, is entirely due to its status as the site of the world's most famous UFO incident – the alleged crash of a real-life flying saucer in the desert nearby, back in July 1947. Whether or not you're a true believer, it's worth coming to Roswell to experience one of America's most enduring and fanatical pop-culture memes. Sure it's about as cheesy as it gets, but conspiracy theorists and X-Files fanatics descend from other worlds into Roswell in real seriousness.

If you're driving east on Hwy 70/380 from the Sacramento Mountains, enjoy the view. Roswell sits at the western edge of the dry plains, and these are the last big mountains you'll see for a while. The 'Staked Plains' extending east into Texas were long home to roaming buffalo and nomadic Native Americans. Anglo settlers and hunters moved in during the 19th century and wiped out the buffalo, killing some 3.5 million in just two years. The region became desolate and empty; only a few groups of Comanche mixed with other tribes out on the plains, hunting and trying to avoid confinement on reservations. Roswell itself, founded in 1871, served as a stopping place for cowboys driving cattle.

◉ Sights & Activities

The main west–east drag through town is 2nd St and the main north–south thoroughfare is Main St; they intersect in the heart of downtown.

★**International UFO Museum & Research Center** MUSEUM
(☏575-625-9495; www.roswellufomuseum.com; 114 N Main St; adult/child $5/2; ⊙9am-5pm) There's a lot of reading to be done here; display panels are covered with witness statements, newspaper cuttings and extended essays, outlining the 1947 Roswell Incident Timeline and explaining the 'great cover-up.' Serious UFO-logists will lap it up; for skeptics and the merely curious, homemade models and gruesome mock-ups provide light relief. The library claims to have the world's most comprehensive collection of UFO-related materials; who are we to doubt them?

★**Roswell Museum & Art Center** MUSEUM
(☏575-624-6744; www.roswellmuseum.org; 100 W 11th St; ⊙9am-5pm Mon-Sat, 1-5pm Sun) FREE Roswell's excellent museum deserves a visit. Seventeen galleries showcase Southwestern artists including Georgia O'Keeffe, Peter Hurd and Henriette Wyeth, along with an eclectic mix of Native American, Hispanic and Anglo artifacts that illustrate the domestic and spiritual lives of the region's inhabitants. There's also a fascinating display on local rocket pioneer Robert H Goddard, who launched the first successful liquid fuel rocket in 1926. The adjoining **Goddard Planetarium** was only open for special events at the time of research.

Historical Center for Southeast New Mexico MUSEUM
(☏575-622-1176; www.hfsenm.com; 200 N Lea Ave; admission by donation; ⊙1-4pm) Housed in the 1912 mansion of local rancher James Phelps White, this property is on the National Reg-

Roswell

◎ **Top Sights**

◎ **Sights**

🛏 **Sleeping**

✴ **Eating**

ister of Historic Places, and its interior has been carefully restored to its original early 20th-century decor, with period furnishings, photographs and art.

THE TRUTH IS OUT THERE...

It's long now since the heady summer of 1947, when an unidentified flying object fell out of the sky and crash-landed in the desert near Roswell, but the little New Mexican town is still cashing in on the mystery. Those who believe aliens are out there are convinced that the US government has gone to great lengths to cover up the fact that the craft truly was of extraterrestrial origin. They certainly have a compelling case.

In its initial 1947 press release, the government identified the object as a crashed disk. A day later, however, it changed its story: now the disk was really just a weather balloon. The feds then confiscated all the previous releases, cordoned off the area as they collected debris, and posted armed guards to escort curious locals from the site of the 'weather balloon' crash. A local mortician fielded calls from the mortuary office at the government airfield inquiring after small, hermetically sealed coffins for preventing tissue contamination and degeneration.

Now, 70-odd years later, the government remains tight-lipped, and Roswell is the story that will never die. There are frequent eyewitness accounts of flying saucers in the sky, and rumor and misinformation continue to swirl about the original crash, fueling all manner of speculation. In the early 2000s, Roswell even spawned its own TV series about alien-mutant hybrid teenagers trying to survive as humans while keeping their alien powers alive and attempting to get home.

Bitter Lake National Wildlife Refuge WILDLIFE RESERVE
(☑ 575-622-6755; www.fws.gov/refuge/Bitter_Lake; 4200 E Pine Lodge Rd; ☺ sunrise-sunset Mon-Fri, closed Sat & Sun) FREE Wintering water birds gather at this 38-sq-mile refuge, 10 miles northeast of Roswell; many birds remain to nest in the summer. Bring your binoculars for the best views of cranes, geese and other species; hiking and biking trails can get you closer. To reach the refuge, follow signs from either Hwy 380 or Hwy 285/70.

★ Festivals & Events

UFO Festival QUIRKY
(www.ufofestivalroswell.com; ☺ Jul) Held on Fourth of July weekend, this celebration of Roswell's 1947 brush with fame attracts visitors from around the planet...and beyond. Interplanetary-travel celebs such as the Duras sisters (Klingon warriors), as well as genuine astronauts, make appearances. Amid enough lectures, films and workshops to make anyone's ears go pointy, don't miss the night parade and alien-costume competitions.

Eastern New Mexico State Fair CULTURAL
(☑ 575-623-9411; http://enmsf.com; ☺ Oct) Early October's State Fair sees rodeo, livestock and agricultural competitions and chile-eating contests.

🛏 Sleeping

There are plenty of chain hotels at the north end of main street, as well as independent (sometimes sketchy) budget motels west along 2nd St.

Budget Inn MOTEL $
(☑ 575-623-6050; www.budgetinnroswell.com; 2101 N Main St; r from $45; ❋ 🐾 🛜) Old-fashioned downtown motel that's just about the best value in town, offering basic but clean rooms, with new pillow-top mattresses and continental breakfast.

Bottomless Lakes State Park CAMPGROUND $
(☑ 575-624-6058; www.nmparks.com; 545a Bottomless Lakes Rd; day-use per vehicle $5, tent/RV sites $8/14) The seven lakes at this much-loved park – technically they're sinkholes – provide welcome relief in summer. Waterfront campgrounds range from primitive campsites to the developed site at Lea Lake, the only place you're allowed to swim, which has bathrooms and showers. They're 10 miles east of Roswell on Hwy 380, then 5 miles south on Hwy 409.

Heritage Inn HISTORIC HOTEL $$
(☑ 575-748-2552; www.artesiaheritageinn.com; 209 W Main St, Artesia; r incl breakfast from $119; ❋ @ 🛜 🐾) The nicest place to stay hereabouts is not in Roswell, but in the sleepy downtown Artesia, 36 miles south toward Carlsbad. If you're in the mood for slightly upscale digs – bearing in mind you're in southeastern New Mexico – this Victorian-era establishment offers 11 Old West–style rooms. Half have both bath and shower, the rest a shower only.

Eating

Cowboy Cafe DINER $
(☎575-622-6363; 1120 E 2nd St; mains $5-12; ⊙6am-2pm Mon-Sat) One of the few truly local joints left in town, this is a good option for a breakfast before hitting the UFO museum or the road.

Martin's Capitol Cafe NEW MEXICAN $
(☎575-624-2111; 110 W 4th St; mains $7-15; ⊙6am-8:30pm Mon-Sat) Roswell holds a fine crop of inexpensive New Mexican restaurants; this one is homestyle and dependable, with all the variations on chile you could hope for.

Mama Tucker's BAKERY $
(☎575-625-1475; 3109 N Main St; doughnuts $1; ⊙5am-5pm Tue-Fri, 5am-1pm Sat-Mon) If you're craving something sweet, head a dozen blocks north of dowtown and treat yourself to homemade doughnuts, cakes and cookies.

Pasta Cafe ITALIAN $$
(☎575-624-1111; www.pastacafeitalianbistro.com; 1208 N Main St; mains $9-22; ⊙11am-9:30pm Sun-Thu, to 10:30pm Fri & Sat) One of Roswell's premier date restaurants, this large bistro delivers reliable pizzas and pasta specials as well as steak and seafood dishes like the tasty oven-broiled scallops.

Wellhead BREWERY $$
(☎575-746-0640; 332 W Main St, Artesia; mains $8-27; ⊙11am-9pm Mon-Sat) Modern brewpub restaurant and bar in a 1905 building in downtown Artesia, halfway between Roswell and Carlsbad. As well as decent pub grub, which round here naturally includes green chile stew, it has a fine array of its own beers, including Crude Oil Stout.

ℹ Information

Eastern New Mexico Medical Center (☎575-622-8170; www.enmmc.com; 405 W Country Club Rd; ⊙24hr emergency)
Police (☎575-624-6770; 128 W 2nd St)
Post office (415 N Pennsylvania Ave)
Visitors Bureau (☎575-624-6860; www.seeroswell.com; 912 N Main St; ⊙8:30am-5:30pm Mon-Fri, 10am-3pm Sat & Sun; 🖳)
Pick up local information and have your picture snapped with an alien at the visitors bureau.

ℹ Getting There & Around

Greyhound (☎575-622-2510; www.greyhound.com; 1100 N Virginia Ave) has daily buses to Las Cruces ($42, four hours), where you can transfer to Albuquerque or El Paso, TX, but no services to Carlsbad.

Carlsbad

POP 27,000 / ELEV 3111FT

Previously a remote and sleepy ranching town, Carlsbad received a huge boost in 1923, when Carlsbad Caverns, a 25-mile drive southwest, became a national monument. Now elevated to national park status, the caverns continue to attract hundreds of thousands of visitors each year. Carlsbad itself, however, currently has other things on its mind. It's in the middle of a huge oil boom that's seeing annual production increases of around 20%. The local economy has hit the roof, and rates for even the cheapest motels have rocketed.

◉ Sights & Activities

Carlsbad stands beside the Pecos River 30 miles north of the Texas state line. Its main thoroughfare, Hwy 285, becomes Canal St in town, and then National Parks Hwy as it heads south toward the caverns.

Living Desert Zoo & Gardens State Park ZOO
(☎575-887-5516; www.nmparks.com; 1504 Miehls Dr N, off Hwy 285; adult/child $5/3; ⊙8am-5pm Jun-Aug, 9am-5pm Sep-May, last zoo entry 3:30pm) Northwest of town, this state park is a great place to see and learn about reptiles and roadrunners, wolves and antelopes, along with desert plants like agave, ocotillo and yucca. A good 1.3-mile trail showcases different habitats of the Chihuahuan Desert.

Lake Carlsbad Beach Park WATERFRONT
A system of dams and spillways on the Pecos River created the 2-mile-long Lake Carlsbad immediately east of downtown, which holds pleasant trails along its two banks. You can swim at the north end of Park Dr (or the east end of Church St), and also rent little individual paddlewheel boats.

Carlsbad Museum & Art Center MUSEUM
(☎575-887-0276; www.nmculture.org; 418 W Fox St; ⊙10am-5pm Mon-Sat) FREE This museum displays Apache artifacts, pioneer memorabilia from the region, and paintings by artists from the Taos School.

🛏 Sleeping

Although Carlsbad holds dozens of chain motels, lined up along Canal St, the current oil boom has seen rates for even the most ordinary rooms remain upwards of $200 per night year-round – and nonetheless be

Carlsbad

Carlsbad's best hotel, in a grand downtown building that started life as the First National Bank in 1892, is now strangely among the cheapest in town. Friendly and family-run, it has an excellent restaurant. The sitting room of one suite is inside the old vault; another still has a bullet hole.

✗ Eating & Drinking

Blue House Bakery & Cafe   BREAKFAST $
(☏ 575-628-0555; 609 N Canyon St; mains $4-10; ⊗ 6am-noon Mon-Sat) This sweet Queen Anne house perks the best espresso in southeast New Mexico. Its baked goods are pretty darn good too, while lunchtime sees good fresh-bread sandwiches. Cheery and family-owned, it also offers outdoor-garden seating.

★ Trinity Restaurant & Wine Bar   AMERICAN $$
(☏ 575-234-9891; www.thetrinityhotel.com; Trinity Hotel, 201 S Canal St; breakfast $6-12, dinner $14-34; ⊗ 7am-9pm Mon-Sat; ✍) This elegant split-level dining room – the ceiling is so high there's room for a mezzanine floor – offers Carlsbad's finest dining, with a menu of steaks, seafood and Italian specialties, and plenty of pastas and salads for vegetarians. Nonkosher carnivores will love the roast pork in a cabernet/green chile reduction. Lightning-fast lunch service makes it a favourite rendezvous for downtown employees.

Lucy's Mexicali Restaurant   MEXICAN $$
(☏ 575-881-7714; www.lucysmexicalirestaurant. com; 701 S Canal St; mains $7-18; ⊗ 11am-9pm Mon-Thu, to 9:30 Fri & Sat) Apart from a great Mexican menu, Lucy's serves up tasty margaritas and a good selection of microbrews – small wonder it's usually packed with devoted locals and visitors.

booked solid months in advance. Don't just turn up expecting to find a cheap room – in fact, if you're on a budget, you'd do best to avoid spending the night in Carlsbad, and instead visit the national park as a *long* day's detour between, say, Roswell and Alamogordo.

Carlsbad KOA   CAMPGROUND $
(☏ 575-457-2000; www.carlsbadkoa.com; 2 Manthei Rd; tent/RV sites from $32/44, cabins $57; ❖❂☂) On Hwy 285 about 18 miles north of central Carlsbad, this friendly site offers the choice of air-conditioned 'kamping kabins' or grassy tent sites. There's also a pool, games room, grocery store, laundry, playground, dog park and showers. Ask hosts Scott and Susan Bacher about free rides for kids in their retired fire truck.

★ Trinity Hotel   BOUTIQUE HOTEL $$
(☏ 575-234-9891; www.thetrinityhotel.com; 201 S Canal St; r from $189; ❊❂) Having declined to raise its rates to match its neighbors,

Red Chimney Pit Barbecue BARBECUE $$
(☑575-885-8744; 817 N Canal St; mains $7-15; ☉11am-2pm & 4:30-8:30pm Mon-Fri) Southern-style, slow-cooked pit barbecue – if quality meats and tasty sauce aren't your thing, how about catfish and fried okra?

ℹ Information

Carlsbad Chamber of Commerce (☑575-887-6516; www.carlsbadchamber.com; 302 S Canal St; ☉9am-5pm Mon, 8am-5pm Tue-Fri) Helpful in-town visitor center.

Carlsbad Medical Center (☑575-887-4100; www.carlsbadmedicalcenter.com; 2430 W Pierce St; ☉24hr emergency)

National Park Service Information Center (☑575-785-2232; 3225 National Parks Hwy; ☉8am-4:30pm Mon-Fri) This office, a mile south of town, is a useful source of information before you set off to Carlsbad Caverns National Park.

Police (☑575-885-2111; 602 W Mermod St)

ℹ Getting There & Away

Greyhound (☑575-887-1108; www.greyhound.com; 1000 S Canal St) buses depart daily for Las Cruces ($65, six hours) and El Paso, TX ($57, three hours); the bus stops at the Allsup's gas station a few miles south of town on Hwy 180.

Carlsbad Caverns National Park

Scores of wondrous caves lie hidden beneath the desert hills at this unique **national park** (☑575-785-2232, bat info 505-785-3012; www.nps.gov/cave; adult/child $10/free; ☉caves 8:30am-5pm late May-early Sep, 8:30am-3:30pm early Sep-late May; 🎫), 25 miles by road southwest of Carlsbad. The cavern formations are a weird wonderland of stalactites and fantastical geological features. To reach them, you can either ride straight down from the visitor center in an elevator that drops the height of the Empire State Building in under a minute, or, more enjoyably, take a spooky 2-mile subterranean walk from the cave mouth. Bear in mind that to ensure that visitors have enough time to see the caves, the last admission is at 5pm in summer, 3:30pm otherwise.

Either way, you'll find yourself in the aptly named **Big Room**, an underground chamber 1800ft long, 255ft high and over 800ft below the surface, where you're free to walk an intricate loop trail past the pick of the amazing sights. Bring long sleeves and closed shoes: it's always chilly down here. All visitors return to the surface by elevator.

The cave's other claim to fame is the 300,000-plus Mexican free-tailed bat colony that roosts here from mid-May to mid-October. Wait at the cave mouth at sunset, to watch them cyclone out for an all-evening insect feast.

Guided tours (☑877-444-6777; www.recreation.gov; adult $7-20, child $3.50-10) of additional sectors of the main caverns are available, and should be reserved well in advance. If you want to scramble to lesser-known areas further afield, ask about Wild Cave tours. Wilderness backpacking trips into the desert are allowed by permit (free); the visitor center sells topographical maps of the 50-plus miles of hiking trails. November to March is the best time for backpacking – summer temperatures are scorching, and the countless rattlesnakes should be sleeping in winter.

Somewhere deep within the park's backcountry lies **Lechuguilla Cave**. With a depth of 1604ft and a mapped length (so far!) of some 136 miles, it's the deepest cave and third-longest limestone cave in North America. Sounds incredible – but it's only open to research and exploration teams, with special permission from the park.

I-40 EAST TO TEXAS

As you head across the eastern half of I-40 toward Texas, it can be pretty tempting to keep the pedal to the metal – or set the cruise control – and power on without stopping. If you have a little time, though, some interesting historical detours beckon you off the interstate, from the days of the dinosaurs to the worst of the Wild West and some classic Route 66 kitsch.

Santa Rosa

POP 2600 / ELEV 4600FT

Settled by Hispanic farmers in the mid-19th century, Santa Rosa's modern claim to fame is, weirdly enough, as the scuba diving capital of the Southwest. There's not much else going on here, though.

◉ Sights & Activities

Take exit 273 from Route 66/I-40 to reach downtown. Having started as Coronado St, the main street becomes Parker Ave through downtown, and then Will Rogers Dr when it passes exits 275 and 277.

Blue Hole
LAKE

(📞 575-472-3763; www.santarosanm.org; Hwy 40/US 66) One of the 10 best dive spots in the US is, surprisingly, right here in li'l ol' Santa Rosa. The bell-shaped, 81ft-deep Blue Hole, downtown, is 80ft in diameter at the surface and widens to 130ft down below, and has a dive shop alongside. Fed by a natural spring flowing at 3000 gallons a minute, the water is both very clear and pretty cool (at around 67°F/17°C). Platforms for divers are suspended about 25ft down.

Route 66 Auto Museum
MUSEUM

(www.route66automuseum.com; 2766 Rte 66; admission $5; ⊙7:30am-6pm Mon-Sat, 10am-5pm Sun Apr-Oct, 8am-5pm Mon-Sat, 10am-5pm Sun Nov-Mar) This museum pays homage to the mother of all roads. Boasting around 35 cars from the 1920s through the 1960s, all in beautiful condition, plus lots of 1950s memorabilia, it's a fun place; enjoy a milkshake at the '50s-style snack shack. If you're in the market for a beautifully restored old Chevy, friendly owner 'Bozo' also deals in antique cars.

Puerto de Luna
HISTORIC SITE

The tiny village of Puerto de Luna, beside the Pecos River 10 miles south of Santa Rosa, was founded in the 1860s. The drive there is pretty, winding through arroyos surrounded by eroded sandstone mesas on Hwy 91. Once you arrive you'll find an old county courthouse, a village church and a bunch of weathered adobe buildings. It's all quite charming, so long as you're not in a hurry to do something else.

🎉 Festivals & Events

Santa Rosa de Lima Fiesta
CULTURAL

(⊙Aug) Homespun, to say the least, the Fiesta has a beauty-queen contest and the bizarre, annual Duck Drop: contestants buy squares and then wait for a duck suspended over the squares to poop – if the poop lands on their square, they win cold cash. Held in the third week of August.

Route 66 Festival
CAR SHOW

(⊙Aug/Sep) In keeping with the Route 66 theme, this auto-centric show, held in August or September, attracts vintage- and classic-car enthusiasts, as well as folks driving strange things on wheels.

🛏 Sleeping & Eating

Main street Santa Rosa holds plenty of family-owned diners and roadside cafes, abounding in Route 66 allure. Chain hotels cluster around the I-40 exits.

Joseph's Route 66 Diner
DINER $$

(📞 575-472-3361; 1775 Historic Route 66; mains $7-21; ⊙8am-10pm) Route 66 nostalgia lines the walls of this popular place, family-run since 1956. The bountiful Mexican and American menu ranges from Santa Fe enchiladas with blue corn tortillas to catfish, burgers and steaks. Joseph's also mixes some serious margaritas.

Silver Moon
DINER $$

(📞 505-472-3162; 2545 Historic Route 66; mains $9-17; ⊙6am-10pm) This trademark Route 66 eatery first opened its doors in 1959, and serves fantastic homemade *chile rellenos* and other tasty diner grub dressed up with a New Mexican twist. It's popular with travelers following Route 66's old roadhouse trail, as well as locals who come for a morning coffee and a plate of bacon and eggs.

ℹ Getting There & Away

Santa Rosa's downtown is at exit 273 on I-40, 120 miles east of Albuquerque.

Tucumcari

POP 5200 / ELEV 4100FT

The largest I-40 town between Albuquerque and Amarillo, TX, Tucumcari is a ranching and farming community sited between the mesas and the plains that's also home to one of the best-preserved sections of Route 66. Not surprisingly, it still caters to travelers, with inexpensive motels, several classic pre-interstate buildings and souvenir shops.

⊙ Sights & Activities

Drive the kids down Tucumcari's main street at night, when dozens of old neon signs cast a blazing glow. Relics of Tucumcari's Route 66 heyday, the bright, flashing signs were installed by business owners in the hope of luring tired travelers to stop for the night. Tucumcari lies barely north of I-40. Old Route 66 is the main west–east thoroughfare between exits 329 and 335, and known as Tucumcari Blvd through downtown. The principal north–south artery is 1st St.

SMOKEY BEAR'S STOMPING GROUNDS

You'll see his likeness in state and national forests all over the US. But did you know that Smokey Bear was a real black bear? Once upon a time (back in 1950), a little cub was found clinging to a tree, paws charred from a 27-sq-mile forest fire in the Capitan Mountains. What better idea than to name him after the cartoon bear who had been the symbol of fire prevention since 1944? Nursed back to health, Smokey spent his remaining days as a living mascot in the National Zoo in Washington, DC. At **Smokey Bear Historical Park** (☏575-354-2748; 118 W Smokey Bear Blvd; adult/child $2/1; ⊙9am-5pm), in the village of Capitan, 12 miles west of Lincoln, you can see his grave and learn tons about forest fires – but don't expect to hike or experience the forest; the park is the size of a small garden. Every Fourth of July, the **Smokey Bear Stampede** features a parade, a rodeo, cookouts and other festivities. **Smokey Bear Days**, celebrated the first weekend in May, includes a street dance, wood-carving contest, and craft and antique-car shows.

There's a good little diner next to the park, naturally enough called **Smokey Bear Restaurant** (☏575-354-2257; www.smokeybearrestaurant.com; mains $5-10; ⊙6am-8pm), and serving all Smokey's personal favorites – who knew bears were partial to chicken quesadillas?

Mesalands Dinosaur Museum MUSEUM
(www.mesalands.edu/community/dinosaur-museum; 222 E Laughlin St; adult/child $6.50/4; ⊙10am-6pm Tue-Sat Mar-Aug, noon-5pm Tue-Sat Sep-Feb; ☻) This engaging museum showcases all manner of prehistoric beasts, from ferocious 40ft crocodiles to battling saber-tooth cats and the T-Rex-like torvosaurus. Dinosaur bones are cast in bronze, which not only shows fine detail, but also makes them works of art. There are plenty of hands-on exhibits for kids; one ancient monster is even fitted with a saddle for photo opportunities.

Tucumcari Historical Museum MUSEUM
(☏575-461-4201; 416 S Adams St; adult/child $5/1; ⊙9am-3pm Tue-Sat) Downtown museum of local history that's eclectic to say the least, with everything from a stuffed eagle and a Japanese flag to an entire firehouse and a fighter plane stranded in the yard. Several rooms feature reconstructions of early Western interiors, such as a sheriff's office, a classroom and a hospital room.

Art Murals WALKING TOUR
(www.tucumcarinm.com/visitor-guide.php) Buildings on and around Route 66 in downtown Tucumcari are adorned with large murals depicting local historical highlights. The life work of artists Doug and Sharon Quarles, they can be appreciated on a mural walk that makes a great way to stretch your legs and experience Tucumcari's Route 66 legacy. Grab a map from the website and get walking.

🛏 Sleeping

While the usual chain motels cluster around the I-40 exits, Tucumcari also boasts cool old independent motels along historic Route 66.

★**Blue Swallow Motel** HISTORIC MOTEL $
(☏575-461-9849; www.blueswallowmotel.com; 815 E Tucumcari Blvd; r from $70; ❄ 🛜 🐾) Spend the night in this beautifully restored Route 66 motel listed on the State and National Registers of Historic Places, and feel the decades melt away. The place has a great lobby, friendly owners and vintage, uniquely decorated rooms with little chairs out on the forecourt, plus a James Dean mural, and a classic neon sign boasting '100% refrigerated air.'

Historic Route 66 Motel MOTEL $
(☏575-461-1212; www.tucumcarimotel.com; 1620 E Route 66; r from $42; ❄ 🛜 🐾) When it comes to budget digs, you can't beat this historic motor-court motel, with giant plate-glass doors and mesa views; look for the light plane outside. It's nothing splashy, but the 25 rooms are cheap and clean, with comfy beds and quality pillows. Small dogs welcome, and it even has a morning-only espresso bar-cafe.

🍴 Eating & Drinking

Kix on 66 DINER $
(☏575-461-1966; www.kixon66.com; 1102 E Tucumcari Blvd; mains $5-10; ⊙6am-2pm; 🛜) Popular morning hangout, within walking distance of the Blue Swallow, serving breakfast in all shapes and sizes, from *huevos rancheros* to biscuits and gravy, plus espresso coffees, doughnuts and lunch sandwiches.

Pow-Wow Restaurant & Lizard Lounge
NEW MEXICAN $$

(☑575-461-2587; www.powwowlizard.com; 801 W Tucumcari Blvd; mains $8-20; ⊙7am-10pm, bar until late Fri & Sat) Though it serves a reasonable food menu of steaks and Mexican specialties, the real draw here is the lounge. Thursday is karaoke night, while on most Saturdays there's live music, with big-name New Mexican bands dropping by to play a few sets.

❶ Information

Visitor Center (☑575-461-1694; www.tucumcarinm.com; 404 W Route 66; ⊙8:30am-5pm Mon-Fri) Useful tourist information from the chamber of commerce.

❶ Getting There & Away

Tucumcari is at the crossroads of Historic Route 66, now superceded by I-40, and US Hwy 54. It is 110 miles west of Amarillo, TX, and 170 miles east of Albuquerque.

Fort Sumner

POP 1800 / ELEV 4032FT

If you have a moment to spare, swing south from the interstate to visit Fort Sumner. The little village that sprang up around old Fort Sumner gets more than a footnote in the history books for two reasons: the ill-starred Bosque Redondo Indian reservation and Billy the Kid's last showdown with Sheriff Pat Garrett.

❍ Sights & Activities

Billy the Kid Museum
MUSEUM

(www.billythekidmuseumfortsumner.com; 1601 E Sumner Ave; adult/child $5/3; ⊙8:30am-5pm, closed Sun Oct–mid-May & first 2 weeks Jan) Home to a private collection of more than 60,000 items, this main-street museum is a veritable shrine to the famous outlaw – don't miss the newly discovered photo of the Kid enjoying a game of croquet (really!). Native American artifacts and items from Wild West frontier life fill several rooms, and there's also a shed filled with classic 1950s cars.

Bosque Redondo Memorial at Fort Sumner Historic Site
MUSEUM

(☑575-355-2573; www.bosqueredondomemorial. com; 3647 Billy the Kid Rd; adult/child $5/free; ⊙8:30am-4:30pm Wed-Mon) The convoluted name sums up the tragic history of this bleak, windswept spot, beside the Pecos River 6 miles southeast of town. Fort Sumner was built in 1862 to guard the Bosque Redondo reservation, a prison to more than 10,000 Navajos forced from their homeland on the Long Walk, plus captured Mescalero Apaches. Over 2000 Navajos died before an 1868 treaty authorized their return home. A modern museum tells the story, while a trail loops through the scant remains.

Old Fort Sumner Museum
MUSEUM

(3501 Billy the Kid Rd; admission $4; ⊙10am-5pm) After the reservation closed, Fort Sumner became the private ranch of Lucien Maxwell, and that's where Sherriff Pat Garrett shot Billy the Kid in 1881. This museum, alongside, tells the whole gory story, along with ephemera like a stuffed two-headed cow. Beside it you'll find **Billy the Kid's Grave**, along with that of Lucien Maxwell. The Kid's tombstone is protected by an iron cage because 'souvenir hunters' kept trying to steal it – even in death he's behind bars.

✴ Festivals & Events

Old Fort Days
CULTURAL

(⊙Jun) Held on the second weekend in June, this festival features rodeo, goat roping, shootouts and athletic events. The purse for the winner of the tombstone race, in which contestants must negotiate an obstacle course while lugging an 80lb tombstone – Billy the Kid's, naturally – is $3500.

⏹ Sleeping & Eating

Super 8
MOTEL $

(☑575-355-7888; www.super8.com; 1559 E Sumner Ave; r from $60) All but next door to the Billy the Kid Museum, this chain motel is the best accommodation option in Fort Sumner.

Fred's Restaurant & Lounge
DINER $

(☑575-355-7500; 1266 E Sumner Ave; ⊙11am-8:30pm Tue-Sat) The best food in town, a couple of blocks west of the museum. As well as a great green chile burger, they serve freshly made sandwiches and burritos, and have a wonderful old wooden bar.

❶ Information

The **chamber of commerce** (☑575-355-7705; http://fortsumnerchamber.com; 707 N 4th St; ⊙9am-4pm Mon-Fri) is helpful.

❶ Getting There & Away

Fort Sumner is on Hwy 60, 45 miles southwest of Santa Rosa, 84 miles north of Roswell, and 60 miles west of Clovis. It is best reached by private vehicle.

Southwestern Colorado

POP (COLORADO) 5 MILLION / AREA

Why Go?

The West at its most rugged, this is a landscape of twisting canyons and ancient ruins, with burly peaks and gusty high desert plateaus. Centuries of boom, bust and boom – from silver to real estate and resorts – tell part of the story. There's also the lingering mystery of its earliest inhabitants, whose relics have been found at the abandoned cliff dwellings in Mesa Verde National Park.

Southwestern Colorado can be a heady place to play. Some of the finest powder skiing in the world melts to reveal winding singletrack and hiking trails in summer. A sense of remove keeps the Old West alive in wooden plank saloons and aboard the chugging Durango railroad.

With all that fresh mountain air, local attitudes – from the ranch hand to the real estate agent – are undoubtedly relaxed. Dally a bit under these ultra-blue skies and you'll know why.

Best Places to Eat

➜ James Ranch (p362)

➜ New Sheridan Chop House (p374)

➜ Secret Stash (p384)

➜ There (p374)

Best Places to Stay

➜ Willowtail Springs (p363)

➜ Kelly Place (p369)

➜ Wiesbaden (p378)

➜ Jersey Jim Lookout Tower (p363)

When to Go
Silverton

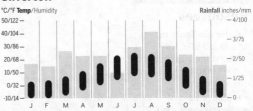

Jun–Aug Prime time for cycling and hiking the legendary San Juans.

Sep–Nov Cool days in the high desert and fewer crowds in Mesa Verde.

Dec–Apr Powder hounds hit the famed slopes of Telluride.

TIME ZONE

Colorado runs on Mountain Time (seven hours behind GMT) and observes daylight saving time.

Fast Facts

→ **Colorado area** 104,247 sq miles

→ **Sales tax** 2.9% state sales tax, plus individual city taxes up to 6%

→ **Durango to Mesa Verde National Park** 66 miles, one hour

→ **Telluride to Ouray** 50 miles, one hour

→ **Durango to Denver** 340 miles, five hours

→ **Pagosa Springs to Santa Fe** 155 miles, two hours

Powered Up

Thanks to Nikola Tesla, Telluride was the first American city to boast electricity – a key development for the mining that continues today, with the town nesting on the country's biggest uranium belt.

Resources

→ **Colorado Tourism** (☑ 800-265-6723; www. colorado.com) Official visitor website, with information in five languages.

→ **Edible** (www. ediblecommunities.com/ sanjuanmountains) Local food and farmers markets.

→ **14ers** (www.14ers.com) Resource for hikers climbing the Rockies' highest summits.

Southwestern Colorado Planning

Summer at high altitude can be chilly – bring warm clothing and sturdy boots. At lower altitudes, the drier desert climate means mild shoulder seasons ideal for camping and mountain biking, while mountain towns like Ouray and Telluride are still buried in snow. In late summer, afternoon mountain thunderstorms are typical, so keep your outings early. Be sure to use caution anywhere above the tree line, and always have plenty of water on hand, since the high-and-dry climate makes it very easy to get dehydrated.

DON'T MISS

In Mesa Verde National Park (p364), ranger-led backcountry hikes offer an exclusive peek at America's most mystifying spot. If you're looking to set hearts racing, **San Juan** four-wheeling offers off-path adrenaline with steep cliff drops, hairpin turns and rugged Rockies views.

Powder hounds can grab great late-season deals in the ski town Shangri-la of **Crested Butte** (p382), and foodies can nosh their way through the locavore towns of **Durango** (p359), **Mancos** (p363) and **Telluride** (p371).

Tips for Drivers

→ US 160, from Durango to Cortez and past Mesa Verde National Park, is the main east–west vein through the region.

→ Further north, the fast and convenient US 50 also crosses the state east–west, linking Montrose with Pueblo on the north–south I-25 route, a major thoroughfare.

→ In winter conditions, chains or snow tires are required on mountain passes.

→ For road conditions, call ☑ 303-639-1111 (recorded message) or visit www.cotrip.org.

History

Six bands of Utes once resided in a vast area stretching between the Yampa and San Juan Rivers. Unlike other tribes, who migrated to Colorado, their presence here stretches back at least a thousand years. Friction started with gold seekers and settlers entering their lands. Chief Ouray (1833–80), remembered for paving the way to peace between the two parties, actually had little choice but to eventually give up most of the Ute territory.

In 1859 the discovery of gold west of Denver launched the mining era. By the 1870s silver took center stage, turning mountain smelter sites into thriving towns almost overnight. Colorado relied heavily on its abundant resources until the 20th century, when many mines shut and cities became ghost towns.

Now, millions of visitors flock to Colorado's national parks, historic cities and ski resorts every year. The state boasts the most terrain for skiing in North America. Along with tourism, the military and high-tech industries are major components of the economy. The state is home to a number of high-profile Defense Department establishments including the US Air Force Academy and NORAD (North American Aerospace Defense Command).

Southwestern Colorado Scenic Routes

Replete with stunning scenic byways (www.coloradobyways.org), this region also has the greatest concentration of old mining roads in Colorado. Among the most beautiful is the paved north–south US 550 (known as the Million Dollar Highway), which connects Durango with Silverton, Ouray and Ridgway.

Some good options for a 4WD trip are the Alpine Loop or Imogene Pass; both start in Ouray. For beautiful desert scenery, check out the Trail of the Ancients, accessible by normal vehicles.

❶ Information

Bureau of Land Management (BLM; ☑303-239-3600; www.co.blm.gov)

Colorado Travel & Tourism Authority (☑800-265-6723; www.colorado.com; PO Box 3524, Englewood) Provides statewide tourism information along with free state highway maps.

Pagosa Springs & Around

POP 1710 / ELEV 7126FT

Pagosa Springs may seem to be a large slice of humble pie, but it has the bragging rights to the biggest snowfall in Colorado – at Wolf Creek Ski Area, nearby. Pagosa, a Ute term for 'boiling water,' refers to the other local draw: hot springs. Natural thermals provide heat for some of the town's 1720 residents.

The town sits east of Durango, on US 160 at the junction with US 84 south to New Mexico. The historic downtown, with most visitor services, is near the intersection of Hot Springs Blvd and US 160. Condos and vacation rentals flank a winding series of roads 2 miles to the west, over a small rise.

◉ Sights & Activities

Fred Harman Art Museum & the Red Ryder Roundup   MUSEUM

(☑970-731-5785; www.harmanartmuseum.com; 85 Harman Park Dr; adult/child $3/0.50; ☺10:30am-5pm Mon-Sat; P⌖) The Red Ryder's image might be lost on today's whippersnappers, but Fred Harman's comic book hero was born in Pagosa Springs, and today Harman's home is a small museum. It's a kitschy and off-beat roadside attraction, but Harman himself is often on hand to show you around his studio.

★ Springs Resort & Spa   HOT SPRING

(☑970-264-4168; www.pagosahotsprings.com; 165 Hot Springs Blvd; adult/child from $25/14; ☺7am-11pm; ⌖☺) These glorious pools along the San Juan River have healing, mineral-rich waters from the Great Pagosa Aquifer, the largest and deepest hot mineral spring in the world. Man-made pools look fairly natural, and the views are lovely. Temperatures vary from 83°F to 111°F (28°C to 44°C).

Pagosa Outside   RAFTING

(☑970-264-4202; www.pagosaoutside.com; 350 Pagosa St; full day Upper Piedra $150; ☺10am-6pm, reduced hours in winter; ⌖) Check out this outfitter's springtime white-water trips (Class III) on the San Juan and Piedra Rivers. The most exciting travels Mesa Canyon, ideal to sight eagles and other wildlife. Rivers mellow in summer and the focus turns to river tubing ($15 for two hours); mountain-biking trips, including a thrilling singletrack route at Turkey Creek; and rentals ($35 per day).

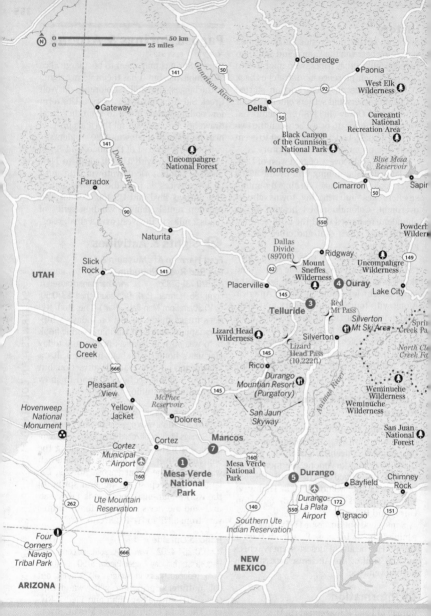

Southwestern Colorado Highlights

❶ Admiring the ages-old cliff dwellings at **Mesa Verde National Park** (p364)

❷ Skiing the trees and glades of spunky **Crested Butte** (p382)

❸ Carving the powder slopes of **Telluride** (p371)

❹ Appreciating the frozen waterfalls and piping hot springs at rugged **Ouray** (p377)

❺ Tasting the bouquet of local brews in **Durango** (p359)

❻ Having fun at **Great Sand Dunes National Park** (p383), nature's most stunning sandbox

Aspen (35mi);
Glenwood
Springs (70mi)

Breckenridge (25mi);
Colorado Springs (50mi);
Denver (80mi);
Boulder (90mi)

2 Crested Butte

Crested
Butte

135

Altmont

Gunnison
National
Forest

Fossil Ridge
Wilderness

Gunnison

Gunnison County
Regional
Airport

50

Monarch

Sargents

Gunnison
National
Forest

114

Continental Divide

Río Grande
National
Forest

La Garita
Wilderness

Creede

149

South Fork

Del Norte

Center

112

La Garita

Wolf
Creek
Pass

*Wolf Creek
Ski Area*

160

Pagosa
Springs

South
San Juan
Wilderness

84

17

Cumbres
Pass
(10,022ft)

Colorado Trail

Buena
Vista

285

San Isabel
National
Forest

291

Monarch

Salida

Poncha
Springs

50

Sangre de
Cristo
Wilderness

Mineral Hot
Springs

Saguache

San Isabel
National
Forest

285

17

Río Grande
National
Forest

15

Alamosa

285

La Jara

142

Antonito

▲Crestone
Peak

69

Arkansas River

Texas
Creek

Pike
National
Forest

67

Cripple
Creek

Victor

Cañon City

*Royal
Gorge
Bridge*

67

96

**Silver
Cliff**

Westcliffe

Crestone

165

69

San Isabel
National
Forest

Gardner

**6 Great
Sand Dunes
National Park**

Mosca

150

▲Blanca Peak
(14,345ft)

160

La Veta

Blanca

Fort
Garland

159

San Luis

159

San Isabel
National
Forest

Cuchara

12

Monument
Park

Stonewall

Rio Grande

7 Poking around friendly and
offbeat **Mancos** (p363)

MARY JANE GOES MAINSTREAM

Now the highest state in multiple ways, Colorado made recreational marijuana legal in November 2012, with the passing of Amendment 64. Stroll the streets of Telluride, Crested Butte or Durango and you might sniff change in the air, but that isn't how regulation wants it; it's still illegal to smoke in public.

Here's the deal: individuals aged 21 and over may possess less than an ounce (28.35 grams) or cultivate up to six plants for personal use. Like alcohol, consumption while driving is regulated, though predicting your impairment is difficult, since, well, you're high! Also, the way pot affects individuals is far less predictable than alcohol. Safe to say, it's best to abstain while driving. Visitors are allowed to buy, but taking your stash out of state (or to Denver International Airport) is illegal.

Note that not all Colorado towns have (or want) dispensaries and that medical marijuana dispensaries (versus their recreational counterparts) do not necessarily sell to the general public. To keep a low profile with minors, dispensaries have nondescript storefronts, usually away from the prime real estate and often off the ground floor.

Meanwhile, other states beyond Washington, which also legalized it, might consider following suit. In January 2014, the first month of legal sales, Colorado made $2 million in tax revenue on recreational bud alone, with school districts slated to get 30% of the haul.

Wolf Creek Ski Area
SNOW SPORTS

(☑ 970-264-5639; www.wolfcreekski.com; lift ticket adult/child $58/31; ☉ Nov–mid-Apr; ⏲)) With more than 450in of snow per year, hitting Wolf Creek on a powder day feels like riding a tidal wave of snow. Located 25 miles north of Pagosa Springs on US 160, this family-owned ski area is one of Colorado's last and best-kept secrets, never crowded and lacking the glitz of larger resorts. Seven lifts service 50 trails, from wide-open bowls to steep tree glades.

Chimney Rock Archaeological Area
ARCHAEOLOGICAL SITE

(☑ off-season 970-264-2287, visitor cabin 970-883-5359; www.chimneyrockco.org; Hwy 151; guided tours adult/child $12/5; ☉ 9am-4:30pm mid-May–late Sep, additional evening hours for special events; ⏲) Like the architects of the elaborate structures in Chaco Canyon – with which this community was connected – the people of the Chimney Rock Archaeological Area were dedicated astronomers and this place held spiritual significance. Remains of 100 permanent structures are at the base of two large red-rock buttes. Today, the rock monuments remain, though the thriving religious and commercial center has been reduced to sketches in stone. The largest pair of buildings, the Great Kiva and Great House, are impressive examples of Chacoan architecture. Designated an Archaeological Area and National Historic Site in 1970, the entire area covers more than 4000 acres of the San Juan National Forest land. If the local politicos get their way, Chimney Rock will soon be designated a National Monument.

🛏 Sleeping & Eating

With the hot springs a year-round draw, hotels hold rates fairly steady, though they are usually cheaper than Durango. Motels and new hotels sprawl out from the city center on US 160. Usually the further away from the hot springs, the better the deal.

Alpine Inn Motel
MOTEL $

(☑ 970-731-4005; www.alpineinnofpagosasprings.com; 8 Solomon Dr; d incl breakfast $69; ⓟ❄@🛜) A converted chain motel, this roadside option is excellent value. The rooms, each with dark carpet and balconies, are a standard size, the owners are great guides to the local area, and there's a deluxe continental breakfast.

★ Fireside Inn Cabins
CABINS $$

(☑ 888-264-9204; www.firesidecabins.com; 1600 E Hwy 160; cabins from $119; ⓟ❄❄🛜) Hands-down our favorite place in town – each log cabin comes with a Weber grill and planters of wildflowers. Pine interiors have immaculate kitchenettes, quilts and flatscreen TVs. The San Juan River flows through the property. Equestrians can use the corral, and the games available at the central office are great for families.

Pagosa Brewing Company
PUB $

(☑ 970-731-2739; www.pagosabrewing.com; 118 N Pagosa Blvd; mains $7-15; ☉ 11am-10pm; ⏲) Brewmaster Tony Simmons is a professional beer judge, and the Poor Richard's Ale is brewed according to historical standards – the corn and molasses mix is inspired by the tipple of Ben Franklin. After a few, move on to a menu of made-from-scratch pub food. Pagosa's fun dinner spot.

ⓘ Information

Pagosa Springs Area Chamber of Commerce (☑ 970-264-2360; www.visitpagosasprings. com; 402 San Juan St; ⊙ 9am-5pm Mon-Fri) A large visitor center across the bridge from US Hwy 160.

USFS Pagosa Ranger Station (☑ 970-264-2268; 180 Pagosa St; ⊙ 8am-4:30pm Mon-Fri)

ⓘ Getting There & Around

Pagosa Springs is at the junction of US 160 and US 84.

Durango

POP 17,200 / ELEV 6580FT

An archetypal old Colorado mining town, Durango is a regional darling that's nothing short of delightful. Its graceful hotels, Victorian-era saloons and tree-lined streets of sleepy bungalows invite you to pedal around soaking up all the good vibes. There is plenty to do outdoors. Style-wise, Durango is torn between its ragtime past and a cool, cutting-edge future in which townie bikes, caffeine and farmers markets rule.

The town's historic central precinct is home to boutiques, bars, restaurants and theater halls. Foodies will revel in the innovative organic and locavore fare that is making it the best place to eat in the state. But there's also interesting galleries and live music that, combined with a relaxed and congenial local populace, make it a great place to visit.

Durango is also an ideal base for exploring the enigmatic ruins at Mesa Verde National Park, 35 miles to the west. Most visitors' facilities are along Main Ave, including the 1882 Durango & Silverton Narrow Gauge Railroad Depot (at the south end of town). Motels are mostly north of the town center. The compact downtown is easy to walk in a few hours.

🏃 Activities

★ Durango & Silverton Narrow Gauge Railroad

RAILWAY

(☑ 970-247-2733, toll-free 877-872-4607; www. durangotrain.com; 479 Main Ave; adult/child return from $85/51; ⊙ departures at 8am, 8:45am & 9:30am; 🚻) Riding the Durango & Silverton Narrow Gauge Railroad is a Durango must. These vintage steam locomotives have been making the scenic 45-mile trip north to Sil-

verton (3½ hours each way) for more than 125 years. The dazzling journey allows two hours for exploring Silverton. This trip operates only from May through October. Check online for different winter options.

Big Corral Riding Stable

HORSEBACK RIDING

(☑ 970-884-9235; www.vallecitolakeoutfitter.com; 17716 County Rd 501, Bayfield) Highly recommended by locals, this outfitter does day rides and overnight horseback camping for the whole family in the gorgeous Weminuche Wilderness. If you're short on time, try the two-hour breakfast ride (including sausage, pancakes and cowboy coffee) with views of Vallecito Lake. Located 25 miles northeast of Durango.

Durango Mountain Resort

SNOW SPORTS

(☑ 970-247-9000; www.durangomountainresort. com; 1 Skier Pl; lift tickets adult/child from $77/45; ⊙ mid-Nov–Mar; 🚻) Durango Mountain Resort, 25 miles north on US 550, is Durango's winter highlight. The resort, also known as Purgatory, offers 1200 skiable acres of varying difficulty and boasts 260in of snow per year. Two terrain parks offer plenty of opportunities for snowboarders to catch big air. Check local grocery stores and newspapers for promotions and two-for-one lift tickets and other promotional ski season specials before purchasing directly from the ticket window.

Trimble Spa & Natural Hot Springs

HOT SPRING, MASSAGE

(☑ 970-247-0111, toll-free 877-811-7111; www.trimblehotsprings.com; 6475 County Rd 203; day pass adult/child $18/12; ⊙ 9am-9pm Sun-Thu, 9am-10pm Fri & Sat; 🚻) If you need a pampering massage or just a soak in some natural hot springs after hitting the ski runs or mountain-bike trails, this is the place. Qualified massage therapists can work out those knotted muscles and tired limbs with treatment ranging from acupressure to trigger-point myotherapy. Five miles north of Durango. Phone or check the website for last-minute specials, which sometimes include two-for-one deals and other discounts.

Mild to Wild Rafting

RAFTING

(☑ 970-247-4789, toll-free 800-567-6745; www. mild2wildrafting.com; 50 Animas View Dr; trips from $51; 🚻) In spring and summer white-water rafting is one of the most popular sports in Durango. Mild to Wild Rafting is one of numerous companies around town offering rafting trips on the Animas River. Beginners

PEDALING DURANGO

Durango is home to some of the world's best cyclists, who regularly ride the hundreds of local trails ranging from steep singletrack to scenic road rides.

Start easy with the **Old Railroad Grade Trail**, a 12.2-mile loop that uses both US Hwy 160 and a dirt road following the old rail tracks. You can shortcut out and back. From Durango, take Hwy 160 west through the town of Hesperus. Turn right into the Cherry Creek Picnic Area, where the trail starts.

For something a bit more technical, try **Dry Fork Loop**, accessible from Lightner Creek just west of town. It has some great drops, blind corners and copious vegetation. Sports shops on Main Ave rent mountain bikes.

should check out the one-hour introduction to rafting, while the more adventurous (and experienced) can run the upper Animas, which boasts Class III to V rapids.

Duranglers   FISHING
(☎970-385-4081, toll-free 800-347-4346; www. duranglers.com; 923 Main Ave; 1-/2-person day trips $350/375) It won't put the trout on your hook, but Duranglers will do everything to bring you to that gilded moment, serving beginners to experts.

🎊 Festivals & Events

San Juan Brewfest   BEER
(Main Ave, btwn 12th & 13th Sts; admission $25; ☺early Sep; 🐾) Showcasing 30-odd specialist brewers from Durango, around Colorado and interstate, this annual festival is a highlight. Official judging takes place late in the afternoon but all attendees ($25; must be aged 21 and over to taste) get to vote for the San Juan Brewfest's People's Choice award. There are bands and food and a carnival atmosphere.

🛏 Sleeping

Adobe Inn   MOTEL $
(☎970-247-2743; www.durangohotels.com; 2178 Main Ave; d $84; ➔❄@🢢) Locally voted the best lodging value, this friendly motel gets the job done with clean, decent rooms and friendly service. You might even be able to talk staff into giving their best rate if you arrive late at night. Check out the Durango tip sheet.

Siesta Motel   MOTEL $
(☎970-247-0741; www.durangosiestamotel.com; 3475 N Main Ave; d $72; P➔❄@🢢) This family-owned motel is one of the town's cheaper options, sparkling clean and spacious but admittedly dated. If you're self-catering, there's a little courtyard with a BBQ grill.

★Rochester House   HOTEL $$
(☎970-385-1920, toll-free 800-664-1920; www. rochesterhotel.com; 721 E 2nd Ave; d $169-229; ➔❄🢢🐾) Influenced by old Westerns (movie posters and marquee lights adorn the hallways), the Rochester is a little bit of old Hollywood in the new West. Rooms are spacious, with high ceilings. Two formal sitting rooms, where you're served cookies, and a breakfast room in an old train car are other perks at this pet-friendly establishment. Check out the free concert series on summer Wednesdays at 4:30pm in the courtyard.

General Palmer Hotel   HOTEL $$
(☎970-247-4747, toll-free 800-523-3358; www. generalpalmer.com; 567 Main Ave; d incl breakfast $150-235; ❄@🢢) With turn-of-the century elegance, this 1898 Victorian has a damsel's taste, with pewter four-post beds, floral prints, and teddies on every bed. Rooms are small but elegant, and if you tire of TV, there's a collection of board games at the front desk. Check out the cozy library and the relaxing solarium.

Strater Hotel   HOTEL $$$
(☎970-247-4431; www.strater.com; 699 Main Ave; d $197-257; ➔❄@🢢) The past lives large in this historical Durango hotel with walnut antiques, hand-stenciled wallpapers and relics ranging from a Stradivarius violin to a gold-plated Winchester. Rooms lean toward the romantic, with comfortable beds amid antiques, crystal and lace. The boast-worthy staff goes out of its way to assist with inquiries. The hot tub is a romantic plus (reserved by the hour), as is the summertime melodrama (theater) the hotel runs. In winter, rates drop by more than 50%, making it a virtual steal. Look online.

🍴 Eating

★Cream Bean Berry   ICE CREAM $
(http://creambeanberry.com; 1309 E 3rd Ave, Smiliey Bldg; ice cream $4; ☺10am-5pm Mon, Wed & Fri) 🍦 Handmade, organic and local, this stuff tastes like happiness. It's also inventive – with flavors, some seasonal, like salted caramel, beet poppyseed and peach cardamom.

It's the love child of journalists who grabbed inspiration sampling the *helados* of Mexico. If you are on the Animas River path, look for their **bicycle freezer cart** (noon to 5:30pm).

Homeslice PIZZA $
(☏970-259-5551; http://homeslicedelivers.com; 441 E College Ave; slices $4; ⊙11am-10pm) Locals pile into this no-frills pizza place for thick pies with bubbly crust and sri-racha sauce on the side. It has patio seating, gluten-free crust options and salads too.

Olde Tymers Café BURGERS $
(☏970-259-2990; www.otcdgo.com; 1000 Main Ave; mains $8-10; ⊙11am-10pm; 🖉🍴) Voted Durango's best burger by the local paper, the Olde Tymers is popular with the college crowd, especially on Monday's $5.50-burger nights. Well-priced American classics are served at cozy booths under pressed-tin ceilings in a big open dining room or on the patio outside. Ask about the cheap daily specials.

Durango Diner DINER $$
(☏970-247-9889; www.durangodiner.com; 957 Main Ave; mains $7-18; ⊙6am-2pm Mon-Sat, 6am-1pm Sun; 🖉🍴) To watch Gary work the grill in this lovable greasy spoon is to be in the presence of greatness. Backed by a staff of button-cute waitresses, Gary's fluid, graceful wielding of a Samurai spatula turns out monstrous plates of eggs, smothered potatoes and plate-sized French toast. The best diner in the state? Yep.

Jean Pierre Bakery FRENCH, BAKERY $$
(☏970-247-7700; www.jeanpierrebakery.com; 601 Main Ave; mains $9-22; ⊙8am-9pm; 🖉🍴) A charming patisserie serving mouthwatering delicacies made from scratch. Breakfasts are all-out while dinner is a much more formal affair. Prices are dear, but the soup-and-sandwich lunch special with a sumptuous French pastry (we recommend the sticky pecan roll) is a deal.

East by Southwest FUSION, SUSHI $$$
(☏970-247-5533; http://eastbysouthwest.com; 160 E College Dr; sushi $4-13, mains $12-24; ⊙11:30am-3pm & 5-10pm Mon-Sat, 5-10pm Sun; 🖉🍴) 🏵 Low-lit but vibrant, it's packed with locals on date nights. Skip the standards for goosebump-good sashimi with jalapeño, or rolls with mango and wasabi honey. Fish is fresh and endangered species are off the menu. Fusion plates include Thai, Vietnamese and Indonesian, well matched with creative martinis or sake cocktails. The best deals are the happy-hour food specials (5pm to 6:30pm).

Cyprus Cafe MEDITERRANEAN $$$
(☏970-385-6884; www.cypruscafe.com; 725 E 2nd Ave; mains $13-29; ⊙11:30am-2:30pm, 5-9pm, closed Sun; 🍴) 🏵 Nothing says summer like live jazz on the patio at this little Mediterranean cafe, a favorite of the foodie press. With a farm-to-table philosophy, it offers locally raised vegetables, wild seafood and natural meats. Favorites include warm duck salad with almonds and oranges, and Colorado trout with quinoa pilaf.

🍷 Drinking & Entertainment

★**Ska Brewing Company** BREWERY
(☏970-247-5792; www.skabrewing.com; 225 Girard St; mains $7-13; ⊙9am-8pm Mon-Fri, 11am-7pm Sat) Big on flavor and variety, these are the best beers in town. Although the small, friendly tasting-room bar was once mainly a production facility, over the years it's steadily climbed in the popularity charts. Today it is usually jam-packed with friends meeting for an after-work beer. Despite the hype, the place remains surprisingly laid-back and relaxed. Ska does weekly BBQs with live music and free food; call for dates – they are never fixed.

Steamworks Brewing BREWERY
(☏970-259-9200; www.steamworksbrewing.com; 801 E 2nd Ave; ⊙11am-midnight Mon-Thu, 11am-2am Fri-Sun) Industrial meets ski lodge at this popular microbrewery, with high sloping rafters and metal pipes. It has a large bar area, as well as a separate dining room with a Cajun-influenced menu (mains $10 to $20). At night there are DJs and live music.

Eno CAFE, WINE BAR
(☏970-385-0105; 723 E 2nd Ave; ⊙8am-10pm Sun-Thu, 8am-11pm Fri & Sat) Serving excellent pour-over coffee by day and dangerous cocktails at night, this tiny house is an intimate spot for socializing. The award-winning 'alpenglow' pairs local rum with muddled cucumber, mint and hibiscus. Tapas ($3 to $5) highlights include deviled eggs and the Colorado cheese plate, though big appetites should go elsewhere. The later happy hour (8pm to 10pm) makes it a good after-dinner spot.

Diamond Belle Saloon BAR
(☏970-376-7150; www.strater.com; 699 Main Ave; ⊙11am-late) A rowdy corner of the historic Strater Hotel, this elegant old-time bar has waitresses flashing Victorian-era fishnets and live ragtime that packs in out-of-town visitors (standing room only) at happy hour (4pm to 6pm). The food isn't an attraction. Also

WORTH A TRIP

JAMES RANCH

A must for those road tripping the San Juan Skyway, this family-run **organic ranch** (☑970-385-9143; http://jamesranch. net; 33800 U.S. 550; ☺11am-7pm Mon-Sat) 🍴 , 10 miles out of Durango, features a market and outstanding farm-stand grill featuring the farm's own grass-fed beef and fresh produce. Steak sandwiches and fresh cheese melts with caramelized onions rock. Kids dig the goats.

Burger and band nights are held every Thursday from July to October (adult/ child $20/10). There's also yoga hosted on the terraces in summer. A two-hour farm tour ($18) is held on Monday and Friday at 9:30am and Tuesday at 4pm.

in Strater, **The Office** serves cocktails in an upscale and much more low-key atmosphere.

White Dragon Tea Room   TEAHOUSE
(☑970-385-7300; http://teadurango.com; 820 Main Ave; ☺10am-6pm Mon-Sat, noon-5pm Sun) A wonderful find, this modern teahouse run by an ex-monk serves organic Chinese and Japanese teas bought direct from farmers. Chocolate lovers shouldn't miss the $5 sipping cups: on offer is Thomas Jefferson's recipe for hot chocolate and a delicious ancho chili cocoa aptly nicknamed 'high as a kite.'

Durango Brewing Co   BREWERY
(☑970-247-3396; www.durangobrewing.com; 3000 Main Ave; ☺tap room 9am-5pm) While the ambience is nothing special, beer fans can appreciate that this place concentrates on the brews. There are tastings and it's open seven days.

Henry Strater Theatre   LIVE MUSIC
(☑970-375-7160; www.henrystratertheatre.com; 699 Main Ave; 🎭) Internationally renowned, producing old-world music-hall shows, live bands, comedy, community theater for 50 years.

🛍 Shopping

Durango may be the best place to shop in the region for sporting gear and outdoor fashions (locals will take prAna over Prada any day). Boutiques and galleries line Main Ave.

Pedal the Peaks   SPORTS
(☑970-259-6880; www.pedalthepeaks.biz; 598b Main Ave; half-day bike rental $15-65; ☺9am-5pm Mon-Sat, 10am-5pm Sun; 🚲) 🚲 This specialist bike store offers the works from moun-

tain- and road-bike sales and rentals to custom-worked cycles, trail maps and accessories. The staff are hardcore riders, and their advice and knowledge are second to none.

2nd Avenue Sports   SPORTING GOODS
(☑970-247-4511; www.2ndavesports.com; 600 E 2nd Ave; ☺9am-6pm Mon-Sat, 9am-5pm Sun) Skiing and extensive cycling and mountainbiking gear for sale and rental.

Maria's Bookshop   BOOKS
(☑970-247-1438; www.mariasbookshop.com; 960 Main Ave; ☺9am-9pm) Maria's is a good general bookstore – independently owned and well stocked. It does e-reader orders too.

ℹ Information

Durango Welcome Center (☑970-247-3500, toll-free 800-525-8855; www.durango.org; 802 Main Ave; ☺9am-7pm Sun-Thu, to 9pm Fri & Sat; 🛜) A great resource, with live help plus iPad guides, in addition to free sunscreen dispensed in big bottles. There is a second visitor center south of town, at the Santa Rita exit from US Hwy 550.

Mercy Regional Medical Center (☑970-247-4311; www.mercydurango.org; 1010 Three Springs Ave) Outpatient and 24-hour emergency care.

San Juan-Rio Grande National Forest Headquarters (☑970-247-4874; www.fs.fed.us/r2/ sanjuan; 15 Burnett Ct; ☺9am-5pm Mon-Sat) Offers camping and hiking information and maps. It's about a half-mile west on US Hwy 160.

ℹ Getting There & Away

Durango lies at the junction of Hwys 160 and 550, 42 miles east of Cortez, 49 miles west of Pagosa Springs and 190 miles north of Albuquerque in New Mexico.

AIR

Durango–La Plata County Airport (DRO; ☑970-247-8143; www.flydurango.com; 1000 Airport Rd) is 18 miles southeast of Durango via Hwys 160 and 172. Both United and Frontier Airlines have direct flights to Denver; US Airways flies to Phoenix.

BUS

Greyhound (www.greyhound.com) buses run daily from the Durango Bus Center north to Grand Junction and south to Albuquerque, NM.

ℹ Getting Around

Check the website of **Durango Transit** (☑970-259-5438; www.getarounddurango.com; 250 W 8th St) for local travel information. All Durango buses are fitted with bicycle racks. Free, the bright-red T shuttle bus trundles up and down Main St.

Mancos

POP 1340 / ELEV 7028FT

At 10am, tiny Mancos may feel like another Colorado ghost town, but poke around and you'll find an offbeat and inviting community. Downtown has historic homes, art and crafts cooperatives and landmark buildings, while the countryside offers spacious views and ranch-style B&B options. Mesa Verde National Park is just 7 miles to the west, so if visiting the park is on your itinerary, staying in Mancos makes an appealing alternative to Cortez's rather nondescript motels.

🛏 Sleeping

★ Jersey Jim Lookout Tower
HISTORIC HOTEL $

(🕿 970-533-7060; r $40; ⊘ mid-May–mid-Oct) How about spending the night in a former fire-lookout tower? Standing 55ft above a meadow 14 miles north of Mancos at an elevation of 9800ft, this place is on the National Historic Lookout Register and comes with an Osborne Fire Finder and topographic map. But (ironically) no water. The tower accommodates up to four adults (bring your own bedding) and must be reserved far in advance; there's also a two-night minimum stay. The reservation office opens on the first workday of March (1pm to 5pm) and the entire season is typically booked within days.

Flagstone Meadows Ranch Bed & Breakfast
B&B $$

(🕿 970-533-9838; http://flagstonemeadows.com; 38080 Rd K-4; d incl breakfast $95-125; ⊜) This elegant ranch is a decidedly more romantic option than any of the motels in town. Guests sit on the deck to enjoy the stars at night, or warm themselves by the field stone fireplace. During the day it's dead quiet; you can take in big views across the plain to Mesa Verde or walk on nearby trails.

★ Willowtail Springs
LODGE, CABINS $$$

(🕿 800-698-0603; www.willowtailsprings.com; 10451 County Rd 39; cabins $249-279; ⊜🕿) Artist Peggy and T'ai Chi master Lee have crafted a setting that inspires you to slow down to the pace of their pond's largemouth bass. These exquisite camps sit within 60 acres of gardens and ponderosa forest. Two immaculate cabins and a spacious lake house (sleeping six) feature warm and exotic decor including a real remnant beehive. There are also clawfoot tubs, Peggy's fabulous original art, a hot tub and a canoe hitched to the dock. Kitchens are stocked with organic goodies, and extras include candlelight chef dinners, catered meals and massages. It's also a wildlife sanctuary (raptors are released here) and, for roamers, a little slice of heaven. It's well outside town; get directions from the website.

🍴 Eating & Drinking

★ Absolute Baking & Cafe
BREAKFAST, SANDWICHES $

(🕿 970-533-1200; 110 S Main St; mains $6-10; ⊘ 7am-2pm; 🕿🌱) 🌱 The screen door is always swinging open at this town hot spot with giant breakfasts. Try the green chile on eggs – it's made from scratch, as are the organic breads and pastries. Lunch includes salads, big sandwiches and local, grass-fed beef burgers. Grab a bag for the trail, but don't forgo a square of gooey, fresh carrot cake.

Olio
CAFE $$$

(114 W Main St; mains $18-28; ⊘ 4-9pm Tue-Sat; 🌱) This friendly, upscale cafe is the spot to hit for a glass of wine and cheese boards with fig jam. Highlights include deviled eggs, watermelon salad, and local lettuce served with shaved fennel, cherries and aged balsamic. In addition to being pretty original, they also cater well to vegan and gluten-free diets.

Fahrenheit Coffee Roasters
CAFE

(201 W Grand Ave; ⊘ 6:30am-5pm Mon-Fri, 7am-5pm Sat; 🕿) Imbued with the aroma of freshly roasted beans, this quality espresso house also serves slices of homemade pie and cheap breakfast burritos to go. It also provides interesting atmosphere, with small-talking locals, outdoor sofas and Oz-like art installations.

Columbine Bar
BAR

(🕿 970-533-7397; 123 W Grand Ave; ⊘ 10am-2am) Established in 1903, one of Colorado's oldest continuously operating bars is still going strong. Think divey old saloon. The mounted animal heads keep watch as you shoot pool.

Mancos Valley Distillery
DISTILLERY

(www.mancosvalleydistillery.com; 116 N Main St; ⊘ 5pm-late Fri & Sat) If you're interested in tasting something *really* local, make your way to this alley-side rum distillery, where artisan distiller Ian James crafts delicate rum. He opens up his distillery to live blues and bluegrass, but generally only for special occasions. Check the website for more information.

ℹ Information

Mancos Valley Visitors Center (🕿 702-533-7434; www.mancosvalley.com; 101 E Bauer St;

⊘ 9am-5pm Mon-Fri) Historic displays and a walking-tour map are available at the visitor center. It also has information on outdoor activities and local ranches that offer horseback rides and Western-style overnight trips.

Mesa Verde National Park

More than 700 years after its inhabitants left, the mystery behind **Mesa Verde** (⌦970 529 4465; www.nps.gov/meve; 7-day car/motorcycle passJun-Aug $15/8, Sep-May $10/5; P⛽🚻) ⌁remains. This civilization of Ancestral Pueblos abandoned the area in 1300. Today their last known home is preserved as Mesa Verde. Amateur anthropologists will love it; the focus on preserving cultural relics makes Mesa Verde unique among American national parks.

Ancestral Pueblo sites are found throughout the canyons and mesas of the park, perched on a high plateau south of Cortez and Mancos, though many remain off-limits to visitors. The NPS strictly enforces the Antiquities Act, which prohibits the removal or destruction of any antiquities and prohibits public access to many of the approximately 4000 known Ancestral Pueblo sites.

If you only have a few hours, the best approach is a stop at the visitor center and a drive around Wetherill Mesa combined with a short walk to the easily accessible Spruce Tree House, the park's best-preserved cliff dwelling. If you have a day or more, take the ranger-led tours of Cliff Palace and Balcony House, explore Wetherill Mesa, linger around the museum or participate in one of the campfire programs run at Morefield Campground.

The park occupies a mesa, with North Rim summit at Park Point (8571ft) towering more than 2000ft above the Montezuma Valley. From Park Point the mesa gently slopes southward to a 6000ft elevation above the Mancos River in the Ute Mountain Tribal Park. Parallel canyons, typically 500ft below the rim, dissect the mesa-top and carry the drainage southward. Mesa Verde National Park occupies 81 sq miles of the northernmost portion of the mesa and contains the largest and most frequented cliff dwellings and surface sites.

The **Mesa Verde Visitor and Research Center** is located just beyond the park entrance. The cutting-edge LEED-certified compound includes a 7000-sq-ft visitor center featuring exhibits and a repository for the park's 3 million artifacts.

History

A US army lieutenant recorded spectacular cliff dwellings in the canyons of Mesa Verde in 1849-50. The large number of sites on Ute tribal land, and their relative inaccessibility, protected the majority of these antiquities from pothunters.

The first scientific investigation of the sites in 1874 failed to identify Cliff Palace, the largest cliff dwelling in North America. Discovery of this 'magnificent city' occurred only when local cowboys Richard Wetherill and Charlie Mason were searching for stray cattle in 1888. The cowboys exploited their discovery for the next 18 years by guiding both amateur and trained archaeologists to the site, particularly to collect the distinctive black-on-white pottery. When artifacts started being shipped overseas, Virginia McClurg of Colorado Springs began a long campaign to preserve the site and its contents. McClurg's efforts led Congress to protect artifacts on federal land, with the passage of the Antiquities Act establishing Mesa Verde National Park in 1906.

The park entrance is off US 160, midway between Cortez and Mancos. The Mesa Verde Visitor and Research Center sits near the park entrance. From here it's about 21 miles to park headquarters, Chapin Mesa Museum and Spruce Tree House. Along the way are Morefield Campground (4 miles), the panoramic viewpoint at Park Point (8 miles) and the Far View Lodge – about 11 miles. Towed vehicles are not allowed beyond Morefield Campground.

South from park headquarters, Mesa Top Rd consists of two one-way circuits. Turn left about a quarter mile from the start of Mesa Top Rd to visit Cliff Palace and Balcony House on the east loop. From the junction with the main road at Far View Visitor Center, the 12-mile mountainous Wetherill Mesa Rd snakes along the North Rim, acting as a natural barrier to tour buses and indifferent travelers.

ℹ PLAN YOUR VISIT

The park is busiest over 4th of July, Memorial Day and Labor Day weekends. On busy days, visitors are allowed one tour only. Assure your spot by buying tickets one day in advance (there is often a 45-minute wait in line in summer). The best information can be found in the latest visitor's guide, available online at www.nps.gov/meve/planyourvisit.

Mesa Verde National Park

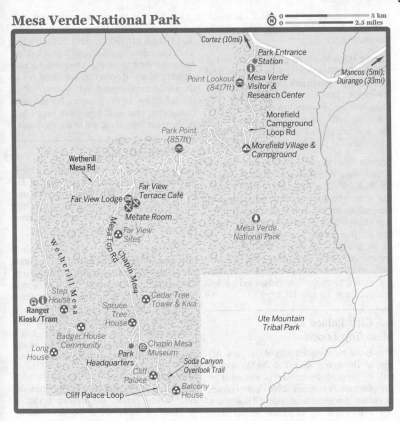

The road is open only from Memorial Day in late May to Labor Day in early September.

◉ Sights

◎ Park Point

With panoramic views, the fire lookout at Park Point (8571ft) has the highest elevation in the park. To the north are the 14,000ft peaks of the San Juan Mountains; in the northeast is the 12,000ft La Plata range; to the southwest, beyond the southward sloping Mesa Verde plateau, is the distant volcanic plug of Shiprock; and to the west is the prone, humanlike profile of Sleeping Ute Mountain.

◎ Chapin Mesa

Chapin Mesa features the most dense clusters of remnants of Ancestral Pueblo settlements. It's a unique opportunity to see and

compare examples of all phases of construction – from pothouses to Pueblo villages to the elaborate multiroom cities tucked into cliff recesses. Pamphlets describing the most excavated sites are available at either the visitor center or Chapin Mesa Museum.

On the upper portion of Chapin Mesa, the **Far View Sites** were the most densely settled area in Mesa Verde after AD 1100. The large-walled Pueblo sites at Far View House enclose a central kiva and planned room layout that was originally two stories high. To the north is a small row of rooms and an attached circular tower that likely used to extend just above the adjacent 'pygmy forest' of piñon pine and juniper trees. This tower is one of 57 in Mesa Verde that may once have served as watchtowers, religious structures or astronomical observatories for agricultural schedules.

South from park headquarters, the 6-mile Mesa Top Rd circuit connects 10 excavated mesa-top sites, three accessible cliff dwellings and many vantages of inaccessible cliff dwellings from the mesa rim. It's open 8am to sunset.

Chapin Mesa Museum
MUSEUM

(☎970-529-4475; www.nps.gov/meve; Chapin Mesa Rd; admission incl with park entry; ⊙8am-6:30pm Apr–mid-Oct, 8am-5pm mid-Oct–Apr; P♿) The Chapin Mesa Museum has exhibits pertaining to the park. It's a good first stop. Staff at the museum provide information on weekends when the park headquarters is closed.

Spruce Tree House
ARCHAEOLOGICAL SITE

(Chapin Mesa Rd; admission incl with park entry; P♿) ✐ This Ancestral Pueblo ruin is the most accessible of the archaeological sites, although the half-mile round-trip access track is still a moderately steep climb. Spruce Tree House was once home to 60 or 80 people and its construction began around AD 1210. Like other sites, the old walls and houses have been stabilized. During winter, there are free ranger-led guided tours at 10am, 1pm and 3:30pm.

◉ Cliff Palace & Mesa Top Loops

This is the most visited part of the park. Access to the major Ancestral Pueblo sites is only by ranger-led tour, and tickets must be pre-purchased in person at the visitors center or online at www.recreation.gov. These tours are well worth it; purchase several days ahead to ensure your spot in high season.

Cliff Palace
ARCHAEOLOGICAL SITE

(www.recreation.gov; Cliff Palace Loop; 1hr guided tour $4; ♿) ✐ The only way to see the superb Cliff Palace is to take the hour-long ranger-led tour. The tour retraces the steps taken by the Ancestral Pueblos – visitors must climb down a stone stairway and four 10ft ladders. This grand engineering achievement, with 217 rooms and 23 kivas, provided shelter for 250 to 300 people. Its inhabitants were without running water. However, springs across the canyon, below Sun Temple, were most likely their primary water sources. The use of small 'chinking' stones between the large blocks is strikingly similar to Ancestral Pueblo construction at Chaco Canyon.

Balcony House
ARCHAEOLOGICAL SITE

(www.recreation.gov; Cliff Palace Loop; 1hr guided tour $4; P♿) ✐ The one-hour guided tour of Balcony House, on the east side of the Cliff Palace Loop, is quite an adventure and will challenge anyone's fear of heights or small places. Visitors descend a 100ft staircase into the canyon, then climb a 32ft ladder, crawl through a 12ft tunnel and climb an additional 60ft of ladders and stone steps to get out. The reward is outstanding views of Soda Canyon, 600ft below the sandstone overhang that once served as the ceiling for 35 to 40 rooms. It's the most challenging tour in the park but might just be the most rewarding, not to mention fun!

◉ Wetherill Mesa

The less-frequented western portion of Mesa Verde offers a comprehensive display of Ancestral Pueblo relics. The Badger House Community consists of a short trail connecting four excavated surface sites depicting various phases of Ancestral Pueblo development.

Long House
ARCHAEOLOGICAL SITE

(www.recreation.gov; Wetherill Mesa Rd; 1hr guided tour $4; ♿) ✐ On the Wetherill Mesa side of the canyon is Long House. It's a strenuous place to visit and can only be done as part of a ranger-led guided tour (organized from the visitor center). Access involves climbing three ladders – two at 15ft and one at 4ft – and a 0.75-mile round-trip hike, and there's an aggregate 130ft elevation to descend and ascend.

Step House
ARCHAEOLOGICAL SITE

(Wetherill Mesa Rd; admission incl with park entry) ✐ Step House was initially occupied by Modified Basketmaker peoples residing in pithouses, and later became the site of a Classic Pueblo–period masonry complex with rooms and kivas. The 0.75-mile trail to Step House involves a 100ft descent and ascent.

🏃 Activities

Hiking

Hiking is a great way to explore the park, but follow the rules. Backcountry access is specifically forbidden and fines are imposed on anyone caught wandering off designated trails or entering cliff dwellings without a ranger. Please respect these necessary regulations, so that these fragile and irreplaceable archaeological sights and artifacts remain protected for centuries to come.

Always carry water and wear appropriate footwear. Trails – some cliffside – can be muddy and slippery after rain or snow. Most, except the Soda Canyon Trail, are strenuous and involve steep elevation changes. Register at the respective trailheads before venturing out.

The 2.8-mile **Petroglyph Loop Trail** is accessed from Spruce Tree House. It follows a path beneath the edge of a plateau before making a short climb to the top of the mesa, where you'll have good views of the Spruce and Navajo Canyons. This is the only trail in the park where you can view petroglyphs. The 2.1-mile **Spruce Canyon Loop Trail** also begins at Spruce Tree House and descends to the bottom of Spruce Canyon. It's a great way to see the canyon bottoms of Mesa Verde.

Cycling

Finding convenient parking at the many stops along Mesa Top Rd is no problem for those with bikes. But only the hardy will want to enter the park by bike and immediately face the grueling 4-mile ascent to Morefield Campground, quickly followed by a narrow tunnel ride to reach the North Rim. An easier option is to unlimber your muscles and mount up at Morefield or park headquarters.

Skiing & Snowshoeing

In winter, Mesa Verde's crowds are replaced with blue skies and snows that drape the cliff dwellings. Sometimes there is enough snow to ski or snowshoe after a snowstorm (although Colorado's dry climate and sunshine cause it to melt quickly). Before setting out, check the current conditions by calling park headquarters. Two park roads have been designated for cross-country skiing and snowshoeing when weather permits. The **Cliff Palace Loop Rd** is a 6-mile relatively flat loop located off the Mesa Top Rd. The road is closed to vehicles after the first snowfall, so you won't have to worry about vehicular traffic. Park at the closed gate and glide 1 mile to the Cliff Palace overlook, continuing on past numerous other scenic stopping points. The **Morefield Campground Loop Rds** offer multiple miles of relatively flat terrain. The campground is closed in winter, but visitors can park at the gate and explore to their heart's content.

☞ Tours

Park concessionaire **Aramark** (www.visitmesaverde.com; adult/child $35/17.50) offers ranger-led bus tours that depart Far View Lodge at 1pm daily.

Highly recommended ranger-led **backcountry hikes** rotate destinations on a yearly basis. The only way to access restricted backcountry, they have proved duly popular, usually selling out. With participants limited to 10 or 12 people, these trips offer a very intimate look at the sites. Some of these trips

UTE MOUNTAIN TRIBAL PARK

If Mesa Verde leaves you intrigued but wanting a more intimate experience, this alternative has been getting rave reviews. The **park** (✆970-749-1452; www.utemountaintribalpark.info; Morning Star Lane; half-day/full-day tours per person $29/48; tent sites $12; ✆by appointment) features a number of fascinating archaeological sites from both Utes and Ancient Pueblos, including petroglyphs and cliff dwellings, accessed only through tours led by Ute tribal members. While half-day tours are suitable to all, full-day tours are physically demanding; visitors hike 3 miles into the backcountry and up ladders to cliff dwellings. It's best to use transportation provided by the tribal park ($12 per person) to avoid 80 miles of wear and tear on your vehicle.

Book in advance or stop by **Ute Mountain Casino, Hotel & Resort** (✆800-258-8007; www.utemountaincasino.com; 3 Weeminuche Dr; r $40-130) near Sleeping Ute Mountain for information. There's also primitive camping and cabin rentals.

are longer and more strenuous than typical ruin visits (think exposed heights and rocky slopes), so they require extra commitment on your part. Purchase tickets ($5 to $25) at the visitor center or online at www.recreation.gov. Check the park website section on backcountry hikes for specific offerings.

★☆ Festivals & Events

12 Hours of Mesa Verde   SPORTS (www.12hoursofmesaverde.com; solo fee $95; ✆May) This annual 12-hour relay-endurance mountain-bike event is popular. Teams race against each other over an incredible network of trails across the national park. There's also a kids' ride. All proceeds raised go to the Montezuma County Partners – a mentoring program for youth at risk.

⌂ Sleeping

Nearby Cortez, Mancos or Durango (36 miles to the east) have plenty of accommodations. Within the national park, visitors can stay at the lodge or camp. Stay overnight to catch sites during the best viewing hours, participate in evening programs and enjoy the sunset over Sleeping Ute Mountain.

SCENIC DRIVE: TRAIL OF THE ANCIENTS

An arid moonscape with cliff dwellings, pottery shreds and rock art, the **Trail of the Ancients** traces the territory of the Ancestral Pueblos. The 114-mile drive uses Hwy 145, Hwy 184 and US 160. Begin in Cortez and either head northwest toward **Hovenweep National Monument** on the Utah border (which, like Mesa Verde, contains dense clusters of Ancestral Pueblo dwellings) or southwest toward Four Corners, where Colorado, Utah, Arizona and New Mexico meet. Allow three hours for driving.

Morefield Campground   CAMPGROUND $
(☑970-529-4465; www.visitmesaverde.com; North Rim Rd; tent/RV sites $30/40; ☺May–early Oct; ☀) ✐ The park's camping option, 4 miles from the entrance gate, also has 445 regular tent sites on grassy grounds conveniently located near Morefield Village. The village has a general store, gas station, restaurant, showers and laundry. It's managed by Aramark. Dry RV campsites (without hookup) cost the same as tent sites.

Far View Lodge   LODGE $$
(☑970-529-4421, toll-free 800-449-2288; www.visitmesaverde.com; North Rim Rd; r $117-177; ☺mid-Apr–Oct; ☒☺❀☎☀) Perched on a mesa top 15 miles inside the park entrance, this tasteful Pueblo-style lodge has 150 Southwestern-style rooms, some with kiva fireplaces. Don't miss sunset over the mesa from your private balcony. Standard rooms don't have air-con (or TV) and summer days can be hot. You can bring your dog for an extra $10 per night.

✗ Eating

Far View Terrace Café   CAFE $
(☑970-529-4421, toll-free 800-449-2288; www.visitmesaverde.com; North Rim Rd; dishes from $6; ☺7-10am, 11am-3pm & 5-8pm May–mid-Oct; ✐❀) Housed in Far View Lodge immediately south of the visitor center, this self-service place offers reasonably priced meals and a convenient espresso bar. Don't miss the house special: the Navajo Taco.

Metate Room   MODERN AMERICAN $$$
(☑800-449-2288; www.visitmesaverde.com; North Rim Rd; mains $18-29; ☺7-10am & 5-7:30pm Apr–mid-Oct, 5-7:30pm mid-Oct–Mar; ✐❀) ✐ With an award in culinary excellence, this upscale restaurant in the Far View Lodge offers an innovative menu inspired by Native American food and flavors. Interesting dishes include stuffed poblano chiles, cinnamon chile pork tenderloin and grilled quail with prickly pear jam.

ⓘ Information

Mesa Verde Museum Association (☑970-529-4445, toll-free 800-305-6053; www.mesaverde.org; Chapin Mesa Rd; ☺8am-6:30pm Apr–mid-Oct, 8am-5pm mid-Oct–Mar; ❀) Attached to the Chapin Mesa Museum, this nonprofit organization sponsors research activities and exhibits. It has an excellent selection of materials on the Ancestral Pueblos and modern tribes in the American Southwest, and has books, posters and glossy calendars for sale.

Mesa Verde Visitor & Research Center (☑800-305-6053, 970-529-5034; www.nps.gov/meve; North Rim Rd; ☺8am-7pm Jun-early Sep, 8am-5pm early Sep–mid-Oct, closed mid-Oct–May; ❀) Visitor information and tickets for tours of Cliff Palace, Balcony House or Long House.

Park Headquarters (☑970-529-4465; www.nps.gov/meve; Chapin Mesa Rd; 7-day park entry per vehicle $15, cyclists, hikers & motorcyclists $8; ☺8am-5pm Mon-Fri; ❀) The Mesa Verde National Park entrance is off US 160, midway between Cortez and Mancos. From the entrance it is 21 miles to the park headquarters. You can get road information and the word on park closures (many areas are closed in winter).

ⓘ Getting There & Around

Mesa Verde is best accessed by private vehicle. In the park, a biodiesel **tram** (☺9:20am-3:30pm, every 30min) shuttles visitors around Wetherill Mesa, starting at the ranger kiosk; park here.

Cortez

POP 8470 / ELEV 6201FT

Cortez fails to beguile but its location, 10 miles west of Mesa Verde National Park, makes it a logical base, and the surrounding area holds quiet appeal. Mountain bikers will covet the hundreds of great singletrack rides nearby.

Typical of small-town Colorado, downtown Cortez is lined with trinket and rifle shops; family-style restaurants dishing up meat and potatoes; and the requisite microbrewery. The edges of the town are jam-packed with independent motels and fast-food outlets. Far-off mountain vistas complete the picture.

◎ Sights & Activities

Cultural Park
MUSEUM

(⊙10am-9pm Mon-Sat summer, to 5pm winter)
FREE The Cultural Park is an outdoor space at the Cortez Cultural Center where Ute, Navajo and Hopi tribe members share their cultures with visitors through dance and crafts demonstrations. Weaving demonstrations and Ute mountain art are also displayed and visitors can check out a Navajo hogan (traditional home).

Cortez Cultural Center
MUSEUM

(⊘702-565-1151; www.cortezculturalcenter.org; 25 N Market St; ⊙10am-9pm Mon-Sat May-Oct, to 5pm Nov-Apr; ⚑) **FREE** Exhibits on the Ancestral Pueblos, as well as visiting art displays, make this museum worthy of a visit if you have a few hours to spare. Summer evening programs feature Native American dances on Tuesday, Friday and Saturday at 6pm, followed by cultural programs at 8pm that often feature Native American storytellers.

Crow Canyon Archaeology Center
ARCHAEOLOGICAL SITE

(⊘800-422-8975, 970-565-8975; www.crowcanyon.org; 23390 Rd K; adult/child $60/35; ⊙9am-5pm Wed & Thu Jun–mid-Sep; ⚑) This cultural center, about 3 miles north of Cortez, offers a day-long educational program that visits an excavation site west of town. Programs teach the significance of regional artifacts and are an excellent way to learn about Ancestral Pueblo culture first-hand.

Travelers who want to stay longer can partake in week-long sessions, where guests share traditional Pueblo hogans and also study excavation field and lab techniques.

Kokopelli Bike & Board
BICYCLE RENTAL

(⊘970-565-4408; www.kokopellibike.com; 130 W Main St; front-suspension bike per day $35; ⊙9am-6pm Mon-Fri, to 5pm Sat) The friendly staff at this local bike shop are happy to talk trail with riders, and also rent and repair mountain bikes. The rental price includes helmet, air pump, water bottle and tools. For some pre-trip planning, visit the shop's website, with great trail descriptions.

🛏 Sleeping

Budget motels dot the main drag; expect winter discounts of around 50%. Sadly, the only campground in town not right next to a highway or dedicated to RVs is the **Cortez-Mesa Verde KOA** (⊘970-565-9301; http://koa.com/campgrounds/cortez; 27432 E Hwy 160; sites from $32-100, cabins $58; ⊙Apr-Oct; 🛜🐾) at the east end of town.

★Kelly Place
B&B $$

(⊘970-565-3125; www.kellyplace.com; 14663 Montezuma County Rd G; r & cabins $125-215, 2-person camp/RV sites $45/55; 🐾🛜) 🌿 A rare gem B&B with archaeological ruins and desert trails with nary a soul in sight. Founded by late botanist George Kelly, this lovely adobe-style lodge sits on 40 acres of orchards, red-rock canyon and Indian ruins abutting Canyon of the Ancients, 15 miles west of Cortez. Rooms are tasteful and rates (even camping) include an enormous buffet breakfast.

Tomahawk Lodge
LODGE $

(⊘970-565-8521, 800-643-7705; www.angelfire.com/co2/tomahawk; 728 S Broadway; r from $65; 🛜🐾) Friendly hosts welcome you at this clean, good-value place. It feels more personable than the average motel, and offers coffee and pastries in the morning. A few rooms allow pets, but they might be a little intimidated by the sweet pony-sized Great Danes kept by the host.

Best Western Turquoise Inn & Suites
HOTEL $$

(⊘970-565-3778; www.bestwestern.com; 535 E Main St; r from $105; 🅿🐾❄🛜) With two swimming pools to keep the young ones entertained, this is a good choice for families (kids stay free, and the restaurant has a kiddy menu). Rooms here are spacious, and bigger families can grab a two-room suite. If you're exploring Mesa Verde all day and just want an affordable and clean, if slightly bland, hotel to crash at for the night, this comfortably laid-out Best Western will do the trick.

🍴 Eating & Drinking

★Farm Bistro
CAFE $

(⊘970-565-3834; www.thefarmbistrocortez.com; 34 W Main St; mains $7-10; ⊙11am-3pm Mon-Wed, 7am-9pm Thu-Sat; ⚑) 🌿 With a mantra of 'mostly local, mostly organic,' this brick cafe with mismatched seat-yourself tables is a hub for healthy appetites. On the menu are grass-fed beef burgers with tomato jam, zucchini fritter salad and homemade green chile with a worthy zing. Ingredients come from an organic farm down the road in Mancos and some fare is vegan or gluten free.

Pepperhead
MODERN SOUTHWESTERN $$

(⊘970-565-3303; www.pepperheadcortez.com; 44 W Main St; mains $7-12; ⊙11am-9pm Tue-Sat; ⚑) A haven of smoky Southwestern spice,

RIDE THE FOUR CORNERS

Billed as the next Moab (to the dismay of locals), unassuming Cortez offers some epic mountain-bike trails among woodland and over the otherworldly slickrock mesa.

With 32 miles of singletrack rolling through piñon juniper, **Phil's World** is the mecca for mountain bikers, located five miles out of Cortez. It's also apt for all levels. Another local fave is **Boggy Draw**, located north of Dolores, with dispersed camping in the ponderosa pines. Want more? Check out **Sand Canyon**, an 18-mile trail starting at the same-named archaeological site west of Cortez. For advanced riders, the 27-mile **Stoner Mesa Loop** has splendid views.

For details, check out *Mountain and Road Bike Routes for the Cortez-Dolores-Mancos Area*. Maps and information are available at helpful Kokopelli Bike & Board (p369).

this newish favorite sits in a colorful room adorned by a beautiful mural. Start with a black cherry margarita – it's tart perfection. Also worthwhile are the *posole* (hominy stew), *tampequeña* (thin steaks) and delicious *chiles rellenos* (stuffed peppers) made with the famous Rocky Ford variety.

Stonefish Sushi & More   JAPANESE $$
(970-565-9244; 16 W Main St; mains $10-16; 11am-2pm Tue & Wed, 11am-2pm & 4:30-10pm Thu-Sat) With blues on the box and a high tin ceiling, this is sushi for the Southwest. Specialties like potstickers with prickly-pear chile and Colorado-rancher seared beef and wasabi liven things up. Cool light fixtures, black tiles and globe-shaped fish tanks behind the bar complete the scene.

ℹ Information

Colorado Welcome Center (970-565-4048; 928 E Main St; 9am-5pm Sep-May, to 6pm Jun-Aug) Maps, brochures and some excellent pamphlets on local activities like fishing and mountain biking.

Southwest Memorial Hospital (970-565-6666; 1311 N Mildred Rd) Emergency services.

ℹ Getting There & Around

Cortez is easier to reach by car from Phoenix, AZ, or Albuquerque, NM, than from Denver (379

miles away by the shortest route). East of Cortez, US 160 passes Mesa Verde National Park on the way to Durango – the largest city in the region.

Cortez Municipal Airport (970-565-7458; 22874 County Rd F) is served by United Express, which offers daily turboprop flights to Denver. The airport is 2 miles south of town off US 160/666.

Dolores

POP 930 / ELEV 6936FT

Scenic Dolores, sandwiched between the walls of a narrow canyon of the same name, has a treasure trove of Native American artifacts and sits near the eponymous sublime river – only rafted in spring. On a more permanent basis, the McPhee Lake boasts the best angling in the southwest. Food and lodging options here are slim.

◉ Sights & Activities

The Bureau of Land Management manages the **Anasazi Heritage Center** (970-882-5600; www.blm.gov/co/st/en/fo/ahc.html; 27501 Hwy 184; admission $3, free Dec-Feb; 9am-5pm Mar-Nov, 10am-4pm Dec-Feb; P ♿) a must-see for anyone touring the area's archaeological sites. It's 3 miles west of town, with hands-on exhibits including weaving, corn grinding, tree-ring analysis and an introduction to the way in which archaeologists examine potsherds. You can walk through the **Dominguez Pueblo**, a roofless site from the 1100s that sits in front of the museum, and compare its relative simplicity to the **Escalante Pueblo**, a Chacoan structure on a nearby hillside.

Reservoir **McPhee Lake** is the second-largest body of water in Colorado. Located in a canyon of the Dolores River, McPhee offers many angling spots accessible only by boat. In skinny, tree-lined side canyons, wakeless boating zones allow for still-water fishing. With the best catch ratio in all of Southwest Colorado, it's a great place to teach younger anglers. Make sure you have a valid Colorado fishing license.

Do-it-yourself crafters will love **Art Girls' Studio** (200 S 4th St; 10am-5pm Tue-Sat), an arts center and crafts shop selling art quilts and exquisite crafting supplies, and teaching courses.

🛏 Sleeping & Eating

Find out about nearby campsites in the San Juan National Forest from the **USFS Dolores Ranger Station** (970-882-7296; www.fs.usda.

gov/sanjuan; 29211 Hwy 184; ⏲8am-5pm Mon-Fri), which has the best options.

Dolores River RV Park
CAMPGROUND $

(☑970-882-7761; 18680 Hwy 145; tent/RV sites $25/37, cabins $50-110) Has pleasant though overpriced sites, 1.5 miles east of town. Cabins turn out to be a good value.

Rio Grande Southern Hotel
HOTEL $

(☑866-882-3026; www.rgshotel.com; 101 S 5th St; r incl breakfast $69-79; 🛜) Norman Rockwell prints and an old-world front desk welcome guests at this National Historic Landmark where Zane Gray wrote *Riders of the Purple Sage* (in room 4). Today it's a bit misshapen; in fact, you might be turned away if the host is napping. Features include a cozy library and small, antique-filled guest rooms.

★ Dolores River Brewery
BREWPUB $

(☑970-882-4677; www.doloresriverbrewery.com; 100 S 4th St; pizzas $9-13; ⏲4pm-late Tue-Sun) Welcome to Dolores nightlife, with live bluegrass bands and cask-conditioned ale. Hickory wood-fired pizzas are the specialty here, with toppings like goat cheese, chipotle peppers and grilled eggplants spicing it up. Drawing patrons from Cortez, it's easily the best pizza in the Four Corners region, and worth the torturous wait (entertain yourself with a pint or two).

Rio Grande Southern Restaurant
GERMAN $$

(☑866-882-3026; www.rgshotel.com; 101 S 5th St; mains $9-15; ⏲7am-8pm Wed-Sat; 🖼) Downstairs from the historic hotel, this welcoming dining room functions as a German restaurant with generous portions of bratwurst and Wiener schnitzel. Repeat customers swear it's the best German food in the region. You can also let off some steam on Karaoke Sunday (2pm to 8pm).

❶ Getting There & Away

Dolores is 11 miles north of Cortez on Hwy 145, also known as Railroad Ave.

San Juan Mountains

In autumn, yellow aspens dot the San Juans and cool air carries the sharp scent of pine. Day-to-day tensions tend to dissipate into serene, blue-sky days as you amble among towering peaks, picturesque towns and old mines.

The 236-mile **San Juan Skyway** climbs to the top of the world as it twists and turns past a series of 'fourteeners' (peaks exceeding 14,000ft). Places like Telluride, Durango and Silverton have storied pasts of boom and bust. The San Juan Skyway leads you past both churling rapids primed for descent and quiet pockets of the Animas River almost made for fly-fishing. In the summer, there's a rousing, rowdy soundtrack of bluegrass, jazz and folk, when local towns host renowned festivals.

From Ridgway follow US 550 south to Ouray and then over Red Mountain Pass to Silverton. Continue heading south on US 550 until you hit Durango. From here, you can head west on US 160 to the ruins at Mesa Verde, then head north on Rte 145 toward Telluride before following Rte 62 back to Ridgway. To drive the entire byway, allow at least one or two days.

Telluride

POP 2300 / ELEV 8750FT

Surrounded on three sides by mastodon peaks, exclusive Telluride is quite literally cut off from the hubbub of the outside world. Once a rough mining town, today it's dirtbag-meets-diva – mixing the few who can afford the real estate with those scratching out a slope-side living for the sport of it. The town center still has palpable old-time charm, though locals often villainize the recently developed Mountain Village, whose ready-made attractions have a touch of Vegas. Yet idealism remains the Telluride mantra. Shreds of paradise persist with the longtime town free box (across from the post office) where you can swap unwanted items, the freedom of luxuriant powder days, and the bonhomie of its infamous festivals.

Colorado Ave, also known as Main St, has most of the restaurants, bars and shops. You can walk everywhere, so leave your car at the intercept parking lot at the south end of Mahoney Dr (near the visitor center) or at your lodgings.

From town you can reach the ski mountain via two lifts and the gondola. The latter also links Telluride with Mountain Village, the base for the Telluride Ski Resort. Located 7 miles from town along Hwy 145, Mountain Village is a 20-minute drive east, but only 12 minutes away by gondola (free for foot passengers). **Ajax Peak**, a glacial headwall, rises up behind the town to form the end of the U-shaped valley. To the right (or south) on Ajax Peak, Colorado's highest waterfall, **Bridal Veil Falls**, cascades 365ft down; a switchback trail leads to a restored Victorian powerhouse atop the falls. To the south, **Mt Wilson** reaches 14,246ft among a group of rugged peaks that form the **Lizard Head Wilderness Area**.

🏃 Activities

Backcountry skiers should look into the incredible San Juan Hut system. In summer, the area has plenty of 4WD routes and some steep but gorgeous hikes.

Telluride Ski Resort   SNOW SPORTS
(📞 970-728-7533, 888-288-7360; www.tellurideskiresort.com; 565 Mountain Village Blvd; adult/child full-day lift ticket $112/67) Covering three distinct areas, Telluride Ski Resort is served by 16 lifts. Much of the terrain is for advanced and intermediate skiers, but there's still ample choice for beginners.

Telluride Ski &
Snowboarding School   SNOW SPORTS
(📞 970-728-7507; www.tellurideskiresort.com; 565 Mountain Village Blvd; 2hr/full-day group lesson $75/170; 👶) If you'd like to sharpen your skills, the Telluride Ski Resort offers private and group lessons with good teachers through this school, which offers classes for children and sessions specific to women, with women instructors.

Telluride Flyfishers   FISHING
(📞 800-294-9269; www.tellurideflyfishers.com; half-day fly-fishing $250) Housed in Telluride Sports, this outfit offers fishing guides and instruction.

Ride with Roudy   HORSEBACK RIDING
(📞 970-728-9611; www.ridewithroudy.com; County Rd 43Zs; 2hr trips adult/child $85/45; ⊙ Mon-Sat; 👶) Offers all-season trail rides through the surrounding hills. Roudy moved here as 'one of the old hippies' in the 1970s and has been leading trips for 30 years. Just don't show up wearing shorts! His rugged hospitality recalls Telluride's yesteryear. Call for an appointment and pricing details.

Telluride Nordic Center   SNOW SPORTS
(📞 970-728-1144; www.telluridetrails.org; 500 E Colorado Ave) There are public cross-country trails in Town Park, as well as along the San Miguel River and the Telluride Valley floor west of town. Instruction and rentals are available from the Telluride Nordic Center.

Paragon Ski & Sport   SPORTS RENTAL
(📞 970-728-4525; www.paragontelluride.com; 213 W Colorado Ave) Has branches at three locations in town and a huge selection of rental bikes. It's a one-stop shop for outdoor activities in Telluride.

Gravity Works   SPORTS RENTAL
(📞 970-728-4143; www.telluridegravityworks.com; 205 E Colorado Ave; full-day bicycle hire $40-85; ⊙ 9am-8pm) This locally owned full-service bike and ski shop sells gear and offers demos and rentals. Kids rentals are also available. As a mountain-sports center, it also boasts an indoor climbing wall and fitness center.

Telluride Food Tours   TOUR
(📞 800-979-3370, 301-758-3555; telluridefoodtours.net; tour $75; ⊙ 3:30pm Wed-Sat; 👶) Run by a young couple, this walking food tour gives visitors a taste of both Telluride and its varied eats. The tour takes two to three hours. After seven to eight tastings with drinks, you may still need to take a walk. Bookings can be made online.

🎉 Festivals & Events

⭐ **Mountainfilm**   FILM
(www.mountainfilm.org; ⊙ May) A four-day screening of outdoor adventure and environmental films, over Memorial Day weekend.

Telluride Bluegrass Festival   MUSIC
(📞 800-624-2422; www.planetbluegrass.com; 4-day pass $205; ⊙ late Jun) This festival attracts thousands for a weekend of top-notch rollicking alfresco bluegrass. Stalls sell all sorts of food and local microbrews to keep you happy, and acts continue well into the night. Camping out for the four-day festival is very popular. Check out the website for info on sites, shuttle services and combo ticket-and-camping packages – it's all very organized!

Telluride Film Festival   FILM
(📞 603-433-9202; www.telluridefilmfestival.com; ⊙ early Sep) National and international films are premiered throughout town, and the event attracts big-name stars. For more information on the relatively complicated pricing scheme, visit the film-festival website.

Brews & Blues Festival   BEER, MUSIC
(www.tellurideblues.com; 3-day pass $185; ⊙ mid-Sep) Telluride's festival season comes to a raucous end at this event, where blues musicians take to the stage and microbrews fill the bellies of fans.

🛏 Sleeping

Aside from camping, there are no cheap places to stay in Telluride. During summer, festival times or winter peak seasons, guests pay dearly. Off-season rates drop by up to 30%.

Some of the huge properties in Mountain Village can offer a decent rate if you book online, but none have the character of the smaller hotels downtown. Most winter visitors stay in vacation rentals – there are scores of them. To book, contact **Telluride Alpine Lodging** (☑888-893-0158; www.tellu-ridelodging.com; 324 W Colorado Ave).

★**New Sheridan Hotel**   HOTEL **$$**
(☑800-200-1891, 970-728-4351; www.newsheri-dan.com; 231 W Colorado Ave; d from $188; ☺☎) Elegant and understated, this historic brick hotel (erected in 1895) provides a lovely base camp for exploring Telluride. High-ceilinged rooms feature crisp linens and snug flannel throws. Check out the hot-tub deck with mountain views. In the bull's eye of downtown, the location is perfect, but some rooms are small for the price.

Victorian Inn   LODGE **$$**
(☑970-728-6601; www.victorianinntelluride.com; 401 W Pacific Ave; r incl breakfast from $124; ☺✳☎) The smell of fresh cinnamon rolls greets visitors at one of Telluride's better deals, offering comfortable rooms (some with kitchenettes) and a hot tub and dry sauna. Best off all, there are fantastic lift-ticket deals for guests. Kids aged 12 and under stay free, and you can't beat the downtown location.

Hotel Columbia   HOTEL **$$$**
(☑970-728-0660, toll-free 800-201-9505; www.columbiatelluride.com; 300 W San Juan Ave; d/ste from $265/365; P☺✳☎≋) Since pricey digs are a given, skiers might as well stay right across the street from the gondola. Locally owned and operated, this stylish and swank hotel pampers. Store your gear in the ski and boot storage and head directly to a room with espresso maker, fireplace and heated tile floors. With shampoo dispensers and recycling, it's also pretty ecofriendly.

Other highlights include a rooftop hot tub and fitness room. Breakfast is included, but food at the connected Cosmopolitan (p374) is also excellent.

Inn at Lost Creek   BOUTIQUE HOTEL **$$$**
(☑970-728-5678; www.innatlostcreek.com; 119 Lost Creek Lane; r $174-349; ☺☎) This lush boutique-style hotel in Mountain Village knows cozy. At the bottom of Telluride's main lift, it's also very convenient. Service is personalized, and impeccable rooms have alpine hardwoods, Southwestern designs

and molded tin. There are also two rooftop spas. Check the website for packages.

Lumière   HOTEL **$$$**
(☑866-530-9466, 907-369-0400; www.lumiereho-tels.com; 118 Lost Creek Lane; d incl breakfast from $250; P☺✳@☎≋) In Mountain Village, this ski-in, ski-out luxury lodge commands breathtaking views of the San Juans. Plush and fluff, it boasts seven-layer bedding, Asian-inspired contemporary design and suites with top-of-the-line appliances that few probably ever use. But even with the hip sushi bar and luxuriant spa menu, its greatest appeal is zipping from the slopes to a bubble bath in minutes.

✖ Eating

Meals and even groceries can be pricey in Telluride, so check out the hot dog stand or taco truck on Colorado Ave for quick fixes. Gaga for sustainability, many local restaurants offer grass-fed beef or natural meat; we indicate those with the greatest commitment to sustainability.

The Butcher & The Baker   CAFE **$**
(☑970-728-3334; 217 E Colorado Ave; mains $10; ☺7am-7pm Mon-Sat, 8am-2pm Sun; 🖼) 🍃 Two veterans of upscale local catering started this heartbreakingly cute cafe, and no one beats it for breakfast. Hearty sandwiches

TELLURIDE CAMPGROUNDS

Right in Telluride Town Park and within walking distance of shops and restaurants, **Telluride Town Park Campground** (☑970-728-2173; 500 E Colorado Ave; campsites with/without vehicle space $23/17; ☺mid-May–mid-Oct; ☎≋) offers 42 campsites, showers and swimming and tennis from mid-May to October. Developed campsites are all on a first-come, first-served basis.

Two campgrounds in the Uncompahgre National Forest are within 15 miles of Telluride on Hwy 145. **Sunshine Campground** (☑970-327-4261; off County Rd 145; sites $20; ☺late May-late Sep) is the nearest and best and offers 15 first-come, first-served campsites; facilities at **Matterhorn Campground** (☑970-327-4261; Hwy 145; sites $22; ☺May-Sep), a bit further up the hill, include showers and electrical hookups for some of the 27 campsites.

with local meats are the perfect takeout for the trail and there are heaps of baked goods and fresh sides.

Baked in Telluride
BAKERY $

(☑ 970-728-4775; www.bakedintelluride.com; 127 S Fir St; mains $6-12; ⊙ 5:30am-10pm) Don't expect ambience. This cafeteria-style Telluride institution serves up XL donuts, mom's meatloaf, sourdough wheat-crust pizza and some hearty soups and salads. The front deck is a fishbowl of local activity and the vibe is happy casual.

Clark's Market
SELF-CATERING $

(www.clarksmarket.com; 700 W Colorado Ave; ⊙ 7am-9pm) Put the condo kitchenette to good use after picking up supplies at Clark's, the nicest market in town. It stocks specialty goods and scores of treats, with fresh fruit and deli meats.

★ There
TAPAS $$

(☑ 970-728-1213; http://therebars.com; 627 W Pacific Ave; mains $6-28; ⊙ 5pm-midnight Mon-Fri, 10am-3pm Sat & Sun) A hip social alcove for cocktails and nibbling, plus weekend brunch. Bigger appetites can dine on shareable mains such as whole Colorado trout. On a comic-book-style menu, East-meets-West in yummy lettuce wraps, duck ramen and sashimi tostadas, paired with original hand-shaken drinks. We liked the jalapeño kiss.

Oak
BARBECUE $$

(The New Fat Alley; ☑ 970-728-3985; www.oakstelluride.com; base of chair 8; mains $11-23; ⊙ 11am-10pm; 🌐) You can pick something off the chalkboard or just take what the other guy has his face in – a cheap and messy delight. Go for the pulled-pork sandwich with cole-slaw on top. Do it right by siding it with a bowl of crispy sweet-potato fries. The can beer specials are outrageous.

Over the Moon
SELF-CATERING $$

(200 W Colorado Ave; cheese plate $12-15; ⊙ 11am-6pm Mon-Tue, 10am-7pm Wed-Sat, noon-5pm Sun) Over the alleyway, this gourmet wine and cheese shop would be a boon to Wallace and Gromit. Cheeses are organized by country of origin, plus it offers fig confit, truffled honey and charcuterie. Sure, it's not without pretension, but its few tables offer travelers the pleasure of fine wines by the glass alongside some exotic cheeses.

La Cocina de Luz
MEXICAN, ORGANIC $$

(www.lacocinatelluride.com; 123 E Colorado Ave; mains $9-19; ⊙ 9am-9pm; 🌐) 🍃 As they lovingly serve two Colorado favorites (organic and Mexican), it's no wonder that the lunch line runs deep at this healthy taqueria. Order the *achiote* pulled pork and you might be full until tomorrow. Delicious details include a salsa and chip bar, handmade tortillas and margaritas with organic lime and agave nectar. With vegan and gluten-free options too.

Brown Dog Pizza
PIZZA $$

(☑ 970-728-8046; www.browndogpizza.net; 10 E Colorado Ave; pizzas $10-22; ⊙ 11am-10pm) The pizza? It's thin crust and fair enough, but the crowd makes the place interesting. Ten minutes after you belly up to the bar for a slice and a cheap pint of Pabst, you'll be privy to all the local dirt. It's one of the most affordable meals on the strip.

Honga's Lotus Petal
ASIAN $$

(☑ 970-728-5134; www.hongaslotuspetal.com; 135 E Colorado Ave; mains $13-32; ⊙ 6pm-late) For pan-Asian cuisine, make your way to this two-story dining space. Prices are dear but the presentation – ranging from sushi to curries – is lovely and the outstanding mojitos have plenty of rock and roll. Korean short ribs just about fall off the bone. So lively and fresh, we can even forgive the pan flutes.

★ New Sheridan Chop House
MODERN AMERICAN $$$

(☑ 970-728-4531; www.newsheridan.com; 231 W Colorado Ave; mains $19-48; ⊙ 5pm-2am) With superb service and a chic decor of embroidered velvet benches, this is an easy pick for an intimate dinner. Start with a cheese plate, but from there the menu gets Western with exquisite elk shortloin and ravioli with tomato relish and local sheep ricotta. Top it off with a flourless dark chocolate cake in fresh caramel sauce. Breakfasts are gourmet and noteworthy too.

Cosmopolitan
MODERN AMERICAN $$$

(☑ 970-728-0660; www.columbiatelluride.com; 300 W San Juan Ave; mains $18-46; ⊙ dinner) The on-site restaurant at the Hotel Columbia is one of Telluride's most respected for fine modern dining with a twist – can you resist Himalayan yak ribeye or lobster corn dogs? The food is certainly inventive, and cheap if you come at happy hour (5pm to 6pm), when sushi and cosmos are half-price.

221 South Oak
MODERN AMERICAN $$$

(☑ 970-728-9505; www.221southoak.com; 221 S Oak St; mains $30-45; ⊙ 5-10pm; 🚗) A great pick, this is an intimate restaurant in a historic home, with a small but innovative menu spinning world flavors with fresh ingredients. Dishes are flavorful and usually based on meat, fish and seafood, with ample vegetable accents. There's also a vegetarian menu with depth and diversity. Tuesday sees two-for-one mains.

La Marmotte FRENCH $$$
(970-728-6232; www.lamarmotte.com; 150 W San Juan Ave; 3-course dinners from $49; 5:30pm-late Tue-Sat) Seasonal plates of French cuisine, white linen and candlelit warmth contrast with this rustic 19th-century icehouse. Dishes like the *coq au vin* with bacon mashed-potatoes are both smart and satisfying. There are some organic options and an extensive wine list. Parents should check out the Friday-night winter babysitting options.

Allreds MODERN SOUTHWESTERN $$$
(970-728-7474; www.allredsrestaurant.com; gondola station St Sophia; mains $29-49; 5:30-9:30pm, bar 5-11:30pm) Midway up the gondola, Allreds stuns with San Juan mountain panoramas – though the bar boasts the best views. Upscale and very exclusive, it emphasizes Colorado and organic ingredients, and has five-course dinners with wine pairings. Smaller budgets can cheat the system: hit the bar for sunset drinks with glorious hand-cut truffle fries and burgers. Summer alpenglow peaks just before 8pm.

🍸 Drinking & Nightlife

Smugglers Brewpub & Grille PUB
(970-728-5620; www.smugglersbrewpub.com; 225 S Pine St; 11am-10pm; 🐾) Beer-lovers will feel right at home at casual Smugglers, a great place to hang out, sample local brew and eat fried stuff. With at least seven beers on tap, it's a smorgasbord, but go for the chocolatey Two Plank Porter or the Smugglers' Scottish Strong Ale.

New Sheridan Bar BAR
(970-728-3911; www.newsheridan.com; 231 W Colorado Ave; 5pm-2am) Well worth a visit in low season for some real local flavor and opinions. At other times, it's a rush hour of beautiful people. But old bullet holes in the wall testify to the plucky survival of the bar itself, even as the adjoining hotel sold off chandeliers and antiques to pay the heating bills when mining fortunes waned.

Last Dollar Saloon BAR
(970-728-4800; www.lastdollarsaloon.com; 100 E Colorado Ave; 3pm-2am) It's all about local color – forget about cocktails and grab a cold can of beer at this longtime late-night favorite, popular when everything else closes. With pool tables and darts.

⭐ Entertainment

Fly Me to the Moon Saloon LIVE MUSIC
(970-728-6666; 132 E Colorado Ave; 3pm-2am) Let your hair down and kick up your heels to the tunes of live bands at this saloon, the best place in Telluride to party hard.

Sheridan Opera House THEATER
(970-728-4539; www.sheridanoperahouse.com; 110 N Oak St; 🐾) This historic venue has a burlesque charm and is always the center of Telluride's cultural life. It hosts the Telluride Repertory Theater, and frequently has special performances for children.

🛍 Shopping

In addition to boutique sporting gear, shoppers will find upscale shops and art galleries (featuring artists of renown) all over town; pick up a local shopping guide.

Telluride Sports SPORTS
(970-728-4477; www.telluridesports.com; 150 W Colorado Ave; 8am-8pm) There are branches and associated shops in Mountain Village, making this the biggest network of outdoor suppliers in town. It covers everything outdoors, has topographical and USFS maps, sporting supplies and loads of local information.

Between the Covers BOOKS
(970-728-4504; www.between-the-covers.com; 224 W Colorado Ave; 9am-7pm Mon-Sat, 9am-6pm Sun) Bookworms flock to this homey shop with a big selection of local interest, creaking floors and a doting staff. Check online for readings and events. Local secret: the coffee counter in back turns out a mean espresso milkshake.

ℹ Information

Telluride Central Reservations (888-355-8743; 630 W Colorado Ave; 9am-5pm Mon-Sat, 10am-1pm Sun) Handles accommodations and festival tickets. Located in the same building as the visitor center.

Telluride Library (970-728-4519; www.telluridelibrary.org; 100 W Pacific Ave; 10am-8pm Mon-Thu, 10am-6pm Fri & Sat, noon-5pm Sun; 📶) With free wi-fi, maps, hiking guides and flyers on local happenings, this is a worthy pitstop, especially with kids. In summer they sponsor a free film series in Mountain Village.

Telluride Medical Center (☑970-728-3848; 500 W Pacific Ave) Handles skiing accidents, medical problems and emergencies.

Telluride Visitor Center (☑970-728-3041, 888-353-5473; www.telluride.com; 630 W Colorado Ave; ☺9am-5pm winter, to 7pm summer) This well-stocked visitor center has local info in all seasons. Restrooms and an ATM make it an all-round useful spot.

ℹ️ Getting There & Around

In ski season Montrose Regional Airport has direct flights to and from Denver (on United), Houston, Phoenix and limited cities on the East Coast.

Gondola (S Oak St; ☺7am-midnight; 🚠) The world's most beautiful commute, this free gondola takes a 15-minute ride up to the Mountain Village through aspen trees.

Telluride Airport (☑970-778-5051; www.tellurideairport.com; Last Dollar Rd) Commuter aircraft serve the mesa-top Telluride Airport, 5 miles east of town – weather permitting. At other times, planes fly into Montrose, 65 miles north.

Telluride Express (☑970-728-6000; www.tellurideexpress.com) Shuttles from the Telluride Airport to town or Mountain Village cost $15. There are also shuttles to Montrose airport (adult/child $50/30); call to arrange pickup.

Ridgway

POP 930 / ELEV 6985FT

Ridgway, with its local quirk, zesty history and scandalous views of Mt Sneffels, is hard to just blow through. Before it got so hip, the town also served as the backdrop for John Wayne's 1969 cowboy classic, *True Grit*.

It sits at the crossroads of US 550, which goes south to Durango, and Hwy 62, which leads to Telluride, but the downtown is tucked away on the west side of the Uncompahgre River. Through town Hwy 62 is called Sherman and all the perpendicular streets are named for his daughters. Ridgway Area Chamber of Commerce has a lot of information about local activities in the area.

👁️ Sights & Activities

⭐**Chicks with Picks**   ROCK CLIMBING
(☑970-623-2442; www.chickswithpicks.net; 163 County Rd 12) This group is dedicated to getting women onto the rocks and ice, giving instruction for all comers (beginners included) about typical male pursuits such as rock-climbing, bouldering and ice-climbing. The programs change frequently and often involve multiday excursions or town-based

COLORADO'S HAUTE ROUTE

An exceptional way to enjoy hundreds of miles of singletrack in summer or virgin powder slopes in winter, **San Juan Hut Systems** (☑970-626-3033; www.sanjuanhuts.com; per person $30) continues the European tradition of hut-to-hut adventures with five backcountry mountain huts. Bring just your food, flashlight and sleeping bag – amenities include padded bunks, propane stoves, wood stoves for heating and firewood.

Mountain-biking routes go from Durango or Telluride to Moab, winding through high alpine and desert regions. Or pick one hut as your base for a few days of backcountry skiing or riding. There's terrain for all levels, though skiers should have knowledge of snow and avalanche conditions or go with a guide.

The website has helpful tips and information on rental skis, bikes and (optional) guides based in Ridgway or Ouray.

courses. Men are included on some activities, but most are women only.

Ridgway Railroad Museum   MUSEUM
(☑970-626-5181; www.ridgwayrailroadmuseum.org; 150 Racecourse Rd; ☺10am-6pm May-Sep, reduced hours Oct-Apr; 🚗) **FREE** Ridgway was the birthplace of the Rio Grande Southern Railroad, a narrow-gauge rail line that connected to Durango with the 'Galloping Goose,' a kind of hybrid train and truck that saved the struggling Rio Grande Southern for a number of years. This museum is dedicated to the plucky rail line.

Rigs Fly Shop & Guide Service   FISHING
(☑970-626-4460, toll-free 888-626-4460; www.fishrigs.com; Suite 2, 565 Sherman St; half-day fishing tours per person from $230; ☺7am-7pm; 🚗) Rigs Fly Shop offers guided fly-fishing tours out of Ridgway from half-day beginners' trips to multiday camp-outs for more experienced anglers. Riggs also does white-water rafting and other soft-adventure itineraries in and around Southwest Colorado. Costs drop significantly as the number of guests increases.

Ridgway State Park & Recreation Area   FISHING
(☑970-626-5822; www.parks.state.co.us/parks/ridgway; 28555 US Hwy 550; admission $7;

⊙ dawn-dusk) Fishing aficionados should head to Ridgway State Park and Recreation Area, 12 miles north of town. The reservoir here is stocked with loads of rainbow trout, as well as German brown, kokanee, yellow perch and the occasional large-mouth bass. There are also hiking trails and campsites.

🛏 Sleeping & Eating

Ridgway State Park & Recreation Area
CAMPGROUND $
(☎ 800-678-2267; www.parks.state.co.us/parks/ ridgway; 28555 US Hwy 550; tent/RV/yurt sites $18/$22/70) With almost 300 sites, the three campgrounds here offer good availability with gorgeous water views, hiking and fishing. Tent campers have 25 walk-in sites, but the path is short and there are wheelbarrows to transport your stuff. Or check out the cool canvas yurts. Rest rooms have coin-op showers and there's a playground for kids. Book online or over the phone.

★ Chipeta Solar Springs Resort
LODGE $$$
(☎ 970-626-3737; www.chipeta.com; 304 S Lena St; r $149-249; ☺) This Southwestern adobe-style lodge is a swank, upscale sleeping option. Rooms feature hand-painted Mexican tiles, rough-hewn log beds and decks with a view. It's very classy and upmarket, and there are wonderful public areas on the property.

Kate's Place
BREAKFAST $$
(☎ 970-626-9800; 615 W Clinton St; mains $9-14; ⊙ 7am-2pm; ⊛) Consider yourself lucky if the morning starts with a chorizo-stuffed breakfast burrito and white cheddar grits from Kate's: it's the best breakfast joint for miles. The restaurant's dedication to local farmers, its cute and colorful interior and the bubbly waitstaff seal the deal.

★ Colorado Boy
PIZZA $$
(602 Clinton St; pizzas $10; ⊙ 4-9pm Tue-Sun) Baking goat's cheese pizzas with fennel sausage and serving craft beer by the barrel, congenial Colorado Boy is a boon to locals, who rush to claim the outdoor picnic tables early. Wash the artisan pizza down with the house-brewed Irish Red, with caramel and toffee notes, or a Mexican Coke.

Thai Paradise
THAI $$
(☎ 970-626-2742; 146 N Cora St; mains $12-16; ⊙ 11am-2pm Mon-Fri, 5-9pm Mon-Sun) Serving up all the standard curries in light, spicy and fragrant preparations, this tiny house of flavor is a hit. Pad Thai, crispy duck and tempura round out the menu, with brown rice and

Asian beers also on offer. If it's warm out, you can enjoy the few tables on the outdoor patio.

True Grit Cafe
AMERICAN $$
(☎ 970-626-5739; 123 N Lena Ave; mains $8-22; ⊙ lunch & dinner; 🛜 ⊛) Scenes from the original *True Grit* were filmed at this appropriately named cafe and watering hole. It's a kind of shrine to John Wayne, with pictures and memorabilia hung on the walls. Quarter-pound burgers, tasty chicken and fried steaks are served, and a crackling fire warms patrons in the winter.

ⓘ Information

Ridgway Area Chamber of Commerce (☎ 800-220-4959, 970-626-5181; www.ridgwaycolorado. com; 150 Racecourse Rd; ⊙ 9am-5pm Mon-Fri)

Ouray & the Million Dollar Highway

POP 1014 / ELEV 7760FT

With gorgeous icefalls draping the box canyon and soothing hot springs dotting the valley floor, Ouray is one privileged place, even for Colorado. For ice-climbers, it's a world-class destination, but hikers and 4WD fans can also appreciate its rugged and sometimes stunning charms. The town is a well-preserved quarter-mile mining village sandwiched between imposing peaks.

Between Silverton and Ouray, US 550 is known as the Million Dollar Hwy because the roadbed fill contains valuable ore. One of the state's most memorable drives, this breathtaking stretch passes old mine headframes and larger-than-life alpine scenery. Though paved, the road is scary in rain or snow, so take extra care.

⊙ Sights

Little Ouray, 'the Switzerland of America,' is very picturesque and littered with old houses and buildings. The visitor center and **museum** (☎ 970-325-4576; www.ouraycountyhistoricalsociety.org; 420 6th Ave; adult/child $6/1; ⊙ hours vary, closed Dec 1-Apr 14; ⊛) issue a free leaflet with details of an excellent walking tour that takes in two-dozen buildings and houses constructed between 1880 and 1904.

Bird-watchers come to Ouray to sight rare birds, including warblers, sparrows and grosbeaks. Box Canyon Falls has the USA's most accessible colony of protected black swifts. The visitor center has resources for bird-watchers.

🏃 Activities

Ouray Ice Park
ICE CLIMBING

(☎970-325-4061; www.ourayicepark.com; Hwy 361; ☺7am-5pm mid-Dec–Mar; 🖝) FREE Enthusiasts from around the globe come to ice climb at the world's first public ice park, spanning a 2-mile stretch of the Uncompahgre Gorge. The sublime (if chilly) experience offers something for all skill levels. Get instruction through a local guide service.

Ouray Hot Springs
HOT SPRING

(☎970-325-7073; www.ourayhotsprings.com; 1200 Main St; adult/child $12/8; ☺10am-10pm Jun-Aug, noon-9pm Mon-Fri & 11am-9pm Sat & Sun Sep-May; 🖝) For a healing soak, try the historic Ouray Hot Springs. The natural springwater is crystal-clear and free of the sulphur smells plaguing other hot springs around here, and the giant pool features a variety of soaking areas at temperatures from 96°F to 106°F (36°C to 41°C). There's a gym and massage service.

Orvis Hot Springs
HOT SPRING

(☎970-626-5324; www.orvishotsprings.com; 1585 County Rd 3; per hour/day $10/14) The attractive rock pools make this outdoor, clothing-optional hot spring hard to resist. Yes, it does get its fair share of exhibitionists, but the variety of soaking areas (100°F to 114°F; 38°C to 45°C) means you can probably scout out the perfect spot. Less appealing are the private indoor pools that feel a little airless. It's 9 miles north of Ouray, outside Ridgway.

San Juan Scenic Jeep Tours
ADVENTURE TOURS, FISHING

(☎970-325-0089; http://sanjuanjeeptours.com; 206 7th Ave; adult/child half-day $59/30; 🖝) The friendly folks at the Historic Western Hotel operate a customized Jeep-touring service. Abandoned ghost towns of the old mining days are popular, as are off-road tours of the nearby peaks and valleys. Hiking, hunting and fishing drop-offs and pick-ups arranged.

San Juan Mountain Guides
ROCK CLIMBING, SKIING

(☎800-642-5389, 970-325-4925; www.ouray-climbing.com; 725 Main St; 🖝) Ouray's own professional guiding and climbing group is certified with the International Federation of Mountain Guides Association (IFMGA). It specializes in ice and rock climbing and wilderness backcountry skiing.

Ouray Mule Carriage Co
TOURS

(☎970-708-4946; www.ouraymule.com; 834 Main St; adult/child $15/5; ☺hourly 1-6pm Jun-Aug; 🖝) The mule-drawn coach you see clip-clopping along Ouray's main streets is the nine-person dray that takes visitors (and locals) around on interpretive tours of the old town. Charters are available for larger groups.

🎉 Festivals & Events

Ouray Ice Festival
ICE CLIMBING

(☎970-325-4288; www.ourayicefestival.com; donation for evening events; ☺Jan; 🖝) The Ouray Ice Festival features four days of climbing competitions, dinners, slide shows and clinics. There's even a climbing wall set up for kids. You can watch the competitions for free, but various evening events require a donation to the ice park. Once inside, you'll get free brews from popular Colorado microbrewer New Belgium.

🛌 Sleeping

Amphitheater Forest Service Campground
CAMPGROUND $

(☎877-444-6777; www.recreation.gov; US Hwy 550; tent sites $20; ☺Jun-Aug) With great tent sites under the trees, this high-altitude campground is a score. On holiday weekends a three-night minimum applies. South of town on Hwy 550, take a signposted left turn.

Historic Western Hotel, Restaurant & Saloon
HOTEL $

(☎970-325-4645; www.historicwesternhotel.com; 210 7th Ave; r without/with bath $55/105; 🅿 🛜) Open by reservation in shoulder season, this somewhat threadbare Wild West boardinghouse serves all budgets. Huge, floral widow's-walk rooms are straight out of a Sergio Leone flick, with saggy beds and a clawfoot tub in room. It's probably wise to skip the cramped shared-bath rooms. The saloon serves affordable meals and grog under a wall of mounted game.

★ Wiesbaden
HOTEL $$

(☎970-325-4347; www.wiesbadenhotsprings.com; 625 5th St; r $132-347; ❄🛜♨) Quirky, quaint and new age, Wiesbaden even boasts a natural indoor vapor cave, which, in another era, was frequented by Chief Ouray. Rooms with quilted bedcovers are cozy and romantic, but the sunlit suite with a natural rock wall tops all. In the morning, guests roam in thick robes, drinking the free organic coffee or tea, post-soak, or awaiting massages.

The on-site Aveda salon also provides soothing facials to make your mountain detox complete. Outside, there's a spacious hot-spring pool (included) and a private, clothing-optional soaking tub with a water-fall, reserved for $35 per hour.

Box Canyon Lodge & Hot Springs LODGE $$

(📞 800-327-5080, 970-325-4981; www.boxcanyonouray.com; 45 3rd Ave; r $120-218; 🐾) It's not every hotel that offers geothermal heated rooms, and pineboard rooms prove spacious and fresh. Spring-fed barrel hot tubs are perfect for a romantic star-gazing soak. With good hospitality that includes free apples and bottled water, it's popular, so book ahead.

Ouray Victoria Inn HOTEL $$

(📞 970-325-7222, toll-free 800-846-8729; www.victorianinnouray.com; 50 3rd Ave; d incl breakfast from $99; P 🐾) Refurbished in 2009, 'The Vic' has a terrific setting next to Box Canyon Park on the Uncompahgre River near Ouray Ice Park. Rooms have cable TV, fridges and coffeemakers, some with balconies and splendid views. Kids will appreciate the deluxe swing set with climbing holds. Rates vary widely by season, but low-season rates are a steal.

St Elmo Hotel HOTEL $$

(📞 970-325-4951, toll-free 866-243-1502; www.stelmohotel.com; 426 Main St; d incl breakfast $125-190; 🐾) Effusively feminine, this 1897 hotel is a showpiece of the Ouray museum's historic walking tour. Nine unique renovated rooms have floral wallpaper and period furnishings. Guests have access to a hot tub and sauna and there's even some of Ouray's best dining, Bon Ton Restaurant (p379), on-site downstairs.

Beaumont Hotel HOTEL $$$

(📞 970-325-7000; www.beaumonthotel.com; 505 Main St; r from $184; P 🐾) With magnificent four-post beds, clawfoot tubs and hand-carved mirrors, this 1886 hotel underwent extensive renovations to revive the glamour it possessed a century ago. Word has it that Oprah stayed here, and you'll probably like it too. It also has a spa and boutiques, but due to the fragile decor, pets and kids under 16 years old are not allowed.

🍴 Eating & Drinking

Buen Tiempo Mexican Restaurant & Cantina MEXICAN $$

(📞 970-325-4544; 515 Main St; mains $7-20; ⊙ 6-10pm; 🐾) This good-time spot bursts with bar-stool squatters and booths of families. From the chili-rubbed sirloin to the *posole* with warm tortillas, Buen Tiempo delivers. Start with a signature margarita with chips and spicy homemade salsa. End with a sat-isfying scoop of deep-fried ice cream. But to find out how the dollars got on the ceiling, it will cost you.

Beaumont Grill MODERN AMERICAN $$

(📞 970-325-7050; http://beaumonthotel.com/dine.html; 507 Main St; mains $16-39; ⊙ 11am-10pm; 🐾) In Colorado, gourmet can also mean a really nice burger, which isn't a bad bet here. With a beautiful courtyard, this contemporary bistro offers everything from rib-eye burgers to homemade mac 'n' cheese, though it is on the pricey side. Choose from the wine cellar's 300 vintages from all over the world.

O'Briens Pub & Grill PUB $$

(📞 970-325-4386; 726 Main St; mains $8-14; ⊙ 11am-midnight) Somewhere between the thick soups and greasy plates, this classic pub fare gets motors started. Perhaps for the lack of pretension, or the very friendly service, it's among the most popular haunts in town, packing in locals and visitors alike. Happy hour is daily from 4pm to 6pm.

Bon Ton Restaurant FRENCH, ITALIAN $$$

(📞 970-325-4951; www.stelmohotel.com; 426 Main St; mains $15-38; ⊙ 5:30-11pm Thu-Mon; 🐾) Bon Ton has been serving supper for a century in a beautiful room under the historic St Elmo Hotel. The French-Italian menu includes specialties like roast duck in cherry peppercorn sauce and tortellini with bacon and shallots. The wine list is extensive and the champagne brunch comes recommended.

Silver Eagle Saloon SALOON

(617 Main St; ⊙ 2pm-2am) With an 1886 bar-back and Wild West attitude to spare, this smoky saloon is a favorite of locals. Unless you're smoking (it's grandfathered into tobacco sale sites), the only thing to do is drink. No food is served but bartenders display an expert pour. It boasts the only pool table in town, though it will take gumption to play.

Ouray Brewery BREWERY

(📞 970-325-7388; ouraybrewery.com; 607 Main St; ⊙ 11am-9pm) With a rooftop deck to spy on Main Street or chairlift bar stools, this pub is something of a flytrap for visitors; in fact, there is a notable lack of locals around. The brewery offers a brew sample tray and growlers to go.

ℹ Information

Ouray Visitors Center (📞 800-228-1876, 970-325-4746; www.ouraycolorado.com; 1230 Main St; ⊙ 10am-5pm Mon-Sat, 10am-3pm Sun;

🛈 📶) Staffed by volunteers, this useful visitor center has brochures and the usual information. It's near the Ouray hot-springs pool.

Post Office (📞970-325-4302; 620 Main St; ⊗9am-4:30pm Mon-Sat)

Buckskin Booksellers (📞970-325-4071; www.buckskinbooksellers.com; 505 Main St; ⊗9am-5pm Mon-Sat; 📶) This excellent bookstore exemplifies the passion locals have for their town and area. Buckskin carries a huge amount of books on local history, mining and geology, as well as birding books, guidebooks and hiking and camping information. There are antique books and collectibles, old photographs and ephemera, as well as a great range of fiction titles.

🛈 Getting There & Away

Ouray is on Hwy 550, 70 miles north of Durango, 24 miles north of Silverton and 37 miles south of Montrose. There are no bus services in the area.

Silverton

POP 630 / ELEV 9318FT

Ringed by snowy peaks and steeped in sooty tales of a tawdry mining town, Silverton would seem more at home in Alaska than the lower 48. But here it is. Whether you're into snowmobiling, biking, fly-fishing, beer on tap or just basking in some very high altitude sunshine, Silverton delivers.

It's a two-street town, but only one is paved. Greene St is where you'll find most businesses. Still unpaved, notorious Blair St runs parallel to Greene and is a blast from the past. During the silver rush, Blair St was home to thriving brothels and boozing establishments.

A tourist town by day in summer, once the final Durango-bound steam train departs it reverts to local turf. Visit in winter for a real treat. Snowmobiles become the main means of transportation, and town becomes a playground for intrepid travelers, most of them serious powder hounds.

One of Silverton's highlights is just getting here from Ouray on the Million Dollar Hwy, an awe-inspiring stretch of road that's one of Colorado's best road trips.

◉ Sights & Activities

★**Silverton Railroad Depot**   RAILWAY
(📞970-387-5416, toll-free 877-872-4607; www.durangotrain.com; 12th St; deluxe/adult/child return from $189/85/51; ⊗departures 1:45pm, 2:30pm & 3pm; 📶) You can buy one-way and return tickets for the brilliant Durango & Silverton Narrow Gauge Railroad at the Silverton terminus. The Silverton Freight Yard Museum is located at the Silverton depot. The train ticket provides admission two days prior to, and two days following, your ride on the train.

The train service offers combination train-bus return trips (the bus route is much quicker). Tickets are also available on the website. Hikers use the train to access the Durango and Weminuche Wilderness trailheads.

★**Silverton Mountain Ski Area**   SKIING
(📞970-387-5706; www.silvertonmountain.com; State Hwy 110; daily lift ticket $49, all-day guide & lift ticket $99) Not for newbies, this is one of the most innovative ski mountains in the US – a single lift takes advanced and expert backcountry skiers up to the summit of an area of ungroomed ski runs. Numbers are limited and the mountain designates unguided and the more exclusive guided days.

Silverton Museum   MUSEUM
(📞970-387-5838; www.silvertonhistoricsociety.org; 1557 Greene St; adult/child $7/3; ⊗10am-4pm Jun-Oct; 🅿📶) Installed in the original 1902 San Juan County Jail, the Silverton Museum has an interesting collection of local artifacts and ephemera.

San Juan Backcountry   TOURS
(📞970-387-5565; toll-free 800-494-8687; www.sanjuanbackcountry.com; 1119 Greene St; 2hr tour adult/child $60/40; ⊗May-Oct; 📶) 🌿 Offering both 4WD tours and rentals, the folks at San Juan Backcountry can get you out and into the brilliant San Juan Mountain wilderness areas around Silverton. The tours take visitors around in modified open-top Chevy Suburbans.

🛏 Sleeping

Silver Summit RV Park   CAMPGROUND $
(📞970-387-0240, toll-free 800-352-1637; www.silversummitrvpark.com; 640 Mineral St; RV sites $36 plus electricity $4; ⊗May 15-Oct 15; 🅿📶) Like so much else in Silverton, Silver Summit is a mixed business running rental Jeeps out of the RV park headquarters (two-/four/four-door Jeep Wranglers $155/185). The park has good facilities, including a laundry, hot tub, fire pit and free wi-fi.

Red Mountain Motel & RV Park   MOTEL, CAMPGROUND $
(📞970-382-5512, toll-free 800-970-5512; www.redmtmotelrvpk.com; 664 Greene St; motel r from $80, cabins from $70, RV/tent sites $38/22; 🅿📶📶) The tiny log cabins stay warm and make good use of their limited space with a double bed, a bunk, a tiny TV and a fully outfitted kitchen-

ette. The managers are friendly and keen to make sure guests and customers have a good time. It's a pet-friendly place that stays open year-round.

Inn of the Rockies at the Historic Alma House
B&B $$

(✆ 970-387-5336, toll-free 800-267-5336; www.innoftherockies.com; 220 E 10th St; r incl breakfast $109-173; P🐾❄) Opened by a local named Alma in 1898, this inn has nine unique rooms furnished with Victorian antiques. The hospitality is first-rate and its New Orleans–inspired breakfasts, served in a chandelier-lit dining room, merit special mention. Cheaper rates are available without breakfast. There's also a garden hot tub for soaking after a long day.

Wyman Hotel & Inn
B&B $$$

(✆ 970-387-5372; www.thewyman.com; 1371 Greene St; d incl breakfast $145-240; ⊙closed Nov; 🐾🛜) A handsome sandstone on the National Register of Historic Places, this 1902 building brims with personality. Local memorabilia lines long halls with room after room of canopy beds, Victorian-era wallpaper and chandelier lamps. Every room is distinct, none more so than the caboose that you can rent out back. Includes a full breakfast plus afternoon wine and cheese tasting.

✕ Eating & Drinking

Stellar
ITALIAN $$

(✆ 970-387-9940; 1260 Blair St; mains $8-20; ⊙4-9:30pm; ♦) This friendly place is a good choice for lunch or dinner. Locals come here for the stellar pizzas, friendly service and easy atmosphere. There's a full bar with beers on tap, and the lasagna and freshly made salads are always good.

Handlebars
AMERICAN $$

(✆ 970-387-5395; www.handlebarssilverton.com; 117 13th St; mains $10-22; ⊙lunch & dinner May-Oct; ♦) Steeped in Wild West kitsch, this place serves worthy baby-back ribs basted in a secret BBQ sauce, and other Western fare. The decor, a mishmash of old mining artifacts, mounted animal heads and cowboy memorabilia, gives this place a ramshackle museum-meets-garage-sale feel. After dinner, kick it up on the dance floor to the sounds of live rock and country music.

★ Montanya Distillers
BAR

(www.montanyadistillers.com; 1309 Greene St; mains $6-14; ⊙noon-10pm) Under new management, this regional favorite still delivers, now in a spacious minimalist bar on Greene St. On a summer day, score a seat on the rooftop deck. Bartenders here can talk you into anything, crafting exotic cocktails with homemade syrups and their very own award-winning rum. It's worth it just for the fun atmosphere. Note: low season hours change.

ℹ Information

Silverton Chamber of Commerce & Visitor Center (✆ 970-387-5654, toll-free 800-752-4494; www.silvertoncolorado.com; 414 Greene St; ⊙9am-5pm; ♦) Staffed by friendly volunteers, this center provides information about the town and surrounds. You can buy tickets for the Durango & Silverton Narrow Gauge Railroad here. Radio KSJC 92.5 FM, a nonprofit community radio station, broadcasts out of an adjoining room in the same building – think about that when you're stomping down the hallway to the public restrooms.

ℹ Getting There & Away

Silverton is on Hwy 550 midway between Montrose, about 60 miles to the north, and Durango, some 48 miles to the south. Other than private car, the only way to get to and from Silverton is by using the Durango & Silverton Narrow Gauge Railroad or the private buses that run its return journeys.

Black Canyon of the Gunnison National Park

The Colorado Rockies are most famous for their mountains, but the **Black Canyon of the Gunnison National Park** (✆ 800-873-0244, 970-249-1915; www.nps.gov/blca; 7-day admission per vehicle $15; ⊙8am-6pm summer, 8:30am-4pm fall, winter & spring; P♦) is the inverse of this geographic feature – a massive yawning chasm etched out over millions of years by volcanic uplift and the flow of the Gunnison River.

A dark, narrow gash above the Gunnison River leads down a 2000ft chasm that's as eerie as it is spectacular. Sheer, deep and narrow, it earned its name because sunlight only touches the canyon floor when the sun is directly overhead. No other canyon in America combines the narrow openings, sheer walls and dizzying depths of the Black Canyon, and a peek over the edge evokes a sense of awe (and vertigo) for most.

Two miles past the park entrance on South Rim Drive, **South Rim Visitor Center** (✆ 800-873-0244, 970-249-1915; www.nps.gov/blca; ⊙8:30am-4pm fall, winter & spring,

8am-6pm summer) is well stocked with books and maps, and enthusiastic National Parks Service staff offer a wealth of information on hiking, fishing and rock climbing.

The park spans 32,950 acres. Head to the 6-mile-long South Rim Rd, which takes you to 11 overlooks at the edge of the canyon, some reached via short trails up to 1.5 miles long (round-trip). At the narrowest part of Black Canyon, **Chasm View** is 1100ft across yet 1800ft deep. Rock climbers are frequently seen on the opposing **North Wall**. Colorado's highest cliff face is the 2300ft **Painted Wall**. To challenge your senses, cycle along the smooth pavement running parallel to the rim's 2000ft drop-off. You get a better feel for the place than when trapped in a car.

In summer the East Portal Rd is open. This steep, winding hairpin route takes you into the canyon and down to the river level where there are picnic shelters and superb views up the gorge and the craggy cliff faces. This area is popular with fly-fishers.

For a surreal experience, visit Black Canyon's **South Rim** in winter. The stillness of the snow-drenched plateau is broken only by the icy roar of the river at the bottom of the canyon, far, far below.

The park has three campgrounds although only one is open all year round. Water is trucked into the park and only the **East Portal Campground** (☑970-249-1915; www.nps.gov/blca; sites $12; ◷ spring to fall) has river-water access. Firewood is not provided and may not be collected in the national park – campers must bring their own firewood into the campgrounds. Rangers at the visitor center can issue a backcountry permit, if you want to descend one of the South Rim's three unmarked routes to the infrequently visited riverside campsites.

The park is 12 miles east of the US Hwy 550 junction with US Hwy 50. Exit at Hwy 347 – well marked with a big brown sign for the national park – and head north for 7 miles.

Crested Butte

POP 1500 / ELEV 8885FT

Powder-bound Crested Butte has retained its rural character better than most Colorado ski resorts. Ringed by three wilderness areas, this remote former mining village is counted among Colorado's best ski resorts (some say *the* best). The old town center features beautifully preserved Victorian-era buildings refitted with hip shops and businesses. Strolling two-wheel traffic matches the laid-back, happy attitude.

In winter, the scene centers around Mt Crested Butte, the conical ski mountain emerging from the valley floor. But come summer, these rolling hills become the state wildflower capital (according to the Colorado State Senate), and many mountain bikers' fave for sweet alpine singletrack.

⊙ Sights & Activities

★**Crested Butte Mountain Heritage Museum** MUSEUM
(☑970-349-1880; www.crestedbuttemuseum. com; 331 Elk Ave; adult/child $4/free; ◷10am-6pm summer, noon-6pm winter; ℙ⬤) In one of the oldest buildings in Crested Butte. It's a worthwhile visit for the Mountain Bike Hall of Fame or to see a terrific model railway. Exhibits range from geology to mining and early home life.

Crested Butte Center for the Arts ARTS CENTER
(☑970-349-7487; www.crestedbuttearts.org; 606 6th St; admission prices vary; ◷10am-6pm; ℙ⬤) With shifting exhibitions of local artists and a stellar schedule of live music and performance pieces, there's always something lively and interesting happening here.

★**Crested Butte Mountain Resort** SKIING
(☑970-349-2222; www.skicb.com; 12 Snowmass Rd; adult/child lift ticket $98/54; ⬤) Catering mostly to intermediates and experts, Crested Butte Mountain Resort sits 2 miles north of the town at the base of Mt Crested Butte. Surrounded by forests, rugged mountain peaks, and the West Elk, Raggeds and Maroon Bells-Snowmass Wilderness Areas, the scenery is breathtaking. It comprises several hotels and apartment buildings, with variable accommodations rates.

Crested Butte Nordic Center SKIING
(☑970-349-1707; www.cbnordic.org; 620 2nd St; adult/child day passes $18/free; ◷8:30am-5pm; ⬤) With 50km of groomed cross-country ski trails around Crested Butte, this center issues day and season passes, manages hut rental and organizes events and races. Ski rentals and lessons are available, in addition to ice-skating, snowshoeing and guided tours of the alpine region.

Adaptive Sports Center OUTDOORS
(☑970-349-2296; www.adaptivesports.org; 10 Crested Butte Way; ⬤) This nonprofit group

is dedicated to providing opportunities for people with disabilities to participate in outdoors activities and adventure sports.

Fantasy Ranch HORSEBACK RIDING
(📞970-349-5425, toll-free 888-688-3488; www.fantasyranchoutfitters.com; 935 Gothic Rd; 1½hr rides $65; ♿) Offers short trail rides (guests over seven years and under 240lbs), wilderness day rides and multiday pack trips. One highlight is a stunning ride from Crested Butte to Aspen round-trip.

Alpineer MOUNTAIN BIKING
(📞970-349-5210; www.alpineer.com; 419 6th St; bike rental per day $20-55; ♿) Serves the mountain-biking mecca with maps, information and rentals. It also rents out skis and hiking and camping equipment.

Crested Butte Guides OUTDOORS
(📞970-349-5430; www.crestedbutteguides.com; off Elk Ave) Guide service for hardcore backcountry skiing, ice climbing or mountaineering. With over a decade of experience, these guys can get you into (and out of) some seriously remote wilderness. They can also provide equipment.

Black Tie Ski Rentals SNOW SPORTS
(📞970-349-0722, toll-free 888-349-0722; www.blacktieskis.com; Unit A/719 4th St; ⏲7:30am-10pm winter; ♿) Black Tie hires out skis, skiing equipment and snowboards.

🛏 Sleeping

Visitors to Crested Butte can stay either in the main town, better for restaurants and nightlife, or in one of the many options at the mountain resort. Some of the Crested Butte Mountain Resort hotels and apartment buildings close over the shoulder sea-sons in spring and fall, but others offer great discounts and longer-stay incentives – check websites, compare prices and bargain. If you've come for the hiking, mountain biking or to enjoy the wildflowers, you can do very well at these times.

Property-management group **Crested Butte Mountain Resort Properties** (CBMR Properties; 📞888-223-2631; www.skicb.com), part of the Crested Butte Mountain Resort, handles reservations for dozens of the lodges, hotels and apartment buildings at Mt Crested Butte.

Crested Butte International Hostel HOSTEL **$**
(📞970-349-0588, toll-free 888-389-0588; www.crestedbuttehostel.com; 615 Teocalli Ave; shared bath dm/d $36/89, r $104-109; 📶) For the privacy of a hotel with the lively ambience of a hostel, grab a room here, one of Colorado's nicest hostels. The best private rooms have their own baths. Dorm bunks come with reading lamps and lockable drawers, and the communal area has a stone fireplace and comfortable couches. Rates vary with the season, with winter being high-season.

⭐ **Ruby of Crested Butte** B&B **$$$**
(📞800-390-1338; www.therubyofcrestedbutte.com; 624 Gothic Ave; d $129-279, ste $199-399; 🅿♿❄📶🐾) Thoughtfully outfitted, down to the bowls of jellybeans and nuts in the stylish communal lounge. Rooms are brilliant, with heated floors, high-definition flatscreen TVs with DVD players (and a library), iPod docks and deluxe linens. It also has a Jacuzzi, a library, a ski-gear drying room, free wi-fi and use of retro townie bikes. Hosts help with dinner reservations and other services. Pets get first-class treatment including their own bed, bowls and treats.

> **WORTH A TRIP**
>
> ## GREAT SAND DUNES NATIONAL PARK
>
> A strange sight, the country's youngest **national park** (📞719-378-6399; www.nps.gov/grsa; 11999 Hwy 150; adult/child $3/free; ⏲visitor center 8:30am-6:30pm summer, shorter hours rest of year) features 55 miles of towering Sahara-like dunes tucked against the looming peaks of the Sangre de Cristo range. Sandboarding, or just running down them at full speed, is heaps of fun. The visitor center provides information. Camp in **Pinyon Flats Campground** (📞888-448-1474; www.recreation.gov; Great Sand Dunes National Park; tent & RV sites $20; 🐾).
>
> The park is 164 miles (approximately 3¼ hours) from Crested Butte and 114 miles (2¼ hours) from Pagosa Springs, Colorado. From Crested Butte, take CO-135 to CO-114 south, then head east toward Mosca and follow the signs to the park. The **visitor center** is 3 miles north of the park entrance; access to the dunes is another mile along the road.

Inn at Crested Butte
BOUTIQUE HOTEL $$$

(☑970-349-2111, toll-free 877-343-211; www.innat-crestedbutte.com; 510 Whiterock Ave; d $199-249; 🅿❄🛜) This refurbished boutique hotel offers intimate lodgings in stylish and luxurious surrounds. With just a handful of rooms, some opening onto a balcony with views over Mt Crested Butte, and all decked out with antiques, flatscreen TVs, coffee-makers and minibars, this is one of Crested Butte's nicest vacation addresses.

Elevation Hotel & Spa
HOTEL $$$

(☑970-349-2222; www.skicb.com; 500 Gothic Rd; r from $139; 🅿) At the base of Crested Butte Mountain Resort and just steps from a major chairlift, this swank address offers oversized luxury rooms ready for first call on powder days. Check online for specials, particularly at the start or end of the season.

✖ Eating & Drinking

Izzy's
CAFE $

(218 Maroon Ave; mains $7-9; ⊙7am-1pm Wed-Mon) Start your day right with breakfast from this buzzing cafe. Latkes, egg dishes and homemade bagels are all done up right. Don't skip the sourdough made with a 50-year-old starter. It's by the creek between Maroon and Elk Aves.

★ Secret Stash
PIZZA $$

(☑970-349-6245; www.thesecretstash.com; 303 Elk Ave; mains $8-24; ⊙8am-late; 🍴🛜) With phenomenal food, the funky-casual Secret Stash is adored by locals, who also dig the original cocktails. The sprawling space was once a general store, but now is outfitted with teahouse seating and tapestries. The house specialty is pizza; its Notorious Fig (with prosciutto, fresh figs and truffle oil) won the World Pizza Championship. Start with the salt-and-pepper fries.

Avalanche Bar & Grill
PUB $$

(www.avalanchebarandgrill.com; off Gothic Rd; mains $9-30; ⊙7:30am-9pm winter, from 11:30am summer; 🍴🛜) One of the favorite après ski venues, Avalanche is right on the slopes and has a big menu of American comfort foods (tuna melts, burgers, club sandwiches, pizzas) as well as an impressive lineup of desserts and beverages. There's a kids' menu too.

Soupçon
FRENCH $$$

(☑970-349-5448; www.soupcon-cb.com; 127 Elk Ave; mains $33-62; ⊙6-10:30pm; 🛜) 🍴 Specializing in seduction, this petite French bistro occupies a characterful old mining cabin with just a few tables. Chef Jason has worked with big NYC names and keeps it fresh with local meat and organic produce. Reserve ahead.

Camp 4 Coffee
CAFE

(www.camp4coffee.com; 402 1/2 Elk Ave; ⊙5am-midnight) Grab your caffeine fix at this serious local roaster, the cutest cabin in town, shingled with license plates (just as local miners once did when they couldn't afford to patch their roofs).

★ Montanya
BAR

(130 Elk Ave; snacks $3-12; ⊙11am-9pm) The original Montanya distillery has moved here, with wide acclaim. Its basiltini, made with basil-infused rum, fresh grapefruit and lime, will have you levitating. It also offers tours, free tastings and worthy mocktails.

Princess Wine Bar
WINE BAR

(☑970-349-0210; 218 Elk St; ⊙8am-midnight; 🛜) Intimate and perfect for conversation while sampling the select regional wine list. There's regular live acoustic music featuring local singer-songwriters. A popular après ski spot.

☆ Entertainment

On CB's lively music scene, most bands play **Eldo Brewery** (☑970-349-6125; www.eldobrewpub.com; 215 Elk Ave; cover charge varies; ⊙3pm-late, music from 10:30pm; 🛜), a popular microbrewery.

The best community theater is **Crested Butte Mountain Theatre** (☑970-349-0366; www.cbmountaintheatre.org; 403 2nd St; prices vary; ⊙vary; 🛜); for bargains check out a dress rehearsal show.

ⓘ Information

Post Office (☑970-349-5568; www.usps.com; 217 Elk Ave; ⊙7:30am-4:30pm Mon-Fri, 10am-1pm Sat)

Visitor Center (☑970-349-6438; www.crestedbuttechamber.com; 601 Elk Ave; ⊙9am-5pm)

ⓘ Getting There & Away

Crested Butte is a 30-minute drive from Gunnison. The trip from Ouray to Crested Butte takes a little less than three hours.

Utah

Best Places to Eat

➡ Red Iguana (p472)

➡ Hell's Backbone Grill (p427)

➡ Crumb Brothers Artisan Bakery (p479)

➡ Copper Onion (p473)

Best Places to Stay

➡ Sundance Resort (p498)

➡ Torrey Schoolhouse B&B (p425)

➡ Valley of the Gods B&B (p392)

➡ Under the Eaves Inn (p452)

Why Go?

Welcome to nature's most perfect playground. From red-rock mesas to skinny slot canyons, powder-bound slopes and slick rock trails, Utah's diverse terrain will stun you. The biking, hiking and skiing are world-class. And with more than 65% of the state lands public, including 12 national parks and monuments, the access is simply superb.

Southern Utah is defined by red-rock cliffs, sorbet-colored spindles and seemingly endless sandstone desert. The pine-forested and snow-covered peaks of the Wasatch Mountains dominate northern Utah. Interspersed are old pioneer remnants, ancient rock art and ruins, and traces of dinosaurs.

Mormon-influenced rural towns can be quiet and conservative, but the rugged beauty has attracted outdoorsy progressives as well. Salt Lake City (SLC) and Park City, especially, have vibrant nightlife and progressive dining scenes. So pull on your boots and stock up on water: Utah's wild and scenic hinterlands await.

When to Go
Salt Lake City

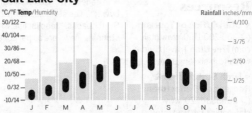

Apr–May Mild weather makes spring an excellent time to hike, especially in southern Utah.

Oct Colorful foliage comes out, but a welcome touch of warmth lingers.

Jan–Mar Powder hounds gear up for the slopes near SLC and Park City mountain resorts.

TIME ZONE

Utah is on Mountain Standard Time (generally seven hours behind GMT), but does follow daylight saving time from mid-March to early November. Note that if you're traveling into Arizona, there's an hour's difference from spring to fall.

Fast Facts

➡ **Population** 2.9 million

➡ **Area** 84,900 sq miles

➡ **Time Zone** Mountain Standard Time

➡ **Sales Tax** 4.7%

➡ **SLC to Moab** 235 miles, four hours

➡ **St George to SLC** 304 miles, 4¼ hours

➡ **Zion to Moab** 359 miles, 5½ hours

Liquor Laws

Although a few unusual liquor laws remain, regulations have relaxed recently. For more information, see p394.

Resources

➡ **Utah Office of Tourism** (☏ 800-200-1160; www.utah.com) Free Utah Travel Guide; website in six languages.

➡ **Utah State Parks & Recreation Department** (☏ 801-538-7220; www.stateparks.utah.gov) Info about the 40-plus state parks.

Utah Planning

Utah is not a large state, but it is largely rural – so unless you're staying in Salt Lake City or Park City, you'll need a car. If you're headed to the parks in southern Utah, your cheapest bet may be to fly into Las Vegas, and rent a ride there.

DON'T MISS

Sure, some of Utah's rugged beauty can be seen roadside. But one of the great things about the state is how much of it is set aside for public use. You'll gain a whole new perspective on, and appreciation of, the terrain if you delve deeper. Not-to-be-missed outdoor adventures are available for all skill levels, and outfitters are there to help. Challenge yourself by rappelling into the narrow canyons around Zion National Park (p445) or mountain biking on the steep and sinister Slick Rock Trail (p399) in Moab. Or take it easy on your body (though not your vehicle) by going off-pavement along one of the state's many 4WD roads. Whether you're rafting on the Colorado River or skiing fresh powder in the Wasatch Mountains, you'll see the state in a whole new way.

Tips for Drivers

➡ Driving between major cities can be quite a speedy affair: the three interstate freeways have a 75mph limit.

➡ Cruising in from Denver on I-70? Make sure you get gas in Green River (345 miles, 5¼ hours). The 104 miles between there and Salina is the largest stretch of US interstate without services.

➡ When traveling between Las Vegas and SLC, consider a scenic detour east on Hwy 9 at St George to Hwy 89 north. It's longer (365 miles, seven hours; compared with 304 miles and 4¼ hours on the I-15), but you'll pass through some stunning red-rock country.

➡ In general, plan to take your time on smaller roads and byways. The state has some daunting geographic features. Switchbacks, steep inclines, reduced speed limits and stunning views are all part of the experience.

History

Traces of the Ancestral Puebloan and Fremont people can today be seen in the rock art and ruins they left behind. But it was the modern Ute, Paiute and Navajo tribes who were living here when European explorers first trickled in. Larger numbers of settlers didn't arrive until after Brigham Young, the second president of the Mormon church, declared 'This is the place!' upon seeing Salt Lake Valley in 1847. The faithful pioneers fled to this territory – then part of Mexico – to escape religious persecution in the east. They then set about attempting to settle every inch of land, no matter how inhospitable, which resulted in skirmishes with Native Americans – and more than one abandoned ghost town. (One group was so determined that it lowered its wagons by rope through a hole in the rock to continue on an impassible mountain trail.)

For nearly 50 years after the United States acquired the land, the Utah Territory's petitions for statehood were rejected due to the Mormon practice of polygamy (the taking of multiple wives). Tensions and prosecutions mounted until 1890, when Mormon leader Wilford Woodruff officially discontinued the practice. In 1896 Utah became the 45th state. About the same time, Utah's remote backcountry served as the perfect hideout for notorious Old West 'bad men', such as native son Butch Cassidy, and the last spike of the first intercontinental railroad was driven here.

Throughout the 20th century the influence of the modern Mormon church, now called the Church of Jesus Christ of Latter-Day Saints (LDS), was pervasive in state government. Though it's still a conservative state, LDS supremacy may be waning – less than 60% of today's population claims church membership (the lowest percentage to date). The urban/rural split may be more telling for future politics: roughly 75% of state residents now live along the urbanized Wasatch Front surrounding Salt Lake City.

Utah Scenic Drives

Roads in Utah are often attractions in and of themselves. State-designated **Scenic Byways** (www.byways.org) twist and turn through the landscape past stunning views. It goes without saying that every main drive in a national park is a knock-out.

Scenic Byway 12 (Hwy 12) The best overall drive in the state for sheer variety: from sculpted slickrock to vivid red canyons and forested mountain tops.

Zion Park Scenic Byway (Hwy 9) Runs through red-rock country and Zion National Park, between I-15 and Hwy 89.

Markagaunt High Plateau Scenic Byway (Hwy 14) High elevation vistas, pine forests and Cedar Breaks National Monument are en route.

Nine Mile Canyon Rd A rough and rugged back road leads to a virtual gallery of ancient rock art and ruins.

Flaming Gorge–Uintas Scenic Byway (Hwy 191) Travel through geologic time on this road: as you head north, the roadside rocks get older.

Burr Trail Rd Dramatic paved backcountry road that skirts cliffs, canyons, buttes, mesas and monoliths on its way to the Waterpocket Fold.

Cottonwood Canyon Rd A 4WD trek through the heart of Grand Staircase–Escalante National Monument.

Mirror Lake Hwy (Rte 150) This high-alpine road cruises beneath 12,000ft peaks before dropping into Wyoming.

Utah Street Layout

Most towns in Utah follow a street grid system, in which numbered streets radiate from a central hub (or zero point) – usually the intersection of Main and Center Sts. Addresses indicate where you are in relation to that hub.

Utah Street Layout

Utah Highlights

1 Achieving the heights of Angels Landing or Observation Point, hiking **Zion National Park** (p445)

2 Stopping at every amphitheater overlook in colorful **Bryce Canyon National Park** (p432)

3 Using tiny rustic towns **Bluff** (p390), **Boulder** (p426) and **Torrey** (p422) as base camps for adventure

4 Cruising the state's incredibly scenic byways, especially **Hwy 12** (p423)

5 Dining in style after a day slopeside in **Park City** (p485)

6 Hiring an outfitter in **Moab** (p401) to guide you into the backcountry by bike or 4WD

MOAB & SOUTHEASTERN UTAH

7 Searching out ancient rock art and ruins at sites such as **Newspaper Rock Recreation Area** (p396)

Newspaper Rock Recreation Area

Blanding

Monticello

Hovenweep National Monument

Bluff

Mexican Hat

San Juan River

Four Corners Navajo Tribal Park

Castle Valley

Thompson Springs

Sego Canyon

Arches National Park

Moab

Canyonlands National Park

Dead Horse Point State Park

The Maze

Glen Canyon National Recreation Area

Colorado River

Abajo Mtns

Edge of the Cedars State Park

Natural Bridges National Monument

Moki Dugway

Goosenecks State Park

Monument Valley

Navajo Indian Reservation

Green River

San Rafael River

Castle Dale

San Rafael Swell

Dinosaur Quarry

Manti

Manti-La Sal National Forest

Palisade State Park

Salina

Hanksville

Goblin Valley State Park

Henry Mountains

Capitol Reef National Park

Caineville

Torrey

Boulder

Calf Creek Recreation Area

Lake Powell

Bullfrog Marina

Page

Richfield

Fishlake National Forest

Fish Lake

Circleville

Panguitch

Escalante

Tropic

Cannonville

Kodachrome Basin State Park

Hwy 12

Grand Staircase–Escalante National Monument

Big Water

Glen Canyon Dam Rd

Paria Canyon-Vermilion Cliffs Wilderness Area

Fremont Indian State Park

Beaver

Parowan

Brian Head

Bryce Canyon National Park

Johnson Canyon Rd

Kanab

Coral Pink Sand Dunes State Park

Cedar Breaks National Monument

Cedar City

Navajo Lake

Zion National Park

Springdale

Hurricane

St George

Snow Canyon State Park

Central

Wah Wah Mountains

Sevier Lake (dry)

ARIZONA

100 km
60 miles

MOAB & SOUTHEASTERN UTAH

Experience the earth's beauty at its most elemental in this rocky-and-rugged desert corner of the Colorado Plateau. Beyond the few pine-clad mountains, there's little vegetation to hide the impressive handiwork of time, water and wind: the thousands of red-rock spans in Arches National Park, the sheer-walled river gorges from Canyonlands to Lake Powell, and the stunning buttes and mesas of Monument Valley. The town of Moab is the best base for adventure, with as much four-wheeling, white-knuckle rafting, outfitter-guided fun as you can handle. Or you can lose the crowd while looking for Ancestral Puebloan rock art and dwellings in miles of isolated and undeveloped lands.

Note that many regional restaurants and shops – and even some motels – close or have variable hours after the May to late-October high season.

Bluff

POP 320 / ELEV 4324FT

Tiny-tot Bluff isn't much more than a spot in the road. But a few great motels and a handful of restaurants, surrounded by stunning red rock, make it a cool little base for exploring the far southeastern corner of the state. From here you can easily reach Moki Dugway (30 miles), Hovenweep National Monument (40 miles), Monument Valley (47 miles) and Natural Bridges National Monument (61 miles) – just to mention a few area sights – as well as explore the surrounding Bureau of Land Management (BLM) wilderness.

There's no visitor center here at the crossroads of Hwys 191 N and 163. You can log onto www.bluff-utah.org, but local business owners and staff are your best resource (they know the hikes better than an office worker could, anyway). To preserve the night sky, Bluff has no streetlights.

ⓘ NO SMOKING ALLOWED

Utah is pretty much a smoke-free state. All lodgings are required to have non-smoking rooms, however most have nothing but (exceptions are noted in the text). Restaurants, and even some bars, also prohibit lighting up.

◉ Sights & Activities

The BLM field office in Monticello has information about the public lands surrounding Bluff. Local motel Recapture Lodge also sells topographic maps for hiking; a public trail leads down from the lodging to the San Juan River.

Bluff Fort   HISTORIC SITE

(www.hirf.org/bluff.asp; 5 E Hwy 191; ◷9am-6pm Mon-Sat) FREE Descendants of the original pioneers have re-created the original log cabin settlement near the few remaining historic buildings in Bluff.

Sand Island Petroglyphs   ARCHAEOLOGICAL SITE

(www.blm.gov; Sand Island Rd, off Hwy 163; ◷24hr) FREE On BLM land 3 miles west of Bluff, these freely accessible petroglyphs were created between 800 and 2500 years ago. The nearby campground boat launch is the starting point for San Juan River adventures.

Far Out Expeditions   HIKING

(☑435-672-2294; www.faroutexpeditions.com; day tours $195) Interested in remote ruins and rock art? Vaughn Hadenfeldt, a longtime canyon expert, leads popular single- and multiday hikes into the desert surrounds.

Wild Rivers Expeditions   RAFTING

(☑800-422-7654; www.riversandruins.com; 101 Main St; day trip adult/child $175/133) Float through the San Juan River canyons with this history- and geology-minded outfitter; you'll also get to stop and see petroglyphs.

Buckhorn Llama   ADVENTURE TOUR

(☑435-672-2466; www.llamapack.com; guided trip per day $400) Llama-supported multiday pack trips into hard-to-reach wilderness.

⏢ Sleeping

★Recapture Lodge   MOTEL $

(☑435-672-2281; www.recapturelodge.com; Hwy 191; r incl breakfast $85; ❄@🛜🐾) This locally owned rustic motel makes the best base for area adventures. Super-knowledgeable staff help out with trip planning and present educational slide shows in season. There's a hot tub and shady pool, and the property has 3½ miles of walking trails.

Kokopelli Inn   MOTEL $

(☑877-342-6099, 435-672-2322; www.kokoinn.com; Hwy 191; r $75-83; ❄🛜🐾) A basic, little 26-room motel with clean rooms and great rates.

Sand Island Campground CAMPGROUND $

(☑ 435-587-1500; www.blm.gov; Sand Island Rd; tent & RV sites $10; ☺ May-Oct) The San Juan River location helps cool things off at these 27 first-come, first-served sites. Pit toilets and drinking water only; no hookups, no showers.

La Posada Pintada B&B $$

(☑ 435-459-2274; www.laposadapintada.com; 239 N 7th E; r incl breakfast $130-150; ✲ 🛜) With cool, airy spaces and whimsical touches of Mexican decor, this family-run inn makes for a comfortable stop. Its six rooms are ample; some feature jet tubs and balconies, and all have minifridges and coffeemakers. Breakfast is served on the back patio.

Desert Rose Inn & Cabins MOTEL $$

(☑ 435-672-2303, 888-475-7673; www.desertroseinn.com; 701 West Main Street; r $140-189, cabins $179-289; ☻✲@🛜) Wraparound porches and log construction add warmth to this big motel at the edge of town, with quilt-covered pine beds in extra large rooms and cabins. There are plans to add a swimming pool.

Far Out Bunkhouse GUESTHOUSE $$

(☑ 435-672-2294; www.faroutexpeditions.com; cnr 7th East & Mulberry Sts; dm/q $95/120) Two private six-bunk rooms available in an attractive guesthouse run by the eponymous hiking outfitter.

✕ Eating

★ Comb Ridge Coffee CAFE $

(www.combridgecoffee.com; 680 S Hwy 191; dishes $3-10; ☺ 7am-9pm Tue-Sat, to 5pm Sun, varies Nov-Feb; 🛜🚲) An adobe gallery and cafe with standout single-pour coffee, blue-corn pancakes and breakfast sandwiches loaded with peppers and eggs. Plans are in the works to add pizzas in the evenings. Service may be slow.

Twin Rocks Cafe & Trading Post NATIVE AMERICAN $$

(913 E Navajo Twins Dr; mains $10-18; ☺ 7am-9pm) Get your fry bread (deep-fried dough) as a breakfast sandwich, wrapped up as a Navajo taco at lunch or accompanying stew with dinner. Beer is also served.

Cottonwood Steakhouse STEAK $$$

(☑ 435-672-2282; www.cottonwoodsteakhouse.com; Hwy 191, cnr Main & 4th East Sts; mains $18-25; ☺ 5:30-9:30pm Mar-Nov) Salad, steak and beans are big on the menu at this Wild West venue with an outdoor grill (closed in windy conditions). For small appetites, it's worth splitting a plate.

Hovenweep National Monument

This area straddling the Utah–Colorado state line was home to a sizeable Ancestral Puebloan population before abandonment in the late 1200s (perhaps because of drought and deforestation). Since 1923, six sets of sites have been protected as a national monument (☑ 970-562-4282, ext 10; www.nps.gov/hove; Hwy 262; 7-day per vehicle $6, tent & RV sites $10; ☺ park dusk-dawn, visitor center 8am-6pm Jun-Sep, 9am-5pm Oct-May).

The **Square Tower Group**, near the visitor center, is what people are generally referring to when speaking of Hovenweep. Pick up the interpretive guide ($1), which is essential for understanding the unexcavated ruins. **Stronghold House** is reachable from a paved, wheelchair-accessible path; from there you overlook the rest of the ruins. To get a closer look, you'll have to hike down into the canyon (and back up); follow the trail clockwise to best see the ruins unfold around every corner. Most of the eight brick towers and unit houses were constructed between 1230 and 1275. The masonry skills it took to piece together such tall structures on such small ledges definitely inspires admiration.

The other sections of the park require 4WD and/or lengthy hikes. Ask for a map at the visitor center, where there's also a nice 31-site **campground** (tent & RV sites $10) with water and toilets (no hookups). Otherwise, there's a whole lotta nothin' out here.

The closest store, **Hatch Trading Post** (County Rd 414), is an atmospheric, white-brick building that sells a few sundries and some Native American crafts. Otherwise, supplies can be found in **Blanding** (a dry town, 45 miles), **Bluff** (40 miles) and **Cortez**, Colorado (43 miles).

The best route to the park is paved Hwy 262. From the turnoff east at Hwy 191 follow the signs; it's a 28-mile drive to the main entrance (past Hatch Trading Post). Use caution traveling on any unpaved roads here: all become treacherous in wet weather. From Hovenweep, Mesa Verde National Park is 75 miles east in Colorado. An interesting route to take into Colorado from here is McElmo Canyon, a gravel road with ruins and a vineyard.

> **ⓘ LOCAL PASSPORTS**
>
> Southeastern Utah national parks sell a **local passport** (per vehicle $25) that's good for a year's entry to Arches and Canyonlands National Parks, plus Hovenweep and Natural Bridges National Monuments. **Federal park passes** (www.nps.gov/findapark/passes.htm; per vehicle adult/senior $80/10), available online and at parks, allow year-long access to all federal recreation lands in Utah and beyond – and are a great way to support the Southwest's amazing parks.

Valley of the Gods

Up and over, through and around: the 17-mile unpaved road (County Rd 242) that leads through Valley of the Gods is like a do-it-yourself roller coaster amid some mind-blowing scenery. In other states, this incredible butte-filled valley would be a national park, but such are the riches of Utah that here it is merely a BLM-administered area (www.blm.gov). Locals call it 'mini–Monument Valley.' The field office in Monticello puts out a BLM pamphlet, available online, identifying a few of the sandstone monoliths and pinnacles, including **Seven Sailors**, **Lady on a Tub** and **Rooster Butte**.

Free, dispersed camping among the rock giants is a dramatic – if shadeless – prospect. In such an isolated, uninhabited place, the night sky is incredible. Or splurge for a secluded refuge at **Valley of the Gods B&B** (☏ 970-749-1164; www.valleyofthegods.cjb.net; off Hwy 261; r incl breakfast $165) 🍴, a 1930s homestead with giant beam-and-post ceilings, stone showers and off-the-grid charm. Homemade breakfasts are monumental and the owners are happy to share hiking and travel tips. It's 6.5 miles north of Hwy 163. Water is trucked in, biofuels are used and solar power is harnessed out of necessity (leave your hair dryer at home).

A high-clearance vehicle is advised for driving the Valley of the Gods. A rental car can make it on a very dry day, but don't go without a 4WD if it has rained recently. Allow an hour for the 17-mile loop connecting Hwys 261 and 163. The nearest services are in Mexican Hat, 7 miles southwest of the Hwy 163 turnoff.

Mexican Hat

POP 31 / ELEV 4244FT

The settlement of Mexican Hat is named after a sombrero-shaped rock off Hwy 163. The town is little more than a handful of simple, somewhat uninspired lodgings, a couple of places to eat and a store or two on the north bank of the San Juan River. The south bank marks the edge of the Navajo Reservation. Monument Valley is 20 miles to the south; Bluff is 27 miles to the east.

The cliffside **San Juan Inn** (☏ 800-447-2022, 435-683-2220; www.sanjuaninn.net; Hwy 163; r $99, apt $295; ❄) perches high above the river. These motel rooms are pretty basic, but they're the nicest in town, with quilted comforters and flat-screen TVs. You can buy Navajo crafts, books and beer at the onsite **trading post** (⊙ 7am-9pm).

The year-round **Old River Grille** (www.sanjuaninn.net; Hwy 163; mains $7-15; ⊙ 7am-11pm) has greasy-spoon cooking and some whopping Navajo tacos (fry bread with chili and taco fixings), plus the only full liquor license for at least 50 miles.

Monument Valley

From Mexican Hat, Hwy 163 winds southwest and enters the Navajo Reservation and – after 22 miles – Monument Valley, on the Arizona state line. Though you'll recognize it instantly from TV commercials and Hollywood movies (it was where Forrest Gump stopped his cross-country run), nothing compares with seeing the sheer chocolate-red buttes and colossal mesas for real. To get close, you must visit Arizona's **Monument Valley Navajo Tribal Park** (p192).

Goosenecks State Park

If instead of heading south to Mexican Hat you turn north on Hwy 261, you'll come to a 4-mile paved road that turns west to Goosenecks State Park. The attraction here is the mesmerizing view of the San Juan River. The serpentine path, carved by years of running water, is dramatically evident from above. You can see how the river snaked back on its course, leaving gooseneck-shaped spits of land untouched. There are pit toilets, picnic tables and free campsites, but frequent high winds discourage staying long. Intrepid hikers can try **Honaker Trail**, a steep, 5-mile round-trip to the canyon floor, with a 1400ft

Southeastern Utah

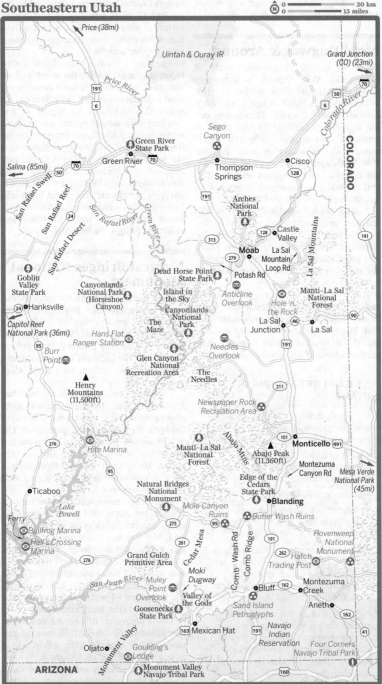

Price (38mi)

Grand Junction (CO) (23mi)

0 — 30 km
0 — 15 miles

Uintah & Ouray IR

Price River

COLORADO

Colorado River

Sego Canyon

Green River State Park

Green River

Thompson Springs

Cisco

Salina (85mi)

San Rafael Swell

San Rafael Reef

San Rafael Desert

San Rafael River

Green River

Arches National Park

Castle Valley

Moab

La Sal Mountain Loop Rd

La Sal Mountains

Dead Horse Point State Park

Potash Rd

Anticline Overlook

Manti-La Sal National Forest

Goblin Valley State Park

Hanksville

Canyonlands National Park (Horseshoe Canyon)

Island in the Sky

Canyonlands National Park

Hole 'n the Rock

La Sal Junction

La Sal

Capitol Reef National Park (36mi)

The Maze

Hans Flat Ranger Station

Glen Canyon National Recreation Area

Needles Overlook

Burr Point

The Needles

Henry Mountains (11,500ft)

Newspaper Rock Recreation Area

Hite Marina

Manti-La Sal National Forest

Abajo Peak (11,360ft)

Monticello

Abajo Mtns

Montezuma Canyon Rd

Mesa Verde National Park (45mi)

Ticaboo

Lake Powell

Natural Bridges National Monument

Mule Canyon Ruins

Edge of the Cedars State Park

Blanding

Butler Wash Ruins

Ferry

Bullfrog Marina

Hall's Crossing Marina

Grand Gulch Primitive Area

Cedar Mesa

Hovenweep National Monument

Hatch Trading Post

San Juan River

Muley Point Overlook

Moki Dugway

Comb Wash Rd

Comb Ridge

Bluff

Montezuma Creek

Goosenecks State Park

Valley of the Gods

Sand Island Petroglyphs

Aneth

Oljato

Goulding's Lodge

Mexican Hat

Navajo Indian Reservation

Monument Valley

Four Corners Navajo Tribal Park

ARIZONA

Monument Valley Navajo Tribal Park

vertical drop; the road approach may require a 4WD on the last mile (or extra walking).

Moki Dugway & Around

Ready for a ride? Eleven miles north of Goosenecks, Moki Dugway is a roughly paved, hairpin-turn-filled section of Hwy 261 that ascends 1100ft in just 3 miles (you descend traveling south). Miners dug out the extreme switchbacks in the 1950s to transport uranium ore. Today this rollercoaster ride offers another route to Lake Powell. Wide pullouts allow a few overviews, but hairpin turns lack good visibility. The Dugway is not for anyone who's sensitive to heights (or for vehicles over 28ft long).

Past the northern end of the Dugway, take the first western-traveling road to **Muley Point Overlook**. This sweeping cliff-edge viewpoint looks south to Monument Valley and other stunning landmarks in Arizona. Pay attention, as the unsigned turnoff is easy to miss.

Follow Hwy 261 further north to the wild and twisting canyons of **Cedar Mesa** and **Grand Gulch Primitive Area** (www.blm.gov), both hugely popular with backcountry hikers. The BLM-administered area also contains hundreds of Ancestral Puebloan sites, many of which have been vandalized by pot hunters. (It bears repeating that all prehistoric sites are protected by law, and authorities are cracking down on offenders.) Some hikes require permits.

The 4-mile, one-way **Kane Gulch** (600ft elevation change) leads to the **Junction Ruin** cliff dwelling. To hike in most canyons you need a $2 day-use permit ($8 overnight). In season (March to June 15, September and October) some walk-in permits are available at the helpful **Kane Gulch Ranger Station** (Hwy 261, 4 miles south of Hwy 95; ⊙8am-noon Mar–mid-Nov), but the number is strictly limited, so make advance reservations by calling the Monticello Field Office (p396). Off season, self-serve permits are available at trailheads. Know that this is difficult country with primitive trails; the nearest water is 10 miles away at Natural Bridges National Monument.

Natural Bridges National Monument

In 1908 **Natural Bridges National Monument** (www.nps.gov/nabr; Hwy 275; 7-day pass per vehicle $6; tent & RV sites $10; ⊙24hr, visitor center 8am-6pm May-Sep, 9am-5pm Oct-Apr) became Utah's first National Park Service (NPS) land. The highlight is a dark-stained, white sandstone canyon with three giant natural bridges.

The oldest – beautifully delicate **Owachomo Bridge** – spans 180ft and rises over 100ft above ground, but is only 9ft thick. **Kachina Bridge** is the youngest and spans 204ft. The 268ft span of **Sipapu Bridge** makes the top five of any 'largest in the US' list (the other four are in Utah, too). All three bridges are visible from a 9-mile, winding loop road with easy-access overlooks.

Most visitors never venture below the canyon rim, but they should. Descents may be a little steep, but distances are short; the longest is just over half a mile one-way. Enthusiastic hikers can take a longer trail that joins all three bridges (8 miles). Don't skip the 0.3-mile trail to the **Horsecollar Ruin** cliff dwelling overlook. The elevation here is 6500ft; trails are open all year, but steeper sections may be closed after heavy rains or snow.

The 12 first-come, first-served sites at the **campground** (☑435-692-1234; www.nps.gov/nabr; Hwy 275; campsites $10), almost half a mile past the visitor center, are fairly sheltered among scraggly trees and red sand. The stars are a real attraction here – this has

❶ CAN I GET A DRINK IN UTAH?

Absolutely. In recent years, laws have relaxed and private club membership bars are no more. Some rules to remember:

➜ Few restaurants have full liquor licenses: most serve beer and wine only. You have to order food to drink.

➜ Minors aren't allowed in bars.

➜ Mixed drinks and wine are available only after midday; 3.2% alcohol beer can be served starting at 10am.

➜ Mixed drinks cannot contain more than 1.5 ounces of a primary liquor, or 2.5 ounces total including secondary alcohol. Sorry, no Long Island Iced Teas or double shots.

➜ Packaged liquor can only be sold at state-run liquor stores; grocery and convenience stores can sell 3.2% alcohol beer and malt beverages. Sales are made from Monday through Saturday only.

been designated an International Dark Sky Park and is one of the darkest in the country. There are pit toilets and grills, but water is available only at the visitor center; there are no hookups. The campground fills on summer afternoons, after which you are directed to camp in a designated area along Hwy 275. No backcountry camping is allowed. Towed trailers are not suitable for the loop drive.

The nearest services are in Blanding, 47 miles to the east. If you continue west on Hwy 95 from Natural Bridges, and follow Hwy 276, the services of Lake Powell's Bullfrog Marina are 140 miles away.

Blanding

POP 3500 / ELEV 6106FT

En route between Bluff (22 miles) and Moab (75 miles), is this aptly named agricultural and mining center. It's worth checking out for its two specialized museums and the nearby outdoors, though it's slim pickings for hotels and restaurants (which do not serve alcohol).

At the **Blanding Visitor Center** (☑435-678-3662; www.blandingutah.org; cnr Hwy 191 N & 200 East; ☺8am-7pm Mon-Sat) the small pioneer artifact collection is worth a look. **Edge of the Cedars State Park Museum** (www.stateparks.utah.gov; 660 W 400 N; adult/child $5/3; ☺9am-5pm Mon-Sat, 10am-4pm Sun) houses a treasure trove of ancient Native American artifacts and pottery gathered from across southeastern Utah. Informative displays provide a good overview of area cultures. Outside, you can climb down into a preserved ceremonial kiva built by the Ancestral Puebloans c 1100. The encroaching subdivision makes you wonder what other sites remain hidden under neighborhood houses.

Born of a private owner's personal collection, the **Dinosaur Museum** (☑435-678-3454; www.dinosaur-museum.org; 754 S 200 West; adult/child $3/1.50; ☺9am-5pm Mon-Sat mid-Apr–mid-Oct) is actually quite large. Mummified remains and fossils come from around the world, but most interesting is the collection of old dinosaur-movie-related exhibits.

Monticello

POP 1980 / ELEV 7070FT

Monticello (mon-ti-*sell*-o) sits up in the foothills of the Abajo (or Blue) Mountains, and is a bit cooler than other towns in the region. As the seat of San Juan County, it's the place to get information about the far southeast

BUTLER WASH & MULE CANYON RUINS

The drive along Hwy 95 between Blanding and Natural Bridges National Monument provides an excellent opportunity to see isolated Ancestral Puebloan ruins. No need to be a backcountry trekker here: it's only a half-mile hike to **Butler Wash Ruins** (14 miles west of Blanding), a 20-room cliff dwelling. Scramble over the slickrock boulders (follow the cairns) and you're rewarded with an overlook of the sacred kivas, habitation and storage rooms that were used c 1300.

Though not as well preserved, the base of the tower, kiva and 12-room **Mule Canyon Ruins** (20 miles west of Blanding) are more easily accessed. Follow the signs to the parking lot just steps from the masonry remains. The pottery found here links the population (c 1000 to 1150) to the Mesa Verde group in southern Colorado; Butler Wash relates to the Kayenta group of northern Arizona. Both are on freely accessible, BLM-administered land.

corner of Utah. Here you're midway between Moab (54 miles) and Bluff (47 miles); both have better places to stay but this is the closest town to the Canyonlands' Needles District.

Just west of town, **Manti–La Sal National Forest** (www.fs.fed.us/r4/mantilasal; off N Creek Rd; ☺24hr) FREE rises to 11,360ft at Abajo Peak. Hundreds of trail miles crisscross the 1.4-million-acre park. Here, spruce- and fir-covered slopes offer respite from the heat – expect about a 10°F (6°C) drop in temperature for every 1000ft you ascend – and spring wildflowers and fall color are a novelty in the arid canyonlands.

Talking Stones (☑435-587-2881; www.talkingstonestours.com; full day from $150) leads rock-art tours and excursions into the Abajo Mountains. The wonderful **Abajo Haven Guest Ranch** (☑435-979-3126; www.abajohaven.com; 5440 N Cedar Edge Ln; cabins $79) is already up in the mountains; guests can have an old-fashioned cook-out. They also organize guided hikes to ancient sites an hour and a half from your cabin. If this sounds great, book ahead – it's popular.

Other places to stay include **Canyonlands Lodge at Blue Mountain** (☑435-220-1050; www.canyonlandslodge.com; Hwy 191; cabins

DON'T MISS

NEWSPAPER ROCK RECREATION AREA

This small, free recreation area showcases a single large sandstone rock panel packed with more than 300 **petroglyphs** attributed to Ute and Ancestral Puebloan groups during a 2000-year period. The many red-rock figures etched out of a black 'desert varnish' surface make for great photos (evening sidelight is best). The site, about 12 miles along Hwy 211 from Hwy 191, is usually visited as a short stop on the way to the Needles section of Canyonlands National Park (8 miles further).

$429-661; [🌐 📶]), a giant log lodge 10 miles south of town and adjacent to the national forest, and the busy **Inn at the Canyons** (📞 435-587-2458; www.monticellocanyonlandsinn. com; 533 N Main St; r from $89; [🌐 📶 🏊]), with modernized motel rooms on the main drag.

A satisfying pit stop, **Peace Tree Juice Café** (516 N Main St; mains $8-20; ⏱ 7:30am-4pm daily, plus 5-9pm May-Sep; 📶) is a great place for full breakfasts, organic espresso, carrot smoothies, lunch wraps or healthy, flavorful dinners (in season).

San Juan Visitor Center (📞 435-587-3235, 800-574-4386; www.southeastutah.com; 117 S Main St; ⏱ 10am-4pm Mon-Fri Nov–mid-Mar, 8am-5pm daily mid-Mar–Oct) has general information on attractions, forest service and other public lands in the region. (Many of its brochures are available online, too.) The **BLM Monticello Field Office** (📞 435-587-1510; 435 N Main St, Monticello; ⏱ 7:45am-noon & 1-4:30pm Mon-Fri) is the place to inquire about area backcountry BLM hiking, driving, camping and permits; you can buy topographic maps here. And if you like to get way, way off the beaten path on multiday hikes, ask about the brilliantly empty **Dark Canyon Primitive Area**.

From Monticello there's a shortcut to Canyonlands National Park's Needles District (22

PUBLIC LANDS

Public lands – national and state parks and monuments, national forests and Bureau of Land Management (BLM) lands – are Utah's most precious natural resource for visitors. Check out www. publiclands.org.

miles instead of the main route's 34 miles). Take County Rd 101 (Abajo Dr) west to Harts Draw Rd (closed in winter); after 17 scenic miles you join Hwy 211 near Newspaper Rock Recreation Area. Befitting the region's religiousness, Hwy 666, which goes to Colorado, was officially renamed Hwy 491 in 2003.

Canyonlands National Park

A 527-sq-mile vision of ancient earth, **Canyonlands National Park** (www.nps.gov/cany; 7-day vehicle/cyclist $10/5) is Utah's largest national park. Vast serpentine canyons tipped with white cliffs loom high over the Colorado and Green Rivers, their waters a stunning 1000ft below the rim rock. Skyward-jutting needles and spires, deep craters, blue-hued mesas and majestic buttes dot the landscape. Overlooks are easy enough to reach. To explore further you'll need to contend with difficult dirt roads, great distances and limited water resources.

The Colorado and Green Rivers form a Y that divides the park into three separate districts, inaccessible to one another from within the park. Cradled atop the Y is the most developed and visited district, **Island in the Sky** (30 miles, 45 minutes from Moab). Think of this as the overview section of the park, where you look down from viewpoints into the incredible canyons that make up the other sections. The thin hoodoos, sculpted sandstone and epic 4WD trails of the **Needles District** are 75 miles and 90 minutes south of Moab. Serious skill is required to traverse the 4WD-only roads of the most inaccessible section, the **Maze** (130 miles, 3½ hours from Moab).

Fees & Permits

In addition to the park entrance fee, permits are required for overnight backpacking, mountain biking, 4WD trips and river trips. Designated camp areas abut most trails; open-zone camping is permitted in some places. Horses are allowed on all 4WD trails. Permits are valid for 14 days and are issued at the visitor center or ranger station where your trip begins. Reservations are available by fax or mail from the **NPS Reservations Office** (📞 435-259-4351; www.nps.gov/cany/ planyourvisit/backcountrypermits.htm; 2282 SW Resource Blvd, Moab; ⏱ 8:30am-noon Mon-Fri) up to two weeks ahead. A few space-available permits may be available same-day, but advanced reservations are essential for spring and fall trips. Costs are as follows:

Backpackers $30 per group of seven

General mountain bike or 4WD day-use $30 for up to three vehicles

Needles Area 4WD day-use $10 per vehicle

River trips $30 per group plus $20 per person fee

Regulations

Canyonlands follows most of the national park hiking and backcountry use regulations. A few rules to note:

➡ No ATVs allowed. Other 4WD vehicles, mountain bikes and street-legal motorbikes are permitted on dirt roads.

➡ Backcountry campfires are allowed only along river corridors; use a fire pan, burn only driftwood or downed tamarisk, and pack out unburnt debris.

➡ Free or clean-aid rock climbing is allowed, except at archaeological sites or on most named features marked on US Geological Survey (USGS) maps. Check with rangers.

➡ New regulations require bear-proof food canisters and human waste removal in some backcountry areas; check with the park for details.

ℹ Information

Island in the Sky and the Needles District have visitor centers. Many of the official park brochures are available online. The information center in Moab also covers the park.

ℹ Getting Around

The easiest way to tour Canyonlands is by car. Traveling between districts takes two to six hours, so plan to visit no more than one per day. Speed limits vary but are generally between 25mph and 40mph.

Outfitters in Moab have hiker shuttles and guide rafting, hiking, biking and 4WD tours in the park.

Island in the Sky

You'll comprehend space in new ways atop the appropriately named Island in the Sky. This 6000ft-high flat-topped mesa drops precipitously on all sides, providing some of the longest, most enthralling vistas of any park in southern Utah. The 11,500ft Henry Mountains bookend panoramic views in the west, and the 12,700ft La Sal Mountains are to the east. Here you can stand beneath a sparkling blue sky and watch thunderheads inundating far-off regions while you contemplate applying more sunscreen. The island sits atop a sandstone bench called the White Rim, which indeed forms a white border 1200ft below the red mesa top and 1500ft above the river canyon bottom. An impressive 4WD road descends from the overlook level.

The complimentary video at the visitor center provides great insight into the nature of the park. Remember to keep your park entry receipt – admission to Island in the Sky includes entry to Needles, too.

Overlooks and trails line each road. Most trails at least partially follow cairns over slickrock. Bring lots of water and watch for cliff edges!

◉ Sights & Activities

Ask rangers about longer hikes off the mesa that are strenuous, steep and require advance planning. There's one major, hard-to-follow backpacking route: the Syncline Loop (8.3 miles, five to seven hours).

White Rim Road MOUNTAIN BIKING, DRIVING TOUR
Blazed by uranium prospectors in the 1950s, primitive White Rim Rd encircling Island in the Sky is the top choice for 4WD and mountain-biking trips. This 70-mile route is accessed near the visitor center via steeply descending Shafer Trail Rd. It generally takes two to three days in a vehicle or three to four days by bike. Since the route lacks any water sources, cyclists should team up with a 4WD support vehicle or travel with a Moab outfitter. Permits are required and rangers do patrol. *A Naturalist's Guide to the White Rim Trail*, by David Williams and Damian Fagon, is a good resource.

IS THIS REAL BEER?

The beer you get in many Utah restaurants, and all grocery stores, doesn't exceed 3.2% alcohol content by weight. However, getting buzzed here may be easier than you think. The alcohol content for beers sold in the US is generally measured by volume, not weight, so a '3.2' beer is actually closer to a 4% beer by volume (a typical Budweiser is 5% by volume) – there's really not that big a difference.

Canyonlands National Park

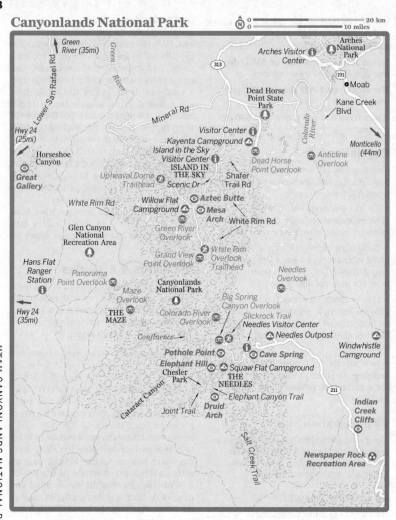

Scenic Driving Tour

From the visitor center the road leads past numerous overlooks and trailheads, ending after 12 miles at **Grand View Point** – one of the Southwest's most sweeping views, rivaled only by the Grand Canyon and nearby Dead Horse Point State Park. Halfway there, a paved spur leads (past **Aztec Butte**) northwest 5 miles to **Upheaval Dome** trailhead. An informative driving tour CD rents for $5 from the visitor center.

Hiking

Several easy trails pack a lot of punch.

Mesa Arch Nature Trail   HIKING

Hike this half-mile loop at sunrise, when the arch, dramatically hung over the very edge of the rim, glows a fiery red.

Upheaval Dome   HIKING

A half-mile spur leads to an overlook of a geological wonder that was possibly the result of a meteorite strike 60 million years ago. Experts can take **Syncline Loop**, the difficult 8-mile hike around the dome, with a spur trail (3 miles round-trip) into its core area – it's considered the park's most challenging trail.

White Rim Overlook Trail   HIKING
A mile before Grand View Point, this is a good spot for a picnic and a 1.8-mile round-trip hike.

Grand View Trail   HIKING
At the end of the road, the trail follows a 2-mile round-trip course at rim's edge. Even if you don't hike, **Grand View Point Overlook** is a must-see.

Aztec Butte Trail   HIKING
Back near the Y in the road, this moderate 2-mile round-trip climbs slickrock to stellar views and an ancient granary ruin.

🛌 Sleeping
Backcountry camping in the Island is mostly open-zone (not in prescribed areas), but is still permit-limited. Nearby Dead Horse Point State Park also has camping; food, fuel and lodging are available in Moab.

Willow Flat Campground   CAMPGROUND $
(tent & RV sites $10) Seven miles from the visitor center, the first-come, first-served, 12-site Willow Flat Campground has vault toilets but no water, and no hookups. Bring firewood and don't expect shade. Arrive early to claim a site during spring and fall.

ℹ Information
Island in the Sky Visitor Center (www.nps.gov/cany/island; Hwy 313; ☉8am-6pm Mar-Oct, 9am-4:30pm Nov-Feb) Get books, maps, permits and campground information here. Schedules are posted daily for ranger-led lectures and hikes.

Needles District
Named for the spires of orange-and-white sandstone jutting skyward from the desert floor, the Needles District's otherworldly terrain is so different from Island in the Sky that it's hard to believe they're both in the same national park. The Needles receives only half as many visitors as the Island since it's more remote – though only 90 minutes from Moab – and there are fewer roadside attractions (but most are well worth the hike). The payoff is huge: peaceful solitude and the opportunity to participate in, not just observe, the vastness of canyon country. Morning light is best for viewing the rock spires.

Needles Visitor Center lies 2.5 miles inside park boundaries and provides drinking water. Hold on to your receipt: admission includes entry to Island in the Sky.

⦿ Sights & Activities
Needles has a couple of short trails (none are wheelchair-accessible), but getting off the beaten path is this section's premier attraction. Many challenging day-hikes connect in a series of loops, some requiring route-finding skills, while 50 miles of 4WD and mountain-biking roads (permit required) crisscross the park. Know what you're doing, though, or risk damaging your vehicle and endangering yourself. Towing fees run from $1000 to $2000 (yes, really). If you're renting a 4WD vehicle, check the insurance policy; you might not be covered here.

Cave Spring Trail   HIKING
Especially popular with kids, the Cave Spring Trail (0.6-mile loop, easy to moderate) leads up ladders and over slickrock to an abandoned cowboy camp. The handprint pictographs on the last cave's walls are haunting.

Slickrock Trail   HIKING
Scamper across slickrock to fabulous views of the canyon; on the return route, you face the district's needles and spires in the distance (2.4-mile loop, moderate).

Chesler Park/Joint Trail Loop   HIKING
Get among the namesake 'needles' formations. An awesome 11-mile route loops across desert grasslands, past towering red-and-white-striped pinnacles and between deep, narrow slot canyons, some only 2ft across. Elevation changes are mild, but the distance makes it an advanced day hike.

Elephant Canyon Trail   HIKING
For gorgeous scenery, the Elephant Canyon Trail (11-mile loop) to Druid Arch is hard to beat. The *National Geographic Trails Illustrated* Canyonlands map should suffice, but if you're inclined to wander, pick up a 7.5-minute quadrangle USGS map at the visitor center.

Elephant Hill   MOUNTAIN BIKING, DRIVING TOUR
This 32-mile round-trip is the most well-known and technically challenging route in the state, with steep grades and tight turns (smell the burning brakes and clutches). If you've always wanted to rock climb on wheels, you've found the right trail. Don't try this as your first 4WD or mountain-bike adventure.

Colorado River Overlook   MOUNTAIN BIKING, DRIVING TOUR
The route to the Colorado River Overlook is easy in a vehicle and moderately easy on

INDIAN CREEK

When driving into the Needles District, look up about 16.5 miles along Hwy 211. Even if you don't rock climb, it's fascinating to watch the experts scaling the narrow cliffside fissures near **Indian Creek** (www.friendsofindiancreek.org). There's a small parking lot from where you can cross the freely accessible Nature Conservancy and BLM grazing land.

a mountain bike. Park and walk the final, steep 1.5-mile descent to the overlook.

Salt Creek Canyon Trail MOUNTAIN BIKING, DRIVING TOUR

Following the district's main drainage, archaeology junkies love the rock art along this 27-mile loop; moderately easy for vehicles and moderate for bikes.

Scenic Driving Tour

Though not much of a drive-by park, the paved road continues almost 7 miles from the visitor center to **Big Spring Canyon Overlook**. Parking areas along the way access several short trails to sights, including arches, **Pothole Point**, Ancestral Puebloan ruins and petroglyphs. All trails listed are off this drive; use the park map you receive on entry to navigate.

🛏 Sleeping & Eating

Backcountry camping, in prescribed areas only, is quite popular, so it's hard to secure an overnight permit without advance reservation. Monticello (34 miles) and Moab (75 miles) are the nearest full-service towns.

Squaw Flat Campground CAMPGROUND $
(www.nps.gov/cany; tent & RV sites $15) This first-come, first-served, 27-site campground 3 miles west of the visitor center fills up every day, spring to fall. It has flush toilets and running water, but no showers, and no hookups. Opt for side A, where many sites (12 and 14, for example) are shaded by juniper trees and cliffs. Maximum allowable RV length is 28ft.

Needles Outpost CAMPGROUND $
(☎ 435-979-4007; www.canyonlandsneedlesoutpost.com; Hwy 211; tent & RV sites $20; ☉ Apr-Nov) If Squaw Flat is full, the dusty private campground at Needles Outpost is an alternative. Shower facilities are $3 for campers, $7 for

noncampers. An on-site store sells limited camping supplies, gasoline and propane. The lunch counter and grill (open 8:30am to 4:30pm) serves sandwiches and burgers.

ℹ️ Information

Needles Visitor Center (☎ 435-259-4711; Hwy 211; ☉ 8am-6pm Mar-Oct, 9am-4:30pm Nov-Feb) A small center, but has similar books and guidance to the one at Island in the Sky.

Horseshoe Canyon

Way far west of Island in the Sky, **Horseshoe Canyon** shelters one of the most impressive collections of millennia-old rock art in the Southwest. The centerpiece is the **Great Gallery** and its haunting Barrier Canyon-style pictographs from between 2000 BC and AD 500. The heroic, bigger-than-life-size figures are magnificent. Artifacts recovered here date back as far as 9000 BC.

That said, it's not easy to get to. The gallery lies at the end of a 6.5-mile round-trip hiking trail descending 750ft from a dirt road. Plan on six hours. Rangers lead hikes here on Saturday and Sunday from April through October; contact the Hans Flat Ranger Station for times. You can camp on BLM land at the trailhead, though it's really a parking lot. There is a single vault toilet, but no water.

From Moab the trip is about 120 miles (2¾ hours). Take Hwy 191 north to I-70 west, then Hwy 24 south. About 25 miles south of I-70, past the turnoff for Goblin Valley State Park, turn east and follow the gravel road 30 miles. Hanksville is 45 miles (1½ hours).

The Maze

A 30-sq-mile jumble of high-walled canyons, the **Maze** is a rare preserve of true wilderness for hardy backcountry veterans. The colorful canyons are rugged, deep and sometimes completely inaccessible. Many of them look alike and it's easy to get turned around – hence the district's name. (Think topographic maps and GPS.) Rocky roads absolutely necessitate reliable, high-clearance 4WD vehicles. Plan on spending at least three days, though a week is ideal.

If you're at all inexperienced with four-wheel driving, stay away. Be prepared to repair your jeep and, at times, the road. There may not be enough money on the planet to get you towed out of here. Most wreckers won't even try.

Predeparture, always contact the **Hans Flat Ranger Station** (435-259-2652; www.nps.gov/cany; Hans Flat Rd, Hwy 24; 8am-4:30pm) for conditions and advice. The station is 136 miles (3½ hours) from Moab, and has a few books and maps, but no other services. Take Hwy 191 north, I-70 west, and then Hwy 24 south. Hans Flat is 16 miles south of Horseshoe Canyon. The few roads into the district are poor and often closed with rain or snow; bring tire chains from October to April.

Around Canyonlands

The BLM **Canyon Rims Recreation Area** (www.blm.gov/utah/moab; Needles Overlook Rd) FREE to the east of the national park has two interesting overlooks, undeveloped hiking and backcountry driving. Turn west off Hwy 191 (32 miles south of Moab, 27 miles north of Monticello); a paved road leads 22 miles to **Needles Overlook** and a panorama of the park. Two-thirds of the way to the overlook, the gravel **Anticline Overlook Rd** stretches 16 miles north to a promontory with awesome views of the Colorado River.

Three miles after the Hwy 191 turnoff is **Windwhistle Campground** (tent & RV sites $15; Mar-Oct). Off a gravel access road, the 20 well-spaced, first-served sites have fire rings and scenic vistas. Pit toilets; water available May through September.

Dead Horse Point State Park

The views at **Dead Horse Point** (www.stateparks.utah.gov; Hwy 313; park day-use per vehicle $10, tent & RV sites $25; park 6am-10pm, visitor center 8am-6pm Mar-Oct, 9am-4pm Nov-Feb) pack a wallop, extending 2000ft down to the winding Colorado River, up to La Sal Mountains' 12,700ft peaks and out 100 miles across Canyonlands' mesmerizing stair-step landscape. (You might remember it from the final scene of *Thelma & Louise*, where they drove off into the abyss.) If you thrive on rare, epic views, you're gonna love Dead Horse.

Drive Hwy 313 south from Hwy 191, 30 miles northwest of Moab, following the road as it turns left into the park (if you go straight you'll reach Island in the Sky). Toward the end of the drive, the road traverses a narrow ridge just 90ft across. Around the turn of the 20th century, cowboys used the mesa top as a sort of natural corral by driving wild horses onto it and blocking the ridge. The story goes that one season ranch hands forgot to release the horses they didn't cull, and the stranded equines supposedly died with a great view of the Colorado River...

The **visitor center** (8am-6pm mid-Mar–mid-Oct, 9am-5pm mid-Oct–mid-Mar) has exhibits, shows on-demand videos and sells books and maps. Rangers lead walks and talks in summer. To escape the small (but sometimes chatty) crowds, take a walk around the mesa rim. Visit at dawn or dusk for the best lighting. South of the vistor center, the 21-site **Kayenta Campground** (800-322-3770; www.stateparks.utah.gov; sites $25) provides limited water and a dump station, but no hookups. Reservations are accepted from March to October, but you can often secure same-day sites by arriving early. Fill RVs with water in Moab.

Moab

POP 5100 / ELEV 4026FT

An island of busy civilization in a sea of desert wilderness, Moab is southern Utah's adventure base camp. Day trippers to Arches or Canyonlands National Parks can return to a hot tub and pub food, a boon after a dusty day on the trail. Unlike the rest of the region, here you can shop for groceries till midnight, buy a bottle of tequila, get a cell signal and even a late dinner.

For those coming from the wilderness, the hubbub can be jarring. Corporate chain motels line Main St, souvenir shops abound and streetlights and neon signs blot out the night sky. Still, there's a distinct sense of fun

UTAH AROUND CANYONLANDS

127 HOURS: BETWEEN A ROCK AND A HARD PLACE

What started out as a day's adventure turned into a harrowing ordeal for one outdoorsman exploring some spectacular slots near Canyonlands National Park in the spring of 2003. Canyoneering southeast of the remote Horseshoe Canyon section in Bluejohn Canyon, Aron Ralston became trapped when a crashing boulder pinned his hand and wrist. The story of how he cut himself out of the situation – literally, as he cut off his own arm with a pocketknife – was first turned into a compelling book, and then the 2010 Oscar-nominated movie *127 Hours*. The film showcases both the amazing beauty of Utah's canyonlands and the brutal reality of its risks.

Moab

A **B** **C** **D**

31 Swanny City Park

100 West

Main St

2

26

Tag-A-Long Expeditions (0.1mi);
Moab Desert Adventures (0.1mi);
Poison Spider Bicycles (0.1mi);
Adventure Inn (0.1mi); Inca Inn (0.2mi);
Holiday Inn Express (1.3mi);
Buck's Grill House (1.4mi);
Portal RV Resort (1.5mi)

8

300 North

1

10
3

28

191

200 North

2

Walnut La

17
29

21

13

27

32

41

100 North

Williams Way

42

30

43

14

Moab
Information
Center

5

35 36

33

Center St

1

24

4

15

34

100 West

Main St

100 East

200 East

300 East

25

39

38

37

100 South

18

Mayor's
House (0.3mi)

4

40

19

200 South

9

300 South

300 South

22

6

Grand St

Mill Creek

11

12

Kane Creek Blvd

Pack Creek

191

23

7

Uranium Ave

Huntridge Dr

Aspen Ave

16

Main St

Canyonlands Campground (100yds);
Chile Pepper Bike Shop (0.1mi);
Moab Brewery (0.1mi); Paradox Pizza (0.1mi);
Rim Tours (1mi); Lazy Lizard Hostel (1.2mi);
Canyonlands Field Institute (1.3mi)

20

7

UTAH MOAB

Moab

in the air. Everyone is here to play in Utah's recreation capital – from the hiker to the four-wheeler, recreationists' enthusiasm borders on fetishism.

Starting in the 1950s, it was miners in search of 'radioactive gold' – uranium – who blazed the network of back roads that laid the groundwork for Moab to become a 4WD mecca. But neither mining nor the hundreds of Hollywood films shot here had as much influence on the character of Moab as the influx of youth-culture, fat-tire, mountain-bike enthusiasts. The town gets overrun March through October, and the impact of all those feet, bikes and 4WDs on the fragile desert is a serious concern (use existing trails). People here love the land, even if they don't always agree about how to protect it. If the traffic irritates you, just remember – you can disappear into the vast desert in no time.

◎ Sights

Between breakfast and dinner there's not much going on in Moab; most people get out of town for activities.

Museum of Moab MUSEUM
(www.moabmuseum.org; 118 E Center St; adult/child $5/free; ☻noon-5pm) Regional exhibits feature everything from paleontology and geology to uranium mining and Native American art. Admission is free on Monday.

Red Cliffs Adventure Lodge MUSEUM
(www.redcliffslodge.com/museum; Mile 14, Hwy 128; ☻8am-10pm) FREE This lodge, 15 miles northeast of town, hosts the Moab Museum of Film & Western Heritage, showing Hollywood memorabilia and posters from all the films shot in the area. There's also a tasting and sales room for its on-site winery.

Spanish Valley Winery WINERY
(www.moab-utah.com/spanishvalleywinery; 4710 S Zimmerman Lane; ☻noon-6pm Mon-Sat Mar-Oct) For some no-frills wine tasting, visit the surprisingly good Spanish Valley Winery, 6 miles south of Moab on Hwy 191.

✦ Activities

The visitor center has a helpful collection of free brochures highlighting rock art, movie locations, driving tours, and 4WD and hiking trails near town. Moab abounds in outfitters for mountain biking, white-water rafting, hiking, and backcountry ATV and jeep tours. Can't choose just one activity? Many operators will help you plan multisport or multiday adventures. The visitor center has a complete list of all outfitters (too numerous to include here).

Mountain Biking

Moab's mountain biking is world-famous. Challenging trails ascend steep slickrock and wind through woods and up 4WD roads. People come from everywhere to ride the famous Slickrock Bike Trail and other challenging routes. If you're a die-hard, ask about trips to the Maze. Bike shop websites and www.discovermoab.com/biking.htm are good trail resources, or pick up *Above & Beyond Slickrock*, by Todd Campbell, and *Rider Mel's Mountain Bike Guide to Moab*. In recent years, the BLM has opened new loops and temporarily closed others. Follow BLM guidelines, avoid all off-trail riding and pack everything out (including cigarette butts). Spring and fall are the busiest seasons. In summer you'd better start by 7am; otherwise, it gets too hot.

For rentals, be sure to reserve in advance. Road and full-suspension bikes cost $40 to $75 per day. Shops are generally open from 8am to 7pm from March through October, and 9am to 6pm November through February. Full-day tours run from $120 to $275 per person including lunch and rental.

Rim Cyclery   MOUNTAIN BIKING
(✆ 435-259-5333; www.rimcyclery.com; 94 W 100 N) Moab's longest-running family-owned bike shop not only does rentals and repairs, it also has a museum of mountain-bike technology.

Poison Spider Bicycles   MOUNTAIN BIKING
(✆ 800-635-1792, 435-259-7882; www.poison-spiderbicycles.com; 497 N Main St; rental per day $45-75) Friendly staff are always busy helping wheel jockeys map out their routes. Well-maintained road and suspension rigs for rent; private guided trips organized in conjunction with Magpie Adventures.

> ### ❶ SHOWERING ESSENTIALS
>
> Area BLM, national and state park campgrounds do not have showers. You can wash up at several in-town campgrounds, and at biking outfitter Poison Spider Bicycles, for a fee (around $6).

Rim Tours   TOUR
(✆ 435-259-5223, 800-626-7335; www.rimtours.com; 1233 S Hwy 191) Well-organized multiday trips cover territory all across southern Utah; day tours are available for top local trails, including Canyonlands. The 18-mile downhill sunrise ride is all adrenaline.

Moab Cyclery   MOUNTAIN BIKING
(✆ 800-451-1133, 435-259-7423; www.moab-cyclery.com; 391 S Main St) Good half-, full-, multiday (and multisport) tours. Rental and sales; biker shuttles available.

Chile Pepper Bike Shop   MOUNTAIN BIKING
(✆ 888-677-4688, 435-259-4688; www.chilebikes.com; 720 S Main St) Rentals and repairs, plus helpful trail maps. Used bikes for sale.

Western Spirit Cycling Adventures   TOUR
(✆ 800-845-2453, 435-259-8732; www.western-spirit.com; 478 Mill Creek Dr) Canyonlands White Rim, Utah and nationwide multiday tours.

White-Water Rafting

Whatever your interest, be it bashing through rapids or gentle floats for studying canyon geology, rafting may prove the highlight of your vacation. Rafting season runs from April to September; jet-boating season lasts longer. Water levels crest in May and June.

Most local rafting is on the Colorado River, northeast of town, including the Class III to IV rapids of **Westwater Canyon**, near Colorado; the wildlife-rich 7-mile Class I float from **Dewey Bridge to Hittle Bottom** (no permit required); and the Class I to II **Moab Daily**, the most popular stretch near town (no permit required; expect a short stretch of Class III rapids).

Rafters also launch north of Moab to get to the legendary Class V rapids of **Cataract Canyon** (NPS permit required). This Colorado River canyon south of town and the Confluence is one of North America's most intense stretches of white water. If you book anything less than a five-day outfitter trip to get here, know that some of the time downstream will be spent in a powered boat. Advanced do-it-yourself rafters wanting to run it will have to book a jet-boat shuttle or flight return.

North of Moab is a Class I float along the **Green River** that's ideal for canoes. From there you can follow John Wesley Powell's 1869 route. (Note that additional outfitters operate out of the town of Green River itself.)

Full-day float trips cost $75 to $90; white-water trips start at $175. Multiday excursions start at $399, while jet-boat trips cost $69. Day trips are often available on short notice, but book overnight trips well ahead. Know the boat you want: an oar rig is a rubber raft that a guide rows; a paddleboat is steered by the guide and paddled by passengers; motor rigs are large boats driven by a guide (such as jet boats).

Do-it-yourselfers can rent canoes, inflatable kayaks or rafts. Canoes and kayaks run $40 to $55 per day and rafts $75 to $185 per day, depending on size. Rentals are discounted for multiday rentals.

Without permits, you'll be restricted to mellow stretches of the Colorado and Green Rivers; if you want to run Westwater Canyon or enter Canyonlands on either river, you'll need a permit. Contact the BLM (p413) or NPS (☑435-259-4351; www.nps.gov/cany/planyourvisit/backcountrypermits.htm), respectively. Reserve equipment, permits and shuttles way in advance.

Sheri Griffith Expeditions　　　RAFTING
(☑800-332-2439; www.griffithexp.com; 2231 S Hwy 191) Operating since 1971, this rafting specialist has a great selection of river trips on the Colorado, Green and San Juan Rivers – from family floats to Cataract Canyon rapids, from a couple hours to a couple weeks.

Canyon Voyages
Adventure Co　　　ADVENTURE SPORTS
(☑800-733-6007, 435-259-6007; www.canyonvoyages.com; 211 N Main St) In addition to half- to five-day mild white-water and kayaking trips, Canyon organizes multisport excursions that include options like hiking, biking and canyoneering. Kayak, canoe and outdoor equipment rental available.

Tag-A-Long Expeditions　　ADVENTURE SPORTS
(☑800-453-3292, 435-259-8946; www.tagalong. com; 452 N Main St) This rafting outfitter offers a little of everything: flat-water jet boat rides, white-water rafting, land safaris, horseback riding, scenic flights, skydiving, Nordic skiing and more. Ask about jet boat return support for Cataract Canyon trips.

Moab Rafting & Canoe Co　　　KAYAKING
(☑435-259-7722; www.moab-rafting.com; 420 Kane Creek Blvd) Small company with guided and self-guided canoe and raft trips.

Adrift Adventures　　　ADVENTURE TOURS
(☑800-874-4483, 435-259-8594; www.adrift.net; 378 N Main St) Rafting, jet boat rides, sport

---

> ### ⓘ WATER REFILLING STATIONS
>
> In addition to the water stations at area national park visitor centers, you can refill your jugs for free at Gear Heads Outdoor Store (p407). Alternatively go to the natural, outdoor tap at **Matrimony Springs** (Hwy 128, 100yd east of Hwy 191 on the right).

boat rides, 4WD land excursions and multisport packages, plus Arches National Park bus tours.

Splore　　　RAFTING
(☑801-484-4128; www.splore.org) If traveling with someone who has a physical or mental disability, book a raft trip with this operator, based in Salt Lake City.

Hiking

Don't limit yourself to the national parks – there's hiking on surrounding public lands as well.

Corona Arch Trail　　　HIKING
(Potash Rd, trailhead 6 miles north) To see petroglyphs and two spectacular arches, hike the moderately easy 3-mile, two-hour walk. You may recognize Corona from a well-known photograph showing an airplane flying through it – this is one big arch.

Negro Bill Canyon Trail　　　HIKING
(Hwy 128, trailhead 3 miles north of Moab) The moderately easy trail includes a 2.5-mile walk along a stream. (The politically incorrect canyon name refers to a prospector who grazed his cows here in the 1800s.) Scoot down a shaded side canyon to find petroglyphs, then continue to the 243ft-wide **Morning Glory Natural Bridge**, at a box canyon. Plan on three to four hours.

La Sal Mountains　　　HIKING
(www.fs.usda.gov; La Sal Mountain Loop) To escape summer's heat, head up Hwy 128 to the Manti–La Sal National Forest lands, in the mountains east of Moab, and hike through white-barked aspens and ponderosa pines.

Canyonlands Field Institute　　　TOUR
(☑800-860-5262, 435-259-7750; www.cfimoab. org; 1320 S Hwy 191) All-ages interpretive hikes and canoe trips – a wonderful introduction to the parks and the area.

TOP MOAB MOUNTAIN-BIKING TRAILS

Slickrock Trail (p399) Moab's legendary trail will kick your ass. The 12.7-mile round-trip, half-day route is for experts only (as is the practice loop).

White Rim Trail Canyonlands National Park's 70-mile, three- to four-day journey around a canyon mesa top is epic.

Bar-M Loop Bring the kids on this easy, 8-mile loop skirting the boundary of Arches, with great views and short slickrock stretches.

Gemini Bridges A moderate, full-day downhill ride past spectacular rock formations, this 13.5-mile one-way trail follows dirt, sand and slickrock.

Klondike Bluffs Trail Intermediates can learn to ride slickrock on this 15.6-mile round-trip trail, past dinosaur tracks to Arches National Park.

Moonlight Meadow Trail Beat the heat by ascending La Sal Mountains to 10,600ft on this moderate 10-mile loop among aspens and pines (take it easy: you *will* get winded).

Park to Park Trail A new paved-road bike path travels one-way from Moab into Arches National Park (30 miles), or you can turn off and follow the Hwy 313 bike lane to the end of Canyonlands' Island in the Sky park (35 miles).

Deep Desert Expeditions HIKING
(☑ 435-260-1696; www.deepdesert.com; half-day from $125) Archaeological hikes, photo treks, multiday guided backpacking, catered camping and Fiery Furnace walks – in winter, too!

Four-Wheel Driving

The area's primitive backroads are coveted by 4WD enthusiasts. You can rent ($200 to $300 per day) or take group 4WD tours, or 'land safaris', in multipassenger-modified, six- to eight-person Humvee-like vehicles (two hours from $81 to $169). Note that rafting companies may have combination land/river trips.

Off-road utility vehicles like Rhinos and Mules (seating two to four), or four-wheelers (straddled like a bicycle) rent from $150 per day. Personal 4WD vehicles and ATVs require an off-highway vehicle (OHV) permit, available at the visitor center. Outfitter hours are generally 7:30am to 7pm March through October, 8am to 5pm November through February. Moab Information Center has good free route info, as well as *Moab Utah Backroads & 4WD Trails* by Charles Wells, and other books for sale. Canyonlands National Park also has some epic 4WD tracks.

If you go four-wheeling, stay on established routes. The desert looks barren, but it's a fragile landscape of complex ecosystems. Biological soil crusts can take up to a century to regenerate after even one tire track (really).

Hell's Revenge DRIVING TOUR
(www.discovermoab.com/sandflats.htm; Sand Flats Rd, Sand Flats Recreation Area) The best-known 4WD road in Moab is in the BLM-administered area east of town, which follows an 8.2-mile route up and down shockingly steep slickrock. For experienced drivers only.

Moab Adventure Center ADVENTURE SPORTS
(☑ 435-259-7019, 866-904-1163; www.moabadventurecenter.com; 225 S Main St) The open-air, canopy-topped land safaris offered here are popular. This megacenter also arranges, alone or in combination, rafting trips, Jeep rental, horseback riding, rock climbing, guided hikes, scenic flights and even Arches National Park bus tours.

High Point Hummer & ATV Tours ADVENTURE SPORTS
(☑ 435-259-2972, 877-486-6833; www.highpointhummer.com; 281 N Main St) Take a two- to four-hour thrill ride up the slickrock on a group Hummer tour; follow a guide as you drive yourself on a four-wheeler or utility vehicle tour; or rent your own ATV.

Dan Mick's Jeep Tours DRIVING TOUR
(☑ 435-259-4567; www.danmick.com) Private Jeep tours and guided drive-your-own-4WD trips with good ol' boy Dan Mick. A highly regarded local operation.

Elite Motorcycle Tours DRIVING TOUR
(☑ 435-259-7621, 888-778-0358; www.elitemotorcycletours.com; 1310 Murphy Lane) Dirt bike and street-legal motorcycle rental and tours.

Farabee's Outlaw Jeep Tours   DRIVING TOUR
([☎]435-259-7494; www.farabeesjeeprentals.com;
35 Grand St) Customized Jeep rental and off-
road ride-along or guide-led tours.

Cliffhanger Jeep Rental   DRIVING TOUR
([☎]435-259-0889; www.cliffhangerjeeprental.com;
40 W Center St) TeraFlex suspension Jeeps,
Rhino two-seaters and four-wheelers for rent.

Coyote Land Tours   DRIVING TOUR
([☎]435-259-6649; www.coyotelandtours.com)
Popular daily tours in a bright-yellow
Mercedes Benz Unimog off-road vehicle
(seats 12); call ahead.

Rock Climbing & Canyoneering

Climb up cliffsides, rappel into rivers and
hike through slot canyons. Half-day canyoneering or climbing adventures run from
around $95 to $165 per person.

Wall Street   ROCK CLIMBING
(Potash Rd) Rock climbers in town gravitate
toward Wall Street; it's Moab's El Capitan, so
it gets crowded.

★**Moab Desert
Adventures**   ADVENTURE SPORTS
([☎]877-765-6622, 435-260-2404; www.moabde-
sertadventures.com; 415 N Main St; half-/full day
from $99) Top-notch climbing tours scale
area towers and walls; the 140ft arch rappel is especially exciting. Canyoneering and
multisport packages available.

Desert Highlights   ADVENTURE SPORTS
([☎]435-259-4433, 800-747-1342; www.de-
serthighlights.com; 50 E Center St; 5hr canyoneering from $95) Canyoneering and combo raft
trips here are big on personal attention.
Offers trips to some worthy, little-known
destinations.

Moab Cliffs & Canyons   ADVENTURE SPORTS
([☎]877-641-5271, 435-259-3317; www.cliffsandcan-
yons.com; 231 N Main St) Canyoneering, climbing and scenic hiking trips. Ask about Fiery
Furnace hikes.

Windgate Adventures   ADVENTURE SPORTS
([☎]435-260-9802; www.windgateadventures.com)
Private guide Eric Odenthal leads guided
climbing, canyoneering, arch-rappelling and
photo trips.

Air Adventures

Moab's airport is 16 miles north of town on
Hwy 191.

Redtail Aviation   SCENIC FLIGHTS
([☎]435-259-7421; www.redtailaviation.com; per
30min $123) Fly high above Arches, Canyon-
lands, Lake Powell, San Rafael Swell, Monument Valley and more.

Skydive Moab   ADVENTURE SPORTS
([☎]435-259-5867; www.skydivemoab.com; tandem
1st jump $225) Skydiving and base-jumping.

Canyonlands Ballooning   BALLOONING
([☎]435-655-1389, 877-478-3544; www.canyon-
landsballooning.com; 4hr $269) Soar over can-
yon country and Manti–La Sal Mountains.

Skiing & Snowshoeing

It's a local secret that La Sal Mountains,
which lord over Moab off Hwy 128, receive
tons of powder, just perfect for cross-country
skiing – and there's a hut-to-hut ski system
($35 per person, per night).

Tag-A-Long Expeditions   SKIING
([☎]800-453-3292, 435-259-8946; www.tagalong.
com; 452 N Main St) Book self-guided nordic
ski packages, snowmobile transfers and hut
lodging here.

Rim Cyclery   SKIING
([☎]435-259-5333; www.rimcyclery.com; 94 W 100
N) Rents skis and provides trail maps.

**Gear Heads Outdoor
Store**   OUTDOOR EQUIPMENT
([☎]888-740-4327, 435-259-4327; www.moabgear.
com; 471 S Main St) Rents snowshoes and provides trail maps.

Other Activities

Red Cliffs Lodge   HORSEBACK RIDING
([☎]866-812-2002, 435-259-2002; www.red-
cliffslodge.com; Mile 14, Hwy 128; half-day $95)
In Castle Valley, 14 miles north of town,
Red Cliffs Lodge provides the area's only
horseback trail rides (March to November),
offered mornings and evenings. If you book
a multisport rafting trip that includes horseback riding, you'll still be coming here.

**Matheson Wetlands
Preserve**   BIRDWATCHING
([☎]435-259-4629; www.nature.org; 934 W Kane
Creek Blvd; ⊙dawn-dusk) [FREE] The Nature
Conservancy oversees the 890-acre preserve
just west of town. At the time of research, a
wildfire had closed sections of the park in-
definitely. Check for updates before heading
out with your binoculars.

Moab Photo Tours PHOTOGRAPHY
(☑ 435-259-4700; www.moabphototours.com)
Area photo workshops and tours by local
photographers.

✨ Festivals & Events

Moab loves a party, and throws them regularly. For a full calendar, consult www.dis-
covermoab.com.

Skinny Tire Festival SPORTS
(www.skinnytirefestival.com) Road cycling festival; first weekend in March.

Jeep Safari SPORTS
(www.rr4w.com) The week before Easter, about
2000 Jeeps (and thousands more people)
overrun the town in the year's biggest event.
Register early; trails are assigned.

Moab Fat Tire Festival SPORTS
(www.moabfattirefest.com) One of Utah's biggest mountain-biking events, with tours,
workshops, lessons, competitions and plenty
of music; in October.

Moab Folk Festival MUSIC
(www.moabfolkfestival.com) Folk music and environmental consciousness combine. This
November festival is 100% wind-powered,
venues are easily walkable and recycling is
encouraged.

🛏 Sleeping

Rates given here are for March to October;
prices drop by as much as 50% outside those
months. Some smaller places close November
through March. Most lodgings have hot tubs
for aching muscles and mini-refrigerators to
store snacks; motels have laundry facilities
to clean up the trail dirt. Cyclists should ask
whether a property provides *secure* bike storage, not just an unlocked closet.

Though Moab has a huge number of
motels, there's often no room at the inn.
Reserve as far ahead as possible in season.
For a full town lodging list, see www.discov-
ermoab.com.

Adventure Inn MOTEL $
(☑ 866-662-2466, 435-259-6122; www.adven-
tureinnmoab.com; 512 N Main St; r incl breakfast
$80-105; ☼ Mar-Oct; ❋ 🤍) A great little in-
die motel, the Adventure Inn has spotless
rooms (some with refrigerators) and decent
linens, as well as laundry facilities. There's
a picnic area on site and the owners prove
helpful.

Inca Inn MOTEL $
(☑ 866-462-2466, 435-259-7261; www.incainn.
com; 570 N Main St; r incl breakfast $59-99; ☼ Feb-
Nov; ❋ 🤍 🏊) Who expects a pool at these
prices? This small mom-and-pop motel has
older but spick-and-span rooms, plus a place
to take a dip. Breakfast is light and snacky.

Lazy Lizard Hostel HOSTEL $
(☑ 435-259-6057; www.lazylizardhostel.com; 1213
S Hwy 191; dm/s/d $10/28/32, cabins $33-54;
❋ @) Hippie hangout with frayed couches,
worn bunks and small kitchen.

★ Cali Cochitta B&B $$
(☑ 888-429-8112, 435-259-4961; www.moabdream
inn.com; 110 S 200 East; cottages incl breakfast $140-
180; ❋ 🤍) Charming and central, these ad-
joining brick cottages offer snug rooms fitted
with smart decor. A long wooden table on the
patio makes a welcome setting for communi-
ty breakfasts. You can also take advantage of
the porch chairs, hammock or backyard hot
tub. The vibe is warm but the innkeepers live
off-site, leaving you alone to enjoy the house.

Castle Valley Inn B&B $$
(☑ 435-259-6012; www.castlevalleyinn.com; 424
Amber Ln, off La Sal Mountain Loop Rd; r & cabins
incl breakfast $105-225; ❋) For tranquility, it's
hard to beat this top option off La Sal Mountain Loop Rd, 15 miles north of Moab. With
cozy quilts and handmade Aspen furniture,
rooms (in the main house or new bungalows) sit amid orchards of apples, plums and
apricots. Bungalows offer full kitchen and
grill; there's also an outdoor hot tub. Ideal
for cycling Castle Valley.

3 Dogs and a Moose B&B $$
(☑ 435-260-1692; www.3dogsandamoosecottages.
com; 171 W Center St; cottages $125-285; ❋ 🤍 🏊)
Lovely and low-key, these four downtown
cottages make an ideal base camp for groups
and families who want a little socializing in
situ. The style is playful modern, with smart
linens, corrugated-tin showers and recycled
doors. Even better, you can pick your own to-
matoes in the landscaped yard, where there's
also hammocks, a bike wash, grill and hot tub.

Sunflower Hill INN $$
(☑ 800-662-2786, 435-259-2974; www.sunflower-
hill.com; 185 N 300 East; r incl breakfast $165-235;
❋ 🤍 🏊) A top-shelf B&B, Sunflower Hill
offers rooms in two inviting buildings – a
cedar-sided early-20th-century home and a
100-year-old farmhouse – amid manicured
gardens and cottonwoods. Rooms have an

elegant country style, with quilt-piled beds and antiques. The staff are eager to please and the hot tub works magic.

Mayor's House
B&B **$$**

(☑ 435-259-6015, 888-791-2345; www.mayorshouse.com; 505 Rose Tree Ln; r incl breakfast $100-140; ✳ @ 🏊) The Brady Bunch would be at home in this prim modern brick house surrounded by lush lilac bushes. But spacious, quiet and immaculate rooms take the vibe down a notch. A lower-level suite is ideal for families and the hosts are quietly welcoming. Plus, it boasts a hot tub and possibly Moab's largest pool.

Adobe Abode
B&B **$$**

(☑ 435-259-7716; www.adobeabodemoab.com; 778 W Kane Creek Rd; r $139-149; ✳) On the upper outskirts of town, this modern adobe pays homage to pioneer style with a mélange of antlers, bear rugs and antique guns. The grounds are xeriscaped and rooms comfortable.

Redstone Inn
MOTEL **$$**

(☑ 435-259-3500, 800-772-1972; www.moabredstone.com; 535 S Main St; r $105-110; ✳ 🛜 🏊) The small pine-paneled rooms here are decorated with rustic wood furniture, lending a cozy feel to their otherwise utilitarian boxiness. The walls are thin, though. There's a bike wash area and storage, guest laundry, on-site hot tub and pool privileges across the street.

Big Horn Lodge
MOTEL **$$**

(☑ 435-259-6171, 800-325-6171; www.moabbighorn. com; 550 S Main St; r $110-120; ✳ 🛜 🏊) OK, so the exterior is kitschy Southwestern style c 1970, but the knotty-pine paneled interiors are cozy, service is taken seriously and there are loads of extras (including a heated swimming pool and hot tub, refrigerators and coffee makers).

Gonzo Inn
MOTEL **$$**

(☑ 800-791-4044, 435-259-2515; www.gonzoinn. com; 100 W 200 South; r 165-349, incl breakfast Apr-Oct; ✳ @ 🛜 🏊) Less an inn than a chain-style motel spruced up with steel accents and sleek cement showers, the Gonzo Inn is friendly, but not quite personal. It does cater well to cyclists, with a bicycle wash and repair station as well as a laundry. Rooms have refrigerators and coffee makers.

Desert Hills
B&B **$$**

(☑ 435-259-3568; www.deserthillsbnb.com; 1989 S Desert Hills Ln; r incl breakfast $125-155; ✳ 🛜) Get away from the traffic in town at this homey B&B in a suburban neighborhood. The four

simple rooms have log beds, pillow-top mattresses and minifridges – and come with friendly, personal service.

Best Western Canyonlands Inn
MOTEL **$$**

(☑ 435-259-2300, 800-649-5191; www.canyonlandsinn.com; 16 S Main St; r $184-224; ✳ 🏊) A comfortable, chain choice at the central crossroads of downtown. Features a fitness room, laundry, playground and outdoor pool.

Holiday Inn Express
HOTEL **$$**

(☑ 800-465-4229, 435-259-1150; www.hiexpress. com/moabut; 1653 Hwy 191 N; r $172-186; ✳ 🏊) Some of the newest, upper midrange rooms in town are at this behemoth chain with a star-shaped pool.

Bowen Motel
MOTEL **$$**

(☑ 435-259-7132, 800-874-5439; www.bowenmotel.com; 169 N Main St; r incl breakfast $122-152; ✳ 🛜 🏊) Basic motel, steps from shops and restaurants. There's a BBQ area, bike washing station and updated rooms.

Sorrel River Ranch
LODGE **$$$**

(☑ 877-359-2715, 435-259-4642; www.sorrelriver.com; Mile 17, Hwy 128; r $429-779; ✳ @ 🏊) Southeast Utah's only full-service luxury resort and gourmet restaurant was originally an 1803 homestead. The lodge and log cabins sit on 240 lush acres, with riding areas and alfalfa fields along the Colorado River. Details strive for rustic perfection, with bedroom fireplaces, handmade log beds, copper-top tables and Jacuzzi tubs. Amenities include an on-site spa (open to the public), fitness facility, salon and hot tub, kitchenettes and horseback riding, and there is a gourmet restaurant. Families welcome.

Red Cliffs Lodge
LODGE **$$$**

(☑ 435-259-2002, 866-812-2002; www.redcliffslodge.com; Mile 14, Hwy 128; ste $150-340; ✳ 🏊) Dude ranch meets deluxe motel. These comfortable rooms feature vaulted knotty-pine ceilings, kitchenettes with dining tables, and private (though cramped) patios, some overlooking the Colorado River. Larger rooms are ideal for families. Also offers horseback riding and a hot tub, an on-site movie museum for Western buffs and wine tasting. Pets are allowed and horse boarding is available.

Aarchway Inn
HOTEL **$$$**

(☑ 800-341-9359, 435-259-2599; www.aarchwayinn.com; 1151 N Hwy 191; r incl breakfast $204; ✳ 🛜 🏊) A boxy prefab with boutique prices. Sure, you could have a conga line in the giant standard bedrooms and family suites. There's also a huge swimming pool and a humongous parking lot to accommodate all-terrain toys. But for the price, you might prefer a more personal option.

Pack Creek Ranch
LODGE $$$

(☎ 888-879-6622; www.packcreekranch.com; off La Sal Mountain Loop Rd; cabins $175-235; 🐾🏊) This hidden Shangri-la's log cabins are tucked beneath mature cottonwoods and willow trees in the La Sal Mountains, 2000ft above Moab. Most feature fireplaces; all have kitchens and gas grills (bring groceries). No TV or phones. Ed Abbey is among the artists and writers who came here for inspiration. Amenities include horseback riding and an indoor hot tub and sauna.

Camping

In addition to the following local campgrounds, there's also camping in nearby national and state parks. Rafting outfitter Canyon Voyages rents tents and sleeping bags.

Up The Creek Campground
CAMPGROUND $

(☎ 435-260-1888; www.moabupthecreek.com; 210 E 300 South; tent sites 1/2 people $25/32; ⏱ Mar-Oct) There's something about this shady, tent-only grove with flower beds, lush lawns and recycling that fosters a sense of community. The 20 sites are within walking distance of downtown. Showers are included, but are also available to nonguests for $6; no fires.

Goose Island Campground
CAMPGROUND $

(www.blm.gov/utah/moab; Hwy 128; campsites $15) Ten no-reservation riverside BLM campgrounds lie along a 28-mile stretch of Hwy 128 that parallels the Colorado River northwest of town. The 19-site Goose Island, just 1.4 miles from Moab, is the closest. Pit toilets, no water.

Canyonlands Campground
CAMPGROUND $

(☎ 435-259-6848; www.canyonlandsrv.com; 555 S Main St; tent sites $27-34, RV sites with hookups $40-47, camping cabins $65; 🐾🏊) Old-growth tree-shaded sites, right in town but still quiet. Includes showers, laundry, store, small pool and playground. Rates are slightly higher for events and holidays.

Portal RV Resort
CAMPGROUND $

(☎ 435-259-6108; www.portalrvresort.com; 1261 N Hwy 191; tent sites $24, RV sites with hookups $36-42; 🐾🏊) The best place for a luxury RV, with long pull-throughs. Has showers, spa, laundry, store and dog run.

Slickrock Campground
CAMPGROUND $

(☎ 435-259-7660, 800-448-8873; www.slickrock-campground.com; 1301½ N Hwy 191; tent sites $26-34, RV sites with hookups $34-39, cabins $54; ⏱ Mar-Nov; 🐾🏊) North of town. Tent sites have canopies; RV sites have 30-amp hookups only. Nonguest showers cost $3; also has hot tubs, heated pool and a store.

Sand Flats Recreation Area
CAMPGROUND $

(www.discovermoab.com/sandflats.htm; Sand Flats Rd; tent & RV sites $10) At the Slickrock Bike trailhead, this mountain-biker special has 120 nonreservable sites, fire rings and pit toilets, but no water and no hookups.

✗ Eating

There's no shortage of places to fuel up in Moab, from backpacker coffeehouses to gourmet dining rooms. Pick up the *Moab Menu Guide* (www.moabmenuguide.com) at area lodgings. Some restaurants close earlier, or on variable days, from December through March.

★ Milt's
BURGERS $

(356 Mill Creek Dr; dishes $4-9; ⏱ 11am-8pm Mon-Sat) Meet greasy goodness. A triathlete couple bought this classic 1954 burger stand and smartly changed nothing. Heaven is one of their honest burgers, jammed with pickles, fresh lettuce, a side of fresh-cut fries and a creamy milkshake. Be patient: the line can get long. It's near the Slickrock Bike Trail.

★ Pantele's Deli
DELI $

(☎ 435-259-0200; 98 E Center St; sandwiches $8-10; ⏱ 11am-4pm Mon-Sat) Doing a brisk business, this deli makes everything fresh and it shows. Salads come in heaping bowls, and high-piled sandwiches are stuffed with fresh roasted turkey or roast beef cooked inhouse. The wait is worth it.

Love Muffin
CAFE $

(www.lovemuffincafe.com; 139 N Main St; dishes $6-8; ⏱ 7am-2pm; 🐾) Early-rising locals buy up many of the daily muffins – like the Breakfast Muffin, with bacon and blueberries. Not to worry, the largely organic menu at this vibrant cafe also includes creative sandwiches, breakfast burritos and inventive egg dishes such as the Verde, with brisket and slow-roasted salsa.

EklectiCafé
ORGANIC $

(352 N Main St; breakfast & sandwiches $9-11; ⏱ 7am-2:30pm Mon-Sat, to 1pm Sun; 🐾🍽) Soy-ginger-seaweed scrambled eggs anyone? This wonderfully quirky cafe lives up

to its eclectic name in food choice and decor. Come for organic coffee, curried wraps and vegetarian salads. Dinner is served some weekend evenings.

Miguel's Baja Grill   MEXICAN $$

(www.miguelsbajagrill.com; 51 N Main St; mains $14-26; ⏰5-10pm) Dine on Baja fish tacos and margaritas in the sky-lit breezeway patio lined with crayon-bright walls. Fajitas, chiles rellenos and seafood mains offer ample portions. For vegetarians, the portobello salad is excellent. And, yes, it does have margaritas.

Sabuku Sushi   JAPANESE, FUSION $$

(☑435-259-4455; www.sabukusushi.com; 90 E Center St; rolls $12-18, small plates $14-19; ⏰5-10pm Tue-Sun; ☑) Its name meaning 'desert' in Japanese, this sushi bar is hot with locals, who especially pile in for the sushi happy hour on Tuesdays and Thursdays (5pm to 6pm). On the menu are inventive vegetarian rolls and small plates such as elk *tataki* (like carpaccio, with an Asian twist). Has outdoor seating.

Jailhouse Café   BREAKFAST $$

(101 N Main St; breakfast $11-14; ⏰7am-noon Mar-Oct) The eggs Benedict here is hard to beat, but the line goes deep on weekends. Wholegrain waffles and ginger pancakes are other temptations. In a former jailhouse, with patio seating.

Singha Thai   THAI $$

(92 E Center St; mains $13-18; ⏰11am-3pm & 5-9:30pm Mon-Sat, plus 5-9:30pm Sun; ☑) Ethnic food is rare as rain in these parts, so locals pile into this authentic Thai cafe for curries and organic basil chicken. Service is sleepy and the ambience generic, but if you're hot for spice, it delivers. No bar.

Paradox Pizza   PIZZA $$

(☑435-259-9999; 729 S Main St; pizzas $14-23; ⏰shop 11am-10pm, delivery 4-10pm) You may want to order your scrumptious locally sourced and organically oriented pizzas to go; the dining area is kinda small and generic.

Moab Brewery   AMERICAN $$

(www.themoabbrewery.com; 686 S Main St; mains $10-22; ⏰11:30am-10pm Mon-Thu, to 11pm Fri & Sat) Choosing from the list of microbrews made in the vats just behind the bar area may be easier than deciding what to eat off the vast and varied menu. Be aware that service isn't their strong suit.

Pasta Jay's   ITALIAN $$

(☑435-259-2900; 4 S Main St; mains $13-17; ⏰11am-9pm) With shady outdoor patio seating and a kid's menu, Jay's serves huge portions of garlicky pasta served with hot homemade bread. Lunch specials are a bargain.

Zax   AMERICAN $$

(96 S Main St; breakfast $6-9, sandwiches $8-10, mains $16-22; ⏰7am-10pm) Dining out in Moab can get expensive, so locals load up at the all-you-can-devour soup, pizza and salad bar ($14) in this semi-generic American eatery.

Eddie McStiff's   AMERICAN $$

(59 S Main St; mains $10-20; ⏰11:30am-midnight, until 1am Fri & Sat) Though it's as much microbrewery-bar as restaurant, the burgers and pizzas (gluten-free available) are almost as popular as the beer here.

★ Desert Bistro   SOUTHWESTERN $$$

(☑435-259-0756; www.desertbistro.com; 36 S 100 West; mains $20-50; ⏰5:30-10pm Tue-Sun Mar-Nov) Stylized preparations of game and fresh, flown-in seafood are the specialty at this welcoming white-tablecloth restaurant inside an old house. Think smoked elk in a huckleberry glaze, pepper-seared scallops and jicama salad with crisp pears. Everything is made on site, from freshly baked bread to delicious pastries. Great wine list, too.

Jeffrey's Steakhouse   STEAK $$$

(☑435-259-3588; 218 N 100 West; mains $22-40; ⏰5-10pm) In a historic sandstone house, Jeffrey's is serious about beef, which comes grain-fed, wagyu-style and (only sometimes) in generous cuts. If the night is too good to end, head upstairs to the upscale Ghost Bar. Reservations advised.

Buck's Grill House   MODERN SOUTHWESTERN $$$

(1394 N Hwy 191; mains $20-42; ⏰5:30-9:30pm) Contemporary Southwestern specialties, such as duck tamales with adobo and elk stew with horseradish cream, are what Buck's does best (there are veggie options, too). Opt for white-tablecloth service in the restaurant, or a more casual evening in the bar.

Self-Catering

Moonflower Market   HEALTH FOOD $

(39 E 100 N; ⏰8am-8pm) Nonprofit health food store with loads of community info.

Moab Farmers Market   MARKET $

(www.moabfarmersmarket.com; 400 N 100 West; ⏰5-8pm Thu May-Oct) Local farms vend their summer produce in Swanny City Park.

ROCK FORMATIONS 101

The magnificent formations you see throughout southern Utah are created by the varying erosion of sandstone, mudstone, limestone and other sedimentary layers. When water freezes and expands in cracks it forms **fins**: thin, soaring, wall-like features like those in the Fiery Furnace at Arches. When portions of the rock break away underneath, an **arch** results. A **bridge** forms when water passes beneath sandstone, causing its erosion. But rivers dry up or change course, so it can sometimes become difficult to tell a bridge from an arch. **Hoodoos** are freestanding pinnacles that have developed from side-eroding fins; layers disintegrate at different rates, creating an irregular profile (often likened to a totem-pole shape).

Though they look stable, rock formations are forever in flux, and eventually they all break and disappear. As you stroll beneath these monuments to nature's power, listen carefully, especially in winter, and you may hear spontaneous popping noises in distant rocks – it's the sound of the future forming.

City Market & Pharmacy   MARKET $
(425 S Main St; ⊙6am-midnight) Moab's largest grocery store, with sandwiches and salad bar to go.

Drinking & Nightlife

The two local brewpub restaurants, Moab Brewery and Eddie McStiff's, are good places to drink as well as eat, and the latter often has live music.

Wake & Bake   CAFE
(59 S Main St, McStiff's Plaza; ⊙7am-7pm; 🛜) Great vibe at this groovy cafe next to a bookstore; ice cream and sandwiches available.

Dave's Corner Market   COFFEE SHOP
(401 Mill Creek Dr; ⊙6am-10pm) Sip shade-grown espresso with locals at the corner convenience store.

Woody's Tavern   BAR
(221 S Main St) Full bar with great outdoor patio; live music Friday and Saturday in season.

Ghost Bar   BAR
(218 N 100 West; ⊙7-11pm) A loungey, dime-sized jazz nook serving wine and a full list of cocktails; upstairs at Jeffrey's Steakhouse.

Red Rock Bakery & Cafe   CAFE
(74 Main St; internet per 30min $2; ⊙7am-6pm; 🛜) This tiny coffeehouse has tasty baked goods – and three internet terminals for web surfing.

☆ Entertainment

Canyonlands by Night & Day   DINNER SHOW
(☎435-259-5261, 800-394-9978; www.canyonlandsbynight.com; 1861 N Hwy 191; adult/child $69/59; ⊙Apr-Oct; 🚸) Start with dinner riverside, then take an after-dark boat ride on the Colorado, with an old-fashioned light show complete with historical narration.

Moab Arts & Recreation Center   CONCERT VENUE
(www.moabcity.state.ut.us/marc; 111 E 100 N) The rec center hosts everything from yoga classes to contra dance parties and poetry gatherings.

🛍 Shopping

Every few feet along downtown's Main St, there's a shop selling T-shirts and Native American–esque knickknacks, but there are some good galleries among the mix. From March to October most stores stay open until 9pm. Every second Saturday in spring and fall there's an evening art walk that includes artist's receptions; contact the **Moab Arts Council** (www.moabartscouncil.org) for more information.

Desert Thread   ARTS & CRAFTS
(www.desertthread.com; 29 E Center St; ⊙10am-5:30pm Mon-Sat) Pick up a gorgeous hand-knitted scarf or bag, or buy supplies to do it yourself.

Back of Beyond Books   BOOKS
(www.backofbeyondbooks.com; 83 N Main St; ⊙9am-6pm; 🛜) Excellent indie bookstore with extensive regional and natural history selection.

ℹ Information

EMERGENCY

Cell phones work in town, but not in canyons or the parks.

Grand County Emergency Coordinator
(☎435-259-8115) Search and rescue.

Police (☎911)

MEDICAL SERVICES

Moab Regional Hospital (☑435-259-7191; 719 W 400 N) For 24-hour emergency medical care.

TOURIST INFORMATION

BLM (Bureau of Land Management; ☑435-259-2100; www.blm.gov/utah/moab) Phone and internet info only.

Moab Information Center (www.discovermoab.com; cnr Main & Center Sts; ☺8am-7pm; ☎) Excellent source of information on area parks, trails, activities, camping and weather. Extensive bookstore and knowledgeable staff. Walk-in only.

WEBSITES

Moab Area Travel Council (www.discover-moab.com) Comprehensive online resource.

Moab Happenings (www.moabhappenings.com) Events listings.

ℹ Getting There & Around

Moab is 235 miles southeast of Salt Lake City, 150 miles northeast of Capitol Reef National Park, and 115 miles southwest of Grand Junction, Colorado.

Delta has regularly scheduled flights to **Canyonlands Airport** (CNY; www.moabairport.com; off Hwy 191), 16 miles north of town, from Salt Lake City. Major car-rental agencies have representatives at the airport. **Roadrunner Shuttle** (☑435-259-9402; www.roadrunnershuttle.com) and **Coyote Shuttle** (☑435-260-2097; www.coyoteshuttle.com) offer on-demand Canyonland Airport, hiker-biker and river shuttles.

Moab Luxury Coach (☑435-940-4212; www.moabluxurycoach.com) operates a scheduled van service to and from SLC (4¾ hours, $159 one-way) and Grand Junction, CO (two hours, $95 one-way), which also has a regional airport.

A private vehicle is pretty much a requirement to get around Moab and the parks.

Arches National Park

Giant sweeping arcs of sandstone frame snowy peaks and desert landscapes at Arches National Park, 5 miles north of Moab. Explore the highest density of rock arches anywhere on Earth: more than 2500 in a 116-sq-mile area. You'll lose all perspective on size at some, such as the thin and graceful Landscape Arch, which us among the largest in the world and which stretches more than 290ft across. The smallest is only 3ft across. An easy drive makes the spectacular arches accessible to all. Fiery Furnace is a not-to-be-missed area of the park, though a guided tour is required to reach it.

◉ Sights & Activities

The **park** (☑435-719-2299; www.nps.gov/arch; Hwy 191; 7-day pass per vehicle $10; ☺24hr; visitor center 7:30am-6:30pm Mar-Oct, 9am-4pm Nov-Feb) has many short hikes; the most popular stops lie closest to the visitor center. Crowds are often unavoidable, and parking areas overflow on weekends, spring to fall. In summer arrive by 9am, when crowds are sparse and temperatures bearable, or visit after 7pm and enjoy a moonlight stroll. July highs average 100°F (38°C); carry at least one gallon of water per person if hiking. Two rugged backroads lead into semi-solitude, but 4WD is recommended – ask at the visitor center.

Rock climbing is allowed only on un-named features. Routes require advanced techniques. No permits are necessary, but ask rangers about current regulations and route closures. For guided canyoneering into the Fiery Furnace, contact an outfitter in Moab.

There are also some fairly easy hikes here, too. Many quick walks lead to named formations, such as **Sand Dune Arch** (0.4-mile round-trip) and **Broken Arch** (1-mile round-trip).

Delicate Arch   HIKING

You've seen this arch before: it's the unofficial state symbol, stamping nearly every Utah tourist brochure in print. The best way to experience the arch is from beneath it. Park near **Wolfe Ranch**, a well-preserved 1908 pioneer cabin. From there a footbridge crosses **Salt Wash** (near Native American rock art) and marks the beginning of the moderate-to-strenuous, 3-mile round-trip trail to the arch itself. The trail ascends slickrock, culminating in a wall-hugging ledge before reaching the arch.

Tip: ditch the crowds by passing beneath the arch and continuing down the rock by several yards to where there's a great view, but fewer folks (bring a picnic). If instead you drive past the ranch to the end of the spur road, there's a 50yd paved path (wheelchair accessible) to the Lower Delicate Arch Viewpoint.

Windows Trail   HIKING

Tight on time? Do part or all of the easy 1-mile round-trip, which brings you up to **North Window**, where you can look out to the canyon beyond. Continue on to **South Window** and castle-like **Turret Arch**. Don't forget to see **Double Arch**, just across the parking lot.

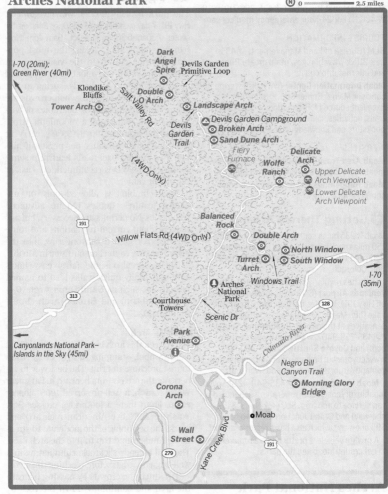

N
0 ——— 5 km
0 ——— 2.5 miles

I-70 (20mi);
Green River (40mi)

Dark Angel Spire

Devils Garden Primitive Loop

Klondike Bluffs

Salt Valley Rd

Double O Arch

Tower Arch

Landscape Arch

Devils Garden Campground

Devils Garden Trail

Broken Arch

Sand Dune Arch

(4WD Only)

Fiery Furnace

Wolfe Ranch

Delicate Arch

Upper Delicate Arch Viewpoint

Lower Delicate Arch Viewpoint

191

Balanced Rock

Willow Flats Rd (4WD Only)

Double Arch

North Window

Turret Arch

South Window

I-70 (35mi)

Arches National Park

Windows Trail

313

Courthouse Towers

Scenic Dr

128

Canyonlands National Park– Islands in the Sky (45mi)

Park Avenue

Colorado River

Negro Bill Canyon Trail

Morning Glory Bridge

Corona Arch

Moab

Kane Creek Blvd

Wall Street

279

191

Fiery Furnace HIKING

(adult/child $10/5; ⊙ Mar-Oct) Advance reservation is usually necessary for the three-hour, ranger-led Fiery Furnace hikes that explore the maze of spectacularly narrow canyons and giant fins. This is no walk in the park. (Well, it is, but...) Be prepared to scramble up and over boulders, chimney down between rocks and navigate narrow ledges. The effort is rewarded with a surprising view – an incredibly thin arch or soaring slot – around every turn. The ranger stops plenty of times to talk (and let hikers rest).

If you're an accomplished route-finder and want to go it alone, you must pay a fee, watch a video and discuss with rangers how to negotiate this confusing jumble of canyons before they'll grant you a permit. A few outfitters in Moab have permits to lead hikes here as well.

Devils Garden Trail HIKING

At the end of the paved road, 19 miles from the visitor center, Devils Garden trailhead marks the beginning of a 2- to 7.7-mile round-trip hike that passes at least eight arches. Most people only go the relatively easy 1.3 miles to **Landscape Arch**, a gravity-defying,

290ft-long behemoth. Further along, the trail gets less crowded, and grows rougher and steeper toward **Double O Arch** and **Dark Angel Spire**. The optional, difficult **Devils Garden Primitive Loop** has narrow-ledge walking and serious slickrock hiking. Ask rangers about conditions before attempting.

Scenic Driving Tour

The park's one main road snakes up ancient Navajo sandstone, past many trailheads and incredible formations, such as **Park Avenue**, a mile-long trail past a giant fin of rock reminiscent of a New York skyline, and **Balanced Rock**, a 3577-ton boulder sitting atop a spindly pedestal, like a fist shooting out of the earth. Don't miss the two small spur roads that veer off to the west (43 miles round-trip in total). Sights listed here are all along this drive; use the park map received on entry to navigate.

🛏 Sleeping & Eating

No food is available in the park. Moab is the place to stock up or dine out.

Devils Garden Campground   CAMPGROUND $
(☑ 877-444-6777; www.recreation.gov; tent & RV sites $20) Surrounded by red rock and scrubby piñons, the park's only campground is 19 miles from the visitor center. From March to October, sites are available by reservation. Book months ahead. Facilities include drinking water, picnic tables, grills and toilets, but no showers (for those, try a place in Moab). RVs up to 30ft are welcome, but generator hours are limited; no hookups.

ℹ Information

Cell phones do not work in most of the park.
Canyonlands Natural History Association (www.cnha.org) Sells area-interest books and maps online, and at national park visitor centers.
Grand County Emergency Coordinator (☑ 435-259-8115) Search and rescue coordinator.
Visitor Center (www.nps.gov/arch; 7-day pass per vehicle $10; ⊙ 24hr, visitor center 7:30am-6:30pm Apr-Oct, 8am-4:30pm Nov-Mar) Watch the informative video, check ranger-led activity schedules and pick up your Fiery Furnace tickets here.

ℹ Getting There & Around

One may be instituted eventually, but as yet the park has no shuttle system and no public buses so you pretty much need your own wheels. Several outfitters in Moab run motorized park tours. Moab Adventure Center and Adrift Adventures have scenic drive van tours; Tag-A-Long Expeditions ventures into the backcountry.

Green River

POP 949 / ELEV 4078FT

Hugging the interstate, Green River offers more utility than charm, but its cheap motels and uncrowded restaurants can be a relief if you're coming from Moab. It's also a useful base for boating the Green River or exploring parts of the San Rafael Swell.

The Colorado and Green Rivers were first explored in 1869 and 1871 by the legendary one-armed Civil War veteran, geologist and ethnologist John Wesley Powell. The town was settled in 1878, and now mainly relies on the limited tourism for income. Moab is 53 miles southeast. If you're passing through on the third weekend in September, be sure to attend the Melon Days festival – this is, after all, the 'world's watermelon capital.'

◎ Sights

Outside of town there's an unpredictable geyser, and fossil track sites; ask at the visitor center for directions.

John Wesley Powell River History Museum   MUSEUM
(☑ 435-564-3427; www.jwprhm.com; 885 E Main St; adult/child $6/2; ⊙ 8am-7pm Apr-Oct, to 4pm

---

WORTH A TRIP

SEGO CANYON

It's rare to see the rock art of three different ancient cultures on display all in one canyon, but that's precisely what you can do at Sego. On the south-facing wall, the Barrier Culture pictographs are the oldest (at least 2000 years old); the wide-eyed anthropomorphic creatures take on a haunted, ghostlike appearance to modern eyes. The Fremont petroglyphs were carved about 1000 years ago. Many of the line-art figures are wearing chunky ornamentation and headdresses (or is it antennae?). The third panel is from the 19th-century Native American Ute tribe; look for the horses and buffalo.

The canyon itself is 4 miles north of I-70 at Thompson Springs (41 miles north of Moab, 26 miles east of Green River). If you drive half a mile further north up the canyon, you come to a little ghost town. The few buildings here were deserted when a mining camp was abandoned in the 1950s.

UTAH GREEN RIVER

Nov-Mar) Learn about John Wesley Powell's amazing travels at this comprehensive museum, with a 20-minute film based on his diaries. It has good exhibits on the Fremont Indians, geology and local history.

Green River State Park PARK
(www.stateparks.utah.gov; Green River Blvd; per car $5; ⏰6am-10pm Mar-Oct, 8am-5pm Nov-Feb) Shady Green River State Park has picnic tables, a boat launch and a nine-hole golf course, but no trails.

🏃 Activities

White-water rafting trips are the most popular, but the Green River is flat between the town and the confluence of the Colorado River, making it good for floats and do-it-yourself canoeing. The current, however, is deceptively strong – swim only with a life jacket.

Holiday River Expeditions RAFTING
(☎800-624-6323, 435-564-3273; www.holidayexpeditions.com; 10 Holiday River St; day trip $165) Offers multiday rafting tours on the Green and Yampa Rivers and day trips through Westwater on the Green; themed trips (naturalist, women-only, mountain biking etc) are available.

WORTH A TRIP

HENRY MOUNTAINS

Southwest of Hanksville, the majestic **Henry Mountains** (11,500ft) were the last range to be named and explored in the lower 48. It's so remote that the area was famous as a hiding place for outlaws, such as Butch Cassidy. The range is home to one of the country's remaining free-roaming (and elusive) wild bison herds; you can expect pronghorn antelopes, mule deer and bighorn sheep as well. Exploring here is for serious adventurers only.

There are two main access roads: from Hanksville, follow 1100 East Street to the south, which becomes Sawmill Basin Rd; from Hwy 95, about 20 miles south of Hanksville, follow the Bull Mountain Scenic Backway west. Both are very rough and rocky dirt roads; flat tires are common and 4WD vehicles are highly recommended. Rangers patrol infrequently. Contact the BLM Field Office in Hanksville for more information.

Colorado River & Trail RAFTING
(☎801-261-1789, 800-253-7328; www.crateinc.com) Though based in Salt Lake City, this outfitter offers several Green River–launched rafting trips.

🛏 Sleeping

Midrange chain motels are surprisingly well represented along Business 70 (Main St).

Robbers Roost Motel MOTEL $
(☎435-564-3452; www.rrmotel.com; 325 W Main St; r from $38; ❄🛜🐕) A steal, with super clean rooms and accommodating staff. Small-and-simple budget rooms are well cared for.

Green River State Park CAMPGROUND $
(☎800-322-3770; http://utahstateparks.reserveamerica.com; tent/RV sites $18/25; cabin $60) Though the 42 green and shady campsites and a few cabins in this riverfront park are open year-round, the restrooms are closed December through February. Water, showers and boat launch on site; no hookups.

Shady Acres RV Park CAMPGROUND $
(☎435-564-8290, 800-537-8674; www.shadyacresrv.com; 350 E Main St; tent sites $20-33, RV sites $37-39, camping cabins $45; 🛜🐕) This 16-acre campground has lots of facilities: a playground, dog run, associated laundromat, internet cafe and sandwich shop.

River Terrace Inn MOTEL $$
(☎435-564-3401, 877-564-3401; www.river-terrace.com; 1880 E Main St; r $106-116; ❄🛜🐕) Ask for a riverfront room, with a terrace overlooking the water. Rooms are well-kept and the swimming pool is a godsend on hot days.

🍴 Eating & Drinking

Roadside stands sell fresh watermelons in summer.

Green River Coffee Co CAFE $
(115 W Main St; breakfast & lunch sandwiches $5-8; ⏰8am-2pm; 🛜) As the sign says, 'We're open when we're here.' Drop in and discuss politics with the local coffee circle, grab a sandwich on thick-sliced wheat bread peppered with veggies, or catch up on your used-book reading at this super-relaxed coffeehouse.

Melon Vine Food Store MARKET $
(76 S Broadway; ⏰8am-7pm Mon-Sat) Grocery store; deli sandwiches available.

Ray's Tavern BURGERS $$
(25 S Broadway; dishes $8-27; ⏰11am-9:30pm) Residents and rafters alike flock to this regionally

famous local beer joint for the best hamburgers and fresh-cut French fries around. The steaks aren't bad, either. Pass the time reading the displayed T-shirts donated by river runners from around the world, or have a game of pool with a Utah microbrew in hand.

ℹ Information

Emery County Visitor Center (☑ 435-564-3600, 888-564-3600; www.emerycounty.com/travel; 885 E Main St; ☺ 8am-8pm Mar-Oct, 8am-4pm Tue-Sun Nov-Feb) Attached to the local museum; pick up info and river guide books and maps here.

ℹ Getting There & Around

Green River is 182 miles southeast of SLC and 53 miles northwest of Moab. It is the only town of note along I-70 between Salina, UT (108 miles west), and Grand Junction, CO (102 miles east), so fuel up.

Amtrak (☑ 800-872-7245; www.amtrak.com; 250 S Broadway) Green River is the only stop in southeastern Utah on the daily California Zephyr train run. Next stop east is Denver, CO (from $59, 10¾ hours).

Greyhound (☑ 435-564-3421, 800-231-2222; www.greyhound.com; 525 E Main St, Rodeway Inn) Buses go to Grand Junction, CO ($36, one hour and 40 minutes).

Moab Luxury Coach (☑ 435-940-4212; www.moabluxurycoach.com; 525 E Main St, Rodeway Inn) Operates a scheduled van service to and from SLC ($149 one-way, 3½ hours) and Moab ($119 one-way, one hour).

Goblin Valley State Park & Around

A Salvador Dalí–esque melted-rock fantasy, a valley of giant stone mushrooms, an otherworldly alien landscape or the results of a cosmological acid trip? No matter what you think the stadium-like valley of stunted hoodoos resembles, one thing's for sure: the 3654-acre **Goblin Valley State Park** (www.stateparks.utah. gov; Goblin Valley Rd, off Hwy 24; per car $8; ☺ park 6am-10pm, visitor center 8am-5pm) is just plain fun. A few trails lead down from the overlooks to the valley floor, but after that there's no path to follow. You can climb down, around and even over the evocative 'goblins' (2ft to 20ft-tall formations) – kids, photographers and Lonely Planet writers especially love it. The park is 46 miles southwest of Green River.

A 19-site **campground** (☑ 800-322-3770; http://utahstateparks.reserveamerica.com; tent & RV sites $20; yurt $80) books up on most weekends. There are small shade shelters and picnic tables, as well as water and no-charge showers, but no hookups. The new 8-person yurts are popular, so reserve well ahead. West of the park off Goblin Valley Rd is BLM land, with good, free dispersed camping, but no services (stay on designated roads).

Twenty miles further south on Hwy 24 is **Hanksville** (population 350, elevation 4300ft); if you don't need gas, there's little reason to stop. It's better to stay in Green River, Torrey or at Lake Powell, depending on where you're headed. The **BLM Field Office** (☑ 435-542-3461; 380 S 100 West; ☺ 8:30am-4:30pm Mon-Fri) has maps and information for surrounding lands, particularly the Henry Mountains. Before continuing south, fill up your car and carry your own food and water. There are no more services until you get to Bullfrog Marina (70 miles) or Mexican Hat (130 miles).

Glen Canyon National Recreation Area & Lake Powell

In the 1960s the construction of a massive dam flooded Glen Canyon, forming Lake Powell, a recreational playground. Almost 50 years later this is still an environmental hot-button topic, but generations of Western families have grown up boating here. Water laps against stunning, multihued cliffs that rise hundreds of feet; narrow channels and tributary canyons twist off in every direction.

Lake Powell stretches for more than 185 miles, surrounded by millions of acres of desert incorporated into the **Glen Canyon National Recreation Area** (7-day pass per vehicle $15). Most of the watery way lies within Utah. However, Glen Canyon Dam itself, the main Glen Canyon National Recreation Area visitor center, the largest and most developed marina (Wahweap) and the biggest town on the lake (Page) are all in Arizona.

In Utah, primary access is 70 miles south of Hanksville; check in at the **Bullfrog Visitor Center** (☑ 435-684-7423; ☺ 9am-5pm May-Aug) for general info. At the end of the road, **Bullfrog Marina** (☑ 435-684-3000; www.lakepowell.com; Hwy 276; ☺ 9am-4pm Mar-Oct) rents out boats – 19ft runabouts ($400) and personal watercraft ($360) – by the day, but houseboats ($600) are its big business. You can rent a 46ft boat that sleeps 12 by the day or week. Invest in the waterproof *Lake Powell Photomap* ($12) so you can pilot your craft to some great canyon hikes.

Landlubbers can spend the night at the marina's waterfront **Defiance House Lodge** (☑ 435-684-3000; www.lakepowell.com; Hwy 276; r $129-159; ☺ Mar-Oct; ❀ ☎) and eat at **Anasazi Restaurant** (Hwy 276; breakfast $8-12, mains $10-28; ☺ 7am-8pm Mar-Oct). The restaurant serves pretty standard all-American fare, but it does try to use local produce and sustainable practices. Also on site: a small convenience store, marine fuel and trailer parking. The 24-space **Bullfrog RV Park & Campground** (☑ 435-684-3000; www.lakepowell.com; Hwy 276; RV sites $51; ☺ Mar-Oct; ☎) is lakeside, with full hookups, showers and grills.

Inland, 12 miles or so from the marina, are a couple of marine-service/gas-station/convenience-store/deli complexes. **Ticaboo Lodge** (☑ 435-788-2110; www.ticaboo.com; Hwy 276; r $70-90; ☺ May-Sep; ☎❀) is a sleeping alternative with a three-meal-a-day restaurant and bar attached.

To continue south along Hwy 276 you have to take the **ferry** (☑ 435-684-3088; www.lakepowell.com; pedestrian/cyclist/car $10/15/25; ☺ closed Dec-Feb) to Hall's Crossing. At the time of research, service was suspended for repairs. Usually the 30-minute trip has four crossings daily between 9am and 4pm, June to August; only two boats run between 9am and 2pm, March through May, and between 10am and 3pm September through November. The **Hall's Crossing marina** (☑ 435-684-7000; www.lakepowell.com; ☺ 8am-4pm Mar-Oct) has a store, boat launch, **campground** (tent & RV sites $49; ☺ Mar-Oct; ☎) and a great playground for kids.

At the time of writing Hite Marina remained closed due to low water levels.

ZION & SOUTHWESTERN UTAH

Wonder at the deep-crimson canyons of Zion National Park; hike among the delicate pink-and-orange minarets at Bryce Canyon; drive past the swirling grey-white-and-purple mounds of Capitol Reef. Southwestern Utah is so spectacular that the vast majority of the territory has been preserved as national park or forest, state park or BLM wilderness. Rugged and remote Grand Staircase–Escalante National Monument (GSENM) is larger than Rhode Island and Delaware put together. The whole area is ripe for outdoor exploration, with narrow slot canyons to shoulder through, pink sand dunes to scale and wavelike sandstone formations for you to seek out.

Several small towns, including artsy Springdale, service these parks. But do note that getting to some of the most noteworthy sites can be quite an uphill hike. Bear in mind that you'll average no more than 35mph to 50mph on scenic highways in the area. Elevation changes in the region – mountainous highs to desert lows – pose an additional weather challenge. In the end, any effort you make usually more than pays off with a stunning view of our eroding and ever-changing Earth.

Capitol Reef National Park

Native Americans once called this colorful landscape of tilted buttes, jumbled rocks and sedimentary canyons the Land of the Sleeping Rainbow. The park's centerpiece is Waterpocket Fold, a 100-mile-long monocline (a buckle in the Earth's crust) that blocked explorers' westward migration as a reef blocks a ship's passage. Known also for its enormous domes – one of which kinda sorta resembles Washington DC's Capitol Dome – Capitol Reef harbors fantastic hiking trails, rugged 4WD roads and 1000-year-old Fremont petroglyph panels. At the park's heart grow the shady orchards of Fruita, a Mormon settlement dating back to the 1870s.

The narrow park runs north–south following the Waterpocket Fold. A little over 100 miles southwest of Green River, Hwy 24 traverses the park. Capitol Reef's central region is the Fruita Historic District. To the far north lies Cathedral Valley, the least-visited section; toward the south you can cross over into Grand Staircase–Escalante National Monument on the Burr Trail Rd. Most services, including food, gas and medical aid, are in the town of Torrey, 11 miles west.

◉ Sights & Activities

There's no fee to enter or traverse the park in general, but the Scenic Drive has an admission fee. Remember that Capitol Reef has little shade. Drink at least one quart of water for every two hours of hiking and wear a hat. Distances listed for hiking are one-way. For backcountry hikes, ask for the information pamphlets at the visitor center or check online. Ranger Rick Stinchfield's *Capitol Reef National Park: The Complete Hiking and Touring Guide* is also a great reference.

Southwestern Utah

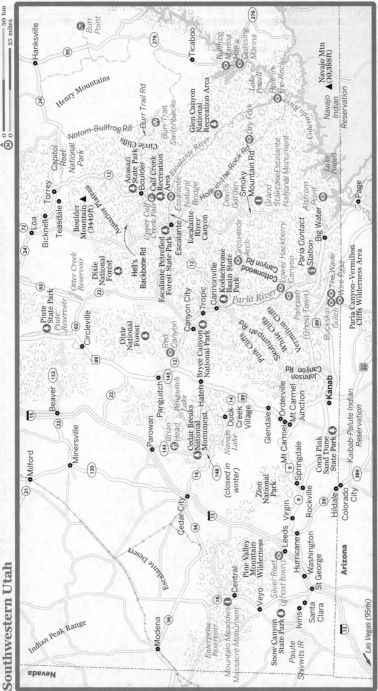

Capitol Reef National Park

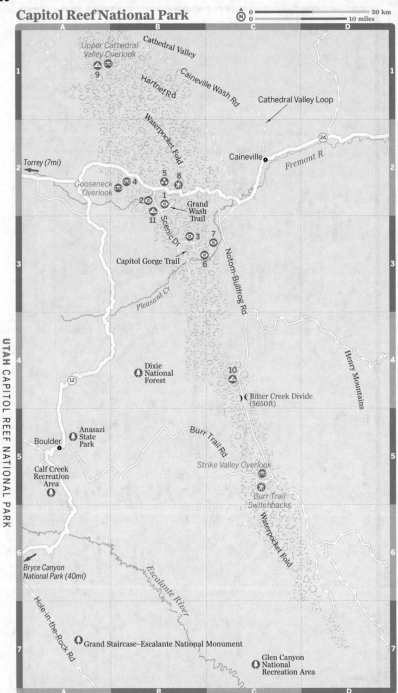

0 — 20 km
0 — 10 miles

Cathedral Valley

Upper Cathedral Valley Overlook
9

Hartnet Rd

Caineville Wash Rd

Cathedral Valley Loop

Waterpocket Fold

24

Caineville

Fremont R

Torrey (7mi)

Gooseneck Overlook
4
5 8
2 1
11
Grand Wash Trail

Scenic Dr

3 7
6
Capitol Gorge Trail

Notom-Bullfrog Rd

Pleasant Cr

Dixie National Forest

12

10
Bitter Creek Divide (5650ft)

Henry Mountains

Boulder

Anasazi State Park

Calf Creek Recreation Area

Burr Trail Rd

Strike Valley Overlook

Burr Trail Switchbacks

Waterpocket Fold

Bryce Canyon National Park (40mi)

Escalante River

Hole-in-the-Rock Rd

Grand Staircase–Escalante National Monument

Glen Canyon National Recreation Area

Capitol Reef National Park

Technical rock climbing is allowed without permits. Note that Wingate Sandstone can flake unpredictably. Follow clean-climbing guidelines, and take all safety precautions. For details, check with rangers or see www.nps.gov/care.

Petroglyphs　　　　ARCHAEOLOGICAL SITE
Just east of the visitor center on Hwy 24, look for the parking lot for freely accessible **petroglyphs**; these are the rock-art carvings that convinced archaeologists that the Fremont Indians were a group distinct from the Ancestral Puebloan. Follow the roadside boardwalk to see several panels.

Panorama Point & Gooseneck Overlook　　　　LOOKOUT
Two miles west of the visitor center off Hwy 24, a short, unpaved road heads to Panorama Point and Gooseneck Overlook. The dizzying 800ft-high viewpoints above serpentine Sulphur Creek are worth a stop. Afternoon light is best for photography.

Fruita Historic District　　　　HISTORIC SITE
(☑ fruit hotline 435-425-3791) Fruita (*froo*-tuh) is a cool, green oasis, where shade-giving cottonwoods and fruit-bearing trees line the Fremont River's banks. The first Mormon homesteaders arrived here in 1880; Fruita's final resident left in 1969. Among the historic buildings, the NPS maintains 2700 cherry, apricot, peach, pear and apple trees planted by early settlers. Visit between June and October to pluck ripe fruit from the trees, for free, from any unlocked orchard. For avail-

ability, ask rangers or call the **fruit hotline**. Pick only mature fruit; leave the rest to ripen.

Near the orchards is a wonderful **picnic area**, with roaming deer and birds in the trees – a desert rarity. Across the road from the blacksmith shop (just a shed with period equipment) is the **Ripple Rock Nature Center** (◎ noon-5pm daily Jun, 10am-3pm Tue-Sat Jul-Aug; ✦), a family-oriented learning center. The **Gifford Homestead** (◎ 8am-5pm Mar-Oct) is an old homestead museum where you can also buy ice cream, Scottish scones or salsas and preserves made from the orchard fruit. Don't skip purchasing one of their famous pies – up to 13 dozen are sold daily (and they usually run out!).

Scenic Drive　　　　DRIVING TOUR
(7-day pass per vehicle/person $5/3; ◎ 24hr) Pay admission at the visitor center or self-service kiosk to go beyond Fruita Campground on the 9-mile-long, paved Scenic Dr. Numbered roadside markers correspond to an interpretive driving tour available at the visitor center or online. The best part is the last 2 miles between the narrow sandstone walls of Capitol Gorge – it'll knock your socks off. To continue south past Pleasant Creek, a 4WD vehicle is advised.

Capitol Gorge Trail　　　　HIKING
At the end of Scenic Dr is Capitol Gorge Trail (1 mile, easy), which leads past petroglyphs. Spur trails lead to **Pioneer Register**, where names carved in the rock date back to 1871, and giant water pockets known as the **Tanks**. Look for the spur to the **Golden Throne** formation off Capitol Gorge Trail (another mile).

Grand Wash Trail　　　　HIKING
Also along Scenic Dr, a good dirt road leads to Grand Wash Trail (2.25 miles, easy), a flat hike between canyon walls that, at one point, tower 80 stories high but are only 15ft apart. You can follow an offshoot of level slickrock to the cool **Cassidy Arch** (2 miles) or continue further to link with other trails.

Hickman Bridge Trail　　　　HIKING
This popular walk (1 mile, moderate) includes a canyon stretch, a stunning natural bridge and wildflowers in spring. Mornings are coolest; it starts about 2 miles east of the visitor center off Hwy 24.

Notom-Bullfrog Rd　　　　DRIVING TOUR
This is a rough, rough road that heads south from Hwy 24 (5 miles east of the visitor

UTAH CAPITOL REEF NATIONAL PARK

MESA FARM MARKET

Dreaming of fresh greens, chèvre and crusty artisan bread? Stop by the desert oasis of **Mesa Farm Market** (☑ 435-487-9711; Hwy 24, Caineville; ⊙ 7am-7pm Mar-Oct) for organic salads, cinnamon rolls, French-style cheeses, sausages, home-grown organic coffee and fresh-squeezed juices. You might also glimpse the goats and meet the farmer. Note that hours do vary. It's about 23 miles east of Capitol Reef's visitor center, near Mile 102.

center) paralleling Waterpocket Fold. Thirty-two miles south, you can turn west toward Hwy 12 and Burr Trail Rd in Grand Staircase–Escalante National Monument. Along the way, **Strike Valley Overlook** has one of the best comprehensive views of the Waterpocket Fold itself. If you instead continue south, you're on the way to Lake Powell and Bullfrog Marina in Glen Canyon National Recreation Area, another 35 miles away.

Cathedral Valley Loop MOUNTAIN BIKING, DRIVING TOUR
(Caineville Wash Rd) Long-distance mountain bikers and 4WDers love this 58-mile route through Cathedral Valley, starting 18.6 miles east of the visitor center. The bumpy, rough-shod backcountry road explores the remote northern area of the park and its alien desert landscapes, pierced by giant sandstone monoliths eroded into fantastic shapes. Before starting, check conditions at the visitor center and purchase an interpretive route guide.

🛏 Sleeping & Eating

The nearest motel lodging and dining are in Torrey.

Free primitive camping is possible year-round at **Cathedral Valley Campground** (☑ 435-425-3791; www.nps.gov/care; cnr Hartnet & Caineville Wash Rds, 38 miles from visitor center; tent sites free; ⊙ year-round), at the end of River Ford Rd, and at **Cedar Mesa Campground** (☑ 435-425-3791; www.nps.gov/care; Notom-Bullfrog Rd, 23 miles south of Hwy 24; tent sites free; ⊙ year-round), about 23 miles south along Notom-Bullfrog Rd.

Fruita Campground CAMPGROUND $
(Scenic Dr; campsites $10) The terrific 71-site Fruita Campground sits under mature cottonwood trees alongside the Fremont River, surrounded by orchards. First-come, first-served

sites have access to water, but no showers. Spring through fall, sites fill up early.

❶ Information

Occasional summer thunderstorms pose a serious risk of flash flooding. Always check weather with rangers at the visitor center. Bugs bite in May and June. Summer temperatures can exceed 100°F (38°C) at the visitor center (5400ft), but it's cooler than Moab. If it's too hot, ascend to Torrey (10°F/6°C cooler) or Boulder Mountain (30°F/17°C cooler).

Visitor Center (☑ 435-425-3791; www.nps.gov/care; cnr Hwy 24 & Scenic Dr; ⊙ 8am-6pm Jun-Aug, 8am-4:30pm Sep-May) Inquire about ranger-led programs, watch the short film, then ooh and aah over the 64-sq-ft park relief map, carved with dental instruments. The bookstore sells several interpretive trail and driving tour maps (50¢ to $2) as well as area-interest books and guides.

❶ Getting Around

Capitol Reef has no public transportation system. Aside from Hwy 24 and Scenic Dr, park routes are dirt roads that are bladed only a few times a year. In summer you may be able to drive Notom-Bullfrog Rd and the Burr Trail in a regular passenger car. Remote regions like Cathedral Valley will likely require a high-clearance 4WD vehicle. Check weather and road conditions with rangers before heading out.

Bicycles are allowed on all park roads but not trails. Cyclists and hikers can arrange drop-off/pick-up shuttle services ($1 to $2 per mile) with Hondoo Rivers & Trails in Torrey.

Torrey

POP 180 / ELEV 6837FT

With shy pioneer charm and quiet streets backed by red-rock cliffs, Torrey is a relaxing stop. A former logging and ranching center, its mainstay now is outdoor tourism. Capitol Reef National Park is only 11 miles east, Grand Staircase–Escalante National Monument is 40 miles south and national forests surround the town. Summer brings a whiff of countercultural sophistication and great dining – but from November to February the town shuts down.

◉ Sights & Activities

Capitol Reef is the major area attraction, but there are other freely accessible public lands nearby. Many of the main street lodgings have Native American arts and crafts for sale in their 'trading posts.'

Fishlake National Forest   PARK
(www.fs.usda.gov/fishlake) More than 300 miles of trails cover the mountainous forest; 4WD roads lead north of town around **Thousand Lake Mountain** (11,306ft). Hwy 72, 17 miles west of town in Loa, is a paved route through the same area. **Fish Lake**, a giant trout fishery, is 21 miles northwest of Loa, off Hwy 25. Check with the **Fremont River/Loa Ranger District Office** (☑ 435-836-2811; www.fs.fed.us/r4/fishlake; 138 S Main St, Loa; ⊙ 9am-5pm Mon-Fri) for info.

Dixie National Forest   PARK
(www.fs.usda.gov/dixie) The expansive Dixie National Forest contains **Boulder Mountain** (11,317ft) to the south of Torrey. Nearby are numerous fishable lakes and streams, as well as campgrounds, hiking, biking and ATV trails. **Teasdale Ranger Station** (☑ 435-425-3702; 138 E Main St, Teasdale; ⊙ 9am-5pm Mon-Fri), 4 miles southwest, is the nearest source of information.

👉 Tours & Outfitters

Guides and outfitters cover the surrounding area well (Capitol Reef, national forest lands, Grand Staircase–Escalante National Monument and beyond). A half-day excursion runs from $90 to $225 per person.

Hondoo Rivers & Trails   ADVENTURE SPORTS
(☑ 800-332-2696, 435-425-3519; www.hondoo.com; 90 E Main St) One of southern Utah's longest-operating backcountry guides, Hondoo offers half- and full-day hiking and driving tours that cover slot canyons and rock art, multiday horseback trail rides, and raft-and-ride combo trips.

Capitol Reef Backcountry Outfitters   ADVENTURE SPORTS
(☑ 435-425-2010; www.backcountryoutfitters.com; 875 E Hwy) In addition to 4WD and hiking packages, Backcountry Outfitters also rents bicycles ($40 per day) and ATVs ($150 per day). Shuttles and guided bike, ATV and horseback rides are available, too.

Thousand Lakes RV Park   DRIVING TOUR
(☑ 435-425-3500, 800-355-8995; www.thousandlakesrvpark.com; 1110 W Hwy 24) Rents 4WD Jeeps from $130 per day.

Boulder Mountain Adventures & Alpine Angler's Flyshop   FISHING
(☑ 435-425-3660; www.alpineadventuresutah.com; 310 W Main St; daytrip fly-fishing $225) Guided fishing trips and multiday excursions that include both horseback riding and fishing.

🎇 Festivals

If you're here on the third weekend in July, don't miss the **Bicknell International Film Festival** (www.thebiff.org), just a couple miles up Hwy 24 in Bicknell. This wacky B-movie spoof on Sundance includes films, parties, a swap meet and the 'fastest parade in America.'

🛏 Sleeping

Camping is available in Capitol Reef National Park and in Dixie and Fishlake National Forests.

DON'T MISS

HWY 12

Arguably Utah's most diverse and stunning route, **Hwy 12 Scenic Byway** (www.scenicbyway12.com) winds through rugged canyonland, from near Capitol Reef southeast past Bryce Canyon – linking several national parks on a 124-mile journey. See how quickly and dramatically the land changes from wooded plateau to red-rock canyon, from slickrock desert to alpine forest, as it climbs over an 11,000ft mountain. Many consider the best section of the road to be the switchbacks and petrified sand dunes between Torrey and Boulder. Then again, the razor-thin Hogback Ridge between Escalante and Boulder is pretty stunning, too.

Pretty much everything between Torrey and Panguitch is on or near Hwy 12. Highlights include foodie-oriented eateries in tiny-tot Boulder; Lower Calf Creek Falls Recreation Area for a picnic; a hike in Grand Staircase–Escalante National Monument; and an incredible drive through arches and Technicolor red rock in Red Canyon. Take time to stop at the many viewpoints and pullouts, especially at Mile 70, where the Aquarius Plateau lords over giant mesas, towering domes, deep canyons and undulating slickrock, all unfurling in an explosion of color.

SCENIC DRIVES: SOUTHERN UTAH

People come from around the world to drive in southern Utah, and Hwy 12 and Burr Trail may be the biggest draws. But from paved desert highways for RV-cruisers to rugged backcountry trails for Jeepsters, there are drives for every taste.

Comb Wash Rd (near Bluff) Straddling Comb Ridge, Comb Wash Rd (or CR 235) is a dirt track that runs for about 20 miles between Hwys 163 and 95 (parallel to Hwy 191) west of Blanding and Bluff. Views are fantastic – bring binoculars – and the ridge contains numerous ancient cliff dwellings. High-clearance 4WD vehicles recommended; in wet weather, this road is impassable.

Colorado River Byway (near Moab) Hwy 128 follows the river northeast to Cisco, 44 miles away just off I-70. Highlights are Castle Rock, the 900ft-tall Fisher Towers, the 1916 Dewey Bridge (one of the first across the Colorado) and sightings of white-water rafters.

La Sal Mountain Loop Rd (near Moab) This road heads south into the Manti–La Sal forest from 15 miles north of Moab, ascending switchbacks (long RVs not recommended) into the refreshingly cool forest, with fantastic views. Connects with Hwy 191, 8 miles south of Moab. The 67-mile (three- to four-hour) paved loop closes in winter.

Loop-the-Fold (near Torrey) This 100-mile loop links several top drives; roughly half is on dirt roads generally accessible to 2WD passenger vehicles. Pick up a driving guide ($2) at the Capitol Reef National Park visitor center. West of the park are the rocky valleys of Hwy 12. It only gets better after turning east along Burr Trail Rd to Strike Valley Overlook. Then take the rough Notom-Bullfrog Rd north to finish the loop at Hwy 24.

Caineville Wash Rd (near Torrey) Just east of Capitol Reef National Park, turn north off Hwy 24 to the otherworldly monoliths like Temple of the Sun and Temple of the Moon on Caineville Wash Rd. Continue on into the northern part of the park and Glass Mountain, a 20ft mound of fused selenite. Two-wheel drive is usually fine for the first 15.5 miles. With a 4WD you can make this a 58-mile Cathedral Valley loop along Hartnet Rd, which fords the Fremont River just before rejoining Hwy 24.

Hell's Backbone Rd (near Boulder) The gravel-strewn 48 miles from Hwy 12 along Hell's Backbone Rd to Torrey is far from a shortcut. You'll twist, you'll turn, you'll ascend and descend hills, but the highlight is a single-lane bridge atop an impossibly narrow ridge called Hell's Backbone.

Hwy 14 (near Cedar City) This paved scenic route leads 42 miles over the Markagunt Plateau, ending in Long Valley Junction at Hwy 89. The road rises to 10,000ft, with splendid views of Zion National Park to the south. Make sure you detour at Cedar Breaks National Monument.

Broken Spur Inn
MOTEL $

(☑435-425-3398, 888-447-4676; www.brokenspurinn.com; 2523 E Hwy 24; r incl breakfast $79-125; ⊙Mar-Nov; ✱🛜🏊🐾) Among the red-rock cliffs east of town near Capitol Reef, this family-owned hilltop place offers remodeled, Western-themed motel rooms with superb sunset vistas (though the stuffed game in the lobby might make some cringe). There's a hot tub and pool. The on-site steakhouse is popular for dinner.

Austin's Chuckwagon Motel
MOTEL $

(☑435-425-3335; www.austinschuckwagonmotel.com; 12 W Main St; r $61-91, cabins $147; ⊙Mar-Oct; ✱🛜🏊🐾) Rustic wood buildings ring the pool and shady grounds here at the town center. Good-value-for-money motel rooms have sturdy, basic furnishings; cabins also have kitchens. The on-site general store, deli and laundromat are a bonus.

Torrey Trading Post
MOTEL $

(☑435-425-3716; www.torreytradingpost.com; 75 W Main St; cabins $40; 🛜) Bare-bones but dirt-cheap cabins with shared bathroom.

Sandcreek RV Park
CAMPGROUND $

(☑435-425-3577; www.sandcreekrv.com; 540 Hwy 24; tent sites/RV sites/cabins $15/30/35; 🐾) Friendly little campground with horseshoe pit, horse pasture ($5 per night) and laundry. Nonguest showers $5.

Thousand Lakes RV Park CAMPGROUND $
(☎435-425-3500, 800-355-8995; www.thousand-lakesrvpark.com; Hwy 24; tent/RV sites $18/33, camping cabins $35-95; ☻Apr-Oct; ☎☲) Twenty-two acres filled with facilities and services, including a heated swimming pool, playground, trading post gift shop, 4WD rental and evening cook-out dinners ($15 to $23). Morning muffins and hot coffee included.

★**Torrey Schoolhouse B&B** B&B $$
(☎435-633-4643; www.torreyschoolhouse.com; 150 N Center St; r incl breakfast $118-148; ☻Apr-Oct; ☀☎) Ty Markham has done an exquisite job of bringing this rambling 1914 schoolhouse back to life as a B&B. Antiques and country elegance contrast with the fascinating black-and-white photos of classes starting from a century back. After a full gourmet breakfast you might need to laze in the garden a while before hiking.

Skyridge Inn B&B $$
(☎435-425-3222, 877-824-1508; www.skyridgeinn.com; 950 E Hwy 24; r incl breakfast $119-169; ☀☎) Sitting on 75 acres, with gorgeous views of red rock from the porch, this country farmhouse provides a relaxing retreat one mile east of Torrey.

Muley Twist Inn B&B B&B $$
(☎435-425-3640, 800-530-1038; www.muleytwistinn.com; 249 W 125 South, Teasdale; r incl breakfast $99-150; ☻Apr-Oct; ☀☎) Set against a towering red-sandstone dome in a Teasdale neighborhood, this big wooden farmhouse with a wraparound verandah looks small. It isn't. Casual rooms at the down-to-earth inn are spacious and bright.

Pine Shadows Cabins BUNGALOW $$
(☎435-425-3939, 800-708-1223; www.pineshadowcabins.net; 195 W 125 South, Teasdale; cabins $110-154; ☀☲) Spacious, modern cabins (two beds and kitchenette) are sheltered among piñon pines at the end of the road, near trails.

Best Western Capitol Reef Resort MOTEL $$
(☎435-425-3761, 888-610-9600; www.bestwesternutah.com; 2600 E Hwy 24; r $108-142; ☀☎☲) Plain-Jane chain, with stunning red-cliff balcony views.

Lodge at Red River Ranch INN $$$
(☎435-425-3322, 800-205-6343; www.redriverranch.com; 2900 W Hwy 24, Teasdale; r incl breakfast $160-245; @☎) In the grand old tradition of Western ranches, the great room here has a three-story open-beam ceiling, timber walls and Navajo rugs. Details are flawless, from the country quilts on high-thread-count sheets to the cowboy memorabilia in the fine-dining room. Wander its 2000-plus acres, or enjoy the star-filled sky from the outdoor hot tub. No room TVs.

✖ Eating & Drinking

The nearest supermarket is 16 miles west, in Loa.

Slacker's Burger Joint BURGERS $
(165 E Main St; burgers $6-8; ☻11am-9pm Fri & Sat, to 8pm Mon-Thu, to 5pm Sun Mar-Oct) Order an old-fashioned burger (beef, chicken, pastrami or veggie), hand-cut fries (the sweet-potato version is delish) and thick milkshake (in a rainbow of cool flavors like cherry cordial), then enjoy – inside, or out at the picnic tables.

Rim Rock Patio PIZZA $
(2523 E Hwy 24; mains $8-10; ☻noon-11pm May-Oct) The best place in Torrey to drink beer also serves up good pizzas, salads, sandwiches and ice cream. Families and friends play darts or disc golf, listen to live bands and hang out.

Castle Rock Coffee & Candy CAFE $
(cnr Hwys 12 & 24; breakfast & sandwiches $4-8; ☻7am-5pm Mar-Oct; ☎) The coffeehouse that serves Utah-roast brews, bakes its own candy and banana bread, and blends up fruit smoothies now also serves breakfast and lunch. Try the Reuben sandwich.

Austin's Chuckwagon General Store MARKET $
(12 W Main St; ☻7am-10pm Apr-Oct) Sells camping supplies, groceries, beer and deli sandwiches to go.

★**Cafe Diablo** SOUTHWESTERN $$$
(☎435-425-3070; www.cafediablo.net; 599 W Main St; lunches $10-14, dinner mains $22-40; ☻11:30am-10pm mid-Apr–Oct; ☝) One of southern Utah's best, with outstanding, highly stylized Southwestern cooking, including vegetarian dishes that burst with flavor. Think stuffed poblano peppers with quinoa and red chile mole (a spicy sauce), Mayan tamales and fire-roasted pork tenderloin on a cilantro waffle. Book ahead; you don't want to miss this one.

Rim Rock Restaurant AMERICAN $$$
(2523 E Hwy 24; mains $18-29; ☻5-9:30pm Mar-Dec) Grilled steaks, pastas and fish come with a million-dollar view of red-rock cliffs. Arrive before sunset for the best show. Full bar.

WORTH A TRIP

BURR TRAIL ROAD

The region's most immediately gratifying, dramatic backcountry drive is a comprehensive introduction to southern Utah's geology. You pass cliffs, canyons, buttes, mesas and monoliths – in colors from sandy-white to deep coral red. Sweeping curves and steep up-and-downs add to the attraction. Just past the **Deer Creek trailhead** look for the towering vertical red-rock slabs of **Long Canyon**. Stop at the crest for views of the sheer **Circle Cliffs**, which hang like curtains above the undulating valley floor. Still snowcapped in summer, the **Henry Mountains** rise above 11,000ft on the horizon.

After 30 paved miles (1½ hours), the road becomes loose gravel as it reaches Capitol Reef National Park and the giant, angled buttes of hundred-mile-long **Waterpocket Fold**. The dramatic **Burr Trail Switchbacks** follow an original wagon route through this monocline. Be sure to see the switchbacks before returning to Boulder. Another option is to turn onto Notom-Bullfrog Rd and continue north to Hwy 24 (32 miles) near Torrey, or south to Glen Canyon and Lake Powell (35 miles). Note that this part of the route is rough, and not generally suited to 2WD.

Robber's Roost Books & Beverages CAFE
(185 W Main St; 8am-4pm Mon-Sat, 1-4pm Sun May-Oct;) Linger over a latte and a scone on comfy couches by the fire at this peaceful cafe-bookstore with bohemian bonhomie. Sells local-interest books and maps; also has three computer terminals (internet access per hour $5) and free wi-fi.

☆ Entertainment

Support the local arts scene by attending an **Entrada Institute** (www.entradainstitute.org; Sat Jun-Aug) event, such as an author reading or evening of cowboy music and poetry, at Robber's Roost Books & Beverages.

ℹ Information

Austin's Chuckwagon General Store has an ATM.
Sevier Valley Hospital (435-896-8271; 1000 N Main St, Richfield) The closest full hospital is 60 miles west on I-70.
Wayne County Travel Council (800-858-7951, 435-425-3365; cnr Hwys 24 & 12; noon-7pm Mon-Sat Apr-Oct) Friendly source of area-wide information.

ℹ Getting There & Around

Rural and remote, Torrey has no public transportation. Activity outfitters can provide hiker shuttles to the national park.

Boulder

POP 220 / ELEV 6703FT

A tiny slice of heaven and a great base to explore the surrounding desert wilderness. Until 1940, this isolated outpost received its mail by mule – it's still so remote that the federal government classifies it as a 'frontier community.' Its diverse population includes artists, ecologists, farmers and cowboys. Though only 32 miles south of Torrey on Hwy 12, you have to traverse 11,317ft-high Boulder Mountain to get here. Note that pretty much all services shut down November through March.

◉ Sights & Activities

Hikes in the northern area of Grand Staircase–Escalante National Monument are near here, but the national forest and BLM lands in the area are also good for hiking and backcountry driving. Burr Trail Rd is the most scenic drive, but Hell's Backbone has its thrills, too.

Anasazi State Park Museum MUSEUM
(www.stateparks.utah.gov; Main St/Hwy 12; admission $5; 8am-6pm Mar-Oct, 9am-5pm Nov-Apr) The pieced-back-together jars and jugs on display are just a few of the many thousands of pottery shards excavated. Today the petite museum protects the Coomb's Site, excavated in the 1950s and inhabited from AD 1130 to 1175. The minimal ruins aren't as evocative as some in southeastern Utah, but the museum is well worth seeing for the re-created six-room pueblo and excellent exhibits about the Ancestral Puebloan peoples. Inside is a seasonal information desk where you can talk to rangers and get backcountry road updates and backcountry permits.

Box–Death Hollow Wilderness Area PARK
(www.blm.gov) This ruggedly beautiful wilderness area surrounds Hell's Backbone Rd. A 16-mile backpack, **Boulder Mail Trail** follows the mule route the post used to take.

Dixie National Forest PARK
(www.fs.usda.gov/dixie) North of Boulder, the
Escalante District of this 2 million-square-
acre forest has trails and campgrounds, including a few up on Boulder Mountain.

👉 Tours & Outfitters

Earth Tours HIKING
(📞 435-691-1241; www.earth-tours.com; trips per person from $75; ⊗ Mar-Oct; 🐾) Founder of Earth
Tours and its main guide, PhD geologist Keith
Watt has an enthusiasm for the area that is
catching. Choose from among the numerous
half- and full-day area hikes offered or take a
4WD trip into the backcountry.

Escalante Canyon Outfitters HIKING
(ECO; 📞 888-326-4453, 435-691-3037; www.
ecohike.com; 2520 S Lower Deer Creek Rd; ⊗ Mar-
Nov) Started by cofounder of the Southern
Utah Wilderness Alliance Grant Johnson,
ECO has well-regarded multiday treks with
canyonland or archaeological-site focus.

Hell's Backbone
Ranch & Trails HORSEBACK RIDING
(📞 435-335-7581; www.bouldermountaintrails.
com; off Hell's Backbone Rd; half-day $90) Head
across the slickrock plateau, into Box–Death
Hollow Wilderness or up the forested mountain on two-hour to full-day area horseback
rides. Or perhaps you'd prefer a multiday
camping trip or cattle drive?

🛌 Sleeping

Pole's Place MOTEL $
(📞 435-335-7422, 800-730-7422; www.polespla-
ceutah.com; Hwy 12; r $76-85; ⊗ late Mar-Oct; 🐾)
Run by a fourth-generation local, this nicely
kept motel has quiet, decent rooms without
wi-fi. There are local menus and historical
news clippings to peruse in each room. Limited TV.

★ Boulder Mountain Lodge LODGE $$
(📞 435-335-7460; www.boulder-utah.com; 20
N Hwy 12; r $135-295; 🐾@🐾🐾) Watch the
birds flit by on the adjacent 15-acre wildlife
sanctuary and stroll through the organic
garden – Boulder Mountain Lodge has a
strong eco-aesthetic. It's an ideal place for
day-hikers who want to return to high-
thread-count sheets, plush terry robes, spa
treatments and an outdoor hot tub. The
onsite Hell's Backbone Grill is a southern
Utah must-eat.

Boulder Mountain Guest Ranch LODGE $$
(📞 435-335-7480; www.bouldermountaingues-
tranch.com; off Hell's Backbone Rd; r $80-115,
cabins $115-125, tipi $55; 🐾🐾) In a peaceful
160-acre wilderness with trails, a waterfall
and outfitter-led hikes and activities. Think
rustic, with a happy hippie vibe. Bunk and
queen rooms in the giant log lodge enjoy a
communal atmosphere; out-cabins are more
private. The dining room has chef-cooked
meals at breakfast and dinner using garden
produce.

🍴 Eating

Hills & Hollows Country Store MARKET $
(Hwy 12; ⊗ 9am-7pm, gas 24hr) Groceries and
organic snacks available year-round, though
hours may be limited November through
February.

★ Burr Trail Grill
& Outpost MODERN SOUTHWESTERN $$
(www.burrtrailgrill.com; cnr Hwy 12 & Burr Trail Rd;
dishes $8-18; ⊗ grill 11:30pm-9:30pm, outpost
8:30am-6pm Mar-Oct; 🐾) The organic vegetable
tarts and eclectic burgers (plus scrumptious
homemade cookies and cakes) at the Grill
rival the more famous restaurant next door.
We like the homey vibe here, where locals
come to chat-and-chew or celebrate friends'
birthdays. It's worth browsing the Outpost
art gallery, gift shop and coffeehouse.

★ Hell's Backbone Grill SOUTHWESTERN $$$
(📞 435-335-7464; www.hellsbackbonegrill.com;
20 N Hwy 12, Boulder Mountain Lodge; breakfast
$8-12, lunch $12-18, dinner $18-27; ⊗ 7:30-11:30am
& 5-9:30pm Mar-Nov) Soulful, earthy preparations of Southwestern dishes include
locally-raised meats and organically grown
produce from their garden. Zen Buddhist
owners Jen Castle and Blake Spalding feed
not only the stomach but the community,
training staff in mindfulness and inviting
the whole town to a 4th of July ice-cream
social and talent show. Dinner reservations
are a must. Save room for the Chimayo-chile
ginger cake with butterscotch sauce.

ℹ Information
The tiny town has no visitor center, but info is
available online at www.boulderutah.com.
Boulder Interagency Desk (📞 435-335-7382;
Hwy 12, Anasazi State Park Museum; ⊗ 9am-
5pm mid-Mar–mid-Nov) BLM and other public-
land trail and camping information.

Escalante

POP 783 / ELEV 5820FT

Your gateway to the north side of the GSENM, Escalante is a mix of ranchers, old-timers, artists and post-monument-creation outdoors lovers. The town itself doesn't exude character, but a friendly selection of lodgings and restaurants make it a decent base camp. Numerous outfitters make this their base for hiking excursions, and you could, too. At the head of several park backroads, it's not far from the most popular GSENM hikes. Escalante is 28 miles south of Boulder, roughly halfway between Capitol Reef (76 miles) and Bryce Canyon (50 miles).

◎ Sights

The Monument is the biggest attraction in the area; hikes off Hwy 12 and Hole-in-the-Rock Rd are within 12 to 30 miles' drive.

Escalante Petrified Forest State Park PARK
(www.stateparks.utah.gov; day use $8; ⊙day use 8am-10pm) Two miles west of town, the centerpiece of this state park is a 130-acre lake. Hike uphill about a mile on an interpretive route to see pieces of colorful petrified wood, millions of years old. Follow another short interpretive trail for further examples. The sites at the **campground** (☑800-322-3770; http://utahstateparks.reserveamerica.com; tent & RV sites with/without hookups $19/25; 🖳🐾) can be reserved; showers available.

Gallery Escalante GALLERY
(www.galleryescalante.com; 425 W Main St; admission free; ⊙9am-8pm) **FREE** An artist-owned local art gallery.

DON'T MISS

KIVA KOFFEEHOUSE

Just past the Aquarius Plateau at Mile 73 on Hwy 12, you reach the singular **Kiva Koffeehouse** (☑435-826-4550; www.kivakoffeehouse.com; Hwy 12, Mile 73; dishes $4-9; ⊙8am-4:30pm Wed-Mon Apr-Oct), whose round structure was built directly into the cliffside. Floor-to-ceiling glass windows, separated by giant timber beams, overlook the expansive canyons beyond. Besides serving barista coffee and yummy baked goods, Kiva also rents two cushy hideaway **cottage rooms** (r $190; 🛜) with whirlpool tubs and fireplaces – and the same stellar views.

☞ Tours & Outfitters

Escalante Outfitters & Cafe ADVENTURE SPORTS
(☑435-826-4266; www.escalanteoutfitters.com; 310 W Main St; natural history tours $45; ⊙8am-9pm) A traveler's oasis, this store and cafe sells area books, topographic maps, camping and hiking gear, liquor, espresso, breakfasts and pizza. Guided fly-fishing trips (from $250 per day) and natural-history tours are available. It also rents out tiny, rustic cabins ($45) and mountain bikes (from $35 per day).

Excursions of Escalante ADVENTURE SPORTS
(☑800-839-7567; www.excursionsofescalante.com; 125 E Main St; full-day from $150; ⊙8am-6pm) For area canyoneering and climbing trips, Excursions is best; offers hiker shuttles and guided photo hikes. At the time of writing, its outfitter store and cafe was under reconstruction.

Escape Goats ADVENTURE SPORTS
(☑435-826-4652; www.escapegoats.us; slot canyons from $110) Take an evening tour or day-hike to dinosaur tracks, slot canyons and ancient sites. Supplies for multiday catered pack-trips are carried by goats. Yes, goats.

Utah Canyons ADVENTURE SPORTS
(☑435-826-4967; www.utahcanyons.com; 325 W Main St; slot canyon hikes from $110) Guided day hikes, multiday supported treks, hiker shuttles and a small outdoors store.

🛏 Sleeping

For a full list of area motels, B&Bs and rentals, check out www.escalante-cc.com.

Circle D Motel MOTEL $
(☑435-826-4297; www.escalantecircledmotel.com; 475 W Main St; r $84-90, ste $112; 🖳🛜🐾) We love the little library of guidebooks and hiking information in the rooms. The friendly proprietor goes out of his way to accommodate guests at this partially updated, older motel. Room microwaves and minifridges are standard.

Canyons Bed & Breakfast B&B $$
(☑866-526-9667, 435-826-4747; www.canyonsbnb.com; 120 E Main St; r incl breakfast $135-165; 🖳🛜) Upscale cabin-rooms with porches surround a shaded terrace and gardens where you can enjoy your gourmet breakfast each morning. Except for a small dining area, the wooden 1905 ranch house on-site is private.

Rainbow Country Bed & Breakfast B&B $$
(☑435-826-4567, 800-252-8824; www.bnbescalante.com; 586 E 300 S; r incl breakfast $74-134;

READER ALL ABOUT IT

The otherworldly beauty of Utah has moved many to words almost as eloquent as the nature itself.

Edward Abbey (1927–89) Abbey became intimate with Arches National Monument when he worked there in the 1950s as a seasonal ranger, prenational park. Environmentalist? Anarchist? It's hard to pin Abbey down. Many of his excellent essay collections are set (in part) in Utah. Start with *Desert Solitaire: A Season in the Wilderness*.

Everett Ruess (1914–34) Artist, poet, writer and adventurer, Everett Ruess set out on his burro into the desert near the Escalante River Canyon at 20 years old, never to be seen again. He left behind scores of letters that paint a vivid portrait of life in canyon country before humans and machines. Pick up a copy of *Everett Ruess: A Vagabond for Beauty*, which includes his letters and an afterword by Edward Abbey.

Craig Childs (b 1967) You'll never see a slot canyon in the same light again after reading the heart-thumping account of flash floods in *Secret Knowledge of Water*, a travelogue that follows naturalist Childs' Utah desert hikes. His *House of Rain* explores ancient ruins in the Four Corners area.

Terry Tempest Williams (b 1955) Born and raised in Utah, Tempest Williams has been both poet and wilderness advocate. In addition to *Red*, an essay collection focused on southeastern Utah, check out *Refuge*, a lyrical elegy for her mother and the Great Salt Lake.

Wallace Stegner (1909–93) A graduate of the University of Utah, Stegner became one of the classic writers of the American West. *Mormon Country* provides an evocative account of the land the Mormons settled and their history; *The Big Rock Candy Mountain* is historical fiction that follows a couple's prosperity-seeking moves to Utah.

Tony Hillerman (1925–2008) Landscape and lore are always woven into Hillerman's whodunits, which take place on Navajo tribal lands similar to those in Utah and New Mexico around Monument Valley.

Mark Sundeen (b 1970) His nonfiction portrait of Daniel Suelo in *The Man Who Quit Money* explores the fascinating life and choices of a Moab resident who rejected the concept of money in 2009 and moved to area caves, where he remains.

⟨✷ 🛜⟩) You couldn't ask for better trail advice than what you receive over big home-cooked breakfasts here. The split-level house on the edge of town is not flashy, just comfortable and homey – with a big TV lounge (no room TVs), guest refrigerator and outdoor hot tub.

🍴 Eating

Griffin Grocery MARKET **$**
(30 W Main St; ⊙8am-7pm Mon-Sat) The only grocery in town.

Esca-Latte Cafe & Pizza PIZZA **$$**
(310 W Main St; breakfast $3-6, pizza $12-22; ⊙8am-9pm Mar-Oct; 🛜) A tiny cafe turning out espresso drinks and decent quick bites. There's granola and quiche at breakfast, and tasty homemade pizza and beer. If you're hiking, you'll wish you had brought along one of their monster cinnamon buns.

Circle D Eatery AMERICAN **$$**
(475 W Main St; mains $9-19; ⊙7am-9:30pm, limited hours Nov-Feb) With attentive service and satisfying burgers with local beef on fresh jalapeno buns and shoestring fries. Smoked meats are a specialty, but there's also pastas, salads and hearty breakfasts.

Cowboy Blues AMERICAN **$$**
(530 W Main St; sandwiches & mains $9-22; ⊙11:30am-10pm) Family-friendly meals here include BBQ ribs, steaks and daily specials like burritos or meatloaf. Has a full bar.

ℹ️ Information

There's no town visitor center; check out www.escalante-cc.com. The nearest hospital is 65 miles west in Panguitch.

Escalante Interagency Office (📞435-826-5499; www.ut.blm.gov/monument; 775 W Main St; ⊙8am-4:30pm daily Apr-Sep, Mon-Fri Oct-Mar) *Information* about area public lands; jointly operated by the BLM, the USFS and NPS.

Grand Staircase– Escalante National Monument

Nearly twice the size of Rhode Island, the 1.9-million-acre Grand Staircase–Escalante National Monument (GSENM; ☑ 435-826-5499; www.ut.blm.gov/monument; ☉24hr) FREE is the largest park in the Southwest and has some of the least visited – yet most spectacular – scenery. Its name refers to the 150-mile-long geological strata that begins at the bottom of the Grand Canyon and rises, in stair steps, 3500ft to Bryce Canyon and Escalante River Canyon. Together the layers of rock reveal 260 million years of history in a riot of colors. Sections of the GSENM have so much red rock that the reflected light casts a pink hue onto the bottom of clouds above.

Established amid some local controversy by President Bill Clinton in 1996, the monument is unique in that it allows some uses that would be banned in a national park (such as hunting and grazing, by permit), but allows fewer uses than other public lands to maintain its 'remote frontier' quality. Tourist infrastructure is minimal and limited to towns on the park's edges. Hwy 12 skirts the northern

---

> ### ❶ BACKROADS SAFETY TIPS
>
> Heading off-trail requires significant route-finding skills; GPS proficiency isn't enough. Know how to use a compass and a topographical map, or risk getting lost. Always check with rangers about weather and road conditions before driving or hiking – after heavy rain or snow, roads may be impassable, even with a 4WD. Some other tips:
>
> ➡ Slot canyons and washes are flash-flood prone. If it starts to rain while you're driving, stop. Storms pass and roads dry quickly, sometimes even within 30 minutes.
>
> ➡ Never park in a wash.
>
> ➡ Carry a gallon of water per person, wear a hat and sunscreen, and carry food, maps and a compass. In an emergency, help will be hard to find.
>
> ➡ Avoid walking on biological soil crusts (the chunky black soil that looks like burnt hamburger meat) – it fixes nitrogen into the ground, changing sand to soil.

---

boundaries between Boulder, Escalante and Tropic. Hwy 89 arcs east of Kanab into the monument's southwestern reaches.

The park encompasses three major geological areas. The Grand Staircase is in the westernmost region, south of Bryce Canyon and west of Cottonwood Canyon Rd. The Kaiparowits Plateau runs north–south in the center of the monument, east of Cottonwood Canyon Rd and west of Smoky Mountain Rd. Canyons of the Escalante lie at the easternmost sections, east of Hole-in-the-Rock Rd and south of the Burr Trail, adjacent to Glen Canyon National Recreational Area.

❍ Sights & Activities

The BLM puts out handy one-page summaries of the most-used day trails. GSENM is also filled with hard-core backcountry treks. Ask rangers about Coyote Gulch (off Hole-in-the-Rock Rd); Escalante River Canyon, Boulder Mail Trail, and the Gulch, off the Burr Trail. Falcon Guide's *Hiking Grand Staircase–Escalante* is the most thorough park-hiking handbook, but we like the more opinionated *Hiking From Here to Wow: Utah Canyon Country*, with great details and color photographs. The waterproof Trails Illustrated/National Geographic map *No 710 Canyons of the Escalante* is good, but to hike the backcountry you'll need USGS 7.5-minute quadrangle maps. Pick these up at any visitor center.

Devils Garden   HIKING
(Mile 12, Hole-in-the-Rock Rd; 🏃) Easy hikes are scarce in GSENM – the closest thing is a foray into Devils Garden, where rock fists, orbs, spires and fingers rise 40ft above the desert floor. A short walk from the car leads to giant sandstone swirls and slabs. From there you have to either walk in the sand or over, among and under the sandstone – like you're in a giant natural playground.

Lower Calf Creek   PARK
(Mile 75, Hwy 12; day use $5; ☉day use dawn-dusk) The most popular and accessible hike lies halfway between Torrey and Boulder. This sandy, 6-mile round-trip track skirts a year-round running creek through a spectacular canyon before arriving at a 126ft waterfall – a joy on a hot day. Pick up the interpretive brochure to help spot ancient granary ruins and pioneer relics.

Escalante Natural Bridge Trail   HIKING
(Hwy 12, 15 miles east of Escalante) Be ready to get your feet wet. You'll crisscross a stream

seven times before reaching a 130ft-high, 100ft-long natural bridge and arch beyond (4.4 miles round-trip).

Upper Calf Creek Falls Trail HIKING
(Hwy 12, btwn Mile 81 & 82) A short (2.2 miles round-trip) but steep and strenuous trail leads down slickrock and through a desert moonscape to two sets of pools and waterfalls, which appear like a mirage at hike's end.

Dry Fork Slot Canyons HIKING
(Mile 26, Hole-in-the-Rock Rd) A remote but popular Hole-in-the-Rock Rd hike leads to four different slot canyons, complete with serpentine walls, incredible narrows and bouldering obstacles. **Dry Fork** is often overlooked as not tight or physically challenging enough, but it's our favorite. You can walk for miles between undulating orange walls, with only a few small boulder step-ups. To get into dramatic **Peekaboo**, you have to climb up a 12ft handhold-carved wall (much easier if you're tall or not alone).

Even narrower **Spooky Gulch** may be too small for some hikers. The farthest, **Brimstone Gulch**, is also the least interesting. Ask rangers for directions and always return the way you came. Climbing up and out of slots, then jumping down the other side, may trap you below the smooth face you've descended.

Cottonwood Canyon Rd DRIVING TOUR
(off Hwys 12 & 89) This 46-mile scenic backway heads east, then south, from Kodachrome Basin State Park, emerging at Hwy 89 near Paria Canyon–Vermilion Cliffs Wilderness Area. It's the closest entry into GSENM from Bryce and an easy (though sometimes rough) drive, passable for 2WD vehicles (RVs not recommended). Twenty miles south of Hwy 12 you'll reach **Grosvenor Arch**, a yellow-limestone double arch, with picnic tables and restrooms.

The road continues south along the west side of the **Cockscomb**, a long, narrow monocline in the Earth's crust. The Cockscomb divides the Grand Staircase from Kaiparowits Plateau to the east; there are superb views. The most scenic stretch lies between Grosvenor Arch and **Lower Hackberry Canyon**, good for hiking. The road then follows the desolate Paria River valley toward Hwy 89.

Hole-in-the-Rock Rd DRIVING TOUR
(off Hwy 12) From 1879 to 1880, more than 200 pioneering Mormons followed this route on their way to settle southeastern Utah. When the precipitous walls of Glen Canyon on the Colorado River blocked their path, they blasted and hammered through the cliff, creating a hole wide enough to lower their 80 wagons through – a feat honored by the road's name today. The final part of their trail lies submerged beneath Lake Powell. History buffs should pick up Stewart Aitchison's *Hole-in-the-Rock Trail* for a detailed account.

The history is often wilder than the scenery along much of this 57-mile, dusty washboard of a road, but it does have several sights and trailheads. The road is passable to ordinary passenger cars when dry, except for the last, extremely rugged 7 miles, which always require 4WD. The road stops short of the actual **Hole-in-the-Rock**, but hikers can trek out and scramble down past the 'hole' to **Lake Powell** in less than an hour. Sorry, no elevators for the climb back up.

Skutumpah & Johnson Canyon Rds DRIVING TOUR
The most westerly route through the monument, the unpaved Skutumpah Rd (scoot‐em‐paw) heads southwest from Cottonwood Canyon Rd near Kodachrome Basin State Park. First views are of the southern end of Bryce Canyon's **Pink Cliffs**. A great little slot-canyon hike, accessible to all, is 6.5 miles south of the turnoff at **Willis Creek**.

After 35 miles (two hours), Skutumpah Rd intersects with the 16-mile paved Johnson Canyon Rd, and passes the **White Cliffs** and **Vermilion Cliffs** areas en route to Hwy 89 and Kanab. Four-wheel drive is recommended; ask GSENM rangers about current conditions.

Tours & Outfitters

Outfitters and guide services that operate in GSENM are based in Boulder, Escalante, Torrey and Kanab.

Sleeping & Eating

Most sleeping and eating is done in Escalante, Boulder or Kanab. The GSENM website lists suggested areas for free dispersed camping. Pick up the required permit at a visitor center.

Remember: water sources must be treated or boiled, campfires are permitted only in certain areas (use a stove instead), and biting insects are a problem in spring and early summer. Watch for scorpions and rattlesnakes.

There are two developed campgrounds in the northern part of the monument.

Calf Creek Campground CAMPGROUND $
(www.ut.blm.gov; Hwy 12; tent & RV sites $10) Beside a year-round creek, Calf Creek Campground is surrounded by red-rock canyons (hot in summer) and has 14 incredibly popular, nonreserveable sites, and drinking water available; no hookups. The campground is near the trailhead to Lower Calf Creek Falls, 15 miles east of Escalante.

Deer Creek Campground CAMPGROUND $
(www.ut.blm.gov; Burr Trail Rd; tent sites $10; ☺mid-May–mid-Sep) This campground, 6 miles southeast of Boulder, has few sites and no water, but does have pit toilets. It sits beside a year-round creek beneath tall trees.

❶ Information

Food, gas, lodging and other services are available in Boulder, Escalante, Torrey and Kanab. For more information about the Monument, consult the Escalante Interoffice Agency (p429).

Big Water Visitor Center (☑435-675-3200; 100 Upper Revolution Way, Big Water; ☺9am-6pm Apr-Oct, 8am-5pm Nov-Mar) Near Lake Powell.

Cannonville Visitor Center (☑435-826-5640; 10 Center St, Cannonville; ☺8am-4:30pm Apr-Oct) Five miles east of Tropic.

Grand Staircase–Escalante Partners (www.gsenm.org) Volunteer opportunities.

Kanab Visitor Center (☑435-644-4680; 745 E Hwy 89, Kanab; ☺7:30am-5:30pm) Park headquarters in the southwestern section.

❶ Getting Around

There is no public transportation in the park. High-clearance 4WD vehicles allow you the most access, since many roads are unpaved and only occasionally bladed. (Most off-the-lot SUVs and light trucks are not high-clearance vehicles.) Heed all warnings about road conditions. Remember to buy gasoline whenever you see it.

Some outfitters in towns around the park have hiker shuttles or 4WD rentals. However, if you plan to do a lot of backroad exploring and are arriving via Las Vegas, it may be cheaper overall to rent from there.

Kodachrome Basin State Park

Petrified geysers and dozens of red, pink and white sandstone chimneys – some nearly 170ft tall – resemble everything from a sphinx to a snowmobile at Kodachrome Basin (☑435-679-8562; www.stateparks.utah.gov; off Cottonwood Canyon Rd; day use per vehicle $8; ☺day use 6am-10pm). The park lies off Hwy 12, 9 miles south of Cannonville and 26 miles southeast of Bryce Canyon National Park. Visit in the morning or afternoon, when shadows play on the red rock.

Most sights are along hiking and mountain-biking trails. The moderately easy, 3-mile round-trip Panorama Trail gives the best overview. Be sure to take the side trails to Indian Cave, where you can check out the handprints on the wall (from 'cowboys' or 'Indians'?), and Secret Passage, a short hike through a narrow slot canyon. Angel Palace Trail (1-mile loop, moderate) has great desert views from on high. Red Canyon Trail Rides (p435), based near Bryce, offers horseback rides.

The 26 well-spaced sites at the reservable park service campground (☑800-322-3770; http://utahstateparks.reserveamerica.com; tent & RV sites with/without hookups $28/19) get some shade from juniper trees. Big showers, too. The four Red Stone Cabins (☑435-679-8536; www.redstonecabins.com; cabins $109; ☺Mar-Oct; ❂❂) are simple, but cozy, with all the essentials (linens, microwave, mini-fridge and coffee maker) and either a king bed or two queens. The same family runs a little camp store (☺8am-6:30pm Sun-Thu, to 8pm Fri & Sat Apr-Oct).

Bryce Canyon National Park & Around

The sorbet-colored, sandcastle-like spires and hoodoos of Bryce Canyon National Park (☑435-834-5322; www.nps.gov/brca; Hwy 63; 7-day pass per vehicle $25; ☺24hr, visitor center 8am-8pm May-Sep, to 4:30pm Oct-Apr) pop like a Dr Seuss picture book creation. Though the smallest of southern Utah's national parks, this is perhaps the most immediately visually stunning, particularly at sunrise and sunset when an orange wash sets the otherworldly rock formations ablaze. Steep trails descend from the rim into the 1000ft amphitheaters of pastel daggers, then continue through a maze of fragrant juniper and undulating high-mountain desert. The location, 77 miles east of Zion and 39 miles west of Escalante, helps make this a must-stop on any southern Utah park itinerary.

Shaped somewhat like a seahorse, the narrow, 56-mile-long park is an extension of the sloping Paunsaugunt Plateau, which rises from 7894ft at the visitor center to 9115ft at Rainbow Point, the plateau's southernmost

Bryce Canyon National Park

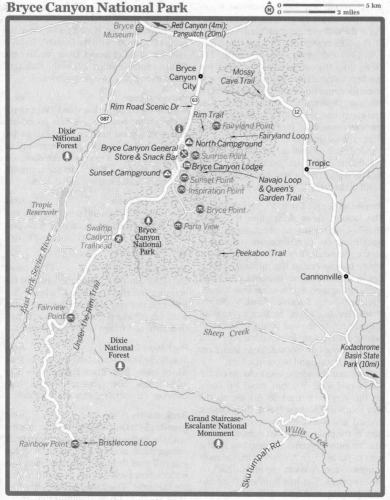

tip. The high altitude means cooler temperatures here than at other Utah parks (80°F, or 27°C, average in July). Crowds arrive in force from May to September, clogging the park's main road (shuttle optional). For solitude, explore trails on the canyon floor. Weatherwise, June and September are ideal; in July and August be prepared for thunderstorms and mosquitoes. In winter, snow blankets the park, but the snowcaps on formations are stunning. Most roads are plowed; others are designated for cross-country skiing and snowshoeing.

You can't enter the park without passing through the townlike sleep-shop-eat-outfit complex, Ruby's Inn, immediately north. The motel has been part of the landscape since 1919, when it was located at the canyon's rim. After the area was declared a national monument in 1923, owner Rueben Syrett moved his business north to his ranch, its current location. In 2007 the 2300-acre resort was officially incorporated as Bryce Canyon City.

◉ Sights & Activities

During summer and early fall, rangers lead canyon-rim walks, hoodoo hikes, geology lectures, campfire programs and kids' ecology walks. If you're here when skies are clear and the moon's full, don't miss the two-hour Moonlight Hike among the hoodoos. Register same-day at the visitor center (p437), but do so early.

The NPS newspaper, *Hoodoo,* lists hikes, activities and ranger-led programs. The views from the overlooks are amazing, but the best thing about Bryce is that you can also experience the weirdly eroding hoodoos up close. Descents and ascents can be long and steep, and the altitude makes them extra strenuous. Take your time: most trails skirt exposed drop-offs.

Additional activities, including mountain-biking trails, are available nearby in Red Canyon, 13 miles west, and Kodachrome Basin State Park, 22 miles east, on Hwy 12.

Rim Road Scenic Drive DRIVING TOUR

The lookout views along along the park's 18-mile-long main road are amazing; navigate using the park brochure you receive at the entrance. **Bryce Amphitheater** – where hoodoos stand like melting sandcastles in shades of coral, magenta, ocher and white, set against a deep-green pine forest – stretches from **Sunrise Point** to **Bryce Point**. For full effect, be sure to walk all the way out to the end of any of the viewpoints; a shaft of sunlight suddenly breaking through clouds as you watch can transform the scene from grand to breathtaking.

Note that the scenic overlooks lie on the road's east side. You can avoid left turns on the very busy road by driving all the way south to **Rainbow Point**, then turning around and working your way back, stopping at the pullouts on your right. From late May to early September a free bus shuttle goes as far as Bryce Amphitheater, the most congested area. You can hop off and back on at viewpoints. The free Rainbow Point bus tour hits the highlights daily at 9am and 1pm; inquire at the visitor center.

Rim Trail HIKING

The easiest hike, this 0.5- to 5.5-mile-long (one-way) trail outlines Bryce Amphitheater from Fairyland Point to Bryce Point. Several sections are paved and wheelchair accessible, the most level being the half-mile between Sunrise and Sunset Points. In the summer, you could easily take the shuttle to any one point and return from another instead of backtracking to a car.

Navajo Loop HIKING

Many moderate trails descend below the rim, but this is one of the most popular. The 1.4-mile trail descends 521ft from Sunset Point and passes through the famous narrow canyon called **Wall Street**. Combine part of the Navajo with the **Queen's Garden Trail** for an easier ascent. Once you hike the 320ft to Sunrise Point, follow the Rim Trail back to your car (2.9-mile round-trip).

Fairyland Loop HIKING

With a trailhead at Fairyland Point north of the visitor center, the 8-mile round-trip makes for a good half-day hike (four to five hours). The tall hoodoos and bridges unfold best if you go in a clockwise direction. On the trail there's a 700ft elevation change, plus many additional ups and downs.

Bristlecone Loop HIKING

The 1-mile Bristlecone Loop, at road's end near **Rainbow Point**, is an easy walk past 1600-year-old bristlecone pines, with 100-mile vistas.

Mossy Cave Trail HIKING

Outside main park boundaries (east of the entrance), off Hwy 12 at Mile 17, take the easy half-mile one-way walk to the year-round waterfall off Mossy Cave Trail – a summertime treat and frozen winter spectacle.

Peekaboo Trail HIKING

The fairly level 7-mile-long Peekaboo Trail, which leaves from Bryce Point, allows dogs and horses. Not recommended in high summer – it doesn't always smell the best.

Backcountry Hikes HIKING

(permits $5-15) Only 1% of all visitors venture onto the backcountry hikes. You won't walk among many hoodoo formations here, but you will pass through forest and meadows with distant views of rock formations. And oh, the quiet. The 23-mile **Under-the-Rim Trail**, south of Bryce Amphitheater, can be broken into several athletic day hikes. The 11-mile stretch between **Bryce Point** and **Swamp Canyon** is one of the hardest and best. Get backcountry permits and trail info from rangers at the visitor center.

Bryce Museum MUSEUM

(www.brycewildlifeadventure.com; 1945 W Hwy 12; admission $8; ☉ 9am-7pm Apr–mid-Nov) Visit this barnlike natural history museum – with more than 400 taxidermied animals, butterflies, and Native American artifacts – then feed the fallow deer and other animals in the yards surrounding. West of the park.

☞ Tours & Outfitters

Ruby's Inn   ADVENTURE SPORTS
(☎435-834-5341, 866-866-6616; www.rubysinn.com; 1000 S Hwy 63) Just outside the park, Ruby's offers guided horseback rides (half-day $85), ATV tours (three hours $120) and mountain-bike rental (half-day $35) – not to mention the rodeo performances, helicopter rides and snowmobiling. Inquire at the inn.

Bryce Wildlife Adventures   ADVENTURE SPORTS
(☎435-834-5555; www.brycewildlifeadventure.com; Bryce Museum, 1945 W Hwy 12; ⊙9am-7pm Apr-Oct) ATV (from $105 for three hours) and mountain-bike ($12.50 per hour) rentals, near public land trails outside the park.

Horseback Riding

Canyon Trail Rides   HORSEBACK RIDING
(☎435-679-8665; www.canyonrides.com; Bryce Canyon Lodge; 2hr/half-day tours $60/80) The national park's only licensed outfitter operates out of the park lodge. You can take a short, two-hour trip to the canyon floor or giddy-up for a half-day through the dramatic hoodoos on Peekaboo Trail.

Red Canyon Trail Rides   HORSEBACK RIDING
(☎435-834-5441, 800-892-7923; www.redcanyontrailrides.com; Hwy 12, Bryce Canyon Pines; 1hr rides $43; ⊙Mar-Nov) Ride for as little as a half-hour or as long as a whole day on private and public lands outside the park, including Red Canyon.

Mecham Outfitters   HORSEBACK RIDING
(☎435-679-8823; www.mechamoutfitters.com; half-day $75) Based in Tropic; leads half- and full-day rides in nearby Dixie National Forest and on GSENM lands.

Cycling

Several companies lead short or four- to six-day, Bryce-to-Zion road cycling tours.

Rim Tours   CYCLING
(☎435-259-5223, 800-626-7335; www.rimtours.com; half-day from $90)

Western Spirit Cyclery   CYCLING
(☎435-259-8732, 800-845-2453; www.westernspirit.com; 6-day trips $1395)

Backroads Bicycle Adventures   CYCLING
(☎800-462-2848; www.backroads.com; 6-day trips from $2498)

✤ Festivals & Events

The park doesn't host any events, but Ruby's Inn does.

Bryce Canyon Winterfest   SPORTS
In early February; includes everything from cross-country skiing and snowmobiling to archery and snow sculpting.

Bryce Canyon Rim Run   SPORTS
Held in August, the run follows a 6-mile course partially along the Bryce Canyon rim outside the park.

🛏 Sleeping

The park has one lodge and two campgrounds. Most travelers stay just north of the park in Bryce Canyon City, near the Hwy 12/63 junction, or 11 miles east in Tropic. Other lodgings are available along Hwy 12, and 24 miles west in Panguitch. Red Canyon and Kodachrome Basin State Park also have campgrounds.

🛏 Inside the Park

Trailers are allowed only as far as Sunset Campground, 3 miles south of the entrance. Backcountry camping permits ($5) are available at the visitor center.

North Campground   CAMPGROUND $
(☎877-444-6777; www.recreation.gov; Bryce Canyon Rd; tent & RV sites $15) The 100-plus NPS campground near the visitor center has a camp store, laundry, showers, flush toilets and water. Loop C is the closest to the rim (sites 59 and 60 have great views, but little privacy). Reservations are accepted early May through late September. No hookups.

Sunset Campground   CAMPGROUND $
(☎877-444-6777; www.recreation.gov; Bryce Canyon Rd; tent & RV sites $15; ⊙Apr-Sep) Though more wooded than North Campground, Sunset has few amenities beyond flush toilets and water. (For laundry, showers and groceries, visit North.) Twenty of the tent sites can be reserved from early May to late August.

Bryce Canyon Lodge   LODGE $$
(☎877-386-4383, 435-834-8700; www.brycecanyonforever.com; Hwy 63, Bryce Canyon National Park; r & cabins $184-213; ⊙Apr-Oct; @) Built in the 1920s, the main park lodge exudes rustic mountain charm, with a large stone fireplace and exposed roof timbers. Most rooms are in two-story wooden satellite buildings

with private balconies. Cabins have inherent charm, with creaky porches and woodsy settings, though furnishings are dated. Be warned: the walls prove thin if the neighbors are noisy. No TVs.

🛏 Outside the Park

A full list of area motels is available at www.brycecanyoncountry.com.

Ruby's RV Park & Campground
CAMPGROUND $

(☎435-834-5301, 866-866-6616; www.rubysinn.com; 1000 S Hwy 63; tent sites $27, tipis $36, RV sites with partial/full hookups $37/43, cabins $57; ⊘Apr-Oct; 🛜🐾) The 200 sites, camping cabins (no linens) and tipis (bring your own sleeping bag and cot) adjacent to all those services at Ruby's Inn are in a fairly forest-like, if commercial, setting. Rates listed are for double occupancy.

★ Bryce Country Cabins
CABINS $$

(☎888-679-8643, 435-679-8643; www.brycecountrycabins.com; 320 N Main St, Tropic; $109-149; ⊘Feb-Oct; ❄🐾) Friendly and family-run, these well-designed pine cabins are centered on an outdoor fire pit, perfect for stargazing around a bonfire. The only drawback is they're right on the main street. Deluxe cabins have cozy furniture and vaulted ceilings. Perks include TVs, coffeemakers, small porches and charm – it's among the best simple accommodations near Bryce.

Ruby's Inn
MOTEL $$

(☎866-866-6616, 435-834-5341; www.rubysinn.com; 1000 S Hwy 63; r $135-180; ❄@🐾) A gargantuan motel complex one mile north of the park entrance, Ruby's has 369 standard rooms. The facilities are the major attraction. The sprawling property includes a grocery store, two gas stations, a post office, coin laundry, a pool and hot tub, a foreign-currency exchange, gift shops, email kiosks, one-hour film processing and a liquor store (a rarity around here).

Bullberry Inn
B&B $$

(☎435-679-8820, 800-249-8126; www.bullberryinn.com; 412 S Hwy 12, Tropic; r incl breakfast $90-125; 🅿🐾) Purpose-built in 1998, this farmhouse-style B&B at the far edge of town has spacious, spotless rooms. The welcoming owners make the bullberry jam that's served with home-baked goodies at the full country breakfast.

Bryce Canyon Resort
MOTEL $$

(☎435-834-5351, 800-834-0043; www.brycecanyonresort.com; cnr Hwys 12 & 63; r $99-189, cabins $159-210; ❄🐾🐾🐾) Four miles from the park, this is the less chaotic alternative to Ruby's Inn. Deluxe rooms include newer furnishings and extra amenities; cabins and cottages have kitchenettes and sleep up to six. Outfitter packages and smoking rooms available.

Bryce View Lodge
MOTEL $$

(☎435-834-5180, 888-279-2304; www.bryceviewlodge.com; r $105-120; ⊘Apr-Oct; 🐾@🐾🐾) Geared toward budget travelers. Rooms are smaller and less spiffy than sister hotel Ruby's, but you have free access to Ruby's pool and hot tub.

Best Western Plus Bryce Grand Canyon Lodge
HOTEL $$

(☎866-866-6634, 435-834-5700; www.brycecanyongrand.com; 30 North 100 East, Bryce Canyon City; r $135-199; ⊘Apr-Oct; ❄@🐾🐾) New in 2009, this Best Western hotel is the best digs in this strip, with stylish, ample rooms and a free breakfast bar. It's operated by Ruby's Inn, so all the amenities at Ruby's are available to guests here.

Bryce Canyon Pines
MOTEL $$

(☎435-834-5441, 800-892-7923; www.brycecanyonmotel.com; Hwy 12; tent/RV sites $20/30, r & cottages $110-325; ⊘Apr-Nov; 🐾) This old, rambling white clapboard motel, 8 miles northwest of the park entrance, has been in the same family for ages. Cottages have the most character; dated standard rooms have simple beds with simple spreads. There's also a homey restaurant, horseback riding and a basic campground on site.

Buffalo Sage B&B
B&B $$

(☎435-679-8443, 866-232-5711; www.buffalosage.com; 980 N Hwy 12, Tropic; r incl breakfast $80-110; ❄🐾) Up on a bluff west of town, three exterior-access rooms lead out to an expansive, upper-level deck or ground-level patio with great views. The owner's background in art is evident in the decor. Note that the communal living area is shared with cats and a dog.

Stone Canyon Inn
INN $$$

(☎435-679-8611, 866-489-4680; www.stonecanyoninn.com; 1220 Stone Canyon Lane, Tropic; r incl breakfast $175, cabins $350; ❄🐾) Backed by natural hills and Technicolor sunsets adjoining backcountry parklands, this stately stone-and-wood inn offers adventure out the back door. New cabins are spacious and luxuriantly private, though they're trumped by the charm of the main-house rooms, which includes hot breakfasts with homemade pastries and breads.

 Eating

Nobody comes to Bryce for the cuisine. Expect so-so Western fare like grilled pork chops and chicken-fried steaks. If you're vegetarian, BYOV or subsist on salad and fries.

Inside the Park

Bryce Canyon General Store & Snack Bar MARKET $
(Bryce Canyon Rd, near Sunrise Point; dishes $3-7; ☺noon-10pm) Sells basic supplies, sandwiches and pizza in season.

Bryce Canyon Lodge MODERN AMERICAN $$$
(☎435-834-5361; Bryce Canyon Rd; breakfast & sandwiches $8-15, dinner $26-42; ☺7am-10pm Apr-Oct) By far the best (and priciest) place to eat inside the park. Meats are perfectly grilled and sauces caringly prepared. Though upscale, the rustic, white-tablecloth-clad dining room is more family-friendly than romantically refined – or quiet, even.

Outside the Park

Most of the area motels have so-so eateries on site.

Clarke's Grocery MARKET $
(121 N Main St, Tropic; sandwiches $5-8; ☺7:30am-8pm Mon-Sat, 2-8pm Sun) Tropic's only grocery store has a deli sandwich counter and homemade baked goods.

Pizza Place PIZZA $$
(21 N Main St, Tropic; pizzas & sandwiches $5-18; ☺noon-9pm Apr-Oct, 5-8:30pm Thu-Sat Nov-Mar) Think wood-fired flatbread piled high with fresh ingredients. When locals eat out, they come to this family-owned joint. Serves pizzas, salads and sandwiches.

Bryce Canyon Pines Restaurant AMERICAN $$
(☎435-834-5441; www.brycecanyonmotel.com; Hwy 12; breakfasts & lunches $5-12, dinner mains $10-19; ☺6:30am-9:30pm Apr-Nov) This supercute diner is classic Utah, with waitstaff that dotes, Naugahyde booths and even a crackling fire on cold days. Expect hearty plates of meat and potatoes, perfect BLTs and meal-size soups. While mains feel run-of-the-mill, locals come for towering wedges of homemade pie, such as banana blueberry creme.

Clarke's Restaurant AMERICAN $$
(121 N Main St, Tropic; breakfast & lunch $4-15, dinner $12-22; ☺7am-10pm Mon-Sat Jun-Sep, variable hours Oct-May; ☎) Beer and wine are available at this full-service, three-meal-a-day option.

Ebenezer's Bar & Grill DINNER SHOW $$$
(☎800-468-8660; www.rubysinn.com; 1000 S Hwy 63; dinner show $26-32; ☺7pm nightly mid-May–Sep) Kitschy but good-natured fun, an evening at Ebenezer's includes live country-and-western music served up beside a big BBQ dinner: steak, pulled pork, chicken or salmon. It's probably the best meal served at the Ruby's complex and is wildly popular, so book ahead.

ℹ **Information**

Some services are just north of the park boundaries on Hwy 63. The nearest town is Tropic, 11 miles northeast on Hwy 12; the nearest hospital is 25 miles northwest in Panguitch.

Bryce Canyon National Park Visitor Center
(☎435-834-5322; www.nps.gov/brca; Hwy 63; ☺8am-8pm May-Sep, to 6pm Oct & Apr, to 4:30pm Nov-Mar) Get information on weather, trails, ranger-led activities and campsite availability; the introductory film is worth seeing. Good selection of maps and books.

Bryce Canyon Natural History Association
(☎435-834-4600; www.brycecanyon.org) Pre-trip online book shopping.

Garfield County Travel Council (☎800-444-6689, 435-676-1160; www.brycecanyoncountry.com) There's no town visitor center, so plan ahead online or by phone.

Ruby's Inn (www.rubysinn.com; 1000 S Hwy 63) Post office, grocery store, showers ($6), free wi-fi and computer terminals ($1 for five minutes).

ℹ **Getting Around**

A private vehicle is the only way around from fall through spring. If you're traveling in summer, ride the voluntary **shuttle** (free; ☺8am-8pm late May–Sep), lest you find yourself stuck without a parking spot. (Note: the park's visitor center parking lot fills up, too.) Leave your car at the Ruby's Inn or Ruby's Campground stops, and ride the bus into the park. The shuttle goes as far as Bryce Point; buses come roughly every 15 minutes, 8am to 8pm. A round-trip without exiting takes 50 minutes. Tune in to 1610AM on your radio as you approach Bryce to learn about current shuttle operations. The *Hoodoo* newspaper shows routes.

No trailers are permitted south of Sunset Point. If you're towing, leave your load at your campsite or in the trailer turnaround lot at the visitor center.

Red Canyon

Impressive, deep-ocher-red monoliths rise up roadside as you drive along Hwy 12, 10 miles west of the Hwy 63/Bryce Canyon turnoff. The aptly named **Red Canyon** (☑435-676-2676; www.fs.usda.gov/recarea/dixie; Scenic Byway 12, Dixie National Forest; ☺park 24hr, visitor center 9am-6pm Jun-Aug, 10am-4pm May & Sep) **FREE** provides super-easy access to these eerie, intensely colored formations. In fact, you have to cross under two blasted-rock arches to continue on the highway. A network of trails leads hikers, bikers and horseback riders deeper into these national-forest-service lands. Check out the excellent geologic displays and pick up trail maps at the **visitor center** (☑435-676-2676; Hwy 12; ☺9am-6pm Jun-Aug, 10am-4pm May & Sep).

Several moderately easy hiking trails begin near the center. The 0.7-mile **Arches Trail** passes 15 arches as it winds through a canyon; the 1-mile **Pink Ledges Trail** winds through red-rock formations. For a harder hike, try the 2.8-mile, two- to four-hour **Golden Wall Trail**. Legend has it that outlaw Butch Cassidy once rode here; a tough 8.9-mile hiking route, **Cassidy Trail**, bears his name.

There are excellent mountain-biking trails in the area; the best is the 7.8-mile **Thunder Mountain Trail**, which cuts through pine forest and red rock. Outfitters near Bryce Canyon National Park rent out mountain bikes and offer horseback rides through Red Canyon.

Surrounded by limestone formations and ponderosa pines, the 37 no-reservation sites at **Red Canyon Campground** (☑435-676-2676; www.fs.usda.gov; Scenic Byway 12; tent & RV sites $15; ☺mid-May–Sep) are quite scenic. Quiet-use trails (no ATVs) lead off from here, making this a good alternative to Bryce Canyon National Park camping. There are showers and a dump station, but no hookups.

If you prefer a roof over your head, continue west. The rooms and log cabins at family-run **Harold's Place** (☑435-676-2350; www.haroldsplace.net; Hwy 12; r & cabins from $80; ☺Mar-Oct; ❄☎), just before the intersection of Hwys 12 and 89, are cozy and spotless. Locals recommend the above-average **restaurant** (breakfast $5-12, dinner $13-24; ☺7-11am & 5-10pm Mar-Nov) for favorites like balsamic chicken and pecan-crusted trout. More food and lodging choices are available in nearby Panguitch and Hatch.

ON BUTCH CASSIDY'S TRAIL

Nearly every town in southern Utah claims a connection to Butch Cassidy (1866–1908?), the Old West's most famous bank and train robber. As part of the Wild Bunch, Cassidy (born Robert LeRoy Parker) pulled 19 heists between 1896 and 1901. Accounts usually describe him with a breathless romanticism, likening him to a kind of Robin Hood. Bring up the subject in these parts and you'll likely be surprised at how many folks' grandfathers had encounters with him. The robber may even have attended a dance in the old **Torrey Schoolhouse**, now a B&B. And many a dilapidated shack or a canyon, just over yonder, served as his hideout. The most credible claim for the location of the famous Robbers' Roost hideout is in the **Henry Mountains**.

In the wee town of **Circleville**, located 28 miles north of Panguitch, stands the honest-to-goodness boyhood home of the gun-slingin' bandit. The cabin is partially renovated but uninhabited, 2 miles south of town on the west side of Hwy 89. When reporters arrived after the release of the film *Butch Cassidy and the Sundance Kid* (1969), they met the outlaw's youngest sister, who claimed that Butch did in fact not die in South America in 1908, but returned for a visit after that. Writers have been digging for the truth to no avail ever since. You can see where they filmed Robert Redford's famous bicycle scene at the **Grafton ghost town** (p455), outside Rockville.

Local lore holds that Cassidy didn't steal much in Utah because this is where his bread was buttered. Whatever the reason, the Wild Bunch's only big heist in the state was in April 1897, when the gang stole more than $8000 from Pleasant Valley Coal Company in Castle Gate, 4 miles north of Helper on Hwy 191. The little **Western Mining & Railroad Museum** (☑435-472-3009; www.wmrrm.com; 296 S Main St, Helper; adult/child $2/1; ☺10am-5pm Mon-Sat May-Aug, 11am-4pm Tue-Sat Sep-Apr), 8 miles north of Price, has exhibits on the outlaws, including photos, in the basement. For more, check out *The Outlaw Trail*, written by Charles Kelly.

Panguitch

POP 1623 / ELEV 6624FT

Founded in 1864, historically Panguitch was a profitable pioneer ranching and lumber community. Since the 1920s inception of the national park, the town has had a can't-live-with-or-without-it relationship with Bryce Canyon, 24 miles east. Lodging long ago became the number-one industry, as it's also used as an overnight stop halfway between Las Vegas (234 miles) and Salt Lake City (245 miles).

Other than some interesting turn-of-the-20th-century brick homes and buildings, it has few attractions. Main Street has an antique store or two, but mostly people fill up with food and fuel, rest up and move on. In a pinch you could use it as a base for seeing Bryce, Zion and Cedar Breaks.

Panguitch is the seat of Garfield County and hosts numerous festivals. Two of the best are in June: the **Quilt Walk Festival** celebrates pioneer history and **Chariots in the Sky** is a huge hot-air balloon festival.

🛏 Sleeping

Panguitch House   B&B $
(☑435-676-2574; www.panguitchhousebandb.com; 259 E Center St; r incl breakfast $85; ❋ �がい) Nicely simple, new B&B rooms in this renovated redbrick home are an excellent alternative to a motel. The price is more than right; friendly hosts provide a big breakfast and advice on area adventures.

Marianna Inn Motel   MOTEL $
(☑435-676-8844, 800-598-9190; www.mariannainn.com; r $55-95; ❋ �がい❋) Rooms in the dollhouse-like, pink-and-lavender motel with the large, shaded swing deck are standard. But the newest additions – deluxe log-style rooms – are worth splurging on. A BBQ grill is available for guests.

Canyon Lodge   MOTEL $
(☑435-676-8292, 800-440-8292; www.canyonlodgemotel.com; 210 N Main St; r $69; ❋ �が) Thoroughly clean, older 10-room motel, with classic neon sign and helpful hosts. Hot tub on site.

Color Country Motel   MOTEL $
(☑435-676-2386, 800-225-6518; www.colorcountrymotel.com; 526 N Main St; r $52-73; ❋) An economical, standard motel with perks – a pool and an outdoor hot tub.

Hitch-N-Post   CAMPGROUND $
(☑435-676-2436; www.hitchnpostrv.com; 420 N Main St; tent/RV sites with hookups $17/29; �がい❋) Small lawns and trees divide RV spaces; tent sites are in a grassy field, but still have BBQ grills. An RV wash and a heavy-duty laundry is on site.

★**Red Brick Inn**   B&B $$
(☑435-690-1048; www.redbrickinn.com; 11161 N 100 West; d incl breakfast $130; ☉Apr-Oct; ❋�が) Chill out swinging in a garden hammock or pedaling a loaner bike. A warm California native, Peggy runs this 1919 charmer that once served as the town hospital. Stories abound, rooms are cozy and comfortable, and there's an outdoor hot tub. Has a two-night minimum; ask first about pets.

Grandma's Cottage   RENTAL $$
(☑435-690-9495; www.grandmascottages.com; 90 N 100 West; rentals $90-145; ☉Mar-Nov; ❋) Excellent for groups and families, these renovated cottages and homes around central Panguitch have been lovingly put together by a semiretired couple. Save for the studio cottage, the decor is nothing like grandma's – think savvy and stylish. Themes vary: there's a 1960s hideout, a country cottage and a historic brick home. All have TV; some feature cooking and laundry facilities.

🍴 Eating & Drinking

Remember that eateries in Hatch, and Harold's Place in Red Canyon, are also close by.

Little L's   BAKERY $
(☑(435) 676-8750; 37 N Main St; mains $4-9; ☉7am-3pm Mon-Sat) Espresso, pastries and donuts with flavors ranging from butterscotch to a sublime raspberry-lime. You're almost guaranteed to leave with sticky fingers. Offers sandwiches, too.

Joe's Main Street Market   MARKET $
(10 S Main St) The town's main grocery store.

Cowboy's Smokehouse BBQ   BARBECUE $$
(95 N Main St; breakfast & lunch $5-12, dinner $15-32; ☉4-8pm Tue-Wed, to 9pm Thu-Sat) Sweet staff serve steaks and brisket with house-made sauce, but the food quality can be erratic. Portions are generous.

ℹ Information

Garfield County Travel Council (☑435-676-1102, 800-444-6689; www.brycecanyoncountry.com) Town and county information.

Garfield Memorial Hospital (☎435-676-8811; 224 N 400 East; ☺24hr) The nearest clinic and emergency room, 25 miles northwest.

Powell Ranger Station (☎435-676-9300; www.fs.fed.us/dxnf; 225 E Center St; ☺8am-4:30pm Mon-Fri) Dixie National Forest camping and hiking info.

Hwy 89 – Panguitch to Kanab

Most people pass through this stretch of Hwy 89 as quickly as possible en route from Zion to Bryce national parks. All the better for you – the tiny old towns along the way have a few restaurant and lodging gems hidden within. (Note that businesses' seasonal closings change with weather and whim.) When reading distances, keep in mind that you'll average between 35mph and 50mph along these roads.

Independent motels and a few eateries line Hwy 89 in **Hatch**, 25 miles southwest of Bryce Canyon and 15 miles south of Panguitch. **Café Adobe** (16 N Main St, Hatch; mains $10-16; ☺8am-8pm Mar–mid-Nov) has long been the residents' fave for gourmet hamburgers, creative sandwiches and tasty Mexican food – and 'locals' here live in Panguitch or Tropic. Don't pass up the homemade tortilla chips and chunky salsa.

A locally-retired Las Vegas developer and his family have single-handedly breathed new life into sleepy Hatch with several seasonal lodgings and eateries. **Galaxy Diner** (177 S Main St, Hatch; mains $5-12; ☺6:30am-2pm mid-Mar–late Oct) is a pseudo-typical 1950s diner and ice cream parlor, next to a Harley Davidson shop. **Hatch Station Dining Car** (177 S Main St; mains $9-20; ☺noon-8pm mid-Mar–late Oct) serves the best prime rib around, in knickknacky surrounds. Next door, there's a convenience store selling used cowboy boots (perfect if you lack the patience to break 'em in), and bargain rooms are available at **Hatch Station Motel** (177 S Main St; r $55-65; ☺mid-Mar–late Oct; ✲ ☏).

Dubbed 'Cowboy-licious' by a wizened ranch hand, **Cottonwood Meadow Lodge** (☎435-676-8950; www.panguitchanglers.com; Mile 123, Hwy 89; cabins & houses $155-295; ☺mid-April–Oct; ☏) delivers open-range dreams. Recycled from a Mormon saw town, this private ranch, two miles south of Hwy 12 near Panguitch, occupies acres of tawny grass and tumbling sagebrush. Cabins range from a rustic-chic bunkhouse with wooden plank floors to stylish farmhouses with gleaming kitchens, blazing hearths and porch rockers. A trout pond stocked with browns and rainbows is in easy reach; otherwise there are miles of roads and open space for country walkers and mountain bikers. Lest they help themselves to the grass-raised beef on-site, pets are not allowed.

Further south, 50 miles from Bryce and 26 miles to Zion, **Glendale** is a historic lit-

---

UTAH IN THE MOVIES

The movie industry has known about the rugged wilds of southern Utah since its early days – in the 1920s, film adaptations of Zane Grey novels were shot here. All told, more than 700 films (and many TV shows) have been shot on location across the state. Iconic movies with Utah cameos include the following:

➤ *Thelma & Louise* – Remember where they drive off the cliff? That was outside Canyonlands National Park at Dead Horse Point. Scenes were also filmed in Arches National Park.

➤ *Forrest Gump* stopped his cross-country run in front of Monument Valley, which straddles the Utah–Arizona line. *Easy Rider* motorcycled through, too, and *2001: A Space Odyssey* used the monoliths to represent outer space.

➤ Disney shot the Johnny Depp version of *The Lone Ranger* in Red Rock country. (Too bad it was a flop.)

➤ *Con Air* and *Independence Day* both have landing scenes shot on the super-smooth Bonneville Salt Flats.

➤ In *High School Musical*, Zac Efron danced his way through East High School in Salt Lake City, just like Kevin Bacon had done at Payson High School (south of Provo) in *Footloose*.

➤ Kanab was the shooting location for heaps of Western movies, with stars such as John Wayne and Clint Eastwood.

tle Mormon town founded in 1871. Today it's an access point for Grand Staircase–Escalante National Monument. From Hwy 89, turn onto 300 North at the faded sign for GSENM; from there it turns into Glendale Bench Rd, which leads to scenic **Johnson Canyon** and **Skutumpah Rds**.

The seven-room **Historic Smith Hotel** (☎800-528-3558, 435-648-2156; www.historicsmithhotel.com; 295 N Main St, Glendale; r incl breakfast $79-89; ✳) is more comfortable than a favorite old sweater; don't let the small rooms turn you off. The proprietors are a great help in planning your day and the big breakfast tables are the place to meet other intrepid travelers from around the globe. Great back decks and garden, too. Next door, **Buffalo Bistro** (☎435-648-2778; www.buffalobistro.net; 305 N Main St, Glendale; mains $8-24; ⊘4-9:30pm Thu-Sun mid-Mar–mid-Oct) conjures a laid-back Western spirit with a breezy porch, sizzling grill and eclectic menu. Try buffalo steaks, wild boar ribs, elk burgers – or pasta. The gregarious owner-chef has a great sense of humor; he sometimes hosts music and events, and sometimes closes early.

In **Mt Carmel**, the **Thunderbird Foundation for the Arts** (☎435-648-2653; www.thunderbirdfoundation.com; Mile 84, Hwy 89, Mt Carmel) runs exhibits and artist retreats in adjacent spaces. The beautiful **Maynard Dixon Home & Studio** (self-guided tour $10; ⊘10am-5pm May-Oct) is where renowned Western painter Maynard Dixon (1875–1946) lived and worked in the 1930s and '40s. Look for a few other galleries, arts-and-crafts and rock shops along the way.

At the turnoff for Hwy 9, **Mt Carmel Junction** has two gas stations (one with a sandwich counter) and a couple of decent sleeping options about 15 slow-and-scenic miles from the east entrance of Zion, and 18 miles north of Kanab. The Navajo lookout on the outside of the **Best Western East Zion Thunderbird Lodge** (☎435-648-2203, 800-780-7234; www.bestwesternutah.com; cnr Hwys 9 & 89, Mt Carmel Junction; r $107-114; ✳ 🖳 ⛾) is just a facade; the rooms within are standard Best Western. The quilt-covered four-poster beds sure are comfy at **Arrowhead Country Inn & Cabins** (☎435-648-2569, 888-821-1670; www.arrowheadbb.com; 2155 S State St, Mt Carmel Junction; r $79-129, cabins $129-269, both incl breakfast; ✳ 🖳 ⛾ ☰). The east fork of the Virgin River meanders behind the inn and a trail leads from here to the base of the white cliffs.

Kanab

POP 4410 / ELEV 4970FT

Vast expanses of rugged desert surround the remote outpost of Kanab. Don't be surprised if it all looks familiar: hundreds of Western movies were shot here. Founded by Mormon pioneers in 1874, Kanab was put on the map by John Wayne and other gun-slingin' celebs in the 1940s and '50s. Just about every resident had something to do with the movies from the 1930s up until the '70s. You can still see a couple of movie sets in the area and hear old-timers talk about their roles. In August, the **Western Legends Roundup** celebrates 'Utah's little Hollywood.'

Kanab sits at a major crossroads: GSENM is 20 miles away, Zion 40 miles, Bryce Canyon 80 miles, Grand Canyon's North Rim 81 miles and Lake Powell 74 miles. It makes a good base for exploring the southern side of GSENM and Paria Canyon–Vermilion Cliffs Wilderness formations such as the Wave. Coral Pink Sand Dunes State Park is a big rompin' playground to the northwest.

Note that local opening hours are often altered by mood and demand, especially off season.

⊙ Sights & Activities

The Kane County Office of Tourism (p444) has an exhibit of area-made movie posters and knowledge about sites.

Best Friends Animal Sanctuary RESCUE CENTER
(☎435-644-2001; www.bestfriends.org; Angel Canyon, Hwy 89; ⊘9:30am-5:30pm; ♿) **FREE** Kanab's most famous attraction is outside of town. Surrounded by more than 33,000 mostly private acres of red-rock desert 5.5 miles north of Kanab, Best Friends is the largest no-kill animal rescue center in the country. The center shows films and gives facility tours four times a day; call ahead for times and reservations. The 1½-hour tours let you meet some of the more than 1700 horses, pigs, dogs, cats, birds and other critters on site.

Volunteers come from around the country to work here. Spending the night in one of eight one-bedroom cottages with kitchenettes ($140) or in a one-room cabin ($92) and volunteering for at least a half-day allows visitors to borrow a dog, cat or pot-bellied pig for the night. (Cottages should be booked well in advance.) They also have RV sites ($45) with hookups.

The sanctuary is located in Angel Canyon (Kanab Canyon to locals), where scores of movies and TV shows were filmed during Kanab's Hollywood heyday. The cliff ridge about the sanctuary is where the Lone Ranger reared up and shouted 'Hi-yo Silver!' at the end of every episode.

Frontier Movie Town & Trading Post
FILM LOCATION

(297 W Center St; ⊙7:30am-11pm Apr-Oct, 10am-5pm Nov-Mar) **FREE** Wander through a bunkhouse, saloon and other buildings used in Western movies filmed locally, including *The Outlaw Josey Wales*, and learn some tricks of the trade. This classic roadside attraction sells all the Western duds and doodads you could care to round up. Lists of movies shot here, and some of the DVDs of the films themselves, are also available.

Parry Lodge
HISTORIC SITE

(www.parrylodge.com; 89 E Center St; ⊙movies 8pm Sat Jun-Aug) **FREE** Parry Lodge became movie central when it was built in the 1930s. Stars stayed here and owner Whit Parry provided horses, cattle and catering for the sets. There are nostalgic photos on lobby and dining room walls, and on summer Saturday nights the hotel shows the old Westerns in a barn out back.

Johnson Canyon
DRIVING TOUR

Heading into GSENM, the paved scenic drive into Johnson Canyon is popular. More movies were filmed here, and 6 miles along you can see in the distance the Western set where the longtime TV classic *Bonanza* was filmed (on private land). Turn north off Hwy 89, 9 miles east of Kanab.

Paria Movie Set
HISTORIC SITE

The movie set at Paria (pa-*ree*-uh), where many Westerns were filmed, burnt down during the 2007 Western Legends Roundup. A 5-mile dirt road leads to a picnic area and an interpretive sign that shows what the set used to look like.

A mile further north, on the other side of the river, it's a hike to look for the little that's left of **Pahreah ghost town**. Floods in the 1880s rang the death knell for the 130-strong farming community. Since then, time and fire have taken the buildings and all but the most rudimentary signs of settlement. But the valley is a pretty introduction to GSENM.

The signed turnoff for Paria Valley is 33 miles from Kanab on Hwy 89.

Moqui Cave
MUSEUM

(adult/child $5/2; ⊙9am-7pm Mon-Sat Mar-Nov) Five miles north of town, this tourist trap is an oddball collection of genuine dinosaur tracks, real cowboy and Native American artifacts, and other flotsam and jetsam collected in the 1950s – all inside a giant cave.

🢂 Tours

★Dreamland Safari
TOURS

(www.dreamlandtours.net; 3hr tour $90) Hikes with naturalist tour guides to gorgeous backcountry sites and slot canyons by 4WD. They also offer nature photography and multiday backpacking trips.

Paria Outpost
ADVENTURE TOUR

(☑928-691-1047; www.paria.com; half-day tour $125) Friendly, flexible and knowledgeable; 4WD tours and guided hikes through the rocks and sand of GSENM and Paria Canyon–Vermillion Cliffs.

Seldom Seen Adventures
ADVENTURE TOUR

(☑888-418-9908; www.seldomseenadventures.net; day hike $129) Family-oriented, personalized tours of the national parks, GSENM and wilderness areas, with canyoneering, 4WD tours, super fat-tire biking and hiking. Also offers transfers.

Windows of the West Hummer Tours
ADVENTURE TOUR

(☑888-687-3006; www.wowhummertours.com; 2hr tour $85) Personalized backcountry excursions (two hours to full-day) to slot canyons, petroglyphs and spectacular red-rock country.

🎉 Festivals & Events

Western Legends Roundup
FILM

(☑800-733-5263; www.westernlegendsroundup.com) The town lives for the annual Western Legends Roundup in late August. There are concerts, gunfights, cowboy poetry, dances, quilt shows, a film festival and more. Take a bus tour to all the film sites, or sign up for a Dutch-oven cooking lesson.

🛏 Sleeping

For a full listing of motels and some house rentals see www.visitsouthernutah.com.

Treasure Trail Motel
MOTEL $

(☑435-577-2645, 800-603-2687; www.treasuretrailkanab.com; 150 W Center St; r $60-90; ❀🢂🢂🢂) Friendly little independent motel; microwaves and mini-refrigerators are standard.

Hitch'n Post Campground　　CAMPGROUND $
(☎435-644-2142, 800-458-3516; www.hitchn-postrvpark.com; 196 E 300 South; tent/RV sites with hookups $18/29, camping cabins $32-36; 🛜🐾) Friendly 17-site campground near the town center; has a laundry and showers.

★**Canyons Lodge**　　MOTEL $$
(☎800-644-5094, 435-644-3069; www.can-yonslodge.com; 236 N 300 West; r incl breakfast $89-169; 🏵@🛜🐾🐾) 🅿 A renovated motel with an art-house Western feel. There's a warm welcome, free cruiser bikes and good traveler assistance. In summer, guests enjoy twice-weekly live music and wine and cheese by the fire pit. Rooms feature original artwork and whimsical touches. Recycles soaps and containers.

Quail Park Lodge　　MOTEL $$
(☎435-215-1447; www.quailparklodge.com; 125 N 300 W; r/ste $155/203; 🏵@🛜🐾🐾) Schwinn Cruiser bicycles stand near vibrant beach balls bobbing in the postage-stamp-size pool, and yellow clamshell chairs wait outside surprisingly plush rooms. A colorful retro style pervades all 13 rooms at this refurbished 1963 motel. Mod cons include free phone calls, microwaves, minifridges and complimentary gourmet coffee.

Victorian Inn　　HOTEL $$
(☎435-644-8660; www.kanabvictorianinn.com; 190 N 300 West; r incl breakfast $119-164; 🏵🛜🐾) From the architecture to appointments, the inn is a modern-day remake of period Victoriana. Ethan Allen furnishings, gas fireplaces and jetted tubs grace every room, but it all looks a little too new. The hot breakfast buffet is shared with guests from the Canyons Lodge next door.

Purple Sage Inn　　B&B $$
(☎435-644-5377, 877-644-5377; www.purplesage-inn.com; r incl breakfast $135-165; 🏵🛜) A former Mormon polygamist's home, this later became a hotel, where Western author Zane Grey stayed. Now it's a B&B with exquisite antique details. Zane's namesake room – with its quilt-covered wood bed, sitting room and balcony access – is our favorite.

Parry Lodge　　MOTEL $$
(☎435-644-2601, 888-289-1722; www.parrylodge.com; 89 E Center St; r $77-125; 🏵🛜🐾🐾) The aura of bygone Westerns is the best feature of this rambling old classic motel. Some rooms bear the names of movie stars who stayed here, like Gregory Peck or Lana Turn-er. If quality is your concern, opt for the L-shaped double queen room, nicely refurbished in cottage decor.

Holiday Inn Express　　HOTEL $$
(☎435-644-3100, 800-315-2621; www.hiex-press/kanabut.com; 217 S 100 E; r/ste $154/171; 🏵@🛜🐾🐾) Newest, nicest chain property.

✖ Eating & Drinking

Numerous themed restaurants, ice-cream parlors and such line Center St.

Escobar's　　MEXICAN $
(mains $7-12; ⏰11am-9:30pm Sun-Fri) Sometimes it feels like all of Kanab is stuffed into this busy, family-run restaurant with swift service and XL portions. Start with the complimentary homemade chips and salsa and move on to a green chile burrito and a chilled mug of beer.

Jakey Leighs　　CAFE $
(4 E Center St; sandwiches $4-8; ⏰7am-10pm Tue-Sat, to 3pm Sun & Mon; 🛜) Come here for tasty quiche and OK coffee on the pleasant patio, or grab a sandwich for the road.

Honey's Marketplace　　MARKET $
(260 E 300 S; ⏰7am-10pm) Full grocery store with deli; look for the 1950s truck inside.

★**Rocking V Cafe**　　AMERICAN $$
(www.rockingvcafe.com; 97 W Center St; lunch $8-18, dinner $15-34; ⏰11:30am-10pm; 🍴) Fresh ingredients star in dishes like hand-cut buffalo tenderloin and chargrilled zucchini with curried quinoa. Local artwork decorating the 1892 brick storefront is as creative as the food. Off-season hours vary.

Houston's Trail's End Restaurant　　AMERICAN $$
(☎435-644-2488; 32 E Center St; breakfast $5-10, mains $7-24; ⏰7am-10pm) Join the locals for chicken-fried steak and razzleberry pie – you know the food must be good if they'll frequent a place where the waitresses wear cowboy boots and toy six-shooters. No alcohol.

Luo's　　CHINESE $$
(365 S 100 E; mains $10-18; ⏰11am-10pm; 🍴) For a change. Surprisingly good Chinese food; great vegetable selection.

Calvin T's Smoking Gun　　BARBECUE $$
(78 E Center St; mains $12-26; ⏰11:30am-10pm; 🍴) Kitschy barbecue, including pulled pork and slabs of ribs, is served cafeteria-style to mixed reviews.

Dog House Tavern PUB
(☑435-644-3636; 98 S 100 E; ☺hours vary) Not your stereotypical watering hole – here the bartenders serve up vegan bar food, smoothies and beer on tap.

★ Entertainment

Crescent Moon Theater THEATER
(☑435-644-2350; www.crescentmoontheater.com; 150 S 100 East; ☺May-Sep) Cowboy poetry, bluegrass music and comedic plays are just some of what is staged here. Monday is Western-movie night.

🛍 Shopping

Western clothing and bric-a-brac are sold, along with Native American knickknacks, at shops along Center St.

**Willow Canyon
Outdoor Co** OUTDOOR EQUIPMENT
(263 S 100 East; ☺7:30am-8pm, off-season hours vary) It's easy to spend hours sipping espresso and perusing the eclectic books here. Before you leave, outfit yourself with field guides, camping gear, USGS maps and hiking clothes.

ℹ Information

As the biggest town around the GSENM, Kanab has several grocery stores, ATMs, banks and services.

BLM Kanab Field Office (☑435-644-4600; 318 N 100 East; ☺8am-4pm Mon-Fri) Provides information and, November 16 through March 14, issues permits for hiking the Wave in Paria Canyon–Vermilion Cliffs Wilderness Area.

GSENM Visitor Center (☑435-644-1300; www.ut.blm.gov/monument; 745 E Hwy 89; ☺8am-4:30pm) Provides road, trail and weather updates for the Grand Staircase–Escalante National Monument.

Kane County Hospital (☑435-644-5811; 355 N Main St; ☺24hr) The closest medical facility to GSENM.

Kane County Office of Tourism (☑800-733-5263, 435-644-5033; www.kaneutah.com; 78 S 100 East; ☺8:30am-6pm Mon-Fri, to 4pm Sat) The main source for area information; great old Western movie posters and artifacts on display.

Local Police (☑435-644-5807; 140 E 100 South)

Visit Kanab (www.visitkanab.com)

Getting There & Around

There is no public transportation to or around Kanab.

Xpress Rent-a-Car (☑435-644-3408; www.xpressrentalcarofkanab.com; 1530 S Alt 89) Car and 4WD rental.

Around Kanab

Coral Pink Sand Dunes State Park

Coral-colored sand is not especially strange in the southern half of GSENM, but seeing it gathered as giant dunes in a 3700-acre state park (☑435-648-2800; http://stateparks.utah.gov; Sand Dunes Rd; day-use $8; ☺day-use dawn-dusk, visitor center 9am-9pm Mar-Oct, to 4pm Nov-Feb) is quite novel. The pinkish hue results from the eroding red Navajo sandstone in the area. Note that 1200 acres of the park are devoted to off-highway vehicles, so it's not necessarily a peaceful experience unless you're here during quiet hours (10pm to 9am), though a 0.5-mile interpretive dune-hike does lead to a 265-acre, ATV-free conservation area.

The same winds that shift the dunes can make tent camping unpleasant at the 22-site campground (☑800-322-3770; http://utahstateparks.reserveamerica.com; tent/RV sites $20/40), with toilets and hot showers; no hookups. Reservations are essential on weekends when off-roaders come to play.

Paria Canyon–Vermilion Cliffs Wilderness Area

With miles of weathered, swirling slickrock and slot-canyon systems that can be hiked for days without seeing a soul, it's no wonder that this wilderness area is such a popular destination for hearty trekkers, canyoneers and photographers. Day-hike permits cost $5 to $7 and several are very tough to get. General information and reservations are available at www.blm.gov/az/st/en/arolrsmain.html. In-season info and permits are picked up at Paria Contact Station (www.blm.gov/az; Mile 21, Hwy 89; ☺8:30am-4pm Mar 15–Nov 15), 44 miles east of Kanab. Rangers at the BLM Kanab Field Office are in charge of permits from November 16 through March 14. Remember that summer is scorching; spring and fall are best – and busiest. Beware of flash floods.

Day hikers fight like dogs to get a North Coyote Buttes permit. This trail-less expanse of slickrock includes one of the Southwest's most famous formations – the Wave.

The nearly magical sight of the slickrock that appears to be seething and swirling in waves is well worth the 6-mile, four- to five-hour round-trip hike. Go online to request advance permits four months ahead; otherwise you can hope for one of the handful of next-day walk-in permits available. Line up for the lottery by 7am in spring and fall.

As an alternative, take the 3.4-mile round-trip hike starting at Wire Pass trailhead, a popular slot-canyon day-hike with self-service trailhead permits. The pass dead-ends where Buckskin Gulch narrows into some thrillingly slight slots. Another option is to start at the Buckskin Gulch trailhead and hike 3 miles one-way to its narrow section.

Trailheads lie along House Rock Valley Rd (4.7 miles west of the contact station); it's a dirt road that may require 4WD. Inquire with rangers.

Two miles south of the contact station along a different dirt road, you come to primitive White House Campground (tent sites $5). The five walk-in sites have pit toilets, but no water and few trees. Overnight backcountry camping permits are easier to get than day-hike ones, and can be reserved online and in person. Use of human-waste carryout bags is encouraged; the contact station provides them for free.

Paria Outpost & Outfitters (☑928-691-1047; www.paria.com; Mile 21, Hwy 89; r incl breakfast $65; ✿✿) has spare B&B rooms at its kicked-back lodge with restaurant, with some basic camping between Kanab and the wilderness area. Outfitter trips and hiker shuttles available.

East Zion

Eighteen miles north of Kanab, the turnoff for Hwy 9 leads about 15 miles to the east entrance of Zion National Park.

Families love activity-rich Zion Ponderosa Ranch Resort (☑800-293-5444, 435-648-2700; www.zionponderosa.com; N Fork Rd, off Hwy 9; tent/RV sites $25/58, cabins $88-200; @ 🛜 ✿), occupying 4000 acres on Zion's eastern, up-country side. Several great backcountry trails lead from 4WD roads here into the national park. But you may never want to leave the property since you can hike, bike, canyoneer, climb, swim, play sports, ride four-wheelers and horses, and eat three meals a day right here (packages available). Wi-fi-enabled camping sites and cabins (linens included) are served by huge showers/

HIKING EAST ZION

East Zion has several little-traveled, up-country hikes that provide an entirely different perspective on the park, leading off from Zion Ponderosa Ranch Resort. **Cable Mountain** and **Deer-trap Mountain**, to name two, have incredible views.

It feels deliciously like cheating to wander through open stands of tall ponderosa pines and then descend 500ft to Observation Point instead of hiking 2500ft uphill from Zion Canyon floor; **East Mesa Trail** (6.4 miles round-trip, moderate difficulty) does just that. It's less legwork because it's a hearty drive. Getting to the trailhead requires a 4WD for the last few miles, but Zion Ponderosa Ranch Resort and outfitters in Springdale can provide hiker shuttles. Ask rangers for details.

Note that at 6500ft, these trails may be closed due to snow from November through March.

bathrooms. North Fork Rd is about 2.5 miles from the park's East Entrance; continue 5 miles north of Hwy 9 from there.

Closer to the highway, **Zion Mountain Ranch** (☑866-648-2555, 435-688-1039, campground 435-648-3302; www.zmr.com; Hwy 9; tent/RV sites $19/29, cabins $159-1155, ste $196-419; ✿@🛜✿) has a similar adventure and lodging set-up, though it's a bit fancier. Buffalo roam (and appear on the dinner menu) at this 6000-acre resort with numerous trails and a slot canyon. In season it runs a restaurant, pizza place and campground with showers, laundry service, wi-fi and full hookups. Registration is 2.5 miles east of the Zion park entrance.

Zion National Park

Get ready for an overdose of awesome. The soaring red-and-white cliffs of Zion Canyon, one of southern Utah's most dramatic natural wonders, rise high over the Virgin River. Hiking downriver through the Narrows or peering beyond Angels Landing after a 1400ft ascent is indeed amazing. But, for all its awe-inspiring majesty, the **park** (www.nps.gov/zion; Hwy 9; 7-day pass per vehicle $25; ⊘24hr, visitor center Jun-Aug 8am-7:30pm, closes earlier Sep-May) also holds more delicate beauties: weeping

Zion National Park

UTAH ZION NATIONAL PARK

rocks, tiny grottoes, hanging gardens and meadows of mesa-top wildflowers. Lush vegetation and low elevation give the magnificent rock formations here a whole different feel from the barren parks in the east.

Most of the 2.7 million annual visitors enter the park along Zion Canyon floor; even the most challenging hikes become congested May through September (shuttle required). But you have other options. Up-country, on the mesa tops (7000ft), it's easy to escape the crowds – and the heat. And the Kolob Canyons section, 40 miles northwest by car, sees one-tenth of the visitors year-round.

Summers are hot (100°F, or 38°C, is common), though summer nighttime temperatures drop into the 70s (low 20s in Celsius). Beware of sudden cloudbursts from July to September. Winter brings some snow, but daytime temperatures can reach up to 50°F (10°C). Wildflowers bloom in May, as do the bugs: bring repellant.

ⓘ Fees & Permits

Park admission is $25 per week, per vehicle, and an annual Zion Pass is $50. Note that you have to pay to drive through the park on Hwy 9, whether you plan to stop or not. Keep your

Zion National Park

receipt: it's good for both the main and Kolob Canyons sections.

Backcountry permits (📋 435-772-0170; www. nps.gov) are required for all overnight trips (including camping and rock climbs with bivouacs), all through-hikes of the Virgin River (including the Narrows top hike) and any canyoneering hikes requiring ropes for descent. Use limits are in effect on some routes to protect the environment. Online permit reservations ($5 reservation fee) are available for many trips, up until 5pm the preceding day. For busy routes there may be a lottery. Twenty-five percent of available permits remain reserved for walk-in visitors the day before or day of a trip. Trying to get a next-day walk-in permit on a busy weekend is like trying to get tickets to a rock concert; lines form at the Backcountry Desk by 6am or earlier.

Permit fees (which are in addition to the reservation fee) are $10 for one to two hikers, $15 for three to seven hikers, and $20 for eight to 12 hikers.

◉ Sights & Activities

The park occupies 147,000 acres. Driving in from east Zion, Hwy 9 undulates past yellow sandstone before getting to tighter turns and redder rock after the Zion–Mt Carmel Tunnel. Zion Canyon – with most of the trailheads and activities – lies off Hwy 9 near the south entrance, and the town of Springdale. No roads within the park directly connect this main section with the Kolob Canyons section in the northwest. Unless you hike, you'll have to drive the 40 miles (an hour) between the two, via Hwy 9, Rte 17 and I-15.

Scenic Drives

Zion Canyon Scenic Dr   DRIVING TOUR
The premier drive in the park leads between towering cliffs of an incredible red-rock canyon and accesses all the major front-country trailheads. A shuttle bus ride is required April through October. If you've time for only one activity, this is it. Your first stop should be the **Human History Museum** (📋435-772-0168; ⏰9am-7pm late May–early Sep, 10am-5pm early Mar–late May & early Sep–Nov, closed Dec–early Mar) **FREE**; the excellent exhibits and 22-minute film are a great introduction to the park. There are shuttle stops, and turn-outs, at viewpoints like the **Court of the Patriarchs**, at the **Zion Lodge**, and the end point, the **Temple of Sinawava**. Use the map you receive at the entrance to navigate. The shuttle takes 45 minutes round-trip; we suggest allowing at least two hours with stops.

Hwy 9   DRIVING TOUR
East of the main park entrance, Hwy 9 rises in a series of six tight switchbacks before the 1.1-mile Zion–Mt Carmel Tunnel, an engineering marvel constructed in the late 1920s. It then leads quickly into dramatically different terrain – a landscape of etched multicolor slickrock, culminating at the mountainous **Checkerboard Mesa**. If you have an RV or trailer, see p451 for more information on vehicle restrictions.

Kolob Canyons Rd   DRIVING TOUR
The less-visited, higher-elevation alternative to Zion Canyon Scenic Dr. Sweeping vistas of cliffs, mountains and finger canyons dominate this stunning, 5-mile red-rock route, rich with overlooks. The scenic road, off I-15, lies 40 miles from the main visitor center.

Hiking
Zion has everything from short day hikes for families to multiday backpacking trips.

UTAH ZION NATIONAL PARK

ANGELS LANDING TRAIL

Among harder trails, the 2.5-mile **Angels Landing Trail** (1490ft ascent) is the one everyone's heard of – and fears. At times the trail is no more than 5ft wide, with 1500ft drop-offs to the canyon floor on both sides. Follow the sandy flood plain until you start ascending sharply. After Walter's Wiggles, the set of 21 stonework zigzags that take you up a cleft in the rock, there's a wide area (with pit toilet) that offers vistas and a place to gather strength. Acrophobes may stop here, before the chain-assist rock climb and the 5ft-wide ridge – with 1000ft-plus drop-offs – that you have to cross. The final push to the top is even steeper, and requires some rock scrambling – but oh, the views from the top...

Trails can be slippery; ask rangers about weather conditions before you depart. There are hundreds of miles of backcountry (overnight) hiking trails with wilderness camping and enough quiet to hear the whoosh of soaring ravens overhead. If you hike the entirety of Zion, north to south, it's a four-day traverse of 50-plus miles. All backcountry hiking and camping requires a permit.

Flash floods occur year-round, particularly in July and August. Check weather and water conditions with rangers before hiking in river canyons. If you hear thunder, if water rises suddenly or goes muddy, or if you feel sudden wind accompanied by a roar, immediately seek higher ground. Climbing a few feet can save your life; if you can't, get behind a rock fin. There's no outrunning a flash flood.

Zion Canyon   HIKING

Spring to fall, the mandatory shuttle stops at all major trailheads along Zion Canyon Scenic Dr, allowing one-way hikes. In low season you can park at these stops, but you'll have to hike back to your car.

Of the easy-to-moderate trails, the mile-long **Riverside Walk** (1 mile) at the end of the road is a good place to start. When the trail ends, you can continue along in the Virgin River for 5 miles to **Big Springs**; this is the bottom portion of the **Narrows** – a difficult backpacking trip. Yes, you'll be hiking in the water (June through October), so be prepared.

A steep, but paved, half-mile trail leads to the lower of the **Emerald Pools**. Here water tumbles from above a steep overhang, creating a desert varnish that resembles rock art. It's worth your while to hike a mile further up the gravel to the more secluded Upper Pool. Note: you will have to scramble up (and back down) some stairlike rocks. The quarter-mile-long **Weeping Rock Trail** climbs 100ft to hanging gardens.

Hidden Canyon Trail has sheer drop-offs and an 850ft elevation change in just over a mile before you reach the narrow, shady canyon. Think of it as an easier test of your fear of heights.

The most work (2150ft elevation change) is rewarded with the best views – at the top of **Observation Point Trail** (4 miles). From here you look down on Angels Landing – heck, the whole park really. A backcountry shortcut, the East Mesa Trail, leads here with much less legwork.

The paved **Pa'rus Trail** parallels the scenic drive from Watchman Campground to the main park junction (about 2 miles). It's the only trail that allows bicycles and dogs.

The only marked trail along Hwy 9 in east Zion is **Canyon Overlook Trail**, a moderately easy half-mile walk, yielding thrilling views 1000ft down into Zion Canyon. But you can also stop at Hwy 9 pullouts where there are some interesting narrow canyon hikes and slickrock scrabbles. In summer, locals park at one turnout, climb down, cross under the road and follow a wash to the river for a cool dip...happy searching! Just be aware of your surroundings, and stay in the wash or on the rock to avoid damaging the desert ecology.

Kolob Terrace Road   HIKING

Fourteen miles west of Springdale, Kolob Terrace Rd takes off north from Hwy 9, weaving in and out of BLM and national park highlands. (The road is closed due to snow from at least November to March.) **Wildcat Canyon Trailhead** lies about 28 miles north, after a hairpin turn.

From here, follow the Wildcat Canyon Trail till you get to the turnoff for **Northgate Peaks Trail**. You'll traipse through meadows (filled with wildflowers in spring) and pine forests before you descend to the viewpoint overlooking the peaks. It's a whole different – and much less visited – side of Zion. Wildcat Canyon to Northgate Peaks overlook is 2.2 miles one-way.

About 5 miles north of Wildcat Canyon is the gravel road to **Lava Point**, where there's a lookout and a campground.

Kolob Canyons Road
HIKING

In the northwestern section of the park, the easiest trail is at the end of the road: **Timber Creek Trail** (0.5 miles) follows a 100ft ascent to a small peak with great views. The main hike is the 2.7-mile-long **Taylor Creek Trail**, which passes pioneer ruins and crisscrosses the creek.

The 7-mile one-way hike to **Kolob Arch** has a big payoff: this arch competes with Landscape Arch in Arches National Park in terms of being one of the biggest in the world. Fit hikers can manage it in a day, or continue on to make it a multiday backcountry trans-park connector.

The Narrows
HIKING

The most famous backcountry route is the unforgettable **Narrows**, a 16-mile journey into skinny canyons along the Virgin River's north fork (June through October). Plan on getting wet: at least 50% of the hike is in the river.

The trip takes 12 hours; split it into two days, spending the night at one of the designated campsites you reserved or finish the hike in time to catch the last park shuttle. The trail ends among the throngs of day hikers on Riverside Walk at the north end of Zion Canyon. A trailhead shuttle is necessary for this and other one-way trips.

Cycling

Zion Canyon Scenic Drive is a great road ride when cars are forbidden in shuttle season. You can even carry your bicycle up to the end of the road on the shuttle and cruise back down. Bikes are only allowed on the scenic drive and on the 2-mile Pa'rus Trail. Mountain biking is prohibited in the park, but there are other public land trails nearby. Rentals and advice are available in Springdale.

Climbing & Canyoneering

If there's one sport that makes Zion special, it's canyoneering. Rappelling over the lip of a sandstone bowl, swimming icy pools, tracing a slot canyon's curves...canyoneering is beautiful, dangerous and sublime all at once. Zion's slot canyons are the park's most sought-after backcountry experience; reserve far in advance.

Zion Canyon also has some of the most famous big-wall rock climbs in America. However, there's not much for beginners or those who like bolted routes. Permits are required

for all canyoneering and climbing. Get information at the Backcountry Desk at the Zion Canyon Visitor Center, which also has route descriptions written by climbers.

Guided trips are prohibited in the park. Outfitters in Springdale hold courses outside Zion, after which students can try out their newfound skills in the park.

The Subway
CANYONEERING

This incredibly popular route (9.5 miles, 1850ft elevation change) has four or five rappels of 20ft or less, and the namesake, tube-looking slickrock formation. Start at the Wildcat Canyon trailhead off Kolob Terrace Rd. Hiker shuttle required.

Mystery Canyon
CANYONEERING

Mystery Canyon lets you be a rock star: the last rappel drops into the Virgin River before admiring crowds hiking the Narrows. It's accessed off Zion Ponderosa Ranch roads in East Zion; ask rangers for more information. Backcountry permit required; hiker shuttle necessary.

Pine Creek Canyon
CANYONEERING

A popular route with moderate challenges and rappels of 50ft to 100ft, Pine Creek has easy access from near the Canyon Overlook Trail. A backcountry permit is required.

Other Activities

Canyon Trail Rides
HORSEBACK RIDING

(☑ 435-679-8665, 435-772-3810; www.canyonrides.com; 3hr rides $75; ☺ Mar-Nov) Zion's official horseback-riding concessionaire operates across from Zion Lodge. Ride on the Sand Bench Trail along the Virgin River.

Tours & Outfitters

Cycling, rock-climbing, canyoneering and driving-tour outfitters from Springdale operate outside the park.

Zion Canyon Field Institute
TOUR

(☑ 800-635-3959, 435-772-3264; www.zionpark.org; half-day from $50) Explore Zion by moonlight, take a wildflower photography class, investigate Kolob Canyon's geology or help clean up the Narrows. All courses and tours include some hiking.

Ride Along With A Ranger
DRIVING TOUR

(☑ 435-772-3256; www.nps.gov/zion; Zion Canyon Visitor Center; ☺ May-Oct) FREE Reservations are usually required for the entertaining, ranger-led Zion Canyon shuttle tour (90 minutes) that makes stops not on the regular route. It's a great nonhiking alternative for those with limited mobility.

Red Rock Shuttle & Tours
DRIVING TOUR

(☎435-635-9104; www.redrockshuttle.com) Offers private van tours of Zion ($100 per person for six hours).

🛏 Sleeping

Both of the park's large, established campgrounds are near the Zion Canyon Visitor Center. For wilderness camping at designated areas along the West Rim, La Verkin Creek, Hop Valley and the Narrows you'll need a permit. More lodging and camping is available in Springdale.

Watchman Campground
CAMPGROUND $

(☎reservations 877-444-6777; www.recreation. gov; Hwy 9, Zion National Park; tent sites $16, RV sites with hookups $20) Towering cottonwoods provide fairly good shade for the 165 well-spaced sites at Watchman (95 have electricity). Reservations are available May through October; book as far in advance as possible to request a riverside site. Fire grates, drinking water and flush toilets; no showers. Note that there are sometimes construction works happening during the winter season.

South Campground
CAMPGROUND $

(Hwy 9, Zion National Park; tent & RV sites $16; ⊘early Mar-Oct) The South Campground has very similar scenery and the same basic facilities as Watchman, except that here limited generator use is allowed because there are no hookups. The 116 first-come, first-served tent sites often fill up by 10am. Note that this ground sits beside the busy Pa'rus Trail.

Lava Point Campground
CAMPGROUND $

(Lava Point Rd, Zion National Park; ⊘Jun-Sep) Six first-come, first-served park sites 35 miles up Kolob Terrace Rd at 7900ft. Pit toilets, but no water.

Zion Lodge
LODGE $$

(☎435-772-7700, 888-297-2757; www.zion-lodge.com; Zion Canyon Scenic Dr; r/cabins/ste $185/$193/$226; ❄@?) We love the stunning red-rock cliffs on all sides, and the coveted location in the middle of Zion Canyon (along with the red permit that allows you to drive to the lodge in shuttle season). Be warned: today's reconstructed lodge is not as grand as other national park lodges (the 1920s original burned down in 1966).

Although they're in wooden buildings with balconies, the motel rooms are just motel rooms: nothing fancy. Carved headboards, wood floors and gas fireplaces do give 'Western cabins' more charm, but be warned that paper-thin walls separate you from neighbors. There are two eateries and a big lawn for lounging outside. No room TVs.

🍴 Eating

The lodge has the only in-park dining; otherwise head to Springdale.

Castle Dome Café
CAFE $

(Zion Canyon Scenic Dr, Zion Lodge; mains $8-15; ⊘11am-5pm Apr-Oct) This counter-service cafe serves sandwiches, pizza, salads, soups, Asian-ish rice bowls and ice cream.

Red Rock Grill
AMERICAN $$$

(☎435-772-7760; Zion Canyon Scenic Dr, Zion Lodge; breakfast & sandwiches $8-14, dinner mains $18-30; ⊘6:30-10:30am, 11:30am-3pm & 5-10pm Mar-Oct, hours vary Nov-Feb) Settle into your replica log chair or relax on the big deck with magnificent canyon views. Though the dinner menu touts its sustainable-cuisine stance for dishes like roast pork loin and flat-iron steak, the results are hit-or-miss. Dinner reservations recommended. Full bar.

ℹ Information

Visitor center hours vary slightly month to month. We list the minimums for each season.

Kolob Canyons Visitor Center (☎435-586-0895; www.nps.gov/zion; Kolob Canyons Rd, Zion National Park; ⊘park 24hr, center 8am-6pm Jun-Sep, to 4:30pm Oct-May) Small, secondary visitor center in the northwest section of the park.

Lonely Planet (www.lonelyplanet.com/usa/southwest/zion-national-park) Planning advice, author recommendations, traveler reviews and insider tips.

National Park Rangers Emergency (☎435-772-3322)

Zion Canyon Backcountry Desk (☎435-772-0170; www.nps.gov/zion/planyourvisit; Zion Canyon Visitor Center; ⊘7am-6pm May-Sep, 8am-4:30pm Oct-Apr) Provides backcountry trail and camping information and permits. Some permits available online.

Zion Canyon Visitor Center (☎435-772-3256; www.nps.gov/zion; Hwy 9, Zion National Park; ⊘8am-7:30pm late May–early Sep, 8am-5pm late Sep–early May) Several rangers are on hand to answer questions at the main visitor center; ask to see the picture binder of hikes to know what you're getting into. The large number of ranger-led activities are listed here.

Zion Lodge (435-772-3213; Zion Canyon Scenic Dr;) Free wi-fi and two free internet terminals in the lobby.

Zion Natural History Association (435-772-3264, 800-635-3959; www.zionpark.org) Runs visitor center bookstores; great online book selection for advance planning.

❶ Getting There & Around

BUS

There is no public transportation to the park.

St George Express (435-652-1100; www.stgeorgeexpress.com) Shared van service to St George ($100, one hour) and Las Vegas ($100, three hours). Powered by natural gas.

PRIVATE VEHICLE

Arriving from the east on Hwy 9, you have to pass through the free Zion–Mt Carmel Tunnel. If your RV or trailer is 7ft 10in wide or 11ft 4in high or larger, it must be escorted through, since vehicles this big need both lanes. Motorists requiring an escort pay $15 over the entrance fee, good for two trips. Between April and October, rangers are stationed at the tunnel from 8am to 8pm daily; at other times, ask at the entrance stations. Vehicles prohibited at all times include those more than 13ft 1in tall or more than 40ft long.

PARK SHUTTLE

How you get around Zion depends on the season. Between April and October, passenger vehicles are not allowed on Zion Canyon Scenic Dr. The park operates two free, linked shuttle loops.

The **Zion Park Shuttle** makes nine stops along the canyon, from the main visitor center to the Temple of Sinawava (a 45-minute round-trip).

The **Springdale Shuttle** makes six regular stops and three flag stops along Hwy 9 between the park's south entrance and the Majestic View Lodge in Springdale, the hotel furthest from the park. You can ride the Springdale Shuttle to Zion Canyon Giant Screen Theatre and walk across a footbridge into the park. The visitor center and the first Zion shuttle stop lie on the other side of the kiosk.

The propane-burning park shuttle buses are wheelchair-accessible, can accommodate large backpacks and carry up to two bicycles or one baby stroller. Schedules change, but generally shuttles operate from at least 6:45am to 10pm, every 15 minutes on average.

OTHER TRANSPORTATION

Outfitters that offer hiker shuttles (from $25 to $60 per person, two-person minimum, reservation required) to backcountry and canyoneering trailheads include:

Red Rock Shuttle & Tours (435-635-9104; www.redrockshuttle.com) Picks up from Zion Canyon Visitor Center.

Zion Adventure Company (435-772-1001; www.zionadventures.com)

Zion Rock & Mountain Guides (435-772-3303; www.zionrockguides.com)

Springdale

POP 547 / ELEV 3898FT

When the cottonwoods are budding against the red cliffs, Springdale is the perfect little park town, though more frequently, it's a bottleneck of traffic entering Zion National Park. The main drag – well, the only drag – features eclectic cafes, galleries and restaurants touting local produce and organic ingredients. Many residents were drawn here for the surroundings, but you will occasionally run into a lifelong local who thinks they're 'just rocks.'

◉ Sights & Activities

Hiking trails in Zion are the area's biggest attraction. There are also some awesome, single-track, slickrock mountain-bike trails as good as Moab's. Ask local outfitters about **Gooseberry Mesa**, **Hurricane Cliffs** and **Rockville Bench**.

The Virgin River is swift, rocky and about knee-deep: more of a bumpy adventure ride than a leisurely float, but tubing (outside the park only) is popular in summer. Note that from June to August, the water only warms to between 55°F and 65°F (13°C to 18°C). Zion Canyon Campground and some other riverside lodgings have good water-play access.

Zion Adventure Company Tubing WATER SPORTS (435-772-1001; www.zionadventures.com; 36 Lion Blvd; rentals $17-39; ⊙tubing 10am-4pm May-Sep) River-tubing packages include tube and water-sock rental, drop-off and pick-up. The float stretches about 2.5 miles, and lasts from 90 minutes to two hours depending on water flow. There's much faster, high-adventure tubing (including safety gear) on offer during spring run-off in May.

Deep Canyon Adventure Spa SPA (435-772-3244; www.deepcanyonspa.com; 428 Zion Park Blvd, Flanigan's Inn; 1hr treatments from $99) After a hard day's hike, the river-stone massage will be your muscles' new best friend.

Zion Canyon Elk Ranch FARM (435-619-2424; 792 Zion Park Blvd; by donation; ⊙dawn-dusk;) You can't miss this ranch right in the middle of town. It offers kids of

UTAH SPRINGDALE

all ages the chance to pet and feed the elk and buffalo. The property has been in the owner's family for more than 100 years.

☞ Tours & Outfitters

The town's two main outfitters, Zion Rock & Mountain Guides and Zion Adventure Company, lead hiking, biking, climbing, rappelling and multisport trips on the every-bit-as-beautiful BLM lands near the park (half-days from $150). We highly recommend canyoneering as a quintessential area experience. Both companies have excellent reputations and tons of experience.

Outfitters are also one-stop shops for adventure needs: they sell ropes and maps, have classes, provide advice and suit you up with rental gear (harnesses, helmets, canyoneering shoes, dry suits, fleece layers, water-proof packs and more). The hiker shuttles and gear rental are especially handy for one-way slot-canyon routes and Narrows hikes.

Zion Rock & Mountain
Guides
ADVENTURE SPORTS

(☑435-772-3303; www.zionrockguides.com; 1458 Zion Park Blvd; 4hr rock climbing tour $125; ☉8am-8pm Mar-Oct, hours vary Nov-Feb) More down-to-business than other outfitters, and especially good for sporty types. All classes and trips are private. Static rope-line rental available.

Bike Zion
MOUNTAIN BIKING

(☑435-772-0320; www.bikingzion.com; Zion Rock & Mountain Guides; full-day rentals $35-50) Zion Rock's on-site sister cycle shop; does rentals ranging from road bikes to full suspension and tours. Showers available.

Zion Adventure Company
ADVENTURE SPORTS

(☑435-772-1001; www.zionadventures.com; 36 Lion Blvd; half-day canyoneering tour $125; ☉8am-8pm Mar-Oct, 9am-noon & 4-7pm Nov-Feb) Slick videos and diagrams help put the tentative at ease; good for young families. Winter snowshoes and crampon rentals available.

Zion Cycles
MOUNTAIN BIKING

(☑435-772-0400; www.zioncycles.com; 868 Zion Park Blvd; full-day rentals $38-55; ☉9am-7pm Feb-Nov) Tandem, road and mountain-bike rentals and sales. No tours.

Red Desert Adventures
ADVENTURE SPORTS

(☑435-668-2888; www.reddesertadventure.com; half-day canyoneering tour from $135) A small company with the experienced area guides;

provides private guided hiking, biking, climbing and canyoneering.

Zion Outback Safaris
ADVENTURE TOUR

(☑866-946-6494; www.zionjeeptours.com; 2hr adult/child $60/45) Backroad 4WD tours in a 12-seat modified truck.

✸ Festivals & Events

Springdale celebrates quite often; contact the Zion Canyon Visitor Center for specifics.

St Patrick's Day
PARADE

The St Patrick's Day (March 17) parade and celebration includes a green Jell-O sculpture competition.

Zion Canyon Music Festival
MUSIC

(www.zioncanyonmusicfestival.com) One weekend in late September is filled with folk and other music.

🛏 Sleeping

Prices listed here are for March through October – rates plummet in the off-season. The lower the address number on Zion Park Blvd, the closer to the park entrance; all lodgings are near shuttle stops. Look for slightly less expensive B&Bs around Zion (in Rockville, for example).

Terrace Brook Lodge
MOTEL $

(☑435-772-3932, 800-342-6779; 990 Zion Park Blvd; r $85-109; ❀ ☎ ☒) This bare-bones basic motel does just fine. The two-bed rooms are newer than the singles.

Zion Canyon Campground & RV
Resort
CAMPGROUND $

(☑435-772-3237; www.zioncamp.com; 479 Zion Park Blvd; tent/RV sites with hookups $39/30; @ ☎ ☒ ❀) Water and tubing access at this 200-site campground are just across the Virgin River from the national park. Attached to the Quality Inn Motel; shared amenities include heated pool, laundry, camp store, playground and restaurant. Not all sites have shade.

★ Under the Eaves Inn
B&B $$

(☑435-772-3457; www.undertheeaves.com; 980 Zion Park Blvd; r incl breakfast $95-185; ❀ ☎) From colorful tractor reflectors to angel art, the owners' collections enliven every corner of this quaint 1930s bungalow. The fireplace suite is huge; other character-filled rooms are snug. Hang out in the arts-and-crafts living room or on Adirondack chairs and swings in the gorgeous gardens. The best room is the upstairs suite with clawfoot tub. Local restaurant coupon for breakfast.

Canyon Ranch Motel
MOTEL **$$**

(☑ 866-946-6276, 435-772-3357; www.canyon-ranchmotel.com; 668 Zion Park Blvd; r $99-139; ✱ 🕾 🛋 🐾) Small, cottage-like buildings surround a shaded lawn with redwood swings, picnic tables and a small pool at this 1930s motor-court motel. Inside, the rooms are thoroughly modern; apartments contain kitchenettes.

Driftwood Lodge
LODGE **$$**

(☑ 435-772-3262, 888-801-8811; www.driftwoodlodge.net; 1515 Zion Park Blvd; r $139-169, ste $169-205; ✱ 🕾 🛋 🐾) Rich textures and dark leathers mold the upscale style of thoroughly remodeled rooms at this eco-minded lodging. Some of the contemporary suites have pastoral sunset views of field, river and mountain beyond. With an expansive pool on the grounds.

Pioneer Lodge
MOTEL **$$**

(☑ 435-772-3233, 888-772-3233; www.pioneerlodge.com; 838 Zion Park Blvd; r $161-298; ✱ @ 🕾 🛋) In the absolute center of town; pine-bed rooms have a rustic feel and the rate feels stiff for what you're getting.

Harvest House
B&B **$$**

(☑ 435-772-3880; www.harvesthouse.net; 29 Canyon View Dr; r incl breakfast $130-165; ✱ 🕾) Modern B&B alternative with full breakfast.

Best Western Zion Park Inn
MOTEL **$$**

(☑ 435-772-3200, 800-934-7275; www.zionparkinn.com; 1215 Zion Park Blvd; r $179-229; ✱ @ 🕾 🛋) Rambling lodge complex includes a great room, putting green, badminton court, two pools, two restaurants and a liquor store.

Canyon Vista Suites B&B
B&B **$$**

(☑ 435-772-3801; www.canyonvistabandb.com; 897 Zion Park Blvd; ste incl breakfast $149-179; ✱ 🕾) All the homey comfort of a B&B, coupled with the privacy of a hotel. Individual entrances lead out from Southwestern or Old World–esque rooms onto a wooden porch or a sprawling patio and lawn with river access. Breakfast coupons; hot tub on-site.

Desert Pearl Inn
HOTEL **$$**

(☑ 435-772-8888, 888-828-0898; www.desertpearl.com; 707 Zion Park Blvd; r $178-198, ste $300; ✱ @ 🕾 🛋) How naturally stylish: twig sculptures decorate the walls and molded metal headboards resemble art. Opt for a spacious riverside king suite to get a waterfront patio.

Red Rock Inn
B&B **$$**

(☑ 435-772-3139; www.redrockinn.com; 998 Zion Park Blvd; cottages incl breakfast $169-209; ✱ 🕾) Five romantic country-contemporary cottages spill down the desert hillside, backed by incredible red rock. Enjoy the full hot breakfast (egg dish and pastries) that appears at the door either on the hilltop terrace or your private patio. One suite features an outdoor hot tub.

Novel House Inn
B&B **$$**

(☑ 435-772-3650, 800-711-8400; www.novelhouse.com; 73 Paradise Rd; r $139-159; ✱) Incredible detail has gone into each of the author-themed rooms: Rudyard Kipling has animal prints and mosquito netting, and a pillow in the Victorian Dickens room reads 'Bah humbug.' Breakfast coupons; hot tub.

Zion Canyon Bed & Breakfast
B&B **$$**

(☑ 435-772-9466; www.zioncanyonbandb.com; 101 Kokopelli Circle; r incl breakfast $135-185; ✱ 🕾) Deep canyon colors echo the scenery and over-the top Southwestern styling. Everywhere you turn there's another gorgeous red-rock view framed perfectly in an oversized window. Full gourmet breakfasts and mini-spa.

Cliffrose Lodge
HOTEL **$$$**

(☑ 800-243-8824, 435-772-3234; www.cliffroselodge.com; 281 Zion Park Blvd; r $179-299; ✱ 🕾 🛋) Kick back in a lounge chair or take a picnic lunch to enjoy on the five gorgeous acres of lawn and flower gardens leading down to the river. High-thread-count bedding and pillow-top mattresses are among upscale touches.

✗ Eating

Note that many places in town limit hours variably – or close entirely – during low season. Those listed as serving dinner have beer and wine only, unless otherwise noted. The saloon at Bit & Spur and the wine bar within Parallel 88 are fine places to drink as well as eat. Springdale is not big on nightlife.

Café Soleil
CAFE **$**

(205 Zion Park Blvd; breakfasts & mains $8-10; ⏱ 6:30am-7pm; 🕾 🍴) The food is every bit as good as the free-trade coffee. Try the Mediterranean hummus wrap or giant vegetable frittata; pizza and salads, too. It's a good spot to grab sandwiches for hiking. Breakfast served till noon.

Park House Cafe
CAFE $

(1880 Zion Park Blvd; breakfasts & sandwiches $5-12; ⊙7:30am-3:30pm Mar-Oct) Wake up as late as you like: Park House Cafe serves their Asiago bagel with egg and avocado – along with other breakfast items – until 2pm. Burgers, sandwiches and salads are all made from the freshest ingredients. Great little walled patio, too. Barbecue is served some summer evenings.

MeMe's Cafe
CAFE $

(www.facebook.com/memescafezion; 975 Zion Park Blvd; dishes $6-10; ⊙7am-9pm) For a coffee and *trés bonnes* crêpes – both sweet and savory – make MeMe's Cafe your first stop of the day. They also serve paninis and waffles, and in season have live music and barbecues on the expansive patio.

★ Whiptail Grill
SOUTHWESTERN $$

(☑435-772-0283; 445 Zion Park Blvd; mains $10-20; ⊙noon-9pm Mar-Nov; 🛜🅿) The old gas-station building isn't much to look at, but deep shade and fresh tastes abound: think gorgeous chile rellenos and *carne asada* tacos grilled to perfection. Desserts are rich with a kick. Outdoor tables fill up quick.

Oscar's Cafe
SOUTHWESTERN $$

(www.cafeoscars.com; 948 Zion Park Blvd; breakfast & burgers $10-15, dinner mains $16-30; ⊙8am-9pm) From green-chile laden omelets to pork *verde* burritos (with a green salsa), expect big servings of Southwestern spice. There's also smoky ribs and shrimp and garlic burgers. The Mexican-tiled patio with twinkly lights (and heaters) is a favorite hang-out in the evening.

Bit & Spur Restaurant & Saloon
SOUTHWESTERN $$

(www.bitandspur.com; 1212 Zion Park Blvd; mains $16-28; ⊙5-11pm daily Mar-Oct, to 10pm Thu-Sat Nov-Feb) Sweet-potato tamales and chile-rubbed rib-eyes are two of the classics at this local institution. Inside, the walls are wild with local art; outside on the deck it's all about the red-rock sunset. Full bar.

Flying Monkey
PIZZA $$

(975 Zion Park Blvd; mains $10-16; ⊙8am-9:30pm) Wood-fired goodness at great prices, though service is slow. Expect interesting ingredients like fennel and yellow squash on your roast veggie pizza or Italian sausage with the prosciutto on your oven-baked sandwich. Also serving breakfast.

Thai Sapa
ASIAN $$

(145 Zion Park Blvd; mains $10-27; ⊙noon-9:30pm Apr-Oct, hours vary Nov-Mar) This mix of Thai, Chinese and Vietnamese cuisine is your only Asian-cuisine option in town; service can be spotty.

Sol Foods Downtown Supermarket
MARKET

(☑435-772-3100; 995 Zion Park Blvd; ⊙7am-11pm Apr-Oct, 9am-8pm Nov-Mar) The 'big' supermarket in Springdale.

Zion Deli
DELI

(866 Zion Park Blvd; ⊙9am-8:30pm) Sharing a space with a souvenir shop, this one-counter wonder turns out good sandwiches (including boxed lunches for the park), breakfasts, chocolates and ice cream, all to go.

Switchback Trading Co
MARKET

(1149 Zion Park Blvd; ⊙noon-9pm Mon-Sat) The only liquor store in town is part of the Best Western complex.

★ Deep Creek Coffee Co
CAFE

(932 Zion Park Blvd; pastries $3-6; ⊙6:30am-2pm; 🛜) The town's best coffee, with espresso drinks and fresh pastries daily.

☆ Entertainment

OC Tanner Amphitheater
THEATER

(☑435-652-7994; www.dixie.edu/tanner; 300 Lion Blvd; ⊙mid-May–Aug) Outdoor amphitheater surrounded by red rock; stages classical, bluegrass, country and other concerts and performances.

Zion Canyon Giant Screen Theatre
THEATER

(www.zioncanyontheatre.com; 145 Zion Park Blvd; adult/child $8/6) Catch the 40-minute *Zion Canyon: Treasure of the Gods* on a six-story screen – it's light on substance but long on beauty.

🔒 Shopping

Eclectic boutiques and souvenir shops are scattered the length of Zion Park Blvd. Beyond the gorgeous nature photography, look for the three-dimensional oil paintings of Anna Weiler Brown and the colorful multimedia works of Deb Durban, both locals. Hours vary off season.

David Petit Gallery
ARTS & CRAFTS

(975 Zion Park Blvd; ⊙10:30am-8pm Wed-Sat, 3-8pm Tue) Our favorite intrepid outdoorsman-photographer. His rock art and ruin photos are unlike any others.

David J West Gallery ARTS & CRAFTS
(801 Zion Park Blvd; ⊙10am-9pm Tue-Sun Mar-Oct, to 8pm Nov-Feb) Iconic local-landscape photography; sells some photo gear.

★**Fatali Gallery** ARTS & CRAFTS
(105 Zion Park Blvd; ⊙11am-7pm Mar-Nov) Otherworldly colors in sensational national-park photography.

De Zion Gallery ARTS & CRAFTS
(1051 Zion Park Blvd; ⊙10am-9pm Wed-Sun Mar-Oct) Large studio, with many Utah artists represented.

Sundancer Books BOOKS
(975 Zion Park Blvd; ⊙10am-8pm Mar-Oct, off-season hours vary) Great selection of area-related interest books.

Redrock Jewelry JEWELERY
(998 Zion Park Blvd; ⊙10am-6pm Mar-Oct, off-season hours vary) Gorgeous, locally crafted jewelry.

ℹ **Information**

There's no town information office; go online to www.zionpark.com and www.zionnationalpark.com. The nearest full service hospital is in St George.
Doggy Dude Ranch (☑435-772-3105; www.doggyduderanch.com; 800 Hwy 9) Most local lodgings don't accept pets; board your pampered pooch 3.7 miles west of the park boundary. They also do pet-checks at area hotels.
Pioneer Lodge Internet Café (Zion Park Blvd; per 25min $2.50; ⊙6:30am-9pm) Two internet terminals.
Zion Canyon Medical Clinic (☑435-772-3226; 120 Lion Blvd; ⊙9am-5pm Tue-Sat Mar-Oct, shorter hours Nov-Feb) Walk-in urgent-care clinic.

ℹ **Getting Around**

There's no public transportation to the town, but from April through October the free Springdale Shuttle runs every 15 minutes between 7am and 8pm, with stops in town and Zion National Park.

Around Zion National Park

Just five miles west of Zion National Park, **Rockville** (no services) seems like a neighborhood extension of Springdale. There are a few old buildings, but otherwise it's mostly housing. B&Bs here can be a slightly cheaper alternative to those nearer the park.

The bicycle scene in *Butch Cassidy and the Sundance Kid* was filmed in the nearby **Grafton ghost town**. You can wander freely around the restored 1886 brick meeting house and general store, and a nearby pioneer cemetery. A few pioneer log homes stand on private property. Getting to Grafton can be tricky. Turn south on Bridge Rd, cross the one-lane bridge and turn right. Bear right at the fork and follow signs for 2 miles to the ghost town.

A landscaped backyard with a riverside pool, hot tub and breakfast terrace make **Desert Thistle Bed & Breakfast** (☑435-772-0251; www.thedesertthistle.com; 37 W Main St; r incl breakfast $115-145; ✴🛜🐾) the top choice, especially for summer. Rooms are posh and the Scottish owner, Maureen, is the consummate host. Penny-pinchers can try **Bunk House at Zion** (☑435-772-3393; www.bunkhouseatzion.com; 149 E Main St; s/d incl breakfast $78/90; 🛜) 🐾, a scruffy but thoroughly green two-bedroom B&B serving organic breakfasts and using 100% renewable energy. Other alternatives include floral-but-modern **Dream Catcher Inn** (☑435-772-3600, 800-953-7326; www.dreamcatcherinnzion.com; 225 E Main St; r incl breakfast $80-110; ✴🛜) and the spartan but pleasant rooms at older **Amber Inn** (☑435-772-9597; www.amber-inn.com; 244 W Main St; r $110-120; ✴🛜).

About 14 miles west of Springdale, the next community is **Virgin**; the turnoff to **Kolob Terrace Rd** and a couple of trading posts are here. Mind your manners – in 2000, the Virgin council passed a law requiring every resident to own a gun. (Locals are fined $500 if they don't.) West of town, a 1.5-mile gravel-and-dirt road leads south to **La Verkin Overlook**. Stop for a fantastic, 360-degree view of the surrounding 40 sq miles, from Zion to Pine Valley Mountains.

Hurricane, 22 miles west of Springdale, has the nearest full-size supermarkets and other services, including car washes.

Cedar City

POP 28,860 / ELEV 5850FT

This sleepy college town comes to life every summer when the Shakespeare festival takes over. Associated events, plays and tours continue into fall. Year-round you can make one of the many B&Bs a quiet homebase for exploring the Kolob Canyons section of Zion National Park or Cedar Breaks National Monument. At roughly 6000ft, cooler temperatures prevail here as compared to Springdale

(60 miles away) or St George (55 miles); there's even the occasional snow in May.

◉ Sights & Activities

Frontier Homestead State Park Museum
MUSEUM

(http://stateparks.utah.gov; 635 N Main St; admission $3; ⊙9am-5pm Mon-Sat; ♿) Kids love the cabins and the brightly painted 19th-century buggies, as well as the garden full of old farm equipment to run through. Living history demos take place June through August.

Cedar Cycle
CYCLING

(☑435-586-5210; www.cedarcycle.com; 38 E 200 South; bike rentals $29-49; ⊙9am-5pm Mon-Fri, to 2pm Sat) After you rent a bike (from $29 per day) the knowledgeable staff can point you to local trails.

✹ Festivals & Events

Cedar City is known for its year-round festivities. For a full schedule, check out www.cedarcity.org.

Utah Shakespearean Festival
THEATER

(☑435-586-7878, 800-752-9849; www.bard.org; Southern Utah University, 351 W Center St; tickets from $28) Southern Utah University has been hosting Cedar City's main event since 1962. From late June into September, three of the bard's plays and three contemporary dramas take the stage. From mid-September into late October three more plays are presented – one Shakespearean, one dramatic and one musical. Productions are well regarded, but don't miss the extras, all free: 'greenshows' with Elizabethan minstrels, literary seminars discussing the plays and costume classes. Backstage and scene-changing tours cost extra.

The venues are the open-air **Adams Shakespearean Theatre**, an 819-seat reproduction of London's Globe Theater; the modern 769-seat **Randall L Jones Theatre**, where backstage tours are held; and the less noteworthy **Auditorium Theatre** used for matinees and rainy days. Make reservations at least a few weeks in advance. At 10am on the day of the show, obscured-view gallery seats for the Adams performance go on sale at the walk-up **ticket office** (cnr 300 W & W Center Sts; ⊙10am-7pm late Jun–Aug & mid-Sep–Oct). Note that children under six are not allowed at performances, but free childcare is available.

Neil Simon Festival
THEATER

(www.simonfest.org) American plays staged mid-July to mid-August.

Groove Fest
MUSIC

(www.groovefestutah.com) A late September weekend grooves with folksy and funky sound.

Cedar City Skyfest
SPORTS

(www.cedarcityskyfest.org) Hot-air balloons, kites and model rockets go off in September.

🛏 Sleeping

Weekends during the Shakespearean Festival may cost more than the high season (March through October). A proliferation of good B&Bs is a boon for couples.

Anniversary House
B&B $$

(☑435-865-1266, 800-778-5109; www.theanniversaryhouse.com; 133 S 100 W; r incl breakfast

---

WORTH A TRIP

FREMONT INDIAN STATE PARK

Sixty miles northwest of Cedar City, off I-70, **Fremont Indian State Park & Museum** (☑435-527-4631; http://stateparks.utah.gov; 3820 W Clear Creek Canyon Rd; admission $6; ⊙9am-6pm, museum closed Sun) is a great introduction to one of Utah's other ancient peoples. Fremont Indians inhabited more northerly areas than the well-known ancient group known as the Anasazi, or Ancestral Puebloans. Indications are that the Fremont were fairly sedentary agriculturalists who tended to settle in small groups. Though much is still up for debate, many sites were probably plowed under on ground settled by Mormon pioneers (farmers do tend to like the same areas).

The park contains one of the largest collections of Fremont Indian rock art in the state – more than 500 panels on 14 interpretive trails. There's also a reconstructed kiva you can climb down into. Be sure to watch the visitor center film and pick up an interpretive brochure for the trails. To learn more, *Traces of Fremont*, by Steven Simms, is an excellent resource. Other Fremont sites include those in Dinosaur National Monument (p501), Nine Mile Canyon (p504) and Sego Canyon (p415).

$99-139; ❋ 🛜 🐾) Remarkably comfortable rooms, a great-to-talk-to-host and thoughtful extras make this one of our faves. Savor freshly baked cake and complimentary beverages in the mission-style dining room or lounge around in the landscaped backyard. Outdoor kennel available.

Garden Cottage B&B
B&B $$

(☑ 435-586-4919, 866-586-4919; www.thegardencottagebnb.com; 16 N 200 W; r incl breakfast $119-129; ❋ 🛜) Romantic vines climb up the steep-roofed cottage walls, and in season a fantasia of blooms grow in encompassing gardens. If you like antiques and quilts, you're going to love Garden Cottage. The owner has done an amazing job displaying family treasures. No room TVs.

Amid Summer's Inn
B&B $$

(☑ 435-586-2600, 888-586-2601; www.amidsummersinn.com; 140 S 100 W; r incl breakfast $115-185; ❋ @ 🛜) Tasteful additions have brought the guest room count to 11 at this 1930s home-based B&B. Common areas and some rooms have a Victorian feel; others are more over-the-top trompe l'oeil fantasies. Accommodating hosts; great breakfasts.

Iron Gate Inn
B&B $$

(☑ 435-867-0603, 800-808-4599; www.theirongateinn.com; 100 N 200 West; r incl breakfast $119-179; ❋ @ 🛜) With an on-site winery, this distinct 1897 Second Empire Victorian house features large, modern-luxury guest rooms, rambling porches and a big yard. Enjoy your breakfast on the large shady patio.

Best Western Town & Country
MOTEL $$

(☑ 435-586-9900, 800-780-7234; 189 N Main St; r incl breakfast $89-109; ❋ @ 🛜 🏊) Rooms are giant and rates are right at this well-cared-for Best Western.

Big Yellow Inn
B&B $$

(☑ 435-586-0960; www.bigyellowinn.com; 234 S 300 W; r incl breakfast $99-199; ❋ @ 🛜) A purpose-built Georgian Revival inn with room to roam: a dining room, a library, a den and many porches. Upstairs rooms are elegantly ornate. Downstairs, the ground-floor walk-out rooms are simpler and a bit more 'country'. The owners also oversee several adjunct B&B properties and vacation rentals around town.

🍴 Eating

Hours are usually extended variably during Shakespeare weekends.

WORTH A TRIP

PAROWAN GAP

People have been passing this way for millennia, and the **Parowan Gap** (www.blm.gov) FREE petroglyphs prove it. Look closely as you continue walking along the road to find panels additional to those signed. Archaeo-astronomers believe that the gap in the rocks opposite the petroglyphs may have been used as part of an ancient, astronomically based calendar. Cedar City's tourism office (p458) has colorful interpretive brochures explaining site details.

Sonny Boy's BBQ
BARBECUE $

(☑ 435-867-8010; 126 N Main St; mains $6-14; ⊙ 11am-9pm Mon-Thu, to 10pm Fri & Sat) Locals love the piles of Texas-style, slow-smoked meat and fun side dishes such as fried pickles. Eat in or take out.

★ Centro
PIZZA $$

(☑ 435-867-8123; 50 W Center St; pizzas $10-14; ⊙ 11am-10pm Mon-Sat) Serving wood-fired Neapolitan pizza and heaping bowls of fresh salad in a sleek atmosphere, Centro is a hub for hedonist appetites. Touches like hand-crushed tomato sauce and homemade fennel sausage up the ante. Though the wine list is basic, there's a good selection of brews. Good service.

Milt's Stage Stop
STEAK $$$

(☑ 435-586-9344; www.miltsstagestop.com; 3560 E Highway 14; mains $16-30; ⊙ 5-9pm) A Western steakhouse in a rustic red-rock setting, Milt's is very popular with locals for special occasions. Five miles east of town.

Grind Coffeehouse
CAFE

(19 N Main St; ⊙ 7am-7pm Mon-Sat, 8am-5pm Sun; 🛜) Hang out with the locals and have a barista-made brew, a great hot sandwich ($7 to $10) or a big salad. Sometimes there's music on the menu.

🔒 Shopping

Groovacious Music Store
MUSIC

(www.groovacious.com; 171 N 100 West; ⊙ 10am-9pm Mon-Sat) The local music store (with awesome vinyl) hosts concerts and other events.

UTAH CEDAR CITY

ℹ Information

Cedar City & Brian Head Tourism & Convention Bureau (☏ 435-586-5124, 800-354-4849; www.scenicsouthernutah.com; 581 N Main St; ☺ 8am-5pm Mon-Fri, 9am-1pm Sat) Area-wide info and free internet use.

Cedar City Ranger Station (☏ 435-865-3200; www.fs.fed.us/r4/dixie; 1789 N Wedgewood Ln; ☺ 8am-5pm Mon-Fri) Provides Dixie National Forest information.

Valley View Medical Center (☏ 435-868-5000; www.intermountainhealthcare.org; 1303 N Main St; ☺ 24hr) Hospital.

Zions Bank (3 S Main St) Currency exchange and ATM.

ℹ Getting There & Around

You'll need private transportation to get to and around Cedar City.

Hwy 14

As scenic drives go, **Hwy 14** is awesome. It leads 42 miles over the Markagunt Plateau, cresting at 10,000ft for stunning vistas of Zion National Park and Arizona. The surrounding area is part of Dixie National Forest (p423). For information, check in with Cedar City Ranger Station. Though Hwy 14 remains open all winter, snow tires or chains are required between November and April.

Hiking and biking trails pass the Cedar Breaks National Monument turnoff on Hwy 14 have tremendous views, particularly at sunset. They include the short (less than a mile one-way) **Cascade Falls** and **Bristlecone Pine Trail** and the 32-mile **Virgin River Rim Trail**. A signed turnoff 24.5 miles from Cedar City leads to jumbled **lava beds**.

Boating and fishing are the activities of choice at **Navajo Lake**, 25 miles east of Cedar City. You can rent canoes ($25) or motorboats ($80 to $175 per day) or stay over in a historic 1920s cabin at **Navajo Lake Lodge** (☏ 702-646-4197; www.navajolakelodge.com; cabins $89-144; ☺ May-Oct). The rustic lodgings include bedding, but no refrigerators.

Five miles further east, **Duck Creek Visitor Center** (☏ 435-682-2432; Hwy 14; ☺ 10am-5pm late May–early Sep) provides information for nearby trails and fishing in the adjacent pond and stream. Here at 8400ft, the 87 pine-shaded sites at **Duck Creek Campground** (☏ 877-444-6777; www.recreation.gov; Hwy 14; tent & RV sites without hookups $15-30; ☺ late May–early Sep) are blissfully cool in summer. The ever-expanding log-cabin town

Duck Creek Village (www.duckcreekvillage.com) has more services, including a couple of restaurants, realty offices, cabin-rental outfits, a laundromat and an internet cafe. The village area is big with off-road enthusiasts – ATVs in summer and snowmobiles in winter.

About 7 miles east of Duck Creek, a signed, passable dirt road leads the 10 miles to **Strawberry Point**, an incredibly scenic overview of red-rock formations and forest lands.

Cedar Breaks National Monument

Sculpted cliffs and towering hoodoos glow like neon tie-dye in a wildly eroded natural amphitheater encompassed by **Cedar Breaks National Monument** (☏ 435-586-0787; www.nps.gov/cebr; Hwy 148; 7-day pass per person $4; ☺ 24hr, visitor center 9am-6pm mid-Jun–mid-Oct). The majestic kaleidoscope of magenta, salmon, plum, rust and ocher rises to a height of 10,450ft atop the Markagunt Plateau. The compact park lies 22 miles east and north of Cedar City, off Hwy 14. (There are no cedar trees here, by the way: early pioneers misidentified the evergreen junipers.)

This altitude gets more than a little snow, and the monument's one road, Hwy 148, is closed from sometime in November through to at least May. Summer temperatures range from only 40°F to 70°F (4°C to 21°C); brief storms drop rain, hail and even powdery white snow. In season, rangers hold geology talks and star parties at the small **visitor center** (☏ 435-586-9451; Hwy 148; ☺ 8am-6pm Jun–mid-Oct).

No established trails descend into the breaks, but the park has five viewpoints off Hwy 148 and there are rim trails. **Ramparts Trail** – one of southern Utah's most magnificent trails – leaves from the visitor center. The elevation change on the 3-mile round-trip is only 400ft, but it can be tiring because of the overall high elevation. **Alpine Pond Trail** is a lovely, though less dramatic, 4-mile loop.

The first-come, first-served **Point Supreme Campground** (tent & RV sites without hookups $14; ☺ late Jun–Sep) has water and restrooms, but no showers; its 28 sites rarely fill.

Brian Head

The highest town in Utah, Brian Head towers over Cedar City, 35 miles southwest. 'Town' is a bit of an overstatement, though: this is basically a big resort. From Thanksgiving through

April, snow bunnies come to test the closest slopes to Las Vegas (200 miles). Snowmobiling in winter and mountain-biking in summer are also popular. The tiny **Brian Head Visitor Center** (☑ 435-677-2810; www.brianheadutah.com; Hwy 148; ⊙ 9am-4:30pm Mon-Fri; ☎) leaves pamphlets out after hours. The tourism office in Cedar City has more info.

Advanced skiers might grow impatient with the short trails (except on a powder day), but there's lots to love for beginners, intermediates and free-riders at **Brian Head Resort** (☑ 435-677-2035; www.brianhead.com; Hwy 143; 1-day lift ticket adult/child $45/32). Lines are usually short and it's the only resort in Utah within sight of the red-rock desert. Here's the lowdown: 1320ft vertical drop; base elevation, 9600ft; 640 acres and seven high-speed triple lifts. A ski bridge connects all the lifts. A highlight is the kickin' six-lane snow-tubing area (with surface lift), and there's a mini-terrain park for snowboarders.

Forty-two miles of cross-country trails surround Brian Head, including semi-groomed trails to Cedar Breaks National Monument.

During July and August the elevation keeps temperatures deliciously cool. Ride the **summer chair-lift** (adult/child $12.50/6.50; ⊙ 9:30am-4:30pm Fri-Sun Jul-Sep) up to 11,000ft for an alpine hike or mountain biking. The visitor center puts out a list of area trails.

The resort's lodges and town's sports shops, such as **Georg's Ski & Bike Shop** (☑ 435-677-2013; www.georgsskishop.com; Hwy 143), rent skis and snowboards, mountain bikes and more. Rent an ATV or a guided snowmobile tour with **Thunder Mountain Sports** (☑ 435-677-2288; www.brianheadthunder.com; 539 N Hwy 143; ⊙ 8:30am-5:30pm); half-days for each run cost $99 to $150.

Check the ski resort website for lodging and skiing packages – two nights in Vegas and two nights in Brian Head can be quite reasonable. A long list of condo rentals is avail-

---

IN SEARCH OF ANCIENT AMERICA

Cliff dwellings, centuries-old rock art and artifacts – the southern part of the state is a great place to explore the ancient Ancestral Puebloan cultures. Top sites include:

➡ Hovenweep National Monument (p391)

➡ Anasazi State Park (p426)

➡ Edge of the Cedars State Park (p395)

➡ Great Gallery, Canyonlands – Horseshoe Canyon (p400)

➡ Newspaper Rock Recreation Area (p396)

➡ Grand Gulch Primitive Area (p394)

But there's far more than that to explore: small ruins and petroglyphs are to be found all across BLM lands. We recommend you hire an outfitter in Bluff, Moab, Torrey, Boulder or Escalante – especially if you're an inexperienced backcountry hiker or don't have a 4WD. Their experience and knowledge will take you far.

If you're stocked with at least a gallon of water per person per day, know how to negotiate rock and sand in your high-clearance SUV and can read a topographic map, you may want to explore on your own. Ask locals for tips (hint: look for the ruin symbols on the *Delorme Utah Atlas & Gazetteer*). In the far southeast, a good place to start is off Comb Wash Rd (linking Hwys 95 and 163) near Bluff, as is Montezuma Canyon Rd, north of Hovenweep.

A few things to keep in mind:

➡ Take only pictures. Do not remove any artifacts you find – it's against the law. Not only will touching or moving items contaminate future study, you'll ruin the amazing experience for the next visitor.

➡ Tread lightly. Though sandstone structures seem sturdy, climbing on building walls causes irreparable damage. Don't do it.

➡ Respect the spiritual and historical value of these places – they are sacred to many Native Americans.

➡ Leave no trace – pack out anything you pack in. You'll have the least effect on the area's ecology if you walk on slickrock or in dry washes.

able on the visitor center website. But for our mountain-lodging buck, it's hard to beat warming by an outdoor fireplace or dining under the giant timber-frame trusses like those at the **Grand Lodge** (☏888-282-3327, 435-677-4242; www.grandlodgebrianhead.com; 314 Hunter Ridge Rd; r $119-195; @🖤🖤). Villa apartments at **Cedar Breaks Lodge & Spa** (☏435-677-900, 877-505-6343; www.cedarbreakslodge.com; 222 Hunter Ridge Rd; apt from $124; @🖤🖤) sleep four to eight and have kitchens – great for families. Both lodgings have spas.

Hawking their famous fruit pies, **Apple Annie's Country Store** (508 Hwy 143; ☺9am-6pm Mon-Sat; 🖤) is also the local grocery store, post office and state liquor store. The Tex-Mex menu at **Mi Pueblo** (406 S Hwy 143; mains $9-20; ☺noon-9pm) has a long list of beef and seafood dishes.

From December through April there's a free ski shuttle that travels around town.

St George

POP 75,561 / ELEV 2860FT

Nicknamed 'Dixie' for its warm weather and southern location, St George has long been attracting winter residents and retirees. (Brigham Young, second president of the Mormon church, was one of the first snowbirds in the one-time farming community here.) An interesting-if-small historic downtown core, area state parks and a dinosaur-tracks museum hold some attraction. But for travelers, the abundant and affordable lodging are what make this an oft-used stop between Las Vegas and Salt Lake City – or en route to Zion National Park after a late-night flight.

The town lies about 41 miles (up to an hour) from Zion National Park's south entrance, 30 miles (25 minutes) from the Kolob Canyons' entrance on I-15, and 57 miles (45 minutes) from Cedar City, to the north.

☉ Sights

Pick up a free, full-color, historic-building walking tour brochure at the visitor center. The intersection of Temple and Main Sts is at the heart of the old town center.

Dinosaur Discovery Site   MUSEUM
(www.dinotrax.com; 2200 E Riverside Dr; adult/child $6/3; ☺10am-6pm Mon-Sat, 11am-5pm Sun) St George's oldest residents aren't retirees from Idaho, but Jurassic-era dinosaurs. Entry gets you an interpretive tour of the huge collection of tracks, beginning with a video. The casts

were first unearthed by a farm plow in 2000 and rare paleontology discoveries, such as dinosaur swim tracks, continue to be made.

Mormon Sites   RELIGIOUS
The soaring 1877 **Mormon Temple** (440 S 300 East; ☺visitor center 9am-9pm) was Utah's first. It has a visitor center, but is otherwise closed to the general public. Built concurrently, the red-brick **Mormon Tabernacle** (cnr Tabernacle & Main Sts; ☺9am-5pm) occasionally hosts free music programs and is open to touring.

Brigham Young Winter Home   MUSEUM
(☏435-673-5181; 67 W 200 N; ☺9am-5pm) FREE A tour of the Mormon leader's seasonal home and headquarters illuminates a lot about early town and experimental-farming history.

Jacob Hamblin Home   MUSEUM
(Santa Clara Dr; ☺9am-5pm) FREE For another evocative picture of the Mormon pioneer experience, head 5 miles north of town to Santa Clara and the 1863 Jacob Hamblin Home, where orchards still grow.

Daughters of Utah Pioneers Museum   MUSEUM
(DUP; www.dupinternational.org; 145 N 100 East; ☺10am-5pm Mon-Sat) FREE Two floors packed full of pioneer artifacts, furniture, photographs, quilts, guns and so on.

🏃 Activities

Trails crisscross St George. Eventually they'll be connected and the trail along the Virgin River will extend to Zion; get a map at the visitor center. Mountain-bike rental costs $30 to 45 per day. And don't forget that Snow Canyon State Park (p463) is nearby.

A handful of local golf courses are open to the public (many more are private). Reserve up to two weeks in advance at www.sgcity.org/golf.

Green Valley Trail   MOUNTAIN BIKING
(off Sunbrook Rd) Also called Bearclaw Poppy, this 6-mile trail offers first-rate, playground-like mountain biking on slickrock.

☞ Tours & Outfitters

Bicycles Unlimited   MOUNTAIN BIKING
(☏435-673-4492; www.bicyclesunlimited.com; 90 S 100 East; ☺9am-6pm Mon-Sat) Rentals available.

Paragon Adventures   ADVENTURE SPORTS
(☏435-673-1709; www.paragonadventure.com) The offerings from this popular outfitter

range from road or mountain-bike tours, rock-climbing, small-group canyoneering, interpretive hikes, and popular zip-line adventures.

Red Rock Bicycle Company   MOUNTAIN BIKING
(☑435-674-3185; www.redrockbicycle.com; 446 W 100 S; ⊙9am-7pm Mon-Sat, to 3pm Sun) Rentals and servicing available.

★☆ Festivals & Events

A full festival list is available at www.stgeorgechamber.com.

Dixie Roundup   SPORTS
(☑435-628-8282) A mid-September weekend full of Western fun, including a parade and rodeo.

St George Marathon   SPORTS
(www.stgeorgemarathon.com) This October event takes over the town, attracting runners from all 50 states.

🛏 Sleeping

Around about Easter time, St George becomes Utah's spring-break capital. Head to St George Blvd and Bluff St near I-15 for chain motels. Pretty much every lodging offers a golf package. Tent campers will do best on nearby public lands.

Chalet Motel   MOTEL $
(☑435-628-6272; www.chaletmotelstgeorge.com; 664 E St George Blvd; s/d $69/79; P⊙❄✿) With a friendly Southern welcome, this impeccable motel stands out among the vast competition. Singles have kitchenettes and all units have updated bathrooms.

Dixie Palm Motel   MOTEL $
(☑435-673-3531, 866-651-3997; www.dixiepalms-motel.com; 185 E St George Blvd; r $85-91; ❋❄✿) It may not look like much outside, but regular maintenance and TLC put the Dixie Palm at the head of the low-budget pack. The 15 rooms have minifridges and microwaves.

America's Best Inn & Suites   MOTEL $
(☑435-652-3030, 800-718-0297; www.beststgeorge.com; 245 N Red Cliffs Dr; r incl breakfast $58-110; ❋@❄✿) With a mammoth campus there's no intimacy here, but it's well positioned off I-15, with good facilities.

Temple View RV Resort   CAMPGROUND $
(☑435-673-6400, 800-776-6410; www.templeviewrv.com; 975 S Main St; tent/RV sites with hookups $31/42; @❄✿) The 260 sites at this mega resort mostly accommodate RVs (up to 45ft),

but there are a few tent spots. Amenities include a rec room, business center, swimming pool, gym, putting green and cable hookups.

★ Seven Wives Inn   B&B $$
(☑800-600-3737, 435-628-3737; www.sevenwivesinn.com; 217 N 100 West; r & ste incl breakfast $109-185; ❋@❄✿) Two 1800s homes and a cottage feature lovely bedrooms and suites surrounded by well-tended gardens and a small pool. The name comes from settler times, when one of the owners harbored fugitive polygamists (including one with seven wives) in the 1880s.

Green Gate Village   INN $$
(☑435-628-6999, 800-350-6999; www.greengatevillageinn.com; 76 W Tabernacle St; r incl breakfast $99-199; ❋❄✿) Book a room or a whole house from among nine historic buildings brought together to make a historic village of sorts, complete with a general store. Antiques such as white-iron beds and ornate carved vanities figure prominently in all the lodgings.

Best Western Coral Hills   MOTEL $$
(☑800-542-7733, 435-673-4844; www.coralhills.com; 125 E St George Blvd; r incl breakfast $80-149; ❋@❄✿) You can't beat being a block or two from downtown restaurants and historic sights. Waterfalls and spiffed-up decor set this locally owned franchise apart.

Red Mountain Resort & Spa   RESORT $$$
(☑435-673-4905, 877-246-4453; www.redmountainspa.com; 1275 E Red Mountain Circle; r from $195; ❋@❄✿❀) A Zen-chic sensibility pervades this low-profile adobe resort, right down to the silk pillows that echo the copper color of surrounding cliffs. Full meals, guided hikes, spa services and fitness classes are available and may be included depending on the accommodation package.

The Inn at Entrada   RESORT $$$
(☑435-634-7100; www.innatentrada.com; 2588 West Sinagua Trail; cottages $179-249; P⊙❋ ❄✿) Nestled in red rock and xeriscaped for low-water consumption, this private country club has luxury adobe cottages with hot tubs, gas fireplaces and ample amenities. Other perks include a golf course, on-site restaurant and spa. There's a $20 resort fee.

Green Valley Spa   RESORT $$$
(☑435-628-8060, 800-237-1068; www.greenvalleyspa.com; 1871 W Canyon View Dr; r $169-399; @✿) Luxury spa and sports resort: 4000-sq-ft golf center, 14 tennis courts and

six swimming pools. Hiking and weight-loss programs feature prominently.

✖ Eating & Drinking

All the big chain restaurants and megamarts you'd expect line up along I-15.

Thomas Judd's General Store   ICE CREAM $
(76 Tabernacle St; ice cream $1.50-3; ⊙ 11am-9pm Mon-Sat) Stop for a sweet scoop of ice cream or piece of nostalgic candy in Green Gate Village.

Bear Paw Café   CAFE $
(75 N Main St; mains $5-9; ⊙ 7am-3pm Mon-Sat) Homey cafe with big breakfasts.

★ Riggatti's Wood Fired Pizza   PIZZA $$
(☎ 435-674-9922; 73 North Main; mains $10-18; ⊙ 11am-8pm Mon-Thu, to 9pm Fri & Sat) With a fanatical local following, this tiny pizzeria is a boon for travelers searching for thin-crust pizzas with bubbling mozzarella and pesto. Grab one of the very few counter seats and save room for hot cinnamon sticks.

Twenty-Five on Main   CAFE $$
(25 N Main St; mains $7-12; ⊙ 8am-9pm Mon-Thu, to 10pm Fri & Sat) A lovely, modern cafe with sidewalk tables. Homemade cupcakes are not all they do well – check out the breakfast panini, the warm salmon salad and the pasta primavera, overflowing with veggies.

Benja Thai & Sushi   ASIAN $$
(W St George Blvd, Ancestor Sq; mains $12-15; ⊙ 11:30am-10pm Mon-Sat, 5-9pm Sun) The pan-Asian menu here is certainly more diverse than most offerings in St George. Eclectic specialty rolls share a menu with pad Thai and teriyaki chicken.

★ Painted Pony   MODERN AMERICAN $$$
(☎ 435-634-1700; www.painted-pony.com; 2 W St George Blvd, Ancestor Sq; sandwiches $9-12, dinner mains $24-35; ⊙ 11am-10pm) Think gourmet comfort food and great salads. At dinner you might choose a juniper-brined pork chop; at lunch, meatloaf with a port-wine reduction and rosemary mashed potatoes.

Xetava Gardens Cafe   MODERN SOUTHWESTERN $$$
(☎ 435-656-0165; www.xetava.com; 815 Coyote Gulch Ct, Ivins; breakfast & sandwiches $6-13, dinner $13-34; ⊙ 8am-4pm daily, plus 5:30-9pm Thu-Sat; ☑) We'd drive much further than 8 miles for the creative Southwestern cuisine served here in a stunning red-rock setting. Try dishes like organic blue-corn waffles and chile-rubbed lamb. Dinner reservations recommended.

Anasazi Steakhouse   STEAK $$$
(☎ 435-674-0095; www.anasazisteakhouse.com; 1234 W Sunset Blvd; mains $17-33; ⊙ 5-9:30pm) Grill your steak (or shrimp, or portabello mushroom...) yourself on a hot volcanic rock.

☆ Entertainment

St George gets pretty quiet after dark. For any area music or events, check listings in free monthly newspaper the *Independent* (www.suindependent.com).

Tuacahn Amphitheater   THEATER
(☎ 800-746-9882, 435-652-3300; www.tuacahn.org) Ten miles northwest in Ivins; hosts musicals in summer and other performances year-round.

St George Musical Theater   THEATER
(☎ 435-628-8755; www.sgmt.org; 37 S 100 West) Puts on musicals year-round.

ℹ Information

Additional information is available at www.utahsdixie.com and www.sgcity.org.

Chamber of Commerce (☎ 435-628-1658; www.stgeorgechamber.com; 97 E St George Blvd; ⊙ 9am-5pm Mon-Fri) The visitor center caters to relocating retirees, and has loads of city info.

Dixie Regional Medical Center (☎ 435-251-1000; www.intermountainhealthcare.org; 1380 E Medical Center Dr; ⊙ 24hr) Hospital.

St George Field Office (☎ 435-688-3200; 345 E Riverside Dr; ⊙ 8am-4pm Mon-Fri) Get interagency information on surrounding public lands: USFS, BLM and state parks. Topographic maps and guides available.

Utah Welcome Center (☎ 435-673-4542; http://travel.utah.gov; 1835 S Convention Center Dr, Dixie Convention Center; ⊙ 8:30am-5:30pm) Statewide information 2 miles south of St George. There's a wildlife museum (think taxidermy) on-site with the same hours.

ℹ Getting There & Around

St George is on I-15 just north of the Arizona border, 120 miles from Las Vegas and 305 miles from SLC.

AIR

Taxis (to downtown, $15) and all the big-chain car-rental companies are represented at the St George airport. Note that Las Vegas McCarran International Airport, 120 miles south, often has better flight and car-rental deals than Utah airports.

Delta (☑ 800-221-1212; www.delta.com) Connects SLC and St George several times daily.

St George Municipal Airport (SGU; www.flysgu.com; 4550 S Airport Parkway) A new airport with expanded service.

United Express (☑ 800-864-8331; www.united.com) Has four weekly flights to and from Los Angeles, CA.

BUS

Greyhound (☑ 435-673-2933; www.greyhound.com; 1235 S Bluff St) Buses depart from the local McDonald's en route to SLC ($65, 5½ hours) and Las Vegas, NV ($30, two hours).

St George Express (☑ 435-652-1100; www.stgeorgeexpress.com; 1040 S Main St) Shuttle service to Las Vegas, NV ($39, two hours) and Zion National Park ($25, 40 minutes).

Around St George

Follow Hwy 18 northwest out of St George and you'll come to a series of parks and attractions before reaching higher elevations and Dixie National Forest. Go northeast of town on I-15 for more parks and a small ghost town.

Snow Canyon State Park

Red and white swirls of sandstone flow like lava, and actual lava lies broken like sheets of smashed marble in this small, accessible park. **Snow Canyon** (☑ 435-628-2255; http://stateparks.utah.gov; 1002 Snow Canyon Dr, Ivins; per vehicle $6; ⊙ day use 6am-10pm; ♿) is a 7400-acre sampler of southwest Utah's famous land features, 11 miles northwest of St George. Easy trails, perfect for kids, lead to tiny slot canyons, cinder cones, lava tubes and fields of undulating slickrock. Summers are blazing hot: visit in early morning or come in spring or fall. The park was named after prominent Utah pioneers Lorenzo and Erastus Snow, not frozen precipitation, but for the record it does snow very occasionally here. Check the website for free park events like hikes and talks.

Hiking trails loop off the main road. **Jenny's Canyon Trail** is an easy 1-mile round-trip to a short slot canyon. Wind through a cottonwood-filled field and past ancient lava flows to a 200ft arch on **Johnson Canyon Trail** (2-mile round-trip). A 1000ft stretch of vegetation-free **sand dunes** serves as a playground for the kiddies, old and young, near a picnic area.

Cycling is popular on the main road through the park, a 17-mile loop from St George (where you can rent bikes). There's also great **rock climbing** in the park, particularly for beginners, with over 150 bolted and sport routes, plus top roping.

Apart from during the unrelenting summer, the 35-site **campground** (☑ 800-322-3770; http://utahstateparks.reserveamerica.com; tent/RV sites with partial hookups $16/20) is great, and so scenic. You can reserve one of the 30 sites (14 with electrical and water hookups) up to four months in advance. Showers and dump station available.

Veyo

POP 483 / ELEV 4485FT

The tiny village of Veyo lies 17 miles north of St George on Hwy 18. A warm, spring-fed swimming pool (about 80°F, or 27°C) on the Santa Clara River is the main attraction at **Veyo Pool & Crawdad Canyon Climbing Park** (☑ 435-574-2300; www.veyopool.com; Veyo Pool Resort Rd; adult/child swim $7/5, climbing $8, camping per person $5; ⊙ 11am-8pm May-Aug). But there's also a cafe, picnicking area and sun deck. Eighty-foot high basalt walls in Crawdad Canyon are perfect for rock climbing and have been equipped with more than 100 bolted routes.

Back on the highway there are competing stores that sell homemade mini-pies.

Mountain Meadows Massacre Monument

About 10 miles north of Veyo on Hwy 18 stands a remote monument to one of the darkest incidents in the Mormon settlement of Utah. In 1857, for reasons that remain unclear, Mormons and local Indians killed about 120 non-Mormon pioneers – including women and children – who were migrating through the area. The simple, freely accessible monument, maintained by the LDS, is well-kept but provides little information. On September 11, 2011 it was declared a national historic landmark, so this may change. In the meantime, if you're interested in finding out more, the book *Massacre at Mountain Meadows*, by Ronald Walker, and documentaries such as *Burying The Past: Legacy of the Mountain Meadows Massacre*, fully illuminate the subject. Honestly, the story is a lot more compelling than the sight.

Pine Valley Mountain Wilderness

Mountains rise sharply in the 70-sq-mile **Pine Valley Wilderness Area** (☑ 435-652-3100; www.fs.fed.us/r4/dixie) in the Dixie

National Forest, 32 miles northwest of St George off Hwy 18. The highest point, **Signal Peak** (10,365ft), remains snow-capped till July, and rushing streams lace the mountainous area. The St George Field Office provides information and free backcountry permits.

When the desert heat blurs your vision, Pine Valley offers cool respite. Most hikes here begin as strenuous climbs. The 5-mile round-trip **Mill Canyon Trail** and the 6-mile **Whipple Trail** are most popular, each linking with the 35-mile **Summit Trail**.

Pine Valley Recreation Complex (☑877-444-6777; www.recreation.gov; tent & RV sites $15, day-use fee varies with group size; ☉May-Sep), 3 miles east of Pine Valley, has a couple of pine-shaded campgrounds at 6800ft. They all have water, but no showers or hookups; bring mosquito repellent.

Silver Reef Ghost Town

A few of the old stone buildings are inhabited, while others are crumbling at this 19th-century silver-mining ghost town. The restored **Wells Fargo building** (☉10am-4pm Mon-Sat) `FREE` houses a museum and art gallery. Diagrams of the rough-and-tumble town and mine give a feel of what it was like back in the day. You do need them because it's hard to imagine, giving the encroaching subdivision. Take exit 23 off I-15, 13 miles northeast of St George (past Leeds).

Hildale–Colorado City

ELEV 5050FT

Just 42 miles southeast of St George on Hwy 9, straddling the Utah–Arizona border, sit the twin towns of Hildale (pop 2921) and Colorado City (pop 4830). Though the official Mormon church eschewed plural marriage in 1890, there are still those who believe it is a divinely decreed practice. The majority of the approximately 7000 residents here belong to the polygamy-practicing Fundamentalist Church of Jesus Christ of Latter-Day Saints (FLDS). The spotlight focused on this religious community when leader Warren Jeffs was convicted of being an accomplice to rape here in 2007. After that, many of the FLDS faithful, including Jeffs, moved to a fenced compound in Texas. There he was convicted of child sexual assault for 'spiritual marriages' resulting in the pregnancies of underage girls, and sentenced to life in a Texas prison in 2011.

Other than residents' old-fashioned clothing and a proliferation of really large houses (for multiple wives and their many children), these look like any other American towns. We recommend you respect their privacy. However, if you walk into a Wal-Mart in Washington or Hurricane and see several varying-age females shopping together wearing pastel-colored, prairie-style dresses and lengthy braids or elaborate up-dos, it's a pretty safe guess that they are sister wives. Other, less conspicuous sects are active in the state as well.

SALT LAKE REGION

The vast Salt Lake Valley is the spot Brigham Young claimed when he announced 'this is the place!' to his pioneering followers in 1847. Today almost 80% of the state's population, nearly 2 million people, live along the eastern edge of the Wasatch Mountains from Ogden to Provo. Salt Lake City (SLC) sits smack in the middle of this concentration, but you'd never know it from the small size of the city.

To the north and west lie the Great Salt Lake and 100 miles of salt flats stretching into Nevada.

Salt Lake City

POP 191,180 / ELEV 4226FT

Utah's capital city, and the only one with an international airport, emanates a small-town feel. Downtown is easy to get around and – outside of entertainment enclaves – come evening it's fairly quiet. You'd never know 1.2 million people live in the metro area. Yes, this is the Mormon equivalent of Vatican City, and the LDS owns a lot of land, but less than half the town's population are church members – the university and the great-outdoors-at-your-doorstep vibe have attracted a wide range of residents. A liberal spirit is evident everywhere, from the coffeehouses to the yoga classes, where elaborate tattoos are the norm. Foodies will find much to love among the multitude of international and organic dining options (think Himalayan and East African). And when the trail beckons, you're a scant 45 minutes from the Wasatch Mountains' brilliant hiking and skiing. Friendly people, great food and outdoor adventure – what could be better?

◎ Sights

Mormon Church–related sights cluster mostly near the downtown centerpoint for SLC addresses: the intersection of Main

Greater Salt Lake City

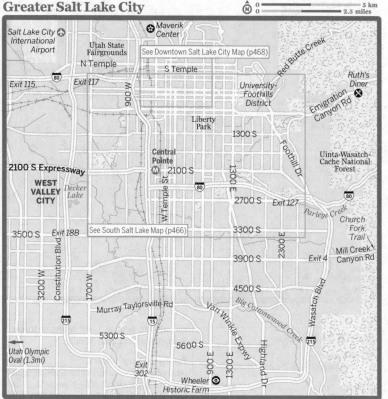

and South Temple St. (Streets are so wide – 132ft – because they were originally built so that four oxen pulling a wagon could turn around.) The downtown hub expects to experience a renaissance with the development of City Creek. To the east, the University-Foothills District has most of the museums and kid-friendly attractions.

Temple Square & Around

Temple Square PLAZA

(Map p468; www.visittemplesquare.com; cnr S Temple & N State Sts; ☺ grounds 24hr, visitor centers 9am-9pm) **FREE** The city's most famous sight occupies a 10-acre block surrounded by 15ft-high walls. LDS docents give free, 30-minute tours continually, leaving from the visitor centers at the two entrances on South and North Temple Sts. Sisters, brothers and elders are stationed every 20ft or so to answer questions. (Don't worry, no one is going to try to convert you –

unless you express interest.) In addition to the noteworthy sights, there are administrative buildings and two theater venues.

Salt Lake Temple RELIGIOUS

(Map p468; Temple Sq; ☺ closed to the public) Lording over Temple Sq is the impressive 210ft-tall Salt Lake Temple. Atop the tallest spire stands a statue of the angel Moroni, who appeared to LDS founder Joseph Smith. Rumor has it that when the place was renovated, cleaners found old bullet marks in one of the gold-plated surfaces. The temple and ceremonies are private, open only to LDS members in good standing.

Tabernacle RELIGIOUS

(Map p468; www.mormontabernaclechoir.org; Temple Sq; ☺ 9am-9pm) **FREE** The domed, 1867 auditorium – with a massive 11,000-pipe organ – has incredible acoustics. A pin dropped in the front can be heard in the back, almost 200ft away. Free daily organ

South Salt Lake

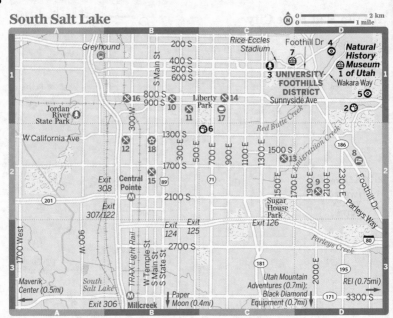

recitals are held at noon Monday through Saturday, and at 2pm Sunday.

Family History Library
LIBRARY
(Map p468; www.lds.org/locations/temple-square-family-history-library; 35 N West Temple St; ⊗ 8am-5pm Mon, to 9pm Tue-Fri, 9am-5pm Sat) FREE Thousands of people come to Salt Lake City every year to research their family history here, the largest genealogical resource on Earth. Because the LDS believes you must pray on your ancestors' behalf to help them along their celestial path, it has acquired a mind-boggling amount of genealogical information to help identify relatives. Volunteers scour the globe microfilming records in the tiniest of villages and then make them freely available here, as well as through libraries across the country.

Joseph Smith Memorial Building
CULTURAL CENTRE
(Map p468; 15 E South Temple St; ⊗ 9am-9pm Mon-Sat) FREE East of the Brigham Young Monument, this building was the elegant Hotel Utah until 1987. Inside, there's a large-screen theater with eight daily screenings of a 65-minute film about Mormon beliefs, entitled *Joseph Smith: The Prophet of the Restoration.*

Beehive House
HISTORIC BUILDING

(Map p468; ☑801-240-2671; www.visittemplesquare.com; 67 E South Temple St; ☺9am-8:30pm Mon-Sat) FREE Brigham Young lived with one of his wives and families in the Beehive House during much of his tenure as governor and church president in Utah. The required tours vary in the amount of historic house detail provided versus religious education offered, depending on the particular LDS docent. The attached 1855 **Lion House**, which was home to a number of Young's other wives, has a self-service restaurant (p472) in the basement. Feel free to look around the dining rooms during mealtimes.

Brigham Young Monument
MONUMENT

(Map p468) On Main St at South Temple St, the Brigham Young Monument marks the zero point for the city.

Museum of Church History & Art
MUSEUM

(Map p468; www.churchhistorymuseum.org; 45 N West Temple St; ☺9am-9pm Mon-Fri, 10am-7pm Sat & Sun) FREE Adjoining Temple Sq, this museum has impressive exhibits of pioneer history and fine art.

◉ Greater Downtown

Salt Lake City Main Library
LIBRARY

(Map p468; www.slcpl.org; 210 E 400 South; ☺9am-9pm Mon-Thu, to 6pm Fri & Sat, 1-5pm Sun) You can do more than read a book at this library. Meander past dramatic glass-walled architecture, stroll through the roof garden or stop by the ground-floor shops (from gardening to comic-book publishing). Occasional concerts are held here, too.

Utah State Capitol
HISTORIC BUILDING

(Map p468; www.utahstatecapitol.utah.gov; 350 N State St; ☺7am-8pm Mon-Fri, 8am-6pm Sat & Sun; visitor center 8:30am-5pm Mon-Fri) FREE The grand, 1916 State Capitol is set among 500 cherry trees on a hill north of Temple Sq. Inside, colorful Works Progress Administration (WPA) murals of pioneers, trappers and missionaries adorn part of the building's dome. Free guided tours (hourly, 9am to 5pm, Monday to Friday) start at the 1st-floor visitor center; self-guided tours are available from the visitor center.

Pioneer Memorial Museum
MUSEUM

(Map p468; www.dupinternational.org; 300 N Main St; ☺9am-5pm Mon-Sat, to 8pm Wed) FREE You'll find relics from the early days at Daughters of Utah Pioneers (DUP) museums throughout Utah, but the Pioneer Memorial Museum is by far the biggest. The vast, four-story treasure trove is like Utah's attic, with a taxidermied two-headed lamb and human-hair artwork in addition to more predictable artifacts.

Clark Planetarium
MUSEUM

(Map p468; ☑801-456-7827; www.clarkplanetarium.org; 110 S 400 West; tickets adult/child $9/7; ☺10:30am-10pm Sun-Thu, to 11pm Fri & Sat) You'll be seeing stars at Clark Planetarium, home to the latest and greatest 3-D sky shows and Utah's only IMAX theater. There are free science exhibits, too. The planetarium is on the edge of the Gateway, a combination indoor-outdoor shopping complex anchored by the old railway depot.

Gilgal Garden
GARDENS

(Map p468; www.gilgalgarden.org; 749 E 500 South; ☺8am-8pm Apr-Sep, 9am-5pm Oct-Mar) Talk about obscure: Gilgal Garden is a quirky little green space hidden in a residential neighborhood. Most notably, this tiny sculpture garden contains a giant stone sphinx wearing Mormon founder Joseph Smith's face.

◉ University-Foothills District

★ Natural History Museum of Utah
MUSEUM

(Map p466; http://nhmu.utah.edu; 301 Wakara Way; adult/child $11/9; ☺10am-5pm Thu-Tue, to 9pm Wed) The stunning architecture of the Rio Tinto Center forms a multistory indoor 'canyon' that showcases exhibits to great effect. Walk up through the layers as you explore both indigenous peoples' cultures and natural history. Past Worlds paleontological displays are the most impressive – an incredible perspective from beneath, next to and above an impressive collection of dinosaur fossils offers the full breadth of pre-history.

This is the Place Heritage Park
HISTORIC SITE

(Map p466; www.thisistheplace.org; 2601 E Sunnyside Ave; adult/child $11/8; ☺9am-5pm Mon-Sat, 10am-5pm Sun; ⊞) Dedicated to the 1847 arrival of the Mormons, the heritage park covers 450 acres. The centerpiece is a living-history village where, June through August, costumed docents depict mid-19th-century life. Admission includes a tourist-train ride and activities. The rest of the year, access is limited to varying degrees at varyingly reduced prices; you'll at

Downtown Salt City

least be able to wander around the exterior of the 41 buildings. Some are replicas, but some are originals, such as Brigham Young's farmhouse.

Red Butte Garden   GARDENS
(Map p466; www.redbuttegarden.org; 300 Wakara Way; adult/child $10/6; ⊙9am-7:30pm) Both landscaped and natural gardens cover a lovely 150 acres, with access to trails in the Wasatch foothills. Check online to see who's playing at the popular, outdoor summer concert series also held here.

Utah Museum of Fine Arts   MUSEUM
(Map p466; ☏801-581-7332; http://umfa.utah.edu; 410 Campus Center Dr; adult/child $9/7; ⊙10am-5pm Tue, Thu & Fri, to 8pm Wed, 11am-5pm Sat & Sun) Soaring galleries showcase permanent collections of tribal, Western and modern art.

Olympic Legacy Cauldron Park   PARK
(Map p466; www.utah.edu; Rice-Eccles Stadium, 451 S 1400 East; ⊙10am-6pm Mon-Sat) The University of Utah, or 'U of U', was the site of the Olympic Village in 2002. This small, on-site park has giant panels detailing the games and also contains the torch. A 10-minute,

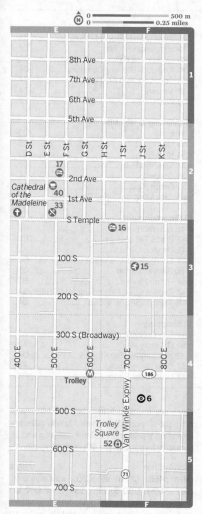

dramatic but heartfelt film booms with artificial fog and sound effects.

🏃 Activities

The best of SLC's outdoor activities are 30 to 50 miles away in the Wasatch Mountains, but gear is available in town. Bicycle rental ranges from $35 to $50 per day. In winter, public transportation links the town with resorts.

The **Utah Heritage Foundation** (☎801-533-0858; www.utahheritagefoundation.com; tours per person $5-20) offers guided tours (some are free in summer) but also puts out a

free, self-guided downtown walking tour brochure, available from the visitor center and online. It also has brochures for several other neighborhoods, and an MP3 downloadable audio tour of the Gateway and Warehouse district.

Church Fork Trail   HIKING
(Mill Creek Canyon Rd, off Wasatch Blvd; day use $3) Looking for the nearest workout with big views? Hike the 6-mile round-trip, pet-friendly trail up to Grandeur Peak (8299ft). Mill Creek Canyon is 13.5 miles southwest of downtown.

Utah Olympic Oval   SKATING
(☎801-968-6825; www.utaholympiclegacy.com; 5662 S 4800 West; adult/child $6/4) You can learn to curl or skate at Utah Olympic Oval, the site of speed-skating events in the 2002 Winter Olympics. Check ahead for public hours, which vary.

Miller Motorsports Park   ADVENTURE SPORTS
(☎435-277-7223; www.millermotorsportspark. com; 2901 N Sheep Lane, Tooele) Feel the need for speed? Head 30 miles west of town, where you can take a lesson and get behind the wheel of a 325-horsepower Mustang GT race model (reservations required), kart race or do a zip-line. Book ahead. The Utah Jazz's late Larry Miller built the raceway.

👉 Tours & Outfitters

REI   OUTDOORS
(☎801-486-2100; www.rei.com; 3285 E 3300 South; ⊙10am-9pm Mon-Fri, 9am-7pm Sat, 11am-7pm Sun) Rents and sells camping equipment, climbing shoes, kayaks and most winter-sports gear. It also stocks a great selection of maps and activity guides, and has an interagency public-lands help desk inside.

Utah Mountain Adventures   ADVENTURE SPORTS
(☎801-550-3986; www.utahmountainadventures. com; cnr 2070 East & 3900 South, #B) Offering everything from backcountry skiing to avalanche education, rock and ice climbing and mountaineering, this reputable outfitter can help you explore the Wasatch safely and with maximum enjoyment. A franchise of Exum Mountain Guides.

Wasatch Touring   ADVENTURE SPORTS
(Map p468; ☎801-359-9361; www.wasatchtour-ing.com; 702 E 100 South) Rents bikes, kayaks, climbing shoes and ski equipment.

Downtown Salt Lake City

◎ Sights
1 Beehive House C2
2 Brigham Young Monument C3
3 Clark Planetarium A3
4 Discovery Gateway A3
5 Family History Library C2
6 Gilgal Garden F4
7 Joseph Smith Memorial Building C2
8 Museum of Church History & Art C2
9 Pioneer Memorial Museum C1
10 Salt Lake City Main Library D4
11 Salt Lake Temple C2
12 Tabernacle C2
13 Temple Square C2
14 Utah State Capitol C1

◉ Activities, Courses & Tours
15 Wasatch Touring F3

◎ Sleeping
16 Anniversary Inn F3
17 Avenues Hostel E2
18 Crystal Inn & Suites B4
19 Ellerbeck Mansion B&B D2
20 Grand America C5
21 Hotel Monaco C3
22 Inn on the Hill C2
23 Peery Hotel C4
24 Rodeway Inn B5

◎ Eating
25 Copper Onion D4
26 Curryer C4

27 Downtown Farmers Market B4
28 Himalayan Kitchen C4
29 Lion House Pantry Restaurant C2
30 Red Rock Brewing Company B4
31 Squatters Pub Brewery B4
32 Takashi C4
33 Wild Grape E2

◎ Drinking & Nightlife
34 Bar X D3
35 Bayou C5
36 Beer Bar D3
37 Beerhive Pub C3
38 Gracie's C4
39 Green Pig C4
40 Jack Mormon Coffee Co E2

◎ Entertainment
41 Assembly Hall C2
42 Burt's Tiki Lounge C5
43 Depot A2
44 Energy Solutions Arena B3
45 Gallivan Center C3
46 Hotel/Elevate B3
47 Rose Wagner Performing Arts Center . B4
48 Tavernacle Social Club D4

◎ Shopping
49 City Creek Center C3
50 Gateway Mall A2
51 Ken Sanders Rare Books D4
52 Sam Weller Books F5
53 Utah Artist Hands C3

Black Diamond Equipment ADVENTURE SPORTS (www.bdel.com; 2092 E 3900 South; ⊙10am-7pm Mon-Sat, 11am-5pm Sun) Retail store for leading manufacturer of climbing and ski gear that headquarters here in SLC.

✪ Festivals & Events

Utah Pride Festival CULTURAL
(www.utahpridefestival.org) Gay pride festival in June, with outdoor concerts, parade and 5km run.

Utah Arts Festival CULTURAL
(www.uaf.org) Concerts, exhibitions and craft workshops over three days; late June.

Days of '47 CULTURAL
(www.daysof47.com) A pioneer parade, rodeo and re-enacted encampment are all part of the July-long festival celebrating the city's first settlers.

⮕ Sleeping

Downtown chain properties cluster around S 200 West near 500 South and 600 South;

there are more in Mid-Valley (off I-215) and near the airport. At high-end hotels rates are lowest on weekends. Look for camping and alternative lodging in the Wasatch Mountains.

Skyline Inn MOTEL $
(Map p466; ☑801-582-5350; www.skylineinn.com; 2475 E 1700 South; r $54-72; ☀@☎☎) A good choice for bargain-hunting skiers and hikers. This indie motel is only 30 minutes from the slopes, and has a hot tub, too. Rooms could use some refurbishment, though.

Rodeway Inn MOTEL $
(Map p468; ☑801-534-0808, 877-424-6423; www.rodewayinn.com; 616 S 200 West; r incl breakfast $59-119; ᐁ☀@☎☎) Solid budget choice within walking distance of downtown.

Avenues Hostel HOSTEL $
(Map p468; ☑801-539-8888, 801-359-3855; www.saltlakehostel.com; 107 F St; dm $19-23, s/d with shared bath $40/47, with private bath $50/57; ☀@☎) Well-worn hostel; a bit halfway-

house-like with long-term residents, but a convenient location.

★ Inn on the Hill   INN $$

(Map p468; ☑ 801-328-1466; www.inn-on-the-hill. com; 225 N State St; r incl breakfast $150-189; P ❋ @ 🛜) Exquisite woodwork and Maxfield Parrish Tiffany glass adorn this sprawling, 1906 Renaissance Revival mansion-turned-inn. Guest rooms are classically comfortable, not stuffy, with Jacuzzi tubs and some fireplaces and balconies. Great shared spaces include patios, a billiard room, a library and a dining room where chef-cooked breakfasts are served. The location is high above Temple Sq; expect great views and an uphill hike back from town.

Peery Hotel   HOTEL $$

(Map p468; ☑ 801-521-4300, 800-331-0073; www.peeryhotel.com; 110 W 300 South; r $99-130; P ❋ @ 🛜) Egyptian-cotton robes and sheets, carved dark-wood furnishings, individually decorated rooms – prepare to be charmed by the 1910 Peery. Small but impeccable bathrooms have pedestal sinks and aromatherapy bath products. This throwback hotel stands smack in the center of the Broadway Ave entertainment district – walking distance to restaurants, bars and theaters. Parking is $12 per day.

Ellerbeck Mansion B&B   B&B $$

(Map p468; ☑ 801-355-2500, 800-966-8364; www.ellerbeckbedandbreakfast.com; 140 North B St; r incl breakfast $99-189) Rambling red-brick mansion with homey, eclectic decor. Walking distance to downtown.

Crystal Inn & Suites   MOTEL $$

(Map p468; ☑ 800-366-4466, 801-328-4466; www.crystalinnssaltlake.com; 230 W 500 South; r incl breakfast $94-179; P ❋ @ 🛜 🏊) Restaurants and Temple Sq are within walking distance of the downtown, multistory branch of Crystal Inns, a Utah-owned chain. Smiling staff here are genuinely helpful and there are lots of amenities for this price point (including a huge, hot breakfast).

Hotel Monaco   BOUTIQUE HOTEL $$$

(Map p468; ☑ 801-595-0000; www.monaco-saltlakecity.com; 15 W 200 South; r $159-260; P ❋ @ 🛜 🏊) Subdued with a dollop of funk, rich colors and plush prints create a whimsical vibe at this boutique chain. Here, pampered-guest pets receive special treatment, and the front desk will loan you a goldfish if you need company. Evening wine

receptions are free, as are cruiser bicycles; parking ($19) is extra.

Anniversary Inn   B&B $$$

(Map p468; ☑ 801-363-4953, 800-324-4152; www.anniversaryinn.com; 678 E South Temple St; ste incl breakfast $199-249; P ❋ @ 🛜) Sleep among the tree trunks of an enchanted forest or inside an Egyptian pyramid: these 3-D themed suites are nothing if not over the top. The quiet location is near a few good restaurants, and not far from Temple Sq.

Grand America   HOTEL $$$

(Map p468; ☑ 800-621-4505; www.grandamerica. com; 555 S Main St; r from $260; P ❋ @ 🛜 🏊) Rooms in SLC's only true luxury hotel are decked out with Italian marble bathrooms, English wool carpeting, tasseled damask draperies and other cushy details. If that's not enough to spoil you, there's always afternoon high tea or the lavish Sunday brunch. Overnight parking is $13.

✕ Eating

What SLC lacks in nightlife it certainly makes up for in dining. Many ethnic and organically-minded restaurants are located within the downtown core. There are also small enclaves in atmospheric neighborhoods 9th and 9th, and 15th and 15th (near

---

THE BOOK OF MORMON (THE MUSICAL)

Singing and dancing Mormon missionaries? You betcha...at least on Broadway. In the spring of 2011 the musical *The Book of Mormon* opened to critical acclaim at the Eugene O'Neill Theatre in New York. The light-hearted satire about LDS missionaries in Uganda came out of the comic minds that also created the musical *Avenue Q* and the animated TV series *South Park*. No wonder people laughed them all the way to nine Tony Awards.

The LDS church's official response? Actually quite measured, avoiding any direct criticism – though it was made clear that their belief is that while 'the Book, the musical' can entertain you, the scriptures of the actual Book of Mormon can change your life.

The show debuts in Salt Lake City in 2015, at the **Capitol Theatre** (www. slccfa.org).

the intersection of 900 East and 900 South, 1500 East and 1500 South), as well as options in the canyons. Food trucks are also invading: look for the Asian-inspired Chow Truck, which gets local raves.

Pho Tay Ho
VIETNAMESE $

(Map p466; ☑801-466-3650; 1766 S Main St; mains $6-8; ⊙11am-4pm & 5-9pm Mon-Sat, 11am-4pm & 5-8pm Sun) For steaming bowls of pho garnished with basil, mint and bean sprout, along with a salty lemonade, it's hard to beat this no-frills, bargain restaurant with three generations of women working together.

Lucky 13
PUB $

(Map p466; www.lucky13slc.com; mains $8-12; ⊙food 10am-midnight, bar to 2am) While no minors are allowed in this divey pub, it's still worth a trip for Salt Lake's best burgers. Yes, these mishappen patties with generous toppings, gooey cheese and a side of garlic fries are messy, but you'll thank us. Behind the stadium.

Chanon
THAI $

(Map p466; ☑801-532-1177; www.chanonthai.com; 278 E 900 S; lunch mains $7-9, dinner $9-13; ⊙11:30am-3pm & 5-9pm Wed-Fri, plus 5-9pm Sat & Sun; ☑) Endorsed by frequenters of Southeast Asia, Chanon specializes in spicy, authentic food with plenty of vegetarian offerings. Look for daily specials, like fresh mango with sticky rice.

Curryer
INDIAN $

(Map p468; 300 South, btwn S State & S Main Sts; dishes $4-8; ⊙11am-2pm; ☑) This former hot-dog cart, modified with a tandoori oven, serves up a tasty range of regional Indian food, from butter chicken to vegan-friendly *aloo matar* (spiced potatoes and peas).

Blue Plate Diner
DINER $

(Map p466; www.facebook.com/blueplatediner; 2041 S 2100 East; breakfasts & burgers $6-9, mains $10-13; ⊙7am-9pm) A hip, retro diner that gets serious about bacon. With a soda fountain, colorful patio and postcards from around the country as decoration.

Lion House Pantry Restaurant
AMERICAN $

(Map p468; www.templesquarehospitality.com; 63 E South Temple St; meals $8-14; ⊙11am-8pm Mon-Sat) Down-home, carb-rich cookin' just like your Mormon grandmother used to make – only it's served cafeteria-style in the basement of an historic house. Several of Brigham Young's wives used to live here (including a previous author's great-great-great grandmother).

Downtown Farmers Market
MARKET $

(Map p468; www.slcfarmersmarket.org; Pioneer Park, cnr 300 South & 300 West; ⊙8am-1pm Sat mid-Jun–late Oct, 4pm-dusk Tue Aug-Sep) Regionally grown produce, ready-to-eat baked goodies and local crafts.

★Red Iguana
MEXICAN $$

(www.rediguana.com; 736 W North Temple; mains $10-16; ⊙11am-10pm) Mexico at its most authentic, aromatic and delicious – no wonder the line is usually snaking out the door at this family-run restaurant. Ask for samples of the mole to decide on one of seven chile- and chocolate-based sauces. The incredibly tender *conchinita pibil* (shredded roast pork) tastes like it's been roasting for days.

Mazza
MIDDLE EASTERN $$

(Map p466; www.mazzacafe.com; 1515 S 1500 East; sandwiches $8-10, dinners $15-25; ⊙11am-3pm & 5-10pm Mon-Sat; ☑) In an inviting ambiance with warm tones and copper highlights, this local favorite consistently delivers well-known fare like kabobs, schwarma and hummus plus wonderful regional specialties, many from Lebanon. We love what they do with lamb and eggplant.

Wild Grape
MODERN AMERICAN $$

(Map p468; www.wildgrapebistro.com; 481 E South Temple; breakfast & lunch $7-15, dinner $13-28; ⊙8am-10pm Mon-Fri, 9am-10pm Sat & Sun) Billing itself as a 'new West' bistro, Wild Grape creates modern versions of country classics. We like the weekend brunch dishes best.

Sage's Cafe
VEGETARIAN $$

(Map p466; 234 W 900 South; sandwiches $7-10, mains $13-16; ⊙11am-2pm & 5-10pm Mon-Fri, 10am-10pm Sat & Sun; ☑) A longtime Salt Lake institution serving creative, mostly vegan and organic meals (think carrot-butter pâté and magical wok curry) in a spacious setting with vinyl booths and wood accents.

Himalayan Kitchen
INDIAN $$

(Map p468; ☑801-328-2077; 360 S State St; mains $8-20; ⊙11:30am-10pm Mon-Sat, 4:30-10pm Sun) A friendly downtown restaurant serving Himalayan classics. Check out the climbing shrine in the back dedicated to Apa Sherpa, an Everest icon and friend of the owner.

Squatters Pub Brewery
AMERICAN $$

(Map p468; www.squatters.com; 147 W Broadway; dishes $10-22; ⊙11am-midnight Sun-Thu, to 1am Fri & Sat) Come for an Emigration Pale Ale, stay for the blackened tilapia salad. In addition to great microbrews, Squatters does a wide range of American casual dishes as well. The lively pub atmosphere is always fun.

Red Rock Brewing Company PUB FOOD $$

(Map p468; ☑ 801-521-7446; www.redrockbrewing. com; 254 S 200 West; sandwiches $7-12, mains $14-18; ⏱ 11am-11pm) Service is so-so, but this brewpub still attracts a crowd for its house beers.

Ruth's Diner DINER $$

(Map p465; www.ruthsdiner.com; 4160 Emigration Canyon Rd; mains $6-16; ⏱ 8am-10pm) Once a railcar diner, Ruth's has expanded into a sprawling institution. We love the canyon surrounds – and the eggs Benedict. Summer concerts sometimes accompany dinner.

★ Copper Onion INTERNATIONAL $$$

(Map p468; ☑ 801-355-3282; www.thecopperonion. com; 111 E Broadway Ave; brunch & small plates $7-15, dinner mains $22-29; ⏱ 11am-3pm & 5-10pm) Locals keep the Copper Onion bustling at lunch (for $10 specials), at dinner, at weekend brunch, at Happy Hour in the bar... And for good reason: small plates like wagyu beef tartare and pasta carbonara call out to be shared. Design-driven rustic decor provides a convivial place to enjoy it all.

Pago ORGANIC $$$

(Map p466; ☑ 801-532-0777; www.pagoslc.com; 878 S 900 East; mains $18-27; ⏱ 11am-3pm Mon-Fri, 5-10pm Mon-Sun, 10am-2:30pm Sat & Sun) 🥬 Earthy and interesting, with seasonal eclectic mains like a Moroccan fried chicken with frisée or a truffle burger. Dine at the few sidewalk tables and you'll feel like part of the chummy neighborhood. Supports local farms. Dinner reservations recommended.

Takashi JAPANESE $$$

(Map p468; ☑ 801-519-9595; 18 W Market St; rolls $10-18, mains $18-30; ⏱ 11:30am-2pm & 5:30-10pm Mon-Sat) Who wouldn't be tempted by 'sex on rice'? The best of a number of surprisingly good sushi restaurants here in landlocked Salt Lake, and often packed. Even LA restaurant snobs rave about the innovative rolls at this ever-so-chic establishment.

Forage MODERN AMERICAN $$$

(Map p466; ☑ 801-708-7834; www.foragerestaurant.com; 370 E 900 South; set menu $87; ⏱ 5:30-10pm Tue-Sat; 🌱) Presenting food as art, with creative minimalist fare that attracts both gourmets and awards. The tasting menu is a three-hour event. The menu changes daily, as do the local sourcing options. Vegetarian-friendly. Reserve well ahead.

SALT LAKE CITY FOR KIDS

Salt Lake is a child-friendly city if there ever was one. In addition to some of the sights already listed, the wonderful hands-on exhibits at the **Discovery Gateway** (Map p468; www.childmuseum.org; 444 W 100 South; admission $8.50; ⏱ 10am-6pm Mon-Thu, to 8pm Fri & Sat, noon-6pm Sun; 🚼) stimulate imaginations and senses.

Kids can help farmhands milk cows, churn butter and feed animals at **Wheeler Historic Farm** (Map p465; www.wheelerfarm.com; 6351 S 900 East, South Cottonwood Regional Park; hay rides $2; ⏱ 9:30am-5:30pm; 🚼) **FREE**, which dates from 1886. There's also blacksmithing, quilting and hay rides in summer.

More than 800 animals inhabit zones such as the Asian Highlands on the landscaped 42-acre grounds at **Hogle Zoo** (Map p466; www.hoglezoo.org; 2600 E Sunnyside Ave; adult/child $15/11; ⏱ 9am-5pm; 🚼). Daily animal encounter programs help kids learn more about their favorite species.

Tracy Aviary (Map p466; www.tracyaviary.org; 589 E 1300 South; adult/child $7/5; ⏱ 9am-5pm; 🚼) lets little ones toss fish to the pelicans as one of its interactive programs and performances. More than 400 winged creatures from around the world call this bird park home.

With 55 acres of gardens, a full-scale working/petting farm, golf course, giant movie theater, museum, dining, shopping and ice-cream parlor, what *doesn't* **Thanksgiving Point** (☑ 801-768-2300; www.thanksgivingpoint.org; 3003 N Thanksgiving Way, Lehi; all-attraction pass adult/child $25/19; ⏱ 10am-8pm Mon-Sat; 🚼) have? The on-site **Museum of Ancient Life** (museum only adult/child $15/12) is one of the highest-tech and most hands-on dinosaur museums in the state. Kids can dig for their own bones, dress up a dinosaur or play in a watery Silurian reef. Lehi is 28 miles south of downtown SLC; to get there take exit 287 off I-15.

🍷 Drinking & Nightlife

Pubs and bars that also serve food are mainstays of SLC's nightlife, and no one minds if you mainly drink and nibble. A complete schedule of local bar music is available in the *City Weekly* (www.cityweekly.net).

★ Beer Bar   PUB
(Map p468; 161 E 200 South; ⊙ 11am-2am Mon-Sat, 10am-2am Sun) With shared wooden tables and over 140 beers and 13 sausage styles, Beer Bar is a little slice of Bavaria in Salt Lake City. The crowd is diverse and far more casual than at Bar X next door (a linked venue). A great place to meet friends and make friends, but it gets pretty loud.

Bar X   COCKTAILS
(Map p468; 155 E 200 S; ⊙ 4pm-2am Mon-Fri, 6pm-2am Sat, 7pm-2am Sun) So low-lit and funky, it's hard to believe you're down the street from Temple Sq. Cozy up to the crowded bar with a Moscow Mule and listen to Motown or funk (or the guy at the next table saying to his date, 'your voice is pretty').

Gracie's   BAR
(Map p468; 326 S West Temple; ⊙ 11am-2am) Even with two levels and four bars, Gracie's trendy bar-restaurant still gets crowded. The two sprawling patios are the best place to kick back. Live music or DJs most nights.

Green Pig   BAR
(Map p468; 31 E 400 South; ⊙ 11am-2am) Your friendly neighborhood watering hole hosts

---

SCENIC DRIVE: PONY EXPRESS TRAIL

Follow more than 130 miles of the original route that horse-and-rider mail delivery took on the **Pony Express Trail Backcountry Byway** (www.byways.org), from Fairfield to Callao. You'll drive through wide-open desert rangeland with stations, many in ruins, placed throughout. The trail begins at one of the former stops, in **Camp Floyd/Stagecoach Inn State Park** (http://stateparks.utah.gov; family/individual $9/3; ⊙ 9am-5pm Mon-Sat), 25 miles southwest of I-15 along Hwy 73. Most of the road is maintained gravel or dirt and is passable to ordinary cars in good weather. In winter, snow may close the route; watch for flash floods in summer.

---

poker tournaments, has live jam sessions and plays sporting events on big screens. Grab some chile verde nachos on the rooftop.

Bayou   PUB
(Map p468; 645 S State St; ⊙ noon-1am) Known almost as much for its Cajun specialties and pub grub as for its vast selection of beer. By day office workers dine here, by night they party. Live jazz on weekends.

Beerhive Pub   PUB
(Map p468; 128 S Main St; ⊙ noon-1am) More than 200 beer choices, including many Utah-local microbrews, are wedged into this downtown storefront bar. Good for drinking and conversation.

★ Jack Mormon Coffee Co   CAFE
(Map p468; www.jackmormoncoffee.com; 82 E St; ⊙ 9am-6pm) Utah's finest roaster also serves mean espresso drinks. When the temps rise, locals binge on a Jack Frost.

Coffee Garden   CAFE
(Map p466; 895 E 900 South; ⊙ 6am-11pm Sun-Thu, to midnight Fri & Sat; 📶) This is perfection in a coffee shop, with substance and style, good treats, desserts and ample seating. At the heart of the eclectic 9th and 9th neighborhood.

☆ Entertainment

We wouldn't say the nightlife here is all that hot; major dance clubs change frequently and few are open more than a couple nights a week. See the *City Weekly* (www.cityweekly.net) for listings. Classical entertainment options, especially around Temple Sq, are plentiful.

Nightclubs

Hotel/Elevate   CLUB
(Map p468; www.thehotelelevate.com; 155 W 200 South; ⊙ 9pm-2am Thu-Sat) Top DJs spin house music and more; live music includes R&B and jazz.

Burt's Tiki Lounge   CLUB
(Map p468; 726 S State St; ⊙ 9pm-2am Thu-Sat) More divey club than tiki lounge. Music may be punk, funk or ska – anything loud.

Live Music & Theater

There are also concerts on Temple Sq, at the Library and in Red Butte Gardens in the summertime. The Salt Lake City Arts Council provides a complete cultural events calendar on its website (www.slcgov.com/

GAY & LESBIAN SLC

In June, 2014, a federal appeals court ruled that Utah's ban on gay marriage was unconstitutional (a Supreme Court ruling is expected). Many from the LGBT community here feel that the state is inevitably headed in a more progressive direction. That said, it is a very conservative state. Salt Lake City has Utah's only gay scene, however limited.

Pick up the free *Q Salt Lake* (www.qsaltlake.com) for listings. Utah Pride Festival (p470), held over one weekend in June, is a big party and parade. The town's closest thing to a gay-ish neighborhood is 9th and 9th (900 South and 900 East), where Coffee Garden is the neighborhood cafe. The Utah Pride Center has the largest LGBT library in the state, housed at the University of Utah Marriott Library.

A nightclub boasting theme nights, a big tube of lipstick and stripper poles, **Paper Moon** (☑ 801-713-0678; 3737 S State St) is SLC's number one – and only – lesbian bar.

calendars). Unless otherwise noted, reserve through **ArtTix** (☑ 888-451-2787, 801-355-2787; www.arttix.org).

Mormon Tabernacle Choir LIVE MUSIC
(☑ 801-570-0080; www.mormontabernaclechoir.org) **FREE** Hearing the world-renowned Mormon Tabernacle Choir is a must-do on any SLC bucket list. A live choir broadcast goes out every Sunday at 9:30am. September through November, and January through May, attend in person at the Tabernacle (p465). Free public rehearsals are held here from 8pm to 9pm Thursday.

From June to August and in December (to accommodate larger crowds) choir broadcasts and rehearsals are held at the 21,000-seat LDS Conference Center. Performance times stay the same, except that an extra organ recital takes place at 2pm, Monday through Saturday.

Gallivan Center CONCERT VENUE
(Map p468; www.thegallivancenter.com; 200 South, btwn State & Main Sts) Bring a picnic to the outdoor concert and movie series at the Gallivan Center, an amphitheater in a garden. Performances run in summer.

Assembly Hall CONCERT VENUE
(Map p468; www.visittemplesquare.com; Temple Sq) A lovely 1877 Gothic building in Temple Sq hosts concerts large and small.

Rose Wagner Performing Arts Center THEATER
(Map p468; www.slccfa.org; 138 W 300 South) Many of SLC Arts Council's dramatic and musical theater performances are staged here.

Depot CONCERT VENUE
(Map p468; ☑ 801-355-5522; www.smithstix.com; 400 W South Temple) Primary concert venue for rock acts.

Tavernacle Social Club CLUB
(Map p468; www.tavernacle.com; 201 E Broadway; ⊙ 5pm-1am Tue-Sat, 8pm-midnight Sun) Dueling pianos or karaoke nightly.

Sports

Utah Jazz BASKETBALL
(☑ 801-325-2500; www.nba.com/jazz) Utah Jazz, the men's professional basketball team, plays at the **Energy Solutions Arena** (Map p468; ☑ 801-355-7328; www.energysolutionsarena.com; 301 W South Temple St), where concerts are also held.

Real Salt Lake SOCCER
(www.realsaltlake.com; 9256 South State St, Rio Tinto Stadium; ⊙ Mar-Oct) Salt Lake's winning Major League Soccer team (pronounced *ree-*AL) has a loyal local following and matches are fun to take in at the new Rio Tinto Stadium.

Utah Grizzlies ICE HOCKEY
(☑ 801-988-7825; www.utahgrizzlies.com) The International Hockey League's Utah Grizzlies plays at the **Maverik Center** (Map p465; ☑ tickets 800-745-3000; www.maverikcenter.com; 3200 S Decker Lake Dr, West Valley City), which hosted most of the men's ice hockey competitions during the Olympics.

Salt Lake Bees BASEBALL
(☑ for tickets 801-325-2273; www.slbees.com) The AAA minor-league affiliate of the Anaheim Angels plays at **Franklin Covey Field** (Map p466; 77 W 1300 South).

🔒 Shopping

An interesting array of boutiques, antiques and cafes line up along Broadway Ave (300 South), between 100 and 300 East. Drawing on Utah pioneer heritage, SLC has quite a few crafty shops and galleries scattered around. A few can be found on the 300 block of W Pierpont Ave. Many participate in the one-day **Craft Salt Lake** (www.craftlakecity. com) expo in August.

Sam Weller Books
BOOKS

(Map p468; ☑ 801-328-2586; 607 Trolley Sq; ☺ 10am-7pm Mon-Sat) The city's biggest and best independent bookstore also has a praise-worthy local rare book selection in its new downtown location.

Utah Artist Hands
ARTS & CRAFTS

(Map p468; www.utahands.com; 61 W 100 South; noon-7pm Mon-Fri, to 5pm Sat) Local artists' work, all made in-state, that runs the gamut from fine art and photography to scarves and pottery.

Ken Sanders Rare Books
BOOKS

(Map p468; www.kensandersbooks.com; 268 S 200 East; ☺ 10am-6pm Mon-Sat) Specializes in Western authors.

City Creek Center
MALL

(Map p468; www.shopcitycreekcenter.com; Social Hall Ave, btwn Regent & Richards Sts) Inaugurated in 2012, this LDS-funded, 20-acre pedestrian plaza has fountains, restaurants, a creek stocked with trout and a retail area with a retractable roof.

Gateway Mall
MALL

(Map p468; 200 South to 50 N, 400 West to 500 West; ☺ 10am-9pm Mon-Sat, noon-6pm Sun) Major-label shopping mall right downtown.

ℹ Information

EMERGENCY

Local Police (☑ 801-799-3000; 315 E 200 South)

MEDIA

City Weekly (www.cityweekly.net) Free alternative weekly with good restaurant and entertainment listings; twice annually it publishes the free *City Guide*.

ℹ CONNECT PASS

Salt Lake City Visitors Bureau (www.visitsaltlake.com) sells one- to three-day discounted attraction passes called Salt Lake Connect Passes ($16 to $40), online and at its visitor center. But unless you plan to visit every child-friendly attraction in the town – and some outside of town – it probably isn't worth your while.

Deseret News (www.desnews.com) Ultraconservative, church-owned paper.

Salt Lake Magazine (www.saltlakemagazine. com) Lifestyle and food.

Salt Lake Tribune (www.sltrib.com) Utah's largest-circulation daily paper.

MEDICAL SERVICES

University Hospital (☑ 801-581-2121; 50 N Medical Dr) For emergencies, 24/7.

MONEY

Note that it can be difficult to change foreign currency in Utah outside SLC.

Wells Fargo (www.wellsfargo.com; 79 S Main St; ☺ 9am-6pm Mon-Fri, to 3pm Sat) Convenient currency exchange and ATM.

POST

Post Office (Map p468; www.usps.com; 230 W 200 South)

TOURIST INFORMATION

Public Lands Information Center (☑ 801-466-6411; www.publiclands.org; REI Store, 3285 E 3300 South; ☺ 10:30am-5:30pm Mon-Fri, 9am-1pm Sat) Recreation information for nearby public lands (state parks, BLM, USFS), including the Uinta-Wasatch-Cache National Forest.

Visit Salt Lake (Map p468; ☑ 801-534-4900; www.visitsaltlake.com; 90 S West Temple, Salt Palace Convention Center; ☺ 9am-6pm Mon-Fri, to 5pm Sat & Sun) Publishes free visitor-guide booklet; large gift shop on site at the visitor center.

WEBSITES

Downtown SLC (www.downtownslc.org) Arts, entertainment and business information about the downtown core.

Lonely Planet (www.lonelyplanet.com/usa/southwest/salt-lake-city) Planning advice, author recommendations, traveler reviews and insider tips.

ℹ Getting There & Away

Springdale and Zion National Park are 308 miles to the south; Moab and Arches National Park are 234 miles south and east.

AIR

Five miles northwest of downtown, **Salt Lake City International Airport** (SLC; Map p465; www.slcairport.com; 776 N Terminal Dr) has mostly domestic flights, though you can fly direct to Canada and Mexico. **Delta** (☑ 800-221-1212; www.delta.com) is the main SLC carrier.

BUS

Greyhound (Map p466; ☑ 800-231-2222; www.greyhound.com; 300 S 600 West) connects SLC with southwestern towns, including St George, UT ($55, six hours); Las Vegas, NV ($62, eight hours); and Denver, CO ($86, 10 hours).

TRAIN

Traveling between Chicago, IL, and Oakland/Emeryville, CA, the California Zephyr from **Amtrak** (☏ 800-872-7245; www.amtrak.com) stops daily at **Union Pacific Rail Depot** (340 S 600 West). Southwest destinations include Denver, CO, (from $79, 15 hours) and Reno, NV (from $70, 10 hours). Schedule delays can be substantial.

❶ Getting Around

Two major interstates cross at SLC: I-15 runs north–south, I-80 east–west. I-215 loops the city. The area around Temple Square is easily walkable, and free public transportation covers much of the downtown core, but to go beyond you will need your own vehicle.

TO/FROM THE AIRPORT

Express Shuttle (☏ 800-397-0773; www. xpressshuttleutah.com) Shared van service; $17 to downtown.

Utah Transit Authority (UTA; www.rideuta. com; one-way $2.50; ☏) With light-rail service to the international airport and free rides within the downtown area. Bus 550 travels downtown from the parking structure between terminals 1 and 2.

Yellow Cab (☏ 801-521-2100) Private taxi to Salt Lake, Park City and area destinations.

CAR & MOTORCYCLE

National rental agencies have SLC airport offices.

Rugged Rental (☏ 801-977-9111, 800-977-9111; www.ruggedrental.com; 2740 W California Ave; ⊙ 8am-6pm Mon-Sat) Rents 4WDs, SUVs and passenger cars. Rates are often better here than at the major companies.

PUBLIC TRANSPORTATION

UTA (www.rideuta.com) Trax, UTA's light-rail system, runs from Central Station (600 W 250 South) west to the University of Utah and south past Sandy. The center of downtown SLC is a free-fare zone. During ski season UTA buses serve the local ski resorts ($4.50 one-way).

BICYCLE

GREENbike (www.greenbikeslc.org; 24hr pass $5) Salt Lake City's bike share program has B-cycle stations all over downtown for rider convenience. Use your credit card at a kiosk to rent.

Antelope Island State Park

The Great Salt Lake is the largest body of water west of the Great Lakes, but it's hard to say just exactly how big it is. Since 1873 the lake has varied from 900 to 2500 sq miles. Maximum depths have ranged from 24ft to 45ft – it's wide and shallow, like a plate. Spring runoff raises levels; summer's sweltering heat lowers them. Evaporation is why the lake is so salty, but its salinity varies drastically, from 6% to 27% (compared with only 3.5% for seawater), depending on location and weather.

The lake is recognized as a Unesco World Heritage Site for its importance for migratory routes. During fall (September to November) and spring (March to May) migrations, hundreds of thousands of birds descend on the park to feast on tiny brine shrimp along the lakeshore en route to distant lands. The best place to experience the lake (and see the birds) is at **Antelope Island State Park** (☏ 801-773-2941; http://stateparks.utah.gov; Antelope Dr; day-use per vehicle $10, tent & RV sites without hookups $15; ⊙ 7am-10pm Jul-Sep, to 7pm Oct-Jun), 25 miles north of SLC. White-sand beaches, birds – and buffalo – are what attract people to the pretty, 15-mile-long park. That's right: the largest island in the Great Salt Lake is home to a 500-strong herd of American bison (buffalo). The **fall round-up**, for veterinary examination, is a thrilling spectacle. Also making their year-round home here are burrowing owls and raptors, as well as namesake antelope, bighorn sheep and deer.

Inquire about the many ranger-led activities, watch an introductory video and pick up a map at the **visitor center** (⊙ 9am-5pm). Nineteen miles of **hiking trails** provide many opportunities to view wildlife; however, some trails are closed during mating and birthing seasons. There is an 8-mile driving loop and a dirt-road spur that leads 11 miles to **Fielding Garr Ranch** (⊙ 9am-5pm). Take a look around what was a working farm from 1848 until 1981, back when the state park was created. Check the park website for ranger tours or cowboy poetry gatherings on-site.

North of the visitor center there's a small marina and the simple **Buffalo Island Grill** (mains $6-15; ⊙ 11am-8pm May-Sep). The white, sandy **beach** to the south on Bridger Bay has showers and flushing toilets that both swimmers and campers use. The 18-site **Bridger Bay Campground** (☏ reservations

800-322-3770; http://utahstateparks.reserveamerica.com; tent & RV sites $15) has shelters for shade, water and pit toilets, but no hookups.

To get to the park, head west from I-15 exit 335 and follow the signs; a 7-mile causeway leads to the island.

Brigham City & Around

POP 18,150 / ELEV 4436FT

Drive north on I-15 from Salt Lake City, past Ogden – the gateway to the Wasatch Mountains ski resorts – and after 50 miles you'll get to the turnoff for Brigham City. The town is pretty small, with a few natural attractions, and one famous restaurant. The stretch of Hwy 89 south of town is known as the 'Golden Spike Fruitway' – from July through September it's crowded with fruit stands vending the abundant local harvest. One week in September Brigham City celebrates 'Peach Days.' Contact **Box Elder County Tourism** (435-734-2634; www.boxelder.org; 1 South Main St; 8am-5pm Mon-Fri) for area information.

West of town, the **Bear River Migratory Bird Refuge** (www.fws.gov/refuge/bear_river_

migratory_bird_refuge; W Forest St; dawndusk) FREE engulfs almost 74,000 acres of marshes on the northeastern shores of the Great Salt Lake. The best time for bird-watchers is during fall (September to November) and spring (March to May) migrations. Birds banded here have been recovered as far away as Siberia and Colombia. Cruising along the 12-mile, barely elevated touring road feels like you're driving on water. You can hear the replicated migratory calls and find out more year round at the **Wildlife Education Center** (435-734-6426; 2155 W Forest St; 10am-5pm Mon-Fri, to 4pm Sat) FREE. The center is just after the I-15 intersection; the driving tour is 16 miles west. Free bird-watching tours leave from here twice daily; reserve ahead.

Get into hot water year-round at **Crystal Hot Springs** (435-279-8104; www.crystalhotsprings.net; 8215 N Hwy 38; pool adult/child $6.50/4.50, slides $10, campground tent/RV sites with hookup $15/25; 10am-10pm Mon-Sat, to 8pm Sun), 10 miles north in Honeyville. Adults float in different-temperature soaking pools, while kids zip down the water slides, which are open shorter hours than the pools from September through May. The log lodge and pools are well taken care of. There's also a small **campground** (tent/RV sites with hookup $15/25).

Brigham City is an easy day trip from Salt Lake, and there are a few motels, including a decent **Days Inn** (435-723-3500, 888-440-2021; www.daysinn.com; 1033 S 1600 West; r incl breakfast $80-90;).

Utahans have been known to travel for hours to eat at **Maddox Ranch House** (435-723-8545; www.maddoxfinefood.com; 1900 S Hwy 89; mains $17-27, lunch from $10; 11:30am-9pm Tue-Fri, to 9:30pm Fri & Sat), where they've been cutting thick beef steaks from locally raised livestock since 1949. You can still see the ranch out back where they originally started in the cattle business. Fried chicken and bison steaks are popular here, too. Don't expect anything fancy – this is a family-owned place, accustomed to serving families. No reservations accepted; expect to wait even if you go early. Out back at **Maddox Drive-In** (1900 S Hwy 89; mains $6-10; 11am-8:30pm Tue-Sat), carhop waiters deliver the famous fried chicken and bison burgers to your car window. Don't miss the homemade sarsaparilla soda.

WORTH A TRIP

LOGAN CANYON SCENIC BYWAY

Pick up a free interpretive trail guide at the Cache Valley Visitor Bureau in Logan before you head off on the 40-mile riverside drive through **Logan Canyon Scenic Byway** (www.logancanyon.com; Hwy 89 btwn Logan & Garden City). Wind your way up through the Bear River Mountains, past Beaver Mountain, before descending to the 20-mile-long Bear Lake, a summer water-sports playground. Along the way there are numerous signposted hiking and biking trails and campgrounds, which are all part of the **Uinta-Wasatch-Cache National Forest** (www.fs.usda.gov). It's beautiful year-round, but July wildflowers and October foliage are particularly brilliant. Note that parts of the route may be closed to snow December through May and campgrounds may not open until late June. Check conditions with the **Logan Ranger District Office** (435-755-3620; 1500 East Hwy 89; 8:30am-4:30pm).

THE REMOTE NORTHWEST

On May 10, 1869, the westward Union Pacific Railroad and eastward Central Pacific Railroad met at Promontory Summit. With the completion of the transcontinental railroad, the face of the American West changed forever. **Golden Spike National Historic Site** (www.nps.gov/gosp; per vehicle $7; ⊘9am-5pm), 32 miles northwest of Brigham City on Hwy 83, has an interesting museum and films, auto tours and several interpretive trails. Steam-engine demonstrations take place June through August. Aside from Golden Spike National Historic Site, few people visit Utah's desolate northwest corner. But while you're here...

At the end of a dirt road (4WD recommended but not required) 15 miles southwest of the Golden Spike visitor center, there's a wonderfully unique outdoor art installation, the **Spiral Jetty** (www.spiraljetty.org). Created by Robert Smithson in 1970, it's a 1500ft coil of rock and earth spinning out into the water. It's a little hard to find – get directions from the visitor center.

Logan & Around

POP 48,900 / ELEV 4350FT

With university charm and pretty rural surroundings, Logan is a quintessential old-fashioned community with strong Mormon roots. It's situated 80 miles north of Salt Lake City in bucolic Cache Valley, which offers year-round outdoor activities. Ask about the possibilities at **Cache Valley Visitor Bureau** (☑435-752-2161, 800-882-4433; www.tourcachevalley.com; 199 N Main St; ⊘9am-5pm Mon-Fri).

The 19th-century frontier comes to life with hands-on, living-history activities at a Shoshone Nation camp and a pioneer settlement at the **American West Heritage Center** (www.awhc.org; 4025 S Hwy 89; ⊘11am-4pm Tue-Sat Jun-Aug, off-season hours vary; ⊕), south of town. The center hosts many popular festivals, including the weeklong **Festival of the American West** in July.

There are a couple of B&Bs around town, and midrange chain motels are well represented on Hwy 89. The comfy **Best Western Weston Inn** (☑435-752-5700, 800-532-5055; www.westoninn.com; 250 N Main; r incl breakfast $105-110; ☎❄) is right downtown. Twenty-five miles east in Logan Canyon, **Beaver Creek Lodge** (☑435-946-3400, 800-946-4485; www.beavercreeklodge.com; Mile 487, Hwy 89; r $109-149) is a great getaway, with horseback riding, snowmobiling, skiing and other activities. Rates are cheapest midweek. No room phones.

For all-American fare and farmboy portions in cool Naugahyde booths, **Angie's Restaurant** (690 N Main St; mains $8-19; ⊘6am-10pm Mon-Thu, to 11pm Fri-Sat, to 9pm Sun) is very popular. Their breakfast menu is extensive. In the evening, upscale **Jack's Pizza** (☑435-754-7523; 256 N. Main; pizzas $10-14; ⊘11:30am-9pm, to 10pm Fri-Sat) fills with Utah hipsters drinking Uintah drafts with exotic thin-crust pizzas that might include house-pickled jalapenos or prosciutto and chipotle peaches. For baked goods that border on ecstasy, **Crumb Brothers Artisan Bakery** (291 S 300 W; mains $3-8; ⊘7am-3pm Mon-Fri, 8am-3pm Sat) delivers, with perfectly-executed European-style pastries and baguettes. They also bake gorgeous, crusty organic breads on-site.

WASATCH MOUNTAINS

Giant saw-toothed peaks stand guard along the eastern edge of Utah's urban centers. When the crush of civilization gets too much, locals escape to the forested slopes. The Wasatch Mountain Range is nature's playground all year long, but in winter a fabulous low-density, low-moisture snowfall (300in to 500in of it a year) blankets the terrain. Perfect snow and thousands of acres of high-altitude slopes helped earn Utah the honor of hosting the 2002 Winter Olympics – the skiing in the Wasatch range is some of the best in North America.

Resort towns cluster near the peaks; Park City, on the eastern slopes, is the most well known and quasi-cosmopolitan of the bunch. Salt Lake City resorts, on the western side, are easiest for townies to reach. Ogden is the sleeper of the bunch and Sundance is known as much for its film festival as its ski trails. Most areas lie within 45 to 60 minutes of the SLC airport, so you can leave New York or Los Angeles in the morning and be skiing by noon.

Wasatch Mountains

N 0 — 20 km
0 — 10 miles

Powder Mountain

165

39

Wolf Mountain

Harrisville • Eden

Pineview Reservoir

Ogden • Huntsville

Snowbasin

Causey Reservoir

Uinta-Wasatch-Cache National Forest

Guilder Peak (8359ft) ▲

Lost Creek Reservoir

Lost Creek State Park

84

80

89

Kaysville

Devil's Slide

189

Morgan

15

Farmington

Porterville

65

Echo

66

Echo Reservoir

Farmington Bay

106

Wasatch Mountains

Coalville

East Canyon State Park

East Canyon Reservoir

65

Salt Lake City International Airport

189

80

Rockport Reservoir

Rockport State Park

Salt Lake City

186

Kimbal Junction

Uinta-Wasatch-Cache National Forest

Canyons Resort

Park City RV Resort

32

Uinta-Wasatch-Cache National Forest

Mill B South Fork Trailhead

Silver Fork Lodge

Utah Olympic Park

Solitude

Park City Mountain Resort

Park City

40

Marion

150

Murray

190

Silver Lake

Nordic Center

248

Deer Valley

Kamas

Mirror Lake Hwy

Twin Peaks (11,330ft) ▲

Redman Campground

Jordanelle Reservoir

209

Lake Blanche

Alta

(closed in winter)

Francis

Sandy

210

Snowbird

Brighton

Albion Basin

32

35

Jordanelle State Park

Riverton

Lone Peak (11,253ft) ▲

Uinta-Wasatch-Cache National Forest

Wasatch Mountain State Park

Midway

Heber City

68

15

Alpine

Soldier Hollow

Uinta-Wasatch-Cache National Forest

92

Alpine Loop Rd

74

Timpanogos Cave NM

Deer Creek State Park

Deer Creek Reservoir

113

Lehi

92

American Fork

Mt Timpanogos (11,750ft) ▲

Mt Timpanogos

Wallsburg

Pleasant Grove

Sundance Resort

40

Utah Lake

189

ℹ Information

SKI SEASON

Ski season runs mid-November to mid-April – only Snowbird stays open much past Easter. However, snow varies: the winter of 2010–11 set an all-time record, when deep powder hung around until June. Saturday is busiest; Sunday ticket sales drop by a third because LDS members are in church. Summer season is from late June until early September.

HOURS

Day lifts usually run from 9am to 4pm.

PRICES

Children's prices are good for ages six to 12; kids under six usually ski for free. All resorts rent out equipment (about $60 per day for mountain bikes, ski or snowboard packages). You can save a few bucks by renting off-mountain, but if there's a problem with the equipment, you're stuck. Ski schools are available at all resorts.

CONDITIONS

Most resorts have jumped into the digital age and have powder reports, blogs and weather-condition updates you can view on their websites or sign up to receive via email.

RULES

No pets are allowed at resorts and four-night minimum stays may be required December through March.

Ski Utah (☑ 800-754-8724; www.skiutah.com) Puts out excellent annual winter vacation guides on paper and online.

DANGERS & ANNOYANCES

Backcountry enthusiasts: heed avalanche warnings! Take a course at a resort, carry proper equipment and check conditions. Drink plenty of fluids, too: dehydrated muscles injure easily.

Road Conditions (☑ 511)

Utah Avalanche Center (☑ 888-999-4019; www.utahavalanchecenter.org)

ℹ Getting Around

Buses and shuttles are widely available, so you don't need to rent a car to reach most resorts. Advanced skiers looking for knock-your-socks-off adventure should definitely consider a backcountry tour.

Ski Utah Interconnect Adventure Tour (☑ 801-534-1907; www.skiutah.com/interconnect; ⊙ mid-Dec–mid-Apr) Six resorts in one day; $295 price tag includes lunch, lift tickets and all transportation.

Salt Lake City Ski Resorts

Because of Great Salt Lake–affected snow, SLC resorts receive almost twice as much snow as Park City. The four resorts east of Salt Lake City sit 30 to 45 miles from the downtown core at the end of two canyons. Follow Hwy 190 up to family-oriented Solitude and skier fave Brighton in Big Cottonwood Canyon. In summer you can continue over the mountain to Heber City and Park City. To the south, Little Cottonwood Canyon is home to the seriously challenging terrain at Snowbird and the all-round ski-purist special, Alta. Numerous summer hiking and biking trails lead off from both canyons.

ℹ Information

For lodging/skiing package deals, see www.visitsaltlake.com or contact resorts directly.

Cottonwood Canyons Foundation (☑ 801-947-8263; www.cottonwoodcanyons.org) USFS ranger–led programs available at Alta, Brighton and Snowbird.

Ski Salt Lake Super Pass (www.visitsaltlake.com/ski/superpass; 4-day pass adult/child $73/38 per day) Pass includes one day's lift ticket for each of the four resorts and all your transportation on UTA ski buses and light rail in town.

ℹ Getting Around

Six ski-service park-and-ride lots are available around town. Buses also run between resorts in the same valley.

Alta Shuttle (☑ 435-274-0225, 866-274-0225; www.altashuttle.com; one-way $37) Shared van service between Salt Lake City and Snowbird or Alta.

Canyon Transportation (☑ 801-255-1841, 800-255-1841; www.canyontransport.com; adult/child one-way $39/25) Shared van service between Salt Lake City and Solitude, Brighton, Snowbird or Alta. Private service available to other destinations.

UTA (☑ 801-743-3882; www.rideuta.com; intercanyon $2.25, ski shuttle $4.50) December through April, reach the resorts via Salt Lake City's public transit system, UTA. Bus route 951 goes from the downtown core to Snowbird and Alta.

Wasatch Park & Ride Lot (6200 S Wasatch Blvd) The most convenient park-and-ride lot, from where you can take bus 960 to Solitude and Brighton or bus 951 or 990 to Snowbird and Alta.

Snowbird Ski & Summer Resort

If you can see it, you can ski it at **Snowbird** (☑800-232-9542; www.snowbird.com; Hwy 210, Little Cottonwood Canyon; day lift-ticket adult/child $95/45), the industrial-strength resort with extreme steeps, long groomers, wide-open bowls (one of them an incredible 500 acres across) and a kick-ass terrain park. The challenging slopes are particularly popular with speed demons and testosterone-driven snowboarders. The 125-passenger **aerial tram** (tram-only round-trip $17; ☺9am-4pm Dec-May, 11am-8pm Jun-Aug, 11am-5pm Sep-Nov) ascends 2900ft in only 10 minutes; die-hards do 'tram laps', racing back down the mountain to re-ascend in the same car they just rode up on. If you like to ski like a teenager, you'll flip out when you see this mountain.

The lowdown: 3240ft vertical drop, base elevation 7760ft; four high-speed quads, six double lifts, one tramway; 2500 acres, 27% beginner, 38% intermediate, 35% advanced. The only conveyor-pull tunnel in the US links the need-for-speed **Peruvian Gulf** area and intermediate terrain in **Mineral Basin**. Wednesday, Friday and Saturday, one lift remains open until 8:30pm for night skiing. Skiers (not boarders) can get an $88 Alta-Snowbird pass, which permits access to both areas, for a total of 4700 skiable acres. Snowbird has the longest season of the four SLC resorts, with skiing usually possible mid-November to mid-May. But that's not all: inquire about snowmobiling, backcountry tours and snowshoeing in winter.

In summer, the Peruvian lift and tunnel offer access to Mineral Basin **hiking** and wildflowers. Good, though strenuous, trails include the **White Pine Lake Trail** (10,000ft), which is just over 3 miles one-way. Watch rocky slopes around the lake for the unique pika – a small, short-eared, tailless lagomorph (the order of mammals that includes rabbits). At the end of the canyon road is **Cecret Lake Trail**, an easy 1-mile loop with spectacular wildflowers (July and August). Pick up basic trail maps at the resort.

An **all-activities pass** (Activity Center; adult/child $39/24; ☺11am-8pm mid-Jun–Aug) includes numerous diversions: take a tramway up to Hidden Peak, ride the luge-like Alpine Slide, zipline down 1000ft, climb a rock wall or trampoline bungee jump. Full suspension mountain bikes can be rented for three hours ($35). Horseback riding,

backcountry 4WD and ATV tours are available, too (from $40 per hour).

Snowbird has five kinds of accommodation, including hotels and condos, all booked through the resort's central phone number and website; packages that include lift tickets are available. In summer, prices drop precipitously. The splashy black-glass-and-concrete 500-room **Cliff Lodge** (www.snowbird.com/lodging/thecllifflodge; r $450-620; @ 🤖 ☒) is like a cruise ship in the mountains, with every possible destination-resort amenity – from flat-screen TVs to a recently remodeled, luxurious full-service spa. Request a 'spa level' room to have unlimited access to the rooftop pool. Otherwise, check out the dramatic 10th-story glass-walled bar and settle for the level-three swimming pool with ski-run views. Right at the heart of the resort's Snowbird Center pedestrian village, this lodge always bustles.

At the other end of the quietness spectrum, we also recommend the **Inn at Snowbird** (r $315-500; 🤖 ☒), with a simpler, almost residential feel to it. Studio rooms have kitchens and wood-burning fireplaces. (Bring groceries and you'll save a bundle.)

Snowbird resort has 15 eating outlets, including standards like a coffee shop, pizza place, steakhouse and aprés-ski bars. **General Gritts** (Snowbird Center; ☺11am-6pm) grocery store has a deli and liquor sales. Everyone loves looking out through 15ft windows to spectacular mountain views at the 10th-floor **Aerie Restaurant** (☑801-933-2160; Cliff Lodge; mains $24-38; ☺7am-11am & 5-10pm Dec-Feb, 6-9pm Apr-Oct). The menu lives up to the fine prices; reservations are a must. The adjacent lounge has a full bar and sushi menu.

The 3000-sq-ft deck at **Creekside Café & Grill** (Gadzoom lift base; breakfast & sandwiches $6-10; ☺9am-2:30pm Dec-Apr) is a great place to grab a sandwich slopeside. The **Plaza Deck**, a huge patio at Snowbird Center, is a favorite place to gather; there's often live music weekend afternoons.

Alta

Dyed-in-the-wool skiers make a pilgrimage to **Alta** (☑801-359-1078, 888-782-9258; www.alta.com; Little Cottonwood Canyon; day lift-pass adult/child $79/42), at the top of the valley. No snowboarders are allowed here, which keeps the snow cover from deteriorating, especially on groomers. Locals have grown up with Alta, a resort filled not with see-and-be-seen types, but rather the see-and-say-hello crowd. Wide-open powder fields, gullies, chutes and glades, such as **East Greeley**, **Devil's Castle** and **High Rustler**, have helped make Alta famous. Warning: you may never want to ski anywhere else.

The lowdown: 2020ft vertical drop, base elevation 8530ft; 2200 skiable acres, 25% beginner, 40% intermediate, 35% advanced; three high-speed chairs, four fixed-grip chairs. You can ski from the Sunnyside lift for free after 3pm, which is great for families with little ones who tire easily (lifts close at 4:30pm). Get the $88 Alta-Snowbird pass, which permits access to both areas for a stunning 4700 acres of skiing. Expert powder hounds, ask about off-piste snow-cat skiing in **Grizzly Gulch** ($325 for five runs).

No lifts run in summer, but there are 10 miles of local trails. From July to August, **Albion Basin** (www.fs.fed.us/wildflowers/regions/intermountain/AlbionBasin) is abloom with wildflowers. July, when an annual wildflower festival is held, is usually peak season.

The lodging options at Alta are like the ski area: simple and just as it's been for decades. Every place here has ski-in, ski-out access and a hot tub. Winter rates, as listed, include breakfast and dinner and require a four-night minimum stay. Lodge restaurants and snack bars are seasonal (December through March) and open to the public.

Alta Lodge (☎801-742-3500, 800-707-2852; www.altalodge.com; dm $127, d $490, d without bath $408-455; @🛜🏊) is a mid-century modernist interpretation of a cozy mountain lodge. The attic bar (open to nonguests) is frequented by intellectuals playing backgammon. Expect to make friends there and at family-style dinners in this classical comfortable Alta lodge.

The granite-block **Snowpine Lodge** (☎801-742-2000; www.thesnowpine.com; male dm $115, r with private/shared bath $250/130), Alta's most basic, is the die-hard skier's first choice. An eight-room expansion overlooks Eagle's Nest and Albion Basin. You'll likely see families with teenagers embarrassed by their parents at the always-fun **Alta Peruvian** (☎801-742-3000, 800-453-8488; www.altaperuvian.com; male dm $132, d with/without bath from $299/239; @🛜🏊). Spacious knotty-pine common areas (movies shown nightly) make up for the tiny rooms. The bar here is Alta's après-ski scene. Neither of these two lodges have room TVs.

Enjoy all the creature comforts of a city hotel at **Rustler Lodge** (☎801-742-2200, 888-532-2582; www.rustlerlodge.com; dm $200, d $625-950, d without bath $380; @🛜🏊). Take

> ### ℹ SKI FOR FREE
>
> After 3pm you ski for free on the Sunny-side lift at Alta. The program is set up to get beginners – or those for whom it's been a while – back on the slopes.

an early-morning stretch class before you hit the slopes and refresh in the eucalyptus sauna afterwards.

Sleep surrounded by July and August wildflowers at **Albion Basin Campground** (☎800-322-3770; www.recreation.gov; Little Cottonwood Canyon Rd; campsites $21; ☺Jul-Sep). The 19 sites sit at 9500ft, among meadows and pine trees, 11 miles up the canyon. Drinking water; no showers, no hookups.

Chef Curtis Kraus uses locally produced ingredients whenever possible on his seasonally changing, ingredient-driven menu at **Shallow Shaft Restaurant** (10199 E Hwy 210, Alta Town; mains $18-40; ☺5-10pm Dec-April, 6-9pm Thu-Sat Jul–early Sep). Mid-mountain, try **Collin's Grill** (Watson's Shelter, Wildcat Base; mains $8-25; ☺11am-2:30pm Dec-Apr) for home-made artisanal soups and French Country mains (make reservations) and **Alf's** (Cecret Lift Base; sandwiches $7-14; ☺9:30am-4pm) for a self-service burger and a look at the antique skis on the walls.

For more general information, see www.discoveralta.com.

Solitude

Though less undiscovered than it once was, sometimes it feels as if you've got the mountain to yourself at **Solitude** (☎801-534-1400; www.skisolitude.com; 12000 Big Cottonwood Canyon Rd; day lift-ticket adult/child $74/46). It's still something of a local secret, so there's room to learn plus lots of speedy, roller-coaster-like corduroy to look forward to once you've gotten your ski legs. They've added three new quads in recent years. If you're an expert, you'll dig the 400 acres of lift-assist cliff bands, gullies, over-the-head powder drifts and super-steeps at off-piste **Honeycomb Canyon**. Everything here, including the expert grooming, is first-class. Some facilities, such as the **ice skating rink** (Village; ☺3-8pm Jan-Mar) FREE, are open only to overnight guests.

The lowdown: 2047ft vertical drop, base elevation 7988ft; 1200 acres, 20% beginner, 50% intermediate, 30% advanced; eight lifts. Ask about helicopter skiing with **Wasatch**

Powderbird Guides (📋 801-742-2800; www. powderbird.com; per day from $1120); they offer scenic flights, too.

North of the resort's lodges, Solitude's **Nordic Center** (day pass adult/child $18/free; ⊙ 8:30am-4:40pm Dec-Mar & Jun-Aug) has 12 miles of groomed classic and skating lanes and 6 miles of snowshoeing tracks through enchanting forests of aspen and pine. In summer the Nordic Center becomes a visitor center and the boardwalk encircling **Silver Lake** becomes the easiest nature trail around, great for children and the mobility-impaired. Ask about guided owl-watching walks and other activities. No swimming, no dogs allowed (this is SLC's watershed).

June through August, the **Sunrise lift** (day pass $20; ⊙ Wed-Sun Jun-Aug) opens for chair-assist mountain-biking and hiking. You can also rent mountain bikes and motorized mountain scooters, and play disc (Frisbee) golf at the resort.

Many hiking trails leave from various trailheads outside the resorts along Hwy 190. Look for trailhead signs. One of the most attractive hikes is the 2-mile round-trip **Lake Blanche Trail**, beginning at the **Mill B South Fork trailhead**, about 5 miles into the canyon.

Most of the 'Village' lodgings at Solitude are atmospheric, Alpine-esque condos. **Central reservations** (📋 800-748-4754; www. skisolitude.com) often has packages that cut room rates by as much as 50%. Of the four full-kitchen properties, we prefer the wood-and-stone rooms at **Creekside Lodge** (apt $318-407; 🛜🞖) with working fireplaces and balconies. The **Inn at Solitude** (r $269-359; @🛜🞖) is the only hotel-style lodging, with an on-site spa and hot tub; no balconies. All accommodations share Club Solitude's heated outdoor pool, sauna, fitness room, games room and movie theater.

Cozy up fireside at **St Bernard's** (📋 801-535-4120; Inn at Solitude; mains $19-36; ⊙ 7:30-11am & 5-10pm Dec-Mar) for wonderful five-course tasting dinners with some local and regional ingredients and wine pairings. For casual dining, there's a grill and pizzeria. You can tip a pint at the **Thirsty Squirrel** (Village; ⊙ 2-9pm Dec-Mar) – though Big Cottonwood Canyon's best après-ski and bar scene is at Brighton. In summer, check out **Wasatch Mountain Table** (📋 801-536-5722; www. skisolitude.com/dining/wasatch_mountain_table. php; Solitude; per person $75; ⊙ Jun-Aug, dates vary), a farm-to-table option that brings fine dining outdoors alongside Wasatch Creek.

For an adventurous treat, hike or snowshoe a mile into the woods for a sumptuous, but unpretentious, five-course meal in a bona-fide canvas yurt at **The Yurt** (📋 801-536-5709; www.skisolitude.com/dining/yurt.php; dinner winter/summer $125/75; ⊙ 5:30pm Tue-Sun Dec-Mar, 6:30pm Wed-Sun Jul-Sep). Be sure to reserve way ahead, and bring your own wine; corkage is included in the price. (There's another yurt dinner at the Canyons in Park City, but this is the original and the best.)

A great alternative to resort or city sleeping, eating and drinking is the classic mountain roadhouse, **Silver Fork Lodge** (📋 801-533-9977, 888-649-9551; www.silverfork-lodge.com; 11332 E Big Cottonwood Canyon; r incl breakfast $165; breakfast & sandwiches $10-13, dinner $11-34 ⊙ 8am-9pm Sun-Thu, to 9:30pm Fri & Sat), a mile west of Solitude. Creative comfort food is served in the rustic dining room, which feels like a cozy log cabin with its crackling fireplace. Western furnishings outfit the twin, queen and bunk-bed rooms simply; the creaking floors only add character. In summer, sit outside and watch hummingbirds buzz across gorgeous alpine scenery. All year, warm up in the hot tub.

Brighton

Slackers, truants and bad-ass boarders rule at **Brighton** (📋 801-532-4731, 800-873-5512; www.brightonresort.com; Big Cottonwood Canyon Rd; day lift-ticket adult/child $68/35). But don't be intimidated: the low-key resort where many Salt Lake residents first learned to ski remains a good first-timers' spot, especially if you want to snowboard. Thick stands of pines line sweeping groomed trails and wide boulevards, and from the top, the views are gorgeous. The whole place is a throwback: come for the ski-shack appeal coupled with high-tech slope improvements and modernized lodge.

The lowdown: 1745ft vertical drop, base elevation 8755ft; 1050 acres, 21% beginner, 40% intermediate, 39% advanced; six chair lifts. One hundred percent of Brighton's terrain is accessible by high-speed quads. There's a half-pipe and terrain park and a liberal open-boundary policy on non-avalanche-prone days. The park has some of the area's best **night skiing** (200 acres, 22 runs), open until 9pm, Monday to Saturday. A magic-carpet slope lift means beginners can just step on and go, or you can leave the kiddies behind at the day-care center.

No lifts operate during summer months, but locals still come up to go hiking in the alpine meadows and to picnic by area lakes.

The 20 basic rooms at **Brighton Lodge** ([✎]801-532-4731, 800-873-5512; www.brightonresort.com; dm $129, r $149-209) go quick; they're retro, but a good deal within spitting distance of the lifts. There are no room TVs, but you can watch more than 200 movies in the common room, or just sit by the fireplace after you've hot-tubbed it. Room prices are crazy low in summer (from $38 including breakfast).

The **Milley Chalet** (⊙8:30am-4:30pm) is the modern ski-lodge base, with various self-service food options. For après-ski drinks and pub grub, you gotta go to the A-frame right on the hill – the runaway favorite of locals, **Molly Green's** (Brighton Manor; pizza $10-24, mains $8-25; ⊙11am-10pm Mon-Sat, 10am-10pm Sun Dec-Mar) has a roaring fire, a gregarious old-school vibe and great slopeside views. Sunday brunch is always a big hit, too. **Brighton Store & Cafe** (11491 Big Cottonwood Canyon Rd; breakfast & sandwiches $6-12; ⊙8am-3pm) serves year-round.

Lands near the top of Big Cottonwood Canyon are part of the **Uinta-Wasatch-Cache National Forest** (www.fs.usda.gov/uwcnf). Camp at 44-site, first-come, first-served **Redman Campground** (www.reserveamerica.com; Solitude Service Rd; campsites $23; ⊙late Jun–Sep) and you'll be sleeping under tall pines at a high-elevation creekside ground (8300ft) near the top of the canyon. Several trails lead off from here and Silver Lake is nearby. Water available; no showers, no hookups.

Park City

POP 7870 / ELEV 6900FT

Century-old buildings line Park City's one main street, looking particularly inviting after a new dusting of snow, or at nightfall when the twinkling lights outline the eaves. It's hard to imagine that this one-time silver boomtown ever went bust. Condos and multimillion-dollar houses abut the valleys and crowd the center of Utah's premier ski village. Fabulous restaurants abound, and the skiing is truly world-class.

Park City skyrocketed to international fame when it hosted the downhill, jumping and sledding events at the 2002 Winter Olympics. Today it's the permanent home base for the US Ski Team; at one time or another most US winter Olympians train at the three ski resorts

OFF THE BEATEN TRACK

SCENIC DRIVE: MIRROR LAKE HWY

This alpine route, also known as Hwy 150, begins about 12 miles east of Park City in **Kamas** and climbs to elevations of more than 10,000ft as it covers the 65 miles into Wyoming. The highway provides breathtaking mountain vistas, passing by scores of lakes, campgrounds and trailheads in the **Uinta-Wasatch-Cache National Forest** (www.fs.fed.us). Note that sections may be closed to traffic well into spring due to heavy snowfall; check online first.

and Olympic Park here. Though the eastern front gets fewer inches per year than the western front of the Wasatch Mountains, there's usually snow from late November through mid-April. Winter is the busy high season.

Come summer, more residents than visitors gear up for hiking and mountain biking among the nearby peaks. June to August, temperatures average in the 70s (low 20s in Celsius); nights are chilly. Spring and fall can be wet and boring; resort services, limited in summer compared with winter, shut down entirely between seasons. Restaurants take extended breaks, especially in May.

◉ Sights & Activities

Skiing is the big area attraction, but there are activities enough to keep you more than busy in both summer and winter. Most are based out of the three resorts: Canyons, Park City Mountain and Deer Valley.

Utah Olympic Park   ADVENTURE SPORTS
([✎]435-658-4200; www.utaholympiclegacy.com; 3419 Olympic Pkwy; museum admission free, tours adult/child $10/7; ⊙10am-6pm, tours 11am-4pm) Visit the site of the 2002 Olympic ski jumping, bobsledding, skeleton, Nordic combined and luge events, which continues to host national competitions. There are 10m, 20m, 40m, 64m, 90m and 120m Nordic ski-jumping hills as well as a bobsled-luge run. The US Ski Team practices here year round – in summer, the freestyle jumpers land in a bubble-filled jetted pool, and the Nordic jumpers on a hillside covered in plastic. Call for a schedule; it's free to observe.

The engaging and interactive **Alf Engen Ski Museum**, also on-site, traces local skiing history and details the 2002 Olympic events.

Park City

N 0 — 200 m
0 — 0.1 miles

Windy Ridge (0.8mi);
White Pine Touring (0.8mi);
Good Karma (1.1mi)

Squatters
Roadhouse
Grill (1mi)

Silver Creek

9th St

Main St

The Shop (0.25mi);
Chateau Apres
Lodge (0.4mi)

Deer Valley Dr

8th St

Town Lift

Park Ave

Old Town Guest
House (0.2mi);
Shadow Ridge
Resort Center (0.7mi);
Park City Mountain
Resort (0.8mi)

16

2

15

Heber Ave

23

6th St

3

J&G Grill (1mi);
St Regis Deer Valley (1.1mi);
Deer Valley (1.1mi)

Deer Valley Dr

Swede Al

13   12

9

11   10

5

Park Ave

Park City
Transit
Center

Marsac Ave

5th St

18

19   6

1

4th St

Visitor
Information
Center

20

22

Main Street
Mall

7

21

Main St

Swede Al

3rd St

Woodside Ave

Park Ave

Norfolk Ave

2nd St

4

14

8

Ontario Canyon

Park City

Experts offer 45-minute **guided tours** on the hour.

Not content to just watch the action? No problem. Reserve ahead and adults can take a 70mph to 80mph **bobsled ride** with up to an incredible 4G to 5G of centrifugal force. The summer **Quicksilver Alpine Slide** is suitable for drivers over eight years old and riders who are three to seven. Clip on a harness and ride the 50mph **Extreme Zipline** or the shorter **Ultra Zipline**. Saturdays in summer there's a **Freestyle Show** that takes off at 1pm. Inquire about bobsled, skeleton, free-jump and freestyle lessons year round.

Skiing, Snowboarding & Sledding

All three resorts and in-town sports shops have equipment rental (ski rental adult/child per day from $60/30) and ski lessons.

Canyons   SNOW SPORTS
(☑ 435-649-5400, 888-604-4169; www.thecanyons.com; 4000 Canyons Resort Dr; lift ticket adult/child $116/94) Bolstered by tens of millions of dollars in improvements, and now owned by Vail Resorts, Canyons' identity has been evolving to compete with the country's best, with its introduction of the first North American 'bubble' lift (enclosed and climate-controlled), along with 300 new acres of advanced skiing acreage and an increased snow-making capability. Lodging properties are expanding on-site and new restaurants are being added. The resort currently sprawls across nine aspen-covered peaks 4 miles outside of town, near the freeway.

The lowdown: 3190ft vertical drop, base elevation 6800ft; 4000 acres, 10% beginner, 44% intermediate, 46% advanced; 19 lifts, in-

cluding a gondola. Varied terrain on 176 trails means there's something for all levels, with wide groomers for beginners and intermediates, three terrain parks and lots of freshies on a powder day. Experts: head to **Ninety-Nine 90**. There's a liberal open-boundary policy (heed avalanche warnings) as well as six natural half-pipes, one of them a whopping mile long, perfect for boarding.

Cross-country skiing and **sleigh rides**, for pleasure or to dinner, are also available. You can even ride or drive a state-of-the-art Snow Cat groomer. Sightseers can take the recently relocated **gondola** (round-trip $20) up not only for the views, but for Belgian waffles or lunch in the **Red Pine** area.

Park City Mountain Resort   SNOW SPORTS
(☑ 435-649-8111, 800-222-7275; www.parkcitymountainresort.com; 1310 Lowell Ave; lift ticket adult/child $108/68; 🅰) From boarder dudes to parents with tots, everyone skis Park City Mountain Resort, host of the Olympic snowboarding and giant slalom events. The awesome terrain couldn't be more family friendly – or more accessible, rising as it does right over downtown.

The lowdown: 3100ft vertical drop, base elevation 6900ft; 3300 acres, 17% beginner, 52% intermediate, 31% advanced; seven high-speed lifts, eight fixed-grip chairs, one magic carpet. Park City's skiable area covers nine peaks, ranging from groomers and wide-open bowls (750 acres of them!) to cotton-mouth-inducing super steeps and the nation's only superpipe. Experts: make a beeline to **Mount Jupiter**; the best open trees are in the **Black Forest**. For untracked powder, take the Eagle lift up to **Vista**. Test your aerial technique on an Olympic-worthy boarding and freestyle course at three amazing terrain parks.

Kids' trails are marked with snowbug statues near the magic-carpet lift and the resort will hook teens up with area locals who provide the lay of the land. Check out the online activity planner at www.mymountainplanner.com. To avoid crowds, stay out late: **night skiing** lasts until 9pm. In winter there's open-air **ice skating** at the Resort Center.

Though the resort has no affiliated hotels, it does offer package lodging/skiing deals with nearby properties, and restaurants and après-ski are on site. The fact that **Town Lift** takes you right from Main St up to the village area makes all downtown accommodations accessible.

Gorgoza Park   SNOW SPORTS
(☑ shuttle 435-645-9388; www.gorgoza.com; 3863 West Kilby Rd, at I-80; tubing per 2hr adult/child $23/12; ☉ 1-8pm Mon-Fri, noon-8pm Sat & Sun mid-Dec–Mar; ☑) Lift-served snow tubing takes place at Park City Mountain's Gorgoza Park, 8 miles north of town, off I-80. Plunge down three beginner or four advanced lanes; for kids under 12 there's a **miniature snowmobile track** ($10), and even littler ones will enjoy the **Fort Frosty play area** ($10, or free with tubing ticket) with carousel. The Park City Mountain Resort–wide **shuttle** will take you out there directly if you reserve.

Deer Valley   SNOW SPORTS
(☑ 435-649-1000, 800-424-3337, snowmobiling 435-645-7669; www.deervalley.com; Deer Valley Dr; day lift-ticket adult/child $111/94, round-trip gondola ride $15; ☉ snowmobiling 9am-5pm) Want to be pampered? Deer Valley, a resort of superlatives, has thought of everything – from tissue boxes at the base of slopes to ski valets. Slalom, mogul and freestyle-aerial competitions in the 2002 Olympics were held here, but the resort is just as famous for its superb dining, white-glove service and uncrowded slopes as meticulously groomed as the gardens of Versailles. Note that there's no snowboarding allowed.

The lowdown: 3000ft vertical drop, base elevation 6570ft; 2026 acres, 27% beginner, 41% intermediate, 32% advanced; one high-speed gondola, 11 high-speed quads, nine fixed-grip chairs. Every trail follows the fall line perfectly, which means you'll never skate a single cat-track. **Lady Morgan** has 200 acres of new terrain (65 acres of which is gladed), well separated from the Jordanelle Gondola area. Only a prescribed number of daily lift tickets are sold, so powder hounds can find hundreds of acres of untracked glades and steeps, days after a storm.

Resort-owned **snowmobiling** ($99 for one hour) takes place 5 miles down the road on Garff Ranch; reserve ahead.

White Pine Touring   SKIING
(☑ 435-649-8710; www.whitepinetouring.com; 1790 Bonanza Dr; 3hr tour $175) Guided cross-country ski trips take you 20 minutes away from Park City and can include yurt camping accommodations. In town, the associated **Nordic Center** (cnr Park Ave & Thaynes Canyon Dr; day pass adult/child $18/10; ☉ 9am-6pm) grooms a 12-mile cross-country course (rental available) with 2-, 3- and 6-mile loops of classic and skating lanes. Skate-skiing lessons are available.

Wasatch Powderbird   SKIING
(☑ 801-742-2800, 800-974-4354; www.powderbird.com; full-day tours from $1190) Advanced skiers can arrange area heli-skiing packages that include six to seven runs.

Other Snow Sports

Activity pick-up service is available from most resorts. Reservations are always a must.

All Seasons Adventures   SNOW SPORTS
(☑ 435-649-9619; www.allseasonsadventures.com) Dog sledding ($375), sleigh rides ($83), cross-country skiing ($95), snowshoe tours (two hours for $75), as well as summer activities. Rates are per person.

Rocky Mountain Recreation of Utah   SNOW SPORTS
(☑ 435-645-7256, 800-303-7256; www.rockymtn-rec.com; sleigh ride $45; 1hr snowmobile tour $95) Snowmobile tours, horse-drawn sleigh rides (to dinner or just around) and dog sledding.

Hiking

You'll feel on top of the world in the peaks over Park City, where over 300 miles of trails crisscross the mountains. Pick up a summer trail map at the visitor center.

Mountain Vista Touring   HIKING
(☑ 435-640-2979; www.parkcityhiking.com; day hike $125; ☉ mid-Apr–mid-Nov) Guided trips include hot springs and moonlight hikes.

Mountain Biking

Park City's big secret is its amazing mountain biking. The visitor center has trail maps and you can rent bikes (from $50 per day) from sports shops in town and at all the resorts; some even have lift-assist riding.

Mid-Mountain Trail   MOUNTAIN BIKING
One of the best for mountain biking is this 15-mile one-way trail, which follows the topography at 8000ft, connecting Deer Valley to Olympic Park. You can also start at Park City Mountain, bike the steep **Spiro Trail** up to Mid-Mountain, then return on roads for a 22-mile loop.

Historic Union Pacific
Rail Trail   MOUNTAIN BIKING
(http://stateparks.utah.gov) A 28-mile multiuse trail that's also a state park. Pick it up at Bonanza Dr just south of Kearns Blvd.

White Pine Touring   CYCLING
(☑ 435-649-8710;   www.whitepinetouring.com; 1790 Bonanza Dr; 3hr tour for 2 people $175) Bike rentals and guided biking tours. Free guided rides are offered every Tuesday for women and for all on Thursdays, with a BBQ included each last week of the month.

Other Summer Activities
Park City Mountain Resort ADVENTURE SPORTS
(☑ 435-649-8111;   www.parkcitymountainresort. com; 1310 Lowell Ave; alpine pass adult/child $70/35) We love the **Town Lift**–served hiking and mountain biking (day pass $21 to $23). The alpine pass is priced by size: those over 54in in height pay the adult fare, which includes access to the alpine slide, lifts and base-area activities. Or you can go á la carte: a 3000ft-long **alpine slide** ($12), where a wheeled sled flies down 550ft along a cement track, as well as a super-long **zipline ride** (2300ft long, 550ft vertical; $20).

Kids not tired yet? Check out the **adventure zone** (admission $14-16) with its climbing wall, spiderweb climb, boulder climb and slide. Note that hours vary depending on the activity and the month.

Canyons   ADVENTURE SPORTS
(☑ 888-226-9667;   www.thecanyons.com;   4000 Canyons Resort Dr; adventure pass adult/child $69/59) Adventure passes cover a range of activities. A scenic ride on the **gondola** (round-trip adult/junior $18/13) is great for sightseers, but hiking trails also lead off from here. Mountain bikers should head over to the **Gravity Bike Park** (day pass adult/junior $32/27), which has varied trails accessed by the High Meadow Lift. Other activities include disc golf, miniature golf, lake pedal-boats and hot-air balloon rides. On

weekends in summer and winter live-music concerts rock the base area.

Deer Valley   ADVENTURE SPORTS
(☑ 800-424-3337;   www.deervalley.com; Deer Valley Dr; scenic chairlift all-day adult/child $23/18) In summer, Deer Valley has more than 50 miles of hiking and mountain-biking trails served by its three operating lifts. Horseback riding and free guided hikes are available by request.

Rocky Mountain
Recreation of Utah   HORSEBACK RIDING
(☑ 435-645-7256, 800-303-7256; www.rockymtn-rec.com; Stillman Ranch, Weber Canyon Rd) Horseback rides (one hour $61), wagon rides with dinner ($74) and guided pack and fly-fishing trips ($285).

All Seasons Adventures   HORSEBACK RIDING
(☑ 435-649-9619; www.allseasonsadventures.com; half-day $65-270) Guided kayaking, hiking, mountain biking, horseback riding, ATV riding and geocaching scavenger races around the area.

National Ability Center   ADVENTURE SPORTS
(NAC;   ☑ 435-649-3991;   www.nac1985.org;   1000 Ability Way) Year-round adapted sports program for people with disabilities and their families: horseback riding, rafting, climbing and biking.

Spas & Massage
When you've overdone it on the slopes, a spa treatment may be just what the doctor ordered. Deer Valley and the Canyons both have swanky spas.

Aura Spa   SPA
(☑ 435-658-2872;   www.auraspaforthespirit.com; 405 Main St; 1hr from $85) Schedule energy-balancing chakra work after your rubdown at in-town Aura Spa.

The Shop   YOGA
(www.parkcityyoga.com; 1167 Woodside Ave; by donation $7 minimum) Stretch out the kinks with an Anusara yoga class at this amazing warehouse space. Walk-ins welcome.

✯✯ Festivals & Events
Sundance Film Festival   FILM
(☑ 888-285-7790; www.sundance.org/festival) Independent films and their makers and movie stars and their fans fill the town to bursting for 10 days in late January. Passes, ticket packages and the few individual tickets sell out well in advance – plan ahead.

🛌 Sleeping

Mid-December through mid-April is high winter season, with minimum stays required; rates rise during Christmas, New Year's and the Sundance Film Festival. With a dearth of budget lodging in Park City in winter, consider staying down in Salt Lake or Heber Valley. Also check resort websites for packages that combine condo or hotel accommodations and lift tickets, which can be a good deal. All three ski resorts have condo rentals that can be booked directly. Resort lodging has ski-in advantages, but staying near nightlife in the old town can be more fun. For a complete list of the more than 100 condos, hotels and resorts in Park City, log onto www.visitparkcity.com.

Rates listed here are for the winter high season. Note that off-season, rates drop 50% or more.

Chateau Apres Lodge HOSTEL $
(☑ 800-357-3556, 435-649-9372; www.chateauapres.com; 1299 Norfolk Ave; dm $45, r $130; 🛜) The only budget-oriented accommodation in town is this basic, 1963 lodge – with a 1st-floor dorm – near the town ski lift. Reserve ahead, as it's very popular with groups and seniors.

Park City RV Resort CAMPGROUND $
(☑ 435-649-8935; www.parkcityrvresort.com; 2200 Rasmussen Rd; tent sites $21, RV sites with hookups $30-45; @🛜🏊) Amenities galore (games room, playground, laundry, hot tub, fishing pond, kids' climbing wall...), 6 miles north of town at I-80.

Treasure Mountain Inn HOTEL $$
(☑ 435-655-4501, 800-344-2460; www.treasuremountaininn.com; 255 Main St; r $158-206, ste from $263; ✳️🛜) 🌱 Park City's first member of the Green Hotel Association utilizes wind energy and serves organic food in its breakfast restaurant. Some of the upscale condos, decorated in earthy tones, have fireplaces, and all have kitchens.

Park City Peaks HOTEL $$
(☑ 800-333-3333, 435-649-5000; www.parkcitypeaks.com; 2121 Park Ave; r $139-189; ✳️@🛜🏊) Comfortable, contemporary rooms include access to heated outdoor pool, hot tub, restaurant and bar. Great deals off season. December through April, breakfast is included.

Park City Crash Pads ACCOMMODATION SERVICES $$
(☑ 435-901-9119, 877-711-0921; www.parkcitycrashpads.com; r from $100) Take advantage of the condo market through this reasonable consolidator. Buildings and facilities may not be the newest, but all rooms have 300-thread-count duvets and iPod clock radios, and many have kitchens. Minimum stays are required.

Shadow Ridge Resort Center HOTEL $$
(☑ 435-649-4300, 800-451-3031; www.shadowridgeresort.com; 50 Shadow Ridge Rd; r $149-199, apt $219-419; 🛜🏊) A hundred yards from Park City Mountain lifts, with both hotel rooms and condo-style apartments with full kitchens, dining areas and fireplaces.

Holiday Inn Express HOTEL $$
(☑ 435-658-1600, 888-465-4329; www.holidayinnexpress.com; 1501 W Ute Blvd; r incl breakfast $111-145; 🛜🏊) Save money by staying outside the downtown area, near Kimball Junction stores and restaurants.

★ Torchlight Inn B&B $$$
(www.torchlightinn.com; r $225-300; P✳️🛜) Right off the traffic circle, this new six-room inn charms with elegant and inviting contemporary spaces, gas fireplaces and flatscreen TVs. There's also a rooftop hot tub, Jeep rentals on-site and two friendly bulldogs to keep you company. With friendly, helpful service, family suites and wheelchair access (including an elevator).

★ Old Town Guest House B&B $$$
(☑ 800-290-6423, 435-649-2642; www.oldtownguesthouse.com; 1011 Empire Ave; r incl breakfast $219-269; ✳️@🛜) Grab the flannel robe, pick a paperback off the shelf and snuggle under a quilt on your lodgepole bed, or kick back on the large deck at this comfy in-town B&B. The host will gladly give you the lowdown on the great outdoors, guided ski tours, mountain biking, and the rest.

Sky Lodge LUXURY HOTEL $$$
(☑ 888-876-2525, 435-658-2500; www.theskylodge.com; 201 Heber Ave; ste $950; ✳️@🛜🏊) The urban-loft-like architecture containing the chic Sky Lodge suites both complements and contrasts the three historic buildings that house the property's restaurants. You can't be more stylish, or more central, if you stay here.

Washington School House BOUTIQUE HOTEL $$$
(☑ 800-824-1672, 435-649-3800; www.washingtonschoolhouse.com; 543 Park Ave; ste incl breakfast $850; ✳️🛜🏊) Architect Trip Bennett oversaw the restoration that turned an 1898 limestone schoolhouse on a hill into a luxurious boutique hotel with 12 suites. How

did the children ever concentrate when they could gaze out at the mountains through 9ft-tall windows instead?

St Regis Deer Valley
LUXURY HOTEL $$$

(☑435-940-5700, 866-932-7059; www.stregis-deervalley.com; 2300 Deer Valley Dr E; r from $999; ✳@🗢🌊) You have to ride a private funicular just to get up to the St Regis, so whether you're lounging by the outdoor fire pits, dining on the terrace or peering from your balcony, the views are sublime. The studied, elegant rusticity here is the height of Deer Valley's luxury lodging. Forget private lessons – where else can you ski with an Olympian?

Hyatt Escala Lodge
HOTEL $$$

(☑435-940-1234, 888-591-1234; www.escalalodge.hyatt.com; 3551 North Escala Ct; r $263-300, ste from $339; ✳🗢🌊🐕) Finished in 2011, the upscale lodge rooms are all meant to have a residential feel. Indeed, suites have full kitchens and a personal grocery shopping service is available throughout. From here you're not more than a few ski strides away from the Canyons resort lifts.

Montage
LUXURY HOTEL $$$

(☑888-604-1301; www.montagehotels.com/deervalley; 9100 Marsac Ave, Empire Pass, Deer Valley; r from $765; P✳@🗢🌊🐕) Among the top area resorts, Montage wows with personalized service and extras like a kids activity center, bowling and a gorgeous spa with trainers and yoga that fills a whole floor. Aprés-ski finds guests, side by side in black tie and robes, enjoying mulled wine and s'mores or braving the heated alpine pool. Rooms go for understated elegance.

Goldener Hirsch
LUXURY HOTEL $$$

(☑435-649-7770, 800-252-3373; www.goldenerhirschinn.com; 7570 Royal St, Deer Valley; r incl breakfast from $529; 🗢) You can tell the Goldener was fashioned after a lodge in Salzburg by the hand-painted Austrian furniture, feather-light duvets and European stone fireplaces. 'Stay & Ski Deer Valley' packages available. A favorite.

Waldorf Astoria
LUXURY HOTEL $$$

(☑435-647-5500; www.parkcitywaldorfastoria.com; 2100 Frostwood Dr; r from $659; @🗢🌊) Top luxury property at the Canyons.

✗ Eating

Park City is well known for exceptional upscale eating – a reasonable meal is harder to find. In the spring and summer, look for half-off main-dish coupons in the *Park Record* newspaper. *Park City Magazine* puts out a full menu guide. The three ski resorts have numerous eating options in season. Assume dinner reservations are required at all top-tier places in winter. Note that from April through November restaurants reduce opening hours variably, and may take extended breaks.

Uptown Fare
CAFE $

(227 Main St; sandwiches $8-11; ⊘11am-3pm) Comforting, house-roasted turkey sandwiches and homemade soups at the hole-in-the-wall hidden below the Treasure Mountain Inn.

Good Karma
INDIAN, FUSION $$

(www.goodkarmarestaurants.com; 1782 Prospector Ave; breakfast $7-12, mains $12-22; ⊘7am-10pm; ☑) 🖉 Whenever possible, local and organic ingredients are used in the Indo-Persian meals at Good Karma. You'll recognize the place by the Tibetan prayer flags flapping out front.

Squatters Roadhouse Grill
PUB $$

(www.squatters.com; 1900 Park Ave; burgers $9-12, mains $10-20; ⊘11am-midnight Mon-Fri, 10am-1am Sat & Sun; ☑) A favorite local hangout and the best of the town brewpubs, as far as food goes. We love the Asiago, cheddar and Havarti mac-and-cheese. Breakfast is served until 2pm daily.

Maxwell's
PIZZA $$

(www.maxwellsece.com; 1456 New Park Blvd; pizza slices $3.50, dishes $10-17; ⊘11am-9pm Sun-Thu, to 10pm Fri & Sat) Eat with the locals at the pizza, pasta and beer joint tucked in a back corner of the stylish outdoor Redstone Mall, north of town. Huge, crispy-crusted 'Fat Boy' pizzas never linger long on the tables. Gluten-free options available.

Windy Ridge Cafe
AMERICAN $$

(www.windyridgefoods.com; 1250 Iron Horse Dr; lunch $10-15, dinner $13-27; ⊘11am-3pm & 5-9pm) Escape the Main St mayhem at this out-of-the-way American cafe. There's a long list of salads to choose from, also available as sides, and comfort food like herb-roasted chicken and baked meatloaf.

Wasatch Brew Pub
PUB $$

(www.wasatchbeers.com; 250 Main St; lunch & sandwiches $10-14, dinner $10-30; ⊘11am-10pm) Pub grub at the top of Main St.

Taste of Saigon VIETNAMESE **$$**
(580 Main St; mains $10-16; ⊘11am-3pm & 5-10pm) Reasonably priced Vietnamese dishes, and even better lunch specials.

Eating Establishment AMERICAN **$$**
(www.theeatingestablishment.net; 317 Main St; breakfast & sandwiches $9-12, dinner $15-20; ⊘8am-10pm) Local institution; service can be hit or miss.

⭐**Riverhorse on Main** MODERN AMERICAN **$$$**
(☑435-649-3536; www.riverhorseparkcity.com; 540 Main St; dinner mains $34-49; ⊘5-10pm Mon-Thu, to 11pm Fri & Sat, 11am-2:30pm & 5-10pm Sun; 🖉) A fine mix of the earthy and exotic, with cucumber quinoa salad, polenta fries and Rocky Mountain rack of lamb. There's a separate menu for vegetarians. A wall-sized window and the sleek modern design creates a stylish atmosphere. Reserve ahead: this is a longtime, award-winning restaurant.

⭐**J&G Grill** AMERICAN **$$$**
(☑435-940-5760; www.jggrilldeercrest.com; 2300 Deer Valley Drive E, Deer Valley Resort; breakfast & lunch mains $14-22, dinner mains $26-55; ⊘7am-9pm) A favorite of locals, who love the tempura onion rings and seared scallops with sweet chili sauce. The bold flavors of meat and fish star here at one of celebrity chef Jean-Georges Vongerichten's collaborative projects. The mid-mountain St Regis setting is spectacular.

Talisker MODERN AMERICAN **$$$**
(☑435-658-5479; www.taliskeronmain.com; 515 Main St; mains $34-39; ⊘5:30-10pm) Talisker elevates superb food to the sublime: lobster hush-puppies, anyone? Settle into one of the four individually designed dining rooms and see what longtime resident and chef Jeff Murcko has to offer on his daily changing menu. The chef also oversees the menus at Canyons Resort.

Wahso ASIAN **$$$**
(☑435-615-0300; www.wahso.com; 577 Main St; mains $30-50; ⊘5:30-10pm Wed-Sun, closed mid-Apr–mid-Jun) Park City's cognoscenti flock to this modern pan-Asian phenomenon, where fine-dining dishes may include lamb vindaloo or Malaysian snapper. Expect to see and be seen.

Silver MODERN AMERICAN **$$$**
(☑435-940-1000; www.silverrestaurant.com; 508 Main St; mains $18-38; ⊘5:30pm-late) With a decor of crushed blue velvet and chain curtains, this is industrial chic. With luxuriant braised leeks and Greek osso bucco, Silver tries for fresh and seasonal fare, paired with a dizzying, 3000-bottle wine list. So far the results have been excellent. Start or end with one of their notable cocktails. There's live DJs and late night dancing.

Viking Yurt EUROPEAN **$$$**
(☑435-615-9878; www.vikingyurt.com; 345 Lowell Avenue for parking; per person 6-course meal & transport $125; ⊘11am & 6pm by reservation) More of an experience than a meal – it isn't every day that a sleigh whisks you to dinner on the mountaintop serenaded by a baby grand. A candlelit dinner includes glogg, hearty Norwegian fare and a cheese course. If you have any allergies, do advise ahead. Dress warm for the ride.

Grappa ITALIAN **$$$**
(☑435-645-0636; 151 Main St; mains $35-40; ⊘5-9pm Thu-Sun, to 10pm Fri & Sat) The rambling old home at the top of the historic downtown hill is perfect for a romantic northern Italian meal. Dine under the soft patio lights in summer, and take advantage of locals' night on Monday, with specials on small plates and wine.

Bistro 412 FRENCH **$$$**
(412 Main St; mains $12-34; ⊘11am-2:30pm & 5-10pm) The cozy dining room and French bistro fare here, including beef Bourguignon and cassoulet (a hearty bean stew made with elk, sausage and lamb bacon), will keep you warm in winter. During summer months, steak *frites* on the outdoor deck might be more appropriate.

Lookout Cabin MODERN AMERICAN **$$$**
(Canyons, 4000 Canyons Resort Dr; mains $18-23; ⊘11:30am-3:30pm Dec-Mar) Gourmet lunch and aprés-ski mid-mountain. Think fondue, grilled vegetables and Wagyu burgers.

Zoom AMERICAN **$$$**
(☑435-649-9108; 660 Main St; mains $22-36; ⊘11:30am-2:30pm & 5-10pm) Earning due acclaim, with an emphasis on regional dishes like seared Utah trout and artisan greens with pear and brie, this atmospheric, Robert Redford–owned restaurant occupies a rehabbed train depot. A perennial Utah-state restaurant award winner.

Shabu FUSION **$$$**
(☑435-645-7253; 442 Main St; small plates & rolls $10-18, mains $14-38; ⊘11am-2:30pm & 5-11pm Thu-Tue) Hip, inventive Asian small plates

and namesake *shabu shabu* (a hot pot of flavorful broth with meat or veggies).

Drinking & Nightlife

Main St is where it's at. In winter there's action nightly; weekends are most lively off-season. For listings, see www.thisweek-inparkcity.com. Several restaurants, such as Bistro 412, Squatters and Wasatch Brew Pub, also have good bars.

High West Distillery & Saloon   BAR
(703 Park St; ☉11am-10pm, tours 3pm & 4pm) A former livery and Model A–era garage is now home to Park City's most happenin' nightspot. You can ski in for homemade rye whiskey at this micro distillery. What could be cooler?

Spur   BAR
(352 Main St; ☉5pm-1am) What an upscale Western bar should be: rustic walls, leather couches, roaring fire. Good grub, too. Live music on weekends.

Sidecar Bar   BAR
(2nd fl, 333 Main St; ☉5pm-1am) Local and regional bands (rock, funk, swing) play to a 20-something crowd.

No Name Saloon & Grill   BAR
(447 Main St; ☉11am-1am) There's a motorcycle hanging from the ceiling and Johnny Cash's 'Jackson' playing on the stereo at this memorabilia-filled bar.

O'Shucks   PUB
(427 Main St; ☉10am-2am) The floor crunches with peanut shells at this hard-drinkin' bar for snowboarders and skiers. Tuesdays see $3 schooners (32 ounces) of beer.

Atticus   CAFE
(738 Main St; ☉7am-7pm) Park City's best espresso bar also serves tea lattes, soup and sandwiches ($4 to $10) – probably the best-value grub in town. Also a bookstore, with little seating.

☆ Entertainment

Symphony, chamber music, bluegrass, jazz and other musical events happen throughout summer and winter; pick up the free *This Week in Park City* (www.parkcityweek.com).

Egyptian Theatre Company   THEATER
(www.egyptiantheatrecompany.org; 328 Main St) The restored 1926 theater is a primary venue for Sundance; the rest of the year it hosts plays, musicals and concerts.

🛍 Shopping

The quality of stores along Main St has improved in recent years. In addition to the typical tourist T-shirts and schlocky souvenirs, you'll find upscale galleries and outdoor clothing brands. **Park City Gallery Association** (www.parkcitygalleryassociation.com) puts out a gallery guide and sponsors art walks.

Tanger Outlet   MALL
(Kimball Junction, Hwy 224) Dozens of outlet and other outdoor mall shops at the junction with I-80 (exit 145).

ℹ Information

Main Street Visitor Center (☎435-649-7457; 528 Main St; ☉10am-7pm Mon-Sat, noon-6pm Sun) Small desk inside the Park City Museum downtown.

Park City Clinic (☎435-649-7640; 1665 Bonanza Dr) Urgent care and 24-hour emergency room.

Park City Magazine (www.parkcitymagazine.com) Glossy magazine with some events listings.

Park Record (www.parkrecord.com) The community newspaper for more than 130 years.

Visitor Information Center (☎435-658-9616, 800-453-1360; www.visitparkcity.com; 1794 Olympic Pkwy; ☉9am-6pm; 🖥) Vast visitor center with a coffee bar, terrace and incredible views of the mountains at Olympic Park. Visitor guides available online.

ℹ Getting There & Away

Downtown Park City is 5 miles south of I-80 exit 145, 32 miles east of SLC and 40 miles from the airport. Hwy 190 (closed October through March) crosses over Guardsman Pass between Big Cottonwood Canyon and Park City.

Park City Transportation (☎800-637-3803, 435-649-8567; www.parkcitytransportation.com), **All Resort Express** (☎435-649-3999, 800-457-9457; www.allresort.com) and **Powder for the People** (☎888-482-7547, 435-649-6648; www.powderforthepeople.com) all run shared van service ($44 one-way) and private-charter vans (from $220 for one to three people) from Salt Lake City International Airport. The latter also has Powder Chaser ski shuttles between Park City and Salt Lake City resorts.

ℹ Getting Around

Traffic can slow you down, especially on weekends; bypass Main St by driving on Park Ave. Parking can also be challenging and meter regulations are strictly enforced. Free lots are available in Swede Alley; those by 4th and 5th Sts are especially convenient.

Better still, forgo the rental and take a shuttle from the airport. The excellent public transit system covers most of Park City, including the three ski resorts, and makes it easy not to need a car.

Park City Transit Center (www.parkcity.org; 558 Swede Alley) Free trolleybuses run one to six times an hour from 8am to 11pm (reduced frequency in summer). There's a downloadable route map online.

Ogden & Around

POP 83,800 / ELEV 4300FT

During Ogden's heyday, historic 25th St was lined with brothels and raucous saloons; today the restored buildings house restaurants, galleries, bakeries and bars. The old town is atmospheric, but the main attraction here is 20 miles east in the Wasatch Mountains of Ogden Valley. Since skiing here is more than an hour's drive from Salt Lake City, most metro area residents head to Park City or the SLC resorts, leaving Snowbasin and Powder Mountain luxuriously empty. The villages of Huntsville and Eden, halfway between town and mountains, are nearest to the resorts.

⊙ Sights

Ogden Eccles Dinosaur Park   MUSEUM
(www.dinosaurpark.org; 1544 E Park Blvd; adult/child $7/6; ⊙10am-8pm Mon-Sat, to 6pm Sun, closed Sun Nov-Mar; ⚑) Prepare for your children to squeal as a couple of animatronic dinosaurs roar to life inside the museum at Ogden Eccles Dinosaur Park. Outside, it's like a giant playground where you can run around, under and over life-size plaster-of-Paris dinosaurs.

Union Station   MUSEUM
(www.theunionstation.org; 2501 Wall Ave; adult/child $6/4; ⊙10am-5pm Mon-Sat) This old train station houses three small museums dedicated to antique autos, natural history and firearms.

🏃 Activities

Snowbasin   SNOW SPORTS
(☑801-620-1100, 888-437-5488; www.snowbasin.com; 3925 E Snowbasin Rd, Huntsville; day lift-ticket adult/child $73/44, gondola day-pass $26; ⊙gondola 9am-6pm Sat & Sun) Snowbasin hosted the 2002 Olympic downhill, and it continues to be a competitive venue today. Terrain varies from gentle slow-skiing zones to wide-open groomers and boulevards, jaw-dropping steeps to gulp-and-go chutes. There are also four terrain parks and a dedicated snow tubing lift and hill. They groom 26 miles of cross-country skiing, both classic and skating; ask about yurt camping.

The lowdown: 3000ft vertical drop, base elevation 6400ft; 3000 acres, 20% beginner, 50% intermediate, 30% expert; one tram, two gondolas, two high-speed quads, four fixed-grip chairs. The lift system is one of the most advanced in the Southwest, but for now Snowbasin remains a hidden gem with fantastic skiing, top-flight service and nary a lift line. The exposed-timber-and-glass Summit Day Lodge (accessible to nonskiers) has a massive four-sided fireplace and a deck overlooking daredevil steeps, in addition to good restaurants.

In summer, the gondola takes you up to **Needles** restaurant and **hiking** and **mountain biking** trails; bike rentals available for $50 per day. Check online for the Sunday afternoon outdoor concert series line-up.

Powder Mountain   SNOW SPORTS
(☑801-745-3772; www.powdermountain.com; Rte 158, Eden; day lift-ticket adult/child $65/35, Snow Cat ride $18) Backcountry enthusiasts groove on Powder Mountain. They've had banner years of late, and its over 7000 skiable acres means there's plenty of elbow room. Half of the area is lift-served by four chairs (one high-speed) and three rope tows. There are two terrain parks and night skiing till 10pm. Best of all, two weeks after a storm, you'll still find powder.

Snow Cat rides access 3000 acres of exclusive bowls, glades and chutes for a day gliding on powder. Inquire about backcountry guided tours and snow-kiting lessons. The rest of the lowdown: 3005ft vertical drop, base elevation 6895ft, 7000 skiable acres; 25% beginner, 40% intermediate, 35% advanced.

Wolf Mountain   SNOW SPORTS
(☑801-745-3511; www.wolfmountainutah.com; 3567 Nordic Valley Way, Eden; day lift-ticket adult/child $45/27; ⚑) The old-fashioned mom-and-pop mountain. At only 1600 skiable acres and with a 1604ft vertical drop, who'd think Wolf Mountain would garner any superlatives? But since all five lifts are lit until 9pm, Wolf Mountain has some of the largest night-skiing terrain in Utah, and the magic-carpet lifts provide good access for young'uns. Runs comprise 25% beginner, 50% intermediate and 25% advanced.

iFly
ADVENTURE SPORTS

(☑801-528-5348; www.iflyutah.com; 2261 Kiesel Ave; per flight $49; ☯noon-10pm Mon-Sat) Take off on an indoor skydiving adventure at iFly; reservations required.

🛏 Sleeping

Cradled by mountains, Ogden Valley is the preferred place to stay. If you choose to stay in town, you'll have more eating and drinking options.

🏨 Ogden Town

Of the standard chain motels near I-15, the Comfort Inn is among the newest.

Ben Lomond Historic Suite Hotel
HOTEL $$

(☑801-627-1900, 877-627-1900; www.benlomondsuites.com; 2510 Washington Blvd; r incl breakfast $105-159; ❋@� ☎❄) Traditional rooms in this 1927 Italian Revival–style downtown hotel could use an update, but you can't beat the local history connection.

Hampton Inn & Suites
HOTEL $$

(☑801-394-9400, 800-426-7866; www.hampton-innogden.com; 2401 Washington Blvd; r $129-160; ❋@☎) Contemporary rooms; short walk to restaurants.

🏨 Ogden Valley

There are no accommodations owned by the ski resorts, but all three have condo partners that offer ski packages; check their websites. The town of Eden is closest to Powder and Wolf Mountains; Huntsville is closest to Snowbasin. For a full lodging list, see www.ovba.org.

Jackson Fork Inn
B&B $

(☑801-745-0051, 800-255-0672; www.jacksonforkinn.com; 7345 E 900 South, Huntsville; r/ste incl breakfast $90/160; ☎) A big ol' white barn has been turned into a simple, seven-room B&B. Downstairs there's a homey restaurant serving dinner and Sunday brunch.

Atomic Chalet B&B
B&B $$

(☑801-745-0538; www.atomicchalet.com; 1st St, Huntsville; r incl breakfast $130; ☎) Down-to-earth and comfy, this cedar-shake cottage makes an excellent home away from home. After a day spent skiing or hiking, relax in the hot tub, watch a film from the video collection or play a game of billiards.

Snowberry Inn
B&B $$

(☑801-745-2634, 888-746-2634; www.snowberry-inn.com; 1315 N Hwy 158, Eden; r incl breakfast $99-139; ❋) A cozy, family-owned log-cabin B&B with wood stoves and game room; no room TVs. Ski packages available.

Alaskan Inn
INN $$

(☑801-621-8600; 435 Ogden Canyon Rd, Ogden; cabins & ste incl breakfast $119-194; ❋☎) Luxury Western-themed suites with in-room Jacuzzi and cabins in the picturesque canyon, just outside Ogden Valley. Wi-fi only reaches to some rooms, so ask ahead.

🍴 Eating & Drinking

Look for restaurants and a handful of bars in Ogden town on historic 25th St between Union Station and Grant Ave.

🍴 Ogden Town

Grounds for Coffee
CAFE $

(www.groundsforcoffee.com; 126 25th St; dishes $2-8; ☯6:30am-8pm Mon-Thu, to 10pm Fri & Sat, 8am-6pm Sun; ☎🐾) Full coffee menu, plus baked goods and some sandwiches, in an artsy, 1800s storefront setting.

Roosters 25th Street Brewing Co
PUB $$

(253 25th St; brunch & sandwiches $8-10, mains $10-20; ☯11am-10pm) Once a house of ill repute, this great old town building is now an upscale gastro brewpub serving Polygamy Porter as a house draft. It has a sister restaurant in Union Station, at the end of the street.

Brewski's
BAR

(244 25th St; ☯10am-1am Mon-Sat, to midnight Sun) More than 20 beers on tap; live-music weekends.

🍴 Ogden Valley

Shooting Star Saloon
PUB $

(7350 E 200 South, Huntsville; burgers $5-8; ☯noon-9pm Wed-Sat, to 8pm Sun) Open since 1879, tiny Shooting Star is Utah's oldest continuously operating saloon. Seek this place out: the cheeseburgers – and cheap beer – are justly famous, though none so much as the starburger, featuring a Polish knockwurst on top. For small appetites, there's a miniburger.

Eats of Eden
ITALIAN $$

(2529 N Hwy 162, Eden; mains $10-20; ☯11:30am-9pm Tue-Sat) Munch on pizza or pasta inside this rustic restaurant, or surrounded by valley on the small patio.

Carlos & Harley's
TEX-MEX $$
(www.carlosandharleys.com; 5510 E 2200 North, Eden; mains $12-20; ⊙11am-9pm) A lively, kitschy Mexican cantina serving margaritas and Tex-Mex inside the old Eden General Store.

Grey Cliff Lodge Restaurant
AMERICAN $$$
(www.grayclifflodge.com; 508 Ogden Canyon, Ogden; brunch $16.50, dinner $18-41; ⊙5-10pm Tue-Sat, 10am-10pm Sun) An old-fashioned resort restaurant, with classics like whole trout, fried chicken and homemade pie. It's an institution in Ogden Canyon.

☆ Entertainment

Motor-Vu Drive-In
THEATER
(www.motorvu.com; 5368 S 1050 West; adult/child $7.50/3.50; ⊙dusk Fri-Sun Mar-Nov) The kids will love piling into the car to catch a flick at this old-time drive-in movie theater. There's a swap-meet here on Saturday at 8am.

❶ Information

Ogden Valley Business Association (www.ovba.org) The online lowdown on Valley activities, eateries and lodging.

Ogden Visitors Bureau (☑800-255-8824, 866-867-8824; www.visitogden.com; 2438 Washington Blvd; ⊙9am-5pm Mon-Fri) Town and area info.

Outdoor Information Center (☑801-625-5306; www.fs.fed.us; 324 25th St; ⊙9am-5pm Mon-Fri year-round, plus 9am-5pm Sat Jun-Sep) Handles USFS and other public lands trail and campground info.

❶ Getting There & Away

Greyhound (☑801-394-5573, 800-231-2222; www.greyhound.com; 2393 Wall Ave) has daily buses traveling between Ogden town and SLC (from $19, 45 minutes), but you really need a car to get around anywhere in the Valley.

Heber City & Midway
ELEV 5600FT

Twenty miles south of Park City, Heber City (population 12,260) and its vast valley make an alternative base for exploring the surrounding mountains. A popular steam-powered railway runs from here. A scant 3 miles east, Midway (population 4020) is modeled after an alpine town, with hand-painted buildings set against the slopes. Here you'll find activity-laden resorts – great for families –

and a thermal crater you can swim in. Resort activities are open to all, and cross-country skiing is available close to both towns.

◉ Sights & Activities

Much of the forested mountains east of the towns have hiking, biking, cross-country skiing, ATV and snowmobile trails that are part of the **Uinta-Wasatch-Cache National Forest** (www.fs.usda.gov).

★Homestead Crater
SWIMMING
(☑435-654-1102; www.homesteadresort.com; Homestead Resort, 700 N Homestead Dr, Midway; admission $16; ⊙noon-8pm Mon-Thu, 10am-8pm Fri & Sat, 10am-6pm Sun) Swim in a 65ft-deep geothermal pool (90°F, or 32°C, year-round) beneath the 50ft-high walls of a limestone cone open to the sky. It's way cool. Reservations required.

Heber Valley Historic Railroad
TRAIN RIDE
(☑435-654-5601; www.hebervalleyrr.org; 450 S 600 West, Heber; adult/child from $20/15) The 1904 Heber Valley Historic Railroad chugs along on scenic trips through the steep-walled Provo Canyon, as well as taking numerous themed trips.

Soldier Hollow
ADVENTURE SPORTS
(☑435-654-2002; www.soldierhollow.com; off Hwy 113; day pass adult/child $18/9, snow tubing adult/child $18/8; ⊙9am-4:30pm, snow tubing noon-8pm Mon-Sat, noon-4pm Sun) A must-ski for cross-country aficionados. Soldier Hollow, 2 miles south of Midway, was the Nordic course used in the 2002 Olympics; its 19 miles of stride-skiing and skating lanes are also open to snowshoeing. For nonskiers, there's a 1201ft-long **snow-tubing hill**; book in advance on weekends, since ticket sales are capped. Snow season is December through March.

From May through October, the resort's gorgeous 36-hole **golf** course, **mountain biking** trails and **horseback riding** are popular. (Equipment rentals are $20 to $40 per day.)

⌂ Sleeping

The standard chain gang of motels are available on Main St in Heber City.

Swiss Alps Inn
MOTEL $
(☑435-654-0722; www.swissalpsinn.com; 167 S Main St, Heber City; r $92; ⊛⊡) This independent motel has huge rooms with hand-painted doors. Guests get a free milkshake from the associated restaurant next door.

SETTING SPEED RECORDS: BONNEVILLE SALT FLATS

Millennia ago, ancient Lake Bonneville covered northern Utah and beyond. Today, all that remains is the Great Salt Lake and 46 sq miles of shimmering white salt. The surface you see is mostly made up of sodium chloride (common table salt) and is 12ft deep in spots, though officials are worried about shrinkage and have started salt reclamation efforts. The Bonneville Salt Flats are now public lands managed by the **BLM** (☑ 801-977-4300; www.blm.gov), and are best known for racing. The flat, hard salt makes speeds possible here that aren't possible anywhere else.

On October 15, 1997, Englishman Andy Green caused a sonic boom on the salt flats by driving the jet-car *ThrustSSC* to 763.035mph, setting the first-ever supersonic world land-speed record. Several clubs hold racing events throughout the year; for a complete list, check the BLM website. Driving up to the Flats is a singular optical experience: the vast whiteness tricks the eye into believing that it's snowed in August, and the inexpressible flatness allows many to see the Earth's curvature. You may recognize scenes from movies, such as *Con Air* and *Independence Day*, that were filmed here.

The Flats are about 100 miles west of SLC on I-80. Take exit 4, Bonneville Speedway, and follow the paved road to the viewing area parking lot (no services). From here you can drive on the hard-packed salt during late summer and fall (it's too wet otherwise). Obey posted signs: parts of the flats are thin and can trap vehicles. Remember, salt is insanely corrosive. If you drive on the flats, wash your car – especially the undercarriage – afterward. If you're traveling west, there's a rest stop where you can walk on the sand (and wash off your shoes in the bathroom). The nearest town is Wendover, on the Utah–Nevada state line.

Homestead Resort RESORT $$
(☑ 435-654-1102, 800-327-7220; www.homestead-resort.com; 700 N Homestead Dr, Midway; r $135-220; @🔊🌊) Most destination family resorts of this caliber faded into obscurity a generation ago. A collection of homey buildings and cottages gathers around the resort's village green. Activities include 18-hole golf, cycling, horseback riding, hot-spring swimming, spa treatments, volleyball, shuffle board and croquet. The restaurants are good, too; some of the packages include meals.

Blue Boar Inn INN $$$
(☑ 435-654-1400, 800-650-1400; www.theblueboarinn.com; 1235 Warm Springs Rd, Midway; r incl breakfast $175-295; @) It's as if an ornate Bavarian inn had been teleported to Utah – everything from the hand-painted exterior to the ornately carved wooden furniture screams Teutonic.

Zermatt Resort & Spa RESORT $$$
(☑ 866-627-1684; www.zermattresort.com; 784 West Resort Dr, Midway; r incl breakfast $175-295; @🔊🌊) The 'Adventure Haus' at this upscale resort not only has mountain-bike rentals; they'll arrange scenic daredevil flights, fly-fishing lessons and boat rental on a nearby lake. Complimentary ski and golf shuttles head to Park City and Sundance.

✕ Eating

Dairy Keen BURGERS $
(☑ 435-654-5336; 199 S Main St, Heber City; burgers $4-8; ⊙ 11am-9pm) Look for the miniature train that travels overhead at this local play on Dairy Queen. The ice-cream sundaes and shakes can't be beat (try the boysenberry).

Snake Creek Grill AMERICAN $$$
(www.snakecreekgrill.com; 650 W 100 South/Hwy 113, Heber City; mains $14-26; ⊙ 5:30-9:30pm Wed-Sat, to 8:30pm Sun) One of northern Utah's best restaurants looks like a saloon from an old Western. The all-American Southwest-style menu features blue-cornmeal crusted trout and finger-lickin' ribs. Located halfway between downtown Heber City and Midway.

Blue Boar Inn INTERNATIONAL $$$
(☑ 435-654-1400, 800-650-1400; www.theblueboarinn.com; 1235 Warm Springs Rd, Midway; breakfast & sandwiches $13, dinner $24-30; ⊙ 7am-10pm) The European-inspired experience at this inn's dining room (open to nonguests) is worth the reservation you need to make.

❶ Information

Most of the services are in Heber City.
Heber Ranger Station (☑ 435-654-0470; 2460 S Hwy 40, Heber City; ⊙ 8am-4pm

Mon-Fri) Information on Uinta-Cache-Wasatch National Forest.

Heber Valley Chamber of Commerce (☑ 435-654-3666; www.hebervalleycc.org; 475 N Main St, Heber City; ☺ 8am-5pm) Pick up information about both towns here.

❶ Getting There & Around

Hwy 190 continues over Guardsman Pass to Big Cottonwood Canyon and SLC (closed in winter). **Greyhound** (☑ 801-394-5573, 800-231-2222; www.greyhound.com; 2393 Wall Ave, Ogden) The Greyhound Station is in Ogden, though some routes make a roadside stop in Heber City (at 1590 S Hwy 40). Prices are the same from either. Daily buses from Ogden to SLC ($19, 55 minutes).

Sundance Resort

Art and nature blend seamlessly at **Sundance** (☑ 800-892-1600, 801-225-4107; www.sundanceresort.com; 9521 Alpine Loop Rd, Provo; r $209-500; ☎), a magical resort-cum-artist-colony founded by Robert Redford, where bedraggled urbanites connect with the land and rediscover their creative spirits. Participate in snow sports, ride horseback, fly-fish, write, do yoga, indulge in spa treatments, climb or hike Mt Timpanogos, nosh at several wonderful eateries and then spend the night in rustic luxury. Day-trippers should ask for trail maps and activity guides at the **general store** (☺ 9am-9pm), which shoppers love for the artisan handicrafts, home furnishings and jewelry (catalog available).

Mt Timpanogos, the second-highest peak in the Wasatch, lords over the **ski resort** (☑ reservations 801-223-4849; day lift-ticket adult/child $55/33), which is family- and newbie-friendly. The 500-skiable-acre hill is primarily an amenity for the resort, but experienced snow riders will groove on the super-steeps. The **Cross Country Center** (☺ 9am-5pm Dec–early Apr) has 16 miles of groomed classic and skating lanes on all-natural snow. You can also snowshoe 6 miles of trails past frozen waterfalls (ask about nighttime owl-watching walks). The woods here are a veritable fairyland.

May through September, there's lift-assist **hiking** and **mountain biking** (trail pass $12, all-day lift use $20); rental is available from $40. Sundance hosts numerous year-round **cultural events**, from its namesake film festival and screenwriting and directing labs to writers' workshops and music seminars. In summer there are outdoor films, plays, author readings and great music series at the **amphitheater**. Don't miss the **art shack** (☺ 10am-5pm), where you can throw pottery and make jewelry.

Lucky enough to be staying over? Rough-hewn **cottage rooms** ($209-500) are secluded, tucked among the trees on the grounds – the perfect place to honeymoon or write your next novel. Decor differs but they've all got pine walls and ever-so-comfy furnishings, plus quilts, paperback books and board games; some have kitchens. Two- to four-bedroom **houses** (from $1025) are also available.

Tree Room (☑ 801-223-4200; mains $25-45; ☺ 5-9pm Tue-Thu, to 10pm Fri & Sat), Sundance's top-flight restaurant, is a study in rustic-mountain chic (and includes, yes, a big tree trunk in the middle of the room). Here the modern American menu items are as artfully presented as the chichi clientele. You'll be hard-pressed to find a better meal this side of San Francisco. The less-exclusive (but still pricey) **Foundry Grill** (breakfast & sandwiches $8-16, dinner $19-39; ☺ 7-11am,

---

GETTING INTO SUNDANCE FILM FESTIVAL

This two-week festival in late January takes over both Park City and Sundance Resort completely. Films screen not just there but at venues in Salt Lake City and Ogden as well. Accommodations rates soar across the Wasatch front, yet rooms are snapped up months in advance – passes ($300 to $3000), ticket packages ($300 to $1000) and individual tickets ($15) are similarly difficult to get. First you need to reserve a timeslot to purchase online at www.sundance.org/festival starting in December (sign up for text-message announcements). You then call during your appointed hour to reserve, but there are no guarantees (note that seats may be a little easier to secure during week two, as week one is generally for the industry). Any remaining tickets are sold a few days ahead online and at the main **Park City Box Office** (Gateway Center, 136 Heber Ave; ☺ 8am-7pm mid-Jan–late Jan). If you don't succeed, do like the locals and go skiing – the slopes are remarkably empty during this two-week period.

11:30am-4pm & 5-9pm Mon-Sat, 9am-2pm & 5-9pm Sun) offers pizzas with artisan greens, Utah steelhead trout and ribeye steaks. For something lighter, pick up a turkey and cranberry-relish panini to go at the **Deli** (sandwiches $9-13; ⊙7am-9pm) and then enjoy it on the grounds.

Built of cast-off barn wood, the centerpiece of the **Owl Bar** (⊙3-11pm Mon-Thu, to 1am Fri, noon-1am Sat, to 11pm Sun) is a century-old bar where the real Butch Cassidy once drank. The place looks like a Wild West roadhouse, but it's full of art freaks, mountain hipsters and local cowboys imbibing by a roaring fireplace. On Friday and Saturday there's often live music.

Provo

POP 115,920 / ELEV 4550FT

The third-largest city in Utah, Provo is a conservative Mormon town. (It's also known as 'Happy Valley,' as more antidepressants are prescribed here than in any other part of Utah.) Remember Donnie and Marie Osmond, the milquetoast 1970s sibling singing sensation? This is their hometown. Unless you're a big fan, the most compelling reason to visit is to see Brigham Young University (BYU) on a day trip from Salt Lake City, 45 miles north. University Ave, Provo's main thoroughfare, intersects Center St in the small old downtown core. Note that the whole place pretty much shuts down on Sunday.

The **BYU campus** (www.byu.edu) is enormous and known for its squeaky-clean student dress codes. Drive 450 East north toward the **Hinckley Alumni & Visitor Center** (☑801-422-4678; cnr W Campus & N Campus Drs; ⊙8am-6pm Mon-Sat) where tours begin (by appointment). The university's what's-this-doing-here **Museum of Art** (☑801-378-2787; 10am-6pm Tue, Wed & Fri, to 9pm Mon & Thu, noon-5pm Sat) FREE is one of the biggest in the Southwest, with a concentration on American art; temporary exhibits are top-notch. BYU sporting events take place at **Lavell Edwards Stadium** (☑801-422-2981; www.byutickets.com; 1700 N Canyon Rd).

You can ice-skate in town at **Peaks Ice Arena** (☑801-377-8777; www.peaksarena.com; 100 N Seven Peaks Blvd; ⊙Mon-Sat), where the Olympic hockey teams faced off in 2002. Free-skate hours vary.

Provo is close enough to SLC for you to easily make it in a day. If you stay over, we

WORTH A TRIP

MT TIMPANOGOS

An incredibly scenic journey, the 16-mile **Alpine Loop Rd** (Hwy 92) makes the journey past **Mt Timpanogos** (11,750ft). At 6800ft, stay overnight at the **Mt Timpanogos Campground** (☑877-444-6777; www.reserveamerica.com; tent & RV sites $21; ⊙May-Oct), which has pit toilets and water, but no hookups. A trailhead leads from here into the surrounding fir-tree-filled wilderness. The paved loop is accessed via the north side of Provo Canyon.

Spectacular, star-like helictite formations are on view at three mid-mountain caverns in **Timpanogos Cave National Monument** (☑801-756-5238; www.nps.gov/tica; off Hwy 92; tour adult/child $8/6; ⊙7am-5:30pm Jun-Aug, 8am-5pm Sep & Oct). Book ahead or get there early for a 90-minute ranger-led tour – they fill up. To get to the caves, it's an uphill hike (that must be done within an hour before your tour time). Hwy 92 is closed December through March.

recommend the 1895 **Hines Mansion B&B** (☑801-374-8400, 800-428-5636; www.hinesmansion.com; 383 W 100 South; r incl breakfast $149-235; @🛜). The 'Library' guest room has a 'secret passage' door to the bathroom.

The historic downtown has numerous little ethnic restaurants, many around the intersection of Center St and University Ave. Garnering regional accolades, **Black Sheep** (☑801-607-2485; www.blacksheepcafe.com; 19 N University Ave; lunch $11-13, dinner $16-24; 🍴) offers cafe food with a Southwestern and Native American influence: offerings include cactus pear salads or green and red chile *posole* with fry bread. **Guru's** (www.guruscafe.com; 45 E Center St; mains $6-11; ⊙8am-9pm Mon-Tue, to 10pm Wed-Sat; 🍴) has an eclectic cafe menu, including rice bowls and tacos, that's popular with both moms and students.

Get information at the **Utah Valley Visitors Bureau** (☑801-851-2100; www.utahvalley.org/cvb; 111 S University Ave; ⊙8:30am-5pm Mon-Fri, 9am-3pm Sat), inside the beautiful courthouse.

UTA (☑801-743-3882, 888-743-3882; www.rideuta.com) runs frequent express buses to SLC ($6), with diminished service on Sunday.

NORTHEASTERN UTAH

A remote and rural area, Northeastern Utah is high-wilderness terrain (much of which is more than a mile above sea level) that has traditionally attracted farmers and miners. Rising oil prices spurred oil and gas development in the rocky valleys, which in turn has led to increased services in towns like Vernal. Most travelers come to see Dinosaur National Monument, but you'll also find other dino dig sites and museums, as well as Fremont Indian rock art and ruins in the area. Up near the Wyoming border, the Uinta Mountains and Flaming Gorge attract trout fishers and wildlife lovers alike.

Vernal & Around

POP 9820 / ELEV 5330FT

A big pink allosaurus welcomes you to the capital of self-dubbed 'Dinoland' – Vernal is the closest town to Dinosaur National Monument (20 miles east). The informative film at the **Utah Field House of Natural History State Park Museum** (☎435-789-3799; http://stateparks.utah.gov; 496 E Main St; adult/child $6/3; ⏰9am-5pm; 👪) is the best all-round introduction to Utah's dinosaurs. Interactive exhibits, video clips and, of course, giant fossils are wonderfully relevant to the area. There's loads to keep the kids entertained, and the museum is still growing.

Ten miles northeast of Vernal on Hwy 191, check out hundreds of fossilized dinosaur tracks at **Red Fleet State Park** (☎435-789-4432; http://stateparks.utah.gov; admission $7; tent/RV campsites $15/25; ⏰6am-10pm Apr-Oct, 8am-5pm Nov & Dec). Eleven miles northwest, the 200ft of **McConkie Ranch Petroglyphs** (Dry Fork Canyon Rd; entry by donation; ⏰dawn-dusk) are well worth checking out. Generous ranch owners built a little self-serve info shack with posted messages and a map, but be advised that the 800-year-old Fremont Indian art requires some rock-scrambling to see. Being on private land has helped; these alien-looking anthropomorphs are in much better shape than the many that have been desecrated by vandals on public lands. Follow 3000 West to the north out of Vernal. You can visit both as part of the 74-mile Red Cloud Loop. For even more rock art and ruins, we recommend the nearby Nine Mile Canyon drive.

SCENIC DRIVE: RED CLOUD LOOP

After you see the dinosaur tracks at Red Fleet State Park, continue on Hwy 191 for 21 miles north of Vernal, then take off west on **Red Cloud Scenic Backway**. The road starts out tame, then rises sharply up to 10,000ft in twists and turns. The one-and-a-half lane road has steep drop-offs and dramatic pine scenery amid the eastern Uinta peaks. Allow three hours to return the full 74 miles back to Vernal via Dry Fork Canyon Rd, where you can stop at the McConkie Ranch Petroglyphs.

There are a number of great drives in the area through public lands and parks, including the road up to the gorgeous rivers and lake of Flaming Gorge, just 35 miles north. The **Dinosaurland Tourist Board** (Vernal Chamber of Commerce; ☎800-477-5558; www.dinoland.com; 134 W Main; ⏰9am-5pm Mon-Fri) provides information on the entire region; pick up driving-tour brochures for area rock art and dino tracks here. The **Vernal Ranger Station** (☎435-789-1181; 355 N Vernal Ave; ⏰8am-5pm Mon-Fri) has details on camping and hiking in Ashley National Forest (p503), to the north.

The Green and Yampa Rivers are the main waterways in the area; both have some rapids and more genteel floats. River trips (May through September) run from day trips to five-day expeditions. Enquire with **Don Hatch River Expeditions** (☎435-789-4316, 800-342-8243; www.donhatchrivertrips.com; 221 N 400 East; one-day adult/child $99/76) or **Dinosaur Expeditions** (☎800-345-7238; www.dinosaurriverexpeditions.com; 550 East Main St; day-trip adult/child $84/68).

Though there's a number of motels, reasonable motel rooms can be hard to find in this town; those at **Econo Lodge** (☎435-789-2000; www.econolodge.com; 311 E Main St; r $79-119) do nicely. Contemporary comforts like deluxe mattresses and flat-screen TVs come standard at **Landmark Inn & Suites** (☎888-738-1800, 435-781-1800; 301 E 100 S; r incl breakfast $110; 📶), with a buffet breakfast and fitness room. One of the town's newer chain hotels, the **Holiday Inn Express** (☎800-315-2621, 435-789-4654; www.holidayinn.com/vernal; 1515 W Hwy 40; r incl breakfast $199-222; ❄📶🏊) has loads of amenities (fitness center, business center, laundry). Kids' laughter usually fills the indoor pool.

For homemade soup, a crusty panini and a good read, stop into **Backdoor Grille** (87 W Main St; mains $5-8; ⏰11am-6pm Mon-Sat),

DINOSAUR DIAMOND

A dual-state national scenic byway, **Dinosaur Diamond** (www.dinosaurdiamond.net) aims to give dinos their due by promoting and protecting paleontology along its 512-mile suggested route in Colorado and Utah. Here are our fossilized favorites in Utah:

Dinosaur National Monument (Vernal; p501) Touch 150-million-year-old bones still in the ground!

Dinosaur Discovery Site (St George; p460) Some of the most amazing dinosaur trackways ever found.

Utah Museum of Natural History (SLC; p467) The new home for the Huntington mammoth.

Utah Field House of Natural History State Park Museum (Vernal) Still growing, but an amazing, kid-friendly Utah dinosaur museum.

Museum of Ancient Life (Lehi; p473) Interactive exhibits provide an overview of world dinosaurs.

Cleveland-Lloyd Dinosaur Quarry (Price; p503) Watch 'em digging up new discoveries daily.

Red Fleet State Park (Vernal; p500) More 200-million-year-old footprints.

And just for fun:

Dinosaur Museum (Blanding; p395) Dino movie memorabilia and models.

Ogden Eccles Dinosaur Park (Ogden; p494) Jurassic-era playground for kids.

at the rear of Bitter Creek Books. Southern US favorites are done right at **The Porch** (www.facebook.com/theporchvernal; 251 E Main St; lunches $8-12, dinner mains $14-23; ⏰11am-2pm & 5-9pm Mon-Fri, 5-9pm Sat): the chicken-fried steak and blackened shrimp taste just like a Louisiana grandmother would make.

Vernal is 145 miles west of Park City and 112 miles north of Price.

Dinosaur National Monument

At the end of desolate stretches in the sparsely populated border with Colorado, **Dinosaur National Monument** (www.nps.gov/dino; off Hwy 40, Vernal; 7-day pass per vehicle $10; ⏰24hr) is one remote destination, but for travelers fascinated by prehistoric life on Earth, it is worth every lonely mile. It's one of the few places that you can reach out and touch a dinosaur skeleton, snarling in its final pose, in situ.

Paleontologist Earl Douglass of Pittsburgh's Carnegie Museum discovered this dinosaur fossil bed, one of the largest in North America, in 1909. The monument's 210,000 acres of starkly eroded canyons provide the visitor with scenic drives, hiking and camping.

Monument headquarters, and most of the land, are actually in Colorado, but the quarry (the only place to see fossils protruding from the earth) is in Utah. River-running trips come through here on the scenic Yampa and Green Rivers. Though each state's section is beautiful, Utah has the bones.

⊙ Sights

Dinosaur Quarry ARCHAEOLOGICAL SITE
(www.nps.gov/dino; per vehicle $10; ⏰8am-7pm Memorial Day–Labor Day, to 4:30pm rest of year) The Jurassic strata containing the fossils give a glimpse of how paleontologists transform solid rock into the beautiful skeletons seen in museums, and how they develop scientifically reliable interpretations of life in the remote past. Ranger-led walks, talks and tours explain the site; information can also be gleaned from brochures, audio-visual programs and exhibits.

There is also a shop selling gifts and books. The Quarry is completely enclosed to protect the fossils from weathering.

Fossil Discovery Trail ARCHAEOLOGICAL SITE
(🚶) This short interpretive trail is excellent for families as it's only 0.75 miles long and you can reach out and touch the bones of dinosaurs. Regardless of your knowledge or understanding of paleontology, this is

a stunning walk through some 65 million years of history.

Walking along the hillside, visitors enter a small canyon, eventually arriving at the Morrison Formation, one of the most spectacular open-air collections of dinosaur bones in the world. The bones in these walls represent 10 species that range in size from about 7in to 76ft.

Activities

Both the Yampa River and Green River offer excellent opportunities for river-running, with plenty of exciting rapids amid splendid scenery. There's flow from mid-May to early September. Trips range from one to five days. There are tour companies in Vernal, Moab and Green River.

Fishing is permitted only with the appropriate state permits, available from sports stores or tackle shops in Dinosaur, CO, or Vernal, UT. Check with park rangers about limits and the best places.

Sleeping

Green River Campground   CAMPGROUND $
(435-781-7700; Blue Mountain Rd; tent & RV sites $12; mid-Apr–early Oct) Dinosaur National Monument's main campground is Green River Campground, 5 miles east of Dinosaur Quarry along Blue Mountain Rd, with 88 sites. It has bathrooms and drinking water, but no showers or hookups. A park host will sell firewood.

Jensen Inn   B&B $$
(435-789-590; 5056 S 9500 East, Jensen; r incl breakfast $95-150; @) If your destination

SCENIC DRIVE: FLAMING GORGE-UINTAS SCENIC BYWAY

Heading north from Vernal, 80 miles into the northeastern Uintas Mountains, Flaming Gorge-Uintas Scenic Byway (Hwy 191) is a drive and a geology lesson all in one. As you climb up switchbacks to 8100ft, the up-tilted sedimentary layers you see represent one billion years of history. Interpretive signs explain what different colors and rock compositions indicate about the prehistoric climate in which they were laid down. It's a great route for fall color and wildlife-watching, too.

is Dinosaur National Monument, book at the comfortable, modern-home Jensen Inn B&B, 3 miles north of Jensen, off Hwy 40. Camp in a tipi ($88) or pitch your tent in the grassy field ($35) and you still get breakfast.

Information

At the town of Dinosaur, a Colorado Welcome Center offers maps and brochures for the entire state. Information is available from Dinosaur National Monument Headquarters Visitor Center (970-374-3000; 4545 E Hwy 40; 8am-4:30pm daily Jun-Aug, Mon-Fri only Dec-Feb), sometimes called the Canyon Visitor Center. It has an audio-visual program, exhibits and a bookstore.

There's also a visitor center at Dinosaur Quarry. Entrance to the monument headquarters' visitor center is free, but entrance to other parts of the monument (including Dinosaur Quarry) is $10 per private vehicle and $5 for cyclists or bus passengers.

Getting There & Away

The monument is 88 miles west of Craig via US 40 and 120 miles east of Salt Lake City, Utah, by I-80 and US 40. Dinosaur Quarry is 7 miles north of Jensen, UT, on Cub Creek Rd (Utah Hwy 149). Monument headquarters is just off US 40 on Harpers Corner Dr, about 4 miles east of the town of Dinosaur, CO.

Flaming Gorge National Recreation Area

Named for its fiery red sandstone canyon, Flaming Gorge provides 375 miles of shoreline around Flaming Gorge Reservoir, which straddles the Utah–Wyoming state line. As with many artificial lakes, fishing and boating are prime attractions. Various records for giant lake trout and Kokanee salmon have been set here.

The area also provides plenty of hiking and camping in summer, and cross-country skiing and snowmobiling in winter. Keep an eye out for common wildlife such as moose, elk, pronghorn antelope and mule deer; you may also see bighorn sheep, black bears and mountain lions. The lake's 6040ft elevation ensures pleasantly warm but not desperately hot summers – daytime highs average about 80°F (27°C).

Information is available from www.flaminggorgecountry.com, the USFS Flaming Gorge Headquarters (435-784-3445; www.fs.usda.gov/ashley; 25 W Hwy 43, Manila; 8am-5pm Mon-Fri) and at the Flaming Gorge

Dam Visitor Center (☑435-885-3135; Hwy 191; ☺9am-5pm May-Sep). Day use of some Flaming Gorge areas costs $5 at self-pay stations.

In **Dutch John**, rent a fishing, pontoon or ski boat ($130 to $280 per day) or get active with a kayak or paddle boat ($30 for three hours) from **Cedar Springs Marina** (☑435-889-3795; www.cedarspringsmarina.com; off Hwy 191; ☺Apr-Oct), 2 miles east of Flaming Gorge Dam. The best fishing is found with a guide; ask at the marina or contact **Trout Creek Flies** (☑435-885-3355; www.fishgreenriver.com; cnr Hwy 191 & Little Hole Rd; half-day fishing $345). Aim to fly-fish late June to early July, before the river is flooded with fun floaters. Trout Creek also rents rafts and kayaks and runs a floater shuttle.

Ashley National Forest (www.fs.usda.gov/ashley) runs more than two dozen May-to-September campgrounds in the area. The 7400ft elevation, ponderosa-pine-forest location and excellent clifftop overlook views of the reservoir make **Canyon Rim Campground** (☑877-444-6777; www.recreation.gov; Red Canyon Rd, off Hwy 44; tent & RV sites $18) a top choice. Keep an eye out for big-horn sheep. Water; no showers or hookups.

Activities at **Red Canyon Lodge** (☑435-889-3759; www.redcanyonlodge.com; 790 Red Canyon Rd, Dutch John; cabins $115-155) include fishing, rowing, rafting and horseback riding, among others; its pleasantly rustic cabins have no TVs. **Flaming Gorge Resort** (☑435-889-3773; www.flaminggorgeresort.com; 155 Greendale/Hwy 191, Dutch John; r/ste $125/165, RV sites $35; ❋☎) has similar water-based fun, and rents motel rooms and suites. Both have decent restaurants. Convenience stores in Dutch John have deli counters.

High Uintas Wilderness Area

The Uinta Mountains are unusual in that they run east–west, unlike all other major mountain ranges in the lower 48. Several peaks rise to more than 13,000ft, including Kings (13,528ft), the highest point in the Southwest. The central summits lie within the **High Uintas Wilderness Area** (www.fs.usda.gov/main/uwcnf), part of Ashley National Forest, which provides 800 sq miles of hiking and horseback riding opportunities. No roads, no mountain biking and no off-road driving permitted. The reward? An incredible, remote mountain experience, one without snack bars or lodges.

STARVATION STATE PARK

No one is quite sure who did the stealing, but either trappers in the area stashed some winter stores in the mountains, or Native Americans did, and then the other group took the food. Advance planners starved when they found no provisions buried under the snow, or so the story goes. In all likelihood bears were to blame for the theft – and the name of **Starvation State Park** (http://stateparks.utah.gov; Hwy 40, Duchesne; day-use $7; ☺6am-10pm Jun-Aug, 8am-5pm Sep-May).

Subsequent homesteaders tried to make a go of it on the Strawberry River, but with a short growing season and frozen ground they had no better luck fending off hunger. Today the park contains a 3500-acre reservoir as well as plenty of picnickers. There's primitive camping and the 60-site **Lower Beach Campground** (☑800-322-3770; http://utahstateparks.reserveamerica.com; tent & RV sites with hookups $18-28; ☺Jun-Sep), with showers and a sandy beach.

Price & San Rafael Swell

POP 8715 / ELEV 5630FT (PRICE)

Though a true Utah backwater, Price can serve as a base for exploring enticing backcountry dinosaur and ancient rock-art sites in the scenic San Rafael Swell and beyond. It's en route from Green River (65 miles) to Vernal (112 miles), so the staff at the **visitor center** (Castle County Travel; ☑435-636-3701; www.castlecountry.com; 710 E 100 N, Courthouse; ☺9am-5pm Mon-Sat) can help you plan out your regional routes. (Note that the temporary 2014 location is at 81 North 200 East, across the parking lot from the museum, but they will move to a courthouse under construction until 2015.) The **College of Eastern Utah Prehistoric Museum** (☑435-613-5060; www.usueastern.edu/museum; 155 East Main St; adult/child $6/3; ☺9am-5pm Mon-Sat) exhibits fossils that were discovered within two hours' drive of the museum. Look for the Utah raptor, first identified in this part of the world, and get directions to the dinosaur quarry.

Thirty miles south of Price you can visit an actual dinosaur dig site. More than 12,000 bones have been taken from the ground at **Cleveland-Lloyd Dinosaur Quarry**

SCENIC DRIVE: NINE MILE CANYON

Abundant rock art is the attraction on the **Nine Mile Canyon National Backcountry Byway** (www.byways.org), billed as the 'longest art gallery in the world'. You can also spot Fremont granaries and structures along the canyon walls (bring binoculars). Many of the petroglyphs are easy to miss; some are on private property. Pick up a free guide at area restaurants or at the Castle Country Travel Desk in Price or the Utah Welcome Center outside Dinosaur National Monument. Allow at least three to five hours for the 70-mile unpaved ride from Wellington (on Hwy 6) to Myton (on Hwy 40). Get gas before you go: there are no services.

About 23 miles northeast along Nine Mile Canyon Byway from the Hwy 6/191 turnoff, you can stay at the simple **Nine Mile Bunk & Breakfast** (☎ 435-637-2572; www.ninemilecanyon.com; r with shared bath $70, camping cabins $55, camping $10), with two big ranchhouse rooms on spacious grounds; plus you can stay in an old pioneer cabin or pitch a tent on-site. The rustic accommodations are run by a 'retired' ranching couple who are the nicest folks you'd ever want to meet. They run canyon tours (half-day from $155), too.

(☎ 435-636-3600; www.blm.gov; off Hwy 10; adult/child $5/2; ⏱ 10am-5pm Thu-Sat late Mar-Oct). A dozen species of dinosaur were buried here 150 million years ago, but the large concentration of meat-eating allosaurus has helped scientists around the world draw new conclusions. Two excavations are on display and the visitor center's exhibits are quite informative. Several hikes lead off from there, too. Take Rte 10 south to the Elmo/Cleveland turnoff and follow signs on the dirt road.

These southern lands between Hwys 10 and 6/24 are the canyons, arches and cliffs of the **San Rafael Swell**. Look for the purples, grays and greens that indicate ancient seabeds, in addition to the oxygenated oranges and reds of this anticline. The area is all BLM land, where free dispersed camping and some four-wheeling is allowed. Sights include a 1200ft canyon drop at **Wedge Overlook**, Barrier Canyon–style pictographs at **Buckhorn Wash**, and a suspension **footbridge**. Ask for a basic map at the town visitor center or the quarry site. For more details contact the **BLM Price Field Office** (☎ 435-636-3600; www.blm.gov; 125 S 600 West; ⏱ 9am-4:30pm Mon-Fri) or go online to www.emerycounty.com/travel.

The well-preserved ancient archaeological sites protected by Wilcox Ranch are now part of **Range Creek Wildlife Management Area** (www.wildlife.utah.gov/range_creek), east of East Carbon (25 miles southeast of

Price); since the family turned the property over to the government, the public has been allowed limited access. The best way to explore is with a full-day 4WD tour ($150 per person) run by **Tavaputs Ranch** (☎ 435-637-1236; www.tavaputsranch.com; Hwy 6 North; per person incl meals & activities $200; ⏱ mid-Jun–Sep). Included in the lodging price are three meals, backcountry hikes, scenic drives and wildlife tours on the 15,000-acre spread; horseback riding is $50 extra.

Free camping is allowed off established roads on the San Rafael Swell BLM lands. The motels off Hwy 6/191 and on Main St aren't exactly exciting, but they are plentiful. **Super 8** (☎ 435-637-8088, 888-288-5081; www.super8.com; 180 N Hospital Dr; r $60-80; ✴ 🖘) has fine, basic rooms. Thirty miles south in Castle Dale, **San Rafael Swell Bed & Breakfast** (☎ 435-381-5689; www.sanrafaelbedandbreakfast.com; 15 E 100 N, Castle Dale; r incl breakfast $65-110; ✴ 🖘) has more of a personal touch and themed rooms; less expensive rooms share a bath.

The place to be and the best place around for grub is **Grogg's Pinnacle Brewing Company** (www.groggspinnaclebrewing.com; 1653 N Carbonville, Helper; mains $9-20; ⏱ 11am-10pm) – it's got friendly staff, tasty casual-American fare and microbrews on tap. (Though barely 3 miles north of Price, it's technically in Helper.) Look for other eateries along Main St.

Understand Southwest USA

Southwest USA Today

Marijuana sales, gay marriage and natural disasters are all hot topics. In 2012 recreational use of marijuana was legalised in Colorado and in 2013 New Mexico became the 17th state to legalize gay marriage. Arizona wasn't so gay-friendly, passing a bill – later vetoed by the governor – allowing businesses to refuse service to gay couples for religious reasons. Climate-related unease continued, stemming from cataclysmic flooding in Colorado's Front Range, devastating fires in Arizona and New Mexico and an ongoing drought across most of the region.

Best Books

The Grapes of Wrath (John Steinbeck; 1939) Dust Bowl migrants follow Route 66 west to California.

Desert Solitaire (Edward Abbey; 1968) Essays about the Southwest and industrial tourism by no-holds-barred eco-curmudgeon.

Bean Trees (Barbara Kingsolver; 1988) Thoughtful look at motherhood and cross-cultural adoption in Tucson.

Blood & Thunder (Hampton Sides; 2007) Traces the life and adventures of mountain man Kit Carson, who traveled across the Southwest

Best Films

Stagecoach (1939) Monument Valley may be the true star of this John Ford western drama.

Butch Cassidy & the Sundance Kid (1969) – Follows the adventures of two real-life outlaws who hid out in Utah.

Thelma & Louise (1991) Two gal pals run from the law and into stunning Southwest scenery.

The Hangover (2009) – It's a bachelor party gone wrong – or right – in Las Vegas.

127 Hours (2010) Aron Ralston's harrowing experience in Utah's redrock country.

It's All About Politics...

Arizona's legislature has crafted two highly controversial pieces of legislation in recent years. In 2010 Arizona lawmakers passed a stringent anti-immigration law requiring police officers to ask for ID from anyone they suspected of being in the country illegally. Sections of the law have been struck down by the courts as unconstitutional, but law enforcement officers can still ask for papers. Immigration remains a hot-button issue, and border patrol agents have a very visible presence in the southern parts of the state. In 2014 the state legislature drafted a bill that would allow business owners to refuse service to gay customers based on the owner's religious beliefs. At the urging of various corporations and sports franchises, Governor Jan Brewer vetoed the measure.

New Mexico took the opposite approach to gay rights, and in 2013 the State Supreme court confirmed the right of gay couples to marry. But the Land of Enchantment is not free of controversy. In Albuquerque there have been 37 police shootings that led to the deaths of 23 people in the last five years. Concerned citizens held demonstrations to protest the shootings in the spring of 2014, and one of these gatherings escalated into a riot.

In Nevada, rancher Cliven Bundy grabbed the spotlight when federal officials tried to impound 900 head of his cattle, an action stemming from Bundy's alleged failure to pay federal grazing fees and fines. But when Bureau of Land Management officials arrived to collect the animals, they were met by Bundy supporters armed with semi-automatic weapons. The BLM backed down, deciding not to ramp up the conflict. Later, conservative pundits, who initially supported Bundy's anti-federal rhetoric, quieted down as his public comments were criticized for being racially tinged.

...or the Weather

The Southwest has been hit hard by forest fires in recent years. The 2011 Wallow Fire was one of the worst in Arizona's history, burning about 538,000 acres. That same year the Las Conchas Fire burned more than 244 sq miles near Los Alamos, NM. In 2014, 19 members of the Granite Mountain Hotshots, an elite team of firefighters, were killed while fighting the devastating Yarnell Hill Fire.

But fire isn't the region's only natural foe. A 14-year drought has left reservoirs along the Colorado River at less than half their capacity. This is troubling because the river supplies drinking water for 36 million people and water for more than 10% of the nation's crops. The good news? An above-average snow pack in 2014 should – at least temporarily – raise water levels in Lake Powell.

At the other extreme, in 2013 severe flooding in Colorado affected a 4500-sq-mile area across the state's Front Range, killing eight people and incurring property damages estimated at about $2 billion.

On the Bright Side

It's not all bad news. The nation's economy isn't exactly booming, but the Southwest's economic landscape is looking less bleak in a handful of places. The purchase and use of recreational marijuana became legal in Colorado in 2014, and the state received $2 million in pot-related tax revenue in the first month alone. In Las Vegas the LINQ entertainment district opened on the Strip in 2014, bringing with it the 550ft-tall High Roller, the world's tallest observation wheel. Online retailer Zappos is also moving its headquarters to downtown Las Vegas and revitalizing the neighborhood in the process.

Environmental issues continue to be a major concern for Southwesterners. Eco-friendly initiatives at Grand Canyon National Park are continuing, including a summer park-and-ride shuttle from Tusayan, AZ, to the visitor center, as well as a bicycle rental service. And Colorado continues to be an environmental hub. Boulder County has passed a Zero Waste Action Plan with a goal to reduce waste to near zero percent, and Denver International Airport has added enough solar panels to power 2595 Denver homes.

POPULATION OF AZ, NM, UT, NV & CO: **22 MILLION**

REGIONAL UNEMPLOYMENT RATE JUNE 2011: **6.3%**

US UNEMPLOYMENT RATE JUNE 2011: **6.3%**

if the Southwest was 100 people

58 would be Caucasian
29 would be Hispanic
4 would be Native American
4 would be African American
5 would be other

belief systems
(% of population)

34 Protestant
19 Mormon
20 Unaffiliated
22 Catholic
❺ Other

population per sq km

Arizona   New Mexico   USA

≈ 17 people

History

Landscape and water have shaped the story of the Southwest. Prehistoric settlers carved out irrigation systems for farming, building communities in the process. Prospectors and pioneers followed, lured by the promise of mineral riches, ranch land, religious freedom, unfettered adventure and self-determination. This resulted in all the trappings of civilization, and the wild was tamed with churches, government and enormous dams. In the 20th and 21st centuries the Southwest proved amenable to big-sky science projects, becoming home to rocket and atomic-bomb test sites, world-class observatories and a very modern spaceport.

In Search of the Old Ones by David Roberts explores the culture of the Ancestral Puebloans and examines the reasons why they may have left their villages. It's a good resource for off-the-beaten-path hiking, too.

The First Americans

Archaeologists believe that the region's first inhabitants were hunters – descendants of those hardy souls who crossed the Bering Strait into North America 25,000 years ago. The population grew and wild game became extinct, forcing hunters to augment their diets with berries, seeds, roots and fruits. After 3000 BC, contact with farmers in what is now central Mexico led to the beginnings of agriculture in the Southwest. Primitive corn was grown, and by 500 BC beans and squash were also cultivated. Between 300 BC and AD 100, distinct groups began to settle in villages in the Southwest.

The Hohokam, Mogollon & Ancestral Puebloans

By about AD 100, three dominant cultures were emerging in the Southwest: the Hohokam of the desert, the Mogollon of the central mountains and valleys, and the Ancestral Puebloans. Archaeologists originally called the Ancestral Puebloans the Anasazi, which comes from a Navajo term meaning 'ancient enemy' and has fallen out of favor.

The Hohokam lived in the deserts of Arizona from 300 BC to AD 1400, adapting to desert life by creating an incredible river-fed irrigation system. They also developed low earthen pyramids and sunken ball courts with sloped earthern walls. These oval-shaped courts, which varied in

TIMELINE	AD 100	1300s	1598
	The region's dominant indigenous cultures emerge. The Hohokam settle in the desert, the Mogollon in the mountains and valleys and Ancestral Puebloans build cliff dwellings around the Four Corners.	The Ancestral Puebloans living in Mesa Verde, CO, abandon a sophisticated city of cliff dwellings.	A large force of Spanish explorers, led by Don Juan de Oñate, stops near present-day El Paso, TX, and declares the land to the north New Mexico for Spain.

size, may have been used for organized games as well as for markets and community gatherings.

The Mogollon people settled near the Mexican border from 200 BC to AD 1400. They lived in small communities, often elevated on isolated mesas or ridge tops, and built pit dwellings, which were simple structures of wood, shrubs and mud erected over a small depression in the ground. Although the Mogollon farmed, they depended more on hunting and foraging for food. Growing villages featured the kiva – a circular, underground chamber used for ceremonies and other communal purposes.

Around the 13th or 14th century, the Mogollon were likely being peacefully assimilated by the Ancestral Puebloan groups from the north. One indication of this is the beautiful black-on-white Mimbres pottery with its distinctive animal and human figures executed in a geometric style reminiscent of Puebloan ware. (The Mimbres were Mogollons who lived in a remote valley area in southwestern New Mexico between 1100 and 1150 AD.) The Gila Cliff Dwellings in New Mexico are a late-Mogollon site with Puebloan features.

The Ancestral Puebloans inhabited the Colorado Plateau – also called the Four Corners area – which comprises parts of northeastern Arizona, northwestern New Mexico, southwestern Colorado and southeastern Utah. This culture left the Southwest's richest archaeological sites and ancient settlements, some of which are still inhabited.

Today, descendants of the Ancestral Puebloans live in Pueblo Indian communities along New Mexico's Rio Grande, and in the Acoma, Zuni and Laguna Pueblos in northwest New Mexico. The oldest links with the Ancestral Puebloans are found among the Hopi tribe of northern Arizona. The mesa-top village of Old Oraibi has been inhabited since the 1100s, making it the oldest continuously inhabited settlement in North America.

By about 1400, the Hohokam had abandoned their villages. There are many theories on this tribe's disappearance, but the most likely explanation involves a combination of factors, including drought, overhunting, conflict among groups and disease. The Mogollon people were more or less incorporated into the Ancestral Puebloans, who had also all but disappeared from their ancestral cliff dwellings at Mesa Verde in southwestern Colorado by the 1400s – their mass exodus began in the 1300s.

Cliff Dwellings

Mesa Verde National Park, CO

Bandelier National Monument, NM

Gila Cliff Dwellings National Monument, NM

Montezuma Castle National Monument, AZ

Walnut Canyon National Monument, AZ

Navajo National Monument, AZ

HISTORY THE SPANIARDS ARRIVE

The Spaniards Arrive

Francisco Vásquez de Coronado led the first major expedition into North America in 1540. It included 300 soldiers, hundreds of Native American guides and herds of livestock. It also marked the first major violence between Spanish explorers and the native people.

1609	1680	1846–48	1847
Santa Fe, America's oldest capital city, is founded. The Palace of Governors is the only remaining 17th-century structure; the rest of Santa Fe was destroyed by a 1914 fire.	During the Pueblo Revolt, northern New Mexico Pueblos drive out the Spanish after the latter's bloody campaign to destroy Puebloan kivas and ceremonial objects.	The battle for the West is waged with the Mexican–American War. The Treaty of Guadalupe Hidalgo ends the fighting, and the US annexes most of Arizona and New Mexico.	Mormons fleeing religious persecution arrive in Salt Lake City by wagon train; over the next 20 years more than 70,000 Mormons will escape to Utah via the Mormon Pioneer Trail.

The expedition's goal was the fabled, immensely rich Seven Cities of Cibola. For two years, they traveled through what is now Arizona, New Mexico and as far east as Kansas, but instead of gold and precious gems, the expedition found adobe pueblos, which they violently commandeered. During the Spaniards' first few years in northern New Mexico, they tried to subdue the Pueblos, resulting in much bloodshed. The fighting started in Acoma Pueblo, in today's New Mexico, when a Spanish contingent of 30 men led by one of the nephews of conquistador Juan de Oñate demanded tax payment in the form of food. The Acoma Indians responded by killing him and about half of his force. Oñate retaliated with greater severity. Relations with the Native Americans, poor

PETROGLYPHS: WRITTEN ON THE LAND

Petroglyphs can be found etched into desert-varnished boulders across the Southwest. This rock art is simple yet mysterious and always leaves us wondering: who did this, and why? What were they trying to say?

Dating from at least 4000 BC to as late as the 19th century, rock art in the Southwest has been attributed to every known ancestral and modern people. In fact, one way archaeologists track the spread of ancestral cultures is by studying their distinctive rock-art styles, which tend to be either abstract or representational and anthropomorphic. Representational rock art is almost always more recent, while abstract designs appear in all ages.

We can only speculate about what it means. This symbolic writing becomes obscure the moment the cultural context for the symbols is lost. Archaeologists believe much of the art was the work of shamans or elders communicating with the divine. Some of the earliest abstract designs may have been created in trance states. Certain figures and motifs seem to reflect a heavenly pantheon, while other rock art may tell stories – real or mythical – of successful hunts or battles. Some etchings may have served as simple agricultural calendars, marking the start of harvest season, for example, by the way a shadow falls across a picture.

Other images may have marked tribal territory, and some may have been nothing more than idle doodling. But no matter what the meaning, each rock-art site – whether a petroglyph (inscribed or pecked into the stone) or pictograph (painted figure) – is irreplaceable, whether as a valuable part of the human archaeological record or the continuing religious traditions and cultural patrimony of contemporary tribes.

Preserve rock-art sites for future generations by observing these rules of etiquette:

➡ Do not disturb or remove any artifacts or features of the site.

➡ Do not trace, repaint, remove graffiti or otherwise touch or apply any materials to the rock art.

➡ Stay back at least 10ft from all rock-art panels, using binoculars or a zoom lens for better views.

1849	1862	1864	1869
A regular stagecoach service starts along the Santa Fe Trail. The 900-mile trail will serve as the country's main shipping route until the arrival of the railroad 60 years later.	Confederate rangers defeat Union cavalry forces at Picacho Peak in Arizona during the Civil War. It is the war's westernmost battle.	Kit Carson captures 9000 Navajo and forces them to walk 400 miles to a camp near Fort Sumner. Hundreds of Native Americans die along 'The Long Walk.'	One-armed Civil War veteran John Wesley Powell leads the first Colorado River descent, a grueling 1000-mile expedition through the Grand Canyon's rapids that kills half of his men.

harvests, harsh weather and accusations of Oñate's cruelty led to many desertions among the colonizers. By 1608, Oñate had been recalled to Mexico. A new governor, Pedro de Peralta, was sent north to found a new capital in 1609. Santa Fe remains the capital of New Mexico today, the oldest capital in what is now the USA.

Almost two centuries later, in an attempt to link Santa Fe with the newly established port of San Francisco and to avoid Native American raids, small groups of explorers pressed into what is now Utah but were turned back by the rugged and arid terrain. The 1776 Dominguez-Escalante expedition was the first to survey Utah, but no attempt was made to settle there until the arrival of the Mormons in the 19th century.

In addition to armed conflict, Europeans introduced smallpox, measles and typhus, to which the Native Americans had no resistance. Pueblo populations were decimated by these diseases, shattering cultures and trade routes and proving a destructive force that far outstripped combat.

Everett Ruess, a 20-year-old artist and vagabond, explored southern Utah and the Four Corners region in the early 1930s. He disappeared under mysterious circumstances outside of Escalante in November 1934. Read his evocative letters in the book *Everett Ruess: A Vagabond for Beauty*.

The Long Walk & Apache Conflicts

For decades, US forces pushed west across the continent, killing or forcibly moving whole tribes of Native Americans who were in their way. The most widely known incident in the Southwest is the forceful relocation of many Navajo in 1864. US forces, led by Kit Carson, destroyed Navajo fields, orchards and houses, and forced the people into surrendering or withdrawing into remote parts of Canyon de Chelly in modern-day Arizona. Eventually starvation forced them out. About 9000 Navajo were rounded up and marched 400 miles east to a camp at Bosque Redondo, near Fort Sumner, NM. Hundreds of Native Americans died from sickness, starvation or gunshot wounds along the way. The Navajo call this 'The Long Walk.'

The last serious conflicts were between US troops and the Apache. This was partly because raiding was the essential path to manhood for the Apache. As US forces and settlers moved into Apache land, they became obvious targets for the raids that were part of the Apache way of life. These continued under the leadership of Mangas Coloradas, Cochise, Victorio and, finally, Geronimo, who surrendered in 1886 after being promised that he and the Apache would be imprisoned for two years and then allowed to return to their homeland. As with many promises made during these years, this too was broken.

Even after the wars were over, Native Americans continued to be treated like second-class citizens for many decades. Non–Native Americans used legal loopholes and technicalities to take over reservation land. Many children were removed from reservations and shipped off to boarding schools where they were taught in English and punished for speaking their own languages or behaving 'like Indians' – this practice continued into the 1930s.

1881	1919	1931	1938
In 1881, Wyatt Earp, along with his brothers Virgil and Morgan, and Doc Holliday, kill Billy Clanton and the McLaury brothers during the OK Corral shoot-out in Tombstone, AZ.	The Grand Canyon becomes the USA's 15th national park. Only 44,173 people visit the park that year, compared to 4.5 million in 2013.	Nevada legalizes gambling and drops the divorce residency requirement to six weeks; this, along with legalized prostitution and championship boxing, carries the state through the Great Depression.	Route 66 becomes the first cross-country highway to be completely paved, including more than 750 miles across Arizona and New Mexico.

Westward Ho!

In 1803 the Louisiana Purchase resulted in the USA acquiring a huge tract of land (from Louisiana to the Rocky Mountains) from the French, doubling the size of the country. The Spanish colonies of the Southwest now abutted US territory and the two countries maintained an uneasy peace.

When Mexico became independent from Spain in 1821, the newly independent Mexicans welcomed US traders and a major trade route was established. This was the infamous Santa Fe Trail between Missouri and Santa Fe, a trail traversed by thousands of people until the railway arrived about 60 years later.

In the 1830s and 1840s, with growing nationalist fervor and dreams of continental expansion, many Americans came to believe it was 'manifest destiny' that all the land should be theirs. In 1836 a group of Texans fomented a revolution against Mexico. Their loss at the Alamo that year was a pivotal event, and 'Remember the Alamo!' became a rallying cry for Texans. Ten years later the US annexed the Texas Republic and when Mexico resisted, the US waged war for it and California, in 1846. In 1848 Mexico was soundly defeated, and the land north of the Gila River was claimed by the state and ceded into the New Mexico Territory. The US soon realized that the best route from the Mississippi River to the burgeoning territory of California lay south of the Gila River, passing through the Mexican town of Tucson. In 1854, pursuant to the $10 million Gadsden Purchase, the US bought this remaining strip of land, which included Tucson south to Tumacacori, AZ and the Mesilla Valley, NM.

Nineteenth-century Southwest history is strongly linked to transportation development. During early territorial days, movement of goods

The cry 'Geronimo!' became popular for skydivers after a training group of US Army paratroopers in 1940 saw the movie *Geronimo* (1939). Afterward they began shouting the great warrior's name for courage during their jumps.

TOP FIVE OLD WEST SITES

OK Corral, Tombstone, AZ Home of the famous 1881 gunfight, with the Earps and Doc Holliday facing Billy Clanton and the McLaury brothers.

Lincoln, NM Shooting grounds of Billy the Kid; he left a still-visible bullet hole in the courthouse wall during a successful escape.

Jerome, AZ Once known as the 'wickedest town in the Old West,' it brimmed with brothels and saloons and is now known for ghosts.

Virginia City, NV Where the silver-laden Comstock Lode was struck; it's now a national historic landmark.

Silverton, CO Old miners' spirit and railroad history with a historical downtown.

1943	1945	1946	1947
High in the northern New Mexican desert, Los Alamos is chosen as the headquarters of the Manhattan Project, the code name for the research and development of the atomic bomb.	The first atomic bomb is detonated in a desolate desert area in southern New Mexico that is now part of the White Sands Missile Range.	The opening of the glitzy Flamingo casino in Vegas kicks off a building spree. Sin City reaches its first golden peak in the '50s.	An unidentified object falls in the desert near Roswell. The government first calls it a crashed disk, but the next day calls it a weather balloon and closes off the area.

and people from the East to the Southwest was very slow. Horses, mule trains and stagecoaches represented state-of-the-art transportation. In addition to the Santa Fe Trail, major routes included the Old Spanish Trail, which ran from Santa Fe into central Utah and across Nevada to Los Angeles, CA. Regular stagecoach services along the Santa Fe Trail began in 1849; the Mormon Trail reached Salt Lake City in 1847.

The arrival of more people and resources via the railroad led to further land exploration and the frequent discovery of mineral deposits. The Civil War distracted most of the country between 1861 and 1865 as Union and Confederate forces clashed bloodily in the East. After the war, in the 1870s and 1880s, many mining towns cropped up across the Southwest. Some are now ghost towns, while others such as Tombstone, AZ, and Silver City, NM, remain active.

The West was officially tamed in 1912, when New Mexico and Arizona became, respectively, the 47th and 48th states in the Union.

The Wild West

Romanticized tales of gunslingers, cattle rustlers, outlaws and train robbers fuel Wild West legends. Good and bad guys were designations in flux – a tough outlaw in one state became a popular sheriff in another. And gunfights were more frequently the result of mundane political struggles in emerging towns than storied blood feuds. New mining towns mushroomed overnight, playing host to rowdy saloons and bordellos where miners would come to brawl, drink, gamble and be fleeced.

Legendary figures Billy the Kid and Sheriff Pat Garrett, both involved in the infamous Lincoln County War, were active in the late 1870s. Billy the Kid reputedly shot and killed more than 20 men in a brief career as a gunslinger – he himself was shot and killed by Garrett at the tender age of 21. In 1881, Wyatt Earp, along with his brothers Virgil and Morgan, and Doc Holliday, shot dead Billy Clanton and the McLaury brothers in a blazing gunfight at the OK Corral in Tombstone, AZ – the showdown took less than a minute. Both sides accused the other of cattle rustling, but the real story will never be known.

Butch Cassidy and the Sundance Kid once roamed much of Utah. Cassidy, a Mormon, robbed banks and trains with his Wild Bunch gang during the 1890s but never killed anyone.

Depression, War & Recovery

While the 1930s saw much of the USA in a major depression, the Southwest remained relatively prosperous.

Las Vegas came on to the scene after the completion of a railroad linking Salt Lake City and Los Angeles in 1902. It grew during the despair of

For fascinating behind-the-scenes stories about Wild West legends, along with their photographs, pick up a copy of the monthly magazine True West (www.truewestmagazine.com) during your trip or check out the website to see who's in the spotlight.

HISTORY THE WILD WEST

1950	1957	1963	1973
A radio game-show host challenges any town to name itself after the show. Tiny Hot Springs, NM accepts the challenge and renames itself Truth or Consequences.	Los Alamos opens its doors to ordinary people for the first time. The city was first exposed to the public after the atomic bomb was dropped on Japan.	The controversial Glen Canyon Dam is finished and Lake Powell begins, eventually covering Ancestral Puebloan sites and rock formations but creating 1960 miles of shoreline and a boater fantasyland.	The debut of the MGM Grand in 1973 signals the dawn of the era of corporate-owned megaresorts and sparks a building bonanza along the Strip that's still going on today.

the '30s and reached its first golden peak (the second came at the turn of the century) during the fabulous '50s, when mob money ran the city and all that glittered really was gold.

During the Depression, the region benefited from a number of federal employment projects, and WWII rejuvenated a demand for metals mined in the Southwest. In addition, production facilities were located in New Mexico and Arizona to protect those states from the vulnerability of attack. Migrating defense workers precipitated population booms and urbanization, which was mirrored elsewhere in the Southwest.

The struggle for an adequate supply of water for the growing desert population marked the early years of the 20th century, resulting in federally funded dam projects such as the 1936 Hoover Dam and, in 1963, Arizona's Glen Canyon Dam and Lake Powell. Water supply continues to be a key challenge to life in this region, with dwindling snow packs and ongoing drought conditions exacerbating the issue.

GUNFIGHT AT THE OK CORRAL

Considering it's the most famous shoot-out in the history of the Wild West, we know pitifully little of what really happened on October 26, 1881. We do know that Ike and Billy Clanton and their cohorts Frank and Tom McLaury belonged to a loose association of rustlers and thieves called the Cowboys. Wyatt Earp was an on-again-off-again lawman with one heck of a mustache, who was serving as a temporary deputy to his brother Virgil, Tombstone's city marshal. Their other brother, Morgan, was also a deputy. Doc Holliday, a dentist, was their good buddy. Neither Wyatt nor Doc was squeaky-clean.

Long-simmering bad blood between the Earp group and the Cowboys began to boil over just before the shoot-out. Earlier that month, Frank McLaury had threatened to kill all of the Earps. On the day of the shoot-out, the Cowboys had come to Tombstone and were apparently in violation of the law requiring them to check their weapons. Virgil was the only one of these gunslingers who wasn't itching for a showdown, preferring to keep the peace. But the situation got out of hand. As the men confronted each other on the street, shots rang out. According to lore, Wyatt shot Frank McLaury at the same time Billy Clanton shot at Wyatt. During this first exchange, Frank was hit but didn't go down and Wyatt escaped unscathed. After about 30 seconds, it was all over. Tom had been felled by the sawn-off shotgun wielded by Doc, Frank was hit again, and Billy Clanton was dropped by a shot to the chest. All three were dead. Doc had been grazed in the hip, Virgil in the calf and Morgan was hit in the back. Wyatt was untouched.

Wyatt and Doc were charged with murder but exonerated, although questions remained about who was really guilty. Soon after, a full-scale vendetta broke out between the Earps and Cowboys. Morgan was shot and killed; Virgil was attacked, lost the use of his left arm, and fled to Tucson. Wyatt and Doc, after doing some damage of their own to the Cowboy clan, moved up to Colorado, each going his own way.

1996	2002	2004	2006
President Bill Clinton establishes Utah's Grand Staircase-Escalante National Monument, which is unique in allowing some activities (such as hunting and grazing by permit) usually banned in national parks.	Salt Lake City hosts the Winter Olympics and becomes the most populated place to ever hold the winter games, as well as the first place women competed in bobsled racing.	Sin City is back! Las Vegas enters its second golden heyday, hosting 37.5 million visitors, starting work on its latest megaresort and becoming the number-one party destination.	Warren Jeffs, leader of the Fundamentalist Church of Jesus Christ of the Latter-Day Saints (FLDS) is charged with aggravated assaults of two underage girls. He is serving a life-plus-20-years sentence.

The Atomic Age

In 1943, Los Alamos, then a boys school perched on a 7400ft mesa, was chosen as the top-secret headquarters of the Manhattan Project, the code name for the research and development of the atomic bomb. The 772-acre site, accessed by two dirt roads, had no gas or oil lines and only one wire service, and it was surrounded by forest.

Isolation and security marked every aspect of life on 'the hill.' Scientists, their spouses, army members providing security, locals serving as domestic help and manual laborers lived together in a makeshift community. They were surrounded by guards and barbed wire and unknown even to nearby Santa Fe; the residents' postal address was simply 'Box 1663, Santa Fe.'

Not only was resident movement restricted and mail censored, there was no outside contact by radio or telephone. Perhaps even more unsettling, most employee-residents had no idea why they were living in Los Alamos. Knowledge was on a 'need to know' basis; everyone knew only as much as their job required.

In just under two years, Los Alamos scientists successfully detonated the first atomic bomb at New Mexico's Trinity site, now White Sands Missile Range.

After the US detonated the atomic bomb in Japan, the secret city of Los Alamos was exposed to the public and its residents finally understood why they were there. The city continued to be clothed in secrecy, however, until 1957 when restrictions on visiting were lifted. Today, the lab is still the town's backbone, and a tourist industry embraces the town's atomic history by selling T-shirts featuring exploding bombs and bottles of La Bomba wine.

Some of the original scientists disagreed with the use of the bomb in warfare and signed a petition against it – beginning the love/hate relationship with nuclear development still in evidence in the Southwest today. Controversies continue over the locations of nuclear power plants as well as the transportation and disposal of nuclear waste, notably at Yucca Mountain, 90 miles from Las Vegas.

The late environmentalist and essayist Edward Abbey wrote that the canyon country of the Colorado Plateau once had a 'living heart' – Glen Canyon, now drowned beneath Lake Powell.

HISTORY THE ATOMIC AGE

Anasazi, a Navajo word meaning 'ancient enemy,' is a term to which many modern Pueblo Indians object; it's no longer used.

2010	2011	2012	2014
Arizona passes controversial legislation requiring police officers to request identification from anyone they suspect of being in the US illegally. Immigration-rights activists call for a boycott of the state.	Jared Loughner is charged with shooting Arizona Congresswoman Gabrielle Giffords outside a Tucson grocery store. Giffords suffers a critical brain injury, six others are killed.	New Mexico and Arizona celebrate 100 years of statehood with special events and commemorative stamps. Arizona was the last territory in the Lower 48 to earn statehood.	On January 1 the legal sale of recreational marijuana begins in Colorado.

The Way of Life

Rugged individuality is the cultural idiom of the Southwest. But the reality? It's a bit more complex. The major identities of the region, centered on a trio of tribes – Anglo, Hispanic and Native American – are as vast and varied as the land that has shaped them. Whether their personal religion involves aliens, art, nuclear fission, slot machines, peyote or Joseph Smith, there's plenty of room for you in this beautiful, barely tamed chunk of America.

The Phoenix Suns protested Arizona's new immigration law in 2010 by changing the team's name on their jerseys to 'Los Suns' (that's Spanglish) for one game.

People of the Southwest

Early Settlers

Although the region's culture as a whole is united by the psychology, mythology and spirituality of its harsh, arid desert landscape, the people here are a sundry assortment of characters not so easily branded. The Southwest has long drawn stout-hearted pioneers pursuing slightly different agendas than those of the average American. Mormons arrived in the mid-1800s seeking religious freedom. Cattle barons staked their claims with barbed wire and remote ranches, luring cowboys in the process. Old mining towns were founded by fierce individualists – prospectors, mining-company executives, gamblers, storekeepers and madams. When the mining industry went bust in the 20th century, boomtowns became ghost towns for a while, before a new generation of idealistic entrepreneurs transformed them into New Age art enclaves and Old West tourist towns. Scientists flocked to the empty spaces to develop and test atomic bombs and soaring rockets.

Residents Today

Today, these places attract folks similar to the original white pioneers – solitary, focused and self-reliant. Artists are drawn to the Southwest's clear light, cheap housing and wide, open spaces. Collectors, in turn, follow artists and gentrify towns such as Santa Fe and Taos in New Mexico, Prescott in Arizona and Durango in Colorado. Near Truth or Consequences, NM, global entrepreneur Richard Branson of Virgin Galactic is fine-tuning a commercial spacecraft that will launch paying customers into space from the scrubby desert. But not all new arrivals are Type A personalities. Mainstream outcasts still come to the Southwest to 'turn on, tune in and drop out.'

For years, these disparate individuals managed to get along with little strife. In recent years, however, state and local governments – and vocal citizens – have clashed with federal agencies and policies, most noticeably in Arizona and Nevada. In Arizona, the state's efforts to stop illegal immigration have destroyed the kumbaya vibe and garnered national headlines. These efforts include Arizona's controversial SB 1070 – a law that requires police officers to ask for ID from anyone they suspect of being in the country illegally – and a simultaneous surge in federal border-patrol agents and checkpoints. The anti-immigration rhetoric isn't common in day-to-day conversation, but heightened press coverage of the most vit-

WHAT'S IN A NAME?

Though the stereotypes that too often accompany racial labels are largely ignored in the Southwest, it's still a challenge for publishers to figure out the most accurate (and politically correct) term for various ethnic groups. Here's the rundown on our terminology:

Native American After introducing themselves to one very confused Christopher Columbus, the original Americans were labeled 'Indians.' The name stuck, and 500 years later folks from Mumbai are still trying to explain that, no, they don't speak a word of Tewa. 'Native American' is recommended by every major news organization, but in the Southwest most tribal members remain comfortable with the term 'Indian.' However, the best term to use is always each tribe's specific name, though this can also get complicated. The name 'Navajo,' for instance, was bestowed by the Spanish; in Athabascan, Navajo refer to themselves as Diné. What to do? Simply try your best, and if corrected, respect each person's preference.

Anglo Though 'Caucasian' is the preferred moniker (even if their ancestors hailed from nowhere near the Caucuses) and 'white' is the broadest and most useful word for European Americans, in this region the label for non-Iberian Europeans is 'Anglo' (of England). Even English speakers of Norwegian-Polish ancestry are Anglo around here, so get used to it.

Hispanic It's common (but sometimes considered offensive) to hyphenate 'Mexican-American,' 'Venezuelan-American,' etc. Obviously it's easier, if less precise, to use 'Latino' to describe people hailing from the Spanish-speaking Americas. Then add to that list 'Chicano,' 'Raza' and 'Hispano,' a de-anglicized term currently gaining popularity, and everyone's confused. But, because this region was part of Spain for 225 years and Mexico for only 25, and many folks can trace an unbroken ancestry back to Spain, 'Hispanic' (of Spain) is the term used throughout this state, sprinkled with 'Spanish' and all the rest.

riolic comments, coupled with the checkpoints and ever-present border patrol vehicles, do cast a pall over the otherwise sunny landscape.

Regional Identity

For the most part, other regions of the Southwest have retained the live-and-let-live philosophy, and residents of the Southwest are more easygoing than their counterparts on the East and West Coasts. They tend to be friendlier too. Even at glitzy restaurants in the biggest cities (with the exception of Las Vegas), you'll see more jeans and cowboy boots than haute couture. Chat with a local at a low-key pub in Arizona or Colorado, and they'll likely tell you they're from somewhere else. They moved out here for the scenery, unpolluted air and slower pace of life. Folks in this region consider themselves environmentally friendly. Living a healthy lifestyle is important, and many residents like to hike, mountain bike, ski and ride the rapids. They might have money, but you won't necessarily know it. It's sort of a faux pas to flaunt your wealth.

In *Finders Keepers* (2010) journalist and naturalist Craig Childs examines the ethics of collecting prehistoric artifacts – whether for study or for sale – discovered in the Southwest.

Las Vegas is a different story. But a place where you can go from Paris to Egypt in less than 10 minutes can't possibly play by the rules. This is a town that's hot and knows it. The blockbuster comedy *The Hangover* stoked its image as party central. The identity here is also a little different – there's an energy to Sin City not found elsewhere in the region. People from Vegas don't say they're from the Southwest, or even from Nevada. They say they're from Las Vegas, dammit.

If Vegas is all about flaunting one's youthful beauty, then Arizona may just be its polar opposite. In the last decade, Arizona has done a great job at competing with Florida for the retiree-paradise award – the warm weather, dry air, abundant sunshine, and lots and lots of space draw more

POLYGAMY & THE MORMON CHURCH

Throughout its history, Utah has been a predominately Mormon state; more than 60% of the current population has church affiliation. But as late church president Gordon Hinckley was fond of saying, the Church of Jesus Christ of Latter-Day Saints (or LDS, as the modern Mormon faith is known) has nothing to do with those practicing polygamy today.

Members of the LDS believe the Bible is the Word of God and that the *Book of Mormon* is 'another testament of Jesus Christ,' as revealed to LDS church founder Joseph Smith. It was in the 1820s that the angel Moroni is said to have led Smith to the golden plates containing the story of a family's exodus from Jerusalem in 600 BC, and their subsequent lives, prophesies, trials, wars and visitations by Jesus Christ in the new world (Central America). Throughout his life he is said to have received revelations from God, including the 1843 visitation that revealed the righteous path of plural marriage to the prophet. Polygamy was formally established as church doctrine in 1852 by the second president, Brigham Young.

For all the impact plural marriage has had, it seems odd that the practice was officially endorsed for less than 40 years. By the 1880s US federal laws had made polygamy a crime. With the threatened seizure of church assets looming, president Wilford Woodruff received spiritual guidance and abdicated polygamy in 1890.

Today the church has more than 15 million members and a missionary outreach that spans the globe. But what happened to polygamy? Well, fundamentalist sects broke off to form their own churches almost immediately; they continue to practice today. The official Mormon church disavows any relationship to these fundamentalists, and shows every evidence of being embarrassed by the past.

The number of people estimated to be still practicing or recognizing polygamy are about 38,000, mostly in Utah and surrounding areas. Some you'd never recognize; they're just large families. Others belong to isolated, cultlike groups such as the FLDS in Hildale-Colorado City on the Utah-Arizona border, which have distinct styles of dress and hair. Some of these sects have become notorious for crimes committed by some of their members.

Though polygamy itself is illegal, prosecution is rare. Without a confession or videotaped evidence, the case is hard to prove. Men typically marry only their first wife legally (subsequent wives are considered single mothers by the state, and are therefore entitled to more welfare). The larger Utah populace is deeply ambivalent about polygamy. Tens – maybe hundreds – of thousands of them wouldn't exist but for the historic practice, including me. My great-great-great grandmother, Lucy Bigelow, was a wife of Brigham Young.

Lisa Dunford

seniors each year. You'll see villages of RV parks surrounding Phoenix and Tucson, and early-bird specials are the plat du jour at many restaurants.

Colorado, Arizona and New Mexico have large Native American and Hispanic populations, and these residents take pride in maintaining their cultural identities through preserved traditions and oral history lessons.

Lifestyle

In a region of such diversity and size, it's impossible to describe the 'typical' Southwestern home or family. What lifestyle commonalities, after all, can be seen in the New Age mystics of Sedona, the businesspeople, lounge singers and casino workers of Las Vegas and the Mormon faithful of Salt Lake City? Half the fun of touring the Southwest is comparing and contrasting all these different identities.

Utah's heavily Mormon population stresses traditional family values; drinking, smoking and premarital sex are frowned upon. You won't see much fast fashion or hear much cursing here.

Family and religion are also core values for Native Americans and Hispanics throughout the region. For the Hopi, tribal dances are such sacred events they were mostly closed to outsiders. And although many Native Americans and Hispanics are now living and working in urban areas, large family gatherings and traditional customs are still important facets of daily life.

Because of its favorable weather and boundless possibilities for outdoor adventures, much of the Southwest is popular with transplants from the East and West coasts. In cities such as Santa Fe, Telluride, Las Vegas, Tucson and Flagstaff, you'll find a blend of students, artists, wealthy retirees, celebrity wannabes and adventure junkies. In urban centers throughout the region (with the exception of Utah) many people consider themselves 'spiritual' rather than religious, and forgo church for Sunday brunch. Women work the same hours as men, and many children attend daycare.

With the exception of Mormon Utah, attitudes toward gays and lesbians in the Southwest are generally open, especially in major cities such as Las Vegas, Santa Fe and Phoenix.

More than 100,000 images documenting the history and people of the Colorado Plateau are viewable online as part of the Colorado Plateau Archives, a collection established by the Cline Library at Northern Arizona University (http://archive.library.nau.edu).

THE WAY OF LIFE SPORTS

Sports

Professional sports teams are based in Phoenix and Salt Lake City. The Arizona Diamondbacks of Phoenix play major league baseball from April through September; the only Southwestern major-league football team, the Arizona Cardinals, play from September through December. Basketball (men play November through April) is more competitive; you can watch hoops with Salt Lake City's Utah Jazz or the Phoenix Suns, both mens' teams. The women's pro basketball team, Phoenix Mercury, plays June through August.

Because pro tickets are hard to get, you'll have a better shot with college sports. Albuquerque teams across the board are quite popular. The University of Arizona Wildcats consistently place among the best basketball teams in the nation.

Several major-league baseball teams (such as the Chicago White Sox) migrate from the cold, wintry north from late February through March for training seasons in warmer Arizona. They play in what is aptly referred to as the Cactus League.

Native American Southwest

Jeff Campbell

The Southwest is sometimes called 'Indian Country,' but this nickname fails to capture the diversity of the tribes that make the region their home. From the Apache to the Zuni, each tribe maintains distinctions of law, language, religion, history and custom. Members within a tribe are linked by common heritage, but follow broadly diverse paths as they navigate the legacy of their ancestors and outside cultures. These differences turn the Southwest's seemingly borderless, painted desert into a kaleidoscopic league of nations.

The People

The US population in 2012 was 312.8 million. Native Americans/Native Alaskans represented about 2% of the total, about 5.2 million people. There were 325 federally recognized Indian reservations.

The cultural traditions and fundamental belief systems of the Southwest's tribes reflect their age-old relationship to the land, the water, the sky and the creatures that inhabit those elements. This relationship is reflected in their crafts, their dances and their architecture.

Culturally, tribes grapple with dilemmas about how to prosper in contemporary America while protecting their traditions from erosion and their lands from further exploitation, and how to lift their people from poverty while maintaining their sense of identity and the sacred.

Apache

The Southwest has four major Apache reservations: New Mexico's Jicarilla Apache reservation and Mescalero Apache reservation, and Arizona's San Carlos Apache reservation and Fort Apache reservation, home to the White Mountain Apache Tribe. All the Apache tribes descend from Athabascans who migrated from Canada around 1400. They were nomadic hunter-gatherers who became warlike raiders, particularly of Pueblo tribes and European settlements, and they fiercely resisted relocation to reservations.

The most famous Apache is Geronimo, a Chiricahua Apache who resisted the American takeover of Indian lands until he was finally subdued by the US Army with the help of White Mountain Apache scouts.

Havasupai

The Havasupai reservation abuts Arizona's Grand Canyon National Park beneath the Canyon's south rim. The tribe's one village, Supai, can only be reached by an 8-mile hike or a mule or helicopter ride from road's end at Hualapai Hilltop.

Havasupai (hah-vah-*soo*-pie) means 'people of the blue-green water,' and tribal life has always been dominated by the Havasu Creek tributary of the Colorado River. Reliable water meant the ability to irrigate fields, which led to a season-based village lifestyle. The deep Havasu Canyon also protected them from others; this extremely peaceful people basically avoided Western contact until the 1800s. Today, the tribe relies on tourism, and Havasu Canyon's gorgeous waterfalls draw a steady stream of visitors. The tribe is related to the Hualapai.

Native American Pueblos & Reservations

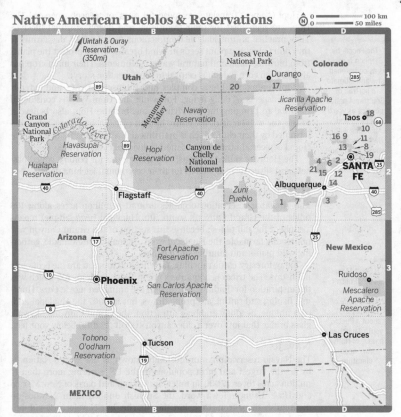

Native American Pueblos & Reservations

Hopi

The Hopi reservation occupies more than 1.5 million acres in the middle of the Navajo reservation. Most Hopi live in 12 villages at the base and on top of three mesas jutting from the main Black Mesa. The village of Moenkopi is to the west. Old Oraibi, on Third Mesa, is considered (along with Acoma Pueblo) the continent's oldest continuously inhabited settlement. Like all Pueblo peoples, the Hopi are descended from the Ancestral Puebloans (formerly known as Anasazi).

Hopi (*ho*-pee) translates as 'peaceful ones' or 'peaceful person.' The Hopi are renowned for their traditional and deeply spiritual lifestyle. They practice an unusual, near-miraculous technique of 'dry farming'; they don't plow, but plant seeds in 'wind breaks', which protect the plants from blowing sand, and natural water catchments. Their main crop has always been corn (which is central to their creation story).

Hopi ceremonial life is complex and intensely private, and extends into all aspects of daily living. Following the 'Hopi Way' is considered essential to bringing the life-giving rains, but the Hopi also believe it fosters the well-being of the entire human race. Each person's role is determined by their clan, which is matrilineal. Even among themselves, the Hopi keep certain traditions of their individual clans private.

The Hopi are skilled artisans; they are famous for pottery, coiled baskets and silverwork, as well as for their ceremonial kachina dolls.

The People by Stephen Trimble is as comprehensive and intimate a portrait of Southwest native peoples as you'd hope to find, bursting with Native American voices and beautiful photos.

Hualapai

The Hualapai reservation occupies around a million acres along 108 miles of the Grand Canyon's south rim. Hualapai (*wah*-lah-pie) means 'people of the tall pines'; because this section of the Grand Canyon was not readily farmable, the Hualapai were originally seminomadic, gathering wild plants and hunting small game.

Today, forestry, cattle ranching, farming and tourism are the economic mainstays. The tribal headquarters are in Peach Springs, AZ, which was the inspiration for 'Radiator Springs' in the animated movie *Cars*. Hunting, fishing and rafting are prime draws, but in 2007 the Hualapai added a unique, headline-grabbing attraction: the Grand Canyon's Skywalk glass bridge that juts over a side canyon 4000ft (1220m) below your feet.

N Scott Momaday's Pulitzer Prize–winning *House Made of Dawn* (1968), about a Pueblo youth, launched a wave of Native American literature.

Navajo

The Navajo reservation, more formally known as the Navajo Nation, is by far the largest and most populous in the US, covering more than 17 million acres (over 27,000 sq miles) in Arizona and parts of New Mexico and Utah. Using a Tewa word, the Spanish dubbed them 'Navajos' to distinguish them from their kin the Apache, but Navajo (*nah*-vuh-ho) call themselves the Diné (dee-*nay;* 'the people') and their land Dinétah.

Nationwide, there are about 300,000 Navajo, making it the USA's second-largest tribe (after the Cherokee). The Navajo's Athabascan tongue is the most spoken Native American language, with 170,000 speakers, despite its notorious complexity. In the Pacific Theater during WWII, Navajo 'code talkers' sent and received military messages in Navajo; Japan never broke the code, and the code talkers were considered essential to US victory.

Like the Apache, the Navajo were feared nomads and warriors who both traded with and raided the Pueblos, and who fought settlers and the US military. They also borrowed generously from other traditions: they acquired sheep and horses from the Spanish, learned pottery and weaving from the Pueblos and picked up silversmithing from Mexico. Today, the Navajo are renowned for their woven rugs, pottery and inlaid silver jewelry. Their intricate sandpainting is used in healing ceremonies.

For decades, traditional Navajo and Hopi have successfully thwarted US industry efforts to strip-mine sacred Big Mountain, but the fight continues. Black Mesa Indigenous Support (www.blackmesais.org) tells their story.

The reservation has significant mineral reserves – Black Mesa, for instance, contains the USA's largest coal deposit, perhaps 21 billion tons – and modern-day mining of coal, oil, gas and uranium has been an important, and controversial, economic resource. Mining has depleted the region's aquifer, contaminated water supplies (leading, some claim, to high cancer rates) and affected sacred places.

Tribal headquarters are in Window Rock, AZ, and the reservation boasts numerous cultural and natural attractions, including Monument

HOPI KACHINAS

In the Hopi religion, maintaining balance and harmony between the spirit world and our 'fourth world' is crucial, and the spirit messengers called kachinas (also spelled katsinas) play a central role. These supernatural beings are spirits of deities, animals and even deceased clan members, and they can bring rain, influence the weather, help in daily tasks and punish violators of tribal laws. They are said to live atop Southwest mountains; on the winter solstice they travel to the Hopi Pueblos, where they reside until the summer solstice.

In a series of kachina ceremonies and festivals, masked dancers impersonate the kachinas; during these rituals, it is believed the dancers are inhabited by and become the kachinas. There are hundreds of kachina spirits: some are kindly, some fearsome and dangerous, and the elaborate, fantastical costumes dancers wear evoke the mystery and religious awe of these beings. In the 1990s, to keep these sacred ceremonies from becoming trivialized as tourist spectacles, the Hopi closed most to the public.

Kachina dolls (*tithu* in Hopi) are brightly painted, carved wooden figures traditionally given to young Hopi girls during certain kachina festivals. The religious icons become treasured family heirlooms. The Hopi now carve some as art meant for the general public.

Valley, Canyon de Chelly National Monument, Navajo National Monument and Antelope Canyon.

Pueblo

There are 19 Pueblo reservations in New Mexico. Four of them lead west from Albuquerque – Isleta, Laguna, Acoma and Zuni – and 15 Pueblos fill the Rio Grande Valley between Albuquerque and Taos: Sandia, San Felipe, Santa Ana, Zia, Jemez, Kewa Pueblo (or Santo Domingo), Cochiti, San Ildefonso, Pojoaque, Nambé, Tesuque, Santa Clara, Ohkay Owingeh (or San Juan), Picuris and Taos. For information about each of the Pueblos, see www.indianpueblo.org.

These tribes are as different as they are alike. Nevertheless, the term 'Pueblo' (Spanish for 'village') is a convenient shorthand for what these tribes share: all are believed to be descended from the Ancestral Puebloans and to have inherited their architectural style and their agrarian, village-based life – often atop mesas.

Pueblos are unique among Native Americans. These adobe structures can have up to five levels, connected by ladders, and are built with varying combinations of mud bricks, stones, logs and plaster. In the central plaza of each pueblo is a kiva, an underground ceremonial chamber that connects to the spirit world.

With a legacy of missionary activity, Pueblos tend to have Catholic churches, and many Pueblo Indians now hold both Christian and native religious beliefs. This unmerged, unconflicted duality is a hallmark of much of Pueblo modern life.

To donate to a cause, consider Black Mesa Weavers for Life and Land (www.blackmesaweavers.org), which helps aid traditional Diné sheep raisers and artisans in Navajoland market handmade weavings, yarn and crafts.

Other Tribes: Paiute, Ute & Tohono O'odham

Paiute

The Kaibab-Paiute reservation is on the Arizona–Utah border. The Kaibab (*cay*-bob) are a band of Southern Paiute (*pie*-oot) who migrated to the Colorado Plateau around 1100. They were peaceful hunter-gatherers who moved frequently across the arid, remote region, basing their movements on seasonal agricultural needs and animal migrations. The tribe's lifestyle changed drastically in the 1850s when Mormons began settling the region, overtaking the land for their farms and livestock. The Kaibab-Paiute reservation, located on the Arizona Strip west of Fredonia, is next to a vitally important regional spring, one that was also important to the

LEGAL STATUS

Although Arizona's major tribes are 'sovereign nations' and have significant powers to run their reservations as they like, their authority – and its limitations – is granted by Congress. While they can make many of their own laws, plenty of federal laws apply on reservations, too. The tribes don't legally own their reservations – it's public land held in trust by the federal government, which has a responsibility to administer it in a way that's beneficial for the tribes. Enter the Bureau of Indian Affairs.

While Native Americans living on reservations have officially been American citizens since 1924, can vote in state and national elections, and serve in the armed forces, they are not covered by the Bill of Rights. Instead, there's the Indian Civil Rights Act of 1968, which does grant reservation dwellers many of the same protections found in the Constitution, but not all. This is not an entirely bad thing. In some ways, it allows tribal governments to do things that federal and state government can't, which helps them create a system more attuned to their culture.

Mormons. Today, near the spring, their reservation runs a public campground (closed at research time for upgrades) and contains Pipe Spring National Monument; the Kaibab-Paiute worked with the National Park Service to create rich displays about Native American life. The tribe is renowned for its basketmaking.

Ute

Along with the Navajo and Apache tribes, Utes helped drive the Ancestral Puebloans from the region in the 1200s. By the time of European contact, seven Ute tribes occupied most of present-day Colorado and Utah (named for the Utes). In the 16th century, Utes eagerly adopted the horse and became nomadic buffalo hunters and livestock raiders.

There are three main Ute reservations. With over 4.5 million acres, the Uintah and Ouray reservation in northeastern Utah is the second largest in the US. Ranching and oil and gas mining are the tribe's main industries. The Ute Mountain Utes (who call themselves the Weeminuche) lead half-day and full-day tours to petroglyph sites and cliff dwellings in Ute Mountain Tribal Park; their reservation abuts Mesa Verde National Park in southwestern Colorado. The Southern Ute Reservation relies in part on a casino for income.

Tohono O'odham

The Tohono O'odham reservation is the largest of four reservations that make up the Tohono O'odham Nation in the Sonoran Desert in southern Arizona. Tohono O'odham (to-ho-no oh-oh-dum) means 'desert people.' The tribe was originally seminomadic, moving between the desert and the mountains seasonally. They were famous for their calendar sticks, which were carved to mark important dates and events, and they remain well known for their baskets and pottery. Today, the tribe runs three casinos and the Mission San Xavier del Bac in southern Arizona.

The Indian Arts and Crafts Board (www.doi.gov/iacb) publishes a directory of Native American–owned businesses, listed by state, and also punishes deceptive merchants.

Arts

Native American art nearly always contains ceremonial purpose and religious significance; the patterns and symbols are woven with spiritual meaning that provides an intimate window into the heart of Southwest people. By purchasing arts from Native Americans, visitors have a direct, positive impact on tribal economies, which depend in part on tourist dollars.

Pottery & Basketry

Pretty much every Southwest tribe has pottery and/or basketry traditions. Originally, each tribe and even individual families maintained distinct styles, but modern potters and basketmakers readily mix, borrow and reinterpret classic designs and methods.

Pueblo pottery is perhaps most acclaimed of all. Typically, local clay determines the color, so that Zia pottery is red, Acoma white, Hopi yellow, Cochiti black and so on. Santa Clara is famous for its carved relief designs, and San Ildefonso for its black-on-black style, which was revived by world-famous potter Maria Martinez. The Navajo and Ute Mountain Utes also produce well-regarded pottery.

Pottery is nearly synonymous with village life, while more portable baskets were often preferred by nomadic peoples. Among the tribes who stand out for their exquisite basketry are the Jicarilla Apache (whose name means 'basketmaker'), the Kaibab-Paiute, the Hualapai and the Tohono O'odham. Hopi coiled baskets, with their vivid patterns and kachina iconography, are also notable.

To learn about Navajo rugs, visit www.gonavajo. com. To see traditional weaving demonstrations, visit the Hubbell Trading Post in Ganado, AZ.

Navajo Weaving

According to Navajo legend, Spider Woman taught humans how to weave, and she seems embodied today in the iconic sight of Navajo women patiently shuttling handspun wool on weblike looms, creating the Navajo's legendary rugs (originally blankets), so tight they held water. Preparation of the wool and sometimes the dyes is still done by hand, and finishing a rug takes months (occasionally years).

Authentic Navajo rugs are expensive, and justifiably so, ranging from hundreds to thousands of dollars. They are not average souvenirs but artworks that will last a lifetime, whether displayed on the wall or the floor. Take time to research, even a little, so you recognize when quality matches price.

Silver & Turquoise Jewelry

Jewelry using stones and shells has always been a native tradition; silverwork did not arrive until the 1800s, along with Anglo and Mexican contact. In particular, Navajo, Hopi and Zuni became renowned for combining these materials with inlaid-turquoise silver jewelry. In addition to turquoise, jewelry often features lapis, onyx, coral, carnelian and shells.

Authentic jewelry is often stamped or marked by the artisan, and items may come with an Indian Arts and Crafts Board certificate; always ask. Price may also be an indicator: a high tab doesn't guarantee authenticity, but an absurdly low one probably signals trickery. A crash course can be had at the August Santa Fe Indian Market.

Etiquette

When visiting a reservation, ask about and follow any specific rules. Almost all tribes ban alcohol, and some ban pets and restrict cameras. All require permits for camping, fishing and other activities. Tribal rules may be posted at the reservation entrance, or visit the tribal office or the reservation's website.

The other thing is attitude and manner. When you visit a reservation, you are visiting a unique culture with perhaps unfamiliar customs. Be courteous, respectful and open-minded, and don't expect locals to share every detail of their lives.

Ask First, Document Later Some tribes restrict cameras and sketching entirely; others may charge a fee, or restrict them at ceremonies or in certain areas. If you want to photograph a person or their property, ask permission; a tip may or may not be expected.

Pueblos are not Museums At Pueblos, the incredible adobe structures are homes. Public buildings will be signed; if a building isn't signed, assume it's private. Don't climb around. Kivas are nearly always off-limits.

Ceremonies are not Performances Treat ceremonies like church services; watch silently and respectfully, without talking, clapping or taking pictures, and wear modest clothing. Powwows are more informal, but remember: unless they're billed as theater, ceremonies and dances are for the tribe, not you.

Privacy and Communication Many Native Americans are happy to describe their tribe's general religious beliefs, but this is not always the case, and details about rituals and ceremonies are often considered private. Always ask before discussing religion and respect each person's boundaries. Also, Native Americans consider it polite to listen without comment; silent listening, given and received, is another sign of respect.

The new Hopi Arts Trail (www. hopiartstrail.com) spotlights artists and galleries on the Hopi reservation. The website has descriptions of participating galleries, with directions, phone numbers and the type of art sold.

Geology & the Land

David Lukas

Blistering deserts. Snow-capped mountains. And every climate zone in between. For proof of the Southwest's ecological diversity, just drive up the Santa Catalina Mountains outside Tucson, where you climb from searing desert to snow-blanketed fir forests within 30 miles, the ecological equivalent of driving 2000 miles from southern Arizona to Canada. Contrasts such as these, often in close proximity, make the Southwest a fascinating place to explore. And that's without mentioning the photogenic aspects of the geologic diversity: red rock buttes, delicate arches, twisted hoodoos, crumbling spires... well, you get the idea.

The Land

Geologic History

It may be hard to imagine now, but the Southwest was once inundated by a succession of seas. There is geological evidence today of deep bays, shallow mud flats and coastal dunes. During this time North America was a young continent on the move, evolving slowly and migrating northward from the southern hemisphere over millions of years. Extremely ancient rocks (among the oldest on the planet) exposed in the deep heart of the Grand Canyon show that the region was under water two billion years ago, and younger layers of rocks in southern Utah reveal that this region was continuously or periodically under water until about 60 million years ago.

At the end of the Paleozoic era (about 245 million years ago), a collision of continents into a massive landmass known as Pangaea deformed the Earth's crust and produced pressures that uplifted an ancestral Rocky Mountains. Though this early mountain range lay to the east, it formed rivers and sediment deposits that began to shape the Southwest. In fact, by 240 millions years ago, erosion had leveled the range, with much of the sediment draining westward into what we now call Utah. Around the same time, a shallow tropical sea teeming with life, including a barrier reef that would later be sculpted into Carlsbad Caverns, covered much of southern New Mexico.

For long periods of time (between episodes of being underwater), much of the Southwest may have looked like northern Egypt today: floodplains and deltas surrounded by expanses of desert. A rising chain of island mountains to the west apparently blocked the supply of wet storms, creating a desert and sand dunes that piled up thousands of feet high. Now preserved as sandstone, these dunes can be seen today in the famous Navajo sandstone cliffs of Zion National Park.

Mountains & Basins

This sequence of oceans and sand ended around 60 million years ago as North America underwent a dramatic separation from Europe, sliding westward over a piece of the Earth's crust known as the East Pacific plate and leaving behind an ever-widening gulf that became the Atlantic

On the evening of July 5, 2011, a mile-high dust storm with an estimated 100-mile width enveloped Phoenix after reaching speeds of 50mph to 60mph. Visibility dropped to between zero and a quarter mile. There were power outages and Phoenix International Airport temporarily closed.

Visit www.publiclands.org for a one-stop summary of recreational opportunities on government-owned land in the Southwest. The site also has maps, a book index, links to relevant agencies and updates on current conditions.

Ocean. This East Pacific plate collided with, and pushed down, the North American plate. This collision, named the Laramide orogeny, resulted in the birth of the modern Rocky Mountains and uplifted an old basin into a highland known today as the Colorado Plateau. Fragments of the East Pacific plate also attached themselves to the leading edge of the North American plate, transforming the Southwest from a coastal area to an interior region increasingly detached from the ocean.

In contrast to the compression and collision that characterized earlier events, the Earth's crust began stretching in an east–west direction about 30 million years ago. The thinner, stretched crust of New Mexico and Texas cracked along zones of weakness called faults, resulting in a rift valley where New Mexico's Rio Grande now flows. These same forces created the stepped plateaus of northern Arizona and southern Utah.

Pages of Stone: Geology of the Grand Canyon & Plateau Country National Parks & Monuments, by Halka and Lucy Chronic, is an excellent way to understand the Southwest's diverse landscape.

Increased pulling in the Earth's crust between 15 and eight million years ago created a much larger region of north–south cracks in western Utah, Arizona and Nevada known as the Basin and Range province. Here, parallel cracks formed hundreds of miles of valleys and mountain ranges that fill the entire region between the Sierra Nevada and the Rocky Mountains.

During the Pleistocene glacial period, large bodies of water accumulated throughout the Southwest. Utah's Great Salt Lake is the most famous remnant of these mighty Ice Age lakes. Basins with now completely dry, salt-crusted lakebeds are especially conspicuous on a drive across Nevada.

For the past several million years the dominant force in the Southwest has probably been erosion. Not only do torrential rainstorms readily tear through soft sedimentary rocks, but the rise of the Rocky Mountains also generates large powerful rivers that wind throughout the Southwest, carving mighty canyons in their wake. Nearly all the contemporary features in the Southwest, from arches to hoodoos, are the result of weathering and erosion.

Geographic Make Up of the Land

The Colorado Plateau is an impressive and nearly impenetrable 130,000-sq-mile tableland lurking in the corner where Colorado, Utah, Arizona and New Mexico join. Formed in an ancient basin as a remarkably coherent body of neatly layered sedimentary rocks, the plateau has remained relatively unchanged, even as the lands around it were compressed, stretched and deformed by powerful forces.

The most powerful indicators of the plateau's long-term stability are the distinct and unique layers of sedimentary rock stacked on top of each other, with the oldest dating back two billion years. In fact, the science of stratigraphy – the reading of Earth history through its rock layers – stemmed from work at the Grand Canyon, where an astonishing set of layers have been

CRYPTOBIOTIC CRUSTS: WATCH YOUR STEP!

Cryptobiotic crusts, also known as biological soil crusts, are living crusts that cover and protect desert soils, literally gluing sand particles together so they don't blow away. Cyanobacteria, one of the Earth's oldest life forms, start the process by extending mucous-covered filaments into dry soil. Over time these filaments and the sand particles adhering to them form a thin crust that is colonized by algae, lichen, fungi and mosses. This crust plays a significant role in desert food chains, and also stores rainwater and reduces erosion.

Unfortunately, the thin crust is easily fragmented under heavy-soled boots and tires. Once broken, the crust takes 50 to 250 years to repair itself. In its absence, winds and rains erode desert soils, and much of the water that would nourish desert plants is lost. Many sites in Utah, in particular, have cryptobiotic crusts. Protect these crusts by staying on established trails.

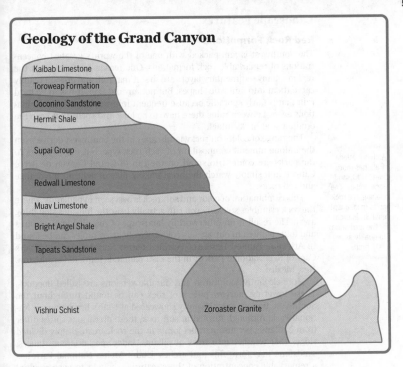

Geology of the Grand Canyon

Kaibab Limestone

Toroweap Formation

Coconino Sandstone

Hermit Shale

Supai Group

Redwall Limestone

Muav Limestone

Bright Angel Shale

Tapeats Sandstone

Vishnu Schist

Zoroaster Granite

laid bare by the Colorado River cutting across them. Throughout the Southwest, and on the Colorado Plateau in particular, layers of sedimentary rock detail a rich history of ancient oceans, coastal mudflats and arid dunes.

All other geographic features of the Southwest seem to radiate out from the plateau. To the east, running in a north–south line from Canada to Mexico, are the Rocky Mountains, the source of the mighty Colorado River, which gathers on the mountains' high slopes and cascades across the Southwest to its mouth in the Gulf of California. East of the Rocky Mountains, the eastern third of New Mexico grades into the Llano Estacado – a local version of the vast grasslands of the Great Plains.

In Utah, a line of mountains known collectively as the Wasatch Line bisects the state nearly in half, with the eastern half on the Colorado Plateau, and the western half in the Basin and Range province. Northern Arizona is highlighted by a spectacular set of cliffs called the Mogollon Rim that run several hundred miles to form a boundary between the Colorado Plateau to the north and the highland region of central Arizona. The mountains of central Arizona decrease in elevation as you travel into the deserts of southern Arizona.

Four deserts – the Sonoran, Mojave, Chihuahuan and Great Basin – stretch across the Southwest. Each is home to an array of well-adapted reptiles, mammals and plants. Look closely to discover everything from fleet-footed lizards to jewel-like wildflowers. As Southwest ecowarrior Edward Abbey wrote in *Desert Solitaire: A Season in the Wilderness,* 'The desert is a vast world, an oceanic world, as deep in its way and complex and various as the sea.' The Southwest's four distinct desert zones are superimposed on an astonishing complex of hidden canyons and towering mountains.

The often-used term 'slickrock' refers to the fossilized surfaces of ancient sand dunes. Pioneers named it slickrock because their metal-shoed horses and iron-wheeled wagons would slip on the surface.

Landscape Features

Red Rock Formations

The Southwest is jam-packed with one of the world's greatest concentrations of remarkable rock formations. One reason for this is that the region's many sedimentary layers are so soft that rain and erosion readily carve them into fantastic shapes. But not any old rain. It has to be hard rain that is fairly sporadic because frequent rain would wash the formations away. Between rains there have to be long arid spells that keep the eroding landmarks intact.

The range of colors on rocky landscapes in the Southwest derive from the unique mineral composition of each rock type, but most visitors to the parks are content to stand on the rim of Grand Canyon or Bryce Canyon and simply watch the breathtaking play of light on the orange and red rocks.

This combination of color and soft rock is best seen in badlands, where the rock crumbles so easily you can actually hear the hillsides sloughing away. The result is an otherworldly landscape of rounded knolls, spires and folds painted in outrageous colors. Excellent examples can be found in Arizona's Painted Desert of Petrified Forest National Park, at Utah's Capitol Reef National Park or in the Bisti Badlands south of Farmington, New Mexico.

More-elegantly sculptured and durable versions are called hoodoos. These towering, narrow pillars of rock can be found throughout the Southwest, but are magnificently showcased at Utah's Bryce Canyon National Park. Although formed in soft rock, these precarious spires differ from badlands because parallel joints in the rock create deeply divided ridges that weather into rows of pillars. Under special circumstances, sandstone may form fins and arches. Utah's Arches National Park has a remarkable concentration of these features, thought to have resulted from a massive salt deposit that was laid down by a sea 300 million years ago. Squeezed by the pressure of overlying layers, this salt body apparently domed up then collapsed, creating a matrix of rock cracked along parallel lines. Erosion along deep vertical cracks left behind fins and narrow walls of sandstone that sometimes partially collapse to create freestanding arches.

Streams cutting through resistant sandstone layers form natural bridges, which are similar in appearance to arches. Three examples of natural bridges can be found in Utah's Natural Bridges National Monument. These formations are the result of meandering streams that double back on themselves to cut at both sides of a rock barrier. At an early stage of development these streams could be called goosenecks as they loop across the landscape. A famous example can be found at the Goosenecks State Park in Utah.

Sandstone Effects

Many of the Southwest's characteristic features are sculpted in sandstone. Laid down in distinct horizontal layers, like a stack of pancakes, these rocks erode into unique formations, like flat-topped mesas. Surrounded by sheer cliffs, mesas represent a fairly advanced stage of erosion in which all of the original landscape has been stripped away except for a few scattered outposts that tower over everything else. The eerie skyline at Monument Valley on the Arizona–Utah border is a classic example.

Where sandstone layers remain fairly intact, it's possible to see details of the ancient dunes that created the sandstone. As sand dunes were blown across the landscape millions of years ago they formed fine layers of cross-bedding that can still be seen in the rocks at Zion National Park. Wind-blown ripple marks and tracks of animals that once walked the

Arches National Park has more than 2000 sandstone arches. The opening in a rock has to measure at least 3ft in order for the formation to qualify as an arch.

For an insight into how indigenous peoples used this landscape, read *Wild Plants and Native Peoples of the Four Corners*, by William Dunmire and Gail Tierney.

WHAT'S THE BLM?

The **Bureau of Land Management** (BLM; www.blm.gov) is a Department of Energy agency that oversees more than 245 million surface acres of public land, much of it in the West. It manages its resources for a variety of uses, from energy production to cattle grazing to recreational oversight. What does that mean for you? All kinds of outdoor fun.

You'll also find both developed camping and dispersed camping. Generally, when it comes to dispersed camping on BLM land, you can camp where you want as long as your campsite is at least 900ft from a water source used by wildlife or livestock. You cannot camp in one spot for more than 14 days. Don't leave campfires unattended and be sure to pack out what you pack in, which means that all of your personal belongings and trash, including food scraps, should be taken with you when you leave. Some regions may have more specific rules, so check the state's camping requirements on the BLM website and call the appropriate district office for specifics. For developed campground information, you can also visit www.recreation.gov.

dunes are also preserved. Modern sand dunes include the spectacular dunes at White Sands National Monument in New Mexico, where shimmering white gypsum crystals thickly blanket 275 sq miles.

Looking beneath the surface, the 85-plus caves at Carlsbad Caverns National Park in southern New Mexico are chiseled deep into a massive 240-million-year-old limestone formation that was part of a 400-mile-long reef similar to the modern Great Barrier Reef of Australia.

Geology of the Grand Canyon

Arizona's Grand Canyon is the best-known geologic feature in the Southwest and for good reason: not only does its immensity dwarf the imagination, but it also records two billion years of geologic history – a huge amount of time considering the earth is just 4.6 billion years old. The Canyon itself, however, is young – a mere five to six million years old. Carved out by the powerful Colorado River as the land bulged upward, the 277-mile-long canyon reflects the differing hardness of the 10-plus layers of rocks in its walls. Shales, for instance, crumble easily and form slopes, while resistant limestones and sandstones form distinctive cliffs.

The layers making up the bulk of the canyon walls were laid during the Paleozoic era, 570 to 245 million years ago. These formations perch atop a group of one- to two-billion-year-old rocks lying at the bottom of the inner gorge of the canyon. Between these two distinct sets of rock is the Great Unconformity, a several-hundred-million-year gap in the geologic record where erosion erased 12,000ft of rock and left a huge mystery.

A summer thunderstorm in 1998 increased the flow of Zion's Virgin River from 200 to 4500 cubic ft per second, scouring out canyon walls 40ft high at its peak flow.

Wildlife

The Southwest's landscape may seem desolate but this doesn't mean it lacks wildlife – on the contrary. However, the plants and animals of North America's deserts are a subtle group and it takes patience to see them, so many visitors will drive through without noticing any at all. While a number of species are widespread, others have adapted to the particular requirements of their local environment and live nowhere else in the world. Deep canyons and waterless wastes limit travel and dispersal opportunities for animals and plants as well as for humans, and all life has to hunker down and plan carefully to survive.

Reptiles & Amphibians

While most people expect to see snakes and lizards in a desert, it's less obvious that frogs and toads find a comfortable home here as well. But

Edward Abbey shares his desert philosophy and insights in his classic *Desert Solitaire: A Season in the Wilderness,* a must-read for desert enthusiasts and conservationists.

on a spring evening, many of the canyons of the Southwest reverberate with the calls of canyon tree frogs or red-spotted toads. With the rising sun, these are replaced by several dozen species of lizards and snakes that roam among rocks and shrubs. Blue-bellied fence lizards are particularly abundant in the region's parks, but visitors can always hope to encounter a rarity such as the strange and venomous 'Gila monster' lizard. Equally fascinating, if you're willing to hang around and watch for a while (but never touch or bother), are the Southwest's many colorful rattlesnakes. Quick to anger and able to deliver a painful or toxic bite, rattlesnakes are placid and retiring if left alone.

Birds

More than 400 species of birds can be found in the Southwest, bringing color, energy and song to every season. There are blue grosbeaks, yellow warblers and scarlet cardinals. There are massive golden eagles and tiny vibrating calliope hummingbirds. In fact, there are so many interesting birds that it's the foremost reason many people travel to the Southwest. Springtime is particularly rewarding, as songbirds arrive from their southern wintering grounds and begin singing from every nook and cranny.

One recent arrival at the Grand Canyon tops everyone's list of must-see wildlife. With a 9ft wingspan, the California condor looks more like a prehistoric pterodactyl than any bird you've ever seen. Pushed to the brink of extinction, these unusual birds are staging a minor comeback at the Grand Canyon. After several decades in which no condors lived in the wild, a few wild pairs are now nesting on the canyon rim.

An estimated nine million free-tailed bats once roosted in Carlsbad Caverns. Though reduced in recent years, the evening flight is still one of the premier wildlife spectacles in North America.

Fall provides another bird-watching highlight when sandhill cranes and snow geese travel in long skeins down the Rio Grande Valley to winter at the Bosque del Apache National Wildlife Refuge in New Mexico. The Great Salt Lake is one of North America's premier sites for migrating birds, including millions of ducks and grebes stopping each fall to feed before continuing south.

Mammals

The Southwest's most charismatic wildlife species were largely exterminated by the early 1900s. A combination of factors has contributed to their decline over the decades, including loss of habitat, overhunting and oil-and-gas development. First to go was the grizzly bear. After that, herds of buffalo, howling wolves and the tropical jaguars that crossed the border out of Mexico also disappeared from the region. Prairie dogs (actually small rodents) vanished with hardly a trace, even though they once numbered in the billions.

Read Marc Reisner's *Cadillac Desert: The American West and Its Disappearing Water* for a thorough account of how exploding populations in the West have utilized every drop of available water.

Like the California condor, however, some species are being reintroduced. A small group of Utah prairie dogs were successfully released in Bryce Canyon National Park in 1974. Mexican wolves were released in the midst of public controversy into the wilds of eastern Arizona in 1998.

Mule deer still roam as widely as ever, and coyote are seen and heard nearly everywhere. Small numbers of elk, pronghorn antelope and bighorn sheep dwell in their favorite habitats (forests for elk, open grasslands for pronghorns and rocky cliffs for bighorns), but it takes a lot of luck or some sharp eyes to spot them. Even fewer people will observe a mountain lion, one of the wildest and most elusive animals in North America.

Plants

Although the Southwest is largely a desert region, the presence of many large mountain ranges creates a remarkable diversity of niches for plants. One way to understand the plants of this region is to understand life zones and the ways each plant thrives in its favored zone.

At the lowest elevations, generally below 4000ft, high temperatures and lack of water create a desert zone where drought-tolerant plants such as cacti, sagebrush and agave survive. Many of these species have greatly reduced leaves to reduce water loss, or they hold water (cacti, for example) to survive long hot spells.

At mid-elevations, from 4000ft to 7000ft, conditions cool a bit and more moisture is available for woody shrubs and small trees. In much of Nevada, Utah, northern Arizona and New Mexico, piñon pines and junipers blanket vast areas of low mountain slopes and hills. Both trees are short and stout to help conserve water.

Nearly pure stands of stately, fragrant ponderosa pine are the dominant tree at 7000ft on many of the West's mountain ranges. In fact, this single tree best defines the Western landscape and many animals rely on it for food and shelter; timber companies also consider it their most profitable tree. High mountain, or boreal, forests composed of spruce, fir, quaking aspen and a few other conifers are found on the highest peaks in the Southwest. This is a land of cool, moist forests and lush meadows with brilliant wildflower displays.

> There are more than 100 species of cacti in the Southwest. The iconic saguaro can grow up to 50ft tall, and a fully hydrated giant saguaro can store more than a ton of water.

Environmental Issues

Forest Fires

Nineteen firefighters, part of the elite Granite Mountain Hotshots, were killed while battling the Yarnell Hill Fire in central Arizona in June 2013. By August 2013, more than 50 large wildfires burned across Western states, including fires in Arizona and Nevada. Evidence indicates that fires in the West are occurring more frequently and are more intense than in previous years. The reasons? Scientists are looking at three connected factors. The first is global warming, which may be contributing to the extended Western drought. Dry conditions are exacerbated when snow packs are low because there is less melting runoff for streams. Also, with higher temperatures, the evaporation of existing water sources happens more quickly. Another factor may be increased development, which leads more people to forest lands. Finally, the long-running forestry practice of fire suppression may have allowed the build-up of more underbrush, which can ignite and fuel the fire.

> Many of the Southwest's most common flowers can be found in *Canyon Country Wildflowers*, by Damian Fagan. Chapters are arranged by the color of the flowers, including white, yellow and blue.

Drought, Dams & Water Loss

Drought conditions have been persistent for the last 14 years. According to the US Drought Monitor, large sections of Arizona, New Mexico and Utah were suffering from moderate to severe drought in the spring of 2014. Severe drought conditions were present for 36% of Arizona. The 2014 National Climate Assessment, released by the White House, states that temperatures in the Southwest in the last decade have, on average, been two degrees higher than historic norms.

DESERT FLOWERS

Some of the Southwest's biggest wildlife surprises are the incredibly diverse flowers that appear each year in the region's deserts and mountains. These include desert flowers that start blooming in February, and late summer flowers that fill mountain meadows after the snow melts or pop out after summer thunderstorms wet the soil. Some of the largest and grandest flowers belong to the Southwest's 100 or so species of cacti; these flowers are one of the reasons collectors seek out cacti for gardens and homes. The claret-cup cacti is composed of small cylindrical segments that produce brilliant red flowers in profusion from all sides of their prickly stems. Even a 50ft-tall giant saguaro, standing like a massive column in the desert, has prolific displays of fragrant yellow flowers that grow high on the stem and can be reached only by bats.

GRAND CANYON DEVELOPMENT: NAVAJO DISCOVERY CENTER

A tram ride to the bottom of the Grand Canyon? It could happen if the Navajo Nation moves forward with plans to develop a 420-acre tourist destination known as Grand Canyon Escalade. The project would include a discovery center, a museum, a multimedia complex, shops, restaurants and up to 900 hotel rooms. The tram would drop 3200ft from the rim of the canyon to a scenic spot at the confluence of the Colorado and Little Colorado Rivers. The complex would be located on the East Rim between Lees Ferry and Grand Canyon National Park. At the time of writing, the bill approving the partnership agreement between the Navajo and the development company had not yet been placed on the legislative agenda of the Navajo Nation Council. If approved, and all goes according to plan, construction would begin in 2018.

As pitched by the developers, the primary benefits of the project would be 1000 to 2000 construction and tourism jobs for tribe members (there would be a Navajo hiring preference), plus an educational opportunity for travelers who want to learn more about the tribe. On the flip side, there are concerns about the negative environmental impact of the project on this remote spot. The development may also affect the Hopi Salt Trail, which leads to a sacred Hopi site at the river. The Hopi oppose the project, and some Navajo have also expressed concerns with various parts of the plan. There is also an argument that the development site is within Grand Canyon National Park's boundaries, which would give the park – and its development restrictions – the ultimate say.

What will happen? There is only one thing we can predict with certainty: lawsuits.

Need visual proof of water loss? Just look at the reservoir for Lake Mead behind the Hoover Dam. The 'bath-tub ring' – where the adjacent canyon walls have been bleached by minerals in the water – grows taller every year as the water level drops.

The construction of dam and human-made water features throughout the Southwest has radically altered the delicate balance of water that sustained life for countless millennia. Dams, for example, halt the flow of warm waters and force them to drop their rich loads of life-giving nutrients. These sediments once rebuilt floodplains, nourished myriad aquatic and riparian food chains, and sustained the life of ancient endemic fish that now flounder on the edge of extinction. In place of rich annual floods, dams now release cold waters in steady flows, favoring the introduced fish and weedy plants that have overtaken the West's rivers.

In other areas, the steady draining of aquifers to provide drinking water for cows and sprawling cities is shrinking the water table and drying up unique desert springs and wetlands that countless animals once depended on during the dry season. Cows further destroy the fragile desert crust with their heavy hooves, and also graze on native grasses and herbs that are soon replaced by introduced weeds. Development is increasingly having the largest impact, as uniquely adapted habitats are bulldozed to make room for more houses.

The region's stately pine and fir forests have largely become thickets of scrawny little trees. The cutting of trees and building of roads in these environments can further dry the soil and make it harder for young trees and native flowers to thrive. Injuries to an ecosystem in an arid environment take a very long time to heal.

A radiation leak contaminated 22 workers at the Waste Isolation Pilot Plant near Carlsbad, NM in 2014. The probable cause of the leak? A chemical reaction between organic kitty litter (used to pack 57 barrels of nuclear waste) and nitrate salts in the waste.

Nuclear Power & Nuclear Waste

Ongoing environmental controversies include the location of nuclear power plants and the transport and disposal of nuclear waste, most notably at Yucca Mountain, 90 miles from Las Vegas. A 2013 headline in the *Las Vegas Review-Journal* summed up the controversy by declaring, 'No end in sight for Yucca legal fight.'

Southwest Cuisine

Whoever advised 'moderation in all things' has clearly never enjoyed a Sonoran dog in Tucson. A Sonoran dog 'moderated' is not a Sonoran dog at all. Same goes for a messy plate of huevo rancheros at a small-town Arizona diner. Or a green-chile cheeseburger at the Owl Bar Café near Socorro, NM. Food in the Southwest is a tricultural celebration not well suited for the gastronomically timid, or anyone on a diet. One or two dainty bites? Impossible! But come on, admit it, isn't the food part of the reason you're here?

Cultural Influences

Three ethnic groups – Mexican, cattle-country Anglo and Native American – influence Southwestern food culture. Spain and Mexico controlled territories from Texas to California well into the 19th century, and when they officially packed up, they left behind their cooking style and many of their best chefs. The American pioneers who claimed these states also contributed to the Southwest style of cooking. Much of the Southwest is cattle country, and whether you are in Phoenix, Flagstaff or Las Vegas you can expect a good steak. Native American cuisine – which goes beyond fry bread – is gaining exposure as locally grown, traditional plants and seasonings are appearing on more menus across the region.

> You can't visit Albuquerque without ordering a Frito pie – a messy concoction of corn chips, beef chile, cheese and sour cream. You can find it in restaurants and it's always served at city festivals.

Staples & Specialties

Huevos rancheros is the quintessential Southwestern breakfast; eggs prepared to order are served on top of two fried corn tortillas, loaded with beans and potatoes, sprinkled with cheese and served swimming in chile. Breakfast burritos are built by stuffing a flour tortilla with eggs, bacon or chorizo, cheese, chile and sometimes beans.

A Southwestern lunch or dinner will probably start with a big bowl of corn chips and salsa. Almost everything comes with beans, rice and your choice of warm flour or corn tortillas, topped with chile, cheese and sometimes sour cream. Blue-corn tortillas are one colorful New Mexican contribution to the art of cooking. Guacamole is also a staple, and many restaurants will mix the avocado, lime, cilantro (coriander), tomato and onion creation right at your table.

Steak & Potatoes

Home, home on the range, where the ranches and the steakhouses reign. Have a hankerin' for a juicy slab of beef with a salad, baked potato and beans? Look no further than the Southwest, where there's a steakhouse for every type of traveler. In Phoenix alone choices range from the old-school Durant's (p127) to the outdoor Greasewood Flat (p129) to the family-friendly Rawhide Western Town & Steakhouse (p121). In Utah, the large Mormon population influences culinary options – good, old-fashioned American food such as chicken, steak, potatoes, vegetables, homemade pies and ice cream prevail.

Mexican & New Mexican Food

In Arizona, Mexican fare is of the Sonoran type, with specialties such as *carne seca* (dried beef). Meals are usually served with refried beans, rice, and flour or corn tortillas; chiles are relatively mild. Tucsonans refer to their city as the 'Mexican food capital of the universe,' which, although hotly contested by a few other places, carries a ring of truth. Colorado restaurants serve Mexican food, but they don't insist on any accolades for it.

New Mexico's food is different from, but reminiscent of, Mexican food. Pinto beans are served whole instead of refried; posole (a corn stew) may replace rice. Chiles aren't used so much as a condiment (like salsa) but more as an essential ingredient in almost every dish. *Carne adobada* (marinated pork chunks) is a specialty.

If a restaurant references red or green chile or chile sauces on the menu, it probably serves New Mexican–style dishes. The state is famous for its chile-enhanced Mexican standards. The town of Hatch, NM, is particularly known for its green chiles.

Mexican food is often hot and spicy, but it doesn't have to be. If you don't like spicy food, go easy on the salsa.

Eat Your Words

Carne seca – beef that is sun-dried before cooking

Fry bread – deep-fried, doughy Native American bread

Mole – spicy chocolate-flavored chile sauce

Sopaipilla – deep-fried puff pastry with honey

Native American Food

Modern Native American cuisine bears little resemblance to that eaten before the Spanish conquest, but it is distinct from Southwestern cuisine. Navajo and Indian tacos – fried bread usually topped with beans, meat, tomatoes, chile and lettuce – are readily available. Chewy *horno* bread is baked in *hornos* (beehive-shaped outdoor adobe ovens) using remnant heat from a fire built inside the oven, then cleared out before cooking.

Most other Native American cooking is game-based and usually involves squash and locally harvested ingredients such as berries and piñon nuts. Though becoming better known, it can be difficult to find, especially in Southwestern Colorado, Utah and Las Vegas. Your best bets are festival food stands, powwows, rodeos, Pueblo feast days, casino restaurants or people's homes at the different pueblos.

For Native American fare, try Albuquerque's Indian Pueblo Cultural Center (p244), the Metate Room (p368) in Southwestern Colorado, Tiwa Kitchen (p303) near Taos Pueblo, the restaurant at the View Hotel (p192) in Monument Valley, the Hopi Cultural Center Restaurant (p195) on the Hopi Reservation and Kai (p127) at Wild Horse Pass Resort in Chandler, AZ.

Fruit & Vegetables

Beyond the chile pepper, Southwestern food is characterized by its use of posole, *sopaipillas* (deep-fried puff pastry) and blue corn. Posole, Spanish for hominy, is dried or frozen kernels of corn processed in a lime solution to remove the hulls. It's served plain, along with pinto beans, as a side dish. Blue-corn tortillas have a heartier flavor than the more com-

EATING GREEN IN THE SOUTHWEST

Numerous restaurants throughout the five-state region are dedicated to serving only organic, and when possible buying local, which helps their community self-sustain. One of the most unique, ecofriendly and wholesome eating experiences in the Four Corners can be enjoyed at Hell's Backbone Grill (p427) in Boulder, UT. It takes four hours on a lonely, potholed stretch of road to reach this super-remote foodie outpost, but those who make the drive will be rewarded. The restaurant is sustainable, growing most of its bounty on its 2-acre organic farm – the vegetables are divine. Owner Jen Castle says her goal for the restaurant is to evoke a little bit of provincial France in off-the-grid Utah.

mon yellow-corn tortillas. Pinto beans, served either whole or refried, are a basic element of most New Mexican dishes.

Beans, long the staple protein of New Mexicans, come in many colors, shapes and preparations. They are usually stewed with onions, chiles and spices and served somewhat intact or refried to a creamy consistency. Avocados are a delightful staple, made into zesty guacamole. 'Guac' recipes are as closely guarded and vaunted by cooks as their bean recipes.

Contemporary Southwestern Cuisine

An eclectic mix of Mexican and Continental (especially French) traditions began to flourish in the late 1970s and continues to grow. Try innovative combinations such as chiles stuffed with lobster or barbecued-duck tacos. But don't expect any bargains here. Southwestern food is usually inexpensive, but as soon as the chef tacks on a 'contemporary' or 'nouvelle' tag, the tab soars as high as a crested butte.

Another trend is foraging locally for ingredients, as they do at the Curious Kumquat (p331) in Silver City, NM, and Coppa Cafe (p157) in Flagstaff, AZ.

Generally speaking, cities such as Phoenix, Tucson, Santa Fe and Albuquerque have the most contemporary Southwestern restaurants.

Beer, Wine & Beyond

Craft Beer & Microbreweries

Microbrewery and craft-beer production has skyrocketed in the US. There are more than 2700 microbreweries across the country and craft-beer sales accounted for 7.8% of the domestic market in 2013. The term microbrew is used broadly these days, and tends to include beer produced by large, well-established brands such as Sam Adams and Sierra Nevada. According to the Brewers Association, however, a true craft brewery must produce no more than six million barrels annually. It must also be independently owned and made with traditional ingredients.

These smaller craft breweries are popping up everywhere across the Southwest, from small towns to urban centers. They are a popular gathering spot for an after-work drink, and often a good meal. Durango, CO, is one regional hub for microbreweries, and Ska Brewery there is one of the best in the state. New breweries have also opened in Flagstaff, AZ, and you can find them easily by following the **Flagstaff-Grand Canyon Ale Trail** (www.flagstaffaletrail.com).

Popular regional beers are often sold in local grocery and liquor stores. Note that many microbrews are considered 'big beers' – meaning they have a high alcohol content.

Wine & Wineries

There are three things a good wine grape needs: lousy soil, lots of sunshine and dedicated caretakers, all of which can be found in New Mexico and Arizona. For a full rundown of New Mexico's 40-plus producers, visit the New Mexico Wine Growers Association at www.nmwine.com. La Chiripada Winery, with a shop just off Taos plaza, is our choice for regional vineyards, serving a fabulous riesling and cabernet sauvignon.

In Arizona, the best-known wine region is in the southern part of the state near Patagonia. The Verde Valley between Phoenix and Flagstaff is close on Patagonia's heels in terms of quality and publicity. Tool lead singer and Jerome resident Maynard James Keenan is actively involved in producing Arizona wines, and he owns two Arizona vineyards. The Arizona Wine Growers Association lists the state's wine producers.

The folks behind the much-lauded cookies at the Jacob Lake Inn, on the road to the Grand Canyon's North Rim, say the lemon-zucchini cookies have a passionate following (www.jacoblake.com).

Kim Jordan cofounded Fort Collins–based New Belgium Brewery with her ex-husband in 1991. Today she is the company's CEO, and New Belgium – famous for its Fat Tire beer – is the eighth-largest brewery in the country. It is regularly named one of the best work environments in the US.

SOUTHWEST CUISINE BEER, WINE & BEYOND

Margaritas

Margaritas are the alcoholic drink of choice and synonymous with the Southwest, especially in heavily Hispanic New Mexico, Arizona and Southwestern Colorado. Margaritas vary in taste depending on the quality of the ingredients used, but all are made from tequila, a citrus liquor (Grand Marnier, Triple Sec or Cointreau) and either fresh squeezed lime or premixed Sweet & Sour.

Our perfect margarita includes fresh squeezed lime (say no to the ultrasugary and high-carb packaged mix), a high-end tequila (skip the gold and go straight to silver or pure agave – we like Patron or Herrendura Silver) and Grand Marnier liquor (better than sickly-sweet Triple Sec). Ask the bartender to add a splash of orange juice if your drink is too bitter or strong.

Margaritas are either served frozen, on the rocks (over ice) or straight up. Most people order them with salt. Traditional margaritas are lime flavored, but these days the popular drink comes in a rainbow of flavors – best ordered frozen. Prickly pear margaritas, made with syrup from prickly pear cacti, are typically bright pink and easily found in Arizona.

Coffee Shops

For something nonalcoholic, you'll find shops serving delicious espresso in the bigger cities and sophisticated small towns; however in rural Arizona or Nevada you're likely to get nothing better than stale, weak diner coffee. Santa Fe, Phoenix, Durango, Truth or Consequences, Flagstaff and Tucson all have excellent coffee shops with comfortable couches for reading or studying. Basically, if the Southwestern town has a college, it will have a good coffee shop. That's a regional given.

Vegetarians & Vegans

Most metro-area eateries offer at least one veggie dish, although few are devoted solely to meatless menus. These days, fortunately, almost every larger town has a natural-food grocer. You may go wanting in smaller hinterland towns, however, where beef still rules. In that case, your best bet is to assemble a picnic from the local grocery store.

'Veggie-heads' will be happiest in New Mexico and Arizona, where they go nuts (or more specifically, go piñon). Thanks to the area's long-standing appeal for hippie types, vegetarians and vegans will have no problem finding something delicious on most menus, even at drive-throughs and tiny dives. One potential pitfall? Traditional Southwestern cuisine uses lard in beans, tamales, *sopaipillas* and flour (but not corn) tortillas, among other things. Be sure to ask – often, even the most authentic places have a pot of pintos simmering for vegetarians.

Favorite Vegetarian Eateries

Green
(Phoenix, AZ)

Lovin' Spoonfuls
(Tucson, AZ)

Macy's
(Flagstaff, AZ)

Annapurna's World Vegetarian Cafe
(Albuquerque, NM)

Veggie Delight
(Las Vegas, NV)

Sage's Cafe
(Salt Lake City, UT)

Arts & Architecture

Art has always been a major part of Southwest culture and one of the most compelling ways for its people to express their heritage and ideologies. The rich history and cultural texture of the Southwest is a fertile source of inspiration for artists, filmmakers, writers, photographers and musicians.

Literature

From the classic Western novels of Zane Grey, Louis L'Amour and Larry McMurtry to contemporary writers such as ecosavvy Barbara Kingsolver and Native American Louise Erdrich, authors imbue their work with the scenery and sensibility of the Southwest. Drawing from the mystical reality that is so infused in Latin literature, Southwestern style can sometimes be fantastical and absurdist, yet poignantly astute.

DH Lawrence moved to Taos in the 1920s for health reasons, and went on to write the essay 'Indians and Englishmen' and the novel *St Mawr*. Through his association with artists like Georgia O'Keeffe, he found some of the freedoms from puritanical society that he'd long sought.

Tony Hillerman, an enormously popular author from Albuquerque, wrote *Skinwalkers, People of Darkness, Skeleton Man* and *The Sinister Pig*. His award-winning mystery novels take place on the Navajo, Hopi and Zuni reservations.

Hunter S Thompson, who committed suicide in 2005, wrote *Fear and Loathing in Las Vegas,* set in the temple of American excess in the desert; it's the ultimate road-trip novel, in every sense of the word.

Edward Abbey, a curmudgeonly ecowarrior who loved the Southwest, created the thought-provoking and seminal works *Desert Solitaire* and *The Journey Home: Some Words in Defense of the American West*. His classic *Monkey Wrench Gang* is a fictional and comical account of real people who plan to blow up Glen Canyon Dam before it floods Glen Canyon.

John Nichols wrote *The Milagro Beanfield War,* part of his New Mexico trilogy. It's a tale of a Western town's struggle to take back its fate from the Anglo land barons and developers. Robert Redford's movie of the novel was filmed in Truchas, NM.

Barbara Kingsolver lived for a decade in Tucson before publishing *The Bean Trees* in 1988. Echoing her own life, it's about a young woman from rural Kentucky who moves to Tucson. Her 1990 novel, *Animal Dreams,* gives wonderful insights into the lives of people from a small Hispanic village near the Arizona–New Mexico border and from an Indian Pueblo.

For chick lit that gives you a feel for the land, adventures and people of the Southwest, read Pam Houston's books. Her collection *Cowboys Are My Weakness* is filled with funny, sometimes sad, stories about love in the great outdoors.

The National Cowboy Poetry Gathering – the bronco of cowboy poetry events – is held in January in Elko, NV. Ropers and wranglers have waxed lyrical here for more than 30 years (www.western-folklife.org).

Cinema & Television

The movie business is enjoying a renaissance in the Southwest, with New Mexico as the star player. Former governor Bill Richardson (2002–10) wooed Hollywood producers and their production teams to the state with a 25% tax rebate on production expenditures. His efforts helped inject more than $3 billion into the economy. On television, the critically acclaimed American TV series *Breaking Bad* (2008–13) was set and filmed in and around Albuquerque. Its spin-off, *Better Call Saul,* also shot in Albuquerque, is set to premiere in the fall of 2014. Joel and Ethan Coen shot the 2007 Oscar winner *No Country for Old Men* almost entirely around Las Vegas, NM (doubling for 1980s west Texas). The Coen brothers returned in 2010 to film their remake of *True Grit,* basing their production headquarters in Santa Fe and shooting on several New Mexico ranches.

Las Vegas, NV, had a starring role in 2009's blockbuster comedy *The Hangover,* an R-rated buddy film that earned more than $467 million worldwide. Visitors line up regularly to try to catch a glimpse of Chumlee and other cast members in *Pawn Stars,* a History Channel reality show set in Gold & Silver Pawn in Las Vegas.

A few places have doubled as film and TV sets so often that they have come to define the American West. In addition to Utah's Monument Valley, popular destinations include Moab, for *Thelma and Louise* (1991), Dead Horse Point State Park, also in Utah, for *Mission Impossible: 2* (2000), Lake Powell, AZ, for *Planet of the Apes* (1968) and Tombstone for the eponymous *Tombstone* (1993). Scenes in *127 Hours* (2010), about Aron Ralston's harrowing experience trapped in Blue John Canyon in Utah's Canyonlands National Park, were shot in and around the canyon.

The region also specializes in specific location shots. Snippets of *Casablanca* (1942) were actually filmed in Flagstaff's Hotel Monte Vista, *Butch Cassidy and the Sundance Kid* (1969) was shot at the Utah ghost town of Grafton and *City Slickers* (1991) was set at Ghost Ranch in Abiquiú, NM.

> In Albuquerque, *Breaking Bad* fans can visit Twisters (4257 Isleta Blvd), which doubles as Gus Fring's Los Pollos Hermanos. Rebel Donut (www.rebeldonut.com; 400 Gold Ave) sells a Blue Sky doughnut with blue sugar crystals – a nod to Walter White's Blue Meth.

Music

The larger cities of the Southwest are the best options for classical music. Choose among Phoenix's Symphony Hall, which houses the Arizona Opera and the Phoenix Symphony Orchestra, the famed Santa Fe Opera, the New Mexico Symphony Orchestra in Albuquerque and the Arizona Opera Company in Tucson and Phoenix.

Nearly every major town attracts country, bluegrass and rock groups. A notable major venue is Flagstaff's Museum Club (p158), with a lively roster of talent. Surprisingly, Provo, UT, has a thriving indie-rock scene, which offers a stark contrast to the Osmond-family image that Utah often conjures. A fabulous festival offering is Colorado's Telluride Bluegrass Festival.

Las Vegas is a mecca for entertainers of every stripe; current headliners include popular icons such as Celine Dion and Shania Twain, but for a little gritty goodness head to the Joint (p85) at Hard Rock Hotel & Casino.

Try to catch a mariachi ensemble (they're typically dressed in ornately sequined, body-hugging costumes) at southern **New Mexico's International Mariachi Conference** (www.lascrucesmariachi.org).

> **Top Places for Art & Culture**
>
> ·············
> Phoenix, AZ
> ·············
> Santa Fe, NM
> ·············
> Taos, NM
> ·············
> Indian Pueblo Cultural Center, Albuquerque, NM
> ·············
> Salt Lake City, UT

Architecture

Not surprisingly, architecture has three major cultural regional influences in the Southwest. First and foremost are the ruins of the Ancestral Puebloans – most majestically their cliff communities – and Taos Pueblo. These traditional designs and examples are echoed in the Pueblo Revival style of Santa Fe's New Mexico Museum of Art and are speckled across the city and the region today. The most traditional structures are adobe – mud mixed with straw, formed into bricks, mortared with mud and smoothed with another layer of mud. This style dominates many New Mexico cityscapes and landscapes.

The mission-style architecture of the 17th and 18th centuries, visible in religious and municipal buildings such as Santa Fe's State Capitol, is also

EARTHSHIP ARCHITECTURE

The eye-catching Earthships, located about 2 miles west of the Rio Grande outside Taos, NM, is the world's premier sustainable, self-sufficient community. Its environmentally friendly architectural form, pioneered in northern New Mexico, consists of auto tires packed with earth, stacked with rebar and turned into livable dwellings (http://earthship. org). The community looks like Mos Eisley Spaceport from *Star Wars*.

The brainchild of architect Mike Reynolds, Earthships are a form of biotecture (biology plus architecture: buildings based on biological systems of resource use and conservation) that maximizes available resources so you'll never have to be on the grid again.

Walls made of old tires are laid out for appropriate passive solar use, packed with tamped earth, and then buried on three sides for maximum insulation. The structures are outfitted with photovoltaic cells and an elaborate gray-water system that collects rain and snow, which filters through several cycles that begin in the kitchen and end in the garden.

Though the Southwest is their home, Earthships have landed in Japan, Bolivia, Scotland, Mexico and beyond, and are often organized into communities.

regularly seen. It is characterized by red-tile roofs, ironwork and stucco walls. The domed roof and intricate designs of Arizona's Mission San Xavier del Bac embody the Spanish Colonial style.

The third influence was 1800s Anglo settlers, who brought many new building techniques and developed Territorial-style architecture, which often includes porches, wood-trimmed doorways and other Victorian influences.

Master architect Frank Lloyd Wright was also a presence in the Southwest, most specifically at Taliesin West in Scottsdale, AZ. More recently, architectural monuments along Route 66 include kitschy motels lit by neon signs that have forever transformed the concept of an American road trip.

Painting, Sculpture & Visual Arts

The region's most famous artist is Georgia O'Keeffe (1887–1986), whose Southwestern landscapes are seen in museums throughout the world. The minimalist paintings of Agnes Martin (1912–2004) began to be suffused with light after she moved to New Mexico. Also highly regarded is Navajo artist RC Gorman (1932–2005), known for sculptures and paintings of Navajo women. Gorman lived in Taos for many years.

Both Taos and Santa Fe, NM, have large and active artist communities considered seminal to the development of Southwestern art. Santa Fe is a particularly good stop for those looking to browse and buy art and native crafts. More than 100 galleries and boutiques line the city's Canyon Rd, and Native American vendors sell high-quality jewelry and crafts beside the plaza.

The vast landscapes of the region have long appealed to large-format black-and-white photographers such as Ansel Adams, whose archives are housed at the Center for Creative Photography (p208) at the University of Arizona.

For something different, pop into art galleries and museums in Las Vegas, specifically the Bellagio, which partners with museums and foundations around the world for knock-out exhibitions, and the new City Center, which hosts art by internationally renowned artists like Jenny Holzer, Maya Lin and Claes Oldenburg.

Acoma Pueblo's 40,000-sq-ft Sky City Cultural Center and Haak'u Museum showcases vibrant tribal culture ongoing since the 12th century.

Jewelry & Crafts

Hispanic and Native American aesthetic influences are evident in the region's pottery, paintings, weavings, jewelry, sculpture, woodcarving and leatherworking. Excellent examples of Southwestern Native American

NAMPEYO

Hopi cultural expression as we think of it today owes much to a woman named Nampeyo. Born on First Mesa in 1859 or 1860 to a Hopi father and Tewa mother, she learned how to work clay from her paternal grandmother. Nampeyo was a natural; as a young woman she earned the reputation as a master and was known for her inspired designs. Influenced by the patterns on shards of ancient pots that her husband brought to her from the ruins at Sikyatki, where he was helping with an archaeological dig, Nampeyo created a style that blended past motifs with her own artistic instincts.

At the time, pottery was a dying craft, as contact with traders enabled the Hopi to buy premade goods. But as Nampeyo's work began to fetch high prices and draw worldwide attention, a renaissance of Hopi arts was sparked, not only in pottery, but also in silver, woodcarving and textiles. Thanks to her influence, the tradition more than lives on – it has been taken to higher levels of artistry than at any time in the tribe's past.

art are displayed in many museums, most notably in Phoenix's Heard Museum (p114) and Santa Fe's Museum of Contemporary Native Arts (p259). Contemporary and traditional Native American art is readily available in hundreds of galleries.

Kitsch & Folk Art

The Southwest is a repository for kitsch and folk art. In addition to the predictable Native American knockoffs and beaded everything (perhaps made anywhere but there), you'll find invariable UFO humor in Roswell and unexpected atomic-age souvenirs at Los Alamos, both in New Mexico. Pick up an Atomic City T-shirt, emblazoned with a red and yellow exploding bomb, or a bottle of La Bomba wine. If you need a shot glass – Route 66 has you covered.

More serious cultural artifacts fill the Museum of International Folk Art (p261) in Santa Fe.

Dance & Theater

Native Americans have a long tradition of performing sacred dances throughout the year. Ceremonial or ritual religious dances are spiritual, reverential community occasions, and many are closed to the public. When these ceremonies are open to the public, some tribes (such as the Zuni) require visitors to attend an orientation; always contact the tribes to confirm arrangements.

The Hotel Monte Vista in Flagstaff, AZ, has hosted numerous famous guests since opening in 1927. Some recognizable names include Humphrey Bogart, Gary Cooper, John Wayne, Jane Russell and Michael Stipe.

Social dances are typically cultural, as opposed to religious, events. They are much more relaxed and often open to the public. They occur during powwows, festivals, rodeos and other times, both on and off the reservation. Intertribal dance competitions (the lively 'powwow trail') are quite popular; the dancing may tell a story or be just for fun, to celebrate a tribe or clan gathering. The public may even be invited to join the dance.

Native Americans also perform dances strictly for the public as theater or art. Though these may lack community flavor, they are authentic and wonderful.

Classical dance options include Ballet West in Salt Lake City and Ballet Arizona in Phoenix. Dance and theater productions are flashy and elaborate in Las Vegas, where they have always been a staple of the city's entertainment platform. In Utah, Park City's George S and Dolores Doré Eccles Center for the Performing Arts hosts varied events.

Survival Guide

Directory A–Z

Accommodations

From bare bones to luxurious to truly offbeat, the Southwest offers a vast array of lodging options. Cookie-cutter chains line the interstates, providing a nice safety net for the less adventurous, but it's the indie-owned places that really shine. Where else but the Southwest can you sleep in a concrete wigwam or a cavern 21 stories underground? For road-trippers, the most comfortable accommodations for the lowest price are usually found in mom-and-pop roadside motels.

Parking icon P Only used in the biggest cities.

Internet icon @Used where a place has computers available for public use or where an innkeeper is OK with people briefly using their personal computer.

Wi-fi icon 🛜 Look for this if you're carrying a laptop.

Family-friendly icons 👪 Child-friendly hotels have their own icon, as do pet-friendly lodgings (🐾).

Top icon ★ Indicates those accommodations that truly stand out.

High season varies depending on the region. In general, the peak travel season is June through August, except in the hottest parts of southern Arizona, when some places slash their prices in half because it's too hot. Mid-December to mid-April is the high season in southern Arizona and for the ski areas of northern Utah – when the snow is best. The ski season varies slightly across the Southwest depending on the location of the ski resort.

Lodging rates increase in resort areas and many parks during holidays. Hotels in larger cities may book up during big conferences and special events. When demand peaks, and during special events no matter the time of year, book rooms well in advance.

If you show up at a hotel or motel without a reservation, always ask if they'll consider a lower rate than what they first quote you. If they're not full, they'll likely knock off a few dollars.

Note cancellation policies when booking. Many accommodations will charge a cancellation fee, or the amount of your first night's stay (in some cases the full stay), if you cancel after the stated date.

Some resorts and B&Bs have age restrictions. If you're traveling with children, inquire before making reservations.

B&Bs & Inns

B&Bs are a good choice for travelers looking for more personal attention and a friendly home base for regional exploration, but they may not work as well for longer stays, especially if you want to cook your own meals.

SLEEPING PRICE RANGES

Accommodations listings are grouped by price then ordered by preference. Rates are based on standard double-occupancy in high season:

$ less than $100

$$ $100 to $200

$$$ more than $200

Unless otherwise noted, breakfast is not included, bathrooms are private and lodging is open year-round. Rates generally don't include taxes, which vary considerably between towns and states. Most places are nonsmoking although some national chains and local budget motels may offer smoking rooms. Ask beforehand; many places charge a hefty fee for smoking in a nonsmoking room.

→ In smaller towns, simple guesthouses may charge $80 to $130 a night for rooms with a shared bathroom, breakfast included.

→ Fancier B&Bs have more charming features, such as kiva fireplaces, courtyards or lounge areas. They typically charge $125 to $195 per night with a private bathroom, although could cost more than $250 per night.

→ Most B&Bs have fewer than 10 rooms, and many don't allow pets or young children.

→ Many B&Bs require a two-night stay on weekends.

Camping

DISPERSED CAMPING

Free dispersed camping (independent camping at non-established sites) is permitted in many backcountry areas including national forests and Bureau of Land Management (BLM) lands, and less often in national and state parks.

Dispersed camping can be particularly helpful in the summer when every motel within 50 miles of the Grand Canyon is full. Try Kaibab National Forest beside the southern and northern boundaries of the national park. Stake your spot among the ponderosas, taking care not to camp within a quarter-mile of any watering hole or within a mile of any developed campgrounds or administrative or recreational sites.

For the latest information about how far you're allowed to drive from the nearest road to pitch camp, see the Travel Management Rule updates for Kaibab National Forest at www.fs.fed.us or check with the appropriate ranger station. Rules may vary by district (Williams, Tusayan, North Kaibab).

CAMPGROUNDS & CAMPSITES

→ The more developed areas (especially national parks) usually require reservations

BOOK YOUR STAY ONLINE

For more accommodation reviews by Lonely Planet authors, check out hotels.lonelyplanet.com. You'll find independent reviews, as well as recommendations on the best places to stay. Best of all, you can book online.

in advance. To reserve a campsite on federal lands, book through Recreation.gov.

→ Many state parks and federal lands allow camping, sometimes free, on a first-come, first-served basis.

→ Developed camping areas usually have toilets, water spouts, fire pits, picnic tables and even wireless internet.

→ Some sites don't have access to drinking water. It is always a good idea to have a few gallons of water in your vehicle when you're out on the road.

→ Some camping areas are open year-round, while others are open only from May through to the first snowfall – check in advance if you're planning to slumber outdoors in winter.

→ Basic tenting usually costs $12 to $25 a night and cabins and tipis are sometimes available.

→ More developed campgrounds may be geared to recreational vehicle travel and cost $25 to $45 a night.

→ **Kampgrounds of America** (KOA; www.koa. com) is a national network of private campgrounds with tent sites averaging $30 to $34 per night plus taxes.

Hostels

Staying in a private double at a hostel is a great way to save money and still have privacy (although you'll usually have to share a bathroom), while a dorm bed allows those in search of the ultimate bargain to sleep cheap under a roof.

→ Dorms cost between $20 and $28, depending on the city and whether or not you are a Hostelling International (HI) member.

→ A private room in a Southwestern hostel costs between $25 and $68.

→ Most hostels in the Southwest are run independently and are not part of **Hostelling International USA** (☏240-650-2100; www.hiusa.org). They often have private or single rooms, sometimes with their own bathrooms. Kitchen, laundry, notice board and TV facilities are typically available.

→ **Hostels.com** (www.hostels. com) lists hostels throughout the world.

Hotels

→ Prices vary tremendously from season to season.

→ Rates don't include state and local occupancy taxes, which can be as high as 13% combined.

→ During high season and special events, prices may rise, but you never know when a convention may take over several hundred rooms and make beds hard to find – and raise prices.

→ Members of the American Association of Retired Persons (AARP) and the American Automobile Association (AAA) often qualify for discounts.

Lodges

→ Normally situated within national parks, lodges are often rustic looking but are usually quite comfy inside. Basic rooms and cabins generally start at $100 but increase as the view and decor improves.

→ Lodges often represent the only noncamping option inside a park, so many are fully booked well in advance.

➡ If you need a room today, call as you might be lucky and hit on a cancellation.

➡ In addition to on-site restaurants, they also offer touring services.

Motels

Budget motels are prevalent throughout the Southwest. In smaller towns, they will often be your only option. Many motels have at-the-door parking, with exterior room doors. These are convenient, though some folks, especially single women, may prefer the more expensive places with safer interior corridors.

Prices advertised by motels are called rack rates and are not written in stone. You may find rates as low as $35, but expect most to fall into the $50 to $75 range; that price range is your best bet if you are expecting a certain basic level of quality, safety and cleanliness. Children are often allowed to stay free with their parents.

Resorts & Guest Ranches

Luxury resorts and guest ranches (often called 'dude ranches') really require a stay of several days to be appreciated and are often destinations in themselves. Start the day with a round of golf or a tennis match, then luxuriate with a massage, swimming, sunbathing and drinking. Many resorts charge a daily resort fee, sometimes as high as $25. Check the fine print when booking to avoid surprises.

Guest ranches can be like whole vacations, with active schedules of horseback riding, cattle roundups, rodeo lessons, cookouts or other Western activities. When planning, be aware that ranches in the desert lowlands may close in summer, while those in the mountains may close in winter or convert into skiing centers. The website of the **Arizona Dude Ranch Association** (www.azdra.com) has a helpful dude-ranch comparison chart for the Grand Canyon State.

Discount Cards

From printable internet coupons to coupons found in tourist magazines, there are price reductions aplenty. For lodging, pick up one of the coupon books stacked outside highway visitor centers. These typically offer some of the cheapest rates out there.

Senior Cards

Travelers aged 50 and older can receive rate cuts and benefits at many places. Inquire about discounts at hotels, museums and restaurants before you make your reservation. US citizens aged 62 and older are eligible for the **Senior Pass** (http://store. usgs.gov/pass; $10), which allows lifetime entry into all national parks and discounts on some services (Golden Age Passports are still valid).

A good resource for travel bargains is the **American Association of Retired Persons** (AARP; ☎888-687-2277; www.aarp.org), an advocacy group for Americans aged 50 years and older.

Electricity

120V/60Hz

Food

Many Utah restaurants are closed on Sunday; when you find one open (even if it's not your first choice), consider yourself among the fortunate.

See the Southwest Cuisine chapter for more information (p535).

Gay & Lesbian Travelers

The most visible gay communities are in major cities. Utah and southern Arizona are typically not as freewheeling as San Francisco. Gay travelers should be careful in predominantly rural areas – simply holding hands might get you assaulted.

The most active gay community in the Southwest is in Phoenix. Santa Fe and Albuquerque have active gay communities, and Las Vegas has an active gay scene. Conservative Utah has almost no visible gay life outside Salt Lake City.

Damron (www.damron.com) Publishes classic gay travel guides.

Gay Yellow Network (www. glyp.com) Has listings for numerous US cities including Phoenix.

National Gay & Lesbian Task Force (☎Washington, DC 202-393-5177; www. thetaskforce.org) The website of this national activist group covers news and politics.

OutTraveler (www.outtraveler.com) This website shares news, tips and in-depth stories about gay travel for destinations around the world.

Purple Roofs (www.purpleroofs.com) Lists gay-owned and gay-friendly B&Bs and hotels.

Health

Altitude Sickness

Visitors from lower elevations undergo rather dramatic physiological changes as they adapt to high altitudes. Symptoms, which tend to manifest during the first day after reaching altitude, may include headache, fatigue, loss of appetite, nausea, sleeplessness, increased urination and hyperventilation due to overexertion. Symptoms normally resolve within 24 to 48 hours. The rule of thumb is, don't ascend until the symptoms descend. More severe cases may display extreme disorientation, ataxia (loss of coordination and balance), breathing problems (especially a persistent cough) and vomiting. People afflicted should descend immediately and get to a hospital.

To avoid the discomfort characterizing the milder symptoms, drink plenty of water and take it easy – at 7000ft, a pleasant walk around Santa Fe can wear you out faster than a steep hike at sea level.

Dehydration

Visitors to the desert may not realize how much water they're losing, as sweat evaporates almost immediately and increased urination (to help the blood process oxygen more efficiently) can go unnoticed. Drink more water than usual – think a gallon (about 4L) a day if you're active. Parents can carry fruit and fruit juices to help keep kids hydrated.

Severe dehydration can easily cause disorientation and confusion, and even day hikers have become lost and then died because they ignored their thirst. So bring plenty of water, even on short hikes, and drink it!

Heat Exhaustion & Heatstroke

Dehydration or salt deficiency can cause heat exhaustion. Take time to acclimatize to high temperatures and make sure you get enough liquids. Salt deficiency is characterized by fatigue, lethargy, head-

aches, giddiness and muscle cramps. Salt tablets may help. Vomiting or diarrhea can also deplete your liquid and salt levels. Anhydrotic heat exhaustion, caused by the inability to sweat, is quite rare. Unlike other forms of heat exhaustion, it may strike people who have been in a hot climate for some time, rather than newcomers. Always use water bottles on long trips. One gallon of water per person per day is recommended if hiking.

Long, continuous exposure to high temperatures can lead to the sometimes-fatal condition heatstroke, which occurs when the body's heat-regulating mechanism breaks down and the body temperature rises to dangerous levels. Hospitalization is essential for extreme cases, but meanwhile get out of the sun, remove clothing, cover the body with a wet sheet or towel and fan continually.

Insurance

It's expensive to get sick, crash a car or have things stolen from you in the US. When it comes to health care, the US has some of the finest in the world. The problem? Unless you have good insurance, it can be prohibitively expensive. It's essential to purchase travel health insurance if your regular policy doesn't cover you when you're abroad. At a minimum you need coverage for medical emergencies and treatment, including hospital

stays and an emergency flight home if necessary.

If your health insurance does not cover you for medical expenses abroad, consider supplemental insurance. Find out in advance if your insurance plan will make payments directly to providers or reimburse you later for overseas health expenditures.

Consult your homeowner's (or renter's) insurance policy before leaving home to confirm whether or not you are insured for theft of items in your car while traveling. You might need liability insurance if driving a rental car, in case of a collision. For more details see (p557).

Worldwide travel insurance is available at www.lonelyplanet.com/travel_services. You can buy, extend and claim online anytime – even if you're already on the road.

International Visitors

US entry requirements continue to change as the country fine-tunes its national security guidelines. All travelers should double check current visa and passport regulations well before coming to the USA.

Entering the Country

Getting into the US can be complicated and the entry requirements continue to evolve. Plan ahead. For up-to-date information about visas and immigration, start with the **US State Department** (☎main switchboard 202-647-4000; www.travel.state.gov).

➡ Apart from most Canadian citizens and those entering under the Visa Waiver Program (VWP), all foreign visitors to the US need a visa. Pursuant to VWP requirements, citizens of certain countries may enter the US for stays of 90 days or fewer without a US visa. This list is subject to continual reexamination and bureaucratic rejigging. Check http://travel.state.gov/content/visas/english/visit/visa-waiver-program.html to see which countries are included under the waiver and for a summary of current VWP requirements.

➡ If you're a citizen of a VWP country you do not need a visa *only if* you have a passport that meets current US standards *and* you get approval from the Electronic System for Travel Authorization (ESTA) in advance. Register online with the Department of Homeland Security at https://esta.cbp.dhs.gov at least 72 hours before arrival. The fee is $14.

Canadians are currently exempt from ESTA.

➡ Visitors from VWP countries must still present at the port of entry all the same evidence as for a nonimmigrant visa application. They must demonstrate that their trip is for 90 days or fewer and that they have a round-trip or onward ticket, adequate funds to cover the trip and binding obligations abroad.

➡ Every foreign visitor entering the USA from abroad needs a passport. In most cases, your passport must be valid for at least another six months after you are due to leave the USA. If your passport doesn't meet current US standards you'll be turned back at the border. If your passport was issued on or after October 26, 2006 it must be an e-passport with a digital photo and an integrated chip containing biometric data.

➡ For step-by-step assistance check out the Visa Wizard on the State Department website (www.travel.state.gov/content/visas/english/general/visa-wizard.html).

Internet Access

➡ Public libraries in most cities and towns offer free internet access, either at computer terminals or through a wireless connection, usually for 15 minutes to an hour (a few may charge a small fee). In some cases you may need to obtain a guest pass or register.

➡ If you can bring your laptop do so, as most places that serve coffee also offer free wi-fi as long as you order a drink. Several national companies – McDonald's, Panera Bread, Barnes & Noble – now provide free wi-fi.

➡ Computers with internet access can be found in small business centers in many chain hotels.

SOUTHWEST WITH PETS

When it comes to pet-friendly travel destinations, the Southwest is one of the best. More and more hotels accept pets these days, although some charge extra per night, others make you leave a deposit and still others have weight restrictions – less than 35lb is usually the standard. To not get hit with an extra $50 in dog-room fees, call the hotel in advance. One of the most unique pet-friendly options in the Southwest is in Santa Fe: head to the swank **Ten Thousand Waves Japanese Resort & Spa** (☑505-982-9304; www.tenthousandwaves.com; 3451 Hyde Park Rd; r from $239; 🅿✳🛜📶🐾).

At national parks, check first before you let your pet off the leash – many forests and park lands have restrictions on dogs. If you're planning a long day in the car, vets recommend stopping at least every two hours to let your dog pee, stretch their legs and have a long drink of water. If your dog gets nervous or nauseated in the car, it is safe and effective to give her Benadryl (or its generic equivalent) to calm her down. The vet-recommended dosage is 1mg per pound.

When stopping to eat during a downtown stroll, don't immediately tie your dog up outside the restaurant. Instead ask about the local laws.

The following websites have helpful pet-travel tips:

Humane Society (www.humanesociety.org/animals/resources/tips/traveling_tips_pets_ships_planes_trains.html) Provides safety information for traveling with your pet by car and airplane.

Best Friends Animal Society (www.bestfriends.org) Has a wealth of general info. If you're volunteering there – working with adoptable dogs, rational horse training, etc – you may be able to bring one of the dogs to your Kanab hotel, and many hotels approve.

→ Airports and campgrounds often offer laptop owners the chance to get online for free or a small fee.

→ You're likely to be charged for wi-fi use in nice hotels and resorts – some places charge up to $13 per day or bundle it into an expensive resort fee.

→ Check www.wififreespot.com for a list of free wi-fi hot spots nationwide.

Legal Matters

→ If you are arrested for a serious offense in the US, you are allowed to remain silent, are entitled to have an attorney present during any interrogation and are presumed innocent until proven guilty.

→ You have the right to an attorney from the very first moment you are arrested. If you can't afford one, the state must provide one for free.

→ All persons who are arrested are legally allowed to make one phone call. If you don't have a lawyer or family member to help you, call your embassy or consulate.

→ If you are stopped by the police for everyday matters, there is no system of paying fines on the spot. The officer should explain to you how the fine can be paid, and many matters can be handled by mail or online.

→ Stiff fines, jail time and penalties can be incurred if you are caught driving under the influence of alcohol or providing alcohol to minors.

Money

Most locals do not carry large amounts of cash for everyday transactions, and rely instead on credit cards, ATMs and debit cards. Small businesses may refuse to accept bills larger than $20. Prices

in this book exclude taxes, unless otherwise noted.

ATMs & Cash

→ ATMs are great for quick cash influxes and can negate the need for traveler's checks entirely. Watch out for ATM surcharges as they may charge $2 to $3 per withdrawal. Some ATMs in Vegas may charge more.

→ The Cirrus and Plus systems both have extensive ATM networks that will give cash advances on major credit cards and allow cash withdrawals with affiliated ATM cards.

→ Look for ATMs outside banks and in large grocery stores, shopping centers, convenience stores and gas stations.

→ To avoid possible account-draining scams at self-serve gas stations, consider paying with cash instead of using your debit card at the pump.

Credit Cards

Major credit cards are widely accepted throughout the Southwest, including at car-rental agencies and most hotels, restaurants, gas stations, grocery stores and tour operators. It's highly recommended that you carry at least one card.

Currency Exchange

→ Banks are usually the best places to exchange currency. Most large city banks offer currency exchange, but banks in rural areas do not.

→ Currency-exchange counters at the airports and in tourist centers typically have the worst rates; ask about fees and surcharges first.

→ **Travelex** (☎877-414-6359; www.travelex.com) is a major currency-exchange company.

→ See p22 for exchange rates.

See p22 for exchange rates.

TIPPING

Airport & hotel porters	$2 per bag, minimum $5 per cart
Bartenders	10-15% per round, minimum per drink $1
Housekeeping	$2-4 per night, left under card provided
Restaurant servers	15-20%, unless gratuity is included in the bill
Taxi drivers	10-15%, rounded up to the next dollar
Valet parking	minimum $2 when keys handed back

National & State Parks

National Parks

Before visiting any national park, check out its website, using the search tool on the National Park Service (NPS) home page (www.nps.gov). On the Grand Canyon's website (www.nps.gov/grca), you can download the seasonal newspaper, the *Guide*, for the latest information on prices, hours and ranger talks. There is a separate edition for both the North and South Rims.

→ At the entrance of a national or state park, be ready to hand over cash (credit cards may not always be accepted). Costs range from nothing at all to $25 per vehicle for a seven-day pass.

→ If you're visiting several parks in the Southwest, you may save money by purchasing the **America the Beautiful** (http://store.usgs.gov/pass; $80) annual pass. It admits all passengers in a vehicle (or four adults at per-person fee areas) to all national parks and federal recreational lands for one

TIPS FOR SHUTTERBUGS

➜ Morning and evening are the best times to shoot. The same sandstone bluff can turn four or five different hues throughout the day, and the warmest hues will be at sunset. Underexposing the shot slightly (by a half-stop or more) can bring out richer details in red tones.

➜ When shooting red rocks, a warming filter added to an SLR lens can enhance the colors of the rocks and reduce the blues of overcast or flat-light days. Achieve the same effect on any digital camera by adjusting the white balance to the automatic 'cloudy' setting (or by reducing the color temperature).

➜ Don't shoot into the sun or include it in the frame; shoot what the sunlight is hitting. On bright days, move your subjects into shade for close-up portraits.

➜ A zoom lens is extremely useful; most SLR cameras have one. Use it to isolate the central subject of your photos. A common composition mistake is to include too much landscape around the person or feature that's your main focus.

➜ For more tips, check out Lonely Planet's *Travel Photography* book.

year. With the pass, children under 16 are admitted free.

➜ US citizens and permanent residents aged 62 and older are eligible for a lifetime Senior Pass.

➜ US citizens and permanent residents with a permanent disability may qualify for a free Access Pass.

➜ Check the park's website for notices about Fee-Free Days, when no admission is charged.

State Parks

Some state parks in Arizona operate on a five-day schedule, closed Tuesdays and Wednesdays. Before visiting an Arizona state park, check its website to confirm opening times.

Opening Hours

Generally speaking, business hours are from 10am to 6pm. In large cities, a few supermarkets and restaurants open 24 hours. In Utah many restaurants are closed on Sunday. The following are normal opening hours:

Banks 8:30am to 4:30pm Monday to Thursday, to 5:30pm Friday; some open 9am to 12:30pm Saturday

Bars 5pm to midnight Sunday to Thursday, to 2am Friday and Saturday

Government offices 9am to 5pm Monday to Friday

Post offices 9am to 5pm Monday to Friday, some open 9am to noon Saturday

Restaurants Breakfast 7am to 10:30am Monday to Friday; brunch 9am to 2pm Saturday and Sunday; lunch 11:30am to 2:30pm Monday to Friday; dinner 5pm to 9:30pm Sunday to Thursday, later Friday and Saturday. In larger cities and resort towns many restaurants serve at least a limited menu from open to close; in Vegas restaurants can stay open 24 hours.

Shops 10am to 6pm Monday to Saturday, noon to 5pm Sunday. Shopping malls may keep extended hours.

Photography

Print film can be found in drugstores and at specialty camera shops. Digital-camera memory cards are available at chain retailers such as Best Buy and Target.

Some Native American reservations prohibit photography and video recording completely; when it's allowed you may be required to purchase a permit. Always ask permission to photograph someone close-up; anyone who agrees may expect a small tip.

Post

➜ The **US Postal Service** (USPS; ☎800-275-8777; www.usps.gov) provides great service for the price. For 1st-class mail sent and delivered within the US, postage rates are 49¢ for letters up to 1oz (21¢ for each additional ounce) and 34¢ for standard-size postcards.

➜ If you have the correct postage, drop your mail into any blue mailbox. To send a package weighing 13oz or more, go to a post office.

➜ International airmail rates are $1.15 for a 1oz letter or postcard.

➜ Call private shippers such as **United Parcel Service** (UPS; ☎800-742-5877; www.ups.com) and **Federal Express** (FedEx; ☎800-463-3339; www.fedex.com) to send more important or larger items.

Public Holidays

New Year's Day January 1

Martin Luther King Jr Day 3rd Monday of January

Presidents Day 3rd Monday of February

Easter March or April

Memorial Day Last Monday of May

Independence Day July 4

Labor Day 1st Monday of September

Columbus Day 2nd Monday of October

Veterans Day November 11

Thanksgiving 4th Thursday of November

Christmas Day December 25

Safe Travel

Southwestern cities generally have lower levels of violent crime than larger cities like New York, Los Angeles and Washington, DC. Nevertheless, violent crime is certainly present.

When exploring the outdoors, travelers should keep an eye out for wildlife, which may not want to be disturbed. Also keep in mind that weather conditions throughout the Southwest can quickly change from fair to foul.

Take the following precautions:

➡ Lock your car doors and don't leave any valuables visible. Smash-and-grab thefts can be a problem at trailhead parking lots.

➡ Avoid walking alone on empty streets or in parks at night.

➡ Avoid being in the open, especially on canyon rims or hilltops, during lightning storms.

➡ Avoid riverbeds and canyons when storm clouds gather in the distance; flash floods are deadly.

➡ When dust storms brew, pull off to the side of the road, turn off your lights and wait it out. They don't usually last long.

➡ Drivers should watch for livestock on highways and on Native American reservations and areas marked 'Open Rangelands.'

➡ When camping where bears are present, place your food inside a food box (one is often provided by the campground).

➡ Watch where you step when you hike – particularly on hot summer afternoons and evenings, when rattlesnakes like to bask on the trail.

➡ Scorpions spend their days under rocks and woodpiles; use caution.

Telephone

➡ Always dial ☏1 before toll-free (☏800, ☏888 etc) and domestic long-distance numbers.

➡ Some toll-free numbers may only work within the region or from the US mainland. But you'll only know if it works by making the call.

➡ All phone numbers in the US consist of a three-digit area code followed by a seven-digit local number.

➡ All five Southwestern states require you to dial the full 10-digit number for all phone calls because each state has more than one area code. You will not be charged for long-distance fees when dialing locally.

➡ When calling a cell phone anywhere in the USA you need to always dial the 10-digit number; however, you do not need to dial the country code (☏1) when calling from within the United States.

➡ Pay phones aren't as readily found now that cell phones are more prevalent. But keep your eyes peeled and you'll find them. If you don't have change, you can use a calling card.

➡ To make international calls direct, dial ☏011 + country code + area code + number. An exception is to Canada, where you dial ☏1 + area code + number. International rates apply for Canada.

THE SWARM

Africanized bees (killer bees) have made it to southern Arizona. Chances are you won't run into any killer-bee colonies, but here are a few things to know:

➡ Bees are attracted to dark colors, so hike in something light.

➡ Forget the perfume, and if a bee starts 'bumping' you, it could be its way of warning you that you're getting too close to the hive.

➡ If you do attract the angry attention of a colony, *run!* Cover your face and head with your clothing, your hands, or whatever you can, and keep running.

➡ Don't flail or swat, as this will only agitate them.

➡ They should stop following you before you make it half a mile. If you can't get that far, take shelter in a building or a car or under a blanket.

➡ Don't go into the water – the swarm will hover above and wait for you to come up for air.

➡ If you do get stung by lots of bees, get medical help. To remove the stingers, scrape them away, don't pull, which will inject more venom.

EMERGENCIES

If you need any kind of emergency assistance, such as police, ambulance or firefighters, call ☏911. Some rural phones might not have this service, in which case dial 0 for the operator and ask for emergency assistance.

➜ For international operator assistance, dial ☏0. The operator can provide specific rate information and tell you which time periods are the cheapest for calling.

➜ If you're calling the Southwest from abroad, the international country code for the US is ☏1. All calls to the Southwest are then followed by the area code and the seven-digit local number.

Cell Phones

➜ In the USA, cell phones use GSM 1900 or CDMA 800, operating on different frequencies than systems in other countries. The only foreign phones that will work in the US are tri- or quad-band models. If you have one of these phones, check with your service provider about using it in the US. Make sure to ask if roaming charges apply; these will turn even local US calls into pricey international calls.

➜ If your phone is unlocked, you may be able to buy a prepaid SIM card for the USA, which you can insert into your international cell phone to get a local number and voicemail.

➜ Even though the Southwest has an extensive cellular network, you'll still find a lot of coverage holes when you're driving in the middle of nowhere. Don't take undue risks thinking you'll be able to call for help from anywhere. Once you get up into the mountains or in isolated areas, cell-phone reception can be sketchy at best.

Phonecards

Private prepaid phonecards are available from convenience stores, supermarkets and pharmacies. AT&T sells a reliable phonecard that is widely available in the US.

Travelers with Disabilities

Travel within the Southwest is getting better for people with disabilities, but it's still not easy. Public buildings are required to be wheelchair accessible and to have appropriate rest-room facilities. Public-transportation services must be made accessible to all and teleph552one companies have to provide relay operators for the hearing impaired. Many banks provide ATM instructions in braille, curb ramps are common, many busy intersections have audible crossing signals, and most chain hotels have suites for guests with disabilities. Still, it's best to call ahead to check.

➜ Disabled US residents and permanent residents may be eligible for the lifetime Access Pass, a free pass to national parks and more than 2000 recreation areas managed by the federal government. Visit http://store.usgs.gov/pass/access.html.

➜ **Accessing Arizona** (www.accessingarizona.com) has information about wheelchair-accessible activities in Arizona. It's slightly out-of-date but still useful.

➜ For reviews about the accessibility of hotels, restaurants and entertainment venues in metropolitan Phoenix, check out www.brettapproved.com.

➜ **Arizona Raft Adventures** (☏800-786-7238, 928-526-8200; www.azraft.com; 6-day Upper Canyon hybrid/paddle trips $2050/2150, 10-day Full Canyon motor trips $3000) ✆ can accommodate disabled travelers on rafting trips through the Grand Canyon.

➜ The Utah tourism office has a list of programs and resources for disabled travelers in Utah at http://travel.utah.gov/publications/onesheets/Accessible_Utah_web.pdf.

➜ **Wheelchair Getaways** (☏Arizona & Las Vegas 888-824-7413, Colorado 800-238-6920, New Mexico 800-408-2626, main office 800-642-2042; www.wheelchairgetaways.com) rents accessible vans in cities across the Southwest including Phoenix, Tucson, Albuquerque, Las Vegas and Boulder City.

A number of organizations specialize in the needs of travelers with disabilities:

Disabled Sports USA (☏301-217-0960; www.disabledsportsusa.org) Offers sport, adventure and recreation programs for those with disabilities. Also publishes *Challenge* magazine.

Mobility International USA (☏541-343-1284; www.miusa.org) Advises travelers with disability about mobility issues, but primarily runs an educational exchange program.

Society for Accessible Travel & Hospitality (SATH; ☏212-447-7284; www.sath.org) Advocacy group providing general information for travelers with disabilities.

Splore (☏801-484-4128; www.splore.org) Runs accessible outdoor adventure trips in Utah.

Transportation

GETTING THERE & AWAY

Most travelers to the Southwest arrive by air and car, with bus running a distant third place. The train service is little used but available. Major regional transportation hubs include Las Vegas, Phoenix, Albuquerque and Salt Lake City.

Flights, tours and rail tickets can be booked online at www.lonelyplanet.com/bookings.

Air

Unless you live in or near the Southwest, flying in and renting a car is the most time-efficient option. Most domestic visitors fly into Phoenix, Las Vegas or Albuquerque. International visitors, however, usually first touch down in Los Angeles, New York, Miami, Denver or Dallas/Fort Worth before catching an onward flight to any number of destinations.

Airports & Airlines

International visitors might consider flying into Los Angeles and driving. **Los Angeles Airport** (LAX; ☑310-646-5252; www.lawa.org/lax) is an easy day's drive from western Arizona or southwestern Utah, via Las Vegas. The following airports are located in the Southwest.

Albuquerque International Sunport (ABQ; ☑505-244-7700; www.cabq.gov/airport; ☎) Serving Albuquerque and all of New Mexico, this is a small and friendly airport that's easy to navigate.

Denver International Airport (DEN; ☑303-342-2000; www.flydenver.com; ☎) Serving southern Colorado, Denver is only four hours from northeastern New Mexico by car.

McCarran International Airport (LAS; ☑702-261-5211; www.mccarran.com; ☎) Serves Las Vegas and southern Utah. Las Vegas is 290 miles from the South Rim of the Grand Canyon and 277 miles from the North Rim.

Salt Lake City International Airport (SLC; ☑801-575-2400; www.slcairport.com; ☎) Serving Salt Lake City and northern Utah, it's also a good choice if you're headed to the North Rim of the Grand Canyon and the Arizona Strip.

Sky Harbor International Airport (PHX; ☑602-273-3300; www.skyharbor.com; ☎) Located in Phoenix, this busy airport is 220 miles from the South Rim of the Grand Canyon and 335 miles from the North Rim.

Tucson International Airport (TUS; ☑520-573-8100; www.tucsonairport.org; ☎) Serving Tucson and southern Arizona, this is a small and easily navigated airport.

Land

Border Crossings

From Yuma, AZ, you can cross into Baja California and

CLIMATE CHANGE & TRAVEL

Every form of transportation that relies on carbon-based fuel generates CO_2, the main cause of human-induced climate change. Modern travel is dependent on airplanes, which might use less fuel per kilometer per person than most cars but travel much greater distances. The altitude at which aircraft emit gases (including CO_2) and particles also contributes to their climate change impact. Many websites offer 'carbon calculators' that allow people to estimate the carbon emissions generated by their journey and, for those who wish to do so, to offset the impact of the greenhouse gases emitted with contributions to portfolios of climate-friendly initiatives throughout the world. Lonely Planet offsets the carbon footprint of all staff and author travel.

Mexico. Nogales, AZ, is also a prime border town. The biggest gateway from New Mexico to reach Ciudad Juárez is El Paso, TX.

Don't forget your passport if you are crossing the border.

Bus

➡ Long-distance buses can get you to major points within the region, but then you will need to rent a car, as public transportation to the national parks, including the Grand Canyon, is nonexistent.

➡ Bus lines don't serve many smaller towns, including

important tourist hubs such as Moab.

➡ Bus terminals are often in more dangerous areas of town. Having said that, **Greyhound** (☏800-231-2222; www.greyhound.com) is the main US bus system. In sketchier terminals, stay alert and be discreet with valuable personal property.

➡ To save money on bus travel, plan seven days in advance, buy tickets online, travel on weekdays, and travel with a companion. Search the internet for special deals. Students,

military personnel, seniors and children under 12 receive discounts.

➡ When you've graduated from **Green Tortoise** (☏800-867-8647; www.greentortoise.com), a fun-loving tour company popular with younger travelers, but you still want to sleep on a bus and hang with like-minded adventurers, look into **Adventure Bus** (☏888-737-5263; www.adventurebus.com). It specializes in travel to the Grand Canyon and the Moab area but also offers an Arizona Desert Explorer trip, a New Mexico Magic trip, and

CROSSING THE MEXICAN BORDER

Travel Advisories

The issue of crime-related violence in Mexico has been front and center in the international press for several years. Nogales, AZ, for example, is safe for travelers, but Nogales, Mexico was a major locus for the drug trade and its associated violence. Ciudad Juárez, located to the south of Las Cruces, NM, and El Paso, TX, has one of the highest murder rates in Mexico. At time of writing the state department had issued travel advisories for both cities. Specific details about safety in these regions can be found at http://travel.state.gov/content/passports/english/alertswarnings/mexico-travel-warning.html.

As such, we cannot safely recommend crossing the border for an extended period to these cities and other areas under an advisory until the security situation changes. Day trips are OK, but anything past that may be risky.

The **US State Department** (http://travel.state.gov) recommends that travelers visit its website before traveling to Mexico. Here you can check for travel updates and warnings and confirm the latest border-crossing requirements. Before leaving, US citizens can sign up for the **Smart Traveler Enrollment Program** (STEP; http://step.state.gov/step) to receive email updates prior to departure.

Western Hemisphere Travel Initiative Requirements

Border-crossing requirements are subject to change. Travelers should double check regulations before arriving at the border. US and Canadian citizens entering the US from Mexico at airports of entry must present a valid passport. To enter by land or sea, US citizens must present a WHTI-compliant document such as a valid passport, US passport card, Trusted Traveler Program card (NEXUS, SENTRI, Global Entry or FAST), or an Enhanced Driver's License. Canadian citizens entering the US by sea or land must present a valid passport issued by the Government of Canada; a Trusted Traveler Program card (NEXUS, FAST or SENTRI); or an Enhanced Driver's License.

US and Canadian citizens under age 16 can also enter using only proof of citizenship, such as a birth certificate or Naturalization Certificate. Visit www.cbp.gov/travel/us-citizens/whti-program-background for current rules.

Driving in Mexico

Driving across the border is a serious hassle. At the border or at the checkpoint 13 miles south of it, you need to pick up a free Mexican tourist card. US or other nations' auto insurance is not valid in Mexico, and we strongly suggest you buy Mexican insurance on the US side of the border. Rates range from $30 to $50 per day, depending on coverage and your car's age, model and value.

an Arizona and New Mexico combo option.

Car & Motorcycle

➡ While the quickest way to get to the Southwest is by plane, the best way to get around is by car. Many places can only be reached by car, and it's nearly impossible to explore the national parks by bus.

➡ If you love driving, you'll be in heaven. Of the 160,000 or so miles in the national highway system, the Southwest has more stunning miles than any other part of the country – just look at all the scenic byway signs.

➡ On scenic drives in the Southwest, don't be surprised if you glance in your rearview mirror and see a pack of motorcycles roaring up behind you. Arizona's backroads are popular with motorcycle riders, and Harleys and other bikes are often lined up like horses in front of watering holes on lonely highways.

➡ Long-distance motorcycle driving can be dangerous because of the fatigue factor that sets in, and there are plenty of lengthy stretches of highway between major cities in the Southwest. Use caution during long hauls.

Train

➡ Three **Amtrak** (☎800-872-7245; www.amtrak.com) trains cut a swath through the Southwest, but they are not connected to one another. Use them to reach the region but not for touring.

➡ The *Southwest Chief* runs daily between Chicago and Los Angeles, via Kansas City. Significant stations include Albuquerque, NM, and Flagstaff and Williams, AZ. On-board guides provide commentary through national parks and Native American regions.

➡ At time of writing Amtrak was considering whether to reroute a section of track

between eastern New Mexico and Colorado to Oklahoma and Texas due to track limitations.

➡ The *California Zephyr* runs daily between Chicago and San Francisco (Emeryville) via Denver, with stops in Salt Lake City and Reno, NV.

➡ The *Sunset Limited* runs thrice weekly from Los Angeles to New Orleans and stops in Tucson, AZ.

➡ Book tickets in advance and look for plenty of available deals. Children, seniors and military personnel receive good discounts.

➡ Amtrak's USA Rail Pass offers coach-class travel for 15 ($449), 30 ($679) and 45 ($879) days, with travel limited to eight, 12 or 18 one-way segments. Changing trains or buses completes one segment. In other words, every time you step off the train to either visit a city or to get on another Amtrak train or vehicle, you use up one of your allotted segments. Plan carefully.

➡ It's not unusual for Amtrak trains, especially on longer routes, to run late.

GETTING AROUND

Once you reach the Southwest, traveling by car is the best way to get around and allows you to reach rural areas not served by public transportation. If you do not relish long drives, you can take buses and trains between a limited number of major destinations and then rent a car. But that's both time-consuming and more expensive than driving yourself and stopping along the way. State laws relating to driving are subject to frequent change, especially those relating to cell-phone use while driving.

Air

Because distances between places in the Southwest are so great, regional airports are located in a number of smaller towns such as Yuma and Flagstaff, AZ, and Carlsbad and Taos, NM. These airports primarily serve residents and businesspeople, and flying between these places is quite expensive and impractical.

Airlines in the Southwest

Great Lakes (☎307-433-2899; www.greatlakesav.com) Direct flights between Prescott, AZ, and Los Angeles, CA, and between Phoenix, AZ, and Page, AZ.

Southwest Airlines (☎800-435-9792; www.southwest.com) Major regional and budget carrier. Flies to Albuquerque, NM, Denver, CO, Phoenix, AZ, Tucson, AZ, Las Vegas, NV, Salt Lake City, UT, and El Paso, TX.

United Express (☎800-864-8331; www.united.com) Flies between Los Angeles International Airport (LAX) and Yuma, AZ.

US Airways (☎800-428-4322; www.usairways.com) Flies between Flagstaff, AZ, and Sky Harbor International Airport in Phoenix.

Bicycle

Cycling is a cheap, convenient, healthy, environmentally sound and fun way to travel. In the Southwest and because of altitude, distance and heat it's also a good workout. Cyclists are generally treated courteously by motorists.

➡ Carry at least a gallon of water and refill bottles at every opportunity. Dehydration is a major problem in the arid Southwest.

➡ Airlines accept bicycles as checked luggage, but since each airline has specific requirements, it's best to contact them for details.

→ Bicycle rentals are readily available. Expect to spend $20 to $40 a day for a beach cruiser or basic mountain bike.

→ Moab is generally considered the mountain-biking capital of the Southwest. The countryside around Sedona is also great for biking.

→ Cyclists are permitted on some interstates in all five Southwestern states, but they may not be allowed if there is a nearby alternative route or frontage road. Cycling on interstates is typically not allowed in urban areas.

→ In New Mexico and in certain counties and localities in Nevada and Arizona (including Flagstaff and Tucson), helmets are required by law for those who under 18. There are no requirements in Colorado and Utah, but helmets should still be worn, to reduce the risk of head injury.

→ Consider your environmental impact. Know your environment and regulations before you ride. Bikes are restricted from entering wilderness areas and some designated trails but may be used in Bureau of Land Management (BLM) singletrack trails and National Park Service (NPS) sites, state parks, national and state forests.

Bus

→ **Greyhound** (☏800-231-2222; www.greyhound.com) is the main carrier to and within the Southwest, operating buses several times a day along major highways between large towns.

→ Greyhound only stops at smaller towns that happen to be along the way, in which case the bus terminal is likely to be a grocery-store parking lot or something similar. To see if Greyhound serves a town, look for the blue and red Greyhound symbol.

→ The best schedules often involve overnight routes; the best fares often require seven days' advance notice.

GETTING TO THE SOUTHWEST

By Bus

FROM	TO	FARE ($)*	DURATION (HOUR)
Chicago, IL	Las Vegas, NV	330-425	38-40
Dallas, TX	Albuquerque, NM	188-259	13-15
Los Angeles, CA	Las Vegas, NV	84-129	6
Portland, OR	Salt Lake City, UT	194-267	18

*Round-trip prices

By Car or Motorcycle

FROM	TO	VIA	DURATION (HOUR)
Dallas, TX	Albuquerque, NM	I-35 & I-40	11½
Denver, CO	Santa Fe, NM	I-25	6½
Los Angeles, CA	Las Vegas, NV	I-15	5
San Diego, CA	Phoenix, AZ	I-8	7
San Francisco, CA	Santa Fe, NM	I-5 & I-40	19

By Train

FROM	TO	FARE ($)*	DURATION (HOUR)
Chicago, IL	Albuquerque, NM	275	26
Chicago, IL	Salt Lake City, UT	275	34
Los Angeles, CA	Flagstaff, AZ	138	10½
Los Angeles, CA	Tucson, AZ	89	9½
San Francisco, CA	Salt Lake City, UT	193	17

*Round-trip prices

BUSES AROUND THE SOUTHWEST

FROM	TO	FARE ($)*	DURATION (HOUR)
Albuquerque, NM	Salt Lake City, UT	165	20
Las Vegas, NV	Phoenix, AZ	60	8½-9
Phoenix, AZ	Tucson, AZ	18	2
Tucson, AZ	Albuquerque, NM	135	12½-17¼

*One-way prices

➡ Greyhound no longer offers service to Santa Fe, NM. Your best bet is to ride to Albuquerque, NM, then hop onto the adjacent Rail Runner train, which takes 90 minutes to get to Santa Fe.

Car & Motorcycle

The interstate system is thriving in the Southwest, but smaller state roads and fine scenic byways offer unparalleled opportunities for exploration.

➡ I-10 runs east–west through southern Arizona

➡ I-40 runs east–west through Arizona and central New Mexico

➡ I-70 runs east–west through central Utah

➡ I-80 runs east–west through northern Utah

➡ I-15 links Las Vegas to Salt Lake City

➡ I-25 runs through central New Mexico to Denver, CO

➡ Route 66 more or less follows the modern-day I-40 through Arizona and New Mexico

Automobile Associations

The **American Automobile Association** (AAA; ☑800-874-7532, towing, roadside assistance 800-222-4357; www.aaa.com) provides members with maps and other information. Members also get discounts on car rentals, air tickets and some hotels and sightseeing attractions, as well as emergency road service and towing. AAA has reciprocal agreements with automobile associations in other countries. Be sure to bring your membership card from your home country.

Emergency breakdown services are available 24 hours.

Driver's Licenses

➡ Foreign visitors can legally drive a car in the USA for up to 12 months using their home country's driver's license.

➡ An IDP (International Driving Permit) will have more credibility with US traffic police, especially if your normal license doesn't have a photo or isn't in English. Your home country's automobile association can issue an IDP, valid for one year. Always carry your license together with the IDP.

➡ To ride a motorcycle in the US, you need either a valid US state motorcycle license or an IDP endorsed for motorcycles.

Fuel

Gas stations are common and many are open 24 hours. Small-town stations may be open only from 7am to 8pm or 9pm.

At most stations, you must pay before you pump. The more modern pumps have credit-/debit-card terminals built into them, so you can pay right at the pump. At more expensive, 'full service' stations, an attendant will pump your gas for you; no tip is expected.

Insurance

➡ Liability insurance covers people and property that you might hit.

➡ For damage to the rental vehicle, a collision damage waiver (CDW) is available for about $27 to $29 per day. If you have collision coverage on your vehicle at home, it might cover damage to rental cars; inquire before departing.

➡ Some credit cards offer reimbursement coverage for collision damages when you use the card to rent a car; check before departing. There may be exceptions for rentals of more than 15 days or for exotic models, jeeps, vans and 4WD vehicles. Check your policy.

➡ Many rental agencies stipulate that damage a car suffers while being driven on unpaved roads is not covered by the insurance they offer. Check with the agent when you make your reservation.

Rental

➡ Rental cars are readily available at all airports and many downtown city locations.

➡ With advance reservations for a small car, the daily rate

INSPECTION STATIONS

When entering California, agricultural inspection stations at the Arizona–California border may ask you to surrender fruit in an attempt to stop the spread of pests associated with produce.

with unlimited mileage is about $25 to $47.

➡ Larger companies don't require a credit-card deposit, which means you can cancel without a penalty if you find a better rate.

➡ Midsize cars are often only a tad more expensive.

➡ Deals abound and the business is competitive so it pays to shop around. Aggregator sites like www. kayak.com can provide a good cross section of options. You can often snag great last-minute deals via the internet; rental reservations made in conjunction with an airplane ticket often yield better rates.

➡ Most companies require that you have a major credit card, are at least 25 years old and have a valid driver's license. Some national agencies may rent to drivers between the ages of 21 and 25 but may charge a daily fee.

➡ If you decide to fly into one city and out of another, you may incur drop-off charges. Check the amount before finalizing your plans. Dropping off the car in another state may raise the rate.

➡ To rent a Harley-Davidson or Honda motorcycle to cruise Arizona's scenic highways, try **Funtime Rentals** (☑480-968-2522) in Phoenix.

Road Conditions & Hazards

Be extra defensive while driving in the Southwest. Everything from dust storms to snow to roaming livestock can make conditions dangerous. Near Flagstaff, watch for elk at sunset on I-17. The animals like to soak up warmth from the blacktop (or so we've heard). You don't want to hit an elk, which can weigh between 500lb and 900lb.

Distances are great in the Southwest and there are long stretches of road without gas stations. Running out of gas on a hot and desolate stretch of highway is no fun, so pay attention to signs that caution 'Next Gas 98 Miles.'

For updates on road conditions within a state, call ☑511. From outside a state, try one of the following:

Arizona (☑888-411-7623; www. az511.com)

Nevada (☑877-687-6237; www. nvroads.com)

New Mexico (☑800-432-4269; http://m.nmroads.com)

Southern Colorado (☑303-639-1111; www.cotrip.org)

Utah (☑866-511-8824; www. commuterlink.utah.gov)

Road Rules

➡ Driving laws are slightly different in each state, but all require the use of safety belts.

➡ In every state, children under five years of age must be placed in a child safety seat secured by proper restraints (p53).

➡ The maximum speed limit on rural interstates in Arizona, Colorado, Nevada and New Mexico is 75mph, and can get as high as 80mph in Utah. That drops to 65mph in urban areas in Southwestern states but obey all traffic signs that require a lower speed. On undivided highways, the speed-limit range is based on local population and other factors.

➡ Bans on cell-phone use and texting while driving are becoming more common.

BORDER PATROL AGENTS & CHECKPOINTS

Officers of the United States Border Patrol (USBP) are ubiquitous in southern Arizona. Border patrol officers are law enforcement personnel who have the ability to pull you over, ask for ID and search your car if they have reasonable cause. Be aware that there's a good chance they'll flash you to the side of the road if you're driving down back roads in a rental or out-of-state car. This is because said roads have been used to smuggle both people and drugs north from Mexico.

➡ Always carry ID, including a valid tourist visa if you're a foreign citizen, and car registration (if it's a rental car, your rental contract should suffice).

➡ Be polite and they should be polite to you.

➡ If they ask, it's best to allow the agents to see inside your trunk (boot) and backseat (assuming you have nothing illegal to hide).

It's almost guaranteed that you'll drive through checkpoints down here. If you've never done so before, the 'stop side' of the checkpoints is the route going from south (Mexico) to north (USA). There's a chance you'll just be waved through the checkpoint; otherwise slow down, stop, answer a few questions (regarding your citizenship and the nature of your visit) and possibly pop your trunk and roll down your windows so officers can peek inside your car. Visitors may consider the above intrusive, but grin and bear it. For better or worse, this is a reality of traveling in southern Arizona.

Currently, you cannot talk on a hand-held device or text while driving in Nevada. In Utah and Colorado cell-phone use for drivers under the age of 18 is prohibited. Texting while driving is banned in Colorado and New Mexico. These laws are becoming stricter and are subject to change.

Motor Home (RV)

➡ Rentals range from ultra-efficient VW campers to plush land yachts.

➡ After the size of the vehicle, consider the impact of gas prices, gas mileage, additional mileage costs, insurance and refundable deposits; these can add up quickly. It pays to shop around and read the fine print.

➡ The base rate for a four-person vehicle can be anywhere from $420 to $1800 weekly in the summer, plus 34¢ for each additional mile not included in your package. Get out a good map and a calculator to determine if it's practical.

➡ Before heading out, consult www.rvtravel.com for tips galore.

➡ Purchase a campground guide from **Woodall's** (www.woodalls.com), which also has a great all-round website, or check the website for **Kampgrounds of America** (KOA; www.koa.com). KOA also publishes a free annual campground directory listing its US and Canadian campgrounds.

For RV rentals contact the following:

Adventure Touring RV Rentals (☎877-778-9569; www.adventuretouring.com) Serving Los Angeles, Las Vegas and Denver. Will rent to those heading to Burning Man.

Cruise America (☎800-671-8042; www.cruiseamerica.com) Locations nationwide, including Las Vegas, Phoenix, Flagstaff, Tucson, Salt Lake City, Albuquerque, Colorado Springs and Denver.

Jucy Rentals (☎800-650-4180; www.jucyrentals.com) These green-and-purple pop-up camper vans have started appearing in the Southwest. Currently they have rental locations in Las Vegas and Los Angeles.

Train

Several train lines provide services using historic steam trains. Although they are mainly for sightseeing, the Williams to Grand Canyon run is a destination in itself. More scenic train rides are located in Clarkdale, AZ, Chama, NM, Santa Fe, NM, and Durango, CO.

Behind the Scenes

SEND US YOUR FEEDBACK

We love to hear from travelers – your comments keep us on our toes and help make our books better. Our well-traveled team reads every word on what you loved or loathed about this book. Although we cannot reply individually to postal submissions, we always guarantee that your feedback goes straight to the appropriate authors, in time for the next edition. Each person who sends us information is thanked in the next edition – the most useful submissions are rewarded with a selection of digital PDF chapters.

Visit **lonelyplanet.com/contact** to submit your updates and suggestions or to ask for help. Our award-winning website also features inspirational travel stories, news and discussions.

Note: We may edit, reproduce and incorporate your comments in Lonely Planet products such as guidebooks, websites and digital products, so let us know if you don't want your comments reproduced or your name acknowledged. For a copy of our privacy policy visit lonelyplanet.com/privacy.

OUR READERS

Many thanks to the travelers who used the last edition and wrote to us with helpful hints, useful advice and interesting anecdotes:

Benjamin Blaise, Doreen Coppens, Richard Crighton, Judy Larquier, John Malone, Joyce Tocher, Gary Turnquist, John-Richard Winn

AUTHOR THANKS

Amy C Balfour

Thank you, Karen Underhill and Jayne Powell for the inside scoop on Flagstaff, and Doug Campbell for Grand Canyon area updates. In Tucson, thank you, Chris and Cheryl Ray family, and Deb Corcoran. Thank you, Nelson Echevarria for great tips about food and brews in Phoenix. Nick Bleser and Birdie Stabel, I enjoyed our lunch in Tubac. Julie Campbell, Deb Armstrong, Sarah Bunn and Sheila Romana – thank you for the leads. Cheers to Carolyn McCarthy and Greg Ward for top-notch text, Chris Pitts for spot-on editing and Alex Howard for skillfully keeping us on track.

Carolyn McCarthy

With a nod to Ed Abbey, Everett Ruess and Daniel Suelo, whose desert roamings still inspire. Thanks to Sandra B for helping me explore more of this magical corner of the planet. For providing needed breaks, my full gratitude goes out to Lance, Drew, Anne Bliss and the Kudos. Thanks also to Chris Rose and Angela Donini for their tips. Virtual craft beers go out to Amy Balfour for steering the ship.

Greg Ward

Thanks to everyone who helped me on the road in New Mexico, especially Steve Horak, Bill Tefft, Heather Arnold, Kelly Ryan and Steve Lewis. Back home, thanks as ever to my wife Samantha Cook.

ACKNOWLEDGMENTS

Climate map data adapted from Peel MC, Finlayson BL & McMahon TA (2007) 'Updated World Map of the Köppen-Geiger Climate Classification', Hydrology and Earth System Sciences, 11, 163344.

Cover photograph: Canyonlands National Park, Utah, Michele Falzone/AWL.

THIS BOOK

This 7th edition of *Southwest USA* was researched and written by Amy C Balfour, Carolyn McCarthy and Greg Ward. The previous edition was written by Amy C Balfour, Michael Benanav, Sarah Chandler, Lisa Dunford and Carolyn McCarthy. The 5th edition was researched and written by Becca Blond, Sara 'Sam' Benson, Lisa Dunford and Andrea Schulte-Peevers. The Native American Southwest USA chapter was

written by Jeff Campbell. The Geology chapter was written by David Lukas. The Travel with Children chapter was based on text by Jennifer Denniston. This guidebook was commissioned in Lonely Planet's London office, and produced by the following:

Destination Editor Alexander Howard

Product Editor Kate Kiely

Senior Cartographer Alison Lyall

Cartographer Gabe Lindquist

Book Designer Wendy Wright

Assisting Editors Justin Flynn, Kellie Langdon, Ali Lemer, Christopher Pitts, Erin Richards

Assisting Cartographer Hunor Csutoros

Cover Researcher Naomi Parker

Thanks to Martine Power, Dianne Schallmeiner, Angela Tinson, Samantha Tyson, Cliff Wilkinson

Index

Map Legend

Sights

- Beach
- Bird Sanctuary
- Buddhist
- Castle/Palace
- Christian
- Confucian
- Hindu
- Islamic
- Jain
- Jewish
- Monument
- Museum/Gallery/Historic Building
- Ruin
- Sento Hot Baths/Onsen
- Shinto
- Sikh
- Taoist
- Winery/Vineyard
- Zoo/Wildlife Sanctuary
- Other Sight

Activities, Courses & Tours

- Bodysurfing
- Diving
- Canoeing/Kayaking
- Course/Tour
- Skiing
- Snorkeling
- Surfing
- Swimming/Pool
- Walking
- Windsurfing
- Other Activity

Sleeping

- Sleeping
- Camping

Eating

- Eating

Drinking & Nightlife

- Drinking & Nightlife
- Cafe

Entertainment

- Entertainment

Shopping

- Shopping

Information

- Bank
- Embassy/Consulate
- Hospital/Medical
- Internet
- Police
- Post Office
- Telephone
- Toilet
- Tourist Information
- Other Information

Geographic

- Beach
- Hut/Shelter
- Lighthouse
- Lookout
- Mountain/Volcano
- Oasis
- Park
- Pass
- Picnic Area
- Waterfall

Population

- Capital (National)
- Capital (State/Province)
- City/Large Town
- Town/Village

Transport

- Airport
- BART station
- Border crossing
- Boston T station
- Bus
- Cable car/Funicular
- Cycling
- Ferry
- Metro/Muni station
- Monorail
- Parking
- Petrol station
- Subway/SkyTrain station
- Taxi
- Train station/Railway
- Tram
- Underground station
- Other Transport

Note: Not all symbols displayed above appear on the maps in this book

Routes

- Tollway
- Freeway
- Primary
- Secondary
- Tertiary
- Lane
- Unsealed road
- Road under construction
- Plaza/Mall
- Steps
- Tunnel
- Pedestrian overpass
- Walking Tour
- Walking Tour detour
- Path/Walking Trail

Boundaries

- International
- State/Province
- Disputed
- Regional/Suburb
- Marine Park
- Cliff
- Wall

Hydrography

- River, Creek
- Intermittent River
- Canal
- Water
- Dry/Salt/Intermittent Lake
- Reef

Areas

- Airport/Runway
- Beach/Desert
- Cemetery (Christian)
- Cemetery (Other)
- Glacier
- Mudflat
- Park/Forest
- Sight (Building)
- Sportsground
- Swamp/Mangrove

OUR STORY

A beat-up old car, a few dollars in the pocket and a sense of adventure. In 1972 that's all Tony and Maureen Wheeler needed for the trip of a lifetime – across Europe and Asia overland to Australia. It took several months, and at the end – broke but inspired – they sat at their kitchen table writing and stapling together their first travel guide, *Across Asia on the Cheap*. Within a week they'd sold 1500 copies. Lonely Planet was born.

Today, Lonely Planet has offices in Franklin, London, Melbourne, Oakland, Beijing and Delhi, with more than 600 staff and writers. We share Tony's belief that 'a great guidebook should do three things: inform, educate and amuse'.

OUR WRITERS

Amy C Balfour

Coordinating author, Arizona Amy has hiked, biked, skied and gambled her way across the Southwest, and she can't stop hiking to the depths of the Grand Canyon. Maybe the beer just tastes better at Phantom Ranch. On this trip she enjoyed an inaugural hike to Fort Bowie and finally tackled the lush West Fork Trail in Oak Creek Canyon. Amy has authored or co-authored 25 books for Lonely Planet and has written for *Backpacker*, BBC.com, theknot.com, *Redbook*, *Southern Living*, *Women's Health*, and the *Los Angeles Times* and *Washington Post*.

Read more about Amy at:
lonelyplanet.com/members/amycbalfour

Carolyn McCarthy

Las Vegas & Nevada, Southwestern Colorado, Utah Carolyn first reached Dead Horse Point one spring break in a vintage Volkswagen bus that barely made the trip. The Southwest remains a favorite destination. This time, she rafted the Grand Canyon, explored lost canyons of ancient ruins and wore her best gear to tatters. Carolyn has contributed to over 25 Lonely Planet titles, specializing in the American West and Latin America, and has written for National Geographic, Outside, Lonely Planet Magazine and other publications. Join her travels at www.carolynswildblueyonder.blogspot.com.

Read more about Carolyn at:
lonelyplanet.com/members/carolynmcc

Greg Ward

New Mexico Since first falling in love with Taos almost 25 years ago, Greg Ward has spent much of the last two decades exploring the deserts of the Southwest. Besides writing several guidebooks to the region, he has amassed copious research for a still-unwritten novel about the first encounters between New Mexico's Pueblo peoples and the earliest Spanish expeditions. His website is gregward.info.

Contributing Authors

Jeff Campbell has been a travel writer for Lonely Planet since 2000. He was the coordinating author of three editions of *USA*, as well as editions of *Southwest USA, Zion & Bryce National Parks*, *Hawaii*, *Florida*, and *Mid-Atlantic Trips*, and he's been a contributor on other titles. He wishes that he called the Southwest home, but next best is meeting and writing about those who do. Jeff wrote the Native American Southwest USA chapter.

David Lukas is a professional naturalist whose travels and writing take him around the American West and further afield. He has contributed environment and wildlife chapters to about 20 Lonely Planet guides. David's favorite Southwest moment was getting up to watch sunrise on the magnificent hoodoos at Bryce Canyon (don't miss it!). David wrote the Geology chapter.

Published by Lonely Planet Publications Pty Ltd
ABN 36 005 607 983
7th edition – March 2015
ISBN 978 1 74220 736 0
© Lonely Planet 2015   Photographs © as indicated 2015
10 9 8 7 6 5 4 3 2
Printed in China